2014
北京统计年鉴
Beijing Statistical Yearbook

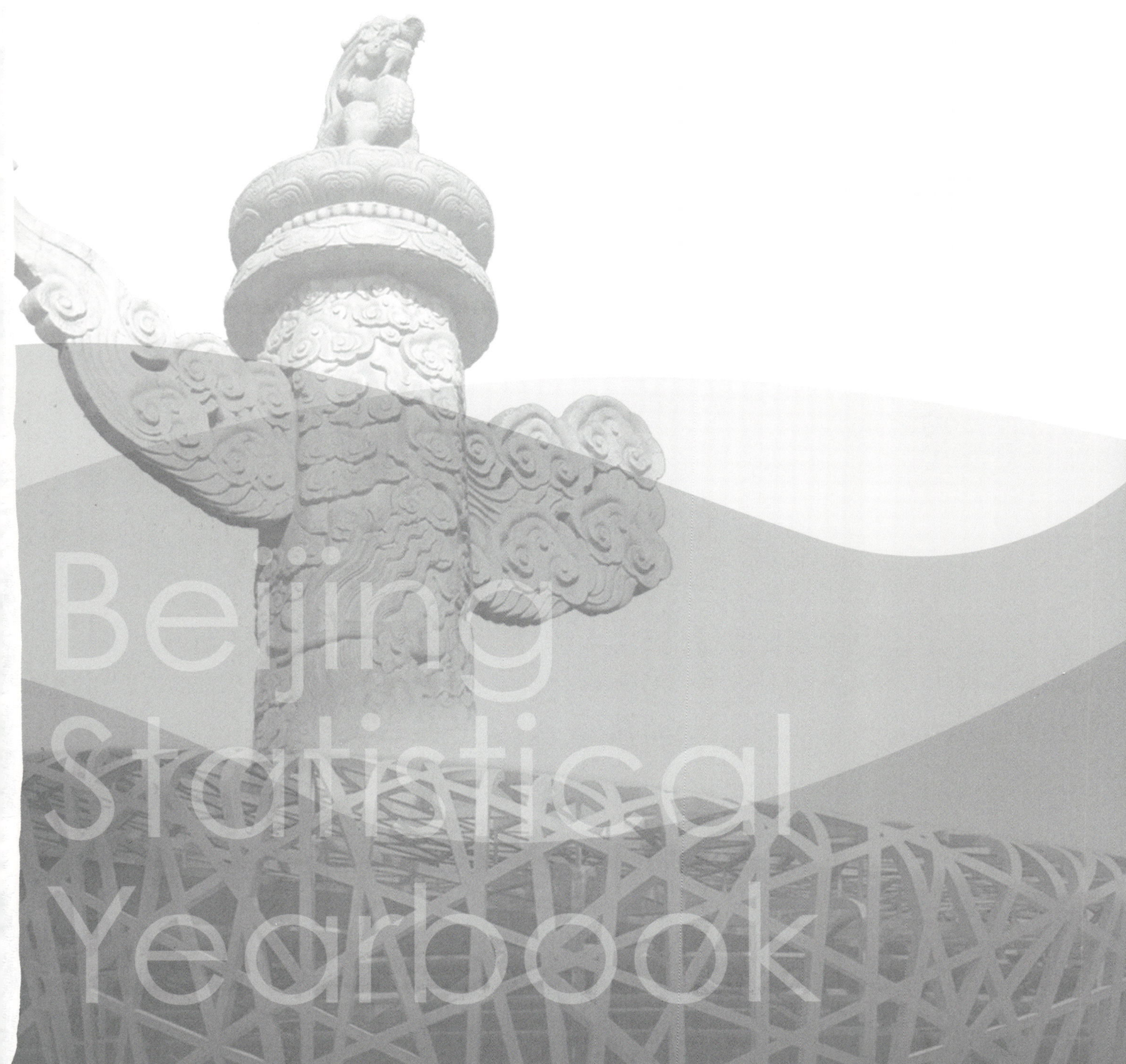

图书在版编目(CIP)数据

北京统计年鉴. 2014 : 汉英对照 / 北京市统计局，国家统计局北京调查总队编. -- 北京 : 中国统计出版社，2014.9

ISBN 978-7-5037-7116-3

Ⅰ. ①北 Ⅱ. ①北 ②国 Ⅲ. ①统计资料 - 北京市 - 2014 - 年鉴 - 汉、英 Ⅳ. ①C832.1-54

中国版本图书馆CIP数据核字(2014)第136853号

北京统计年鉴-2014

作　　者/北京市统计局　国家统计局北京调查总队
责任编辑/郭　栋　　李　冲
封面设计/高　立
出版发行/中国统计出版社
通信地址/北京市丰台区西三环南路甲6号　邮政编码/100073
电　　话/邮购（010）63376909　书店（010）68783171
网　　址/http://csp.stats.gov.cn
印　　刷/北京画中画印刷有限公司
经　　销/新华书店
开　　本/880mm×1230mm　1/16
字　　数/1200千字
印　　张/38印张　彩插/1.5印张
版　　别/2014年9月第1版
版　　次/2014年9月第1次印刷
定　　价/350.00元

本书附同版本CD-ROM一张，光盘内容以书面文字为准。
如有印装差错，由本社发行部调换。

2013年是全面贯彻落实党的十八大精神的第一年。全市人民在党中央、国务院和市委、市政府的坚强领导下，同心同德、脚踏实地、攻坚克难，加快转变经济发展方式，全市经济持续健康发展，社会和谐稳定。

The year of 2013 was the first year in fully implementing the guiding principles of the Eighteenth National Congress of the CPC. Under the firm leadership of the Party Central Committee, the State Council and the Municipal Party Committee and Beijing Municipal Government, people of the Capital worked with one heart and one mind, united as one to tackle difficult problems in a down-to-earth manner. By accelerating transformation of the mode of economic development, Beijing witnessed a sustainable and healthy economic development as well as a harmonious and stable social environment.

2013年的北京 Beijing in 2013

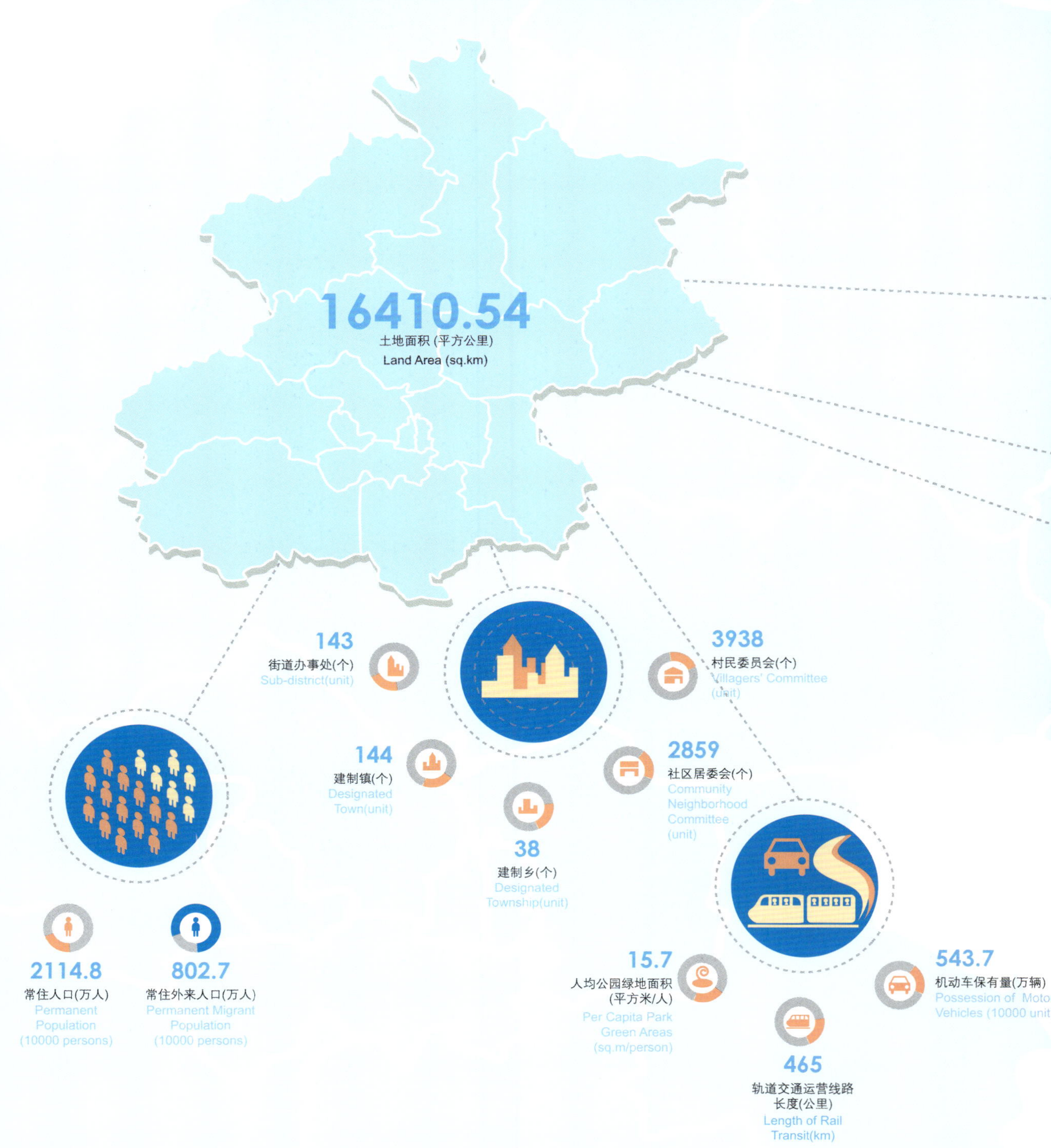

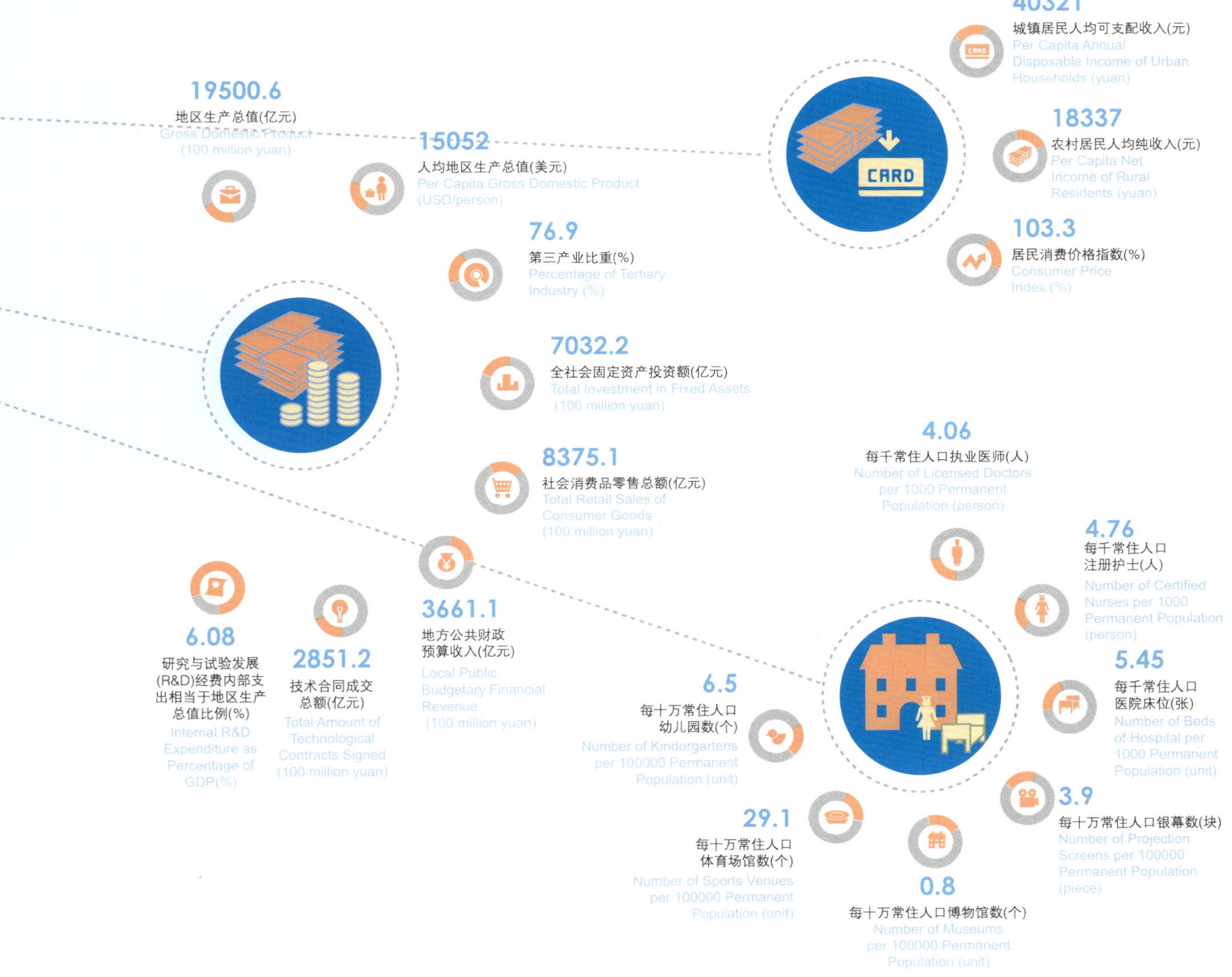
19500.6
地区生产总值(亿元)
Gross Domestic Product
(100 million yuan)
15052
人均地区生产总值(美元)
Per Capita Gross Domestic Product
(USD/person)
76.9
第三产业比重(%)
Percentage of Tertiary
Industry (%)
7032.2
全社会固定资产投资额(亿元)
Total Investment in Fixed Assets
(100 million yuan)
8375.1
社会消费品零售总额(亿元)
Total Retail Sales of
Consumer Goods
(100 million yuan)
3661.1
地方公共财政
预算收入(亿元)
Local Public
Budgetary Financial
Revenue
(100 million yuan)
2851.2
技术合同成交
总额(亿元)
Total Amount of
Technological
Contracts Signed
(100 million yuan)
6.08
研究与试验发展
(R&D)经费内部支
出相当于地区生产
总值比例(%)
Internal R&D
Expenditure as
Percentage of
GDP(%)
40321
城镇居民人均可支配收入(元)
Per Capita Annual
Disposable Income of Urban
Households (yuan)
18337
农村居民人均纯收入(元)
Per Capita Net
Income of Rural
Residents (yuan)
103.3
居民消费价格指数(%)
Consumer Price
Index (%)
CARD
4.06
每千常住人口执业医师(人)
Number of Licensed Doctors
per 1000 Permanent
Population (person)
4.76
每千常住人口
注册护士(人)
Number of Certified
Nurses per 1000
Permanent Population
(person)
5.45
每千常住人口
医院床位(张)
Number of Beds
of Hospital per
1000 Permanent
Population (unit)
3.9
每十万常住人口银幕数(块)
Number of Projection
Screens per 100000
Permanent Population
(piece)
0.8
每十万常住人口博物馆数(个)
Number of Museums
per 100000 Permanent
Population (unit)
29.1
每十万常住人口
体育场馆数(个)
Number of Sports Venues
per 100000 Permanent
Population (unit)
6.5
每十万常住人口
幼儿园数(个)
Number of Kindergartens
per 100000 Permanent
Population (unit)

北京一日 A Day In Beijing

每日创造 Daily Production

152495.4
地方财政收入(万元/日)
Local Financial Revenue (10000 yuan/day)

165463.6
地方财政支出(万元/日)
Local Financial Expenditure (10000 yuan/day)

9074.3
发电量(万千瓦时/日)
Electricity (10000 kwh/day)

5584
汽车生产量(辆/日)
Output of Motor Vehicles(unit/day)

514614
移动电话机生产量(台/日)
Output of Mobile Telephone(unit/day)

2335.4
实际利用外资(万美元/日)
Foreign Capital Actually Used (USD 10000/day)

30326
微型计算机生产量(台/日)
Output of Micro-computers (unit/day)

117792.2
海关进出口总值(万美元/日)
Total Value of Imports and Export at Customs (USD 10000/day)

4432.9
第一产业(万元/日)
Primary Industry(10000 yuan/day)

119241.1
第二产业(万元/日)
Secondary Industry(10000 yuan/day)

410589.0
第三产业(万元/日)
Tertiary Industry(10000 yuan/day)

534263.0
地区生产总值(万元/日)
Gross Domestic Product (10000 yuan/day)

3512
机动车销售量(辆/日)
Sales of Motor Vehicles(unit/day)

100445.3
国内旅游收入(万元/日)
Earnings From Domestic Tourists (10000 yuan/day)

1326.9
公共电汽车客运量(万人次/日)
Passengers Carried by Buses and Trolley Buses (10000 Person-times/day)

67.8
接待国内旅游者人数(万人次/日)
Domestic Tourists (10000 Person-times/day)

1313.6
旅游外汇收入(万美元/日)
Foreign Exchange Earnings from Tourism (USD 10000/day)

1.2
接待入境旅游人数(万人次/日)
International Tourists (10000 Person-times/day)

1556
首都机场飞机起降次数(架次/日)
Takeoff and Landing of Airplanes in Beijing Capital International Airport(unit/day)

878.0
轨道交通客运量(万人次/日)
Passengers Carried by Rail Transit (10000 Person-times/day)

1 人均地区生产总值(美元/人)
Per Capita Gross Domestic Product(USD/person)

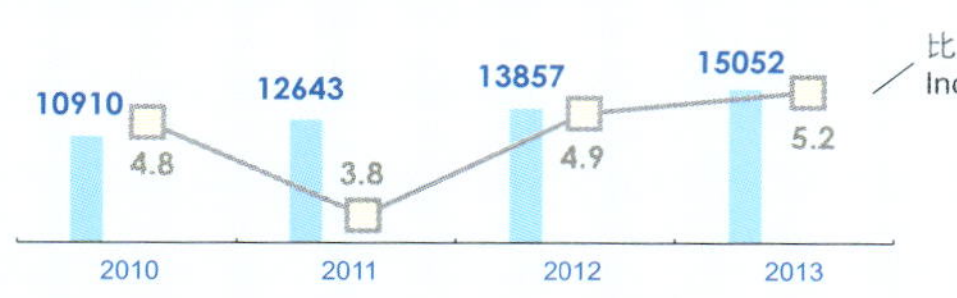

2 常住人口(万人)
Permanent Population (10000 persons)

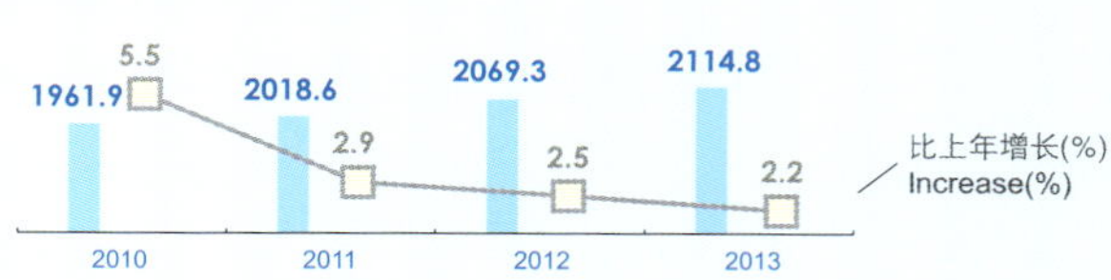

历史数据 Historical Data

每日生活 Daily Life

常住出生人口（人/日）
Birth Population (Permanent Population) (person/day)

常住死亡人口（人/日）
Death Population (Permanent Population) (person/day)

登记结婚对数（对/日）
Marriage Registered (couple/day)

离婚对数（对/日）
Registered Divorces (couple/day)

医院诊疗人次（万人次/日）
Patients Treated in Hospitals (10000 Person-times/day)

污水处理量（万立方米/日）
Disposal Volume of Waste Water (10000 cu.m/day)

城镇居民人均可支配收入(元/日)
Per Capita Disposable Income of Urban Residents(yuan/day)

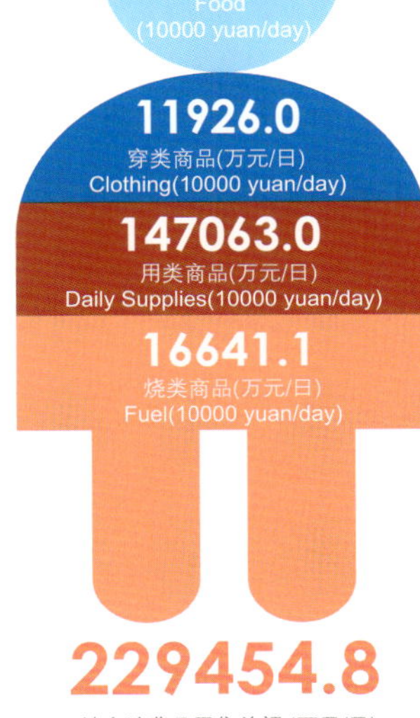

229454.8
社会消费品零售总额（万元/日）
Retail Sales of Consumer Goods (10000 yuan/day)

生活垃圾清运量（万吨/日）
Domestic Waste Removed and Transported (10000 tons/day)

城镇居民人均消费性支出(元/日)
Per Capita Living Expenditures of Urban Residents(yuan/day)

城乡居民生活用电量（万千瓦时/日）
Residential Electricity Consumption (10000 kwh/day)

农村居民人均纯收入(元/日)
Per Capita Net Income of Rural Residents(yuan/day)

居民家庭用天然气（万立方米/日）
Natural Gas for Living Use (10000 cu.m/day)

居民家庭用自来水（万立方米/日）
Tap Water for Living Use (10000 cu.m/day)

专业艺术剧团演出场次（场次/日）
Performance of Professional Art Troupes (time/day)

电影放映场次（场次/日）
Film Show Times (Times/day)

农村居民人均生活消费支出(元/日)
Per Capita Living Expenditures of Rural Residents(yuan/day)

③ 轨道交通运营线路长度(公里) Operating Routes Length of Rail Transit (km)
轨道交通客运量(亿人次) Passenger Traffic of Rail Transit (100 million times)

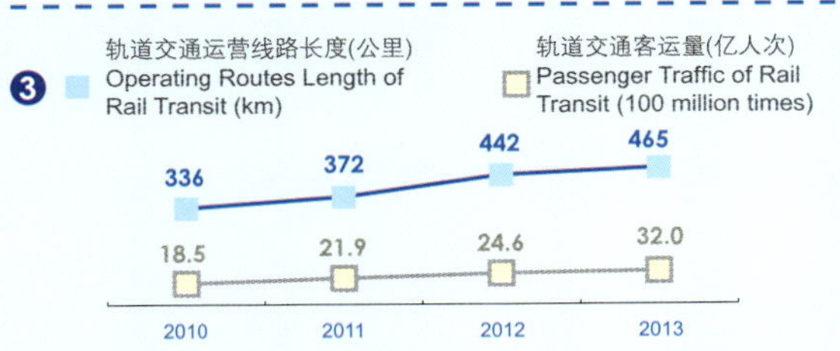

④ 公共电汽车运营线路长度(公里) Operating Routes Length of Buses and Trolley Buses (km)
公共电汽车客运量(亿人次) Passenger Traffic of Buses and Trolley Buses (100 million times)

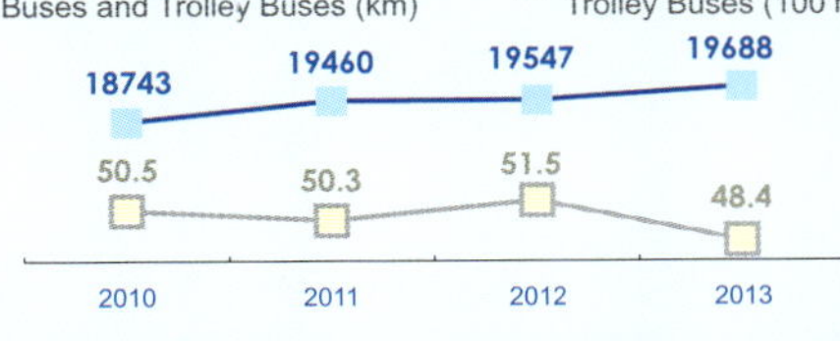

经济运行总体平稳、稳中有进

Economy maintained steady development and grew at a moderate pace

经济运行总体平稳
Economy maintained steady development

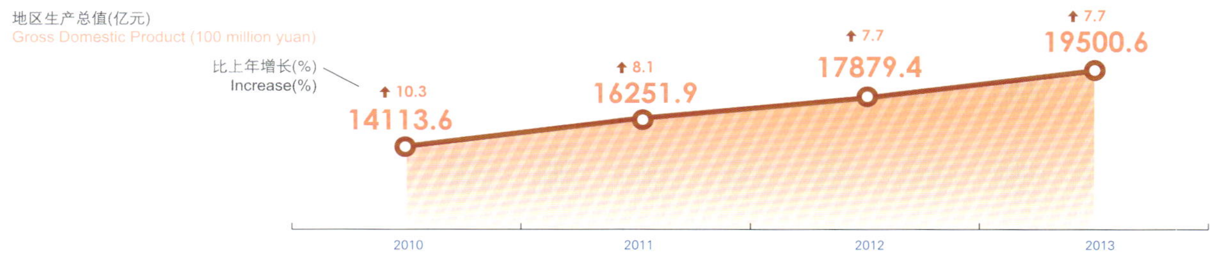

居民消费价格涨幅总体可控
CPI growth was generally under control

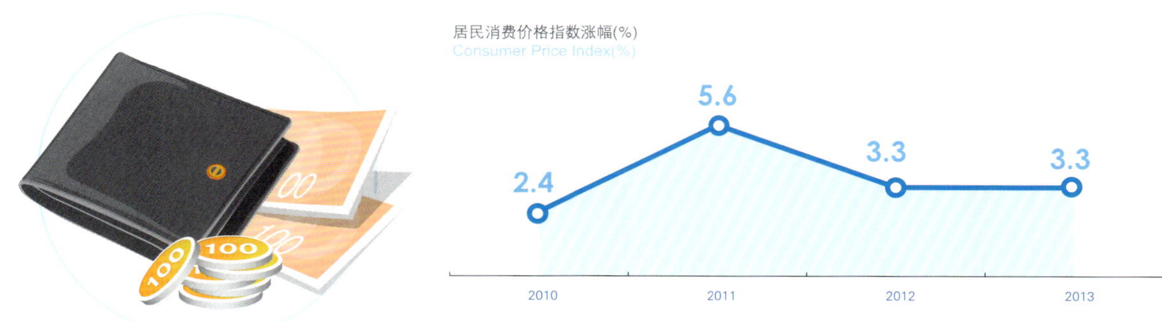

就业形势保持稳定
Employment remained stable

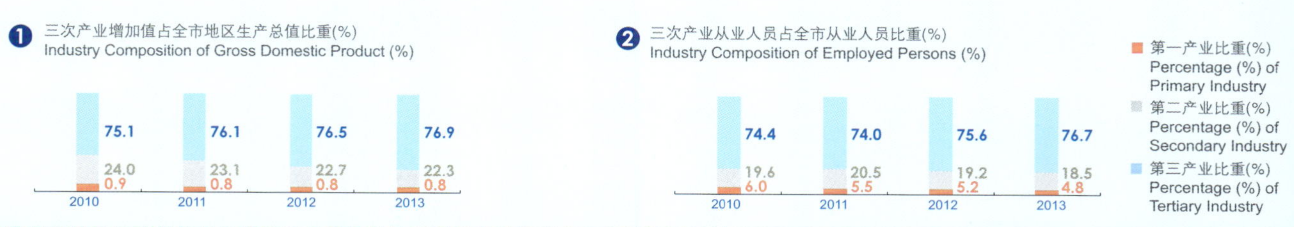

投资消费内部结构继续改善
Internal structure of investment and consumption continued to be improved

民间投资(亿元)
Private Investment in Fixed Assets (100 million yuan)

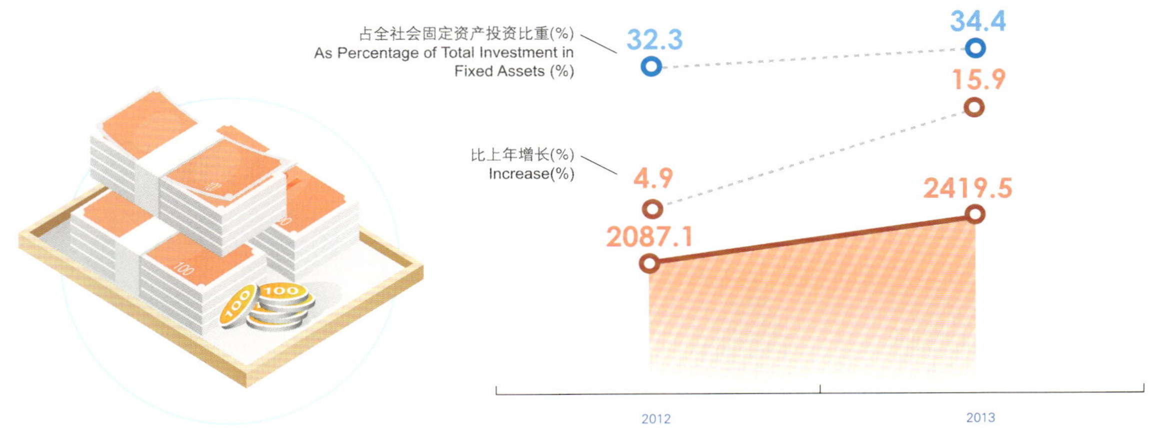

限额以上批发零售企业网上零售额(亿元)
Online Retail Sales of Wholesale and Retail Enterprises above Designated Size (100 million yuan)

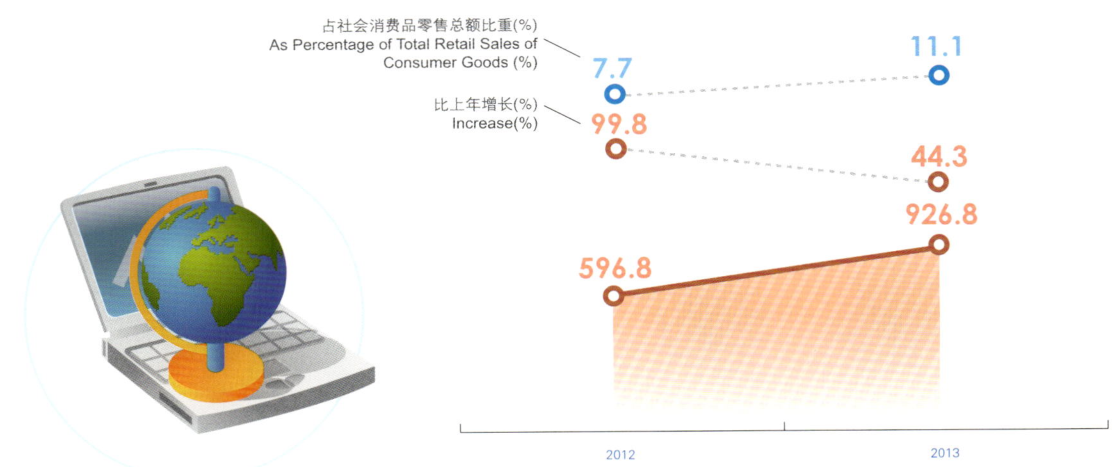

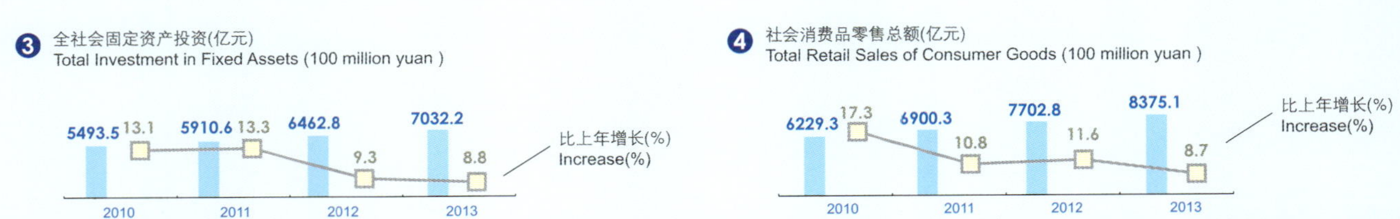

总体经济“服务型、创新型、集约型、集聚化”特征明显

The overall economy grew more service-oriented, creative, intensive and centralized

第三产业比重达到76.9%
Added Value of Tertiary Industry Represented 76.9%

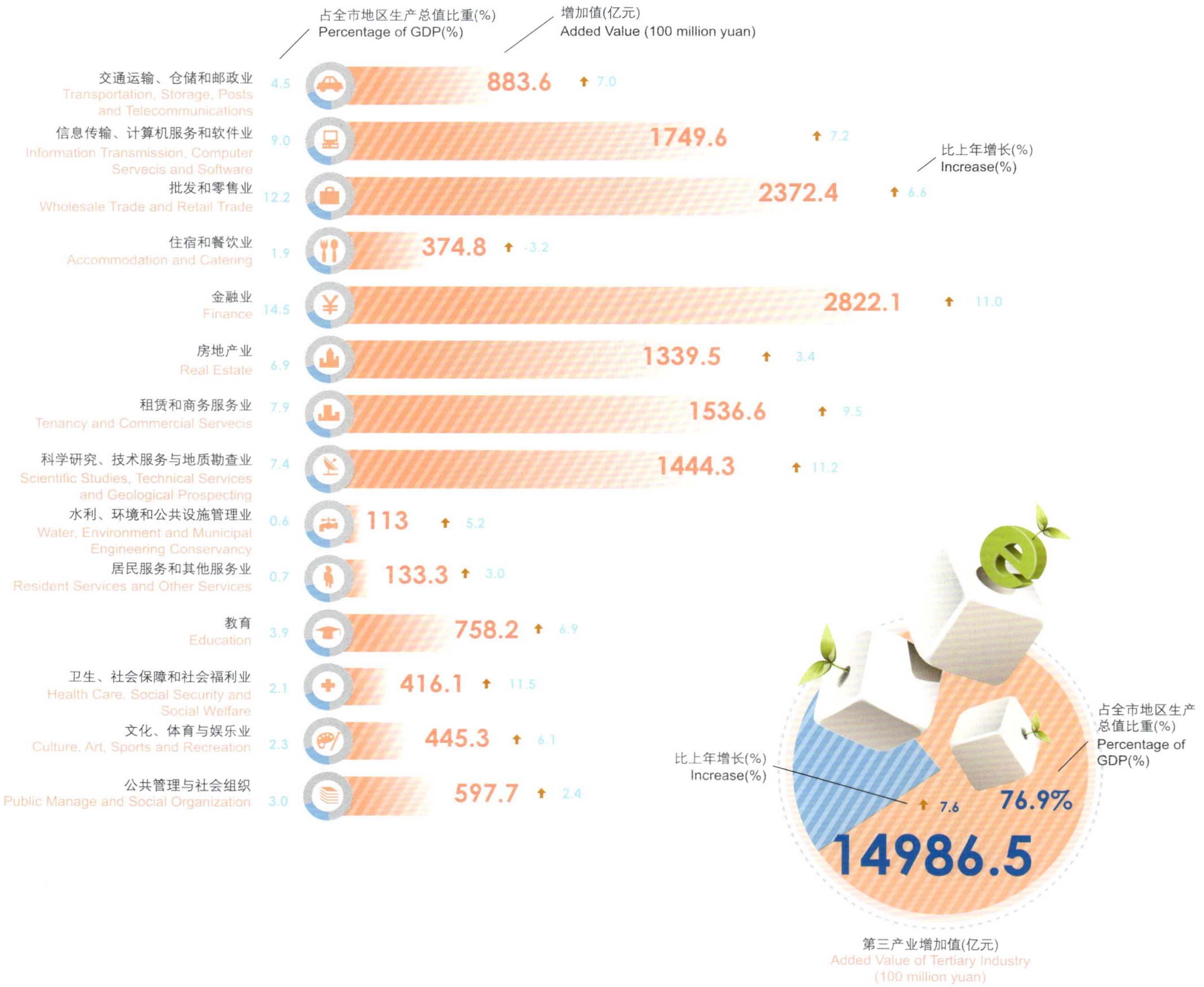

占全市地区生产总值比重(%)
Percentage of GDP(%)
增加值(亿元)
Added Value (100 million yuan)
比上年增长(%)
Increase(%)
交通运输、仓储和邮政业
Transportation, Storage, Posts and Telecommunications
4.5
883.6
7.0
信息传输、计算机服务和软件业
Information Transmission, Computer Servecis and Software
9.0
1749.6
7.2
批发和零售业
Wholesale Trade and Retail Trade
12.2
2372.4
6.6
住宿和餐饮业
Accommodation and Catering
1.9
374.8
-3.2
金融业
Finance
14.5
2822.1
11.0
房地产业
Real Estate
6.9
1339.5
3.4
租赁和商务服务业
Tenancy and Commercial Servecis
7.9
1536.6
9.5
科学研究、技术服务与地质勘查业
Scientific Studies, Technical Services and Geological Prospecting
7.4
1444.3
11.2
水利、环境和公共设施管理业
Water, Environment and Municipal Engineering Conservancy
0.6
113
5.2
居民服务和其他服务业
Resident Services and Other Services
0.7
133.3
3.0
教育
Education
3.9
758.2
6.9
卫生、社会保障和社会福利业
Health Care, Social Security and Social Welfare
2.1
416.1
11.5
文化、体育与娱乐业
Culture, Art, Sports and Recreation
2.3
445.3
6.1
公共管理与社会组织
Public Manage and Social Organization
3.0
597.7
2.4
比上年增长(%)
Increase(%)
7.6
76.9%
14986.5
占全市地区生产总值比重(%)
Percentage of GDP(%)
第三产业增加值(亿元)
Added Value of Tertiary Industry (100 million yuan)

❶ 第三产业增加值(亿元)
Added Value of Tertiary Industry (100 million yuan)

75.1
76.1
76.5
76.9
10600.8
12363.1
13669.9
14986.5
9.3
8.7
7.9
7.6
2010
2011
2012
2013
占全市地区生产总值比重(%)
Percentage of GDP(%)
比上年增长(%)
Increase(%)

❷

信息传输、计算机服务和软件业增加值占全市地区生产总值比重(%)
Added Value of Information Transmission, Computer Service and Software Sectors as % of Beijing's GDP
金融业增加值占全市地区生产总值比重(%)
Added Value of Finance Sector as % of Beijing's GDP
房地产业增加值占全市地区生产总值比重(%)
Added Value of Real Estate Sector as % of Beijing's GDP
8.6
13.2
7.1
9.2
13.6
6.6
9.1
14.2
7.0
9.0
14.5
6.9
2010
2011
2012
2013

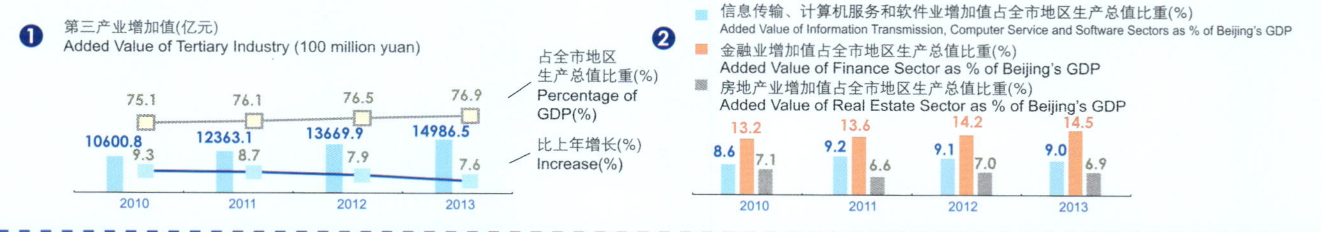

中关村国家自主创新示范区创新发展活动后劲增强
Innovative development gathered more and more momentum in Zhongguancun National Innovation Demonstration Zone

中关村国家自主创新示范区研究与试验发展经费支出快速增长
Faster Growth in R&D Expenditures

中关村国家自主创新示范区研究与试验发展经费支出(亿元)
R&D Expenditures (100 million yuan)

比上年增长(%) Increase(%)

	2010	2011	2012	2013
R&D Expenditures (100 million yuan)	260.4	313.5	381.3	456.3
比上年增长(%) Increase(%)	10.6	20.4	21.6	19.7

中关村国家自主创新示范区科技创新成果丰富
Scientific and technological innovation was fruitful in Zhongguancun National Innovation Demonstration Zone

中关村国家自主创新示范区专利申请数(件)
Patent Applications (unit)

2010	2011	2012	2013
18515	24894	34192	44275

中关村国家自主创新示范区专利授权数(件)
Patent Granted (unit)

2010	2011	2012	2013
13151	12951	17969	22308

中关村国家自主创新示范区获奖成果数(个)
Number of Prize-winning Achievements (unit)

2010	2011	2012	2013
1811	2329	2509	2852

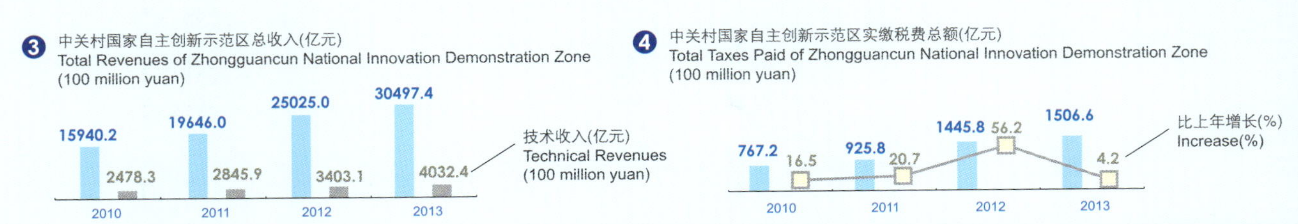

3 中关村国家自主创新示范区总收入(亿元)
Total Revenues of Zhongguancun National Innovation Demonstration Zone (100 million yuan)

	2010	2011	2012	2013
Total Revenues	15940.2	19646.0	25025.0	30497.4
技术收入(亿元) Technical Revenues (100 million yuan)	2478.3	2845.9	3403.1	4032.4

4 中关村国家自主创新示范区实缴税费总额(亿元)
Total Taxes Paid of Zhongguancun National Innovation Demonstration Zone (100 million yuan)

	2010	2011	2012	2013
Total Taxes Paid	767.2	925.8	1445.8	1506.6
比上年增长(%) Increase(%)	16.5	20.7	56.2	4.2

总体经济“服务型、创新型、集约型、集聚化”特征明显

The overall economy grew more service-oriented, creative, intensive and centralized

高耗能行业节能降耗效果显著

Energy-intensive industry made great progress in energy saving and consumption reduction

第二产业能源消耗持续下降
Energy consumption of secondary industry was on the steady decline

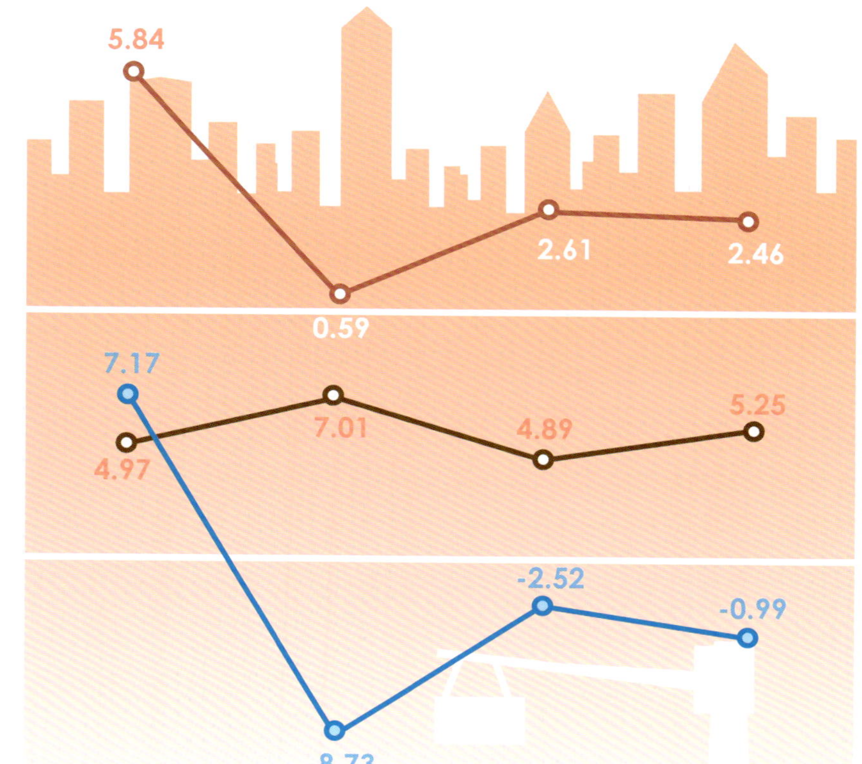

第二产业比上年增长(%)
Energy Consumption of Secondary Industry up by (%) over the Previous Year

第三产业比上年增长(%)
Energy Consumption of Tertiary Industry up by (%) over the Previous Year

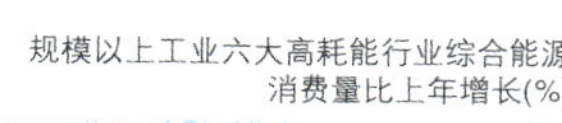

❶ 万元地区生产总值水耗(立方米)
Water Consumption per 10000 yuan GDP (cu.m)

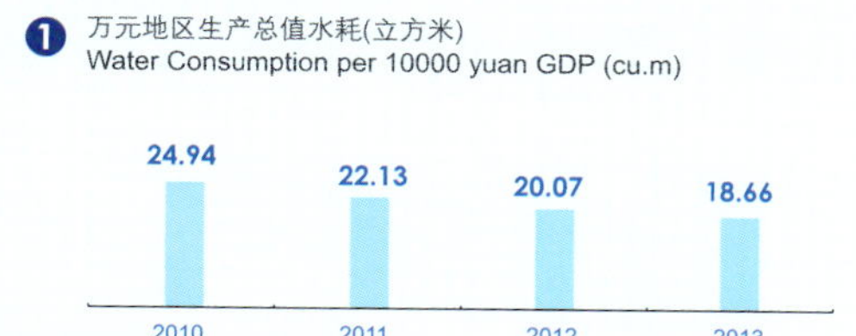

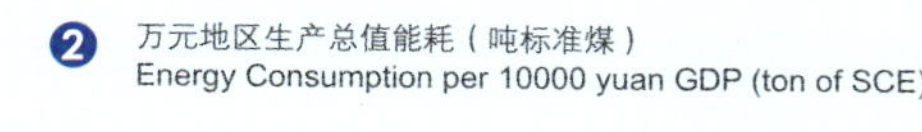

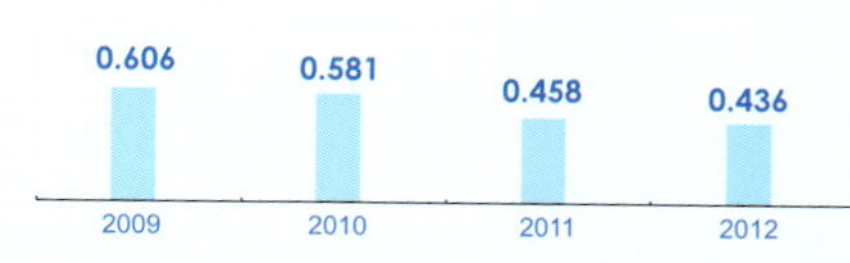

六大高端产业功能区经济保持平稳增长
Economy in Six Major High-tech Industry Functional Zone kept Stable Growth

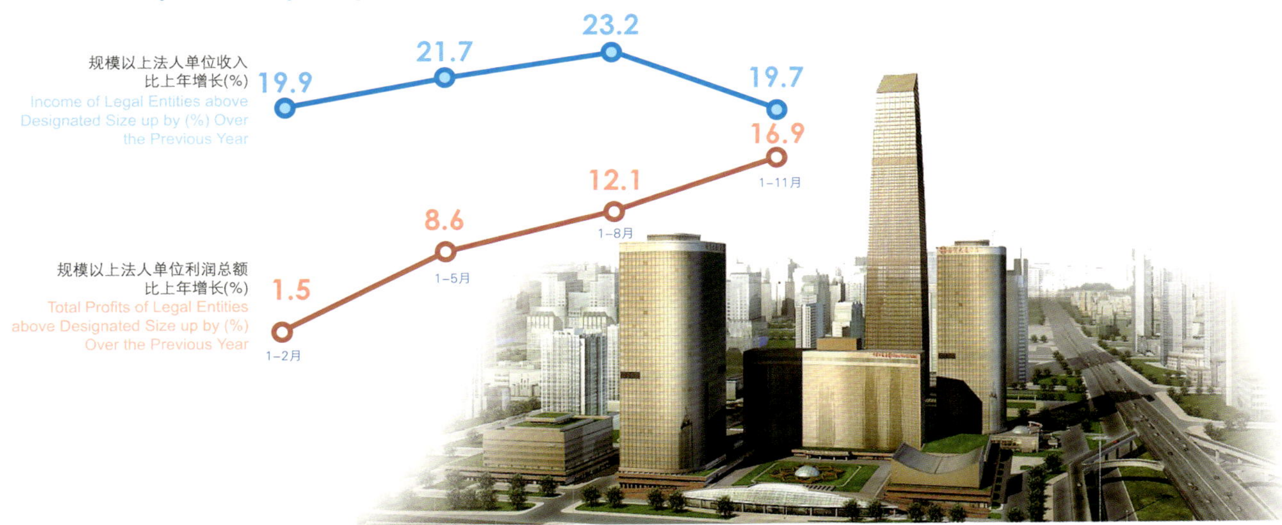

高端产业集聚明显
High-end industry showed clear agglomeration effects

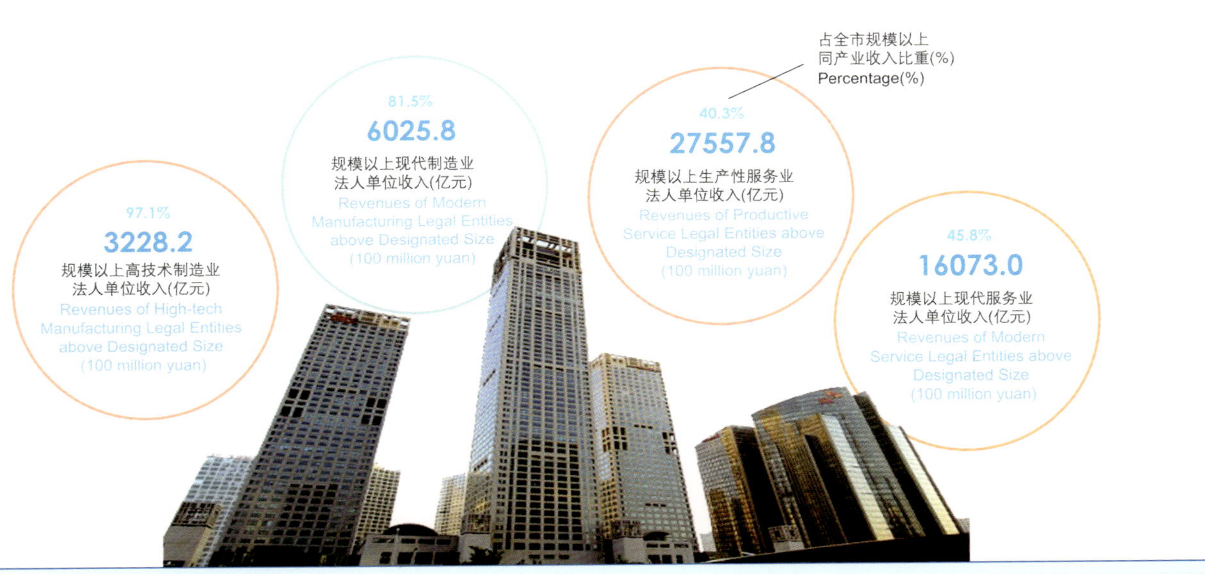

高新技术产品出口份额总体稳定 利用外资稳步增长

Proportion of exports of high-tech industry remained stable and Amount of foreign capital utilized maintained steady growth

高新技术产品出口份额总体稳定
Proportion of exports of high-tech industry remained stable

北京地区海关进出口总值(亿美元)
Total Value of Imports and Exports (USD 100 million)

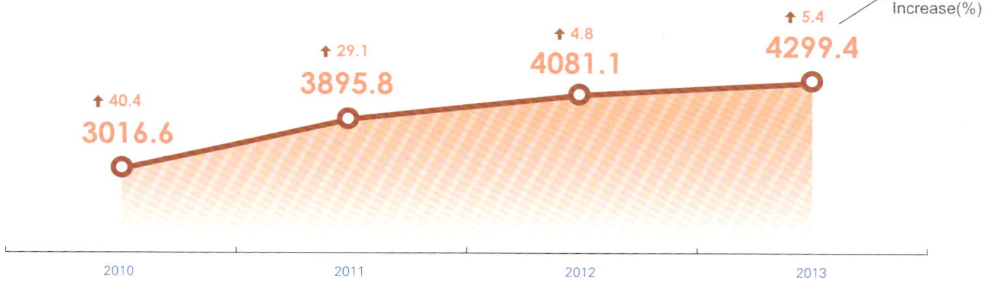

比上年增长(%)
Increase(%)

↑40.4
3016.6
↑29.1
3895.8
↑4.8
4081.1
↑5.4
4299.4

2010
2011
2012
2013

高新技术产品出口值(亿美元)
Exports of High-tech Products (USD 100 million)

占出口总值比重(%)
As Percentage of Exports

34.9
30.7
31.9
32.3

193.7
181.2
190.2
203.6

2010
2011
2012
2013

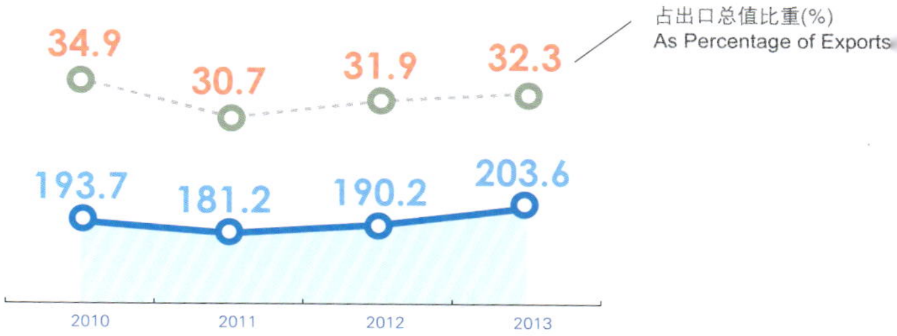

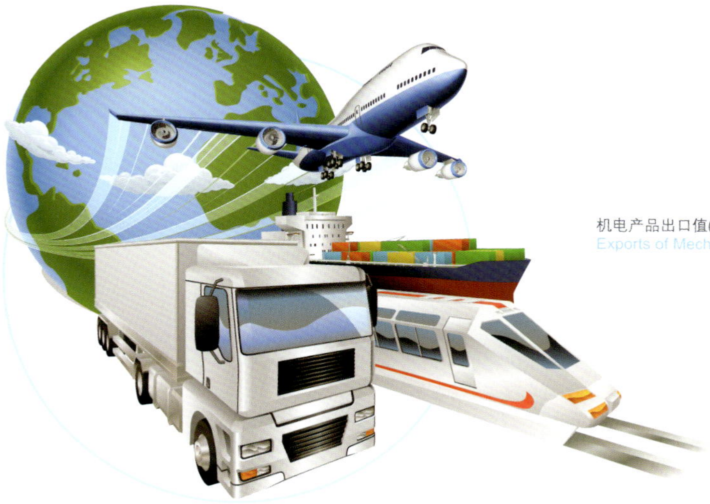

机电产品出口值(亿美元)
Exports of Mechanical and Electrical Products (USD 100 million)

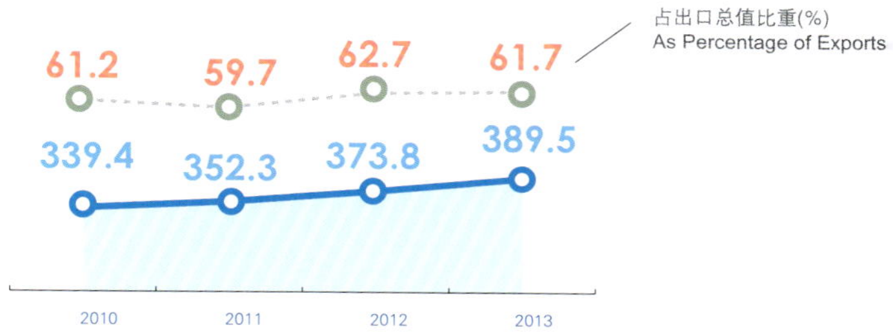

占出口总值比重(%)
As Percentage of Exports

61.2
59.7
62.7
61.7

339.4
352.3
373.8
389.5

2010
2011
2012
2013

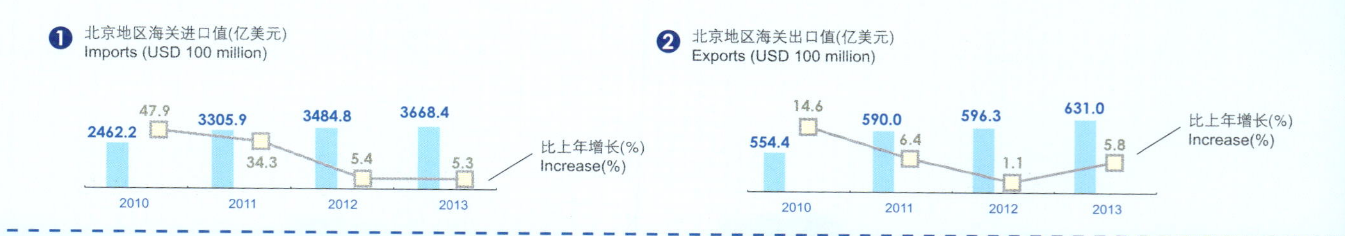

利用外资稳步增长
Amount of foreign capital utilized maintained steady growth

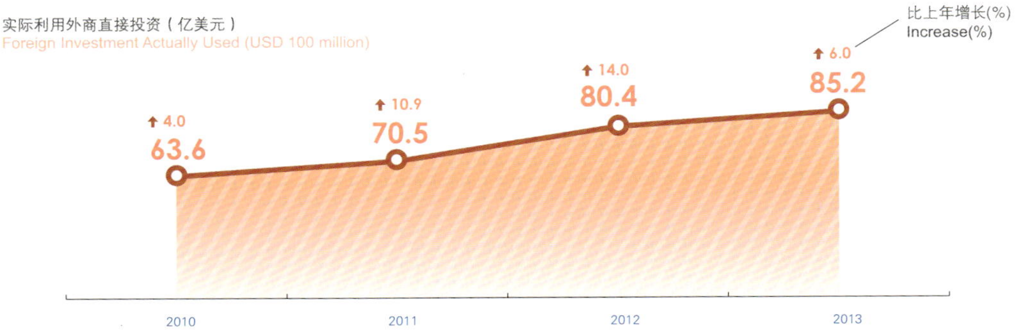

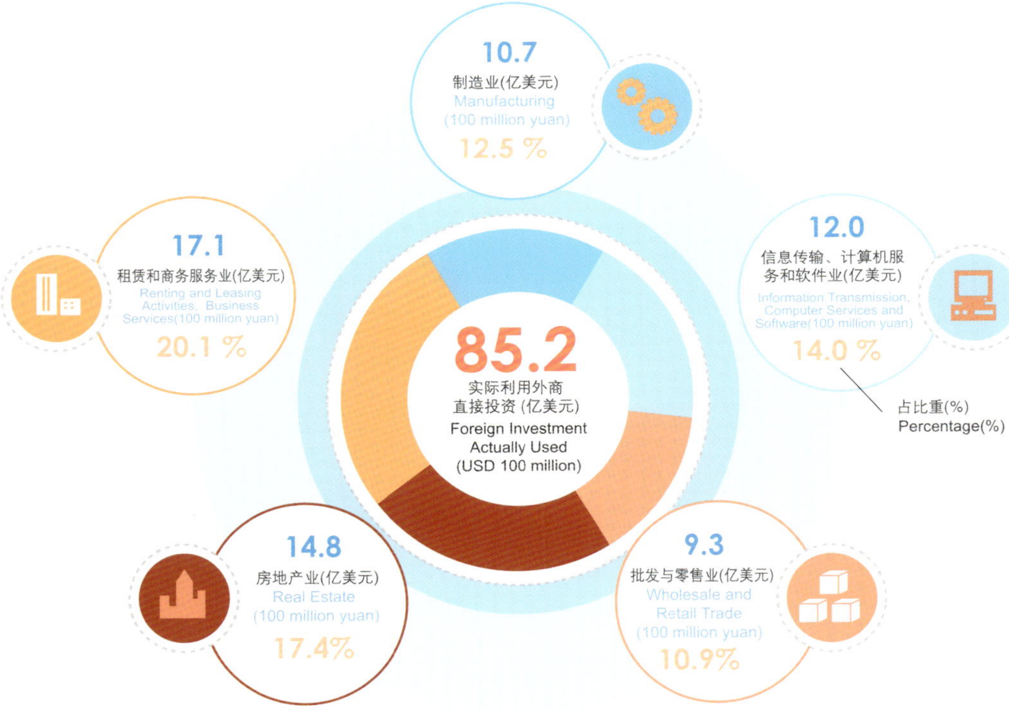

❸ 外商直接投资项目(合同)个数(个)
Number of Contracts of Foreign Economic Cooperation(unit)

❹ 对外经济合作合同额(亿美元)
Contract Value of Foreign Economic Cooperation (USD 100 million)

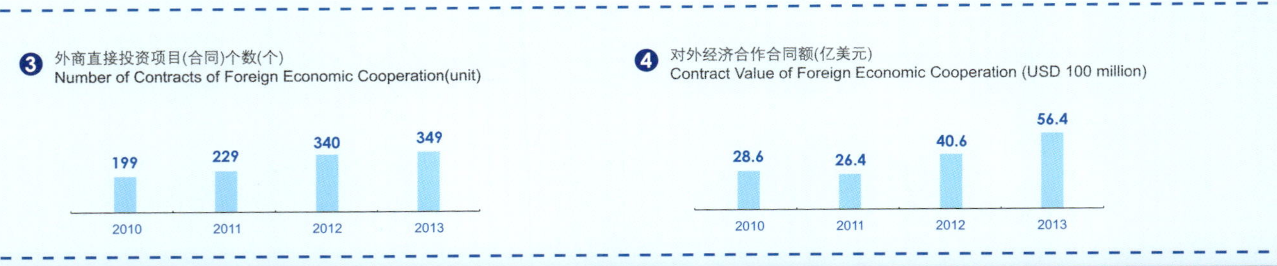

人口增长有所放缓 环境指标有所改善

Population growth slowed down and environmental indexes were improved

常住人口年均增量逐年减少，增速持续放缓
Average annual increment of permanent population continued to decrease year by year with a lower growth rate

常住人口(万人)
Permanent Population (10000 persons)

↑ 2.2
2114.8
2013年

常住人口 (万人)
Permanent Population (10000 persons)

	2010	2011	2012	2013
常住人口(万人) Permanent Population (10000 persons)	1961.9	2018.6	2069.3	2114.8
比上年增长(%) Increase(%)	5.5	2.9	2.5	2.2
比上年增量(万人) Increase (10000 persons)	101.9	56.7	50.7	45.5

常住外来人口 (万人)
Permanent Migrant Population (10000 persons)

	2010	2011	2012	2013
常住外来人口(万人) Permanent Migrant Population (10000 persons)	704.7	742.2	773.8	802.7
占全市常住人口比重(%) As Percentage of Permanent Population (%)	35.9	36.8	37.4	38.0

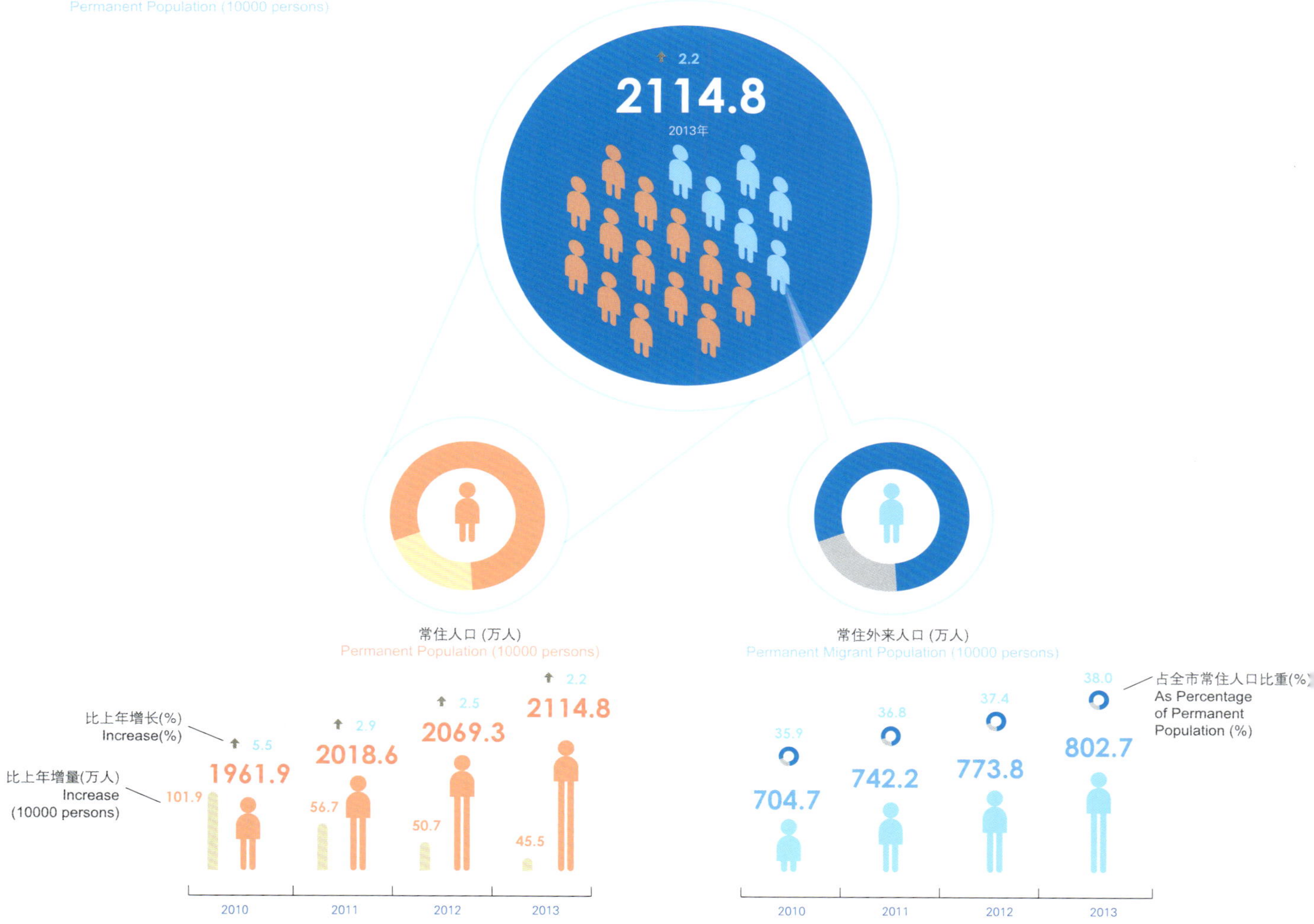

❶ 60岁及以上人口占全市常住人口比重(%)
People of Age 60 and above as Percentage of Permanent Population (%)

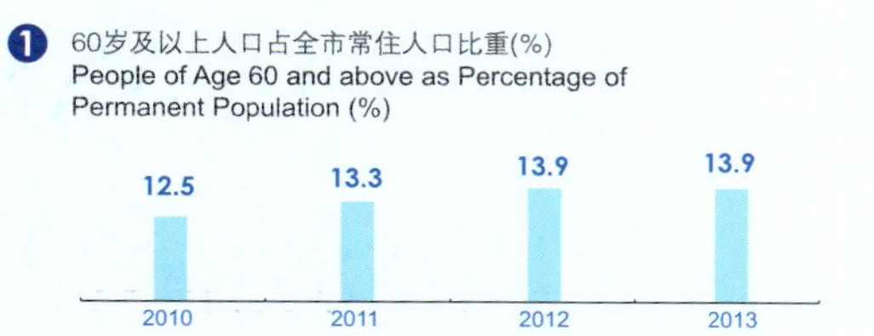

❷ 65岁及以上人口占全市常住人口比重(%)
People of Age 65 and above as Percentage of Permanent Population (%)

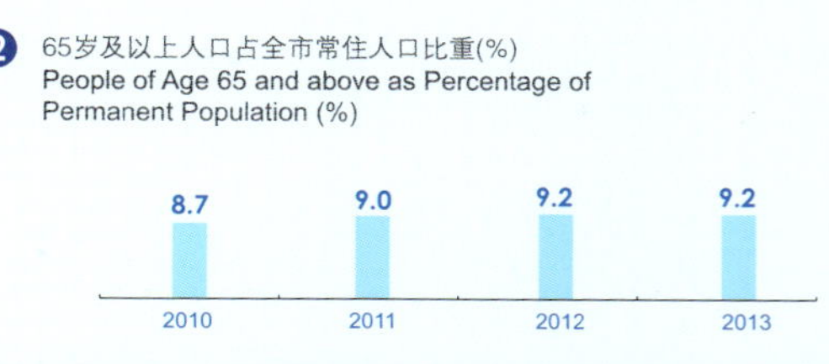

主要污染物年均浓度总体下降
Annual concentration of major pollutants was generally on the decline

生活环境指标进一步改善
Indexes of living environment continued to be improved

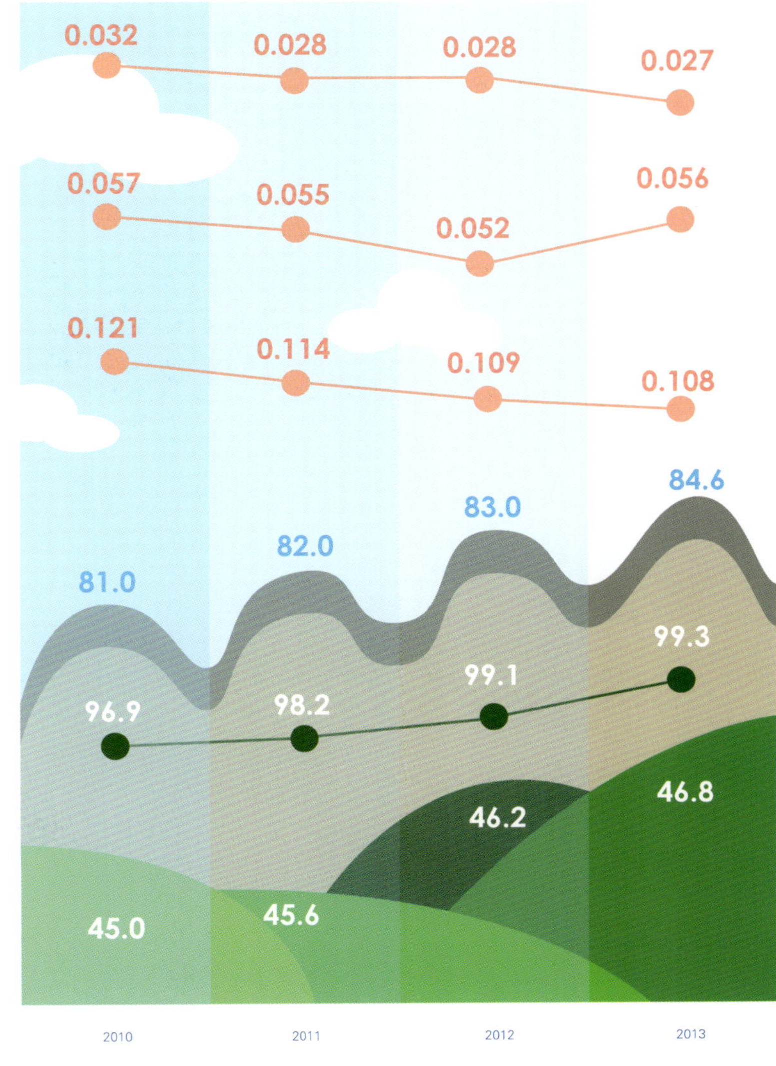

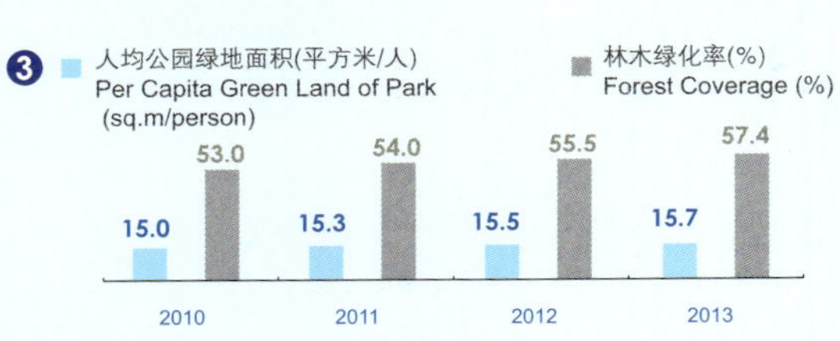

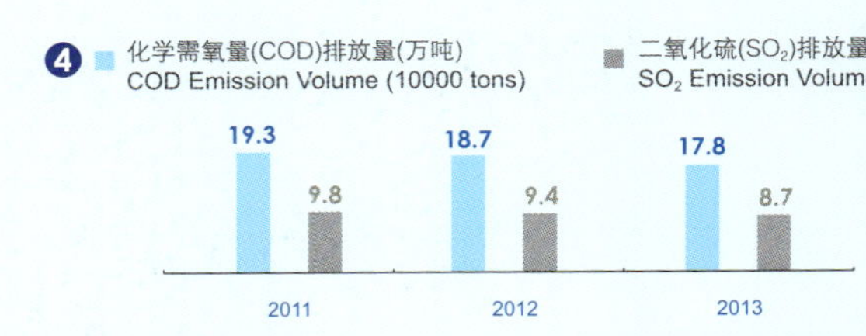

城乡居民收入平稳增长 相对差距缩小

Income of urban and rural residents maintained steady growth and relative income gap was narrowed

城乡居民人均收入稳步增长

Per capital income of urban and rural residents increased in a steady way

城镇居民人均可支配收入(元)
Per Capita Disposable Income of Urban Residents(yuan)

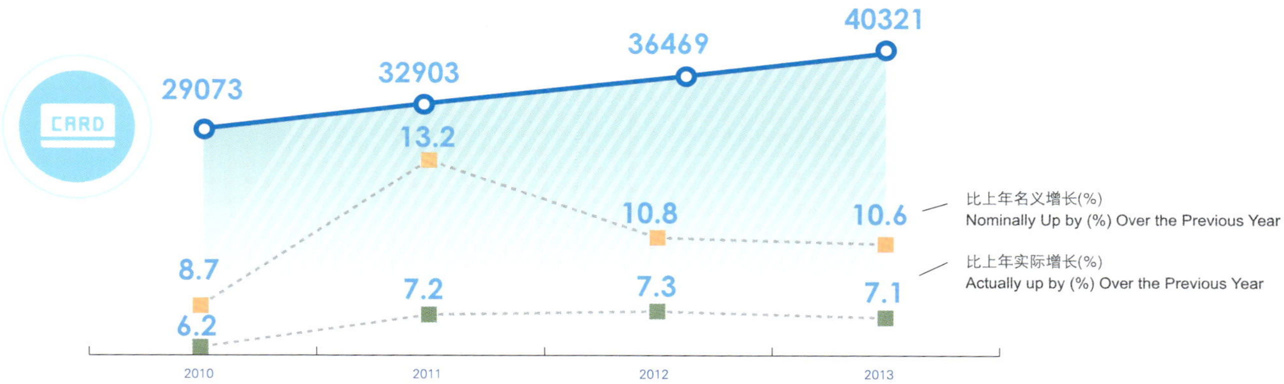

	2010	2011	2012	2013
城镇居民人均可支配收入(元)	29073	32903	36469	40321
比上年名义增长(%) Nominally Up by (%) Over the Previous Year	8.7	13.2	10.8	10.6
比上年实际增长(%) Actually up by (%) Over the Previous Year	6.2	7.2	7.3	7.1

农村居民人均纯收入(元)
Per Capita Net Income of Rural Residents (yuan)

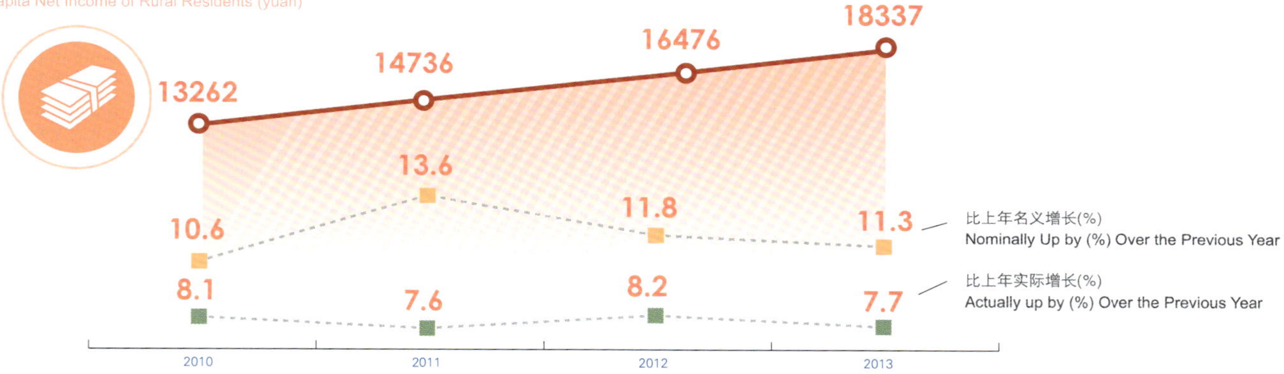

	2010	2011	2012	2013
农村居民人均纯收入(元)	13262	14736	16476	18337
比上年名义增长(%) Nominally Up by (%) Over the Previous Year	10.6	13.6	11.8	11.3
比上年实际增长(%) Actually up by (%) Over the Previous Year	8.1	7.6	8.2	7.7

城乡居民收入之比(以农村居民收入为1)
Income of urban residents to rural residents ratio (income of rural residents as 1)

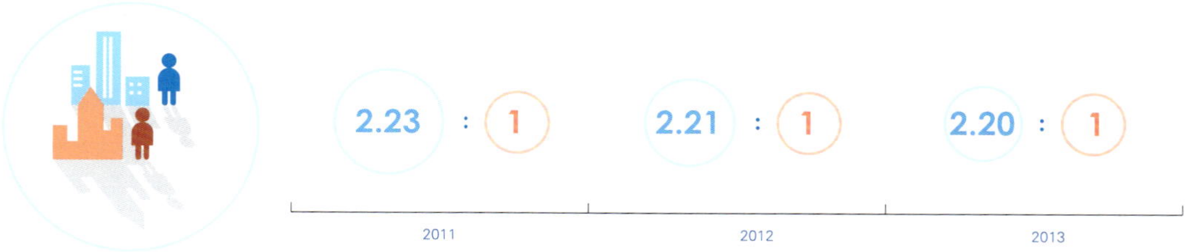

2011	2012	2013
2.23 : 1	2.21 : 1	2.20 : 1

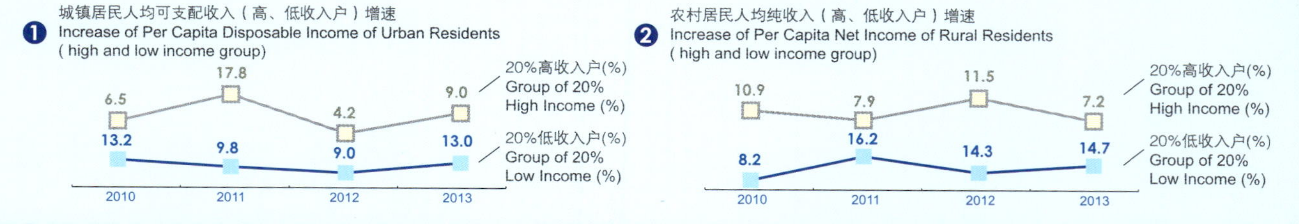

工资性收入占比稳定，转移性收入占比上升
Proportion of wage income remained stable, while the proportion of transfer income increased

城镇居民人均总收入构成
Composition of Per Capita Total Income of Urban Residents

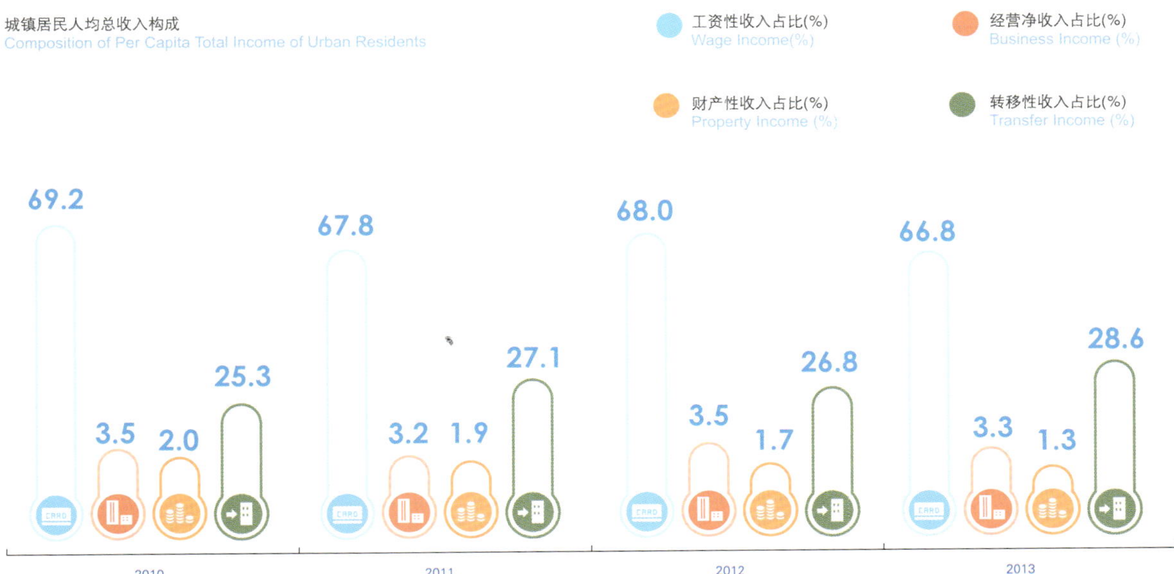

农村居民人均纯收入构成
Composition of Per Capita Net Income of Rural Residents

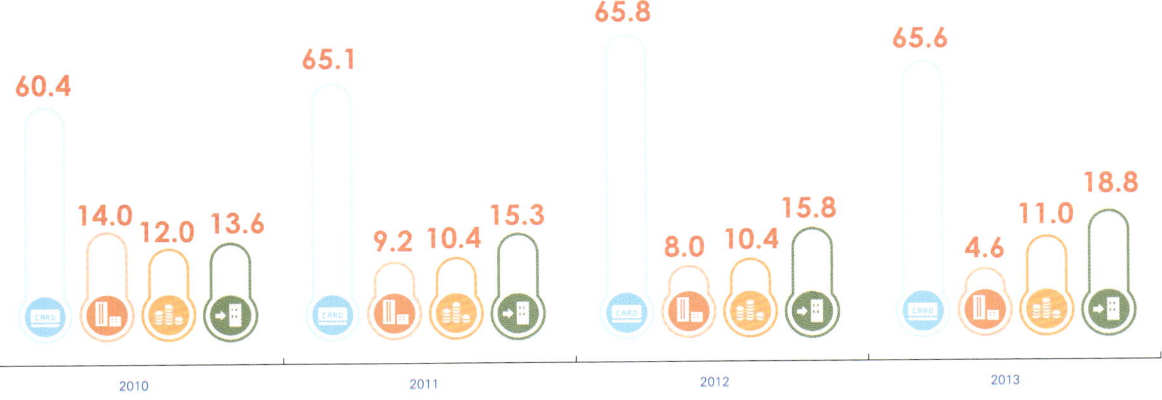

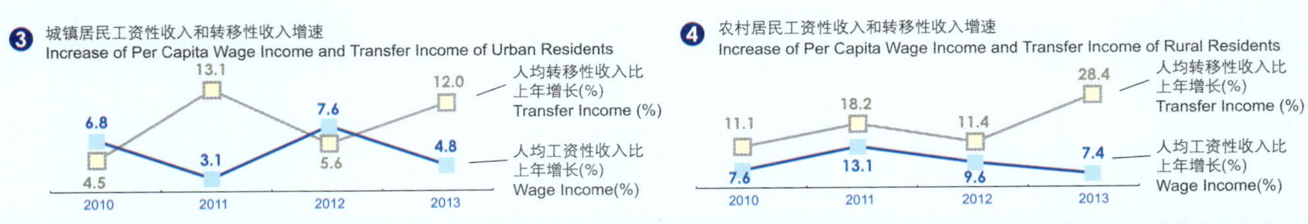

城乡居民消费结构继续升级

Consumption patterns of urban and rural residents went through notable upgrading

城乡居民服务性消费支出占比在三成左右
Proportion of service living expenditure of urban and rural residents was about 30%

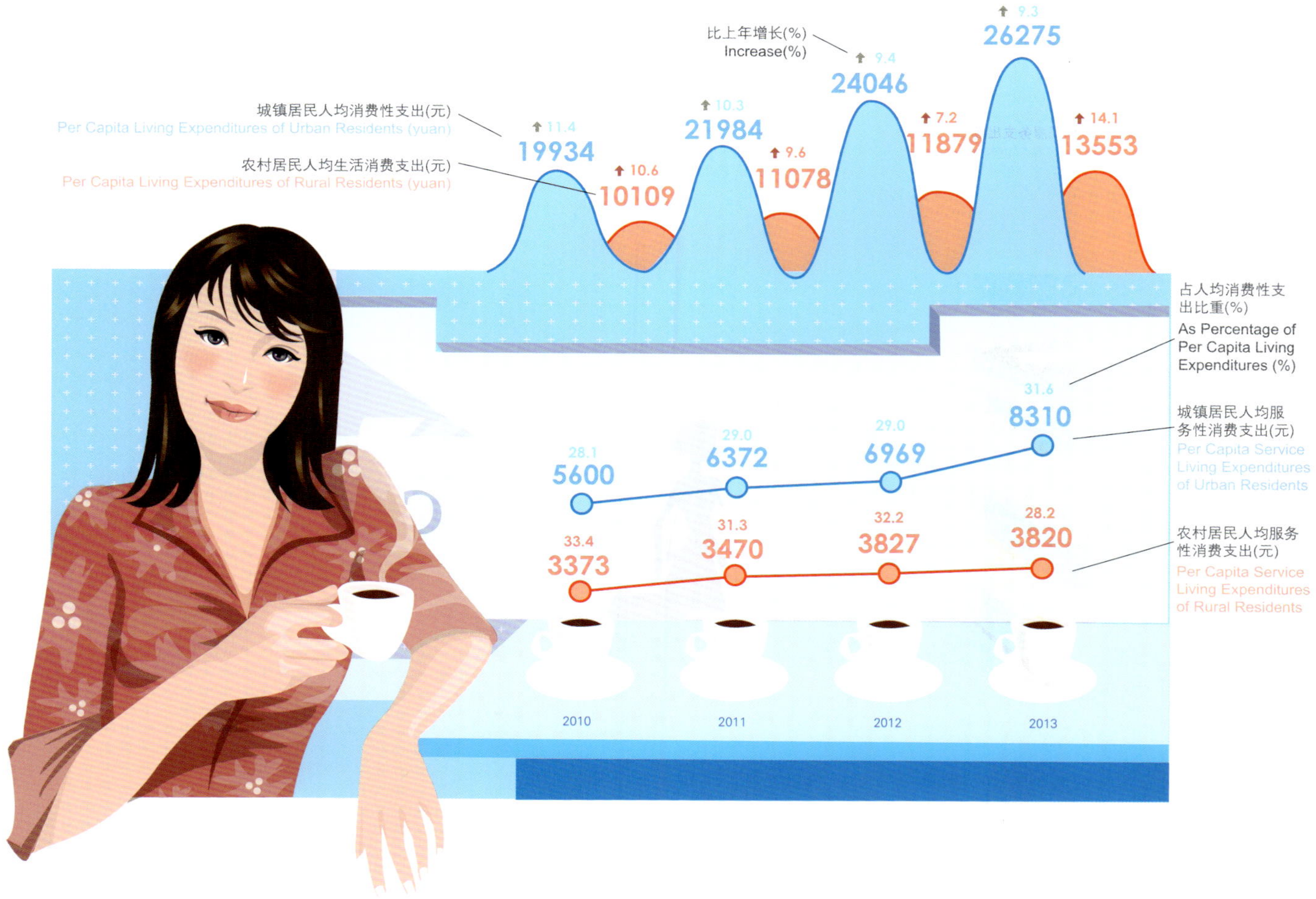

比上年增长(%)
Increase(%)
城镇居民人均消费性支出(元)
Per Capita Living Expenditures of Urban Residents (yuan)
农村居民人均生活消费支出(元)
Per Capita Living Expenditures of Rural Residents (yuan)
11.4
19934
10.6
10109
10.3
21984
9.6
11078
9.4
24046
7.2
11879
9.3
26275
14.1
13553
占人均消费性支出比重(%)
As Percentage of Per Capita Living Expenditures (%)
城镇居民人均服务性消费支出(元)
Per Capita Service Living Expenditures of Urban Residents
农村居民人均服务性消费支出(元)
Per Capita Service Living Expenditures of Rural Residents
28.1
5600
29.0
6372
29.0
6969
31.6
8310
33.4
3373
31.3
3470
32.2
3827
28.2
3820
2010
2011
2012
2013

❶ 每百户城乡居民家庭拥有家用汽车(辆)
Number of Motor Vehicles Per 100 Urban and Rural Households (unit)

34
16
38
19
42
21
43
34
2010
2011
2012
2013

❷ 每百户城乡居民家庭拥有家用电脑(台)
Number of Computers Per 100 Urban and Rural Households (unit)

104
64
104
63
112
67
110
74
2010
2011
2012
2013

❸ 每百户城乡居民家庭拥有移动电话(部)
Number of Mobile Phones Per 100 Urban and Rural Households (unit)

221
224
215
231
226
235
225
221
2010
2011
2012
2013

城镇家庭 Urban Households
农村家庭 Rural Households

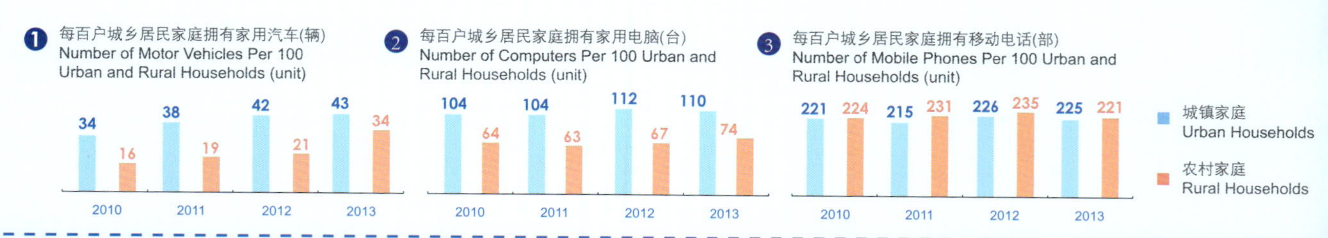

城乡居民文化娱乐服务支出比重稳步提升
Proportion of cultural and recreational expenditures grew steadily for urban and rural residents

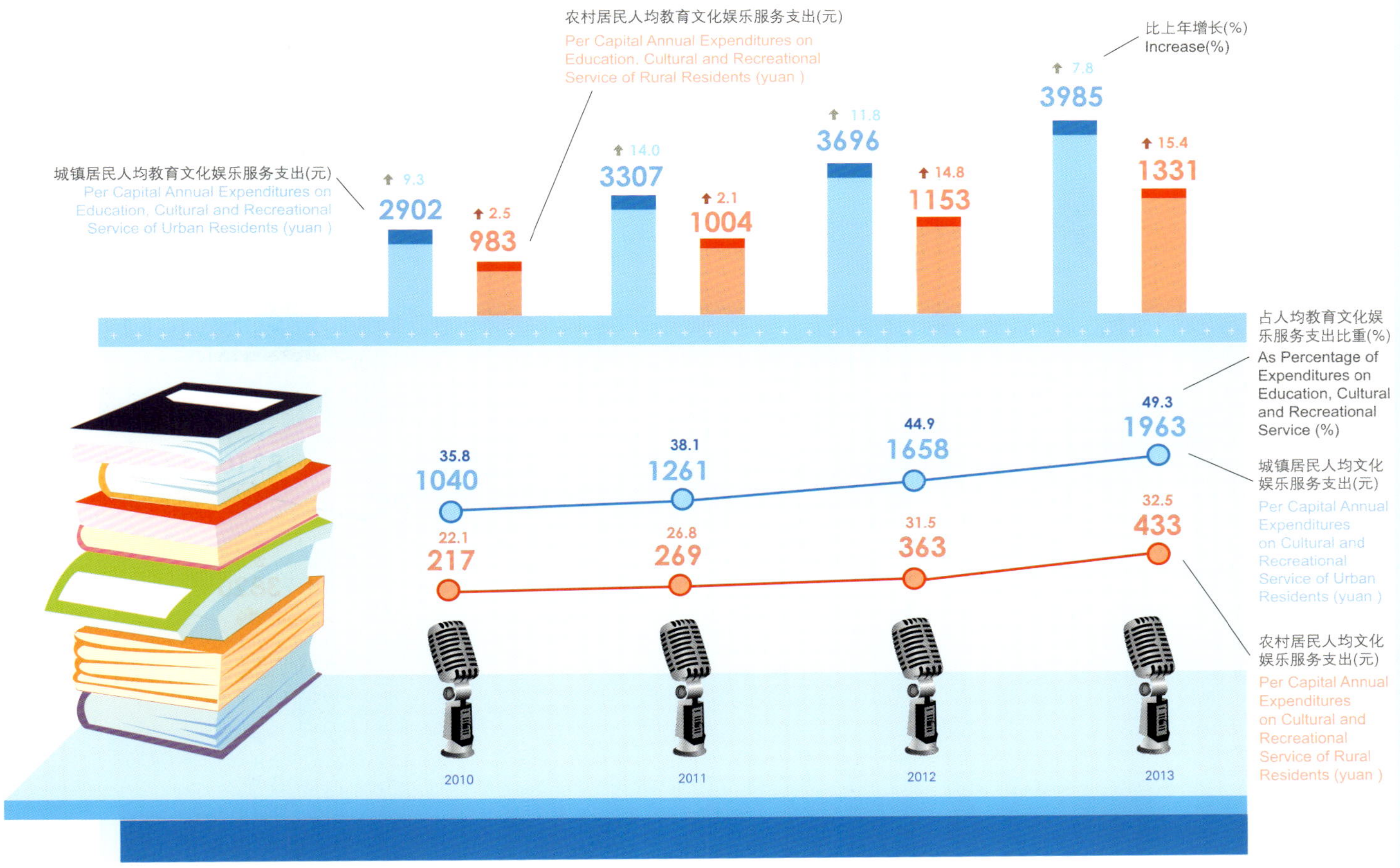

城镇居民人均教育文化娱乐服务支出(元)
Per Capital Annual Expenditures on Education, Cultural and Recreational Service of Urban Residents (yuan)

农村居民人均教育文化娱乐服务支出(元)
Per Capital Annual Expenditures on Education, Cultural and Recreational Service of Rural Residents (yuan)

比上年增长(%)
Increase(%)

	2010	2011	2012	2013
城镇居民人均教育文化娱乐服务支出(元)	2902	3307	3696	3985
比上年增长(%)	9.3	14.0	11.8	7.8
农村居民人均教育文化娱乐服务支出(元)	983	1004	1153	1331
比上年增长(%)	2.5	2.1	14.8	15.4

占人均教育文化娱乐服务支出比重(%)
As Percentage of Expenditures on Education, Cultural and Recreational Service (%)

城镇居民人均文化娱乐服务支出(元)
Per Capital Annual Expenditures on Cultural and Recreational Service of Urban Residents (yuan)

农村居民人均文化娱乐服务支出(元)
Per Capital Annual Expenditures on Cultural and Recreational Service of Rural Residents (yuan)

	2010	2011	2012	2013
城镇居民人均文化娱乐服务支出(元)	1040	1261	1658	1963
占比重(%)	35.8	38.1	44.9	49.3
农村居民人均文化娱乐服务支出(元)	217	269	363	433
占比重(%)	22.1	26.8	31.5	32.5

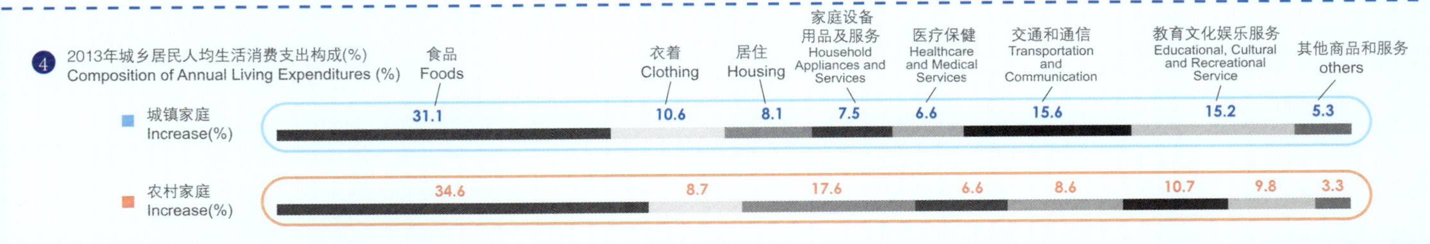

基本公共服务支出总体稳定 社会保障标准继续提高

Expenditures of basic public services were generally stable and standards of social security were further upgraded

基本公共服务支出占比近六成
Proportion of expenditures in basic public services was about 60%

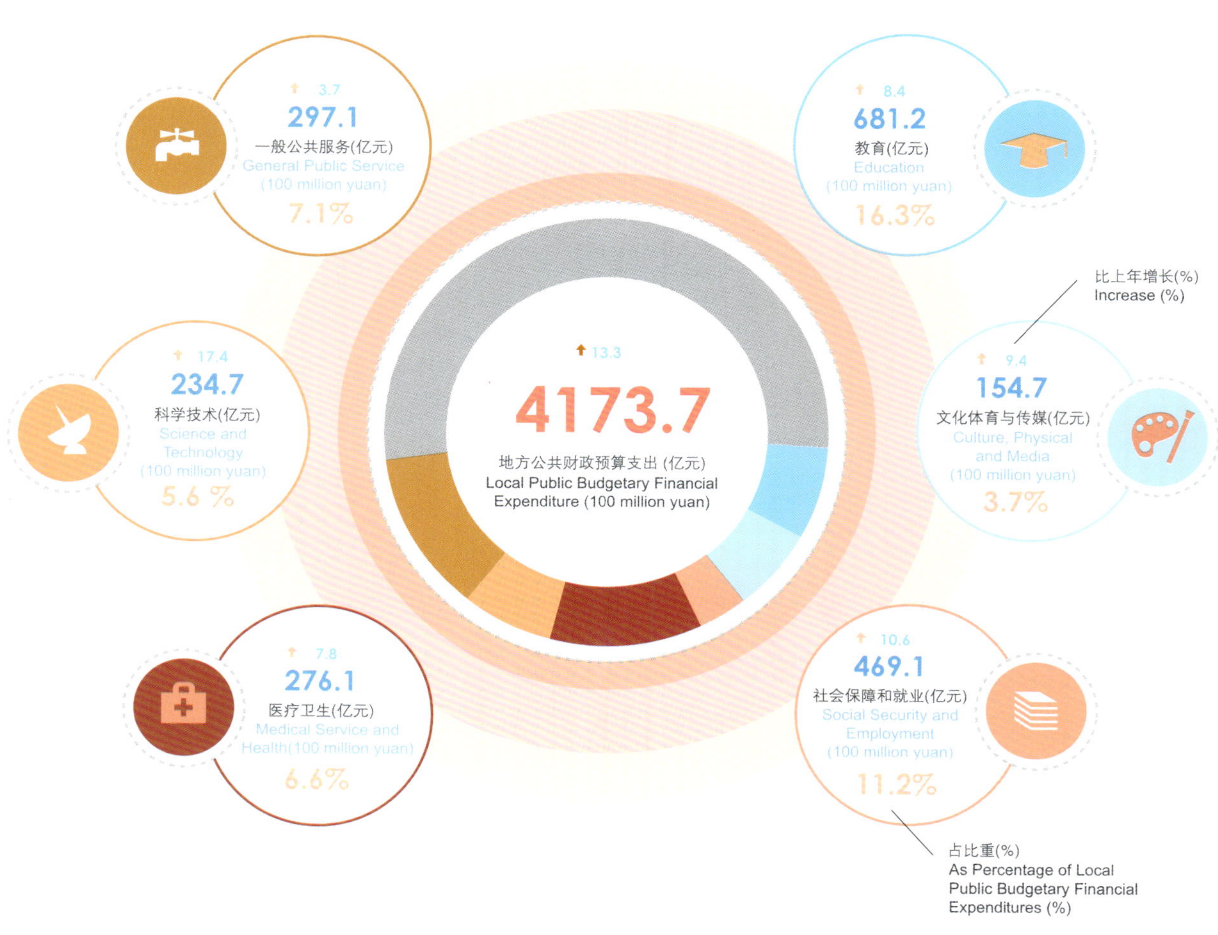

社会保障标准继续提高
Social Security Payment Increased Continuously

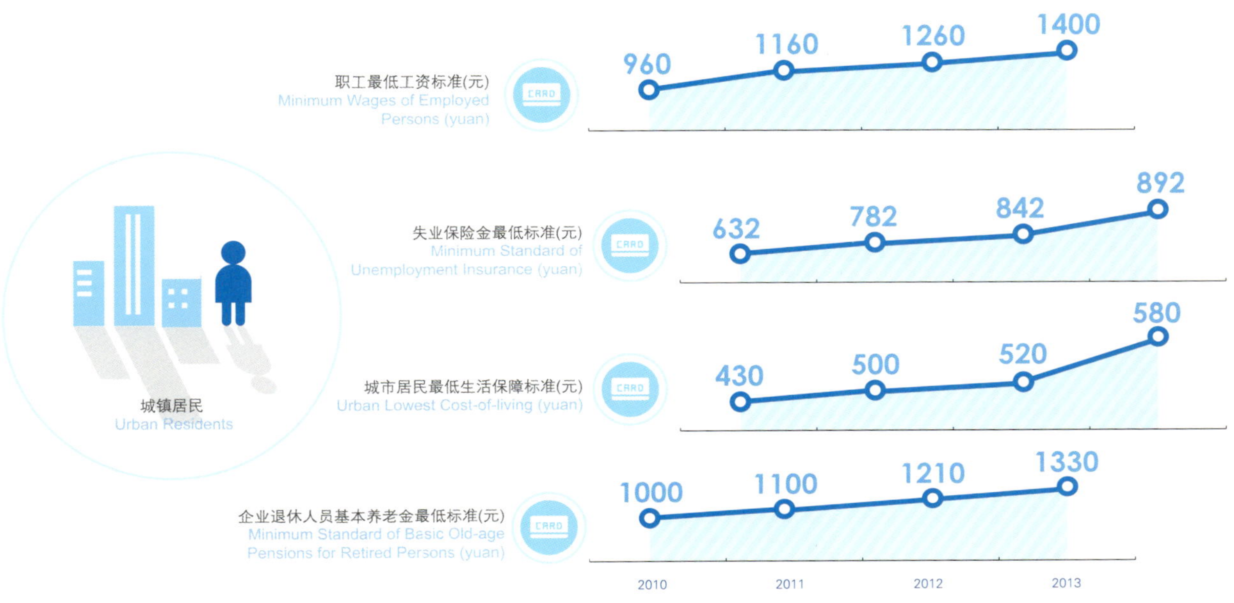

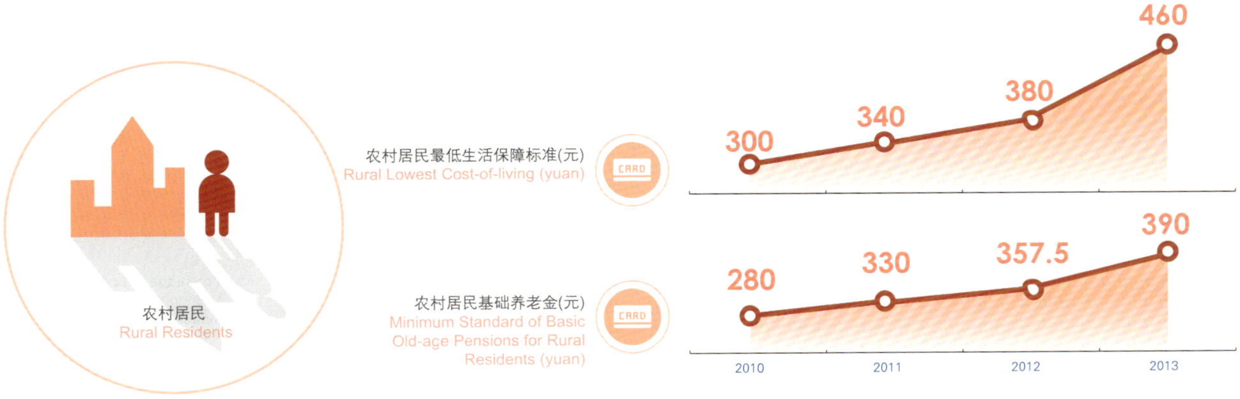

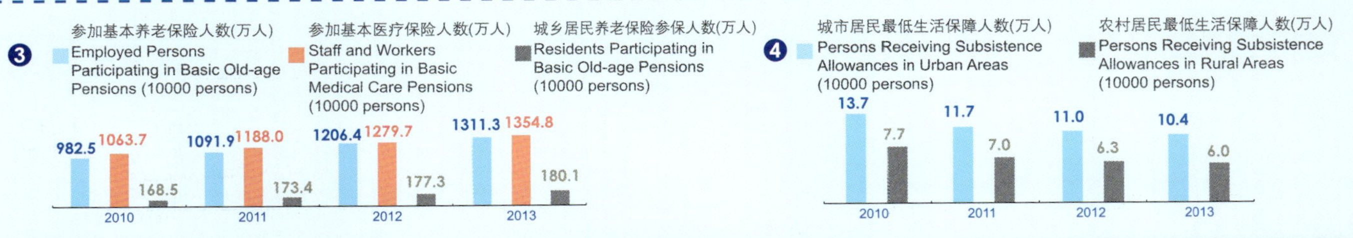

文化领域繁荣活跃

Prosperity and vitality prevailed in cultural sector

文化创意产业发展稳健
Cultural and creative industry developed soundly

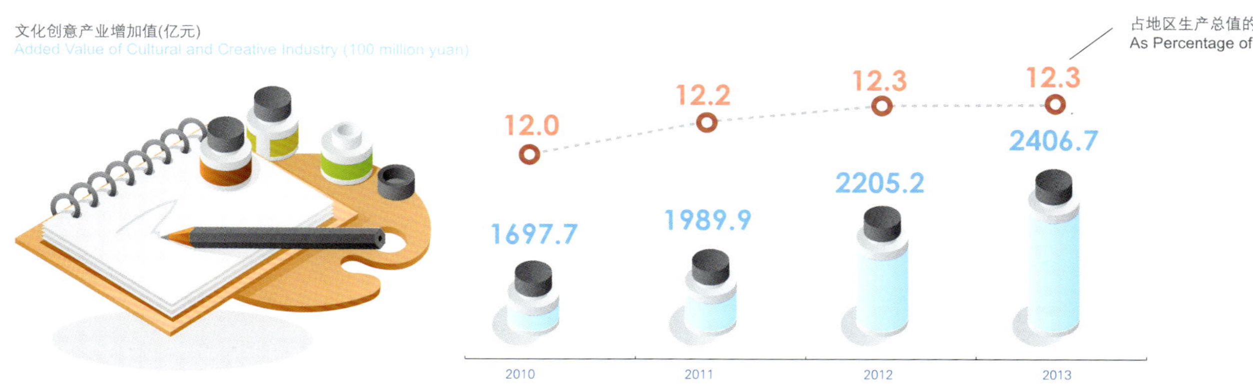

文化生活丰富多彩
Cultural life was rich and colorful

比上年增长(%)
Increase (%)

25
公共图书馆(个)
Public Libraries (unit)

↑ 25.2
325
书刊外借(万人次)
Person-times Borrowing Books, Magazines, and Documents (10000 person-times)

↑ 2.7
13016
演出场次(场)
Performance (times)

35
专业艺术剧团(个)
Professional Art Troupes (unit)

20
群众艺术馆、文化馆(个)
Mass Art Centers and Cultural Centers (unit)

↑ 23.9
4769
组织文艺活动(次)
Art Activities Organized (times)

↑ 8.4
4288.5
观影人次(万人)
Audience (10000 person-times)

820
电影院总银幕数(块)
Total Screens (unit)

↑ 14.9
137.8
放映场次(万场)
Show times (10000 times)

52
免费开放(所)
Museums Open for Free (unit)

167
博物馆(个)
Museums (unit)

3500
参观人次(万人次)
Visitors (10000 person-times)

《北京统计年鉴—2014》

编辑委员会及编辑工作人员

使用指南

《北京统计年鉴》是一部按年连续出版的大型统计资料。本年鉴通过大量的统计数据，真实地记录了北京市一年来经济社会发展变化情况，是国内外各界人士了解北京、认识北京的重要资料工具书。

一、关于框架结构

（一）总体结构

《北京统计年鉴》整体框架基本保持稳定，一般包括两部分：文章选编和统计表。

文章选编：主要登载各种大型普查或专项调查公报，例如，人口普查、经济普查、农业普查，以及 R&D 资源清查公报等。

统计表：包括 24 个章节，分别为综合，国民经济核算，人口与就业，能源、资源和环境，全社会固定资产投资和房地产开发，财政与税收，价格指数，人民生活，城市公用事业，农业及农村经济，工业，建筑业，交通运输邮电，批发和零售业、住宿和餐饮业，对外经济贸易，旅游业，金融和保险，教育、文化，科技，卫生、体育，社会福利、社区、政法及其他，第三产业，企业景气指数、消费者信心指数，开发区等 24 章。从多行业、多领域反映全市经济和社会发展情况。

（二）章节结构

章节设置：主要是参照统计制度，排列顺序具有一定的内在逻辑，大体为先综合指标、后分行业或分领域；先经济领域、后社会领域。

章节内结构：每一章节由《简要说明》、《统计表》和《主要统计指标解释》三部分组成。《简要说明》在每一章节首页，主要介绍该章节的主要内容、资料来源、统计范围、指标口径和历史数据调整方法；《主要统计指标解释》在每章节页尾，主要对本章节内所涉及的主要指标、计算方法等做简要解释；《统计表》是各章节的核心内容。

统计表排列：每一章节注重从反映该领域主要情况出发，编排统计表内容。统计表的排列顺序一般先是主要指标历史数据表，后为当年数据表。

二、关于使用要领

（一）年份

按照惯例，书名中标注的年份为出版年份，年鉴中统计表内所表示的最新数据则为上一年数据。例如，书名为《北京统计年鉴 2014》表示此本年鉴为 2014 年出版，年鉴中最新数据年份截至 2013 年。

统计表名中的“年份”大致会有三种标识方法，分别代表三种含义。一是统计表名为“****** （1978-2013 年）”字样（其中，“******”代表该统计表反映的内容，下同），表示表内所列数据是从 1978 年到 2013 年；二是统计表名中未显示年份，表示表内所列数据为当年和上年两年数据；三是统计表名为“******（2013 年）”，表示表内所列数据为 2013 年的数据。

（二）符号

统计表中常见符号如下：

：代表表中的总量指标与分组指标呈依次缩进的格式。其中，有“#”号的分组指标表示其为总量指标的一部分；无“#”号的分组指标则反映全部分组指标数据之和为总指标数据。

‖ ：宾栏中的“‖”为分组符号，代表某个指标存在几种分组数据。

…：表示该数据不足该表最小计量单位数。

空格：表示该项指标数据不详或没有数据。

*** ：表示为使个别单位的数据得以保密，该数据不予公布。

（三）文字说明

文字说明包括《使用指南》、《目录》、《简要说明》和表下注解等。《使用指南》在《目录》之前，是对年鉴整体框架进行介绍，对主要调整内容进行说明；《简要说明》在每一章节首页，主要介绍该章节的主要内容、资料来源、统计范围、指标口径和历史数据调整方法等；统计表下的注释则是对部分统计指标口径、方法、范围等内容的说明。

（四）数据

一般情况下，每一章节的前几张表均为该专业或该领域核心指标的历史数据。历史数据如果按年份连续反映在一张表内的，一般是可以连续使用的，但也需要留意表下的注释，以便对指标内涵有更详尽的了解；如果历史数据分成若干张表显示，则表示相关指标统计有过重大调整，需要分段反映。

此外，最新出版的年鉴上发布的部分历史数据会与以往年鉴上的数据有调整，存在差异，因此，在查询和使用历史数据时应以最新出版的年鉴为准。

（五）电子光盘

《北京统计年鉴》配有电子光盘，包括中文版和英文版两种语言的版本，辅助用户对数据进行加工处理。

（六）本年鉴中部分数据合计数或相对数由于计量单位取舍不同而产生的计算误差，均未作机械调整。

三、关于 2014 年版《北京统计年鉴》说明

与 2013 年版《北京统计年鉴》相比较，本年鉴在内容上主要做了如下修订:

1．关于行业划分标准。本年鉴中，除国民经济核算和部门资料仍执行 2002 年《国民经济行业分类标准》（GB/T 4754-2002）外，其他涉及行业分组的数据均执行 2011 年《国民经济行业分类标准》（GB/T 4754-2011）。

2．关于 2013 年数据。一是由于第三次全国经济普查数据尚未对外公布，本年鉴中“国民经济核算”章节登载的 2013 年数据为初步核算结果；收入法地区生产总值和新产业增加值的最新数据截止时间仍为 2012 年；在“能源资源环境”章节中，2013 年能源消费总量为初步核算结果，登载的有关能源平衡表的最新数据截止时间仍为 2012 年。二是由于有些部门 2013 年的数据尚未发布，所以本年鉴中登载的最新数据截止时间仍为 2012 年。

3．优化调整统计表。一是为了方便用户使用年鉴，调整原“商品交易市场基本情况”和“商品交易市场成交额”表，形成新的“商品交易市场基本情况”、“商品交易市场经营情况”和“亿元及以上商品交易市场基本情况”表；调整原“北京市金融机构（含外资）存贷款余额”和 “北京市中资金融机构存贷款余额”表，形成新的“北京市金融机构(含外资)存贷款余额”表。二是根据需求情况取消原“按登记注册类型分限额以上批发和零售企业商品零售额”和“商品交易市场主要商品成交量”表。

4．增加或补充有关内容。根据新需求，增加《规模以上高技术制造业主要科技指标》表和《耕地面积》的历史数据表。增加反映商品交易市场情况的摊位数、成交额，餐余垃圾处理量，再生水利用量，人工造林面积，平原造林面积等指标。

5．继续加强规范统一。包括对简要说明、统计表格式、统计分组的规范，以及英文翻译一致性和准确性的统一规范。

USER GUIDE

Beijing Statistical Yearbook is a large statistical book published continuously on a chronological basis. With a great deal of statistical data, this Yearbook gives a true reflection of the social and economic development and changes in Beijing over the past year. It serves as an important reference book for domestic and foreign personnel in all circles to understand and know Beijing.

I. Overall Framework

(I) Overall Structure

The overall structure of Beijing Statistical Yearbook remains basically stable. Generally, it consists of two parts: article selections and statistical tables.

Article Selections: mainly include various large censuses and special investigation communiques, such as population census, economic census, agricultural census, as well as R&D resource check communique, etc.

Statistical Tables: include 24 chapters, i.e. General Survey; National Accounts; Population and Employment; Energy, Resources and Environmental Protection; Total Investment in Fixed Assets and Real Estate Development; Government Finance and Tax Revenues; Price Index; People's Livelihood; Public Utilities; Agriculture and Rural Economy; Industry; Construction; Transport, Post and Telecommunication Service; Wholesale and Retail Trade, Accomodation and Restaurants; Foreign Trade; Tourism; Finance and Insurance; Education and Culture; Science and Technology; Health and Sports; Social Welfare, Community, Law and Others; Tertiary Industry; Enterprise Prosperity Index and Consumer Confidence Index; and Development Zones, 24 chapters in total, reflecting the economic and social development situation across the city through multiple industries and fields.

(II) Structure of Chapters

Setting of chapters: The chapters are set in keeping with the statistical system, with certain inherent logic. Generally speaking, general indicators come first, followed by indicators in specific industries and fileds. economic indicators cone before social indicators.

Internal structure of chapters: Each chapter is composed of the Brief Introduction, Statistical Tables and Explanatory Notes to Main Statistical Indicators. Brief Introduction appears on the first page of each chapter, mainly introducing the main content, source of data, statistical scope, indicator standards, method of adjustment to historical data in each chapter; Explanatory Notes to Main Statistical Indicators come on the last page of each chapter, mainly giving a brief explanation to the calculation method of main indicators involved in the chapter; Statistical Tables are the core content of each chapter.

Arrangement of statistical tables: In each chapter, statistical tables are arranged for the purpose of reflecting the main conditions in the field. Generally speaking, historical statistical tables come before current year statistical tables.

II. How to Use

(I) Years

Conventionally, the year indicated in the book is the year of publication The latest data indicated in the statistical tables in the yearbook are data in the previous years. For example, this book is titled 2014 Bejing Statistical Yearbook, which means it will be published in 2014 while the lastest data in the book is from the end of 2013.

"Years" in the statistical tables are marked in three ways, each indicating a different meaning. Firstly, the statistical table is named "******(1978-2013)" (of which, "******" represents the content reflected in the statistical table, the same below), indicating that the data listed in the table are those from 1978 to 2013; Secondly, the statistical table contains no years, indicating that the data listed in the table are those of the current year and the previous year; Thirdly, the statistical table is named "****** (2013)", indicating that the data listed in the table are those of 2013.

(II) Symbols

Symbols in statistical tables include:

#: means that the aggretate indicator and grouped indicators are indented. Grouped indicators marked with # are part of the aggregate indicator, while grouped indicators not marked with # indicate that the aggregate indicator is the sum of all group indicators.

||: means that there are multiple ways of grouping the indicators.

…: means that the figure is less than the minimum measurement unit of the table.

Blank: mean that the figure is unknown or unavailable.

***: means that the figure is not disclosed for secrecy reasons.

(III) Explanations

Explanations include User Guide, Table of Contents, Brief Introduction, and notes under the tables. User Guide appears before the Table of Contents, giving an introduction to the overall framework of the yearbook, and explaining the main adjustments; Brief Introduction appears on the first page of each chapter, giving an introduction to the chapter's main content, source of data, statistical scope, standards of indicators, adjustment method of historical data, etc; Notes under the tables make an explanation on stadard of some indicators, method, scope, etc.

(IV) Data

In general cases, the first tables in each chapter contain historical data of core indicators in the area or field. Generally speaking, historical data that are shown in one table continuously by year can be used continuously. But it is also necessary to refer to the notes under the table in order to have a full understanding of the connation of indicators; historical data that are shown in several tables indicate that there were major adjustments to relevant indicators, and they need to be reflected by sections.

In addition, some of the historical data in the latest yearbook may have been adjusted over data in previous yearbooks. Therefore, please refer to the latest yearbook when enquiring or using historical data.

(V) Electronic CD-ROM

Beijing Statistical Yearbook is provided with a CD-ROM, which containes Chinese and English versions of the yearbook. The CD-ROM helps users in working with and processing the data.

(VI) The sum of some statistics or some relative numbers in this yearbook might have certain calculation errors because of the choice of different units of measurement. All the statistics have not undergone mechanical adjustment.

III. About Beijing Statistical Yearbook 2014

Compared with Beijing Statistical Yearbook 2013, the following revisions have been made:

1. Classification of Sectors. In this year book, Apart from data for national economic accounting and several sectors that still follow the *Standand for Classification of National Economic Sectors 2002 (GB/T 4754-2002)*, other data involving industrial classification are all calculated according to *Standard for Classification of National Economic Sectors 2011 (GB/T 4754-2011)*.

2. The Statistics in 2013. Firstly, the statistics for the Third National Economic Census have not been officially released yet, so the data for 2013 in the chapter National Economic Accounting are prelinimary data; latest data for GDP and added value of Beijing by income approach was gathered in 2012; in the chapter Energy, Resources and Environment, the total energy consumption is preliminary data and the latest data of energy balance dates back to 2012. Secondly, some sectors still haven't released data for 2013. Therefore, the latest data of those sectors comes from 2012.

3. Optimization of Statistical Table. Firstly, to help readers better use the yearbook, the original tables of commodity transaction markets and volume of business for commodity transaction markets have been changed into commodity transactoin markets, tables of operation of commodity transactoin markets and statistics for commodity transactoin markets above 1 billion yuan; the tables of deposit and loan balance of financial institutions (including foreign banks) and deposit and loan balance of domestically-funded financial institutions have been integrated into a new table of deposit and loan balance of financial institutions (including foreign banks). Secondly, the tables of volume of retail sales for wholesale and retail enterprises above designated size by type of registration and trading volume of major commodities in commodity transaction markets are cancelled according to demands.

4. Addtion of relevant contents. According to new requests, the tables of historical statistics for major science and techonology indicators of high-tech manufacuring above designated size and arable land area are added in this yearbook. Indicators reflecting the situation of commodity transaction markets, such as number of booths, trading volume, volume of kitchen waste, volume of recycled water used, artificial afforestation area and affroestation area on the plain are added.

5. Enhancement of unification and improvement of standard includes unified regulations on brief introduction, format of statistical tables, standards of statistical grouping and consistency of English translation

目 录
Contents

一、综合
GENERAL SURVEY

二、国民经济核算
NATIONAL ACCOUNTS

三、人口与就业
POPULATION AND EMPLOYMENT

四、能源、资源和环境

ENERGY, RESOURCES AND ENVIRONMENT

五、全社会固定资产投资和房地产开发
TOTAL INVESTMENT IN FIXED ASSETS AND REAL ESTATE DEVELOPMENT

六、财政与税收
GOVERNMENT FINANCE AND REVENUES

七、价格指数
PRICE INDEX

八、人民生活
PEOPLE'S LIVELIHOOD

九、城市公用事业
PUBLIC UTILITIES

十、农业及农村经济
AGRICULTURE AND RURAL ECONOMY

十一、工业
INDUSTRY

十二、建筑业
CONSTRUCTION

十三、交通运输邮电
TRANSPORT, POST AND TELECOMMUNICATION SERVICES

十四、批发和零售业、住宿和餐饮业
WHOLESALE AND RETAIL TRADE, ACCOMMODATION AND RESTAURANTS

十五、对外经济贸易
FOREIGN ECONOMY AND TRADE

十六、旅游业
TOURISM

十七、金融和保险
FINANCE AND INSURANCE

十八、教育、文化
EDUCATION AND CULTURE

十九、科技
SCIENCE AND TECHNOLOGY

二十、卫生、体育
HEALTH AND SPORTS

二十一、社会福利、社区、政法及其他
SOCIAL WELFARE, COMMUNITY, LAW AND OTHERS

二十二、第三产业
TERTIARY INDUSTRY

二十三、企业景气指数、消费者信心指数
ENTERPRISE PROSPERITY INDEX AND CONSUMER CONFIDENCE INDEX

二十四、开发区
DEVELOPMENT ZONES

综 合
GENERAL SURVEY

简要说明

一、本章资料的主要内容

本章主要包括北京市行政区划、法人及产业活动单位数、私营个体、非公经济、中小微型企业基本情况、全市社会经济发展的主要指标以及“十二五”时期监测指标等。

二、本章资料的数据来源

北京市行政区划情况来自北京市民政局；全市法人及产业活动单位情况来自北京市统计局；全市私营个体经济基本情况来自北京市工商行政管理局、北京市地方税务局、北京市国家税务局；非公经济数据和中小微型企业数据来自北京市统计局、国家统计局北京调查总队；全市社会经济主要指标及“十二五”时期主要监测指标资料由北京市统计局及国家统计局北京调查总队根据相关资料整理取得。

三、有关统计标准的变化说明

（一）《国民经济行业分类与代码》（GB/T 4754-2002版）与原（GB/T 4754-1994版）的主要框架结构变化：

增加的门类：a).信息传输、计算机服务和软件业 b).租赁和商务服务业 c).住宿和餐饮业 d).水利、环境和公共设施管理业 e).教育 f).国际组织

名称或范围进行调整的门类：a).农、林、牧、渔业 b).采矿业 c).制造业 d).交通运输、仓储和邮政业 e).批发和零售业 f).金融业 g).科学研究、技术服务和地质勘查业 h).居民服务和其他服务业 i).卫生、社会保障和社会福利业 j).文化、体育和娱乐业 k).公共管理和社会组织

取消的门类：a).地质勘查、水利管理 b).其它行业

（二）《国民经济行业分类》（GB/T 4754-2011版）与原（GB/T 4754-2002版）的主要框架结构变化：

门类名称调整：(1)“电力、燃气及水的生产和供应业”更名为“电力、热力、燃气及水生产和供应业”；(2)“信息传输、计算机服务和软件业”更名为“信息传输、软件和信息技术服务业”；(3)“科学研究、技术服务和地质勘查业”更名为“科学研究和技术服务业”；(4)“居民服务和其他服务业”更名为“居民服务、修理和其他服务业”；(5)“卫生、社会保障和社会福利业”更名为“卫生和社会工作”；(6)“公共管理和社会组织”更名为“公共管理、社会保障和社会组织”。

门类位次调整：(1)“批发和零售业”调至“建筑业”后面；(2)“住宿和餐饮业”调至“交通运输、仓储和邮政业”后面。

门类范围调整：A农、林、牧、渔业；C制造业；G交通运输、仓储和邮政业；I信息传输、软件和信息技术服务业；J金融业；L租赁和商务服务业；M科学研究和技术服务业；O居民服务、修理和其他服务业；P教育；Q卫生和社会工作；R文化、体育和娱乐业；S公共管理、社会保障和社会组织。

Brief Introduction

I. Main Content

Statistics in this chapter mainly show the basic information of administrative divisions of Beijing, number of corporate and industrial entities, non-public economy, small-, medium and micro-sized enterprises, main indicators for social and economic development of the city, and monitoring indicators for the 12th Five-Year Plan, etc.

II. Source of Statistics

Statistics on administrative divisions of Beijing are from Beijing Municipal Bureau of Civil Affairs. Statistics on municipal corporate and industrial entities are from Beijing Municipal Bureau of Statistics. Statistics on private and self-employment economy in the city are from Beijing Administration for Industry and Commerce, Beijing Municipal Bureau of Local Tax and Beijing Municipal Bureau of State Tax. Statistics on non-public economy, small-, medium and micro-sized enterprises are from National Bureau of Statistics Survey Office in Beijing and Beijing Municipal Bureau of Statistics. Statistics on social and economic indicators and main monitoring indicators for the 12th Five-Year Plan of the city are sorted out by Beijing Municipal Bureau of Statistics and National Bureau of Statistics Survey Office in Beijing on the basis of relevant statistics.

III. Adjustment to Historical Statistics According to New Industrial Standards

(I) Changes to the main framework of the Classification and Codes of Sectors in National Economy Version (GB/T 4754-2002) as compared with the previous Version (GB/T 4754-1994):

Sectors added: a). information transmission, computer service and software, b). renting and leasing activities and business services, c). accommodation and restaurants, d). management of water conservancy, environment and public facilities, e). education, f). international organizations.

Sectors with name or range changed: a).farming, forestry, animal husbandry and fishery, b). mining, c). manufacturing, d). transport, storage and post, e). wholesale and retail trade, f). finance, g). scientific research, technical service, geological prospecting, h). resident service and other service, i). health, social security, and social welfare, j). culture, sports and recreation, k). public administration and social organizations.

Sectors cancelled: a). geological prospecting, water conservancy management, b). other sectors.

（II）Compared with the previous (GB/T 4754-2002) version, the Industrial Classification for National Economic Activities (GB/T 4754-2011) mainly involves the following framework changes:

Changes to the name of category: (1) The "electric power, gas and water production and supply" is renamed "electric power, heating power, gas and water production and supply"; (2) the "information transmission, computer service and software" is renamed "information transmission, software and information technology services"; (3) the "scientific research, technical service and geological prospecting" is renamed "scientific research and development technical services"; (4) the "resident service and other service" is renamed "resident services, repair and other services"; (5) the "health, social security and social welfare" is renamed "health care and social works"; (6) "public administration and social organization" is renamed "public administration, social security and social organizations".

Changes to the place of category: (1) the "wholesale and retail trade" is put after the "construction"; (2) the "accommodation and restaurants" is put after the "transport, storage and post".

Changes to the scope of category: A. Agriculture, Forestry, Animal production and Hunting, Fishing; C. Manufacturing; G. Transport, Storage and Post; I. Information Transmission, Software and Information Technology Services; J. Finance; L. Renting and Leasing Activities and Business Services; M. Scientific Research and Development Technical Service; O. Resident Services, Repair and Other Services; P. Education; Q. Health care and Social Works; R. Culture, Sports and Entertainment; S. Public Administration, Social Security and Social Organizations.

1-1 行政区划(2013年)
ADMINISTRATIVE DIVISIONS (2013)

单位：个 (unit)

地 区	District	街道办事处 Sub-district	建制镇 Designated Town	建制乡 Designated Township	社区居委会 Community Neighborhood Committee	村民委员会 Villagers' Committee
全 市	**Total**	**143**	**144**	**38**	**2859**	**3938**
首都功能核心区	**Core Functional Area of the Capital**	**32**			**442**	
东 城 区	Dongcheng District	17			187	
西 城 区	Xicheng District	15			255	
城市功能拓展区	**Urban Function Extension Area**	**70**	**9**	**22**	**1401**	**303**
朝 阳 区	Chaoyang District	23		19	388	154
丰 台 区	Fengtai District	16	2	3	297	65
石景山区	Shijingshan District	9			146	
海 淀 区	Haidian District	22	7		570	84
城市发展新区	**New Area of Urban Development**	**28**	**72**	**7**	**698**	**2190**
房 山 区	Fangshan District	8	14	6	124	459
通 州 区	Tongzhou District	4	10	1	110	475
顺 义 区	Shunyi District	6	19		95	426
昌 平 区	Changping District	5	15		192	303
大 兴 区	Daxing District	5	14		177	527
生态涵养发展区	**Ecological Conservation Area**	**13**	**63**	**9**	**318**	**1445**
门头沟区	Mentougou District	4	9		119	178
怀 柔 区	Huairou District	2	12	2	32	284
平 谷 区	Pinggu District	2	14	2	29	273
密 云 县	Miyun County	2	17	1	92	334
延 庆 县	Yanqing County	3	11	4	46	376

资料来源：北京市民政局。
Source: Beijing Municipal Bureau of Civil Affairs

1-2 规模(限额)以上法人单位基本情况(2013年)
NUMBER OF LEGAL ENTITIES AND ABOVE DESIGNATED SIZE (2013)

单位：个 (unit)

项 目	Item	法人单位数合计 Total Number of Legal Entities	单产业法人 Single-industry Legal Entities	多产业法人 Multi-industry Legal Entities
合 计	**Total**	**43976**	**37153**	**6823**
按登记注册类型分	**By Registration Type**			
内 资	Domestically-invested Enterprises	39603	33873	5730
国 有	State-owned Enterprises	6666	5817	849
集 体	Collectively-owned Enterprises	756	661	95
股份合作	Joint-equity Cooperative Enterprises	525	449	76
联 营	Associated Enterprises	44	38	6
有限责任公司	Limited Liability Companies	14242	11877	2365
股份有限公司	Companies Limited by Shares	1178	851	327
私 营	Private Enterprises	15788	13806	1982
其 他	Others	404	374	30
港澳台商投资	Hong Kong, Macao and Taiwan-invested Enterprises	1623	1231	392
与港澳台商合资经营	Joint Ventures	532	421	111
与港澳台商合作经营	Cooperative Enterprises	131	115	16
港澳台商独资	Solely-funded Enterprises	927	678	249
港澳台商投资股份有限公司	Companies Limited by Shares	33	17	16
其他港澳台商投资	Others			
外商投资	Foreign-invested Enterprises	2750	2049	701
中外合资经营	Joint Ventures	809	640	169
中外合作经营	Cooperative Enterprises	115	96	19
外资企业	Solely-funded Enterprises	1782	1286	496
外商投资股份有限公司	Companies Limited by Shares	42	27	15
其他外商投资	Others	2		2
按隶属关系分	**By Affiliation**			
中 央	Central	4687	3964	723
地 方	Local	39289	33189	6100
按机构类型分	**By Organization Type**			
企 业	Enterprises	38385	32124	6261
事业单位	Institutions	3603	3331	272
机 关	Government Agencies and Organizations	1152	937	215
社会团体	Social Organizations	282	221	61
其他机构	Others	554	540	14

注：本表为2013年年报规模(限额)以上法人单位数据。
Note: This table covers legal entities above designated size in the 2013 annual report.

1-3 国民经济各行业规模(限额)以上法人单位情况(2013年)
NUMBER OF LEGAL ENTITIES IN DIFFERENT SECTORS OF THE NATIONAL ECONOMY ABOVE DESIGNATED SIZE (2013)

单位：个 (unit)

行业	Sector	法人单位数合计 Total Number of Legal Entities	单产业法人 Single-industry Legal Entities	多产业法人 Multi-industry Legal Entities
合 计	**Total**	**43976**	**37153**	**6823**
农、林、牧、渔业	**Agriculture, Forestry, Animal Production and Hunting, Fishing**			
采矿业	**Mining and Quarrying**	**22**	**16**	**6**
煤炭开采和洗选业	Mining and Washing of Coal	4	2	2
石油和天然气开采业	Extraction of Petroleum and Natural Gas	2		2
黑色金属矿采选业	Mining of Ferrous Metal Ores	7	6	1
有色金属矿采选业	Mining of Non-Ferrous Metal Ores			
非金属矿采选业	Mining and Processing of Nonmetal Ores	4	4	
开采辅助活动	Mining Support Service Activities	5	4	1
其他采矿业	Mining of Other Ores			
制造业	**Manufacturing**	**3518**	**2975**	**543**
农副食品加工业	Processing of Food from Agricultural Products	140	116	24
食品制造业	Manufacture of Foods	121	100	21
酒、饮料和精制茶制造业	Manufacture of Wine, Beverage and Refined Tea	43	30	13
烟草制品业	Manufacture of Cigarettes and Tobacco	1		1
纺织业	Manufacture of Textile	36	33	3
纺织服装、服饰业	Manufacture of Textile, Wearing Apparel and Ornament	153	118	35
皮革、毛皮、羽毛及其制品和制鞋业	Manufacture of Leather, Fur, Feather and Its Products, and Footwear	18	17	1
木材加工和木、竹、藤、棕、草制品业	Processing of Timbers, Manufacture of Wood, Bamboo, Rattan, Palm and Straw Products	20	18	2
家具制造业	Manufacture of Furniture	66	57	9
造纸和纸制品业	Manufacture of Paper and Paper Products	41	38	3
印刷和记录媒介复制业	Printing, Reproduction of Recording Media	119	113	6
文教、工美、体育和娱乐用品制造业	Manufacture of Articles for Culture, Education, Artwork, Sport and Entertainment Activities	33	25	8
石油加工、炼焦和核燃料加工业	Processing of Petroleum, Coking, Processing of Nucleus Fuels	22	20	2
化学原料和化学制品制造业	Manufacture of Chemical Raw Materials and Chemical Products	217	192	25
医药制造业	Manufacture of Medicines	188	152	36
化学纤维制造业	Manufacture of Chemical Fibers	3	2	1
橡胶和塑料制品业	Manufacture of Rubber and Plastics Products	119	104	15
非金属矿物制品业	Manufacture of Non-metallic Mineral Products	252	217	35
黑色金属冶炼和压延加工业	Manufacture and Pressing of Ferrous Metals	32	30	2

注：1．本表为2013年年报规模(限额)以上法人单位数据。
2．本表行业划分执行2011年国民经济行业分类标准(GB/T 4754-2011)。

Note: a) This table covers legal entities above designated size in the 2013 annual report.
b) Sectors in this table are classified in accordance with the Standard for Classification of National Economic Sectors 2011 (GB/T 4754-2011).

1-3 续表 1 Continued 1

单位：个 (unit)

行业	Sector	法人单位数合计 Total Number of Legal Entities	单产业法人 Single-industry Legal Entities	多产业法人 Multi-industry Legal Entities
有色金属冶炼和压延加工业	Manufacture and Processing of Non-ferrous Metals	36	33	3
金属制品业	Manufacture of Fabricated Metal Products	226	195	31
通用设备制造业	Manufacture of General-Purpose Machinery	256	208	48
专用设备制造业	Manufacture of Special-Purpose Machinery	318	268	50
汽车制造业	Manufacture of Motor Vehicles	216	196	20
铁路、船舶、航空航天和其他运输设备制造业	Manufacture of Railway Locomotives, Building of Ships and Boats, Manufacture of Air and Spacecrafts and Other Transportation Equipment	64	55	9
电气机械和器材制造业	Manufacture of Electrical Machinery and Equipment	260	226	34
计算机、通信和其他电子设备制造业	Manufacture of Computers, Communication Equipment and Other Electronic Equipment	296	239	57
仪器仪表制造业	Manufacture of Measuring Instrument and Meter	170	130	40
其他制造业	Other Manufacturing	29	23	6
废弃资源综合利用业	Waste Rrecycling and Recovery	8	8	
金属制品、机械和设备修理业	Repair of Fabricated Metal Products, Machinery and Equipment	15	12	3
电力、热力、燃气及水生产和供应业	**Production and Distribution of Electricity, Heating Power, Gas and Water**	**101**	**83**	**18**
电力、热力生产和供应业	Production and Distribution of Electricity and Heating Power	59	51	8
燃气生产和供应业	Production and Distribution of Gas	23	17	6
水的生产和供应业	Production and Distribution of Water	19	15	4
建筑业	**Construction**	**3717**	**3031**	**686**
房屋建筑业	Construction of Building	649	427	222
土木工程建筑业	Civil Engineering Construction	580	442	138
建筑安装业	Construction Installation	879	754	125
建筑装饰和其他建筑业	Building Completion, Finishing and Other Construction	1609	1408	201
批发和零售业	**Wholesale and Retail Trade**	**7470**	**6117**	**1353**
批发业	Wholesale	4980	4243	737
零售业	Retail Trade	2490	1874	616
交通运输、仓储和邮政业	**Transport, Storage and Post**	**1090**	**873**	**217**
铁路运输业	Transport via Railway	16	14	2
道路运输业	Transport via Road	544	461	83
水上运输业	Water Transport	6	4	2
航空运输业	Air Transport	17	14	3
管道运输业	Transport via Pipeline	2	2	
装卸搬运和运输代理业	Loading, Unloading, Portage and Other Transport Services	342	239	103
仓储业	Storage	132	120	12
邮政业	Post	31	19	12
住宿和餐饮业	**Accommodation and Restaurants**	**2935**	**2363**	**572**
住宿业	Accommodation	1113	928	185
餐饮业	Restaurants	1822	1435	387
信息传输、软件和信息技术服务业	**Information Transmission, Software and Information Technology Services**	**2803**	**2281**	**522**
电信、广播电视和卫星传输服务	Telecommunications, Broadcasting, Television and Satellite Transmission Services	263	195	68
互联网和相关服务	Internet and Related Services	260	210	50
软件和信息技术服务业	Software and Information Technology Services	2280	1876	404

1-3 续表 2 Continued 2

单位：个 (unit)

行 业	Sector	法人单位数合计 Total Number of Legal Entities	单产业法人 Single-industry Legal Entities	多产业法人 Multi-industry Legal Entities
金融业	**Finance**	**1783**	**1548**	**235**
货币金融服务	Monetary Financial Services	524	456	68
资本市场服务	Capital Market Services	461	420	41
保险业	Insurance	456	366	90
其他金融业	Other Financial Services	342	306	36
房地产业	**Real Estate**	**4654**	**3984**	**670**
租赁和商务服务业	**Renting and Leasing Activities, Business Services**	**6253**	**5479**	**774**
租赁业	Renting and Leasing Activities	136	109	27
商务服务业	Business Services	6117	5370	747
科学研究和技术服务业	**Scientific Research and Development, Technical Services**	**3400**	**2933**	**467**
研究和试验发展	Research and Experimental Development	602	554	48
专业技术服务业	Professional Technique Services	1708	1414	294
科技推广和应用服务业	Technique Generalization and Application Services	1090	965	125
水利、环境和公共设施管理业	**Management of Water Conservancy, Environment and Public Facilities**	**543**	**493**	**50**
水利管理业	Management of Water Conservancy	48	43	5
生态保护和环境治理业	Ecological Protection and Environmental Control	63	53	10
公共设施管理业	Management of Public Facilities	432	397	35
居民服务、修理和其他服务业	**Resident Services, Repair and Other Services**	**481**	**418**	**63**
居民服务业	Resident Services	174	141	33
机动车、电子产品和日用产品修理业	Repair of Motor Vehicles, Electronics and Household Appliances	141	122	19
其他服务业	Other Services	166	155	11
教育	**Education**	**1539**	**1409**	**130**
卫生和社会工作	**Health Care and Social Works**	**619**	**504**	**115**
卫生	Health Care	571	458	113
社会工作	Social Work Activities	48	46	2
文化、体育和娱乐业	**Culture, Sports and Entertainment**	**1289**	**1173**	**116**
新闻和出版业	Journalism and Publishing	537	485	52
广播、电视、电影和影视录音制作业	Radio Broadcasting, Television, Movies, Videos and Sound Recording	225	208	17
文化艺术业	Culture and Arts	237	223	14
体育	Sports Activities	188	162	26
娱乐业	Entertainments	102	95	7
公共管理、社会保障和社会组织	**Public Administration, Social Security and Social Organizations**	**1759**	**1473**	**286**
中国共产党机关	Organs of Communist Party of China	49	43	6
国家机构	Organs of State	1294	1080	214
人民政协、民主党派	Peole's Political Consultative Conference and Democratic Parties	25	24	1
社会保障	Social Security	10	10	
群众团体、社会团体和其他成员组织	Mass Communities, Social Organizations and Other Membership Organizations	326	264	62
基层群众自治组织	Grass Roots Self-Government Organization	55	52	3
国际组织	**International Organizations**			

1-4 规模(限额)以上企业法人单位情况(2013年)

NUMBER OF CORPORATE ENTERPRISES ABOVE DESIGNATED SIZE (2013)

单位：个 (unit)

项　目	Item	法人单位合　计 Total Number of Legal Entities
合　计	**Total**	**38385**
按开业时间分	**By Openning Time**	
1949年以前	Before 1949	35
1950-1965	Between 1950 and 1965	304
1966-1979	Between 1966 and 1979	175
1980-1989	Between 1980 and 1989	1508
1990年以后	After 1990	36363
按登记注册类型分	**By Registration Type**	
内资企业	Domestically-invested Enterprises	34017
国有企业	State-owned Enterprises	1848
集体企业	Collectively-owned Enterprises	663
股份合作企业	Joint-equity Cooperative Enterprises	519
联营企业	Associated Enterprises	36
有限责任公司	Limited Liability Companies	14238
股份有限公司	Companies Limited by Shares	1178
私营企业	Private Enterprises	15533
其他内资企业	Other Domestically-invested Enterprises	2
港澳台商投资企业	Hong Kong, Macao and Taiwan-invested Enterprises	1622
与港澳台商合资经营	Joint Ventures	532
与港澳台商合作经营	Cooperatives	131
港澳台商独资	Solely-funded Enterprises	926
港澳台商投资股份有限公司	Companies Limited by Shares	33
其他港澳台商投资	Others	
外商投资企业	Foreign-invested Enterprises	2746
中外合资经营	Joint Ventures	809
中外合作经营	Cooperatives	112
外资企业	Solely-funded Enterprises	1781
外商投资股份有限公司	Companies Limited by Shares	42
其他外商投资	Other	2
按控股情况分	**By Share Holding Status**	
国有控股	Stated Holding	7656
集体控股	Collective Holding	1931
私人控股	Privately Holding	24299
港澳台商控股	Hong Kong, Macao and Taiwan-invested Holding	1469
外商控股	Foreign-invested Holding	2497
其　他	Others	533

注：本表为2013年年报规模(限额)以上企业法人单位数据。

Note: This table covers legal entities above designated size in the 2013 annual report.

1-5 全市私营个体经济基本情况
STATISTICS FOR PRIVATE AND INDIVIDUAL ECONOMY

单位：万元 (10000 yuan)

项 目	Item		私 营 Private			个 体 Individual		
			2013	2012	2013年为2012年% 2013 as % of 2012	2013	2012	2013年为2012年% 2013 as % of 2012
工商登记注册*	Registered at Administration for Industry and Commerce							
户 数 （户）	Number of Business Entities	(unit)	673436	600354	112.2	664306	691066	96.1
从业人员 （人）	Number of Employed Persons	(person)	5278964	3710912	142.3	1123814	1066883	105.3
注册资本	Registered Capital		178551821	136694192	130.6	1854185	1712269	108.3
国税、地税入库税收合计	Taxes Put into Local and National Treasury		5043474	4640961	108.7	2360744	1339440	176.2

注：*为期末时点数。
资料来源：北京市工商行政管理局、北京市地方税务局、北京市国家税务局。
Note: Figures with * indicate the accumulative figures at end of the year.
Source: Beijing Administration for Industry and Commerce, Beijing Municipal Bureau of Local Taxation, Beijing Municipal Bureau of State Taxation

1-6 规模以上非公经济主要指标(2012年)
MAIN STATUS OF NON-PUBLIC ECONOMICS ABOVE DESIGNATED SIZE (2012)

项目	Item	单位数 (个) Number of Enterprises (unit)	收入合计 (亿元) Total Income (100 million yuan)	利润总额 (亿元) Total Profits (100 million yuan)	应交税金合计 (亿元) Total Tax (100 million yuan)	从业人员平均人数 (万人) Average Number of Persons Employed (10000 persons)
合计	**Total**	**29059**	**37827.3**	**2879.8**	**1782.4**	**321.7**
按登记注册类型分	**Grouped by Registration Status**					
内资	Domestic Investment Economy	25032	19429.3	816.4	910.7	209.3
私营独资	Private Wholly-Funded	143	39.4	2.0	1.1	1.2
私营合伙	Private Partnership	355	141.9	70.4	15.5	2.2
私营有限责任公司	Private Limited Liability Companies	14601	8043.8	172.6	256.5	93.7
私营股份有限公司	Private Joint-Stock Companies	558	372.0	38.6	20.9	6.0
私人投资控股	Private Holding Companies	9375	10832.2	532.9	616.7	106.3
港澳台商投资	Units with Funds from Hongkong, Macao and Taiwan	1451	4585.8	419.7	302.9	39.8
港澳台商独资	Hongkong, Macao and Taiwan Enterprises	874	3349.4	262.5	165.9	24.8
港澳台商投资控股	Enterprises Funded and Controlled by Hongkong, Macaoand Taiwan Companies	577	1236.4	157.2	137.0	15.0
外商投资	Foreign Funded Units Funded Share Holding Corporations	2576	13812.2	1643.7	568.8	72.5
外商独资	Foreign Enterprises	1777	10964.4	1426.0	428.4	47.7
外商投资控股	Foreign Funded and Controlled Corporations	799	2847.8	217.7	140.4	24.9
按规模分	**Grouped by Size**					
大型企业	Large-sized Enterprises	867	16984.1	1287.1	873.9	115.2
中小微型企业	Mini-, Small-, Mediume-sized Enterprises	27938	20709.6	1592.7	906.9	203.1
中型	Medium Size	5163	11722.5	1300.2	558.3	103.5
小型	Small Size	16511	7979.9	340.4	298.6	91.1
微型	Mini Size	6264	1007.2	-47.8	49.9	8.5
按行业分	**Grouped by Sector**					
#制造业	Manufacturing	2706	6781.2	439.0	298.9	62.5
建筑业	Construction	2822	1722.3	44.3	66.1	19.4
批发和零售业	Wholesale and Retail Trade	6573	16627.6	390.0	368.9	49.5
交通运输、仓储和邮政业	Transport, Storage and Post	749	717.2	30.5	25.3	16.0
住宿和餐饮业	Accommodation and Restaurants	2291	641.8	12.7	47.8	27.7
信息传输、软件和信息技术服务业	Information Transmission,Software and Information Technology Services	2303	3355.6	1084.5	243.4	45.5
金融业	Finance	1033	650.6	78.9	161.4	5.6
房地产业	Real estate	2946	1838.7	326.0	317.9	22.7
租赁和商务服务业	Renting and Leasing Activities and Business Services	4383	3681.2	321.3	157.0	37.2
科学研究和技术服务业	Scientific Research and Development, Technical Services	1867	956.3	89.6	56.4	16.1
水利、环境和公共设施管理业	Management of Water Conservancy, Environment and Public Facilities	170	139.1	13.8	7.6	1.5
居民服务、修理和其他服务业	Resident Services, Repair and Other Services	335	131.0	3.1	7.4	6.4
教育	Education	250	141.8	7.3	6.6	6.0
卫生和社会工作	Health Care and Social Works	112	48.3	4.2	1.2	1.5
文化、体育和娱乐业	Culture, Sports and Entertainment	381	121.9	7.7	10.2	2.7
公共管理和社会组织	Pulic Administration, Social Security and Social Organizations	108	73.5		0.7	0.4

注：1. 本表私人投资控股包含内资中除私营独资、私营合伙、私营有限责任公司和私营股份有限公司以外的非公有经济，港澳台商投资控股包含除港澳台独资以外的港澳台商投资经济，外商投资控股包含除外商独资以外的外商投资经济。本表不包含个体经营户数据。
2. 应交税金合计主要包括应交增值税、应交所得税、营业税金及附加和管理费用中的税金等。
3. 按规模分组中，各类型非公经济是指执行企业会计制度的非公企业数据，不包含执行事业会计制度的非公单位数据，因此，规模分组合计数不等于其他分组合计数。

Note: a) Private holding companies include non-public economies in domestically funded enterprises other than wholly private-funded, private cooperative, private liability limited and private joint-stock companies. Enterprises funded and controlled by Hongkong, Macao and Taiwan companies include economies funded by Hongkong, Macao and Taiwan companies other than those wholly funded by Hongkong, Macao and Taiwan companies. Foreign funded and controlled corporations include foreign funded economies other than wholly foreign-funded companies.
b) Total Tax mainly includes payable VAT,payable income tax, business tax and surtax, and tax in management expenses, etc.
c) In the group by size, figures of various types of non-public economies are those of non-public enterprises implementing enterprise accounting system, excluding those of non-public entities implementing public institution accounting system. Therefore, total amounts in the group by size are not equal to total amounts of other groups.

1-7 规模以上中小微型企业主要指标(2012年)
MAIN STATUS OF MINI- SMALL- AND MEDIUM-SIZED ENTERPRISES ABOVE DESIGNATED SIZE (2012)

项 目	Item	单位数 (个) Number of Enterprises (unit)	收入合计 (亿元) Total Income (100 million yuan)	利润总额 (亿元) Total Profits (100 million yuan)	应交税金合计 (亿元) Total Tax (100 million yuan)	从业人员平均人数 (万人) Average Number of Persons Employed (10000 persons)
合 计	**Total**	**37166**	**50698.0**	**7638.7**	**1839.6**	**309.0**
按规模分	**Grouped by Size**					
中型	Medium Size	8124	33122.3	5195.5	1120.1	174.6
小型	Small Size	21254	13354.5	1101.9	546.6	123.0
微型	Mini Size	7788	4221.2	1341.3	172.9	11.4
按登记注册类型分	**Grouped by Registration Status**					
内 资	Domestic Investment Economy	33286	44729.6	6534.5	1488.7	259.5
港澳台商投资	Units with Funds from Hongkong, Macao and Taiwan	1407	2131.8	103.4	125.0	19.0
外商投资	Foreign Funded Economy	2473	3836.6	1000.8	225.9	30.5
按行业分	**Grouped by Sector**					
#制造业	Manufacturing	3421	5549.7	405.3	303.4	63.9
建筑业	Construction	3401	2198.0	89.8	83.0	25.4
批发和零售业	Wholesale and Retail Trade	7771	23003.1	272.5	315.1	35.6
交通运输、仓储和邮政业	Transport, Storage and Post	1028	961.7	-13.6	23.1	14.3
住宿和餐饮业	Accommodation and Restaurants	2971	513.1	-8.2	36.2	25.9
信息传输、软件和信息技术服务业	Information Transmission,Software and Information Technology Services	2530	1907.7	909.6	83.1	27.2
金融业	Finance	1678	5761.1	4647.7	265.9	6.3
房地产业	Real estate	4500	2487.8	410.5	377.3	27.0
租赁和商务服务业	Renting and Leasing Activities and Business Services	5477	4086.0	622.1	200.0	51.2
科学研究和技术服务业	Scientific Research and Development, Technical Services	2454	1872.0	179.6	84.0	15.9
水利、环境和公共设施管理业	Management of Water Conservancy, Environment and Public Facilities	294	151.9	12.1	6.9	1.8
居民服务、修理和其他服务业	Resident Services, Repair and Other Services	361	119.1	2.5	6.3	3.0
教育	Education	169	50.8	3.9	4.0	1.6
卫生和社会工作	Health Care and Social Works	111	34.3	2.2	0.7	1.1
文化、体育和娱乐业	Culture, Sports and Entertainment	895	409.8	47.9	30.9	6.1

注：1. 本表中的企业规模划型标准执行国家统计局《关于统计上大中小微型企业划分办法》(国统字〔2011〕75号)。
2. 行业划分执行2011年国民经济行业分类标准(GB/T 4754-2011)。

Note: a) In this table, enterprise size is identified in accordance with the provisions concerning the Statistical Division Standards of Mini-, Small-, Mediume- and Large-sized Enterprises in the Notice of the National Bureau of Statistics Concerning Printing and Issuing Measures for Statistical Division of Mini-, Small-, Mediume- and Large-sized Enterprises (GTZ (2011) No.75).

b) Sectors in this table are classified in accordance with the Standard for Classification of National Economic Sectors 2011 (GB/T 4754-2011).

1-8 主要经济指标增长速度(1979-2013年)

单位：%

年份 Year	地区生产总值比上年增长 YoY Growth Rate of Gross Domestic Product	全社会固定资产投资比上年增长 YoY Growth Rate of Fixed Asset Investment	房地产开发投资比上年增长 YoY Growth Rate of Real Estate Development Investment	地方公共财政预算收入比上年增长 YoY Growth Rate of Public Finance Budget Revenue	社会消费品零售总额比上年增长 YoY Growth Rate of Retail Sales of Consumer Goods	进出口总值比上年增长 YoY Growth Rate of Gross Value of Imports & Exports
1979	9.7	17.3			20.6	
1980	11.8	25.3			17.8	
1981	-0.5	10.2			12.6	
1982	7.4	5.5			6.6	
1983	16.4	32.9			14.6	
1984	17.4	29.2			22.5	16.3
1985	8.7	41.8			27.0	-8.6
1986	8.0	13.0			15.3	-6.0
1987	9.6	28.2			21.9	-12.7
1988	12.8	19.7			35.5	11.9
1989	4.4	-14.4			15.2	-4.3
1990	5.2	28.5			17.1	-17.4
1991	9.9	7.1	6.7		18.3	2.5
1992	11.3	38.5	40.4		23.2	3.1
1993	12.3	54.3	73.3		21.5	11.7
1994	13.7	58.1	70.4		25.4	3.5
1995	12.0	29.7	254.6		24.0	28.2
1996	9.0	4.2	-7.0		11.7	-20.8
1997	10.1	9.6	0.6		13.8	3.7
1998	9.5	20.2	14.3	20.0	13.7	0.4
1999	10.9	1.3	11.7	22.6	9.9	12.6
2000	11.8	10.8	23.9	22.7	9.9	43.8
2001	11.7	18.0	50.1	31.6	10.4	4.2
2002	11.5	18.5	26.2	25.9	9.5	2.0
2003	11.1	18.9	21.5	18.2	14.5	30.5
2004	14.1	17.2	22.5	29.7	14.4	38.1
2005	12.1	11.8	3.5	23.5	10.9	32.7
2006	13.0	19.3	12.8	21.5	13.2	25.9
2007	14.5	17.6	16.0	33.6	16.4	22.1
2008	9.1	-3.0	-4.4	23.1	21.1	40.8
2009	10.2	26.2	22.5	10.3	14.3	-20.9
2010	10.3	13.1	24.1	16.1	17.3	40.4
2011	8.1	13.3	10.1	27.7	10.8	29.1
2012	7.7	9.3	3.9	10.3	11.6	4.8
2013	7.7	8.8	10.5	10.4	8.7	5.4

注：1. 自2011年起全社会固定资产投资统计起点发生变化，但2011年全社会固定资产投资增长速度和房地产开发投资增长速度均按可比口径计算。
2. 2002-2004年地方公共财政预算收入增长速度是按可比口径计算。
3. 城镇居民人均可支配收入和农村居民人均纯收入实际增长速度是指扣除物价后的实际增长速度。

YOY GROWTH RATE OF MAIN INDICATORS (1979-2013)

(%)

农林牧渔业总产值比上年增长 YoY Growth Rate of Gross Output Value of Agriculture, Forestry, Animal Production and Hunting, Fishing	规模以上工业总产值比上年增长 YoY Growth Rate of Gross Output Value of Industrial Enterprises Above Designated Size	居民消费价格指数(上年=100) Consumer Price Index (Preceding=100)	城镇居民人均可支配收入 Per-capita Disposable Income of Urban Households		农村居民人均纯收入 Per-capita Net Income of Rural Households	
			比上年名义增长 Nominal Growth Rate	比上年实际增长 Real Growth Rate	比上年名义增长 Normal Growth Rate	比上年实际增长 Real Growth Rate
7.0		101.8	13.6	11.6	11.1	10.9
16.3		106.0	20.8	14.0	23.2	22.1
4.2		101.3	2.5	1.2	17.2	17.1
12.8		101.8	9.1	7.2	19.1	17.3
16.7		100.5	5.2	4.7	20.7	20.9
13.3		102.2	17.5	15.0	27.9	25.7
16.7	17.4	117.6	30.8	11.3	16.7	14.5
8.5	3.8	106.8	17.6	10.1	6.2	3.7
22.4	15.2	108.6	10.7	1.9	11.3	6.5
52.9	27.9	120.4	21.6	1.0	16.0	3.1
14.8	21.6	117.2	11.1	-5.2	15.8	2.2
16.2	3.8	105.4	11.9	6.2	5.4	2.1
9.0	16.7	111.9	14.2	2.1	9.6	1.7
10.5	17.8	109.9	15.8	5.4	10.3	2.0
18.8	35.7	119.0	39.4	17.1	18.2	5.1
43.7	35.1	124.9	43.5	14.9	30.6	9.1
13.9	-5.3	117.3	24.0	5.7	32.5	6.3
2.7	6.5	111.6	17.3	5.1	11.1	4.8
0.9	14.4	105.3	13.5	7.8	5.6	5.1
2.5	7.0	102.4	8.4	5.9	7.1	6.7
3.3	12.1	100.6	8.4	7.8	7.1	7.2
4.4	30.2	103.5	12.7	8.9	8.6	7.3
7.2	15.1	103.1	11.9	8.5	12.5	8.7
5.6	10.7	98.2	13.5	15.6	11.5	12.3
5.2	21.8	100.2	11.4	11.2	10.5	11.5
4.5	30.0	101.0	12.6	11.5	10.4	9.2
1.9	21.2	101.5	12.9	11.2	9.6	8.1
0.4	18.2	100.9	13.2	12.2	9.7	8.7
13.4	17.5	102.4	13.9	11.2	10.9	8.2
11.6	7.9	105.1	12.4	7.0	12.4	6.5
3.6	6.0	98.5	8.1	9.7	11.5	13.4
4.1	24.1	102.4	8.7	6.2	10.6	8.1
10.7	5.9	105.6	13.2	7.2	13.6	7.6
9.0	7.5	103.3	10.8	7.3	11.8	8.2
6.6	11.4	103.3	10.6	7.1	11.3	7.7

Note: a) The statistical starting point for Fixed Asset Investment was changed in 2011. But the growth rates of Fixed Asset and Real Estate Development Investment in 2011 are calculated with the same coverage.

b) The growth rates of public finance budget revenue in 2002-2004 are calculated with the same coverage.

c) The growth rates of per-capita disposable income of urban households and per capita net income of rural households mean the real growth rate after the price influence is eliminated.

1-9 主要年份国民经济和社会发展总量与速度指标

项目		Item		1990	1995
人口与就业		**Population and Employment**			
人 口		**Population**			
年末全市常住人口	(万人)	Year-end Permanent Population	(10000 persons)	1086.0	1251.1
按性别分		By Sex			
男性人口		Male		545.0	627.0
女性人口		Female		541.0	624.1
按城乡分		By Urban Area and Rural Area			
城镇人口		Urban Population		798.0	946.2
乡村人口		Rural Population		288.0	304.9
年末户籍人口	(万人)	Year-end Registed Population	(10000 persons)	1032.2	1070.3
就 业		**Employment**			
从业人员年末人数	(万人)	Year-end Employed Persons	(10000 persons)	627.1	665.3
#城镇单位在岗职工人数		On-the-job Staff and Workers		454.9	470.9
年末实有城镇登记失业人员	(万人)	Registered Unemployed Persons in Urban Areas at Year End	(10000 persons)	1.7	2.2
宏观经济		**Macro Economy**			
国民经济核算		**National Accounts**			
地区生产总值	(亿元)	Gross Domestic Product	(100 million yuan)	500.8	1507.7
第一产业		Primary Industry		43.9	73.5
第二产业		Secondary Industry		262.4	645.8
第三产业		Tertiary Industry		194.5	788.4
人均地区生产总值	(元/人)	Per Capita Gross Domestic Product	(yuan/person)	4635.0	12690.0
固定资产投资		**Fixed Asset Investment**			
全社会固定资产投资	(亿元)	Total Fixed Asset Investment	(100 million yuan)	179.2	841.5
#房地产开发投资		Real Estate Development		22.5	352.8
#国有单位		State-Owned Entities		154.2	514.2
全社会房屋施工面积	(万平方米)	Floor Space of Houses under Construction	(10000 sq.m)	2864.9	5524.3
全社会房屋竣工面积	(万平方米)	Floor Space of Houses Completed	(10000 sq.m)	1081.2	1530.2
财 政		**Government Finance**			
地方财政收入	(亿元)	Local Finance Revenue	(100 million yuan)	74.0	115.3
#地方公共财政预算收入		Local Public Finance Budget Revenue			
地方财政支出	(亿元)	Local Finance Expenditure	(100 million yuan)	66.5	154.4
#地方公共财政预算支出		Local Public Finance Budget Expenditure			
价格指数(上年=100)		**Price Indices (Preceding Year=100)**			
居民消费价格指数	(%)	Consumer Price Index	(%)	105.4	117.3
商品零售价格指数	(%)	Retail Price Index	(%)	104.1	112.6
农产品生产价格指数	(%)	Farm Product Price Index	(%)	101.9	130.6
工业生产者出厂价格指数	(%)	Producer Price Index for Industrial Products	(%)	107.9	107.3
工业生产者购进价格指数	(%)	Purchase Price Index for Industrial Products	(%)	114.8	106.7
固定资产投资价格指数	(%)	Price Index of Investment in Fixed Asset	(%)		113.9
能源消费总量	**(万吨标准煤)**	**Total Energy Consumption**	**(10000 tons of SCE)**	**2709.7**	**3533.3**
产 业		**Industry**			
农村经济		**Rural Economy**			
耕地面积	(万公顷)	Cultivated Areas	(10000 hectare)	41.3	39.4
农林牧渔业总产值(现价)	(亿元)	Gross Output Value of Agriculture, Animal Production and Hunting, Fishing (at current prices)	(100 million yuan)	70.2	164.4
主要农产品产量	(万吨)	Yield of Agricultural and Sideline Products	(10000 tons)		
粮 食		Grain		264.6	259.8
蔬菜及食用菌		Vegetables and Edible Mushrooms		356.1	397.3
禽 蛋		Poultry Eggs		25.8	28.5
牛 奶		Milk		21.7	20.6
肉 类		Meat		26.8	39.8

注：1. 地区生产总值绝对值按现价计算，发展速度按可比价格计算；2006-2010年人均地区生产总值根据第六次人口普查数据进行修正。2013年地区生产总值数据为初步核算数。

2. 2007年及以前在岗职工人数包括乡及乡以上独立核算法人单位，不包括乡镇企业、私营单位和个体工商户；2008年及以后包括乡镇企业。

3. 从2011年起，根据国家统计局相关规定，固定资产投资起点由50万元调整至500万元。

AGGREGATE INDICATORS AND SPEED INDICATORS ON NATIONAL ECONOMIC AND SOCIAL DEVELOPMENT IN KEY YEARS

总量指标 Aggregate Indicator					速度指标(%) Speed Indicator (%) 指 数(2013年为以下各年) Index (2013 as Percentage of the Following Year)					
2000	2005	2010	2012	2013	1990	1995	2000	2005	2010	2012
1363.6	1538.0	1961.9	2069.3	2114.8	194.7	169.0	155.1	137.5	107.8	102.2
710.9	778.7	1013.0	1068.1	1090.7	200.1	174.0	153.4	140.1	107.7	102.1
652.7	759.3	948.9	1001.2	1024.1	189.3	164.1	156.9	134.9	107.9	102.3
1057.4	1286.1	1686.4	1783.7	1825.1	228.7	192.9	172.6	141.9	108.2	102.3
306.2	251.9	275.5	285.6	289.7	100.6	95.0	94.6	115.0	105.2	101.4
1107.5	1180.7	1257.8	1297.5	1316.3	127.5	123.0	118.9	111.5	104.7	101.5
619.3	878.0	1031.6	1107.3	1141.0	181.9	171.5	184.2	130.0	110.6	103.0
434.2	448.4	587.7	670.4	695.5	152.9	147.7	160.2	155.1	118.3	103.7
3.3	10.6	7.7	7.2	6.8	407.8	311.0	205.1	64.4	88.1	94.6
3161.7	6969.5	14113.6	17879.4	19500.6	1085.3	620.5	380.9	215.1	125.4	107.7
79.3	88.7	124.4	150.2	161.8	131.8	126.3	117.9	114.8	107.3	103.0
1033.3	2026.5	3388.4	4059.3	4352.3	880.0	525.4	334.7	195.4	124.0	108.1
2049.1	4854.3	10600.8	13669.9	14986.5	1460.2	727.2	412.1	225.5	126.2	107.6
24127.4	45992.8	73856.0	87475.0	93213.0	559.6	352.0	238.5	155.8	114.5	105.2
1297.4	2827.2	5493.5	6462.8	7032.2	3924.2	835.7	542.0	248.7	128.0	108.8
522.1	1525.0	2901.1	3153.4	3483.4	15481.8	987.4	667.2	228.4	120.1	110.5
765.8	897.7	1907.3	2248.2	2382.0	1544.7	463.2	311.0	265.3	124.9	106.0
6995.9	14096.2	15572.1	20045.4	21526.0	751.4	389.7	307.7	152.7	138.2	107.4
2358.2	4679.2	3908.4	3723.5	3989.7	369.0	260.7	169.2	85.3	102.1	107.1
398.4	1007.4	3810.9	4573.7	5566.1	7520.7	4829.2	1397.1	552.5	146.1	121.7
345.0	919.2	2353.9	3314.9	3661.1			1061.2	398.3	155.5	110.4
490.3	1137.3	4065.0	4866.4	6039.4	9079.1	3911.5	1231.7	531.0	148.6	124.1
443.0	1058.3	2717.3	3685.3	4173.7			942.1	394.4	153.6	113.3
103.5	101.5	102.4	103.3	103.3						
98.9	99.7	100.4	100.6	99.8						
95.0	102.9	106.5	104.7	104.7						
102.5	101.3	102.2	98.4	97.4						
100.0	111.4	110.5	98.7	97.8						
101.0	100.7	102.5	101.3	99.9						
4144.0	**5521.9**	**6954.1**	**7177.7**	**7354.2**	**271.4**	**208.1**	**177.5**	**133.2**	**105.8**	**102.5**
32.9	23.3	22.4	22.1							
188.6	239.3	328.0	395.7	421.8	600.8	256.6	223.6	176.3	128.6	106.6
144.2	94.9	115.7	113.8	96.1	36.3	37.0	66.6	101.3	83.1	84.5
466.3	373.1	303.0	279.9	266.9	75.0	67.2	57.2	71.5	88.1	95.3
16.0	16.0	15.1	15.2	17.5	67.8	61.4	109.4	109.4	115.9	114.8
30.3	64.2	64.1	65.1	61.5	283.4	298.5	203.0	95.8	96.0	94.5
50.5	53.3	46.3	43.2	41.8	155.9	105.1	82.8	78.4	90.3	96.8

Note: a) Figures in value terms on GDP are calculated at current prices, whereas growth rates are calculated at comparable prices.Per Capita Gross Domestic Product from 2006 to 2010 were adjusted according to the 6th population census.Figures of GDP in 2013 were preliminary statistics.

b) Urban entities in and before 2007 mean business entities keeping separate accounts at and above the township level, excluding township enterprises, private entities and self-employed operators. Urban entities in and after 2008 mean business entities keeping separate accounts excluding private entities and self-employed operators.

c) From 2011, the starting point of fixed asset investment is changed from RMB 500,000 to RMB 5 million according to relevant regulations of National Bureau of Statistics.

1-9 续表 1

项　目		Item		1990	1995
工　业		**Industry**			
工业增加值(现价，规模以上)	(亿元)	Added Value of Industry (at Current Prices, Above Designated Size)	(100 million yuan)		473.1
工业总产值(现价，规模以上)	(亿元)	Gross Output Value of Industry (at Current Prices, Above Designated Size)	(100 million yuan)	625.9	1493.3
轻工业		Light Industry		262.2	472.2
重工业		Heavy Industry		363.7	1021.1
工业企业主要经济指标(规模以上)		Main Indicators of Industrial Enterprises (Above Designated Size)			
资产总计	(亿元)	Total Asset	(100 million yuan)	498.3	2582.6
负债总额	(亿元)	Total Liability	(100 million yuan)		1528.8
主营业务收入	(亿元)	Revenue from Core Operations	(100 million yuan)	610.5	1590.4
利润总额	(亿元)	Total Profit	(100 million yuan)	48.9	85.3
建　筑		**Construction**			
建筑业施工企业总产值	(亿元)	Gross Output Value	(100 million yuan)	94.7	426.6
建筑业施工企业年末从业人员	(万人)	Year-end Employed Persons	(10000 persons)	60.2	82.6
运　输		**Transport**			
货物周转量	(亿吨公里)	Total Freight Turnover	(100 million ton-km)	268.8	323.1
铁　路		Railway		206.7	239.3
公　路		Road		57.5	76.2
民　航		Civil Aviation		4.5	7.5
管　道		Pipeline		0.2	0.1
旅客周转量	(亿人公里)	Total Passenger Turnover	(100 million passenger-km)	119.8	207.7
邮　电		**Post and Telecommunication Services**			
邮电业务总量	(亿元)	Business Volume of Post and Telecommunications	(100 million yuan)	11.9	56.1
固定电话用户	(万户)	Fixed Telephone Subscribers	(10000 subscribers)	33.3	150.5
固定电话主线普及率	(线/百人)	Penetration Rate of Main Line	(lines/100 persons)	3.1	12.0
移动电话用户	(万户)	Mobile Telephone Subscribers	(10000 subscribers)	0.3	16.9
移动电话普及率	(户/百人)	Penetration Rate of Mobile Telephone	(sets/100 persons)	0.0	1.4
商　业		**Commerce**			
社会消费品零售总额	(亿元)	Retail Sales of Consumer Goods	(100 million yuan)	345.1	950.4
对外经济贸易和旅游		**Foreign Trade and Tourism**			
北京地区进出口总值	(亿美元)	Total Value of Imports and Exports	(USD 100 million)	236.4	370.4
进口值		Imports		192.3	267.9
出口值		Exports		44.1	102.5
实际利用外商直接投资额	(亿美元)	Paid-in Foreign Investment	(USD 100 million)	2.8	14.0
接待入境旅游者人数	(万人次)	Inbound Tourists	(10000 persons)	100.0	207.0
旅游外汇收入	(亿美元)	Foreign Exchange Earning from Tourism	(USD 100 million)	6.6	21.8
金融保险		**Finance and Insurance**			
金融机构(含外资)本外币存款余额	(亿元)	Deposits of Financial Institutions (Including Foreign Institutions)	(100 million yuan)		
金融机构(含外资)本外币贷款余额	(亿元)	Loans of Financial Institutions (Including Foreign Institutions)	(100 million yuan)		
原保险保费收入	(亿元)	Premiums Revenue	(100 million yuan)		

注：1. 工业增加值按生产法计算。
2. 邮电业务总量2000年及以前按1990年不变价格计算，2010年及以前按2000年不变价格计算,从2011年开始按2010年不变价计算。

1-9 Continued 1

总量指标 Aggregate Indicator					速度指标(%) Speed Indicator (%)					
					指 数(2013年为以下各年) Index (2013 as Percentage of the Following Year)					
2000	2005	2010	2012	2013	1990	1995	2000	2005	2010	2012
776.0	1627.0	2751.7	3033.3	3432.1						
2842.0	6946.2	13699.8	15596.2	17370.9	2775.3	1163.3	611.2	250.1	126.8	111.4
719.3	1164.9	2000.0	2402.1	2541.5	969.3	538.2	353.3	218.2	127.1	105.8
2122.7	5781.3	11699.8	13194.1	14829.4	4077.4	1452.3	698.6	256.5	126.7	112.4
4612.7	12829.8	22750.6	28613.2	30800.7	6181.5	1192.6	667.7	240.1	135.4	107.6
2676.4	4706.7	11548.1	14837.2	16208.0		1060.2	605.6	344.4	140.4	109.2
2821.4	7279.1	14807.1	16905.1	18688.6	3061.4	1175.1	662.4	256.7	126.2	110.6
127.1	413.5	1028.3	1267.9	1282.9	2621.5	1504.1	1009.5	310.3	124.8	101.2
812.5	1894.0	5196.0	6588.3	7459.6	7877.1	1748.6	918.1	393.9	143.6	113.2
56.6	67.2	59.9	49.2	49.3	81.9	59.7	87.1	73.4	82.3	100.2
299.6	457.7	513.7	638.3	680.9	253.3	210.7	227.2	148.8	132.6	106.7
200.2	310.8	257.5	307.6	323.2	156.3	135.0	161.4	104.0	125.5	105.1
82.6	85.5	101.6	139.8	156.2	271.8	205.0	189.0	182.7	153.7	111.7
16.8	28.2	48.2	49.0	49.2	1101.3	656.3	293.3	174.6	101.9	100.4
0.04	33.3	106.4	141.9	152.3				458.0	143.2	107.3
314.0	838.1	1399.5	1595.8	1498.8						
214.7	413.0	1108.9	546.5	652.5	5487.7	1162.4	303.8	158.0	152.3	119.4
451.2	943.5	885.6	883.1	867.6	2605.8	576.4	192.3	92.0	98.0	98.2
33.1	61.3	45.1	42.7	41.0						
347.2	1459.8	2129.8	3168.0	3373.8			971.7	231.1	158.4	106.5
25.5	94.9	108.6	153.1	159.5						
1658.7	2911.7	6229.3	7702.8	8375.1	2426.9	881.2	504.9	287.6	134.4	108.7
494.0	1255.1	3016.6	4081.1	4299.4	1818.3	1160.9	870.3	342.6	142.5	105.4
374.3	946.4	2462.2	3484.8	3668.4	1907.5	1369.6	980.0	387.6	149.0	105.3
119.7	308.7	554.4	596.3	631.0	1429.7	615.6	527.2	204.4	113.8	105.8
24.6	35.3	63.6	80.4	85.2	3077.8	607.7	346.8	241.7	134.0	106.0
282.1	362.9	490.1	500.9	450.1	450.1	217.4	159.6	124.0	91.8	89.9
27.7	36.2	50.4	51.5	47.9	729.7	219.7	173.2	132.4	95.1	93.1
11526.0	28969.9	66584.6	84837.3	91660.5			795.3	316.4	137.7	108.0
6407.9	15335.5	36479.6	43189.5	47880.9			747.2	312.2	131.3	110.9
93.4	498.2	966.5	923.1	994.4			1064.2	199.6	102.9	107.7

Note: a) Added value of industry is calculated with the production approach.

b) Business volumes of post and telecommunications before and in 2000 were calculated at 1990's constant price, those since 2000 were calculated at 2000's constant price, and those since 2011 were calculated at 2010's constant price.

1-9 续表 2

项　　目		Item		1990	1995
教育、文化、科技、卫生		**Education, Culture, Science and Technology and Health Care**			
教　育		**Education**			
在校学生数	(万人)	Students Enrollment	(10000 persons)		238.0
专任教师数	(万人)	Full-time Teachers	(10000 persons)		17.7
文　化		**Culture**			
公共图书馆总藏数	(万册、万件)	Collection of Public Libraries	(10000 volumes)	2205	2629
专业艺术剧团国内演出场次	(场)	Performances of Domestic Art Troupes	(time)	7527	6728
科　技		**Science and Technology**			
研究与试验发展经费内部支出	(亿元)	Expenditures on Research and Development	(100 million yuan)		
技术合同成交总额	(亿元)	Volume of Technical Contract	(100 million yuan)	20.3	41.2
专利授权量	(件)	Patent Grants	(case)	2268	4025
卫　生		**Health Care**			
卫生机构个数	(个)	Health Care Institutions	(unit)	4953	4955
卫生机构病床数	(万张)	Beds at Health Care Institutions	(10000 beds)	5.9	6.7
卫生技术人员数	(万人)	Medical Personnel	(10000 persons)	11.2	11.6
#执业(助理)医师		Certified Doctors		5.1	5.4
注册护师(士)		Registered Nurses		3.5	3.7
生活与环境		**People's Living and Environment**			
婚　姻		**Marriages and Divorces**			
登记结婚对数	(万对)	Number of Registered Marriages	(10000 couples)	9.30	8.55
离婚对数	(万对)	Number of Divorces	(10000 couples)	1.47	2.02
居　住		**Housing**			
城镇居民人均住房建筑面积	(平方米)	Per Capita Living Space for Urban Residents	(sq.m)		
农村居民人均住房面积	(平方米)	Per Capita Living Space for Rural Residents	(sq.m)	20.62	24.74
生　活		**People's Livelihood**			
城镇居民人均可支配收入	(元)	Per Capita Annual Disposable Income of Urban Residents	(yuan)	1787	5868
农村居民人均纯收入	(元)	Per Capita Net Income of Rural Residents	(yuan)	1297	3209
金融机构(含外资)储蓄存款余额	(亿元)	Saving Deposits of Financial Institutions (including foreign institutions)	(100 million yuan)		
工　资		**Wages**			
城镇单位在岗职工工资总额	(亿元)	Total Wage of On-the-job Staff and Workers	(100 million yuan)	118.9	382.0
城镇单位在岗职工平均工资	(元)	Average Wage of On-the-job Staff and Workers	(yuan)	2653	8144
市政建设		**Municipal Construction**			
全社会用电量	(亿千瓦时)	Total Electricity Consumption	(100 million kwh)	150.5	222.6
自来水销售总量	(亿立方米)	Sales of Tap Water	(100 million cu.m)	5.3	6.8
居民燃气用户	(万户)	Households with Access to Gas	(10000 households)	176.1	219.8
城市公共交通客运量	(亿人次)	Passengers Carried by Urban Public Transport	(100 million person-times)	33.5	37.2
环　境		**Environment**			
城市绿化覆盖率	(%)	Urban Green Area Coverage	(%)	28.0	32.7
污水处理率	(%)	Sewage Treatment Rate	(%)	7.3	19.4

注：1. 北京地区用电量来源于北京市电力公司，2000年以前工业用电量不包含输配损失和发电企业自产自用电量。
2. 从2001年开始，有关职工的指标调整为在岗职工的指标。2007年及以前城镇单位在岗职工工资包括乡及乡以上独立核算法人单位，不包括乡镇企业、私营单位和个体工商户；2008年及以后包括乡镇企业。
3. 离婚对数包括在民政部门登记的对数和经法院调离和判离的对数。
4. 2010年及以前，本表中卫生机构数据都不包含村卫生室及驻京部队医院情况。2011年开始，包含村卫生室情况。2012年开始，卫生机构数、卫生技术人员数据中包含驻京部队医院，床位数不包含。2013年开始，本表所有数据均包含驻京部队医院情况。
5. 城镇居民人均住房建筑面积改为城镇住户抽样调查数据。

1-9 Continued 2

总量指标 Aggregate Indicator					速度指标(%) Speed Indicator (%)					
					指 数(2013为以下各年) Speed Indicator (2013 as Percentage of the Following Year)					
2000	2005	2010	2012	2013	1990	1995	2000	2005	2010	2012
229.9	226.4	330.0	356.8	373.6		157.0	162.5	165.0	113.2	104.7
16.7	17.5	20.7	20.5	21.6		122.6	129.6	124.0	104.8	105.7
3020	3626	4613	5556	5316	241.0	202.2	176.0	146.6	115.2	95.7
7610	8934	10483	11675	12084	160.5	179.6	158.8	135.3	115.3	103.5
155.7	379.5	821.8	1063.4	1185.0			761.1	312.2	144.2	111.4
140.3	434.4	1579.5	2458.5	2851.2	14066.1	6925.4	2032.4	656.4	180.5	116.0
5905	10100	33511	50511	62671	2763.3	1557.0	1061.3	620.5	187.0	124.1
6176	4818	6539	9974	10141						
7.1	7.9	9.3	10.0	12.3						
11.6	12.0	17.1	22.0	23.0						
5.2	5.1	6.6	8.2	8.6						
4.0	4.3	6.7	9.5	10.1						
8.02	9.66	13.81	17.41	16.37	176.0	191.4	204.1	169.4	118.5	94.0
2.66	3.42	4.40	4.86	6.46	438.1	320.5	242.8	188.7	146.9	133.0
	22.03	28.94	29.26	31.31						
28.91	36.94	40.62	49.08	51.35						
10349.7	17653	29073	36469	40321	2256.2	687.1	389.6	228.4	138.7	110.6
4687	7860	13262	16476	18337	1413.7	571.5	391.2	233.3	138.3	111.3
	8315.8	17585.2	22298.6	23747.6				285.6	135.0	106.5
695.5	1520.1	3789.1	5657.9	6502.0	5468.5	1702.1	934.9	427.7	171.6	114.9
15726	34191	65683	85307	93997	3543.0	1154.2	597.7	274.9	143.1	110.2
384.4	570.5	809.9	874.3	913.1	606.8	410.2	237.5	160.0	112.7	104.4
7.5	7.2	8.9	9.4	9.8	186.2	144.6	130.3	137.1	110.1	104.6
291.9	462.6	634.2	713.5	737.4	418.7	335.5	252.6	159.4	116.3	103.4
40.7	51.8	69.0	76.2	80.5	240.5	216.6	197.9	155.4	116.7	105.7
36.5	42.0	45.0	46.2	46.8						
39.4	62.4	81.0	83.0	84.6						

Note: a) Figures on electricity eonsumption are provided by Beijing Electric Power Corporation. Before 2000, electricity consumption by industry excluded transmission and distribution losses and electricity generated and consumed by power generating enterprises.

b) From 2001, indicators related to the "staff and workers " have been changed to those of "on-the-job staff and workers". In and before 2007, figures on wages of urban on-the-job staff and workers covered corporate entities keeping separate accounts at and above the township level, excluding township enterprises, private entities and self-employed operators; in and after 2008, such figures included township enterprises.

c) Registered divorces include those registered with civil affair authorities and those mediated and ruled in courts.

d) From 2010, figures on health centers were emerged with other health institutions such as community health service centers (stations).From 2011,health care institutions included village health centers.

e) Figures on per-capita floor space of urban residents are from spot check figures of urban households.

1-10 主要年份国民经济和社会发展结构指标
STRUCTURAL INDICATORS ON NATIONAL ECONOMIC AND SOCIAL DEVELOPMENT IN KEY YEARS

单位：% (%)

项目	Item	1990	1995	2000	2005	2010	2012	2013
人口与就业	**Population and Employment**							
常住人口	**Permanent Population**							
按性别分	By Sex							
男	Male	50.2	50.1	52.1	50.6	51.6	51.6	51.6
女	Female	49.8	49.9	47.9	49.4	48.4	48.4	48.4
按城乡分	By Urban Area and Rural Area							
城　镇	Urban	73.5	75.6	77.5	83.6	86.0	86.2	86.3
乡　村	Rural	26.5	24.4	22.5	16.4	14.0	13.8	13.7
就　业	**Employment**							
从业人员年末人数	Year-end Employed Persons							
第一产业	Primary Industry	14.5	10.6	11.8	7.1	6.0	5.2	4.8
第二产业	Secondary Industry	44.9	40.7	33.6	26.3	19.6	19.2	18.5
第三产业	Tertiary Industry	40.6	48.7	54.6	66.6	74.4	75.6	76.7
宏观经济	**Macro Economy**							
国民经济核算	**National Accounts**							
地区生产总值	Gross Domestic Product							
第一产业	Primary Industry	8.8	4.9	2.5	1.3	0.9	0.8	0.8
第二产业	Secondary Industry	52.4	42.8	32.7	29.1	24.0	22.7	22.3
第三产业	Tertiary Industry	38.8	52.3	64.8	69.6	75.1	76.5	76.9
投　资	**Investment**							
全社会固定资产投资	Fixed Asset Investment							
城　镇	Urban	88.2	94.4	91.9	91.8	91.1	90.6	90.3
农　村	Rural	9.7	4.8	6.5	8.2	8.9	9.4	9.7
资金来源结构	Source of Capital							
国家预算内资金	State Budgetary Appropriation	25.3	7.7	7.4	2.8	1.2	1.7	1.5
国内贷款	Domestic Loans	16.7	13.4	26.0	23.2	26.6	23.9	24.1
利用外资	Foreign Investment	11.2	20.5	3.6	1.6	0.5	0.3	0.2
债券、自筹和其他资金	Securities, Fundraising and Other Investment	46.8	58.4	63.0	72.4	71.6	74.1	74.2
财　政	**Government Finance**							
地方公共财政预算收入主要税种	Main Taxes of Public Finance Budget Revenue							
#增值税	Value Added Tax			13.3	10.6	8.9	9.5	15.7
营业税	Business Tax			43.2	41.7	36.3	34.8	28.3
企业所得税	Corporate Income Tax			16.8	17.9	21.8	22.7	21.9
个人所得税	Private Income Tax			16.3	9.2	9.1	8.5	9.1
能源消费总量	**Energy Consumotion**							
第一产业	Primary Industry	3.9	3.4	2.5	1.6	1.4	1.4	1.4
第二产业	Secondary Industry	63.5	65.9	58.5	48.9	39.2	33.8	32.7
第三产业	Tertiary Industry	19.0	17.9	26.1	34.8	41.7	45.3	46.5
生活消费	Living Consumption	13.6	12.8	12.9	14.7	17.7	19.5	19.4

注：自2012年开始，从业人员年末人数和能源消费总量三次产业分组口径根据国家统计局规定进行了调整。

Note: From 2012, The grouping standards for Year-end Employed Persons and Energy Consumption of three industries were changed according to provisions of the National Bureau of Statistics.

1-10 续表 1 Continued

单位：% (%)

项 目	Item	1990	1995	2000	2005	2010	2012	2013
产 业	**Industry**							
农 业	**Agriculture**							
农林牧渔业产值结构	Structure of Gross Output Value of Agriculture							
农 业	Agriculture	55.6	52.8	46.7	38.0	47.0	42.0	40.4
林 业	Forestry	1.3	1.7	2.8	5.2	5.1	13.8	18.0
牧 业	Animal Production and Hunting	39.8	41.8	46.4	50.5	42.6	39.0	36.7
渔 业	Fishing	3.3	3.7	4.1	3.6	3.5	3.3	3.0
农林牧渔服务业	Service Activities for Agriculture, Forestry, Animal Production and Hunting, Fishing				2.7	1.8	1.9	1.9
工 业	**Industry**							
规模以上工业主要行业增加值结构	Structure of Added Value of Industry by Sector (Above Designated Size)							
#医药制造业	Manufacture of Medicines		1.6	3.6	3.0	5.6	7.3	7.4
黑色金属冶炼和压延加工业	Smelting and Pressing of Ferrous Metals		20.1	8.9	14.0	1.1	0.2	0.4
汽车制造业	Manufacture of Motor Vehicles		9.4	3.7	8.7	16.6	16.9	21.3
计算机、通信和其他电子设备制造业	Manufacture of Computer, Communication Equipment and Other Electronic Equipment		9.9	24.7	16.7	8.7	8.0	8.9
电力、热力的生产和供应业	Production and Distribution of Electricity and Heating Power		7.0	6.4	11.8	14.9	17.7	17.5
建筑业	**Construction**							
建筑业总产值结构	Stucture of Gross Output Value of Construction							
#国有企业	State-owned Enterprises	68.7	69.1	44.8	27.4	6.3	5.7	5.1
集体企业	Collectively-owned Enterprises	31.3	26.4	21.7	4.7	2.0	1.8	1.7
港澳台商投资企业	Hong Kong, Macao and Taiwan-invested Enterprises		1.4	1.4	1.2	1.8	1.5	0.9
外商投资企业	Foreign-invested Enterprises		1.2	2.0	1.7	1.0	0.8	0.7
交通运输业	**Transport**							
货运量结构(按运输方式分)	Structure of Freignt (By Means of Transportation)							
铁 路	Railway	11.4	9.2	8.5	6.1	6.6	4.3	3.8
公 路	Road	87.5	90.4	91.2	92.4	85.1	87.0	87.1
民 航	Civil Aviation	0.04	0.05	0.1	0.2	0.5	0.5	0.5
管 道	Pipeline	1.0	0.3	0.2	1.2	7.7	8.2	8.6
客运量结构(按运输方式分)	Structure of Passenger (By Means of Transportation)							
铁 路	Railway	50.4	45.1	24.2	9.5	6.3	6.9	16.3
公 路	Road	46.7	47.7	70.7	85.3	89.7	88.8	73.9
民 航	Civil Aviation	2.9	7.2	5.1	5.2	4.0	4.3	9.8
国内贸易	**Domestic Trade**							
社会消费品零售总额结构	Structure Retail Sales of Consumer Goods							
吃类商品	Food	39.6	42.7	28.4	25.8	21.4	21.8	20.0
穿类商品	Clothing	13.2	14.6	12.0	9.7	8.8	9.3	8.7
用类商品	Daily Use Articles	44.8	40.8	56.2	56.5	62.4	60.7	64.1
烧类商品	Fuels	2.4	1.9	3.4	8.1	7.5	8.1	7.3
对外贸易	**Foreign Trade**							
地区出口商品结构	Structure of Export Commodities							
#一般贸易	General Trade		70.6	65.9	54.5	45.0	48.0	43.2
加工贸易	Processing Trade		21.3	29.6	39.6	42.1	37.5	40.5
地区进口商品结构	Structure of Import Commodities							
#一般贸易	General Trade		84.4	87.3	85.2	88.7	89.4	89.2
加工贸易	Processing Trade		5.2	3.5	8.2	5.9	4.8	5.6
国际旅游	**International Tourism**							
接待海外旅游人数结构	Structure of Inbound Tourist							
外国人	Foreigners	63.7	80.5	84.4	85.9	86.0	86.7	86.1
港澳台同胞	Compatriots from Hong Kong, Macao and Taiwan	34.6	17.6	15.6	14.1	14.0	13.3	13.9

1-10 续表 2 Continued

单位：% (%)

项　目	Item	1990	1995	2000	2005	2010	2012	2013
教育、科技、文化、卫生	**Education, Science and Technology, Culture, Health Care**							
教　育	**Education**							
在校学生结构	Structure of Students Enrollment							
#高等教育	Higher Education	8.3	9.0	14.0	46.2	49.5	49.8	50.4
中等教育	Secondary Education	32.5	41.0	48.7	29.7	22.1	20.5	18.9
小学教育	Primary Education	59.0	49.6	36.8	16.9	19.8	20.1	21.1
专任教师结构	Structure of Full-time Teachers							
#高等教育	Higher Education	24.6	22.7	22.2	32.7	35.9	31.3	32.2
中等教育	Secondary Education	38.3	38.6	40.5	33.6	29.1	32.5	31.5
小学教育	Primary Education	36.7	37.9	36.8	25.3	23.9	22.8	22.5
科　技	**Science and Technology**							
研究与试验发展(R&D)人员折合全时当量结构	Structure of R&D Personnel							
基础研究	Basic Research				12.9	15.2	14.7	14.8
应用研究	Applied Research				29.8	27.1	24.6	24.5
试验发展	Experimental Development				57.3	57.7	60.8	60.7
研究与试验发展(R&D)经费内部支出结构	Structure of Internal R&D Expenditures							
基础研究	Basic Research				10.1	11.6	11.8	11.6
应用研究	Applied Research				27.8	26.4	22.7	21.8
试验发展	Experimental Development				53.1	62.0	65.4	66.6
卫　生	**Health Care**							
卫生技术人员结构	Structure of Medical Personnel							
#执业(助理)医师	Certified Doctors	45.6	46.7	44.6	42.2	38.5	37.4	37.4
注册护士	Registered Nurses	31.0	31.7	34.5	35.8	39.3	43.3	43.8
生活与环境	**People's Livelihood and Environment**							
生　活	**People's Livelihood**							
城镇居民消费结构	Consumption Structure of Urban Residents							
食品(恩格尔系数)	Food (Engel Coefficient)	54.2	48.5	36.3	31.8	32.1	31.3	31.1
衣　着	Clothing	14.8	15.1	8.9	8.9	10.4	11.0	10.6
居　住	Housing	3.5	4.5	6.9	7.9	7.9	8.2	8.1
家庭设备用品及服务	Household Appliances and Services	10.4	8.8	12.9	6.4	6.9	6.7	7.5
医疗保健	Health Care and Medical Services	1.4	2.9	6.9	9.8	6.7	6.9	6.6
交通和通信	Transport and Communications	1.5	4.7	7.1	14.7	17.2	15.7	15.6
教育文化娱乐服务	Education, Cultural and Entertainment Services	11.5	10.2	15.1	16.5	14.6	15.4	15.2
其他商品和服务	Qther Goods and Services	2.7	5.2	5.8	4.0	4.2	4.8	5.3
农村居民消费结构	Consumption Structure of Rural Residents							
食品(恩格尔系数)	Food (Engel Coefficient)	50.7	49.6	36.7	32.8	30.9	33.2	34.6
衣　着	Clothing	9.5	10.9	7.6	7.8	7.7	8.0	8.7
居　住	Housing	19.2	9.7	15.7	16.2	21.8	18.5	17.6
家庭设备用品及服务	Household Appliances and Services	8.0	7.6	7.3	6.2	5.6	6.5	6.6
医疗保健	Health Care and Medical Services	3.8	4.8	8.0	9.0	8.9	9.5	8.6
交通和通信	Transport and Communications	1.7	4.1	6.3	11.0	13.1	11.8	10.7
文教娱乐用品及服务支出	Education, Cultural and Entertainment Services	6.6	10.6	14.4	15.1	9.7	9.7	9.8
其他商品和服务	Qther Goods and Services	0.6	2.8	4.0	1.9	2.4	2.8	3.3
环　境	**Environment**							
林木绿化率	Green Area Coverage	28.3	36.3	42.0	50.5	53.0	55.5	57.4

1-11 国民经济和社会发展比例和效益指标
INDICATORS ON PROPORTIONS AND EFFICIENCY IN NATIONAL ECONOMIC AND SOCIAL DEVELOPMENT

项 目	Item	2013	2012
人口与就业	**Population and Employment**		
人 口	**Population**		
常住人口出生率 (‰)	Birth Rate of Permanent Population (‰)	8.93	9.05
常住人口死亡率 (‰)	Death Rate of Permanent Population (‰)	4.52	4.31
常住人口自然增长率 (‰)	Natural Growth Rate of Permanent Population (‰)	4.41	4.74
就 业	**Employment**		
城镇登记失业率 (%)	Registered Unemployment Rate in Urban Areas (%)	1.21	1.27
宏观经济	**Macro Economy**		
国民经济核算	**National Accounts**		
地区生产总值构成 (%)	Structure of Gross Domestic Product (%)	100.0	100.0
第一产业	Primary Industry	0.8	0.8
第二产业	Secondary Industry	22.3	22.7
第三产业	Tertiary Industry	76.9	76.5
全社会劳动生产率 (元/人)	Overall Labor Productivity (yuan/person)	173470	164257
第一产业	Primary Industry	28713	25808
第二产业	Secondary Industry	205540	188018
第三产业	Tertiary Industry	175066	167852
固定资产投资	**Fixed Asset Investment**		
全社会固定资产投资相当于地区生产总值比例 (%)	Proportion of Fixed Asset Investment to Gross Domestic Product (%)	36.1	36.1
财 政	**Government Finance**		
地方财政收入相当于地区生产总值比例 (%)	Proportion of Local Finance Revenue to Gross Domestic Product (%)	28.5	25.6
地方财政支出相当于地区生产总值比例 (%)	Proportion of Local Finance Expenditure to Gross Domestic Product (%)	31.0	27.2
能源消费	**Energy Consumption**		
能源消费弹性系数	Energy Consumption Elasticity Coefficient	0.32	0.34
电力消费弹性系数	Electricity Consumption Elasticity Coefficient	0.51	0.88
万元地区生产总值能耗(可比价) (吨标准煤)	Energy Consumption per 10000 yuan of GDP (Comparable Price) (ton of SCE)		0.436
万元地区生产总值水耗(现价) (立方米)	Water Consumption per 10000 yuan of GDP (Current Price) (cu.m)	18.66	20.07
产 业	**Industry**		
规模以上工业企业效益	**Efficiency of Industrial Enterprises Above Designated Size**		
综合效益指数 (%)	General Efficiency Index (%)	275.80	253.53
总资产贡献率 (%)	Ratio of Profits to Average Assets (%)	7.79	7.98
资产保值增值率 (%)	Capital Maintenance and Appreciation Rate (%)	105.93	109.67

1-11 续表 Continued

项 目		Item		2013	2012
资产负债率	(%)	Ratio of Debts to Assets	(%)	52.62	51.85
流动资产周转率	(次)	Turnover of Working Capital	(time)	1.55	1.59
成本费用利润率	(%)	Ratio of Profits to Total Industrial Cost	(%)	7.24	7.91
全员劳动生产率	(元/人)	Overall Labor Productivity	(yuan/person)	295513	252465
产品销售率	(%)	Ratio of Sales to Gross Output Value	(%)	98.94	99.04
建筑业		**Construction**			
产值竣工率	(%)	Rate of Buildings Completed (by Output Value)	(%)	47.9	49.8
面积竣工率	(%)	Rate of Buildings Completed (by Floor Space)	(%)	18.2	20.2
邮电通信业		**Post and Communications**			
移动电话普及率	(户/百人)	Penetration Rate of Mobile Phone	(sets/100 persons)	159.5	153.1
固定电话主线普及率	(线/百人)	Penetration Rate of Main Line of Fixed Telephone	(line/100 persons)	41.0	42.7
国内贸易		**Domestic Trade**			
人均社会消费品零售总额	(元)	Per Capita Retail Sales of Consumer Goods	(yuan)	40033	37686
教育、科技、文化、卫生		**Education, Science and Technology, Culture and Health Care**			
教 育		**Education**			
学龄儿童入学率	(%)	Enrollment Rate of Children at School-Age	(%)	99.99	99.99
平均每一专任教师负担学生数		Average Number of Students Instructed by a Full-time Teacher			
#普通中学	(人)	Ordinary Secondary Education	(person)	9.5	9.7
小学学校	(人)	Primary Education	(person)	14.4	13.7
科 技		**Science and Technology**			
研究与试验发展经费内部支出相当于地区生产总值比例	(%)	Internal R&D Expenditures as % of GDP	(%)	6.08	5.95
文 化		**Culture**			
每万人拥有公共图书馆	(个)	Public Libraries per 10,000 persons	(library)	0.01	0.01
每万人拥有博物馆	(个)	Museums per 10,000 persons	(museum)	0.08	0.08
卫 生		**Health Care**			
婴儿死亡率	(‰)	Infant Mortality Rate	(‰)	2.33	2.87
孕产妇死亡率	(1/10万)	Maternal Mortality Rate	(1/100,000)	9.45	6.05
平均每千人口拥有执业医师数(常住人口)	(人)	Certified Doctors per 1,000 Persons (Permanent Resident)	(person)	4.06	3.97
平均每千人口拥有医院床位数(常住人口)	(张)	Hospital Beds per 1,000 Persons (Permanent Resident)	(bed)	5.45	4.48
家庭、生活、环境、灾害		**Household, Livelihood, Environment and Accidents**			
家 庭		**Household**			
少儿抚养比(常住人口)	(%)	Child-age Dependency Rate (Permanent Population)	(%)	11.64	11.55
老年抚养比(常住人口)	(%)	Old-age Dependency Rate (Permanent Population)	(%)	11.31	11.31
生 活		**Livelihood**			
城镇与农村居民收入比例(以农村居民收入为1)		Ratio of Urban Residents' Income to Rural Residents' Income (Rural Residents' Income = 1)		2.20	2.21
城镇居民人均住房建筑面积	(平方米)	Per Capita Living Space for Urban Residents	(sq.m)	31.31	29.26
农村居民人均住房面积	(平方米)	Per Capita Living Space for Rural Residents	(sq.m)	51.35	49.08
环境、灾害		**Environment and Accidents**			
人均公园绿地面积	(平方米)	Per Capita Park and Green Area	(sq.m)	15.70	15.50
平均每起火灾直接经济损失	(元)	Average Direct Losses per Fire Accident	(yuan)	12496	8706
平均每起交通事故直接经济损失	(元)	Average Direct Losses per Traffic Accident	(yuan)	9158	9443
食品安全监测抽查合格率(含烟酒等)	(%)	Pass Rate in Food Safety Spot Check (tobacco and wine included)	(%)	96.94	95.29
药品抽验合格率	(%)	Pass Rate in Medicine Spot Check	(%)	99.88	99.71

1-12 北京一日
A DAY IN BEIJING

项 目		Item		2013	2012
每天创造的财富		**Daily Production**			
地区生产总值	(万元)	Gross Domestic Product	(10000 yuan)	534263.0	488508.2
第一产业		Primary Industry		4432.9	4103.8
第二产业		Secondary Industry		119241.1	110909.8
工 业		Industry		96901.4	90008.2
建筑业		Construction		22339.7	20901.6
第三产业		Tertiary Industry		410589.0	373494.5
#交通运输、仓储和邮政业		Transport, Storage and Post		24208.2	22303.3
地方财政收入	(万元)	Local Public Finance Budget Revenue	(10000 yuan)	152495.4	124965.2
地方财政支出	(万元)	Local Public Finance Budget Expenditure	(10000 yuan)	165463.6	132962.7
发电量	(万千瓦时)	Electricity Generated	(10000 kwh)	9074.3	7945.9
汽车生产量	(辆)	Output of Motor Vehicles	(vehicle)	5584	4564
移动电话机生产量	(台)	Output of Mobile Telephones	(set)	514614	545064
每天收入与消费量		**Daily Income and Consumption**			
城镇居民人均可支配收入	(元)	Per Capita Disposable Income of Urban Residents	(yuan)	110.5	99.6
城镇居民人均消费性支出	(元)	Per Capita Living Expenditures of Urban Residents	(yuan)	72.0	65.7
农村居民人均纯收入	(元)	Per Capita Net Income of Rural Residents	(yuan)	50.2	45.1
农村居民人均生活消费支出	(元)	Per Capita Living Expenditures of Rural Residents	(yuan)	37.1	32.5
城镇单位在岗职工平均工资	(元)	Average Wage of On-the-job Staff and Workers	(yuan)	257.5	233.1
社会消费品零售总额	(万元)	Retail Sales of Consumer Goods	(10000 yuan)	229454.8	210459.5
机动车销售量	(辆)	Sales of Motor Vehicles	(vehicle)	3512	3511
居民生活用电量	(万千瓦时)	Resident Electricity Use	(10000 kwh)	4302.4	4421.7
居民家庭用自来水	(万立方米)	Resident Tap Water Use	(10000 cu.m)	135.0	126.5
每天其他活动		**Other Daily Activities**			
地区出口值	(万美元)	Exports of Local Enterprises	(USD 10000)	17287.0	16292.9
旅游外汇收入	(万美元)	Foreign Exchange Earning from Tourism	(USD 10000)	1313.6	1406.8
国内旅游收入	(万元)	Domestic Tourism Earnings	(10000 yuan)	100445.3	90199.5
接待入境旅游人数	(人次)	Inbound Tourists	(person-time)	12332	13686
接待国内旅游者人数	(人次)	Domestic Tourists	(person-time)	677776	618407
市内公共交通客运量	(万人次)	Urban Public Transport Turnover	(10000 person-times)	2204.9	2080.8
报刊、图书印数量	(万份、万册、万张)	Printed Copies of Newspaper, Magazines and Books	(10000 copies)	3454.5	3342.8
每天人口和婚姻变动		**Daily Population and Marriage Changes**			
出生人口(常住人口)	(人)	Births (Permanent Residence)	(person)	512	505
死亡人口(常住人口)	(人)	Deaths (Permanent Residence)	(person)	259	241
登记结婚对数	(对)	Registered Marriages	(couple)	448	476
离婚对数	(对)	Divorces	(couple)	177	133

注：离婚对数包括在民政部门登记的对数和经法院调离和判离的对数。
Note: Divorces include those registered with civil affair authorities and those mediated and ruled in courts.

1-13 “十二五”时期经济社会发展主要监测指标
MAIN MONITORING INDICATORS OF SOCIAL AND ECONOMIC DEVELOPMENT IN THE 12TH FIVE-YEAR PLAN PERIOD

项目		Item		2013	2012
地区生产总值比上年增长	(%)	Annual Growth Rate of GDP	(%)	7.7	7.7
第三产业占地区生产总值比重	(%)	Tertiary Industry as % of GDP	(%)	76.9	76.5
最终消费率	(%)	Final Consumption Rate	(%)	61.3	59.6
地方公共财政预算收入		Annual Growth Rate of Local Public			
比上年增长	(%)	Finance Budget Revenue	(%)	10.4	10.3
城镇居民人均可支配收入		Annual Growth Rate of Per-capita Disposable			
实际增长	(%)	Income of Urban Residents	(%)	7.1	7.3
农村居民人均纯收入实际增长	(%)	Annual Growth Rate of Per-capita Net		7.7	8.2
		Income of Rural Residents	(%)		
城镇登记失业率	(%)	Urban Registered Unemployment Rate	(%)	1.21	1.27
食品安全监测抽查合格率	(%)	Up-to-standard Rate of Food Security Monitor Spot Check			
（含烟酒等）		(tobacco and wine included)	(%)	96.94	95.29
药品抽验合格率	(%)	Pass Rate of Medicines Spot Check	(%)	99.88	99.71
全社会研究与试验发展经费支出		R&D Expenditure as % of GDP	(%)		
占地区生产总值的比例	(%)			6.08	5.95
万元地区生产总值能耗降低	(%)	Decrease of Energy Consumption			4.75
		per 10000 yuan of GDP	(%)		
万元地区生产总值水耗降低	(%)	Decrease of Water Consumption		5.85	7.38
		per 10000 yuan of GDP	(%)		
林木绿化率	(%)	Green Area Coverage	(%)	57.4	55.5

主要统计指标解释

法人单位 指有权拥有资产、承担负债，并独立从事社会经济活动（或与其他单位进行交易）的组织。法人单位应同时具备以下条件：（1）依法成立，有自己的名称、组织机构和场所，能够独立承担民事责任；（2）独立拥有（或授权使用）资产或者经费，承担负债，有权与其他单位签订合同；（3）具有包括资产负债表在内的账户，或者能够根据需要编制账户。

单产业法人 指仅包含一个产业活动单位的法人单位，该法人单位同时也是一个产业活动单位。

多产业法人 指由两个及以上产业活动单位组成的法人单位，这些产业活动单位接受法人单位的管理和控制。

登记注册类型 企业法人或企业产业活动单位的登记注册类型，按其在工商行政管理机关登记注册的类型填写。如企业登记注册类型发生变化，但未及时到工商部门变更登记，企业应根据变化后的实际情况填写。其他法人和产业活动单位的登记注册类型，按其主要经费来源和管理方式，根据实际情况，比照《企业登记注册类型与代码》填写。

国有企业 指企业全部资产归国家所有，并按《中华人民共和国企业法人登记管理条例》规定登记注册的非公司制的经济组织。不包括有限责任公司中的国有独资公司。

集体企业 指企业资产归集体所有，并按《中华人民共和国企业法人登记管理条例》规定登记注册的经济组织。

股份合作企业 指以合作制为基础，由企业职工共同出资入股，吸收一定比例的社会资产投资组建，实行自主经营，自负盈亏，共同劳动，民主管理，按劳分配与按股分红相结合的一种集体经济组织。

联营企业 指两个及两个以上相同或不同所有制性质的企业法人或事业单位法人，按自愿、平等、互利的原则，共同投资组成的经济组织称为联营企业。联营企业包括国有联营企业、集体联营企业、国有与集体联营企业和其他联营企业。

有限责任公司 指根据《中华人民共和国公司登记管理条例》规定登记注册，由两个以上，五十个以下的股东共同出资，每个股东以其所认缴的出资额对公司承担有限责任，公司以其全部资产对其债务承担责任的经济组织。有限责任公司包括国有独资公司、其他有限责任公司。

私营企业 指由自然人投资设立或由自然人控股，以雇佣劳动为基础的营利性经济组织。包括按照《公司法》、《合伙企业法》、《私营企业暂行条例》、《个人独资企业法》规定登记注册的私营独资企业、私营合伙企业、私营有限责任公司、私营股份有限公司和个人独资企业。

其他企业 指上述类型之外的其他内资经济组织。

港澳台商投资企业 指港澳台地区投资者依照中华人民共和国有关涉外经济的法律、法规成立的企业，包括与港澳台商合资经营企业、与港澳台商合作经营企业、港澳台商独资经营企业、港澳台商投资股份有限公司、其他港澳台商投资企业。

外商投资企业 指外国企业或外国人依照中华人民共和国有关涉外经济的法律、法规成立的企业，包括中外合资经营企业、中外合作经营企业、外资企业、外商投资股份有限公司、其他外商投资企业。

非公经济 指资产由我国私人控股、港澳台商控股、外商控股的“非公有控股”的企业法人单位，以及主要经费来源于私人、港澳台资和外资的非企业法人单位和个体工商户。其中，私人、港澳台及外商控股是指由其绝对控股和相对控股的经济成分。

Explanatory Notes on Main Statistical Indicators

Legal Entity refers to any organization that has the right to own assets and bear liabilities, and conducts social and economic activities independently (or conducts transactions with other entities). A business entity shall meet all of such conditions as: (1) established in accordance with law, having its own name, organization and site, capable of assuming civil responsibilities independently; (2) independently owning and using (or using under authorization) assets or outlays, assuming liabilities, having the right to sign contracts with other entities; (3) maintaining accounts including balance sheet, or capable of preparing accounts as needed.

Single-industry Legal Entity refers to any business entity conducting only one industrial activity. Such business entity is also an industrial activity entity.

Multi-industry Legal Entity refers to any business entity composed of two or more industrial activity entities which are managed and controlled by the business entity.

Registration type of an enterprise as legal person or as industrial activity entity shall be completed according to the type registered at the administration for industry and commerce. In the event of any change in registration type, and no registration alteration is made with administration for industry and commerce in good time, the registration type shall be completed according to the actual situation. Registration type for other legal persons and industrial activity entities shall be completed according to the main source of outlays and management manner, pursuant to the actual conditions, and by referring to the Type of Enterprise Registration and Code.

State-owned Enterprise refers to non-corporation economic organizations where the entire assets are owned by the state and which have registered in accordance with the Regulation of the People's Republic of China on the Management of Registration of Corporate Enterprises, excluding solely state-funded corporations in limited liability companies.

Collectively-owned Enterprise refer to economic organizations where the assets are owned collectively and which have registered in accordance with the Regulation of the People's Republic of China on the Management of Registration of Corporate Enterprises.

Joint-equity Cooperative Enterprise refers to a form of collective economic organizations based on cooperative system, where capitals come mainly from employees as their shares, with certain proportion of capital from the public, where production is organized on the basis of independent operation, independent accounting for profits and losses, joint work, democratic management, and where the distribution system integrates distribution according to work with distribution according to capital share.

Associated Enterprise refers to economic organizations established by two or more corporate legal persons or institutional legal persons of the same or different ownership, through joint investment on the basis of equality, voluntary participation and mutual benefits. They include state-owned associated enterprises, collectively-owned associated enterprises, state-collective associated enterprises and other associated enterprises.

Limited Liability Company refers to economic organizations established with investment from 2-50 shareholders and registered in accordance with the Regulation of the People's Republic of China on the Management of Registration of Corporations, each shareholder bearing limited liability to the corporation depending on its share of investment, and the corporation bearing liability to its debt to the maximum of its total assets. Limited liability companies include solely state-funded limited liability companies and other limited liability companies.

Private Enterprise refers to profit-making economic organizations established by natural persons or controlled by natural persons using employed labor. Private enterprises include private solely-funded enterprises, private partnership enterprises, private limited liability companies, private companies limited by shares, and private-funded enterprises registered in accordance with provisions in the Corporation Law, Partnership Enterprises Law, Interim Regulations on Private Enterprises and Sole Proprietorship Enterprise Law.

Other Enterprise refers to domestically funded economic organizations other than those mentioned above.

Hong Kong, Macao and Taiwan-invested Enterprise refers to enterprises established by investors from Hong Kong, Macao and Taiwan in accordance with laws and rules of the People's Republic of China on foreign-related economy. They include joint ventures with investors from Hong Kong, Macao and Taiwan, cooperative enterprises with investors from Hong Kong, Macao and Taiwan, enterprises wholly funded by investors from Hong Kong, Macao and Taiwan, companies limited by shares funded by investors from Hong Kong, Macao and Taiwan, and other enterprises funded by investors from Hong Kong, Macao and Taiwan.

Foreign-invested Enterprise refers to enterprises established by foreign enterprises or foreigners in accordance with laws and regulations of the People's Republic of China on foreign-related economy. They include Sino-foreign joint ventures, Sino-foreign cooperative enterprises, foreign wholly-funded enterprises, foreign-funded companies limited by shares, and other foreign-funded enterprises.

Non-public Economy means enterprises as business entities whose shares are controlled by "non-public entities" and whose assets are controlled by individuals, investors from Hong Kong, Macao and Taiwan, and foreign investors, along with enterprises not as business entities and self-employed operators whose main funds are from individuals, investors from Hong Kong, Macao and Taiwan, and foreign investors. Here, enterprises controlled by individuals, investors from Hong Kong, Macao and Taiwan, and foreign investors mean economic sectors with absolute or relative control by such companies.

国民经济核算
NATIONAL ACCOUNTS

简要说明

一、本章资料的主要内容

本章主要包括历年北京市地区生产总值、部分新兴产业增加值、各行业增加值、居民消费水平、全社会劳动生产率、三次产业的贡献率等资料。其中，地区生产总值是由北京市统计局根据统计资料、会计资料和部门财务资料采用不同方法核算的数据。

二、本章中关于历史数据调整的问题

本章中 1997-2008 年地区生产总值的数据及其分组资料，按照国家统一规定，根据"北京市第二次全国经济普查"和"北京市第二次全国农业普查"的数据结果进行了修正。

人均地区生产总值按年平均常住人口计算。同时，根据全国第六次人口普查数据对 2006-2010 年人均地区生产总值数据进行了修正。

鉴于第三次全国经济普查数据尚未对外公布，本章中 2013 年的相关数据均为初步核算数据。

三、关于按照新行业标准调整历史数据的问题

2002 年 10 月，国家统计局新修订的《国民经济行业分类》（GB/T 4754-2002）经国家质量监督检验检疫总局批准正式实施。本章中凡涉及行业及三次产业分组的数据（含历史资料）均已按此行业标准做出调整。

Brief Introduction

I. Main Content

Statistics in this chapter include the GDP of Beijing, added value of some emerging sectors, added value of different sectors, residents' consumption level, total productivity, contribution rate of three industries in previous years. Among them, the GDP of Beijing is calculated by Beijing Municipal Bureau of Statistics using different measures according to statistical data, accounting data and financial data of different sectors.

II. Adjustment to Historical Statistics

Figures of GDP 1997-2008 and grouping data have been corrected in accordance with the national uniform regulation and the results of Beijing 2nd National Economic Census and Beijing National 2nd Agricultural Census.

Per-capita Gross Regional Product is calculated at the annual permanent population. And 2006-2010 per-capita GDP figures were adjusted according to figures from the national 6th census.

The statistics for the Third National Economic Census have not been officially released yet, so the data of 2013 in this chapter are preliminary ones.

III. Adjustment to Historical Statistics According to New Industrial Standards

In October 2002, the Classification of National Economic Sectors revised by the National Bureau of Statistics (GB/T 4754-2002) became formally authorized by the State Administration for Quality Supervision, Inspection and Quarantine. In this chapter, all statistics related to sectors and grouping of three industries (including historical statistics) have been adjusted according to the new industrial standards.

2-1 地区生产总值(1978-2013年)
GROSS DOMESTIC PRODUCT (1978-2013)

单位：亿元 (100 million yuan)

年份 Year	地区生产总值 Gross Domestic Product	第一产业 Primary Industry	第二产业 Secondary Industry	工业 Industry	建筑业 Construction	第三产业 Tertiary Industry	人均地区生产总值(元/人) Per Capita Gross Domestic Product (yuan/person)	人均地区生产总值(美元/人) Per Capita Gross Domestic Product (USD/person)
1978	108.8	5.6	77.4	70.2	7.2	25.8	1257	797
1979	120.1	5.2	85.2	77.4	7.8	29.7	1358	908
1980	139.1	6.1	95.8	86.9	8.9	37.2	1544	1009
1981-1985	**950.9**	**62.3**	**589.4**	**515.5**	**73.9**	**299.2**		
1981	139.2	6.6	92.5	82.7	9.8	40.1	1526	895
1982	154.9	10.3	99.8	89.3	10.5	44.8	1671	883
1983	183.1	12.8	112.7	98.8	13.9	57.6	1943	983
1984	216.6	14.8	130.7	114.0	16.7	71.1	2262	972
1985	257.1	17.8	153.7	130.7	23.0	85.6	2643	900
1986-1990	**1978.7**	**162.9**	**1084.3**	**917.3**	**167.0**	**731.5**		
1986	284.9	19.1	165.8	141.2	24.6	100.0	2836	821
1987	326.8	24.3	182.6	154.5	28.1	119.9	3150	846
1988	410.2	37.1	221.3	189.5	31.8	151.8	3892	1046
1989	456.0	38.5	252.2	212.8	39.4	165.3	4269	1134
1990	500.8	43.9	262.4	219.3	43.1	194.5	4635	969
1991-1995	**4847.2**	**289.6**	**2220.4**	**1833.5**	**386.9**	**2337.2**		
1991	598.9	45.8	291.5	255.6	35.9	261.6	5494	1032
1992	709.1	49.1	345.9	293.0	52.9	314.1	6458	1171
1993	886.2	53.7	419.6	339.2	80.4	412.9	8006	1389
1994	1145.3	67.5	517.6	417.9	99.7	560.2	10240	1188
1995	1507.7	73.5	645.8	527.8	118.0	788.4	12690	1520
1996-2000	**12084.0**	**387.8**	**4277.7**	**3450.5**	**827.2**	**7418.5**		
1996	1789.2	75.0	714.7	576.2	138.5	999.5	14254	1714
1997	2077.1	77.2	781.8	635.9	145.9	1218.1	16621	2005
1998	2377.2	77.9	840.6	670.4	170.2	1458.7	19128	2310
1999	2678.8	78.4	907.3	724.0	183.3	1693.1	21407	2586
2000	3161.7	79.3	1033.3	844.0	189.3	2049.1	24127	2915
2001-2005	**26032.9**	**423.4**	**7759.7**	**6446.2**	**1313.5**	**17849.8**		
2001	3708.0	80.8	1142.4	938.8	203.6	2484.8	26980	3260
2002	4315.0	82.4	1250.0	1021.2	228.8	2982.6	30730	3713
2003	5007.2	84.1	1487.2	1224.5	262.7	3435.9	34777	4202
2004	6033.2	87.4	1853.6	1554.7	298.9	4092.2	40916	4943
2005	6969.5	88.7	2026.5	1707.0	319.5	4854.3	45993	5615
2006-2010	**55346.2**	**545.6**	**13571.1**	**11103.4**	**2467.7**	**41229.5**		
2006	8117.8	88.8	2191.4	1821.8	369.6	5837.6	51722	6488
2007	9846.8	101.3	2509.4	2082.8	426.6	7236.1	60096	7903
2008	11115.0	112.8	2626.4	2131.7	494.7	8375.8	64491	9286
2009	12153.0	118.3	2855.5	2303.1	552.4	9179.2	66940	9799
2010	14113.6	124.4	3388.4	2764.0	624.4	10600.8	73856	10910
2011	16251.9	136.3	3752.5	3048.8	703.7	12363.1	81658	12643
2012	17879.4	150.2	4059.3	3294.3	765.0	13669.9	87475	13857
2013	19500.6	161.8	4352.3	3536.9	815.4	14986.5	93213	15052

注：1. 本表数据按当年价格计算。
2. 本表中地区生产总值三次产业数据按国家2002年版国民经济行业分类标准核算。
3. 人均地区生产总值按年平均常住人口计算。同时，根据全国第六次人口普查数据对2006年至2010年人均地区生产总值进行了调整（下同）。
4. 2013年数据为初步核算数。

Note: a) Figures in this table are calculated at current year's prices.
b) Figures in the table on three industries of GDP follows the classification standard of national economy sectors 2002 edition.
c) Per capita GDP is calculated at average permamnent population. Per capita GDP 2006-2010 were adjusted according to the 6th National Population Census (the same below).
d) Figures for 2013 were preliminary statistics.

2-2 地区生产总值指数(上年=100)(1978-2013年)
INDICES OF GROSS DOMESTIC PRODUCT (PRECEDING YEAR=100) (1978-2013)

单位：% (%)

年份 Year	地区生产总值 Gross Domestic Product	第一产业 Primary Industry	第二产业 Secondary Industry			第三产业 Tertiary Industry	人均地区生产总值 Per Capita Gross Domestic Product
				工业 Industry	建筑业 Construction		
1978	110.5	109.0	115.1	112.4	153.0	97.7	109.1
1979	109.7	105.0	109.2	110.1	108.4	113.2	107.4
1980	111.8	109.3	110.1	110.1	110.3	118.5	109.8
1981	99.5	109.1	96.3	95.3	106.4	106.0	98.3
1982	107.4	113.4	105.8	105.8	106.1	109.9	105.6
1983	116.4	107.5	113.6	111.5	132.3	124.2	114.5
1984	117.4	106.8	116.1	115.7	118.8	121.8	115.6
1985	108.7	106.3	111.0	109.1	124.7	104.4	106.9
1986	108.0	100.1	104.8	105.0	103.7	115.7	104.6
1987	109.6	113.4	105.6	105.5	106.3	116.7	106.1
1988	112.8	111.2	112.1	113.0	106.5	114.1	111.0
1989	104.4	101.1	108.9	108.4	112.2	97.3	103.1
1990	105.2	103.3	101.1	101.9	95.6	113.3	104.0
1991	109.9	103.7	107.5	112.6	81.6	114.5	108.9
1992	111.3	103.1	112.2	110.3	125.7	111.9	110.5
1993	112.3	103.2	113.0	110.5	128.5	113.1	111.4
1994	113.7	102.8	114.1	113.5	117.0	115.0	112.5
1995	112.0	92.0	107.7	107.7	107.6	120.5	105.4
1996	109.0	97.2	106.2	106.1	107.0	113.4	103.1
1997	110.1	102.9	108.1	108.7	105.1	113.2	110.6
1998	109.5	101.1	109.6	108.7	114.2	110.1	110.1
1999	110.9	102.8	112.0	112.8	108.0	110.6	110.1
2000	111.8	103.1	111.4	113.2	102.1	112.9	106.8
2001	111.7	103.7	109.5	110.2	106.6	113.1	106.5
2002	111.5	102.7	108.4	107.8	110.9	113.3	109.1
2003	111.1	98.9	112.0	112.2	110.7	111.2	108.3
2004	114.1	99.4	117.0	119.3	106.3	113.1	111.4
2005	112.1	98.1	110.1	110.9	106.3	113.4	109.1
2006	113.0	100.6	110.5	109.5	116.0	114.3	109.1
2007	114.5	102.2	112.7	113.1	110.9	115.4	109.7
2008	109.1	101.1	100.8	100.2	103.7	112.5	103.7
2009	110.2	104.6	110.4	108.8	118.5	110.2	104.6
2010	110.3	98.4	113.7	114.9	108.3	109.3	104.8
2011	108.1	100.9	106.7	107.5	102.9	108.7	103.8
2012	107.7	103.2	107.5	107.0	109.7	107.9	104.9
2013	107.7	103.0	108.1	107.8	109.6	107.6	105.2

注：1.本表按可比价格计算。
2.2013年数据为初步核算数。

Note: a) Statistics in this table are calculated at comparable prices.
b) Figures for 2013 were preliminary statistics.

2-3 地区生产总值指数(1978年=100)(1978-2013年)
INDICES OF GROSS DOMESTIC PRODUCT (YEAR OF 1978=100) (1978-2013)

单位：% (%)

年份 Year	地区生产总值 Gross Domestic Product	第一产业 Primary Industry	第二产业 Secondary Industry	工业 Industry	建筑业 Construction	第三产业 Tertiary Industry	人均地区生产总值 Per Capita Gross Domestic Product
1978	100.0	100.0	100.0	100.0	100.0	100.0	100.0
1979	109.7	105.0	109.2	110.1	108.4	113.2	107.4
1980	122.6	114.8	120.2	121.2	119.6	134.1	117.9
1981	122.0	125.2	115.8	115.5	127.2	142.2	115.9
1982	131.1	142.0	122.5	122.2	135.0	156.3	122.4
1983	152.6	152.6	139.2	136.3	178.6	194.1	140.2
1984	179.1	163.0	161.6	157.7	212.1	236.4	162.0
1985	194.7	173.3	179.3	172.0	264.5	246.8	173.2
1986	210.3	173.5	187.9	180.6	274.3	285.5	181.2
1987	230.4	196.7	198.5	190.6	291.6	333.2	192.2
1988	259.9	218.7	222.5	215.3	310.6	380.2	213.4
1989	271.4	221.1	242.3	233.4	348.5	369.9	220.0
1990	285.5	228.4	244.9	237.9	333.1	419.2	228.8
1991	313.8	236.9	263.3	267.8	271.8	479.9	249.1
1992	349.2	244.2	295.4	295.4	341.7	537.0	275.3
1993	392.2	252.0	333.8	326.4	439.1	607.4	306.7
1994	445.9	259.1	380.9	370.5	513.7	698.5	345.0
1995	499.4	238.4	410.2	399.0	552.8	841.7	363.7
1996	544.3	231.7	435.7	423.4	591.5	954.5	374.9
1997	599.3	238.4	471.0	460.2	621.7	1080.5	414.6
1998	656.2	241.0	516.2	500.2	710.0	1189.6	456.5
1999	727.7	247.7	578.1	564.2	766.8	1315.7	502.8
2000	813.6	255.4	644.0	638.7	782.9	1485.4	536.8
2001	908.8	264.8	705.2	703.8	834.6	1680.0	571.7
2002	1013.3	271.9	764.4	758.7	925.6	1903.4	623.9
2003	1125.8	268.9	856.1	851.3	1024.6	2115.9	676.0
2004	1284.5	267.3	1001.6	1015.6	1089.1	2393.1	753.1
2005	1440.3	262.2	1102.8	1126.3	1157.7	2714.9	821.5
2006	1627.5	263.8	1218.6	1233.3	1342.9	3102.0	896.3
2007	1863.3	269.6	1373.4	1394.9	1489.3	3580.0	983.2
2008	2033.0	272.6	1384.4	1397.7	1544.4	4027.6	1019.6
2009	2240.4	285.2	1528.7	1520.8	1829.4	4437.6	1066.5
2010	2471.2	280.6	1738.1	1747.4	1981.2	4850.3	1117.7
2011	2671.4	283.1	1854.6	1878.5	2038.7	5272.3	1160.2
2012	2877.1	292.2	1993.7	2010.0	2236.5	5688.8	1217.0
2013	3098.6	301.0	2155.2	2166.8	2451.2	6121.1	1280.3

注：1.本表按可比价格计算。
2. 2013年数据为初步核算数。

Note: a) Statistics in this table are calculated at comparable prices.
b) Figures for 2013 were preliminary statistics.

2-4 地区生产总值构成(1978-2013年)
COMPOSITION OF GROSS DOMESTIC PRODUCT (1978-2013)

单位：% (%)

年份 Year	地区生产总值 Gross Domestic Product	第一产业 Primary Industry	第二产业 Secondary Industry	工业 Industry	建筑业 Construction	第三产业 Tertiary Industry
1978	100.0	5.2	71.1	64.5	6.6	23.7
1979	100.0	4.3	70.9	64.4	6.5	24.8
1980	100.0	4.4	68.9	62.5	6.4	26.7
1981	100.0	4.7	66.5	59.4	7.1	28.8
1982	100.0	6.7	64.4	57.6	6.8	28.9
1983	100.0	7.0	61.5	53.9	7.6	31.5
1984	100.0	6.9	60.3	52.6	7.7	32.8
1985	100.0	6.9	59.8	50.8	9.0	33.3
1986	100.0	6.7	58.2	49.6	8.6	35.1
1987	100.0	7.4	55.9	47.3	8.6	36.7
1988	100.0	9.0	54.0	46.2	7.8	37.0
1989	100.0	8.5	55.3	46.7	8.6	36.2
1990	100.0	8.8	52.4	43.8	8.6	38.8
1991	100.0	7.6	48.7	42.7	6.0	43.7
1992	100.0	6.9	48.8	41.3	7.5	44.3
1993	100.0	6.1	47.3	38.3	9.0	46.6
1994	100.0	5.9	45.2	36.5	8.7	48.9
1995	100.0	4.9	42.8	35.0	7.8	52.3
1996	100.0	4.2	39.9	32.2	7.7	55.9
1997	100.0	3.7	37.6	30.6	7.0	58.7
1998	100.0	3.3	35.4	28.2	7.2	61.3
1999	100.0	2.9	33.9	27.0	6.9	63.2
2000	100.0	2.5	32.7	26.7	6.0	64.8
2001	100.0	2.2	30.8	25.3	5.5	67.0
2002	100.0	1.9	29.0	23.7	5.3	69.1
2003	100.0	1.7	29.7	24.5	5.2	68.6
2004	100.0	1.4	30.8	25.8	5.0	67.8
2005	100.0	1.3	29.1	24.5	4.6	69.6
2006	100.0	1.1	27.0	22.4	4.6	71.9
2007	100.0	1.0	25.5	21.2	4.3	73.5
2008	100.0	1.0	23.6	19.2	4.4	75.4
2009	100.0	1.0	23.5	19.0	4.5	75.5
2010	100.0	0.9	24.0	19.6	4.4	75.1
2011	100.0	0.8	23.1	18.8	4.3	76.1
2012	100.0	0.8	22.7	18.4	4.3	76.5
2013	100.0	0.8	22.3	18.1	4.2	76.9

注：2013年数据为初步核算数。
Note: Figures for 2013 were preliminary statistics.

2-5 地区生产总值指数(2000年=100)(2000-2013年)
INDICES OF GROSS DOMESTIC PRODUCT (YEAR OF 2000=100) (2000-2013)

单位：% (%)

年份 Year	地区生产总值 Gross Domestic Product	第一产业 Primary Industry	第二产业 Secondary Industry	工业 Industry	建筑业 Construction	第三产业 Tertiary Industry	人均地区生产总值 Per Capita Gross Domestic Product
2000	100.0	100.0	100.0	100.0	100.0	100.0	100.0
2001	111.7	103.7	109.5	110.2	106.6	113.1	106.5
2002	124.5	106.5	118.7	118.8	118.2	128.1	116.2
2003	138.3	105.3	132.9	133.3	130.8	142.4	125.9
2004	157.8	104.7	155.5	159.0	139.0	161.1	140.3
2005	176.9	102.7	171.2	176.3	147.8	182.8	153.0
2006	199.9	103.3	189.2	193.0	171.4	208.9	166.9
2007	228.9	105.6	213.2	218.3	190.1	241.1	183.1
2008	249.8	106.8	214.9	218.7	197.1	271.2	189.9
2009	275.3	111.7	237.3	238.0	233.5	298.8	198.6
2010	303.7	109.9	269.8	273.5	252.9	326.6	208.1
2011	328.3	110.9	287.9	294.0	260.2	355.0	216.0
2012	353.6	114.4	309.5	314.6	285.4	383.0	226.6
2013	380.8	117.8	334.6	339.1	312.8	412.1	238.4

注：1. 本表按可比价格计算。
2. 2013年数据为初步核算数。

Note: a) Statistics in this table are calculated at comparable prices.
b) Figures for 2013 were preliminary statistics.

2-6 按行业分地区生产总值(2000-2013年)

单位：亿元

项　目	Item	2000	2001
地区生产总值	**Gross Domestic Product**	**3161.7**	**3708.0**
第一产业	**Primary Industry**	**79.3**	**80.8**
第二产业	**Secondary Industry**	**1033.3**	**1142.4**
工　业	Industry	844.0	938.8
建筑业	Construction	189.3	203.6
第三产业	**Tertiary Industry**	**2049.1**	**2484.8**
交通运输、仓储和邮政业	Transportation, Storage and Post	220.6	254.2
信息传输、计算机服务和软件业	Information Transmission, Computer Servecis and Software	164.4	210.1
批发与零售业	Wholesale and Retail Trade	372.5	424.1
住宿和餐饮业	Accommodation and Restaurants	81.2	97.2
金融业	Finance	425.2	487.5
房地产业	Real Estate	144.0	203.6
租赁和商务服务业	Renting and Leasing Activities and Business Services	118.8	137.0
科学研究、技术服务与地质勘查业	Scientific Research, Technical Services and Geological Prospecting	123.0	178.7
水利、环境和公共设施管理业	Management of Water Conservancy, Environment, and Public Facilities	23.4	25.2
居民服务和其他服务业	Resident Services and Other Services	36.2	42.2
教　育	Education	102.3	148.8
卫生、社会保障和社会福利业	Health Care, Social Security and Social Welfare	55.3	67.7
文化、体育与娱乐业	Culture, Sports and Entertainment	84.5	96.9
公共管理与社会组织	Public Manage and Social Organization	97.7	111.6

注：1.本表按当年价格计算；行业按国家2002年版国民经济行业分类标准核算。
2.2013年数据为初步核算数。

2-7 按行业分地区生产总值指数(上年=100)(2000-2013年)

单位：%

项　目	Item	2000	2001
地区生产总值	**Gross Domestic Product**	**111.8**	**111.7**
第一产业	**Primary Industry**	**103.1**	**103.7**
第二产业	**Secondary Industry**	**111.4**	**109.5**
工　业	Industry	113.2	110.2
建筑业	Construction	102.1	106.6
第三产业	**Tertiary Industry**	**112.9**	**113.1**
交通运输、仓储和邮政业	Transportation, Storage and Post		103.8
信息传输、计算机服务和软件业	Information Transmission, Computer Servecis and Software		112.3
批发与零售业	Wholesale and Retail Trade		112.4
住宿和餐饮业	Accommodation and Restaurants		109.0
金融业	Finance		113.1
房地产业	Real Estate		131.1
租赁和商务服务业	Renting and Leasing Activities and Business Services		104.5
科学研究、技术服务与地质勘查业	Scientific Research, Technical Services and Geological Prospecting		130.1
水利、环境和公共设施管理业	Management of Water Conservancy, Environment, and Public Facilities		94.8
居民服务和其他服务业	Resident Services and Other Services		102.9
教　育	Education		125.0
卫生、社会保障和社会福利业	Health Care, Social Security and Social Welfare		115.6
文化、体育与娱乐业	Culture, Sports and Entertainment		104.3
公共管理与社会组织	Public Manage and Social Organization		105.3

注：1.本表按当年价格计算；行业按国家2002年版国民经济行业分类标准核算。
2.2013年数据为初步核算数。

GROSS DOMESTIC PRODUCT BY SECTOR (2000-2013)

(100 million yuan)

2002	2003	2004	2005	2006	2007	2008	2009	2010	2011	2012	2013
4315.0	**5007.2**	**6033.2**	**6969.5**	**8117.8**	**9846.8**	**11115.0**	**12153.0**	**14113.6**	**16251.9**	**17879.4**	**19500.6**
82.4	**84.1**	**87.4**	**88.7**	**88.8**	**101.3**	**112.8**	**118.3**	**124.4**	**136.3**	**150.2**	**161.8**
1250.0	**1487.2**	**1853.6**	**2026.5**	**2191.4**	**2509.4**	**2626.4**	**2855.5**	**3388.4**	**3752.5**	**4059.3**	**4352.3**
1021.2	1224.5	1554.7	1707.0	1821.8	2082.8	2131.7	2303.1	2764.0	3048.8	3294.3	3536.9
228.8	262.7	298.9	319.5	369.6	426.6	494.7	552.4	624.4	703.7	765.0	815.4
2982.6	**3435.9**	**4092.2**	**4854.3**	**5837.6**	**7236.1**	**8375.8**	**9179.2**	**10600.8**	**12363.1**	**13669.9**	**14986.5**
281.1	309.0	356.8	403.3	455.2	497.5	498.9	556.6	712.0	809.0	816.3	883.6
278.6	378.0	449.6	586.6	696.4	870.5	999.1	1066.5	1214.1	1493.4	1621.8	1749.6
463.0	515.5	587.7	704.3	872.0	1098.2	1426.7	1525.0	1888.5	2139.7	2229.8	2372.4
122.0	112.6	163.3	182.3	218.4	245.0	274.4	262.5	317.3	348.4	373.1	374.8
561.9	635.6	713.8	840.2	982.4	1302.8	1519.2	1603.6	1863.6	2215.4	2536.9	2822.1
298.0	341.9	436.1	493.7	658.3	821.5	844.6	1062.5	1006.5	1074.9	1244.2	1339.5
214.2	231.6	276.6	360.7	447.1	623.6	765.3	809.6	953.2	1162.1	1340.6	1536.6
209.2	246.2	276.5	347.4	438.6	566.2	706.7	816.9	941.1	1135.5	1268.4	1444.3
27.3	30.5	34.6	40.5	47.0	51.8	59.1	67.2	75.3	86.3	101.3	113.0
54.7	64.1	79.6	80.2	85.3	82.1	74.9	73.9	99.3	112.1	124.3	133.3
159.6	206.2	267.4	289.4	320.6	365.2	402.1	444.1	516.2	605.9	681.8	758.2
73.7	87.2	105.9	118.2	140.3	162.6	187.8	213.0	254.5	311.5	363.6	416.1
111.6	125.0	142.7	170.2	189.0	223.1	247.4	259.0	294.6	339.4	402.6	445.3
127.7	152.5	201.6	237.3	287.0	326.0	369.6	418.8	464.6	529.5	565.2	597.7

Note: a) Data in this table are calculated at current prices.This table follows the classification standard of national economy sectors 2002 edition.
b) Figures for 2013 were preliminary statistics.

INDICES OF GROSE DOMESFIC PRODUCT BY SECTOR (PRECEDING YEAR=100) (2000-2013)

(%)

2002	2003	2004	2005	2006	2007	2008	2009	2010	2011	2012	2013
111.5	**111.1**	**114.1**	**112.1**	**113.0**	**114.5**	**109.1**	**110.2**	**110.3**	**108.1**	**107.7**	**107.7**
102.7	**98.9**	**99.4**	**98.1**	**100.6**	**102.2**	**101.1**	**104.6**	**98.4**	**100.9**	**103.2**	**103.0**
108.4	**112.0**	**117.0**	**110.1**	**110.5**	**112.7**	**100.8**	**110.4**	**113.7**	**106.7**	**107.5**	**108.1**
107.8	112.2	119.3	110.9	109.5	113.1	100.2	108.8	114.9	107.5	107.0	107.8
110.9	110.7	106.3	106.3	116.0	110.9	103.7	118.5	108.3	102.9	109.7	109.6
113.3	**111.2**	**113.1**	**113.4**	**114.3**	**115.4**	**112.5**	**110.2**	**109.3**	**108.7**	**107.9**	**107.6**
104.1	104.0	108.7	105.9	107.6	108.0	104.1	103.0	111.7	106.2	106.9	107.0
119.2	126.3	111.2	121.2	113.1	116.8	114.9	106.8	110.6	122.9	106.8	107.2
109.1	111.2	112.0	117.7	118.3	122.3	124.9	109.3	120.9	108.9	104.0	106.6
117.2	90.7	136.6	106.9	115.5	107.6	98.0	96.7	115.2	102.3	99.7	96.8
112.4	110.6	107.1	113.2	111.4	121.4	107.8	106.4	108.6	107.6	112.7	111.0
130.4	110.8	119.2	108.3	121.9	105.2	94.8	122.0	85.8	93.2	113.7	103.4
132.2	103.2	110.1	121.6	117.3	123.8	123.3	111.6	110.0	118.3	109.5	109.5
111.5	112.4	108.9	117.4	119.4	121.1	125.6	121.9	107.9	110.4	107.1	111.2
102.0	103.8	104.7	113.0	110.3	104.3	114.5	119.9	104.7	105.5	106.7	105.2
111.8	108.6	115.0	97.4	100.6	91.9	91.7	104.1	125.5	112.3	104.2	103.0
108.8	129.0	125.2	106.3	107.4	111.2	110.5	109.0	108.5	103.6	105.2	106.9
106.4	112.1	116.7	111.2	113.1	108.7	113.9	113.6	111.6	107.9	108.4	111.5
107.7	106.7	108.6	115.4	107.8	109.7	113.6	107.3	106.2	106.1	109.5	106.1
108.1	112.4	125.0	113.6	116.6	109.6	108.3	110.9	105.3	102.1	103.4	102.4

Note: a) Data in this table are calculated at current prices.This table follows the classification standard of national economy sectors 2002 edition.
b) Figures for 2013 were preliminary statistics.

2-8 部分新兴产业增加值(2004-2012年)
ADDED VALUE OF SOME EMERGING INDUSTRIES (2004-2012)

单位：亿元 (100 million yuan)

项 目	Item	2004	2005	2006	2007	2008
地区生产总值	**Gross Domestic Product**	**6033.2**	**6969.5**	**8117.8**	**9846.8**	**11115.0**
文化创意产业	**Cultural and Creative Industry**	**573.0**	**674.1**	**823.2**	**1008.3**	**1346.4**
文化艺术	Culture and Arts	22.6	32.2	35.3	38.8	42.7
新闻出版	Journalism and Publishing	108.1	106.8	135.3	142.2	153.7
广播、电视、电影	Radio Broadcasting, Television and Movies	54.9	78.0	73.5	102.7	120.1
软件、网络及计算机服务	Software, Internet and Computer Services	229.2	266.6	375.5	483.4	703.1
广告会展	Advertising and Exhibitions	47.8	51.0	52.2	64.9	112.2
艺术品交易	Artwork Trading	11.5	7.1	10.1	13.8	20.5
设计服务	Design Service	29.9	31.6	40.2	49.2	52.8
旅游、休闲娱乐	Tourism, Leisure and Entertainment	27.0	37.6	48.4	50.2	58.4
其他辅助服务	Other Auxiliary Service	42.0	63.2	52.7	63.1	82.9
信息产业	**Information Industry**	**867.3**	**1152.7**	**1344.5**	**1668.3**	**1759.8**
电子信息设备制造	Manufacture of Electronic Information Equipment	216.6	303.5	343.5	391.6	331.5
电子信息设备销售和租赁	Sales and Renting of Electronic Information Equipment	87.7	127.7	157.2	229.7	233.1
电子信息传输服务	Electronic Information Transmission Service	285.7	355.6	381.7	462.8	382.6
计算机服务和软件业	Computer Service and Software	163.9	231.0	314.7	407.8	616.5
其他信息相关服务	Other Information-related Service	113.4	134.9	147.4	176.4	196.1
高技术产业	**High-tech Industry**	**370.6**	**504.4**	**606.4**	**729.6**	**852.3**
核燃料加工	Manufacture of Nucleus Fuels	0.2	0.2		-0.4	
信息化学品制造	Manufacture of Information Chemical Products	1.5	1.1	1.7	1.7	2.7
医药制造业	Manufacture of Medicines	46.2	49.7	56.4	78.1	114.4
航空航天器制造	Manufacture of Aircrafts and Spacecrafts	16.8	17.7	23.8	25.2	27.0
电子及通信设备制造业	Manufacture of Electronic and Comminication Equipment	144.3	214.8	248.3	265.9	234.1
电子计算机及办公设备制造业	Manufacture of Computers and Office Equipments	48.4	65.3	63.6	88.2	64.8
医疗设备及仪器仪表制造业	Manufacture of Medical Equipment and Measuring Instrument and Meter	53.3	52.0	73.5	82.7	86.6
公共软件服务	Public Software Service	59.9	103.6	139.1	188.2	322.7
现代制造业	**Modern Manufacturing Industry**		**602.7**	**679.7**	**779.3**	**836.2**
电子类	Electronics		260.5	289.1	323.0	268.8
机电类	Electromechanical		132.6	154.2	169.6	212.0
交通类	Transport		130.0	142.7	178.3	206.5
医药类	Pharmaceutical		55.0	66.1	84.6	124.1
其他类	Other		24.6	27.6	23.8	24.8
现代服务业	**Modern Service Industry**	**2669.6**	**3206.8**	**3870.0**	**4933.1**	**5660.0**
信息传输、计算机服务和软件业	Information Transmission, Computer Service and Software	449.6	586.6	696.4	870.5	999.1
金融业	Finance	713.8	840.2	982.4	1302.8	1519.2
科学研究、技术服务和地质勘查业	Scientific Research and Development, Technical Services and Geologic Exploration	276.5	347.4	438.6	566.2	706.7
卫生和社会保障业	Health Care and Social Security	100.7	112.9	133.8	155.1	171.2
文化、体育和娱乐业	Culture, Sports and Entertainment	142.7	170.2	189.0	223.1	247.4
房地产业	Real Estate	436.1	493.7	658.3	821.5	844.6
商务服务业	Business Services	268.7	350.4	434.1	608.8	748.7
环境管理业	Environmental Management	14.1	16.0	16.8	19.9	21.0
教　育	Education	267.4	289.4	320.6	365.2	402.1
生产性服务业	**Producer Services**	**2261.0**	**2802.1**	**3409.4**	**4425.2**	**5355.3**
流通服务	Logistical Services	544.5	667.2	844.9	1062.1	1365.0
信息服务	Information Service	449.6	586.6	696.4	870.5	999.1
金融服务	Financial Service	713.8	840.2	982.4	1302.8	1519.2
商务服务	Business Service	276.6	360.7	447.1	623.6	765.3
科技服务	Scientific and Technological Services	276.5	347.4	438.6	566.2	706.7
信息服务业	**Inforamtion Service**		**721.5**	**843.8**	**1047.0**	**1195.2**
信息传输服务	Inforamtion Transmission Service		308.4	309.4	375.6	265.7
信息技术服务	Information Technology Service		231.0	314.7	407.8	616.5
信息内容服务	Information Content Service		182.1	219.7	263.6	313.0
物流业	**Logistics**			**368.0**	**383.5**	**423.4**
交通运输、邮政、仓储业	Transport, Post, Storage			306.2	318.1	324.2
流通加工、配送、包装业	Circulation and Processing, Delivery, Packaging			61.8	65.4	99.2

2-8 续表 continued

单位：亿元 (100 million yuan)

项目	Item	2009	2010	2011	2012
地区生产总值	**Gross Domestic Product**	**12153.0**	**14113.6**	**16251.9**	**17879.4**
文化创意产业	**Cultural and Creative Industry**	**1489.9**	**1697.7**	**1989.9**	**2205.2**
文化艺术	Culture and Arts	48.8	53.7	68.0	76.0
新闻出版	Journalism and Publishing	159.8	171.8	191.9	208.3
广播、电视、电影	Radio Broadcasting, Television and Movies	124.5	138.6	154.0	177.6
软件、网络及计算机服务	Software, Internet and Computer Services	710.5	847.1	1042.2	1190.3
广告会展	Advertising and Exhibitions	98.5	127.4	159.0	168.6
艺术品交易	Artwork Trading	30.9	43.0	56.4	59.2
设计服务	Design Service	76.4	84.2	90.6	97.4
旅游、休闲娱乐	Tourism, Leisure and Entertainment	60.7	69.5	78.6	83.4
其他辅助服务	Other Auxiliary Service	179.8	162.4	149.2	144.4
信息产业	**Information Industry**	**1762.9**	**1989.2**	**2377.7**	**2560.7**
电子信息设备制造	Manufacture of Electronic Information Equipment	260.2	282.5	297.0	374.6
电子信息设备销售和租赁	Sales and Renting of Electronic Information Equipment	235.1	261.4	320.5	245.2
电子信息传输服务	Electronic Information Transmission Service	445.6	480.0	613.5	661.5
计算机服务和软件业	Computer Service and Software	620.8	734.1	879.9	960.7
其他信息相关服务	Other Information-related Service	201.2	231.2	266.8	318.7
高技术产业	**High-tech Industry**	**778.4**	**888.8**	**1043.2**	**1240.3**
核燃料加工	Manufacture of Nucleus Fuels				
信息化学品制造	Manufacture of Information Chemical Products	2.0	3.3	2.2	1.5
医药制造业	Manufacture of Medicines	127.2	150.1	175.8	221.3
航空航天器制造	Manufacture of Aircrafts and Spacecrafts	28.6	34.6	41.3	46.8
电子及通信设备制造业	Manufacture of Electronic and Comminication Equipment	189.4	204.3	199.1	257.5
电子计算机及办公设备制造业	Manufacture of Computers and Office Equipments	33.2	36.4	44.3	56.1
医疗设备及仪器仪表制造业	Manufacture of Medical Equipment and Measuring Instrument and Meter	89.0	88.3	105.6	116.0
公共软件服务	Public Software Service	309.0	371.8	474.9	541.1
现代制造业	**Modern Manufacturing**	**895.2**	**1082.3**	**1234.9**	**1396.1**
电子类	Electronics	202.9	222.9	226.6	295.7
机电类	Electromechanical	243.5	263.3	279.6	288.0
交通类	Transport	279.0	400.7	494.6	533.0
医药类	Pharmaceutical	141.6	165.7	200.8	244.1
其他类	Other	28.2	29.7	33.3	35.3
现代服务业	**Modern Service Industry**	**6264.7**	**7026.3**	**8311.3**	**9435.3**
信息传输、计算机服务和软件业	Information Transmission, Computer Service and Software	1066.5	1214.0	1493.4	1621.8
金融业	Finance	1603.6	1863.6	2215.4	2536.9
科学研究、技术服务和地质勘查业	Scientific Research and Development, Technical Services and Geologic Exploration	816.9	941.1	1135.5	1268.4
卫生和社会保障业	Health Care and Social Security	192.9	226.3	286.0	335.2
文化、体育和娱乐业	Culture, Sports and Entertainment	259.0	294.6	339.4	402.6
房地产业	Real Estate	1062.5	1006.5	1074.9	1244.2
商务服务业	Business Services	791.7	930.9	1126.6	1302.2
环境管理业	Environmental Management	27.5	33.1	34.2	42.2
教　育	Education	444.1	516.2	605.9	681.8
生产性服务业	**Producer Services**	**5676.1**	**6705.0**	**8124.8**	**8890.8**
流通服务	Logistical Services	1379.5	1733.0	2118.4	2123.1
信息服务	Information Service	1066.5	1214.1	1493.4	1621.8
金融服务	Financial Service	1603.6	1863.6	2215.4	2536.9
商务服务	Business Service	809.6	953.2	1162.1	1340.6
科技服务	Scientific and Technological Services	816.9	941.1	1135.5	1268.4
信息服务业	**Inforamtion Service**	**1267.6**	**1445.3**	**1760.2**	**1940.9**
信息传输服务	Inforamtion Transmission Service	319.6	309.4	371.3	355.0
信息技术服务	Information Technology Service	620.8	734.1	879.9	960.7
信息内容服务	Information Content Service	327.2	401.8	509.0	625.2
物流业	**Logistics**	**427.7**	**493.7**	**562.5**	**598.5**
交通运输、邮政、仓储业	Transport, Post, Storage	326.1	382.9	429.9	452.7
流通加工、配送、包装业	Circulation and Processing, Delivery, Packaging	101.6	110.8	132.6	145.8

2-9 收入法地区生产总值(1978-2012年)
INCOME APPROACH COMPONENTS OF GROSS DOMESTIC PRODUCT (1978-2012)

单位: 亿元 (100 million yuan)

年 份 Year	地区生产总值 Gross Domestic Product	劳动者报酬 Compensation for Labors	生产税净额 Net Taxes on Production	固定资产折旧 Depreciation of Fixed Assets	营业盈余 Operating Surplus
1978	108.8	37.1	16.5	11.5	43.7
1979	120.1	42.0	18.3	13.4	46.4
1980	139.1	48.9	21.0	15.4	53.8
1981-1985	**950.9**	**350.9**	**142.8**	**111.0**	**346.2**
1981	139.2	52.9	22.0	16.9	47.4
1982	154.9	57.4	23.2	17.7	56.6
1983	183.1	66.0	26.8	20.7	69.6
1984	216.6	79.1	31.8	25.4	80.3
1985	257.1	95.5	39.0	30.3	92.3
1986-1990	**1978.7**	**773.7**	**290.5**	**244.9**	**669.6**
1986	284.9	107.8	43.4	34.9	98.8
1987	326.8	125.4	48.0	40.9	112.5
1988	410.2	153.9	59.7	49.9	146.7
1989	456.0	179.3	66.5	57.1	153.1
1990	500.8	207.3	72.9	62.1	158.5
1991-1995	**4847.2**	**2102.6**	**717.3**	**608.1**	**1419.2**
1991	598.9	254.2	86.4	75.7	182.6
1992	709.1	304.7	103.3	89.5	211.6
1993	886.2	387.7	131.4	109.0	258.1
1994	1145.3	508.1	168.9	140.2	328.1
1995	1507.7	647.9	227.3	193.7	438.8
1996-2000	**12084.0**	**5112.5**	**1761.0**	**1664.8**	**3545.7**
1996	1789.2	760.9	264.9	236.9	526.5
1997	2077.1	880.1	302.6	275.0	619.4
1998	2377.2	1008.5	341.3	319.6	707.8
1999	2678.8	1135.3	388.1	375.3	780.1
2000	3161.7	1327.7	464.1	458.0	911.9
2001-2005	**26032.9**	**11244.4**	**3999.7**	**4091.6**	**6697.2**
2001	3708.0	1538.7	549.8	559.7	1059.8
2002	4315.0	1810.6	643.0	680.3	1181.1
2003	5007.2	2119.7	753.1	791.5	1342.9
2004	6033.2	2595.5	960.4	960.5	1516.8
2005	6969.5	3179.9	1093.4	1099.6	1596.6
2006-2010	**55346.2**	**26740.5**	**8959.8**	**7893.4**	**11752.5**
2006	8117.8	3657.3	1286.7	1268.3	1905.5
2007	9846.8	4405.8	1625.8	1383.0	2432.2
2008	11115.0	5615.8	1896.6	1608.4	1994.2
2009	12153.0	6141.6	1953.5	1707.7	2350.2
2010	14113.6	6920.0	2197.2	1926.0	3070.4
2011	16251.9	7992.4	2566.1	2155.8	3537.6
2012	17879.4	9102.6	2894.6	2269.6	3612.6

2-10 收入法地区生产总值(2012年)
INCOME APPROACH COMPONENTS OF GROSS DOMESTIC PRODUCT (2012)

单位：亿元 (100 million yuan)

项　目	Item	地区生产总值 Gross Regional Product	劳动者报酬 Renumeration of Labor	生产税净额 Net Production Tax	固定资产折旧 Depreciation of Fixed Asset	营业盈余 Operating Surplus
地区生产总值	**Gross Regional Product**	**17879.4**	**9102.6**	**2894.6**	**2269.6**	**3612.6**
第一产业	**Primary Industry**	**150.2**	**102.8**	**1.1**	**24.2**	**22.1**
第二产业	**Secondary Industry**	**4059.3**	**1731.9**	**901.1**	**635.0**	**791.3**
工　业	Industry	3294.3	1312.1	692.0	560.8	729.4
建筑业	Construction	765.0	419.8	209.1	74.2	61.9
第三产业	**Tertiary Industry**	**13669.9**	**7267.9**	**1992.4**	**1610.4**	**2799.2**
交通运输、仓储和邮政业	Transportation, Storage and Post	816.3	469.4	76.1	289.9	-19.1
信息传输、计算机服务和软件业	Information Transmission, Computer Service and Software	1621.8	867.7	176.5	203.8	373.8
批发与零售业	Wholesale and Retail Trade	2229.8	859.2	761.0	114.4	495.2
住宿和餐饮业	Accomodation and Restaurants	373.1	255.6	60.6	43.1	13.8
金融业	Finance	2536.9	689.2	261.2	80.2	1506.3
房地产业	Real Estate	1244.2	346.6	278.9	375.4	243.3
租赁和商务服务业	Renting and Leasing Activities and Business Services	1340.6	1083.6	132.1	170.7	-45.8
科学研究、技术服务与地质勘查业	Scientific Research, Technical Services and Geological Prospecting	1268.4	839.2	148.4	110.6	170.2
水利、环境和公共设施管理业	Management of Water Conservancy, Environment and Public Facilities	101.3	71.7	8.0	11.7	9.9
居民服务和其他服务业	Resident Service and Other Service	124.3	105.1	10.8	6.6	1.8
教　育	Education	681.8	582.1	11.7	73.2	14.8
卫生、社会保障和社会福利业	Health Care, Social Security and Social Welfare	363.6	327.8	1.1	29.3	5.4
文化、体育与娱乐业	Culture, Sports and Entertainment	402.6	271.3	61.6	40.1	29.6
公共管理与社会组织	Public Management and Social Organization	565.2	499.4	4.4	61.4	

2-11 支出法地区生产总值(1978-2013年)
GROSS DOMESTIC PRODUCT BY EXPENDITURE APPROACH (1978-2013)

单位：亿元 (100 million yuan)

年份 Year	地区生产总值 Gross Domestic Product	最终消费支出 Final Consumption Expenditure	居民消费 Households Consumption	政府消费 Government Consumption	资本形成总额 Gross Capital Formation	固定资本形成总额 Completed Fixed Assets	存货增加 Changes in Inventories	货物和服务净流出 Net Outflow of Goods and Services	最终消费率(消费率)(%) Final Consumption Rate (%)	资本形成率(投资率)(%) Capital Formation Rate (%)
1978	108.8	53.0	28.6	24.4	31.7	24.9	6.8	24.1	48.7	29.1
1979	120.1	55.4	31.5	23.9	37.0	29.1	7.9	27.7	46.1	30.8
1980	139.1	57.3	39.6	17.7	45.1	36.5	8.6	36.7	41.2	32.4
1981	139.2	61.8	44.2	17.6	50.5	40.2	10.3	26.9	44.4	36.3
1982	154.9	68.6	48.8	19.8	51.8	42.3	9.5	34.5	44.3	33.4
1983	183.1	77.6	54.6	23.0	62.9	56.1	6.8	42.6	42.4	34.4
1984	216.6	96.5	64.8	31.7	84.7	72.5	12.2	35.4	44.6	39.1
1985	257.1	127.1	88.7	38.4	150.6	102.7	47.9	-20.6	49.4	58.6
1986	284.9	161.1	109.9	51.2	178.8	116.0	62.8	-55.0	56.5	62.8
1987	326.8	181.5	124.3	57.2	201.2	148.6	52.6	-55.9	55.5	61.6
1988	410.2	222.6	161.9	60.7	251.1	177.7	73.4	-63.5	54.3	61.2
1989	456.0	244.0	176.1	67.9	271.5	151.9	119.6	-59.5	53.5	59.5
1990	500.8	269.7	194.1	75.6	296.5	195.0	101.5	-65.4	53.9	59.2
1991	598.9	302.6	225.7	76.9	327.3	208.8	118.5	-31.0	50.5	54.7
1992	709.1	341.5	260.7	80.8	414.6	289.0	125.6	-47.0	48.2	58.5
1993	886.2	445.6	354.9	90.7	535.0	445.5	89.5	-94.4	50.3	60.4
1994	1145.3	614.1	504.2	109.9	787.5	703.8	83.7	-256.3	53.6	68.8
1995	1507.7	844.2	672.8	171.4	1036.0	912.0	124.0	-372.5	56.0	68.7
1996	1789.2	1022.7	815.5	207.2	1034.8	949.6	85.2	-268.3	57.2	57.8
1997	2077.1	1215.5	927.0	288.5	1235.1	1040.1	195.0	-373.5	58.5	59.5
1998	2377.2	1335.5	988.5	347.0	1360.3	1249.4	110.9	-318.6	56.2	57.2
1999	2678.8	1510.4	1075.9	434.5	1533.9	1264.6	269.3	-365.5	56.4	57.3
2000	3161.7	1688.0	1155.8	532.2	1697.4	1400.4	297.0	-223.7	53.4	53.7
2001	3708.0	1911.7	1244.8	666.9	1936.5	1602.1	334.4	-140.2	51.6	52.2
2002	4315.0	2300.3	1528.0	772.3	2332.7	1951.9	380.8	-318.0	53.3	54.1
2003	5007.2	2636.5	1729.7	906.8	2737.8	2437.9	299.9	-367.1	52.7	54.7
2004	6033.2	3085.3	1979.5	1105.8	3167.5	2844.3	323.2	-219.6	51.1	52.5
2005	6969.5	3486.5	2221.8	1264.7	3580.9	3204.7	376.2	-97.9	50.0	51.4
2006	8117.8	4138.5	2587.6	1550.9	3936.7	3551.2	385.5	42.6	51.0	48.5
2007	9846.8	5108.7	3040.0	2068.7	4469.3	4022.6	446.7	268.8	51.9	45.4
2008	11115.0	6026.4	3466.5	2559.9	4722.9	3989.5	733.4	365.7	54.2	42.5
2009	12153.0	6930.4	3998.2	2932.2	5049.9	4435.0	614.9	172.7	57.0	41.6
2010	14113.6	8032.8	4774.0	3258.8	6059.7	5342.4	717.3	21.1	56.9	42.9
2011	16251.9	9488.2	5525.0	3963.2	6683.6	5953.9	729.7	80.1	58.4	41.1
2012	17879.4	10655.1	6203.3	4451.8	7409.6	7032.8	376.8	-185.3	59.6	41.4
2013	19500.6	11946.1	6974.3	4971.8	7868.4	7595.4	273.0	-313.9	61.3	40.3

注：1. 根据全国第六次人口普查数据对2006年-2010年的数据进行了调整。
2. 2013年数据为初步核算数。

Note: a) Figures for 2006-2010 are revised according to the results of the Sixth National Population Census.
b) Figures for 2013 were preliminary statistics.

2-12 支出法地区生产总值
GROSS DOMESTIC PRODUCT BY EXPENDITURE APPROACH

单位：亿元 (100 million yuan)

项　目	Item	2013	2012	2013年为2012年% 2013 as % of 2012
地区生产总值	**Gross Domestic Product**	**19500.6**	**17879.4**	**107.7**
最终消费支出	**Final Consumption Expenditure**	**11946.1**	**10655.1**	**108.7**
居民消费	Households Consumption	6974.3	6203.3	109.1
城镇居民	Urban Resident	6466.2	5790.1	108.2
农村居民	Rural Resident	508.1	413.2	121.0
政府消费	Government Consumption	4971.8	4451.8	108.2
资本形成总额	**Gross Capital Formation**	**7868.4**	**7409.6**	**107.0**
固定资本形成总额	Completed Fixed Asset	7595.4	7032.8	108.6
存货增加	Changes in Inventories	273.0	376.8	77.8
货物和服务净流出	**Net Outflow of Goods and Services**	**-313.9**	**-185.3**	**-**

注：1.发展速度按可比价格计算。
2. 2013年数据为初步核算数。

Note: a) Figures of 2013 as % of 2012 are calculated at comparable prices.
b) Figures for 2013 were preliminary statistics.

2-13 三大需求对地区生产总值增长的拉动(2001-2013年)
CONTRIBUTION OF THREE DEMANDS TO GROWTH OF GDP (2001-2013)

年　份 Year	最终消费支出 Final Consumption Expenditure		资本形成总额 Gross Capital Formation		货物和服务净流出 Net Outflow of Goods and Services	
	贡献率(%) Contribution Rate(%)	拉　动(百分点) Impetus (Percentage Points)	贡献率(%) Contribution Rate(%)	拉　动(百分点) Impetus (Percentage Points)	贡献率(%) Contribution Rate(%)	拉　动(百分点) Impetus (Percentage Points)
2001	32.4	3.8	43.2	5.1	24.4	2.8
2002	77.0	8.8	61.6	7.1	-38.6	-4.4
2003	40.7	4.5	66.3	7.4	-7.0	-0.8
2004	40.2	5.7	37.3	5.3	22.5	3.1
2005	37.2	4.5	45.7	5.5	17.1	2.1
2006	60.0	7.8	24.6	3.2	15.4	2.0
2007	61.1	8.9	21.0	3.0	17.9	2.6
2008	81.6	7.4	9.0	0.8	9.4	0.9
2009	76.4	7.8	39.0	4.0	-15.4	-1.6
2010	65.8	6.8	47.7	4.9	-13.5	-1.4
2011	83.4	6.8	12.7	1.0	3.9	0.3
2012	73.0	5.6	43.8	3.4	-16.8	-1.3
2013	68.0	5.2	37.3	2.9	-5.3	-0.4

注：1．三大需求指支出法地区生产总值的三大构成项目，即最终消费支出、资本形成总额、货物和服务净流出。
2．贡献率指三大需求增量与支出法地区生产总值增量之比。
3．拉动指地区生产总值增长速度与三大需求贡献率的乘积。
4．本表按可比价格计算。
5．根据全国第六次人口普查数据对2006年-2010年的数据进行了调整。2013年数据为初步核算数。

Note: a) Three demands of GDP by expenditure method are final consumption expenditure,gross capital formation and net outflow of goods and services.
b) Contribution rate of the three demands to GDP growth refers to the proportion of the increment of the each component of GDP by expenditure method to the increment of GDP.
c) Impetus of the three demands to GDP growth refers to the growth rate of GDP multiplied by the contribution share of the three demands.
d) Figures in this table are calculated at comparable prices.
e) Figures for 2006-2010 are revised according to the results of the Sixth National Population Census. Figures for 2013 were preliminary statistics.

2-14 居民消费水平(1978-2013年)
HOUSEHOLDS CONSUMPTION EXPENDITURE (1978-2013)

年份 Year	居民消费水平(元) Level(yuan) 全市 All Households	城镇居民 Urban Households	农村居民 Rural Households	城乡消费水平对比(农村居民=1) Uban/Rural Consumption Ratio(Rural Households=1)	指数(1978年=100) Index(1978=100) 全市 All Households	城镇居民 Urban Households	农村居民 Rural Households	指数(上年=100) Index(Preceding=100) 全市 All Households	城镇居民 Urban Households	农村居民 Rural Households
1978	330	451	185	2.4	100.0	100.0	100.0	112.3	110.1	122.6
1979	356	464	221	2.1	117.5	114.5	120.8	117.5	114.5	120.8
1980	440	562	280	2.0	147.6	140.0	159.0	125.6	122.1	131.5
1981	485	590	338	1.7	160.3	144.8	189.4	108.6	103.6	119.2
1982	526	622	384	1.6	170.6	149.7	211.2	106.4	103.4	111.5
1983	579	674	432	1.6	175.4	151.2	222.6	102.8	101.0	105.4
1984	677	789	494	1.6	201.4	173.9	250.4	114.8	115.0	112.5
1985	912	1101	585	1.9	263.2	235.3	289.2	130.7	135.3	115.5
1986	1094	1284	749	1.7	312.9	272.0	365.8	118.9	115.6	126.5
1987	1198	1391	827	1.7	316.7	272.0	375.3	101.2	100.0	102.6
1988	1536	1779	1046	1.7	367.7	313.3	435.7	116.1	115.2	116.1
1989	1648	1874	1169	1.6	398.2	337.1	472.7	108.3	107.6	108.5
1990	1797	2045	1186	1.7	466.7	393.4	527.5	117.2	116.7	111.6
1991	2071	2330	1345	1.7	528.3	440.2	587.1	113.2	111.9	111.3
1992	2375	2696	1456	1.9	553.7	465.3	583.0	104.8	105.7	99.3
1993	3206	3743	1634	2.3	619.6	529.0	588.8	111.9	113.7	101.0
1994	4508	5307	2114	2.5	717.5	618.4	630.6	115.8	116.9	107.1
1995	5663	6497	3101	2.1	774.2	656.7	737.2	107.9	106.2	116.9
1996	6497	7477	3420	2.2	814.5	693.5	742.4	105.2	105.6	100.7
1997	7418	8594	3638	2.4	928.5	795.4	791.4	114.0	114.7	106.6
1998	7954	9195	3874	2.4	949.9	812.9	797.7	102.3	102.2	100.8
1999	8598	9916	4163	2.4	1025.9	876.3	855.1	108.0	107.8	107.2
2000	8820	10145	4277	2.4	1031.0	878.9	860.2	100.5	100.3	100.6
2001	9057	10301	4695	2.2	1026.9	865.7	915.3	99.6	98.5	106.4
2002	10882	12505	5020	2.5	1204.6	1026.7	952.8	117.3	118.6	104.1
2003	12014	13826	5275	2.6	1267.2	1082.1	954.7	105.2	105.4	100.2
2004	13425	15438	5713	2.7	1371.1	1169.8	1000.5	108.2	108.1	104.8
2005	14662	16478	6602	2.5	1442.4	1202.6	1105.6	105.2	102.8	110.5
2006	16487	18185	7580	2.4	1579.4	1292.8	1236.1	109.5	107.5	111.8
2007	18553	20320	8984	2.3	1691.5	1375.5	1389.4	107.1	106.4	112.4
2008	20113	21872	10375	2.1	1777.8	1436.0	1547.8	105.1	104.4	111.4
2009	22023	23812	11917	2.0	1928.9	1550.9	1742.8	108.5	108.0	112.6
2010	24982	26949	13392	2.0	2116.0	1696.7	1896.2	109.7	109.4	108.8
2011	27760	30037	13659	2.2	2243.0	1805.3	1835.5	106.0	106.4	96.8
2012	30350	32857	14664	2.2	2391.0	1922.6	1958.5	106.6	106.5	106.7
2013	33337	35836	17663	2.0	2548.8	2032.2	2320.8	106.6	105.7	118.5

注：根据全国第六次人口普查数据对2006年-2010年的数据进行了调整。2013年数据为初步核算数。

Note: Figures for 2006-2010 are revised according to the results of the Sixth National Population Census. Figures for 2013 were preliminary statistics.

2-15 社会劳动生产率(1978-2013年)
OVERALL LABOR PRODUCTIVITY (1978-2013)

单位：元/人 (yuan/person)

年 份 Year	社会劳动生产率 Overall Labor Productivity	第一产业 Primary Industry	第二产业 Secondary Industry	第三产业 Tertiary Industry
1978	2504	444	4496	1896
1979	2626	421	4567	2019
1980	2914	510	4760	2379
1981	2795	561	4325	2408
1982	2959	887	4445	2451
1983	3368	1102	4808	2983
1984	3909	1296	5355	3630
1985	4580	1680	6048	4253
1986	5002	1942	6339	4769
1987	5669	2580	6932	5479
1988	7046	4106	8324	6718
1989	7742	4292	9447	7114
1990	8203	4832	9578	7916
1991	9498	5047	10387	10095
1992	11051	5602	12325	11491
1993	13878	7179	14959	14577
1994	17728	9761	18767	18605
1995	22679	10223	23778	24538
1996	26997	10482	26914	30692
1997	31567	10760	30203	37205
1998	37202	10933	34764	44752
1999	43179	10740	41036	51888
2000	51082	10760	48695	61525
2001	59414	11214	53874	73082
2002	65974	11873	55408	83069
2003	72437	12909	64507	86864
2004	77478	14074	80837	83977
2005	80475	14341	87368	84828
2006	90313	14498	96009	95800
2007	105743	16716	110668	112388
2008	115565	18208	120615	122794
2009	122807	18898	140319	126872
2010	139057	20129	168451	140968
2011	154684	22622	177886	158613
2012	164257	25808	188018	167852
2013	173470	28713	205540	175066

注：1. 本表按可比价格计算。
2. 2013年数据为初步核算数。

Note: a) Figures in this table are calculated at comparable prices.
b) Figures for 2013 were preliminary statistics.

2-16 三次产业贡献率(2001-2013年) CONTRIBUTION SHARE OF THREE INDUSTRIES TO THE INCREASE OF GDP (2001-2013)

单位：% (%)

年份 Year	地区生产总值 Gross Domestic Product	第一产业 Primary Industry	第二产业 Secondary Industry	工业 Industry	建筑业 Construction	第三产业 Tertiary Industry
2001	100.0	0.8	26.7	23.3	3.4	72.5
2002	100.0	0.5	23.4	18.0	5.4	76.1
2003	100.0	-0.2	33.4	28.0	5.4	66.8
2004	100.0	-0.1	37.9	35.4	2.5	62.2
2005	100.0	-0.3	26.9	24.1	2.8	73.4
2006	100.0	0.1	23.5	17.9	5.6	76.4
2007	100.0	0.2	24.9	21.4	3.5	74.9
2008	100.0	0.1	2.4	0.6	1.8	97.5
2009	100.0	0.4	26.5	18.6	7.9	73.1
2010	100.0	-0.1	34.4	30.7	3.7	65.7
2011	100.0	0.1	19.7	18.1	1.6	80.2
2012	100.0	0.3	22.9	17.6	5.3	76.8
2013	100.0	0.3	24.9	19.6	5.3	74.8

注：1. 产业贡献率指各产业增加值增量与地区生产总值增量之比。
2. 本表按可比价格计算。
3. 2013年数据为初步核算数。

Note: a) Share of the contributions of the three industries to the increase of the GDP refers to the proportion of the increment of the value-added of each industry to the increment of GDP.
b) Figures in this table are calculated at comparable prices.
c) Figures for 2013 were preliminary statistics.

2-17 三次产业对地区生产总值增长的拉动(2001-2013年) IMPETUS OF THREE INDUSTRIES TO GDP GROWTH (2001-2013)

单位：百分点 (%)

年份 Year	地区生产总值 Gross Domestic Product	第一产业 Primary Industry	第二产业 Secondary Industry	工业 Industry	第三产业 Tertiary Industry
2001	11.7	0.1	3.1	2.7	8.5
2002	11.5	0.1	2.7	2.1	8.7
2003	11.1	…	3.7	3.1	7.4
2004	14.1	…	5.3	5.0	8.8
2005	12.1	…	3.2	2.9	8.9
2006	13.0	…	3.1	2.3	9.9
2007	14.5	…	3.6	3.1	10.9
2008	9.1	…	0.2	0.1	8.9
2009	10.2	…	2.7	1.9	7.5
2010	10.3	…	3.5	3.2	6.8
2011	8.1	…	1.6	1.5	6.5
2012	7.7	…	1.8	1.4	5.9
2013	7.7	…	1.9	1.5	5.8

注：1. 三次产业拉动指地区生产总值增长速度与各产业贡献率之乘积。
2. 本表按可比价格计算。
3. 2013年数据为初步核算数。

Note: a) Contribution of the three industries to GDP growth refers to the growth rate of GDP multiplied by the industrial shares.
b) Figures in this table are calculated at comparable prices.
c) Figures for 2013 were preliminary statistics.

主要统计指标解释

地区生产总值 是按市场价格计算的地区生产总值的简称。它是一个地区所有常住单位在一定时期内生产活动的最终成果。地区生产总值有三种表现形式，即价值形态、收入形态和产品形态。从价值形态看，它是所有常住单位在一定时期内所生产的全部货物和服务价值超过同期投入的全部非固定资产货物和服务价值的差额，即所有常住单位的增加值之和；从收入形态看，它是所有常住单位在一定时期内所创造并分配给常住单位和非常住单位的初次分配收入之和；从产品形态看，它是最终使用的货物和服务减去进口货物和服务。在实际核算中，地区生产总值的三种表现形态表现为三种计算方法，即生产法、收入法和支出法。三种方法分别从不同的方面反映地区生产总值及其构成。

三次产业 根据社会生产活动历史发展的顺序对产业结构的划分，产品直接取自自然界的部门称为第一产业，对初级产品进行再加工的部门称为第二产业，为生产和消费提供各种服务的部门称为第三产业。它是世界上通用的产业结构分类，但各国的划分不尽一致。我国2002年版国民经济行业分类标准：

第一产业：农、林、牧、渔业（包括农业、林业、畜牧业、渔业和农、林、牧、渔服务业）。

第二产业：工业（包括采矿业、制造业、电力、燃气及水的生产及供应业）和建筑业。

第三产业：除第一、第二产业以外的其他各业。

$$\text{最终消费率（消费率）}=\frac{\text{最终消费支出}}{\text{地区生产总值}}\times 100$$

$$\text{资本形成率（投资率）}=\frac{\text{资本形成总额}}{\text{地区生产总值}}\times 100$$

部分新兴产业统计划分标准

1. 文化创意产业 北京市文化创意产业指以创作、创造、创新为根本手段，以文化内容和创意成果为核心价值，以知识产权实现或消费为交易特征，为社会公众提供文化体验的具有内在联系的行业集群。北京市文化创意产业标准是在《国民经济行业分类》(GB/T 4754-2002）的基础上，根据文化创意活动的特点将行业分类中相关的类别重新进行的组合。适用于统计及政策管理中对文化创意相关活动的分类。内容上主要包括9个行业大类、27个中类、88个小类。

2. 信息产业 信息相关产业主要是指与电子信息相关联的各种活动的集合。信息产业标准是国家统计局在《国民经济行业分类》(GB/T 4754-2002）的基础上，参考了联合国的《全部经济活动的国际标准产业分类》，并结合我国的实际情况制定的。北京市从2004年开始执行国家信息产业统计标准。

3. 高技术产业 高技术产业主要是指与高技术产品相关联的各种活动的集合。高技术产业标准是国家统计局在《国民经济行业分类》(GB/T4754-2002）的基础上，根据高技术产业的特性，结合我国的实际情况制定的。北京市从2006年开始执行国家高技术产业统计标准。

4. 现代制造业 现代制造业是指用现代科学技术武装起来的制造业，是现代科学技术与制造业相结合的产物。现代制造业是应用现代制造技术、现代生产组织系统和现代管理理念所进行的以现代集成制造为特征、知识密集为特色、高效制造为特点的技术含量高、附加值大、产业链长的产业组织体系。现代制造业产业标准是北京市统计局在《国民经济行业分类》(GB/T4754-2002）的基础上，根据现代制造业的特性，将符合基本要求的行业归并，结合北京市的实际情况制定的。北京市从2005年开始执行现代制造业统计标准。

5. 现代服务业 现代服务业是相对于传统服务业而言，是适应现代人和现代城市发展的需求，而产生和发展起来的具有高技术含量和高文化含量的服务业。现代服务业有新服务领域、新服务模式、高文化品位和高技术含量的特征。现代服务业标准是北京市统计局在《国民经济行业分类》(GB/T4754-2002）的基础上，根据现代服务业的特性，将符合基本要求的行业归并，结合北京市的实际情况制定的。北京市从2005年开始执行现代服务业统计标准。

6. 生产性服务业 指以市场化的中间投入服务为主导的行业，生产性服务业具有经营性和可贸易性的特点，不仅为制造业提供中间投入服务，也为第一产业和第三产业提供中间投入服务。北京市生产性服务业分类标准涉及《国民经济行业分类》(GB/T 4754-2002）中交通运输、仓储和邮政业，信息传输、计算机服务和软件业，批发与零售业，金融业，租赁和商务服务业，科学研究、技术服务和地质勘查业等6个行业门类、22个行业大类，共包括148个行业小类，根据业务活动特点将生产性服务业划分为流通服务、信息服务、金融服务、商务服务、科技服务五大类别。

7. 信息服务业 指以信息资源为基础，利用现代信息技术，对信息进行生产、收集、处理、输送、存储、传播、使用并提供信息产品和服务的产业。本分类涉及《国民经济行业分类》(GB/T 4754-2002）中信息传输、计算机服务和软件业，文化、体育和娱乐业2个行业门类、6个行业大类、17

个行业中类和28个行业小类。根据信息服务业的概念和活动性质，将信息服务业划分为信息传输服务、信息技术服务和信息内容服务三大领域。

8．**物流业**　指为物品及其信息流动提供相关服务的经济活动。按照国家发改委、国家统计局、中国物流与采购联合会联合制定的《社会物流统计核算与报表制度（试行方案）》中的相关规定，物流业统计范围为：在工商登记注册时企业（单位）名称中具有“物流”、“配送”“快运”、“储运”、“货运”等物流功能，且业务经营范围以配送、流通加工、包装、仓储、运输等物流业务为主的单位。

Explanatory Notes on Main Statistical Indicators

Gross Domestic Product is a short name for the GDP calculated at market prices. It represents the final results of all resident units in an area from their productive activities over a given period of time. It is expressed in three different perspectives, namely value, income, and products respectively. GDP in its value perspective refers to the total value of all goods and services produced by all resident units during a certain period of time, minus the total value of input of goods and services of the nature of non-fixed assets; in other words, it is the sum of added value of all resident units. GDP from the perspective of income is the sum of primary incomes created by all resident units and distributed to resident and non-resident units. GDP from the perspective of products means the finally used goods and services minus the imported goods and services. In the practice of national accounting, gross domestic product is calculated with three approaches, namely production approach, income approach and expenditure approach, which reflect the gross domestic product and its composition from different angles.

Three Strata of Industry means the division of industrial structure according to the historical sequence of social productive activities. The sector which receives products directly from the nature is called the primary industry. The sector which re-processes primary products is called the secondary industry. The sector which offers various services for production and consumption is called the tertiary industry. This is a world universal classification of industrial structure. But it is different in different countries. As stated in China's standards on Classification of Sectors in National Economy Version 2002:

Primary Industry: agriculture, forestry, animal husbandry and fishery (including agriculture, forestry, animal husbandry and fishery sectors and services in support of these industries.

Secondary Industry: industry (including mining, manufacturing, production and supply of electricity, water and gas) and construction.

Tertiary Industry: any sector other than the primary or secondary industries.

Final Consumption Rate (Consumption Rate)

Final Consumption Rate (Consumption Rate) = Final Consumption / GDP × 100%

Capital Formation Rate (Investment Rate)

Capital Formation Rate (Investment Rate) = Total Capital Formation /GDP ×100%

Statistical Classification of some emerging Industries

1. Cultural and Creative Industry The cultural creation sector in Beijing means an internal correlative cluster of sectors with invention, creation and innovation as fundamental means, cultural content and creative fruits as core value, realization and consumption of intellectual property rights as transaction features, which provide cultural experience for the public. It is a new combination of related sectors in the industrial classification according to the characteristics of cultural creation activities on the basis of Classification of Sectors in National Economy (GB/T 4754-2002). It consists of 88 small categories, 27 middle categories and 9 major categories of sector.

2. Information Industry Information industry mainly means the set of activities related to electronic information. It is classified by the National Bureau of Statistics on the basis of Classification of Sectors in National Economy (GB/T 4754-2002) by reference to the International Standard Classification of Industries for All Economic Activities of the United Nations, combining the actual situation of China. The national statistical standard for information industry was effective in 2004 in Beijing.

3. High-tech Industry High-tech Industry mainly means the set of activities related to high-tech products. It is classified by the National Bureau of Statistics on the basis of Classification of Sectors in National Economy (GB/T 4754-2002) pursuant to the features of high-tech industry and combining the actual situation of China. The national statistical standard for information industry was effective in 2006 in Beijing.

4. Modern Manufacturing Industry Modern manufacturing industry mainly means the manufacturing industry equipped with modern sciences and technologies. Modern manufacturing is an industrial organization system with large content of technology, great added value and long industrial chain, with features of modern integrated manufacturing, intensive knowledge, efficient manufacturing, using modern manufacturing technologies, modern production organization system and modern management concepts. It is a combination of modern sciences, technologies and manufacturing. It is classified by the Beijing Municipal Bureau of Statistics on the basis of Classification of Sectors in National Economy (GB/T 4754-2002) pursuant to the features of modern manufacturing industry, merging the sectors meeting basic requirements and combining the actual situation of Beijing. The national statistical standard for information industry was effective in 2005 in Beijing.

5. Modern Service Industry Modern service is relative to conventional service. It is a service sector with great content of high technology and great content of culture, which has occurred and evolved to meet the need of modern people and modern cities' development. Modern service industry has new service fields, new service modes, high-grade culture and great content of high technology. It is classified by the Beijing Municipal Bureau of Statistics on the basis of Classification of Sectors in National Economy (GB/T 4754-2002) pursuant to the features of modern service industry, merging the sectors meeting basic requirements and combining the actual situation of Beijing.

The national statistical standard for modern service industry was effective in 2005 in Beijing

6. Productive Service means the sector dominant with intermediate input services. Productive service is operating and tradable. It offers intermediate input services for manufacturing industry, and for the primary and secondary industries. The productive service sector of Beijing covers 148 small categories, 22 major categories, 6 sectors in the Classification of Sectors in National Economy (GB/T 4754-2002), including transport, warehouse storage, post and telecom service, information transmission, computer service and software, wholesale and retail trades, financing, leasing and business service, scientific research, technical service, and geological survey. By the features of business activities, productive service falls into five categories, i.e. circulation service, information service, financial service, business service, science and technology service.

7. Information Service means the sector producing, collecting, processing, delivering, storing, transmitting and using information, and providing information products and services on the basis of information resource and by using modern IT. This sector involves 28 small categories, 17 middle categories, 6 major categories, and 2 industries in the Classification of Sectors in National Economy (GB/T 4754-2002), including information transmission, computer service and software, culture, sports and entertainment. Pursuant to the concept and nature of activities, the information service sector consists of three fields, i.e. information transmission service, information technology service, and information content service.

8. Logistics means economic activities offering relevant services for goods and information movement. Under relevant provisions in the Statistical Calculation and Reporting System (Tryout) for Social Logistics developed jointly by the State Development and Reform Commission, National Bureau of Statistics, China Federation of Logistics and Procurement, logistics statistics apply for: companies specializing in delivery, circulation processing, package, storage, transport and other logistics service, with their names registered for industry and commerce containing such terms as “logistics”, “delivery”, “fast transport”, “storage and transport”, “cargo transport”, and so on.

人口与就业
POPULATION AND EMPLOYMENT

简要说明

一、本章资料的主要内容

本章人口部分包括历年北京市常住人口和户籍人口的分组资料；建国以来已开展的六次人口普查的北京市人口数据；1990年以后的人口变动情况抽样调查数据；北京市计划生育数据。

本章劳动力部分包括北京市三次产业从业人员情况；法人单位从业人员及平均工资情况；城镇单位在岗职工人数及工资的分组情况；城镇登记失业情况等。

二、本章数据资料的来源

本章人口部分中，"户籍人口"数据来自于北京市公安局；"土地面积"数据来自于北京市国土资源局；计划生育情况来自于北京市卫生和计划生育委员会；其余资料均来自北京市统计局。

本章劳动力部分中，城镇登记失业情况由北京市人力资源和社会保障局提供，其他资料来源于北京市统计局。

三、有关统计标准的变化说明

（一）关于行业划分。根据国家统计局规定，自 2012 年开始执行《国民经济行业分类》（GB/T 4754-2011）标准。

（二）关于三次产业划分。根据国家统计局《三次产业划分规定》（国统字[2012]108 号），该规定对三次产业的范围进行了调整。其中第一产业是指农、林、牧、渔业（不含农、林、牧、渔服务业）；第二产业是指采矿业（不含开采辅助活动），制造业（不含金属制品、机械和设备修理业），电力、热力、燃气及水生产和供应业，建筑业；第三产业是指除第一产业、第二产业以外的其他行业。2012 年及以后开始执行此标准。

（三）关于统计上城乡划分标准

2008 年 7 月，国务院批复了国家统计局与民政部、住房城乡建设部、公安部、财政部、国土资源部、农业部共同制定的《关于统计上划分城乡的规定》（国函[2008]60 号文件和国家统计局令第 14 号），以后每年国家统计局都会出台《统计用区划代码和城乡分类代码》。本章中"城镇人口"和"乡村人口"的确定均执行当年的城乡分类标准。

Brief Introduction

I. Main Content

Population statistics in this chapter include classified data for permanent population and registered population in Beijing in previous years; statistics of population in Beijing from six national population censuses since the founding of the People's Republic of China; statistics from National Sample Survey on Population Changes after 1990 and statistics on family planning in Beijing.

Employment statistics in this chapter include information on employed persons in three industries in Beijing; employees and average wages in business entities; classified statistics for the number and wage of fully employed staff and workers in urban entities; registered unemployment in urban areas.

II. Source of Statistics

In the population section of this chapter, statistics on "registered population" are from Beijing Municipal Bureau of Public Security; statistics on "land area" are from Beijing Municipal Bureau of Land and Resources; family planning statistics are from Beijing Municipal Commission of Health and Family Planning; other statistics are from Beijing Municipal Bureau of Statistics.

In the employment section in this chapter, urban registered unemployment statistics are from Beijing Municipal Bureau of Human Resources and Social Security; other statistics are from Beijing Municipal Bureau of Statistics.

III. Changes in Relevant Statistical Standards

(I) Classification of Sectors. According to relevant provisions of the National Bureau of Statistics, the Standard for Classification of National Economic Sectors (GB/T 4754-2011) was implemented in 2012.

(II) Classification of Three Industries. According to the Provisions of the National Bureau of Statistics on Classification of Three Industries (GTZ [2012] No. 108), the scope of three industries was changed. The primary industry refers to agriculture, forestry, animal production and hunting, fishing (excluding service for agriculture, forestry, animal production and hunting, fishing); the secondary industry refers to mining and quarrying (excluding mining support activities), manufacturing (excluding metal products, machinery and equipment repair), production and distribution of electricity, heating power, gas and water, and construction; the tertiary industry refers to sectors other than the primary and secondary industries. The Provisions of the National Bureau of Statistics on Classification of Three Industries (GTZ [2012] No. 108) came into effect in 2012.

(III) Urban-Rural Statistical Definition

In July 2008, the State Council approved the Regulations on Urban-Rural Statistical Definition jointly developed by the National Bureau of Statistics, Ministry of Civil Affairs, Ministry of Housing and Urban-Rural Development, Ministry of Public Security, Ministry of Finance, Ministry of Land and Resources and Ministry of Agriculture. In the population section, new definition applies for the figures of "urban population" and "rural population".

3-1 六次人口普查人口基本情况
BASIC STATISTICS ON POPULATION CENSUS IN 1953, 1964, 1982, 1990, 2000 AND 2010

项 目	Item	1953	1964	1982	1990	2000	2010
常住人口 (万人)	**Permanent Population (10000 persons)**	**276.8**	**759.7**	**923.1**	**1081.9**	**1356.9**	**1961.2**
按性别分	**By Sex**						
男	Male	159.8	391.1	467.1	559.3	707.4	1012.6
女	Female	117.0	368.6	456.0	522.6	649.5	948.6
性别比(女=100)	Sex Ratio(Female=100)	136.5	106.1	102.4	107.0	108.9	106.8
按城乡分	**By Urban Area and Rural Area**						
城镇人口	Urban Population	205.8	425.8	597.0	794.5	1052.2	1685.9
乡村人口	Rural Population	71.0	333.9	326.1	287.4	304.7	275.3
家庭户规模 (人/户)	**Average Family Size (person/household)**			**3.7**	**3.2**	**2.9**	**2.5**
各年龄组人口比重 (%)	**Composition by Age Group (%)**						
0-14	Age 0-14	30.1	41.5	22.4	20.2	13.6	8.6
15-59	Age 15-59	64.3	51.9	69.1	69.7	73.9	78.9
60岁及以上	Age 60 and Above	5.6	6.6	8.5	10.1	12.5	12.5
#65岁及以上	Age 65 and Above	3.3	4.1	5.6	6.3	8.4	8.7
总抚养比 (%)	**Gross Dependency Ratio (%)**	**50.2**	**83.8**	**38.9**	**36.1**	**28.2**	**20.9**
老年抚养比	Old-age Dependency Ratio	5.0	7.5	7.8	8.6	10.8	10.5
少儿抚养比	Child Dependency Ratio	45.2	76.3	31.1	27.5	17.4	10.4
民族人口	**Population by Ethnic Group**						
汉族 (万人)	Han Chinese (10000 persons)	260.0	731.2	890.8	1040.5	1298.4	1881.1
占常住人口比重 (%)	Percentage in Permanent Population (%)	93.9	96.2	96.5	96.2	95.7	95.9
少数民族 (万人)	Ethnic Minority (10000 persons)	16.8	28.5	32.3	41.4	58.5	80.1
占常住人口比重 (%)	Percentage in Permanent Population (%)	6.1	3.8	3.5	3.8	4.3	4.1
每十万人口拥有的各种受教育程度人口 (人)	**Population with Various Education Attainment Per 100000 Persons (person)**						
大专及以上	Junior College and Above		4359	4866	9300	16839	31499
高中和中专	Senior Secondary/Secondary Technical School		4513	17646	18978	23165	21220
初 中	Junior Secondary School		11768	29086	30551	34380	31396
小 学	Primary School		31883	26197	22579	16963	9956
文盲人口及文盲率	**Illiterate Population and Illiteracy Rate**						
文盲人口 (万人)	Illiterate Population (10000 persons)		168.9	114.7	94.3	57.8	33.3
文盲率 (%)	Illiteracy Rate (%)		34.2	16.0	10.9	4.9	1.9
平均受教育年限 (年)	**Average Education Years (year)**		**5.3**	**7.8**	**8.6**	**10.0**	**11.5**
平均预期寿命 (岁)	**Average Life Expectancy (year old)**			**71.9**	**72.9**	**76.1**	**80.2**

注：1. 1964年的文盲人口数为12周岁及以上文盲和半文盲人口，1982年、1990年、2000年、2010年的文盲人口数为15周岁及以上文盲和半文盲人口。文盲率是指15周岁及以上人口中，文盲人口和半文盲人口所占比重。

2. 本表与表3-2相同的指标数据不同，是因为本表数据为普查时点数，表3-2为年末时点数。1953年普查时点为7月1日零时；1964年普查时点为7月1日零时；1982年普查时点为7月1日零时；1990年普查时点为7月1日零时；2000年普查时点为11月1日零时；2010年普查时点为11月1日零时。

Note: a) Statistics on illiterate population covered the illiterate and semi-illiterate people at 12 and over in 1964, and those at 15 and over in 1982, 1990, 2000, and 2010. Illiteracy rate means the share of illiterate and semi-illiterate people in the population at 15 and over.

b) This table has the same indicators but different figures from Table 3-2, because this table uses the data at the time point of the census, while Table 3-2 uses the year end as the time point. The time point of the census in 1953 was 12 o'clock midnight, July 1st; in 1964 the time point was 12 o'clock midnight, July 1st; in 1982 the time point was 12 o'clock midnight, July 1st; the time point in 1990 was 12 o'clock midnight, July 1st; the time point in 2000 was 12 o'clock midnight, November 1st; the time point in 2010 was 12 o'clock midnight, November 1st.

3-2 常住人口(1978-2013年)
PERMANENT POPULATION (1978-2013)

年 份 Year	常住人口(万人) Permanent Population (10000 persons)	#常住外来人口 Permanent Migrant Population	按性别分 By Sex 男 Male	女 Female	按城乡分 By Urban Area and Rural Area 城镇人口 Urban Population	乡村人口 Rural Population	常住人口出生率(‰) Birth Rate (‰)	常住人口死亡率(‰) Death Rate (‰)	常住人口自然增长率(‰) Natural Growth Rate (‰)
1978	871.5	21.8	443.2	428.3	479.0	392.5	12.93	6.12	6.81
1979	897.1	26.5	454.6	442.5	510.3	386.8	13.67	5.92	7.75
1980	904.3	18.6	457.8	446.5	521.1	383.2	15.56	6.30	9.26
1981	919.2	18.4	465.9	453.3	533.3	385.9	16.93	6.02	10.91
1982	935.0	17.2	474.0	461.0	544.0	391.0	20.04	5.68	14.36
1983	950.0	16.8	483.0	467.0	557.0	393.0	15.63	5.49	10.14
1984	965.0	19.8	491.0	474.0	570.0	395.0	16.74	5.53	11.21
1985	981.0	23.1	500.0	481.0	586.0	395.0	15.45	5.75	9.70
1986	1028.0	56.8	524.0	504.0	621.0	407.0	15.82	4.47	11.35
1987	1047.0	59.0	525.0	522.0	637.0	410.0	17.29	5.40	11.89
1988	1061.0	59.8	534.0	527.0	650.0	411.0	14.43	5.08	9.35
1989	1075.0	53.9	538.0	537.0	664.0	411.0	12.84	5.35	7.49
1990	1086.0	53.8	545.0	541.0	798.0	288.0	13.04	5.81	7.23
1991	1094.0	54.5	547.0	547.0	808.0	286.0	8.03	5.82	2.21
1992	1102.0	57.1	554.0	548.0	819.0	283.0	9.22	6.11	3.11
1993	1112.0	60.8	559.0	553.0	831.0	281.0	9.35	6.16	3.19
1994	1125.0	63.2	564.0	561.0	846.0	279.0	8.96	5.76	3.20
1995	1251.1	180.8	627.0	624.1	946.2	304.9	7.92	5.12	2.80
1996	1259.4	181.7	639.0	620.4	957.9	301.5	8.02	5.34	2.68
1997	1240.0	154.5	628.7	611.3	948.3	291.7	7.91	6.02	1.89
1998	1245.6	154.1	630.6	615.0	957.7	287.9	6.00	5.30	0.70
1999	1257.2	157.4	636.4	620.8	971.7	285.5	6.50	5.60	0.90
2000	1363.6	256.1	710.9	652.7	1057.4	306.2	6.20	5.30	0.90
2001	1385.1	262.8	722.1	663.0	1081.2	303.9	6.10	5.30	0.80
2002	1423.2	286.9	743.1	680.1	1118.0	305.2	6.60	5.73	0.87
2003	1456.4	307.6	761.2	695.2	1151.3	305.1	5.06	5.15	-0.09
2004	1492.7	329.8	779.9	712.8	1187.2	305.5	6.13	5.39	0.74
2005	1538.0	357.3	778.7	759.3	1286.1	251.9	6.29	5.20	1.09
2006	1601.0	403.4	817.6	783.4	1350.2	250.8	6.22	4.94	1.28
2007	1676.0	462.7	850.8	825.2	1416.2	259.8	8.16	4.83	3.33
2008	1771.0	541.1	900.2	870.8	1503.6	267.4	7.89	4.59	3.30
2009	1860.0	614.2	949.8	910.2	1581.1	278.9	7.66	4.33	3.33
2010	1961.9	704.7	1013.0	948.9	1686.4	275.5	7.27	4.29	2.98
2011	2018.6	742.2	1040.7	977.9	1740.7	277.9	8.29	4.27	4.02
2012	2069.3	773.8	1068.1	1001.2	1783.7	285.6	9.05	4.31	4.74
2013	2114.8	802.7	1090.7	1024.1	1825.1	289.7	8.93	4.52	4.41

注：1. 1978-1981年为户籍统计数，含暂住人口；1982-1989年数据是根据1982、1990年两次人口普查数据调整的；1990年以后数据为人口变动情况抽样调查推算数,其中1995、2005年为1%人口抽样调查推算数；2000年为第五次人口普查快速汇总推算数；2010年为第六次人口普查推算数。2006-2009年常住人口、出生率、死亡率等数据又根据2010年人口普查数据进行了调整。

2. "按城乡分"栏包括的"城镇人口"和"乡村人口"，1978-1989年数据为户籍管理统计中的"非农业人口"和"农业人口"口径；1990-1999年数据是根据1990年、2000年两次人口普查数据调整的；2000年数据为国家统计局1999年发布的《关于统计上划分城乡的规定(试行)》中的"城镇人口"和"乡村人口"口径，2001-2005年数据为该口径的推算数；2006-2008年数据为国家统计局2006年发布的《关于统计上划分城乡的暂行规定》中的"城镇人口"和"乡村人口"口径的推算数；2009年以后数据为《国务院关于统计上划分城乡规定的批复》中的"城镇人口"和"乡村人口"口径的推算数。

Note: a) Statistics for 1978-1981 were figures of registered residents, including temporary residents; statistics for 1982-1989 were adjusted from population censuses in 1982 and 1990. Data after 1990 were estimated from sample surveys on population changes; data for 1995 and 2005 were estimated from sample surveys on 1% of the population. Data for 2000 were estimated from fast summarizing of the fifth population census. Data for 2010 were estimated from fast summarizing of the 6th population census. Data of permanant population, birth rate, death rate and natural growth rate from 2006 to 2009 were adjusted from population census in 2010.

b) In classification by rural and urban areas, the "urban population" and "rural population" from 1978 to 1989 were non-agricultural population and agricultural population respectively in household registration. Data from 1990-1999 were adjusted from the censuses conducted in 1990 and 2000, and those in 2000 were on the basis of statistical classification of rural and urban population stated by the State Statistical Bureau in 1999. Statistics from 2001 to 2005 were estimated on the same basis. Figures from 2006 to 2008 were the estimated figures of "urban population" and "rural population", of which the statistical range was provided in Provisional Regulations on Statistical Division of Rural and Urban Areas issued by the State Statistics Bureau in 2006. Figures after 2009 were the estimated figures of "urban population" and "rural population", of which the statistical range was provided in the Official Reply of the State Council Concerning the Statistical Division of Rural and Urban Areas.

3-3 常住人口总量（按区县分）(2013年)
TOTAL NUMBER OF PERMANENT POPULATION (BY DISTRICT) (2013)

单位：万人 (10000 persons)

地区	District	常住人口 Permanent Population	#常住外来人口 Permanent Migrant Population	城镇人口 Urban Population	乡村人口 Rural Population
全市	**Total**	**2114.8**	**802.7**	**1825.1**	**289.7**
首都功能核心区	**Core Funtional Area of the Capital**	**221.2**	**55.4**	**221.2**	
东城区	Dongcheng District	90.9	21.0	90.9	
西城区	Xicheng District	130.3	34.4	130.3	
城市功能拓展区	**Urban Function Extension Area**	**1032.2**	**426.0**	**1022.4**	**9.8**
朝阳区	Chaoyang District	384.1	176.1	383.1	1.0
丰台区	Fengtai District	226.1	85.0	224.6	1.5
石景山区	Shijingshan District	64.4	21.4	64.4	
海淀区	Haidian District	357.6	143.5	350.3	7.3
城市发展新区	**New Area of Urban Development**	**671.5**	**289.6**	**464.5**	**207.0**
房山区	Fangshan District	101.0	24.6	70.4	30.6
通州区	Tongzhou District	132.6	53.6	84.5	48.1
顺义区	Shunyi District	98.3	37.3	53.2	45.1
昌平区	Changping District	188.9	100.6	154.4	34.5
大兴区	Daxing District	150.7	73.5	102.0	48.7
生态涵养发展区	**Ecological Conservation Area**	**189.9**	**31.7**	**117.0**	**72.9**
门头沟区	Mentougou District	30.3	5.0	26.0	4.3
怀柔区	Huairou District	38.2	10.6	26.2	12.0
平谷区	Pinggu District	42.2	5.3	22.9	19.3
密云县	Miyun County	47.6	7.2	26.3	21.3
延庆县	Yanqing County	31.6	3.6	15.6	16.0

注：本表数据为人口抽样调查推算数据，为年末数。
Note: Figures in this table are estimated figures from sample survey on population.

3-4 常住人口密度（按区县分）(2013年)
PERMANENT POPULATION DENSITY (BY DISTRICT) (2013)

地　区	District	土地面积 (平方公里) Land Area (sq.km)	常住人口 (万人) Permanent Population (10000 persons)	常住人口密度 (人/平方公里) Permanent Population Density (person/sq.km)
全　市	**Total**	**16410.54**	**2114.8**	**1289**
首都功能核心区	**Capital Core Functional Area**	**92.39**	**221.2**	**23942**
东 城 区	Dongcheng District	41.86	90.9	21715
西 城 区	Xicheng District	50.53	130.3	25787
城市功能拓展区	**Urban Function Extension Area**	**1275.93**	**1032.2**	**8090**
朝 阳 区	Chaoyang District	455.08	384.1	8440
丰 台 区	Fengtai District	305.80	226.1	7394
石景山区	Shijingshan District	84.32	64.4	7638
海 淀 区	Haidian District	430.73	357.6	8302
城市发展新区	**Urban Development New Area**	**6295.57**	**671.5**	**1067**
房 山 区	Fangshan District	1989.54	101.0	508
通 州 区	Tongzhou District	906.28	132.6	1463
顺 义 区	Shunyi District	1019.89	98.3	964
昌 平 区	Changping District	1343.54	188.9	1406
大 兴 区	Daxing District	1036.32	150.7	1454
生态涵养发展区	**Ecological Conservation Area**	**8746.65**	**189.9**	**217**
门头沟区	Mentougou District	1450.70	30.3	209
怀 柔 区	Huairou District	2122.62	38.2	180
平 谷 区	Pinggu District	950.13	42.2	444
密 云 县	Miyun County	2229.45	47.6	214
延 庆 县	Yanqing County	1993.75	31.6	158

注：本表常住人口数据为人口抽样调查数据推算数据，为年末数。

资料来源：本表"土地面积"由北京市国土资源局提供。

Note: Figures of permanent population in this table are estimated figures from the sample survey on population.

Source: Figures of land area were provided by Beijing Municipal Bureau of Land Resources.

3-5 常住人口自然变动（按区县分）(2013年)
NATURAL CHANGE OF PERMANENT POPULATION (BY DISTRICT) (2013)

地　区	District	出生人数(人) Number of Births (person)	死亡人数(人) Number of Deaths (person)	自然增加人数(人) Natural Increase of Population (person)	出生率(‰) Birth Rate (‰)	死亡率(‰) Death Rate (‰)	自然增长率(‰) Natural Growth Rate (‰)
全　市	**Total**	**186886**	**94510**	**92376**	**8.93**	**4.52**	**4.41**
首都功能核心区	**Capital Core Functional Area**	**22927**	**12904**	**10023**	**10.40**	**5.86**	**4.54**
东城区	Dongcheng District	9585	5022	4563	10.55	5.53	5.02
西城区	Xicheng District	13342	7882	5460	10.30	6.09	4.21
城市功能拓展区	**Urban Function Extension Area**	**87969**	**37970**	**49999**	**8.62**	**3.72**	**4.90**
朝阳区	Chaoyang District	35304	13857	21447	9.31	3.65	5.66
丰台区	Fengtai District	15668	8551	7117	7.00	3.82	3.18
石景山区	Shijingshan District	5027	3005	2022	7.84	4.68	3.16
海淀区	Haidian District	31970	12557	19413	9.06	3.56	5.50
城市发展新区	**Urban Development New Area**	**59438**	**28914**	**30524**	**8.98**	**4.37**	**4.61**
房山区	Fangshan District	9390	5583	3807	9.41	5.59	3.82
通州区	Tongzhou District	10548	5535	5013	8.06	4.23	3.83
顺义区	Shunyi District	9658	5461	4197	9.98	5.64	4.34
昌平区	Changping Ddistrict	15174	6191	8983	8.16	3.33	4.83
大兴区	Daxing District	14668	6144	8524	9.85	4.13	5.72
生态涵养发展区	**Ecological Conservation Area**	**16552**	**14722**	**1830**	**8.75**	**7.78**	**0.97**
门头沟区	Mentougou District	2540	2524	16	8.45	8.40	0.05
怀柔区	Huairou District	3407	2747	660	8.98	7.24	1.74
平谷区	Pinggu District	4007	3021	986	9.52	7.18	2.34
密云县	Miyun County	4137	3979	158	8.71	8.38	0.33
延庆县	Yanqing County	2461	2451	10	7.78	7.74	0.04

注：本表数据为人口抽样调查推算数据。
Note: Figures in this table are estimated figures from the sample survey on population.

3-6 常住人口年龄构成(2013年)
PERMANENT POPULATION BY AGE COMPOSITION (2013)

年龄组 Age Group	常住人口数(万人) Permanent Population (10000 persons)	比重(%) Percentage(%)
总 计 Total	**2114.8**	**100.0**
0-4	85.3	4.0
5-9	66.7	3.2
10-14	48.2	2.3
15-19	97.8	4.6
20-24	252.7	11.9
25-29	266.4	12.6
30-34	239.0	11.3
35-39	165.0	7.8
40-44	176.4	8.3
45-49	155.7	7.4
50-54	137.7	6.5
55-59	131.0	6.2
60-64	98.4	4.7
65-69	75.1	3.6
70-74	50.0	2.4
75-79	38.3	1.8
80-84	20.1	1.0
85岁及以上 85 and over	11.0	0.5

注：本表数据为人口抽样调查推算数据，为年末数。
Note: Figures in this table are estimated figures from the sample survey on population.

3-7 常住人口受教育程度(2013年)
EDUCATION ATTAINMENT OF PERMANENT POPULATION (2013)

单位：人 (person)

项 目	Item	调查人口合计 Total	男 Male	女 Female
6岁及以上人口	**Population at 6 and above**	**143310**	**73477**	**69833**
#小 学	Primary School	15067	7075	7992
初 中	Junior Secondary School	46046	24447	21599
高 中	Senior Secondary School	29644	15662	13982
大学专科	Junior College	19617	9307	10310
大学本科	4-year Unversity Education	23864	12390	11474
研究生	Postgraduate	6787	4039	2748

注：本表数据为人口抽样调查样本数据。
Note: Figures in this table are sample figures from the sample survey on population.

3-8 常住人口家庭户规模(2013年)
FAMILY SIZE OF PERMANENT POPULATION (2013)

地 区	Area	调查家庭总户数(户) Total Number of Households (household)	家庭户规模所占比重(%) Percentage of Various Sized Family(%) 一人户 One Person	二人户 Two Persons	三人户 Three Persons	四人户 Four Persons	五人及以上户 Five Persons and above
全 市	**Total**	**50064**	**20.7**	**30.7**	**29.7**	**10.6**	**8.2**
城 镇	Urban	38685	20.7	30.5	31.3	10.3	7.2
乡 村	Rural	11379	20.7	31.5	24.4	11.7	11.7

注：本表数据为人口抽样调查样本数据。
Note: Figures in this table are sample figures from the sample survey on population.

3-9 户籍人口(1978-2013年)
REGISTERED POPULATION (1978-2013)

单位：万人 (10000 persons)

年份 Year	户籍户数(万户) Registered Households (10000 households)	户籍人口 Registered Population	#60岁及以上人口 Population at 60 and over	按性别分 By Sex: 男 Male	按性别分 By Sex: 女 Female	按户籍性质分 By Type of Household Register: 非农业户 Non-Agricultural	按户籍性质分 By Type of Household Register: 农业户 Agricultural	户籍人口出生人数 Births of Registered Population	户籍人口死亡人数 Deaths of Registered Population	户籍人口自然增加人数 Natural Increase of Registered Population
1978	205.5	849.7		432.1	417.5	467.0	382.6	10.9	5.2	5.7
1979	214.6	870.6		441.1	429.4	495.2	375.4	11.8	5.1	6.7
1980	223.2	885.7		448.4	437.3	510.4	375.3	13.7	5.5	8.2
1981	234.8	900.8		456.6	444.2	522.6	378.2	15.1	5.4	9.7
1982	245.0	917.8		465.5	452.3	534.0	383.8	18.2	5.2	13.1
1983	255.1	933.2		474.7	458.5	547.1	386.0	14.5	5.1	9.4
1984	263.1	945.2		481.2	464.0	558.1	387.0	13.2	5.1	8.1
1985	274.1	957.9		488.0	469.9	572.5	385.4	11.8	5.2	6.6
1986	284.6	971.2		495.5	475.7	586.8	384.4	12.9	5.2	7.8
1987	299.4	988.0		504.1	483.9	601.0	387.0	16.9	5.3	11.6
1988	310.8	1001.2		510.4	490.8	614.3	387.0	15.3	5.5	9.8
1989	322.5	1021.1		520.3	500.8	630.6	390.5	19.0	5.7	13.3
1990	335.0	1032.2		525.3	507.0	640.2	392.1	14.0	6.3	7.7
1991	343.1	1039.5		528.5	511.1	648.4	391.2	9.2	5.7	3.5
1992	349.3	1044.9		530.8	514.1	656.3	388.6	8.3	6.2	2.2
1993	354.6	1051.2		533.9	517.3	668.7	382.5	7.9	6.3	1.6
1994	360.3	1061.8		538.9	522.8	683.8	377.9	8.5	6.3	2.2
1995	365.7	1070.3		543.0	527.3	696.9	373.5	8.5	6.2	2.3
1996	370.9	1077.7		546.8	530.9	709.7	368.0	7.8	6.7	1.2
1997	375.7	1085.5		550.4	535.1	722.7	362.9	7.6	6.7	0.9
1998	383.4	1091.5		552.6	538.9	733.6	357.8	6.7	7.5	-0.8
1999	390.3	1099.8		556.7	543.1	747.2	352.6	6.3	6.2	0.1
2000	397.9	1107.5		560.1	547.4	760.7	346.8	7.2	7.8	-0.5
2001	405.3	1122.3		567.3	555.0	780.2	342.2	6.0	5.3	0.7
2002	416.3	1136.3		574.7	561.6	806.9	329.4	6.0	5.2	0.8
2003	427.6	1148.8		581.0	567.9	830.8	318.0	4.5	5.8	-1.3
2004	439.8	1162.9		587.2	575.7	854.7	308.2	6.6	6.2	0.4
2005	451.7	1180.7		596.0	584.7	880.2	300.5	7.5	7.0	0.5
2006	463.7	1197.6		604.2	593.4	905.4	292.2	7.7	5.1	2.6
2007	473.0	1213.3	210.3	612.0	601.3	929.0	284.3	9.9	5.2	4.8
2008	481.2	1229.9	218.6	620.0	609.9	950.7	279.2	10.6	5.1	5.5
2009	488.7	1245.8	228.7	627.5	618.9	971.9	273.9	10.9	6.2	4.7
2010	496.1	1257.8	237.2	632.8	625.0	989.5	268.3	10.2	9.1	1.1
2011	503.1	1277.9	250.5	642.4	635.6	1013.8	264.2	12.5	5.3	7.2
2012	509.2	1297.5	266.1	651.7	645.8	1039.3	258.2	14.5	5.7	8.8
2013	516.2	1316.3	283.2	660.4	655.9	1065.0	251.4	13.6	5.7	7.9

资料来源：北京市公安局。
Source: Beijing Municipal Bureau of Public Security.

3-10 户籍户数及人口数（按区县分）(2013年)
REGISTERED HOUSEHOLDS AND POPULATION (BY DISTRICT) (2013)

地　区	District	户籍户数及人口 Registered Households and Population					
		户数（万户） Households (10000 households)			人口数(万人) Population (10000 persons)		
		合　计 Total	非农业户 Non-Agricultural	农业户 Agricultural	合　计 Total	非农业户 Non-Agricultural	农业户 Agricultural
全　市	**Total**	**516.2**	**405.8**	**110.5**	**1316.3**	**1065.0**	**251.4**
首都功能核心区	**Capital Core Functional Area**	**82.1**	**82.1**		**238.2**	**238.2**	
东城区	Dongcheng District	34.6	34.6		97.4	97.4	
西城区	Xicheng District	47.5	47.5		140.8	140.8	
城市功能拓展区	**Urban Function Extension Area**	**209.1**	**193.8**	**15.3**	**585.4**	**554.1**	**31.4**
朝阳区	Chaoyang District	78.1	72.0	6.2	201.2	188.5	12.7
丰台区	Fengtai District	46.1	41.0	5.1	111.4	100.9	10.5
石景山区	Shijingshan District	14.2	14.2		37.6	37.6	
海淀区	Haidian District	70.7	66.6	4.1	235.3	227.1	8.2
城市发展新区	**Urban Development New Area**	**148.3**	**89.2**	**59.1**	**328.8**	**188.8**	**140.1**
房山区	Fangshan District	36.7	21.7	15.0	78.6	45.1	33.5
通州区	Tongzhou District	33.7	19.5	14.2	69.3	37.4	31.9
顺义区	Shunyi District	26.7	15.8	10.9	60.1	33.9	26.1
昌平区	Changping District	25.4	16.7	8.7	57.3	38.4	18.9
大兴区	Daxing District	25.8	15.4	10.3	63.6	33.9	29.7
生态涵养发展区	**Ecological Conservation Area**	**76.7**	**40.7**	**36.0**	**163.9**	**84.0**	**79.9**
门头沟区	Mentougou District	11.9	9.2	2.8	24.9	19.9	5.0
怀柔区	Huairou District	13.4	6.3	7.1	27.9	13.0	14.9
平谷区	Pinggu District	16.9	9.3	7.6	39.9	20.8	19.1
密云县	Miyun County	20.6	9.2	11.4	43.1	18.0	25.1
延庆县	Yanqing County	13.9	6.7	7.2	28.1	12.3	15.8

资料来源：北京市公安局。
Source: Beijing Municipal Bureau of Public Security.

3-11 户籍人口年龄构成(2013年)
AGE COMPOSITION OF REGISTERED POPULATION (2013)

年龄组 Age Group	户籍人口(万人) Registered Population (10000 persons)			占人口比重(%) Percentage(%)		
	合计 Total	男 Male	女 Female	合计 Total	男 Male	女 Female
总计 Total	**1316.3**	**660.4**	**655.9**	**100.0**	**50.2**	**49.8**
0-4	57.8	29.8	28.0	4.4	2.3	2.1
5-9	43.7	22.6	21.2	3.3	1.7	1.6
10-14	33.5	17.2	16.3	2.5	1.3	1.2
15-19	51.0	25.6	25.4	3.9	1.9	1.9
20-24	90.0	45.5	44.5	6.8	3.5	3.4
25-29	114.5	58.4	56.1	8.7	4.4	4.3
30-34	116.0	58.7	57.3	8.8	4.5	4.4
35-39	80.3	40.6	39.7	6.1	3.1	3.0
40-44	104.0	52.9	51.1	7.9	4.0	3.9
45-49	105.0	53.3	51.7	8.0	4.0	3.9
50-54	122.1	62.3	59.8	9.3	4.7	4.5
55-59	115.3	57.3	58.1	8.8	4.4	4.4
60-64	87.5	42.9	44.6	6.6	3.3	3.4
65-69	54.1	26.0	28.1	4.1	2.0	2.1
70-74	44.3	20.5	23.8	3.4	1.6	1.8
75-79	46.0	21.9	24.1	3.5	1.7	1.8
80-84	30.1	14.8	15.3	2.3	1.1	1.2
85-89	14.1	6.8	7.3	1.1	0.5	0.6
90岁及以上 90 and above	7.1	3.3	3.8	0.5	0.3	0.3

资料来源：北京市公安局。
Source: Beijing Municipal Bureau of Public Security.

3-12 户籍人口性别构成及性别比（按区县分）(2013年)
SEX COMPOSITION AND SEX RATIO OF REGISTERED POPULATION (BY DISTRICT) (2013)

地 区	District	户籍人口(万人) Registered Population (10000 persons)			性别比 (女=100)
		合 计 Total	男 Male	女 Female	Sex Ratio (female=100)
全 市	**Total**	**1316.3**	**660.4**	**655.9**	**100.7**
首都功能核心区	**Capital Core Functional Area**	**238.2**	**118.5**	**119.7**	**99.0**
东城区	Dongcheng District	97.4	48.2	49.2	97.8
西城区	Xicheng District	140.8	70.3	70.5	99.8
城市功能拓展区	**Urban Function Extension Area**	**585.4**	**295.1**	**290.3**	**101.7**
朝阳区	Chaoyang Dsitrict	201.2	100.9	100.3	100.6
丰台区	Fengtai District	111.4	56.5	54.9	103.0
石景山区	Shijingshan District	37.6	19.4	18.2	106.7
海淀区	Haidian District	235.3	118.3	116.9	101.2
城市发展新区	**Urban Development New Area**	**328.8**	**164.2**	**164.6**	**99.8**
房山区	Fangshan District	78.6	39.4	39.1	100.7
通州区	Tongzhou District	69.3	34.4	34.9	98.7
顺义区	Shunyi District	60.1	29.8	30.3	98.3
昌平区	Changping District	57.3	28.9	28.4	101.7
大兴区	Daxing District	63.6	31.7	31.9	99.6
生态涵养发展区	**Ecological Conservation Area**	**163.9**	**82.6**	**81.3**	**101.6**
门头沟区	Mentougou Dsitrict	24.9	12.7	12.1	104.9
怀柔区	Huairou District	27.9	14.0	13.9	100.5
平谷区	Pinggu District	39.9	20.1	19.8	101.4
密云县	Miyun County	43.1	21.6	21.5	100.3
延庆县	Yanqing County	28.1	14.2	13.9	102.2

资料来源：北京市公安局。
Source: Beijing Municipal Bureau of Public Security.

3-13 户籍人口变动情况
CHANGES OF REGISTERED POPULATION

单位：人 (person)

项　　目	Item	2013	2012
自然变动	**Natural Changes**		
自然增加	Natural Increase	78673	88200
非农业人口	Non-agricultural Population	86948	94812
农业人口	Agricultural Population	-8275	-6612
出　生	Births	135925	145067
非农业人口	Non-agricultural Population	121743	129071
农业人口	Agricultural Population	14182	15996
死　亡	Deaths	57252	56867
非农业人口	Non-agricultural Population	34795	34259
农业人口	Agricultural Population	22457	22608
机械变动	**Non-natural Changes**		
机械增加	Non-natural Increase	109656	107072
非农业人口	Non-agricultural Population	99284	97875
农业人口	Agricultural Population	10372	9197
市外迁入	Inflow	198869	190510
非农业人口	Non-agricultural Population	186990	180355
农业人口	Agricultural Population	11879	10155
迁往市外	Outflow	89213	83438
非农业人口	Non-agricultural Population	87706	82480
农业人口	Agricultural Population	1507	958

资料来源：北京市公安局。
Source: Beijing Municipal Bureau of Public Security.

3-14 户籍人口自然变动情况(按区县分)
NATURAL CHANGES OF REGISTERED POPULATION (BY DISTRICT)

单位：人 (person)

地 区	District	出生人数 Number of Births		死亡人数 Number of Deaths		自然增加人数 Number of Natural Increase	
		2013	2012	2013	2012	2013	2012
全 市	**Total**	**135925**	**145067**	**57252**	**56867**	**78673**	**88200**
首都功能核心区	**Capital Core Functional Area**						
东 城 区	Dongcheng District	9426	9838	3884	3685	5542	6153
西 城 区	Xicheng District	13925	14864	5419	5121	8506	9743
城市功能拓展区	**Urban Function Extension Area**						
朝 阳 区	Chaoyang District	22211	23581	7445	7324	14766	16257
丰 台 区	Fengtai District	10819	11691	4641	4732	6178	6959
石景山区	Shijingshan District	3549	3882	1506	1460	2043	2422
海 淀 区	Haidian District	21922	23787	5454	5403	16468	18384
城市发展新区	**Urban Development New Area**						
门头沟区	Mentougou District	2050	2358	1491	1760	559	598
房 山 区	Fangshan District	8201	8623	4576	4653	3625	3970
通 州 区	Tongzhou District	7993	8370	4155	4099	3838	4271
顺 义 区	Shunyi District	6670	7514	3629	3750	3041	3764
昌 平 区	Changping District	7240	7856	2723	2796	4517	5060
大 兴 区	Daxing District	8759	8696	3114	3019	5645	5677
生态涵养发展区	**Ecological Conservation Area**						
怀 柔 区	Huairou District	2694	3160	1887	2019	807	1141
平 谷 区	Pinggu District	4037	4100	2564	2504	1473	1596
密 云 县	Miyun County	3727	4223	2955	2742	772	1481
延 庆 县	Yanqing County	2702	2524	1809	1800	893	724

资料来源：北京市公安局。
Source: Beijing Municipal Bureau of Public Security.

3-15 计划生育状况 FAMILY PLANNING

项 目	Item	2013	2012	2013年比2012年增、减 Increase/Decrease in 2013 over 2012
已婚育龄妇女人数（户籍） （人）	**Number of Married Women of Child-bearing Age (registered) (person)**	**2058882**	**2063395**	**-4513**
非农业户口	Non-agricultural Population	1525923	1488644	37279
农业户口	Agricultural Population	532959	574751	-41792
实际采取节育措施人数(户籍) （人）	**Number of Women Actually Taking Birth Control Measures (registered) (person)**	**1625911**	**1735866**	**-109955**
非农业户口	Non-agricultural Population	1162549	1224668	-62119
农业户口	Agricultural Population	463362	511198	-47836
计划内生育（户籍） （人）	**Planned Births (registered) (person)**	**127473**	**123364**	**4109**
计划生育率（户籍） (%)	**Rate of Planned Births (registered) (%)**	**98.14**	**98.31**	**-0.17**
非农业户口	Non-agricultural Population	98.64	98.84	-0.20
农业户口	Agricultural Population	95.00	95.07	-0.07
独生子女领证率（户籍） (%)	**Acceptance Rate of Only-child Certificate (registered) (%)**	**45.44**	**53.09**	**-7.65**
非农业户口	Non-agricultural Population	41.43	50.06	-8.63
农业户口	Agricultural Population	56.91	60.95	-4.04

资料来源：北京市卫生和计划生育委员会。
Source: Beijing Municipal Commission of Health and Family Planning.

3-16 三次产业从业人员年末人数及构成(1978-2013年)
EMPLOYED PERSONS IN THREE INDUSTRIES AND THEIR COMPOSITION (1978-2013)

年 份 Year	从业人员年末人数 (万人) Year-end Employed Persons (10000 persons)				构 成(%)(合计=100) Composition (Total=100)		
		第一产业 Primary Industry	第二产业 Secondary Industry	第三产业 Tertiary Industry	第一产业 Primary Industry	第二产业 Secondary Industry	第三产业 Tertiary Industry
1978	444.1	125.9	177.9	140.3	28.3	40.1	31.6
1979	470.5	121.4	195.2	153.9	25.8	41.5	32.7
1980	484.2	118.0	207.3	158.9	24.4	42.8	32.8
1981	511.7	117.2	220.4	174.1	22.9	43.1	34.0
1982	535.2	115.1	228.6	191.5	21.5	42.7	35.8
1983	552.0	117.1	240.2	194.7	21.2	43.5	35.3
1984	556.2	111.3	247.9	197.0	20.0	44.6	35.4
1985	566.5	100.6	260.4	205.5	17.7	46.0	36.3
1986	572.7	96.1	262.7	213.9	16.8	45.9	37.3
1987	580.2	92.3	264.1	223.8	15.9	45.5	38.6
1988	584.1	88.4	267.6	228.1	15.1	45.8	39.1
1989	593.9	91.0	266.3	236.6	15.3	44.9	39.8
1990	627.1	90.7	281.6	254.8	14.5	44.9	40.6
1991	634.0	90.8	279.7	263.5	14.3	44.1	41.6
1992	649.3	84.5	281.6	283.2	13.0	43.4	43.6
1993	627.8	65.1	279.4	283.3	10.4	44.5	45.1
1994	664.3	73.2	272.2	318.9	11.0	41.0	48.0
1995	665.3	70.6	271.0	323.7	10.6	40.7	48.7
1996	660.2	72.5	260.1	327.6	11.0	39.4	49.6
1997	655.8	71.0	257.6	327.2	10.8	39.2	50.0
1998	622.2	71.5	226.0	324.7	11.5	36.3	52.2
1999	618.6	74.5	216.2	327.9	12.1	34.9	53.0
2000	619.3	72.9	208.2	338.2	11.8	33.6	54.6
2001	628.9	71.2	215.9	341.8	11.3	34.3	54.4
2002	679.2	67.6	235.3	376.3	10.0	34.6	55.4
2003	703.3	62.7	225.8	414.8	8.9	32.1	59.0
2004	854.1	61.5	232.8	559.8	7.2	27.3	65.5
2005	878.0	62.2	231.1	584.7	7.1	26.3	66.6
2006	919.7	60.3	225.4	634.0	6.6	24.5	68.9
2007	942.7	60.9	228.1	653.7	6.5	24.2	69.3
2008	980.9	63.0	207.4	710.5	6.4	21.2	72.4
2009	998.3	62.2	199.6	736.5	6.2	20.0	73.8
2010	1031.6	61.4	202.7	767.5	6.0	19.6	74.4
2011	1069.7	59.1	219.2	791.4	5.5	20.5	74.0
2012	1107.3	57.3	212.6	837.4	5.2	19.2	75.6
2013	1141.0	55.4	210.9	874.7	4.8	18.5	76.7

注：1. 2010年及以前，劳务派遣人员按照"谁发工资谁统计"进行统计。2011年以后，劳务派遣人员按照"谁用工谁统计"进行统计。
2. 自2012年开始，三次产业划分执行国家统计局《三次产业划分规定》(国统字〔2012〕108号)。

Note: a) In 2010 and before, dispatched personnel of labor service were calculated by "wage payers". After 2011, dispatched personnel of labor service were calculated by "employers".

b) Since 2012, the three industries have been classified according to the Regulations of the National Bureau of Statistics on the Classification of the Three Industries (GTZ [2012] No. 108).

3-17 按登记注册类型分从业人员年末人数(1978-2013年)
EMPLOYED PERSONS BY TYPE OF REGISTRATION(1978-2013)

单位：万人 (10000 persons)

年份 Year	合计 Total	#城镇 Urban	#国有单位 State-owned Enterprises	#集体单位 Collectively-owned Enterprises	#联营单位 Associated Enterprises	#有限责任公司 Limited Liability Companies	#股份有限公司 Companies Limited By Shares	#外商投资 Foreign-invested	#港澳台商投资 Hong Kong, Macao and Taiwan-invested	#私营 Private Enterprises	#个体 Individual Economy
1978	444.1	291.6	240.9	50.7							
1979	470.5	311.9	254.2	57.8							
1980	484.2	326.8	269.4	57.1							0.3
1981	511.7	345.2	283.1	61.3							
1982	535.2	361.1	293.0	67.1							
1983	552.0	373.8	303.4	68.5							
1984	556.2	377.6	302.5	71.6				1.3			
1985	566.5	392.6	308.1	72.6				1.6			2.5
1986	572.7	400.5	324.4	71.1				2.4			2.6
1987	580.2	408.3	331.8	70.7				2.8			3.1
1988	584.1	413.9	336.4	69.9	0.2			3.4			3.5
1989	593.9	424.0	343.8	67.4	3.4			3.7			5.6
1990	627.1	461.2	357.9	86.8	5.1			4.6			6.3
1991	634.0	477.2	367.8	89.0	0.5			7.7	0.2		7.2
1992	649.3	490.6	371.5	90.5	0.4			11.4	0.2		14.0
1993	627.8	481.4	362.3	79.7	2.8			11.0	6.4		14.0
1994	664.3	492.7	363.5	73.3	3.5			15.0	9.4		20.9
1995	665.3	492.7	358.2	72.1	3.7			17.4	10.0		21.9
1996	660.2	495.7	355.1	68.6	3.4			20.7	10.1		22.9
1997	655.8	498.7	354.7	68.5	3.2			21.2	10.2		21.2
1998	622.2	463.2	308.1	51.0	5.2	13.7	10.8	21.2	13.1		20.1
1999	618.6	456.1	287.6	49.7	4.8	24.0	12.2	20.6	13.5		23.7
2000	619.3	456.3	266.2	48.3	4.0	34.2	14.0	23.8	14.2		24.4
2001	628.9	464.2	246.3	45.8	4.1	50.6	17.3	22.4	12.9		24.8
2002	679.2	513.6	224.8	36.8	4.1	85.0	27.1	29.2	17.0	4.8	33.1
2003	703.3	533.7	212.8	30.1	3.8	102.3	33.4	31.5	17.3	5.2	37.2
2004	854.1	682.7	199.5	28.2	3.5	134.5	37.9	45.0	18.3	134.2	45.7
2005	878.0	694.0	195.0	23.8	2.4	149.4	36.4	49.6	21.7	131.2	57.2
2006	919.7	734.2	189.3	18.8	2.1	165.1	35.5	57.3	23.5	154.8	65.6
2007	942.7	745.4	189.3	17.3	1.9	179.5	38.7	69.3	28.8	133.8	67.2
2008	980.9	813.7	187.8	24.8	2.2	196.4	46.4	72.9	33.5	159.6	65.1
2009	998.3	856.6	185.7	24.3	0.9	215.7	58.4	71.2	36.6	172.2	67.5
2010	1031.6	905.4	189.0	22.7	0.9	228.2	64.7	74.9	42.4	193.5	65.3
2011	1069.7	955.8	188.8	20.1	0.7	243.0	75.9	90.1	50.6	210.6	59.3
2012	1107.3	996.1	188.3	19.8	0.7	261.6	83.2	92.7	54.3	227.9	50.8
2013	1141.0	1073.0	189.5	17.5	0.7	278.0	85.4	96.1	56.1	265.9	64.8

资料来源：表中私营和个体从业人员数据来源于北京市工商行政管理局。

Source: Figures of employed persons in private enterprises and individual economy in this table were from Beijing Administration for Industry and Commerce.

3-18 全市法人单位从业人员年末人数和平均工资
EMPLOYED PERSONS IN LEGAL ENTITIES AND AVERAGE WAGES

项目	Item	从业人员年末人数（万人） Year-end Employed Persons (10000 persons)		从业人员平均工资（元） Average Wage (yuan)	
		2013	2012	2013	2012
合计	**Total**	**981.9**	**951.4**	**82045**	**74464**
按登记注册类型分	**By Registration Type**				
内资	Domestically-invested Enterprises	829.7	804.4	75121	67876
国有	State-owned Enterprises	189.5	188.3	94173	87299
集体	Collectively-owned Enterprises	17.5	19.8	42502	38552
股份合作	Joint-equity Cooperative Enterprises	6.8	7.2	38149	34146
联营	Associated Enterprises	0.7	0.7	48850	63030
有限责任公司	Limited Liability Companies	278.0	261.6	74007	67006
股份有限公司	Companies Limited By Shares	85.4	83.2	125033	109537
私营	Private Enterprises	239.6	234.0	48027	42882
其他	Others	12.2	9.6	54442	44253
港、澳、台商投资	Hong Kong, Macao and Taiwan-invested Enterprises	56.1	54.3	104819	96608
外商投资	Foreign-invested Enterprises	96.1	92.7	128513	118777
按国民经济行业分	**By Sector**				
农、林、牧、渔业	Agriculture, Forestry, Animal Production and Hunting, Fishing	3.9	3.1	45286	37156
采矿业	Mining and Quarrying	6.8	6.9	82239	78038
制造业	Manufacturing	133.2	136.3	66218	58839
电力、热力、燃气及水生产和供应业	Production and Distribution of Electricity, Heating Power, Gas and Water	9.1	9.2	97934	90345
建筑业	Construction	60.8	58.5	60713	54924
批发和零售业	Wholesale and Retail Trade	122.6	124.6	66681	60593
交通运输、仓储和邮政业	Transport, Storage and Post	65.5	64.4	68379	63064
住宿和餐饮业	Accommodation and Restaurants	46.2	47.7	41708	38725
信息传输、软件和信息技术服务业	Information Transmission, Software and Information Technology Services	79.4	73.2	119766	113390
金融业	Finance	40.5	39.5	200529	181886
房地产业	Real Estate	52.0	47.6	69020	60767
租赁和商务服务业	Renting and Leasing Activities and Business Services	109.5	101.1	81934	74710
科学研究和技术服务业	Scientific Research and Development, Technical Services	79.1	73.9	99072	90514
水利、环境和公共设施管理业	Management of Water Conservancy, Environment and Public Facilities	11.4	10.7	56201	52287
居民服务、修理和其他服务业	Resident Service, Repair and Other Service	17.8	16.4	39390	35752
教育	Education	49.5	48.0	85406	80447
卫生和社会工作	Health Care and Social Works	26.1	24.3	106907	94796
文化、体育和娱乐业	Culture, Sports and Entertainment	23.0	21.2	99851	92424
公共管理、社会保障和社会组织	Public Administration, Social Security and Social Organizations	45.5	44.8	73552	70272
国际组织	International Organizations				

注：行业划分执行2011年国民经济行业分类标准(GB/T 4754-2011)。
Note: Sectors in this table are classified in accordance with the Standard for Classification of National Economic Sectors 2011 (GB/T 4754-2011).

3-19 城镇单位在岗职工年末人数及工资总额(1978-2013年)
NUMBER AND WAGES OF FULLY EMPLOYED STAFF AND WORKERS IN URBAN ENTITIES (1978-2013)

年份 Year	在岗职工年末人数(万人) Year-end Fully Employed Staff and Workers (10000 persons)	国有单位 State-owned	集体单位 Collectively-owned	其他单位 Others	在岗职工工资总额(亿元) Total Wages of Fully Employed Staff and Workers (yuan)	国有单位 State-owned	集体单位 Collectively-owned	其他单位 Others
1978	291.6	240.9	50.7		18.7	16.2	2.5	
1979	311.9	254.2	57.7		22.4	19.4	3.0	
1980	326.5	269.4	57.1		26.9	23.3	3.6	
1981-1985					**183.7**	**153.7**	**29.6**	**0.4**
1981	344.4	283.1	61.3		28.3	24.2	4.1	
1982	360.1	293.0	67.1		30.5	25.9	4.6	
1983	371.9	303.4	68.5		33.8	28.5	5.3	
1984	375.4	302.5	71.6	1.3	40.4	33.7	6.6	0.1
1985	382.3	308.1	72.6	1.6	50.7	41.5	9.0	0.3
1986-1990					**421.1**	**349.7**	**64.4**	**7.0**
1986	397.9	324.4	71.1	2.4	58.0	48.5	9.1	0.4
1987	405.2	331.8	70.7	2.7	66.7	56.0	10.1	0.6
1988	410.4	336.4	69.9	4.1	81.2	68.1	12.1	1.0
1989	418.4	343.8	67.4	7.2	96.3	81.0	13.4	1.9
1990	454.9	357.9	86.8	10.2	118.9	96.1	19.7	3.1
1991-1995					**1198.1**	**950.3**	**156.6**	**91.2**
1991	470.0	367.8	89.0	13.2	132.2	106.1	21.5	4.6
1992	476.6	371.5	90.5	14.6	158.5	128.6	23.9	6.0
1993	467.3	362.3	79.6	25.4	218.9	176.6	28.5	13.8
1994	471.8	363.5	73.4	34.9	306.5	243.4	36.2	26.9
1995	470.9	358.2	72.1	40.6	382.0	295.6	46.5	39.9
1996-2000					**2825.4**	**1988.5**	**236.5**	**600.4**
1996	460.6	349.0	64.8	46.8	442.4	339.4	46.2	56.8
1997	465.3	348.7	65.0	51.6	514.8	383.6	53.8	77.4
1998	450.1	321.7	50.8	77.6	558.2	391.9	45.0	121.3
1999	438.0	303.0	49.6	85.4	614.5	420.0	44.8	149.7
2000	434.2	283.0	46.0	105.2	695.5	453.6	46.7	195.2
2001-2005					**5662.3**	**2872.7**	**184.6**	**2605.0**
2001	400.3	235.9	40.0	124.4	777.3	477.8	44.8	254.7
2002	434.2	212.6	32.7	188.9	950.9	508.8	40.0	402.1
2003	436.3	197.6	26.1	212.6	1098.9	565.5	35.0	498.4
2004	446.4	183.7	24.8	237.9	1315.1	625.7	34.0	655.4
2005	448.4	178.5	20.7	249.2	1520.1	694.9	30.8	794.4
2006-2010					**13890.4**	**4904.7**	**219.9**	**8765.8**
2006	453.1	172.9	16.4	263.8	1805.5	738.0	30.5	1037.0
2007	478.9	172.7	15.4	290.8	2194.3	862.4	31.2	1300.7
2008	526.1	171.0	22.7	332.4	2874.3	1008.8	48.2	1817.3
2009	560.4	170.9	22.4	367.1	3227.2	1074.3	53.3	2099.6
2010	587.7	175.1	21.1	391.5	3789.1	1221.2	56.7	2511.2
2011	640.3	177.1	18.7	444.5	4778.6	1421.1	62.3	3295.2
2012	670.4	177.3	18.6	474.5	5657.9	1582.5	71.6	4003.8
2013	695.5	178.4	16.5	500.6	6502.0	1724.7	70.2	4707.1

注：1. 2007年及以前城镇单位是指乡及乡以上独立核算法人单位，不包括乡镇企业、私营单位和个体工商户。2008年及以后城镇单位是指不包括私营单位和个体工商户的独立核算法人单位(下表同)。

2. 表中2000年及以前数据为职工口径，职工包括在岗职工和不在岗职工(下表同)。

Note: a) Urban entities in and before 2007 referred to legal entities with independent accounting at and above township level, excluding township enterprises, private entities and self-employed businesses. Urban entities in and after 2008 referred to legal entities with independent accounting excluding private entities and self-employed businesses (the same to the follow Tables).

b) Figures before 2001 were counted by the statistical range of employees including on-the-job and off-the-job ones (the same to the follow tables).

3-20 城镇单位在岗职工平均工资(1978-2013年) AVERAGE WAGES OF FULLY EMPLOYED STAFF AND WORKERS IN URBAN ENTITIES (1978-2013)

单位：元 (yuan)

年份 Year	在岗职工平均工资 Average Wage of Fully Employed Staff and Workers	国有单位 State-owned Enterprises	集体单位 Collectively-owned Enterprises	其他单位 Others
1978	673	703	471	
1979	742	778	556	
1980	848	889	635	
1981	837	880	685	
1982	863	896	715	
1983	931	964	785	
1984	1086	1127	946	1170
1985	1343	1367	1231	1768
1986	1488	1530	1287	2080
1987	1670	1712	1449	2267
1988	2000	2048	1738	2661
1989	2312	2366	1992	2761
1990	2653	2713	2334	3243
1991	2877	2937	2504	3713
1992	3402	3500	2828	4289
1993	4780	4920	3834	5469
1994	6540	6695	5009	8179
1995	8144	8237	6516	10278
1996	9579	9645	7133	13851
1997	11019	10917	8259	15370
1998	12285	11971	8800	15989
1999	13778	13483	8928	17748
2000	15726	15483	9844	19165
2001	19155	19776	11063	20594
2002	21852	23754	11997	21432
2003	25312	28464	13580	23769
2004	29674	34009	13422	28026
2005	34191	39067	14695	32324
2006	40117	43298	17781	39513
2007	46507	50524	20379	45508
2008	54913	59361	20990	54983
2009	58140	63239	23553	57911
2010	65683	70320	26607	65755
2011	75834	81215	32469	75584
2012	85307	90456	38596	85234
2013	93997	97356	42482	94513

3-21 城镇单位在岗职工年末人数
NUMBER OF FULLY EMPLOYED STAFF AND WORKERS IN URBAN ENTITIES AT YEAR-END

单位：人 (person)

项　目	Item	2013	2012	2013年为2012年% 2013 as % of 2012
合　计	**Total**	**6954597**	**6703514**	**103.7**
按登记注册类型分	**By Registration Type**			
内　资	Domestically-invested Enterprises	5524082	5322816	103.8
国　有	State-owned Enterprises	1783445	1772818	100.6
集　体	Collectively-owned Enterprises	165345	185642	89.1
股份合作	Joint-equity Cooperative Enterprises	63766	67876	93.9
联　营	Associated Enterprises	6469	6073	106.5
有限责任公司	Limited Liability Companies	2626320	2473332	106.2
股份有限公司	Companies Limited By Shares	781099	741926	105.3
其　他	Others	97638	75149	129.9
港、澳、台商投资	Hong Kong, Macao and Taiwan-invested Enterprises	533924	517641	103.1
外商投资	Foreign-invested Enterprises	896591	863057	103.9
按国民经济行业分	**By Sector**			
农、林、牧、渔业	Agriculture, Forestry, Animal Production and Hunting, Fishing	30589	24804	123.3
#农　业	Agriculture	10974	6536	167.9
采矿业	Mining and Quarrying	67397	68613	98.2
制造业	Manufacturing	1007050	1050690	95.8
电力、热力、燃气及水生产和供应业	Production and Distribution of Electricity, Heating Power, Gas and Water	85403	88135	96.9
建筑业	Construction	412088	400995	102.8
批发和零售业	Wholesale and Retail Trade	647356	646861	100.1
批发业	Wholesale	341847	347716	98.3
零售业	Retail Trade	305509	299145	102.1
交通运输、仓储和邮政业	Transport, Storage and Post	577387	555438	104.0
#铁路运输业	Transport via Railway	98182	99876	98.3
道路运输业	Transport via Road	269597	265648	101.5
邮政业	Post	77134	65327	118.1
住宿和餐饮业	Accomodation and Restaurants	271133	279594	97.0
住宿业	Accommodation	133707	143891	92.9
餐饮业	Restaurants	137426	135703	101.3
信息传输、软件和信息技术服务业	Information Transmission, Software and Information Technology Services	570199	512081	111.3
金融业	Finance	321056	308109	104.2
房地产业	Real Estate	378727	343734	110.2
租赁和商务服务业	Renting and Leasing Activities and Business Services	625960	580253	107.9
租赁业	Renting and Leasing Activities	18147	7955	228.1
商务服务业	Business Services	607813	572298	106.2
科学研究和技术服务业	Scientific Research and Development, Technical Services	547380	495463	110.5
水利、环境和公共设施管理业	Management of Water Conservancy, Environment and Public Facilities	92830	88906	104.4
居民服务、修理和其他服务业	Resident Services, Repair and Other Services	85358	79999	106.7
#居民服务业	Resident Services	28886	26660	108.3
教　育	Education	415072	396645	104.6
卫生和社会工作	Healthcare and Social Works	234651	216540	108.4
#卫　生	Health care	223300	207332	107.7
文化、体育和娱乐业	Culture, Sports and Entertainment	170225	160205	106.3
#文化艺术业	Cultures and Arts	34937	29536	118.3
体　育	Sports Activities	22917	22693	101.0
公共管理、社会保障和社会组织	Public Administration, Social Security and Social Organizations	414736	406449	102.0
国际组织	International Organizations			

注：行业划分执行2011年国民经济行业分类标准（GB/T 4754-2011）。
Note: Sectors in this table are classified in accordance with the Standard for Classification of National Economic Sectors 2011 (GB/T 4754-2011).

3-22 城镇单位在岗职工工资总额
TOTAL WAGES OF FULLY EMPLOYED STAFF AND WORKERS IN URBAN ENTITIES

单位：万元 (10000 yuan)

项目	Item	2013	2012	2013年为2012年% 2013 as % of 2012
合计	**Total**	**65020386**	**56579220**	**114.9**
按登记注册类型分	**By Registration Type**			
内资	Domestically-invested Enterprises	48623030	42264987	115.0
国有	State-owned Enterprises	17247256	15825113	109.0
集体	Collectively-owned Enterprises	702385	716187	98.1
股份合作	Joint-equity Cooperative Enterprises	241660	230019	105.1
联营	Associated Enterprises	31636	39769	79.5
有限责任公司	Limited Liability Companies	19698696	16638129	118.4
股份有限公司	Companies Limited By Shares	10199839	8511668	119.8
其他	Others	501558	304102	164.9
港、澳、台商投资	Hong Kong, Macao and Taiwan-invested Enterprises	5454356	4867678	112.1
外商投资	Foreign-invested Enterprises	10943000	9446555	115.8
按国民经济行业分	**By Sector**			
农、林、牧、渔业	Agriculture, Forestry, Animal Production and Hunting, Fishing	153878	99564	154.6
#农业	Agriculture	40314	23189	173.8
采矿业	Mining and Quarrying	559621	543038	103.1
制造业	Manufacturing	7318327	6647951	110.1
电力、热力、燃气及水生产和供应业	Production and Distribution of Electricity, Heating Power, Gas and Water	881792	811538	108.7
建筑业	Construction	2867294	2448888	117.1
批发和零售业	Wholesale and Retail Trade	5444375	4953977	109.9
批发业	Wholesale	3704126	3438786	107.7
零售业	Retail Trade	1740249	1515191	114.9
交通运输、仓储和邮政业	Transport, Storage and Post	4077794	3592690	113.5
#铁路运输业	Transport via Railway	834737	763203	109.4
道路运输业	Transport via Road	1222995	1078562	113.4
邮政业	Post	528828	432496	122.3
住宿和餐饮业	Accomodation and Restaurants	1298478	1223503	106.1
住宿业	Accommodation	692415	670818	103.2
餐饮业	Restaurants	606063	552685	109.7
信息传输、软件和信息技术服务业	Information Transmission,Software and Information Technology Services	7601404	6383564	119.1
金融业	Finance	7414384	6278276	118.1
房地产业	Real Estate	2753756	2198063	125.3
租赁和商务服务业	Renting and Leasing Activities and Business Services	5908539	4945253	119.5
租赁业	Renting and Leasing Activities	89477	36442	245.5
商务服务业	Business Services	5819062	4908811	118.5
科学研究和技术服务业	Scientific Research and Development, Technical Services	6298432	5330821	118.2
水利、环境和公共设施管理业	Management of Water Conservancy, Environment and Public Facilities	555050	480722	115.5
居民服务、修理和其他服务业	Resident Services, Repair and Other Services	377374	315273	119.7
#居民服务业	Resident Services	122159	103661	117.8
教育	Education	3750880	3436122	109.2
卫生和社会工作	Health Care and Social Works	2574247	2119431	121.5
#卫生	Health Care	2515513	2072759	121.4
文化、体育和娱乐业	Culture, Sports and Entertainment	1955010	1725996	113.3
#文化艺术业	Cultures and Arts	281876	229944	122.6
体育	Sports Activities	143288	126214	113.5
公共管理、社会保障和社会组织	Public Administration, Social Security and Social Organizations	3229751	3044550	106.1
国际组织	International Organizations			

注：行业划分执行2011年国民经济行业分类标准（GB/T 4754-2011）。
Note: Sectors in this table are classified in accordance with the Standard for Classification of National Economic Sectors 2011 (GB/T 4754-2011).

3-23 城镇单位在岗职工平均工资
AVERAGE WAGES OF FULLY EMPLOYED STAFF AND WORKERS IN URBAN ENTITIES

单位：元 (yuan)

项目	Item	2013	2012	2013年为2012年% 2013as % of 2012
合计	**Total**	**93997**	**85307**	**110.2**
按登记注册类型分	**By Registration Type**			
内资	Domestically-invested Enterprises	88486	80266	110.2
国有	State-owned Enterprises	97356	90456	107.6
集体	Collectively-owed Enterprises	42482	38596	110.1
股份合作	Joint-equity Cooperative Enterprises	37960	33876	112.1
联营	Associated Enterprises	48109	65658	73.3
有限责任公司	Limited Liability Companies	75356	68004	110.8
股份有限公司	Companies Limited By Shares	131357	115693	113.5
其他	Others	51560	40967	125.9
港、澳、台商投资	Hong Kong, Macao and Taiwan-invested Enterprises	103059	93616	110.1
外商投资	Foreign-invested Enterprises	122538	111542	109.9
按国民经济行业分	**By Sector**			
农、林、牧、渔业	Agriculture, Forestry, Animal Production and Hunting, Fishing	48836	39664	123.1
#农业	Agriculture	35447	33941	104.4
采矿业	Mining and Quarrying	82729	78460	105.4
制造业	Manufacturing	71812	63148	113.7
电力、热力、燃气及水生产和供应业	Production and Distribution of Electricity, Heating Power, Gas and Water	100677	92489	108.9
建筑业	Construction	69525	62079	112.0
批发和零售业	Wholesale and Retail Trade	84535	76642	110.3
批发业	Wholesale	109711	98978	110.8
零售业	Retail Trade	56794	50684	112.1
交通运输、仓储和邮政业	Transport, Storage and Post	71958	65321	110.2
#铁路运输业	Transport via Railway	85481	76960	111.1
道路运输业	Transport via Road	46319	40830	113.4
邮政业	Post	69943	68579	102.0
住宿和餐饮业	Accommodation and Restaurants	47217	43517	108.5
住宿业	Accommodation	50502	46166	109.4
餐饮业	Restaurants	43951	40685	108.0
信息传输、软件和信息技术服务业	Information Transmission, Software and Information Technology Service	135346	127707	106.0
金融业	Finance	234497	209483	111.9
房地产业	Real Estate	73578	64696	113.7
租赁和商务服务业	Renting and Leasing Activities, Business Services	95525	88054	108.5
租赁业	Renting and Leasing Activities	51297	47333	108.4
商务服务业	Business Services	96809	88620	109.2
科学研究和技术服务业	Scientific Research and Development, Technical Services	116571	109302	106.7
水利、环境和公共设施管理业	Management of Water Conservancy, Environment and Public Facilities	59276	53840	110.1
居民服务、修理和其他服务业	Resident Services, Repair and Other Services	44023	39186	112.3
#居民服务业	Resident Services	41868	38886	107.7
教育	Education	91166	87579	104.1
卫生和社会工作	Health Care and Social Works	112293	100081	112.2
#卫生	Health Care	115402	102295	112.8
文化、体育和娱乐业	Culture, Sports and Entertainment	115062	108910	105.6
#文化艺术业	Cultures and Arts	81717	78875	103.6
体育	Sports Activities	61837	56376	109.7
公共管理、社会保障和社会组织	Pulic Administration,Social Security and Social Organizations	78310	75242	104.1
国际组织	International Organizations			

注：行业划分执行2011年国民经济行业分类标准（GB/T 4754-2011）。
Note: Sectors in this table are classified in accordance with the Standard for Classification of National Economic Sectors 2011 (GB/T 4754-2011).

3-24 国民经济各行业城镇单位在岗职工平均工资(2013年)
AVERAGE WAGES OF URBAN ENTITIES FULLY EMPLOYED STAFF AND WORKERS IN DIFFERENT SECTORS OF NATIONAL ECONOMY (2013)

单位：元 (yuan)

项目	Item	平均工资 Average Wages	国有单位 State-owned	集体单位 Collectively-Owned	其他单位 Others
合计	**Total**	**93997**	**97356**	**42482**	**94513**
农、林、牧、渔业	**Agriculture, Forestry, Animal Production and Hunting, Fishing**	**48836**	**62017**	**27490**	**47244**
#农、林、牧、渔服务业	Service Activities for Agriculture, Forestry, Animal Production and Hunting, Fishing	94084	63877	34153	125952
采矿业	**Mining and Quarrying**	**82729**		**65597**	**82906**
煤炭开采和洗选业	Mining and Washing of Coal	76075			76075
石油和天然气开采业	Extraction of Petroleum and Natural Gas	96081			96081
黑色金属矿采选业	Mining and Processing of Ferrous Metal Ores	75713		72407	75790
有色金属矿采选业	Mining and Processing of Non-Ferrous Metal Ores	36000			36000
非金属矿采选业	Mining and Processing of Nonmetal Ores	46237		26592	51209
开采辅助活动	Mining Support Service Activities	94362			94362
其他采矿业	Mining of Other Ores	62333			62333
制造业	**Manufacturing**	**71812**	**85591**	**35529**	**72071**
农副食品加工业	Processing of Food from Agricultural Products	53007	47042	26174	53953
食品制造业	Manufacture of Foods	59402	41193	22089	59656
酒、饮料和精制茶制造业	Manufacture of Wine, Beverage and Refined Tea	58237	60087	26974	58111
烟草制品业	Manufacture of Cigarettes and Tobacco	181128	181128		
纺织业	Manufacture of Textile	44251	63504	25738	43922
纺织服装、服饰业	Manufacture of Textile, Wearing Apparel and Ornament	42246	40803	31809	42910
皮革、毛皮、羽毛及其制品和制鞋业	Manufacture of Leather, Fur, Feather and Its Products, and Footwear	38105	39714	26030	38844
木材加工和木、竹、藤、棕、草制品业	Processing of Timbers, Manufacture of Wood, Bamboo, Rattan, Palm and Straw Products	42518	101500	23449	43373
家具制造业	Manufacture of Furniture	42289	32111	23538	42682
造纸和纸制品业	Manufacture of Paper and Paper Products	44823	46257	28148	47536
印刷和记录媒介复制业	Printing, Reproduction of Recording Media	56417	63630	48937	55544
文教、工美、体育和娱乐用品制造业	Manufacture of Articles for Culture, Education, Artwork, Sport and Entertainment Activities	46841	29976	28706	47872
石油加工、炼焦和核燃料加工业	Processing of Petroleum, Coking, Processing of Nucleus Fuels	74513	76968	23160	74656
化学原料和化学制品制造业	Manufacture of Chemical Raw Materials and Chemical Products	66757	88208	30002	66126
医药制造业	Manufacture of Medicines	111327	80756	36131	112630
化学纤维制造业	Manufacture of Chemical Fibers	46856			46856
橡胶和塑料制品业	Manufacture of Rubber and Plastics Products	47300	61635	39993	47687
非金属矿物制品业	Manufacture of Non-metallic Mineral Products	54954	51604	31479	56091
黑色金属冶炼和压延加工业	Manufacture and Pressing of Ferrous Metals	57791	64074	32052	58689

注：行业划分执行2011年国民经济行业分类标准(GB/T 4754-2011)。
Note: Sectors in this table are classified in accordance with the Standard for Classification of National Economic Sectors 2011 (GB/T 4754-2011).

3-24 续表 1 Continued 1

单位：元 (yuan)

行业	Sector	平均工资 Average Wages	国有单位 State-owned	集体单位 Collectively-Owned	其他单位 Others
有色金属冶炼和压延加工业	Manufacture and Pressing of Nonferrous Metals	57365	85727	28805	58044
金属制品业	Manufacture of Fabricated Metal Products	54534	40151	33156	56247
通用设备制造业	Manufacture of General-Purpose Machinery	72334	100425	38628	72931
专用设备制造业	Manufacture of Special-Purpose Machinery	76191	109768	39534	74181
汽车制造业	Manufacture of Motor Vehicles	74189	42962	36600	74544
铁路、船舶、航空航天和其他运输设备制造业	Manufacture of Railway Locomotives, Building of Ships and Boats, Manufacture of Air and Spacecrafts and Other Transportation Equipment	89043	121574	47979	76159
电气机械和器材制造业	Manufacture of Electrical Machinery and Equipment	77345	65932	35292	78222
计算机、通信和其他电子设备制造业	Manufacture of Computers, Communication Equipment and Other Electronic Equipment	87075	58597	40154	87782
仪器仪表制造业	Manufacture of Measuring Instruments and Meters	86300	78060	44718	87334
其他制造业	Other Manufacturing	84867	107527	35454	80721
废弃资源综合利用业	Waste Recrecycling and Recovery	60364	91730	30478	63029
金属制品、机械和设备修理业	Repair of Fabricated Metal Products, Machinery and Equipment	109407	56437	27258	111552
电力、热力、燃气及水生产和供应业	**Production and Distribution of Electricity, Heating Power, Gas and Water**	**100677**	**108364**	**35618**	**98383**
电力、热力生产和供应业	Production and Distribution of Electricity and Heating Power	108109	112728	33703	106584
燃气生产和供应业	Production and Distribution of Gas	88649	64876		92190
水的生产和供应业	Production and Distribution of Water	71416	72976	40311	71949
建筑业	**Construction**	**69525**	**78124**	**53214**	**69485**
房屋建筑业	Construction of Buildings	71649	66651	47978	73629
土木工程建筑业	Civil Engineering Construction	74649	91228	65844	72228
建筑安装业	Construction Installation	64771	50589	69689	65201
建筑装饰和其他建筑业	Building Completion, Finishing and Other Constructions	56487	89029	39717	55117
批发和零售业	**Wholesale and Retail Trade**	**84535**	**118729**	**43628**	**83534**
批发业	Wholesale	109711	147528	45633	108290
零售业	Retail Trade	56794	65043	42050	56764
交通运输、仓储和邮政业	**Transport, Storage and Post**	**71958**	**79772**	**31060**	**70680**
铁路运输业	Transport via Railway	85481	87024		80408
道路运输业	Transport via Road	46319	23430	23319	46960
水上运输业	Water Transport	164317			164317
航空运输业	Air Transport	157434	43556		157450
管道运输业	Transport via Pipeline	132319			132319
装卸搬运和运输代理业	Loading, Unloading, Portage and Other Transport Services	74728	64130	52677	75739
仓储业	Storage	59622	65748	29944	58994
邮政业	Post	69943	68347		70746
住宿和餐饮业	**Accommodation and Restaurants**	**47217**	**50438**	**40049**	**46905**
住宿业	Accommodation	50502	50518	43002	51055
餐饮业	Restaurants	43951	49409	30226	44039
信息传输、软件和信息技术服务业	**Information Transmission, Software and Information Technology Services**	**135346**	**118683**	**35257**	**135815**
电信、广播电视和卫星传输服务	Telecommunications, Broadcasting, Television and Satellite Transmission Services	136478	133608	30305	136707
互联网和相关服务	Internet and Related Services	114802	107210	24000	115016
软件和信息技术服务业	Software and Information Technology Services	138465	118127	37069	139010

3-24 续表 2 Continued 2

单位：元 (yuan)

行 业	Sector	平均工资 Average Wages	国有单位 State-owned	集体单位 Collective-Owned	其他单位 Others
金融业	**Finance**	**234497**	**185076**	**130000**	**236131**
货币金融服务	Monetary Financial Services	253699	188136		256139
资本市场服务	Capital Market Services	244994	140664	60000	250709
保险业	Insurance	159181	246760		157925
其他金融业	Other Financial Services	252054	339743	144000	251258
房地产业	**Real Estate**	**73578**	**68577**	**41483**	**75494**
租赁和商务服务业	**Renting and Leasing Activities and Business Services**	**95525**	**77502**	**30800**	**107823**
租赁业	Renting and Leasing Activities	51297	75737	24337	51441
商务服务业	Business Services	96809	77511	30951	110026
科学研究和技术服务业	**Scientific Research and Development, Technical Services**	**116571**	**127784**	**73284**	**110607**
研究和试验发展	Research and Experimental Development	123392	123452	88933	125646
专业技术服务业	Professional Technique Services	115805	136880	66833	110534
科技推广和应用服务业	Technique Generalization and Application Services	107695	127300	59543	104394
水利、环境和公共设施管理业	**Management of Water Conservancy, Environment and Public Facilities**	**59276**	**60999**	**30946**	**59825**
水利管理业	Management of Water Conservancy	73386	74280	48735	74952
生态保护和环境治理业	Ecological Protection and Environmental Control	93954	87680	31111	96294
公共设施管理业	Management of Public Facilities	55068	58240	29424	52852
居民服务、修理和其他服务业	**Resident Services, Repair and Other Services**	**44023**	**52489**	**28257**	**44302**
居民服务业	Resident Services	41868	52104	28242	40909
机动车、电子产品和日用产品修理业	Repair of Motor Vehicles, Electronics and Household Appliances	50876	54238	31711	52082
其他服务业	Other Services	41863	52243	26522	41821
教育	**Education**	**91166**	**99402**	**62496**	**60532**
卫生和社会工作	**Health Care and Social Works**	**112293**	**120721**	**73710**	**68233**
卫生	Health Care	115402	122764	78783	73156
社会工作	Social Works	52138	65013	32956	32711
文化、体育和娱乐业	**Culture, Sports and Entertainment**	**115062**	**132384**	**43420**	**86713**
新闻和出版业	Journalism and Publishing	124620	122895	60964	131734
广播、电视、电影和影视录音制作业	Radio Broadcasting, Television, Movies, Videos and Sound Recording	173014	210960	38167	98044
文化艺术业	Culture and Arts	81717	88534	47056	66159
体育	Sports Activities	61837	88266	23200	51237
娱乐业	Entertainment	66545	104142	28239	61317
公共管理、社会保障和社会组织	**Public Administration, Social Security and Social Organizations**	**78310**	**83986**	**32369**	**30220**
中国共产党机关	Organs of Communist Party of China	87976	87976		
国家机构	Organs of State	82847	83148	41858	28202
人民政协、民主党派	Peole's Political Consultative Conference and Democratic Parties	96300	96300		
社会保障	Social Security	79065	85549	89000	50816
群众团体、社会团体和其他成员组织	Mass Communities, Social Organizations and Other Membership Organizations	90757	99114	46740	80321
基层群众自治组织	Grass Roots Self-Government Organization	17048		19018	16990
国际组织	**International Organizations**				

3-25 城镇登记失业人员和新增就业人数(1979-2013年)
NUMBER OF REGISTERED UNEMPLOYED PERSONS AND NEWLY EMPLOYED PERSONS IN URBAN AREA (1979-2013)

单位：万人 (10000 persons)

年 份 Year	年末实有城镇登记失业人员 Number of Actual Registed Unemployed Persons in Urban Area Year-end	城镇登记失业率(%) Registered Unemployment Rate in Urban Area	城镇新增就业人数 Newly Employed Persons in Urban Area
1979	4.96	1.60	
1980	8.67	1.60	
1981	8.36	1.28	
1982	7.03	1.62	
1983	4.20	1.09	
1984	2.03	0.54	
1985	1.61	0.40	
1986	1.25	0.30	
1987	2.24	0.45	
1988	1.58	0.40	
1989	1.71	0.40	
1990	1.67	0.30	
1991	1.92	0.40	
1992	1.72	0.36	
1993	1.92	0.41	
1994	1.91	0.41	
1995	2.19	0.46	
1996	2.80	0.58	
1997	3.29	0.73	
1998	2.95	0.66	
1999	2.80	0.62	
2000	3.32	0.76	
2001	5.19	1.18	
2002	6.02	1.35	
2003	6.96	1.43	
2004	6.46	1.30	
2005	10.57	2.11	31.50
2006	10.40	1.98	34.39
2007	10.63	1.84	40.71
2008	10.33	1.82	41.97
2009	8.16	1.44	42.44
2010	7.73	1.37	44.64
2011	7.89	1.39	44.69
2012	7.20	1.27	43.89
2013	6.81	1.21	42.87

资料来源：北京市人力资源和社会保障局。
Source: Beijing Municipal Bureau of Human Resource and Social Security.

主要统计指标解释

户籍人口 指公民依照《中华人民共和国户口登记条例》已在其经常居住地的公安户籍管理机关登记了常住户口的人。

常住人口 指在某地区实际居住半年以上的人口。

常住外来人口 指不具有本市户籍户口，来自北京市行政区划以外的省、自治区、直辖市，且在京居住半年以上的人口。

出生率 指在一定时期内（通常为一年）出生人数与同期平均人数(或期中人数)之比，一般用千分比表示。计算公式：

$$出生率=\frac{年出生人数}{年平均人数}\times1000‰$$

出生人数是指活产，即脱离母体时（不管怀孕月数），有过呼吸或其他生命现象的活婴儿总和。年平均人数是年初、年末人口数的平均数，也可用年中人口数代替。

死亡率 指在一定时期内（通常为一年）死亡人数与同期平均人数（或期中人数）之比，一般用千分比表示。计算公式：

$$死亡率=\frac{年死亡人数}{年平均人数}\times1000‰$$

自然增长率 指在一定时期内（通常为一年）人口自然增加数（出生人数减死亡人数）与该时期内平均人数（或期中人数）之比，一般用千分比表示。计算公式：

$$自然增长率=\frac{年出生人数-年死亡人数}{年平均人数}\times1000‰$$

人口自然增长率=人口出生率－人口死亡率

从业人员 指在各级国家机关、党政机关、社会团体及企业、事业单位中工作，取得工资或其他形式的劳动报酬的全部人员。包括：在岗职工、聘用的离退休人员以及在单位中工作的港澳台及外籍人员、兼职人员、借用的外单位人员和第二职业者。不包括本单位的不在岗职工。

在岗职工 指在本单位工作并由单位支付工资的人员，以及有工作岗位，但由于学习、病伤产假（六个月以内）等原因暂未工作，仍由单位支付工资的人员。

在岗职工工资总额 与"在岗职工"指标相对应，根据1990年1月1日的国家统计局令（一号）修订，指单位在报告期内直接支付给本单位在岗职工的劳动报酬总额。包括基础工资、职务工资、级别工资、工龄工资、计件工资、奖金、各种津贴和补贴、交通补贴、洗理费、书报费、旅游费、过节费、伙食补助、住房补贴、住房提租补贴、由单位从个人工资中直接为其代扣或代缴的个人所得税、房水电费以及住房公积金和社会保险基金个人缴纳部分等。

在岗职工平均工资 指企业、事业、机关等单位的在岗职工在一定时期内的人均劳动报酬。它表明一定时期在岗职工工资收入的高低程度，是反映在岗职工工资水平的主要指标。计算公式为：

$$在岗职工平均工资=\frac{报告期实际支付的全部在岗职工工资总额}{报告期全部在岗职工平均人数}$$

从业人员平均工资 指企业、事业、机关等单位的从业人员在一定时期内的人均劳动报酬。计算公式为：

$$从业人员平均工资=\frac{报告期实际支付的全部从业人员劳动报酬总额}{报告期全部从业人员平均人数}$$

年末实有城镇登记失业人员 指年末实有的城镇登记失业人员数（包括全部正在领取失业保险金的失业人员）。

城镇登记失业率 指城镇登记失业人数与城镇从业人数和城镇登记失业人数二者之和的比。计算公式如下：

$$城镇登记失业率=\frac{年末实有登记失业人数}{城镇从业人数+年末实有登记失业人数}\times100\%$$

Explanatory Notes on Main Statistical Indicators

Registered Population refers to persons who have registered their permanent residence with the public security register authority of their habitual residence.

Permanent Population refers to persons actually living for more than half a year at a place.

Permanent Migrant Population refers to persons who have no permanent residence registration in Beijing, come from other provinces, autonomous regions and municipalities, and have stayed in Beijing for more than half a year.

Birth Rate refers to the ratio of the number of births to the average population (or mid-period population) during a certain period of time (usually a year), which is often expressed in ‰. The following formula is used:

Birth Rate = Annual Number of Births/Annual Average Number of Population×1000‰

Number of births refers to live births i.e. the births when babies had shown any vital phenomena regardless of the length of pregnancy.

Annual average number of population is the average of the number of population at the beginning of the year and that at the end of the year. Sometimes it is substituted with the mid-year population.

Death Rate refers to the ratio of the number of deaths to the average population (or mid-period population) during a certain period of time (usually a year), which is often expressed in ‰. The following formula is used:

Death Rate= Annual Number of Deaths/Annual Average Number of Population×1000‰

Natural Growth Rate refers to the ratio of the natural growth of population (births minus deaths) to the average population (or mid-period population) during a certain period of time (usually a year), which is often expressed in ‰. The following formula is used:

Natural Growth Rate of Population = (Annual Number of Births - Annual Number of Deaths)/Annual Average Number of Population×1000‰

Natural Growth Rate of Population = Birth Rate - Death Rate

Employed Persons refer to all persons working in government agencies, Party and political organs, social groups, enterprises and public institutions at all levels, and receiving wages or labor remuneration in other forms. They include: fully employed staff and workers, retired persons employed, persons from Hong Kong, Macao, Taiwan and foreign countries who are employed, part-time employees, employees transferred from other entities, and employees with a second job. They exclude employees that are not on the job in the entity.

Fully Employed Staff and Workers refer to persons working in the entity and paid by the entity, as well as persons having a job in the entity, but not working temporarily due to study, illness, injury or maternity leaves (less than 6 months) and other reasons, and still paid by the entity.

Total Wages of Fully Employed Staff and Workers corresponds to the indicator Fully Employed Staff and Workers. The indicator was revised in accordance with Decree 1 of the National Bureau of Statistics dated January 1, 1990, referring to the total wages directly paid by an entity to fully employed staff and workers of the entity during the reporting period.

It consists of basic wage, position-based wage, post wage, wage of a rank, piece rate wage, bonus, allowances and subsidies, traffic subsidy, washing and haircutting allowance, books and newspaper allowance, travel benefit, festival bonus, food subsidy, housing subsidy, subsidy for incremental house rent, as well as personal income tax, water and electricity fees and the personally payable portion of housing accumulation fund and social security fund withheld directly by the employer from the employee's wage.

Average Wage of Fully Employed Staff and Workers refers to the per-capita labor remuneration of on-the-job staff and workers in enterprises, public institutions and government agencies within a given period of time. It shows the level of wage income of fully employed staff and workers within a given period of time, serving as a main indicator reflecting the level of wage of fully employed staff and workers. The following formula is used:

Average Wage of Fully Employed Staff and Workers = Total Wages of Fully Employed Staff and Workers Actually Paid in the Reporting Period / Total Number of Fully Employed Staff and Workers in the Reporting Period

Average Wage of Employed Persons refers to the per-capita labor remuneration of employed persons in enterprises and government agencies within a given period of time. The following formula is used:

Average Wage of Employed Persons = Total Wages of All Employed Persons Actually Paid in the Reporting Period / Total Number of Employed Persons in the Reporting Period

Number of Actual Registered Unemployed Persons in Urban Area at Year-end refers to the actual number of unemployed persons registered at the year end (including all unemployed persons receiving unemployment insurance benefit).

Registered Unemployment Rate in Urban Area refers to the ratio of urban registered unemployed persons to the sum of urban staff and workers and urban registered unemployed persons. The following formula is used:

Registered Unemployment Rate in Urban Area

= Number of Actual Registered Unemployed Persons at Year-end / (Urban Employed Persons + Number of Actual Registered Unemployed Persons at Year-end) × 100%

能源、资源和环境
ENERGY, RESOURCES AND ENVIRONMENT

简要说明

一、本章资料的主要内容

本章包括的主要内容有：北京市能源生产量、能源消费量、万元地区生产总值能耗、能源消费的行业构成和品种构成、能源平衡表、能源消费弹性系数、人均及日均能源消费量和北京地区用电量情况；土地利用情况；气象情况、水资源情况、排水及节水情况；园林绿化及森林情况；大气环境、固体废物处置情况等环境保护资料。

二、本章资料的统计范围

本章能源部分统计范围为全社会口径。

三、本章资料的数据来源

本章能源部分由北京市统计局、国家统计局北京调查总队提供；土地利用情况由北京市国土资源局提供；气象资料由北京市气象局提供；水资源、排水及节水情况由北京市水务局提供；城市环境卫生由北京市市政市容管理委员会提供；其他资料由北京市环境保护局提供。

四、本章中关于历史数据调整的问题

按照国家统计局统一要求和统一方法，本章中 1995 至 2003 年的能源消费总量数据已根据“北京市第一次全国经济普查”的数据结果，采用“趋势离差法”进行修正。2004 年能源消费总量为第一次经济普查数据。

本章中 1997-2007 年的万元地区生产总值能耗及下降率、万元地区生产总值水耗及下降率、能源消费弹性系数、平均每万元地区生产总值能源消费量中使用的地区生产总值数据，已根据第二次经济普查和第二次农业普查结果进行了修正。

本章中人均生活用能、人均水资源按年平均常住人口计算；同时，根据全国第六次人口普查数据对 2006-2010 年的人均指标数据进行了修正。

由于第三次经济普查数据尚未对外公布，有些数据的报告期仍为 2012 年；已列示 2013 年的数据为初步统计结果。

五、有关统计标准的变化说明

（一）关于行业划分。根据国家统计局规定，自 2012 年开始执行《国民经济行业分类》GB/T 4754-2011 标准。

（二）关于三次产业划分。根据国家统计局《三次产业划分规定》（国统字[2012]108 号），对三次产业的范围进行了调整。其中第一产业是指农、林、牧、渔业（不含农、林、牧、渔服务业）；第二产业是指采矿业（不含开采辅助活动），制造业（不含金属制品、机械和设备修理业），电力、热力、燃气及水生产和供应业，建筑业；第三产业是指除第一产业、第二产业以外的其他行业。自 2012 年开始执行此规定。

六、全市能源统计的内容及能源消费量的测算方法

全市能源统计主要内容包括第二、三产业限额以上法人单位能源消费情况全面调查；限额以下法人单位能源消费情况抽样调查；农业生产能源消费统计；居民生活能源消费情况抽样调查；能源供应部门的能源供应情况等。

全市能源消费总量包括三次产业能源消费量（生产消费）和居民生活能源消费量。其中，三次产业能源消费量根据各产业能源统计资料分别测算，居民生活能源消费量根据居民能源消费抽样调查资料测算。

从全市范围看，各能源品种的生产量、供应量和消费量应存在平衡关系。因此，在利用上述方法进行生产和居民生活的能源消费量测算时，还应根据全市各能源品种的生产量、供应量和供应结构进行平衡修正。

Brief Introduction

I. Main Content

This chapter consists of statistics for volume of energy production and energy consumption in Beijing, energy consumption per 10,000 yuan of GDP, energy consumption by sector and by type, energy balance sheet, energy consumption elasticity coefficient, per-capita and daily energy consumption and electricity consumption in Beijing; land utilization; meteorology, water resources, water drainage and water saving; landscaping and forest; atmospheric environment, solid waste disposal and other environmental protection data.

II. Scope of Statistics

In this chapter, statistics on energy cover the entire society.

III. Source of Statistics

Energy statistics are from Beijing Municipal Bureau of Statistics, and the NBS Survey Office in Beijing; statistics on land utilization are from Beijing Municipal Bureau of Land and Resources; meteorology statistics are from Beijing Municipal Bureau of Meteorology; water resources, water drainage and water saving statistics are from Beijing Water Authority; urban environment and sanitation statistics are from Beijing Municipal Commission of City Administration and Environment; other statistics are from Beijing Municipal Bureau of Environmental Protection.

IV. Adjustment to Historical Statistics

In accordance with requirements and uniform method of the National Bureau of Statistics, total energy figures in 1995-2003 in this chapter have been corrected with "trend deviation method" based on the results from the "first national economic census". Statistics on total energy consumption in 2004 are those of the first economic census.

Figures of GDP of Beijing used in the 1997-2007 energy consumption per 10,000 yuan of GDP, water consumption per 10,000 yuan of GDP and decrease rate, energy consumption elasticity coefficient, and energy consumption per 10,000 yuan of GDP by different energy have been corrected in accordance with results from the second economic census and the second agricultural census.

In this chapter, the per-capita energy consumption for living, per-capita water resources are calculated by average permanent population; at the same time, per-capita figures in 2006-2010 have been corrected in accordance with the sixth national population census.

Statistics for the Third National Economic Census have not been officially released yet, so the reporting period of some statistics is still the year of 2012 and the 2013 statistics filled in the tables are preliminary figures.

V. Changes in Relevant Statistical Standards

(I) Classification of Sectors. According to relevant provisions of the National Bureau of Statistics, the Standard for Classification of National Economic Sectors (GB/T4754-2011) came into effect in 2012.

(II) Classification of Three Industries. According to the provision of the National Bureau of Statistics on Classification of Three Industries (GTZ[2012]No.108), the scope of three industries has been changed. The primary industry means farming, forestry, animal husbandry and fishery (excluding service for farming, forestry, animal husbandry and fishery); the secondary industry means mining (excluding mining support activities), manufacturing (excluding metal products, machinery and equipment repair), electricity, heating power, fuel gas and water production and service sectors, and construction industry; the tertiary industry means industries other than the primary and secondary industries. The Provisions of the National Bureau of Statistics on Classification of Three Industries (GTZ [2012] No. 108) came into effect in 2012.

Ⅵ .Content of Energy Statistics in Beijing and Calculation Method of Energy Consumption

Energy statistics in Beijing include complete survey on energy consumption in entities above designated size in the secondary and tertiary industries; sample survey on energy consumption in entities below designated size; statistics on energy consumption in agricultural production; sample survey on energy consumption in residents' living and energy supply in energy supply departments, etc.

Total energy consumption in Beijing includes energy consumption in three industries (in production) and residents' living, in which, the energy consumption in three industries is calculated according to energy statistics for each industry, and that in residents' living is calculated according to statistics from sample survey on residents' energy consumption.

In terms of the whole city, the volume of production, supply and consumption shall be balanced among all types of energy. Therefore, in the calculation of energy consumption in production and residents' living by using the above-mentioned method, a correction shall be made for balance according to the volume of production, supply and consumption of all types of energy in the city.

4-1 能源生产量(2000-2013年) ENERGY PRODUCTION (2000-2013)

项目		Item		2000	2001	2002	2003	2004	2005	2006
一次能源	**(万吨标准煤)**	**Primary Energy**	**(10000 tons of SCE)**	**523.7**	**597.4**	**632.1**	**686.3**	**765.0**	**679.5**	**460.6**
#原煤	(万吨)	Raw Coal	(10000 tons)	690.0	831.9	881.0	957.3	1067.9	945.2	642.1
二次能源	**(万吨标准煤)**	**Secondary Energy**	**(10000 tons of SCE)**	**2461.4**	**2362.0**	**2388.6**	**2470.5**	**2850.8**	**2832.1**	**2714.4**
#汽油	(万吨)	Gasoline	(10000 tons)	146.2	146.7	154.1	151.4	169.8	156.5	159.3
煤油	(万吨)	Kerosene	(10000 tons)					8.1	12.4	11.6
柴油	(万吨)	Diesel Oil	(10000 tons)	183.9	186.7	174.1	170.2	180.7	176.8	185.9
燃料油	(万吨)	Fuel Oil	(10000 tons)	78.6	67.4	64.4	64.5	68.2	68.9	64.0
液化石油气	(万吨)	Liquefied Petroleum Gas	(10000 tons)	40.0	39.7	41.7	38.4	43.3	47.3	40.5
热力	(万百万千焦)	Heat	(10 billion kilo-joules)	8758.8	8608.2	9064.0	9616.6	10973.9	11335.7	12181.6
电力	(亿千瓦时)	Electricity	(100 million kwh)	180.7	174.5	180.3	188.3	200.4	209.8	209.7

4-1 续表 Continued

项目		Item		2007	2008	2009	2010	2011	2012	2013
一次能源	**(万吨标准煤)**	**Primary Energy**	**(10000 tons of SCE)**	**466.1**	**414.2**	**475.7**	**481.1**	**482.0**	**501.8**	**536.8**
#原煤	(万吨)	Raw Coal	(10000 tons)	648.8	578.5	641.3	500.1	500.1	493.1	500.1
二次能源	**(万吨标准煤)**	**Secondary Energy**	**(10000 tons of SCE)**	**2895.2**	**3213.3**	**3346.7**	**3457.3**	**3209.1**	**3267.2**	**3170.9**
#汽油	(万吨)	Gasoline	(10000 tons)	176.5	215.5	272.6	257.1	251.2	261.9	243.3
煤油	(万吨)	Kerosene	(10000 tons)	36.4	85.2	111.6	116.1	126.4	132.9	99.4
柴油	(万吨)	Diesel Oil	(10000 tons)	268.2	373.3	364.2	350.4	355.7	319.1	247.1
燃料油	(万吨)	Fuel Oil	(10000 tons)	41.9	42.1	29.6	34.9	21.4	24.0	22.8
液化石油气	(万吨)	Liquefied Petroleum Gas	(10000 tons)	66.2	50.0	40.3	32.9	30.2	35.0	35.7
热力	(万百万千焦)	Heat	(10 billion kilo-joules)	12951.1	13846.2	14476.1	15710.9	15127.7	15632.4	14935.1
电力	(亿千瓦时)	Electricity	(100 million kwh)	224.4	244.9	242.0	263.3	257.3	284.7	328.1

4-2 能源消费总量及万元地区生产总值能耗(1980-2013年)
TOTAL ENERGY CONSUMPTION AND ENERGY CONSUMPTION PER 10000 YUAN OF GDP (1980-2013)

单位：万吨标准煤 (10000 tons of SCE)

年 份 Year	能源消费总量 Total Energy Consumption	第一产业 Primary Industry	第二产业 Secondary Industry	#工业 Industry	第三产业 Tertiary Industry	生活消费 Residential Consumption	万元地区生产总值能耗（吨标准煤） Energy Consumption per 10000 yuan of GDP (ton of SCE)	万元地区生产总值能耗下降率(%) Decrease Rate of Energy Consumption per 10000 yuan GDP(%)
1980	1907.7	66.8	1400.3	1385.0	297.6	143.0	13.715	
1981	1902.6	53.3	1339.4	1326.1	334.9	175.0	13.668	-0.23
1982	1920.4	55.7	1346.2	1330.8	338.0	180.5	12.398	6.02
1983	1984.7	73.4	1379.4	1359.5	313.6	218.3	10.839	11.22
1984	2144.1	85.8	1470.9	1451.6	347.3	240.1	9.899	7.98
1985	2211.4	90.7	1488.3	1463.9	351.6	280.8	8.601	5.12
1986	2400.0	95.7	1612.0	1586.5	380.4	311.9	8.424	-0.49
1987	2475.8	89.0	1647.8	1619.8	424.7	314.3	7.576	5.88
1988	2612.6	111.7	1748.1	1719.7	412.2	340.6	6.369	6.45
1989	2653.2	114.4	1735.9	1700.0	427.0	375.9	5.818	2.73
1990	2709.7	105.7	1720.1	1686.4	515.3	368.6	5.411	2.92
1991	2872.0	126.7	1807.6	1773.7	542.0	395.7	4.795	3.56
1992	2987.5	143.6	1888.1	1851.6	552.4	403.4	4.213	6.54
1993	3264.6	133.6	2150.9	2106.9	561.0	419.1	3.684	2.69
1994	3385.9	143.6	2234.1	2198.1	574.8	433.4	2.956	8.78
1995	3533.3	120.4	2328.4	2282.4	632.7	451.8	2.344	6.83
1996	3734.5	110.8	2477.0	2430.7	698.1	448.6	2.087	2.75
1997	3719.2	95.7	2369.6	2312.3	799.8	454.1	1.792	9.55
1998	3808.1	96.2	2400.5	2343.1	856.4	455.0	1.603	6.49
1999	3906.6	86.9	2370.7	2308.5	971.8	477.2	1.459	7.49
2000	4144.0	104.8	2424.8	2356.4	1080.9	533.5	1.311	5.12
2001	4229.2	105.4	2366.6	2287.7	1196.2	561.0	1.198	8.62
2002	4436.1	103.0	2414.6	2325.4	1334.5	584.0	1.127	5.93
2003	4648.2	99.9	2476.7	2380.2	1391.0	680.6	1.062	5.73
2004	5139.6	85.6	2664.2	2550.2	1638.0	751.8	1.029	3.09
2005	5521.9	86.3	2702.5	2599.1	1918.7	814.4	0.986 (0.792)	4.17
2006	5904.1	92.3	2773.1	2670.1	2129.3	909.4	0.750	5.37
2007	6285.0	96.4	2793.8	2685.0	2389.5	1005.3	0.697	7.02
2008	6327.1	96.9	2550.5	2430.8	2610.5	1069.2	0.643	7.74
2009	6570.3	99.0	2544.2	2392.4	2760.3	1166.8	0.606	5.76
2010	6954.1	100.3	2726.7	2559.7	2897.4	1229.7	0.581 (0.493)	4.04
2011	6995.4	100.3	2488.7	2329.7	3100.5	1305.9	0.458	6.95
2012	7177.7	100.8	2426.1	2275.7	3252.1	1398.7	0.436	4.75
2013	7354.2	102.6	2402.2	2238.5	3422.9	1426.5		

注：1. 本表能源消费量指标按等价值计算，万元地区生产总值能耗下降率按可比价计算。
2. 2000年及以前万元地区生产总值能耗按当年价格计算；2000年以后按可比价格计算，可比价格每五年调整一次基期，更换基期年份计算两个可比价数据，括号内数据是按新基期价格计算。
3. 由于第三次经济普查数据尚未发布，所以表内2013年数据空缺。

Note: a) Enery consumption in this table is at equivalent prices. Reduction rate of Energy Consumption per 10000 yuan of GDP is calculated at comparable prices.
b) Energy consumption per 10000 yuan of GDP befor 2000 was calculated at the price of that year; figures after 2000 were calculated at comparable prices. The base period of comparable prices is changed every five years. Two figures at comparable prices were calculated for the year in which the base period is changed. Figures in brackets were calculated at the price of new base period.
c) As the data of the Third National Economic Census has not been released yet, data for 2013 were not filled in this table.

4-3 按行业分能源消费总量(2005-2012年)
TOTAL ENERGY CONSUMPTION BY SECTOR (2005-2012)

单位：万吨标准煤 (10000 tons of SCE)

项 目	Item	2005	2006	2007	2008	2009	2010	2011	2012
能源消费总量	**Total Energy Consumption**	**5521.9**	**5904.1**	**6285.0**	**6327.1**	**6570.3**	**6954.1**	**6995.4**	**7177.7**
第一产业	**Primary Industry**	**86.3**	**92.3**	**96.4**	**96.9**	**99.0**	**100.3**	**100.3**	**100.8**
第二产业	**Secondary Industry**	**2702.5**	**2773.1**	**2793.8**	**2550.5**	**2544.2**	**2726.7**	**2488.7**	**2426.1**
工业	Industry	2599.1	2670.1	2685.0	2430.8	2392.4	2559.7	2329.7	2275.7
建筑业	Construction	103.4	103.0	108.8	119.7	151.8	167.0	159.0	150.4
第三产业	**Tertiary Industry**	**1918.7**	**2129.3**	**2389.5**	**2610.5**	**2760.3**	**2897.4**	**3100.5**	**3252.1**
批发和零售业	Wholesale and Retail Trade	157.6	162.7	202.9	195.2	206.9	192.7	211.5	221.7
交通运输、仓储和邮政业	Transport, Storage and Post	563.4	717.6	840.8	993.9	1025.2	1104.8	1185.9	1235.1
住宿和餐饮业	Accommodation and Restaurants	199.9	202.5	249.7	218.0	220.8	239.4	253.1	262.3
信息传输、软件和信息技术服务业	Information transmission,software and information technology services	52.3	59.0	73.2	88.3	96.0	107.5	124.0	129.6
金融业	Finance	27.5	28.1	34.0	39.1	40.8	43.3	50.9	54.3
房地产业	Real Estate	306.7	308.9	318.4	346.0	364.2	389.6	391.2	411.5
租赁和商务服务业	Renting and Leasing Activities and Business Services	115.3	121.9	127.8	165.5	191.2	182.5	182.6	196.3
科学研究和技术服务业	Scientific research and development, technical services	85.5	94.1	101.7	116.9	123.1	122.7	144.7	163.9
水利、环境和公共设施管理业	Management of Water Conservancy, Environment and Public Facilities	23.4	27.4	38.7	35.7	37.8	40.2	47.0	46.5
居民服务、修理和其他服务业	Resident Services, Repair and Other Services	64.9	72.5	58.7	31.9	33.6	34.2	46.2	47.1
教 育	Education	143.7	153.7	157.9	165.1	183.0	199.6	205.8	222.9
卫生和社会工作	Healtlcare and Social Works	52.4	54.6	52.6	58.0	64.6	66.9	71.7	74.1
文化、体育和娱乐业	Culture, Sports and Entertainment	43.8	45.3	45.1	53.5	59.3	60.1	69.8	71.5
公共管理、社会保障和社会组织	Public Administration, Social Security and Social Organizations	82.3	81.0	88.0	103.4	113.8	114.0	116.1	115.3
生活消费	**Residential Consumption**	**814.4**	**909.4**	**1005.3**	**1069.2**	**1166.8**	**1229.7**	**1305.8**	**1398.7**

注：1. 行业划分执行《国民经济行业分类》(GB/T 4754—2011)标准(下同)。
2. 2012年开始执行国家统计局《三次产业划分规定》，具体调整内容见本章简要说明(下同)。

Note: a) Sectors in this table are classified in accordance with Standard for Classification of National Economic Sectors 2011 (GB/T 4754-2011) (the same below).
b) From 2012, the provisions of National Bureau of Statistics on Classification of Three Industires became effective. See Brief Introduction of this chapter for detailed changes (the same below).

4-4 按三次产业分万元地区生产总值能耗及能耗下降率(2001-2012年)
ENERGY CONSUMPTION PER 10000 YUAN OF GDP AND DECREASE RATE (2001-2012)

单位：吨标准煤 (ton of SCE)

项 目 Item	万元地区生产总值能耗 Energy Consumption per 10000 yuan of GDP	第一产业 Primary Industry	第二产业 Secondary Industry	#工业 Industry	第三产业 Tertiary Industry
2001	1.198	1.282	2.091	2.460	0.516
2002	1.127	1.220	1.968	2.318	0.508
2003	1.062	1.196	1.803	2.114	0.476
2004	1.029	1.031	1.658	1.898	0.496
2005	0.986	1.060	1.527	1.745	0.512
	(0.792)	(0.973)	(1.334)	(1.523)	(0.395)
2006	0.750	1.035	1.238	1.429	0.384
2007	0.697	1.058	1.107	1.271	0.373
2008	0.643	1.052	1.002	1.148	0.362
2009	0.606	1.028	0.906	1.038	0.348
2010	0.581	1.058	0.853	0.967	0.334
	(0.493)	(0.806)	(0.805)	(0.926)	(0.273)
2011	0.458	0.799	0.689	0.784	0.269
2012	0.436	0.778	0.624	0.716	0.262

4-4 续表 Continued

单位：% (%)

项 目 Item	万元地区生产总值能耗下降率 Decrease Rate of Energy Consumption per 10000 yuan of GDP	第一产业 Primary Industry	第二产业 Secondary Industry	#工业 Industry	第三产业 Tertiary Industry
2001	8.62	2.98	10.90	11.91	2.13
2002	5.93	4.83	5.88	5.75	1.56
2003	5.73	1.96	8.39	8.80	6.23
2004	3.09	13.79	8.04	10.22	-4.08
2005	4.17	-2.80	7.89	8.07	-3.25
2006	5.37	-6.35	7.15	6.17	2.87
2007	7.02	-2.26	10.61	11.06	2.76
2008	7.74	0.57	9.43	9.67	2.89
2009	5.76	2.29	9.66	9.55	4.03
2010	4.04	-2.96	5.74	6.88	3.96
2011	6.95	0.89	14.46	15.34	1.55
2012	4.75	2.61	9.30	8.71	2.75

注：1. 万元地区生产总值能耗按可比价格计算，可比价格每五年调整一次基期，更换基期年份计算两个可比价数据，括号内数据是按新基期价格计算。

2. 表内万元地区生产总值能耗下降率按可比价格计算。

Note: a) Energy consumption per 10000 yuan of GDP were calculated at comparable prices. The base period of comparable prices is changed every five years. Two figures at comparable prices were calculated for the year in which the base period is changed. Figures in brackets were calculated at the price of new base period.

b) Energy consumption per 10000 yuan of GDP decrease rate is at comparable prices.

4-5 电力平衡表(2004-2012年)
ELECTRICITY BALANCE (2004-2012)

单位：亿千瓦时 (100 million kwh)

项　　目	Item	2004	2005	2006	2007	2008	2009	2010	2011	2012
可供本地区消费的能源量	**Total Energy Available for Local Consumption**	**308.50**	**358.26**	**409.33**	**449.46**	**462.09**	**512.97**	**558.13**	**596.49**	**627.21**
加工转换投入(-)产出(+)量	**Input(-) or Output(+) in Processing and Conversion**	**200.40**	**209.80**	**209.65**	**224.43**	**244.86**	**242.02**	**263.34**	**257.28**	**284.73**
火力发电	Thermal Power	200.40	209.80	209.65	224.43	244.86	242.02	263.34	257.28	284.73
供　热	Heating									
煤炭洗选	Washing of Coal									
炼　焦	Coking									
炼油及煤制油	Oil Refining and Coal to Liquid									
#油品再投入量(-)	Oil Product Re-input(-)									
制　气	Gas Production									
#焦炭再投入量(-)	Coke Re-input(-)									
煤制品加工	Coal Product Processing									
回收能	**Energy Recycled**									
损失量	**Losses**	**40.65**	**41.23**	**43.64**	**46.85**	**47.36**	**54.86**	**49.68**	**46.82**	**51.02**
#运输和输配损失	In Transportation and Transmission	40.65	41.23	43.64	46.85	47.36	54.86	49.68	46.82	51.02
终端消费量	**End-use Energy Consumption**	**469.46**	**525.81**	**575.35**	**628.24**	**660.79**	**703.99**	**781.22**	**806.86**	**860.92**
第一产业	Primary Industry	10.42	11.43	12.26	13.36	13.61	15.73	16.89	17.04	18.14
第二产业	Secondary Industry	216.39	224.57	242.19	249.60	247.09	248.09	279.70	265.56	272.01
工　业	Industry	196.18	209.91	227.49	234.08	230.18	227.99	256.15	240.42	246.12
#用作原料、材料	Use as Materials									
建筑业	Construction	20.21	14.66	14.70	15.52	16.91	20.10	23.55	25.14	25.89
第三产业	Tertiary Industry	162.11	200.89	225.03	258.6	283.79	311.37	345.30	379.53	408.93
生活消费	Residential Consumption	80.54	88.92	95.87	106.68	116.30	128.80	139.33	144.74	161.83
城镇	Urban	64.75	70.64	76.89	86.26	95.01	98.32	95.38	95.48	137.09
乡村	Rural	15.79	18.28	18.98	20.42	21.29	30.47	43.95	49.26	24.74
平衡差额	Balance	-1.21	1.02	-0.01	-1.20	-1.20	-3.86	-9.44	0.09	
消费量合计	**Total Energy Consumption**	**510.11**	**567.04**	**618.99**	**675.09**	**708.15**	**758.85**	**830.90**	**853.68**	**911.94**

4-6 综合能源平衡表(标准量)(2004-2012年)
COMPREHENSIVE ENERGY BALANCE (STANDARD VOLUME) (2004-2012)

单位：万吨标准煤 (10000 tons of SCE)

项　目	Item	2004	2005	2006	2007	2008	2009	2010	2011	2012
可供本地区消费的能源量	**Total Energy Available for Consumption**	**5169.57**	**5481.04**	**5650.63**	**5984.79**	**6144.99**	**6412.80**	**6777.08**	**6934.04**	**7179.42**
加工转换投入(-)产出(+)量	**Input(-) or Output(+) in Processing and Conversion**	**-35.52**	**-15.29**	**-27.81**	**-31.99**	**-24.24**	**-31.69**	**-73.50**	**-121.51**	**-119.05**
火力发电	Thermal Power				-1.60	-2.08	-3.20			
供　热	Heating							-48.71	-99.05	-106.65
煤炭洗选	Washing of Coal					-1.08	-0.55	-1.12	-1.10	-1.15
炼　焦	Coking	-35.24	-15.29	-12.82	-3.73	-3.10	-1.06	-2.12		
炼油及煤制油	Oil Refining and Coal to Liquid	-0.05		-13.62	-24.00	-16.45	-24.33	316.11	324.79	325.94
#油品再投入量(-)	Oil Product Re-input(-)							-335.89	-345.08	-344.14
制　气	Gas Production	139.97	131.64	116.98	113.55	69.01	67.54	-0.43	-0.41	-0.36
#焦炭再投入量(-)	Coke Re-input(-)	-139.97	-131.64	-116.98	-113.55	-69.01	-67.54			
煤制品加工	Coal Product Processing	-0.23		-1.37	-2.65	-1.53	-2.56	-1.35	-0.66	-1.01
回收能	**Energy Recycled**							**92.14**		**8.33**
损失量	**Losses**	**176.05**	**183.59**	**194.09**	**175.54**	**184.47**	**211.23**	**211.77**	**202.87**	**218.91**
#运输和输配损失	In Transportation and Transmission	176.05	183.18	194.09	175.54	184.47	211.23	207.70	192.22	211.17
终端消费量	**End-use Energy Consumption**	**4927.98**	**5323.07**	**5682.22**	**6077.51**	**6118.42**	**6327.41**	**6668.79**	**6671.01**	**6839.73**
第一产业	Primary Industry	85.60	86.35	92.30	96.44	96.90	99.01	100.25	100.33	100.75
第二产业	Secondary Industry	2476.85	2556.15	2606.52	2620.85	2383.95	2348.86	2501.93	2217.68	2149.53
工　业	Industry	2362.78	2452.70	2503.80	2512.05	2264.18	2196.98	2334.92	2058.62	1999.08
#用作原料、材料	Use as Materials	444.59	454.24	439.20	377.89	395.56	355.47	346.53	418.89	365.08
建筑业	Construction	114.07	103.45	102.72	108.80	119.77	151.88	167.01	159.06	150.45
第三产业	Tertiary Industry	1613.80	1866.20	2073.96	2354.96	2568.34	2712.74	2836.90	3047.16	3190.70
生活消费	Residential Consumption	751.73	814.37	909.44	1005.26	1069.23	1166.81	1229.71	1305.84	1398.75
城　镇	Urban	564.38	630.67	682.11	764.67	864.95	904.59	921.67	959.49	1115.45
乡　村	Rural	187.35	183.70	227.33	240.59	204.28	262.22	308.04	346.35	283.31
平衡差额	Balance	30.02	-40.91	-253.49	-300.25	-182.14	-157.55	-84.83	-61.36	1.74
消费量合计	**Total Energy Consumption**	**5139.55**	**5521.94**	**5904.11**	**6285.04**	**6327.13**	**6570.34**	**6954.05**	**6995.40**	**7177.68**

注：2004-2009年，热力按等价热值计算，“加工转换投入产出量”中的供热没有损失量；从2010年起热力按当量热值计算，“加工转换投入产出量”中的供热有损失量。

Note: Heating power in 2004-2009 was calculated in equivalent caloricity. There were no losses of heating in the "input or output in processing and transformation" . Heating power in 2010 was calculated as equivalent heat value. There were losses of heating in the "input or output in processing and transformation" .

4-7 能源平衡表(实物量简表)(2012年)
ENERGY BALANCE (PHYSICAL VOLUME) (SIMPLE EDITION) (2012)

单位：万吨　　(10000 tons)

项　目	Item	原煤 Coal	洗精煤 Washed Coal	其他洗煤 Other Washed Coal	煤制品 Coal Products	煤矸石 Coal Slack	焦炭 Coke	焦炉煤气(亿立方米) Coking Gas (100 million cu.m)
可供本地区消费的能源量	**Total Energy Available for Local Consumption**	**2264.79**	**1.77**		**3.32**		**32.26**	**3.58**
加工转换投入(-)产出(+)量	**Input(-) or Output(+) in Procesing and Conversion**	**-1256.90**	**-1.70**		**2.25**			
火力发电	Thermal Power	-649.56			-1.48			
供　热	Heating	-586.16			-20.18			
煤炭洗选	Washing of Coal	-17.44	12.57					
炼　焦	Coking							
炼油及煤制油	Oil Refining and Coal to Liquid							
#油品再投入量(-)	Oil Product Re-input(-)							
制　气	Gas Production	-1.60						
#焦炭再投入量(-)	Coke Re-input(-)							
煤制品加工	Coal Product Processing	-2.14	-14.27		23.91			
回收能	**Energy Recycled**							
损失量	**Losses**							
#运输和输配损失	In Transportation and Transmission							
终端消费量	**End-use Energy Consumption**	**1007.89**	**0.06**		**5.59**		**32.27**	**3.58**
第一产业	Primary Industry	44.60						
第二产业	Secondary Industry	407.46	0.06		1.06		32.27	3.58
工　业	Industry	395.97	0.06		0.70		32.26	3.58
#用作原料、材料	Use as Materials	0.09						
建筑业	Construction	11.49			0.36			
第三产业	Tertiary Industry	283.60			4.53			
生活消费	Residential Consumption	272.23						
城　镇	Urban	62.23						
乡　村	Rural	210.00						
平衡差额	Balance	-0.004	0.01		-0.02		-0.01	
消费量合计	**Total Energy Consumption**	**2264.79**	**14.34**		**27.25**		**32.27**	**3.58**

4-7 续表 1 Continued 1

单位：万吨 (10000 tons)

项　目	Item	高炉煤气（亿立方米）Blast Furnace Gas (100 million cu.m)	转炉煤气（亿立方米）Converter Gas (100 million cu.m)	其它煤气（亿立方米）Other Gas (100 million cu.m)	其它焦化产品 Other Carbonized Products	原油 Crude Oil	汽油 Gaso-line	煤油 Kero-sene
可供本地区消费的能源量	**Total Energy Available for Local Consumption**	**1.39**				**1075.77**	**154.04**	**310.44**
加工转换投入(-)产出(+)量	**Input(-) or Output(+) in Procesing and Conversion**			**0.64**		**-1075.01**	**261.86**	**132.92**
火力发电	Thermal Power							
供　热	Heating							
煤炭洗选	Washing of Coal							
炼　焦	Coking							
炼油及煤制油	Oil Refining and Coal to Liquid					-1075.01	261.86	132.92
#油品再投入量(-)	Re-inputs of Oil Products							
制　气	Gas Production			0.64				
#焦炭再投入量(-)	Coke Re-input(-)							
煤制品加工	Coal Product Processing							
回收能	**Energy Recycled**							
损失量	**Losses**					**0.76**		
#运输和输配损失	In Transportation and Transmission							
终端消费量	**Final Consumption Industry**	**1.39**		**0.64**			**415.90**	**443.33**
第一产业	Primary Industry						5.05	
第二产业	Secondary Industry	1.39		0.64			28.99	0.13
工　业	Industry	1.39		0.64			19.38	0.13
#用作原料、材料	Use in Materials						0.20	0.04
建筑业	Construction						9.61	
第三产业	Tertiary Industry						121.58	443.21
生活消费	Residential Consumption						260.27	
城　镇	Urban						252.35	
乡　村	Rural						7.92	
平衡差额	Balance							0.02
消费量合计	**Total Energy Consumption**	**1.39**		**0.64**		**1075.77**	**415.90**	**443.33**

4-7 续表 2 Continued 2

单位：万吨 (10000 tons)

项 目	Item	柴油 Diesel Oil	燃料油 Fuel Oil	石脑油 Naphtha	润滑油 Grease Oil	石蜡 Oilfin	溶剂油 Solvent Oil	石油沥青 Oil Asphalt	石油焦 Petroleum Coal
可供本地区消费的能源量	**Total Energy Available for Local Consumption**	**-102.98**	**54.15**	**61.26**	**25.11**	**-9.42**	**0.10**	**10.57**	**-25.68**
加工转换投入(-)产出(+)量	**Input(-) or Output(+) in Procesing and Conversion**	**318.59**	**-45.10**	**-0.08**		**9.60**		**8.95**	**25.81**
火力发电	Thermal Power	-0.10	-0.13						-5.69
供 热	Heating	-0.38	-1.86						-20.15
煤炭洗选	Washing of Coal								
炼 焦	Coking								
炼油及煤制油	Oil Refining and Coal to Liquid	319.08	24.01	114.82		9.60		8.95	51.65
#油品再投入量(-)	Oil Product Re-input(-)		-67.12	-114.90					
制 气	Gas Production								
#焦炭再投入量(-)	Coke Re-input(-)								
煤制品加工	Coal Product Processing								
回收能	**Energy Recycled**								
损失量	**Losses**								
#运输和输配损失	In Transportation and Transmission								
终端消费量	**End-use Energy Consumption**	**215.34**	**9.05**	**61.18**	**25.22**	**0.18**	**0.10**	**19.52**	
第一产业	Primary Industry	3.81			0.10				
第二产业	Secondary Industry	71.53	6.79	61.18	25.12	0.18	0.10	19.52	
工 业	Industry	44.73	6.79	61.18	25.12	0.18	0.10	19.52	
#用作原料、材料	Use in Materials	0.24	3.50	61.18	25.12	0.18	0.10	19.52	
建筑业	Construction	26.80							
第三产业	Tertiary Industry	139.45	2.27						
生活消费	Residential Consumption	0.56							
城 镇	Urban								
乡 村	Rural	0.56							
平衡差额	Balance	0.27			-0.11				0.13
消费量合计	**Total Energy Consumption**	**215.82**	**78.16**	**176.08**	**25.22**	**0.18**	**0.10**	**19.52**	**25.84**

4-7 续表 3 Continued 3

单位：万吨 (10000 tons)

项目	Item	液化石油气 Liquefied Petroleum Gas	炼厂干气 Refinery Gas	其它石油制品 Other Petroleum Products	天然气（亿立方米） Natural Gas (100 million cu.m)	热力（万百万千焦） Heat (10000 million kilo-joule)	电力（亿千瓦时） Electricity (100 million kwh)	其它能源（万吨标准煤） Others (10000 tons of SCE)
可供本地区消费的能源量	**Total Energy Available for Local Consumption**	**10.60**		**-29.38**	**92.07**	**1433.55**	**627.21**	**33.73**
加工转换投入(-)产出(+)量	**Input(-) or Output(+) in Procesing and Conversion**	**32.32**	**75.02**	**216.17**	**-34.78**	**15632.37**	**284.73**	**-11.34**
火力发电	Thermal Power		-0.48	-0.60	-21.22		284.73	-19.67
供热	Heating	-0.04	-4.55	-7.19	-13.56	15632.37		
煤炭洗选	Washing of Coal							
炼焦	Coking							
炼油及煤制油	Oil Refining and Coal to Liquid	34.99	80.05	283.00				
#油品再投入量(-)	Oil Product Re-input(-)	-2.63		-59.03				
制气	Gas Production							
#焦炭再投入量(-)	Coke Re-input(-)							
煤制品加工	Coal Product Processing							
回收能	**Energy Recycled**							**8.33**
损失量	**Losses**	**3.88**			**4.68**		**51.02**	
#运输和输配损失	In Transportation and Transmission				4.68		51.02	
终端消费量	**Final Consumption Industry**	**39.12**	**74.09**	**186.80**	**52.61**	**17065.92**	**860.92**	**22.39**
第一产业	Primary Industry	0.07			0.01		18.14	
第二产业	Secondary Industry	2.59	74.09	186.80	10.89	5016.16	272.01	3.64
工业	Industry	1.88	74.09	186.80	10.40	4890.54	246.12	3.47
#用作原料、材料	Use in Materials	0.23	3.21	164.39				
建筑业	Construction	0.71			0.49	125.62	25.89	0.16
第三产业	Tertiary Industry	17.37			30.18	8648.76	408.93	11.75
生活消费	Residential Consumption	19.10			11.54	3401.00	161.83	7.00
城镇	Urban	11.21			11.27	3401.00	137.09	
乡村	Rural	7.89			0.27		24.74	7.00
平衡差额	Balance	-0.08	0.93					
消费量合计	**Total Energy Consumption**	**45.67**	**79.12**	**253.62**	**92.07**	**17065.92**	**911.94**	**42.06**

4-8 能源平衡表(标准量简表)(2012年)
ENERGY BALANCE (STANDARD VOLUME) (SIMPLE EDITION) (2012)

单位：万吨标准煤 (10000 tons of SCE)

项 目	Item	合计 Total	原煤 Coal	洗精煤 Washed Coal	其他洗煤 Other Washed Coal	煤制品 Coal Products	煤矸石 Coal Slack	焦炭 Coke	焦炉煤气 Coking Gas
可供本地区消费的能源量	**Total Energy Available for Local Consumption**	**7179.42**	**1765.39**	**1.75**		**2.14**		**31.34**	**21.98**
加工转换投入(-)产出(+)量	**Input(-) or Output(+) in Proce-ssing and Transformation**	**-119.05**	**-962.18**	**-1.68**		**0.68**			
火力发电	Thermal Power		-525.43			-0.96			
供 热	Heating	-106.65	-420.12			-12.99			
煤炭洗选	Washing of Coal	-1.15	-13.57	12.42					
炼 焦	Coking								
炼油及煤制油	Oil Refining and Coal to Liquid	325.94							
#油品再投入量(-)	Oil Product Re-input(-)	-344.14							
制 气	Gas Production	-0.36	-1.51						
#焦炭再投入量(-)	Coke Re-input(-)								
煤制品加工	Coal Product Processing	-1.01	-1.53	-14.10		14.63			
回收能	**Energy Recycled**	**8.33**							
损失量	**Losses**	**218.91**							
#运输和输配损失	In Transportation and Transmission	211.17							
终端消费量	**Final Consumption Industry**	**6839.73**	**803.21**	**0.06**		**2.82**		**31.34**	**22.01**
第一产业	Primary Industry	100.75	34.17						
第二产业	Secondary Industry	2149.53	318.05	0.06		0.54		31.34	21.98
工 业	Industry	1999.08	309.01	0.06		0.35		31.34	21.98
#用作原料、材料	Use as Materials	365.08	0.07						
建筑业	Construction	150.45	9.04			0.18			
第三产业	Tertiary Industry	3190.70	218.18			2.29			0.03
生活消费	Residential Consumption	1398.75	232.81						
城 镇	Urban	1115.45	58.67						
乡 村	Rural	283.31	174.14						
平衡差额	Balance	1.74		0.01		-0.01		-0.01	-0.03
消费量合计	**Total Energy Consumption**	**7177.68**							

注：从2010年起，热力调整为按当量热值计算，电力仍然按等价热值计算。
Note: From 2010, heating power is calculated as equivalent heat value. Electrivity is still calculated in equivalent caloricity.

4-8 续表 1 Continued 1

单位：万吨标准煤 (10000 tons of SCE)

项　目	Item	高炉煤气(亿立方米) Furnace Gas (100 million cu.m)	转炉煤气(亿立方米) Converter Gas (100 million cu.m)	其它煤气 Other Gas	其它焦化产品 Other Carbonized Products	原油 Crude Oil	汽油 Gaso-line	煤油 Kero-sene
可供本地区消费的能源量	**Total Energy Available for Local Consumption**	**1.55**				**1536.85**	**226.65**	**456.78**
加工转换投入(-)产出(+)量	**Input(-) or Output(+) in Proce-ssing and Transformation**			**1.15**		**-1535.76**	**385.30**	**195.57**
火力发电	Thermal Power							
供　热	Heating							
煤炭洗选	Washing of Coal							
炼　焦	Coking							
炼油及煤制油	Oil Refining and Coal to Liquid					-1535.76	385.30	195.57
#油品再投入量(-)	Oil Product Re-input(-)							
制　气	Gas Production			1.15				
#焦炭再投入量(-)	Coke Re-input(-)							
煤制品加工	Coal Product Processing							
回收能	**Energy Recycled**							
损失量	**Losses**					**1.08**		
#运输和输配损失	In Transportation and Transmission							
终端消费量	**Final Consumption Industry**	**1.55**		**1.15**			**611.95**	**652.32**
第一产业	Primary Industry						7.44	
第二产业	Secondary Industry	1.55		1.15			42.66	0.19
工　业	Industry	1.55		1.15			28.52	0.19
#用作原料、材料	Use as Materials						0.29	0.05
建筑业	Construction						14.15	
第三产业	Tertiary Industry						178.90	652.13
生活消费	Residential Consumption						382.96	
城　镇	Urban						371.31	
乡　村	Rural						11.65	
平衡差额	Balance							0.03
消费量合计	**Total Energy Consumption**							

4-8 续表 2　Continued 2

单位：万吨标准煤　　(10000 tons of SCE)

项　目	Item	柴油 Diesel Oil	燃料油 Fuel Oil	石脑油 Naphtha	润滑油 Grease Oil	石蜡 Oilfin	溶剂油 Solvent Oil	石油沥青 Oil Asphalt	石油焦 Petroleum Coal
可供本地区消费的能源量	**Total Energy Available for Local Consumption**	**-150.05**	**77.36**	**91.89**	**35.51**	**-12.86**	**0.15**	**14.07**	**-28.04**
加工转换投入(-)产出(+)量	**Input(-) or Output(+) in Proce -ssing and Transformation**	**464.22**	**-64.38**	**-0.12**		**13.11**		**11.91**	**28.17**
火力发电	Thermal Power	-0.14	-0.18						-6.20
供　热	Heating	-0.56	-2.61						-21.97
煤炭洗选	Washing of Coal								
炼　焦	Coking								
炼油及煤制油	Oil Refining and Coal to Liquid	464.93	34.30	172.23		13.11		11.91	56.34
#油品再投入量(-)	Oil Product Re-input(-)		-95.89	-172.35					
制　气	Gas Production								
#焦炭再投入量(-)	Coke Re-input(-)								
煤制品加工	Coal Product Processing								
回收能	**Energy Recycled**								
损失量	**Losses**								
#运输和输配损失	In Transportation and Transmission								
终端消费量	**Final Consumption Industry**	**313.78**	**12.98**	**91.76**	**35.67**	**0.25**	**0.15**	**25.98**	
第一产业	Primary Industry	5.55			0.14				
第二产业	Secondary Industry	104.23	9.73	91.76	35.53	0.25	0.15	25.98	
工　业	Industry	65.17	9.73	91.76	35.53	0.25	0.15	25.98	
#用作原料、材料	Use as Materials	0.35	5.02	91.76	35.53	0.25	0.15	25.98	
建筑业	Construction	39.05							
第三产业	Tertiary Industry	203.19	3.25						
生活消费	Residential Consumption	0.81							
城　镇	Urban								
乡　村	Rural	0.81							
平衡差额	Balance	0.40		0.01	-0.15			-0.01	0.13
消费量合计	**Total Energy Consumption**								

4-8 续表 3 Continued 3

单位：万吨标准煤 (10000 tons of SCE)

项　　目	Item	液　化 石油气 Liquefied Petroleum Gas	炼厂 干气 Refinery Gas	其它石油 制　　品 Other Petroleum Products	天然气 Natural Gas (100 million cu.m)	热力 Heat	电力 Electricity	其它 能源 Others
可供本地区消费的能源量	**Total Energy Available for Local Consumption**	**18.17**		**-33.04**	**1197.83**	**48.88**	**1841.38**	**33.73**
加工转换投入(-)产出(+)量	**Input(-) or Output(+) in Processing and Transformation**	**55.41**	**117.88**	**260.48**	**-446.46**	**533.06**	**835.90**	**-11.34**
火力发电	Thermal Power		-0.75	-0.79	-281.78		835.90	-19.67
供　热	Heating	-0.06	-7.15	-9.57	-164.68	533.06		
煤炭洗选	Washing of Coal							
炼　焦	Coking							
炼油及煤制油	Oil Refining and Coal to Liquid	59.99	125.79	342.23				
#油品再投入量(-)	Oil Product Re-input(-)	-4.51		-71.38				
制　气	Gas Production							
#焦炭再投入量(-)	Coke Re-input(-)							
煤制品加工	Coal Product Processing							
回收能	**Energy Recycled**							**8.33**
损失量	**Losses**	**6.65**			**61.38**		**149.80**	
#运输和输配损失	In Transportation and Transmission				61.38		149.80	
终端消费量	**Final Consumption Industry**	**67.07**	**116.43**	**227.45**	**689.96**	**581.95**	**2527.49**	**22.39**
第一产业	Primary Industry	0.12			0.08		53.25	
第二产业	Secondary Industry	4.44	116.43	227.45	142.80	171.05	798.57	3.64
工　业	Industry	3.23	116.43	227.45	136.43	166.77	722.57	3.47
#用作原料、材料	Use as Materials	0.39	5.05	200.17				
建筑业	Construction	1.21			6.37	4.28	76.00	0.16
第三产业	Tertiary Industry	29.78			395.73	294.92	1200.55	11.75
生活消费	Residential Consumption	32.74			151.34	115.97	475.12	7.00
城　镇	Urban	19.22			147.80	115.97	402.48	
乡　村	Rural	13.52			3.55		72.64	7.00
平衡差额	Balance	-0.14	1.46		0.04		-0.01	
消费量合计	**Total Energy Consumption**							

4-9 分行业能源消费总量和主要能源品种消费量(2012年)

单位：万吨

项 目	Item	能源消费总量(万吨标准煤) Total Energy Consumption (10000 tons of SCE)	煤 炭 Coal	焦 炭 Coke
合 计	**Total**	**7177.68**	**2269.89**	**32.27**
农、林、牧、渔业	Agriculture, Forestry, Animal Production and Hunting, Fishing	100.75	44.60	
采矿业	Mining and Quarrying	195.12	47.34	27.73
煤炭开采和洗选业	Mining and Washing of Coal	6.44	1.34	
石油和天然气开采业	Extraction of Petroleum and Natural Gas	0.77		
黑色金属矿采选业	Mining and Processing of Ferrous Metal Ores	150.94	44.53	27.73
有色金属矿采选业	Mining and Processing of Non-Ferrous Metal Ores			
非金属矿采选业	Mining and Processing of Nonmetal Ores	1.81	0.14	
开采辅助活动	Mining Support Service Activities	35.16	1.33	
其他采矿业	Mining of Other Ores			
制造业	Manufacturing	1640.46	391.77	4.54
农副食品加工业	Processing of Food from Agricultural Products	30.85	17.66	
食品制造业	Manufacture of Foods	32.70	7.89	
酒、饮料和精制茶制造业	Manufacture of Wine, Beverage and Refined Tea	46.09	30.76	
烟草制品业	Manufacture of Cigarettes and Tobacco	2.40	0.01	
纺织业	Manufacture of Textile	8.86	4.30	
纺织服装、服饰业	Manufacture of Textile Wearing Apparel and Ornament	22.65	13.83	
皮革、毛皮、羽毛及其制品和制鞋业	Manufacture of Leather, Fur, Feather and Its Products, and Footwear	1.39	0.38	
木材加工和木、竹、藤、棕、草制品业	Processing of Timbers, Manufacture of Wood, Bamboo, Rattan, Palm, and Straw Products	5.49	0.66	
家具制造业	Manufacture of Furniture	8.52	2.12	
造纸和纸制品业	Manufacture of Paper and Paper Products	15.31	8.66	
印刷和记录媒介复制业	Printing, Reproduction of Recording Media	30.29	3.80	
文教、工美、体育和娱乐用品制造业	Manufacture of Articles for Culture, Education, Artwork, Sport and Entertainment Activities	5.89	1.76	
石油加工、炼焦和核燃料加工业	Processing of Petroleum, Coking, Processing of Nucleus Fuel	564.68	3.29	
化学原料和化学制品制造业	Manufacture of Chemical Raw Materials and Chemical Products	158.36	71.24	0.01
医药制造业	Manufacture of Medicines	33.05	11.95	
化学纤维制造业	Manufacture of Chemical Fibers	1.72	0.03	
橡胶和塑料制品业	Manufacture of Rubber and Plastics Products	34.65	8.21	
非金属矿物制品业	Manufacture of Non-Metallic Mineral Products	235.20	152.13	2.15

注：1. 各行业能源总消费量为各行业终端消费量与各行业分摊的损失量和加工转换损失量之和，不等于分品种能源消费量(标准煤)的合计。

2. 行业划分执行《国民经济行业分类》(GB/T 4754—2011)标准。

CONSUMPTION OF TOTAL ENERGY AND MAIN ENERGY VARIETIES BY SECTOR (2012)

(10000 tons)

汽　油 Gasoline	煤　油 Kerosene	柴　油 Diesel Oil	燃料油 Fuel Oil	液　化 石油气 Liquefied Petroleum Gas	天然气 (亿立方米) Natural Gas (100 million cu.m)	热　力 (万百万千焦) Heat (10 billion kilo-joule)	电　力 (亿千瓦时) Electricity (100 million kwh)
415.90	**443.33**	**215.82**	**78.16**	**45.67**	**92.07**	**17065.92**	**911.94**
5.05		3.81		0.07	0.01		18.14
0.91		25.88	0.01	0.04	0.32	165.57	19.40
0.07		0.10				1.16	1.72
0.01					0.06		0.26
0.13		4.41	0.01		0.24	162.85	16.34
0.03		0.56				1.51	0.24
0.67		20.81		0.04	0.02	0.05	0.84
16.71	0.13	18.25	73.90	4.45	9.88	4439.60	175.62
0.54		0.46	0.03	0.05	0.12	47.06	3.97
0.62		0.53		0.25	0.45	101.72	4.86
0.36		0.59		0.01	0.09	102.38	5.46
0.01					0.12		0.26
0.12		0.03		0.02	0.03	18.97	1.35
0.80		0.23		0.03	0.03	35.25	2.09
0.08		0.01				1.96	0.19
0.14		0.08			0.02	1.05	1.11
0.50		0.10	0.01	0.02	0.01	14.32	1.38
0.36		0.19	0.01	0.02	0.06	8.71	1.95
0.90	0.01	0.23		0.03	0.30	75.78	5.92
0.19		0.04		0.02	0.04	26.88	0.71
0.05		0.08	67.12	2.66	2.62	1594.33	17.38
0.98		0.86	3.51	0.25	0.29	1113.76	17.02
0.53		0.30		0.02	0.35	113.07	4.87
0.02					0.02	9.52	0.37
0.62		0.25		0.11	0.09	84.78	7.25
0.98		10.00	3.18	0.11	0.98	33.17	21.45

Note: a) Total energy consumption in each sector is the end consumption of each sector plus losses shared by each sector and losses from processing in each sector, but not equal to sum of consumption (SCE equivalent) of all sorts of energy.

b) Sectors in this table are classified in accordance with Standard for Classification of National Economic Sectors 2011 (GB/T 4754-2011).

4-9 续表

单位：万吨

项目	Item	能源消费总量（万吨标准煤）Total Energy Consumption (10000 tons of SCE)	煤炭 Coal
黑色金属冶炼及压延加工业	Manufacture and Pressing of Ferrous Metals	32.23	1.31
有色金属冶炼及压延加工业	Manufacture and Pressing of Non-Ferrous Metals	8.47	1.32
金属制品业	Manufacture of Fabricated Metal Products	37.66	6.78
通用设备制造业	Manufacture of General-purpose Machinery	38.37	6.65
专用设备制造业	Manufacture of Special-purpose Machinery	26.03	5.14
汽车制造业	Manufacture of Motor Vehicles	98.84	9.15
铁路、船舶、航空航天和其他运输设备制造业	Manufacture of Railway Locomotives, Building of Ships and Boats, Manufacture of Air and Spacecrafts and Other Transportation Equipment	17.46	11.48
电气机械和器材制造业	Manufacture of Electrical Machinery and Equipment	28.95	6.65
计算机、通讯和其他电子设备制造业	Manufacture of Computer, Communication Equipment and Other Electronic Equipment	82.79	0.68
仪器仪表制造业	Manufacture of Measuring Instruments and Meters	8.97	0.65
其他制造业	Other Manufacturing	6.52	0.08
废弃资源综合利用业	Waste recycling and recovery	1.59	0.38
金属制品、机械和设备修理业	Repair of Fabricated Metal Products, Machinery and Equipment	14.48	2.82
电力、燃气及水的生产和供应业	Production and Distribution of Electricity, Gas and Water	440.08	1213.97
电力、热力生产和供应业	Production and Distribution of Electricity and Heating Power	400.38	1213.53
燃气生产和供应业	Production and Distribution of Gas	10.92	
水的生产和供应业	Production and Distribution of Water	28.78	0.44
建筑业	Construction	150.45	11.85
批发和零售业	Wholesale Trade and Retail Trade	221.68	11.53
交通运输、仓储和邮政业	Transport, Storage and Post	1235.05	15.86
住宿和餐饮业	Accommodation and Restaurants	262.34	27.77
信息传输、软件和信息技术服务业	Information transmission,software and information technology services	129.64	1.14
金融业	Finance	54.26	0.96
房地产业	Real Estate Trade	411.54	90.02
租赁和商务服务业	Renting and Leasing Activities and Business Services	196.26	44.50
科学研究和技术服务业	Scientific Research and Development, Technical Services	163.92	14.48
水利、环境和公共设施管理业	Water, Environment and Municipal Engineering Conservancy	46.51	4.16
居民服务、修理和其他服务业	Resident services, repair and other services	47.13	16.84
教育	Education	222.87	33.30
卫生和社会工作	Healthcare and Social Works	74.05	10.26
文化、体育和娱乐业	Culture, Sports and Entertainment	71.47	2.60
公共管理、社会保障和社会组织	Public Administration, Social Security and Social Organizations	115.35	14.71
生活消费	Residential Consumption	1398.75	272.23
城镇	Urban	1115.44	62.23
乡村	Rural	283.31	210.00

4-9 Continued

(10000 tons)

焦炭 Coke	汽油 Gasoline	煤油 Kerosene	柴油 Diesel Oil	燃料油 Fuel Oil	液化石油气 Liquefied Petroleum Gas	天然气（亿立方米）Natural Gas (100 million cu.m)	热力（万百万千焦）Heat (10 billion kilo-joule)	电力（亿千瓦时）Electricity (100 million kwh)
0.79	0.09		0.39		0.02	0.91	13.13	5.86
0.06	0.11		0.05		0.01	0.01	19.41	2.05
0.06	1.13		0.48		0.51	0.44	46.43	6.56
0.91	1.16	0.02	0.56		0.10	0.19	143.71	6.16
0.03	1.03		0.31	0.01	0.01	0.12	106.44	4.54
0.46	1.78	0.03	1.71	0.03	0.12	1.88	185.36	18.15
0.02	0.22		0.23		0.01	0.05	112.74	2.24
0.02	1.18		0.09		0.03	0.15	95.12	4.86
	0.70		0.09		0.02	0.28	217.16	23.37
	0.62		0.04			0.06	55.16	1.27
	0.13		0.10		0.01	0.02	37.11	0.90
	0.02		0.05				1.42	0.35
0.03	0.74	0.07	0.17		0.01	0.15	23.70	1.72
	1.77		1.07	1.99	3.94	34.98	285.37	102.13
	1.35		0.91	1.99	0.05	34.49	253.71	92.42
	0.23		0.06		3.88	0.43	6.68	0.80
	0.19		0.10		0.01	0.06	24.98	8.91
	9.61		26.80		0.71	0.49	125.62	25.89
	26.00		6.09	0.03	0.63	0.62	690.58	45.27
	44.03	442.79	117.34	1.28	0.34	8.22	663.38	69.11
	1.77		0.94	0.03	14.07	4.67	653.59	43.62
	3.96		0.44		0.04	0.14	317.93	37.24
	2.54		0.24		0.04	0.10	254.27	13.42
	4.46		1.45	0.89	0.37	8.21	1332.85	60.29
	10.61		2.92	0.01	0.20	2.03	722.34	30.63
	9.40	0.41	1.49		0.13	3.07	782.88	23.40
	2.05		4.42		0.15	0.20	41.03	9.88
	1.50		0.84	0.01	0.15	0.91	110.15	5.04
	3.45		1.76		0.47	3.97	1618.13	27.02
	1.07		0.23		0.18	1.14	379.87	11.59
	2.03		0.40		0.23	0.85	393.30	13.76
	8.71		0.89	0.01	0.36	0.72	688.46	18.66
	260.27		0.56		19.10	11.54	3401.00	161.83
	252.35				11.21	11.27	3401.00	137.09
	7.92		0.56		7.89	0.27		24.74

4-10 能源消费弹性系数(2000-2013年)
ELASTICITY COEFFICIENT OF ENERGY CONSUMPTION (2000-2013)

项 目 Item	能源消费比上年增长 (%) Growth Rate of Energy Consumption over the Preceding Year	电力消费比上年增长(%) Growth Rate of Electricity Consumption over the Preceding Year	地区生产总值比上年增长(%) Growth Rate of Gross Domestic Product(GDP) over the Preceding Year	能源消费弹性系数 Elasticity Coefficient of Energy Consumption	电力消费弹性系数 Elasticity Coefficient of Electricity Consumption
2000	6.08	9.53	11.8	0.51	0.81
2001	2.06	5.68	11.7	0.18	0.49
2002	4.89	9.54	11.5	0.43	0.83
2003	4.78	5.71	11.1	0.43	0.51
2004	10.57	10.60	14.1	0.75	0.75
2005	7.44	11.16	12.1	0.61	0.92
2006	6.92	9.16	13.0	0.53	0.71
2007	6.45	9.06	14.5	0.45	0.63
2008	0.67	4.90	9.1	0.07	0.54
2009	3.84	7.15	10.2	0.38	0.70
2010	5.84	9.49	10.3	0.57	0.92
2011	0.59	2.74	8.1	0.07	0.34
2012	2.61	6.82	7.7	0.34	0.88
2013	2.46	3.95	7.7	0.32	0.51

注：1.地区生产总值增长速度按可比价计算。
2.2013年数据为初步核算数。

Note: a)The groth rates of GDP are calculated at comparable prices.
b)Figures for 2013 were preliminary statistics.

4-11 平均每万元地区生产总值能源消费量(2001-2012年)
ENERGY CONSUMPTION PER 10000 YUAN OF GROSS DOMESTIC PRODUCT (2001-2012)

项 目 Item	能源总消费量 (吨标准煤) Total (ton of SCE)	煤 炭 (吨) Coal (ton)	电 力 (千瓦时) Electricity (kwh)	石 油 (吨) Petroleum (ton)
2001	1.20	0.77	1127.91	0.23
2002	1.13	0.66	1108.09	0.25
2003	1.06	0.63	1053.83	0.22
2004	1.03	0.59	1021.65	0.20
2005	0.99	0.55	1012.86	0.20
	(0.79)	(0.44)	(813.60)	(0.16)
2006	0.75	0.39	786.01	0.15
2007	0.70	0.33	748.74	0.15
2008	0.64	0.28	719.84	0.14
2009	0.61	0.25	700.03	0.13
2010	0.58	0.22	694.69	0.12
	(0.49)	(0.19)	(588.72)	(0.10)
2011	0.46	0.15	559.28	0.10
2012	0.44	0.14	554.57	0.09

注：本表中每万元地区生产总值能源消费量按可比价格计算，可比价格每五年调整一次基期，更换基期年份计算两个可比价数据，括号内数据是按新基期价格计算。

Note: Energy consumption per 10000 yuan of GDP were calculated at comparable prices. The base period of comparable prices is changed every five years. Two figures at comparable prices were calculated for the year in which the base period is changed. Figures in brackets were calculated at the price of new base period.

4-12 人均生活用能源(2000-2012年)
PER CAPITA ENERGY CONSUMPTION FOR NON-PRODUCTIVE PURPOSE (2000-2012)

年份 Year	合计 (千克标准煤) Total (kg of SCE)	煤炭 (千克) Coal (kg)	电力 (千瓦时) Electricity (kwh)	液化石油气 (千克) Liquefied Petroleum Gas(kg)	天然气 (立方米) Natural Gas (cu.m)	汽油 (升) Gasoline (liter)
2000	407.1	223.6	363.6	13.7	16.4	31.4
2001	408.2	209.6	392.5	13.1	18.7	38.4
2002	415.8	156.0	445.8	16.3	24.1	50.7
2003	472.7	187.8	488.2	20.2	28.4	61.8
2004	509.8	167.6	546.2	22.2	32.9	72.2
2005	537.4	154.1	586.8	20.8	37.4	93.5
2006	579.4	169.9	610.8	15.2	53.5	113.5
2007	613.5	169.1	651.1	16.8	54.8	136.5
2008	620.4	148.4	674.8	12.8	53.1	153.8
2009	642.7	150.7	709.4	12.5	54.3	162.1
2010	643.5	145.9	729.1	11.3	53.1	164.9
2011	656.1	140.5	727.2	10.7	52.7	167.6
2012	684.3	133.2	791.8	9.3	56.5	174.4

注：本表人均生活用能源按常住人口年平均数计算。2006-2010年数据根据全国第六次人口普查进行了修正。

Note: Per-capita energy consumption for non-productive prupose is calculated by average permanent population. Figures for 2006-2010 have been revised in accordance with the 6th national population census.

4-13 主要能源日均消费量(2000-2012年)
DAILY CONSUMPTION OF MAIN ENERGY VARIETIES(2000-2012)

年份 Year	合计 (万吨标准煤) Total (10000 tons of SCE)	煤炭 (吨) Coal (ton)	焦炭 (吨) Coke (ton)	原油 (吨) Crude Oil (ton)	汽油 (吨) Gasoline (ton)	煤油 (吨) Kerosene (ton)	柴油 (吨) Diesel Oil (ton)	燃料油 (吨) Fuel Oil (ton)	电力 (万千瓦时) Electricity (10000 kwh)	天然气 (万立方米) Natural Gas (10000 cu.m)
2000	11.3	76598.4	12270.5	20620.2	3046.4	3213.1	2303.3	2448.1	10297.8	352.5
2001	11.6	74331.5	11769.9	19191.8	3997.3	3542.5	2972.6	2147.9	10912.3	457.5
2002	12.2	70726.0	10353.4	20501.4	4380.8	3978.1	3145.2	1950.7	11953.4	569.9
2003	12.7	75274.0	12008.2	19909.6	4772.6	3778.1	3194.5	1811.0	12635.6	580.8
2004	14.0	80404.4	12451.6	22114.8	5420.8	4994.5	3603.8	1830.6	13937.2	737.7
2005	15.1	84081.4	10887.7	21906.8	6444.7	5187.9	3859.2	1804.9	15535.3	877.8
2006	16.2	83717.0	9551.2	21811.5	7620.8	6407.1	4862.7	1316.4	16958.6	1113.7
2007	17.2	81771.8	9813.4	26052.3	8896.4	7591.8	5260.8	1174.0	18495.6	1277.8
2008	17.3	75073.8	6363.4	30513.7	9314.2	8699.5	6207.7	699.5	19349.7	1658.5
2009	18.0	73005.5	5807.4	31861.1	9961.9	9367.9	6580.3	1161.6	20790.4	1901.4
2010	19.1	72181.1	6039.7	30583.3	10178.9	10757.0	6504.4	1826.8	22764.4	2048.8
2011	19.2	64809.3	911.8	30276.2	10679.2	11503.6	6605.8	2045.2	23388.5	2015.3
2012	19.6	62018.9	881.7	29392.6	11363.4	12112.8	5896.7	2135.5	24916.4	2515.6

4-14 全社会用电量(1978-2013年)
TOTAL ELECTRICITY CONSUMPTION IN BEIJING (1978-2013)

单位：万千瓦时 (10000 kwh)

年 份 Year	全社会用电量 Electricity Consumption	第一产业 Primary Industry	第二产业 Secondary Industry	工 业 Industry	建筑业 Construction	第三产业 Tertiary Industry	城乡居民生活用电 Residential Electricity Consumption	城 市 Urban	乡 村 Rural
1978	735000	48993	570621	570621		94555	20831	11022	9809
1979	802317	52134	620262	620262		107437	22484	11495	10989
1980	854638	65283	648496	648496		116947	23912	12441	11471
1981	867153	80027	643976	643976		121883	21267	9452	11815
1982	925700	104842	657060	657060		139403	24395	10820	13575
1983	956293	92601	687937	687937		151290	24465	12320	12145
1984	1029420	105234	716653	716653		177455	30078	16025	14053
1985	1106255	111110	746324	746324		210622	38199	22479	15720
1986	1181155	105688	851519	835725	15794	175090	48858	31008	17850
1987	1285023	77909	923797	899760	24037	224747	58570	35063	23507
1988	1378574	83809	970885	943383	27502	248446	75434	48624	26810
1989	1421817	100151	979216	949629	29587	258067	84383	56120	28263
1990	1504785	93049	1014037	986356	27681	302775	94924	65262	29662
1991	1613977	93256	1061207	1032064	29143	348769	110745	77575	33170
1992	1759611	101985	1155514	1123835	31679	375874	126238	88621	37617
1993	1924978	107010	1243115	1206001	37114	429835	145018	103579	41439
1994	2054504	101134	1307898	1262961	44937	479679	165791	119025	46766
1995	2225922	102099	1403864	1341398	62466	538936	181022	130897	50125
1996	2443709	111904	1496968	1422590	74378	617286	217551	158474	59077
1997	2636078	120444	1529201	1449129	80072	721774	264659	196641	68018
1998	2762080	108267	1548485	1457149	91336	811283	294045	220543	73502
1999	2972629	121242	1581977	1478523	103454	912834	356576	276642	79934
2000	3844266	130865	2172604	2066892	105712	1064322	476475	385396	91079
2001	3999415	131811	2105819	1978673	127146	1222471	539314	439058	100256
2002	4399637	137370	2293735	2145292	148443	1342490	626042	517386	108656
2003	4676056	107372	2418419	2250525	167894	1447344	702921	574623	128298
2004	5131804	104234	2593504	2391414	202090	1628731	805335	647474	157861
2005	5705364	114308	2795753	2605832	189921	1906093	889210	706405	182805
2006	6115719	122550	2943550	2744127	199423	2090888	958731	768884	189847
2007	6670089	133557	3091374	2881807	209567	2378399	1066759	862604	204155
2008	6897189	136065	2943893	2763399	180494	2654140	1163091	949878	213213
2009	7391465	157310	3027974	2853018	174956	2918229	1287952	982720	305232
2010	8099029	168992	3278682	3081364	197319	3258009	1393346	951811	441535
2011	8217055	170368	3109174	2894464	214708	3490143	1447370	945588	501782
2012	8742835	181391	3209078	2980645	228430	3734022	1618344	1370932	247412
2013	9131113	185749	3345854	3110626	235229	4029145	1570365	1347401	222964

注：1. 1985年以前农、林、牧、渔和水利业用电量中，只包含农业排灌、农副业和社队企业的用电量。
2. 1980年以前的城市居民用电量以全市市政用电量的1/10计算。
3. 2000年以前工业用电量不包含输配损失和发电企业自产自用电量。

资料来源：北京市电力公司。

Note: a) Before 1985, electricity consumption by agriculture, forestry, animal production and hunting, fishing and water conservancy only included the electricity consumption by farming irrigation, agricultural and sideline products, and village enterprises.
b) Before 1980, electricity consumption by urban residents was one-tenth of the total electricity consumption by municipal administration in Beijing.
c) Before 2000, electricity consumption by industry excluded transmission and distribution losses and electricity generated and consumed by power generating enterprises.

Source: Beijing Electric Power Corporation.

4-15 主要土地利用状况(2009-2012年)
LAND UTILIZATION (2009-2012)

单位：公顷 (hectare)

年 份 Year	耕地面积 Arable Land	园地面积 Garden Plot	林地面积 Forest Land	草地面积 Grass Land	城镇村及工矿用地面积 Land for Urban, Rural,Industrial and Mining Use	交通运输用地面积 Land for Transportation	水域及水利设施用地面积 Water Areas and Land for Water Conservancy Facilities
2009	227170.43	141617.22	743696.19	84843.14	284791.79	44446.42	80235.85
2010	223779.38	139298.50	742018.50	85827.05	290782.01	45335.78	79774.99
2011	221956.16	138072.99	740730.87	85651.69	295116.72	45452.68	79380.05
2012	220856.16	137117.72	739633.48	85491.29	297758.79	46327.98	79088.32

注：表中2009年数据为第二次全国土地调查数据，2010-2012年为各年土地变更调查数据。

资料来源：北京市国土资源局。

Note: Statistics for 2009 were from the 2nd National Land Survey, and statistics for 2010-2012 were survey data of land changed.

Source: Beijing Municipal Bureau of Land Resources.

4-16 水资源情况(2001-2013年)

单位：亿立方米

项目	Item	2001	2002	2003	2004
全年水资源总量	**Total Volume of Water Resource in the Year**	**19.2**	**16.1**	**18.4**	**21.4**
地表水资源量	Volume of Surface Water Resource	7.8	5.3	6.1	8.2
地下水资源量	Volume of Underground Water Resource	15.7	14.7	14.8	16.5
人均水资源(立方米)	**Per-capita Water Resource(cu.m)**	**139.7**	**114.7**	**127.8**	**145.1**
全年供水(用水)总量	**Total Volume of Water Supplied (Consumed) in the Year**	**38.9**	**34.6**	**35.8**	**34.6**
按来源分	By Source				
地表水	Surface Water	11.7	10.4	8.3	5.7
地下水	Underground Water	27.2	24.2	25.4	26.8
再生水	Recycled Water			2.1	2.0
南水北调	Water Transit from South to North				
应急供水	Emergent Water Supply				
按用途分	By Purpose				
农业用水	Water Used by Agriculture	17.4	15.5	13.8	13.5
工业用水	Water Used by Industry	9.2	7.5	8.4	7.7
生活用水	Domestic Water	12.0	10.8	13.0	12.8
环境用水	Water for the Environment	0.3	0.8	0.6	0.6
万元地区生产总值水耗(立方米)	**Water Consumption per 10000 yuan GDP (cu.m)**	**104.91**	**80.19**	**71.50**	**57.35**
万元地区生产总值水耗下降率(%)	**Decrease Rate of Water Consumption per 10000 yuan GDP (%)**	**13.79**	**20.22**	**6.91**	**15.29**

注：1. 万元地区生产总值水耗按现价计算，下降率按可比价计算，如按可比价计算，2013年万元地区生产总值水耗为20.55立方米。

2. 本表人均水资源按常住人口年平均数计算。2006-2010年数据根据全国第六次人口普查进行了修正。

3. 2013年万元GDP水耗按初步核算的地区生产总值计算。

资料来源：除人均数据和万元地区生产总值水耗以外其它数据来自北京市水务局。

STATISTICS FOR WATER RESOURCES (2001-2013)

(100 million cu.m)

2005	2006	2007	2008	2009	2010	2011	2012	2013
23.2	**22.1**	**23.8**	**34.2**	**21.8**	**23.1**	**26.8**	**39.5**	**24.8**
7.6	6.7	7.6	12.8	6.8	7.2	9.2	18.0	9.4
15.6	15.4	16.2	21.4	15.1	15.9	17.6	21.6	15.4
153.1	**140.6**	**145.3**	**198.5**	**120.3**	**120.8**	**134.7**	**193.3**	**118.6**
34.5	**34.3**	**34.8**	**35.1**	**35.5**	**35.2**	**36.0**	**35.9**	**36.4**
6.4	5.7	5.0	4.7	3.8	3.9	4.8	4.4	3.9
23.1	22.2	21.6	20.5	19.7	19.1	18.8	18.3	17.9
2.6	3.6	5.0	6.0	6.5	6.8	7.0	7.5	8.0
			0.7	2.6	2.6	2.6	2.8	3.5
2.5	2.8	3.2	3.2	2.9	2.9	2.7	2.9	3.0
13.2	12.8	12.4	12.0	12.0	11.4	10.9	9.3	9.1
6.8	6.2	5.8	5.2	5.2	5.1	5.0	4.9	5.1
13.4	13.7	13.9	14.7	14.7	14.8	15.6	16.0	16.2
1.1	1.6	2.7	3.2	3.6	4.0	4.5	5.7	5.9
49.50	**42.25**	**35.34**	**31.58**	**29.92**	**24.94**	**22.13**	**20.07**	**18.66**
11.07	**12.01**	**11.38**	**7.56**	**8.12**	**10.14**	**5.49**	**7.38**	**5.85**

Note: a) Water consumption per 10000 yuan GDP is at current prices,and decrease rate is at comparable prices.Caculated at comparable prices, the water consumption per 10000 yuan GDP in 2013 is 20.55 cubic metres.

b) Per-capita water resource are calculated by average permanent population.Per-capita figures 2006-2010 have been corrected in accordance with the Sixth Population Census.

c) Water consumption per 10000 yuan GDP for 2013 is calculated by GDP of preliminary statistics.

Source: Except for per-capita figures and water consumption per 10000 yuan GDP,other figures are from Beijing Water Authority.

4-17 气象情况(1978-2013年)
METEOROLOGY (1978-2013)

年 份 Year	降水量(毫米) Precipitation (mm)	平均气温(℃) Average Temperature (℃)	最高 Highest	最低 Lowest	日照时数(时) Hours of Sunshine (hours)	平均风速(米/秒) Average Wind Speed (meter/second)	平均气压(百帕) Average Air Pressure (100 pa)	大风日数(日) Days of Strong Wind (day)	雨日数(日) Days of Rain (day)
1978	664.8	11.6	37.5	-14.4	2865.4	2.6	1012.8	35	64
1979	718.4	11.1	35.9	-15.4	2667.4	2.5	1012.2	33	63
1980	380.7	11.0	35.1	-15.4	2920.8	2.5	1012.7	29	83
1981	393.2	12.3	38.1	-14.0	2803.9	2.5	1010.8	15	92
1982	544.4	12.8	37.3	-14.3	2825.1	2.6	1010.5	26	92
1983	489.9	13.0	37.2	-15.0	2844.3	2.4	1010.3	29	100
1984	488.8	11.9	36.1	-14.9	2767.6	2.4	1010.6	18	90
1985	721.0	11.5	35.1	-15.2	2511.9	2.2	1010.4	12	104
1986	665.3	12.1	38.5	-15.4	2804.1	2.3	1010.7	21	96
1987	683.9	12.3	36.1	-15.5	2631.9	2.4	1010.3	23	102
1988	673.3	12.7	38.1	-13.2	2558.1	2.4	1010.8	17	96
1989	442.2	13.2	35.8	-11.0	2626.2	1.9	1011.1	3	78
1990	697.3	12.7	37.5	-14.8	2325.0	1.9	1010.6	12	113
1991	747.9	12.5	35.7	-12.6	2536.6	2.1	1010.8	8	98
1992	541.5	12.8	37.5	-8.7	2712.5	2.2	1011.0	6	100
1993	506.7	13.0	35.8	-13.0	2669.8	2.6	1010.8	12	91
1994	813.2	13.7	37.2	-11.5	2470.5	2.5	1010.1	9	92
1995	572.5	13.3	35.0	-9.2	2519.1	2.6	1010.3	16	89
1996	700.9	12.7	36.0	-10.0	2418.7	2.6	1011.0	16	103
1997	430.9	13.1	38.2	-14.0	2596.5	2.5	1012.9	11	76
1998	731.7	13.1	37.2	-14.2	2420.7	2.3	1012.5	10	93
1999	266.9	13.1	41.9	-12.2	2594.0	2.4	1012.5	7	86
2000	371.1	12.8	39.4	-15.0	2667.2	2.5	1012.7	10	83
2001	338.9	12.9	39.6	-17.0	2611.7	2.4	1012.9	10	78
2002	370.4	13.2	41.1	-12.8	2588.4	2.3	1012.7	15	84
2003	444.9	12.9	37.6	-15.0	2260.2	2.5	1013.3	6	93
2004	483.5	13.5	38.9	-12.9	2515.4	2.4	1012.6	12	94
2005	410.7	13.2	38.9	-11.5	2576.1	2.4	1012.8	5	79
2006	318.0	13.4	37.3	-14.7	2192.7	2.2	1012.5	5	86
2007	483.9	14.0	37.3	-11.7	2351.1	2.2	1012.6	5	78
2008	626.3	13.4	36.3	-13.5	2391.4	2.2	1012.6	8	100
2009	480.6	13.3	39.6	-12.2	2511.8	2.2	1011.9	15	86
2010	522.5	12.6	40.6	-16.7	2382.9	2.3	1012.2	14	88
2011	720.6	13.4	35.9	-11.6	2485.7	2.2	1013.2	3	82
2012	733.2	12.9	38.0	-13.7	2450.2	2.2	1012.2	3	85
2013	578.9	12.8	38.2	-14.1	2371.1	2.1	1012.2	3	71

资料来源：北京市气象局。
Source: Beijing Municipal Bureau of Meteorology.

4-18 气象(2013年)
METEOROLOGY (2013)

月 份 Month	降水量 (毫米) Precipitation (mm)	平均气温(℃) Average Temperature (℃)	日照时数(时) Hours of Sunshine (hours)	平均风速(米/秒) Average Wind Speed (meter/second)	平均气压(百帕) Average Air Pressure (100 pa)	大风日数(日) Days of Strong Wind (day)	雨日数(日) Days of Rain (day)
全 年 Total	**578.9**	**12.8**	**2371.1**	**2.1**	**1012.2**	**3**	**71**
1	3.0	-4.7	138.9	1.8	1024.1		4
2	3.4	-1.4	159.6	2.3	1022.6		3
3	10.7	6.2	213.1	2.5	1014.6		3
4	5.5	12.6	264.2	3.0	1010.2		3
5	23.6	21.9	244.8	2.4	1004.8		4
6	91.0	23.8	132.4	2.1	1001.6		12
7	235.4	27.4	216.4	1.9	997.5		12
8	118.6	27.3	223.8	1.9	1000.8		11
9	71.1	20.7	164.8	1.7	1011.0		12
10	16.4	13.6	203.9	1.8	1018.0	1	6
11	0.2	6.3	201.2	2.2	1018.8	1	1
12		0.1	208.0	2.0	1022.0	1	

注：1. 无霜期270天。

2. 年极端最高气温38.2℃，出现日期7月24日。

3. 年极端最低气温-14.1℃，出现日期1月5日。

资料来源：北京市气象局。

Note: a) Annual frost-free period is 270 days.

b) Annual utmost highest air temperature is 38.2℃, seen on the 24th of July.

c) Annual utmost lowest air temperature is -14.1℃, seen on the 5th of January.

Source: Beijing Municipal Bureau of Meteorology.

4-19 污水处理及环境卫生(1978-2013年)
SEWAGE DISPOSAL AND ENVIRONMENTAL SANITATION (1978-2013)

年份 Year	污水管道长度(公里) Length of Sewage Pipes (km)	污水处理能力(万立方米/日) Sewage Treatment Capacity (10000 cu.m/day)	污水处理率(%) Sewage Treatment Rate (%)	再生水利用量(万立方米) Volume of Recycled Water Used (10000 cu.m)	生活垃圾无害化处理能力(吨/日) Harmless Disposal Capacity of Domestic Waste (ton/day)	生活垃圾产生量(万吨) Output of Domestic Garbage (10000 tons)	生活垃圾清运量(万吨) Domestic Waste Removed and Transported (10000 tons)	生活垃圾无害化处理率(%) Rate of Harmless Disposal of Domestic Waste (%)	粪便清运量(万吨) Excrement Removed and Transported (10000 tons)
1978	290	23	7.6				107.20		88.9
1979	309	23	10.2				128.00		89.4
1980	334	23	9.4				147.00		95.1
1981	347	25	10.8				174.00		97.6
1982	365	25	10.9				204.70		99.3
1983	411	25	10.2				221.40		99.5
1984	568	25	10.0				235.40		98.8
1985	706	25	10.0				248.10		142.2
1986	747	26	8.9				274.40		167.5
1987	805	26	7.7				298.30		181.0
1988	770	26	7.4				319.90		190.0
1989	860	26	6.6				337.00		196.0
1990	904	30	7.3				384.10		210.0
1991	968	30	6.6				397.10		210.3
1992	1036	5	1.2				430.90		216.0
1993	1064	5	3.1				446.30		220.6
1994	1122	25	9.6				467.20		238.1
1995	1065	59	19.4				483.90		258.4
1996	1597	59	21.2				483.00		268.0
1997	1635	59	22.0				490.00		279.0
1998	1712	59	22.5				495.10		295.6
1999	1754	59	25.0				505.00		298.0
2000	1852	129	39.4		6550		295.56	56.4	274.0
2001	2163	144	42.0		6750		309.27	82.2	301.0
2002	2658	181	45.0		8750		321.35	86.4	311.7
2003	2903	215	50.1		9400		361.36	91.3	268.0
2004	2909	255	53.9		10050	495.46	405.86	93.8	175.0
2005	2521	324	62.4	23815.7	10350	536.93	454.59	96.0	171.7
2006	3398	331	73.2	36088.0	10350	585.13	538.32	92.5	175.7
2007	4357	348	76.2	49501.0	10350	619.49	600.93	95.7	189.1
2008	4458	329	78.9	60000.0	12148	672.82	656.61	97.7	206.8
2009	4495	356	80.3	64999.0	13680	669.13	656.12	98.2	211.2
2010	4479	365	81.0	68014.0	16680	634.86	632.98	96.9	194.4
2011	4765	369	82.0	71012.0	16930	634.35	634.35	98.2	207.5
2012	5735	389	83.0	75003.0	17530	648.31	648.31	99.1	207.2
2013	6363	393	84.6	80108.0	21971	671.69	671.69	99.3	220.7

注：1. 污水处理能力等指标1992年及以后为污水无害化处理情况，1992年以前为污水简易处理情况。
2. 生活垃圾无害化处理率按清运量计算。

资料来源：北京市水务局、北京市市政市容管理委员会。

Note: a) Disposal capacity and other indicators were about harmless disposal in and after 1992, and simple disposal before 1992.
b) The harmless disposal rate of domestic waste is calculated with the volume of waste cleared and transported.

Source: Beijing Water Authority，Beijing Municipal Commission of City Administration and Environment.

4-20 排水及节水
WATER DRAINAGE AND SAVING

项目		Item		2013	2012
排　水		**Water Drainage**			
污水处理能力	(万立方米/日)	Sewage Treatment Capacity	(10000cu.m/day)	393	389
#二三级	(万立方米/日)	Grade-II and III Treatment	(10000cu.m/day)	393	389
污水年处理量	(万立方米)	Annual Treatment Volume of Sewage	(10000 cu.m)	131401	126411
#污水厂	(万立方米)	Treated by Sewage Treatment Plants	(10000 cu.m)	128746	125241
#二三级	(万立方米)	Grade-II and III Treatment	(10000 cu.m)	128746	125241
污水处理率	(%)	Sewage Treatment Rate	(%)	84.6	83.0
#集中处理率	(%)	Rate of Concentrated Treatment	(%)	84.6	83.0
污水排放总量	(万立方米)	Total Volume of Sewage Drainage	(10000 cu.m)	155317	152010
排水管道长度	(公里)	Length of Drainage Pipelines	(km)	13505	12665
污水管	(公里)	Sewage Pipes	(km)	6363	5735
雨水管	(公里)	Rain Pipes	(km)	5038	4808
雨污合流管	(公里)	Rain-sewage Sewer	(km)	2104	2122
再生水利用量	(万立方米)	Volume of Recycled Water Used	(10000 cu.m)	80108	75003
节　水		**Water Saving**			
节水量	(万立方米)	Volume Saved	(10000 cu.m)	11322	11311
节水措施	(项)	Water Saving Measures Implemented	(unit)	207	219

资料来源：北京市水务局。
Source: Beijing Water Authority.

4-21 环境卫生
MUNICIPAL ENVIRONMENT AND SANITATION

项目		Item		2013	2012
工作量		**Work Load**			
清扫街道面积	(万平方米/日)	Area of Cleaned Streets	(10000 sq.m/day)	14234	14346
生活垃圾无害化处理能力	(吨/日)	Harmless Disposal Capacity of Domestic Waste	(ton/day)	21971	17530
生活垃圾产生量	(万吨)	Output of Domestic Waste	(10000 tons)	671.7	648.3
生活垃圾清运量	(万吨)	Domestic Waste Removed and Transported	(10000 tons)	671.7	648.3
生活垃圾无害化处理量	(万吨)	Volume of Harmless Disposal of Domestic Waste	(10000 tons)	667.0	642.6
生活垃圾无害化处理率 (按清运量计算)	(%)	Rate of Harmless Disposal of Domestic Waste (Calculated by Volume of Waste Cleared and Transported)	(%)	99.3	99.1
餐余垃圾处理量	(万吨)	Kitchen Waste Removed and Transported	(10000 tons)	20.0	18.6
粪便清运量	(万吨)	Excrement Removed and Transported	(10000 tons)	220.7	207.2
环卫机械数量	**(辆)**	**Number of Environmental Sanitation Machinery**	**(unit)**	**9797**	**9384**
环卫设施		**Environmental Sanitation Facilities**			
公共厕所	(座)	Public Lavatories	(unit)	5563	5773

资料来源：北京市市政市容管理委员会。
Source: Beijing Municipal Commission of City Administration and Environment.

4-22 环境保护(2000-2013年) ENVIRONMENTAL PROTECTION (2000-2013)

年 份 Year	可吸入颗粒物年日均值(毫克/立方米) Daily Average of Inspiratory Particulate Matter in the Year (mg/cu.m)	二氧化硫年日均值(毫克/立方米) Daily Average of Sulfur Dioxide in the Year (mg/cu.m)	二氧化氮年日均值(毫克/立方米) Daily Average of Nitrogen Dioxide (mg/cu.m)	化学需氧量(COD)排放量(万吨) COD Emission Volume (10000 tons)	二氧化硫(SO_2)排放量(万吨) SO_2 Emission Volume (10000 tons)	区域环境噪声平均值(分贝) Average Value of Noises in Regional Environment (db)	道路交通干线噪声平均值(分贝) Average Value of Noises in Road Transportation (db)
2000	0.162	0.071	0.071	17.9	22.4	53.9	71.0
2001	0.165	0.064	0.071	17.0	20.1	53.9	69.6
2002	0.166	0.067	0.076	15.3	19.2	53.5	69.5
2003	0.141	0.061	0.072	13.4	18.3	53.6	69.7
2004	0.149	0.055	0.071	13.0	19.1	53.8	69.6
2005	0.142	0.050	0.066	11.6	19.1	53.2	69.5
2006	0.161	0.053	0.066	11.0	17.6	53.9	69.7
2007	0.148	0.047	0.066	10.7	15.2	54.0	69.9
2008	0.122	0.036	0.049	10.1	12.3	53.6	69.6
2009	0.121	0.034	0.053	9.9	11.9	54.1	69.7
2010	0.121	0.032	0.057	9.2	11.5	54.1	70.0
2011	0.114	0.028	0.055	19.3	9.8	53.7	69.6
2012	0.109	0.028	0.052	18.7	9.4	54.0	69.2
2013	0.108	0.027	0.056	17.8	8.7	53.9	69.1

注：化学需氧量(COD)排放量和二氧化硫排放量(SO_2)指标自2011年起调整统计口径和核算方法.

资料来源：北京市环境保护局。

Note: From 2011, statistical standard and calculation method are adjusted for COD emission volume and SO_2 emission volume.

Source: Beijing Municipal Bureau of Environmental Protection.

4-23 环境保护
ENVIRONMENTAL PROTECTION

项　目		Item		2013	2012
水环境		**Water Environment**			
废水排放总量	(万吨)	Total Discharge of Sewage	(10000 tons)	144579.93	140273.59
#工业废水排放量		Industrial Waste Water Discharge Volume		9486.42	9189.93
化学需氧量(COD)排放量	(吨)	COD Emission Volume	(ton)	178475	186501
#工业废水中COD排放量		Emission of COD in Industrial Waster Water		6055	6266
氨氮排放量	(吨)	Ammonia Nitrogen Discharge		19704	20483
#工业废水中氨氮排放量		Ammonia Nitrogen Discharge in Industrial Waster Water	(ton)	330	352
大气环境		**Atmosphere Environment**			
二氧化硫(SO2)排放量	(吨)	SO2 Emission Volume	(ton)	87042	93849
#工业二氧化硫排放量		Emission of Industrial SO2		52041	59330
氮氧化物排放量	(吨)	Smoke and Dust Emission	(ton)	166329	177495
#工业氮氧化物排放量		Emission of Industrial Smoke and Dust		75297	85331
烟(粉)尘排放量	(吨)	Smoke and Dust Emission	(ton)	59286	66829
#工业烟(粉)尘排放量		Emission of Industrial Smoke and Dust		27182	30844
固体废物		**Solid Waste**			
一般工业固体废物产生量	(万吨)	General Industrial Solid Waste Generated	(10000 tons)	1044.12	1104.05
一般工业固体废物综合利用量	(万吨)	General Industrial Solid Waste Recycled	(10000 tons)	904.46	871.73
一般工业固体废物处置量	(万吨)	General Industrial Solid Waste Disposed	(10000 tons)	140.16	219.49
危险废物产生量	(吨)	Hazardous Wastes Generated	(ton)	132177	134130
危险废物综合利用量	(吨)	Hazardous Wastes Recycled	(ton)	57879	44990
危险废物处置量	(吨)	Hazardous Wastes Disposed	(ton)	68126	89130
生态环境		**Ecological Environment**			
自然保护区个数	(个)	Number of Nature Reserves	(unit)	20	20
#国家级自然保护区		State-level Nature Reserves		2	2
自然保护区面积	(万公顷)	Area of Nature Reserves	(10000 hectares)	13.41	13.41

数据来源：北京市环境保护局。
Source: Beijing Municipal Bureau of Environmental Protection.

4-24 园林绿化及森林情况(1978-2013年)

年份 Year	年末公园绿地面积(公顷) Green Land and Park (year-end) (hectare)	人均公园绿地面积(平方米/人) Per Capita Green Land and Park (sq.m/person)	城市绿化覆盖率(%) Green Land Coverage (%)	林木绿化率(%) Forest Coverage (%)	年末园林绿地面积(公顷) Green Area (year-end) (hectare)
1978	2693	5.07	22.30		
1979	2693	5.07	22.30		
1980	2746	5.14	20.10	16.6	
1981	2751	5.14	20.10	16.6	
1982	2779	5.14	20.10	16.6	
1983	2823	5.14	20.10	16.6	
1984	2878	5.14	20.10	16.6	
1985	3263	4.94	22.10	16.6	
1986	3606	5.07	22.86	16.6	
1987	3570	5.07	22.90	16.6	
1988	4074	5.80	25.00	16.6	
1989	6910	6.00	26.00	16.6	
1990	7110	6.14	28.00	28.3	
1991	4279	6.41	28.43	28.3	
1992	4213	6.65	30.33	28.3	
1993	4452	7.76	31.33	28.3	
1994	5221	7.89	32.39	28.3	
1995	5017	7.48	32.68	36.3	
1996	5147	7.54	33.24	36.3	
1997	5408	7.80	34.22	36.3	
1998	6351	9.00	35.60	36.3	
1999	6457	9.10	36.30	36.3	
2000	7140	9.66	36.50	42.0	26680
2001	7554	10.07	38.78	44.0	30224
2002	7907	10.66	40.57	45.5	32572
2003	9115	11.43	40.87	47.5	38475
2004	10446	11.45	41.91	49.5	36755
2005	11365	12.00	42.00	50.5	38877
2006	11788	12.00	42.50	51.0	45495
2007	12101	12.60	43.00	51.6	46320
2008	12316	13.60	43.50	52.1	46993
2009	18070	14.50	44.40	52.6	61695
2010	19020	15.00	45.00	53.0	62672
2011	19728	15.30	45.60	54.0	63541
2012	21178	15.50	46.20	55.5	65540
2013	22215	15.70	46.80	57.4	67048

资料来源：北京市园林绿化局。

LANDSCAPING, AND STATISTICS FOR FORESTS (1978-2013)

森林面积 (公顷) Forest Area (hectare)	森林覆盖率 (%) Forest Coverage Rate (%)	活立木蓄积量 (万立方米) Total Stock of Standing Trees (10000 cu.m)	森林蓄积量 (万立方米) Forest Stock (10000 cu.m)	森林火灾次数 (次) Number of Forest Fires (unit)	森林火灾经济损失 (万元) Economic Loss of Forest Fires (10000 yuan)
619243.2		1521.4	1295.3	9	11.4
626006.3	35.9	1521.4	1295.3	13	96.7
636565.7	36.5	1559.5	1368.9	8	28.1
641368.3	36.5	1574.0	1394.4		
658914.1	36.7	1810.3	1406.2	2	…
666050.7	37.0	1854.7	1435.4	4	1.4
673411.8	37.6	1899.4	1468.7	3	1.7
691341.1	38.6	1943.3	1499.0	1	
716456.1	40.1	1993.4	1536.8		

Source: Beijing Municipal Bureau of Landscape and Forestry.

主要统计指标解释

能源生产量 能源生产量是反映能源生产规模、构成、生产成果的重要指标。按能源的成因分为一次能源（亦称天然能源）生产量和二次能源（亦称人工能源）生产量。

一次能源生产量 指报告期内生产一次能源的企业将自然界现存的能源资源经过开采而产出的合格产品，主要包括原煤、原油、天然气、水电等。

二次能源生产量 指报告期内将一次能源经过各种加工转换设备生产出的另一种形式的各种合格的能源产品。如火电、热力、洗煤、焦炭、各种石油制品、焦炉煤气、其他煤气等。

能源消费总量 指一定地域（行政或地理区域）内，国民经济各行业和居民家庭在一定时期所消费的各种能源的总和。能源消费总量包括终端能源消费量、能源加工转换损失量、能源运输和管理过程的损失量三部分。

能源消费总量（等价值） 是电力、热力按等价热值计算的能源消费总量。等价热值是能源统计中经常使用的一个热值概念，是指加工转换产出的某种二次能源所投入的一次能源的量，即获得一个度量单位的某种二次能源所消耗的以热值表示的一次能源。

能源加工转换投入产出量 能源具有由一种能量形式转换为另一种能量形式及耗用过程中可用一种能源替代另一种能源的特征。为提高能源的利用价值和效率，对能源进行加工、转换，产出适合生产和生活需要的更高级的能源产品。在加工转换投入(-)产出(+)量中，“-”表示能源加工转换的投入量，“+”表示二次能源的产出量。

投入量 是指为生产二次能源产品，所投入到能源加工转换设备的各种能源数量。在表中以负数表示。

产出量 是指各种能源（一次能源或少量再投入的二次能源）经过加工转换后，产出的各种二次能源产品（包括不作为能源使用的副产品，联产品）数量。

加工转换损失量 是指在能源加工、转换过程中损失的能量（能源），即能源加工、转换过程中投入的能源和产出的二次能源之间的差额。

损失量 指能源在经营管理和生产、输送、分配、储存等过程中发生的损失以及由于自然因素等原因造成的损失数量。不包括加工转换损失量。

终端消费量 是指能源消费环节的最后一个环节的能源消费，包括直接用作燃料、原材料和动力的各种能源的消费。它们的消费过程体现了能源消费的终止，不会再重新作为能源投入使用。终端消费量不包括用于能源加工转换投入量、加工转换损失量和损失量。

能源消费弹性系数 指能源消费总量增长率与地区生产总值增长率的比值。

电力消费弹性系数 指电力消费量增长率与地区生产总值增长率的比值。

平均每万元地区生产总值能源消费量 能源总消费量或分品种能源消费量与地区生产总值之比。

人均生活用能量 指用于生活消费的各种能源数量与人口总数之比。

日均能源消费量 指各品种能源消费量与当年实际天数之比。

垃圾无害化处理能力 指垃圾无害化处理场（厂）按工艺设计每天所能处理生活垃圾的数量。垃圾无害化处理场（厂）必须是按照有关技术、环境、卫生标准和规范进行设计、建设、运行、维护和管理的各种生活垃圾处理设施，主要包括卫生填埋场、堆肥厂和焚烧厂等。

水资源总量 指降水形成的地表和地下水总量，不包括过境水量。

排水管道长度 指所有排水总管、干管、支管、检查井及连接井进出口等长度之和。计算时应按单管计算，即在同一条街道上如有两条或两条以上并排的排水管道时，应按每条排水管道的长度相加计算。

污水处理能力 指污水处理厂（或处理装置）每昼夜处理污水量的设计能力。

按污水处理的程度，一般可分为一级处理、二级处理和三级处理。

一级处理是以沉淀为主体的处理工艺。指去除污水中的漂浮物和悬浮物的净化过程，主要为沉淀。

二级处理是以生物处理为主体的处理工艺。指污水经一级处理后，用生物处理方法继续除去污水中胶体和溶解性有机物的净化过程。

三级处理也称高级处理或深度处理。指进一步去除二级处理不能完全去除的污水中的污染物的处理工艺。

污水处理量 指污水处理厂和处理装置实际处理的污水量。包括物理处理量、生物处理量和化学处理量。

污水处理率 指污水处理量与污水排放总量的比率。计算公式:

$$污水处理率 = \frac{污水处理量}{污水排放总量} \times 100\%$$

生活垃圾清运量 指报告期内收集和运送到各垃圾处理场（厂）的垃圾的数量。

粪便清运量 指报告期内收集和运送到各粪便处理场（厂）的粪便的数量。

生活垃圾无害化处理量 指报告期内简易处理场和各种垃圾无害化处理场（厂）处理垃圾的总量。垃圾简易处理量指垃圾简易填埋场所处理的垃圾总量。垃圾无害化处理量指垃圾无害化处理场（厂）所处理的垃圾总量。

生活垃圾无害化处理率 指报告期垃圾无害化处理量与垃圾产生量的比率。计算公式:

$$垃圾无害化处理率=\frac{垃圾无害化处理量}{垃圾产生量}\times 100\%$$

在统计时，如果生活垃圾产生量不易取得，可用清运量代替。

化学需氧量（COD）排放量 指工业废水中 COD 排放量与生活污水中 COD 排放量之和。指用化学氧化剂氧化水中有机污染物时所需的氧量。COD 值越高，表示水中有机污染物污染越重。

二氧化硫（SO_2）排放量 指报告期内工业 SO_2 排放量与生活 SO_2 排放量之和。

工业固体废物综合利用量 指报告期内企业通过回收、加工、循环、交换等方式，从固体废物中提取或者使其转化为可以利用的资源、能源和其他原材料的固体废物量（包括当年利用的往年工业固体废物贮存量）。如用做农业肥料、生产建筑材料、筑路等。

公园绿地 指向公众开放，以游憩为主要功能，兼具生态、美化、防灾等作用，其绿地率达到 65%以上，配有多种乔灌木及地被植物，有一定设施和艺术布局的绿地。包括公园、社区公园、街旁绿地、其他公园绿地。人均公园绿地面积计算口径为户籍非农业人口。

绿化覆盖率 指报告期末区域内绿化覆盖面积与区域面积的比率。

计算公式:

$$绿化覆盖率=\frac{区域内绿化覆盖面积}{区域面积}\times 100\%$$

森林面积 指由乔木树种构成，郁闭度 0.20 以上(含 0.20)的林地或冠幅宽度 10 米以上的林带的面积，即有林地面积。它是反映森林资源总面积的重要指标。森林面积包括天然起源和人工起源的针叶林面积、阔叶林面积、针阔混交林面积和竹林面积。

活立木蓄积量 指一定范围土地上全部树木蓄积的总量，包括森林蓄积、疏林蓄积、散生木蓄积和四旁树蓄积。

森林蓄积量 指一定森林面积上存在着的林木树干部分的总材积，以立方米为计量单位。

森林火灾次数 指发生在城市市区外的一切森林、林木和林地的火灾次数，包括森林火警、一般灾害、重大灾害和特大灾害。

Explanatory Notes on Main Statistical Indicators

Energy Production is an important indicator reflecting the size, composition and results of energy production. By the cause of formation, it consists of the production of primary energy (also known as natural energy) and that of secondary energy (also known as artificial energy).

Production of Primary Energy means up-to-grade products produced by primary energy producers in the reporting period through extraction of existing energy in the nature, mainly including raw coal, crude oil, natural gas, hydroelectricity, etc.

Production of Secondary Energy means various up-to-grade energy products in another form that are made from primary energy with various processing and converting equipment in the reporting period, including thermal power, heating power, washed coal, coke, various petroleum products, coke oven gas and other gases, etc.

Total Energy Consumption means the total consumption of various energies by national economic sectors and resident households in a specific region (administrative or geographic). Total energy consumption can be divided into three parts: end-use energy consumption, loss during energy processing and conversion and loss during energy transport and management.

Total Energy Consumption (in Equivalent Caloricity) means the total consumption of electric power and heating power calculated in equivalent caloricity. Equivalent caloricity is a caloricity concept frequently used in statistics of energy. It means the quantity of primary energy input for a secondary energy produced through processing and conversion, i.e. the primary energy in terms of caloricity which is consumed to produce one measuring unit of a secondary energy.

Input and Output of Energy Processing and Conversion One form of energy can be converted into another form of energy. And in consumption, one sort of energy can be replaced with another. In order to improve the energy use value and efficiency, energy is processed and converted to produce energy products at higher levels which are suitable for productive and living needs. In the processing and conversion input (-) and output (+), "-" means the input for energy processing and conversion. And "+" means the output from energy processing and conversion.

Input means the volume of energy put into the energy processing and converting equipment in order to produce secondary energy products.

Output means the volume of secondary energy products (including byproducts and multi-products that cannot be used as energy) from processing and conversion of energy sources (primary energy or a small amount of secondary energy re-input).

Loss during Processing and Conversion means the energy lost in the processing and conversion of energy, namely the difference between the energy input and the secondary energy output during energy processing and conversion.

Energy Loss means the loss of energy during operation, management, production, transportation, distribution and storage, as well as the loss due to natural factors and other reasons. It excludes the loss during processing and conversion.

End-use Energy Consumption means the energy consumption in the last section of energy consumption, including the consumption of various energy sources used as fuel, raw materials and power. Such consumption represents the end of energy consumption, and the energy will not be put into use again as energy. End-use energy consumption does not include the input for energy processing and conversion, loss during the processing and conversion of energy, and energy loss.

Elasticity Coefficient of Energy Consumption means the ratio of growth rate of total energy consumption to the growth rate of GDP.

Elasticity Coefficient of Electric Power Consumption means the ratio of growth rate of electric power consumption to the growth rate of GDP.

Average Energy Consumption per 10000 yuan of GDP means the ratio of total energy consumption or energy consumption by variety to GDP.

Per-capital Energy Consumption by Households means the ratio of quantity of energy consumed by households to the total population.

Daily Energy Consumption means the ratio of energy consumption to the actual days in the same year.

Harmless Disposal Capacity of Waste means the quantity of domestic waste that can be disposed at harmless disposal facilities (sites) according to the process designed. Harmless disposal facilities (sites) must be domestic waste disposal facilities, including landfills, manure yards, incineration facilities and so on, which are designed, built, operated and managed in accordance with relevant technological, environmental, and sanitary standards and criterion.

Total Water Resources means the total volume of surface water and underground water caused by rainfall, excluding passing-by water.

Length of Sewage Pipes means the total length of all main drainage pipes, trunk pipes, branch pipes, access manholes, and connector well entrances and exits, and so on. The length of single pipes shall be included, i.e. if there are two or more drainage pipes parallel on a street, the length of every pipe shall be included.

Sewage Treatment Capacity means the designed capacity of sewage disposal for a sewage disposal plant (or facility).

In terms of extent, sewage disposal consists of primary disposal, secondary disposal and tertiary disposal.

Primary Disposal is a disposal process focusing on precipitation. It means a purification process removing the floating and suspended substances in sewage, mostly precipitation.

Secondary Disposal is a disposal process focusing on biological disposal. It means a purification process further removing the colloids and resolvable organic substances in sewage after the process of primary disposal.

Tertiary Disposal is also known as senior or deep disposal. It means a disposal process further removing any pollutants that cannot be removed completely in the process of secondary disposal.

Volume of Sewage Treated means the volume of sewage actually disposed by sewage disposal plants and facilities, consisting of physical volume, biological volume and chemical volume of waste water disposed.

Sewage Treatment Rate means the ratio of sewage disposed to the total discharge of sewage. The formula is:

Sewage Disposal Rate = Volume of Sewage Disposed / Total Discharge of Sewage × 100%

Domestic Waste Removed and Transported means the quantity of waste collected and transported to waste treatment sites (plants) in the reporting period.

Excrement Removed and Transported means the quantity of excrement collected and transported to waste treatment sites (plants) in the reporting period.

Volume of Harmless Disposal of Domestic Waste means the total volume of waste disposed by simple disposal sites and harmless waste disposal sits (plants) in the reporting period. Simple disposal of waste means the total volume of waste by simple landfills. Harmless waste disposal means the total volume of waste disposed by harmless waste disposal sites (plants).

Rate of Harmless Disposal of Domestic Waste means the ratio of harmless waste disposal to the waste produced in the reporting period. The formula is:

Rate of Harmless Disposal of Domestic Waste = Harmless Waste Disposal / Waste Produced × 100%

In practical statistics, if it is hard to get figures on the volume of domestic waste produced, the volume removed and transported may be used.

COD Emission Volume means the sum of COD emission in industrial sewage and in domestic waste water. It means the amount of oxygen required when chemical oxidants are used to oxidize organic pollutants in water. A higher value of COD corresponds to more serious pollution by organic pollutants.

SO_2 Emission Volume means the sum of industrial SO_2 emission and domestic SO_2 emission in the reporting period.

Industrial Solid Waste Utilized means the volume of solid wastes from which useful materials can be extracted or which can be converted into usable resources, energy or other materials by means of reclamation, processing, recycling and exchange (including utilizing in the year the stocks of industrial solid wastes of the previous year). Examples of such utilizations include fertilizers, building materials and road materials.

Green Land and Parks means the green land open to the public, with main function of recreation, together with ecological, landscaping and disaster preventing functions, and with more than 65% green coverage, provided with multiple arbors, shrubs and ground-cover plants, along with certain facilities and artistic layouts. They include parks, community parks, street-side green land and other green land in gardens.

Green Land Coverage means the ratio of area of green land in a region to the total area of the region in the reporting period. The formula is:

Green Land Coverage = Area of Green Land in a Region / Total Area of the Region × 100%

Forest Area means the area of forest where arbor trees grow with canopy density above 0.2 (and at 0.2) or forest area with crown width more than 10m, i.e. the area of land with forest. It is an important indicator reflecting the total area of forest resources. Forest Area includes the area of coniferous forest, broad leaf forest, mixed coniferous-broad-leaf forest and bamboo forest from both natural and artificial origins.

Total Stock of Standing Trees mean the total stock of all trees on specific area of land, including trees in forest, trees in sparse forest, scattered trees and trees planted by the side of villages, farm houses and along roads and rivers.

Forest Stock means the total volume of timber of forest tree trunks growing on specific area of forest, which are measured in cubic meters.

Number of Forest Fires means the number of all fires occurring in forests, woods, woodlands outside the urban districts, including forest fires, general fires, severe fires and fire disasters.

北京统计年鉴2014 BEIJING STATISTICAL YEARBOOK

全社会固定资产投资和房地产开发

TOTAL INVESTMENT IN FIXED ASSETS AND REAL ESTATE DEVELOPMENT

简要说明

一、本章资料的主要内容

本章资料包括历年北京市全社会固定资产投资、房地产开发的主要分组数据、保障性安居工程建设等情况。

二、本章资料的统计范围

1996 年及以前固定资产投资统计起点为 5 万元以上，1996 年以后调整为 50 万元及以上，从 2011 年开始调整为 500 万元及以上。

三、有关统计标准的变化说明

（一）关于行业划分。根据国家统计局规定，自 2012 年开始执行《国民经济行业分类》（GB/T 4754-2011）标准。

（二）关于三次产业划分。根据国家统计局《三次产业划分规定》（国统字[2012]108 号），该规定对三次产业的范围进行了调整。其中第一产业是指农、林、牧、渔业（不含农、林、牧、渔服务业）；第二产业是指采矿业（不含开采辅助活动），制造业（不含金属制品、机械和设备修理业），电力、热力、燃气及水生产和供应业，建筑业；第三产业是指除第一产业、第二产业以外的其他行业。自 2012 年开始执行此规定。

四、本章资料的数据来源

本章资料来源于北京市统计局、国家统计局北京调查总队。

五、本章的统计调查方法

除农户固定资产投资统计采用抽样调查方法外，其他均为全面调查。

Brief Introduction

I. Main Content

Statistics in this chapter include figures on fixed assets investment in Beijing and its main grouped figures as well as figures on government-subsidized housing projects.

II. Scope of Statistics

Before and in 1996, the threshold of fixed assets statistics was RMB 50,000; after 1996, it was increased to RMB 500,000; since 2011, the figure has been set at RMB 5 million.

III. Changes in Relevant Statistical Standards

(I) Classification of Sectors. According to relevant provisions of the National Bureau of Statistics, the Standard for Classification of National Economic Sectors (GB/T 4754-2011) came into effect in 2012.

(II) Classification of Three Industries. According to the Provision of National Bureau of Statistics on Classification of Three Industries (GTZ [2012] No.108), the scope of three industries has been adjusted. The primary industry refers to agriculture, forestry, animal production and hunting, fishing (excluding services for agriculture, forestry, animal production and hunting, fishing); the secondary industry refers to mining (excluding mining support activities), manufacturing (excluding metal products, machinery and equipment repair), production and distribution of electricity, heating power, gas and water, and construction; the tertiary industry refers to sectors other than the primary and secondary industries. the Provision of National Bureau of Statistics on Classification of Three Industries (GTZ [2012] No.108) came into effect in 2012.

Ⅳ. Source of Statistics

Statistics in this chapter are from the Beijing Municipal Bureau of Statistics and NBS Survey Office in Beijing.

Ⅴ. Method of Statistical Survey

Sample survey is used for the statistics on investment of rural households in fixed assets. For other statistics, the complete survey is conducted.

5-1 全社会固定资产投资和增长速度情况(1978-2013年)
TOTAL INVESTMENT IN FIXED ASSETS AND GROWTH RATE (1978-2013)

单位：亿元 (100 million yuan)

年 份 Year	全社会固定资产投资 Total Investment in Fixed Assets	城镇固定资产投资 Investment in Urban Fixed Assets	#房地产开发投资 Investment in Real Estate Development	农村固定资产投资 Investment in Rural Fixed Assets	#基础设施投资 Infrastructure Investment	#建筑安装投资 Construction and Installation Investment	新增固定资产 Incremental Fixed Assets
1978	22.6	22.6			5.4		16.9
1979	26.5	26.5			5.8		21.2
1980	33.2	33.2			6.0		23.2
1981-1985	**286.8**	**234.4**		**50.8**	**40.6**		**184.4**
1981	36.6	31.4		5.2	5.8		30.9
1982	38.6	34.5		4.1	6.1		26.3
1983	51.3	38.5		12.8	6.7		32.5
1984	66.3	52.2		14.1	8.8		47.1
1985	94.0	77.8		14.6	13.2		47.6
1986-1990	**724.1**	**634.9**	**22.5**	**76.5**	**117.9**		**417.4**
1986	106.2	94.5		10.4	14.5		58.5
1987	136.2	121.4		12.7	22.1		79.9
1988	163.0	138.7		21.3	23.2		77.3
1989	139.5	122.2		14.7	26.5		79.6
1990	179.2	158.1	22.5	17.4	31.6		122.1
1991-1995	**2358.7**	**2181.5**	**568.4**	**154.1**	**494.9**	**1297.1**	**1229.1**
1991	192.0	168.4	24.0	21.0	35.2	107.3	139.0
1992	266.0	234.7	33.7	27.2	58.8	136.2	157.8
1993	410.4	376.6	58.4	30.0	91.4	232.0	201.6
1994	648.8	607.4	99.5	35.7	153.4	362.6	356.0
1995	841.5	794.4	352.8	40.2	156.1	459.0	374.7
1996-2000	**5461.7**	**5063.8**	**1979.5**	**322.7**	**1382.1**	**3069.5**	**4051.2**
1996	876.9	825.6	328.2	43.6	188.8	515.8	592.5
1997	961.2	912.4	330.3	40.6	218.3	546.2	637.9
1998	1155.6	1060.3	377.4	75.8	320.4	626.9	759.3
1999	1170.6	1072.9	421.5	78.2	302.7	679.1	949.5
2000	1297.4	1192.6	522.1	84.5	351.9	701.5	1112.0
2001-2005	**10857.4**	**10033.6**	**5974.0**	**755.4**	**2260.0**	**5926.2**	**6897.4**
2001	1530.5	1417.1	783.8	93.7	356.4	801.6	1177.0
2002	1814.3	1688.2	989.4	102.5	411.9	964.9	1251.0
2003	2157.1	1999.9	1202.5	132.1	417.8	1151.3	1165.9
2004	2528.3	2333.0	1473.3	195.3	463.2	1438.9	1455.1
2005	2827.2	2595.4	1525.0	231.8	610.7	1569.5	1848.4
2006-2010	**21538.5**	**19678.6**	**10863.2**	**1859.9**	**6137.3**	**9860.6**	**11666.8**
2006	3371.5	3086.3	1719.9	285.2	935.3	1836.0	1972.1
2007	3966.6	3656.7	1995.8	309.9	1175.8	2117.9	2004.9
2008	3848.5	3554.8	1908.7	293.7	1160.7	1798.8	2666.8
2009	4858.4	4378.2	2337.7	480.2	1462.0	1983.0	2457.2
2010	5493.5 (5218.3)	5002.6	2901.1	490.9	1403.5	2124.9	2565.8
2011	5910.6	5463.9	3036.3	446.7	1400.2	2585.3	2382.0
2012	6462.8	5853.1	3153.4	609.8	1789.2	3076.6	2570.4
2013	7032.2	6352.6	3483.4	679.6	1785.7	3482.2	3163.8

注：1. 根据国家统计局有关规定，从2004年起，全社会固定资产投资中不包括零星购置投资。
2. 2004年起,新增固定资产、基础设施投资、建筑安装投资中包含农村投资。
3. 根据国家统计局有关规定，2011年起投资统计起点调整为500万元，为便于比较2010年的相应数据也作了调整，未加括号的为原口径数，括号内为调整后的数据，当年固定资产投资等增长速度均按可比口径计算。

Note: a) According to regulations of National Bureau of Statistics, since 2004, total investment in fixed assets has not included investment in acquiring minor items.

b) Since 2004, rural investment has been counted in incremental fixed assets, infrastructure investment, construction and installation investment.

c) Since 2011, the statistical threshold of investment has been adjusted to 5 million yuan according to the National Bureau of Statistics. For comparison, relevant figures in 2010 were adjusted accordingly. Figures with no brackets are based on the former standard. Figures in brackets are data after adjustment. Growth rates of fixed assets investment in respective years are calculated in comparable terms.

5-1 续表 Continued

单位：% (%)

年份 Year	全社会固定资产投资比上年增长 Growth rate of Total Investment in Fixed Assets	城镇固定资产投资 Growth rate of Investment in Urban Fixed Assets	#房地产开发投资 Growth rate of Investment in Real Estate Development	农村固定资产投资 Growth rate of Investment in Rural Fixed Assets	#基础设施投资 Growth rate of Infrastructure Investment	#建筑安装投资 Growth rate of Construction and Installation Investment
1978						
1979	17.3	17.3			7.4	
1980	25.3	25.3			3.4	
1981-1985	**18.8**	**11.7**			**10.3**	
1981	10.2	-5.4			-3.3	
1982	5.5	9.9		-21.2	5.2	
1983	32.9	11.6		212.2	9.8	
1984	29.2	35.6		10.2	31.3	
1985	41.8	49.0		3.5	50.0	
1986-1990	**14.8**	**16.8**		**1.5**	**20.0**	
1986	13.0	21.5		-28.8	9.8	
1987	28.2	28.5		22.1	52.4	
1988	19.7	14.3		67.7	5.0	
1989	-14.4	-11.9		-31.0	14.2	
1990	28.5	29.4		18.4	19.2	
1991-1995	**34.2**	**36.0**	**59.9**	**19.7**	**40.8**	
1991	7.1	6.5	6.7	20.7	11.4	
1992	38.5	39.4	40.4	29.5	67.0	26.9
1993	54.3	60.5	73.3	10.3	55.4	70.3
1994	58.1	61.3	70.4	19.0	67.8	56.3
1995	29.7	30.8	254.6	12.6	1.8	26.6
1996-2000	**8.9**	**8.2**	**3.9**	**16.2**	**19.7**	**9.9**
1996	4.2	3.9	-7.0	8.5	20.9	12.4
1997	9.6	10.5	0.6	-6.9	15.6	5.9
1998	20.2	16.2	14.3	86.7	46.8	14.8
1999	1.3	1.2	11.7	3.2	-5.5	8.3
2000	10.8	11.2	23.9	8.1	16.3	3.3
2001-2005	**17.7**	**17.9**	**29.0**	**20.1**	**8.5**	**18.0**
2001	18.0	18.8	50.1	10.9	1.3	14.3
2002	18.5	19.1	26.2	9.4	15.6	20.4
2003	18.9	18.5	21.5	28.9	1.4	19.3
2004	17.2	16.7	22.5	47.8	10.9	25.0
2005	11.8	11.2	3.5	18.7	31.8	9.1
2006-2010	**14.4**	**14.2**	**12.0**	**16.2**	**24.2**	**7.7**
2006	19.3	18.9	12.8	23.0	53.2	17.0
2007	17.6	18.5	16.0	8.7	25.7	15.4
2008	-3.0	-2.8	-4.4	-5.2	-1.3	-15.1
2009	26.2	23.2	22.5	63.5	26.0	10.2
2010	13.1	14.3	24.1	2.2	-4.0	7.2
2011	13.3	14.8	10.1	-2.9	0.3	22.4
2012	9.3	7.1	3.9	36.5	27.8	19.0
2013	8.8	8.5	10.5	11.5	-0.2	13.2

5-2 按登记注册类型分全社会固定资产投资(1978-2013年)
TOTAL INVESTMENT IN FIXED ASSETS BY REGISTRATION TYPE (1978-2013)

单位：亿元 (100 million yuan)

年份 Year	全社会固定资产投资 Total Investment in Fixed Assets	国有 State-owned	集体 Collectively-owned	股份制 Joint-stock	港澳台商 Hong Kong, Macao and Taiwan	外商 Foreign	私营个体 Private	其他 Others
1978	22.6							
1979	26.5							
1980	33.2							
1981-1985	**286.8**	**223.8**	**22.6**				**40.4**	
1981	36.6	30.1	1.3				5.2	
1982	38.6	33.0	1.5				4.1	
1983	51.3	37.1	1.4				12.8	
1984	66.3	50.0	2.2				14.1	
1985	94.0	73.6	16.2				4.2	
1986-1990	**724.1**	**609.6**	**83.1**				**31.4**	
1986	106.2	88.7	13.3				4.2	
1987	136.2	115.8	15.2				5.2	
1988	163.0	133.2	21.4				8.4	
1989	139.5	117.7	15.1				6.7	
1990	179.2	154.2	18.1				6.9	
1991-1995	**2358.7**	**1764.2**	**188.7**				**24.8**	
1991	192.0	165.0	20.2				6.8	
1992	266.0	230.1	27.3				8.6	
1993	410.4	340.1	37.4				2.0	
1994	648.8	514.8	44.6				3.1	
1995	841.5	514.2	59.2				4.3	
1996-2000	**5461.7**	**3380.8**	**261.8**				**155.3**	
1996	876.9	545.7	57.6				4.8	
1997	961.2	605.7	54.7				4.0	
1998	1155.6	727.9	48.7				30.9	
1999	1170.6	735.7	55.8				36.1	
2000	1297.4	765.8	45.0				79.5	
2001-2005	**10857.4**	**3922.4**	**303.3**				**809.4**	
2001	1530.5	752.6	45.8				110.9	
2002	1814.3	771.5	53.9				150.6	
2003	2157.1	745.1	62.4				201.3	
2004	2528.3	755.5	69.5	1063.8	204.5	198.8	176.4	59.8
2005	2827.2	897.7	71.7	1211.8	164.1	274.1	170.2	37.6
2006-2010	**21538.5**	**8162.9**	**398.0**	**9206.8**	**903.8**	**1480.8**	**1121.2**	**265.0**
2006	3371.5	1207.2	69.3	1384.5	180.9	315.9	174.9	38.8
2007	3966.6	1343.0	80.4	1679.0	236.4	378.9	209.0	39.9
2008	3848.5	1388.6	66.8	1688.5	145.3	274.9	242.2	42.2
2009	4858.4	2316.8	68.9	1728.5	172.2	273.0	233.0	66.0
2010	5493.5	1907.3	112.6	2726.3	169.0	238.1	262.1	78.1
2011	5910.6	1903.3	99.4	3053.2	224.1	266.8	278.4	85.4
2012	6462.8	2248.2	106.8	3280.9	208.8	300.2	231.7	86.1
2013	7032.2	2382.0	151.4	3318.4	464.2	321.7	317.0	77.5

注：1. 根据国家统计局有关规定，从2004年起，全社会固定资产投资中不包括零星购置投资。
2. 国有包括登记注册类型为国有、国有联营及国有独资公司的单位。
3. 集体包括登记注册类型为集体和集体联营的单位。

Note: a) According to regulations of National Bureau of Statistics, since 2004, total investment in fixed assets has not included investment in acquiring minor items.
b) State-owned units include state-owned enterprises, state-owned associated enterprises and wholly state-owned enterprises.
c) Collectively-owned units include collectively-owned enterprises and collectively-owned associated enterprises.

5-3 按产业分全社会固定资产投资(1978-2013年)
INVESTMENT IN FIXED ASSETS BY INDUSTRY (1978-2013)

单位: 亿元 (100 million yuan)

年 份 Year	全社会固定资产投资 Total Investment in Fixed Assets	第一产业 Primary Industry	第二产业 Secondary Industry	第三产业 Tertiary Industry
1978	22.6	1.4	10.8	10.4
1979	26.5	1.0	12.0	13.5
1980	33.2	0.7	15.7	16.8
1981-1985	**286.8**	**5.9**	**98.1**	**130.4**
1981	36.6	0.6	13.6	17.2
1982	38.6	1.2	15.4	17.9
1983	51.3	1.2	16.4	20.9
1984	66.3	1.3	20.3	30.6
1985	94.0	1.6	32.4	43.8
1986-1990	**724.1**	**9.4**	**218.8**	**384.2**
1986	106.2	1.5	41.4	51.6
1987	136.2	1.6	46.9	72.9
1988	163.0	2.0	48.8	87.9
1989	139.5	1.9	38.4	81.9
1990	179.2	2.4	43.3	89.9
1991-1995	**2358.7**	**15.5**	**624.1**	**973.5**
1991	192.0	2.7	51.3	90.4
1992	266.0	3.9	82.9	114.2
1993	410.4	2.1	150.4	165.7
1994	648.8	3.7	185.8	318.4
1995	841.5	3.1	153.7	284.8
1996-2000	**5461.7**	**9.9**	**914.3**	**2160.2**
1996	876.9	2.8	174.9	319.7
1997	961.2	0.9	201.1	380.1
1998	1155.6	1.5	201.7	479.7
1999	1170.6	1.7	179.4	470.4
2000	1297.4	3.0	157.2	510.3
2001-2005	**10857.4**	**63.4**	**1410.6**	**9383.4**
2001	1530.5	8.4	154.2	1367.9
2002	1814.3	7.5	185.0	1621.8
2003	2157.1	21.0	260.7	1875.4
2004	2528.3	14.6	401.0	2112.7
2005	2827.2	11.9	409.7	2405.6
2006-2010	**21538.5**	**159.9**	**2172.8**	**19205.8**
2006	3371.5	14.5	363.2	2993.8
2007	3966.6	16.7	484.1	3465.8
2008	3848.5	28.1	386.0	3434.4
2009	4858.4	57.4	411.4	4389.5
2010	5493.5	43.2	528.1	4922.3
2011	5910.6	47.2	762.2	5101.3
2012	6462.8	145.4	719.8	5597.5
2013	7032.2	175.5	755.0	6101.7

注：1. 根据国家统计局有关规定，从2004年起，全社会固定资产投资中不包括零星购置投资。
2. 2000年及以前按产业划分中，不含房地产开发投资及农村投资。2000年以后含房地产开发投资及农村固定资产投资。
3. 自2012年起，三次产业划分执行国家统计局《三次产业划分规定》（国统字〔2012〕108号）。

Note: a) According to regulations of National Bureau of Statistics, since 2004, total investment in fixed assets has not included investment in acquiring minor items.
b) Data of investment in fixed assets grouped by industry excluded investment in real estate development and rural investment in 2000 and before. After 2000, data of investment in fixed assets included investment in real estate development and rural fixed assets.
c) Since 2012, the three industries have been classified according to the Regulations of the National Bureau of Statistics on the Classification of the Three Industries (GTZ [2012] No. 108).

5-4 全社会固定资产投资资金来源情况(1978-2013年)
TOTAL INVESTMENT IN FIXED ASSETS BY SOURCE OF FUNDS (1978-2013)

单位：亿元 (100 million yuan)

年份 Year	上年末结余资金 Surplus Funds by the Year End of the Preceding Year	本年资金来源小计 Subtotal of Funds at Current Year	国家预算内资金 State Budgets	国内贷款 Domestic Loans	债券 Bonds	利用外资 Foreign Investment	自筹资金 Self-raised Funds	其他资金 Others
1978		22.5	16.9					
1979		26.5	19.2					
1980		33.2	18.5					
1981		31.4	15.4					
1982		34.5	14.1					
1983		38.5	16.0					
1984		52.2	22.5					
1985		77.8	30.4					
1986		94.5	33.0					
1987		126.2	43.1					
1988		149.4	37.4					
1989		123.1	35.0	12.8		18.2	44.5	12.6
1990		136.2	34.4	22.8		15.2	52.3	11.5
1991		151.1	35.5	28.2		13.9	65.5	8.0
1992		216.7	42.2	40.1		14.9	109.9	9.6
1993	54.3	425.2	47.1	79.2	1.6	28.0	205.2	64.1
1994	71.1	695.7	64.1	91.5	0.8	96.9	331.2	111.2
1995	200.8	915.8	70.3	122.7	1.1	187.3	339.8	194.6
1996	204.9	926.1	76.7	152.8	1.0	161.2	330.5	203.9
1997	183.1	1016.7	86.3	194.3		139.2	383.4	213.5
1998	207.1	1140.1	98.4	223.8	17.0	132.1	450.2	218.6
1999	212.1	1183.8	136.2	262.2	1.4	82.7	461.3	240.0
2000	293.1	1439.1	107.0	373.8	0.6	51.5	505.6	400.6
2001	325.5	1796.8	136.7	429.4	2.5	35.6	595.6	597.0
2002	433.2	2075.3	108.5	543.8	1.9	41.5	672.8	706.8
2003	542.7	2674.0	78.4	755.2		52.6	887.9	899.9
2004	654.6	3712.8	118.6	804.7		120.5	1245.7	1423.3
2005	924.4	4553.7	128.8	1055.8		70.9	1452.8	1845.4
2006	1043.8	4927.3	126.4	1347.5	32.7	76.2	1532.2	1812.3
2007	1202.2	6193.0	102.2	1513.3	22.4	82.8	2195.6	2276.7
2008	1469.5	5184.7	104.2	1394.2	35.5	80.0	2016.4	1554.5
2009	1321.7	8702.2	118.1	3038.5	17.5	39.3	2441.3	3047.4
2010	2109.1	8327.8	99.5	2218.7	4.3	43.8	3209.1	2752.4
2011	2341.4	8235.4	71.7	1853.6	85.4	29.8	3588.6	2606.3
2012	2830.7	9156.0	156.1	2186.3	12.7	24.9	3478.4	3297.6
2013	3133.1	10580.3	159.6	2554.1	0.8	23.5	4295.2	3547.2

注：1978-1992年不含房地产开发和农村投资；1993-2003年不含农村投资。

Note: Figures from 1978 to 1992 did not include investment in real estate development and rural investment; figures from 1993 to 2003 did not include rural investment.

5-5 全社会基础设施投资(1978-2013年)

单位：亿元

年 份 Year	基础设施投资 Infrastructure Investment	#能 源 Energy	电 力 Electricity	供 热 Heating	供 气 Gas	供 水 Water	#公共服务业 Public Services	#园林绿化 Landscaping	#环境卫生 Environmental Sanitation	#市政工程管理 Municipal Project Management
1978	5.4	1.4	0.7				0.6			
1979	5.8	1.1	0.4				1.3			
1980	6.0	0.9	0.6				2.3			
1981-1985	**40.6**	**9.4**	**5.4**				**11.2**			
1981	5.8	1.3	0.6				2.0			
1982	6.1	1.4	0.9				1.9			
1983	6.7	1.5	0.9				1.9			
1984	8.8	1.4	0.7				3.0			
1985	13.2	3.8	2.3				2.5			
1986-1990	**117.9**	**39.8**	**21.1**				**25.3**			
1986	14.5	4.8	2.3				2.1			
1987	22.1	8.0	4.1				3.1			
1988	23.2	8.8	4.1				5.3			
1989	26.5	9.2	5.2				6.6			
1990	31.6	9.0	5.3				8.3			
1991-1995	**494.9**	**134.1**	**84.6**	**12.3**	**15.2**	**22.0**	**62.9**	**2.9**		**57.3**
1991	35.2	12.4	6.4	2.0	1.3	2.7	7.5	0.3		6.8
1992	58.8	17.7	9.0	4.0	2.6	2.1	8.2	0.4		7.2
1993	91.4	19.3	11.4	1.4	2.6	3.9	4.1	1.6		1.7
1994	153.4	38.0	22.7	2.5	5.0	7.8	27.2	0.3		26.5
1995	156.1	46.7	35.1	2.4	3.7	5.5	15.9	0.3		15.1
1996-2000	**1382.1**	**363.4**	**239.7**	**45.2**	**41.4**	**37.1**	**321.0**	**14.2**	**27.1**	**275.9**
1996	188.8	59.2	48.2	3.4	4.1	3.5	29.1	2.3	0.1	25.4
1997	218.3	75.6	52.1	10.3	7.8	5.4	24.3	1.7	2.8	19.8
1998	320.4	85.1	54.2	14.2	6.7	10.0	38.0	3.0	1.9	33.1
1999	302.7	90.3	58.6	11.2	10.3	10.2	75.0	5.4	2.9	64.7
2000	351.9	53.2	26.6	6.1	12.5	8.0	154.6	1.8	19.4	132.9
2001-2005	**2260.0**	**301.7**	**165.2**	**52.7**	**53.9**	**29.9**	**668.6**	**23.1**	**79.9**	**511.4**
2001	356.4	40.8	19.3	7.2	11.0	3.3	114.6	6.7	22.4	85.4
2002	411.9	49.5	26.0	7.2	13.2	3.0	101.6	3.5	17.0	81.1
2003	417.8	36.1	10.6	11.3	10.8	3.4	152.8	1.9	17.0	103.6
2004	463.2	73.0	39.3	14.8	6.9	12.0	139.3	5.5	16.3	100.8
2005	610.7	102.3	70.0	12.2	12.0	8.1	160.3	5.5	7.2	140.6
2006-2010	**6137.3**	**780.3**	**443.6**	**176.9**	**57.6**	**102.1**	**1640.0**	**44.8**	**349.4**	**1117.7**
2006	935.3	113.4	72.8	18.7	11.0	10.9	265.3	3.4	55.4	194.8
2007	1175.8	200.2	121.0	43.0	11.2	25.0	289.5	8.0	75.7	187.3
2008	1160.7	144.1	88.4	25.9	8.1	21.7	291.6	8.0	82.2	188.7
2009	1462.0	165.4	88.9	40.1	10.5	25.8	434.5	15.9	77.7	314.0
2010	1403.5	157.2	72.5	49.2	16.8	18.7	359.1	9.5	58.4	232.9
2011	1400.2	171.1	90.1	25.3	17.0	38.8	379.4	8.1	40.5	267.8
2012	1789.2	231.9	106.3	64.8	27.3	33.5	508.1	22.0	23.5	361.6
2013	1785.7	270.2	133.7	53.6	38.1	44.8	451.3	18.2	53.6	318.3

注：2004年及以后基础设施投资包括农村基础设施投资。

TOTAL INVESTMENT IN INFRASTRUCTURE (1978-2013)

(100 million yuan)

#交通运输 Transportation	#铁路 Railway	#公路 Road	#城市公共交通业 Urban Public Transportation	#航空 Aviation	#邮政电信 Post & Telecommunications	邮政 Post	电信 Telecommunications	基础设施投资占全社会固定资产投资比重 (%) Infrastructure Investment as Percentage of Total Investment in Fixed Assets (%)
1.7	0.8	0.4		0.5	0.4			23.9
1.7	0.4	0.4		0.8	0.4			21.9
2.3	1.1	0.7		0.5	0.5			17.9
11.1	**3.9**	**5.5**		**1.7**	**5.2**			
1.8	0.6	0.9		0.3	0.4			15.8
1.9	0.8	0.8		0.3	0.4			15.8
2.6	1.2	1.0		0.4	0.6			13.1
2.3	0.7	1.3		0.3	1.1			13.3
2.6	0.7	1.6		0.4	2.7			14.0
28.3	**5.0**	**19.3**		**4.0**	**20.3**			
3.1	1.0	1.5		0.6	3.5			13.7
6.6	1.2	4.0		1.3	3.2			16.2
4.7	1.4	3.0		0.4	3.0			14.2
5.2	0.7	3.9		0.6	5.2			19.0
8.7	0.7	6.9		1.1	5.4			17.6
123.0	**50.8**	**30.6**	**22.4**	**4.6**	**137.3**	**9.5**	**127.8**	
9.3	0.8	5.6	2.3	0.5	5.8	5.0	0.8	18.3
20.1	4.7	10.7	4.0	0.7	12.3	1.1	11.2	22.1
29.4	11.2	4.7	4.7	1.1	24.2	1.7	22.5	22.3
30.0	13.6	3.6	5.7	1.0	48.6	0.9	47.7	23.6
34.2	20.5	6.0	5.7	1.3	46.4	0.8	45.6	18.6
337.4	**26.0**	**131.3**	**80.0**	**3.2**	**299.6**	**6.0**	**293.6**	
54.0	11.7	15.8	6.0	1.2	44.1	0.9	43.2	21.5
51.2	6.0	11.1	9.1	0.2	60.3	2.1	58.2	22.7
104.6	8.0	42.1	24.4		77.5	1.8	75.7	27.7
63.0		30.1	20.7		54.0	0.4	53.6	25.9
64.6	0.3	32.2	19.8	1.8	63.7	0.8	62.9	27.1
766.2	**23.2**	**294.0**	**302.8**	**137.6**	**384.0**	**6.2**	**377.9**	
104.4	1.5	52.8	45.1	2.0	84.8	2.2	82.6	23.3
159.7	1.4	107.0	44.6	1.4	78.7	1.6	77.1	22.7
129.2	9.3	55.3	48.8	15.8	82.2	0.9	81.3	19.4
148.8	7.2	38.2	51.1	52.3	68.5	1.0	67.5	18.3
224.1	3.9	40.7	113.2	66.2	69.9	0.5	69.4	21.6
3010.9	**358.7**	**732.8**	**1456.7**	**457.7**	**462.9**	**8.2**	**454.4**	
439.6	25.1	140.6	201.0	72.2	72.3	1.2	71.1	27.7
548.0	65.7	189.6	202.4	87.5	84.8	…	84.7	29.6
604.2	75.9	170.5	215.8	141.8	86.7	0.3	86.3	30.2
698.6	114.9	134.8	426.7	21.9	124.9	3.3	121.5	30.1
720.5	77.1	97.3	410.8	134.3	94.2	3.4	90.8	25.5
680.7	43.6	107.7	351.3	176.6	82.3	2.7	79.6	23.7
712.0	43.0	98.2	391.0	178.1	122.0	4.6	117.4	27.7
664.5	36.9	127.5	310.9	162.5	132.9	3.5	129.4	25.4

Note: Investment in infrastructure in and after 2004 includes that in rural infrastructure investment.

5-6 全社会基础设施投资(2013年)
TOTAL INVESTMENT IN INFRASTRUCTURE (2013)

项目	Item	投资额(万元) Investment (10000 yuan) 全市 Beijing Municipality	#城镇 Urban	比重(%) Percentage (%) 全市 Beijing Municipality	#城镇 Urban
合计	**Total**	**17857332**	**14388190**	**100.0**	**100.0**
能源	**Energy**	**2701631**	**2518211**	**15.1**	**17.5**
电力	Electricity	1336673	1248330	7.5	8.7
供热	Heating	536062	534015	3.0	3.7
供气	Gas	381352	372938	2.1	2.6
供水	Water	447544	362928	2.5	2.5
公共服务业	**Public Services**	**4513456**	**3560158**	**25.3**	**24.7**
园林绿化	Landscaping	182342	162714	1.0	1.1
环境卫生	Environmental Sanitation	535505	317698	3.0	2.2
市政工程管理	Municipal Project Management	3182572	2858611	17.8	19.9
其他公共服务业	Others	613037	221135	3.4	1.5
交通运输	**Transportation**	**6644671**	**6357982**	**37.2**	**44.2**
铁路	Railway	368652	368652	2.1	2.6
公路	Road	1275202	1020945	7.1	7.1
管道运输	Pipeline	266508	266508	1.5	1.9
城市公共交通业	Urban Public Transportation	3109401	3077269	17.4	21.4
#公交电汽车客运	Buses and Electirc Cars	93107	91917	0.5	0.6
出租汽车	Taxis	77231	70536	0.4	0.5
航空	Aviation	1624608	1624608	9.1	11.3
其他	Others	300			
邮政电信	**Post and Telecommunications**	**1328968**	**1285512**	**7.4**	**9.0**
邮政	Post	35343	26377	0.2	0.2
电信	Telecommunications	1293625	1259135	7.2	8.8
其他	**Others**	**2668606**	**666327**	**15.0**	**4.6**
#水利	Water Conservancy	1271798	572198	7.1	4.0

5-7 全社会固定资产投资及新增固定资产(按行业分)(2013年)
TOTAL INVESTMENT IN FIXED ASSETS AND ITS INCREMENTAL FIXED ASSETS (GROUPED BY SECTOR) (2013)

单位：万元 (10000 yuan)

项目	Item	投资额 Investment			新增固定资产 Incremental Fixed Assets		
		合计 Total	中央 Central	地方 Local	合计 Total	中央 Central	地方 Local
合计	**Total**	**70321895**	**9792533**	**60529362**	**31638183**	**5704123**	**25934060**
农、林、牧、渔业	**Agriculture, Forestry, Animal Production and Hunting, Fishing**	**1734307**	**6398**	**1727909**	**1085835**	**715**	**1085120**
农业	Agriculture	219397	4447	214950	137850		137850
林业	Forestry	1391228		1391228	855115		855115
畜牧业	Animal Production and Hunting	26806		26806	20060		20060
渔业	Fishing	1690		1690	1060		1060
农、林、牧、渔服务业	Service Activities for Agriculture, Forestry, Animal Production and Hunting, Fishing	95186	1951	93235	71750	715	71035
采矿业	**Mining and Quarrying**	**91031**	**11075**	**79956**	**38649**		**38649**
煤炭开采和洗选业	Mining and Washing of Coal	34975	11075	23900	7875		7875
黑色金属矿采选业	Mining of Ferrous Metal Ores	56056		56056	30774		30774
制造业	**Manufacturing**	**4663748**	**756636**	**3907112**	**4916622**	**645397**	**4271225**
农副食品加工业	Processing of Food from Agricultural Products	72107		72107	40186		40186
食品制造业	Manufacture of Foods	106938	15322	91616	67283		67283
酒、饮料和精制茶制造业	Manufacture of Wines, Beverage and Refined Tea	72753		72753	44452		44452
烟草制品业	Manufacture of Cigarettes and Tobacco	6043	6043		25164	25164	
纺织业	Manufacture of Textile	8494		8494	6570		6570
纺织服装、服饰业	Manufacture of Textile Wearing Apparel and Ornament						
皮革、毛皮、羽毛及其制品和制鞋业	Manufacture of Leather, Fur, Feather and Its Products, and Footwear	1772		1772	11160		11160
木材加工及木、竹藤、棕、草制品	Processing of Timbers, Manufacture of Wood, Bamboo, Rattan, Palm and Straw Products	2085		2085	2700		2700
家具制造业	Manufacture of Furniture	31661		31661	29477		29477
造纸及纸制品业	Manufacture of Paper and Paper Products	9261		9261	9046		9046
印刷和记录媒介复制业	Printing, Reproduction of Recording Media	74797	23798	50999	59832	22753	37079
文教、工美、体育和娱乐用品制造业	Manufacture of Articles for Culture, Education, Artwork, Sport and Entertainment Activities	27616	1226	26390	17829	1226	16603
石油加工、炼焦及核燃料加工业	Processing of Petroleum, Coking, Processing of Nucleus Fuel	113856	110146	3710	192470	191318	1152
化学原料及化学制品制造业	Manufacture of Chemical Raw Materials and Chemical Products	272130	186339	85791	357689	312522	45167
医药制造业	Manufacture of Medicines	541261	126207	415054	119285		119285
化学纤维制造业	Manufacture of Chemical Fibers	11083		11083	2224		2224
橡胶和塑料制品业	Manufacture of Rubber and Plastic Products	11522		11522	3288		3288
非金属矿物制品业	Manufacture of Non-metallic Mineral Products	89367	276	89091	180759		180759
黑色金属冶炼及压延加工业	Manufacture and Pressing of Ferrous Metals	4035		4035			
有色金属冶炼及压延加工业	Manufacture and Pressing of Non-ferrous Metals	2670		2670	2037		2037
金属制品业	Manufacture of Fabricated Metal Products	162984	50055	112929	108713	28040	80673
通用设备制造业	Manufacture of General-Purpose Machinery	74246		74246	68592		68592

注：1. 本表分行业数据不含农户投资。
2. 行业划分执行2011年国民经济行业分类标准（GB/T 4754-2011）。

Note: a) The figures of grouping exclude investment of rural households.
b) Sectors are classified in accordance with the Standard for Classification of National Economic Sectors 2011 (GB/T 4754-2011).

5-7 续表 1 Continued 1

单位：万元 (10000 yuan)

项目	Item	投资额 Investment			新增固定资产 Incremental Fixed Assets		
		合计 Total	中央 Central	地方 Local	合计 Total	中央 Central	地方 Local
专用设备制造业	Manufacture of Special-Purpose Machinery	207987	5937	202050	116125	9613	106512
汽车制造业	Manufacture of Motor Vehicles	1576392	12999	1563393	375705	12952	362753
铁路、船舶、航空航天和其他运输设备制造业	Manufacture of Railway Locomotives, Building of Ships and Boats, Manufacture of Air and Spacecrafts and Other Transportation Equipment	255515	192328	63187	18581	14781	3800
电气机械及器材制造业	Manufacture of Electrical Machinery and Equipment	77889	49	77840	99306	49	99257
计算机、通信和其他电子设备制造业	Manufacture of Computer, Communication Equipment and Other Electronic Equipment	726604	18692	707912	2810405	25868	2784537
仪器仪表制造业	Manufacture of Measuring Instrument and Meter	71789	4311	67478	75942	351	75591
其他制造业	Other Manufacturing	12329	2783	9546	1801	760	1041
废弃资源综合利用业	Waste Recycling and Recovery	1480		1480	4850		4850
金属制品、机械和设备修理业	Repair of Fabricated Metal Products, Machinery and Equipment	125	125				
电力、热力、燃气及水生产和供应业	**Production and Distribution of Electricity, Heating Power, Gas and Water**	**2703631**	**165269**	**2538362**	**1634243**	**567**	**1633676**
电力、热力的生产和供应业	Production and Supply of Electric Power and Heat Power	1874735	165269	1709466	1551467	567	1550900
燃气生产和供应业	Production and Distribution of Gas	381352		381352	31849		31849
水的生产和供应业	Production and Distribution of Water	447544		447544	50927		50927
建筑业	**Construction**	**73652**	**5839**	**67813**	**90763**	**37855**	**52908**
房屋建筑业	Construction of Building	17142	5839	11303	51855	37855	14000
土木工程建筑业	Civil Engineering Construction	28473		28473	19138		19138
建筑安装业	Construction Installation	7167		7167	2470		2470
建筑装饰和其他建筑业	Building Completion, Finishing and Other Construction	20870		20870	17300		17300
批发和零售业	**Wholesale and Retail Trade**	**507453**	**197740**	**309713**	**259135**	**15976**	**243159**
批发业	Wholesale	380565	197740	182825	78176	15976	62200
零售业	Retail Trade	126888		126888	180959		180959
交通运输、仓储和邮政业	**Transport, Storage and Post**	**6814391**	**2263179**	**4551212**	**4683874**	**2977073**	**1706801**
铁路运输业	Transport via Railway	368652	367181	1471	1268738	1268738	
道路运输业	Transport via Road	4389211	2260	4386951	1629063		1629063
水上运输业	Water Transport						
航空运输业	Air Transport	1624608	1617297	7311	1587197	1587197	
管道运输业	Transport via Pipeline	266508	263308	3200			
装卸搬运和运输代理业	Loading, Unloading, Portage and Other Transport Services	880		880	2480		2480
仓储业	Storage	129189	2734	126455	44604	1658	42946
邮政业	Post	35343	10399	24944	151792	119480	32312
住宿和餐饮业	**Accommodation and Restaurants**	**781313**	**217786**	**563527**	**39658**	**824**	**38834**
住宿业	Accommodation	752129	217786	534343	35190	824	34366
餐饮业	Restaurants	29184		29184	4468		4468
信息传输、软件和信息技术服务业	**Information Transmission, Software and Information Technology Services**	**2097423**	**615891**	**1481532**	**712403**	**220947**	**491456**
电信、广播电视和卫星传输服务	Telecommunications, Broadcasting, Television and Satellite Transmission Services	1116794	276225	840569	372873	143911	228962
互联网和相关服务	Internet and Related Services	269003		269003	168623		168623
软件和信息技术服务业	Software and Information Technology Services	711626	339666	371960	170907	77036	93871
金融业	**Finance**	**573857**	**437504**	**136353**	**344528**	**276851**	**67677**
货币金融服务	Monetary Financial Services	300223	298179	2044	236353	235074	1279
资本市场服务	Capital Market Services	32485		32485	40922		40922
保险业	Insurance	112797	47583	65214	67253	41777	25476
其他金融业	Other Financial Services	128352	91742	36610			

5-7 续表 2 Continued 2

单位：万元 (10000 yuan)

项　目	Item	投资额 Investment			新增固定资产 Incremental Fixed Assets		
		合计 Total	中央 Central	地方 Local	合计 Total	中央 Central	地方 Local
房地产业	**Real Estate**	**38651990**	**2691498**	**35960492**	**12633666**	**510358**	**12123308**
租赁和商务服务业	**Renting and Leasing Activities and Business Services**	**504850**	**41982**	**462868**	**106955**	**11061**	**95894**
租赁业	Renting and Leasing Activities	16782		16782	17462		17462
商务服务业	Business Services	488068	41982	446086	89493	11061	78432
科学研究和技术服务业	**Scientific Research and Ddevelopment, Technical Services**	**1274042**	**1053992**	**220050**	**665410**	**605142**	**60268**
研究与试验发展	Research and Experimental Development	794544	721319	73225	487089	445040	42049
专业技术服务业	Professional Technique Services	169871	122374	47497	46959	34130	12829
科技推广和应用服务业	Technique Generalization and Application Services	309627	210299	99328	131362	125972	5390
水利、环境和公共设施管理业	**Management of Water Conservancy, Environment and Public Facilities**	**5155569**	**41680**	**5113889**	**2133150**		**2133150**
水利管理业	Management of Water Conservancy	1300015	4768	1295247	399855		399855
生态保护和环境治理业	Ecological Protection and Environmental Control	163856		163856	61219		61219
公共设施管理业	Management of Public Facilities	3691698	36912	3654786	1672076		1672076
居民服务、修理和其他服务业	**Resident Services, Repair and Other Services**	**146443**		**146443**	**108092**		**108092**
居民服务业	Resident Services	14003		14003	17535		17535
机动车、电子产品和日用产品修理业	Repair of Motor Vehicles, Electronics and Household Applicances	5489		5489	1161		1161
其他服务业	Other Services	126951		126951	89396		89396
教　育	**Education**	**1427356**	**623625**	**803731**	**707911**	**221886**	**486025**
卫生和社会工作	**Health Care and Social Works**	**608930**	**180615**	**428315**	**119511**	**17488**	**102023**
卫　生	Health Care	520591	180615	339976	74198	17488	56710
社会工作	Social Work activities	88339		88339	45313		45313
文化、体育和娱乐业	**Culture, Sports and Entertainment**	**1116274**	**297614**	**818660**	**565537**	**130108**	**435429**
新闻出版业	Journalism and Publishing	91572	87100	4472	1998	741	1257
广播、电视、电影和影视录音制作业	Radio Broadcasting, Television,Movies, Videos and Sound Recording	301937	173875	128062	164279	110871	53408
文化艺术业	Culture and Arts	307872	34435	273437	308554	15499	293055
体　育	Sports Activities	68391	2204	66187	63706	2997	60709
娱乐业	Entertainment	346502		346502	27000		27000
公共管理、社会保障和社会组织	**Public Administration, Social Security and Social Organizations**	**900436**	**184210**	**716226**	**314489**	**31875**	**282614**
中国共产党机关	Organs of Communist Party of China	93367	93367		31875	31875	
国家机构	Organs of State	585007	17090	567917	196514		196514
社会保障	Social Security	80524	58750	21774	17672		17672
群众团体、社会团体和其他成员组织	Mass Communities, Social Organizations and Other Membership Organizations	125945	15003	110942	58030		58030
基层群众自治组织	Grass Roots Self-government Organizations	15593		15593	10398		10398

5-8 全社会房屋建筑施工及竣工面积(1978-2013年)
FLOOR SPACE OF BUILDINGS UNDER CONSTRUCTION AND COMPLETED (1978-2013)

单位：万平方米 (10000 sq.m)

年 份 Year	施工面积 Floor Space of Buildings under Construction	#住 宅 Residential Buildings	竣工面积 Floor Space of Buildings Completed	#住 宅 Residential Buildings	中 央 Central	地 方 Local
1978	956.3	456.8	407.0	190.4	158.7	248.3
1979	1340.6	780.2	537.6	304.9	235.2	302.4
1980	1704.1	1037.0	648.4	396.9	315.8	332.6
1981-1985			**3941.6**	**2383.4**	**1723.2**	**2218.4**
1981	1875.8	1189.9	726.9	462.6	327.2	399.7
1982	1938.6	1210.1	728.3	463.8	303.7	424.6
1983	1952.1	1163.6	775.5	514.0	312.3	463.2
1984	2351.9	1327.1	818.7	437.6	352.7	466.0
1985	2802.7	1599.2	892.2	505.4	427.3	464.9
1986-1990			**5142.4**	**2939.9**	**2635.1**	**2507.3**
1986	2760.7	1557.4	906.5	532.7	424.5	482.0
1987	2578.0	1273.2	1042.2	608.9	507.8	534.4
1988	2642.2	1226.2	1065.6	623.5	499.6	566.0
1989	2450.8	1167.8	1046.9	601.8	565.8	481.1
1990	2864.9	1561.9	1081.2	573.0	637.4	443.8
1991-1995			**6206.7**	**3707.2**	**1869.2**	**4337.5**
1991	2818.0	1612.0	1036.4	601.8	396.2	640.2
1992	3126.8	1784.7	1111.4	681.2	399.3	712.1
1993	3607.5	1866.4	1158.0	654.8	320.5	837.5
1994	4460.9	2315.1	1370.7	832.1	366.8	1003.9
1995	5524.3	2897.6	1530.2	937.3	386.4	1143.8
1996-2000			**9644.3**	**5979.9**	**2726.7**	**6917.6**
1996	5633.2	2696.9	1517.5	870.4	452.0	1065.5
1997	5819.4	2881.3	1625.7	996.8	492.2	1133.5
1998	6496.1	3473.7	1821.5	1093.1	508.4	1313.1
1999	6556.5	3754.8	2321.4	1519.9	655.3	1666.1
2000	6995.9	4083.3	2358.2	1499.7	618.8	1739.4
2001-2005			**17781.6**	**11992.2**	**1733.0**	**16048.6**
2001	8203.3	5226.4	2554.6	1804.9	490.6	2064.0
2002	9697.7	6193.3	3121.8	2191.4	441.8	2680.0
2003	11262.2	7011.3	3222.8	2322.3	242.1	2980.7
2004	13121.9	7513.1	4203.2	2649.5	301.9	3901.3
2005	14096.2	8043.2	4679.2	3024.1	256.6	4422.6
2006-2010			**20059.1**	**10993.8**	**2002.6**	**18056.4**
2006	14069.2	7113.0	4191.0	2391.6	388.6	3802.4
2007	14146.7	6788.8	3866.4	2098.0	399.6	3466.8
2008	14145.3	6656.3	3840.7	1871.1	496.8	3343.9
2009	14380.6	7058.4	4252.6	2369.6	388.4	3864.2
2010	15572.1	7932.9	3908.4	2263.5	329.2	3579.1
2011	18065.2	8817.1	4032.9	2121.8	425.5	3607.4
2012	20045.4	9217.8	3723.5	1992.5	216.9	3506.6
2013	21526.0	9469.0	3989.7	2154.8	255.2	3734.4

注：2007年及以前，表中数据不包含农村农户房屋施工和竣工面积。
Note: Figures in and before 2007 excluded buildings under construction and completed in rural areas.

5-9 全社会房屋建筑施工及竣工面积
FLOOR SPACE OF BUILDINGS UNDER CONSTRUCTION AND COMPLETED

单位：万平方米 (10000 sq.m)

项　目	Item	2013	2012	占竣工面积比重(%) Proportion in Completed Floor Space (%)	
				2013	2012
施工总面积	**Floor Space of Buildings under Construction**	**21526.0**	**20045.4**		
竣工总面积	**Floor Space of Buildings Completed**	**3989.7**	**3723.5**	**100.0**	**100.0**
按隶属关系分	**By Affiliation**				
中　央	Central	255.2	216.9	6.4	5.8
地　方	Local	3734.4	3506.6	93.6	94.2
#国　有	State-owned	692.0	471.1	17.3	12.7
集　体	Collectively-owned	34.7	67.5	0.9	1.8
按功能区分	**By Functional Zone**				
首都功能核心区	Capital Core Functional Area	93.4	153.3	2.3	4.1
城市功能拓展区	Urban Function Extension Area	1137.8	1352.5	28.5	36.3
城市发展新区	Urban Development New Area	2181.9	1710.1	54.7	45.9
生态涵养发展区	Ecological Conservation Area	576.6	507.6	14.5	13.6

5-10 房地产开发面积(1990-2013年)

单位：万平方米

年份 Year	商品房施工面积 Floor Space of Commercial Buildings under Construction	#本年新开工面积 Floor Space of Buildings Newly Started Floor	住宅 Residential Houses	#经济适用房 Affordable Houses	#公寓别墅 Apartments & Villas	办公楼(写字楼) Office Buildings	商业、非公益用房及其他 Buildings for Commercial Use, Non-public Buildings and Others	商品房竣工面积 Floor Space of Comnmercial Buildings Completed	住宅 Residential Houses	#经济适用房 Affordable Houses	#公寓别墅 Apartments & Villas
1990	774.0	249.1	643.4			17.4	41.2	271.6	226.5		
1991	815.1	317.6	692.1			2.1	57.6	275.2	240.4		
1992	1021.1	508.6	865.4			7.6	54.8	331.4	300.8		
1993	1262.0	524.8	887.6					356.4	280.6		
1994	1593.2	659.4	1107.6					445.7	385.6		
1995	2810.2	1012.2	1728.7		334.8	462.7	252.6	653.0	506.3		55.6
1996	2824.6	578.7	1520.7		316.8	638.7	283.9	663.4	470.8		43.3
1997	2869.6	848.4	1541.1		335.7	637.7	260.8	682.3	478.3		99.8
1998	3499.1	1193.4	2107.2		368.3	590.7	297.7	842.8	588.7		57.0
1999	3784.0	1061.8	2447.9	301.4	390.7	484.4	281.3	1208.5	908.3	114.1	93.2
2000	4455.0	1676.9	2971.6	296.6	537.8	449.1	281.3	1365.6	1013.7	184.9	164.2
2001	5966.7	2789.8	4349.6	563.1	494.4	495.5	330.6	1707.4	1393.4	214.0	150.8
2002	7510.7	3206.0	5397.5	660.2	550.8	672.5	400.3	2384.4	1926.2	228.4	161.9
2003	9070.7	3433.8	6352.9	802.5	705.0	901.3	557.7	2593.7	2080.8	322.8	127.9
2004	9931.3	3054.3	6759.4	793.2	776.0	1122.4	641.8	3067.0	2343.9	298.8	153.2
2005	10748.5	2965.9	7283.4	783.4	1023.5	1209.8	809.2	3770.9	2841.4	325.6	342.7
2006	10483.5	3179.4	6311.3	551.9	913.8	1245.8	1403.0	3193.9	2193.3	270.1	255.6
2007	10438.6	2557.4	5914.5	440.1	1009.2	1364.6	1482.1	2891.7	1854.0	188.6	239.6
2008	10014.3	2337.2	5538.2	544.9	954.7	1287.2	1429.8	2558.0	1399.3	101.1	233.0
2009	9719.1	2246.6	5551.9	628.7	840.9	1132.2	1323.4	2678.6	1613.2	98.2	213.7
2010	10300.9	2974.2	6176.0	572.7	830.0	1054.8	1229.3	2386.7	1498.5	144.6	183.2
2011	12065.4	4246.1	7168.1	444.8	754.8	1422.7	1187.5	2245.2	1316.1	74.6	133.0
2012	13122.5	3224.2	7510.4	435.1	642.2	1711.9	1236.9	2390.9	1522.7	188.5	135.1
2013	13886.9	3577.5	7406.9	310.5	530.1	2114.1	4365.9	2666.4	1692.0	95.7	133.5

注：1. 2005年及以前的商品房销售面积为竣工后的全部商品房销售面积，2006年及以后为期房与现房销售面积之和。

2. 2010年起，商品房销售面积中包含定向安置房数据。

3. 2012年及以前商业、非公益用房及其他只包括商业及服务性等营业性用房。自2013年起包括：厂房、仓库、商业营业用房、服务业用房、教育用房、文化体育用房、医疗用房、科研用房及其他用房。

STATISTICS FOR FLOOR SPACE OF REAL ESTATE DEVELOPENT (1990-2013)

(10000 sq.m)

办公楼（写字楼） Office Buildings	商业、非公益用房及其他 Buildings for Commercial Use, Non-public Buildings and Others	商品房销售面积 Floor Space of Commercial Buildings Sold	住宅 Residential Houses	#经济适用房 Affordable Houses	公寓别墅 Apartments & Villas	办公楼（写字楼） Office Buildings	商业、非公益用房及其他 Buildings for Commercial Use, Non-public Buildings and Others	年末商品房待售面积 Floor Space of Vacant Commercial Buildings at the Year End	#住宅 Residential Houses	#一年以内 Less than One Year	#三年以上 Over Three Years
9.7	13.3	142.2									
0.9	10.9	154.0	152.5								
2.7	8.3	159.1	153.0								
		182.0	182.0								
		168.6	149.0			17.2	1.1				
27.9	43.5	191.9	180.0		16.7	4.0	4.5	81.5			
79.0	38.3	215.3	183.1		24.9	13.7	14.4	214.8	179.6		
80.9	42.4	290.9	256.2		53.5	18.8	8.0	298.3	258.9		
92.3	69.8	409.2	377.0		40.0	23.2	7.0	334.8	262.9		
108.8	43.1	544.4	484.7	45.8	55.1	48.0	6.8	624.3	529.1		
97.2	48.7	956.9	898.2	166.5	107.6	41.2	6.1	627.4	515.1		
98.0	48.2	1205.0	1127.5	185.2	120.8	49.8	17.4	774.0	634.1	429.4	84.6
97.4	82.9	1708.3	1604.4	220.7	153.6	44.0	32.9	919.0	763.2	557.9	96.4
94.0	117.5	1895.8	1771.1	320.0	131.9	38.1	50.8	1123.4	896.9	745.5	109.8
153.9	225.3	2472.0	2285.8	306.3	172.7	92.5	60.2	1044.1	723.8	744.4	72.9
287.8	180.9	2803.2	2566.0	304.0	302.1	131.2	66.9	1374.2	799.7	993.5	75.8
304.4	289.2	2607.6	2205.0	176.3	276.9	260.3	108.6	1039.7	494.1	628.3	106.9
314.8	315.1	2176.6	1731.5	100.1	319.3	265.7	134.8	1136.2	411.8	697.2	203.1
364.6	313.1	1335.4	1031.4	108.3	164.6	139.4	112.4	1438.3	522.7	945.1	209.8
316.6	322.4	2362.3	1880.5	82.2	339.8	255.8	157.1	1351.4	426.8	768.0	229.9
198.4	271.9	1639.5	1201.4	49.5	175.9	208.1	142.1	1482.7	511.9	810.4	239.7
245.2	232.4	1440.0	1035.0	39.4	93.3	211.4	108.7	1792.6	699.8	1021.5	298.3
226.8	240.1	1943.7	1483.4	85.9	116.9	253.5	114.0	1911.8	789.5	958.7	309.0
273.1	701.3	1903.1	1363.7	106.6	87.8	317.9	221.5	1861.4	829.3	922.3	337.7

Note: a) Floor space of commercial buildings sold in 2005 and before was the floor space of completed commercial buildings, and after 2006, the figure is the sum of completed commercial buildings and those under construction.

b) Since 2010, the floor space of completed commercial buildings has included figures of targeted resettlement buildings.

c) In and Before 2012, buildings for commercial use, non-public buildings and others only included business and commercial buildings. Since 2013, it has included: factory buildings, warehouses, commercial buildings, buildings for service industy, education buildings, cultural and sports buildings, medical buildings, scientific research buildings and others.

5-11 房地产开发情况(1990-2013年)
STATISTICS FOR REAL ESTATE DEVELOPENT (1990-2013)

年份 Year	房地产开发企业个数(个) Number of Real Estate Development Enterprises (unit)	房地产开发投资额(亿元) Investment in Real Estate Development (100 million yuan)	#土地购置费 Land Purchase Cost	按用途分 By Purpose of Investment: 住宅 Residential Buildings	写字楼(办公楼) Office Buildings	商业、非公益用房及其他 Buildings for Commercial Use, Non-public Buildings and Others	按投资构成分 By Investment Structure: #建筑安装工程 Construction and Installation Projects	#设备工器具购置 Purchase of Equipment, Tools and Devices
1990		22.5		12.3			18.4	
1991-1995		**568.4**		**264.8**			**341.9**	
1991	40	24.0		14.0			16.8	
1992	42	33.7		20.0			20.7	
1993	74	58.4	2.5	38.1			43.4	0.4
1994	81	99.5	4.0	50.3			69.3	0.9
1995	623	352.8	52.4	142.4	71.5	35.2	191.7	8.4
1996-2000		**1979.5**	**161.5**	**950.7**	**351.5**	**161.3**	**1280.6**	**95.5**
1996	554	328.2	15.0	124.9	84.2	35.2	222.0	17.0
1997	601	330.3	23.9	132.9	91.1	29.2	208.0	19.8
1998	585	377.4	28.4	168.0	78.5	36.1	250.7	20.7
1999	716	421.5	36.6	236.6	52.5	30.2	278.6	16.8
2000	893	522.1	57.6	288.3	45.2	30.6	321.3	21.2
2001-2005		**5974.0**	**993.6**	**3239.5**	**696.1**	**368.3**	**3498.9**	**137.8**
2001	1142	783.8	115.6	464.2	72.0	41.7	438.0	22.3
2002	1508	989.4	149.2	586.7	97.3	57.6	572.7	31.5
2003	1546	1202.5	213.2	633.0	142.7	61.3	716.2	24.3
2004	2704	1473.3	275.8	776.0	187.9	94.8	872.1	35.4
2005	3123	1525.0	239.8	779.5	196.2	112.9	881.8	42.3
2006-2010		**10863.2**	**3642.0**	**5211.5**	**1055.2**	**1270.8**	**4550.5**	**255.0**
2006	2882	1719.9	477.9	863.6	216.7	226.0	953.2	55.5
2007	2688	1995.8	644.7	991.7	242.2	267.4	1015.3	58.9
2008	3433	1908.7	639.0	940.6	170.5	240.4	829.6	48.6
2009	3171	2337.7	587.7	906.6	166.7	200.7	841.6	45.7
2010	3190	2901.1	1292.7	1509.0	259.1	336.3	910.8	46.3
2011	3069	3036.3	1301.2	1778.3	363.8	296.7	1235.1	38.5
2012	2960	3153.4	1102.7	1628.0	384.8	275.9	1383.1	65.7
2013	2927	3483.4	1159.5	1724.6	611.7	1147.1	1510.0	53.0

注：2012年及以前商业、非公益用房及其他只包括商业及服务性等营业性用房。自2013年起包括：厂房、仓库、商业营业用房、服务业用房、教育用房、文化体育用房、医疗用房、科研用房及其他用房。

Note: In and Before 2012, buildings for commercial use, non-public buildings and others only included business and commercial buildings. Since 2013, it has included: factory buildings, warehouses, commercial buildings, buildings for service industy, education buildings, cultural and sports buildings, medical buildings, scientific research buildings and others.

5-12 房地产开发企业经营情况(2013年)
REAL ESTATE DEVELOPMENT ENTERPRISES (2013)

项　目	Item	企业单位个数(个) Number of Enterprises (unit)	实收资本合计(万元) Paid-in Capital (10000 yuan)	资产总计(万元) Total Assets (10000 yuan)	主营业务收入(万元) Main Business Income (10000 yuan)	利润总额(万元) Total Profits (10000 yuan)	年末从业人员(人) Number of Staff at the Year End (person)
合　计	**Total**	**2927**	**52368500**	**390374393**	**38148592**	**7311005**	**93628**
按企业登记注册类型分	**By Registration Type**						
内资企业	Domestically-Funded Enterprises	2668	42972033	340139871	32025813	5411138	80119
国有企业	State-owned Enterprises	68	3921250	13346860	533728	132359	5844
集体企业	Collectively-owned Enterprises	19	71940	1401010	37898	22694	430
私营企业	Private Enterprises	625	2108361	22206340	1362046	-179314	10232
股份合作企业	Joint-equity Cooperative Enterprises	2	7000	91337		-1702	80
股份有限公司	Companies Limited by Shares	65	5028066	32834191	2334038	957375	3742
有限责任公司	Limited Liability Companies	1889	31835417	270260134	27758103	4479725	59791
港澳台商投资企业	Hong Kong, Macao and Taiwan-invested Enterprises	157	5984033	31164839	4237249	1251793	8173
港澳台合资经营	Joint Ventures	60	1941010	8062391	1968249	522113	2460
港澳台合作经营	Cooperative	58	1348962	8837679	1162035	345043	2754
港澳台商独资企业	Solely-funded Enterprises	39	2694061	14264768	1106965	384637	2959
港澳台商投资股份有限公司	Companies Limited by Shares						
外商投资企业	Foreign-invested Enterprises	102	3412433	19069683	1885531	648074	5336
中外合资经营	Joint Ventures	40	1323839	7197504	532141	144456	2233
中外合作经营	Cooperative	41	704522	4442774	935665	293839	1702
外资(独资)企业	Solely-funded Enterprises	18	1043494	4169473	258643	164721	916
外商投资股份有限公司	Companies Limited by Shares	3	340578	3259933	159081	45059	485
按隶属关系分	**By Affiliation**						
中　央	Central	111	5277082	30018796	2935043	770170	4544
地　方	Local	2816	47091417	360355597	35213549	6540835	89084
按资质等级分	**By Qualification Grade**						
一　级	First-grade	116	8296080	83904782	6938934	2226753	13085
二　级	Second-grade	201	6426787	58181167	5794497	1455712	14038
三　级	Third-grade	258	4050091	39172752	4393230	618674	10054
四　级	Fourth-grade	1217	15181170	117234307	12465747	1674617	31497
暂　定	Provisional	557	10983406	61124362	6802471	970992	14934
其　他	Others	578	7430966	30757023	1753712	364257	10020
按营业状况分	**By Operating Condition**						
营　业	Operating	2704	51262754	385811514	38056090	7312643	92770
停　业	Closed	199	864674	3775769	60868	-20856	675
筹　建	In Preparation						
当年关闭	Closed in the Present Year	11	24000	76775	31457	19707	5
当年破产	Bankrupted in the Present Year						
其　他	Others	13	217072	710335	177	-489	178

5-13 房地产开发企业开发建设情况(2013年)
DEVELOPMENT OF REAL ESTATE ENTERPRISES (2013)

单位：万元、平方米 (10000 yuan,sq.m)

项目	Item	全市合计 Total	#国有企业 State-owned	#三资企业 Foreign Funded	按隶属关系分 By Affiliation 中央 Central	地方 Local
计划总投资	**Total Planned Investment**	**205217817**	**14647866**	**19045925**	**11869100**	**193348717**
开始建设至本年度累计	**Accumulative Investment Completed**					
完成投资	**from Beginning to the End of This Year**	**144732472**	**10908508**	**13753429**	**8506686**	**136225786**
本年完成投资合计	**Investment Completed in the Year**	**34834045**	**2358559**	**3022320**	**1449596**	**33384449**
#土地购置费	Land Purchase Cost	11594732	348058	1526288	314792	11279940
本年完成投资按用途分	**Grouped by Purpose of Investment**					
住宅	Residential Buildings	17245610	1378657	914619	893279	16352331
#普通住房	Ordinary Residential Houses					
别墅、高档公寓	Villas, High-end Apartments	1356381	29525	192565	52905	1303476
办公楼(写字楼)	Office Buildings	6117479	125496	943914	139522	5977957
商业、非公益用房及其他	Buildings for Commercial Use, Non-public Buildings and Others	11470956	854406	1163787	416795	11054161
本年购置土地面积	**Land Space Purchased This Year**	**9321334**	**722910**	**34822**	**299287**	**9022047**

5-14 保障性安居工程建设情况
CONSTRUCTION OF GOVERNMENT-SUBSIDIZED HOUSING PROJECTS

单位：亿元、万平方米 (100 million yuan,10000sq.m)

项　　目	Item	2013	2012	2013年为2012年% 2013as % of 2012
完成投资额	**Investment Completed**	**729.7**	**857.5**	**85.1**
经济适用房	Affordable Houses	45.5	61.2	74.3
限价房	Price-capped Houses	112.3	153.9	73.0
公租(廉租)房	Public Rental (Low-rent) Houses	77.9	49.3	158.0
定向安置房	Targeted Resettlement Houses	494.0	593.1	83.3
施工面积	**Floor Space Under Construction**	**4857.1**	**4821**	**100.7**
经济适用房	Affordable Housing	380.7	557.7	68.3
限价房	Price-capped Housing	599.2	689.6	86.9
公租(廉租)房	Public Rental (Low-rent) Housing	352.2	296.3	118.9
定向安置房	Resettlement Housing	3525.0	3277.4	107.6
竣工面积	**Floor Space Completed**	**1079.2**	**752.6**	**143.4**
经济适用房	Affordable Houses	115.3	241.0	47.8
限价房	Price-capped Houses	196.2	197.7	99.2
公租(廉租)房	Public Rental (Low-rent) Houses	78.0	37.8	206.3
定向安置房	Targeted Resettlement Houses	689.7	276.1	249.8
本年新开工面积	**Floor Space Newly Started in the Year**	**964.9**	**1112.3**	**86.7**
经济适用房	Affordable Houses	57.9	74.8	77.4
限价房	Price-capped Houses	101.2	142.2	71.2
公租(廉租)房	Public Rental (Low-rent) Houses	119.5	109.8	108.8
定向安置房	Targeted Resettlement Houses	686.3	785.5	87.4

主要统计指标解释

全社会固定资产投资 包括城镇固定资产投资（含房地产开发投资）和农村固定资产投资。

城镇固定资产投资 是指城镇各种登记注册类型的企业、事业、行政单位及个体户进行的计划总投资在500万元及以上的建设项目投资。镇及镇以上各级政府及主管部门直接领导、管理的建设项目和企事业单位的投资均为城镇固定资产投资。

农村固定资产投资 农村投资统计以投资项目建设地址所在的地域为界定农村投资统计的范围，即农村投资是指各种投资主体建设的建设项目地址在农村区域范围内的、以满足农村居民生产、生活需要为主要目的的各种投资活动。农村固定资产投资包括农户和非农户固定资产投资。

新增固定资产投资 是指报告期内交付使用的固定资产价值。包括本年内建成投入生产或交付使用的工程投资和达到固定资产标准的设备、工具、器具的投资及有关应摊入的费用。属于增加固定资产价值的其他建设费用，应随同交付使用的工程一并计入新增固定资产。

基础设施投资 是指能够为企业提供作为中间投入用于生产的基本需求；能够为消费者提供所需的基本消费服务；能够为社区提供用于改善不利的外部环境的服务等建设的投资，包括固定资产投资中用于市政工程、电信工程、公共设施和水利环保等建设的投资。

上年末结余资金 是指上年资金来源中没有形成固定资产投资额而结余的资金。包括尚未用到工程上去的材料价值、未开始安装的需要安装设备价值及结存的现金和银行存款等。

本年资金来源小计 是指固定资产投资单位在报告期收到的，用于固定资产投资的各种货币资金。包括国家预算内资金、国内贷款、债券、利用外资、自筹资金和其他资金。

国家预算内资金 分为财政拨款和财政安排的贷款两部分。包括中央财政的基本建设基金(分经营性基金和非经营性基金两部分)、专项支出(如煤代油专项等)、收回再贷、贴息资金，财政安排的挖潜改造和新产品试制支出、城建支出、商业部门简易建筑支出、不发达地区发展基金等资金中用于固定资产投资的资金；地方财政中由国家统筹安排的资金等。

国内贷款 是指报告期固定资产投资项目单位向银行及非银行金融机构借入的用于固定资产投资的各种国内借款，包括银行利用自有资金及吸收存款发放的贷款、上级主管部门拨入的国内贷款、国家专项贷款(包括煤代油贷款、劳改煤矿专项贷款等)，地方财政专项资金安排的贷款、国内储备贷款、周转贷款等。

利用外资 是指报告期收到的用于固定资产建造和购置投资的境外资金(包括设备、材料、技术在内)。包括外商直接投资、对外借款(外国政府贷款、国际金融组织贷款、出口信贷、外国银行商业贷款、对外发行债券和股票)及外商其他投资(包括利用外商投资收益在国内进行固定资产再投资活动的资金)。不包括我国自有外汇资金(包括国家外汇、地方外汇、留成外汇、调剂外汇和国内银行自有资金发行的外汇贷款等)。

自筹资金 指固定资产投资单位报告期收到的，由各地区、各部门及企业、事业单位筹集用于固定资产投资的预算外资金，包括中央各部门、各级地方和企业、事业单位的自有资金。

其他资金来源 是指在报告期收到的除以上各种资金之外其他用于固定资产投资的资金。包括社会集资、个人资金、无偿捐赠的资金及其他单位拨入的资金等。

住宅建设投资 是指专供居住使用的房屋，包括职工家属宿舍、职工单身宿舍、学生宿舍和经济适用房等房屋建造的投资，不包括购置的商品住宅。

建筑安装工程投资（建筑安装工作量） 是指各种房屋、建筑物的建造工程，各种设备、装置的安装工程，又称建筑安装工作量。建筑工程投资必须经过兴工动料，通过施工活动才能实现。在安装工程中，不包括被安装设备本身价值。

设备工器具购置 是指建设单位或企、事业单位购置或自制的，达到固定资产标准的设备、工具、器具的价值。

房地产开发投资 指从本年1月1日起至本年最后一天止完成的全部用于房屋建设工程和土地开发工程的投资额，以及公益性建筑和土地购置费等投资。

土地购置费 通过各种方式取得土地使用权而支付的费用（包括开发补偿费）。土地购置费包括：（1）通过“划拨”方式取得的土地使用权所支付的土地补偿费、附着物和青苗补偿费、安置补偿费及土地征收管理费等；竣工后计入新增固定资产。（2）通过“出让”方式（包括协议出让、招、拍、挂出让）取得的土地使用权所支付的费用；竣工后不计入新增固定资产。土地购置费按当期实际发生额计入投资。土地购置费为分期付款的，应分期计入投资。

经济适用住房 指政府提供政策优惠，限定套型面积和销售价格，按照合理标准建设，面向城镇低收入住房困难家庭供应的具有保障性质的政策性住房。

限价商品住房 指政府控制土地出让价格，限定销售价格和套型面积，向城镇中等收入家庭供应的普通商品住房。

公共租赁住房 指政府提供财政投入和政策支持，限定套型建筑面积标准，按照合理标准组织建设，或通过长期租赁等方式筹集，按照当地政府规定的供应标准，面向城镇中等偏下收入住房困难家庭、新就业职工和有稳定职业并在城镇居住一定年限的外来务工人员供应的保障性住房。

廉租住房 指政府提供财政投入和政策支持，限定套型建筑面积标准，按照合理标准组织建设，或通过购买、改建和租赁等方式筹集，按照当地政府规定的供应标准，面向城镇低收入住房困难家庭供应的具有保障性质的住房。

房屋施工面积 是指报告期内施工的全部房屋建筑面积。包括本期新开工的面积和上年开工跨入本期继续施工房屋面积，以及上期已停建在本期恢复施工的房屋面积。本期竣工和本期施工后又停建、缓建的房屋面积仍包括在施工面积中，多层建筑应填各层建筑面积之和。

房屋竣工面积 是指报告期内房屋建筑按照设计要求已全部完工，达到住人和使用条件，经验收鉴定合格（或达到竣工验收标准），可正式移交使用的各栋房屋建筑面积的总和。

待售面积 指报告期末已竣工的可供销售或出租的商品房屋建筑面积中，尚未销售或出租的商品房屋建筑面积，包括以前年度竣工和本期竣工的房屋面积，但不包括报告期已竣工的拆迁还建，统建代建，公共配套建筑、房地产公司自用及周转房等不可销售或出租的房屋面积。

Explanatory Notes on Main Statistical Indicators

Total Investment in Fixed Assets includes urban investment in fixed assets (including the investment in real estate development) and rural investment in fixed assets.

Investment in Urban Fixed Assets refers to investment in construction projects with a total planned investment over 5,000,000 yuan (inclusive) by enterprises with various types of registration, institutions, administrative units and individuals in urban areas. The investment in construction projects under the direct leadership and management of government agencies at and above town levels and investment by enterprises and public institutions are also calculated in investment in urban fixed assets.

Investment in Rural Fixed Assets refers to all investment activities that are conducted in rural areas to meet the production and living needs of the rural residents. Investment in rural fixed assets consists of investment in fixed assets by rural and non-rural households.

Incremental Fixed Assets means the value of fixed assets put into use in the reporting period, including investment in projects completed and put into use within the year, and investment in equipment, tools and appliances that reach the standard of fixed assets, together with expenses incurred in these activities. Other construction costs adding value to fixed assets shall be calculated in the incremental fixed assets together with the projects put into use.

Infrastructure Investment refers to investment that provides intermediate inputs for enterprise to meet their basic production needs, provides consumers with basic consumer services needed, or provides communities with services for improving external environment, which includes the investment in municipal projects, telecom projects, public facilities, water conservancy and environmental protection.

Surplus Funds by the Year End of the Preceding Year refers to the fund in the previous year that was not included in the investment in fixed assets, including the value of materials not yet used for projects, value of equipment to be installed, and balance of cash and bank deposits.

Subtotal of Funds at Current Year refers to monetary capital received by investors that was used for investment in fixed assets, including funds from state budgetary funds, domestic loans, bonds, foreign investment, self-raised funds and other funds.

State Budgets consists of budgetary appropriation and government loans. More specifically, it consists of infrastructure fund from the central government (operating fund and non-operating fund), earmarked expenditures (e.g. expenditures on replacing oil with coal), refinancing, discount interest funds, expenditures on technical updates, transformation and new products promotion, expenses on urban construction, expenses on temporary construction from business departments, development funds for less developed areas, as well as local budgetary funds transferred from the central budget.

Domestic Loans refer to loans of various forms borrowed by fixed assets investment project entities from banks and non-bank financial institutions for the purpose of investment in fixed assets during the reporting period, including loans issued by banks from their equity funds and deposits, loans appropriated by higher authorities, special loans allocated by the central government (including loans for replacing oil with coal, and special loans for labor camp coal mines), loans arranged by local government from special funds, domestic reserve loans and revolving loans.

Foreign Investment refers to foreign funds received during the reporting period for the investment in construction and purchase of fixed assets (including equipment, materials and technologies), including foreign direct investment, foreign loans (loans from foreign governments and international financial institutions, export credit, commercial loans from foreign banks, issued bonds and stocks overseas), and other foreign investments (including funds for domestic re-investment in fixed assets by earnings from foreign investment). It does not include foreign exchanges owned by China (foreign exchanges owned by the central and local governments, foreign exchanges retained, foreign exchange swap, loans in foreign exchanges issued by the domestic banks with their own funds, etc.).

Self-raised Funds refer to non-budgetary funds for investment in fixed assets received during the reporting period by different regions, departments, enterprises and public institutions, including self-owned funds of central departments, local authorities, enterprises and public institutions.

Other Funds refer to funds for investment in fixed assets received from sources other than those listed above, including social funds, personal funds, donated funds and funds transferred from other institutions.

Investment in Construction of Residential Buildings refer to the investment in houses specially used for residence, including employee family's dormitories, single employees' dormitories, student dormitories, and affordable houses, excluding purchased commercial residences.

Construction and Installation Investment (Workload of Construction and Installation) refers to the investment in construction projects of various houses and buildings, and installation projects of various equipment and devices, also known as the workload of construction and installation. It can only be realized through construction work and consumption of materials. For installation projects, the value of equipment installed is not included.

Purchase of Equipment, Tools and Devices refers to the value of equipment, tools and devices purchased or made by construction companies, enterprises or public institutions, which reach the specified amount of fixed assets.

Real Estate Development Investment refers to all investment used for housing projects and land development projects, together with public welfare buildings and land purchase costs spent from January 1st to the last day of the year.

Land Purchase Cost refers to expenses on acquiring the land use right, including development compensation. It includes: (1) Expenses on land use right by allocation, including land compensation fees, compensation fees for its attached objects and crops; after completion, these expanses will be included in incremental fixed assets. (2) Expenses on land use right by transfer, including fees for agreement transfer, bid invitation, auction and listing; after completion, these expanses will not be included in incremental fixed assets. Land purchase expense shall be accounted according to actual amount paid. If paid by installment, it should be included in investment by stages.

Affordable Houses refer to government-subsidized houses that are supplied to urban low-income households and built in line with reasonable standards, limited size and fixed pricing.

Price-capped Houses refer to ordinary commercial houses with limited size and fixed pricing that are supplied to middle-income urban households, and their land transfer price is controlled by the government.

Public Rental Houses refer to government-subsidized houses that are built in line with reasonable standards and limited size, and can be rented by lower middle-income urban households with housing difficulties, new employees and migrant workers with stable jobs and have lived in the urban area for a certain period.

Low-rent Houses refer to government-subsidized houses that are built in line with reasonable standards and limited size, with funds raised by purchasing, reconstruction or leasing, and can be rented by low-income urban households with housing difficulties.

Floor Space of Buildings under Construction refers to the total floor space of all houses and buildings under construction during the reference period, including floor space of newly started buildings in current period, floor space of construction extended from the previous period to the current period, and floor space of construction suspended during the previous period and resumed in the current period. Floor space of construction completed in the current period, and floor space of construction started and then suspended in the current period are also included in the floor space under construction. For multi-storey buildings, the sum of floor space of all floors shall be calculated.

Floor Space of Buildings Completed refers to the total floor space of all houses and buildings fully completed as required in the design plan during the reference period, which have been examined as qualified for living and use, and can be handed over and put into use.

Floor Space of Vacant Commercial Buildings refers to total floor space of commercial buildings for sale or for renting by the end of the reference period. It consists of the floor space of completed buildings in previous years and in the current year, but does not include relocated houses or buildings of unified construction or agent contract, as well as houses not for sale or renting such as public facilities, houses used by real estate companies and temporary houses.

北京统计年鉴2014 BEIJING STATISTICAL YEARBOOK

财政与税收
GOVERNMENT FINANCE AND REVENUES

一、本章资料的主要内容

本章资料包括北京市财政收支情况，北京市国税、地税税收(费)收入情况。其中财政收支包括历年财政收入、支出及相当于地区生产总值比例等情况；税收（费）收入包括国税、地税税收（费）收入分组情况。

二、本章资料的数据来源

本章财政收支数据由北京市财政局提供；税收（费）数据由北京市国家税务局、北京市地方税务局提供。

Brief Introduction

I. Main Content

Statistics in this chapter include fiscal revenues and expenditures, and state and local tax revenues of Beijing Municipality. Figures of fiscal revenues and expenditures include fiscal revenues, expenditures and their proportions to GDP of Beijing in previous years; figures of tax revenues include the grouped figures of state and local tax revenues.

II. Source of Data

Data of fiscal revenues and expenditures are from Beijing Municipal Bureau of Finance; data of tax revenues are from Beijing Municipal Bureau of State Tax and Beijing Municipal Bureau of Local Tax.

6-1 地方财政收支(1978-2013年)
LOCAL FISCAL REVENUE AND EXPENDITURES (1978-2013)

单位：亿元 (100 million yuan)

年份 Year	地方财政收入 Local Financial Revenue	#地方公共财政预算收入 Local Public Budgetary Revenue	税收收入 Tax Revenue	#增值税 Value-added Tax	#营业税 Operation Tax	#个人所得税 Individual Income Tax	#企业所得税 Company Income Tax	#城市维护建设税 Urban Maintenance and Construction Tax	非税收入 Non-tax Revenue	#政府性基金预算收入 Governmental Fund Budgetary Revenue
1978	50.46		18.25							
1979	47.75		19.41							
1980	51.29		21.22							
1981-1985	**234.27**		**191.96**	**8.34**	**11.46**	**0.61**	**43.77**	**2.16**		
1981	49.12		24.22			0.02	1.76			
1982	47.25		25.81	0.05		0.05	1.43			
1983	39.84		38.03	1.30		0.07	11.70			
1984	45.62		43.91	2.20	1.23	0.13	12.70			
1985	52.44		59.99	4.79	10.23	0.34	16.18	2.16		
1986-1990	**337.13**		**397.96**	**65.02**	**103.00**	**7.29**	**116.89**	**16.67**		
1986	60.34		60.83	7.61	13.19	0.97	20.46	2.51		
1987	63.62		67.77	9.09	15.42	1.54	21.87	2.70		
1988	68.11		84.04	15.10	21.11	1.23	27.70	3.37		
1989	71.05		91.09	16.75	25.33	1.53	24.31	3.74		
1990	74.01		94.23	16.47	27.95	2.02	22.55	4.35		
1991-1995	**456.48**		**643.24**	**136.88**	**228.80**	**35.46**	**105.24**	**34.07**		
1991	77.02		100.58	19.53	30.78	2.56	20.59	4.77		
1992	80.25		110.54	22.29	35.86	3.15	19.08	5.13		
1993	84.10		148.19	42.30	52.07	4.30	14.20	6.57		
1994	99.85		120.53	25.54	45.63	9.24	21.70	7.18		
1995	115.26		163.40	27.22	64.46	16.21	29.67	10.42		
1996-2000	**1341.65**		**1397.26**	**185.46**	**570.06**	**190.18**	**223.71**	**70.84**		
1996	150.90		201.32	29.53	81.61	22.67	37.22	11.36		
1997	209.91	182.32	235.82	32.67	97.54	28.76	41.05	12.74	-53.50	27.59
1998	262.01	229.45	272.23	37.58	113.00	36.49	41.42	14.12	-42.78	32.56
1999	320.44	281.37	315.10	39.72	128.86	45.88	45.99	15.27	-33.74	39.07
2000	398.39	345.00	372.79	45.96	149.05	56.38	58.03	17.35	-27.79	53.39
2001-2005	**3611.96**	**3244.40**	**3216.46**	**367.43**	**1389.75**	**355.88**	**566.23**	**147.84**	**27.94**	**367.57**
2001	507.68	454.17	475.00	59.00	181.35	79.52	86.07	20.53	-20.83	53.51
2002	600.96	533.99	539.87	66.69	227.79	61.29	100.00	24.91	-5.88	66.97
2003	665.94	592.54	588.96	75.26	263.69	57.21	93.70	28.85	3.58	73.40
2004	830.03	744.49	726.50	68.88	333.16	73.34	121.70	34.72	17.99	85.55
2005	1007.35	919.21	886.13	97.60	383.76	84.52	164.76	38.83	33.08	88.14
2006-2010	**11889.54**	**8827.85**	**8453.62**	**800.72**	**3321.83**	**801.97**	**1965.28**	**317.03**	**374.23**	**3061.69**
2006	1235.78	1117.15	1076.82	117.80	460.99	102.28	213.86	45.17	40.33	118.63
2007	1882.04	1492.64	1435.67	134.84	601.06	135.20	309.34	56.63	56.97	389.40
2008	2282.04	1837.32	1775.58	158.34	651.78	171.33	497.52	63.95	61.75	444.71
2009	2678.77	2026.81	1913.97	179.73	752.60	177.84	430.42	71.28	112.84	651.96
2010	3810.91	2353.93	2251.59	210.01	855.40	215.33	513.09	80.00	102.34	1456.98
2011	4359.10	3006.28	2854.63	237.76	1071.51	272.90	683.71	145.65	151.65	1352.82
2012	4573.72	3314.93	3124.75	314.00	1152.74	281.49	752.47	160.34	190.18	1197.92
2013	5566.08	3661.11	3514.52	574.89	1034.79	333.84	802.12	177.41	146.59	1841.76

注：1. 地方财政收支数为决算数。
2. 2011年开始，原指标"地方一般预算收入"和"地方一般预算支出"更名为"地方公共财政预算收入"和"地方公共财政预算支出"(下同)。
3. 自2012年开始，地方财政收支包含三部分内容，即地方财政公共预算收支、政府性基金预算收支和国有资本经营预算收支(下同)，历史数据仅包含前两部分内容。

资料来源：北京市财政局。

Note: a) Local government revenue and expenditures are final accounts.
b) Since 2011, "local general budgetary revenue" and "local general budgetary expenditure" is renamed as "local public budgetary revenue" and "local public budgetary expenditure" (the same below).
c) Since 2012, local financial revenue has included three parts: local public budgetary financial revenue and expenditures, governmental fund budgetary revenue and expenditures and budgetary revenue and expenditures of state-owned capital operation(the same below).

Source: Beijing Municipal Bureau of Finance.

6-1 续表

单位：亿元

年 份 Year	地 方 财政支出 Local Government Expenditures	#地方公共财政预算支出 Local Public Budgetary Expenditures	#一般公共服务 General Public Service	#教 育 Education	#科学技术 Science and Technology	#文化体育与传媒 Culture, Sports and Media	#社会保障和就业 Social Security and Employment
1978	20.38						
1979	20.06						
1980	14.87						
1981-1985	**111.40**						
1981	14.85						
1982	16.80						
1983	19.61						
1984	27.15						
1985	32.99						
1986-1990	**272.89**						
1986	44.27						
1987	49.67						
1988	52.93						
1989	59.50						
1990	66.52						
1991-1995	**473.64**						
1991	67.98						
1992	71.74						
1993	80.99						
1994	98.53						
1995	154.40						
1996-2000	**1646.07**						
1996	187.45						
1997	262.20	236.39					
1998	307.55	280.68					
1999	398.53	355.19					
2000	490.34	443.00					
2001-2005	**4219.74**	**3878.85**					
2001	614.92	559.11					
2002	683.98	628.35					
2003	809.39	734.80					
2004	974.17	898.28					
2005	1137.28	1058.31					
2006-2010	**12765.99**	**9942.31**	**987.56**	**1604.40**	**578.30**	**309.36**	**1048.02**
2006	1411.58	1296.84	159.95	209.21	70.14	40.51	149.22
2007	2067.65	1649.50	179.56	263.00	90.74	53.62	179.28
2008	2400.93	1959.29	196.27	316.30	112.19	61.11	209.33
2009	2820.86	2319.37	212.21	365.67	126.31	74.75	234.29
2010	4064.97	2717.32	239.57	450.22	178.92	79.36	275.90
2011	4574.94	3245.23	261.38	520.08	183.07	87.01	354.88
2012	4866.43	3685.31	286.57	628.65	199.94	141.37	424.31
2013	6039.42	4173.66	297.12	681.18	234.67	154.71	469.13

6-1 continued

(100 million yuan)

#医疗卫生 Healthcare	#节能环保 Energy Conservation and Environmental Protection	#交通运输 Transportation	#城乡社区事务 Urban and Rural Community Affairs	#农林水 Agriculture, Forestry and Water Conservancy	#政府性基金预算支出 Governmental Fund Budgetary Expenditure
718.40	**199.77**	**422.53**	**1182.65**	**613.55**	**2823.69**
100.95	20.14	7.05	153.26	88.62	114.74
118.95	29.27	33.09	187.43	102.51	418.15
145.05	35.47	80.35	199.84	121.77	441.64
166.63	54.04	147.07	347.82	142.01	501.50
186.82	60.85	154.99	294.30	158.64	1347.65
225.49	94.51	199.12	339.27	187.34	1329.71
256.06	113.54	243.76	430.76	222.69	1118.45
276.13	138.17	231.79	510.67	297.62	1798.81

6-2 地方财政收支增长速度及相当于地区生产总值比例(1978-2013年)
GROWTH RATE OF LOCAL GOVERNMENT REVENUE AND EXPENDITURES AND THEIR SHARE IN GDP (1978-2013)

单位: % (%)

年 份 Year	增长速度(上年=100) Growth Rate (Preceding Year=100)				相当于地区生产总值比例 Share in GDP			
	地方财政收 入 Local Financial Revenue	#地方公共财政预 算 收 入 Local Public Budgetary Revenue	地方财政支 出 Local Financial Expenditures	#地方公共财政预 算 支 出 Local Public Budgetary Expenditures	地方财政收 入 Local Government Revenue	#地方公共财政预 算 收 入 Local Public Budgetary Revenue	地方财政支 出 Local Government Expenditures	#地方公共财政预 算 支 出 Local Public Budgetary Expenditures
1978	18.0		27.6		46.4		18.7	
1979	-5.4		-1.6		39.8		16.7	
1980	7.4		-25.9		36.9		10.7	
1981-1985					**24.6**		**11.7**	
1981	-4.2		-0.1		35.3		10.7	
1982	-3.8		13.1		30.5		10.8	
1983	-15.7		16.7		21.8		10.7	
1984	14.5		38.4		21.1		12.5	
1985	14.9		21.5		20.4		12.8	
1986-1990					**17.0**		**13.8**	
1986	15.1		34.2		21.2		15.5	
1987	5.4		12.2		19.5		15.2	
1988	7.1		6.6		16.6		12.9	
1989	4.3		12.4		15.6		13.0	
1990	4.2		11.8		14.8		13.3	
1991-1995					**9.4**		**9.8**	
1991	4.1		2.2		12.9		11.4	
1992	4.2		5.5		11.3		10.1	
1993	4.8		12.9		9.5		9.1	
1994	9.9		21.7		8.7		8.6	
1995	21.8		56.7		7.6		10.2	
1996-2000					**11.1**		**13.6**	
1996	30.9		21.4		8.4		10.5	
1997	25.5		39.9		10.1	8.8	12.6	11.4
1998	24.8	20.0	17.4	18.7	11.0	9.7	12.9	11.8
1999	22.3	22.6	29.6	26.5	12.0	10.5	14.9	13.3
2000	24.3	22.7	23.0	24.7	12.6	10.9	15.5	14.0
2001-2005					**13.9**	**12.5**	**16.2**	**14.9**
2001	27.4	31.6	25.4	26.2	13.7	12.2	16.6	15.1
2002	25.8	25.9	11.2	12.4	13.9	12.4	15.9	14.6
2003	17.2	18.2	18.3	16.9	13.3	11.8	16.2	14.7
2004	28.3	29.7	20.4	22.3	13.8	12.3	16.1	14.9
2005	21.4	23.5	16.7	17.8	14.5	13.2	16.3	15.2
2006-2010					**21.5**	**16.0**	**23.1**	**18.0**
2006	22.7	21.5	24.1	22.5	15.2	13.8	17.4	16.0
2007	52.3	33.6	46.5	27.2	19.1	15.2	21.0	16.8
2008	21.3	23.1	16.1	18.8	20.5	16.5	21.6	17.6
2009	17.4	10.3	17.5	18.4	22.0	16.7	23.2	19.1
2010	42.3	16.1	44.1	17.2	27.0	16.7	28.8	19.3
2011	14.4	27.7	12.5	19.4	26.8	18.5	28.2	20.0
2012	4.9	10.3	6.4	13.6	25.6	18.5	27.2	20.6
2013	21.7	10.4	24.1	13.3	28.5	18.8	31.0	21.4

注: 2002-2004年地方财政收入增长速度按可比口径计算。
资料来源: 北京市财政局。
Note: The growth rate of local government revenue in 2002-2004 is calculated in comparable figures.
Source: Beijing Municipal Bureau of Finance.

6-3 地方财政收入
LOCAL FINANCIAL REVENUE

项目	Item	绝对数(万元) Absolute Value (10000 yuan) 2013	2012	2013年为2012年% 2013 as % of 2012	构成(%) Composition (%) 2013	2012
合计	**Total**	**55660805**	**45737247**	**121.7**	**100.0**	**100.0**
地方公共财政预算收入	**Local Public Budgetary Revenue**	**36611097**	**33149340**	**110.4**	**65.8**	**72.5**
#增值税	Value-added Tax	5748900	3139994	183.1	10.3	6.9
营业税	Business Tax	10347918	11527384	89.8	18.6	25.2
个人所得税	Personal Income Tax	3338449	2814872	118.6	6.0	6.2
城市维护建设税	Urban Maintenance and Construction Tax	1774052	1603445	110.6	3.2	3.5
固定资产投资方向调节税	Tax on the Adjustment of the Investment in the Fixed Assets		107			
耕地占用税	Arable Land Occupation Tax	89964	102719	87.6	0.2	0.2
企业所得税	Company Income Tax	8021152	7524673	106.6	14.4	16.5
国有资本经营收入	Operation Income of State-owned Assets	-602398	-305024			
罚没收入	Income of Fines and Confiscations	344880	430571	127.6	0.6	0.9
行政事业性收费收入	Administrative Fees	416928	458964	105.2	0.7	1.0
政府性基金预算收入	**Government Fund Budgetary Revenue**	**18417585**	**11979238**	**153.7**	**33.1**	**26.2**
国有资本经营预算收入	**Budgetary Revenue of State-owned Capital Operation**	**632123**	**608669**	**103.9**	**1.1**	**1.3**

资料来源：北京市财政局。
Source: Beijing Finance Bureau.

6-4 地方财政支出
LOCAL GOVERNMENT EXPENDITURES

项目	Item	绝对数(万元) Value (10000 yuan) 2013	2012	2013年为2012年% 2013 as % of 2012	构成(%) Composition (%) 2013	2012
合计	**Total**	**60394197**	**48664329**	**124.1**	**100.0**	**100.0**
地方公共财政预算支出	**Local Public Budgetary Expenditures**	**41736563**	**36853076**	**113.3**	**69.1**	**75.7**
#一般公共服务	General Public Service	2971203	2865685	103.7	4.9	5.9
教育	Education	6811775	6286510	108.4	11.3	12.9
科学技术	Science and Technology	2346742	1999444	117.4	3.9	4.1
文化体育与传媒	Culture, Sports and Media	1547082	1413733	109.4	2.6	2.9
社会保障和就业	Social Security and Employment	4691317	4243122	110.6	7.8	8.7
医疗卫生	Healthcare	2761274	2560626	107.8	4.6	5.3
节能环保	Energy Conservation and Environmental Protection	1381672	1135370	121.7	2.3	2.3
交通运输	Transportation	2317948	2437624	95.1	3.8	5.0
城乡社区事务	Urban and Rural Community Affairs	5106691	4307560	118.6	8.5	8.9
农林水事务	Agriculture, Forestry and Water Conservancy	2976191	2226932	133.6	4.9	4.6
政府性基金支出合计	**Total Expenditures of Governmental Funds**	**17988141**	**11184472**	**160.8**	**29.8**	**23.0**
国有资本经营预算支出	**Budgetary Expenditure of State-owned Capital Operation**	**669493**	**626781**	**106.8**	**1.1**	**1.3**

资料来源：北京市财政局。
Source: Beijing Municipal Bureau of Finance.

6-5 地税税费收入分税种、分行业完成情况(2007-2013年)
LOCAL TAX REVENUE BY CATEGORY AND INDUSTRY (2007-2013)

单位：亿元 (100 million yuan)

项目	Item	2007	2008	2009	2010	2011	2012	2013
地税税费收入	**Local Tax Revenue**	**1366.14**	**1578.02**	**1771.87**	**2104.89**	**2666.62**	**2865.25**	**3061.60**
按税种分	**By Category**							
#营业税	Business Tax	601.06	651.78	749.90	855.40	1071.51	1152.74	1032.35
企业所得税	Coporate Income Tax	150.64	161.06	142.24	173.18	210.52	221.02	258.07
个人所得税	Personal Income Tax	308.24	409.62	436.49	536.27	681.27	703.48	834.47
按行业分	**By Sector**							
第一产业	Primary Industry	1.66	2.05	2.57	3.67	3.90	4.94	4.98
第二产业	Secondary Industry	198.90	216.00	209.91	235.20	303.14	326.20	348.54
#制造业	Manufacturing	74.52	94.87	88.62	101.75	138.36	150.45	160.70
电力、燃气及水的生产和供应业	Production and Distribution of Electricity, Gas and Water	12.00	14.96	15.46	15.69	19.37	21.18	25.20
建筑业	Construction	108.51	97.19	98.64	109.88	134.37	144.65	153.99
第三产业	Tertiary Industry	1165.57	1359.97	1559.39	1866.00	2359.58	2534.11	2708.14
#交通、运输仓储及邮政业	Transport, Storage and Post	37.78	45.90	46.43	51.41	63.95	60.58	38.14
信息传输、计算机服务和软件业	Information Transmission, Computer Servicesand Software	64.63	82.03	85.87	98.02	125.48	132.76	123.65
批发和零售业	Wholesale and Retail Trade	66.80	85.20	89.24	111.40	159.35	169.30	188.84
金融业	Finance	142.17	211.13	228.57	276.40	366.35	446.67	477.99
房地产业	Real Estate	317.19	282.32	371.28	437.40	520.36	525.44	659.25

资料来源：北京市地方税务局。
Source: Beijing Municipal Bureau of Local Taxation.

6-6 国税税收收入分税种、分行业完成情况(2007-2013年)
STATE TAX REVENUE BY CATEGORY AND INDUSTRY (2007-2013)

单位：亿元 (100 million yuan)

项目	Item	2007	2008	2009	2010	2011	2012	2013
国税税收收入	**State Tax Revenue**	**3030.6**	**3861.7**	**4561.1**	**4346.8**	**5332.5**	**6339.4**	**7470.9**
按税种分	**By Category**							
#增值税	Value-added Tax	574.1	652.4	749.7	868.3	961.7	1096.0	1456.3
营业税	Business Tax	196.6	225.3	160.6	145.4	161.3	191.3	203.7
企业所得税	Corporate Income Tax	1874.9	2526.3	3116.5	2642.0	3506.5	3609.4	4365.2
按行业分	**By Sector**							
第一产业	Primary Industry	0.4	1.0	4.0	5.8	0.7	0.3	2.6
第二产业	Secondary Industry	684.8	602.6	627.8	779.1	881.1	843.8	1069.3
#制造业	Manufacturing	402.4	419.3	563.6	623.2	709.2	764.6	832.0
电力、燃气及水的生产和供应业	Production and Distribution of Electricity, Gas and Water	76.4	124.1	84.3	105.2	103.5	131.0	261.4
建筑业	Construction	7.4	14.6	20.4	30.1	45.3	54.8	57.0
第三产业	Tertiary Industry	2345.4	3258.1	3929.3	3561.9	4450.8	5495.3	6399.0
#交通、运输仓储及邮政业	Transport, Storage and Post	151.6	173.2	134.2	157.9	209.2	212.1	245.1
信息传输、计算机服务和软件业	Information Transmission, Computer Services and Software	116.6	126.2	208.4	30.8	105.9	245.9	373.2
批发和零售业	Wholesale and Retail Trade	719.2	842.8	820.5	1081.6	1410.8	1314.6	1451.0
金融业	Finance	1090.5	1768.6	2396.0	1831.2	2158.0	3034.0	3500.2
房地产业	Real Estate	67.3	106.3	77.0	107.6	122.3	111.6	157.0

资料来源：北京市国家税务局。
Source: Beijing Municipal Bureau of State Taxation.

主要统计指标解释

财政部分

地方财政收入 指国家财政参与社会产品分配所得的收入，是实现国家职能的财力保证。包括地方公共财政预算收入、政府性基金预算收入和国有资本经营预算收入。

地方公共财政预算收入 是通过一定的形式和程序，由各级财政部门组织并纳入预算管理的各项收入。

政府性基金预算收入 是按规定收取，转入或通过当年财政安排，由财政管理并具有指定用途的政府性基金预算收入等。

国有资本经营预算 是指国家以所有者身份取得国有资本收益，并对所得收益进行分配而发生的各项收支预算，是政府预算的重要组成部分。

税收收入 包括增值税、营业税、企业所得税、个人所得税、资源税、城市维护建设税、房产税、印花税、城镇土地使用税、土地增值税、车船税、耕地占用税、契税等。

非税收收入 包括专项收入、行政事业性收费、罚没收入和其他收入。

地方财政支出 是以国家为主体，以财政的事权为依据进行的一种财政资金分配活动，集中反映了国家的职能活动范围及其所发生的耗费，包括地方公共财政预算支出和基金预算支出。

地方公共财政预算支出 是各级财政部门对集中的一般预算收入有计划地分配和使用而安排的支出。

政府性基金预算支出 是各级财政部门用基金预算收入安排的支出。

一般公共服务支出 指政府提供基本公共管理与服务的支出，包括人大事务、政协事务、政府办公厅(室)及相关机构事务、发展与改革事务、统计信息事务、财政事务、税收事务、审计事务、海关事务、人力资源事务、纪检监察事务、人口与计划生育事务、商贸事务、知识产权事务、工商行政管理事务、国土资源事务、海洋管理事务、测绘事务、地震事务、气象事务、民族事务、宗教事务、港澳台侨事务、档案事务、共产党事务、民主党派事务及工商联事务、群众团体事务、彩票事务等。

教育支出 指政府教育事务支出，包括教育行政管理、学前教育、小学教育、初中教育、普通高中教育、普通高等教育、初等职业教育、中专教育、技校教育、职业高中教育、高等职业教育、广播电视教育、留学生教育、特殊教育、干部继续教育、教育机关服务等。

科学技术支出 指用于科学技术方面的支出，包括科学技术管理事务、基础研究、应用研究、技术研究与开发、科技条件与服务、社会科学、科学技术普及、科技交流与合作等。

文化教育与传媒支出 指政府在文化、文物、体育、广播影视、新闻出版等方面的支出。

社会保障和就业支出 指政府在社会保障与就业方面的支出，包括社会保障和就业管理事务、民政管理事务、财政对社会保险基金的补助、补充全国社会保障基金、行政事业单位离退休、企业改革补助、就业补助、抚恤、退役安置、社会福利、残疾人事业、城市居民最低生活保障、其他城镇社会救济、农村社会救济、自然灾害生活救助、红十字事务等。

医疗卫生支出 指政府医疗卫生方面的支出，包括医疗卫生管理事务支出、医疗服务支出、医疗保障支出、疾病预防控制支出、卫生监督支出、妇幼保健支出、农村卫生支出等。

节能环保支出 指政府环境保护支出，包括环境保护管理事务支出、环境监测与监察支出、污染治理支出、自然生态保护支出、天然林保护工程支出、退耕还林支出、风沙荒漠治理支出、退牧还草支出、已垦草原退耕还草、能源节约利用、污染减排、可再生能源和资源综合利用等支出。

交通运输支出 指政府交通运输和邮政业方面的支出，包括公路运输支出、水路运输支出、铁路运输支出、民用航空运输支出、邮政业支出等。

城乡社区事务支出 指政府城乡社区事务支出，包括城乡社区管理事务支出、城乡社区规划与管理支出、城乡社区公共设施支出、城乡社区住宅支出、城乡社区环境卫生支出、建设市场管理与监督支出等。

农林水事务支出 指政府农林水事务支出，包括农业支出、林业支出、水利支出、扶贫支出、农业综合开发支出等。

税收部分

税费收入 指由各级地方税务局征缴的各项税收收入和罚没收入。包括营业税、企业所得税、个人所得税、资源税、房产税、契税、城市维护建设税等。

税收收入 指由各级国家税务局征缴的各项税收收入。包括增值税、消费税、营业税、企业所得税、个人所得税、城市维护建设税等。

营业税 是对在中华人民共和国境内提供应税劳务、转让无形资产或者销售不动产的单位和个人，就其取得营业额征收的一种税。

企业所得税 是对中国境内全部企业的生产经营所得和其他所得征收的一种税。

增值税 指以商品或劳务销售额为计税依据并实行扣除已征税款制度的一种流转税。

个人所得税 是对个人（自然人）取得的各项应税所得征收的一种税。

Explanatory Notes on Main Statistical Indicators

Finance

Local Financial Revenue refers to the revenue for the national finance through participating in the distribution of social products. It is the financial guarantee to ensure the functions and powers of the government. The local financial revenue includes local public budgetary revenue, governmental fund budgetary revenue and budget of state-owned capital operation.

Local Public Budgetary Revenue refers to the revenue organized by finance authorities at all levels in certain form and through certain procedures and involved in budgetary management.

Governmental Fund Budgetary Revenue refers to governmental fund budgetary revenues collected, transferred or allocated by government finance in the current year in accordance with regulations, and regulated by government finance and used for specific purpose.

Budget of State-owned Capital Operation refers to the state-owned capital income of the country as the owner and all kinds of income and expenditure budgets resulted from the allocation of the income. It is an important part of governmental budget.

Tax Revenue includes value-added tax, business tax, corporate income tax, individual income tax, resource tax, urban maintenance and construction tax, house property tax, stamp tax, urban land use tax, land appreciation tax, tax on vehicles and boat operation, farm land occupation tax, deed tax, etc.

Non-tax Revenue includes special program receipts, charge of administrative and institutional units, income of fines and confiscation, and other non-tax revenues.

Local Government Expenditure refers to the allocation of financial funds by the state based on the financial administration, which demonstrates the scope of government functioning and the expenditures incurred. It includes local public budgetary expenditure and fund budgetary expenditure.

Local Public Budgetary Expenditure refers to the expenditure arranged by finance authorities at all levels from the general budgetary revenue according to the planned distribution .

Governmental Fund Budgetary Expenditure refers to the expenditure arranged by finance authorities at all levels according to the fund budget revenue.

Expenditure for General Public Services refers to the spending on the basic public management and services provided by the government, including the expenses on affairs of Beijing Municipal People's Congress, CPC Beijing Municipal Committee, General Office of Beijing Municipal Government and relative institutions, development and reform, statistical information, finance, taxation, audit, customs, human resources, discipline inspection and supervision, population and family planning, commerce and trade, intellectual property, administration for industry and commerce, land and resources, oceanic administration, surveying and mapping, earthquake, weather, ethnics, religions, Hong Kong, Macao, Taiwan, and Overseas Chinese, archive administration, Chinese Communist Party, democratic parties, federation of industry and commerce, mass organizations, and lottery, etc.

Expenditure for Education refers to the spending of government on education, including the expenses on the administration of education, pre-school education, primary education, junior high school education, senior high school education, general higher education, primary vocational education, secondary vocational education, technical school education, vocational senior high school education and higher vocational education, radio and television education, overseas student education, special education, continuing education for management personnel, and services for education authorities, etc.

Expenditure for Science and Technology refers to the spending on science and technology (S&T), including the expense on the administration of S&T, basic research, applied research, research and development, conditions and services of S&T, popularization of social science and S&T, exchanges and cooperation of S&T, etc.

Expenditure for Cultural Education and Media refers to the spending on culture, cultural relics, sports, radio, films, television, press and publication, etc.

Expenditure for Social Security and Employment refers to the spending on social security and employment, including the expenses on social security and employment administration affairs, civil affairs, budgetary subsidy on the social insurance funds, subsidy on National Social Security Fund, subsidy on retirees of administrative and institutional units, subsidy on enterprise reform, subsidy on employment, pension, reemployment of ex-serviceman, social welfare, the handicapped undertakings, subsistence allowances for urban residents, other urban social relief, rural social relief, relief for natural disasters, affairs of Red Cross, etc.

Expenditure for Medical and Health Care refers to the spending on medical and health care, including the expenses on medical and health administration, medical services, medical guarantee, disease prevention and control, health inspection and supervision, women and children's health care, rural health care, etc.

Expenditure for Energy Conservation and Environmental Protection refers to the spending of government on environmental protection, including the expenses on administration of environmental protection, environment monitoring and supervision, pollution control, natural and ecological protection, projects of natural forest protection, reforestation, control of sand storms, grassland rehabilitation, energy conservation and utilization, emission reduction, comprehensive utilization of renewable energy and resources, etc.

Expenditure for Transportation refers to the spending of government on transportation and postal services, including the expenses on highway transportation, waterway transportation, railway transportation, civil aviation transportation and postal services, etc.

Expenditure for Urban and Rural Community Affairs refers to the spending of government on urban and rural community affairs, including the expenses on administration of urban and rural communities, planning and management of urban and rural communities, public facilities in urban and rural communities, residential houses in urban and rural communities, sanitation in urban and rural communities, management and supervision of construction markets, etc.

Expenditure for Agriculture, Forestry and Water Conservancy Affairs refers to the spending of government on agriculture affairs, forestry affairs, water conservancy affairs, poverty alleviation and comprehensive agricultural development, etc.

Revenues

Local Tax Revenue refers to the revenue of taxes, fines and confiscations levied and collected by local tax bureaus at all levels, including business tax, corporate income tax, personal income tax, resource tax, house property tax, deed tax, urban maintenance and construction tax, etc.

State Tax Revenue refers to the revenue of taxes levied and collected by state tax bureaus at all levels, including value-added tax, excise tax, business tax, corporate income tax, individual income tax, urban maintenance and construction tax, etc.

Business Tax is a kind of tax levied against the business income of entities and individuals providing taxable labor services, transferring intangible assets or selling real estate within the territory of PRC.

Corporate Income Tax is a sort of tax levied against income of China domestic enterprises from their production and operation and other income.

Value-Added Tax is a sort of commodity turnover tax based on commodity and service sales, with a system of deduction of tax levied.

Personal Income Tax is a sort of tax levied against taxable income earned by individuals (natural persons).

价格指数
PRICE INDEX

简要说明

一、本章资料的主要内容

本章价格指数资料，反映生产、流通、消费与投资的价格变动趋势和变动幅度。主要包括居民消费价格指数；商品零售价格指数；农产品生产价格指数；工业生产者出厂价格指数；工业生产者购进价格指数；固定资产投资价格指数；住宅销售价格指数。

二、本章资料的数据来源

本章资料由国家统计局北京调查总队、北京市统计局提供。

三、调查方法

（一）居民消费价格指数和商品零售价格指数

编制居民消费价格指数、商品零售价格指数的资料采用抽样调查和重点调查相结合的方法取得，即在全市选择不同的区域，按照布局合理的原则抽选价格调查点，由国家确定调查商品和服务项目，在此基础上按照消费量大、价格变动趋势有较强代表性的原则选择调查样本，对其市场价格进行定期调查，以样本推算总体。现将指数编制过程按下列几个步骤进行说明。

抽选价格调查点。按照布局合理等原则，将不同区域各种类型的商场、农贸市场、服务网点分别按销售额、成交额和经营规模为标志，从高到低排队，依据所需调查点的数量进行等距抽样。

选择代表规格品。代表商品和服务项目由国家确定，代表规格品由各省市按照有关原则选择。选择原则：（1）消费量较大；（2）价格变动趋势和变动程度有较强的代表性，即选中规格品的价格变动特征与未选中规格品之间价格变动的相关性愈高愈好；（3）选中的规格品之间，性质相隔愈远愈好，价格变动特征的相关性愈低愈好；选中的工业消费品必须是合格产品，产品包装上有注册商标、产地、规格等级等标识。

目前，居民消费价格调查按用途划分为 8 大类，262 个基本分类，国家规定大城市调查规格品数量应在 600 种左右，北京市由于编制分收入层居民消费价格指数，代表规格品数量增加到 1661 种。商品零售价格指数划分为 16 个大类，229 个基本分类，北京市代表规格品数量为 1308 种。

价格资料的采集。采取定人、定点、定时直接调查的方法采集价格资料。

权数资料来源与计算。居民消费价格指数的权数根据城市居民家庭生活消费支出调查资料整理计算。商品零售价格指数的权数根据商业统计中社会消费品零售总额计算。

（二）工业生产者出厂价格指数和工业生产者购进价格指数

工业生产者出厂价格是工业品第一次出售时的出厂价格。该项调查采用重点调查与典型调查相结合的调查方法。重点调查对象为选中的全年主营业务收入 2000 万元及以上的工业法人样本单位及部分生产特定产品的全年主营业务收入 2000 万元以下的工业法人样本单位。

工业生产者购进价格是工业企业作为中间投入的价格。调查对象从填报工业生产者出厂价格的企业中选择。

选择代表企业的原则：（1）按工业行业选择调查企业，各中类行业原则上都要有调查企业；（2）大型企业应尽量都选占相当大比重企业；（3）选择生产正常、稳定的企业作为调查对象；（4）选择企业时要兼顾不同所有制形式。

选择代表产品的原则：（1）按工业行业选择代表产品；（2）选择对国计民生影响大的产品；（3）选择生产较为稳定的产品；（4）选择有发展前景的产品；（5）选择具有地方特色的产品。

除了以上原则及方法外，工业生产者购进价格调查还要考虑到特殊性，即调查企业要填报其生产中消耗的主要原材料、燃料、动力，不填报消耗较少、在生产投入中比重较小的原材料、燃料、动力。

权数的确定。编制工业生产者出厂价格指数所用的权数，用工业品销售产值算。计算资料来自于经济普查的工业数据。若近期没有经济普查，采用工业统计年度资料计算。编制工业生产者购进价格指数所用的权数来自工业部门各种物质消耗额，计算资料为经济普查资料结合一次性产品调查数据。权数一般五年更换一次。

（三）固定资产投资价格指数

固定资产投资价格调查采用重点调查与典型调查相结合的方法。固定资产投资价格调查所涉及的价格是构成固定资产投资额实体的实际购进价格（或结算价格）。调查的内容包括构成当年建筑工程实体的钢材、木材、水泥、地方建筑材料、电料、化工材料等主要建筑材料价格；投入的劳动力价格（单位工资）和各种施工机械使用费用；设备工器具购置和其他费用投资价格。

选择建筑安装工程调查点的原则：（1）样本单位应具有一定覆盖面；（2）投资经济活动代表性强；（3）兼顾不同经济类型；（4）选择重点工程；（5）兼顾不同工程类别。

选择其他费用调查点的原则：在选择其他费用调查点时，所遵循的原则与建筑安装工程调查点的原则基本相同，特别是要注意选择那些投资额大的工程。但由于其他费用不易取得，所以在实际操作过程中，应同时在建设单位、施工单位开展重点调查，并辅以典型调查（从有关管理部门取得资料）。

权数的确定。固定资产投资价格指数的计算权数是建筑安装工程、设备工器具购置和其他费用三者前三年投资完成额的平均比重。

（四）住宅销售价格指数是反映住宅销售价格总水平变动趋势和程度的相对数。包括新建住宅销售价格指数和二手住宅销售价格指数。

新建住宅销售价格的调查方法：目前我国住宅销售价格调查在 70 个大中城市开展。新建住宅销售价格、面积、金额等资料直接采用当地房地产管理部门的网签数据。新建住宅的网签数据内容主要包括：住宅在建项目（楼盘）名称、项目地址、幢号、总层数、所在层数、住宅结构、建筑面积、成交总价（合同金额）、签约时间等。

二手住宅销售价格的调查方法：二手住宅销售价格调查为非全面调查，采用重点调查与典型调查相结合的方法，按照房地产经纪机构上报、房地产管理部门提供与调查员实地调查相结合的方式收集基础数据。

（五）农产品生产价格指数

农产品生产价格调查采取抽样调查和重点调查相结合的调查方法。抽取 323 个农产品生产和出售的农业生产经营单位和行政村作为调查对象。对一些区域性比较强的农产品采取在主产区主观选样的方法选择农业生产经营单位和行政村作为调查对象。

被调查单位及行政村在辅助调查员的指导下将在报告期出售的农产品的名称、出售数量、价格、金额即时记入农产品生产价格调查台账，并上报，由市级超级汇总。

Brief Introduction

I. Main Content

Price indexes in this chapter reflect the trend and rate of changes in prices of production, circulation, consumption and investment, mainly consisting of consumer price index (CPI), retail price index (RPI), producer price index for agricultural products, producer price index for industrial products (PPI); purchasing price index for industrial products; price index for investment in fixed assets; and selling price index for residential houses.

II. Source of Statistics

Statistics in this chapter are from NBS Survey Office in Beijing and Beijing Municipal Bureau of Statistics.

III. Survey Methods

1.Consumer Price Index (CPI) and Retail Price Index (RPI)

Data for compilation of the consumer price index and retail price index are collected through a combination of sample surveys and surveys of key units. Different areas are selected across the city as the sample areas and representative commodities with large amount of consumption and price changes are selected as the sample commodities in reasonable layout. Commodity and service items are identified by the central government. Regular surveys are conducted to collect data on their market prices. General indexes are inferred on the basis of the sample data. The process of CPI development is described as the following steps.

The selection of price survey sites: By adopting the principle of reasonable layout, an equidistant sampling is conducted for department stores, agricultural product trade markets and service outlets in different types and in different areas by their sales value, transaction value and operational scale, which will be ranked in a descending order based on the number of survey sites required.

The selection of representative commodities: Representative commodity and service items are determined by the country. Representative commodities are selected by provinces and cities according to relevant principles. Principles for selection: (1) large quantity of consumption; (2) strongly representative trend and extent of price changes, which means the characteristics of price changes of selected commodities shall be highly correlated with price changes of those that are not selected; (3) selected commodities shall be different in their nature and least correlated in the characteristics of price changes between each other; the selected industrial products must be qualified products, with registered trademark, origin, specifications, grade and other marks on the their package.

At present, data are collected over 600 specifications each month under 262 basic headings in 8 categories in the consumer price surveys. In Beijing, due to the development of CPI by income class, representative commodities have increased to 1661 specifications. Retail price index consists of 16 categories, 229 basic headings and 1308 specifications of representative commodities.

Method of data collection: Price data are collected through direct surveys by designated personnel at designated sites on periodic basis.

Source and calculation of the weights: CPI weights are calculated according to survey information on living expenditures of urban residents. RPI weights are calculated according to the total retail sales of commodities.

2．Producer Price Index for Industrial Products (PPI); Purchasing Price Index for Industrial Products

The producer price index for industrial products refers to the producer's price of industrial products when sold for the first time. The survey program is a combination of the key units' survey and typical units' survey methods. Key units refer to industrial enterprises with annual turnover from primary activities at and above 20 million yuan. Typical units refer to the industrial enterprises with annual revenue from the primary activities below 20 million yuan.

Purchasing price for Industrial Products refers to the price of intermediate inputs of industrial enterprise. Enterprises for survey are selected among those that have submitted the ex-factory prices of industrial products.

Principles for selecting the representative enterprises: (1) Enterprises to be covered in the survey are selected by industrial sectors. In principle, every branch should have enterprises selected; (2) All (or a majority of) large-sized enterprises should be selected; (3) Enterprises selected should be those with normal and stable production; (4) Enterprises selected should include those with different ownerships.

Principles for selecting representative products: (1) Representative products are be selected by industrial sectors; (2) The selected products should have significant impact on the national economy and people's livelihood: (3) The production of the goods selected should be relatively more stable; (4) The prospects of the goods selected should be promising; (5) The products selected shall represent the localities.

In addition to the above-mentioned principles, a special condition shall be taken into account in the survey of producer price index for industrial products. Namely, enterprises under survey shall report main raw materials, fuel and power consumed in production.

Determination of weights: Weights used for compiling producer price index for industrial products (PPI) are calculated according to sales value of industrial products. Data for calculation are industrial data from economic census. If no economic census is conducted recently, data from annual industrial statistics will be used. Weights for compiling the purchasing price index for industrial products are from consumption value of different materials. Data for calculation are data from economic census combined with data from primary product survey; the weights are changed every five years.

3. Price Index for Investment in Fixed Assets

A combined method of key survey and typical survey is used for the collection of data on prices of investment in fixed assets. The prices collected in the surveys of investment in fixed assets are the actual purchasing prices (or settlement prices) of entities of investment in fixed assets. The survey covers the prices of main construction materials that constitute the architectural engineering entities in the year, such as steel, timber, cement, local construction materials, electric parts and chemical materials in construction projects; prices of labor input (wages) and costs of use of construction machines; purchasing price of equipment, tools and devices as well as other expenditures.

Principles for selecting survey sites of construction and installation projects: (1) The sample unit shall have certain coverage; (2) The economic activity of investment should have strong representativeness; (3) Different types of registration should be considered; (4) Key projects shall be selected; (5) Attention should be given to various types of projects.

Principles for selecting survey sites of other expenditures: in the selection of survey sites of other expenditures, the same principles shall be followed as in the selection of survey sites of building and installation projects. Especially projects with larger amount of investment shall be selected. Since it is not easy to obtain data on other expenditures, during the actual data operations, survey on key builders and construction units is to be conducted concurrently with survey on typical units (with information from administration units).

Determination of weights. Weights used for calculating the fixed assets investment price index are determined according to the average proportion of investment amount of construction and installation projects, purchase of equipment, tools and instruments and other expenditures completed in the previous three years.

4. Selling Price Index for Residential Houses is a relative number reflecting the trend and extent of overall level of house selling prices. It includes selling price index for new houses and second-hand houses.

Survey method of new house selling price:

At present, real estate price survey is conducted in 70 medium and large-sized cities across the country. For new houses, selling price, area, amount and other data are taken directly from the online data recorded by local real estate authorities. Online data of new house transaction mainly consist of the name of construction project in process, project location, building number, total number of floors, floor number, house structure, building area, total price of transaction (contractual amount), and date of contract signing, etc.

Survey method of second-hand house selling price:Survey of second-house selling price is incomplete survey conducted with the combined method of key survey and typical survey. Basic data are collected in a combined manner of reporting by real estate broker agencies, providing by real estate authorities and field survey by investigators.

5. Producer Price Index for Agricultural Products

A combined method of sample survey and key survey was used for the survey of producer prices of agricultural products. 323 entities and administrative villages producing and selling agricultural products are sampled. For some regional agricultural products, data on agricultural entities and administrative villages are collected with the method of subjective sampling in main production areas.

Under the instruction of assistant investigators, the surveyed entities and administrative villages will record the name, quantity, price and amount of agricultural products sold during the reporting period onto the log book and report them for summarization at the municipal level.

7-1 各种价格指数(1978-2013年)
PRICE INDEXES (1978-2013)

(上年=100) (preceding year=100)

年份 Year	居民消费价格指数 Consumer Price Index	商品零售价格指数 Retail Price Index	农产品生产价格指数 Producer Price Index for Agricultural Products	工业生产者出厂价格指数 Producer Price Index for Industrial Products (PPI)	工业生产者购进价格指数 Purchasing Price Index for Industrial Products	固定资产投资价格指数 Price Index for Investment in Fixed Assets
1978	100.6	100.6				
1979	101.8	101.8	109.5			
1980	106.0	106.7	105.5			
1981	101.3	101.4	109.4			
1982	101.8	102.0	101.9			
1983	100.5	100.6	101.8			
1984	102.2	102.1	102.3			
1985	117.6	118.6	117.6			
1986	106.8	106.7	108.1			
1987	108.6	108.7	116.1			
1988	120.4	121.9	123.2			
1989	117.2	118.5	106.8			
1990	105.4	104.1	101.9	107.9	114.8	
1991	111.9	108.5	101.7	105.8	111.7	107.3
1992	109.9	108.3	102.4	100.9	103.3	112.2
1993	119.0	116.9	107.0	121.8	133.2	126.6
1994	124.9	117.9	133.4	112.9	118.7	116.2
1995	117.3	112.6	130.6	107.3	106.7	113.9
1996	111.6	107.3	101.5	100.7	100.3	108.2
1997	105.3	103.8	92.8	101.1	103.4	102.7
1998	102.4	98.3	93.6	95.1	98.1	100.8
1999	100.6	98.8	97.5	97.7	95.8	99.9
2000	103.5	98.9	95.0	102.5	100.0	101.0
2001	103.1	98.8	102.0	99.4	100.5	100.6
2002	98.2	98.4	92.4	96.6	97.1	100.4
2003	100.2	98.2	102.5	101.5	104.7	102.2
2004	101.0	99.2	106.2	103.0	114.2	104.3
2005	101.5	99.7	102.9	101.3	111.4	100.7
2006	100.9	100.2	99.1	99.1	105.5	100.4
2007	102.4	100.8	114.4	99.7	105.0	102.8
2008	105.1	104.4	112.3	103.3	115.8	107.8
2009	98.5	97.8	98.3	94.4	88.6	97.1
2010	102.4	100.4	106.5	102.2	110.5	102.5
2011	105.6	103.2	110.7	102.3	108.4	105.7
2012	103.3	100.6	104.7	98.4	98.7	101.3
2013	103.3	99.8	104.7	97.4	97.8	99.9

注：工业生产者出厂价格指数原指标为"工业品出厂价格指数"；工业生产者购进价格指数原指标为"原材料、燃料、动力购进价格指数"(下同)。

Note: Producer Price Index for Industrial Products (PPI) was formerly counted as "Producer's Price Index for Manufactured Products"; Purchasing Price Index for Industrial Products was formerly counted as "Purchasing Price Index for Raw Materials, Fuels and Power" (the same below).

7-2 各种价格定基指数(1978-2013年)
FIXED-BASE PRICE INDEXES (1978-2013)

年份 Year	居民消费价格指数 Consumer Price Index (1978=100)	商品零售价格指数 Retail Price Index (1978=100)	工业生产者出厂价格指数 Producer Price Index for Industrial Products (1990=100)	工业生产者购进价格指数 Purchasing Price Index for Industrial Products (1990=100)	固定资产投资价格指数 Price Index for Investment in Fixed Assets (1990=100)
1978	100.0	100.0			
1979	101.8	101.8			
1980	107.9	108.6			
1981	109.3	110.1			
1982	111.3	112.3			
1983	111.8	113.0			
1984	114.3	115.4			
1985	134.4	136.8			
1986	143.5	145.9			
1987	155.8	158.6			
1988	187.6	193.3			
1989	219.9	229.1			
1990	231.8	238.5	100.0	100.0	100.0
1991	259.4	258.8	105.8	111.7	107.3
1992	285.1	280.3	106.8	115.4	120.4
1993	339.3	327.7	130.0	153.7	152.4
1994	423.8	386.4	146.8	182.4	177.1
1995	497.1	435.1	157.5	194.7	201.7
1996	554.8	466.9	158.6	195.2	218.3
1997	584.2	484.6	160.4	201.9	224.2
1998	598.2	476.4	152.5	198.0	226.0
1999	601.8	470.7	149.0	189.7	225.7
2000	622.9	465.5	152.7	189.7	228.0
2001	642.2	459.9	151.8	190.7	229.4
2002	630.6	452.5	146.6	185.1	230.3
2003	631.9	444.4	148.8	193.8	235.3
2004	638.2	440.8	153.3	221.4	245.5
2005	647.8	439.5	155.3	246.6	247.2
2006	653.6	440.4	153.9	260.2	248.2
2007	669.3	443.9	153.5	273.3	255.1
2008	703.4	463.4	158.6	316.3	275.0
2009	692.8	453.2	149.8	280.3	266.9
2010	709.4	455.0	153.1	309.7	273.6
2011	749.1	469.6	156.6	335.7	289.2
2012	773.8	472.4	154.1	331.3	293.0
2013	799.3	471.5	150.1	324.0	292.7

7-3 八大类居民消费价格指数(1978-2013年)

(上年=100)

年份 Year	居民消费价格指数 Consumer Price Index	#服务项目价格指数 Price Index of Services	食品 Food	#粮食 Grain	#油脂 Oil or Fat	#肉禽及其制品 Meat, Poultry and Their Processed Products	#水产品 Aquatic Products
1978	100.6	100.0	101.2	100.0	100.0		100.6
1979	101.8	101.2	102.2	100.0	100.0		107.2
1980	106.0	95.5	108.2	100.0	100.0		131.3
1981	101.3	100.4	102.9	100.0	100.0		100.0
1982	101.8	100.1	104.2	100.0	100.0		100.0
1983	100.5	100.3	101.5	100.0	100.0		100.0
1984	102.2	103.1	102.8	99.3	100.6		106.6
1985	117.6	108.1	126.6	104.6	116.3		235.3
1986	106.8	107.9	109.6	103.6	132.4		129.7
1987	108.6	107.6	111.3	104.6	103.5		116.1
1988	120.4	106.0	123.9	114.4	120.7		144.9
1989	117.2	104.6	112.5	109.5	129.2		114.5
1990	105.4	118.2	103.7	104.5	101.9		101.7
1991	111.9	142.9	111.2	132.2	137.4		102.0
1992	109.9	122.8	111.5	134.3	110.9		101.8
1993	119.0	133.8	120.7	134.6	111.8		109.3
1994	124.9	136.1	126.7	144.0	133.8	138.2	125.6
1995	117.3	128.3	121.1	135.2	109.0	123.2	111.1
1996	111.6	120.0	107.7	112.2	90.8	101.5	104.5
1997	105.3	117.5	102.2	96.8	100.7	107.0	109.7
1998	102.4	121.3	97.1	96.4	103.3	93.2	94.8
1999	100.6	107.9	97.7	97.9	99.4	92.3	95.5
2000	103.5	116.2	97.9	91.4	85.8	98.4	107.3
2001	103.1	115.9	101.5	95.0	87.5	102.6	96.9
2002	98.2	99.4	98.0	98.5	94.7	98.9	95.7
2003	100.2	100.7	103.2	99.1	114.1	100.9	102.5
2004	101.0	101.8	104.8	120.6	117.0	110.1	107.1
2005	101.5	101.3	104.9	104.6	98.0	103.8	104.7
2006	100.9	101.2	102.8	101.6	101.5	99.4	101.9
2007	102.4	101.3	109.2	107.4	117.3	128.7	108.8
2008	105.1	99.9	116.1	108.9	121.3	125.1	120.1
2009	98.5	94.8	102.4	105.6	83.9	95.2	104.5
2010	102.4	103.7	105.5	109.6	100.9	101.2	110.6
2011	105.6	106.4	110.6	110.8	114.2	121.8	109.5
2012	103.3	104.2	106.6	102.6	104.5	106.7	104.8
2013	103.3	105.5	104.7	104.4	99.8	106.7	103.4

EIGHT CATEGORIES OF CONSUMER PRICE INDEX (1978-2013)

(preceding year=100)

#鲜菜 Fresh Vegetables	#鲜果 Fresh Fruits	烟酒及用品 Tobacco, Liquor and Related Articles	衣着 Clothing	家庭设备用品及维修服务 Household Facilities, Articles and Repair Services	医疗保健和个人用品 Healthcare and Personal Articles	交通和通信 Transportation and Communication	娱乐教育文化用品及服务 Recreational, Educational, Cultural Articles and Services	居住 Residence
114.5	101.6		100.0		100.4		100.1	
100.2	99.5		99.3		103.7		104.5	
114.1	106.7		99.5		101.5		100.8	
111.4	100.8		99.4		101.4		100.3	
104.7	94.3		96.7		101.4		100.1	
104.9	119.1		97.0		103.0		98.1	
106.8	112.1		101.2		107.4		100.0	
162.0	148.6		103.0		106.5		101.6	
106.7	121.4		101.3		102.2		100.8	
118.4	124.0		104.0		103.1		103.5	
133.5	124.4		125.1		131.5		114.4	
105.1	112.0		126.2		119.5		133.1	
107.1	98.6		110.3		111.0		93.5	
118.4	111.1		105.7		105.0		94.4	
115.1	104.6		103.3		114.8		92.8	
114.5	109.2		109.2		115.1		99.7	
128.5	114.9		124.7	112.7	113.2	104.9	118.7	124.1
124.3	129.5		117.5	108.3	102.6	100.3	100.8	113.2
113.7	104.6		119.1	104.6	110.1	102.1	110.1	129.2
95.0	94.0		102.9	105.4	105.2	100.3	98.1	121.2
93.9	89.5		105.9	97.5	108.6	99.0	97.8	104.7
106.2	101.4		99.4	96.5	115.8	98.3	98.8	101.0
98.4	88.4		102.6	96.3	113.5	92.3	97.8	117.9
100.2	101.5	101.5	100.4	97.0	98.7	100.8	114.2	104.2
84.7	94.5	100.6	95.9	97.0	100.2	99.5	96.6	101.9
145.4	111.4	100.2	97.1	97.7	100.1	97.8	98.3	101.6
95.0	104.1	101.2	98.9	96.9	99.2	95.7	101.5	101.4
111.9	111.0	100.0	100.1	99.7	98.0	97.5	99.7	105.9
112.8	112.0	99.9	99.7	101.2	101.1	99.3	98.7	101.4
109.9	100.8	101.8	100.0	100.4	100.3	95.7	99.2	103.5
108.1	112.9	106.0	99.1	104.4	102.0	97.6	98.0	103.0
111.9	109.4	102.2	98.4	100.3	99.9	95.9	97.6	89.8
124.0	112.3	101.1	98.4	99.4	101.5	100.8	99.4	105.0
97.3	112.1	102.5	102.7	104.2	103.7	101.5	99.7	108.5
114.5	101.6	102.2	100.9	102.8	101.5	99.1	102.3	103.9
108.7	107.2	100.1	101.5	101.7	100.2	99.0	103.9	105.6

7-4 多基期居民消费价格指数(2013年)
CONSUMER PRICE INDEX WITH MULTIPLE BASE PERIODS (2013)

项 目	Item	1978=100	1980=100	1990=100	2000=100	2005=100	2010=100
居民消费价格指数	**Consumer Price Index**	**799.3**	**740.7**	**344.7**	**128.3**	**123.4**	**112.7**
#服务项目价格指数	**Price Index of Services**	**3067.9**	**3060.0**	**1317.4**	**140.8**	**117.7**	**117.0**
食 品	**Food**	**1270.1**	**1150.1**	**460.7**	**196.3**	**173.8**	**123.4**
#粮 食	Grain	1228.5	1228.5	832.2	191.1	163.3	118.7
油 脂	Oil and Fat	805.0	805.0	316.2	157.9	145.7	119.1
肉禽及其制品	Meat, Poultry and Their Processed Products	1564.2	1265.8	543.3	250.1	213.7	138.7
水产品	Aquatic Products	3076.9	2185.6	343.4	194.4	182.7	118.7
菜	Vegetables	3212.8	2842.4	781.9	279.3	220.2	120.5
#鲜 菜	Fresh Vegetables	3585.1	3137.8	779.7	295.2	225.1	121.1
干菜及菜制品	Dried Vegetables and Vegetable Products	818.5	788.7	379.2	159.1	169.3	121.9
调味品	Flavoring	1025.3	1055.6	519.9	148.4	141.0	114.0
干鲜瓜果	Dried and Fresh Melons and Fruits	1347.9	1259.7	345.6	213.0	179.6	119.4
烟酒及用品	**Tobacco, Liquor and Related Articles**	**452.9**	**452.9**	**206.7**	**121.0**	**116.8**	**104.9**
衣着	**Clothing**	**353.2**	**361.2**	**216.1**	**93.2**	**100.6**	**105.2**
#服 装	Garments	369.9	381.6	223.9	94.2	101.6	105.4
衣着材料	Clothing Materials	310.7	311.9	219.7	118.9	126.7	122.3
鞋袜帽	Footwear, Hosiery and Hats	366.4	371.9	217.2	87.7	96.7	103.9
家庭设备用品及维修服务	**Household Facilities, Articles and Repair Services**	**301.7**	**300.0**	**158.0**	**102.3**	**115.2**	**108.9**
医疗保健和个人用品	**Healthcare and Personal Articles**	**676.0**	**621.5**	**275.7**	**106.5**	**110.5**	**105.5**
交通和通信	**Transportation and Communication**	**105.2**	**105.2**	**88.7**	**81.8**	**89.2**	**99.6**
娱乐教育文化用品及服务	**Recreational, Educational, Cultural Commodities and Services**	**227.4**	**222.1**	**117.2**	**108.3**	**98.5**	**106.0**
居 住	**Residence**	**720.1**	**968.0**	**709.5**	**140.4**	**121.3**	**119.0**
#住房租金	House Rent	1976.8	3125.6	3100.8	158.6	138.6	121.2
水、电、燃料	Water, Electricity, and Fuels	757.2	757.2	624.4	166.1	112.2	105.5

7-5 居民消费价格分类指数(2013年)
CONSUMER PRICE INDEX BY CATEGORY (2013)

项目	Item	2012 =100
居民消费价格指数	**Consumer Price Index**	**103.3**
#非食品价格指数	**Non-food Price Index**	**102.7**
#服务项目价格指数	**Price Index for Services**	**105.5**
#消费品价格指数	**Price Index for Consumer Goods**	**101.9**
食　品	**Food**	**104.7**
粮　食	Grain	104.4
淀粉及制品	Starches and Their Products	105.0
干豆类及豆制品	Beans and Their Products	105.0
油　脂	Oil and Fat	99.8
肉禽及其制品	Meat, Poultry and Their Products	106.7
蛋	Eggs	103.7
水产品	Aquatic Products	103.4
菜	Vegetables	109.6
调味品	Flavoring	103.8
糖	Sugar	101.4
茶及饮料	Tea and Beverages	101.1
干鲜瓜果	Dried and Fresh Melons and Fruits	105.7
糕点饼干面包	Cake, Biscuits and Bread	102.4
液体乳及乳制品	Liquid Milk and Dairy Products	106.2
在外用膳食品	Foods Eaten Externally	104.0
其他食品	Other Foods	97.6
烟酒及用品	**Tobacco, Liquor and Related Articles**	**100.1**
烟　草	Tobacco	99.8
酒	Liquor	100.5
衣　着	**Clothing**	**101.5**
服　装	Garments	101.8
衣着材料	Clothing Materials	103.1
鞋袜帽	Footwear, Hosiery and Hats	100.8
衣着加工服务费	Clothing Processing Services	105.3
家庭设备用品及维修服务	**Households Facilities, Articles and Repairing Services**	**101.7**
耐用消费品	Durable Consumer Goods	100.8
室内装饰品	Interior Decorations	102.0
床上用品	Bedding	98.9
家庭日用杂品	Daily Groceries for Households	100.3
家庭服务及加工维修服务	Households Services and Maintenance Services	109.8
医疗保健和个人用品	**Healthcare and Personal Articles**	**100.2**
医疗保健	Health Care	101.2
医疗器具及用品	Medical Apparatus and Supplies	100.1
中药材及中成药	Traditional Chinese Medicial Materials and Chinese Patent Drugs	103.8
西　药	Western Medicines	99.9
保健器具及用品	Healthcare Appliances and Articles	103.0
医疗保健服务	Healthcare Services	100.0
个人用品及服务	Personal Articles and Services	98.4
化妆美容用品	Cosmetics	97.0
清洁类化妆品	Cosmetics for Cleaning	100.7
个人饰品	Personal Accessories	92.3
个人服务	Personal Services	108.8
交通和通信	**Transportation and Communication**	**99.0**
交　通	Transportation	100.4
交通工具	Vehicles	97.6
车用燃料及零配件	Fuels and Vehicle Parts	99.0
车辆使用及维修费	Fees for Use and Maintenance of Vehicles	104.9
市区公共交通费	Incity Public Traffic	103.2
城市间交通费	Intercity Traffic	101.3
通　信	Communication	96.1
通信工具	Communication Devices	74.4
通信服务	Communication Services	99.5
娱乐教育文化用品及服务	**Recreational, Educational, Cultural Articles and Related Services**	**103.9**
文娱用耐用消费品及服务	Durable Consumer Goods for Cultural and Recreation Use and Services	92.2
教　育	Education	107.2
文化娱乐类	Culture and Entertainment	102.7
旅　游	Tourism	105.6
居　住	**Residence**	**105.6**
建房及装修材料	Building and Decoration Materials	100.8
住房租金	House Rent	106.0
自有住房	Private Housing	106.8
水、电、燃料	Water, Electricity and Fuels	103.4

7-6 商品零售价格分类指数(2013年)
RETAIL PRICE INDEX BY CATEGORY (2013)

项　　目	Item	2012 =100	项　　目	Item	2012 =100
商品零售价格指数	**Retail Price Index**	**99.8**	床上用品	Bedding	98.8
食　品	**Food**	**104.9**	**家用电器及音像器材**	**Household Appliances, and Audio Equipment**	**95.7**
粮　食	Grain	104.4	家庭设备	Household Appliances	98.9
淀粉及制品	Starches and Their Products	105.0	文娱用耐用消费品	Durable Consumer Goods for Cultural and Recreation Use	91.9
干豆类及豆制品	Beans and Their Products	105.0	专业音响器材	Professional Audio Equipment	98.1
油　脂	Oil and Fat	99.8	**文化办公用品**	**Cultural and Office Ariticles**	**95.6**
肉禽及其制品	Meat, Poultry and Their Products	106.7	**日用品**	**Domestic Commodities**	**100.8**
食用畜肉及副产品	Meat and Sideline Products	108.6	日用百货	General Merchandise	100.8
禽	Pourtry	101.7	日用杂品	Groceries for Daily Use	99.8
加工肉禽	Processed Meat and Poultry	103.8	洗涤用品	Washing Products	101.4
蛋	Eggs	103.7	其他日用品	Other Domestic Commodities	100.9
水产品	Aquatic Products	103.4	**体育娱乐用品**	**Sports and Entertainment Articles**	**101.9**
鱼	Fish	102.0	体育用品	Sports Articles	102.0
其他水产品	Other Aquatic Products	104.8	娱乐用品	Entertainment Articles	101.6
菜	Vegetables	109.6	**交通、通信用品**	**Transportation and Communication Articles**	**94.5**
调味品	Flavoring	103.8	交通运输机械	Transportation Machinery	97.3
糖	Sugar	101.4	通信器材	Communication Devices	76.7
干鲜瓜果	Dried and Fresh Melons and Fruits	105.7	**家　具**	**Furnitures**	**103.2**
糕点饼干面包	Cake, Biscuits and Bread	102.4	**化妆品**	**Cosmetics**	**99.1**
液体乳及乳制品	Liquid Milk and Dairy Products	106.2	**金银珠宝**	**Gold, Silver and Jewelry**	**88.9**
在外用膳食品	Foods Eaten Externally	104.0	**中西药品及医疗保健用品**	**Traditional Chinese and Western Medicines and Healthcare Articles**	**101.6**
其他食品	Other Foods	97.6	医疗器具及用品	Medical Apparatus and Articles	100.1
饮料、烟酒	**Beverages, Tobacco and Liquor**	**100.6**	中药材及中成药	Traditional Chinese Medicial Materials and Chinese Patent Drugs	103.8
茶及饮料	Tea and Beverages	101.1	西　药	Western Medicines	99.9
茶　叶	Tea	99.9	保健器具及用品	Healthcare Apparatus and Articles	103.0
饮　料	Beverages	102.0	**书报杂志及电子出版物**	**Books, Newspapers, Magazines and Electronic Publications**	**100.8**
烟　草	Tobacco	99.8	教材及参考书	Teaching Materials and Reference Books	100.3
酒	Liquor	100.5	书报杂志	Books and Magazines	101.0
服装、鞋帽	**Garments, Footwear, and Hats**	**101.5**	电子音像制品	Electronic Publications	103.3
服　装	Garments	101.8	**燃　料**	**Fuels**	**100.6**
男式服装	Clothing for Men	100.4	煤炭及制品	Coal and Coal Products	102.8
女式服装	Clothing for Women	102.5	石油及制品	Petroleum and Related Products	100.4
儿童服装	Clothing for Children	105.8	**建筑材料及五金电料**	**Building Materials and Hardware**	**100.4**
鞋袜帽	Footwear, Hosiery and Hats	100.8	建筑装璜材料	Building and Decoration Materials	100.5
鞋	Shoes	100.8	五金电料	Hardware	99.8
袜　子	Hosiery	101.5			
帽　子	Hats	94.8			
其　他	Others	102.7			
纺织品	**Textiles**	**99.3**			
衣着材料	Clothing Materials	103.1			

7-7 农产品生产价格指数
PRODUCER PRICE INDEX FOR ARICULTURAL PRODUCTS

(上年=100) (preceding year=100)

项　　目	Item	2013	2012
总指数	**General Index**	**104.7**	**104.7**
农业产品	Agricultural Products	105.5	107.9
#粮　食	Grain	102.9	105.7
蔬菜及食用菌	Vegetable and Edible Fungus	107.0	107.9
林业产品	Forestry Products	111.3	107.8
牧业(畜产品)	Animal Husbandry Products	104.2	100.7
#肉　牛	Beef Cattle	113.1	114.4
肉　羊	Mutton Sheep	106.0	110.1
奶产品	Milk Products	111.3	99.7
猪	Hogs	98.3	93.5
肉禽(毛重)	Poultry (Gross Weight)	104.4	104.8
禽　蛋	Eggs	105.1	100.5
渔　业	Fishing	99.0	112.6

7-8 工业生产者出厂价格及购进价格指数(2000-2013年)

(上年=100)

年 份 Year	工业生产者出厂价格指数 Producer Price Index for Industrial Products (PPI)	轻工业 Light Industry	重工业 Heavy Industry	生产资料 Capital Goods	生活资料 Living Goods	工业生产者购进价格指数 Purchasing Price Index for Industrial Products	燃料、动力类 Fuels and Power
2000	102.5	98.0	104.2	103.4	98.8	100.0	104.3
2001	99.4	99.6	99.4	99.4	99.6	100.5	101.7
2002	96.6	97.6	96.4	96.4	97.9	97.1	102.3
2003	101.5	98.0	104.5	102.2	99.1	104.7	109.6
2004	103.0	100.2	105.3	103.7	100.6	114.2	120.0
2005	101.3	98.7	103.3	101.9	99.1	111.4	117.1
2006	99.1	97.9	99.6	99.0	99.3	105.5	113.1
2007	99.7	100.7	99.2	99.3	101.3	105.0	105.1
2008	103.3	101.8	104.0	103.8	101.3	115.8	132.3
2009	94.4	96.2	93.6	93.3	99.1	88.6	85.1
2010	102.2	98.7	103.8	102.7	100.3	110.5	121.3
2011	102.3	104.6	102.0	102.5	101.6	108.4	117.8
2012	98.4	101.1	98.0	97.8	101.0	98.7	99.0
2013	97.4	100.7	96.9	96.7	100.5	97.8	96.4

PRODUCER PRICE INDEX AND PURCHASING PRICE INDEX FOR INDUSTRIAL PRODUCTS (2000-2013)

(preceding year=100)

黑色金属材料类 Ferrous Metal Materials	有色金属材料和电线类 Nonferrous Metal Materials and Electric Wires	化工原料类 Chemical Raw Materials	木材及纸浆类 Timber and Paper Pulp	建筑材料及非金属矿类 Construction Materials and Nonmetal Ores	其他工业原材料及半成品类 Other Industrial Materials and Semi-finished Products	农副产品类 Agricultural Products	纺织原料类 Textile Raw Materials
100.5	106.9	103.4	94.8	101.9	98.4	94.5	91.5
100.3	97.9	97.6	98.3	99.5	98.8	103.5	100.6
96.4	96.1	99.3	102.5	97.6	92.3	93.6	97.8
110.9	101.4	107.3	100.6	99.0	95.2	114.3	98.1
124.5	120.9	111.1	100.7	105.8	103.8	122.3	102.8
108.3	123.3	114.9	103.6	101.8	102.8	96.3	106.2
96.7	138.3	104.1	100.3	99.4	98.0	101.3	100.9
115.6	112.2	106.7	101.7	103.5	95.3	138.6	99.2
128.5	97.9	108.3	108.5	115.2	94.9	132.6	101.5
79.8	81.1	82.3	97.0	99.4	95.3	88.2	97.6
115.4	121.6	111.7	104.2	102.7	99.0	106.6	102.8
112.7	115.2	112.7	105.7	103.0	98.9	128.8	108.2
92.2	96.7	102.5	99.0	93.9	98.8	98.5	100.8
94.6	92.1	98.6	98.4	94.2	98.9	102.2	99.6

7-9 工业生产者出厂价格指数
PRODUCER PRICE INDEX FOR INDUSTRIAL PRODUCTS

(上年=100) (preceding year=100)

项目	Item	2013	2012
总指数	**General Index**	**97.4**	**98.4**
按轻、重工业分	**By Light Industry and Heavy Industry**		
轻工业	Light Industry	100.7	101.1
以农产品为原料	Using Farming Products as Raw Materials	102.0	102.6
以非农产品为原料	Using Non-agricultural Products as Raw Materials	99.0	98.7
重工业	Heavy Industry	96.9	98.0
采　掘	Excavation	87.7	93.9
原　料	Raw Materials	99.6	101.8
加　工	Processing	96.3	96.6
按生产、生活资料分	**By Capital Goods and Living Goods**		
生产资料	Capital Goods	96.7	97.8
采　掘	Excavation	87.7	93.9
原　料	Raw Materials	99.6	101.8
加　工	Processing	95.9	96.2
生活资料	Living Goods	100.5	101.0
食　品	Foods	102.9	103.3
衣　着	Clothing	97.7	98.8
一般日用品	Articles for Daily Use	99.1	100.2
耐用消费品	Durable Consumer Goods	99.8	99.9

7-10 工业生产者出厂价格指数(按行业分)
PRODUCER PRICE INDEX FOR INDUSTRIAL PRODUCTS(BY SECTOR)

(上年=100) (preceding year=100)

项 目	Item	2013	2012
总指数	**General Index**	**97.4**	**98.4**
煤炭开采和洗选业	Mining and Washing of Coal	86.8	94.7
黑色金属矿采选业	Mining and Processing of Ferrous Metal Ores	99.1	80.5
非金属矿采选业	Mining and Processing of Nonmetal Ores	100.0	99.5
农副食品加工业	Processing of Food from Agriculture Products	105.8	102.1
食品制造业	Manufacture of Foods	101.6	107.8
酒、饮料和精制茶制造业	Manufacture of Wines, Beverage and Refined Tea	101.4	101.8
烟草制品业	Manufacture of Cigarettes and Tobacco	100.1	100.3
纺织业	Manufacture of Textile	96.8	96.5
纺织服装、服饰业	Manufacture of Textile Wearing Apparel and Ornament	99.3	100.5
皮革、毛皮、羽毛及其制品和制鞋业	Manufacture of Leather, Fur, Feather and Its Products, and Footwear	100.4	99.9
木材加工和木、竹、藤、棕、草制品业	Processing of Timbers, Manufacture of Wood, Bamboo, Rattan, Palm and Straw Products	100.1	102.7
家具制造业	Manufacture of Furniture	102.4	102.2
造纸和纸制品业	Manufacture of Paper and Paper Products	97.7	101.6
印刷和记录媒介复制业	Printing, Reproduction of Recording Media	99.6	99.8
文教、工美、体育和娱乐用品制造业	Manufacture of Articles for Culture, Education, Artwork, Sports and Entertainment Activity	97.1	99.8
石油加工、炼焦和核燃料加工业	Processing of Petroleum, Coking, Processing of Nucleus Fuel	98.0	103.8
化学原料和化学制品制造业	Manufacture of Chemical Raw Material and Chemical Products	99.0	94.6
医药制造业	Manufacture of Medicines	99.6	100.3
化学纤维制造业	Manufacture of Chemical Fibres	99.8	99.3
橡胶和塑料制品业	Manufacture of Rubber and Plastics Products	98.0	98.4
非金属矿物制品业	Manufacture of Non-Metallic Mineral Products	98.0	98.0
黑色金属冶炼和压延加工业	Manufacture and Processing of Ferrous Metals	92.1	90.8
有色金属冶炼和压延加工业	Manufacture and processing of Non-Ferrous Metals	89.2	103.5
金属制品业	Manufacture of Fabricated Metal Products	96.9	99.9
通用设备制造业	Manufacture of General-Purpose Machinery	98.7	99.6
专用设备制造业	Manufacture of Special-Purpose Machinery	100.0	100.5
汽车制造业	Manufacture of Motor Vehicles	99.2	99.3
铁路、船舶、航空航天和其他运输设备制造业	Manufacture of Railway Locomotives, Building of Ships and Boats, Manufacture of Air and Spacecrafts and Other Transportation Equipments	98.2	98.9
电气机械和器材制造业	Manufacture of Electrical Machinery and Equipment	97.8	95.9
计算机、通信和其他电子设备制造业	Manufacture of Computer, Communication Equipment and Other Electronic Equipment	92.4	92.4
仪器仪表制造业	Manufacture of Measuring Instrument and Meter	99.3	99.6
其他制造业	Other Manufacturing	100.7	103.1
废弃资源综合利用业	Waste Recycling and Recovery	98.5	95.2
金属制品、机械和设备修理业	Repair of Fabricated Metal Products,Machinery and Equipment	103.4	99.3
电力、热力生产和供应业	Production and Supply of Electricity and Heating Power	100.2	102.2
燃气生产和供应业	Production and Distribution of Gas	104.8	97.8
水的生产和供应业	Production and Distribution of Water	100.0	105.5

注：根据国家统计局规定，2012年起执行2011年国民经济行业分类标准（GB/T 4754-2011）。

Note: According to provisions of the National Bureau of Statistics, since 2012, sectors have been classified in accordance with the Standard for Classification of National Economic Sectors 2011(GB/T 4754-2011).

7-11 工业生产者购进价格指数
PURCHASING PRICE INDEX FOR INDUSTRIAL PRODUCTS

(上年=100) (preceding year=100)

项目	Item	2013	2012
总指数	**General Index**	**97.8**	**98.7**
燃料、动力类	Fuels and Power	96.4	99.0
黑色金属材料类	Ferrous Metal Materials	94.6	92.2
#钢材	Steel Products	94.3	91.1
其他	Others	95.9	95.9
有色金属材料和电线类	Nonferrous Metal Materials and Electric Wires	92.1	96.7
化工原料类	Chemical Raw Materials	98.6	102.5
木材及纸浆类	Timber and Paper Pulp	98.4	99.0
建筑材料及非金属矿类	Construction Materials and Nonmetal Ores	94.2	93.9
其他工业原材料及半成品类	Other Industrial Materials and Semi-finished Products	98.9	98.8
农副产品类	Agricultural Products	102.2	98.5
纺织原料类	Textile Raw Materials	99.6	100.8

7-12 固定资产投资价格指数(2013年)
PRICE INDEX FOR INVESTMENT IN FIXED ASSETS (2013)

项目	Item	1992 =100	1993 =100	1994 =100	2000 =100	2004 =100	2005 =100	2006 =100	2007 =100	2008 =100	2009 =100	2010 =100	2011 =100	2012 =100
总指数	**General Index**	**243.2**	**192.2**	**165.3**	**128.3**	**119.3**	**118.4**	**118.0**	**114.8**	**106.5**	**109.6**	**107.0**	**101.2**	**99.9**
建筑安装、装饰工程	Construction, Installation and Decoration Projects	299.1	228.0	190.2	139.4	120.9	120.2	120.7	115.8	103.6	109.9	105.7	96.3	97.3
人工费	Labor Cost	980.6	693.3	479.3	210.3	181.0	174.0	167.3	157.6	144.4	138.5	130.3	116.7	106.4
材料费	Cost of Materials	239.2	177.3	150.8	129.8	111.1	111.3	113.0	108.7	96.2	104.8	100.9	91.8	95.1
机械使用费	Cost of Machinery Use				123.2	119.8	119.8	118.2	116.3	110.6	109.8	108.0	104.4	101.3
设备、工器具购置	Purchase of Equipment, Tools and Instruments	104.2	90.6	88.8	71.1	85.8	87.2	87.5	88.5	90.2	93.3	94.1	95.2	97.7
其他费用	Others	208.3	170.6	138.2	130.7	127.0	124.7	122.5	119.9	114.4	113.4	111.3	107.0	102.9

7-13 住宅销售价格指数(2013年各月)
SELLING PRICE INDEX OF RESIDENTIAL HOUSES (EACH MONTH OF 2013)

(上年同月=100) (preceding year=100)

项 目	Item	1月 JAN	2月 FEB	3月 MAR	4月 APR	5月 MAY	6月 JUN
新建住宅	**New Residential Houses**	**103.3**	**105.9**	**108.6**	**110.3**	**111.8**	**112.9**
#新建商品住宅	New Commercial Residential Houses	104.3	107.7	111.2	113.4	115.2	116.7
90平方米及以下	90sq.m and below	104.3	108.0	111.9	114.5	116.2	118.0
90-144平方米	90-144sq.m	104.3	107.5	110.8	113.0	114.9	116.3
144平方米以上	144sq.m over	104.2	107.5	110.9	112.9	114.8	116.3
二手住宅	**Second-hand Residential Houses**	**103.5**	**106.0**	**109.1**	**110.9**	**112.8**	**114.1**
90平方米及以下	90sq.m and below	104.0	106.8	110.3	112.3	113.7	114.9
90-144平方米	90-144sq.m	103.0	105.2	108.1	109.7	112.1	113.6
144平方米以上	144sq.m over	103.1	105.0	107.4	109.0	111.6	112.7

7-13 续表 Continued

(上年同月=100) (preceding year=100)

项 目	Item	7月 JUL	8月 AUG	9月 SEP	10月 OCT	11月 NOV	12月 DEC
新建住宅	**New Residential Houses**	**114.1**	**114.9**	**116.0**	**116.4**	**116.3**	**116.0**
#新建商品住宅	New Commercial Residential Houses	118.3	119.3	120.6	121.2	121.1	120.6
90平方米及以下	90sq.m and below	119.6	120.6	122.1	122.7	122.5	121.7
90-144平方米	90-144sq.m	117.7	118.8	120.1	120.8	120.8	120.1
144平方米以上	144sq.m over	117.8	118.8	120.0	120.4	120.2	120.2
二手住宅	**Second-hand Residential Houses**	**115.3**	**116.4**	**117.8**	**119.0**	**120.1**	**119.7**
90平方米及以下	90sq.m and below	116.4	117.4	119.0	120.3	121.4	120.8
90-144平方米	90-144sq.m	114.7	115.7	117.1	118.6	119.7	119.5
144平方米以上	144sq.m over	113.5	114.7	115.5	116.3	117.5	117.4

主要统计指标解释

居民消费价格指数 是度量消费商品及服务项目价格水平随着时间而变动的相对数，反映居民家庭购买的消费品及服务价格水平的变动情况。居民消费价格指数变动率通常被用来作为反映通货膨胀（或紧缩）程度的指标。

商品零售价格指数 是度量工业、商业、餐饮业和其他零售企业向城乡居民、机关团体出售生活消费品和办公用品价格水平随着时间而变动的相对数，反映市场商品零售价格的变动程度。

工业生产者出厂价格指数 是反映全部工业产品出厂价格总水平变动程度的相对数。其中包括工业企业售给商业、外贸、物资部门的产品，还包括售给工业和其他部门的生产资料以及直接售给居民的生活消费品。通过工业生产价格指数能观察工业产品出厂价格变动对工业总产值的影响。

工业生产者购进价格指数 是反映全部工业原材料、燃料、动力购进价格总水平变动程度的相对数。用其可以观察和研究工业企业原材料价格变动对生产的影响，以及企业对原材料涨价的消化能力和承受能力，为制定价格政策提供依据。

固定资产投资价格指数 是反映固定资产投资额价格变动程度的相对数。固定资产投资额由建筑安装装饰工程投资完成额，设备、工器具购置投资完成额和其他费用投资完成额三部分组成。编制固定资产投资价格指数应首先分别编制上述三部分投资的价格指数，然后采用加权算术平均法求出固定资产投资价格总指数。编制固定资产投资价格指数可以准确地反映固定资产投资中涉及的各类商品和取费项目价格变动幅度，消除按现价计算的固定资产投资指标中的价格变动因素，真实地反映固定资产投资的规模、速度、结构和效益，为国家科学地制定、检查固定资产投资计划，提高宏观调控水平，为完善国民经济核算体系提供科学、可靠的依据。

住宅销售价格指数 是反映住宅销售价格总水平变动趋势和程度的相对数。包括新建住宅销售价格指数和二手住宅销售价格指数。

农产品生产价格指数 是指农产品生产价格总水平变动程度的相对数。农产品生产价格是指农产品生产者第一次出售其产品时的单位产品价格。

Explanatory Notes on Main Statistical Indicators

Consumer Price Index (CPI) is a relative number measuring the changes in prices of consumer goods and service purchased by consumers over time. CPI is usually used for reflecting the level of inflation (or deflation).

Retail Price Index is a relative number measuring the changes in prices of consumer goods and office supplies provided by industrial, commercial, catering and other retail businesses over time. It reflects the extent of changes in retail prices of commodities in the market.

Producer Price Index for Industrial Products (PPI) is a relative number reflecting the degree of changes in general producer prices of all industrial products, including products sold by industrial enterprises to commercial, foreign trade and materials companies, as well as production materials sold to industrial and other enterprises, and consumer goods directly sold to consumers. It can be used to analyze the impact of producer prices of industrial products on gross industrial output value.

Purchasing Price Index for Industrial Products is a relative number reflecting the degree of changes in the overall level of prices of all industrial materials, fuels and power. It can be used to observe and analyze the effect of changes in prices of raw materials in industrial enterprises on their production, as well as the enterprises' capacity of digesting and bearing the rising prices of raw materials, thus providing basis for formulating price policies.

Price Index for Investment in Fixed Assets is a relative number reflecting the degree of changes in prices of investment in fixed assets. The investment in fixed assets consists of three components, i.e. the investment in construction and installation, the investment in purchasing equipment and instrument, and the investment in other items. Price index for investment in fixed assets is calculated as the weighted arithmetic mean of the price indices of the three components of investment in fixed assets. Removing the factor of price change in the aggregates of investment at current prices, this indicator shows the changes in the prices of commodities and fees involved in the investment of fixed assets, and can be used to observe the actual size, growth, structure, and efficiency of investment in fixed assets and provides reliable and scientific basis for government planning on and examination of fixed assets investment, thus to improve overall adjustment and controlling skill, and further improve the national accounting system.

Selling Price Index of Residential Houses is a relative number reflecting the trend and degree of changes in the overall level of house selling prices, including new house selling price index and second-hand house selling price index.

Producer Price Index for Agricultural Products is a relative number reflecting the degree of changes in the overall production prices of agricultural products. Producer price of agricultural products refers to the price of unit product at which the producers of agricultural products sell their products for the first time.

北京统计年鉴2014　BEIJING STATISTICAL YEARBOOK

人民生活
PEOPLE'S LIVELIHOOD

简要说明

一、本章资料的主要内容

本章资料反映北京市居民生活现状及变化情况，分为城镇居民生活和农村居民生活两部分。调查内容主要包括家庭基本情况、家庭收入和消费支出情况、主要商品购买数量及支出金额、居住状况和耐用消费品拥有量等。

二、本章资料的数据来源

城乡居民生活状况的数据来源于国家统计局北京调查总队、北京市统计局。

三、本章资料的调查方法

城乡居民生活状况调查方法和方案由国家统计局统一制定，采用抽样调查的方法，按对全市及分区县居民主要收支指标有代表性的原则在全市城乡住户中抽取样本，并按一定的周期对样本进行轮换以保证其代表性。对抽中的住户采用日记账和问卷相结合的方式采集数据。

四、本章资料的调查范围

城镇住户调查的口径范围：2000-2003 年为 1000 户城市居民，覆盖城八区；2004-2006 年为 2000 户城市居民，覆盖城八区；2007 年为 3000 户城镇居民，覆盖所有区县；2008-2012 年为 5000 户城镇居民，覆盖所有区县。

农村住户调查的口径范围：2000-2002 年为 2710 户，覆盖 14 个郊区县；2003 年为 2670 户（石景山区全部农民转居民，40 个样本取消），覆盖 13 个郊区县；2004-2012 年为 3000 户，覆盖 13 个郊区县。

城乡住户调查一体化：2013 年，根据国家统计局实施城乡住户调查一体化改革的要求和《住户收支与生活状况调查方案》的有关规定，国家统计局北京调查总队、北京市统计局对全市城乡住户进行了统一的样本抽取，城乡住户调查样本量共计 10000 户。

五、五等分组的含义

要客观的反映不同收入层次家庭的收支及生活状况，必须按不同收入水平进行分组来观察和分析。“五等分组”即城镇住户按人均可支配收入、农村住户按人均纯收入从低到高排队分别分成五等份，即低收入组、中低收入组、中等收入组、中高收入组和高收入组五部分，各组的户数均占总户数的 20%。通过对调查户的分组，可以分别计算各组人均收入、消费性支出的情况，以观察不同收入组之间的差距和存在的问题。

Brief Introduction

I. Main Content

Statistics in this chapter reflect the living conditions of residents in Beijing and their changes, consisting of two parts, one for urban residents, and the other for rural residents. Figures include the basic family situation, household income and expenditures in cash, purchase quantity and expenditures of main commodities, housing conditions and number of durable consumer goods in possession.

II. Source of Statistics

Statistics on the living conditions of urban and rural residents are from NBS Survey Office in Beijing, and Beijing Municipal Bureau of Statistics.

Ⅲ. Method of Survey

Methods and plans of survey for living conditions of urban and rural residents are designated by National Bureau of Statistics. The method of sampling survey is adopted to take samples across Beijing Municipality following the principle of selecting representative residents in terms of major income and expenditure indicators. Samples are changed in certain periods to ensure their representativeness. For selected residents, statistics are gathered through journals and questionnares.

Ⅳ. Scope of Survey

Scope of survey for urban residents: In 2000-2003, the survey covered 1,000 urban households in 8 urban districts; in 2004-2006, covered 2,000 urban households in 8 urban districts; in 2007 covered 3,000 urban households in all districts and counties; in 2008-2012, covered 5,000 households in all districts and counties.

Scope of survey for rural residents: In 2000-2002, the survey covered 2,710 households in 14 suburban districts and counties; in 2003, covered 2,670 households (All rural residents became urban residents in Shijingshan District, so 40 samples were cancelled.); in 2004-2012 covered 3,000 households in 13 suburban districts and counties.

Integration of survey on urban and rural residents. In 2013, according to the requirements of the National Bureau of Statistics on carrying out integrated reforms of urban and rural resident survey, and Survey Plan on Income and Expenditure, and Living Conditions of Households, the NBS Survey Office in Beijing and Beijing Municipal Bureau of Statistics took a total of 10,000 samples of urban and rural residents in an integrated way.

V. Meaning of Five-level Grouping

It is necessary to have groups at different levels for observation and analysis to reflect the income and payment and living conditions of households at different income levels. "Five-level grouping" means that urban households are divided into five groups in a low-to-high order regarding the per capita disposable income, while rural households are grouped by net per capita income. These five groups are the low-income, middle-low-income, middle-income, middle-high-income and high-income groups. The number of households in each group accounts for 20% of the total. Through grouping of the households under survey, we can calculate the per capital income and consumptive expenditures of each group so as to observe the differences between different income groups and existing problems.

8-1 人民生活基本情况(1978-2013年)
PEOPLE'S LIFE (1978-2013)

年份 Year	城镇居民家庭基本情况 Basic Information on Urban Household Lives							
	人均家庭总收入(元) Per Capita Total Income (yuan)	人均可支配收入(元) Per Capita Disposable Income (yuan)	人均可支配收入实际增长(%) Actual Growth Rate of Per Capita Disposable Income (%)	人均消费性支出(元) Per Capita Living Expenditures (yuan)	#食品 Foods	城镇居民家庭恩格尔系数(%) Engel Coefficient of Urban Households (%)	每一城镇就业者负担人数(人) Dependents Per Urban Employee (person)	城镇居民人均住房建筑面积(平方米) Per Capita Floor Space of Houses in Urban Areas (sq.m)
1978	450.2	365.4		359.9	211.2	58.7	1.86	
1979	491.5	415.0	11.6	408.7	236.7	57.9	1.83	
1980	599.4	501.4	14.0	490.4	271.0	55.3	1.80	
1981	619.6	514.1	1.2	511.4	295.1	57.7	1.72	
1982	668.1	561.1	7.2	534.8	317.6	59.3	1.66	
1983	716.6	590.5	4.7	574.1	337.7	58.8	1.65	
1984	837.7	693.7	15.0	666.8	379.1	56.8	1.63	
1985	1158.8	907.7	11.3	923.3	466.9	50.6	1.66	
1986	1317.3	1067.5	10.1	1067.4	543.4	50.9	1.66	
1987	1413.2	1181.9	1.9	1147.6	605.0	52.7	1.65	
1988	1767.7	1437.0	1.0	1455.6	743.4	51.1	1.71	
1989	1899.6	1597.1	-5.2	1520.4	841.3	55.3	1.52	
1990	2067.3	1787.1	6.2	1646.1	892.2	54.2	1.52	
1991	2359.9	2040.4	2.1	1860.2	1016.8	54.7	1.47	
1992	2813.1	2363.7	5.4	2134.7	1126.3	52.8	1.43	
1993	3935.4	3296.0	17.1	2939.6	1404.7	47.8	1.42	
1994	5585.9	4731.2	14.9	4134.1	1919.0	46.4	1.41	
1995	6748.7	5868.4	5.7	5019.8	2436.5	48.5	1.41	
1996	7945.8	6885.5	5.1	5729.5	2671.5	46.6	1.41	
1997	8741.7	7813.1	7.8	6531.8	2854.4	43.7	1.43	
1998	10098.2	8472.0	5.9	6970.8	2865.7	41.1	1.40	
1999	10654.8	9182.8	7.8	7498.5	2959.2	39.5	1.41	
2000	12560.3	10349.7	8.9	8493.5	3083.4	36.3	1.41	
2001	13768.8	11577.8	8.5	8922.7	3229.3	36.2	1.39	
2002	13253.3	12463.9	15.6	10285.8	3472.5	33.8	1.41	19.22
2003	14959.3	13882.6	11.2	11123.8	3522.7	31.7	1.39	19.71
2004	17116.5	15637.8	11.5	12200.4	3925.5	32.2	1.44	21.49
2005	19533.3	17653.0	11.2	13244.2	4215.6	31.8	1.39	22.03
2006	22417.0	19978.0	12.2	14825.0	4561.0	30.8	1.40	23.65
2007	24576.0	21989.0	11.2	15330.0	4934.0	32.2	1.40	24.77
2008	27678.0	24725.0	7.0	16460.0	5562.0	33.8	1.40	26.90
2009	30674.0	26738.0	9.7	17893.0	5936.0	33.2	1.40	27.69
2010	33360.0	29073.0	6.2	19934.0	6393.0	32.1	1.40	28.94
2011	37124.0	32903.0	7.2	21984.0	6905.0	31.4	1.50	29.38
2012	41103.0	36469.0	7.3	24046.0	7535.0	31.3	1.40	29.26
2013	45274.0	40321.0	7.1	26275.0	8170.0	31.1	1.50	31.31

注：表内城镇居民人均住房建筑面积为城镇住户抽样调查数据。

Note: Per capita floor space of houses in urban areas in this table is the data of sampling survey on urban households.

8-1 续表 Continued

年份 Year	农村居民家庭基本情况 Basic Information on Rural Households Lives							居民储蓄存款余额(亿元) Balance of Deposits (100 million yuan)	人均储蓄(元) Per Capita Deposits (yuan)
	人均纯收入(元) Per Capita Net Income (yuan)	人均纯收入实际增长(%) Actual Growth Rate of Per Capita Net Income (%)	人均总支出(元) Per Capita Total Expenditures (yuan)	人均生活消费支出(元) Per Capita Living Expenditures (yuan)	#食品 Foods	农村居民家庭恩格尔系数(%) Engel Coefficient of Rural Households (%)	每一农村劳动力负担人数(人) Dependents Per Rural Labor Force (person)	农村居民人均住房面积(平方米) Per Capita Living Space of Rural Residents (sq.m)		
1978	224.8		219.0	185.4	116.7	63.2	2.15	9.20	9.33	110
1979	250.0	10.9	235.0	204.7	131.1	63.9	2.16	9.67	11.07	127
1980	308.1	22.1	290.0	256.8	140.2	54.1	2.13	10.09	14.39	162
1981	361.4	17.1	350.5	307.2	160.6	52.3	2.14	12.35	17.39	193
1982	430.2	17.3	411.2	345.5	181.1	52.4	1.97	13.01	21.77	237
1983	519.5	20.9	498.5	384.4	193.8	50.4	1.82	14.24	29.81	319
1984	664.2	25.7	559.3	435.0	222.5	51.1	1.79	14.22	38.82	411
1985	775.1	14.5	726.0	510.0	240.5	47.1	1.64	16.48	51.70	540
1986	823.1	3.7	857.0	645.3	292.4	45.3	1.66	17.41	68.58	706
1987	916.4	6.5	943.0	705.5	340.9	48.3	1.64	18.38	92.90	940
1988	1062.6	3.1	1246.0	883.3	407.9	46.2	1.63	19.23	111.60	1115
1989	1230.7	2.2	1356.0	976.3	484.3	49.6	1.62	20.09	162.01	1587
1990	1297.1	2.1	1372.0	980.7	497.0	50.7	1.61	20.62	226.62	2196
1991	1422.3	1.7	1585.0	1100.1	537.0	48.8	1.59	21.92	299.23	2879
1992	1568.8	2.0	1684.0	1179.0	573.8	48.7	1.58	22.67	389.79	3730
1993	1854.8	5.1	1714.0	1308.9	611.7	46.8	1.51	23.70	562.54	5351
1994	2422.1	9.1	2175.0	1676.5	824.8	49.2	1.49	24.42	853.21	8036
1995	3208.5	6.3	3080.0	2433.0	1206.0	49.6	1.47	24.74	1253.95	11716
1996	3562.7	4.8	3272.0	2655.5	1233.1	46.4	1.45	25.74	1706.98	15839
1997	3762.4	5.1	3379.0	2795.4	1248.4	44.7	1.48	27.39	1975.26	18197
1998	4028.9	6.7	3617.0	2945.5	1241.9	42.2	1.44	27.64	2287.19	20955
1999	4316.4	7.2	3938.0	3132.5	1253.5	40.0	1.43	28.65	2680.66	24374
2000	4687.0	7.3	4517.9	3441.4	1263.6	36.7	1.51	28.91	2923.21	26395
2001	5274.3	8.7	5098.8	3871.5	1353.2	34.9	1.52	31.01	3536.32	31510
2002	5880.1	12.3	5548.7	4206.0	1386.6	33.0	1.48	32.58	4389.69	38631
2003	6496.3	11.5	5886.6	4655.3	1475.6	31.7	1.45	33.95	5293.53	46079
2004	7172.1	9.2	6275.2	4886.4	1592.3	32.6	1.46	34.21	6122.35	52647
2005	7860.0	8.1	7181.2	5515.0	1807.0	32.8	1.45	36.94	7477.59	49346
2006	8620.0	8.7	7935.0	6061.0	1937.0	32.0	1.42	39.10	8703.29	55453
2007	9559.0	8.2	8866.0	6828.0	2190.0	32.1	1.40	39.54	9113.49	55621
2008	10747.0	6.5	10166.0	7656.0	2629.0	34.3	1.40	39.40	11869.91	68871
2009	11986.0	13.4	11814.0	9141.0	2961.0	32.4	1.39	39.42	14566.30	80233
2010	13262.0	8.1	12805.0	10109.0	3121.0	30.9	1.39	40.62	16876.30	88314
2011	14736.0	7.6	14503.0	11078.0	3593.0	32.4	1.38	48.63	18924.64	95087
2012	16476.0	8.2	15196.0	11879.0	3945.0	33.2	1.40	49.08	21419.28	104794
2013	18337.0	7.7	16994.0	13553.0	4696.0	34.6	1.49	51.35	22929.60	109604

注：1. 本表中"居民储蓄存款余额"为中资金融机构人民币储蓄存款余额。
2. 本表中计算"人均储蓄"使用的人口标准:2004年及以前年份使用北京市户籍人口，2005年开始使用北京市年平均常住人口。
3. 2011年农村居民人均纯收入及其分组数据按国家统计局方案进行了口径调整，2011年增长速度为同口径增速。

资料来源：表中"居民储蓄存款余额"数据来自中国人民银行营业管理部。

Note: a) In this table, the "balance of deposits" is the balance of deposits in RMB for domestic-funded financial institutions.
b) Population figures used for "per capital deposits" in this table are the population for residents registered in Beijing before 2004, and since 2005, the figures are the annual permanent residents population in Beijing.
c) Since 2011, coverage of figures for per capita net income of rural households and their grouping are adjusted in accordance with plans of the National Bureau of Statistics. Growth rate in 2011 are figures with the same coverage.

Source: Figures of Balance of Deposits in the table are from the Banking Administration Department of the People's Bank of China.

8-2 城镇居民家庭基本情况(按收入水平分)(2013年)
BASIC DATA ON URBAN HOUSEHOLDS (BY INCOME LEVEL) (2013)

项目		Item		全市平均 Auerage	低收入户20% Low Income	中低收入户20% Medium-Low Income	中等收入户20% Medium Income	中高收入户20% Medium-High Income	高收入户20% High Income
平均每户家庭人口	(人)	Average Population Per Household	(person)	2.6	2.9	2.8	2.5	2.5	2.1
平均每户就业人口数	(人)	Average Empolyee Per Household	(person)	1.3	1.2	1.3	1.0	1.2	1.4
平均每一就业者负担人数	(人)	Dependents Per Employee Person	(person)	1.5	1.9	1.5	1.4	1.3	1.1
平均每人年可支配收入	(元)	Per Capita Annual Disposable Income	(yuan)	40321	18514	28312	35479	44631	71914
平均每人年消费性支出	(元)	Per Capita Annual Living Expenditures	(yuan)	26275	15236	19112	24349	28335	42779

8-3 城镇居民家庭人均收入(2013年)
PER CAPITA ANNUAL INCOME OF URBAN HOUSEHOLDS (2013)

单位：元 (yuan)

项目	Item	全市平均 Average	低收入户 20% Low Income	中低收入户 20% Medium-Low Income	中等收入户 20% Medium Income	中高收入户 20% Medium-High Income	高收入户 20% High Income	2013年为2012年% 2013 as % of 2012
家庭总收入	**Total Income of Households**	**45274**	**21161**	**31329**	**38752**	**49264**	**82493**	**110.1**
#可支配收入	Annual Disposable Income	40321	18514	28312	35479	44631	71914	110.6
工资性收入	Wage Income	30273	13566	18098	19898	30617	62246	108.3
工资及补贴收入	Wage and Subsidies	28966	12803	17753	19120	29792	58481	105.9
其他劳动收入	Other Income from Work	1307	763	345	778	825	3765	210.5
经营净收入	Business Income	1487	825	916	983	991	3554	104.0
财产性收入	Property Income	575	216	372	265	410	1667	109.5
利息收入	Interest Income	144	37	95	132	133	406	208.7
股息与红利收入	Dividend Income	49	14	12	16	23	175	76.6
保险收益	Insurance Proceeds	15			20	19	32	375.0
其他投资收入	Other Income from Investment	17	…		2	1	82	29.8
出租房屋收入	House Rent Income	327	111	265	95	234	908	109.4
其他财产性收入	Other Property Income	23	54	…	…		64	127.8
转移性收入	Transfer Income	12939	6554	11943	17606	17246	15026	115.7
#养老金或离退休金	Annuities and Pensions	11928	5895	11375	16924	16355	12813	115.9
社会救济收入	Social Relief Income	18	59	24				78.3
辞退金	Dismissal Income	32			43	13	102	246.2
保险收入	Insurance Income	6	31					120.0
#失业保险金	Unemployment Insurance Income	6	31					200.0
赡养收入	Alimony Income	128	74	59	112	195	189	93.4
捐赠收入	Donation Income	215	94	120	134	179	534	112.0
提取住房公积金	Money Drawing from Public Reserve Fund for Housing	243	11	32	48	171	923	110.0
记账补贴	Account Subsidy	291	285	285	304	271	308	111.5
出售财物收入	**Income from Property Sales**	**23**	**…**	**5**	**5**	**2**	**102**	**63.9**
借贷收入	**Loan Income**	**6545**	**3815**	**4667**	**6030**	**6887**	**10946**	**37.4**

注：城镇居民人均可支配收入实际增长7.1%。
Note: Real growth rate of the per capita annual disposable income is 7.1%.

8-4 城镇居民家庭人均总支出(2013年)
PER CAPITA ANNUAL EXPENDITURES OF URBAN HOUSEHOLDS (2013)

单位：元 (yuan)

项目	Item	全市平均 Average	低收入户20% Low Income	中低收入户20% Medium-Low Income	中等收入户20% Medium Income	中高收入户20% Medium-High Income	高收入户20% High Income	2013年为2012年% 2013 as % of 2012
家庭总支出	**Total Expenditures of Households**	**33035**	**18725**	**23503**	**29552**	**35447**	**55918**	**107.2**
消费性支出	Living Expenditures	26275	15236	19112	24349	28335	42779	109.3
#服务性消费支出	Service Living Expenditures	8310	4526	5423	7363	8979	14701	119.2
购房与建房支出	Expenditures for Purchasing and Building Houses	273	153	208	56	157	780	62.5
购房	Purchasing Houses	270	149	202	56	153	780	62.4
建房	Building Houses	3	4	6		4		75.0
转移性支出	Transfer Expenditures	2272	1004	1287	1937	2367	4586	100.5
缴纳个人所得税	Individual Income Tax	486	38	45	170	406	1707	123.0
捐赠支出	Donation Expenditures	1295	709	944	1403	1391	1950	95.9
购买彩票	Lottery Expenditures	6	3	5	3	10	9	54.5
赡养支出	Alimony Expenditures	252	138	115	137	318	528	87.5
各种非储蓄性保险支出	Non-depositing Insurance Expenditures	191	97	149	177	200	322	100.0
#车辆保险支出	Automotive Insurance	105	45	59	85	92	237	72.9
其他转移性支出	Others	42	19	29	47	42	70	168.0
财产性支出	Property Expenditures	38	8	30	12	33	109	35.5
社会保障支出	Social Security Expenditures	4177	2324	2866	3198	4555	7664	105.0
个人交纳的养老基金	Contribution to Annuities	1618	1069	1149	1282	1696	2812	113.1
个人交纳的住房公积金	Contribution to Public Reserve Fund for Housing	1989	834	1281	1476	2266	3918	97.6
个人交纳的医疗基金	Contribution to Medical Funds	505	369	386	399	528	822	108.8
个人交纳的失业基金	Contribution to Unemployment Funds	48	31	35	36	51	83	104.3
其他社会保障支出	Others	17	21	15	5	14	29	1700.0
借贷支出	**Credit Expenditures**	**11843**	**4282**	**7125**	**10438**	**12198**	**24173**	**42.8**
#存入储蓄款	Deposits	11115	4070	6865	9608	11730	22351	41.1
归还借款	Repayment of Loans	40	16	8	35	48	90	39.2
储蓄性保险支出	Depositing Insurance Costs	121	57	80	93	137	230	99.2
购买有价证券	Purchase of Securities	116	3	12	508	20	34	527.3
归还住房贷款	Repayment of Housing Loan	314	72	139	122	158	1057	133.6
归还汽车贷款	Repayment of Automobile Loans	11		1	5	43	4	78.6

8-5 城镇居民家庭人均消费性支出(2013年)
PER CAPITA ANNUAL LIVING EXPENDITURES OF URBAN HOUSEHOLDS (2013)

单位：元 (yuan)

项目	Item	全市平均 Average	低收入户20% Low Income	中低收入户20% Medium-Low Income	中等收入户20% Medium Income	中高收入户20% Medium-High Income	高收入户20% High Income	2013年为2012年% 2013 as % of 2012
消费性支出	**Living Expenditures**	**26275**	**15236**	**19112**	**24349**	**28335**	**42779**	**109.3**
食品	Foods	8170	5714	6892	8045	8583	11285	108.4
衣着	Clothing	2795	1484	1921	2463	3025	4894	105.9
居住	Housing	2126	1452	1429	1997	2126	3532	107.9
家庭设备用品及服务	Household Appliances and Services	1974	1064	1490	1856	2121	3215	122.5
医疗保健	Healthcare and Medical Services	1718	1112	1360	1930	1812	2295	103.6
交通和通信	Transportation and Communication	4106	1745	2591	3301	4712	7831	108.6
教育文化娱乐服务	Educational, Cultural and Recreational Services	3985	2076	2579	3593	4330	7072	107.8
其他商品和服务	Other Goods and Services	1401	589	850	1164	1626	2655	121.4

注：城镇居民人均消费性支出实际增长5.8%。
Note: Real growth rate of the per capita living expenditures is 5.8%.

8-6 城镇居民家庭人均消费性支出构成(2013年)
COMPOSITION OF ANNUAL LIVING EXPENDITURES OF URBAN HOUSEHOLDS (2013)

单位：% (%)

项目	Item	全市平均 Average	低收入户20% Low Income	中低收入户20% Medium-Low Income	中等收入户20% Medium Income	中高收入户20% Medium-High Income	高收入户20% High Income
消费性支出	**Living Expenditures**	**100.0**	**100.0**	**100.0**	**100.0**	**100.0**	**100.0**
食品（恩格尔系数）	Foods (Engel Coefficient)	31.1	37.5	36.1	33.0	30.3	26.4
衣着	Clothing	10.6	9.7	10.1	10.1	10.7	11.4
居住	Housing	8.1	9.5	7.4	8.2	7.5	8.3
家庭设备用品及服务	Household Appliances and Services	7.5	7.0	7.8	7.6	7.5	7.5
医疗保健	Healthcare and Medical Services	6.6	7.3	7.1	7.9	6.4	5.4
交通和通信	Transportation and Communication	15.6	11.5	13.6	13.6	16.6	18.3
教育文化娱乐服务	Educational, Cultural and Recreational Services	15.2	13.6	13.5	14.8	15.3	16.5
其他商品和服务	Other Goods and Services	5.3	3.9	4.4	4.8	5.7	6.2

8-7 城镇居民家庭人均食品支出(2013年)
PER CAPITA ANNUAL EXPENDITURES ON FOOD OF URBAN HOUSEHOLDS (2013)

单位: 元 (yuan)

项 目	Item	全市平均 Average	低收入户 20% Low Income	中低收入户 20% Medium-Low Income	中等收入户 20% Medium Income	中高收入户 20% Medium-High Income	高收入户 20% High Income
食 品	**Foods**	**8170**	**5714**	**6892**	**8045**	**8583**	**11285**
粮油类	Grain and Oil	786	695	760	838	795	836
肉禽蛋及水产品类	Meat, Poultry and Aqnatio Products	1636	1321	1484	1770	1690	1878
蔬菜类	Vegetables	638	559	585	666	663	710
调味品	Flavoring	135	115	130	142	143	144
糖烟酒饮料类	Sugar, Tabacco and Beverage	1150	740	875	1105	1180	1794
干鲜瓜果类	Nuts, Fresh Melons and Fruits	774	585	673	803	823	960
糕点、奶及奶制品	Cake, Milk and Dairy Products	697	521	614	705	749	871
其他食品	Others	147	112	124	119	155	228
饮食服务	Catering Services	2207	1066	1647	1897	2385	3864

8-8 城镇居民家庭人均衣着、居住支出(2013年)
PER CAPITA ANNUAL EXPENDIATURES ON CLOTHING AND HOUSING OF URBAN HOUSEHOLDS (2013)

单位：元 (yuan)

项目	Item	全市平均 Average	低收入户 20% Low Income	中低收入户 20% Medium-Low Income	中等收入户 20% Medium Income	中高收入户 20% Medium-High Income	高收入户 20% High Income
衣着	**Clothing**	**2795**	**1484**	**1921**	**2463**	**3025**	**4894**
服装	Garments	1935	1005	1302	1668	2136	3428
衣着材料	Clothing Materials	13	10	11	17	11	16
鞋类	Footwear	726	399	521	678	758	1229
其他衣着用品	Others	109	62	80	89	110	200
衣着加工服务费	Service Fees for Clothing Processing	12	8	7	11	10	21
居住	**Housing**	**2126**	**1452**	**1429**	**1997**	**2126**	**3532**
住房	Housing	1063	582	567	1002	972	2132
#租赁房房租	Renting	488	334	199	381	350	1160
住房装潢支出	Decoration	468	194	308	497	511	792
维修用建筑材料	Building Materials for Maintenance	98	51	53	117	100	163
水电燃料及其他	Water, Electricity, Fuels and Others	898	784	772	866	937	1104
#水费	Water	122	102	102	131	132	140
电费	Electricity	365	327	315	361	386	429
燃料	Fuels	192	154	181	188	178	255
#罐装液化石油气	Bottled LPG	14	21	17	15	8	10
管道液化石油气	Pipeline LPG	2	2	1	4	2	…
管道天然气	Pipeline Natural Gas	167	119	149	163	156	242
居住服务费	Residential Service Fees	165	86	90	129	217	296

8-9 城镇居民家庭人均家庭设备用品及服务、医疗保健、交通和通信支出(2013年)

PER CAPITA ANNUAL EXPENDITURE ON HOUSEHOLDS APPLICANCES AND SERVICES, MEDICAL SERVICES, TRANSPORTATION AND COMMUNICATION OF URBAN HOUSEHOLDS (2013)

单位：元 (yuan)

项目	Item	全市平均 Average	低收入户20% Low Income	中低收入户20% Medium-Low Income	中等收入户20% Medium Income	中高收入户20% Medium-High Income	高收入户20% High Income
家庭设备用品及服务	**Household Applicances and Services**	**1974**	**1064**	**1490**	**1856**	**2121**	**3215**
耐用消费品	Durable Consumer Goods	864	409	697	816	954	1381
家　具	Furniture	361	161	268	289	439	615
家庭设备	Household Appliances	503	248	429	527	515	766
室内装饰品	Interior Decorations	79	35	48	83	73	148
床上用品	Bedding	205	101	142	198	223	347
家庭日用杂品	Daily Groceries for Households	670	446	539	631	721	983
家具材料	Furnitures	7	4	8	7	12	7
家庭服务	Household Services	149	69	56	121	138	349
医疗保健	**Healthcare and Medical Services**	**1718**	**1112**	**1360**	**1930**	**1812**	**2295**
医疗器具	Medical Apparatus	29	14	27	35	38	32
保健器具	Healthcare Apparatus	38	16	29	31	57	51
药品费	Medicine Fees	436	377	423	553	393	440
滋补保健品	Healthcare Products	356	117	175	378	326	755
医疗费	Medical Expenses	859	588	706	933	998	1017
其他医疗保健支出	Others						
交通和通信	**Transportation and Communication**	**4106**	**1745**	**2591**	**3301**	**4712**	**7831**
交　通	Transportation	3066	1109	1720	2304	3548	6359
家庭交通工具	Vehiles for Households	882	174	378	587	1077	2080
车辆用燃料及零配件	Fuels and Vehicle Parts	887	411	580	609	1055	1706
交通工具服务支出	Expenditure on Vehicle Services	394	160	215	355	425	787
交通费	Transportation Expenses	903	364	547	753	991	1786
通　信	Communication	1040	636	871	997	1164	1472
通信工具	Communication Devices	352	202	289	352	408	487
通信服务	Communication Services	688	434	582	645	756	985

8-10 城镇居民家庭人均教育文化娱乐服务、其他商品和服务支出(2013年)
PER CAPITA ANNUAL EXPENDITURES ON EDUCATIONAL, CULTURAL, RECREATIONAL SERVICES AND OTHER GOODS AND SERVICES OF URBAN HOUSEHOLDS (2013)

单位：元 (yuan)

项目	Item	全市平均 Average	低收入户 20% Low Income	中低收入户 20% Medium-Low Income	中等收入户 20% Medium Income	中高收入户 20% Medium-High Income	高收入户 20% High Income
教育文化娱乐服务	**Educational, Cultural and Recreational Services**	**3985**	**2076**	**2579**	**3593**	**4330**	**7072**
文化娱乐用品	Cultural and Recreational Articles	949	397	703	939	1018	1624
文化娱乐服务	Cultural and Recreational Services	1963	704	1112	1789	2161	3882
教　育	Education	1073	975	764	865	1151	1566
教　材	Teaching Materials	29	28	24	27	28	38
教育费用	Educational Expenses	1044	947	740	838	1123	1528
#非义务教育学杂费	Tuition for Non-compulsory Education	96	154	110	63	56	106
义务教育学杂费	Tuition for Compulsory Education	39	35	25	20	37	76
成人教育费	Tuition for Adult Education	217	124	75	170	256	442
培训班	Training Courses	361	300	267	336	444	446
其他商品和服务	**Other Goods and Services**	**1401**	**589**	**850**	**1164**	**1626**	**2655**
其他商品	Other Goods	1041	368	626	901	1212	2000
其他服务	Other Services	360	221	224	263	414	655

8-11 城镇居民家庭每百户主要耐用消费品拥有量(1978-2013年)
NUMBER OF MAIN DURABLE CONSUMER GOODS PER 100 URBAN HOUSEHOLDS (1978-2013)

年份 Year	淋浴热水器(台) Shower Heaters (unit)	洗衣机(台) Washing Machines (unit)	彩色电视机(台) Color TV Sets (unit)	电冰箱(台) Refrige-rators (unit)	照相机(架) Cameras (unit)	空调器(台) Air Conditioners (unit)	计算机(台) Computers (unit)	移动电话(部) Mobile Phones (unit)	家用汽车(辆) Motor Vehicles (unit)
1978					8				
1979		…			10				
1980		2		…	11				
1981		12	2	2	13				
1982		19	2	3	17				
1983		29	4	7	21				
1984		42	8	15	29				
1985		58	32	42	35				
1986		76	51	62	47				
1987		83	58	72	56				
1988		86	70	81	60				
1989		90	81	89	62				
1990		93	91	96	67				
1991		93	97	102	73	…			
1992	17	96	101	101	77	1			
1993	23	100	107	101	82	2			
1994	39	103	112	104	85	5			
1995	45	100	114	104	87	12			
1996	52	101	119	105	87	14			
1997	58	101	124	104	88	27	12	1	1
1998	65	102	133	105	95	34	15	3	1
1999	67	100	141	103	95	50	24	13	3
2000	74	103	146	107	96	70	32	28	3
2001	78	102	149	107	101	90	45	62	3
2002	84	99	148	102	100	107	56	94	4
2003	85	99	147	100	103	119	68	134	7
2004	94	102	151	103	100	136	79	165	13
2005	97	105	153	104	109	147	89	190	14
2006	98	107	155	105	113	157	96	206	18
2007	99	102	147	108	99	157	92	207	20
2008	95	99	134	103	82	152	86	191	23
2009	98	100	138	104	89	163	97	213	30
2010	98	100	140	103	92	169	104	221	34
2011	97	100	138	103	85	171	104	215	38
2012	99	101	141	103	90	179	112	226	42
2013	99	100	140	103	85	180	110	225	43

8-12 城镇居民家庭每百户主要耐用消费品拥有量(2013年)
NUMBER OF MAIN DURABLE CONSUMER GOODS PER 100 URBAN HOUSEHOLDS (2013)

项目		Item		全市平均 Average	低收入户 20% Low Income	中低收入户 20% Medium-Low Income	中等收入户 20% Medium Income	中高收入户 20% Medium-High Income	高收入户 20% High Income
洗衣机	(台)	Washing Machines	(unit)	100	94	94	98	99	102
电冰箱	(台)	Refrigerators	(unit)	103	100	101	100	101	105
微波炉	(台)	Microwave Ovens	(unit)	85	81	85	86	92	81
空调器	(台)	Air Conditioners	(unit)	180	150	158	160	171	189
淋浴热水器	(台)	Showers	(unit)	99	92	94	94	96	103
消毒碗柜	(台)	Disinfectors	(unit)	5	4	4	5	6	6
洗碗机	(台)	Dishwashers	(unit)	2	1	…	1	2	3
摩托车	(辆)	Motorcyles	(unit)	2	2	3	2	2	1
助力车	(辆)	Powered Bicycles	(unit)	10	13	12	10	10	9
家用汽车	(辆)	Motor Vehicles	(unit)	43	34	33	33	46	53
移动电话	(部)	Mobile Phones	(unit)	225	217	216	216	227	231
#接入互联网的移动电话	(部)	Mobile Phones Accessed to the Internet	(unit)	92	88	96	82	84	105
彩色电视机	(台)	Color TV Sets	(unit)	140	120	129	134	138	146
#接入有线电视网络的电视机	(台)	TV Sets Accessed to Cable TV Network	(unit)	111	104	112	110	119	109
计算机	(台)	Computers	(unit)	110	85	98	92	110	121
#接入互联网的计算机	(台)	Computers Accessed to the Internet	(unit)	100	77	87	78	91	106
组合音响	(套)	Audio Systems	(set)	10	6	7	9	12	14
摄像机	(架)	Video Cameras	(unit)	24	8	19	22	29	35
照相机	(架)	Cameras	(unit)	85	55	70	75	86	90
健身器材	(套)	Fitness Equipment	(set)	7	4	4	7	6	10

8-13 城镇居民家庭居住构成情况(2013)
COMPOSITION OF HOUSING CONDITIONS FOR URBAN HOUSEHOLDS(2013)

项　　目	Item	构成(%) Composition(%)
房屋产权情况	**Housing Property Right**	
租赁公房	Public Houses Rented	11.2
租赁私房	Private Houses Rented	8.7
原有私房	Private Houses Formerly Owned	9.4
房改私房	Private Houses from Housing Reform	31.2
商品房	Commercial Houses	37.4
借用房	Borrowed Houses	1.6
其　他	Others	0.5
住宅建筑式样	**Style of House Construction**	
单栋住宅	Individual Storied Buildings	0.5
四居室	Four-bedroom	4.0
三居室	Three-bedroom	23.9
二居室	Two-bedroom	50.3
一居室	One-bedroom	9.7
普通楼房	Ordinary Storied Buildings	8.7
平房及其他	Single-story Buildings and Others	2.9
饮水情况	**Water Drinking**	
自来水	Tap Water	94.5
矿泉水	Mineral Water	
纯净水	Purified Water	1.4
井、河水	Well Water and River Water	
其　他	Others	4.1
用水情况	**Water Using**	
独用自来水	Tap Water for Separate Use	98.3
公用自来水	Public Tap Water	1.7
井、河水	Well Water and River Water	
其　他	Others	
卫生设备拥有情况	**Possession of Sanitary Equipment**	
无卫生设备	No Sanitary Equipment	8.0
有厕所浴室	Having Bathrooms and Lavatories	90.1
有厕所无浴室	Having Lavatories and No Bathroom	0.4
公　用	Public Sanitary Equipment	1.5
炊用燃料使用情况	**Using of Cooking Fuels**	
煤　炭	Coal	…
罐装液化石油气	Bottled LPG	12.1
管道液化石油气	Pipeline LPG	0.9
管道煤气	Pipeline Gas	
管道天然气	Pipeline Natural Gas	86.4
柴　油	Diesel Oil	
其他燃料	Others	0.6

8-14 全市国有土地上房屋总量情况(2007-2013年)
STATISTICS FOR HOUSES ON STATE-OWNED LAND (2007-2013)

单位：万平方米 (10000 sq.m)

项 目	Item	2007	2008	2009	2010	2011	2012	2013
年末实有房屋建筑面积	Floor Space of Houses(year-end)	66918	70993	74715	77772	80986	83510	88219
年末实有住宅建筑面积	Floor Space of Residential Buildings(year-end)	37981	39852	41756	43431	44113	45627	47610

注：统计范围为全市国有土地上的全部房屋，其中2007-2010年数据为根据房屋初始备案登记信息调整修订后的数据，2011-2013年为房屋全生命周期平台年末时点数据。

数据来源：北京市住房和城乡建设委员会。

Note: These statistics covered all houses on state-owned land of Beijing, of which figures of 2011 and 2013 were year-end figures on life-cycle platform, and figures of 2007-2010 were adjusted and revised according to the original house registration information.

Source: Beijing Municipal Commission of Housing and Urban-Rural Development.

8-15 农村居民家庭基本情况(按收入水平分)(2013年)
BASIC DATA ON RURAL HOUSEHOLDS (BY INCOME LEVEL) (2013)

项 目	Item	全市平均 Average	低收入户 20% Low Income	中低收入户 20% Low-Medium Income	中等收入户 20% Medium Income	中高收入户 20% Medium-High Income	高收入户 20% High Income
平均每户常住人口 (人)	Permanent Population Per Household (person)	3.05	3.17	3.22	3.14	2.98	2.70
平均每户整半劳动力 (个)	Full/Semi Labor Force Per Household (person)	2.05	1.90	2.13	2.10	2.13	1.97
平均每一劳动力负担人口 (人)	Dependents Per Labor Force (person)	1.49	1.67	1.51	1.50	1.40	1.37
人均生产性固定资产原值 (元)	Original Value of Per Capita Productive Fixed Assets (yuan)	5060	15987	2473	2071	1758	2624
人均住房面积 (平方米)	Per Capita Living Space (sq.m)	51.35	49.83	45.51	47.24	52.15	63.93
人均总收入 (元)	Per Capita Total Income (yuan)	20418	13948	15230	18812	23044	33413
#现金收入 (元)	Cash Income (yuan)	20356	13916	15190	18728	22950	33335
人均纯收入 (元)	Per Capita Net Income (yuan)	18337	8052	13824	17901	22489	32036
人均生活消费支出 (元)	Per Capita Annual Living Expenditures (yuan)	13553	9223	10483	12943	15169	21230
#现金支出 (元)	Cash Expenditures (yuan)	13470	9122	10339	12862	15103	21442
平均每个劳动力创造纯收入 (元)	Average Net Income Created by Each Labor Force (yuan)	23038	12255	19385	23171	25241	33516
农村居民家庭恩格尔系 (%)	Engel Coefficient of Rural Household (%)	34.6	37.7	37.1	34.6	36.8	30.0

8-16 农村居民家庭人均纯收入(2013年)
PER CAPITA ANNUAL NET INCOME OF RURAL HOUSEHOLDS (2013)

单位：元 (yuan)

项目	Item	全市平均 Average	低收入户20% Low Income	中低收入户20% Low-Medium Income	中等收入户20% Medium Income	中高收入户20% Medium-High Income	高收入户20% High Income	2013年为2012年% 2013 as % of 2012
合计	**Total**	**18337**	**8052**	**13824**	**17901**	**22489**	**32036**	**111.3**
生产性收入	**Productive Income**	**12868**	**5190**	**10618**	**12931**	**16384**	**20985**	**105.8**
工资性收入	Wage Income	12035	4987	9793	12074	15570	19107	111.0
家庭经营纯收入	Net Income from Family Business	833	203	825	857	814	1878	63.2
第一产业收入	From Primary Industry	268	19	226	364	244	760	36.7
#牧业收入	From Animal Husbandry	-28	-115	1	21	30	150	
第二产业收入	From Secondary Industry	39	-79	36	59	14	196	
第三产业收入	From Tertiary Industry	526	263	563	434	556	922	83.9
#交通运输业收入	From Transportation	251	237	392	215	274	161	106.4
非生产性收入	**Non-productive Income**	**5469**	**2862**	**3206**	**4970**	**6105**	**11051**	**126.7**
转移性收入	Transfer Income	3446	2231	2338	3288	3601	6165	132.6
财产性收入	Property Income	2023	631	868	1682	2504	4886	117.8

注：农村居民人均纯收入实际增长7.7%。
Nate: Real growth rate of the per capita annual net income of rural households is 7.7%.

8-17 农村居民家庭人均生活消费支出(2013年)
PER CAPITA ANNUAL LIVING EXPENDITURES OF RURAL HOUSEHOLDS (2013)

单位：元 (yuan)

项目	Item	全市平均 Average	低收入户20% Low Income	中低收入户20% Low-Medium Income	中等收入户20% Medium Income	中高收入户20% Medium-High Income	高收入户20% High Income	2013年为2012年% 2013 as % of 2012
合计	**Total**	**13553**	**9223**	**10483**	**12943**	**15169**	**21230**	**114.1**
食品	Foods	4696	3476	3890	4476	5580	6375	119.0
衣着	Clothing	1173	670	865	1072	1550	1838	123.7
居住	Housing	2387	1670	1901	2099	2108	4456	108.5
家庭设备用品及服务	Household Applicaneas and Services	898	520	757	856	1043	1404	116.2
医疗保健	Healthcare and Medical Services	1167	1097	1010	1162	974	1634	103.7
交通和通讯	Transportation and Communication	1452	799	1001	1571	1540	2515	103.8
文教娱乐用品及服务	Cultural, Educational and Recreational Articles and Services	1331	772	808	1320	1786	2127	115.4
其他商品及服务	Other Commodities and Services	449	219	251	387	588	881	133.6

注：农村居民人均生活消费支出实际增长10.5%。
Nate: Real growth rate of the per capita annual living expen ditures of rural households is 10.5%.

8-18 农村居民家庭人均消费性支出构成(2013年)
COMPOSITION OF PER CAPITA ANNUAL LIVING EXPENDITURES OF RURAL HOUSEHOLDS (2013)

单位：% (%)

项目	Item	全市平均 Average	低收入户20% Low Income	中低收入户20% Medium-Low Income	中等收入户20% Medium Income	中高收入户20% Medium-High Income	高收入户20% High Income
消费性支出	**Living Expenditures**	**100.0**	**100.0**	**100.0**	**100.0**	**100.0**	**100.0**
食　品（恩格尔系数）	Foods (Engel Coefficient)	34.6	37.7	37.1	34.6	36.8	30.0
衣　着	Clothing	8.7	7.3	8.3	8.3	10.2	8.7
居　住	Housing	17.6	18.1	18.1	16.2	13.9	21.0
家庭设备用品及服务	Household Applicaneas and Services	6.6	5.6	7.2	6.6	6.9	6.6
医疗保健	Healthcare and Medical Services	8.6	11.9	9.6	9.0	6.4	7.7
交通和通信	Transportation and Communication	10.7	8.7	9.5	12.1	10.2	11.8
教育文化娱乐服务	Educational, Cultural and Recreational Services	9.8	8.4	7.7	10.2	11.8	10.0
其他商品和服务	Other Goods and Services	3.3	2.4	2.4	3.0	3.9	4.1

8-19 农村居民家庭人均食品、衣着、居住、家庭设备用品及服务支出(2013年)
PER CAPITA ANNUAL EXPENDIATURES ON FOOD, CLOTHING, RESIDENCE, HOUSEHOLD FACILITIES, ARTICLES AND SERVICES OF RURAL HOUSEHOLDS (2013)

单位：元 (yuan)

项目	Item	全市平均 Average	低收入户20% Low Income	中低收入户20% Low-Medium Income	中等收入户20% Medium Income	中高收入户20% Medium-High Income	高收入户20% High Income
食　品	**Foods**	**4696**	**3476**	**3890**	**4476**	**5580**	**6375**
#谷　物	Grain	397	366	368	390	418	452
蔬菜及制品	Vegetables and Related Products	462	356	400	429	545	612
肉、禽、蛋、奶及制品	Meat, Poultry, Egg, Milk and Related Products	1225	948	1011	1202	1451	1589
衣　着	**Clothing**	**1173**	**670**	**865**	**1072**	**1550**	**1838**
#服　装	Garments	769	427	555	699	1020	1230
居　住	**Housing**	**2387**	**1670**	**1901**	**2099**	**2108**	**4456**
#住　房	Housing	920	418	684	827	470	2394
燃　料	Fuels	750	705	716	662	786	908
家庭设备用品及服务	**Household Applicaneas and Services**	**898**	**520**	**757**	**856**	**1043**	**1404**
#耐用消费品	Durable Consumer Goods	456	216	385	426	552	754
家庭日用杂品	Daily Groceries for Households	287	214	253	277	307	405

8-20 农村居民家庭人均医疗保健、交通和通讯、文教娱乐用品及服务、其他商品及服务支出(2013年)

PER CAPITA ANNUAL EXPENDIATURES ON HEALTHCARE AND MEDICAL SERVICES, CULTURAL, EDUCATIONAL AND RECREATION ARTICLES AND SERVICES AND OTHER COMMODITIES AND SERVICES OF RURAL HOUSEHOLDS (2013)

单位：元

项 目	Item	全市平均 Average	低收入户 20% Low Income	中低收入户 20% Low-Medium Income	中等收入户 20% Medium Income	中高收入户 20% Medium-High Income	高收入户 20% High Income
医疗保健	**Healthcare and Medical Services**	**1167**	**1097**	**1010**	**1162**	**974**	**1634**
#药 品	Medicines	449	464	388	440	347	634
医疗费	Medical Expenses	656	593	593	679	572	847
交通和通讯	**Transportation and Communication**	**1452**	**799**	**1001**	**1571**	**1540**	**2515**
#交通工具	Vehicles	326	136	184	467	141	758
通讯工具	Communication Devices	136	61	104	146	145	240
通讯费	Communication Fees	282	183	260	264	330	389
文教娱乐用品及服务	**Cultural, Educational and Recreational Articles and Services**	**1331**	**772**	**808**	**1320**	**1786**	**2127**
#文娱用机电消费品	Mechanical and Electrical Consumer Goods for Cultural and Recreational Use	226	142	110	201	274	437
书报杂志	Books, Newspapers and Magazines	20	13	14	25	21	31
学杂费	Tuition and Incidentals	299	236	181	284	499	317
文娱费	Recreation	433	172	232	346	596	903
其他商品及服务	**Other Commodities and Services**	**449**	**219**	**251**	**387**	**588**	**881**
#服务性支出	Services Expenditures	109	68	62	113	150	168

8-21 农村居民家庭人均粮食收支情况(2013年)
PER CAPITA GRAIN BALANCE OF RURAL HOUSEHOLDS (2013)

单位：公斤 (kg)

项 目	Item	全市平均 Average	低收入户 20% Low Income	中低收入户 20% Low-Medium Income	中等收入户 20% Medium Income	中高收入户 20% Medium-High Income	高收入户 20% High Income
年内粮食收入实物量	**Grain Collected in the Year**	**254.7**	**526.7**	**182.5**	**201.8**	**177.2**	**170.2**
家庭经营生产	Household-based Production	66.0	113.7	70.3	83.9	38.6	16.3
购 买	Purchased	188.7	413.0	112.2	117.9	138.6	153.9
年内粮食消费及出售量	**Grain Consumed and Sold in the Year**	**256.3**	**571.8**	**188.4**	**188.2**	**148.9**	**160.7**
生活用粮	Grain for Domestic Use	103.0	101.0	98.5	101.0	104.3	110.8
#稻 谷	Rice	37.1	36.6	34.5	35.4	39.5	39.6
小 麦	Wheat	49.5	48.4	48.6	49.2	48.3	53.1
出售粮食	Grain Sold	71.8	131.8	87.3	80.9	23.5	21.9
其 他	Others	81.5	339.0	2.6	6.3	21.2	28.0

8-22 农村居民家庭主要食品人均消费量(2013年)
PER CAPITA CONSUMPTION OF MAJOR FOODS OF RURAL HOUSEHOLDS (2013)

项 目		Item		全市平均 Average	低收入户 20% Low Income	中低收入户 20% Low-Medium Income	中等收入户 20% Medium Income	中高收入户 20% Medium-High Income	高收入户 20% High Income
粮 食	(公斤)	Grain	(kg)	103.0	101.0	98.5	101.0	104.3	110.8
豆制品	(公斤)	Bean Products	(kg)	7.9	7.5	7.3	8.2	8.0	8.4
蔬 菜	(公斤)	Vegetables	(kg)	102.8	95.5	96.7	96.2	112.3	119.1
植物油	(公斤)	Vegetable Oil	(kg)	9.5	8.8	8.5	8.7	10.2	12.0
猪 肉	(公斤)	Pork	(kg)	16.2	14.1	13.7	16.3	19.0	18.6
牛羊肉	(公斤)	Beef and Mutton	(kg)	5.1	3.2	3.8	4.8	6.7	7.5
家 禽	(公斤)	Poultry	(kg)	5.2	4.3	4.2	4.8	6.1	6.7
蛋 类	(公斤)	Eggs	(kg)	11.7	10.2	10.7	11.9	13.0	12.6
奶及奶制品	(公斤)	Milk and Diary Products	(kg)	16.8	11.9	13.3	17.7	21.2	20.6
水产品	(公斤)	Aquatic Products	(kg)	6.9	5.1	5.4	6.0	8.4	10.3
食 糖	(公斤)	Sugar	(kg)	1.0	1.1	1.0	0.9	1.1	1.2
酒 类	(公斤)	Liquor	(kg)	15.5	12.8	15.6	15.2	17.5	16.6
茶 叶	(公斤)	Tea	(kg)	0.6	0.5	0.5	0.6	0.7	0.8
干鲜瓜果	(公斤)	Melons and Fruits	(kg)	49.0	37.6	42.3	47.1	56.7	63.8

8-23 农村居民家庭每百户主要耐用消费品拥有量(1978-2013年) NUMBER OF MAIN DURABLE CONSUMER GOODS PER 100 RURAL HOUSEHOLDS (1978-2013)

年份 Year	移动电话 (部) Mobile Phones (unit)	空调机 (台) Air Conditioners (unit)	彩色电视机 (台) Color TV Sets (unit)	家用计算机 (台) Computers (unit)	照相机 (架) Cameras (unit)	洗衣机 (台) Washing Machines (unit)	电冰箱 (台) Refrigerators (unit)	家用汽车 (辆) Motor Vehicles (unit)
1978								
1979								
1980								
1981								
1982								
1983								
1984								
1985			7		2	23	2	
1986			12		4	39	5	
1987			15		5	48	9	
1988			20		7	56	14	
1989			25		8	61	19	
1990			29		8	63	23	
1991			42		11	69	36	
1992			46		14	73	40	
1993			56		15	76	47	
1994		1	65		17	80	53	
1995		2	74		21	81	63	
1996		2	79		21	83	67	
1997		3	85		25	84	72	
1998		5	92		26	85	75	
1999		9	101		29	86	81	
2000	14	20	107	7	26	85	84	3
2001	30	27	112	12	29	91	86	5
2002	52	35	116	16	32	94	91	6
2003	77	39	116	22	32	94	94	6
2004	102	47	119	27	35	96	96	8
2005	139	63	129	36	37	97	100	10
2006	161	72	131	41	38	97	100	10
2007	182	78	134	46	37	99	104	11
2008	201	89	137	52	39	101	104	12
2009	212	98	138	58	42	101	105	12
2010	224	107	139	64	42	103	107	16
2011	231	108	134	63	37	99	104	19
2012	235	113	136	67	37	99	103	21
2013	221	123	132	74	32	95	102	34

8-24 农村居民家庭每百户主要耐用消费品拥有量(2013年) NUMBER OF MAIN DURABLE CONSUMER GOODS PER 100 RURAL HOUSEHOLDS (2013)

项目		Item		全市平均 Average	低收入户20% Low Income	中低收入户20% Low-Medium Income	中等收入户20% Medium Income	中高收入户20% Medium-High Income	高收入户20% High Income
洗衣机	(台)	Washing Machines	(unit)	95	91	97	96	99	94
电冰箱	(台)	Refrigerators	(unit)	102	99	102	101	106	103
摩托车	(辆)	Motorcycles	(unit)	12	11	13	13	9	11
家用汽车	(辆)	Motor Vehicles	(unit)	34	23	26	34	38	47
彩色电视机	(台)	Color TV Sets	(unit)	132	124	124	140	139	134
照相机	(架)	Cameras	(unit)	32	17	23	29	44	47
抽油烟机	(台)	Smoke Exhausters	(unit)	73	54	70	74	81	85
微波炉	(台)	Microwave Ovens	(unit)	59	43	53	57	72	71
热水器	(台)	Water Heaters	(unit)	94	87	90	97	99	98
固定电话	(部)	Fixed-line Telephones	(unit)	81	76	78	79	86	85
移动电话	(部)	Mobile Phones	(unit)	221	199	220	221	246	219
#接入互联网	(部)	Accessed to the Internet	(unit)	81	63	77	71	89	105
家用计算机	(台)	Computers	(unit)	74	55	71	69	87	87
#接入互联网	(部)	Accessed to the Internet	(unit)	57	43	56	51	67	68
空调机	(台)	Air Conditioners	(unit)	123	85	102	131	145	150

8-25 农村居民家庭居住情况(2013年)
LIVING CONDITIONS OF RURAL HOUSEHOLDS(2013)

项目		Item		2013
年内建房户数比重	**(%)**	**Households with Newly Built Houses within the Year**	**(%)**	**1.3**
户均住房价值	**(元)**	**Housing Value Per Household**	**(yuan)**	**873961**
住房类型		**Type of Housing**		
楼房面积占比重	(%)	Storied Buildings	(%)	19.3
砖瓦平房面积占比重	(%)	Single-storey Brick-and-Tile Housing	(%)	80.7
其他面积占比重	(%)	Others	(%)	
饮用水来源情况		**Source of Drinking Water**		
自来水户数占比重	(%)	Tap Water Users	(%)	99.9
深井水户数占比重	(%)	Deep-well Water Users	(%)	
浅井水户数占比重	(%)	Shallow-well Water Users	(%)	0.1
住房卫生设备使用情况		**Use of Sanitation Facilities**		
无厕所户数占比重	(%)	Households Without Washroom	(%)	1.5
使用旱厕户数占比重	(%)	Households Using Dry Toilet	(%)	19.7
使用卫生厕所户数占比重	(%)	Households Using Sanitary Washroom	(%)	78.8
炊事使用的主要能源		**Main Energy Used in Cooking**		
使用液化气的户数占比重	(%)	Households Using LPG	(%)	90.5
使用煤炭的户数占比重	(%)	Households Using Coal	(%)	1.5
使用柴草的户数占比重	(%)	Households Using Firewood	(%)	2.7
使用电的户数占比重	(%)	Households Using Electricity	(%)	4.0
使用其他燃料的户数占比重	(%)	Households Using Other Fuels	(%)	1.3
住宅外道路路面状况		**Pavement Conditions of Roads Outside Houses**		
水泥或柏油路面的户数占比重	(%)	Cement or Tar-coated Surface	(%)	92
沙石或石板等硬质路面的户数占比重	(%)	Hard Surface Paved with Sand and Stones or Slates	(%)	7.6
其它路面的户数占比重	(%)	Other Pavements	(%)	0.4

主要统计指标解释

城镇部分

平均每一就业者负担人数 是由家庭人口数与离退休人口数之差，再除以就业人口数计算得到的。计算公式为:

$$平均每一就业者负担人数=\frac{(家庭人口数-离退休人口数)}{就业人口数}$$

家庭总收入 指调查户中生活在一起的所有家庭成员在调查期得到的工资性收入、经营净收入、财产性收入、转移性收入的总和，不包括出售财物和借贷收入。收入的统计标准以实际发生的数额为准，无论收入是补发还是预发，只要是调查期得到的都应如实计算。

可支配收入 指调查户可用于最终消费支出和其他非义务性支出以及储蓄的总和，即居民家庭可以用来自由支配的收入。它是家庭总收入扣除交纳的个人所得税、个人交纳的社会保障支出以及调查户的记账补贴后的收入。计算公式为:

可支配收入＝家庭总收入－交纳个人所得税－个人交纳的社会保障支出－记账补贴

工资性收入 指就业人员通过各种途径得到的全部劳动报酬，包括所从事主要职业的工资以及从事第二职业、其他兼职和零星劳动得到的其他劳动收入。

工资及补贴收入 指劳动者从工作单位得到的全部劳动报酬和各种福利。

其他劳动收入 指家庭成员从事第二职业、兼职、零星劳动等劳动所得的报酬。

经营净收入 指家庭成员从事生产经营活动所获得的净收入，是全部生产经营收入中扣除生产成本和税金（但不扣除个人所得税）后所得的收入。如当期收入小于生产费用的开支，冲减成本后直接计入即可。

财产性收入 指家庭拥有的动产(如银行存款、有价证券)、不动产(如房屋、土地等)所获得的收入。包括出让财产使用权所获得的利息、租金、专利收入；财产营运所获得的红利收入、财产增值收益等。不包括出售财物获得的收入。

保险收益 指家庭参加储蓄性保险，扣除缴纳的保险本金后，所获得的保险净收益。不包括保险责任人对保险人给予的保险理赔收入。

其他投资收入 指家庭从事股票、保险以外的投资行为所获得的投资收益。如出售艺术品、邮票等收藏品超过原购买价的那部分收入；如投资各种经营活动（自己不参与经营）所获得的利润；财产转让溢价部分收入，包括出售住房增值部分的收入。

转移性收入 指国家、单位、社会团体对居民家庭的各种转移支付和居民家庭间的收入转移。包括政府对个人收入转移的离退休金、失业救济金、赔偿等；单位对个人收入转移的辞退金、保险理赔、住房公积金、家庭间的赠送和赡养等。

保险收入 指参加保险的住户得到的保险收入，包括从保险公司得到的保险理赔款以及其他责任赔款。如人身意外事故赔偿、财产损失赔偿和住院医疗赔偿等。不包括人寿保险返回的年金。

记账补贴 指调查户因承担记账工作从统计部门、工作单位和其他途径所得到的现金。不包括实物部分。

出售财物收入 指调查户出售家庭财物所得到的收入。由于出售财物是家庭财产从实物形态转为货币形态，家庭财产总量不变，因此不计入可支配收入中。

借贷收入 指家庭资产不发生增减的周转性非生产经营性收入。包括提取银行存款、借入款、收回借出款、兑售有价证券、收回投资本金、贷款等。

家庭总支出 指家庭除借贷支出以外的全部实际支出。包括消费性支出、购房与建房支出、转移性支出、财产性支出、社会保障支出。支出统计是以实际购得的商品或服务的总价值填报，不论其付款方式是一次付清、分期付款、还是赊购，只要商品或服务已被消费就要按其总价值计量。如果采用分期付款或赊购形式，则要在借贷收入类相应的项目填入实付款与总的应付款的差额。

消费性支出 指调查户用于满足家庭日常生活消费需要的全部支出，包括食品、衣着、居住、家庭设备用品及服务、医疗保健、交通和通信、教育文化娱乐服务、其他商品和服务等八大类。包括用于赠送的商品或服务。消费性支出构成是按照商品或服务的用途进行分类，如果消费支出的目的与用途不一致时，必须按照用途归入相应类内。

服务性消费支出 指调查户用于本家庭支付社会提供的各种文化和生活方面的非商品性服务费用。包括为别人付款的服务。服务消费与商品消费不同，其特点在于其劳动过程和消费过程在时间与空间上的统一。

购房与建房支出 指调查户购买住房、建房时的全部支出。

转移性支出 指调查户对国家、单位、住户、个人的转移支付。包括交纳的税款、捐赠和赡养支出等。

财产性支出 指家庭购买或维护财产所支付的利息等有关费用。

社会保障支出 指调查户家庭成员参加国家法律、法规规定的社会保障项目中由个人交纳的保障支出。不包括职工所在单位交纳的那部分社会保障金。

现住房总建筑面积 指调查户现住房的总建筑面积。现住房计算总建筑面积时以房屋产权证或租赁证为准，建筑面积也可按使用面积 × 1.333 计算得出。应扣除住房中专门用于出租的建筑面积。

农村部分

平均每一劳动力负担人口 是由调查户常住人口除以整半劳动力计算得到的。计算公式为:

$$平均每一劳动力负担人口=\frac{调查户常住人口}{整半劳动力}$$

农村居民家庭整半劳动力 指农村常住居民家庭成员中有劳动能力并经常参加实际劳动的人员。是生产的基本要素指标之一，是发展生产增加农民家庭收入的重要源泉。按规定，农村男18周岁至50周岁、女18周岁至45周岁为整劳动力；男16周岁至17周岁、51周岁到60周岁，女16周岁到17周岁、46周岁至55周岁为半劳动力。农民家庭整半劳动力既包括在上述规定劳动年龄内和在劳动年龄以外有劳动能力并经常参加实际劳动的男女整半劳动力，也包括农民家庭常住人员中属于职工的劳动力。但不包括在劳动年龄内已丧失劳动能力的人员。

农村居民家庭总收入 指报告期内农村住户和住户成员以各种来源渠道得到的收入总和。按收入的性质分为工资性收入、家庭经营性收入、财产性收入和转移性收入。

纯收入 指农村住户当年从各个来源得到的总收入相应地扣除所发生的费用后的收入总和。纯收入主要用于再生产投入和当年生活消费支出，也可用于储蓄和各种非义务性支出。“农民人均纯收入”是按人口平均的纯收入水平，反映的是一个地区或一个农户农村居民的平均收入水平。计算方法:

纯收入＝总收入－家庭经营费用支出－税费支出－
生产性固定资产折旧－农村内部亲友赠送收入

农村居民家庭生活消费支出 指农村住户用于物质生活和精神生活方面的支出。包括食品、衣着、居住、家庭设备用品及服务、医疗保健、交通和通讯、文化教育娱乐用品及服务、其他商品和服务等消费支出。

恩格尔系数 随着家庭和个人收入增加，收入中用于食品方面的支出比例将逐渐减小，这一定律被称为恩格尔定律，反映这一定律的系数被称为恩格尔系数。计算公式为:

$$恩格尔系数=\frac{食品支出总额}{家庭或个人消费支出总额}\times 100\%$$

Explanatory Notes on Main Statistical Indicators

Urban Households

Dependents Per Employed Pesron refers to the difference between the total number of persons and the number of retired persons in an urban household, which is divided by the number of employed persons in an urban household. The formula is:

Dependents Per Urban Employee = (total number of persons - the number of retired persons in an urban household) / the number of employed persons in the household

Total Income of Household refers to the sum of wage income; net business income; income from properties; and income from transfers of members of the households. Income from selling of properties and income from borrowing are not included. Income is calculated on actual basis. Any income paid in the survey period, no matter it is repaid or prepaid, should be included.

Disposable Income refers to the actual income at the disposal of members of the households, which can be used for final consumption, other non-compulsory expenditures and savings. This equals to total income minus income tax, personal contribution to social security and subsidies for keeping accounts in a sampled household. The following formula is used:

Disposable Income = Total Income of Household – Personal Income Tax - Personal Contribution to Social Security - Subsidies for Keeping Accounts for a Sampled Household

Wage Income refers to income earned by employed persons through all channels, including other earnings from main job, second job, part-time job, and casual work.

Wages and Subsidies refers to all rewards and welfares received by an employee from the employer.

Other Income from Work refers to the rewards received by family members from any second job, part-time job, and casual work.

Business Income refers to the net income of family members from productive and operating activities. It is the income of all productive and operating income deducting the production cost and tax. If the income in the period is smaller than the production cost, the difference is counted in the "Other Expenditure on Lending".

Property Income refers to the income earned from personal estates (such as bank deposits, securities) and real estates (such as house and land) owned by households, including the interest, rent, and patent income gained from transfer of use right of any property; bonus from property operation and property premium; it does not include the income from selling of any property.

Insurance Proceeds refers to the net proceeds of insurance gained by households for participating in depositing insurance after the paid insurance principal is deducted, excluding the income of insurance claim paid by the responsible person under the insurance program.

Other Income from Investment refers to the return of investment earned by households from investment activities other than stock transactions and insurance, such as income from selling artworks, stamps and other collections in excess of their original purchase costs; any profit from investment in operating activities (without personally participating in the operation); premium from property transfer, including the added value earned from house sales.

Transfer Income refers to various transfer payment from the nation, enterprises, companies, and social groups to households, along with income transfer between households, including such government's transfer of personal income as retirement pension, unemployment relief payment, and compensations; transfer of personal income from enterprises and companies such as dismissal pay, insurance claim, public housing funds, and donation and support between households.

Insurance Income refers to the insurance income obtained by households participating in insurance programs, including any claim payment and other agreed compensation from an insurance company, such as compensation for personal incidence, compensation for property loss, and compensation for hospitalization costs, excluding annuity paid from life insurance.

Account Subsidy refers to the cash paid by authorities of statistics, employers and other channels to the sampled household for its responsibility of accounts keeping, excluding any allowance in kind.

Income from Property Sales refers to the income received by the sampled household for selling any household properties. As the sale of household property is a conversion of physical form of household property to monetary form, and the total amount of household properties remains unchanged, the income from selling property is not included in the disposable income.

Loan Income refers to the non-productive and non-operating income which causes no change in the amount of household property, including withdrawal of bank deposits, borrowings, lending repaid, conversion and sale of securities, returned principal of investment, loans, etc.

Household Expenditures refers to all expenditures of households except credit expenditures. It includes expenditure on consumption; on purchasing or building houses; on transfers; on properties; and on social security. Expenditure is calculated with the total value of goods and services actually purchased. Whether they are purchased with lump-sum payment, installment, or on credit basis, the goods and services are measured at their total value so long as they are consumed. In the case of installment or credit-based purchase, the difference between the actually made payment and the payables shall be counted in the relevant item of income from borrowing and lending.

Living Expenditures refers to total expenditures of households for consumption in daily life, including eight major categories, i.e. expenditures on foods, clothing, housing, household articles, appliances and services, healthcare and medical services, transportion and communication, recreational, educational and cultural services; and other goods and services. It includes any good or service for donation. Components of consumption expenditures are classified according to the purpose of goods and services. In the event of any discrepancy in the aim and purpose of consumption expenditures, it must be involved in relevant category according to the purpose of goods and services.

Service Living Expenditures refers to expenditure of households on various kinds of non-commercial services provided by society, including services paid for other persons. Not like commodity consumption, service consumption is completed in a consistent period and space.

Expenditures for Purchasing and Building Houses refers to all expenditures for purchase and construction of houses by the sampled households.

Transfer Expenditures refers to the transfer payment made by the sampled households to the State, enterprises and companies, households and individuals, including tax payment, donation and support payments, etc.

Property Expenditures refers to relevant costs including interest paid by the sampled households for purchasing or maintaining properties.

Social Security Expenditures refers to the personal payment made by members of the sampled family for any social security program stated in national laws and regulations, excluding the payment made by employers for social security.

Total Building Area of Current Houses refers to the total building area of house resided by the surveyed households, which is calculated on the basis of the property ownership certificate or lease certificate. The building area can also be calculated as the usable floor space multiplied by 1.333, which shall deduct the building area of the house specially used for lease.

Rural Households

Dependents Per Labour Force refers to the number of permanent population in the sampled household divided by the number of full/semi labourers. It is calculated with the following formula:

Dependents Per Laborer = Number of Permanent Population in the Sampled Households / Number of Full/Semi laborers

Full/Semi Labour Force in Rural Households refers to persons among permanent family members in rural households who are capable of working and work frequently. This is one of the indicators for basic production elements, and an important source for production development and increase of farmer's household income. As stated in regulations, rural males aged 18-50 and females aged 18-45 are full labours. Males aged 16-17 and 51-60 and females aged 16-17 and 46-55 are semi labor force. Full/Semi Labour Force in Rural Households includes the male and female full/semi labour force within the above-mentioned range age as well as those beyond such range of ages who are capable of working and work frequently; also include labourers among permanent members in rural households who are employees. But it exclude persons who are within the range of labour age but incapable of working.

Total Income of Rural Households refers to the total income earned from various sources by the rural households and their members during the reporting period, and by the nature of income. It consists of income from wages and salaries, income from household operations, income from properties and transfer income.

Net Income refers to the total income of rural households from all sources minus all corresponding expenses. Net income is mainly used as input for reinvestment in production and as consumption expenditure of the year, and also used for savings and non-compulsory expenses of various forms. "Per capita net income of farmers" is the level of net income averaged by population, reflecting the average income level of rural households in a given area. It is calculated as follows:

Net Income = Total Income - Household Operation Expenses - Taxes and Fees Paid - Taxes and Fees - Depreciation of Fixed Assets for Production – Income from Donation by Relatives and Friends In Rural Areas

Living Expenditures of Rural Households refers to spending by rural households on material life and cultural life, including consumption spending on food, clothes, housing, household appliance and service, medical service and health care, transport and communication, cultural, educational and entertainment supplies and services, other goods and services.

Engel's Coefficient Along with the increase in household and personal income, a gradually smaller portion of income is used for purchase of food. This law is called Engel's law, and the coefficient reflecting such law is called Engel's Coefficient. It is calculated as following:

$$\text{Engels Coefficient} = \frac{\text{expenditure on food}}{\text{total consumption expenditure}} \times 100\%$$

城市公用事业
PUBLIC UTILITIES

简要说明

一、本章资料的主要内容

本章资料反映北京市城市公用事业的综合水平，主要内容包括四部分:

1. 历年城市公用事业基本情况;
2. 水、气、热等供应及消费情况;
3. 城市公交、出租车情况;
4. 市政主要设施情况。

二、本章资料的数据来源

本章城市供热、供气情况由北京市市政市容管理委员会提供；自来水情况由北京市水务局提供；城市公交、出租车情况由北京市交通委员会提供；道路及市政主要设施情况由北京市交通委员会、北京市公安交通管理局、北京市路灯管理中心提供。

Brief Introduction

I. Main Content

Statistics in this chapter show the overall level of urban public utilities in Beijing, which consist of four parts:

1. Basic statistics for urban public utilities in previous years;
2. Water, gas and heating supply and consumption;
3. Urban public transport and taxi services;
4. Main public facilities.

II. Source of Data

Data on urban heating and gas supply were provided by Beijing Municipal Commission of City Administration and Environment; data on tap water were provided by Beijing Water Authority; data on urban public transport and taxi services were provided by Beijing Municipal Commission of Transport; data on roads and main public facilities were provided by Beijing Municipal Commission of Transport, Beijing Traffic Management Bureau and Street Lighting Administration Center Of Beijing.

9-1 公路、城市道路及桥梁(1978-2013年)
HIGHWAYS, URBAN ROADS AND BRIDGES (1978-2013)

年份 Year	境内道路总里程(公里) Total Length of Highways and Roads (km)	公路里程(公里) Total Length of Highways (km)	#高速公路 Express-ways	城市道路里程(公里) Length of Urban Roads (km)	#快速路 Rapid Roads	#主干路 Trunk Roads	城市道路面积(万平方米) Area of Urban Roads (10000 sq.m)	城市道路桥梁(座) Number of Bridges (unit)	#立交桥 Overpasses
1978		6562		2078			1611	351	2
1979		7278		2131			1618	348	2
1980		7487		2185			1664	351	6
1981		7566		2234			1742	342	8
1982		7683		2671			2098	408	9
1983		8058		2820			2265	431	10
1984		8271		2928			2393	440	11
1985		8482		2979			2485	460	16
1986		8995		3038			2559	479	16
1987		9103		3087			2631	510	22
1988		9124		3151			2701	522	23
1989		9371		3235			2815	552	27
1990		9648	35	3276			2905	562	33
1991		10259	63	3308			3134	569	40
1992		10827	71	3189			3212	595	55
1993		11260	99	3285			3398	596	64
1994		11532	112	3316			3470	616	75
1995		11811	113	3194			3494	582	84
1996		12084	114	3665			3807	646	133
1997		12306	144	3637			4061	693	140
1998		12498	190	3721			4214	715	138
1999		12825	230	3753			4353	787	141
2000		13600	268	4126			4921	834	149
2001		13891	335	4312			6062	891	160
2002		14359	463	5444			7645	1051	180
2003	18942	14453	499	3055			5345	848	119
2004	19010	14630	525	4067	219	834	6417	949	271
2005	19015	14696	548	4073	239	922	7437	964	304
2006	25377	20503	625	4419	232	955	7258	1079	376
2007	25765	20754	628	4460	236	960	7632	1230	377
2008	26921	20340	777	6186	242	755	8941	1738	381
2009	27436	20755	884	6247	242	805	9179	1765	393
2010	27907	21114	903	6355	263	874	9395	1855	411
2011	28446	21347	912	6258	263	861	9164	1885	418
2012	28585	21492	923	6271	263	865	9236	1950	413
2013	28808	21673	923	6295	269	953	9611	1998	414

注：1. 境内道路总里程为全市道路和公路里程之和(剔除道路、公路交叉重复部分)。
2. 道路及桥梁1978年-1981年统计范围为城八区及通县；1982年-2002年统计范围为城八区及14个县城；2003年-2010年统计范围为城八区和北京经济技术开发区。2011年起城市道路及其附属设施统计范围为城六区。
3. 2008年道路数据为北京市城市道路普查数据。

资料来源：北京市交通委员会。

Note: a) Total length of highways and roads means the sum of roads and highways across the city (excluding intersections of roads and highways)
b) Statistics for roads and bridges covered 8 urban districts and Tongzhou County in 1978-1981; the coverage was extended to 8 urban districts and 14 counties in 1982-2002; in 2003-2010, the coverage included 8 central urban districts and Beijing Economic-Technological Development Zone; since 2011, statistics for urban roads and the auxiliary facilities have been confined to 6 urban districts.
c) Statistics for roads and highways in 2008 were from Beijing Urban Road Census.

Source: Beijing Municipal Commission of Transport.

9-2 城市公共交通(1978-2013年)

年 份 Year	公共交通运营线路条数(条) Number of Operating Public Transport Routes (line)	公共电汽车 Buses and Trolley Buses	轨道交通 Rail Transit	公共交通运营线路长度(公里) Length of Operating Public Transport Lines (km)	公共电汽车 Buses and Trolley Buses	轨道交通 Rail Transit	公共交通运营车辆(辆) Number of Operating Public Transport Vehicles in Operation (vehicle)
1978	119	118	1	1427	1403	24	2743
1979	121	120	1	1469	1446	24	2997
1980	123	122	1	1479	1455	24	3113
1981	127	126	1	1525	1501	24	3375
1982	139	138	1	1678	1654	24	3620
1983	151	150	1	1820	1797	24	3907
1984	164	162	2	1939	1899	40	4221
1985	191	189	2	2312	2272	40	4583
1986	200	198	2	2574	2534	40	4576
1987	194	192	2	2382	2342	40	4776
1988	199	197	2	2445	2405	40	4787
1989	207	205	2	2525	2485	40	4890
1990	216	214	2	2654	2614	40	5160
1991	223	221	2	2755	2715	40	5182
1992	262	260	2	3379	3338	42	5223
1993	268	266	2	3532	3491	42	5213
1994	284	282	2	4117	4075	42	5319
1995	300	298	2	4538	4497	42	5367
1996	399	397	2	7317	7276	42	6828
1997	667	665	2	14011	13969	42	10479
1998	690	688	2	14929	14888	42	10819
1999	750	748	2	16566	16513	54	12509
2000	682	680	2	15639	15585	54	14191
2001	555	553	2	13180	13126	54	15420
2002	592	589	3	15835	15760	75	17580
2003	620	616	4	16131	16017	114	17445
2004	621	617	4	15247	15133	114	19343
2005	626	622	4	18328	18214	114	19471
2006	624	620	4	18582	18468	114	20489
2007	649	644	5	17495	17353	142	20525
2008	679	671	8	18057	17857	200	23221
2009	701	692	9	18498	18270	228	23730
2010	727	713	14	19079	18743	336	24011
2011	764	749	15	19832	19460	372	24478
2012	795	779	16	19989	19547	442	25831
2013	830	813	17	20153	19688	465	27590

注：自2006年5月1日起，公共电汽车、轨道交通售票采取刷卡方式，并陆续进行了票制票价改革，客运量统计口径方法相应调整，因此与历史数据不可比。

资料来源：本表2005年及以后数据来源于北京市交通委员会。

URBAN PUBLIC TRANSPORT (1978-2013)

		公共交通			出租小汽车 Taxis Service	
公共电汽车 Buses and Trolley Buses	轨道交通 Rail Transit	客运量（万人次） Passengers Carried by Public Transport (10000 person-times)	公共电汽车 Buses and Trolley Buses	轨道交通 Rail Transit	运营车辆（辆） Operating Vehicles (vehicle)	客运量（万人次） Passenger Traffic (10000 persons)
2627	116	172559	169465	3094		
2889	108	205703	200918	4785		
3001	112	236998	231477	5521		
3259	116	263944	257478	6466		
3500	120	284175	276922	7253		
3753	154	302501	294301	8200		
4037	184	324437	314132	10305		
4398	185	335227	321264	13963		
4371	205	328770	312990	15780		
4524	252	330417	311190	19227		
4535	252	337094	306396	30698		
4587	303	306435	275383	31052		
4857	303	334673	296495	38178		
4877	305	344525	307438	37087		
4900	323	348770	305959	42811		
4890	323	335378	286268	49110		
4984	335	353289	299993	53296		
4984	383	371579	315777	55802		
6427	401	349847	305433	44414		
10044	435	391182	346676	44507		
10382	437	418825	372494	46331		
12018	491	426706	378483	48223		
13604	587	406691	363213	43478		
14803	617	449720	402850	46870		
16939	641	492122	443880	48242		
16753	692	426628	379380	47248		
18451	892	499830	439130	60700		
18503	968	517769	449793	67976	66000	65000
19522	967	468225	397919	70306	66646	64121
19395	1130	488138	422645	65493	66646	64111
21507	1714	592523	470863	121660	66646	69000
21716	2014	658785	516517	142268	66646	68000
21548	2463	689788	505144	184645	66646	69000
21628	2850	722552	503272	219280	66646	69600
22146	3685	761578	515416	246162	66646	69862
23592	3998	804775	484306	320469	67046	69946

Note: From May 1, 2006, buses, trolley buses and rail transit tickets were sold by card swiping. Ticket system and prices were also reformed successively. The statistical coverage and methods for passenger traffic were adjusted accordingly, so these figures were incomparable with historical data.

Source: After 2005, data in this table were provided by Beijing Municipal Commission of Transport.

9-3 城市供水、供气及供热(1978-2013年)
URBAN WATER SUPPLY, GAS SUPPLY AND HEAT SUPPLY (1978-2013)

年份 Year	全市集中供热管道长度(公里) Total Length of Pipelines for Centralized Heating (km)	全市集中供热面积(万平方米) Centralized Heating Area in Beijing (10000 sq.m)	#住宅 Residence	煤气销售量(万立方米) Sales Volume of Coal Gas (10000 cu.m)	液化石油气销售量(吨) Sales Volume of Liquefied Petroleum Gas (ton)	天然气销售量(万立方米) Sales Volume of Natural Gas (10000 cu.m)
1978				32687	97255	
1979				32113	114350	
1980				34935	128990	
1981				36309	134771	
1982				36748	149805	
1983				37319	150058	
1984				38710	156421	
1985				41678	169720	
1986				44542	182239	
1987				47594	178205	
1988				49595	177112	287
1989				56056	175814	1805
1990		3702		59508	172688	3544
1991		4560		66111	174326	5062
1992		5281		73615	174694	6040
1993		5730		80163	177065	6702
1994		7056		80409	173105	7623
1995		7537		85201	177637	11003
1996		7838		88356	185304	13504
1997		8399		76429	172879	16565
1998		9102		68998	174464	32619
1999		9992		61846	188450	64833
2000		10860		46719	190571	95919
2001		14729		33960	182188	150585
2002		18172		21077	234680	176504
2003		25108		23991	311657	208837
2004		28150	18962	17714	431660	250326
2005	6272	31736	22218	16776	356551	294279
2006	7013	34977	23158	9763	415268	389202
2007	10424	37203	23697		319631	441327
2008	11948	42501	26738		289576	578626
2009	12156	44240	27694		332693	645356
2010	12224	46715	32305		299392	677009
2011	11734	50794	34563		394437	726229
2012	11031	52555	35104		379371	883385
2013	11192	54591	36806		453546	956852

注：1. 2006年6月开始全市煤气家庭用户已全部置换为天然气用户，因此2007年以后煤气销售量无数据。
2. 自2012年起，自来水数据口径调整为城镇公共供水。
资料来源：北京市市政市容管理委员会、北京市水务局。

Note: a) Since June 2006, all households using coal gas have started to use natual gas. Therefore, there are no data on coal gas sales volume since 2007.
b) Relevant figures of tap water for 2012 were changed to cover urban public water supply.
Source: Beijing Municipal Commission of City Administration and Environment and Beijing Water Authority.

9-3 续表 Continued

年 份 Year	居 民 燃气用户 (万户) Gas Using Households (10000 households)	自来水综合 生产能力 (万立方米/日) Gereral Production Capacity of Tap Water (10000 cu.m/day)	自来水供水 管线长度 (公里) Length of Tap Water Supply Pipelines (km)	自 来 水 销售总量 (万立方米) Total Sales Volume of Tap Water (10000 cu.m)
1978	65.2	134	2926	32664
1979	76.7	151	3083	36232
1980	80.3	163	3272	38933
1981	85.1	167	3435	41634
1982	88.0	164	4216	41136
1983	90.9	166	4452	42778
1984	96.9	167	4622	43716
1985	102.3	176	4927	45601
1986	153.6	188	5079	46695
1987	160.9	185	5257	47680
1988	165.4	189	5550	50059
1989	172.6	206	5647	50145
1990	176.1	215	5770	52718
1991	184.7	221	5947	56107
1992	192.4	226	6130	58704
1993	197.5	234	6367	60794
1994	210.3	242	6727	67977
1995	219.8	264	6907	67877
1996	188.1	266	6907	69684
1997	243.0	302	6339	79046
1998	254.4	330	6989	75969
1999	259.8	357	7179	78098
2000	291.9	367	7610	75364
2001	310.0	371	8146	69807
2002	336.4	428	8555	79322
2003	406.0	429	9278	71583
2004	438.6	399	9981	82986
2005	462.6	348	9831	71600
2006	540.2	373	11899	74970
2007	556.4	391	13133	77778
2008	591.0	404	14118	80792
2009	600.0	424	14791	86881
2010	634.2	445	16144	89185
2011	644.1	473	16963	94622
2012	713.5	411	14029	93826
2013	737.4	444	14495	98178

9-4 全市集中供热
CENTRAL HEATING SUPPLY

项 目		Item		2013	2012	2013年为2012年% 2013 as % of 2012
供热面积	**(万平方米)**	**Total Area of Heating Supply**	**(10000 sq.m)**	**54591**	**52555**	**103.9**
#住 宅		Residence		36806	35104	104.8
供热能力	**(兆瓦)**	Heating Supply Capacity	**(megawatt)**	**38585**	**38298**	**100.7**
热电厂供热		Heating from Thermal Power Plants		7199	7187	100.2
锅炉房供热		Heating from Boiler Houses		31386	31111	100.9
供热总量	**(万吉焦)**	**Total Heating Supply**	**(10000 giga joules)**	**33960**	**35222**	**96.4**
热电厂供热		Heating from Thermal Power Plants		5268	5752	91.6
锅炉房供热		Heating from Boiler Houses		28692	29470	97.4
供热管道长度	**(公里)**	**Length of Pipelines**	**(km)**	**11192**	**11031**	**101.5**

资料来源：北京市市政市容管理委员会。
Source: Beijing Municipal Commission of City Administration and Environment.

9-5 液化石油气及天然气
LIQUEFIED PETROLEUM GAS AND NATURAL GAS

项 目		Item		2013	2012	2013年为2012年% 2013 as % of 2012
液化石油气		**Liquefied Petroleum Gas**				
供气总量	(吨)	Gas Supply	(ton)	472980	418156	113.1
销售气量	(吨)	Gas Sales	(ton)	453546	379371	119.6
#家庭用量	(吨)	Domestic Consumption	(ton)	202468	190975	106.0
家庭用户	(万户)	Domestic Consumers	(10000 households)	190.5	194.1	98.1
天然气		**Natural Gas**				
供气总量	(万立方米)	Gas Supply	(10000 cu.m)	994222	924763	107.5
销售气量	(万立方米)	Gas Sales	(10000 cu.m)	956852	883385	108.3
#家庭用量	(万立方米)	Domestic Consumption	(10000 cu.m)	119406	115401	103.5
家庭用户	(万户)	Domestic Consumers	(10000 households)	546.9	519.4	105.3
居民燃气用户	**(万户)**	**Household Gas Users**	**(10000 households)**	**737.4**	**713.5**	**103.4**

注：本表天然气、液化石油气用量中包含燕山石化用气量。
资料来源：北京市市政市容管理委员会、中国石化集团北京燕山石化有限公司。
Note: Data on natural gas consumption and liquefied petroleum gas consumption in this table include the consumption of Yanshan Petrochemical.
Source: Beijing Municipal Commission of City Administration and Environment, and SINOPEC Beijing Yanshan Petrochemical Co., Ltd.

9-6 自来水及自备水源
TAP WATER AND SELF-PROVIDED SOURCES OF WATER

项目		Item		2013	2012
自来水		**Tap Water**			
综合生产能力	(万立方米/日)	General Production Capacity	(10000cu.m/day)	444	411
供水管道长度	(公里)	Length of Water Supply Pipelines	(km)	14495	14029
销售总量	(万立方米)	Total Sales Volume	(10000 cu.m)	98178	93826
#生产运营用	(万立方米)	For Production Use	(10000 cu.m)	12161	12045
公共服务用	(万立方米)	For Public Service Use	(10000 cu.m)	36045	34710
居民家庭用	(万立方米)	For Domestic Use	(10000 cu.m)	49268	46303
自备井水		**Self-provided Well Water**			
用水量	(万立方米)	Consumption	(10000 cu.m)	69634	69145
#生产运营用	(万立方米)	For Production Use	(10000 cu.m)	15705	15416
公共服务用	(万立方米)	For Public Service Use	(10000 cu.m)	19158	19487
居民家庭用	(万立方米)	For Domestic Use	(10000 cu.m)	26854	28087

注：自来水数据口径为城镇公共供水。2013年起自备井水相关数据的填报范围调整为市区、卫星城、中心镇、一般建制镇，不含农业，并对2012年数据进行了同口径调整。

资料来源：北京市水务局。

Note: Statistical scope for the data on tap water were urban public water supply. Since 2013, statistical scope for the data on self-provided well water were changed to cover city center, satellite city, central town, common town, except agriculture, and the data of 2012 were adjusted as the same statistical scope

Source: Beijing Water Authority.

9-7 公共交通及客运出租小轿车
PUBLIC TRANSPORT AND TAXI SERVICES

项目		Item		2013	2012
公共交通		**Public Transportation**			
运营车辆	(辆)	Operating Vehicles	(unit)	27590	25831
公共电汽车	(辆)	Buses and Trolley Buses	(unit)	23592	22146
轨道交通	(辆)	Rail Transit	(unit)	3998	3685
运营线路条数	(条)	Number of Operating Routes	(line)	830	795
公共电汽车	(条)	Buses and Trolley Buses	(line)	813	779
轨道交通	(条)	Rail Transit	(line)	17	16
运营线路长度	(公里)	Length of Operating Routes	(km)	20153	19989
公共电汽车	(公里)	Buses and Trolley Buses	(km)	19688	19547
轨道交通	(公里)	Rail Transit	(km)	465	442
客运量	(万人次)	Passenger Traffic	(10000 person-times)	804775	761578
公共电汽车	(万人次)	Buses and Trolley Buses	(10000 person-times)	484306	515416
轨道交通	(万人次)	Rail Transit	(10000 person-times)	320469	246162
客运出租小轿车		**Taxi Services**			
年末运营车辆	(辆)	Vehicles in Operation (year-end)	(unit)	67046	66646
客运量	(万人次)	Passenger Traffic	(10000 person-times)	69946	69862

资料来源：北京市交通委员会。

Source: Beijing Municipal Commission of Transport.

9-8 市政设施情况
BASIC STATISTICS FOR MUNICIPAL FACILITIES

项目	Item	2013	2012
境内道路总里程 (公里)	Total Length of Highways and Roads (km)	28808	28585
高速公路里程 (公里)	Length of Expressways (km)	923	923
城市道路里程 (公里)	Length of Urban Roads (km)	6295	6271
#快速路 (公里)	Rapid Roads (km)	269	263
#主干路 (公里)	Trunk Roads (km)	953	865
城市道路面积 (万平方米)	Coverage of Urban Roads (10000 sq.m)	9611	9236
#铺装步道 (万平方米)	Paved Roads (10000 sq.m)	1639	1605
城市道路立交桥数 (座)	Number of Overpasses in City (unit)	414	413
城市过街天桥数 (座)	Number of Pedestrain Overpasses in City (unit)	520	512
城市地下通道数 (座)	Number of Underpasses in City (unit)	211	210
备案停车场个数 (个)	Number of Parking Lots Recorded (unit)	5964	6273
备案停车场车位总数 (个)	Total Capacity of Parking Lots Recorded (unit)	1574126	1611372
路口电视监视点位 (台)	TV Monitors at Crossings (unit)	1235	1235
城六区照明线路长度 (公里)	Length of Lighting Lines in 6 Urban District (km)	6194	5948

注：1. 本表统计范围为城六区。

2. 表中“备案停车场个数”和“备案停车场车位总数”为原指标“经营性停车场个数”和“经营性停车场车位总数”。

资料来源：北京市交通委员会、北京市公安交通管理局、北京市路灯管理中心。

Note: a) Data in this table covers 6 urban districts .

b) In the table, the "Parking Lots Recorded" and "Total Capacity of Parking Lots Recorded" are the original indicators "Operational Parking Lots" and "Total Capacity of Operational Parking Lots".

Source: Beijing Municipal Communission of Transport, Beijing Administration for Public Security & Traffic, Beijing Street Lamp Administration Center.

主要统计指标解释

自来水综合生产能力 指按供水设施取水、净化、送水、出厂输水干管等环节实际测定计算的综合生产能力。不包括供水高峰阶段，超负荷增加的生产能力。计算时，以四个环节中最薄弱的环节为主确定能力。

自来水供水管道长度 指从送水泵至用户水表之间所有管道的长度。不包括新安装尚未使用的管道。

生产运营用水 指在城市范围内生产、运营的农、林、牧、渔业、工业、建筑业、交通运输业等单位在生产、运营过程中的用水。

公共服务用水 指为城市社会公共生活服务的用水。包括行政事业单位、部队营区和公共设施服务、社会服务业、批发零售贸易业、旅馆饮食业以及社会服务业等单位的用水。

居民家庭用水 指城市范围内所有居民家庭的日常生活用水。包括城市居民家庭、农民家庭、公共供水站用水。

公共交通年末运营车辆 指公交企业（单位）用于运营业务的全部车辆数。

运营线路总长度 指全部运营线路长度之和。计算公式:

$$运营线路长度=\sum 各条运营线路长度$$

$$=\sum\left[\begin{pmatrix}上行起点至终点里程+下行起点至终点里程\\+上下行终点掉头里程\end{pmatrix}\right]$$

公路里程 指公路的长度，凡达到《公路工程技术标准（JTGB01-2003)》规定的技术等级的公路，均统计公路里程，包括大、中城市的郊区公路里程，公路通过城镇（指县城、集镇）街道的里程和公路桥梁长度、隧道长度、渡口的宽度以及分期修建的公路已验收交付使用的里程。国道、省道、县道、乡道和专用公路中新增的人工修建的、路基宽度在4.5米以上的等外路里程也纳入公路里程统计。按技术等级公路可分为高速公路、一级公路、二级公路、三级公路、四级公路和等外公路。

道路里程 指道路长度和与道路相通的桥梁、隧道的长度，按车行道中心线计算。城市道路由车行道和人行道两部分组成。在统计时只统计路面宽度在3.5米（含3.5米）以上的各种铺装道路，包括开放型工业区和住宅区道路在内。

道路面积 指道路面积和与道路相通的广场、桥梁、隧道的面积（统计时，将人行道面积单独统计）。人行道面积按道路两侧面积相加计算。包括步行街和广场，不含人车混行的道路。

Explanatory Notes on Main Statistical Indicators

General Production Capacity of Tap Water means the comprehensive production capacity of water facilities calculated by on-site measurement, including capacity of the water in-taking, treatment, transmission and delivery; while overloaded capacity during water supply peak hours are not included. Calculation of the capacity was mainly dependent upon the weakest link of the whole production process.

Length of Tap Water Supply Pipelines means the length of all pipes linking between the water outlet pumps and users' water meters, excluding the ones newly installed and not yet put into use.

Water for Production Use means the water used for production and operation of business entities within the city, covering sectors including farming, forestry, animal husbandry, fishery, industry, construction, transportation, etc.

Water for Public Service Use means the water used for urban public services, including water supply for administrative and public institutions, military units, public facilities, social services, wholesale and retail trades, hotels and catering, and social service organizations.

Water for Domestic Use means the water used for daily life of all households in urban area, including the water used for urban residents, rural households, and public water supply stations.

Year-end Public Transport Vehicles in Operation means the number of all vehicles used for operational businesses in public transit enterprises (institutions).

Total Length of Public Transport Routes means the sum of all lines in operation. It is calculated with the formula:

Length of Public Transit Lines = ∑ Length of all lines in operation = ∑ [(mileage from the upward starting point to the end point + mileage from the downward starting point to the end point + mileage of double back from upward and downward end points)]

Total Length of Highways means the length of highways. Such statistics apply for any highway reaching the technical grade stated in *Highway Engineering Technical Standards (JTGB01-2003)*, including the mileage of highways in suburbs of middle and large cities, mileage of highways passing through streets in towns (counties and townships), length of highway bridges, length of tunnels, width of ferries, and mileage of highways constructed in several phases and put into use. The mileage of non-graded new highways built manually onto national highways, provincial highways, county highways, township highways and special highways, with roadbed width of 4.5m and above, are also incorporated. In terms of technical grade, highways fall into expressways, first-grade highways, second-grade highways, third-grade highways, fourth-grade highways, and non-graded highways.

Length of Highways and Roads means the length of roads and bridges and tunnels connecting with roads, calculated by the central lines of carriage ways. Urban roads consist of carriageways and sidewalks. Statistics only cover paved roads with width of pavement above 3.5m (including 3.5m), roads in open industrial zones and residential zones included.

Area of Roads means the area of roads and the area of squares, bridges and tunnels connecting to the roads (the area of sidewalks is calculated separately). The area of sidewalks is the sum of area on both sides of roads, including pedestrian streets and squares, excluding roads passable for both pedestrians and vehicles.

10

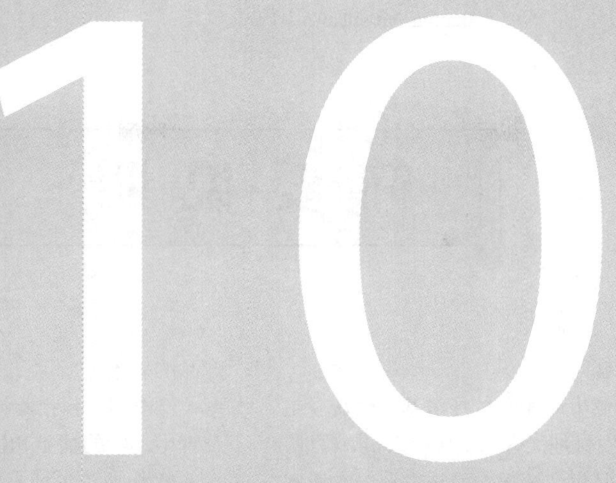

北京统计年鉴2014　BEIJING STATISTICAL YEARBOOK

农业及农村经济
AGRICULTURE AND RURAL ECONOMY

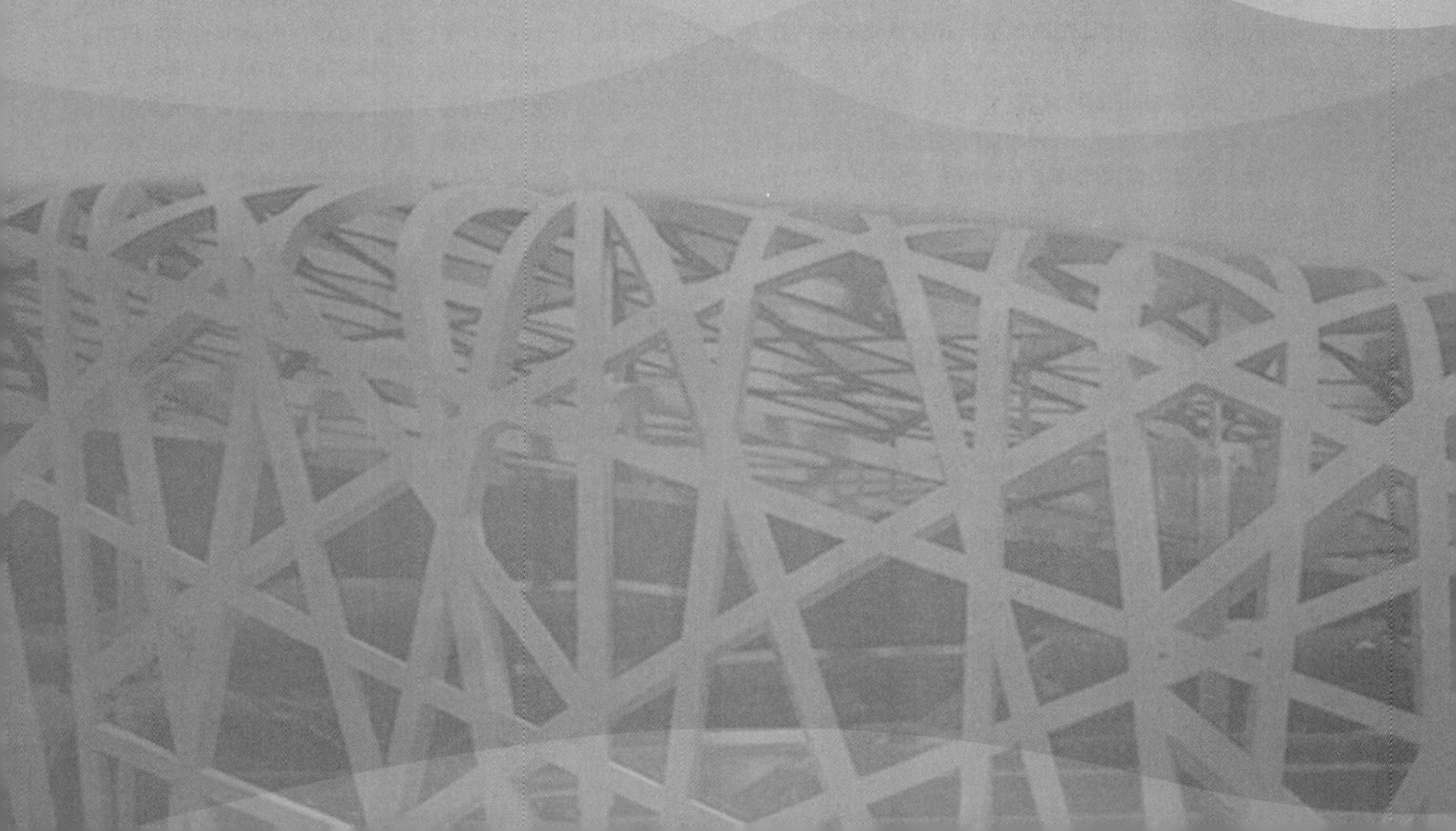

简要说明

一、本章资料的主要内容

本章资料反映北京市农业生产和农村经济基本情况，主要包括农村基层组织情况、农村地区人口、从业人员、耕地、农林牧渔业产值及主要农产品生产情况、设施农业、农业观光园、民俗旅游、农村固定资产投资、乡镇企业情况、农村经济收入与分配情况等。

二、本章资料的统计范围

农林牧渔业统计范围包括辖区内全部农林牧渔业生产单位、非农行业单位附属的农林牧渔业生产活动单位以及农户的农业生产活动。军委系统的农林牧渔业生产（除军马外）也应包括在内，但不包括农业科学试验机构进行的农业生产。

1. 农业：指各种农作物的种植活动。包括谷物、豆类、薯类、棉花、油料、糖料、麻类、烟叶、蔬菜、食用菌及花卉盆景园艺产品、水果、坚果、饲料和香料作物、药材及其它作物的种植。

2. 林业：包括林木的栽培(不包括茶园、桑园和果园的栽培、管理和收获等活动)、木材和竹材的采运、林产品的采集。

3. 畜牧业：包括牲畜饲养和放牧、家禽饲养以及野生动物的捕猎和饲养。

4. 渔业：分为淡水养殖和海水养殖，包括水生动物和海藻类植物的养殖和捕捞。

农村社会经济统计范围包括所有乡镇辖区内的社会经济活动。

三、本章资料的数据来源

乡镇企业数据由北京市经济和信息化委员会提供。农村经济收入分配数据由北京市农村经济研究中心农村合作经济经营管理站提供，耕地数据由北京市国土资源局提供，林业数据由北京市园林绿化局提供，水产品数据由北京市农业局提供，农村基层组织资料由北京市民政局提供。其余资料均由北京市统计局、国家统计局北京调查总队提供。

四、本章资料的调查方法和核算方法

根据农业生产特点，农林牧渔业总产值的核算采用“产品法”计算，即用产品产量乘以价格求出各种产品的产值，按产品产值类别分别汇总，计算出农林牧渔各业的产值，各业相加为农林牧渔业总产值。

(1)农业：包括谷物和其他作物；蔬菜、食用菌及花卉盆景园艺产品；水果、坚果、饮料、香料；中药材。

(2)林业：包括林木的培育和种植；木材、竹材采运；林产品的采集。

(3)牧业：包括除渔业养殖以外的一切动物饲养和放牧以及野生动物的捕猎和饲养。

(4)渔业：包括水生动物和海藻类植物的养殖和捕捞。

(5)服务业：产值等于农林牧渔服务业营业收入。

1957 年以前的农业总产值中包括了厩肥和农民自给性手工业（如农民自制衣服、鞋、袜，自己从事粮食初步加工等）。1958 年及以后的林业产值中增加了村及村以下竹木采伐产值；牧业中取消了厩肥产值；副业中取消了农民自给性手工业产值；渔业中增加了海洋捕捞水产品产值。1980 年及以后的农业总产值，在副业中增加了农民家庭兼营工业商品部分的产值。从 1984 年起村及村以下办工业产值划归工业。从 1993 年起，取消副业，将野生动物的捕猎划入牧业，野生植物采集和农民家庭兼营商品性工业划归农业。从 2003 年起按照新的《国民经济济行业分类》标准取消了“其它农业”；将农林牧渔服务业产值纳入农林牧渔业总产值中；从农林牧渔业总产值中取消了“家庭兼营商品性工业”；将村以上木材和竹材的采运划入了林业；产值计算采用生产者价格，即生产者第一次出售农产品的价格。2004 年国家统计局报表制度规定农林牧渔业总产值增加按可比价计算的产值及发展速度（计算方法：用现价产值的中类数据除以中类缩减指数求得各中类的可比价产值，各中类相加得大类的可比价产值，最后用大类数据相加得农业可比价总产值，可比价产值除以上年现价产值得发展速度）。从 2005 年起，取消了按 1990 年价格计算的农业产值。由于 2006 年农业普查后对农业生产历史数据进行了修订，新修订的农业产值数据只到大类，如果按大类缩减计算农业可比价总产值不符合国家报表制度要求，故 2005 年及以前年度没有按可比价计算的发展速度。2010 年起，根据新的《统计用产品分类目录》将原林业产值中的核桃、栗子、白果、松子等干果产值调整至农业产值中，为同口径对比，将 2009 年年报数据也作了相应调整。

主要粮食播种面积数据通过卫星遥感测量方法取得,粮食产量数据通过抽样调查方法取得。农林牧渔业生产统计采取全面调查方法，村级起报。

五、本章中关于历史数据调整的问题

根据 2006 年第二次农业普查结果，北京市统计局、国家统计局北京调查总队按照国务院农普办要求，依照国际通用做法，已对 1997—2005 年的相关指标历史数据进行了修订。

Brief Introduction

I. Main Content

Statistics in this chapter show basic situation of agricultural production and rural economy in Beijing, mainly consisting of statistics for rural grass-root organizations, population and employment, arable land, output of agriculture, forestry, animal production and hunting, fishing, production of main agricultural products, facility agriculture, agricultural sightseeing gardens, folk-custom tourism, investment in fixed assets in rural areas, township enterprises, income and distribution of rural economy.

II. Scope of Statistics

Statistics on agriculture, forestry, animal production and hunting, fishing cover all related producing entities, producers affiliated to non-agricultural departments, as well as farmers' agricultural production activities. Production by the military commission system shall also be included (except for army horse breeding), but the production by scientific testing agencies is not included.

1. Agriculture: It refers to the growing of various agricultural crops, including grains, beans, potatoes, cotton, oil plants, sugar plants, fiber plants, tobacco leaves, vegetables, edible fungus, flower bonsai and gardening products, fruits, nuts, feedstuff, and spice crops, herbs, and other crops.

2. Forestry: It includes tree planting (except for the cultivation, management and harvest of tea gardens, mulberry fields, and orchards), the logging of timber and bamboo, and the collection of forestry products.

3. Animal production and hunting: It includes the breeding and grazing of livestock, poultry agriculture, as well as hunting and breeding of wildlife.

4. Fishing: It falls into two parts: freshwater agriculture and mariculture, including the cultivation and fishing for aquatic animals and algae.

Statistics for social and economic development in rural areas cover social and economic activities of all villages and towns within the jurisdiction.

Ⅲ. Source of Statistics

Statistics on township enterprises were provided by Beijing Municipal Commission of Economy and Information Technology. Statistics on income distribution in rural economy were provided by the Operation and Management Station of Rural Cooperative Economy, Beijing Research Center for Rural Economy. Statistics on arable land were provided by Beijing Municipal Bureau of Land and Resources. Forestry statistics were provided by Beijing Municipal Bureau of Landscape and Forestry. Statistics on aquatic products were provided by Beijing Municipal Bureau of Agriculture. Statistics on rural basic organization were provided by Beijing Municipal Bureau of civil Affairs. All other statistics were provided by Beijing Municipal Bureau of Statistics and National Bureau of Statistics Survey Office in Beijing.

Ⅳ. Method for Survey and Counting

Based on agricultural production characteristics, the gross output value of agriculture, forestry, animal production and hunting, fishing was calculated by the "product approach"--that is to multiply production volume by the unit price, so as to get output value of each product, then sum it up by category, namely agriculture, forestry, animal production and hunting, fishing; and the sum total of these categories will be gross output value of the whole sector.

(1) Agriculture: including cereal and other crops; vegetables, edible mushrooms, flower bonsai and gardening products; fruits, nuts, beverage, spices, and herbs.

(2) Forestry: including the cultivation and planting of forest trees; logging of timber and bamboo; and collection of forestry products.

(3) Animal production and hunting: including the breeding and grazing of animals other than fish breeding, as well as hunting and breeding of wildlife.

(4) Fishing: including cultivation and catching of aquatic animals and seaweed plants.

(5) Service: the output value equals the operating income of services in support of, forestry, animal production and hunting, fishing.

Prior to 1957, China's gross agricultural output value included the output of barnyard manure and handicraft products for self-consumption (e.g. clothes, shoes, socks, and primary grain processing by peasants). Since 1958, output value of bamboo and timber logging by villages and units subordinated to villages has been included in the statistics of forestry; output value of barnyard manure has been excluded from animal production and hunting statistics; subsistence handicrafts has been excluded from sideline products output value; and the output value of aquatic products by marine fishing has been added to fishing. Since 1980, the output value of industrial commodities operated by rural households has been included in the output value of sideline products. Since 1984, industrial output value produced by villages and units subordinated to villages has been added in the sector of industry. In 1993, the group "sideline products" was cancelled; the hunting of wild animals has been classified as animal production and hunting, and the gathering of wild plants and commercial industrial businesses run by rural households have been included in agriculture. A new *Standard for Classification of National Economic Sectors* was introduced in 2003. According to the new classification, the group "other agricultural activities" was cancelled; the output value of services in support of agriculture, forestry, animal production and hunting, fishing is included in the gross output value of agriculture; the value of industrial output by households is excluded; output value of wood and bamboo logging is included in forestry statistics; the output value is calculated at the producer's price, namely the price at which producers sell their agricultural products for the first time; the 2004 Reporting System of National Bureau of Statistics states that, for incremental gross output value of agriculture, forestry, animal production and hunting, fishing, the output value and growth rate shall be calculated at comparable prices (calculation method: use the output value of groups at present prices to divide the groups' deflator, so as to get the output value at comparable prices; then add up the groups' output value to get the whole division's output value at comparable prices; in the end, add up all divisions' output value to get the gross output value at comparable prices for agriculture sector and divide the output value at comparable prices by the output value at current prices in the previous year to get the growth rate). Since 2005, the practice of using prices of 1990 as reference numbers to calculate agricultural output value has been cancelled. As historical data of agricultural production were revised after the agricultural census in 2006, revised agricultural production output value figures were presented only in divisions; and it does not meet the requirements of national reporting system to calculate the gross agricultural output value at comparable prices by divisions' deflator. Therefore, there were no figures of growth rate at comparable prices in and prior to 2005. Since 2010, the output value of nuts such as walnuts, chestnuts, gingkoes and pine nuts formerly included in forestry has been added in the output value of framing according to the new *Catalog on Statistical Product Classification*. In order to conduct same-caliber comparison, data in the 2009 *annual report* have also been adjusted accordingly.

Data on the sown area of major grain were collected by satellite remote sensing; data on grain yield were gathered through sampling survey; and the production figures on agriculture, forestry, animal production and hunting, fishing sectors were added up by complete survey, starting from the village level.

Ⅴ. Adjustments to Historical Statistics

Based on results of the second agricultural census 2006, Beijing Municipal Bureau of Statistics and NBS Survey Office in Beijing revised related historical statistics during 1997-2005 as required by the Agricultural Census Office of the State Council and in accordance with the international practice.

10-1 农村基本情况(1978-2013年)
BASIC STATISTICS FOR RURAL AREAS (1978-2013)

年 份 Year	乡政府 (个) Township Governments (unit)	镇政府 (个) Town Governments (unit)	村民委员会 (个) Villagers' Committees (unit)	乡镇及行政村常住户数 (万户) Number of Permanent Households in Towns and Administrative Villages (10000 households)	乡镇及行政村常住人口 (万人) Permanent Population in Towns and Administrative Villages (10000 persons)	乡镇及行政村从业人员 (万人) Employed Persons in Towns and Administrative Villages (10000 persons)
1978				91.9	382.1	165.3
1979				92.9	374.7	165.1
1980				95.0	374.3	167.4
1981				98.9	377.6	172.9
1982				103.2	381.8	179.4
1983				106.6	384.0	184.6
1984				108.9	385.6	188.9
1985	350	15	4394	111.8	387.2	190.0
1986	327	15	4400	113.1	386.9	189.5
1987	324	14	4326	115.7	388.9	189.8
1988	321	13	4111	118.6	389.6	189.2
1989	322	14	4483	121.5	390.0	186.1
1990	252	77	4481	124.5	392.0	184.3
1991	209	77	4480	125.5	390.7	182.1
1992	209	77	4229	126.2	387.6	178.7
1993	192	81	4476	126.5	382.4	176.0
1994	174	92	4464	124.9	376.0	171.6
1995	166	100	4355	125.0	371.5	163.6
1996	166	100	4357	124.6	368.9	164.2
1997	132	108	4348	124.6	365.3	161.2
1998	126	105	4032	125.9	364.4	161.0
1999	125	103	4040	125.9	363.9	165.3
2000	70	142	4039	126.8	363.7	165.8
2001	52	139	4010	127.6	361.6	165.3
2002	51	141	4005	128.0	357.6	165.6
2003	45	142	3985	131.1	360.6	169.6
2004	42	142	3985	132.8	359.9	171.4
2005	43	142	3953	142.2	381.8	184.0
2006	41	142	3957	143.6	501.6	316.9
2007	41	142	3955	176.9	510.0	313.4
2008	40	142	3951	189.8	547.4	321.3
2009	40	142	3950	203.8	572.5	338.7
2010	40	142	3943	216.0	589.4	347.8
2011	38	144	3941	212.4	574.8	338.3
2012	38	144	3940	215.2	582.5	341.7
2013	38	144	3938	221.9	599.5	353.5

注：1. 从业人员指标1998年以前为乡村劳动力。
2. 乡政府个数、镇政府个数、村民委员会个数由北京市民政局提供。
3. 2006年乡镇及行政村人口和从业人员为农业普查数据；2007年以后乡镇及行政村人口和从业人员为农业普查口径，包含居住半年以上外来人口。
4. 2006年乡镇及行政村户数为农业普查数据，为自然户口径；2007年以后为居住一年以上的户口径。

Note: a) Employed persons before 1998 were rural labor force.
b) Numbers of township governments, town governments, villagers' committees are provided by Beijing Municipal Bureau of Civil Affairs.
c) Population and employed persons in towns and administrative villages were agriculture census data in 2006. Statistical range of agriculture census data have covered population and employed persons in towns and administrative villages since 2007 including migrant population residing for over 6 months.
d) Number of households in towns and administrative villages in 2006 was from agricultural census, using natural households as the caliber; since 2007, the caliber was changed into households residing for over a year.

10-2 农业生产条件(1978-2013年)
CONDITIONS FOR AGRICULTURAL PRODUCTION (1978-2013)

年份 Year	年末实有耕地面积(万公顷) Actual Area of Arable Land (year-end) (10000 hectares)	有效灌溉面积(千公顷) Effective Irrigation Area (1000 hectares)	农业机械总动力(万千瓦) Total Power of Agricultural Machinery (10000 kw)	农村用电量(万千瓦小时) Rural Electricity Consumption (10000 kwh)	化肥施用量(万吨) Consumption of Chemical Fertilizers (10000 tons)
1978	42.9	341.7	189.4	58802	11.6
1979	42.7	340.8	212.2	63124	11.3
1980	42.6	340.3	234.6	76753	12.3
1981	42.5	341.3	244.8	91844	11.2
1982	42.4	339.4	242.2	96961	12.0
1983	42.3	343.3	261.8	104608	12.0
1984	42.2	342.6	290.8	119289	10.7
1985	42.1	338.4	320.4	126830	8.2
1986	41.9	337.9	345.5	180640	9.1
1987	41.8	337.9	388.4	159450	10.0
1988	41.6	338.1	399.7	163986	10.6
1989	41.4	338.4	423.9	128414	11.8
1990	41.3	335.1	416.2	122711	14.4
1991	41.1	328.7	384.8	111347	14.4
1992	40.9	331.1	399.8	143963	14.4
1993	40.6	314.7	450.5	169911	14.9
1994	40.2	323.4	459.2	172042	19.8
1995	39.4	292.4	468.1	201731	18.8
1996	34.4	301.9	468.4	275871	18.9
1997	34.2	323.3	433.2	301655	19.7
1998	34.1	323.7	415.5	290859	19.3
1999	33.8	322.1	410.4	330069	19.0
2000	32.9	322.7	399.2	572257	17.9
2001	29.2	322.7	394.9	619806	15.7
2002	27.5	219.7	381.8	414248	14.9
2003	26.0	178.9	366.9	427266	14.3
2004	23.6	186.7	340.3	383954	14.5
2005	23.3	181.5	337.7	421680	14.8
2006	23.3	181.5	325.5	416459	14.8
2007	23.2	173.6	300.5	411238	14.0
2008	23.2	171.8	267.0	427377	13.6
2009	22.7	165.2	271.5	439099	13.8
2010	22.4	162.6	276.0	443774	13.7
2011	22.2	163.1	265.2	454009	13.8
2012	22.1	159.2	241.1	473121	13.7
2013		154.4	207.7	485320	12.8

注：1. 化肥施用量为折纯量。
2. 2003年以前农村用电量由原北京市供电局提供。
3. 农业机械总动力数据由北京市农业局提供。
4. 1991-2001年有效灌溉面积由北京市水务局提供。

Note: a) Data on consumption of chemical fertilizers were net amount.
b) Figures of rural electricity consumption before 2003 were provided by the former Beijing Electric Power Supply Bureau.
c) Figures of total power of agricultural machinery were provided by Beijing Municipal Bureau of Agriculture.
d) Figures of irrigated area 1991-2001 were provided by Beijing Water Authority.

10-3 农作物播种面积和造林面积(1978-2013年) SOWN AND AFFORESTATION AREA (1978-2013)

年 份 Year	农作物播种面积(万公顷) Sown Area (10000 hectares)	#粮食作物 Grain Crops	#玉米 Corn	#小麦 Wheat	#油料 Oil-bearing Crops	#蔬菜及食用菌 Vegetables and Edible Mushrooms	#瓜类及草莓 Melons & Strawberries	#饲料 Forage	造林面积(万公顷) Afforestation Area (10000 hectares)
1978	69.1	56.1	16.9	19.2	3.3	5.6	0.2	2.0	1.4
1979	67.7	56.0	18.2	19.7	3.0	5.4	0.3	2.0	1.6
1980	65.7	54.9	19.7	18.8	2.8	5.1	0.4	1.8	2.4
1981	64.4	53.0	19.8	18.4	2.7	5.5	0.6	1.7	2.7
1982	64.2	52.7	19.7	18.1	2.4	5.9	0.8	1.6	2.8
1983	63.8	53.0	20.1	18.7	1.9	5.7	0.5	1.5	3.3
1984	63.3	52.3	20.6	19.5	1.8	5.8	0.7	1.5	3.2
1985	61.8	51.1	21.7	19.1	2.0	5.4	0.9	1.3	3.0
1986	60.5	49.9	21.6	18.5	2.0	5.8	1.1	1.0	1.5
1987	59.8	49.5	22.3	18.3	1.6	6.0	0.9	1.1	2.0
1988	59.5	48.8	22.2	18.6	1.5	6.3	1.0	1.2	1.6
1989	58.9	48.3	21.9	18.5	1.3	6.8	0.8	1.1	0.8
1990	59.0	48.4	22.4	18.8	1.2	7.0	0.6	1.1	1.3
1991	59.0	48.3	22.3	19.2	1.2	7.3	0.5	1.0	1.5
1992	58.5	47.7	22.4	19.2	1.2	7.5	0.5	0.8	1.5
1993	56.5	45.6	21.8	17.8	1.3	7.8	0.5	0.7	4.8
1994	55.1	43.0	20.6	16.4	1.2	9.1	0.6	0.6	5.5
1995	55.3	43.4	20.8	17.2	1.2	9.1	0.5		4.7
1996	53.8	42.7	20.8	17.1	1.1	8.8	0.5	0.5	4.0
1997	53.6	42.5	20.6	17.1	1.0	8.9	0.5	0.5	3.8
1998	53.5	42.3	20.8	17.1	1.0	9.0	0.5	0.5	3.7
1999	52.6	41.0	19.8	16.8	1.0	9.2	0.5	0.5	3.0
2000	45.4	30.8	13.6	12.2	1.5	10.4	0.8	1.2	2.6
2001	38.0	21.4	10.0	7.3	1.4	11.3	0.9	1.9	3.2
2002	33.5	16.9	8.7	4.7	1.6	11.5	0.9	1.8	4.8
2003	30.1	14.1	7.5	3.6	1.4	10.8	0.9	1.9	4.7
2004	30.4	15.4	9.4	3.9	1.1	9.1	0.8	2.8	3.2
2005	30.8	19.2	12.0	5.3	0.9	7.9	0.8	1.5	1.2
2006	32.0	22.0	13.6	6.3	0.7	7.1	0.9	0.6	1.3
2007	29.5	19.7	13.9	4.1	0.7	7.0	0.9	0.4	1.1
2008	32.2	22.6	14.6	6.4	0.7	6.8	0.8	0.4	0.9
2009	32.0	22.6	15.1	6.1	0.6	6.8	0.8	0.4	1.8
2010	31.7	22.3	15.0	6.2	0.5	6.8	0.8	0.5	1.4
2011	30.3	20.9	14.1	5.8	0.5	6.7	0.8	0.5	2.1
2012	28.3	19.4	13.2	5.2	0.5	6.4	0.8	0.3	3.6
2013	24.2	15.9	11.4	3.6	0.3	6.2	0.7	0.2	4.4

注：1．蔬菜播种面积2006年为农业普查衔接数据，1997年-2005年为历史修订数据。

2．造林面积2009年以前为人工造林面积，2009年起调整为荒山荒(沙)地造林面积，包括人工造林、无林地和疏林地新封面积。

Note: a) Figures of vegetable sown area in 2006 were from agricultural census, and figures in 1997-2005 were historically revised data.

b) Afforestation area before 2009 was artificial afforestation area, and after 2009 it became barren mountains and barren (sand) afforestation area, including the area of artificial forests, non-forest land and newly enclosed forest land.

10-4 农林牧渔业总产值(1978-2013年)
GROSS OUTPUT VALUE OF AGRICULTURE, FORESTRY, ANIMAL PRODUCTION AND HUNTING, FISHING (1978-2013)

年份 Year	农林牧渔业总产值(亿元) Gross Output Value of Agriculture, Forestry, Animal Production and Hunting, Fishing (100 million yuan)	农业 Agriculture	林业 Forestry	牧业 Animal Production and Hunting	渔业 Fishing	农林牧渔服务业 Related Service Industry	农林牧渔业总产值比上年增长(%) Growth Rate (%) 按现价计算 Calculated at Current Price	按可比价计算 Calculated at Comparable Price
1978	11.5	8.9	0.2	2.4	0.01			
1979	12.3	8.8	0.2	3.3	0.02		7.0	
1980	14.3	9.8	0.5	3.9	0.05		16.3	
1981-1985	**99.4**	**64.6**	**3.9**	**30.1**	**0.8**			
1981	14.9	10.1	0.7	4.1	0.05		4.2	
1982	16.8	11.3	0.7	4.7	0.05		12.8	
1983	19.6	12.7	0.8	6.0	0.1		16.7	
1984	22.2	14.4	0.9	6.7	0.2		13.3	
1985	25.9	16.1	0.8	8.6	0.4		16.7	
1986-1990	**245.7**	**142.1**	**4.1**	**91.6**	**7.9**			
1986	28.1	17.2	0.8	9.4	0.7		8.5	
1987	34.4	20.3	0.8	12.3	1.0		22.4	
1988	52.6	31.4	0.9	18.6	1.7		52.9	
1989	60.4	34.2	0.7	23.3	2.2		14.8	
1990	70.2	39.0	0.9	28.0	2.3		16.2	
1991-1995	**570.1**	**293.2**	**11.2**	**244.6**	**21.1**			
1991	76.5	39.6	1.5	32.8	2.6		9.0	
1992	84.5	43.2	1.6	36.3	3.4		10.5	
1993	100.4	51.1	2.3	42.7	4.3		18.8	
1994	144.3	72.5	3.1	64.0	4.7		43.7	
1995	164.4	86.8	2.7	68.8	6.1		13.9	
1996-2000	**883.4**	**441.8**	**18.2**	**388.5**	**34.9**			
1996	168.9	89.2	2.8	71.1	5.8		2.7	
1997	170.5	86.8	2.9	74.6	6.2		0.9	
1998	174.8	88.3	3.2	75.8	7.5		2.5	
1999	180.6	89.4	4.1	79.5	7.6		3.3	
2000	188.6	88.1	5.2	87.5	7.8		4.4	
2001-2005	**1114.6**	**423.2**	**57.0**	**567.3**	**45.6**			
2001	202.2	84.7	9.0	99.3	9.2		7.2	
2002	213.5	83.5	11.9	108.6	9.5		5.6	
2003	224.7	80.9	12.3	114.3	9.3	7.9	5.2	
2004	234.9	83.1	11.4	124.3	8.9	7.2	4.5	
2005	239.3	91.0	12.4	120.8	8.7	6.4	1.9	
2006-2010	**1459.4**	**648.4**	**87.1**	**643.7**	**51.5**	**28.7**		
2006	240.2	104.5	14.8	105.1	9.8	6.0	0.4	0.9
2007	272.3	115.5	17.8	122.4	10.1	6.5	13.4	0.8
2008	303.9	128.1	20.5	140.5	9.8	5.0	11.6	0.8
2009	315.0	146.1	17.2	136.1	10.3	5.3	3.6	5.5
2010	328.0	154.2	16.8	139.6	11.5	5.9	4.1	-1.7
2011	363.1	163.4	18.9	162.7	11.5	6.6	10.7	0.9
2012	395.7	166.3	54.8	154.2	13.0	7.5	9.0	2.9
2013	421.8	170.4	75.9	154.8	12.8	8.0	6.6	2.1

注：1. 农林牧渔业总产值绝对数按现价计算，从2003年起执行新《国民经济行业分类标准》，农林牧渔业总产值中含农林牧渔服务业产值。
2. 2003年以后，计算农林牧渔业总产值使用的价格从农产品综合平均价调整为农产品生产价格。
3. 2006年为与农业普查衔接的数据，1997-2005年为历史修订数据。
4. 2010年按照新的《统计用产品分类目录》，将原归属林业产值的核桃、板栗等林产品调整至农业产值，并对2009年数据作了调整。

Note: a) The absolute number of agricultural gross output value are calculated at current prices. In the year of 2003, new Standard for Classification of National Economic Sectors was implemented, and gross output value of agriculture, forestry, animal production and hunting, fishing has included the output value of services for agriculture, forestry, animal production and hunting, fishing.
b) After 2003, the prices used for calculating the output value of agriculture, forestry, animal production and hunting, fishing have been changed f comprehensive average price of agricultural products to production price of agricultural products.
c) Figures for 2006 were from agricultural census, and figures in 1997-2005 were historically revised data.
d) Output value of forestry productions such as walnuts and chestnuts was transferred to that of the agriculture sector in 2010 according to the new Catalog of Product Classification Used for Statistics. Figures of 2009 were adjusted accordingly.

10-5 主要农业产品产量(1978-2013年)
OUTPUT OF MAJOR AGRICULTURAL PRODUCTS (1978-2013)

单位：万吨 (10000 tons)

年份 Year	粮食 Grain	油料 Oil-bearing Crops	蔬菜及食用菌 Vegetables and Edible Mushroom	干鲜果品 Nuts and Fresh Fruits	牛奶 Milk	肉类 Meat	#猪牛羊肉 Pork, Beef and Mutton	禽蛋产量 Poultry and Eggs	水产品 Aquatic Products
1978	186.0	2.6	164.5	17.5	5.4	11.9	11.9	2.1	0.2
1979	172.8	2.6	181.3	15.8	6.0	13.1	13.1	3.1	0.3
1980	186.0	3.1	175.9	15.9	6.8	15.1	15.1	3.4	0.4
1981-1985	**1004.8**	**13.1**	**1002.2**	**86.7**	**53.3**	**69.0**	**69.0**	**44.3**	**4.0**
1981	180.7	2.2	172.8	15.6	7.6	13.2	13.2	3.7	0.4
1982	185.5	2.3	208.3	13.8	8.9	13.9	13.9	5.4	0.4
1983	201.5	2.1	199.1	18.2	10.6	14.9	14.9	8.9	0.6
1984	217.4	2.6	218.0	20.2	12.6	13.4	13.4	12.2	1.0
1985	219.7	3.9	204.0	18.9	13.5	13.6	13.6	14.1	1.6
1986-1990	**1181.9**	**15.2**	**1422.2**	**119.3**	**89.7**	**90.8**	**78.3**	**103.8**	**18.8**
1986	216.5	3.0	222.7	18.7	14.6	13.3	13.3	14.7	2.2
1987	227.0	3.3	241.1	22.5	15.5	12.9	12.9	16.8	3.0
1988	234.6	3.0	271.3	23.8	18.0	14.5	14.5	21.8	3.9
1989	239.2	2.8	331.0	26.7	19.9	23.3	17.2	24.7	4.6
1990	264.6	3.1	356.1	27.6	21.7	26.8	20.4	25.8	5.1
1991-1995	**1354.7**	**17.6**	**1915.9**	**198.5**	**113.7**	**180.7**	**134.0**	**139.3**	**34.7**
1991	279.7	3.3	368.4	29.3	23.9	33.9	24.8	27.9	5.6
1992	281.9	3.4	381.4	34.0	24.5	35.9	27.3	30.0	6.4
1993	284.1	3.8	418.8	39.6	22.5	36.7	28.2	31.4	7.0
1994	249.2	3.8	350.0	48.8	22.2	34.4	24.8	31.2	7.6
1995	259.8	3.3	397.3	46.8	20.6	39.8	28.9	28.5	8.1
1996-2000	**1059.4**	**15.0**	**2101.9**	**291.8**	**120.2**	**218.1**	**146.5**	**98.2**	**38.2**
1996	237.4	2.9	403.2	51.3	21.0	38.2	27.3	24.7	7.8
1997	237.5	2.7	408.8	54.8	22.2	39.9	27.8	23.8	7.7
1998	239.3	2.8	403.8	59.5	22.7	43.4	30.3	17.9	7.6
1999	201.0	2.8	419.8	60.2	24.0	46.1	30.2	15.8	7.6
2000	144.2	3.8	466.3	66.0	30.3	50.5	30.9	16.0	7.5
2001-2005	**410.3**	**18.5**	**2302.3**	**419.5**	**295.5**	**287.8**	**169.1**	**78.9**	**35.0**
2001	104.9	4.3	491.0	71.9	42.9	55.9	33.0	15.6	7.4
2002	82.3	4.6	507.4	78.7	55.1	60.9	35.2	15.2	7.4
2003	58.0	3.3	486.7	84.1	63.3	60.6	35.2	16.2	7.1
2004	70.2	2.9	444.1	90.9	70.0	57.4	34.0	15.9	6.7
2005	94.9	2.5	373.1	93.9	64.2	53.3	31.7	16.0	6.4
2006-2010	**577.3**	**10.0**	**1622.7**	**445.3**	**322.1**	**231.7**	**135.0**	**76.5**	**29.6**
2006	109.2	2.2	341.2	88.7	61.9	45.3	26.9	15.2	5.4
2007	102.1	2.2	340.1	91.1	62.2	47.9	27.1	15.6	6.0
2008	125.5	2.2	321.3	89.8	66.4	45.1	25.9	15.2	6.1
2009	124.8	1.8	317.1	90.3	67.4	47.2	27.6	15.4	5.8
2010	115.7	1.6	303.0	85.4	64.1	46.3	27.5	15.1	6.3
2011	121.8	1.4	296.9	87.8	64.0	44.4	27.6	15.1	6.1
2012	113.8	1.3	279.9	84.3	65.1	43.2	27.3	15.2	6.4
2013	96.1	1.0	266.9	79.5	61.5	41.8	27.9	17.5	6.4

注：1. 蔬菜、干鲜果品、猪牛羊肉产量2006年为农业普查衔接数据，1997年-2005年为历史修订数据。
2. 肉类产量1988年及以前为猪牛羊肉产量。
3. 2006年及以前水产品产量为淡水鱼产量，2007年以后含远洋捕捞量。水产品数据由北京市农业局提供。

Note: a) Figures of output for vegetables, nuts and fresh fruits, pork, beef and mutton in 2006 were from agricultural census, and figures in 1997-2005 were historically revised data.
b) Output of meat in and before 1988 was the output of pork, beef and mutton.
c) Output of aquatic products was output of fresh water fish in and before 2006, and long-range fishing has been included since 2007. Figures of aquatic products were provided by Beijing Municipal Bureau of Agriculture.

10-6 平均每一从业人员创造农、林、牧、渔业产值(1990-2013年)
AVERAGE OUTPUT VALUE OF AGRICULTURE, FORESTRY, ANIMAL PRODUCTION AND HUNTING, FISHING CREATED BY EACH PERSON (1990-2013)

单位：元 (yuan)

年 份 Year	农林牧渔业总产值 Total Output Value of Agriculture, Forestry, Animal Production and Hunting, Fishing	#农 业 Agriculture	#林 业 Forestry	#畜牧业 Animal Production and Hunting	#渔 业 Fishing
1990	8507	5537	1540	54837	22729
1991	9523	5722	2807	68268	26442
1992	11329	6678	3826	78905	33689
1993	13859	8271	4558	92901	39518
1994	21002	12461	6507	139136	39182
1995	25110	15760	5750	156332	47266
1996	25250	15504	6741	173404	53133
1997	26101	15605	6886	169541	56211
1998	25817	15653	7724	124279	68379
1999	25396	15621	8398	101869	63684
2000	27061	16454	8416	99481	65223
2001	29772	16838	12287	109151	76321
2002	33313	18193	15209	116799	86784
2003	37770	19579	14634	129862	92879
2004	40569	20934	12376	153518	98619
2005	40834	22700	12496	156911	96184
2006	36559	21147	17398	166889	195867
2007	44276	25892	19324	177359	126998
2008	49175	28405	22031	212910	122318
2009	51750	33061	18507	215008	128750
2010	54579	35130	17886	228814	164441
2011	62556	38613	20344	285988	155637
2012	70258	40585	59852	282916	175234
2013	77516	43643	81323	294659	179937

注：1. 2006年从业人员为农普数据，2007年以后为农业普查口径，含居住半年以上的外来人口。
2. 2006年农林牧渔业总产值及分行业产值为与农业普查衔接的数据，1997-2005年为历史修订数据。
3. 2010年按照新的《统计用产品分类目录》，将原归属林业产值的核桃、板栗等林产品调整至农业产值，并对2009年数据作了调整。

Note: a) Figures of employed persons in 2006 were from agriculture census. These figures are from agriculture census and include migrant population who have resided for over half a year since 2007.
b) Figures of output value for agriculture, forestry, animal production and hunting, fishing in 2006 were from agricultural census, and figures in 1997-2005 were historically revised data.
c) Output value of forestry, such as walnuts and chestnuts, was transferred to the farming sector in 2010 according to the new Catalog of Product Classification Used for Statistics. Figures in 2009 were adjusted accordingly.

10-7 耕地面积(2009-2012年)
ARABLE LAND AREA (2009-2012)

单位：公顷 (hectare)

项　　目	Item	2009	2010	2011	2012
年初耕地总资源	**Total Arable Land Resources at the Beginning of the Year**		**227170.4**	**223779.4**	**221956.2**
年内增加	**Increase in the Year**		**11.1**	**521.5**	**545.4**
#土地整理	Land Consolidation				429.6
土地复垦	Land Rehabilitation				
土地开发	Land Development			4.8	
农业结构调整	Agricultural Structure Adjustment			489.8	42.8
其　他	Others		11.1	26.9	73.1
年内减少	**Decrease in the Year**		**3402.1**	**2344.7**	**1645.4**
#建设占用	Occupied by Construction		3038.2	1917.0	1302.3
灾害损毁	Disaster Damage				172.9
生态退耕	Farmland Converted for Ecological Preservation				
农业结构调整	Agricultural Structure Adjustment		321.0	412.7	83.6
其　他	Others		43.0	15.0	86.7
年末耕地面积	**Total Arable Land Resources at the End of the Year**	**227170.4**	**223779.4**	**221956.2**	**220856.2**
水　田	Paddy Field	2240.5	2207.9	2155.2	2121.1
水浇地	Irrigable Land	171983.2	169205.7	167694.0	166562.7
其　他	Others	52946.8	52365.7	52107.0	52172.4

注：表中2009年耕地面积相关数据为第二次全国土地调查数据，2010-2012年为各年土地变更调查数据。

资料来源：北京市国土资源局。

Note: Related statistics for Arable land area in 2009 were from the 2nd National Land Survey, and statistics for 2010-2012 were survey data of land changed.

Source: Beijing Municipal Bureau of Land and Resources.

10-8 农村固定资产投资情况(2013年)
INVESTMENT IN FIXED ASSETS IN RURAL AREAS (2013)

单位：万元、万平方米 (10000 yuan, 10000 sq.m)

项目	Item	合计 Total	非农户 Non-Agricultural	农户 Agricultural
本年固定资产投资完成额	**Investment in Fixed Assets Completed in the Year**	**6795910**	**6300711**	**495199**
按投资方向分	**By Use of Funds**			
农、林、牧、渔业	Agriculture, Forestry, Animal Production and Hunting, Fishing	1646913	1626503	20410
采矿业	Mining and Quarrying	24802	24802	
制造业	Manufacturing	562566	548096	14470
电力、热力、燃气及水生产和供应业	Production and Distribution of Electricity, Heating Power, Gas and Water	183447	183420	27
建筑业	Construction	7947	4146	3801
批发和零售业	Wholesale and Retail Trade	80309	73645	6664
交通运输、仓储和邮政业	Transport, Storage and Post	399190	360710	38480
住宿和餐饮业	Accommodation and Restaurants	83369	82858	511
信息传输、软件和信息技术服务业	Information Transmission, Software and Information Technology Services	37187	37187	
金融业	Finance			
房地产业	Real Estate	1135705	725082	410623
租赁和商务服务业	Renting and Leasing Activities and Business Services	132508	132508	
科学研究和技术服务业	Scientific Research and Development, Technical Services	8136	8136	
水利、环境和公共设施管理业	Management of Water Conservancy, Environment and Public Facilities	1658031	1658031	
居民服务、修理和其他服务业	Resident Services, Repair and Other Services	16554	16341	213
教育	Education	192725	192725	
卫生和社会工作	Healthcare and Social Works	45919	45919	
文化、体育和娱乐业	Culture, Sports and Entertainment	459111	459111	
公共管理、社会保障和社会组织	Public Administration, Social Security and Social Organizations	121491	121491	
上年末结余资金	**Balance by the End of Last Year**	**855395**	**855395**	
本年资金来源小计	**Total Source of Funds in the Year**	**5822878**	**5327679**	**495199**
国家资金	State Funds	21922	21922	
国内贷款	Domestic Loan	532805	532805	
债券	Bonds	7928	7928	
利用外资	Foreign Funds	4049	4049	
自筹资金	Self-raised Funds	4843065	4347866	495199
其他资金	Other Funds	413109	413109	
本年施工房屋面积	**Floor Space of Buildings under Construction in the Year**	**2111**	**1748**	**363**
#住宅	Residential Buildings	1017	674	343
本年竣工房屋面积	**Floor Space of Buildings Completed in the Year**	**625**	**277**	**348**
#住宅	Residential Buildings	411	83	328
本年竣工房屋投资完成额	**Investment of Buildings Completed in the Year**	**409430**		**409430**
#住宅	Residential Buildings	392568		392568
本年新增固定资产	**Original Value of Incremental Fixed Assets in the Year**	**3723713**	**3245961**	**477752**

注：1.本表非农户固定资产投资为全面调查；农户固定资产投资为抽样调查。
2.行业划分执行2011年国民经济行业分类标准（GB/T 4754-2011）。

Note: a) Figures of Investment by non-agricultural households in fixed assets in this table are from comprehensive survey; investment by agricultural households in fixed assets is from sample survey.
b) Sectors are classified in accordance with the Standard for Classification of National Economic Sectors 2011 (GB/T 4754-2011).

10-9 农业生产条件
PRODUCTIVE CONDITIONS OF AGRICULTURE

项目		Item		2013	2012	2013年为2012年% 2013 as % of 2012
主要农业机械拥有量		**Possession of Major Agricultural Machinery**				
农业机械总动力	(万千瓦)	Total Power of Agricultural Machinery	(10000 kw)	207.7	241.1	86.2
大中型拖拉机	(混合台)	Large and Medium-sized Tractors	(unit)	6461	7426	87.0
小型拖拉机	(台)	Mini Tractors	(unit)	2421	7270	33.3
机引农具	(台)	Tractor-propelled Farm Tools	(unit)	14406	20655	69.7
机动喷雾器	(部)	Motorized Sprayers	(unit)	22205	29505	75.3
联合收割机	(台)	Combine Harvesters	(unit)	2172	2172	
机动脱粒机	(台)	Motorized Shellers	(unit)	4066	4236	96.0
米面加工机	(台)	Processing Machines of Rice and Flour	(unit)	4067	4620	88.0
机动挤奶器	(台)	Motorized Milkers	(unit)	1727	1293	133.6
饲料粉碎机	(台)	Fodder Grinders	(unit)	3912	4368	89.6
载重汽车	(辆)	Motor Trucks	(unit)	2320	3804	61.0
农业机械作业面积		**Operation Area of Agricultural Machinery**				
机耕面积	(公顷)	Cultivated Area by Machinery	(hectare)	72603	81425	89.2
占全部耕地面积比重	(%)	Share in the Total Arable Land	(%)	87.8	82.9	
机播面积	(公顷)	Sown Area by Machinery	(hectare)	147491	183689	80.3
占播种面积比重	(%)	Share in the Total Sown Area	(%)	66.8	68.0	
机收面积	(公顷)	Harvest Area by Machinery	(hectare)	128629	157139	81.9
占收获面积比重	(%)	Share in the Total Harvest Area	(%)	56.3	56.5	
农村用电量及小水电		**Rural Electricity Consumption and Small Hydropower Stations**				
农村用电量	(万千瓦小时)	Rural Electricity Consumption	(10000 kwh)	485320	473121	102.6
农村小水电站	(处)	Rural Small Hydropower Stations	(unit)	19	19	
农村小水电站发电量	(万千瓦小时)	Energy Generated by Rural Small Hydropower Statio	(10000 kwh)	333.1	422.6	78.8
农田水利		**Irrigation and Water Conservancy**				
排灌用动力机械	(台)	Irrigation Machinery	(unit)	39694	41193	96.4
排灌用动力机械动力	(万千瓦)	Power of Irrigation Machinery	(10000 kw)	43.9	46.2	95.0
机(电)井	(眼)	Motor-pumped Wells	(unit)	32586	49000	66.5
#已配套	(眼)	Completed Sets	(unit)	30645	47000	65.2
扬水站(固定机电排灌站)	(处)	Pumping Stations (Drainage and Irrigation Stations with Fixed Machinery)	(unit)	1573	1573	
有效灌溉面积	(公顷)	Effective Irrigation Area	(hectare)	154421	159236	97.0
化肥施用量(折纯)		**Consumption of Chemical Fertilizers (converted into net amount)**				
化肥施用量	(吨)	Consumption of Chemical Fertilizers	(ton)	127809	136707	93.5
#氮　肥	(吨)	Nitrogenous Fertilizers	(ton)	59373	64858	91.5
磷　肥	(吨)	Phosphate Fertilizers	(ton)	7415	7825	94.8
钾　肥	(吨)	Potash Fertilizers	(ton)	6722	7012	95.9

注：1. 农村小水电站是指乡村两级小水电站实有数。
2. 主要农业机械拥有量、农业机械作业面积、排灌动力机械数据由北京市农业局提供。
3. 机(电)井和扬水站数据由北京市水务局提供。

Note: a) Figures of rural small hydropower stations refer to actual number of small hydropower stations at township and village level.
b) Figures of possession of major agricultural machinery, operation area of agricultural machinery and irrigation machinery are provided by Beijing Municipal Bureau of Agriculture.
c) Figures of motor-pumped wells are provided by Beijing Water Authority.

10-10 农林牧渔业总产值
GROSS OUTPUT VALUE OF AGRICULTURE, FORESTRY, ANIMAL PRODUCTION AND HUNTING, FISHING

单位：万元 (10000 yuan)

项 目	Item	总产值 Gross Output Value		2013年为2012年% 2013 as % of 2012
		2013	2012	
合 计	**Total**	**4217827.9**	**3957128.8**	**106.6**
农 业	**Agriculture**	**1704065.2**	**1662890.9**	**102.5**
谷 物	Cereal	207507.1	235780.0	88.0
豆 类	Beans	5287.5	5493.2	96.3
经济作物	Cash Crops	8488.3	12815.3	66.2
蔬菜、食用菌	Vegetables and Edible Mushromms	688039.0	623672.0	110.3
水果（含瓜果类）	Fruits (including melons)	565617.8	543067.7	104.2
其 他	Others	229125.5	242062.7	94.7
林 业	**Forestry**	**758857.3**	**548252.5**	**138.4**
牧 业	**Animal Production and Hunting**	**1547519.2**	**1541607.2**	**100.4**
牲畜饲养	Animal Breeding	446670.6	418170.4	106.8
养 猪	Hogs	540726.6	527536	102.5
家禽饲养	Poultry	483513.8	511970.8	94.4
#禽 蛋	Poultry Eggs	227924.5	203250.1	112.1
其 他	Others	76608.2	83930.0	91.3
渔 业	**Fishing**	**127809.5**	**129778.2**	**98.5**
农林牧渔服务业	**Services for Agriculture, Forestry, Animal Production and Hunting, Fishing**	**79576.7**	**74600.0**	**106.7**

10-11 主要农作物播种面积及产量
SOWN AREA AND YIELD OF MAJOR CROPS

项目	Item	2013 播种面积(公顷) Sown Areas (hectare)	2013 单产(公斤/公顷) Yield Per Unit (kg/hectare)	2013 总产量(吨) Total Yield (ton)	2012 播种面积(公顷) Sown Areas (hectare)	2012 单产(公斤/公顷) Yield Per Unit (kg/hectare)	2012 总产量(吨) Total Yield (ton)
粮 食	**Grain**	**158911.1**	**6049.0**	**961259.8**	**193874.5**	**5868.4**	**1137733.6**
按季节分	By Season						
夏 粮	Summer Grain	36241.3	5170.3	187377.3	52212.5	5257.5	274507.4
秋 粮	Autumn Grain	122669.7	6308.7	773882.5	141662.0	6093.6	863226.2
按品种分	Grouped by Variety						
稻 谷	Rice	188.9	6913.2	1305.9	202.1	6442.9	1302.1
冬小麦	Winter Wheat	36196.4	5172.1	187213.2	52183.0	5258.1	274383.4
玉 米	Corn	114486.4	6567.0	751832.2	132021.4	6330.9	835814.3
薯 类	Tubers	1436.9	5412.0	7776.5	2132.6	5740.7	12242.6
大 豆	Soybeans	4110.1	1960.1	8056.1	4716.3	1880.8	8870.5
棉 花	**Cotton**	**140.9**	**1071.0**	**150.9**	**239.3**	**1135.4**	**271.7**
油 料	**Oil-bearing Crops**	**3418.0**	**2856.1**	**9762.1**	**4531.2**	**2958.3**	**13404.6**
#花 生	Peanuts	3024.9	3003.3	9084.7	4038.8	3070.3	12400.4
药 材	**Medical Materials**	**2260.9**	**850.4**	**1922.7**	**2465.9**	**852.7**	**2102.7**
蔬菜及食用菌	**Vegetables and Edible Mushrooms**	**61984.7**	**43052.4**	**2668593.0**	**64090.4**	**43673.0**	**2799019.5**
瓜类及草莓	**Melons & Strawberries**	**6953.5**	**42763.0**	**297352.4**	**7659.8**	**44415.1**	**340210.7**
#西 瓜	Watermelons	5777.3	46387.8	267996.1	6473.7	47843.8	309726.5
饲 料	**Forage**	**2250.9**			**3388.0**		
#牧 草	Forage Grass	363.8			771.9		
花 卉	**Flowers**	**3833.9**			**3412.9**		

10-12 林业及干鲜果品生产
FORESTRY, NUTS AND FRESH FRUIT PRODUCTION

项目	Item	2013	2012	2013年为2012年% 2013 as % of 2012
林业生产	**Forestry**			
荒山荒(沙)地造林面积 (公顷)	Afforestation Area for Barren Mountains and Barren (Sand) Land (hectare)	43823	35752	122.6
#人工造林面积 (公顷)	Artificial Afforestation Area (hectare)	30808	22171	139.0
#平原造林面积 (公顷)	Afforestation Area on the Plain (hectare)	24284	16974	143.1
育苗面积 (公顷)	Seedling Growing Area (hectare)	17736	9744	182.0
#本年新育 (公顷)	Newly Growing in the Year (hectare)	1643	985	166.8
果类生产	**Fruits**			
干鲜果总产量 (吨)	Output of Nuts and Fresh Fruit (ton)	795071	842580	94.4
干 果 (吨)	Nuts (ton)	53936	46744	115.4
#核 桃 (吨)	Walnuts (ton)	12280	11840	103.7
板 栗 (吨)	Chinese Chestnuts (ton)	35782	29737	120.3
鲜 果 (吨)	Fresh Fruits (ton)	741135	795836	93.1
#苹 果 (吨)	Apples (ton)	87330	103017	84.8
梨 (吨)	Pears (ton)	147628	162632	90.8
葡 萄 (吨)	Grapes (ton)	36709	41316	88.8
柿 子 (吨)	Persimmons (ton)	43036	44235	97.3
桃 (吨)	Peaches (ton)	358519	373295	96.0
年末实有果园面积 (公顷)	**Actual Orchard Area (year-end) (hectare)**	**60183**	**62469**	**96.3**

资料来源：林业生产数据由北京市园林绿化局提供。
Source: Figures of forestry are from Beijing Municipal Bureau of Landscape and Forestry.

10-13 牲畜饲养及畜产品产量
LIVESTOCK BREEDING AND OUTPUT

项　　目		Item		2013	2012	2013年为2012年% 2013 as % of 2012
畜禽存栏		**Amount of Livestock and Poultry on Hand**				
大牲畜	(万头)	Large Animals	(10000 heads)	21.09	22.28	94.7
#役　畜	(万头)	Draught Animals	(10000 heads)	0.27	0.40	67.5
#牛	(万头)	Cattle and Buffaloes	(10000 heads)	20.35	21.36	95.3
猪	(万头)	Hogs	(10000 heads)	189.23	187.39	101.0
羊	(万只)	Sheep	(10000 units)	59.47	58.07	102.4
山　羊	(万只)	Goats	(10000 units)	15.80	16.63	95.0
绵　羊	(万只)	Sheep	(10000 units)	43.67	41.43	105.4
家　禽	(万只)	Poultry	(10000 units)	2524.88	2596.35	97.2
#产蛋鸡	(万只)	Hens	(10000 units)	1628.83	1569.60	103.8
肉　鸡	(万只)	Chickens	(10000 units)	582.57	685.10	85.0
鸭	(万只)	Ducks	(10000 units)	289.25	329.08	87.9
兔	(万只)	Rabbits	(10000 units)	6.00	4.66	128.8
畜禽出栏		**Amount of Livestock and Poultry Marketed**				
牛	(万头)	Cattle	(10000 heads)	11.24	11.88	94.6
猪	(万头)	Hogs	(10000 heads)	314.39	306.11	102.7
羊	(万只)	Sheep	(10000 units)	70.77	71.80	98.6
畜禽产品产量		**Output of Livestock and Poultry Products**				
肉类产量	(万吨)	Output of Meat	(10000 tons)	41.80	43.19	96.8
#猪　肉	(万吨)	Pork	(10000 tons)	24.63	23.94	102.9
牛　肉	(万吨)	Beef	(10000 tons)	2.05	2.17	94.5
羊　肉	(万吨)	Mutton	(10000 tons)	1.20	1.21	99.8
牛奶产量	(万吨)	Milk	(10000 tons)	61.46	65.05	94.5
禽　蛋	(万吨)	Poultry Eggs	(10000 tons)	17.50	15.24	114.8
#鸡　蛋	(万吨)	Eggs	(10000 tons)	17.12	14.95	114.5
蜂　蜜	(吨)	Honey	(ton)	2757	2554	107.9

10-14 水产品生产 AQUATIC PRODUCTS

项 目	Item	2013	2012	2013年为2012年% 2013 as % of 2012
渔业水域面积 (公顷)	**Area of Fishery Waters (hectare)**	**21276**	**20789**	**102.3**
#淡水养殖面积 (公顷)	Freshwater Agriculture (hectare)	4221	4364	96.7
#水 库 (公顷)	Reservoirs (hectare)			
池 塘 (公顷)	Puddles and Ponds (hectare)	4143	4254	97.4
水产品产量 (吨)	**Output of Aquatic Products (ton)**	**63610**	**63842**	**99.6**
#淡水鱼产量 (吨)	Output of Freshwater Fish (ton)	56603	54262	104.3
#大水库 (吨)	Large Reservoirs (ton)	2264	2241	101.0
中、小水库 (吨)	Medium and Small Reservoirs (ton)	1427	1581	90.3
池 塘 (吨)	Puddles and Ponds (ton)	47837	45494	105.2

资料来源：北京市农业局。
Source: Beijing Municipal Bureau of Agriculture.

10-15 农业观光园、民俗旅游、种业和设施农业(2005-2013年) AGRICULTURAL SIGHTSEEING GARDENS, FOLK-CUSTOM TOURISM, BREEDING OF SEEDS AND FACILITY AGRICULTURE (2005-2013)

项 目	Item	2005	2006	2007	2008
农业观光园	**Agricultural Sightseeing Gardens**				
农业观光园个数 (个)	Number of Agricultural Sightseeing Gardens (unit)	1012	1230	1302	1332
生产高峰期从业人员 (人)	Employed Persons in Peak Production Period (person)	40729	52828	51392	49366
接待人次 (万人次)	Visits Received (10000 person-times)	892.5	1210.6	1446.8	1498.2
经营总收入 (亿元)	Total Operating Income (100 million yuan)	7.88	10.49	13.15	13.58
民俗旅游	**Folk-Custom Tourism**				
从事民俗旅游实际经营接待户 (户)	Number of Actual Operating Households in Folk-Custom Tourism Receiption (household)	7268	8726	10323	9151
期末从业人员 (人)	Number of Employed Persons at the End of the Term (person)	14070	18253	20750	19421
民俗旅游接待人次 (万人次)	Number of Visits Received by Folk-Custom Tourism (10000 person-times)	758.9	982.5	1167.6	1205.6
民俗旅游总收入 (亿元)	Total Income of Folk-Custom Tourism (100 million yuan)	3.14	3.65	4.96	5.29
种 业	**Seed Industry**				
种业收入 (亿元)	Income (100 million yuan)	5.94	7.75	9.91	10.93
#销往外埠收入 (亿元)	Sales To Other Areas (100 million yuan)			3.99	5.78
#牧业收入 (亿元)	Income from Animal Production and Hunting (100 million yuan)			8.27	9.27
设施农业	**Facility Agriculture**				
设施农业实际利用占地面积 (公顷)	Actual Area Utilized by Facility Agriculture (hectare)	15645	17832	18022	17051
设施农业播种面积 (公顷)	Sown Area of Facility Agriculture (hectare)			30331	33889
设施农业收入 (亿元)	Income of Facility Agriculture (100 million yuan)	18.62	21.11	28.12	28.17

10-15 续表 Continued

项 目	Item	2009	2010	2011	2012	2013
农业观光园	**Agricultural Sightseeing Gardens**					
农业观光园个数 (个)	Number of Agricultural Sightseeing Gardens (unit)	1294	1303	1300	1283	1299
生产高峰期从业人员 (人)	Employed Persons in Peak Production Period (person)	49504	42561	46038	48906	50406
接待人次 (万人次)	Visits Received (10000 person-times)	1597.4	1774.9	1842.9	1939.9	1944.4
经营总收入 (亿元)	Total Operating Income (100 million yuan)	15.24	17.80	21.72	26.88	27.36
民俗旅游	**Folk-Custom Tourism Receiption**					
从事民俗旅游实际经营接待户 (户)	Number of Actual Operating Households in Folk-Custom Tourism Receiption (household)	8705	7979	8396	8367	8530
期末从业人员 (人)	Number of Employed Persons at the End of the Term (person)	19790	16856	18232	18705	19578
民俗旅游接待人次 (万人次)	Number of Visits Received by Folk-Custom Tourism (10000 person-times)	1393.1	1553.6	1668.9	1695.8	1806.5
民俗旅游总收入 (亿元)	Total Income of Folk-Custom Tourism (100 million yuan)	6.09	7.35	8.68	9.05	10.20
种 业	**Seed Industry**					
种业收入 (亿元)	Income (100 million yuan)	12.84	14.57	18.12	16.09	13.98
#销往外埠收入 (亿元)	Sales To Other Areas (100 million yuan)	7.28	8.05	11.68	9.70	8.23
#牧业收入 (亿元)	Income from Animal Production and Hunting (100 million yuan)	10.56	12.13	15.09	13.63	12.59
设施农业	**Facility Agriculture**					
设施农业实际利用占地面积 (公顷)	Actual Area Utilized by Facility Agriculture (hectare)	18762	18323	18616	19059	18852
设施农业播种面积 (公顷)	Sown Area of Facility Agriculture (hectare)	36203	36811	38006	37797	38763
设施农业收入 (亿元)	Income of Facility Agriculture (100 million yuan)	33.91	40.72	45.58	51.98	57.32

10-16 农业观光园
STATISTICS FOR AGRICULTURAL SIGHTSEEING GARDENS

项 目	Item	2013	2012	2013年为2012年% 2013 as % of 2012
农业观光园个数 (个)	Number of Agricultural Sightseeing Gardens (unit)	1299	1283	101.2
生产高峰期从业人员 (人)	Employed Persons in Peak Production Period (person)	50406	48906	103.1
接待人次 (万人次)	Visits Received (10000 person-times)	1944.4	1939.9	100.2
经营总收入 (万元)	Total Operating Income (10000 yuan)	273600.0	268820.9	101.8

10-17 民俗旅游
STATISTICS FOR FOLK-CUSTOM TOURISM

项 目		Item		2013	2012	2013年为2012年% 2013 as % of 2012
从事民俗旅游实际		Number of Actual Operating Households in				
经营接待户	(户)	Folk-Custom Tourism Receiption	(household)	8530	8367	101.9
期末从业人员	(人)	Number of Employed Persons at the End o	(person)	19578	18705	104.7
民俗旅游接待人次	(万人次)	Number of Visits Received by Folk-Custor	(10000 person-times)	1806.5	1695.8	106.5
民俗旅游总收入	(万元)	Total Income of Folk-Custom Tourism	(10000 yuan)	101958.7	90548.4	112.6

10-18 种业生产
STATISTICS FOR PRODUCTION OF SEED INDUSTRY

项 目		Item		产 量 Output			收 入(万元) Income (10000 yuan)		
				2013	2012	2013年为2012年% 2013 as % of 2012	2013	2012	2013年为2012年% 2013 as % of 2012
合 计		**Total**					**139807.6**	**160947.9**	**86.9**
农 业		**Agriculture**					**5368.3**	**8671.6**	**61.9**
#小麦种	(公斤)	Wheat Seeds	(kg)	4434263	5700925	77.8	850.5	1210.9	70.2
玉米种	(公斤)	Corn Seeds	(kg)	486735	1113903	43.7	290.8	606.6	47.9
蔬菜种	(公斤)	Vegetable Seeds	(kg)	91055	200029	45.5	1290.1	2403.2	53.7
林 业		**Forestry**					**5622.2**	**8541.5**	**65.8**
#树 苗	(百株)	Saplings	(100 units)	13939.0	29742.0	46.9	5443.3	8000.3	68.0
牧 业		**Animal Production and Hunting**					**125936.0**	**136286.3**	**92.4**
#种 猪	(头)	Boars	(head)	261970	255546	102.5	57225.0	54657.7	104.7
种雏禽	(万只)	Breeding Birds	(10000 units)	3037.4	3429.0	88.6	19227.6	33720.3	57.0
种 蛋	(万枚)	Breeding Eggs	(10000 units)	35556.2	35725.5	99.5	39700.3	40128.0	98.9
渔 业		**Fishing**					**2881.1**	**7448.5**	**38.7**
#种鱼苗	(万尾)	Breeding Fish Fry	(10000 units)	5939.5	12180.2	48.8	2564.3	6889.2	37.2

10-19 设施农业(2013年)
FACILITY AGRICULTURE (2013)

项　目	Item	设施农业播种面积（公顷）Sown Area of Facility Agriculture (hectare)	设施农业产量（吨）Output of Facility Agriculture (ton)	设施农业收入（万元）Income of Facility Agriculture (10000 yuan)
合 计	**Total**	**38763**		**573197.0**
温 室	**Greenhousse**	**22691**		**410570.9**
蔬菜及食用菌	Vegetables and Edible Mushrooms	20302	749162	296857.4
花卉苗木	Flowers and Saplings	917		36217.4
#切 花	Cut Flowers	215	2283	5665.8
盆 花	Potted Flowers	678	7967	29831.1
瓜果类	Melons	987	23586	62335.4
水 果	Fruits	340	4280	9797.4
其 它	Others	145		5363.3
大 棚	**Greenhouse Garden**	**12078**		**130918.4**
蔬菜及食用菌	Vegetables and Edible Mushrooms	9046	338364	88505.9
花卉苗木	Flowers and Sapling	157		5266.3
#切 花	Cut Flowers	25	524	645.9
盆 花	Potted Flowers	115	2492	4456.5
瓜果类	Melons	2625	120391	33414.9
水 果	Fruits	171	1458	2783.2
其 它	Other	79		948.1
中小棚	**Medium and Small Shed**	**3994**		**31707.7**
蔬菜及食用菌	Vegetables and Edible Mushrooms	1959	65074	15184.5
花卉苗木	Flowers and Sapling	24		446.0
#切 花	Cut Flowers	1	20	51.1
盆 花	Potted Flowers	12	210	349.9
瓜果类	Melons	1952	78593	15904.6
水 果	Fruits			
其 它	Other	60		172.6

注：切花产量的计量单位是万枝，盆花产量的计量单位是万盆。

Note: Cut flowers are measured in 10000 ones; and potted flowers, 10000 pots.

10-20 乡镇企业各业基本情况(2013年)
BASIC STATISTICS FOR TOWN AND TOWNSHIP ENTERPRISES IN DIFFERENT SECTORS (2013)

项目	Item	企业个数(个) Number of Enterprises (unit)		从业人员(人) Employed Persons (person)		总收入(万元) Total Income (10000 yuan)		利润总额(万元) Total Profits (10000 yuan)	
		数量 Number	构成(%) Composition (%)	数量 Number	构成(%) Composition (%)	数量 Number	构成(%) Composition (%)	数量 Number	构成(%) Composition (%)
合计	**Total**	**149544**	**100.0**	**1229627**	**100.0**	**52718678**	**100.0**	**3085543**	**100.0**
农业	Agriculture	2738	1.8	24593	2.0	567471	1.1	53952	1.7
工业	Industry	19974	13.4	538973	43.8	27086217	51.4	1593634	51.6
建筑业	Construction	6730	4.5	184457	15.0	5537116	10.5	278554	9.0
交通运输业	Transportation	23777	15.9	89185	7.3	4081560	7.7	314165	10.2
批发零售业	Wholesale and Retail Trade	37984	25.4	116073	9.4	8752955	16.6	357698	11.6
住宿及餐饮业	Accommodation and Restaurants	13478	9.0	61481	5.0	1357116	2.6	110265	3.6
居民服务、其它服务和娱乐业	Household Services, Other Services and Entertainment	27965	18.7	182175	14.8	3095272	5.9	274613	8.9
其他	Others	16898	11.3	32690	2.7	2240971	4.3	102662	3.3

资料来源：北京市经济和信息化委员会。
Source: Beijing Municipal Commission of Economy and Information Technology.

10-21 农村经济收入与分配
INCOME AND DISTRIBUTION OF RURAL ECONOMY

单位：万元 (10000 yuan)

项 目	Item	2013	2012	2013年为2012年% 2013 as % of 2012
营业收入	**Operation Income**	**50911573.0**	**48129713.4**	**105.8**
农 业	Agriculture	1168971.8	1162659.8	100.5
#粮 食	Grain	310323.2	305752.2	101.5
林 业	Forestry	243406.7	214391.2	113.5
牧 业	Animal Production and Hunting	1207972.1	1174299.9	102.9
渔 业	Fishing	111721.3	98683.3	113.2
工 业	Industry	14366190.6	14226578.0	101.0
建筑业	Construction	6150834.4	5657689.8	108.7
交通运输业	Transportation	3038449.7	2555781.1	118.9
商业、饮食业	Commerce and Catering	10345381.6	9834460.9	105.2
服务业	Services	10369376.8	9411390.7	110.2
其 他	Others	3909268.0	3793778.7	103.0
营业成本	**Operation Costs**	**45241887.0**	**42740806.4**	**105.9**
农 业	Agriculture	1146066.6	1133488.0	101.1
#粮 食	Grain	308073.3	305721.2	100.8
林 业	Forestry	239624.5	210266.7	114.0
牧 业	Animal Production and Hunting	1191249.3	1163534.2	102.4
渔 业	Fishing	108011.4	96343.9	112.1
工 业	Industry	12589806.6	12512204.1	100.6
建筑业	Construction	5478480.8	5052260.9	108.4
交通运输业	Transportation	2931553.0	2477162.4	118.3
商业、饮食业	Commerce and Catering	9418878.3	8981789.8	104.9
服务业	Services	8687548.2	7757250.6	112.0
其 他	Others	3450668.3	3356505.8	102.8
营业利润	**Operating Profits**	**1372018.5**	**1132259.4**	**121.2**
利润总额	**Total Profits**	**1895094.3**	**1623797.3**	**116.7**
税后利润	**After-tax Profits**	**1651419.5**	**1399396.5**	**118.0**
可供分配的利润	**Profits Available for Distribution**	**1888185.0**	**1733207.7**	**108.9**
未分配利润	**Undistributed Profits**	**1258879.2**	**1046237.2**	**120.3**

资料来源：北京市农村经济研究中心农村合作经济经营管理站。
Source: Operation and Management Station for Rural Cooperative Economy of Beijing Rural Economy Research Center.

10-22 乡镇企业出口供货情况
GOODS SUPPLIES FOR EXPORT OF TOWN AND TOWNSHIP ENTERPRISES

单位：万元 (10000 yuan)

项 目	Item	2013	2012
合 计	**Total**	**1210724**	**1452479**
化 工	Chemical Products	57063	66813
机 械	Machinery	203836	254339
矿 产	Mineral Products	11288	13071
轻 工	Light Industry	183072	218407
食 品	Food	131239	159773
土产畜产	Local and Livestock Products	28248	31955
纺织服装	Textile and Garments	411622	476948
工艺品	Artworks	29535	33411
其 他	Others	154821	197762

资料来源：北京市经济和信息化委员会。
Source: Beijing Municipal Commission of Economy and Information Technology.

主要统计指标解释

农林牧渔业总产值 是以货币表现的农林牧渔业的全部产品总量和对农林牧渔业生产活动进行的各种支持性服务活动的价值。

耕地 指种植农作物的土地，包括熟地，新开发、复垦、整理地，休闲地（含轮歇地、轮作地）；以种植农作物（含蔬菜）为主，间有零星果树、桑树或其他树木的土地；平均每年能保证收获一季的已垦滩地和海涂。耕地中包括南方宽度<1.0米、北方宽度<小于2.0米固定的沟、渠、路和地坎(埂)；临时种植药材、草皮、花卉、苗木等的耕地，以及其他临时改变用途的耕地。

农作物播种面积 指实际播种或移植有农作物的面积。凡是实际种植有农作物的面积，不论种植在耕地上还是种植在非耕地上，均包括在农作物播种面积中。在播种季节基本结束后，因遭灾而重新改种和补种的农作物面积，也包括在内。

有效灌溉面积 指具有一定的水源，地块比较平整，灌溉工程或设备已经配套，在一般年景下当年能够进行正常灌溉的耕地面积。

设施农业 指以工厂化生产方式，建造人工设施，改变气候条件，提高农作物抵御自然灾害的能力，改良生物特性，使作物实现错季或反季节生产，达到农作物均衡生产的目的。

农业机械总动力 指主要用于农、林、牧、渔业的各种动力机械的动力总和。包括耕作机械、排灌机械、收获机械、农用运输机械、植物保护机械、牧业机械、渔业机械和其他农用机械[内燃机按引擎马力折成瓦（特）计算，电动机按功率折成瓦（特）计算]。不包括专门用于乡、镇、村、组办工业、基本建设、非农业运输、科学实验和教学等非农业生产方面用的动力机械与作业机械。

农村用电量 指本年度内，扣除在农村中的国有经济工业交通、基建等单位的用电量以后的农村生产和生活的全年用电总量（计量单位千瓦小时，按全年累计数统计），即包括国家电网供电，也包括农村自办电站供电量。

农用化肥施用量 指本年度内实际用于农业生产的化学肥料数量，包括氮肥、磷肥、钾肥和复合肥。施用量要求按折纯量计算数量，即各类化学肥料的实际施用数量按其含氮、含五氧化二磷、含氧化钾的比例折成百分之百计算。

折纯量＝实物量×某种化肥有效成份含量的百分比

乡镇及行政村单位常住户数 指长期（一年以上）居住在乡镇（不包括城关镇）行政管理区域内的住户，还包括居住在城关镇所辖行政村范围内的农村住户。户口不在本地而在本地居住一年及以上的住户也包括在本地农村住户内；有本地户口，但举家外出谋生一年以上的住户，无论是否保留承包耕地都不包括在本地农村住户范围内。不包括乡村地区内的国有经济的机关、团体、学校、企业、事业单位的集体户。

乡镇及行政村常住人口 指乡村地区常住居民户数中的常住人口数，即经常在家或在家居住6个月以上，而且经济和生活与本户连成一体的人口。外出从业人员在外居住时间虽然在6个月以上，但收入主要带回家中，经济与本户连为一体，仍视为家庭常住人口；在家居住，生活和本户连成一体的国家职工、退休人员也为家庭常住人口。但是现役军人、中专及以上（走读生除外）的在校学生、以及常年在外（不包括探亲、看病等）且已有稳定的职业与居住场所的外出从业人员，不应当作家庭常住人口。

乡镇及行政村从业人员 指全部乡镇及行政村人口中16岁以上实际参加生产经营活动并取得实物或货币收入的人员，既包括劳动年龄内经常参加劳动的人员，也包括超过劳动年龄但经常参加劳动的人员。但不包括户口在家的在外学生、现役军人和丧失劳动能力的人，也不包括待业人员和家务劳动者。从业人员按从事主业时间最长（时间相同按收入）分为农业从业人员，工业从业人员，建筑业从业人员，交通运输仓储及邮政业从业人员，信息传输、计算机服务和软件业，批发与零售业从业人员，住宿和餐饮业从业人员，其它从业人员。

Explanatory Notes on Main Statistical Indicators

Gross Output Value of Agriculture, Forestry, Animal Production and Hunting, Fishing refers to the monetary value of all products of agriculture, forestry, animal production and hunting, fishing, as well as the monetary value of services provided in support of all the above-mentioned sectors.

Arable Land refers to the land suitable for growing crops, including cultivated land; any land newly opened up, reclaimed and cultivated; fallow land(including swidden and rotated land); land mostly for growing crops(including vegetables), supplemented by mulberry trees, fruit trees, and other trees; cultivated bottomland and shallows that can secure an average of one harvest annually. Arable land includes furrows, ditches, paths and field ridges less than 1m wide in the southern part of China, or less than 2m wide in the northern part. It also covers arable land that is temporarily for growing medicinal materials, turf, flowers, nursery stock and other uses.

Sown Area refers to the area of all lands actually sown or transplanted with crops, including both the cultivated and non-cultivated land. Area of lands re-planted after seedtime has passed due to natural disasters is also included.

Effective Irrigation Area refers to the area of arable lands that can be effectively irrigated in a normal harvest year, i.e. relatively level land, with certain water sources and complete sets of irrigation facilities.

Facility Agriculture means to produce in an industrialized manner, put in place facilities of manual intervention, change climate conditions, increase the crops' capability to resist natural disasters, and improve the crops' biological property, so as to stagger harvest seasons, create anti-season production, and achieve balanced production of crops.

Total Power of Agricultural Machinery refers to the total power of motive power machines used in agriculture, forestry, animal production and hunting, fishing sectors, including machinery for ploughing, irrigation and drainage, harvesting, agricultural transport, plant protection, animal production and hunting, fishing and other farm machinery (The horsepower of internal combustion engines is converted into watts, and the output of electric motors is also converted into watts). Motive power machines and operating machines exclusively used for non-agricultural production activities, such as industrial operations run by counties, towns, villages and teams, capital construction, non-agricultural transport, scientific experiments and teaching, are not included.

Rural Electricity Consumption refers to the total rural production and rural residents' electricity consumption in the whole year (unit of measurement: kilowatt-hour; the data representing accumulative usage of the year), deducting the consumption by entities like state-owned industry, transport, and infrastructure construction. The data cover both power supplies by the State Grid and by the rural self-run power stations.

Consumption of Chemical Fertilizers refers to the total quantity of chemical fertilizers applied in agricultural production within the year, including nitrogenous fertilizer, phosphate fertilizer, potash fertilizer, and compound fertilizer. The amount of chemical fertilizers applied is calculated in terms of net amount, that is, to use the gross weight of the respective fertilizers in calculating the quantity of effective ingredients (e.g. nitrogen content in nitrogenous fertilizer, phosphorous pent oxide content in phosphate fertilizer, and potassium oxide content in potash fertilizer).

Net Amount = Physical Quantity× Content (%) of Effective Ingredients in Certain Chemical Fertilizer

Number of Resident Households in Towns and Administrative Villages refer to households living in the administrative areas of towns and villages (excluding township government premises) on a long-term basis (more than one year), including those living in administrative villages within township government premises. Households with non-local household registration but having been living locally for more than one year are also counted as local rural households; while households with local household registration but left to make a living elsewhere for more than one year, with or without contract lands, are not counted as local rural households. Collective households of state-owned organs, groups, schools, enterprises, and public institutions, as well as households living in grouped commercial residential quarters in rural areas are not included.

Permanent Population in Towns and Administrative Villages refers to the population of permanent households in rural areas, namely those who stay home regularly or live at home for more than 6 months with their economic life and livelihood incorporated into the household. Migrant workers who live away from home for more than 6 months but taking most of their earnings back home, with their economic life still incorporated into the household, are also counted as permanent population of the household; state employees and retirees who live locally with their life incorporated into the household are also considered permanent population. But soldiers in active service, enrolled students (externs excluded) in technical secondary schools or above, as well as migrant workers who lived away from home for years (excluding those who travel to visit their families or to seek medical care) with a stable job and residence elsewhere, are not regarded as permanent population.

Employ Persons in Towns and Administrative Villages

refer to persons above 16 in all towns and administrative villages, who actually participate in productive and operating activities and earn incomes in kind or cash, including persons within the range of labor age and regularly participating in labor, and persons beyond the range of labor age but regularly participating in labor; while local registered students who left home for education, soldiers in active service, and people who lost the ability to work are not included, neither are the people waiting for employment or domestic workers. In terms of the length of employment period (or in terms of income if the employment periods are identical), employment falls into the following categories: agriculture, industry, construction, transportation, storage and post, information transmission, software and information technology services, wholesale and retail trade, accommodation and restaurants, and other sectors.

11

北京统计年鉴2014　BEIJING STATISTICAL YEARBOOK

工　业
INDUSTRY

简 要 说 明

一、本章统计的主要内容

本章资料反映北京市工业方面的基本情况，主要包括按登记注册类型、轻重工业、企业规模、工业行业大类等分组的主要经济指标数据，还包括国有控股工业企业、股份制工业企业、港澳台及外商投资工业企业、大中型工业企业的主要经济指标数据。

具体指标包括单位数、工业总产值、工业增加值、资产总计、负债合计、主营业务收入、主营业务成本、主营业务税金及附加、利润总额、应交增值税、总资产贡献率、资产负债率、成本费用利润率、主要工业产品产量等。

二、本章资料的统计范围

1984 年以前农村的村及村以下办工业归属农业，1984 年以后划归工业。

1999 年以前，工业的统计范围按隶属关系划分为乡及乡以上独立核算工业企业和非独立核算生产单位、村办工业、城镇合作工业、农村合作工业、城镇个体工业、农村个体工业六大部分（1984 年以前村办工业不在工业统计范围内）。

2000 年-2006 年，工业统计调查范围由按隶属关系划分，改变为按企业规模划分。2000 年至 2006 年，分为全部国有及年主营业务收入在 500 万元及以上非国有工业企业（简称“规模以上”）和年主营业务收入在 500 万元以下非国有工业企业和全部个体经营工业单位（简称“规模以下”）两部分。

2007 年-2010 年，分为年主营业务收入在 500 万元及以上法人工业企业（简称“规模以上”）和年主营业务收入在 500 万元以下法人工业企业和全部个体经营工业单位（简称“规模以下”）两部分。

2011 年及以后，分为年主营业务收入在 2000 万元及以上法人工业企业（简称“规模以上”）和年主营业务收入在 2000 万元以下法人工业企业和全部个体经营工业单位（简称“规模以下”）两部分。

三、数据来源和调查方法

本章工业企业统计数据来源于北京市统计局、国家统计局北京调查总队。其中，规模以上数据为全面调查，规模以下数据为抽样调查。

四、有关统计标准的变化说明

（一）关于行业划分：本章资料中工业行业分类 2002-2011 年期间执行 2002 年《国民经济行业分类标准》(GB/T 4754-2002)划分标准，2012 年开始执行 2011 年《国民经济行业分类》(GB/T 4754-2011)划分标准；

（二）关于企业标准划分：2010 年以前企业大中小型划分执行《统计上大中小型企业划分办法（暂行）》标准，自 2011 年开始，大中小微型企业划分标准执行国家统计局《关于统计上大中小微型企业划分办法》（国统字[2011]75 号）。

五、本章中关于历史数据调整的问题

按照国家统计局统一要求和统一方法，规模以上工业总产值及增加值历史资料已根据“北京市第一次全国经济普查”的结果采用“趋势离差法”进行了修正。调整历史区间为 1993 年至 2003 年。2004 年为第一次经济普查数据，2008 年为第二次经济普查数据。

Brief Introduction

I. Main Content

Data in this chapter show the basic situation of industry in Beijing, including: major economic indicators grouped by type of registration, light or heavy industry, enterprise scale, and industrial sector. and also includes main economic indicators for state-holding industrial enterprises, industrial enterprises limited by shares, Hong Kong, Macao, Taiwan and foreign-invested enterprises, and the large and medium-sized industrial enterprises.

Indicators include: unit number, gross industrial output value, industrial added value, total assets, total liabilities, main business income, main business cost, main business tax and surtax, total profits, payable VAT, contribution rate to total assets, asset-liability ratio, cost-profit ratio, and output of main industrial products, etc.

II. Scope of Statistics

Prior to 1984, the rural industrial production run by villages and units subordinated to villages was classified as agriculture. Since 1984, it has been grouped into industry.

Before 1999, industrial statistics coverage was divided into six parts by registration type, i.e. industrial enterprises at the township-level and above with and without independent accounting, village-run industry, urban cooperative industry, rural cooperative industry, urban individual operated industry, and rural individual operated industry (village-run industry was not included in the industrial statistics before 1984).

2000-2006, the scope of industrial statistics was grouped by enterprise scale instead of registration type. From 2000 to 2006, industrial enterprises fell into two classes. One class includes all state-owned enterprises and non-state-owned ones with annual main business income of RMB5 million and above ("above designated size"), while the other class covers all individual operations and non-state-owned enterprises with annual main business income below RMB5 million ("below designated size").

2007-2010, industrial enterprises fell into two classes. One includes corporate industrial enterprises with main business income of RMB5 million and above ("above designated size"), the other includes corporate industrial enterprises with main business income below RMB5 million and all individual operations ("below designated size").

In and after 2011, industrial enterprises fell into two classes. One includes corporate industrial enterprises with main business income of RMB20 million and above ("above designated size"), the other includes corporate industrial enterprises with main business income below RMB20 million and all individual operations ("below designated size").

III. Source of Data and Methods of Survey

Data on industrial enterprises in this chapter were provided by Beijing Municipal Bureau of Statistics and NBS Survey Corps in Beijing. Data on industrial enterprises above designated size were gathered through complete survey, and data on those below designated size were obtained through sampling survey.

IV. Changes in Relevant Statistical Standards

(I) Classification of Industrial Sectors: In this chapter, classification of industrial sectors during 2002-2011 was based on the Standard for Classification of National Economic Sectors 2002 (GB/T 4754-2002). Standard for Classification of National Economic Sectors 2011 (GB/T 4754-2011) began to be enforced in 2012;

(II) Classification of Enterprises: Before 2010, small, medium and large-sized enterprises were classified by standards of Measures for Statistical Classification of Small, Medium and Large-sized Enterprises (Temporary). Since 2011, the classification of micro, small, medium and large-sized enterprises has been in line with standards of Circular by National Bureau of Statistics on Printing and Issuing the Measures for Statistical Classification of Micro, Small, Medium and Large-sized Enterprises (GTZ [2011] No.75).

V. About the Adjustment to Historical Data

In accordance with the unified requirements and methods of the National Bureau of Statistics, data on total output value and added value of industrial enterprises above designated size were based on results from the "first national economic census in Beijing" after revision through the "trend deviation method".. The time span of the revised data is from 1993 to 2003. The first economic census was carried out in 2004 and the second in 2008.

11-1 规模以上工业总产值(1984-2013年)
GROSS OUTPUT VALUE OF INDUSTRY ABOVE DESIGNATED SIZE (1984-2013)

单位：亿元 (100 million yuan)

年 份 Year	合 计 Total	轻工业 Light Industry	重工业 Heavy Industry	#大中型工业 Medium and Large-sized Industry
1984	276.2	118.0	158.2	178.7
1985	324.2	135.8	188.4	213.7
1986-1990	**2448.3**	**1039.7**	**1408.6**	**1691.2**
1986	336.5	140.8	195.7	231.6
1987	387.6	160.1	227.5	272.1
1988	495.6	212.5	283.1	345.4
1989	602.7	264.1	338.6	408.3
1990	625.9	262.2	363.7	433.8
1991-1995	**5826.7**	**1936.6**	**3890.1**	**3770.8**
1991	730.2	298.1	432.1	507.4
1992	860.0	306.5	553.5	587.4
1993	1166.6	361.9	804.7	747.6
1994	1576.6	497.9	1078.7	990.7
1995	1493.3	472.2	1021.1	937.7
1996-2000	**10382.8**	**3026.2**	**7356.6**	**5765.7**
1996	1590.6	509.1	1081.5	962.3
1997	1819.7	577.8	1241.9	999.6
1998	1947.0	598.2	1348.8	1059.8
1999	2183.5	621.8	1561.7	1090.9
2000	2842.0	719.3	2122.7	1653.1
2001-2005	**23980.6**	**4911.1**	**19069.5**	**16858.4**
2001	3270.1	842.4	2427.7	2298.4
2002	3620.2	882.4	2737.8	2434.7
2003	4410.8	936.7	3474.1	3183.9
2004	5733.3	1084.7	4648.6	3699.3
2005	6946.2	1164.9	5781.3	5242.1
2006-2010	**53010.4**	**8204.7**	**44805.7**	**40357.2**
2006	8210.0	1258.2	6951.8	6237.9
2007	9648.4	1505.5	8142.9	7365.9
2008	10413.1	1674.3	8738.8	7898.9
2009	11039.1	1766.7	9272.4	8349.3
2010	13699.8	2000.0	11699.8	10505.3
2011	14513.6	2227.2	12286.4	11289.3
2012	15596.2	2402.1	13194.1	12239.6
2013	17370.9	2541.5	14829.4	13941.3

注：1. 工业总产值按现价计算。
2. 规模以上工业：2000年以前各年为乡及乡以上工业口径；2000-2006年调整为全部国有及年主营业务收入在500万元及以上非国有工业口径；2007年-2010年调整为年主营业务收入500万元及以上的全部法人工业企业；2011年及以后调整为年主营业务收入2000万元及以上的全部法人工业企业(下同)。
3. 自2011年开始，大中型企业划分标准执行国家统计局《关于统计上大中小微型企业划分办法》(国统字[2011]75号)(下同)。

Note: a) Gross output value is calculated at current prices.
b) Data on industry above designated size covered enterprises at and above the township level before 2000, 2000-2006 covered all State-owned enterprises and non-State-owned enterprises with main business income of over 5 million yuan annually, 2007-2010 covered all corporate industrial enterprises with main business income of over 5 million yuan annually, and from 2011 covered all corporate industrial enterprises with main business income over 20 million yuan (the same below).
c) From 2011, the classification of medium and large-sized enterprises complies with Circular of the National Bureau of Statistics on Printing and Issuing Measures for the Statistical Classification of Micro, Small, Medium, and Large-Sized Enterprises (the same below).

11-2 规模以上工业企业主要指标(1978-2013年)
MAIN INDICATORS FOR INDUSTRIAL ENTERPRISES ABOVE DESIGNATED SIZE (1978-2013)

年 份 Year	企业单位个数(个) Number of Enterprises (unit)	从业人员平均人数(万人) Average Number of Employed Persons (10000 persons)	资产总计(万元) Total Assets (10000 yuan)	负债合计(万元) Total Liabilities (10000 yuan)	固定资产原价(万元) Original Value of Fixed Assets (10000 yuan)	主营业务收入(万元) Main Business Income (10000 yuan)	利润总额(万元) Total Profits (10000 yuan)	利税总额(万元) Total Taxes & Profits (10000 yuan)
1978	4225	114.79			1305271	1098279	370551	501588
1979	3746	116.79	1417223		1371335	1186497	414344	554895
1980	3733	140.91	1547267		1495083	1987967	453147	604241
1981-1985						**12561630**	**2404751**	**3383077**
1981	3778	152.90	1650869		1622035	2054862	440753	599452
1982	3867	158.70	1748915		1750727	2183458	440000	604372
1983	4011	161.98	1846698		1886857	2408893	469364	642437
1984	4291	165.50	2003625		2045344	2728866	505249	707360
1985	4458	165.63	2338194		2337082	3175551	549385	829456
1986-1990						**24054442**	**2924045**	**4825016**
1986	5461	169.85	2720485		2627346	3385055	523961	813979
1987	5746	170.52	3147157		3008917	3935004	570760	885303
1988	5932	170.54	3607173		3412765	5032042	701574	1081370
1989	6175		4343353		3890267	5597829	638385	1087017
1990	6272	173.46	4982746		4382462	6104512	489365	957347
1991-1995						**57731437**	**4241285**	**8051832**
1991	6344	172.39	5672894		5052285	7271529	583381	1106009
1992	6205	175.48	6409037		5754181	8526860	748098	1347058
1993	10320	167.90	15209851		9986886	12822058	1095165	1811556
1994	10889	179.50	19692285		9648050	13207344	961715	1857476
1995	10712	176.16	25826309	15287699	13900296	15903646	852926	1929733
1996-2000						**103617473**	**3188809**	**8655552**
1996	16905	166.63	28755517	17220941	16319878	15801389	330539	1225314
1997	19387	157.52	34083006	20496564	18503218	17070867	405129	1405499
1998	18089	167.11	40129028	24839166	22213387	20345380	484460	1617338
1999	19682	161.10	42540707	25863159	23121446	22186280	697807	1846310
2000	16027	145.60	46127325	26763977	25316408	28213557	1270874	2561091
2001-2005						**233471075**	**13486920**	**23453788**
2001	4356	108.02	44482243	24595592	25036546	30068965	1369794	2795203
2002	4551	107.56	47429487	25278299	26554117	31827790	1655153	3219863
2003	4019	100.81	51779832	27511740	27559571	38856527	2352909	4189859
2004	6872	113.60	120495094	41430793	39221838	59926564	3974076	6417537
2005	6301	117.06	128298350	47067350	44340413	72791229	4134988	6831326
2006-2010						**576103251**	**35550064**	**57599572**
2006	6400	117.36	142444009	55423362	50306165	89141630	5311453	8479249
2007	6398	119.25	162155043	65083476	58148433	104401683	6956067	10552194
2008	7206	123.38	168024206	80850104	65745860	112758173	5569968	9379138
2009	6891	120.41	195407033	98746128	70836396	121730618	7429216	12699472
2010	6885	124.15	227505774	115480740	79360648	148071147	10283360	16489519
2011	3740	117.87	253217462	126486073	86208174	157533565	11294991	18061726
2012	3692	120.15	286131557	148372202	102771932	169051357	12678868	20104385
2013	3641	116.14	308007299	162079598	107885887	186886314	12828840	21252443

注：规模以上指:2000年以前统计范围为独立核算工业企业；2000-2006年为全部国有及年主营业务收入500万元及以上非国有企业；2007年-2010年调整为年主营业务收入500万元及以上的全部法人工业企业；2011年及以后调整为年主营业务收入2000万元及以上的全部法人工业企业。

Note: "Above designated size" covered industrial enterprises with independent accounting system before 2000; 2000-2006, covered all State-owned enterprises and non-State-owned enterprises with main business income of and over 5 million yuan annually; 2007-2010 covered all corporate industrial enterprises with main business income of and over 5 million yuan annually; from 2011, covered all corporate industrial enterprises with main business income over 20 million yuan .

11-3 规模以上工业增加值(1993-2013年)

单位：亿元

年 份 Year	增加值 Added Value of Industry	轻工业 Light Industry	重工业 Heavy Industry	#计算机、通信和其他电子设备制造业 Manufacture of Computers, Communication Equipment and Other Electronic Equipment	#汽车制造业 Manufacture of Motor Vehicles	#电力、热力生产和供应业 Production and Supply of Electric Power and Heat Power	#黑色金属冶炼和压延加工业 Manufacture and Pressing of Ferrous Metals
1993	304.1	98.3	205.8	22.6	28.4	4.6	54.3
1994	374.6	138.0	236.6	30.9	29.7	9.5	56.4
1995	473.1	112.3	360.8	46.7	44.4	33.0	94.9
1996-2000	**3058.8**	**981.7**	**2077.1**	**622.0**	**180.7**	**170.4**	**264.5**
1996	500.2	168.8	331.4	66.6	38.1	-12.1	75.6
1997	558.0	170.1	387.9	75.7	58.0	45.8	62.2
1998	588.2	197.2	391.0	133.8	30.0	41.5	22.4
1999	636.5	200.6	435.9	154.5	25.6	45.4	35.4
2000	776.0	245.0	531.0	191.4	29.0	49.8	68.9
2001-2005	**6153.4**	**1549.4**	**4604.0**	**1078.7**	**505.4**	**564.2**	**696.3**
2001	866.3	265.2	601.0	203.6	39.0	52.4	87.4
2002	960.7	306.6	654.1	177.8	54.8	66.6	71.2
2003	1174.7	304.8	869.9	228.3	126.0	78.3	98.2
2004	1524.7	332.6	1192.1	197.5	144.2	174.4	211.3
2005	1627.0	340.2	1286.8	271.5	141.4	192.5	228.2
2006-2010	**11071.1**	**2366.2**	**8704.9**	**1423.7**	**1329.5**	**1705.0**	**687.9**
2006	1840.2	370.1	1470.1	329.7	155.1	254.6	240.0
2007	2159.4	427.6	1731.9	363.6	194.9	355.2	235.8
2008	2037.6	482.3	1555.3	289.4	211.1	358.4	110.9
2009	2282.2	529.4	1752.8	201.2	310.6	327.3	71.9
2010	2751.7	556.8	2194.8	239.8	457.8	409.5	29.3
2011	2899.1	619.2	2279.9	204.5	562.1	448.8	1.6
2012	3033.3	681.3	2352.0	243.6	512.6	536.0	7.2
2013	3432.1	749.7	2682.4	304.4	732.3	602.3	13.0

注：1. 本表增加值均按生产法计算，2004年以前数据为根据全国第一次经济普查数据调整后的数据。

2. 2012年开始行业划分执行2011年国民经济行业分类标准（GB/T 4754-2011）；表中2012年前，汽车制造业为原“交通运输设备制造业”数据，计算机、通信和其它电子设备制造业为原“通信设备、计算机及其他电子设备制造业”的数据。

ADDED VALUE OF INDUSTRY ABOVE DESIGNATED SIZE (1993-2013)

(100 million yuan)

#化学原料和化学制品制造业 Manufacture of Chemical Raw Materials and Chemical Products	#通用设备制造业 Manufacture of General-Purpose Machinery	#专用设备制造业 Manufacture of Special-Purpose Machinery	#电气机械和器材制造业 Manufacture of Electrical Machinery and Equipment	#仪器仪表制造业 Manufacture of Measuring Instruments and Meters	#医药制造业 Manufacture of Medicines	#非金属矿物制品业 Manufacture of Non-Metallic Mineral Products	#石油加工、炼焦和核燃料加工业 Processing of Petroleum, Coking, Processing of Nuclear Fuel
15.5	13.0	10.0	10.1	3.2	5.5	14.8	12.5
19.7	15.9	26.4	11.6	4.5	5.3	21.2	14.2
28.9	17.2	12.1	9.8	9.0	7.5	17.7	45.9
136.2	**73.1**	**114.5**	**99.5**	**52.6**	**90.3**	**139.4**	**194.5**
26.0	18.1	16.9	15.4	10.6	11.8	28.4	37.9
21.4	13.2	19.3	17.3	7.5	15.6	25.7	42.3
25.3	17.5	22.9	21.0	10.9	12.6	30.9	31.4
24.0	8.2	22.9	19.0	11.1	22.7	19.6	42.3
39.5	16.1	32.5	26.8	12.4	27.6	34.8	40.6
381.2	**200.8**	**263.7**	**257.8**	**142.2**	**225.4**	**230.1**	**215.6**
44.1	25.7	29.2	36.5	17.0	31.0	34.4	35.8
55.3	25.5	56.3	38.7	19.0	47.2	47.2	53.9
76.3	36.6	49.8	54.9	21.6	53.2	48.5	29.6
141.8	56.5	67.7	65.1	38.3	44.7	52.0	19.7
63.7	56.5	60.7	62.6	46.4	49.3	48.0	76.6
331.2	**495.2**	**526.7**	**497.0**	**313.6**	**543.0**	**333.5**	**461.6**
56.9	72.6	86.6	57.1	57.2	57.0	53.5	49.6
72.6	84.7	84.7	85.8	70.6	81.6	52.7	56.9
60.5	99.1	111.9	92.9	58.7	115.3	55.2	-2.3
57.1	97.4	112.3	126.4	61.0	135.8	85.8	172.5
84.1	141.4	131.2	134.8	66.1	153.3	86.3	184.9
77.7	153.1	139.8	137.1	63.6	184.2	80.7	122.8
56.1	130.2	130.4	124.8	59.6	222.2	79.5	126.2
55.8	125.0	158.1	135.4	64.9	254.2	80.5	98.2

Note: a) Added value in this table is calculated with production method. Figures before 2004 are adjusted according to the national first economic censu

b) The Standard for Classification of National Economic Sectors 2011 (GB/T 4754-2011) became effective in 2012; in this table, figures of "manufacture of motor vehicles" in 2012 were figures of the former "manufacture of transportation equipment", and figures of "manufacture of computers, communication equipment and other electronic equipment" were figures of the former "manufacture of communication equipment, computers and other electronic equipment".

11-4 规模以上工业产品产量(1978-2013年)
OUTPUT OF INDUSTRIAL PRODUCTS ABOVE DESIGNATED SIZE (1978-2013)

年份 Year	布 (万米) Cloth (10000 m)	机制纸及纸板 (万吨) Machine-made Paper and Paperboard (10000 tons)	饮料酒 (万千升) Alcoholic Beverage (10000 kl)	乳制品 (万吨) Dairy Products (10000 tons)	家用电冰箱 (万台) Household Refrigerators (10000 units)	照相机 (万台) Camera (10000 units)	家具 (万件) Furniture (10000 pieces)	原煤 (万吨) Raw Coal (10000 tons)	原油加工量 (万吨) Crude Oil Processed (10000 tons)	乙稀 (万吨) Ethylene (10000 tons)	发电量 (万千瓦时) Electricity Generation (10000 kwh)
1978	25436	12.1	8.4			0.5	137.8	818.7			990750
1979	27297	13.9	9.9		2.0	0.7	171.3	711.1			1042870
1980	28940	14.0	11.6		2.6	1.0	200.2	791.0	591.1		1065060
1981-1985	**142080**	**86.9**	**87.3**	**2.0**	**41.6**	**25.7**	**1348.4**	**4269.1**	**2811.3**	**132.3**	**5101356**
1981	28635	14.5	13.4		3.1	4.2	217.7	788.7	533.5	24.7	993071
1982	29758	15.8	14.9	0.2	4.5	0.9	243.5	811.3	533.5	25.6	1003446
1983	30068	17.1	17.4	0.3	6.4	2.8	254.2	840.5	563.8	27.3	1028826
1984	27621	18.9	20.3	0.6	10.3	5.3	297.9	884.3	589.4	26.9	1038842
1985	25998	20.6	21.3	0.9	17.3	12.5	335.1	944.3	591.1	27.8	1037171
1986-1990	**153032**	**120.5**	**131.4**	**4.7**	**96.4**	**74.6**	**2096.6**	**4745.3**	**3210.5**	**141.8**	**5656282**
1986	27503	21.9	21.5	0.7	18.1	15.9	303.8	917.2	619.0	25.3	1043208
1987	29738	24.1	22.7	0.8	19.4	16.5	283.0	899.8	640.2	27.0	1057493
1988	32262	23.3	23.9	1.0	23.6	15.8	347.1	906.0	645.0	30.3	1110758
1989	32271	25.8	28.7	1.0	24.7	13.5	572.1	1016.8	651.9	29.1	1191269
1990	31258	25.4	34.6	1.2	10.7	12.9	590.6	1005.5	654.4	30.1	1253554
1991-1995	**133994**	**116.5**	**347.3**	**5.9**	**27.0**	**450.8**	**3261.0**	**4851.0**	**3269.9**	**172.2**	**6772732**
1991	31497	27.2	43.8	1.3	7.1	5.4	602.0	996.5	653.4	31.1	1318000
1992	29717	22.6	56.6	1.2	9.1	4.2	570.0	1015.2	662.5	32.8	1423000
1993	26816	19.1	72.6	1.6	4.2	39.3	729.0	835.4	664.0	27.2	1410900
1994	21440	21.0	83.1	0.3	6.6	158.8	605.0	1008.5	642.0	28.1	1298718
1995	24524	26.6	91.2	1.5		243.1	755.0	995.4	648.0	53.0	1322114
1996-2000	**96005**	**70.0**	**436.6**	**7.3**	**15.9**	**706.5**	**1986.8**	**4360.0**	**3336.5**	**306.0**	**7330814**
1996	22585	15.3	102.2	1.2	6.3	234.3	510.6	1013.7	633.6	57.5	1415555
1997	25185	18.1	...	1.7	...	157.7	469.4	1011.7	657.0	58.0	1464302
1998	21299	13.1		0.9	0.3	177.7	348.5	989.5	602.3	57.0	1566621
1999	14753	13.0	148.8	1.4	5.8	81.6	386.2	792.1	701.9	68.0	1431772
2000	12183	10.6	185.6	2.1	3.6	55.2	272.1	553.0	741.7	65.5	1452564
2001-2005	**38411**	**59.5**	**700.9**	**119.7**	**189.7**	**685.0**	**2036.9**	**4359.5**	**3624.5**	**430.7**	**8369923**
2001	11353	8.8	135.8	3.7	5.9	61.3	370.6	690.2	647.9	54.3	1326588
2002	10314	6.2	138.7	1.4	16.2	220.7	368.3	880.9	695.2	90.4	1419754
2003	8393	7.9	132.8	1.3	22.8	238.3	323.8	822.6	701.1	88.8	1451197
2004	4081	19.6	148.0	56.4	63.1	116.8	567.7	1067.9	783.4	98.2	2038933
2005	4270	17.0	145.6	56.9	81.7	47.9	406.5	897.9	796.9	99.0	2133451
2006-2010	**4508**	**64.0**	**906.9**	**270.8**	**447.0**	**189.1**	**3765.4**	**2971.5**	**5143.2**	**455.6**	**11960020**
2006	930	14.0	170.8	63.5	74.1	49.2	893.4	629.2	828.9	99.1	2136918
2007	536	10.4	189.1	57.9	73.1	34.7	638.8	633.3	915.0	90.9	2278658
2008	1583	14.9	180.0	44.9	79.0	49.0	690.9	567.7	1114.6	85.4	2431255
2009	965	14.1	181.1	52.2	128.7	27.1	719.4	641.3	1161.3	84.1	2424839
2010	495	10.6	185.8	52.3	92.1	29.2	822.8	500.0	1123.4	96.2	2688350
2011	339	10.0	187.0	58.6	73.5	26.6	750.2	500.1	1103.1	89.6	2628331
2012	351	11.3	191.7	56.6	80.4	18.2	720.1	493.1	1075.0	84.0	2908214
2013	361	10.0	198.0	58.5	83.7	17.9	995.9	500.1	881.6	72.3	3312116

11-4 续表 Continued

年 份 Year	粗 钢 (万吨) Crude Steel (10000 tons)	钢 材 (万吨) Rolled Steel (10000 tons)	水 泥 (万吨) Cement (10000 tons)	交 流 电动机 (万千瓦) Alternator (10000 kw)	汽 车 (万辆) Motor Vehicles (10000 units)	#轿 车 Sedan Cars	移动通信手持机 (万台) Mobile Phones (10000 units)	微型计算机设 备 (万台) Micro-Computers (10000 units)	数控金属切削机床 (台) CNC Metal Cutting Lathe (unit)	显示器 (万台) Displays (10000 units)	集 成 电 路 (亿块) IC (100 million units)
1978	191.0	116.8	191.5	152.5	1.8						
1979	196.5	137.5	196.9	179.7	2.4						
1980	200.9	152.1	217.4	142.7	2.8						
1981-1985	**1114.2**	**907.9**	**1355.7**	**713.0**	**17.2**			**2.0**			
1981	190.3	149.5	225.7	104.0	2.7						
1982	200.4	159.4	249.1	123.3	2.8						
1983	214.1	177.9	270.8	148.3	3.1			0.3			
1984	241.7	200.1	291.6	165.4	3.6			1.2			
1985	267.7	221.0	318.5	172.0	5.0			0.5			
1986-1990	**1837.8**	**1556.7**	**1649.3**	**889.7**	**39.5**			**6.9**			
1986	303.6	255.5	310.5	178.4	5.8			0.5			
1987	335.5	283.4	319.6	196.4	7.4			0.9			
1988	369.0	314.9	334.3	199.5	9.0			3.0			
1989	386.0	327.9	345.9	163.8	8.5			1.3			
1990	443.7	375.0	339.0	151.6	8.8			1.2			
1991-1995	**3411.0**	**2613.9**	**2364.7**	**824.3**	**70.8**			**32.3**			
1991	499.7	402.9	377.6	156.7	11.0			1.7			
1992	575.0	438.3	403.0	174.9	13.8			3.0			
1993	702.7	525.3	477.9	162.3	13.4			4.1			
1994	828.7	617.6	531.7	165.0	14.7			4.3			
1995	804.9	629.8	574.2	165.4	17.9			19.2			
1996-2000	**3937.5**	**3343.3**	**3758.9**	**753.3**	**57.7**			**686.6**	**2238**		**5.4**
1996	794.7	654.3	666.0	151.9	13.4			28.1	326		0.5
1997	801.7	652.4	700.9	148.7	11.0			59.8	433		0.6
1998	803.2	676.1	762.0	149.7	8.5			160.9	430		0.6
1999	734.5	663.8	803.0	142.0	12.3	1.0		180.0	481		1.3
2000	803.4	696.7	827.0	161.0	12.5	0.5	1549.6	257.8	568		2.4
2001-2005	**4113.3**	**4096.9**	**4963.3**	**1169.8**	**179.6**	**45.7**	**21081.2**	**2407.0**	**5783**		**33.0**
2001	824.9	727.3	809.0	175.1	14.3	0.5	2163.4	339.7	1004		2.1
2002	816.9	750.0	884.0	199.3	18.1	0.7	2280.1	415.7	912		2.5
2003	816.4	785.0	882.0	253.1	34.7	7.3	3334.5	469.3	1188		4.7
2004	827.5	868.3	1204.5	279.4	53.9	15.0	4172.1	532.7	1024		11.1
2005	827.6	966.3	1183.8	262.9	58.6	22.2	9131.1	649.6	1655		12.6
2006-2010	**2988.1**	**4267.1**	**5443.8**	**1160.6**	**492.9**	**191.6**	**106256.6**	**4052.3**	**23256**	**3205.7**	**90.2**
2006	818.1	1016.3	1269.4	269.0	68.3	27.0	14068.0	736.1	1875	680.7	11.8
2007	810.8	1030.4	1167.3	281.9	70.7	20.3	22719.9	843.3	2382	513.6	15.7
2008	466.8	656.8	880.8	259.7	76.6	28.3	20725.5	691.7	3108	478.1	19.1
2009	464.9	769.6	1077.4	159.0	127.1	53.8	21355.3	842.7	6125	655.6	18.3
2010	427.5	794.0	1049.0	191.1	150.3	62.2	27388.0	938.6	9766	877.8	25.3
2011	2.9	287.0	911.5	146.0	150.5	67.1	25962.3	1083.7	12537	851.4	32.0
2012	2.6	253.8	874.5	117.1	167.0	78.5	19949.3	1074.5	13332	796.9	31.9
2013	2.3	221.8	868.4	145.4	203.8	94.5	18783.4	1106.9	6983	305.3	38.4

11-5 规模以上工业企业主要经济指标(2013年)

单位：万元

项目	Item	企业单位个数(个) Number of Enterprises (unit)	#亏损企业 Loss-Suffering Enterprises	工业总产值(当年价格) Gross Output Value of Industry (at current year's prices)	工业增加值 Added Value of Industry	工业销售产值(当年价格) Sales Value of Industry (at current)	#出口交货值 Delivery Value of Exports
合　计	**Total**	**3641**	**640**	**173708872**	**34321299**	**171866014**	**15067218**
在合计中:	**Of the Total:**						
中央企业	Central Enterprises	234	42	62394150	10396866	62090516	420864
地方企业	Local Enterprises	3407	598	111314722	23924433	109775498	14646354
在合计中:	**Of the Total:**						
内资企业	Domestially-Invested Enterprises	2753	455	106143995	20139847	104932866	2748695
国有企业	State-owned Enterprises	96	15	31242708	5322562	31170160	46236
集体企业	Collectively-owned Enterprises	52	10	360046	112473	354492	7039
股份合作企业	Joint-equity Cooperative Enterprises	70	14	803037	113034	816388	26430
联营企业	Associated Enterprises	1	***	***	***	***	***
有限责任公司	Limited Liability Companies	1239	247	43280080	7790273	42606830	1371761
股份有限公司	Companies Limited by Shares	215	38	21263669	4907029	21096460	911975
私营企业	Private Enterprises	1079	130	9189535	1893596	8883718	385253
其他企业	Others	1		***	***	***	***
港澳台商投资企业	Hong Kong, Macao and Taiwan-invested Enterprises	223	52	11689034	1888814	11619798	1425419
港澳台合资经营	Joint Ventures	114	23	3576460	942032	3553178	402079
港澳台合作经营	Cooperatives	9	2	53034	18364	50669	
港澳台商独资企业	Solely-funded Enterprises	90	25	7062077	839531	6890028	843791
港澳台商投资股份有限公司	Companies Limited by Shares	10	2	997464	88886	1125923	179550
外商投资企业	Foreign-invested Enterprises	665	133	55875844	12292639	55313351	10893104
中外合资经营	Joint Ventures	263	49	35393959	7865553	34965851	8219888
中外合作经营	Cooperatives	13	3	213986	89005	210085	35516
外资(独资)企业	Solely-funded Enterprises	374	77	19205780	3975619	19097858	2565549
外商投资股份有限公司	Companies Limited by Shares	15	4	1062118	362461	1039556	72151
在合计中:	**Of the Total:**						
#农村企业	Rural Enterprises	81	19	1089075	241977	1088403	27387
在合计中:	**Of the Total:**						
#国有控股	State-holding Enterprises	775	175	100544376	19865519	99977936	2370352
集体控股	Collectively-holding Enterprises	139	24	2904086	642654	2767261	98737
私人控股	Private-holding Enterprises	1971	274	23718054	5517166	23039788	994945
港澳台控股	Hong Kong, Macao, and Taiwan-holding Enterprises	163	44	9391988	1325495	9206522	1187121
外商控股	Foreign-Investor-holding Enterprises	564	115	36769764	6883878	36510039	10402823
在合计中:	**Of the Total:**						
轻工业	Light Industry	1261	241	25415108	7496694	24790502	1790631
重工业	Heavy Industry	2380	399	148293765	26824605	147075512	13276588
在合计中:	**Of the Total:**						
#大中型企业	Medium and Large-sized Enterprises	777	128	139412608	28809659	137994456	13437468

注：1. 工业增加值按生产法计算。
　　2. 应交税金合计包括应交增值税、应交所得税、营业税金及附加和管理费用中的税金。

MAIN ECONOMIC INDICATORS OF INDUSTRIAL ENTERPRISES ABOVE DESIGNATED SIZE (2013)

(10000 yuan)

从业人员平均人数(人) Average Number of Employed Persons (person)	资产负债 Assets and Liabilities						
	资产总计 Total Assets	流动资产合计 Total Current Assets	#存货 Inventories	#产成品 Finished Products	#应收账款 Accounts Receivable (Net)	固定资产合计 Total Fixed Assets	固定资产原价 Total Original Value of Fixed Assets
1161413	**308007299**	**127305911**	**22181833**	**6868929**	**33151258**	**60602824**	**107885887**
180350	143346149	35999525	4440182	1003887	7887409	29018385	56053294
981063	164661150	91306386	17741651	5865042	25263849	31584440	51832592
758368	243619044	87726054	13853227	4336926	22240972	48557434	85425480
50880	109525975	20475642	1225877	167619	2882040	20632643	37917775
8681	402523	291974	94733	49778	60371	89178	164741
10432	614293	454436	132306	63549	151791	110863	181067
***	***	***	***	***	***	***	***
362643	81830047	37441536	6477822	2021921	11692372	21530717	35247906
180694	40074060	21223562	3896489	1290898	4755871	4546500	9404023
144917	11166654	7834705	2024445	742825	2697129	1646306	2508307
***	***	***	***	***	***	***	***
90058	14668627	10748005	2453835	547188	3129340	1860007	3674882
42231	3995400	2283799	528235	214816	781724	1206899	2438960
1191	178005	156916	14065	7710	18613	14976	29102
38959	6222116	4996533	907290	291891	1036650	538414	1018152
7677	4273106	3310757	1004244	32770	1292353	99718	188668
312987	49719627	28831852	5874771	1984815	7780946	10185384	18785524
144158	28203616	16501122	3262065	1037642	3298662	4880127	8925718
6588	311491	231669	18493	4393	54722	58776	148705
146183	18741649	11168581	2445489	887930	4192448	4858710	8997897
16058	2462872	930481	148725	54851	235115	387771	713205
16847	1120663	852642	211956	81558	380735	195019	356087
486569	227855562	73426596	10444680	2891897	15678736	48403547	86403994
30448	3551208	2643790	611777	203967	1115240	449251	720625
328566	37311918	25240302	5513659	1890928	7918417	4226855	6429178
66483	9591435	7057071	1241675	409225	1681663	1080713	1972005
243728	28848328	18264507	4260554	1444528	6555776	6356440	12222981
368938	34571785	20941664	5173115	2292476	4407071	6657499	12150868
792475	273435514	106364247	17008718	4576452	28744187	53945326	95735019
841007	265122188	98397315	15610816	4418315	23287768	54289327	97262966

Note: a) Added value of industry is calculated with production method.
b) Total tax payable mainly includes VAT payable, income tax payable, business tax and surtax, and tax in management expenses.

11-5 续表

单位：万元

项目	Item	负债合计 Total Liabilities	#流动负债合计 Total Current Liabilities	#应付账款 Accounts Receivable	所有者权益合计 Total Owner's Equity	#实收资本 Paid-up Capital
		资产负债 Assets and Liabilities				
合计	**Total**	**162079598**	**103186279**	**35301415**	**145916320**	**66084476**
在合计中：	**Of the Total:**					
中央企业	Central Enterprises	73830830	36850388	9687856	69515319	29473712
地方企业	Local Enterprises	88248768	66335892	25613559	76401002	36610764
在合计中：	**Of the Total:**					
内资企业	Domestically-funded Enterprises	127395769	73704405	21717338	116218586	51309263
国有企业	State-owned Enterprises	54466323	20273937	3653724	55059652	20998216
集体企业	Collectively-owned Enterprises	251703	219879	88845	150820	43281
股份合作企业	Joint-equity Cooperative Enterprises	425249	377533	179654	189044	101906
联营企业	Associated Enterprises	***	***	***	***	***
有限责任公司	Limited Liability Companies	47529689	32411385	11344228	34296669	21282236
股份有限公司	Companies Limited by Shares	18376121	14558269	4197518	21697939	6723029
私营企业	Private Enterprises	6344470	5861317	2252861	4821184	2159701
其他企业	Others	***	***	***	***	***
港澳台商投资企业	Hong Kong, Macao and Taiwan-invested Enterprises	9173744	8418722	3981218	5494883	2725648
港澳台合资经营	Joint Ventures	2148128	1990497	747244	1847272	1048535
港澳台合作经营	Cooperatives	20671	19887	7045	157334	44729
港澳台商独资企业	Solely-funded Enterprises	4565588	4417226	2366476	1656528	914356
港澳台商投资股份有限公司	Companies Limited by Shares	2439358	1991113	860453	1833748	718028
外商投资企业	Foreign-invested Enterprises	25510085	21063152	9602860	24202852	12049565
中外合资经营	Joint Ventures	15113762	12172818	5862727	13089854	6311140
中外合作经营	Cooperatives	171227	158333	73535	140264	163326
外资(独资)企业	Solely-funded Enterprises	9593517	8188640	3484342	9141442	4807320
外商投资股份有限公司	Companies Limited by Shares	631580	543361	182257	1831292	767780
在合计中：	**Of the Total:**					
#农村企业	Rural Enterprises	751932	680486	303744	368731	162276
在合计中：	**Of the Total:**					
#国有控股	State-holding Enterprises	119139801	64890296	19130723	108715761	49366247
集体控股	Collectively-holding Enterprises	1962844	1795491	895270	1588364	585607
私人控股	Private-holding Enterprises	19205282	17007647	5960109	18101947	7317193
港澳台控股	Hong Kong, Macao, and Taiwan-holding Enterprises	6564567	6216252	3061441	3026869	1622226
外商控股	Foreign-Investor-holding Enterprises	14778001	12881166	6112688	14063636	7018139
在合计中：	**Of the Total:**					
轻工业	Light Industry	17422435	15140051	4053874	17149350	8256920
重工业	Heavy Industry	144657164	88046228	31247541	128766970	57827556
在合计中：	**Of the Total:**					
#大中型企业	Medium and Large-sized Enterprises	138068519	81922347	26557719	127053668	55295118

11-5 Continued

(10000 yuan)

损益 Profits and Loss								应交税金合计			
营业收入 Business Income	#主营业务收入 Main Business Income	营业成本 Business Cost	#主营业务成本 Main Business Cost	销售费用 Sales Expenses	管理费用 Management Expenses	财务费用 Financial Expenses	利润总额 Total Profits	应交税金合计 Total Tax	#营业税金及附加 Business Tax and Surtax	#主营业务税金及附加 Main Business Tax and Surtax	#应交增值税 Value Added Tax Payable
190586792	**186886314**	**161248037**	**158335883**	**8251126**	**8683248**	**2036516**	**12828840**	**10749532**	**2840694**	**2813921**	**5371656**
65314378	64257579	59760969	58839938	452845	1577263	1180246	3849283	3352093	1105496	1099863	1553821
125272414	122628735	101487068	99495945	7798281	7105985	856270	8979557	7397439	1735198	1714058	3817835
115783040	113579952	101160943	99372178	3123727	5410708	1784374	7100416	5833526	1529509	1509212	3060873
31554795	31408335	28805576	28705874	156734	342662	943050	3260199	1788238	417768	416084	887342
364850	354143	302278	295487	16124	33084	29	18312	25556	3937	3765	17780
878258	866857	766756	764801	39550	38813	5353	24863	27653	3512	3512	19709
***	***	***	***	***	***	***	***	***	***	***	***
49667946	48523791	44636922	43698310	1135298	2605812	540261	1357081	1673973	189143	177053	1089053
23705721	22959807	19007714	18370267	1164482	1574283	220305	1902405	1885032	874265	868762	757258
9606640	9462202	7637387	7533131	611481	815617	75365	537563	432656	40872	40023	289610
***	***	***	***	***	***	***	***	***	***	***	***
15538372	15080972	12937135	12568679	1241808	775188	67071	502270	472599	48105	47834	297187
4032892	3843544	3196838	3031097	263886	229505	34291	316026	253229	25405	25302	148011
70230	69826	53322	53105	7320	8098	142	1738	5575	459	458	3909
9952570	9867799	8416802	8389531	908881	440516	-16638	225168	172982	13454	13288	108978
1482681	1299803	1270172	1094946	61721	97070	49276	-40662	40814	8786	8786	36290
59265380	58225391	47149958	46395025	3885591	2497353	185071	5226154	4443406	1263080	1256876	2013596
35977658	35627225	28844851	28647441	1712558	1278930	114191	3453734	3010364	1144237	1138567	1110490
404585	394792	333294	325889	41082	17967	-1941	14780	25678	1974	1974	17276
21714164	21089653	17165244	16659411	2008332	1103340	62358	1536535	1318812	109937	109415	834063
1168973	1113721	806570	762284	123620	97115	10463	221105	88552	6932	6920	51767
1139867	1109239	970849	953065	28464	71049	10741	75542	61253	5484	5453	35244
108458228	106441958	95148105	93517461	2347441	3869663	1723178	7142424	6785504	2485870	2462197	2910091
2997321	2948528	2425807	2404392	162352	237388	10405	211481	151728	16869	16212	95919
25097646	24626580	19138553	18767781	1849347	2166801	231587	2111566	1330796	135653	134231	875238
12868086	12552677	10863426	10628363	1039728	605070	11758	392835	315284	28300	28122	189484
40595416	39754767	33199320	32548743	2827048	1769226	53182	2941688	2144536	172222	171547	1289238
28925823	28160389	19862277	19320214	4118136	2226617	188869	2460038	2485950	553202	550726	1395726
161660970	158725925	141385759	139015669	4132990	6456632	1847647	10368802	8263581	2287492	2263196	3975930
152611823	149562961	129128105	126655188	6753021	6180051	1777191	10849858	9160890	2689540	2666311	4421617

11-6 规模以上工业企业主要经济指标(按行业分)(2013年)

单位：万元

项目	Item	企业单位个数(个) Number of Enterprises (unit)	#亏损企业 Loss-Suffering Enterprises	工业总产值(当年价格) Gross Output Value of Industry (at current year's prices)	工业增加值 Added Value of Industry
合计	**Total**	**3641**	**640**	**173708872**	**34321299**
煤炭开采和洗选业	Mining and Washing of Coal	4		7131795	459050
石油和天然气开采业	Extraction of Petroleum and Natural Gas	2	***	***	***
黑色金属矿采选业	Mining and Processing of Ferrous Metal Ores	7		1655920	403827
非金属矿采选业	Mining and Processing of Nonmetal Ores	4		23224	5964
开采辅助活动	Mining Support Service Activities	5	2	2086699	908918
农副食品加工业	Processing of Food from Agricultural Products	140	38	3788262	468424
食品制造业	Manufacture of Foods	121	26	2601593	393103
酒、饮料和精制茶制造业	Manufacture of Wines, Beverage and Refined Tea	43	15	2103232	653117
烟草制品业	Manufacture of Cigarettes and Tobacco	1		***	***
纺织业	Manufacture of Textile	36	5	336654	46414
纺织服装、服饰业	Manufacture of Textile Wearing Apparel and Ornament	153	31	1503202	569004
皮革、毛皮、羽毛及其制品和制鞋业	Manufacture of Leather, Fur, Feather and Its Products, and Footwear	18	3	120947	28699
木材加工和木、竹、藤、棕、草制品业	Processing of Timbers, Manufacture of Wood, Bamboo, Rattan, Palm, and Straw Products	20	4	133253	25486
家具制造业	Manufacture of Furniture	66	8	763431	206671
造纸和纸制品业	Manufacture of Paper and Paper Products	41	7	639170	199545
印刷和记录媒介复制业	Printing, Reproduction of Recording Media	119	21	1224709	517685
文教、工美、体育和娱乐用品制造业	Manufacture of Articles for Culture, Education, Artwork, Sport and Entertainment Activities	33	8	895197	98594
石油加工、炼焦和核燃料加工业	Processing of Petroleum, Coking, Processing of Mucleus Fuels	22	3	7671873	982346
化学原料和化学制品制造业	Manufacture of Chemical Raw Materials and Chemical Products	217	38	3495538	557912
医药制造业	Manufacture of Medicines	188	28	5991489	2542172
化学纤维制造业	Manufacture of Chemical Fibres	3		***	***
橡胶和塑料制品业	Manufacture of Rubber and Plastics Products	119	23	1095806	253117
非金属矿物制品业	Manufacture of Non-metallic Mineral Products	252	37	4910553	804988
黑色金属冶炼和压延加工业	Manufacture and Pressing of Ferrous Metals	32	8	1527066	129655
有色金属冶炼和压延加工业	Manufacture and Pressing of Non-ferrous Metals	36	4	683433	119161
金属制品业	Manufacture of Fabricated Metal Products	226	40	3003411	569650
通用设备制造业	Manufacture of General-purpose Machinery	256	47	5169300	1250143
专用设备制造业	Manufacture of Special-purpose Machinery	318	40	6146718	1580859
汽车制造业	Manufacture of Motor Vehicles	216	44	32692487	7323034
铁路、船舶、航空航天和其他运输设备制造业	Manufacture of Railway Locomotives, Building of Ships and Boats, Manufacture of Air and Spacecrafts and Other Transportation Equipment	64	6	2619740	716678
电气机械和器材制造业	Manufacture of Electrical Machinery and Equipment	260	47	7140550	1354177
计算机、通信和其他电子设备制造业	Manufacture of Computers, Communication Equipment and Other Electronic Equipment	296	56	22170113	3043769
仪器仪表制造业	Manufacture of Measuring Instruments and Meters	170	17	2457819	648574
其他制造业	Other Manufacturing	29	4	780769	218207
废弃资源综合利用业	Waste Recycling and Recovery	8	3	75972	9641
金属制品、机械和设备修理业	Repair of Fabricated Metal Products, Machinery and Equipment	15		359861	162780
电力、热力生产和供应业	Production and Distribution of Electricity and Heating Powe	59	16	37391250	6022854
燃气生产和供应业	Production and Distribution of Gas	23	6	2323289	475942
水的生产和供应业	Production and Distribution of Water	19	4	434069	177360

注：1. 行业划分执行2011年国民经济行业分类标准(GB/T 4754-2011)。
2. 应交税金合计包括应交增值税、应交所得税、营业税金及附加和管理费用中的税金。

MAIN ECONOMIC INDICATORS OF INDUSTRIAL ENTERPRISES ABOVE DESIGNATED SIZE (BY SECTOR) (2013)

(10000 yuan)

工业销售产值(当年价格)	#出口交货值	从业人员平均人数(人)	资产负债 Assets and Liabilities						
			资产总计	流动资产合计	#存货	#产成品	#应收账款	固定资产合计	固定资产原价
Sales Value of Industry (at current year's prices)	Delivery Value of Exports	Average Number of Employed Persons (person)	Total Assets	Total Current Assets	Inventories	Finished Products	Accounts Receivable	Total Fixed Assets	Total Original Value of Fixed Assets
171866014	**15067218**	**1161413**	**308007299**	**127305911**	**22181833**	**6868929**	**33151258**	**60602824**	**107885887**
7137701	152343	15640	2869814	1719912	60510	58495	864187	61389	198027
***	***	***	***	***	***	***	***	***	***
1655223		26119	19616856	6280456	303479	50162	1443599	3731328	4753491
22900		337	55812	34930	3094	1713	11450	6131	7913
2054978	156039	23838	4989642	2498288	353092	10926	1020777	1181576	2321077
3736911	94554	34613	3423428	2382158	520716	255573	300025	432518	704711
2495052	147959	51888	3067747	1860392	376500	177022	459232	682054	1197055
2085668	18733	33246	3818358	1660900	319749	103177	160816	666379	1328802
***	***	***	***	***	***	***	***	***	***
341508	58282	5917	619085	389909	87459	57128	79060	120394	193559
1366547	300594	49218	1710599	1300259	618001	360367	236828	214923	379741
121499	25710	2487	95922	77705	39336	15613	15069	9800	17111
133251	7434	2498	168976	96090	25448	5753	24186	51490	103637
753136	44492	15317	861382	552212	160992	74560	147050	176689	248934
631222	47974	6202	619522	378769	96848	25229	129848	171250	345664
1232828	9834	26902	1945546	1066719	259417	97590	196034	642272	1470951
876606	83500	7796	895109	712322	366917	263533	142315	117885	185680
7691912		15552	2958338	1342131	795776	205491	157913	847595	2774023
3454485	116821	35309	5007103	3013035	459057	183412	696432	1089069	2370335
5930381	59767	69807	9075039	5696136	1319127	544507	1286769	1248860	1981599
***	***	***	***	***	***	***	***	***	***
1101689	141854	20644	1660941	929697	197778	102706	261250	317568	573477
4896068	132313	59645	8393131	5909094	1074322	249716	2973655	1121453	2095109
1507738	92631	9546	2695981	626742	237970	79837	162572	889421	[illegible]
671899	153831	5749	684299	473118	128838	48019	136879	96242	158543
3028197	193532	38705	4709391	2890546	814104	266455	738999	746519	1288465
5093111	782693	58219	8442058	6165982	1869112	563314	1598095	1122892	1943142
6001527	691570	74079	13885788	9185083	1789290	500643	2535048	1058137	1706512
32371928	495893	130051	28576101	15476295	2313398	1130502	3704723	5504447	8064184
2545368	11217	18499	4700260	3356546	1284414	117193	1031369	944450	1126717
6989658	595639	58791	11446432	9043569	1893705	367489	4037789	730566	1387652
21735141	10203466	134742	23702977	15519368	3070364	764085	3973299	4453447	8846620
2438715	127415	31310	4099976	3085973	799220	135218	943855	343651	537632
642080	24730	3636	1298489	802714	165430	27104	295682	289682	513512
75706		934	111590	46670	6710	2472	10581	53107	75256
362526	75919	7309	504154	283798	83555	4004	137701	190665	340579
37378691		61488	120265803	19600890	135845	1411	2693191	26996549	50245287
2320444		11509	3960720	997312	13198	8199	304539	1308786	1779211
422534		10458	5375273	1455335	10684	4403	213934	2708132	4208935

Note: a) Sectors in this table are classified in accordance with the Standard for Classification of National Economic Sectors 2011 (GB/T 4754-2011).
b) Total tax payable mainly includes VAT payable, income tax payable, business tax and surtax, and tax in management expenses.

11-6 续表

单位：万元

项目	Item	资产负债 Assets and Liabilities			
		负债合计 Total Liabilities	#流动负债合计 Total Current Liabilities	#应付账款 Accounts Payable	所有者权益合计 Total Owner's Equity
合 计	**Total**	**162079598**	**103186279**	**35301415**	**145916320**
煤炭开采和洗选业	Mining and Washing of Coal	1423042	1278921	799724	1446772
石油和天然气开采业	Extraction of Petroleum and Natural Gas	***	***	***	***
黑色金属矿采选业	Mining of Ferrous Metal Ores	11449198	3757866	1085562	8167658
非金属矿采选业	Mining and Processing of Nonmetal Ores	31865	31865	8163	23947
开采辅助活动	Mining Support Service Activities	2075712	1914064	691958	2913930
农副食品加工业	Processing of Food from Agricultural Products	2099259	1917620	298312	1324170
食品制造业	Manufacture of Foods	1968711	1808463	264937	1099036
酒、饮料和精制茶制造业	Manufacture of Wines,Beverage and Refined Tea	1727790	1592589	292340	2090568
烟草制品业	Manufacture of Cigarettes and Tobacco	***	***	***	***
纺织业	Manufacture of Textile	334142	257270	88650	284943
纺织服装、服饰业	Manufacture of Textile Wearing Apparel and Ornament	1065118	988392	319889	645481
皮革、毛皮、羽毛及其制品和制鞋业	Manufacture of Leather, Fur, Feather and its Products	55084	53864	12406	40838
木材加工和木、竹、藤、棕、草制品业	Processing of Timbers, Manufacture of Wood, Bamboo, Rattan, Palm, and Straw Products	93040	88757	21800	75936
家具制造业	Manufacture of Furniture	481375	426463	113505	380007
造纸和纸制品业	Manufacture of Paper and Paper Products	329102	312676	104139	290421
印刷和记录媒介复制业	Printing,Reproduction of Recording Media	810439	705323	238710	1135107
文教、工美、体育和娱乐用品制造业	Manufacture of Articles for Culture, Education, Artwork, Sport and Entertainment Activity	559566	522885	234014	335543
石油加工、炼焦和核燃料加工业	Processing of Petroleum ,Coking,Processing of Mucleus Fuel	1719369	1716077	743457	1238969
化学原料和化学制品制造业	Manufacture of Chemical Raw Material and Chemical Products	2857925	2524517	510320	2149178
医药制造业	Manufacture of Medicines	4061890	3413441	1023333	5013149
化学纤维制造业	Manufacture of Chemical Fibres	***	***	***	***
橡胶和塑料制品业	Manufacture of Rubber and Plastics Products	833091	709420	195276	827850
非金属矿物制品业	Manufacture of Non-metallic Mineral Products	5188341	4853933	2148246	3204790
黑色金属冶炼和压延加工业	Manufacture and Processing of Ferrous Metals	1572910	696223	287808	1116380
有色金属冶炼和压延加工业	Manufacture and Processing of Non-ferrous Metals	300755	285609	109691	382544
金属制品业	Manufacture of Fabricated Metal Products	2443110	2157180	682810	2266281
通用设备制造业	Manufacture of General-purpose Machinery	3942523	3647751	1294453	4499536
专用设备制造业	Manufacture of Special-purpose Machinery	7511098	6240402	2253144	6374690
汽车制造业	Manufacture of Motor Vehicles	16452846	13741586	6795285	12123255
铁路、船舶、航空航天和其他运输设备制造业	Manufacture of Railway Locomotives, Building of Ships and Boats, Manufacture of Air and Spacecrafts and Other Transportation Equipments	3063090	2574044	903339	1637170
电气机械和器材制造业	Manufacture of Electrical Machinery and Equipment	6843721	6101345	2555923	4599022
计算机、通信和其他电子设备制造	Manufacture of Computer, Communication Equipment and Other Electronic Equipment	12800275	10323621	4857259	10902702
仪器仪表制造业	Manufacture of Measuring Instrument and Meter	2043430	1908249	796086	2056546
其他制造业	Other Manufacturing	534120	407489	223554	764370
废弃资源综合利用业	Waste Recycling and Recovery	62368	34111	10389	49222
金属制品、机械和设备修理业	Repair of Fabricated Metal Products, Machinery and Equipment	265835	262600	49761	238319
电力、热力生产和供应业	Production and Supply of Electric Power and Heat Power	60568474	23512860	4962521	59697329
燃气生产和供应业	Production and Distribution of Gas	1427451	1229539	119149	2533269
水的生产和供应业	Production and Distribution of Water	2316558	864362	60851	3058715

11-6 Continued

(10000 yuan)

	损益 Profits and Losses											
#实收资本 Paid-up Capital	营业收入 Business Income	#主营业务收入 Main Business Income	营业成本 Business Cost	#主营业务成本 Main Business Cost	销售费用 Sales Expenses	管理费用 Management Expenses	财务费用 Financial Expenses	利润总额 Total Profits	应交税金合计 Total Tax Payable	#营业税金及附加 Business Tax and Surtax	#主营业务税金及附加 Main Business Tax and Surtax	#应交增值税 Value Added Tax Payable
66084476	**190586792**	**186886314**	**161248037**	**158335883**	**8251126**	**8683248**	**2036516**	**12828840**	**10749532**	**2840694**	**2813921**	**5371656**
691325	7173358	7151761	6879683	6875156	50364	66967	12869	178678	170210	27466	27360	**90183**
***	***	***	***	***	***	***	***	***	***	***	***	***
2862794	4789581	4579591	4482929	4271928	4409	116973	120020	113373	139876	22660	18517	104200
6200	36914	34750	29899	29176	438	2990	-127	2145	2055	409	328	1077
2543890	2093861	2081286	1962398	1952725	10459	83718	31281	-77769	67241	31130	31045	24575
607264	4139258	4109975	3496876	3479651	257627	167366	37526	157692	164999	77834	77815	53657
1014041	4149939	4071424	2770433	2703019	959546	242215	11857	176421	281703	24902	24816	205163
851868	2403042	2280675	1704819	1604093	398059	130149	15891	99577	259013	90989	90631	136735
***	***	***	***	***	***	***	***	***	***	***	***	***
232575	476504	469222	412671	409744	10134	36166	6682	12229	12867	1985	1745	6412
321905	1578384	1562293	1075498	1066078	232443	150879	12597	105009	109230	9218	9203	76989
13406	137345	135560	118716	117079	4231	6636	674	7060	6160	448	445	3487
79374	144506	141011	124292	122509	8909	9267	898	4670	6918	868	542	5109
196675	729629	717227	570783	563482	56375	59398	7412	42227	42673	4715	4583	29342
193176	749863	736842	599848	590569	23371	35374	-170	106602	60650	3017	2949	30681
664199	1351080	1298445	1009967	979131	41551	163373	1434	129456	115090	9618	9281	68384
211704	1033728	1017596	946317	941077	27071	48350	11042	281	15973	2331	1857	11527
86873	8777227	8186339	7899037	7317908	68592	241293	26952	-118121	806987	614152	612984	161349
1676788	3750574	3681757	3127197	3072255	263590	278502	46152	12618	169145	19560	19418	115439
1682934	6330207	6096890	2983052	2792747	1663440	618158	84676	1099319	771060	61667	61479	515059
***	***	***	***	***	***	***	***	***	***	***	***	***
446884	1386661	1335747	1168180	1132106	42418	88840	18680	74611	64391	5605	5468	39972
1528659	5425307	5313488	4602563	4516722	239926	345354	73732	220197	180787	26495	25541	107139
651917	1638471	1617607	1552421	1538100	47251	36238	20917	11765	32235	2722	2530	18075
121528	821058	757239	713806	654483	12444	44612	8202	38791	34145	13952	13888	13995
1090694	3496603	3323857	2914206	2778877	115251	261118	31388	200402	129144	17843	15810	74029
1922520	5771514	5630163	4533661	4444871	325885	448412	5298	439815	331152	26492	26229	194906
2639845	6964593	6686177	5236694	5049474	403161	722906	56942	780042	444209	46974	46284	294388
5279608	33542488	32876113	27702417	27185349	1240632	1155865	58191	2914231	2850160	1147593	1141555	1002824
721404	2764155	2737180	2228666	2210937	51053	254418	19631	220737	118735	9655	9527	72315
2417140	7598907	7389712	6136249	5937314	380715	519808	80530	457399	335239	33023	32795	218727
6545532	26177596	25938472	22869964	22752493	1018062	1389371	63542	1138429	505114	53154	51066	268408
682013	2906374	2865368	2078759	2058437	203395	327868	10437	357499	197449	17346	16943	121403
295059	796601	790261	603995	600549	30352	87931	-428	78227	39635	3065	3060	23309
20632	84682	83165	77488	76725	1198	4833	78	4728	4679	376	345	2901
163623	380328	370703	266477	262746	6035	88279	3892	29477	25749	1631	1592	15079
24038406	37537066	37428866	35513789	35431693	7019	195037	1140832	3434993	1730214	175974	172297	1041713
626312	2366172	2338700	2107299	2089745	29224	121977	16200	310244	189404	18867	17902	145933
2654930	522284	513839	515153	510176	2973	61713	-2948	48029	30380	2731	2157	15310

11-7　规模以上工业企业主要经济效益指标(2013年)

单位：%

项　目	Item	工业经济效益综合指数 Aggregate Index of Industrial Economic Efficiency	企业亏损面 Loss-Suffering Enterprises as % of Total	总资产贡献率 Contribution Rate of Total Assets	资产保值增值率 Rate of Assets Preservation and Appreciation
合　计	**Total**	**275.80**	**17.58**	**7.79**	**105.93**
在合计中:	**Of the Total:**				
中央企业	Central Enterprises	440.72	17.95	5.46	104.26
地方企业	Local Enterprises	249.44	17.55	9.87	107.50
在合计中:	**Of the Total:**				
内资企业	Domestically-funded Enterprises	248.63	16.53	5.67	103.20
国有企业	State-owned Enterprises	739.85	15.63	5.09	103.83
集体企业	Collectively-Owned Enterprises	166.23	19.23	9.73	91.58
股份合作企业	Joint-equity Cooperative Enterprises	155.86	20.00	9.17	121.43
联营企业	Associated Enterprises	72.85	100.00	0.39	27.89
有限责任公司	Limited Liability Companies	200.96	19.94	4.10	104.74
股份有限公司	Company Limited by Shares	265.59	17.67	9.33	96.94
私营企业	Private Enterprises	172.63	12.05	9.14	116.86
其他企业	Others	55.15			
港澳台商投资企业	Hong Kong, Macao and Taiwan-invested Enterprises	205.12	23.32	6.54	97.28
港澳台合资经营	Joint Ventures	247.20	20.18	13.33	97.73
港澳台合作经营	Cooperatives	155.28	22.22	3.48	97.80
港澳台商独资企业	Solely-funded Enterprises	211.41	27.78	6.06	99.08
港澳台商投资股份有限公司	Companies Limited by Shares	104.45	20.00	1.24	95.23
外商投资企业	Foreign-invested Enterprises	374.37	20.00	19.16	124.22
中外合资经营	Joint Ventures	483.09	18.63	23.53	138.11
中外合作经营	Cooperatives	171.07	23.08	9.86	109.62
外资(独资)企业	Solely-funded Enterprises	279.93	20.59	14.14	111.12
外商投资股份有限公司	Companies Limited by Shares	296.02	26.67	12.75	110.91
在合计中:	**Of the Total:**				
#农村企业	Rural Enterprises	189.55	23.46	12.09	103.23
在合计中:	**Of the Total:**				
#国有控股	State-holding Enterprises	340.33	22.58	6.42	103.18
集体控股	Collectively-holding Enterprises	224.45	17.27	9.40	104.83
私人控股	Private-holding Enterprises	207.76	13.90	9.96	124.95
港澳台控股	Hong Kong, Macao, and Taiwan-holding Enterprises	203.92	26.99	7.18	98.03
外商控股	Foreign-Investor-holding Enterprises	292.40	20.39	15.94	108.19
在合计中:	**Of the Total:**				
轻工业	Light Industry	238.84	19.11	13.85	111.40
重工业	Heavy Industry	299.19	16.76	7.03	105.24
在合计中:	**Of the Total:**				
#大中型企业	Medium and Large-sized Enterprises	281.08	17.58	8.35	122.11

MAIN INDICATORS OF ECONOMIC BENEFITS OF INDUSTRIAL ENTERPRISES ABOVE DESIGNATED SIZE (2013)

(%)

资 产 负债率 Assets-Liabilities Ratio	流动资产 周转率 (次) Turnover of Current Assets (times)	成 本 费 用 利润率 Ratio of Profits to Costs	全员劳动 生 产 率 (元/人) Overall Labor Productivity (yuan/person)	产 品 销售率 Sales Rate of Products	增 加 值 率 Value-added Rate	人均销售 收 入 (元) Sales Revenue Per Capita (yuan)	流动比率 (倍) Liquidity Ratio (times)	速动比率 (倍) Quick Ratio (times)
52.62	**1.55**	**7.24**	**295513**	**98.94**	**19.76**	**1609129**	**1.23**	**1.02**
51.51	1.86	6.20	576483	99.51	16.66	3562938	0.98	0.86
53.59	1.43	7.79	243862	98.62	21.49	1249958	1.38	1.11
52.29	1.37	6.47	265568	98.86	18.97	1497689	1.19	1.00
49.73	1.64	10.81	1046101	99.77	17.04	6173022	1.01	0.95
62.53	1.21	5.31	129563	98.46	31.24	407952	1.33	0.90
69.23	2.03	2.93	108353	101.66	14.08	830960	1.20	0.85
13.51	0.28	-2.59	84151	91.63	27.95	275885	6.02	4.38
58.08	1.33	2.83	214819	98.44	18.00	1338059	1.16	0.96
45.86	1.17	8.92	271566	99.21	23.08	1270646	1.46	1.19
56.82	1.34	5.95	130668	96.67	20.61	652939	1.34	0.99
84.17		3.00	28651	106.84	3.53	868080	0.88	0.39
62.54	1.46	3.43	209733	99.41	16.16	1674584	1.28	0.99
53.77	1.53	8.88	223066	99.35	26.34	910124	1.15	0.88
11.61	0.79	2.53	154192	95.54	34.63	586279	7.89	7.18
73.38	2.26	2.32	215491	97.56	11.89	2532868	1.13	0.93
57.09	0.38	-3.12	115783	112.88	8.91	1693113	1.66	1.16
51.31	2.16	9.87	392752	98.99	22.00	1860313	1.37	1.09
53.59	2.39	10.88	545620	98.79	22.22	2471401	1.36	1.09
54.97	1.65	3.86	135101	98.18	41.59	599259	1.46	1.35
51.19	1.94	7.75	271962	99.44	20.70	1442688	1.36	1.07
25.64	1.15	22.26	225720	97.88	34.13	693561	1.71	1.44
67.10	1.40	7.10	143632	99.94	22.22	658419	1.25	0.94
52.29	1.53	7.04	408278	99.44	19.76	2187603	1.13	0.97
55.27	1.19	7.51	211066	95.29	22.13	968381	1.47	1.13
51.47	1.11	9.17	167917	97.14	23.26	749517	1.48	1.16
68.44	1.95	3.20	199373	98.03	14.11	1888103	1.14	0.94
51.23	2.20	7.91	282441	99.29	18.72	1631112	1.42	1.09
50.39	1.40	9.52	203197	97.54	29.50	763282	1.38	1.04
52.90	1.58	6.85	338491	99.18	18.09	2002914	1.21	1.01
52.62	1.76	7.24	295513	98.94	19.76	1609129	1.23	1.02

11-8 规模以上国有控股工业企业主要经济指标(2013年)

单位：万元

项 目	Item	企业单位个数(个) Number of Enterprises (unit)	#亏损企业 Loss-Suffering Enterprises	工业总产值(当年价格) Gross Output Value of Industry (at current year's prices)	工业增加值 Added Value of Industry	工业销售产值(当年价格) Sales Value of Industry (at current year's prices)
合　计	**Total**	**775**	**175**	**100544376**	**19865519**	**99977936**
在合计中：	**Of the Total:**					
中央企业	Central Enterprises	226	42	62182568	10383716	61881753
地方企业	Local Enterprises	549	133	38361808	9481803	38096183
在合计中：	**Of theTotal:**					
轻工业	Light Industry	203	34	7259050	2378086	7203738
重工业	Heavy Industry	572	141	93285326	17487432	92774198
在合计中：	**Of the Total:**					
#大中型企业	Medium and Large-sized Enterprises	288	66	87446642	18626531	86990293

注：2013年从业人员平均人数口径有变化，与往年数据不可比。

11-8 续表

单位：万元

项 目	Item	资产负债 Assets and Liabilities				
		负债合计 Total Liabilities	#流动负债合计 Total Current Liabilities	#应付账款 Accounts Payable	所有者权益合计 Total Owner's Equity	#实收资本 Paid-up Capital
合　计	**Total**	**119139801**	**64890296**	**19130723**	**108715761**	**49366247**
在合计中：	**Of the Total:**					
中央企业	Central Enterprises	73279066	36420669	9556951	69149683	29385884
地方企业	Local Enterprises	45860735	28469627	9573772	39566077	19980363
在合计中：	**Of the Total:**					
轻工业	Light Industry	6503667	5116284	959500	8016192	3212433
重工业	Heavy Industry	112636134	59774012	18171223	100699569	46153814
在合计中：	**Of the Total:**					
#大中型企业	Medium and Large-sized Enterprises	110719474	58141775	16347063	102502959	45119094

MAIN ECONOMIC INDICATORS OF STATE-OWNED AND STATE-CONTROLLED INDUSTRIAL ENTERPRISES ABOVE DESIGNATED SIZE (2013)

(10000 yuan)

#出口交货值 Delivery Value of Exports	从业人员平均人数（人） Average Number of Employed Persons (person)	资产负债 Assets and Liabilities: 资产总计 Total Assets	流动资产合计 Total Current Assets	#存货 Inventories	#产成品 Finished Products	#应收账款 Accounts Receivable	固定资产合计 Total Fixed Assets	固定资产原价 Total Original Value of Fixed Assets
2370352	**486569**	**227855562**	**73426596**	**10444680**	**2891897**	**15678736**	**48403547**	**86403994**
393184	176207	142428749	35518583	4397831	984083	7803419	28977856	55968659
1977168	310362	85426812	37908013	6046849	1907814	7875317	19425691	30435335
136461	96258	14519859	7793445	1791725	716778	1233053	3001788	5740999
2233890	390311	213335703	65633151	8652955	2175120	14445683	45401759	80662995
2165596	418777	213222433	64864255	8797632	2196465	12691625	46080726	82507747

Note: The statistical scope of average number of employed persons changed in 2013, so data of 2013 are not comparable with past ones.

11-8 Continued

(10000 yuan)

损益 Profits and Losses: 营业收入 Business Income	#主营业务收入 Main Business Income	营业成本 Business Cost	#主营业务成本 Main Business Cost	销售费用 Sales Expenses	管理费用 Management Expenses	财务费用 Financial Expenses	利润总额 Total Profits	应交税金合计 Total Tax Payable	#营业税金及附加 Business Tax and Surtax	#主营业务税金及附加 Main Business Tax and Surtax	#应交增值税 Value Added Tax Payable
108458228	**106441958**	**95148105**	**93517461**	**2347441**	**3869663**	**1723178**	**7142424**	**6785504**	**2485870**	**2462197**	**2910091**
64833423	63865865	59331315	58492274	441314	1550552	1168633	3832156	3337059	1104243	1098611	1543626
43624806	42576093	35816789	35025187	1906127	2319110	554546	3310268	3448445	1381627	1363586	1366465
8375954	8177800	6129666	6000251	612003	678407	44841	743855	958291	417791	416423	391183
100082274	98264159	89018439	87517210	1735438	3191255	1678338	6398569	5827213	2068079	2045774	2518907
93862399	92076018	81851657	80369125	2057722	3240034	1598539	6645536	6324243	2434945	2413630	2650400

11-9 规模以上国有控股工业企业主要经济指标(按行业分)(2013年)

单位：万元

项目	Item	企业单位个数(个) Number of Enterprises (unit)	#亏损企业 Loss-Suffering Enterprises	工业总产值(当年价格) Gross Output Value of Industry (at current year's prices)	工业增加值 Added Value of Industry
合计	**Total**	**775**	**175**	**100544376**	**19865519**
煤炭开采和洗选业	Mining and Washing of Coal	4		7131795	459050
石油和天然气开采业	Extraction of Petroleum and Natural Gas	2	***	***	***
黑色金属矿采选业	Mining and Processing of Ferrous Metal Ores	4		1579195	374034
开采辅助活动	Mining Support Service Activities	3	***	***	***
农副食品加工业	Processing of Food from Agricultural Products	23	5	1802341	222226
食品制造业	Manufacture of Foods	14	3	465466	70251
酒、饮料和精制茶制造业	Manufacture of Wines, Beverage and Refined Tea	8	2	645345	274859
烟草制品业	Manufacture of Cigarettes and Tobacco	1		***	***
纺织业	Manufacture of Textile	16	3	131120	14993
纺织服装、服饰业	Manufacture of Textile Wearing Apparel and Ornament	8	2	49949	15276
皮革、毛皮、羽毛及其制品和制鞋业	Manufacture of Leather, Fur, Feather and Its Products, and Footwear	3	***	***	***
木材加工和木、竹、藤、棕、草制品业	Processing of Timbers, Manufacture of Wood, Bamboo, Rattan, Palm, and Straw Products	1		***	***
家具制造业	Manufacture of Furniture	4		53724	9675
造纸和纸制品业	Manufacture of Paper and Paper Products	4	1	34127	4985
印刷和记录媒介复制业	Printing, Reproduction of Recording Media	35	6	587809	280828
文教、工美、体育和娱乐用品制造业	Manufacture of Articles for Culture, Education, Artwork, Sport and Entertainment Activities	7	3	359510	32021
石油加工、炼焦和核燃料加工业	Processing of Petroleum, Coking, Processing of Mucleus Fuels	8	2	7006182	905673
化学原料和化学制品制造业	Manufacture of Chemical Raw Materials and Chemical Products	36	12	1412448	22503.86
医药制造业	Manufacture of Medicines	34	3	1346770	658072
化学纤维制造业	Manufacture of Chemical Fibres	2		***	***
橡胶和塑料制品业	Manufacture of Rubber and Plastics Products	14	3	199481	52564
非金属矿物制品业	Manufacture of Non-metallic Mineral Products	64	14	1618892	277929
黑色金属冶炼和压延加工业	Manufacture and Pressing of Ferrous Metals	7	2	946685	23997
有色金属冶炼和压延加工业	Manufacture and Pressing of Non-ferrous Metals	10		348000	48831
金属制品业	Manufacture of Fabricated Metal Products	32	12	1036494	142199
通用设备制造业	Manufacture of General-purpose Machinery	46	17	858133	172687
专用设备制造业	Manufacture of Special-purpose Machinery	60	8	1870966	472845
汽车制造业	Manufacture of Motor Vehicles	39	15	20655058	5552701
铁路、船舶、航空航天和其他运输设备制造业	Manufacture of Railway Locomotives, Building of Ships and Boats, Manufacture of Air and Spacecrafts and Other Transportation Equipment	31	4	2214804	582645
电气机械和器材制造业	Manufacture of Electrical Machinery and Equipment	33	10	1666131	89324
计算机、通信和其他电子设备制造业	Manufacture of Computers, Communication Equipment and Other Electronic Equipment	81	12	4151918	1081819
仪器仪表制造业	Manufacture of Measuring Instruments and Meters	47	9	867795	174255
其他制造业	Other Manufacturing	12		680984	196403
废弃资源综合利用业	Waste Recycling and Recovery	3	***	***	***
金属制品、机械和设备修理业	Repair of Fabricated Metal Products, Machinery and Equipment	5		299701	132342
电力、热力生产和供应业	Production and Distribution of Electricity and Heating Power	45	14	37257119	6027697
燃气生产和供应业	Production and Distribution of Gas	13	6	304186	35414
水的生产和供应业	Production and Distribution of Water	15	2	403200	164744

注：1. 行业划分执行2011年国民经济行业分类标准(GB/T 4754-2011)。
2. 应交税金合计包括应交增值税、应交所得税、营业税金及附加和管理费用中的税金。
3. 2013年从业人员平均人数口径有变化，与往年数据不可比。

MAIN ECONOMIC INDICATORS OF STATE-OWNED AND STATE-CONTROLLED INDUSTIRAL ENTERPRISES ABOVE DESIGNATED SIZE (BY SECTOR) (2013)

(10000 yuan)

工业销售产值(当年价格) Sales Value of Industry (at current year's prices)	#出口交货值 Delivery Value of Exports	从业人员平均人数(人) Average Number of Employed Persons (person)	资产负债 Assets and Liabilities: 资产总计 Total Assets	流动资产合计 Total Current Assets	#存货 Inventories	#产成品 Finished Products	#应收账款 Accounts Receivable	固定资产合计 Total Fixed Assets	固定资产原价 Total Original Value of Fixed Assets
99977936	**2370352**	**486569**	**227855562**	**73426596**	**10444680**	**2891897**	**15678736**	**48403547**	**86403994**
7137701	152343	15640	2869814	1719912	60510	58495	864187	61389	198027
***	***	***	***	***	***	***	***	***	***
1578166		24919	19533955	6236382	290626	48762	1441040	3696873	4704145
***	***	***	***	***	***	***	***	***	***
1796862	8581	12702	1767323	1317947	231610	138689	86140	171963	271799
455452	5896	10664	617446	233783	43387	21777	76605	142157	216697
637616	4396	12161	2165857	924916	150028	40453	45562	204663	508640
***	***	***	***	***	***	***	***	***	***
119320	34735	3619	390168	221004	47846	29578	24402	89776	126508
53615	14962	2720	90504	59462	35058	22413	5095	22803	44169
***	***	***	***	***	***	***	***	***	***
***	***	***	***	***	***	***	***	***	***
56424	2233	1764	130315	64527	17972	10212	8901	30373	46549
34625		408	74164	50510	13082	3126	19444	13730	20753
597476	732	13390	991686	509732	114975	47728	68419	349055	853467
352295	8183	2342	489060	403712	216511	173530	99322	70344	95359
7026774		13964	2775875	1196419	751305	195495	119709	825821	2733285
1417046	8910	11754	2726762	1481389	178386	71926	183931	615468	1489547
1458201	10956	19605	3363215	2023021	557170	182917	395483	383915	695710
***	***	***	***	***	***	***	***	***	***
195442	37224	4770	269519	160722	43288	26436	31356	73300	127645
1605366	29949	23519	3348407	2216153	269176	94570	1143494	553973	1034477
934557	43011	4964	2267626	320602	134437	39596	36198	821216	1864276
347188	100973	2889	372354	266841	74981	26609	61619	66553	104283
1053093	118947	10606	2042046	965573	276849	74665	189443	381047	618896
879606	81754	15782	2344256	1666673	655193	161546	332065	233949	455104
1817587	61854	25921	4404589	3101934	770315	214665	1008665	495378	817893
20496672	271964	76218	21183869	10568967	1438035	716922	1157756	3934621	5693655
2145137	9773	14096	4019096	2816570	1172612	89135	814230	888741	1037782
1631647	89259	10840	4903226	3995986	924076	37389	1869247	109377	236512
3922857	1004634	33809	9862669	5296771	921541	270507	1069059	2400109	4145769
870299	8954	8778	1164603	913485	273212	53315	249036	97206	175505
545887		2015	1182850	719000	152096	21005	260961	270802	468442
***	***	***	***	***	***	***	***	***	***
305162	74897	6461	399557	206856	67877	414	109621	175198	312818
37252707		59197	120037392	19467732	101176	1171	2672675	26931185	50155750
301340		3429	385838	220630	9568	7749	36403	146069	242037
392186		9856	5297110	1415133	10110	4070	205552	2684116	4169835

Note: a) Sectors in this table are classified in accordance with the Standard for Classification of National Economic Sectors 2011 (GB/T 4754-2011).

b) Total tax payable mainly includes VAT payable, income tax payable, business tax and surtax, and tax in management expenses.

c) The statistical scope of average number of employed persons changed in 2013, so data of 2013 are not comparable with past ones.

11-9 续表

单位：万元

项目	Item	资产负债 Assets and Liabilities 负债合计 Total Liabilities	#流动负债合计 Total Current Liabilities	#应付账款 Accounts Payable	所有者权益合计 Total Owner's Equity
合计	**Total**	**119139801**	**64890296**	**19130723**	**108715761**
煤炭开采和洗选业	Mining and Washing of Coal	1423042	1278921	799724	1446772
石油和天然气开采业	Extraction of Petroleum and Natural Gas	***	***	***	***
黑色金属矿采选业	Mining and Processing of Ferrous Metal Ores	11407180	3718602	1076940	8126776
开采辅助活动	Mining Support Service Activities	***	***	***	***
农副食品加工业	Processing of Food from Agricultural Products	1207161	1091124	63482	560161
食品制造业	Manufacture of Foods	352183	300914	81965	265263
酒、饮料和精制茶制造业	Manufacture of Wines, Beverage and Refined Tea	751783	721343	29757	1414073
烟草制品业	Manufacture of Cigarettes and Tobacco	***	***	***	***
纺织业	Manufacture of Textile	202483	128589	29244	187686
纺织服装、服饰业	Manufacture of Textile Wearing Apparel and Ornament	86072	85819	8015	4432
皮革、毛皮、羽毛及其制品和制鞋业	Manufacture of Leather, Fur, Feather and Its Products, and Footwear	***	***	***	***
木材加工和木、竹、藤、棕、草制品业	Processing of Timbers, Manufacture of Wood, Bamboo, Rattan, Palm, and Straw Products	***	***	***	***
家具制造业	Manufacture of Furniture	68478	45879	14896	61837
造纸和纸制品业	Manufacture of Paper and Paper Products	34455	27234	10163	39709
印刷和记录媒介复制业	Printing, Reproduction of Recording Media	334413	273665	64745	657274
文教、工美、体育和娱乐用品制造业	Manufacture of Articles for Culture, Education, Artwork, Sport and Entertainment Activities	328491	307441	174881	160569
石油加工、炼焦和核燃料加工业	Processing of Petroleum, Coking, Processing of Mucleus Fuels	1652248	1649070	701045	1123627
化学原料和化学制品制造业	Manufacture of Chemical Raw Materials and Chemical Products	1861209	1614641	222095	865553
医药制造业	Manufacture of Medicines	1208886	877714	199597	2154329
化学纤维制造业	Manufacture of Chemical Fibres	***	***	***	***
橡胶和塑料制品业	Manufacture of Rubber and Plastics Products	162819	153310	22536	106700
非金属矿物制品业	Manufacture of Non-metallic Mineral Products	2050330	1926168	713541	1298077
黑色金属冶炼和压延加工业	Manufacture and Pressing of Ferrous Metals	1309648	478001	190615	957977
有色金属冶炼和压延加工业	Manufacture and Pressing of Non-ferrous Metals	107746	100146	41553	264608
金属制品业	Manufacture of Fabricated Metal Products	1043838	850977	288454	998208
通用设备制造业	Manufacture of General-purpose Machinery	1352776	1249114	293893	991480
专用设备制造业	Manufacture of Special-purpose Machinery	2611978	2305016	817455	1792611
汽车制造业	Manufacture of Motor Vehicles	12123321	9836646	4188920	9060548
铁路、船舶、航空航天和其他运输设备制造业	Manufacture of Railway Locomotives, Building of Ships and Boats, Manufacture of Air and Spacecrafts and Other Transportation Equipment	2734153	2250749	752432	1284943
电气机械和器材制造业	Manufacture of Electrical Machinery and Equipment	3242899	2725225	1115263	1660327
计算机、通信和其他电子设备制造业	Manufacture of Computers, Communication Equipment and Other Electronic Equipment	4656476	3279351	997467	5206193
仪器仪表制造业	Manufacture of Measuring Instruments and Meters	643141	577289	230287	521462
其他制造业	Other Manufacturing	474916	350671	191899	707934
废弃资源综合利用业	Waste Recycling and Recovery	***	***	***	***
金属制品、机械和设备修理业	Repair of Fabricated Metal Products, Machinery and Equipment	226669	223893	33596	172888
电力、热力生产和供应业	Production and Distribution of Electricity and Heating Power	60378912	23382875	4924266	59658480
燃气生产和供应业	Production and Distribution of Gas	192282	186553	46921	193555
水的生产和供应业	Production and Distribution of Water	2281348	839208	52786	3015762

11-9 Continued

(10000 yuan)

	损益 Profits and Losses											
#实收资本 Paid-up Capital	营业收入 Business Income	#主营业务收入 Main Business Income	营业成本 Business Cost	#主营业务成本 Main Business Cost	销售费用 Sales Expenses	管理费用 Management Expenses	财务费用 Financial Expenses	利润总额 Total Profits	应交税金合计 Total Tax Payable	#营业税金及附加 Business Tax and Surtax	#主营业务税金及附加 Main Business Tax and Surtax	#应交增值税 Value Added Tax Payable
49366247	**1.08E+08**	**106441958**	**95148105**	**93517461**	**2347441**	**3869663**	**1723178**	**7142424**	**6785504**	**2485870**	**2462197**	**2910091**
691325	7173358	7151761	6879683	6875156	50364	66967	12869	178678	170210	27466	27360	90183
***	***	***	***	***	***	***	***	***	***	***	***	***
2860729	4712033	4507778	4424923	4219881	3065	107433	119342	107608	130539	20280	16136	97965
***	***	***	***	***	***	***	***	***	***	***	***	***
182338	2084524	2077652	1737919	1736346	141670	64493	20941	62918	126745	75938	75929	35817
194001	546337	533283	415294	404427	99035	36288	4538	-534	24467	2145	2145	18328
117235	771119	723428	557424	520408	63871	41978	7570	48320	130614	72651	72477	49650
***	***	***	***	***	***	***	***	***	***	***	***	***
175205	179988	173926	150402	148316	2347	24814	3615	-1650	5006	1374	1139	1903
53036	84983	84236	78035	77517	1729	6978	974	-5815	3016	393	392	2136
***	***	***	***	***	***	***	***	***	***	***	***	***
***	***	***	***	***	***	***	***	***	***	***	***	***
27945	67975	64554	45787	44321	11711	7707	1358	4375	5874	629	517	3994
10417	93635	92697	87974	87742	856	3518	-151	2031	1607	151	103	764
432262	696663	654617	487150	462643	12500	107786	-1260	87646	67029	5938	5606	37316
137839	403209	400612	371986	371149	14100	14546	6553	-11756	3681	707	688	3995
63034	7978772	7390153	7182878	6603362	45604	228010	26957	-160509	778579	610798	609648	147467
1087254	1512055	1474369	1443909	1414565	33754	138190	39126	-151138	20017	3022	2918	22839
606322	1505883	1490300	820838	811083	186726	164052	13854	393720	198632	15918	15789	124163
***	***	***	***	***	***	***	***	***	***	***	***	***
82823	310830	286526	265204	249712	8032	22597	2866	13882	14477	1494	1411	9335
744347	1866473	1815864	1612428	1575164	71146	136497	32556	68607	66400	9117	8186	40247
574438	1033973	1018121	1018434	1006412	30383	16575	19639	-21623	8040	712	577	4897
73438	451483	391796	390127	334484	5443	23282	2701	15939	24487	13282	13218	8688
525746	1332164	1252254	1155047	1095893	24145	104002	9329	42445	31320	4690	3296	16986
603307	1129514	1100751	954323	934117	37807	110745	5526	27302	52593	4972	4731	37184
883450	2120889	2083409	1585761	1568661	115054	251375	18014	146268	124567	14097	13482	81203
3896874	20671886	20371257	16262029	16073178	999624	752912	58409	2128209	2307493	1115009	1109127	712373
599064	2311206	2290987	1921979	1908510	29429	203944	17732	149757	79681	6707	6582	49518
969856	1799211	1687087	1605411	1497732	100228	127105	53829	-94791	20467	5010	4926	26058
3534399	4834265	4735930	3792019	3730288	180717	442199	77415	528076	143754	19817	17967	72326
240848	991411	975593	802093	792846	35104	103008	2984	78190	48051	5041	4869	32267
264695	694648	690306	532859	530506	14329	78159	-1376	74495	35281	2489	2483	20395
***	***	***	***	***	***	***	***	***	***	***	***	***
146565	313565	304696	227576	223980	2332	79079	3474	9775	16343	1053	1014	10027
24015446	37402904	37296469	35376483	35295038	4054	182294	1137877	3428847	1728396	175735	172059	1041051
184870	320969	307339	324893	318268	3851	29954	-942	8309	17121	2031	1496	10442
2628871	491432	483089	493929	488967	1456	56373	-3917	46389	27681	2368	1794	13399

11-10 规模以上股份制工业企业主要经济指标(2013年)

单位：万元

项目	Item	企业单位个数(个) Number of Enterprises (unit)	#亏损企业 Loss-Suffering Enterprises	工业总产值(当年价格) Gross Output Value of Industry (at current year's prices)	工业增加值 Added Value of Industry	工业销售产值(当年价格) Sales Value of Industry (at current year's prices)	#出口交货值 Delivery Value of Exports
合　计	**Total**	**1454**	**285**	**64543748**	**12697302**	**63703289**	**2283736**
在合计中：	**Of the Total:**						
中央企业	Central Enterprises	167	36	31300469	4964510	31070072	274349
地方企业	Local Enterprises	1287	249	33243280	7732792	32633217	2009387
在合计中：	**Of the Total:**						
轻工业	Light Industry	441	83	9355994	2749769	8969238	190668
重工业	Heavy Industry	1013	202	55187755	9947534	54734051	2093069
在合计中：	**Of the Total:**						
#大中型企业	Medium and Large-sized Enterprises	361	75	46248552	10341896	45656691	1911143

注：2013年从业人员平均人数口径有变化，与往年数据不可比。

11-10 续表

单位：万元

项目	Item	资产负债 Assets and Liabilities					
		固定资产原价 Total Original Value of Fixed Assets	负债合计 Total Liabilities	#流动负债合计 Total Current Liabilities	#应付账款 Accounts Payable	所有者权益合计 Total Owner's Equity	#实收资本 Paid-up Capital
合　计	**Total**	**44651929**	**65905810**	**46969654**	**15541746**	**55994609**	**28005265**
在合计中：	**Of theTotal:**						
中央企业	Central Enterprises	17396985	19702560	16851627	6019600	14758140	7892581
地方企业	Local Enterprises	27254943	46203249	30118027	9522146	41236469	20112684
在合计中：	**Of the Total:**						
轻工业	Light Industry	5875869	8416048	6880391	1578030	8439728	3909650
重工业	Heavy Industry	38776060	57489762	40089264	13963717	47554881	24095615
在合计中：	**Of the Total:**						
#大中型企业	Medium and Large-sized Enterprises	39883669	53978958	35978498	10984994	47003619	22781307

注：应交税金合计包括应交增值税、应交所得税、营业税金及附加和管理费用中的税金。

MAIN ECONOMIC INDICATORS OF SHARE-HOLDING INDUSTRIAL ENTERPRISES ABOVE DESIGNATED SIZE (2013)

(10000 yuan)

从业人员平均人数(人) Average Number of Employed Persons (person)	资产负债 Assets and Liabilities					
	资产总计 Total Assets	流动资产合计 Total Current Assets	#存货 Inventories	#产成品 Finished Products	#应收账款 Accounts Receivable	固定资产合计 Total Fixed Assets
543337	**121904107**	**58665098**	**10374311**	**3312818**	**16448243**	**26077217**
135742	34460700	16329295	3273306	863186	4917812	8116980
407595	87443407	42335803	7101004	2449633	11530431	17960237
129620	16855776	9847947	2254470	1045377	1713995	3332262
413717	105048331	48817151	8119840	2267442	14734248	22744955
410161	100982577	44209297	7385798	2141117	11220123	23169771

Note: The statistical scope of average number of employed persons changed in 2013, so data of 2013 are not comparable with past ones.

11-10 Continued

(10000 yuan)

损益 Profits and Losses								应交税金合计 Total Tax Payable	#营业税金及附加 Business Tax and Surtax	#主营业务税金及附加 Main Business Tax and Surtax	#应交增值税 Value Added Tax Payable
营业收入 Business Income	#主营业务收入 Main Business Income	营业成本 Business Cost	#主营业务成本 Main Business Cost	销售费用 Sales Expenses	管理费用 Management Expenses	财务费用 Financial Expenses	利润总额 Total Profits				
73373666	**71483597**	**63644636**	**62068577**	**2299780**	**4180095**	**760565**	**3259486**	**3559005**	**1063408**	**1045815**	**1846311**
33773800	32903189	31078235	30303477	342291	1197179	212776	521357	1560087	716900	712584	651736
39599866	38580408	32566401	31765100	1957489	2982916	547789	2738129	1998917	346508	333231	1194575
10367440	10182396	7541925	7434072	961975	889069	61904	1080168	786852	162551	160614	429245
63006226	61301201	56102711	54634506	1337805	3291026	698661	2179318	2772153	900857	885201	1417066
53049607	51463704	45831453	44458432	1713783	3054211	624114	2383283	2850749	986228	970972	1435912

Note: Total tax payable mainly includes VAT payable, income tax payable, business tax and surtax, and tax in management expenses.

11-11 规模以上股份制工业企业主要经济指标(按行业分)(2013年)

单位：万元

项目	Item	企业单位个数(个) Number of Enterprises (unit)	#亏损企业 Loss-Suffering Enterprises	工业总产值(当年价格) Gross Output Value of Industry (at current year's prices)	工业增加值 Added Value of Industry
合计	**Total**	**1454**	**285**	**64543748**	**12697302**
煤炭开采和洗选业	Mining and Washing of Coal	4		7131795	459050
石油和天然气开采业	Extraction of Petroleum and Natural Gas	2	***	***	***
黑色金属矿采选业	Mining and Processing of Ferrous Metal Ores	5		1609893	383176
非金属矿采选业	Mining and Processing of Nonmetal Ores	2		***	***
开采辅助活动	Mining Support Service Activities	3	***	***	***
农副食品加工业	Processing of Food from Agricultural Products	58	17	2065851	295644
食品制造业	Manufacture of Foods	36	8	494149	122464
酒、饮料和精制茶制造业	Manufacture of Wines, Beverage and Refined Tea	11	6	168984	72784
纺织业	Manufacture of Textile	19	3	190861	24140
纺织服装、服饰业	Manufacture of Textile Wearing Apparel and Ornament	34	7	451441	213974
皮革、毛皮、羽毛及其制品和制鞋业	Manufacture of Leather, Fur, Feather and Its Products, and Footwear	8	2	37122	4378
木材加工和木、竹、藤、棕、草制品业	Processing of Timbers, Manufacture of Wood, Bamboo, Rattan, Palm, and Straw Products	8	1	49340	15410
家具制造业	Manufacture of Furniture	16	1	130009	26958
造纸和纸制品业	Manufacture of Paper and Paper Products	15	4	100121	15409
印刷和记录媒介复制业	Printing, Reproduction of Recording Media	37	6	562338	264782
文教、工美、体育和娱乐用品制造业	Manufacture of Articles for Culture, Education, Artwork, Sport and Entertainment Activities	14	4	734732	61957
石油加工、炼焦和核燃料加工业	Processing of Petroleum, Coking, Processing of Mucleus Fuels	9	2	6926341	901014
化学原料和化学制品制造业	Manufacture of Chemical Raw Materials and Chemical Products	75	14	1573638	149292
医药制造业	Manufacture of Medicines	88	12	2521521	1089524
化学纤维制造业	Manufacture of Chemical Fibres	2		***	***
橡胶和塑料制品业	Manufacture of Rubber and Plastics Products	32	10	351656	55010
非金属矿物制品业	Manufacture of Non-metallic Mineral Products	129	22	3335751	502209
黑色金属冶炼和压延加工业	Manufacture and Pressing of Ferrous Metals	17	5	1052543	55136
有色金属冶炼和压延加工业	Manufacture and Pressing of Non-ferrous Metals	13	1	407527	68086
金属制品业	Manufacture of Fabricated Metal Products	80	16	1409204	237319
通用设备制造业	Manufacture of General-purpose Machinery	81	22	994214	249338
专用设备制造业	Manufacture of Special-purpose Machinery	124	11	3496054	926921
汽车制造业	Manufacture of Motor Vehicles	64	23	5116202	1042956
铁路、船舶、航空航天和其他运输设备制造业	Manufacture of Railway Locomotives, Building of Ships and Boats, Manufacture of Air and Spacecrafts and Other Transportation Equipment	39	5	1606506	448753
电气机械和器材制造业	Manufacture of Electrical Machinery and Equipment	111	20	3792735	566972
计算机、通信和其他电子设备制造业	Manufacture of Computers, Communication Equipment and Other Electronic Equipment	148	30	4563715	1078710
仪器仪表制造业	Manufacture of Measuring Instruments and Meters	84	12	1285432	371351
其他制造业	Other Manufacturing	14		703501	199893
废弃资源综合利用业	Waste Recycling and Recovery	4	1	41320	2376
金属制品、机械和设备修理业	Repair of Fabricated Metal Products, Machinery and Equipment	7		41562	18663
电力、热力生产和供应业	Production and Distribution of Electricity and Heating Power	35	10	8815769	1635149
燃气生产和供应业	Production and Distribution of Gas	13	5	336666	64163
水的生产和供应业	Production and Distribution of Water	13	2	386027	150130

注：1. 行业划分执行2011年国民经济行业分类标准(GB/T 4754-2011)。
2. 应交税金合计包括应交增值税、应交所得税、营业税金及附加和管理费用中的税金。
3. 2013年从业人员平均人数口径有变化，与往年数据不可比。

MAIN ECONOMIC INDICATORS OF SHARE-HOLDING INDUSTRIAL ENTERPRISES ABOVE DESIGNATED SIZE (BY SECTOR) (2013)

(10000 yuan)

工业销售产值(当年价格) Sales Value of Industry (at current year's prices)	#出口交货值 Delivery Value of Exports	从业人员平均人数(人) Average Number of Employed Persons (person)	资产负债 Assets and Liabilities: 资产总计 Total Assets	流动资产合计 Total Current Assets	#存货 Inventories	#产成品 Finished Products	#应收账款 Accounts Receivable	固定资产合计 Total Fixed Assets
63703289	**2283736**	**543337**	**121904107**	**58665098**	**10374311**	**3312818**	**16448243**	**26077217**
7137701	152343	15640	2869814	1719912	60510	58495	864187	61389
***	***	***	***	***	***	***	***	***
1609345		25189	19562039	6251230	294746	49160	1441672	3706921
***	***	***	***	***	***	***	***	***
***	***	***	***	***	***	***	***	***
2040640	2183	16135	2522502	1762219	267539	142320	164791	237753
472603	39194	11712	752419	505783	94072	29804	93706	117247
156222	1658	3897	488910	288125	94353	43391	43984	111133
193062	30314	3789	503905	310229	61946	42235	45571	93165
374115	32762	14731	626563	432636	208376	133960	66931	74915
37294	15733	709	18495	16584	9046	4105	3156	1626
49949		1472	79784	50402	12829	2857	12192	11252
129929	2745	3497	223965	130638	48796	26925	26013	49140
99186	1593	2086	111551	50938	15841	5717	18014	36848
570001	3535	11217	883912	467969	118025	44975	59549	313004
712763	7172	4059	695013	546335	290947	210502	106699	99238
6958279		13917	2720492	1169793	720375	170324	120412	807841
1557492	7703	15475	2749692	1672442	196010	77576	240160	460251
2455544	13876	34397	5379005	3091440	673498	256316	570891	750999
***	***	***	***	***	***	***	***	***
355694	67036	6558	866889	417158	80559	42459	70928	122294
3312989	81005	39798	6002882	4262277	732470	166412	2191794	756416
1031474	48306	7332	2404169	396800	166899	54754	51982	861072
396602	96388	3253	396099	256095	77286	28871	60239	59187
1407077	104415	15410	2503916	1328374	408243	119723	314305	443357
954837	47434	19715	3023530	1931997	504110	187485	538469	357851
3387119	168135	37276	8788147	5640183	1012963	288112	1376040	564604
5134216	273344	50388	8101553	3611603	639905	340852	813646	1398628
1586647	11003	14640	2847956	2110615	617529	79614	819910	398536
3678213	33438	26840	5847027	4446354	681330	180550	2278831	334546
4402139	840022	48481	12264148	7113759	1256683	407116	1681588	2377407
1269065	33761	17168	2389677	1720816	455967	82463	501499	196868
568904	3721	2075	1220792	747110	154877	22229	272679	273099
41000		586	79001	29063	6128	2312	736	41778
38628		650	95235	57370	22027	661	20517	22000
8815791		38220	13491932	2182582	60296	1171	367759	6943129
336666		2033	249913	147331	905	25	36418	75350
375524		9278	5185350	1352600	9433	4070	205565	2638060

Note: a) Sectors in this table are classified in accordance with the Standard for Classification of National Economic Sectors 2011 (GB/T 4754-2011).
b) Total tax payable mainly includes VAT payable, income tax payable, business tax and surtax, and tax in management expenses.
c) The statistical scope of average number of employed persons changed in 2013, so data of 2013 are not comparable with past ones.

11-11 续表

单位：万元

项目	Item	资产负债 Assets and Liabilities			
		固定资产原价 Total Original Value of Fixed Assets	负债合计 Total Liabilities	#流动负债合计 Total Current Liabilities	#应付账款 Accounts Payable
合计	**Total**	**44651929**	**65905810**	**46969654**	**15541746**
煤炭开采和洗选业	Mining and Washing of Coal	198027	1423042	1278921	799724
石油和天然气开采业	Extraction of Petroleum and Natural Gas	***	***	***	***
黑色金属矿采选业	Mining and Processing of Ferrous Metal Ores	4717102	11416702	3727775	1077445
非金属矿采选业	Mining and Processing of Nonmetal Ores	***	***	***	***
开采辅助活动	Mining Support Service Activities	***	***	***	***
农副食品加工业	Processing of Food from Agricultural Products	363180	1514182	1374260	115148
食品制造业	Manufacture of Foods	179259	586405	513598	93837
酒、饮料和精制茶制造业	Manufacture of Wines, Beverage and Refined Tea	155553	298117	290078	17325
纺织业	Manufacture of Textile	132436	263780	189887	70229
纺织服装、服饰业	Manufacture of Textile Wearing Apparel and Ornament	138665	338004	322721	96289
皮革、毛皮、羽毛及其制品和制鞋业	Manufacture of Leather, Fur, Feather and Its Products, and Footwear	2980	9421	9421	1584
木材加工和木、竹、藤、棕、草制品业	Processing of Timbers, Manufacture of Wood, Bamboo, Rattan, Palm, and Straw Products	31228	50213	48930	8793
家具制造业	Manufacture of Furniture	73125	123880	94583	29176
造纸和纸制品业	Manufacture of Paper and Paper Products	51413	65194	63281	26703
印刷和记录媒介复制业	Printing, Reproduction of Recording Media	705532	303517	283494	91876
文教、工美、体育和娱乐用品制造业	Manufacture of Articles for Culture, Education, Artwork, Sport and Entertainment Activities	151552	446851	410772	197663
石油加工、炼焦和核燃料加工业	Processing of Petroleum, Coking, Processing of Mucleus Fuels	2713883	1620474	1617182	697312
化学原料和化学制品制造业	Manufacture of Chemical Raw Materials and Chemical Products	1279740	1795738	1647125	210671
医药制造业	Manufacture of Medicines	1193650	2202596	1783112	456559
化学纤维制造业	Manufacture of Chemical Fibres	***	***	***	***
橡胶和塑料制品业	Manufacture of Rubber and Plastics Products	199323	452725	349239	45791
非金属矿物制品业	Manufacture of Non-metallic Mineral Products	1371743	3791311	3503927	1485399
黑色金属冶炼和压延加工业	Manufacture and Pressing of Ferrous Metals	1942921	1400685	563870	209345
有色金属冶炼和压延加工业	Manufacture and Pressing of Non-ferrous Metals	98152	183057	173142	50517
金属制品业	Manufacture of Fabricated Metal Products	699950	1280648	1070866	388374
通用设备制造业	Manufacture of General-purpose Machinery	591717	1350018	1214758	324243
专用设备制造业	Manufacture of Special-purpose Machinery	881138	4602835	3581663	1203850
汽车制造业	Manufacture of Motor Vehicles	1823616	4871399	4016193	1360855
铁路、船舶、航空航天和其他运输设备制造业	Manufacture of Railway Locomotives, Building of Ships and Boats, Manufacture of Air and Spacecrafts and Other Transportation Equipment	662327	1732952	1459491	635447
电气机械和器材制造业	Manufacture of Electrical Machinery and Equipment	566105	3881638	3656064	1348110
计算机、通信和其他电子设备制造业	Manufacture of Computers, Communication Equipment and Other Electronic Equipment	3511168	5623155	4129958	1265745
仪器仪表制造业	Manufacture of Measuring Instruments and Meters	304280	1083039	1016140	387487
其他制造业	Other Manufacturing	471269	489386	364820	193589
废弃资源综合利用业	Waste Recycling and Recovery	53398	55782	27545	3184
金属制品、机械和设备修理业	Repair of Fabricated Metal Products, Machinery and Equipment	30619	40983	39895	19586
电力、热力生产和供应业	Production and Distribution of Electricity and Heating Power	12734107	7709637	5236385	1782430
	Production and Distribution of Gas				
燃气生产和供应业	Production and Distribution of Water	98782	161932	161932	51085
水的生产和供应业	Production and Distribution of Wwater	4089117	2240345	804496	58443

11-11 Continued

(10000 yuan)

所有者权益合计 Total Owner's Equity	#实收资本 Paid-up Capital	损益 Profits and Losses: 营业收入 Business Income	#主营业务收入 Main Business Income	营业成本 Business Cost	#主营业务成本 Main Business Cost	销售费用 Sales Expenses	管理费用 Management Expenses	财务费用 Financial Expenses	利润总额 Total Profits	应交税金合计 Total Tax Payable	#营业税金及附加 Business Tax and Surtax	#主营业务税金及附加 Main Business Tax and Surtax	#应交增值税 Value Added Tax Payable
55994609	**28005265**	**73373666**	**71483597**	**63644636**	**62068577**	**2299780**	**4180095**	**760565**	**3259486**	**3559005**	**1063408**	**1045815**	**1846311**
1446772	691325	7173358	7151761	6879683	6875156	50364	66967	12869	178678	170210	27466	27360	90183
***	***	***	***	***	***	***	***	***	***	***	***	***	***
8145337	2862184	4743631	4537616	4448374	4240947	3466	110954	119504	110690	133474	21386	17242	99755
***	***	***	***	***	***	***	***	***	***	***	***	***	***
***	***	***	***	***	***	***	***	***	***	***	***	***	***
1008320	410824	2340175	2327173	1897865	1891291	157230	103799	25432	116420	135795	76144	76133	37762
166014	157548	544916	536396	425046	418271	58856	38636	7634	18421	30541	2183	2113	20194
190793	118507	244792	241054	189670	188126	8471	18767	7555	-6814	47827	35123	35075	10897
240125	202010	311591	305147	270666	268272	4681	28027	5013	5053	7608	1389	1149	3921
288559	136734	509783	503727	293735	291822	95527	58600	1903	57635	48827	4313	4308	34239
9074	4520	38122	38058	33756	33749	1958	2056	231	101	1126	181	178	830
29571	24457	59092	55770	45394	43621	4158	5582	411	6059	3991	588	262	2713
100086	54163	143532	140126	107933	106483	16539	12811	1941	7061	10192	972	860	6905
46356	38685	133874	128205	121088	116004	3768	8129	702	494	2728	233	233	1980
580395	356027	626818	604988	440744	431332	11704	85302	-435	88763	60805	4384	4055	33180
248162	187803	861735	846831	806443	801735	18074	34091	8923	-4969	7626	1454	979	5866
1100019	39772	7884101	7294595	7103421	6523164	38452	222535	25226	-161105	772893	610479	609329	144055
953954	1041719	1667949	1628690	1496795	1465149	55423	148893	32415	-78264	35962	4005	3904	31509
3176409	970623	2531144	2486435	1260404	1231118	479126	278200	9369	626229	313982	24409	24239	199177
***	***	***	***	***	***	***	***	***	***	***	***	***	***
414164	212424	541389	510237	468851	447706	11964	31138	16278	15361	18872	1987	1882	12220
2211571	1037652	3757889	3676652	3237584	3165586	139938	232036	59384	138076	110827	19869	18936	61637
1003484	595728	1140356	1122106	1104308	1091709	32339	26099	21907	-15101	13593	1253	1061	8808
213042	65730	500491	445998	430825	379190	6106	25724	6955	26704	27144	13287	13250	9639
1223268	618904	1592968	1535908	1336130	1301513	27541	129172	15946	85072	48067	8758	7363	23305
1673512	805687	1236696	1191185	981690	952592	62321	138806	6429	54076	59148	5809	5630	40543
4185312	1841464	3667538	3556480	2813956	2721821	191571	336623	34504	497688	249397	30887	30600	172601
3230154	1469897	5635959	5435938	5070937	4914535	170014	365907	5976	173251	192675	42734	42346	105279
1115004	585791	1750006	1733006	1430672	1421435	39256	158122	14438	116279	74654	5974	5848	49107
1961700	1196282	3883766	3840201	3238921	3197525	198789	286286	50001	161543	140371	14885	14730	93255
6640993	3741609	5758216	5663362	4493923	4434091	297611	628502	80326	533417	218111	23373	21440	129204
1306639	409195	1448571	1425502	1029811	1017404	84569	195490	7953	196316	95609	8673	8443	62566
731406	270995	716910	712562	550502	548149	15852	79015	-1003	76297	35857	2684	2678	20998
23219	17650	48838	48418	45132	44896	621	4342	115	2286	2850	257	257	2125
54252	26572	40758	40068	23758	23586	2842	7706	445	11130	3628	259	258	2220
5782296	2487658	8951431	8876846	8825409	8767119	4645	141608	156840	258224	366848	32382	29521	276222
87981	78325	354228	342667	315614	309707	4530	16084	-159	16305	18956	1952	1509	10848
2945006	2592365	473167	465455	483043	478342	591	50209	-3585	43090	25547	2178	1603	12285

11-12 规模以上港澳台及外商投资工业企业主要经济指标(2013年)

单位：万元

项目	Item	企业单位个数(个) Number of Enterprises (unit)	#亏损企业 Loss-Suffering Enterprises	工业总产值(当年价格) Gross Output Value of Industry (at current year's prices)	工业增加值 Added Value of Industry	工业销售产值(当年价格) Sales Value of Industry (at current year's prices)	#出口交货值 Delivery Value of Exports
合计	**Total**	**888**	**185**	**67564877**	**14181452**	**66933148**	**12318523**
在合计中：	**Of the Total:**						
中央企业	Central Enterprises	13	2	1096946	345831	1101422	105681
地方企业	Local Enterprises	875	183	66467931	13835622	65831727	12212843
在合计中：	**Of the Total:**						
轻工业	Light Industry	331	92	10697941	3106140	10591990	1387724
重工业	Heavy Industry	557	93	56866936	11075313	56341158	10930800
在合计中：	**Of the Total:**						
#大中型企业	Medium and Large-sized Enterprises	270	39	59572168	12462155	58954875	11337105

注：2013年从业人员平均人数口径有变化，与往年数据不可比。

11-12 续表

单位：万元

项目	Item	固定资产原价 Total Original Value of Fixed Assets	负债合计 Total Liabilities	#流动负债合计 Total Current Liabilities	#应付账款 Accounts Payable	所有者权益合计 Total Owner's Equity	#实收资本 Paid-up Capital
		资产负债 Assets and Liabilities					
合计	**Total**	**22460406**	**34683829**	**29481875**	**13584077**	**29697734**	**14775213**
在合计中：	**Of the Total:**						
中央企业	Central Enterprises	1816789	1166342	973912	234538	1674528	920202
地方企业	Local Enterprises	20643618	33517487	28507963	13349539	28023206	13855011
在合计中：	**Of the Total:**						
轻工业	Light Industry	4096299	5615895	5245638	1657464	5266614	3381914
重工业	Heavy Industry	18364107	29067934	24236236	11926614	24431120	11393299
在合计中：	**Of the Total:**						
#大中型企业	Medium and Large-sized Enterprises	19051806	28544486	24596807	11460235	23768173	11261797

MAIN ECONOMIC INDICATORS OF HONGKONG, MACAO, TAIWAN AND FOREIGN-INVESTED INDUSTRIAL ENTERPRISES ABOVE DESIGNATED SIZE (2013)

(10000 yuan)

从业人员平均人数（人）合 计 Average Number of Employed Persons	资产负债 Assets and Liabilities					
	资产总计 Total Assets	流动资产合计 Total Current Assets	#存货 Inventories	#产成品 Finished Products	#应收账款 Accounts Receivable	固定资产合计 Total Fixed Assets
403045	**64388254**	**39579857**	**8328605**	**2532003**	**10910286**	**12045391**
12299	2840871	918354	116205	21366	317892	769865
390746	61547384	38661504	8212400	2510637	10592394	11275526
148525	10882510	7141402	1774976	811218	1910886	2112726
254520	53505745	32438455	6553630	1720785	8999400	9932665
328121	52312659	32224596	6519930	1921871	8594543	10154963

Note: The statistical scope of average number of employed persons changed in 2013, so data of 2013 are not comparable with past ones.

11-12 Continued

(10000 yuan)

损益 Profits and Loss								应交税金合计 Total Tax Payable			
营业收入 Business Income	#主营业务收入 Main Business Income	营业成本 Business Cost	#主营业务成本 Main Business Cost	销售费用 Sales Expenses	管理费用 Management Expenses	财务费用 Financial Expenses	利润总额 Total Profits		#营业税金及附加 Business Tax and Surtax	#主营业务税金及附加 Main Business Tax and Surtax	#应交增值税 Value Added Tax Payable
74803752	**73306362**	**60087093**	**58963704**	**5127399**	**3272541**	**252142**	**5728424**	**4916005**	**1311184**	**1304710**	**2310783**
1402676	1296838	1128334	1037897	32815	135979	26830	137421	100442	7271	7233	62173
73401077	72009525	58958759	57925807	5094585	3136561	225312	5591003	4815563	1303913	1297477	2248610
13024923	12564822	8264282	7915628	2722465	907231	95752	1021716	1096522	102321	102108	720911
61778829	60741541	51822812	51048077	2404934	2365310	156390	4706708	3819483	1208863	1202602	1589872
65723108	64430833	52851284	51872801	4621557	2592774	191096	5004614	4379691	1271860	1265697	1998355

11-13 规模以上港澳台及外商投资工业企业主要经济指标(按行业分)(2013年)

单位：万元

项目	Item	企业单位个数(个) Number of Enterprises (unit)	#亏损企业 Loss-Suffering Enterprises	工业总产值(当年价格) Gross Output Value of Industry (at current year's prices)	工业增加值 Added Value of Industry
合计	**Total**	**888**	**185**	**67564877**	**14181452**
开采辅助活动	Mining Support Service Activities	2		***	***
农副食品加工业	Processing of Food from Agricultural Products	28	12	678256	98539
食品制造业	Manufacture of Foods	44	10	1800843	205230
酒、饮料和精制茶制造业	Manufacture of Wines, Beverage and Refined Tea	24	8	1407384	372016
纺织业	Manufacture of Textile	9	2	90540	14951
纺织服装、服饰业	Manufacture of Textile Wearing Apparel and Ornament	36	12	372730	114492
皮革、毛皮、羽毛及其制品和制鞋业	Manufacture of Leather, Fur, Feather and Its Products, and Footwear	2		***	***
木材加工和木、竹、藤、棕、草制品业	Processing of Timbers, Manufacture of Wood, Bamboo, Rattan, Palm, and Straw Products	1	***	***	***
家具制造业	Manufacture of Furniture	13	3	273156	77757
造纸和纸制品业	Manufacture of Paper and Paper Products	15	2	490691	177512
印刷和记录媒介复制业	Printing, Reproduction of Recording Media	21	6	249298	101745
文教、工美、体育和娱乐用品制造业	Manufacture of Articles for Culture, Education, Artwork, Sport and Entertainment Activities	14	2	123520	31969
石油加工、炼焦和核燃料加工业	Processing of Petroleum, Coking, Processing of Mucleus Fuels	3		***	***
化学原料和化学制品制造业	Manufacture of Chemical Raw Materials and Chemical Products	49	14	1043839	288451
医药制造业	Manufacture of Medicines	35	8	2824352	1217413
橡胶和塑料制品业	Manufacture of Rubber and Plastics Products	27	6	385379	128762
非金属矿物制品业	Manufacture of Non-metallic Mineral Products	30	7	587291	177572
黑色金属冶炼和压延加工业	Manufacture and Pressing of Ferrous Metals	5	1	418064	70469
有色金属冶炼和压延加工业	Manufacture and Pressing of Non-ferrous Metals	5	1	80680	7221
金属制品业	Manufacture of Fabricated Metal Products	42	10	848667	205901
通用设备制造业	Manufacture of General-purpose Machinery	93	15	3417533	824904
专用设备制造业	Manufacture of Special-purpose Machinery	91	20	1629005	387508
汽车制造业	Manufacture of Motor Vehicles	110	12	27189588	6214308
铁路、船舶、航空航天和其他运输设备制造业	Manufacture of Railway Locomotives, Building of Ships and Boats, Manufacture of Air and Spacecrafts and Other Transportation Equipment	8		133022	42151
电气机械和器材制造业	Manufacture of Electrical Machinery and Equipment	47	9	2478590	637427
计算机、通信和其他电子设备制造业	Manufacture of Computers, Communication Equipment and Other Electronic Equipment	73	17	16939243	1779093
仪器仪表制造业	Manufacture of Measuring Instruments and Meters	36	3	773741	182521
其他制造业	Other Manufacturing	9	4	37539	10989
金属制品、机械和设备修理业	Repair of Fabricated Metal Products, Machinery and Equipment	5		296451	134486
电力、热力生产和供应业	Production and Distribution of Electricity and Heating Pow	4		586389	129984
燃气生产和供应业	Production and Distribution of Gas	6		1909092	429371
水的生产和供应业	Production and Distribution of Water	1		***	***

注：1. 行业划分执行2011年国民经济行业分类标准(GB/T 4754-2011)。
2. 应交税金合计包括应交增值税、应交所得税、营业税金及附加和管理费用中的税金。
3. 2013年从业人员平均人数口径有变化，与往年数据不可比。

FOREIGN-INVESTED INDUSTRIAL ENTERPRISES ABOVE DESIGNATED SIZE (BY SECTOR) (2013)

(10000 yuan)

工业销售产值(当年价格) Sales Value of Industry (at current year's prices)	#出口交货值 Delivery Value of Exports	从业人员平均人数(人) Average Number of Employed Persons (person)	资产负债 Assets and Liabilities: 资产总计 Total Assets	流动资产合计 Total Current Assets	#存货 Inventories	#产成品 Finished Products	#应收账款 Accounts Receivable	固定资产合计 Total Fixed Assets
66933148	**12318523**	**403045**	**64388254**	**39579857**	**8328605**	**2532003**	**10910286**	**12045391**
***	***	***	***	***	***	***	***	***
650628	64245	9922	481856	309854	134189	47917	71417	118332
1720589	101882	32014	2028668	1171260	217491	127829	321344	503975
1404096	14337	20135	1476885	671535	133750	46069	101464	380689
96916	23209	1434	87040	57616	19040	11291	24765	23936
350901	212917	14458	410193	344030	161132	83624	64580	43677
***	***	***	***	***	***	***	***	***
***	***	***	***	***	***	***	***	***
269761	26101	4245	204375	138436	42706	21388	43218	49109
483165	46382	3395	418881	276474	72760	17023	89912	114646
251244	4042	4915	341558	224584	41175	18616	57953	101451
128232	61900	3095	155071	132254	70615	51259	20447	13096
***	***	***	***	***	***	***	***	***
1027164	67731	10621	1291161	726210	118166	48176	217920	459018
2876502	38005	25907	2789657	2073622	517944	243813	562914	327036
383277	65820	7674	399560	261242	57124	30328	91330	108604
597372	37632	8660	833640	572516	171451	30250	218539	172942
411410	40438	1533	235043	187917	61771	21528	96578	16967
79527	16734	929	120943	84223	23856	7263	20358	20827
879683	68251	9895	1310329	901657	223163	58606	251679	195372
3411195	682642	26600	4376523	3498955	1180397	316157	793853	630384
1607103	444836	18925	3089972	2140236	429919	107181	620498	269797
26904905	215675	74658	20139399	11629898	1609325	770208	2802980	4032621
133314	214	922	154752	140870	34195	12219	54141	11089
2492383	555548	19049	4243629	3571911	989335	93997	1464079	258466
16693059	9341140	76391	10568009	7710195	1640361	308164	2036749	2008839
779725	81434	7847	1039415	852247	207939	32654	303941	67981
34608	18717	1002	29746	16212	6185	2864	4073	10060
303392	75919	6258	381821	202672	54871	2646	105554	166656
586389		1388	3600396	516140	13831		108396	674644
1909092		7847	3537319	754240	4330	890	267047	1160382
***	***	***	***	***	***	***	***	***

Note: a) Sectors in this table are classified in accordance with the Standard for Classification of National Economic Sectors 2011 (GB/T 4754-2011).
b) Total tax payable mainly includes VAT payable, income tax payable, business tax and surtax, and tax in management expenses.
c) The statistical scope of average number of employed persons changed in 2013, so data of 2013 are not comparable with past ones.

11-13 续表

单位：万元

项目	Item	资产负债 Assets and Liabilities 固定资产原价 Total Original Value of Fixed Assets	负债合计 Total Liabilities	#流动负债合计 Total Current Liabilities	#应付账款 Accounts Payable
合计	**Total**	**22460406**	**34683829**	**29481875**	**13584077**
开采辅助活动	Mining Support Service Activities	***	***	***	***
农副食品加工业	Processing of Food from Agricultural Products	223269	322860	304358	111493
食品制造业	Manufacture of Foods	927981	1198730	1129323	117827
酒、饮料和精制茶制造业	Manufacture of Wines, Beverage and Refined Tea	744312	855171	760600	240676
纺织业	Manufacture of Textile	56108	51817	51470	13137
纺织服装、服饰业	Manufacture of Textile Wearing Apparel and Ornament	91069	293222	286091	88349
皮革、毛皮、羽毛及其制品和制鞋业	Manufacture of Leather, Fur, Feather and Its Products, and Footwear	***	***	***	***
木材加工和木、竹、藤、棕、草制品业	Processing of Timbers, Manufacture of Wood, Bamboo, Rattan, Palm, and Straw Products	***	***	***	***
家具制造业	Manufacture of Furniture	68672	102558	97593	22886
造纸和纸制品业	Manufacture of Paper and Paper Products	267050	209071	206643	67995
印刷和记录媒介复制业	Printing, Reproduction of Recording Media	252457	104322	97940	33819
文教、工美、体育和娱乐用品制造业	Manufacture of Articles for Culture, Education, Artwork, Sport and Entertainment Activities	25141	76718	76521	24403
石油加工、炼焦和核燃料加工业	Processing of Petroleum, Coking, Processing of Mucleus Fuels	***	***	***	***
化学原料和化学制品制造业	Manufacture of Chemical Raw Materials and Chemical Products	781902	562977	421194	138307
医药制造业	Manufacture of Medicines	545662	1332842	1210310	415996
橡胶和塑料制品业	Manufacture of Rubber and Plastics Products	230368	169440	167296	72825
非金属矿物制品业	Manufacture of Non-metallic Mineral Products	388879	418398	406647	151677
黑色金属冶炼和压延加工业	Manufacture and Pressing of Ferrous Metals	55617	123559	87424	67619
有色金属冶炼和压延加工业	Manufacture and Pressing of Non-ferrous Metals	35866	20927	19108	12280
金属制品业	Manufacture of Fabricated Metal Products	403095	558464	506779	137390
通用设备制造业	Manufacture of General-purpose Machinery	1147596	2093784	1955626	788617
专用设备制造业	Manufacture of Special-purpose Machinery	449435	1820428	1661098	653445
汽车制造业	Manufacture of Motor Vehicles	6134384	11346779	9506755	5329327
铁路、船舶、航空航天和其他运输设备制造业	Manufacture of Railway Locomotives, Building of Ships and Boats, Manufacture of Air and Spacecrafts and Other Transportation Equipment	20282	108611	108611	49743
电气机械和器材制造业	Manufacture of Electrical Machinery and Equipment	622240	2179380	1831612	969896
计算机、通信和其他电子设备制造业	Manufacture of Computers, Communication Equipment and Other Electronic Equipment	5226365	6769013	5818217	3454789
仪器仪表制造业	Manufacture of Measuring Instruments and Meters	144042	584537	567592	306634
其他制造业	Other Manufacturing	22491	11546	11406	5110
金属制品、机械和设备修理业	Repair of Fabricated Metal Products, Machinery and Equipment	305556	212936	210789	24249
电力、热力生产和供应业	Production and Distribution of Electricity and Heating Power	1584781	1605884	677274	95662
燃气生产和供应业	Production and Distribution of Gas	1533461	1219354	1027171	66457
水的生产和供应业	Production and Distribution of Water	***	***	***	***

11-13 Continued

(10000 yuan)

所有者权益合计 Total Owner's Equity	#实收资本 Paid-up Capital	损益 Profits and Loss								应交税金合计 Total Tax Payable	#营业税金及附加 Business Tax and Surtax		#应交增值税 Value Added Tax Payable
		营业收入 Business Income	#主营业务收入 Main Business Income	营业成本 Business Cost	#主营业务成本 Main Business Cost	销售费用 Sales Expenses	管理费用 Management Expenses	财务费用 Financial Expenses	利润总额 Total Profits			#主营业务税金及附加 Main Business Tax and Surtax	
29697734	**14775213**	**74803752**	**73306362**	**60087093**	**58963704**	**5127399**	**3272541**	**252142**	**5728424**	**4916005**	**1311184**	**1304710**	**2310783**
***	***	***	***	***	***	***	***	***	***	***	***	***	***
158996	136078	723584	709094	617194	607079	58647	38437	7612	5464	16997	1248	1248	11011
829937	804501	3270722	3204600	2082811	2025191	866282	180987	1800	144487	233475	21261	21261	171802
621714	716785	1585003	1512277	1106579	1043514	328088	82706	8025	54548	128697	20175	19991	86799
35223	27678	110089	109252	93368	92835	3009	6251	1550	5571	3877	469	469	1585
116971	92420	419383	413725	322697	317314	45896	38951	5140	8590	16917	1342	1331	10172
***	***	***	***	***	***	***	***	***	***	***	***	***	***
***	***	***	***	***	***	***	***	***	***	***	***	***	***
101818	39098	212454	204848	153260	148322	23381	20026	1613	12760	11219	1845	1845	7972
209810	141206	519989	514361	388990	385043	18780	23186	-987	104221	56053	2596	2596	27652
237236	138718	265108	260174	198776	196525	13863	23809	-125	25361	27067	1820	1820	16259
78353	15761	132645	131635	106670	106285	6855	11321	1497	4758	7598	739	739	5180
***	***	***	***	***	***	***	***	***	***	***	***	***	***
728184	463506	1077689	1069350	755993	750920	167456	72920	6652	63530	100591	12589	12589	60847
1456814	559326	3186917	3003843	1376156	1219448	1101945	249016	71093	380772	399833	32802	32786	276927
230120	146267	447461	432868	357868	346115	21040	32240	700	37794	30758	2393	2393	18263
415242	245550	620727	612073	486394	481773	32160	48101	7492	47343	42343	3816	3812	27978
104793	43806	431732	430139	386950	385407	12441	7302	-3141	27292	17175	1255	1255	8157
100016	28112	86653	79479	79767	73223	1588	4708	264	1239	1375	71	44	953
751865	285652	1106837	1034551	887255	821616	62096	74118	8548	98702	56909	3971	3971	35758
2282739	921201	3731470	3648473	2940512	2886315	212683	221417	-7124	336879	226570	15842	15841	122092
1269544	487796	2178343	2028686	1620822	1532890	129488	239218	12253	197382	128857	9290	9260	78227
8792621	3760651	27550089	27090598	22316448	21960367	1060898	766607	49557	2735060	2645323	1103852	1098349	888702
46142	20584	150158	148480	112167	111096	4019	9343	-251	25128	12947	811	811	6305
2064249	862685	2821314	2667898	2169079	2021515	136319	157036	22428	260219	156628	15214	15143	98223
3798997	2635669	19688275	19556810	17873698	17822696	668613	652126	-22596	526987	242866	25289	25251	111460
454878	171496	973387	961426	705857	701043	90262	69889	1258	107729	70436	5612	5543	39357
18200	17598	35581	35563	29344	29344	2020	4767	474	-1153	1259	196	196	856
168885	135812	314541	305756	226994	223560	1775	77088	3301	13983	18760	1157	1120	10983
1994512	1269348	593774	587226	502461	498649		29840	54138	159087	56800	4203	4203	34446
2317965	430482	1928679	1914615	1677942	1666579	23411	91697	17185	292149	167433	16523	16041	133720
***	***	***	***	***	***	***	***	***	***	***	***	***	***

11-14 大中型工业企业主要经济指标(2013年)

单位：万元

项 目	Item	企业单位个数(个) Number of Enterprises (unit)	#亏损企业 Loss-Suffering Enterprises	工业总产值(当年价格) Gross Output Value of Industry (at current year's prices)	工业增加值 Added Value of Industry
合 计	**Total**	**777**	**128**	**139412608**	**28809659**
在合计中：	**Of the Total:**				
中央工业	Central Industry	108	20	53606764	9871734
地方工业	Local Industry	669	108	85805844	18937925
在合计中：	**Of the Total:**				
内资企业	Domestially-Invested Enterprises	507	89	79840440	16347504
国有企业	State-owned Enterprises	38	5	30694456	5194358
集体企业	Collectively-owned Enterprises	4		99520	57669
股份合作企业	Joint-equity Cooperative Enterprises	2	***	***	***
联营企业	Associated Enterprises				
有限责任公司	Limited Liability Companies	253	59	26737888	5837342
股份有限公司	Companies Limited by Shares	108	16	19510665	4504554
私营企业	Private Enterprises	102	8	2710512	701234
港澳台商投资企业	Hong Kong, Macao and Taiwan-invested Enterprises	69	13	9867722	1426085
港澳台合资经营	Joint Ventures	35	6	2577830	676554
港澳台合作经营	Cooperatives	2	***	***	***
港澳台商独资企业	Solely-funded Enterprises	25	5	6332880	659149
港澳台商投资股份有限公司	Companies Limited by Shares	7	1	929724	76037
外商投资企业	Foreign-invested Enterprises	201	26	49704447	11036070
中外合资经营	Joint Ventures	83	5	33130819	7422323
中外合作经营	Cooperatives	4	1	161205	78652
外资(独资)企业	Solely-funded Enterprises	105	18	15418503	3183239
外商投资股份有限公司	Companies Limited by Shares	9	2	993919	351856
在合计中：	**Of the Total:**				
#农村企业	Rural Enterprises	13	3	604550	114872
在合计中：	**Of the Total:**				
轻工业	Light Industry	287	47	17465440	5642485
重工业	Heavy Industry	490	81	121947169	23167174
在合计中：	**Of the Total:**				
#大型企业	Large Enterprises	164	24	109655442	21814950

注：2013年从业人员平均人数口径有变化，与往年数据不可比。

MAIN ECONOMIC INDICATORS OF LOCAL MEDIUM AND LARGE-SIZED INDUSTRIAL ENTERPRISES (2013)

(10000 yuan)

工业销售产值（当年价格） Sales Value of Industry (at current year's prices)	#出口交货值 Delivery Value of Exports	从业人员平均人数（人） Average Number of Employed Persons (person)	资产负债 Assets and Liabilities: 资产总计 Total Assets	流动资产合计 Total Current Assets	#存货 Inventories	#产成品 Finished Products	#应收账款 Accounts Receivable	固定资产合计 Total Fixed Assets
137994456	**13437468**	**841007**	**265122188**	**98397315**	**15610816**	**4418315**	**23287768**	**54289327**
53406252	407876	163271	138490169	32443831	3715214	632624	6487493	28617964
84588204	13029592	677736	126632019	65953484	11895603	3785691	16800276	25671363
79039581	2100363	512886	212809529	66172718	9090886	2496445	14693226	44134365
30648898	42547	43102	108333482	19684220	1122263	121196	2696015	20391019
96351		2829	104173	71131	16678	2287	5915	27068
***	***	***	***	***	***	***	***	***
26303473	1172109	246571	64758601	25454272	3966834	1041011	7271336	18959619
19353218	739034	163590	36223976	18755026	3418964	1100105	3948787	4210152
2539605	131335	53876	3288433	2140016	540756	210357	757772	517453
9808126	1201889	71122	11689078	8593154	1990604	352861	2515549	1434441
2563575	262643	31401	2603721	1336190	328776	121443	491079	946057
***	***	***	***	***	***	***	***	***
6162536	759695	31882	5026047	4098407	684360	196797	787706	394649
1055710	179550	7122	4032671	3135563	972429	30298	1226945	90092
49146748	10135216	256999	40623582	23631442	4529326	1569010	6078994	8720522
32683960	7962937	121209	23016574	14105674	2731648	879576	2641987	4191610
157532	27494	5705	251919	194493	6740	1359	45518	40689
15332211	2076899	114998	14991543	8461155	1661776	642723	3182897	4121226
973045	67886	15087	2363546	870120	129162	45352	208592	366998
607369	16775	7917	449190	351388	59108	18400	234344	76685
17008965	1218890	253093	23846476	13735518	3137597	1331495	2750877	4661175
120985490	12218578	587914	241275711	84661797	12473219	3086820	20536892	49628152
108826095	11120467	512709	219020399	69316320	9103173	2704230	13460575	46407329

Note: The statistical scope of average number of employed persons changed in 2013, so data of 2013 are not comparable with past ones.

11-14 续表

单位：万元

项目	Item	资产负债 Assets and Liabilities				
		固定资产原价 Total Original Value of Fixed Assets	负债合计 Total Liabilities	#流动负债合计 Total Current Liabilities	#应付账款 Accounts Payable	所有者权益合计 Total Owner's Equity
合计	**Total**	**97262966**	**138068519**	**81922347**	**26557719**	**127053668**
在合计中：	**Of the Total:**					
中央工业	Central Industry	55089163	70872607	34046555	8268320	67617562
地方工业	Local Industry	42173803	67195913	47875793	18289400	59436106
在合计中：	**Of the Total:**					
内资企业	Domestially-Invested Enterprises	78211160	109524033	57325541	15097484	103285496
国有企业	State-owned Enterprises	37430097	53814851	19819731	3521741	54518631
集体企业	Collectively-owned Enterprises	63561	43896	41492	9220	60277
股份合作企业	Joint-equity Cooperative Enterprises	***	***	***	***	***
联营企业	Associated Enterprises					
有限责任公司	Limited Liability Companies	30965576	36969988	22670297	7218383	27788613
股份有限公司	Companies Limited by Shares	8918093	17008970	13308201	3766611	19215006
私营企业	Private Enterprises	794474	1644264	1458864	570299	1644169
港澳台商投资企业	Hong Kong, Macao and Taiwan-invested Enterprises	2866508	7665503	6964821	3368722	4023574
港澳台合资经营	Joint Ventures	1945587	1449278	1321968	496416	1154443
港澳台合作经营	Cooperatives	***	***	***	***	***
港澳台商独资企业	Solely-funded Enterprises	740264	3930428	3805301	2086697	1095619
港澳台商投资股份有限公司	Companies Limited by Shares	174705	2281675	1833429	784818	1750996
外商投资企业	Foreign-invested Enterprises	16185298	20878983	17631986	8091513	19744598
中外合资经营	Joint Ventures	7707197	12443973	10582359	5284602	10572601
中外合作经营	Cooperatives	109948	135528	124075	59026	116391
外资(独资)企业	Solely-funded Enterprises	7683581	7713703	6423011	2585425	7277840
外商投资股份有限公司	Companies Limited by Shares	684572	585779	502541	162460	1777766
在合计中：	**Of the Total:**					
#农村企业	Rural Enterprises	136693	311388	279573	151662	137802
在合计中：	**Of the Total:**					
轻工业	Light Industry	8736906	11542985	9757140	2299627	12303491
重工业	Heavy Industry	88526060	126525534	72165207	24258093	114750177
在合计中：	**Of the Total:**					
#大型企业	Large Enterprises	83588899	113267462	61166358	18826023	105752937

注：应交税金合计包括应交增值税、应交所得税、营业税金及附加和管理费用中的税金。

11-14 Continued

(10000 yuan)

	损益 Profits and Losses											
#实收资本 Paid-up Capital	营业收入 Business Income	#主营业务收入 Main Business Income	营业成本 Business Cost	#主营业务成本 Main Business Cost	销售费用 Sales Expenses	管理费用 Management Expenses	财务费用 Financial Expenses	利润总额 Total Profits	应交税金合计 Total Tax Payable	#营业税金及附加 Business Tax and Surtax	#主营业务税金及附加 Main Business Tax and Surtax	#应交增值税 Value Added Tax Payable
55295118	**152611823**	**149562961**	**129128105**	**126655188**	**6753021**	**6180051**	**1777191**	**10849858**	**9160890**	**2689540**	**2666311**	**4421617**
28221023	55821211	54854232	50813685	49948641	338787	1387278	1145462	3622460	3163201	1090980	1085817	1450826
27074095	96790612	94708729	78314420	76706548	6414234	4792773	631729	7227398	5997690	1598560	1580495	2970791
44033320	86888715	85132127	76276821	74782388	2131464	3587277	1586095	5845243	4781199	1417680	1400615	2423262
20714864	30860262	30733623	28240490	28149846	131967	270586	942375	3220273	1749590	413840	412497	864899
11403	98522	92434	71274	66037	5572	13327	-830	7290	13579	1945	1945	10135
***	***	***	***	***	***	***	***	***	***	***	***	***
16975828	31553551	30641636	28509697	27713963	660727	1689873	427979	692202	1084836	136557	126684	741163
5805479	21496056	20822068	17321756	16744470	1053057	1364338	196136	1691081	1765913	849671	844288	694750
513746	2780330	2743500	2079853	2054577	260313	241366	20244	216544	157285	14863	14396	104683
1874340	13363875	12943402	11270208	10925652	1097405	605760	60916	309704	319900	36969	36792	207327
645015	2952216	2776078	2403870	2244987	172563	139107	26340	207762	169885	18830	18819	99208
***	***	***	***	***	***	***	***	***	***	***	***	***
545184	8971390	8910294	7624471	7614193	867292	375207	-13852	149045	110681	9475	9309	72705
677373	1399731	1216855	1213177	1037952	54290	87011	48317	-50829	35304	8304	8304	32414
9387457	52359233	51487431	41581076	40947149	3524152	1987014	130180	4694911	4059792	1234891	1228905	1791028
4713188	33432922	33150209	26799529	26653680	1584223	1060316	60692	3237655	2864135	1132376	1126828	1022457
145207	350821	341659	288634	281779	39580	11960	-2611	12822	22535	1764	1764	15337
3782381	17478972	16952366	13741829	13304692	1781161	825297	62411	1228282	1086907	94011	93585	703104
746681	1096518	1043197	751084	706997	119188	89441	9689	216152	86215	6740	6728	50131
58655	616058	603775	544568	534187	14500	33221	5010	24945	27307	2626	2626	16948
5314500	19952769	19335482	12760108	12312012	3516848	1504902	134973	1935865	2025449	510833	508986	1103714
49980618	132659054	130227479	116367996	114343177	3236173	4675150	1642218	8913993	7135441	2178707	2157325	3317902
44690206	119579272	117747960	103151595	101639571	4707630	3624734	1504030	8428331	7021282	2279586	2260495	3234847

Note: Total tax payable mainly includes VAT payable, income tax payable, business tax and surtax, and tax in management expenses.

11-15 大中型工业企业主要经济指标(按行业分)(2013年)

单位：万元

项目	Item	企业单位个数(个) Number of Enterprises (unit)	#亏损企业 Loss-Suffering Enterprises	工业总产值(当年价格) Gross Output Value of Industry (at current year's prices)	工业增加值 Added Value of Industry
合计	**Total**	**777**	**128**	**139412608**	**28809659**
煤炭开采和洗选业	Mining and Washing of Coal	1		***	***
石油和天然气开采业	Extraction of Petroleum and Natural Gas	2	***	***	***
黑色金属矿采选业	Mining and Processing of Ferrous Metal Ores	6		1625222	394685
开采辅助活动	Mining Support Service Activities	4	2	2074316	901664
农副食品加工业	Processing of Food from Agricultural Products	27	5	2407960	372926
食品制造业	Manufacture of Foods	40	8	1961317	246665
酒、饮料和精制茶制造业	Manufacture of Wines, Beverage and Refined Tea	15	4	1918314	607369
烟草制品业	Manufacture of Cigarettes and Tobacco	1		***	***
纺织业	Manufacture of Textile	4	1	16712	-2831
纺织服装、服饰业	Manufacture of Textile Wearing Apparel and Ornament	44	13	990025	439331
皮革、毛皮、羽毛及其制品和制鞋业	Manufacture of Leather, Fur, Feather and Its Products, and Footwear	3		***	***
木材加工和木、竹、藤、棕、草制品业	Processing of Timbers, Manufacture of Wood, Bamboo, Rattan, Palm, and Straw Products	3		***	***
家具制造业	Manufacture of Furniture	11	1	470211	146239
造纸和纸制品业	Manufacture of Paper and Paper Products	6		412662	151489
印刷和记录媒介复制业	Printing, Reproduction of Recording Media	19	1	625620	295801
文教、工美、体育和娱乐用品制造业	Manufacture of Articles for Culture, Education, Artwork, Sport and Entertainment Activities	7	1	417701	35868
石油加工、炼焦和核燃料加工业	Processing of Petroleum, Coking, Processing of Mucleus Fuels	5	2	7074286	955717
化学原料和化学制品制造业	Manufacture of Chemical Raw Materials and Chemical Products	24	7	1674958	315766
医药制造业	Manufacture of Medicines	52	4	4751667	2103330
化学纤维制造业	Manufacture of Chemical fibres	1		***	***
橡胶和塑料制品业	Manufacture of Rubber and Plastics Products	17	2	507744	140846
非金属矿物制品业	Manufacture of Non-metallic Mineral Products	43	5	2838956	536511
黑色金属冶炼和压延加工业	Manufacture and Pressing of Ferrous Metals	6	1	1007124	38428
有色金属冶炼和压延加工业	Manufacture and Pressing of Non-ferrous Metals	5		198709	52686
金属制品业	Manufacture of Fabricated Metal Products	34	4	1574773	292607
通用设备制造业	Manufacture of General-purpose Machinery	45	8	3547131	883655
专用设备制造业	Manufacture of Special-purpose Machinery	53	7	3925804	1007452
汽车制造业	Manufacture of Motor Vehicles	63	8	30130543	6883613
铁路、船舶、航空航天和其他运输设备制造业	Manufacture of Railway Locomotives, Building of Ships and Boats, Manufacture of Air and Spacecrafts and Other Transportation Equipment	19	4	1942043	525716
电气机械和器材制造业	Manufacture of Electrical Machinery and Equipment	50	11	5056927	938751
计算机、通信和其他电子设备制造业	Manufacture of Computers, Communication Equipment and Other Electronic Equipment	89	15	19927237	2551878
仪器仪表制造业	Manufacture of Measuring Instrument and Meter	34	2	1230015	341148
其他制造业	Other Manufacturing	8		655114	188842
金属制品、机械和设备修理业	Repair of Fabricated Metal Products, Machinery and Equipment	1		***	***
电力、热力生产和供应业	Production and Distribution of Electricity and Heating Power	28	10	36815652	6003001
燃气生产和供应业	Production and Distribution of Gas	3	***	***	***
水的生产和供应业	Production and Distribution of Water	4		356565	136397

注：1. 行业划分执行2011年国民经济行业分类标准(GB/T 4754-2011)。
2. 应交税金合计包括应交增值税、应交所得税、营业税金及附加和管理费用中的税金。
3. 2013年从业人员平均人数口径有变化，与往年数据不可比。

MAIN ECONOMIC INDICATORS OF MEDIUM AND LARGE-SIZED INDUSTRIAL ENTERPRISES (BY SECTOR) (2013)

工业销售产值(当年价格) Sales Value of Industry (at current year's prices)	#出口交货值 Delivery Value of Exports	从业人员平均人数(人) Average Number of Employed Persons (person)	资产负债 Assets and Liabilities: 资产总计 Total Assets	流动资产合计 Total Current Assets	#存货 Inventories	#产成品 Finished Products	#应收账款 Accounts Receivable	固定资产合计 Total Fixed Assets	固定资产原价 Total Original Value of Fixed Assets
137994456	**13437468**	**841007**	**265122188**	**98397315**	**15610816**	**4418315**	**23287768**	**54289327**	**97262966**
***	***	***	***	***	***	***	***	***	***
***	***	***	***	***	***	***	***	***	***
1624043		25849	19588772	6265608	299359	49764	1442968	3721280	4740534
2042595	156039	23705	4971487	2485061	352663	10926	1009373	1176649	2315191
2388113	31872	23301	2531172	1752410	305189	166250	164845	270405	449386
1869735	102025	41427	2196160	1270493	233739	128114	347350	535640	945083
1910484	18292	29443	3158951	1337963	236438	64676	110241	495524	1080298
***	***	***	***	***	***	***	***	***	***
19135	2019	1955	231550	143630	19131	8054	6369	54112	80855
882393	215943	34315	1062913	814517	373551	236940	142522	126014	226495
***	***	***	***	***	***	***	***	***	***
***	***	***	***	***	***	***	***	***	***
464681	25288	9368	500444	286126	64139	28785	86282	121071	158185
403991	17604	2519	292788	192277	58627	13362	36218	69984	182719
633533	6489	13934	944593	471575	125896	50448	79579	360046	849469
408589	37011	4301	270317	172624	70938	49867	23218	54138	99889
7105097		14510	2792580	1226444	728510	170715	133468	814150	2718629
1641333	37309	20101	2895633	1713998	185359	76902	277406	527242	1463879
4729199	42519	51911	6942019	4305083	1044024	441733	957347	860651	1356068
***	***	***	***	***	***	***	***	***	***
515681	104830	11112	880777	423643	70592	37504	96409	128780	239588
2826520	105187	36515	5348916	3579239	740278	137214	1652911	675612	1227701
992243	73498	6759	2310071	343128	155471	46533	52860	839562	1920107
196609	57062	2929	277514	188581	54546	17956	68062	44248	70926
1617311	140361	17732	2789694	1554588	407463	104959	324833	433332	701185
3451469	598388	35280	5707809	4172674	1289722	387884	1031423	786286	1399355
3822274	509012	44417	9785623	6029854	1024534	293454	1480608	696565	1159705
29877494	444894	110232	26480552	13921983	1942241	969318	3070647	5158560	7532595
1876852	4586	12702	3650931	2522550	1089237	62184	706321	828759	961481
4942860	562173	36365	8200166	6457637	1410411	200179	3041125	487288	973497
19563043	9843826	109872	19878107	12852713	2461225	518179	3234090	4149049	8348606
1215652	48186	15063	1847600	1361655	374255	75618	357857	168304	291599
522193		1560	1162297	700484	146693	19201	254869	269005	464957
***	***	***	***	***	***	***	***	***	***
									***
36815842		58302	116758506	18756318	107592	1171	2438107	26188481	48839249
***	***	***	***	***	***	***	***	***	***
348154		8257	4955068	1240577	8617	4070	203501	2566683	3966698

Note: a) Sectors in this table are classified in accordance with the Standard for Classification of National Economic Sectors 2011 (GB/T 4754-2011).
b) Total tax payable mainly includes VAT payable, income tax payable, business tax and surtax, and tax in management expenses.
c) The statistical scope of average number of employed persons changed in 2013, so data of 2013 are not comparable with past ones.

11-15 续表

单位：万元

项目	Item	资产负债 Assets and Liabilities			
		负债合计 Total Liabilities	#流动负债合计 Total Current Liabilities	#应付账款 Accounts Payable	所有者权益合计 Total Owner's Equity
合计	**Total**	**138068519**	**81922347**	**26557719**	**127053668**
煤炭开采和洗选业	Mining and Washing of Coal	***	***	***	***
石油和天然气开采业	Extraction of Petroleum and Natural Gas	***	***	***	***
黑色金属矿采选业	Mining and Processing of Ferrous Metal Ores	11439675	3748693	1085057	8149097
开采辅助活动	Mining Support Service Activities	2070755	1909107	691472	2900732
农副食品加工业	Processing of Food from Agricultural Products	1491099	1355629	136671	1040073
食品制造业	Manufacture of Foods	1383171	1275009	148155	812989
酒、饮料和精制茶制造业	Manufacture of Wines, Beverage and Refined Tea	1400713	1298546	252377	1758238
烟草制品业	Manufacture of Cigarettes and Tobacco	***	***	***	***
纺织业	Manufacture of Textile	101642	30000	5063	129908
纺织服装、服饰业	Manufacture of Textile Wearing Apparel and Ornament	609757	572826	185867	453156
皮革、毛皮、羽毛及其制品和制鞋业	Manufacture of Leather, Fur, Feather and Its Products, and Footwear	***	***	***	***
木材加工和木、竹、藤、棕、草制品业	Processing of Timbers, Manufacture of Wood, Bamboo, Rattan, Palm, and Straw Products	***	***	***	***
家具制造业	Manufacture of Furniture	269057	221344	51014	231387
造纸和纸制品业	Manufacture of Paper and Paper Products	174046	173924	48805	118742
印刷和记录媒介复制业	Printing, Reproduction of Recording Media	296908	278988	78064	647685
文教、工美、体育和娱乐用品制造业	Manufacture of Articles for Culture, Education, Artwork, Sport and Entertainment Activities	144431	114734	32754	125886
石油加工、炼焦和核燃料加工业	Processing of Petroleum, Coking, Processing of Mucleus Fuels	1623737	1620559	703581	1168843
化学原料和化学制品制造业	Manufacture of Chemical Raw Materials and Chemical Products	1739351	1571857	172217	1156281
医药制造业	Manufacture of Medicines	3124566	2550397	726868	3817453
化学纤维制造业	Manufacture of Chemical fibres	***	***	***	***
橡胶和塑料制品业	Manufacture of Rubber and Plastics Products	427440	329754	77855	453337
非金属矿物制品业	Manufacture of Non-metallic Mineral Products	3065974	2817958	1066927	2282942
黑色金属冶炼和压延加工业	Manufacture and Pressing of Ferrous Metals	1320525	486167	217683	989546
有色金属冶炼和压延加工业	Manufacture and Pressing of Non-ferrous Metals	100986	94424	48008	176528
金属制品业	Manufacture of Fabricated Metal Products	1328897	1113173	335034	1460797
通用设备制造业	Manufacture of General-purpose Machinery	2476242	2305077	837907	3231567
专用设备制造业	Manufacture of Special-purpose Machinery	5265921	4191082	1473020	4519701
汽车制造业	Manufacture of Motor Vehicles	15192829	12554205	6068669	11287723
铁路、船舶、航空航天和其他运输设备制造业	Manufacture of Railway Locomotives, Building of Ships and Boats, Manufacture of Air and Spacecrafts and Other Transportation Equipment	2516084	2047966	636061	1134847
电气机械和器材制造业	Manufacture of Electrical Machinery and Equipment	4944518	4434986	1806524	3255648
计算机、通信和其他电子设备制造业	Manufacture of Computers, Communication Equipment and Other Electronic Equipment	11017144	8691119	4121359	8860963
仪器仪表制造业	Manufacture of Measuring Instrument and Meter	904493	807736	306001	943108
其他制造业	Other Manufacturing	464338	340641	188075	697959
金属制品、机械和设备修理业	Repair of Fabricated Metal Products, Machinery and Equipment	***	***	***	***
电力、热力生产和供应业	Production and Distribution of Electricity and Heating Power	58497954	22493462	4729760	58260551
燃气生产和供应业	Production and Distribution of Gas	***	***	***	***
水的生产和供应业	Production and Distribution of Water	2101283	689873	42481	2853784

11-15 Continued

(10000 yuan)

#实收资本 Paid-up Capital	损益 Profits and Losses: 营业收入 Business Income	#主营业务收入 Main Business Income	营业成本 Business Cost	#主营业务成本 Main Business Cost	销售费用 Sales Expenses	管理费用 Management Expenses	财务费用 Financial Expenses	利润总额 Total Profits	应交税金合计 Total Tax Payable	#营业税金及附加 Business Tax and Surtax	#主营业务税金及附加 Main Business Tax and Surtax	#应交增值税 Value Added Tax Payable
55295118	**1.53E+08**	**149562961**	**1.29E+08**	**126655188**	**6753021**	**6180051**	**1777191**	**10849858**	**9160890**	**2689540**	**2666311**	**4421617**
***	***	***	***	***	***	***	***	***	***	***	***	***
***	***	***	***	***	***	***	***	***	***	***	***	***
2861339	4757983	4549753	4459478	4250862	4009	113452	119858	110290	136941	21554	17411	102410
2537251	2081478	2068903	1956373	1946700	9946	81639	31335	-81459	66677	30994	30909	24154
443633	2575771	2560763	2072899	2066202	190838	110272	25815	133542	148128	76975	76964	44486
804520	3421083	3352852	2184382	2125049	910451	186173	5642	145657	244901	21971	21901	179860
574922	2128488	2011148	1467438	1369096	379742	111392	10185	109455	241769	85068	84783	128523
***	***	***	***	***	***	***	***	***	***	***	***	***
90747	47996	43940	35976	35297	453	13278	943	-3275	2526	749	552	956
176909	991853	980521	592752	585819	188278	103557	6925	96479	86754	6955	6944	60178
***	***	***	***	***	***	***	***	***	***	***	***	***
***	***	***	***	***	***	***	***	***	***	***	***	***
76322	420455	410938	314490	308071	37527	35441	5082	32627	29537	3487	3406	20419
54088	442068	432016	320638	312038	17267	18714	-334	95906	47787	2426	2426	22129
378697	677027	638596	497039	474044	17771	96279	-858	67192	61723	5172	4843	36673
82013	513175	502109	475764	474668	9152	26584	5049	4094	6942	1175	720	3586
45041	8102240	7513739	7258882	6679537	58011	227013	24279	-123646	795256	612835	611685	154429
1016289	1731066	1701859	1393648	1371009	164368	152830	29149	-30581	86677	12877	12812	65033
1072447	5079034	4858651	2302647	2118258	1469976	432819	84415	906993	638961	51798	51621	426273
***	***	***	***	***	***	***	***	***	***	***	***	***
187001	602106	592372	476880	469208	18782	45942	14906	46602	33907	2741	2729	21761
885577	3226363	3146096	2680281	2610628	143748	209965	52006	182951	118199	20239	19433	69314
593174	1078350	1063779	1041146	1029440	39230	23111	21358	-17231	10497	1184	1124	6290
36800	222575	214911	185849	179957	4347	16090	2405	13419	6170	630	603	3288
583140	1933002	1838218	1562984	1491407	62503	157245	17154	157255	70838	9011	7334	38169
1225686	3755866	3657465	2965033	2899209	209864	251380	-6126	317358	217847	17631	17514	124132
1802899	4393158	4154535	3388195	3218816	245497	425625	42638	512501	281160	30181	29831	195680
4853738	30743589	30163170	25269229	24823012	1180527	1015609	55285	2755305	2731500	1139572	1133681	935493
509735	2023186	2005206	1688750	1677298	23232	181677	15065	127026	65978	5756	5653	40933
1643910	5279468	5112167	4254114	4090309	290615	326196	60533	316018	227415	23639	23636	153068
5528714	23518604	23307670	20785198	20682821	901719	1083976	50870	982225	374431	42178	40252	190373
296268	1449730	1431617	1043852	1033302	107548	144547	5098	206295	103384	9000	8848	61004
260917	663475	660143	509487	507904	13655	74072	-1402	71527	33396	2333	2328	19350
***	***	***	***	***	***	***	***	***	***	***	***	***
23107479	36959796	36857204	34936143	34855200	4733	163077	1074714	3281270	1680675	172994	169327	1017582
***	***	***	***	***	***	***	***	***	***	***	***	***
2537251	442671	437405	453347	449841	591	43023	-3397	43578	24801	1992	1479	12076

11-16 规模以上工业企业主要工业产品生产能力(2013年)
CAPACITY OF MAIN INDUSTRIAL PRODUCTS IN INDUSTRIAL ENTERPRISES ABOVE DESIGNATED SIZE (2013)

主要工业产品名称		Name of Main Industrial Products		年末生产能力 Year-end Capacity
原油加工能力	(吨)	Crude Oil Processing Capacity	(ton)	14000000
硅酸盐水泥熟料	(吨)	Portland Cement Chamotte	(ton)	6690000
发电设备容量总计	(万千瓦)	Total Capacity of Power Generation Equipment	(10000 KW)	787
火电设备容量	(万千瓦)	Capacity of Thermal Power Equipment	(10000 KW)	674
水电设备容量	(万千瓦)	Capacity of Hydropower Equipment	(10000 KW)	98
风电设备容量	(万千瓦)	Capacity of Wind Power Equipment	(10000 KW)	15
原　煤	(吨)	Raw Coal	(ton)	5200000
卷　烟	(万支)	Cigarette	(10000 units)	4347000
棉纺锭	(锭)	Knitting Spindles (Ring Spindle Spinning)	(unit)	19360
气流纺锭	(头)	Air Spinning Spindles (Rotating-cup Spinning)	(unit)	1656
棉布织机	(台)	Cotton Cloth Weaver	(unit)	66
水　泥	(吨)	Cement	(ton)	9740000
钢　材	(吨)	Rolled Steel	(ton)	1789316
金属切削机床	(台)	Metal-Cutting Machine Tools	(unit)	23579
汽　车	(辆)	Motor Vehicles	(unit)	2594500
#基本型乘用车(轿车)	(辆)	Basic-type Passenger Vehicles (Sedans)	(unit)	902000
家用电冰箱	(台)	Household Refrigerators	(unit)	1500000
移动通信手持机(手机)	(台)	Mobile Communication Handsets (Mobile Phones)	(unit)	149560318
微型计算机设备	(台)	Micro-computers	(unit)	20325104

11-17 主要工业产品产量(2013年)
OUTPUT OF MAIN INDUSTRIAL PRODUCTS (2013)

工业产品名称		Name of Main Industrial Product		2013
单晶硅	(千克)	Monocrystalline Silicon	(kg)	148918.1
中成药	(万吨)	Finished Traditional Chinese Herbal Medicines	(10000 tons)	4.0
沥青和改性沥青防水卷材	(万平方米)	Asphalt and Modified Asphalt Waterproof Roll Materia	(10000 sq.m)	6428.0
纤维增强塑料制品	(万吨)	Fiber-reinforced Plastic Products	(10000 tons)	2.1
耐火材料制品	(万吨)	Products Made from Fire-resistant Materials	(10000 tons)	50.9
冷轧薄宽钢带	(万吨)	Cold-rolled Thin Broad Steel Bands	(10000 tons)	111.4
单一稀土金属	(千克)	Single Rare Earth Metals	(kg)	136799.0
发动机	(万千瓦)	Engines	(10000 KW)	11482.8
气动元件	(万件)	Pneumatic Components	(10000 units)	19373.4
数控金属切削机床	(台)	Digital Metal Cutting Tools	(unit)	6983
机床数控装置	(套)	CNC Units of Lathe	(unit)	87114
工业电炉	(台)	Industrial Electric Cookers	(unit)	137
环境污染防治专用设备	(台套)	Special Equipment for Prevention and Control of Environmental Pollution	(set)	100223
汽　车	(万辆)	Automobiles	(10000 units)	203.8
#基本型成用车(轿车)	(万辆)	Including: Basic-type Passenger Vehicles (Sedans)	(10000 units)	94.5
运动型多用途乘用车(SUV)	(万辆)	Sport Utility Vehicles(SUV)	(10000 units)	32.9
载货汽车	(万辆)	Freight Trucks	(10000 units)	62.5
改装汽车	(万辆)	Refitted Automobiles	(10000 units)	1.6
风力发电机组	(万千瓦)	Wind Power Generator Units	(10000 KW)	411.6
锂离子电池	(万只)	Lithiums Ion Batteries	(10000 units)	7832.1
移动通信手持机(手机)	(万台)	Mobile Communication Handsets (Mobile Phones)	(10000 units)	18783.4
微型计算机设备	(万台)	Micro-computer Equipment	(10000 units)	1107.0
服务器	(台)	Servers	(unit)	117397
液晶显示模组	(万套)	Liquid Crystal Display Modules	(10000 units)	659.0
显示器	(万台)	Displays	(10000 units)	305.3
集成电路	(亿块)	Integrated Circuits	(100 million pieces)	38.4
彩色电视机	(万台)	Color TV Sets	(10000 units)	100.0

11-18 规模以上高技术制造业主要经济指标(2013年)
MAIN ECONOMIC INDICATORS OF HIGH-TECH MANUFACTURING ENTERPRISES ABOVE DESIGNATED SIZE (2013)

单位: 亿元 (100 million yuan)

项目	Item	工业总产值 Gross Output Value of Industry	主营业务收入 Main Business Income	利润总额 Total Profits	应交税金 Tax Payable
合计	**Total**	**3292.1**	**3719.9**	**287.2**	**156.9**
按登记注册类型分	**Grouped by Registration Type**				
内资	Domestially-Invested Enterprises	1141.0	1272.6	173.1	81.0
国有	State-owned Enterprises	63.4	65.8	6.4	2.6
集体	Collectively-owned Enterprises	1.3	1.3	0.03	0.04
股份合作企业	Joint-equity Cooperative Enterprises	4.1	4.4	0.2	0.3
联营企业	Associated Enterprises				
有限责任公司	Limited Liability Companies	577.0	629.0	58.4	33.3
股份有限公司	Companies Limited by Shares	332.2	403.1	87.3	32.3
私营企业	Private Enterprises	163.0	169.1	20.7	12.4
其他	Others				
港澳台商投资	Hong Kong, Macao and Taiwan-invested Enterprises	653.7	924.5	27.1	12.7
外商投资	Foreign-invested Enterprises	1497.4	1522.8	87.1	63.2
按高技术领域分	**Grouped by Field of High Technology**				
信息化学品制造	Information Chemical Manufacturing	0.5	0.4	0.3	0.1
医药制造业	Pharmaceutics	599.1	609.7	109.9	77.1
航空航天器制造	Aircraft and Spacecraft Manufacturing	87.3	87.4	6.9	0.7
电子及通信设备制造业	Electronic and Communication Equipment Manufacturing	1841.3	1926.0	96.5	46.0
电子计算机及办公设备制造业	Electronic Computer and Office Equipment Manufacturing	406.2	698.5	19.4	5.2
医疗设备及仪器仪表制造业	Medical Equipment, Apparatus and Instrument Manufacturing	355.4	395.6	53.9	27.7
其他	Others	2.2	2.3	0.3	0.1

注: 应交税金合计包括应交增值税、应交所得税、营业税金及附加和管理费用中的税金。

Note: Total tax payable mainly includes VAT payable, income tax payable, business tax and surtax, and tax in management expenses.

11-19 规模以下工业主要指标(2013年)
MAJOR INDICATORS FOR INDUSTRIAL ENTERPRISES BELOW DESIGNATED SIZE (2013)

项目	Item	单位个数(个) Number of Enterprises (unit)	从业人员平均人数(人) Average Number of Employed Persons (person)	工业总产值(当年价格, 万元) Gross Output Value (at year's current prices, 10000 yuan)
合计	**Total**	**27040**	**283502**	**7009286**
法人工业企业	Corporate Industrial Enterprises	18133	241054	6505288
个体经营工业单位	Individual Operated Business	8907	42448	503998

注: 规模以下工业企业指年主营业务收入2000万元以下的法人工业企业和全部个体经营工业单位。

Note: Industrial enterprises below designed size refers to corperate industrial enterprises with main business income below 20 million yuan and all individual operated business.

主要统计指标解释

工业 指从事自然资源的开采，对采掘品和农产品进行加工和再加工的物质生产部门。具体包括：（1）对自然资源的开采，如采矿、晒盐、森林采伐等（但不包括禽兽捕猎和水产捕捞）；（2）对农副产品的加工、再加工，如粮油加工、食品加工、扎花、纺织、制革等；（3）对采掘品的加工、再加工，如炼铁、炼钢、化工生产、石油加工、机器制造、木材加工等，以及电力、自来水、煤气的生产和供应等；（4）对工业品的修理、翻新，如机器设备的修理。

轻工业 指主要提供生活消费品和制作手工工具的工业。按其所使用的原料不同，可分为两大类：（1）以农业为原料的轻工业，是指直接或间接以农产品为基本原料的轻工业。主要包括食品制造、饮料制造、烟草加工、纺织、缝纫、皮革和毛皮制作、造纸以及印刷等工业；（2）以非农产品为原料的轻工业，是指以工业品为原料的轻工业。主要包括文教体育用品、化学药品制造、合成纤维制造、日用化学制品、日用玻璃制品、日用金属制品、手工工具制造、医疗器械制造、文化和办公用机械制造等工业。

重工业 是指为国民经济各部门提供物质技术基础的主要生产资料的工业。按其生产性质和产品用途，可以分为下列三类：（1）采掘（伐）工业，是指对自然资源的开采，包括石油开采、煤炭开采、金属矿开采、非金属矿开采和木材采伐等工业；（2）原材料工业，指向国民经济各部门提供基本材料、动力和燃料的工业。包括金属冶炼及加工、炼焦及焦炭化学、化工原料、水泥、人造板以及电力、石油和煤炭加工等工业；（3）加工工业，是指对工业原材料进行再加工制造的工业。包括装备国民经济各部门的机械设备制造工业、金属结构、水泥制品等工业，以及为农业提供的生产资料如化肥、农药等工业。

根据上述划分原则，修理业中以重工业产品为修理作业对象的划为重工业，反之划为轻工业。

工业总产值 指工业企业在报告期内生产的以货币形式表现的工业最终产品和提供工业劳务活动的总价值量。它包括：在本企业内不再进行加工，经检验、包装入库（规定不需包装的产品除外）的成品价值，对外加工费收入，自制半成品、在制品期末期初差额价值。工业总产值采用“工厂法”计算，即以工业企业作为一个整体，按企业生产活动的最终成果来计算，企业内部不允许重复计算，不能把企业内部各个车间（分厂）生产的成果相加。但在企业之间、行业之间、地区之间存在着重复计算。

轻重工业总产值的划分也是按“工厂法”计算的，即一个工业企业在正常情况下生产的主要产品的性质属于轻工业，则该企业的全部总产值作为轻工业总产值；一个工业企业生产的主要产品的性质属于重工业，则该企业的全部总产值作为重工业总产值。

工业增加值 是指工业企业在报告期内以货币形式表现的工业生产活动的最终成果，反映企业生产过程中新创造的价值。

工业销售产值 是以货币形式表现的，工业企业在报告期内销售的本企业生产的工业产品或提供工业性劳务价值的总价值量。包括企业在报告期内实际销售（包括本期生产和非本期生产）的全部成品、半成品的总价值，报告期内完成的对外承接的工业品加工的加工费收入，对外工业品修理作业可获取的加工费收入和对内非工业部门提供的加工修理、设备安装等收入。已销售的成品、半成品不论是本期生产的、还是非本期生产的，只要是本期销售出去的均包括在内。企业为本单位基本建设部门、生活福利部门等提供的产品和工业性作业及自制设备也应视同销售，这部分也应作为销售统计。

工业销售产值的计算价格和计算方法与工业总产值一致，但两者计算的基础不同，工业销售产值计算的基础是产品销售总量，工业总产值计算的基础是工业产品生产总量。工业销售产值不包括自制半成品、在制品期末期初差额价值，而工业总产值包括这部分内容。

资产总计 指企业过去的交易或者事项形成的、由企业拥有或者控制的、预期会给企业带来经济利益的资源。资产一般按流动性分为流动资产和非流动资产。其中流动资产可分为货币资金、交易性金融资产、应收票据、应收账款、预付款项、其他应收款、存货等；非流动资产可分为长期股权投资、固定资产、无形资产及其他非流动资产等。

（1）流动资产合计 资产满足以下条件之一应归为流动资产：①预计在一个正常营业周期中变现、出售或耗用，主要包括存货、应收账款等；②主要为交易目的而持有；③预计在资产负债表日起一年内（含一年）变现；④自资产负债表日起一年内，交换其他资产或清偿负债的能力不受限制的现金或现金等价物。包括货币资金、应收票据、应收账款、存货等项目。

（2）固定资产合计 指企业为生产商品、提供劳务、出租或经营管理而持有的，使用寿命超过一个会计年度的有形资产。包括使用期限超过一年的房屋、建筑物、机器、机械、运输工具以及其他与生产、经营有关的设备、器具、工具等。固定资产合计是时点指标，表示固定资产经过扣减折旧、减值准备等后的期末余额。

负债合计 指企业过去的交易或者事项形成的，预期会导致经济利益流出企业的现时义务。负债一般按偿还期长短分为流动负债和非流动负债。

(1) 流动负债合计 负债满足下列条件之一的应归为流动负债：①预计在一个正常营业周期中清偿；②主要为交易目的而持有；③自资产负债表日起一年内到期应予清偿；④企业无权自主地将清偿推迟至资产负债表日后一年以上。包括短期借款、应付票据、应付账款、应付职工薪酬、应交税费等项目。

(2) 非流动负债合计 指流动负债之外的负债。包括长期借款、应付债券等。

所有者权益合计 指企业资产扣除负债后由所有者享有的剩余权益。公司的所有者权益又称股东权益。包括实收资本、资本公积、盈余公积、未分配利润等。

实收资本 指企业各投资者实际投入的资本（或股本）总额，包括货币、实物、无形资产等各种形式的投入。实收资本按投资主体可分为国家资本、集体资本、法人资本、个人资本、港澳台资本和外商资本。

主营业务收入 指企业确认的销售商品、提供劳务等主营业务的收入。

主营业务成本 指企业经营主要业务所发生的成本总额。

主营业务税金及附加 指企业经营主要业务应负担的营业税、消费税、城市维护建设税、教育费附加等。

营业利润 指企业从事生产经营活动所取得的利润。

利润总额 指企业在一定会计期间的经营成果，是生产经营过程中各种收入扣除各种耗费后的盈余，反映企业在报告期内实现的亏盈总额。

应交增值税 指企业按税法规定，从事货物销售或提供加工、修理修配劳务等增加货物价值的活动本期应交纳的税金。

应交增值税=销项税额-（进项税额-进项税额转出）-出口抵减内销产品应纳税额-减免税款+出口退税

应交增值税不含期初未抵扣税额。

工业产品销售率 指报告期工业销售产值与工业总产值之比。计算公式：

$$工业产品销售率(\%)=\frac{报告期现价工业销售产值}{报告期现价工业总产值}\times100\%$$

工业增加值率 指报告期工业增加值占工业总产值的比重，反映降低中间消耗的经济效益。计算公式：

$$工业增加率(\%)=\frac{报告期现价工业增加值}{报告期现价工业总产值}\times100\%$$

工业成本费用利润率 指在一定时期内实现的利润与成本费用之比，是反映工业生产成本及费用投入的经济效益指标，同时也是反映降低成本的经济效益的指标。计算公式：

$$工业成本费用利润率(\%)=\frac{利润总额}{成本费用总额}\times100\%$$

工业全员劳动生产率 指根据产品的价值量指标计算的平均每一个职工在单位时间内创造的工业生产最终成果。是考核企业经济活动的重要指标，是企业生产技术水平、经济管理水平、职工技术熟练程度和劳动积极性的综合表现。

$$工业全员劳动生产率（元/人）=\frac{工业增加值（现价）}{从业人员平均人数}$$

流动资产周转次数 指在一定时期内流动资产完成的周转次数，反映流动资产的周转速度。计算公式：

$$流动资产周转次数(次)=\frac{产品销售收入}{流动资产平均余额}$$

流动比率 是反映企业每百元流动负债中，有多少元流动资产作后盾。计算公式：

$$流动比率(倍)=\frac{流动资产总额}{流动负债总额}$$

速动比率 是衡量企业流动资产中可以立即用于偿付流动负债的能力。计算公式：

$$速动比率(倍)=\frac{流动资产总额-存货}{流动负债总额}$$

资产负债率 反映在企业资产总额中有多少资产是通过借债而得的，也可以用于衡量企业利用债权人提供资金进行经营活动的能力以及企业在清算时保护债权人利益的程度。计算公式：

$$资产负债率=\frac{负债总额}{资产总额}\times100\%$$

总资产贡献率 反映企业全部资产的获利能力，是企业经营业绩和管理水平的集中体现，是评价和考核企业盈利能力的核心指标。计算公式为：

总资产贡献率=(利润总额+税金总额+利息支出)÷平均资产总额×100%

其中：税金总额为主营业务税金及附加、管理费用中的税金与应交增值税之和；平均资产总额为期初期末资产总计的算术平均值。

资本保值增值率 反映企业净资产的变动状况，是企业发展能力的集中体现。计算公式为：

$$资本保值增值率=\frac{报告期期末所有者权益}{上年同期期末所有者权益}\times100\%$$

高技术制造业 在高技术产业中扣除软件开发业以外的全部行业。

Explanatory Notes on Main Statistical Indicators

Industry refers to the material production sector which is engaged in extraction of natural resources and processing and reprocessing of minerals and agricultural products, including (1) extraction of natural resources, such as mining, salt production, logging (but not including animal hunting and fishing); (2) processing and reprocessing of agricultural products, such as grain and oil processing, food processing, embroidery, textile manufacturing, and leather making; (3) processing and reprocessing of mining products, such as iron making, steel making, chemical production, petroleum processing, machine building, timber processing; and production and supply of electric power, tap water and gas; (4) repair and refurbishment of industrial products, such as the repair of machinery equipment.

Light Industry refers to the industries that produce consumer goods and hand tools. It falls into two categories, based on different raw materials:

(1) Industries basing the raw materials on agriculture, which directly or indirectly use farm products as basic raw materials, mainly include the manufacture of foods and beverages, tobacco processing, textile manufacturing, tailoring, fur and leather manufacturing, paper making, printing, etc.

(2) Industries using non-agricultural products as raw materials, which means the manufactured goods are used as raw materials, mainly include the manufacture of cultural, educational articles and sports goods, chemical medicines, synthetic fiber, daily chemical products, glass products for daily use, metal products for daily use, hand tools, medical appliances and instruments, as well as stationery and office machinery.

Heavy Industry refers to the industries that provide material and technical foundation as key means of production for various sectors of the national economy. It falls into the following three categories according to the purpose of production or the use of products:

(1) Mining, quarrying and logging industry refers to the industry that extracts natural resources, including the extraction of petroleum, coal, metal and non-metal ores and logging.

(2) Raw material industry refers to the industry that provides various sectors of the national economy with basic materials, fuels and power. It includes smelting and processing of metals, coking and coke chemistry, chemical materials, cement, artificial boards, as well as power generation, petroleum refining and coal processing.

(3) Processing industry refers to the industry that reprocesses raw materials. It includes machine manufacturing, which equips various sectors of the national economy, metal structure, cement products, and chemical fertilizer and pesticide industry that provide means of production for agriculture.

According to the above principle of classification, the repair services for products of heavy industry are classified as heavy industry, while the repair services for products of light industry are classified as light industry.

Gross Output Value of Industry is the total value in monetary terms for final industrial products and industrial labor service provided by industrial enterprises during the reporting period. It includes the value of the finished products, which will not be further processed in the enterprises and have been inspected, packed and put in storage (except for products required not to be packed), the revenue from processing products for others, the value of semi-finished products, and the price spread between the finished products and products at the initial stage. The gross industrial output value is calculated with "factory method"; that is, to take an industrial enterprise as a whole. It calculates the final products created by the enterprise, instead of double counting or simply adding up productions of all workshops or branches within the enterprise. However, double counting does occur among different enterprises, sectors and regions.

Output value of light and heavy industries is also calculated with the "factory method"; that is, if the major products produced under normal circumstances by an industrial enterprise are light industry products in nature, the gross output value of that enterprise will be considered as part of light industry output; otherwise, it will be considered as heavy industry output.

Added Value of Industry refers to the final results of industrial production by industrial enterprises in monetary terms during the reporting period. It shows the newly created value generated in production by the enterprises.

Sales Value of Industry refers to the total value of industrial products sold or labor service provided by an industrial enterprise during the reporting period in monetary terms. It includes the total value of all finished and semi-finished products actually sold by the enterprise (including products produced in current period and noncurrent period), revenue from processing products for others, repairing industrial products for others, as well as processing, repairing, and installing equipment for internal non-industrial departments in the reporting period. All finished and semi-finished products sold in the current period will be counted, regardless of whether they were produced in the current period or not. The value of products, industrial work and home-built equipment provided by the enterprise for its capital construction department and welfare department will also be included in the industrial sales value.

Sales value of industry is calculated by the same price and method as the calculation of gross output value of industry. But they are calculated on different bases. The calculation of sales value of industry is based on the total sales volume of products, while that of the gross industrial output value is based on the total output of industrial products. The sales value of industry does not cover semi-finished products and the price spread between the finished products and products at the initial stage, while the gross industrial output value does cover this part.

Total Assets refer to resources formed by previous transactions or matters of an enterprise, owned or controlled by the enterprise, and expected to bring economic benefits to the enterprise. Classified by the liquidity, assets fall into current assets and non-current assets. Current assets include monetary capital, tradable financial assets, notes receivable, accounts receivable, prepayment, other receivables, and inventory; while non-current assets include long-term equity investment, fixed assets, intangible assets, and other non-current assets.

(1)Total Current Assets Assets that meet any of the following requirements are considered current assets: a. assets expected to be cashed in, sold or consumed in a normal operating cycle, which mainly includes inventory and accounts receivable; b. assets held mainly for transaction; c. assets expected to be cashed in within one year (including one year) from the balance sheet date; d. cash or cash equivalents with unrestricted capacity of exchanging for other assets or paying off debts within one year from the balance sheet date, which include monetary capital, notes receivable, accounts receivable, inventory, etc.

(2)Total Fixed Assets refer to tangible assets held by an enterprise for producing commodities, rendering labor services, leasing or management, with service life exceeding one fiscal year, which include houses and buildings, apparatus, machinery, means of transport, as well as other equipment, instruments and tools related to production and operation, which have a service life exceeding one year. Total Fixed Assets is a time point indicator, showing the ending balance of fixed assets after deduction and discount, and impairment provision, etc.

Total Liabilities refer to the present obligations formed by previous transactions or matters of an enterprise, expected to lead the flow of economic benefits out of the enterprise. By the term of payment, liabilities generally include current liabilities and non-current liabilities.

(1) Total Current liabilities Liabilities that meet any of the following requirements are considered current liabilities: a. assets expected to be paid off within one normal operating cycle; b. assets held mostly for the purpose of transaction; c. assets expected to be due and paid off within one year from the balance sheet date; d. assets that the enterprise has no right to delay the payment to more than one year after the balance sheet date on its own. They include short-term loans, notes payable, accounts payable, wages payable, taxes and fees payable, etc.

(2) Total Non-current Liabilities refer to liabilities other than current liabilities, including long-term borrowings, bonds payable, etc.

Total Owner's Equity refers to the remaining equity of assets in an enterprise held by owners after deducting the liabilities. Owner's equity of a company is also called shareholders' equity, including paid-up capital, capital reserves, operating surplus reserves, non-distributed profits, etc.

Paid-up Capital refers to the total capital (or equity) actually contributed by investors to an enterprise, including input in various forms, such as monetary investment, physical investment and intangible assets. Categorized by investors, paid-up capital includes state capital, collective capital, legal person's capital, personal capital, capital from Hong Kong, Macao and Taiwan, and foreign capital.

Main Business Income refers to the income from main business of selling commodities and rendering services recognized by the enterprise.

Main Business Cost refers to the total cost incurred by the enterprise during its operation of main business.

Main Business Tax and Surtax refers to the business tax, excise tax, urban maintenance and construction tax, educational surcharge to be levied against the main business operated by an enterprise.

Operating Profits refer to the profits reaped by an enterprise from its productive and operating activities.

Total Profits refer to the operating results of an enterprise during certain accounting period, representing the surplus of various incomes from production and operation deducting various expenses, reflecting the total gains and losses realized by the enterprise during the reporting period.

VAT Payable refer to the tax payable by an enterprise in current period according to provisions in Law of Tax for its activities of adding value to goods, such as selling the goods, providing labor service for processing, repair and replacement.

VAT Payable = Output Tax – (Input Tax – Transfer-out of Input Tax) – Tax Payable Deducted by Export from Output Tax of Domestically Sold Products – Tax Concession + Export Rebate

VAT Payable excludes the taxes not deducted at the beginning of the period.

Sales Rate of Industrial Products refers to the ratio of industrial sales output to the gross output value of industry during the reporting period. It is calculated as follows:

Sales Rate of Industrial Products (%) = Sales Value of Industry at Present Value During the Reporting Period / Gross Output Value of Industry at Present Value During the Reporting Period × 100%

Rate of Industrial Added Value refers to the ratio of added value of industry to the gross output value of industry during the reporting period. It indicates the economic benefits from reduction of intermediate consumption. It is calculated as follows:

Rate of Industrial Added Value = Added Value of Industry at Present Value During the Reporting Period / Gross Output Value of Industry at Present Value During the Reporting Period × 100%

Rate of Profits to Total Industrial Costs refers to the ratio of profits realized in a given period to the total costs in the same period, which reflects the economic efficiency of industrial production input. It is calculated as follows:

Rate of Profits to Total Industrial Cost (%) = (Total Profits/ Total Costs) ×100%

Overall Labor Productivity of Industry refers to the average final result of industrial production created by each employee within a unit time, measured with the value of products. It is an important indicator evaluating the economic activities of an enterprise, and it reflects the level of production technology and economic management of the enterprise, employees' skills, as well as enthusiasm for work.

Overall Labor Productivity of Industry (RMB/person) = Added Value of Industry (at present value) / Average Number of Employees

Turnover of Current Assets refer to the number of times for current assets turnover within a given period of time. It reflects the turnover velocity of current assets. It is calculated as follows:

Turnover of Current Assets (No. of times) = Product Sales Income / Average Balance of Current Assets

Liquidity Ratio reflects how many current assets are backing up every RMB100 of current liabilities in an enterprise. It is calculated as follows:

Liquidity Ratio (times) = Total Current Assets / Total Current Liabilities

Quick Ratio indicates the capacity of an enterprise's current assets for paying off current liabilities immediately.

Quick Ratio (times) = (Total Current Assets – Inventory) / Total Current Liabilities

Assets-liabilities Ratio reflects how many assets—out of the total assets of the enterprise, are obtained by borrowing. It can be used to evaluate the enterprise's capability of operating by using the funds provided by creditors, and to what extent the enterprise will be able to protect the creditors' interests in the case of liquidation. It is calculated as follows:

Ratio of Liabilities to Assets = Total Liabilities / Total Assets × 100%

Contribution Rate of Total Assets indicates the profitability of all assets in an enterprise, reflecting the operating performance and management of the enterprise. It serves as a core indicator evaluating the enterprise's profitability. It is calculated with the following formula:

Total Assets Contribution rate = (Total Profit + Total Tax + Total Interest Expenses) ÷ Average Total Assets × 100%

Note: the total tax is the sum of main business tax and surtax, tax in management expenses, and VAT payable; average total assets are represented by the arithmetic average of total assets at the beginning and the end of the period.

Rate of Assets Preservation and Appreciation reflects the changes in the net assets of an enterprise. It reflects the growth potential of the enterprise. The formula for calculation is:

Capital Preservation and Appreciation Rate = Owner's Equity at the End of the Reporting Period / Owner's Equity at the End of the Same period in the Previous Year × 100%

High-tech Manufacturing Sector refers to all sectors in the high-tech industry other than software development.

12

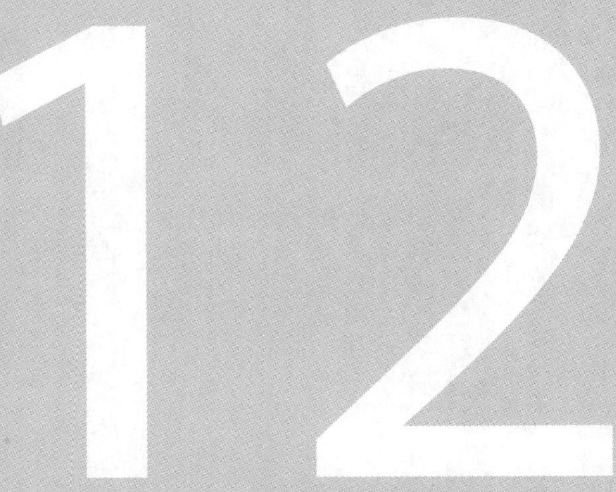

北京统计年鉴2014　BEIJING STATISTICAL YEARBOOK

建筑业
CONSTRUCTION

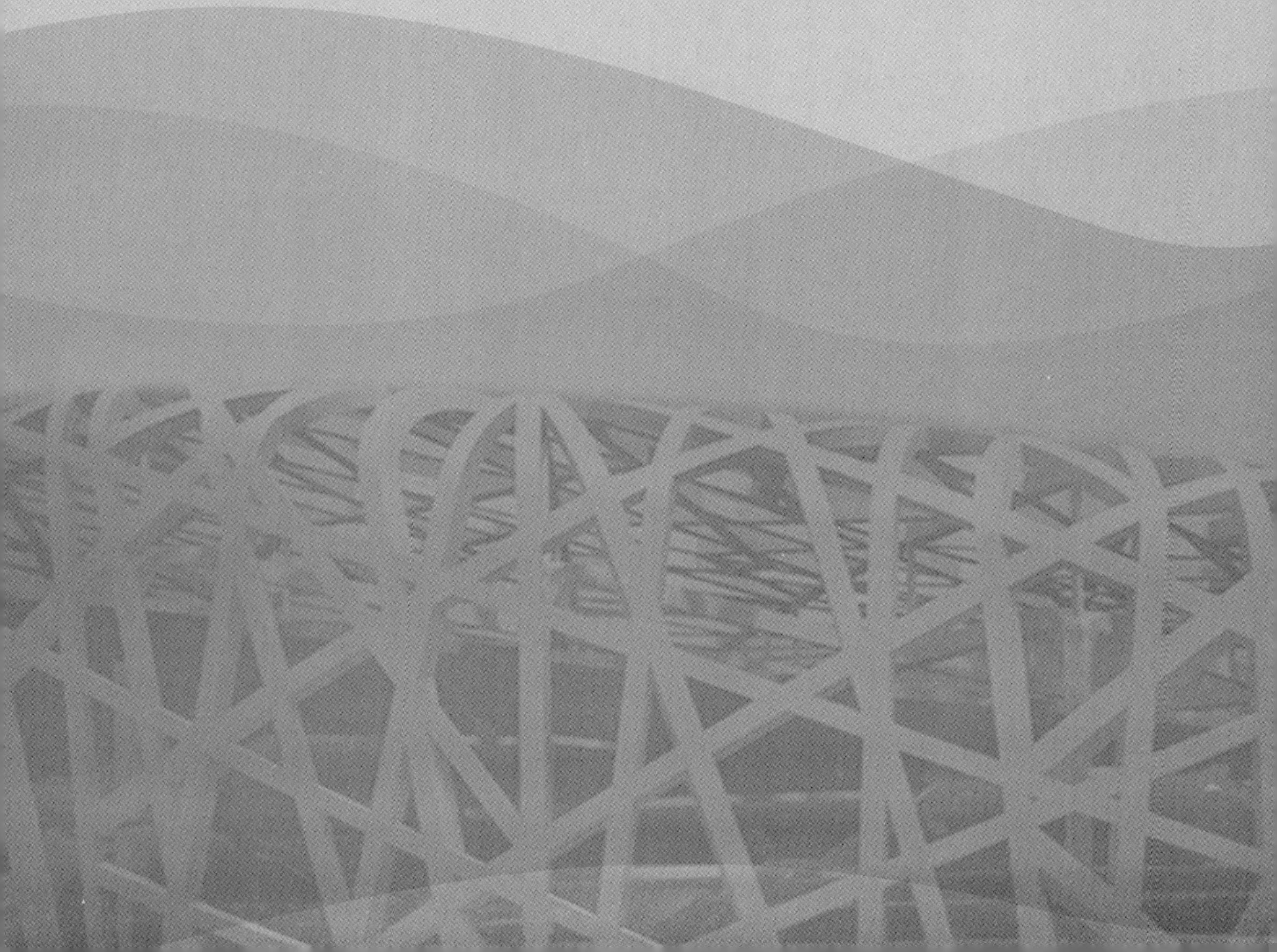

简 要 说 明

一、本章资料的主要内容

本章资料主要反映北京市建筑业企业基本情况和生产经营情况。主要指标包括企业个数、从业人员、建筑业总产值、建筑业企业房屋建筑面积、利润、税金等。

二、本章资料的统计范围

建筑业统计范围从 2004 年起，由原具有建筑业资质等级四级及四级以上的独立核算的建筑业企业调整为具有施工总承包、专业承包资质的所有法人建筑业企业。

三、本章资料的数据来源及调查方法

本章建筑业企业统计数据根据国家统计局制定的《建筑业统计报表制度》整理汇总。建筑业统计数据采取全面调查的方法。资料由北京市统计局、国家统计局北京调查总队提供。

四、有关统计标准的变化说明

本章资料中建筑业行业分类 2002-2011 年期间执行 2002 年《国民经济行业分类标准》(GB/T 4754-2002)划分标准，2012 年开始执行 2011 年《国民经济行业分类》(GB/T 4754-2011)划分标准。

五、本章中关于历史数据调整的问题

由于 2004 年开展了“北京市第一次全国经济普查”，按照国家统计局统一要求和统一方法，历史资料要根据普查结果进行修正。本章中 1993 至 2003 年的建筑业总产值数据采用“趋势离差法”进行了调整，2004 年为第一次经济普查数据，2008 年为第二次经济普查数据。

Brief Introduction

I. Main Content

Data in this chapter reflect the basic situation and operation of construction enterprises in Beijing. Main indicators include number of enterprises, employees, total output value of the construction sector, as well as floor space, profits, and tax of construction enterprises.

II. Scope of Statistics

Since 2004, data on construction sector, which previously covered construction enterprises with independent accounting at or above Level-4 in construction qualifications, have been adjusted to cover all construction enterprises with qualifications of general and specialized contracting.

III. Source of Data and Methods of Survey

Data on construction enterprises in this chapter were gathered based on *Statistical Statement System for Construction Sector* developed by the National Bureau of Statistics. The figures were gained through complete survey, and were provided by Beijing Municipal Bureau of Statistics and NBS Survey Office in Beijing.

IV. Changes in Relevant Statistical Standards

In this chapter, classification of construction sectors during 2002-2011 was based on the *Standard for Classification of National Economic Sectors 2002* (GB/T 4754-2002). *Standard for Classification of National Economic Sectors 2011* (GB/T 4754-2011) began to be enforced in 2012.

V. About the Adjustment to Historical Data

As “The First National Economic Census in Beijing” was conducted in 2004, in accordance with the principles of unified requirements and methods by the National Bureau of Statistics, historical data must be revised on basis of the census result. Data of total output value of construction sector during 1993-2003 were revised by “trend deviation method”. The first economic census was in 2004, and the second was in 2008.

12-1 建筑业企业基本情况(1978-2013年)
BASIC STATISTICS FOR ENTERPRISES IN THE CONSTRUCTION INDUSTRY (1978-2013)

年份 Year	建筑施工企业单位数(个) Construction Enterprises (unit)	建筑施工企业年末从业人员(万人) Employed Persons (year-end) (10000 persons)	建筑施工企业总产值(亿元) Gross Output Value (100 million yuan)	主营业务收入(亿元) Main Business Income (100 million yuan)	建筑施工企业利润总额(亿元) Total Profits (100 million yuan)	建筑施工企业房屋建筑面积(万平方米) Floor Space of Buildings (10000 sq.m) 施工面积 Floor Space under Construction	竣工面积 Floor Space Completed
1978	64	25.4	10.5		0.7		
1979	70	26.4	12.7		0.9		
1980	71	27.8	14.7		1.5		
1981	71	27.0	14.5		1.6		
1982	91	30.7	17.3		1.7		
1983	116	37.2	22.6		2.5		
1984	2765	53.0	33.4		3.2		
1985	2549	63.9	43.9		3.9		
1986	2361	61.3	51.3		3.3		
1987	2292	64.4	67.0		4.1		
1988	1659	64.2	81.6		3.9		
1989	1545	60.0	89.0		3.8		
1990	994	60.2	94.7		3.4		
1991	922	60.3	99.6		2.8	2495	1172
1992	976	62.7	122.6		3.1	2774	1227
1993	1098	75.9	215.5	205.5	6.1	3499	1428
1994	1259	73.4	336.0	289.4	9.4	4035	1437
1995	1332	82.6	426.6	337.6	7.8	4602	1593
1996	1292	82.5	494.7	431.3	8.9	5328	1967
1997	1297	80.3	556.4	481.1	10.4	5801	2117
1998	1482	75.6	678.6	579.3	12.4	6525	2225
1999	1588	62.0	750.6	645.8	13.6	6824	2632
2000	1697	56.6	812.5	706.8	16.4	7247	2809
2001	1811	57.8	1055.4	906.9	18.7	8919	3198
2002	2122	57.0	1211.3	1094.0	24.7	10241	3827
2003	2419	59.1	1521.2	1329.9	31.5	12160	4486
2004	2623	51.2	1659.8	1936.0	40.0	14424	5258
2005	2752	67.2	1894.0	2206.9	67.3	15418	4862
2006	2800	66.9	2167.9	2666.2	112.8	16202	4786
2007	2845	51.7	2576.8	3351.3	115.7	18225	4946
2008	3527	47.0	3066.2	3856.8	84.5	19537	4803
2009	3556	56.2	4059.7	5081.1	217.4	22721	5225
2010	3594	59.9	5196.0	6545.0	265.2	29440	5933
2011	3667	49.6	6046.3	7565.9	219.6	36507	6456
2012	3572	49.2	6588.3	8125.2	293.0	41660	8414
2013	3522	49.3	7459.6	9404.3	385.8	49259	8950

注：1. 1996-2003年全部指标的统计口径为四级及四级以上的法人建筑施工企业。
2. 2004年开始全部指标的统计口径为建筑施工总承包、专业承包的建筑业企业。
3. 建筑施工企业房屋建筑面积包括在本市和外省完成的施工、竣工面积。

Note: a) Data from 1996 to 2003 cover the corporate construction enterprises at Grade IV and above.
b) Data from 2004 cover general contracting and specialized contracting construction enterprises.
c) Data on floor space cover buildings under construction and completed in Beijing and other provinces.and outside the city.

12-2 建筑业施工企业基本情况(2013年)
BASIC STATISTICS FOR CONSTRUCTION ENTERPRISES (2013)

项 目	Item	建筑施工企业单位数 (个) Construction Enterprises (unit)	总产值 (万元) Gross Output Value (10000 yuan)	年末从业人员 (人) Employed Persons (year-end) (person)	年末自有机械设备 Machines and Equipment Owned (year-end) 净值 (万元) Net Value (10000 yuan)	总台数 (台) Total Number (set)	总功率 (千瓦) Total Power (kw)
合 计	**Total**	**3522**	**74596041**	**493201**	**1088199**	**127068**	**4478393**
按企业登记注册类型分	**Grouped by Registration Type of Enterprises**						
内资企业	Domestically-funded Enterprises	3433	73358008	481099	1081416	125473	4440543
国有企业	State-owned Enterprises	99	3834759	28232	49209	9622	268134
集体企业	Collectively-owned Enterprises	126	1305213	15819	7173	5161	67751
私营企业	Private Enterprises	1860	5753284	98403	113231	24593	503888
联营企业	Associate Enterprises	2	1206	41			
股份有限公司	Companies Limited by Shares	61	5795006	20837	78227	6789	398644
有限责任公司	Limited Liability Companies	1223	56263866	310727	827165	75910	3125832
股份合作企业	Joint-equity Cooperative Enterprises	62	404674	7040	6411	3398	76294
其他企业	Others						
外商投资企业	Foreign-invested Enterprises	41	554197	6058	4298	843	32450
港、澳、台商投资企业	Hong Kong, Macao and Taiwan-invested Enterprises	48	683836	6044	2485	752	5400
按隶属关系分	**Grouped by Affiliation**						
中 央	Central	194	39531257	170206	587237	38085	2065447
地 方	Local	3328	35064784	322995	500962	88983	2412946
按行业分	**Grouped by Sector**						
房屋建筑业	Construction of Buildings	611	39685197	192517	309417	41363	1361898
土木工程建筑业	Civil Engineering Construction	562	21943335	122797	630546	42517	2374137
建筑安装业	Construction Installation	825	6206289	83659	67063	22473	458715
建筑装饰和其他建筑业	Building Decoration and Other Construction	1524	6761220	94228	81173	20715	283643

注：1. 统计范围为施工总承包、专业承包的法人建筑业企业（下表同）。
2. 行业划分执行2011年国民经济行业分类标准（GB/T 4754-2011）。

Note: a) Statistics covers general contracting and specialized contracting corporate construction enterprises(same as the following table).
b) Sectors in this table are classified in accordance with the Standard for Classification of National Economic Sectors 2011 (GB/T 4754-2011).

12-3 建筑业施工企业主要财务指标(2013年)

单位：万元

项目	Item	企业单位个数(个) Number of Enterprises (unit)	资产负债 Assets and Liabilities 资产总计 Total Assets	流动资产合计 Total Current Assets	#应收账款 Accounts Receivable	固定资产合计 Total Fixed Assets	固定资产原价 Total Original Value of Fixed Assets	负债合计 Total Liabilities	#流动负债合计 Total Current Liabilities
合计	**Total**	**3522**	**151963023**	**99645218**	**21230709**	**4938680**	**7725092**	**104205325**	**89773209**
按企业登记注册类型分	**By Registration Type**								
内资企业	Domestically-funded Enterprises	3433	150161552	97978380	20791280	4892319	7635464	102800027	88393062
国有企业	State-owned Enterprises	99	8562520	6081517	1086276	517262	852362	5174583	4617627
集体企业	Collectively-owned Enterprises	126	1794874	1406791	95798	118337	186510	1477407	1437095
私营企业	Private Enterprises	1860	7291962	6061626	1448979	592663	877467	4379026	4286774
联营企业	Associate Enterprises	2	***	***	***	***	***	***	***
股份有限公司	Companies Limited by Shares	61	41047152	10938234	1607090	360643	458355	16831287	8930560
有限责任公司	Limited Liability Companies	1223	91004889	73079394	16489008	3269772	5196876	74637901	68837923
股份合作企业	Joint-Equity Cooperative Enterprises	62	458621	409333	63137	33592	63694	297754	281014
其他企业	Others								
外商投资企业	Foreign-invested Enterprises	41	1014110	948321	277260	22451	47986	756985	749628
港、澳、台商投资企业	Hong Kong, Macao and Taiwan-invested Enterprises	48	787361	718517	162169	23910	41642	648313	630519
按隶属关系分	**By Affiliation**								
中央	Central	194	102472842	58567353	11866056	2629176	3915288	65945137	53940031
地方	Local	3328	49490181	41077865	9364653	2309503	3809805	38260188	35833178
按国民经济行业分	**Grouped by Sector**								
房屋建筑业	Construction of Buildings	611	65013564	46768202	11763236	1806109	2845723	47749031	42006226
土木工程建筑业	Civil Engineering Construction	562	68668470	37653401	5924408	1735635	3081745	43081939	35025672
建筑安装业	Construction Installation	825	9540566	7976340	1733682	548226	787009	7218192	6857887
建筑装饰和其他建筑业	Building Decoration and Other Construction	1524	8740423	7247275	1809383	848710	1010615	6156163	5883424

注：1. 行业划分执行2011年国民经济行业分类标准(GB/T 4754-2011)。
2. 应交税金合计包括应交增值税、应交所得税、营业税金及附加和管理费用中的税金。

MAIN FINANCIAL INDICATORS OF CONSTRUCTION ENTERPRISES (2013)

(10000 yuan)

#应付账款 Accounts Payable	所有者权益合计 Total Owner's Equity	#实收资本 Paid-up Capital	损益 Profits and Loss: 营业收入 Business Income	#主营业务收入 Main Business Income	营业成本 Business Cost	#主营业务成本 Main Business Cost	管理费用 Management Expenses	财务费用 Financial Expenses	利润总额 Total Profits	应交税金合计 Total Tax	#营业税金及附加 Business Tax and Surtax	#主营业务税金及附加 Main Business Tax and Surtax
32524191	**47757698**	**23169331**	**94730118**	**94043177**	**86706883**	**85661026**	**3395229**	**598492**	**3857640**	**3059557**	**2333728**	**2306088**
32135618	47361525	22905127	92745569	92087856	84947949	83915706	3292232	598658	3811704	2992274	2286428	2259148
1027640	3387937	1609756	6319673	6215567	5855473	5762658	230190	-5019	322291	201931	126458	125748
284681	317467	198770	1386022	1375496	1223609	1213518	95608	-2124	29233	52145	42512	42012
1354143	2912936	2947372	7056774	6975532	6054612	5987112	488243	13848	110560	266136	219066	214990
***	***	***	***	***	***	***	***	***	***	***	***	***
2411754	24215865	7699487	7964998	7871180	7366999	6761602	256327	127078	1448543	224537	155716	154115
27010321	16366988	10352486	69594473	69230780	64068641	63815277	2204713	462515	1888682	2229289	1728192	1707979
46653	160867	96556	422538	418210	377652	374576	16735	2360	12701	18202	14463	14283
252315	257125	132651	1063021	1043742	928083	923388	58657	-809	34439	39606	24360	24220
136258	139048	131553	921528	911579	830851	821932	44340	643	11497	27677	22940	22720
21279717	36527705	15102710	53764683	53436817	50014424	49212558	1517454	343511	2961608	1608530	1156606	1147205
11244474	11229993	8066621	40965435	40606360	36692459	36448468	1877775	254982	896031	1451027	1177122	1158883
17997058	17264533	8426864	44696659	44401308	41349255	41141565	1293896	356914	1630166	1403556	1131971	1121021
10562920	25586531	10776426	32422445	32204345	29839855	29135395	1136197	207112	1729243	1039298	748987	740701
2244433	2322374	1599199	9250010	9154200	8234336	8165817	506954	5665	225908	273811	210136	207317
1719780	2584260	2366842	8361004	8283324	7283437	7218249	458182	28801	272323	342892	242634	237049

Note: a) Sectors in this table are classified in accordance with the Standard for Classification of National Economic Sectors 2011 (GB/T 4754-2011).

b) Total tax payable mainly includes VAT payable, income tax payable, business tax and surtax, and tax in management expenses.

12-3 续表 Continued

项 目	Item	#应交所得税 Value Income Tax Payable	#应交增值税 Value Added Tax Payable	流动比率(倍) Current Ratio (times)	速动比率(倍) Quick Ratio (times)	资产负债率(%) Assets-Liabilities Ratio (%)	资本金利润率(%) Capital-Profit Ratio (%)
合 计	**Total**	**538976**	**136234**	**1.11**	**0.78**	**68.6**	**16.6**
按企业登记注册类型分	**By Registration Type**						
内资企业	Domestically-funded Enterprises	525445	131197	1.11	0.77	68.5	16.6
国有企业	State-owned Enterprises	57923	13969	1.32	0.98	60.4	20.0
集体企业	Collectively-owned Enterprises	8438	127	0.98	0.55	82.3	14.7
私营企业	Private Enterprises	29755	8348	1.41	1.14	60.1	3.8
联营企业	Associate Enterprises	2	***	***	***	***	***
股份有限公司	Companies Limited by Shares	53254	10867	1.22	0.59	41.0	18.8
有限责任公司	Limited Liability Companies	372598	97855	1.06	0.78	82.0	18.2
股份合作企业	Joint-Equity Cooperative Enterprises	3475	19	1.46	0.95	64.9	13.2
其他企业	Others						
外商投资企业	Foreign-invested Enterprises	10120	4390	1.27	1.10	74.6	26.0
港、澳、台商投资企业	Hong Kong, Macao and Taiwan-invested Enterprises	3411	647	1.14	0.93	82.3	8.7
按隶属关系分	**By Affiliation**						
中 央	Central	337421	94080	1.09	0.74	64.4	19.6
地 方	Local	201555	42154	1.15	0.84	77.3	11.1
按国民经济行业分	**Grouped by Sector**						
房屋建筑业	Construction of Buildings	238307	11961	1.11	0.77	73.4	19.3
土木工程建筑业	Civil Engineering Construction	193546	83143	1.08	0.74	62.7	16.0
建筑安装业	Construction Installation	40325	15284	1.16	0.87	75.7	14.1
建筑装饰和其他建筑业	Building Decoration and Other Construction	66798	25846	1.23	0.98	70.4	11.5

12-4 建筑业施工企业竣工率
PROJECT COMPLETION RATE OF CONSTRUCTION ENTERPRISES

单位：% (%)

项 目	Item	产值竣工率 Completion Rate by Output Value		面积竣工率 Completion Rate by Floor Space	
		2013	2012	2013	2012
合 计	**Total**	**47.9**	**49.8**	**18.2**	**20.2**
按企业登记注册类型分	**By Registration Type**				
内资企业	Domestic Funded Enterprises	47.8	49.4	18.2	20.3
国有企业	State-Owned Enterprises	75.4	59.8	19.0	19.2
集体企业	Collectively-owned Enterprises	47.7	64.1	21.4	26.0
私营企业	Private Enterprises	63.3	60.1	26.3	28.2
联营企业	Associate Enterprises				
股份有限公司	Companies Limited by Shares	32.4	33.3	15.1	22.8
有限责任公司	Limited Liability Companies	45.8	48.7	18.1	19.7
股份合作企业	Joint-Equity Cooperative Enterprises	63.0	96.8	29.2	37.2
其他企业	Others				
外商投资企业	Foreign-invested Enterprises	49.6	46.5	38.3	15.5
港、澳、台商投资企业	Hong Kong, Macao and Taiwan-invested Enterprises	60.9	80.5	6.0	16.0
按隶属关系分	**By Affiliation Relationship**				
中 央	Central	43.9	43.2	16.6	16.8
地 方	Local	52.5	57.2	21.0	25.7
按国民经济行业分	**Grouped by Sector**				
房屋建筑业	Construction of Buildings	58.0	55.0	18.5	20.2
土木工程建筑业	Civil Engineering Construction	30.0	37.5	9.9	20.6
建筑安装业	Construction Installation	45.1	54.6	17.2	20.2
建筑装饰和其他建筑业	Building Completion, Finishing and Other Construction	49.3	53.4	1.0	14.3

注：行业划分执行2011年国民经济行业分类标准(GB/T 4754-2011)。

Note: Sectors in this table are classified in accordance with the Standard for Classification of National Economic Sectors 2011 (GB/T 4754-2011).

主要统计指标解释

建筑业总产值 是以货币表现的建筑业企业在一定时期内生产的建筑产品和服务的总和。它包括建筑工程产值、设备安装工程产值、其他产值三部分内容。

(1)建筑工程产值 指列入建筑工程预(概)算内的各种工程价值。

(2)安装工程产值 指为设备安装而发生的安装工程费用，在设备安装产值中，不得包括被安装设备本身价值。

(3)其他产值 建筑业总产值中除建筑工程、安装工程以外的产值，包括房屋构筑物修理产值、非标准设备制造产值、总包企业向分包企业收取的管理费，以及不能明确划分的施工活动所完成的产值。

年末从业人员 指年末最后一日24小时在本单位工作，并取得工资或其他形式劳动报酬的人员数。该指标为时点指标，不包括最后一日当天及以前与单位解除劳动合同关系的人员，是在岗职工、劳务派遣人员及其他从业人员之和。

房屋施工面积 指报告期内施过工的全部房屋建筑面积，包括：本期新开工的房屋面积、上期施工跨入本期继续施工的房屋面积、上期停缓建本期复工的房屋面积、本期开工又停缓建和本期竣工的房屋面积。

房屋竣工面积 指在报告期内房屋建筑按照设计要求已全部完工，达到了住人和使用条件，经检查验收鉴定合格或达到竣工验收标准，可正式移交使用的房屋建筑面积。

自有机械设备净值 指本企业(或单位)自有机械设备经过使用、磨损后实际存在的价值，即原值减去累计折旧后的净额。

自有机械设备年末总台数 指年末本企业(或单位)自有的直接用于工程施工的各种机械设备的台数。不包括附属辅助生产机械设备、运输机械设备、生产试验机械设备的台数。

自有机械设备年末总功率 指年末本企业(或单位)自有的直接用于工程施工的各种机械设备年末总功率，按设定能力或查定能力计算。包括施工机械本身的动力和为该机械服务的单独动力设备，如电动机等。但不包括附属辅助生产机械设备、运输机械设备、生产试验机械设备的功率。计量单位用千瓦，动力换算可按1马力＝0.735千瓦折合成千瓦数。电焊机、变压器、锅炉不计算动力。

主营业务收入 指企业确认的销售商品、提供劳务等主营业务的收入。

主营业务成本 指企业经营主要业务所发生的成本总额。

主营业务税金及附加 指企业经营主要业务应负担的营业税、消费税、城市维护建设税、教育费附加等。

主营业务利润 指企业经营主要业务实现的利润。

利润总额 指企业在一定会计期间的经营成果，是生产经营过程中各种收入扣除各种耗费后的盈余，反映企业在报告期内实现的亏盈总额。

Explanatory Notes on Main Statistical Indicators

Gross Output Value of Construction refers to total of construction products and services, expressed in money terms, completed by construction and installation enterprises during a given period of time. It includes: output value of construction works, output value of installation works and other output value.

(1)Output Value of Construction Works means the value of works involved in project budgets.

(2)Output Value of Installation Works means the costs of installation works incurred for equipment installation. The calculation is based on the construction targets of construction enterprises, instead of the industrial sector of construction enterprises.

(3)Other Output Value means, of the total output value of construction, the output value other than that of construction and installations works. It includes the repair output value of houses and structures, manufacturing output value of non-standard equipment, management charges collected by general contracting enterprises from subcontracting enterprises, as well as the output value of construction activities falling in no specific categories.

Year-end Employed Persons refers to the number of employed persons who work during the 24 hours of the last day in a year and acquire wage or other forms of labor income. This time-spot index, which does not include persons who terminate their labor contracts at or before the last day of the year, is the sum of fully employed persons, dispatched personnel of labor service and other employed persons.

House Construction Area means the building area of all houses in the reporting period, including: the area of houses newly started in current period, area of houses built in the previous period and continued in current period, area of houses suspended in the previous period and restarted in current period, area of houses started and suspended in current period, and area of houses completed in current period.

Area of Houses Completed means the area of houses and buildings entirely completed in line with requirements of design, meeting conditions of use, satisfactorily accepted by relevant authorities in the reporting period.

Net Value of Machinery and Equipment Owned means the actual value of machinery and equipment owned by an enterprise (or entity) after use and wear, i.e. the net amount of original value minus the accumulated depreciation. Leased equipment for operation is not included as construction machinery and equipment owned. Leased equipment for financing is included as construction machinery and equipment owned by a construction enterprise.

Year-end Total Number of Machinery and Equipment Owned means the number of various machines and equipment owned by an enterprise (or entity) directly used for project construction. It excludes the number of auxiliary productive machines and equipment, transport machines and equipment, production test machines and equipment. Leased equipment for operation is not included as construction machinery and equipment owned. Leased equipment for financing is included as construction equipment owned by a construction enterprise.

Year-end Total Power of Machinery and Equipment Owned means the total power of machinery and equipment owned by an enterprise (entity) at the year end and directly used for project construction, calculated at the verified capacity, including the power of construction machines themselves and the power of any separate equipment serving the machine, such as motors, but excluding the power of auxiliary productive machines and equipment, transport machines and equipment, production test machines and equipment. machinery and equipment for construction, production and transportation. The unit used for the calculation of power is kilowatt, with horsepower converted to kilowatt by 1 horsepower=0.735 kilowatt. The power of welders, transformers and boilers is not included. Leased equipment for operation is not included as construction machinery and equipment owned. Leased equipment for financing is included as construction equipment owned by a construction enterprise.

Main Business Income means the income recognized by an enterprise from main business such as sale of commodities and rendering of service.

Main Business Cost means the total cost incurred in an enterprise for the operation of main business.

Main Business Tax and Surtax means the sales tax, excise, urban maintenance and construction tax, educational surcharge, etc. to be paid by an enterprise for the operation of main business.

Main Business Profit means the profit reaped by an enterprise in its operation of main business.

Total Profits mean the operating result of an enterprise in certain accounting period. It is the surplus of all revenues deducting all costs in its production and operation, reflecting its total profit and loss realized in the reporting period.

北京统计年鉴2014 BEIJING STATISTICAL YEARBOOK

交通运输邮电

TRANSPORT, POST AND TELECOMMUNICATON SERVICES

简 要 说 明

一、本章资料的主要内容

本章资料反映北京市交通运输业和邮政电信业发展的基本状况。

交通运输业资料主要包括：铁路、公路、民航、管道四种运输方式的线路条数、里程、总运量及周转量、主要技术经济指标（不含管道）；机动车拥有情况。

邮政电信业资料主要包括：邮电业务完成情况、邮政电信发展水平等资料。

二、各部分资料的调查范围及数据来源

1. 铁路资料：主要是国家铁路运营情况，不含地方铁路、合资铁路和军用铁路及由厂矿企事业单位自建的铁路专用线和专用铁道，资料来源于北京铁路局。

2. 公路资料：(1)公路里程为年末通车里程数，不含在建和未正式投入使用的公路里程；(2)公路运输统计范围包括在北京市注册从事公路货运的全部企事业单位和私人(包括个体联户)，资料来源于北京市交通委员会。

3. 管道运输资料：包括输送原油、成品油、天然气以及其他气体的管线长度、输送能力及完成的运输量。管道运输统计数据主要来源于中石油北京天然气管道有限公司和中国石油化工股份有限公司北京燕山分公司所属的管道运输企业，由两家集团公司分别负责收集审核本部门统计数据。

4. 民航运输资料：不包括在京运输飞行的外省市及外国航空公司。统计范围为各航空公司从事国内运输、港澳台运输、国际运输的定期航班航线条数及里程、运输量等。2009年及以前数据主要来源于中国国际航空公司、新华航空有限责任公司，2010年起为北京地区的民航运输法人单位。

5. 邮政电信资料：包括邮政和电信运营企业为社会公众提供的各类邮政和电信服务，不含专用网业务资料。邮电业务量按业务种类分为邮政业务量和电信业务量。数据主要来源于北京市邮政公司、中国联合网络通信有限公司北京市分公司、中国移动通信集团北京有限公司、中国铁通集团有限公司北京分公司、中国电信股份有限公司北京分公司。

6. 民用汽车拥有量资料：民用汽车指在公安交通管理部门已注册登记领有民用车辆牌照的全部汽车数量。民用汽车根据汽车结构分为载客汽车、载货汽车及其他汽车；根据汽车所有者不同分为私人汽车、单位汽车。民用汽车数据来自于北京市公安局公安交通管理局。

Brief Introduction

I. Main Content

Figures in this chapter show the basic situation of development of transport, post and telecommunication in Beijing.

Transportation statistics include the number of lines, mileage, total volume of transport, turnover and main technological and economic indicators (excluding pipelines) for four transport modes, i.e. railway, highway, civil aviation, and pipeline,; and number of motor vehicles.

Post and telecommunication statistics include: performance of post and telecom services, development level of post and telecommunication sector, and so on.

II. Scope of Survey and Source of Data

1. Data on railways: including the operation of national railways, excluding local railways, railways built by joint ventures, military railways, and dedicated lines and railways built by factories, mines, enterprises and public institutions. These data are from Beijing Railway Bureau.

2. Data on highways: (1) highway mileage covers highways open to traffic at the year end, excluding those under construction and not put into use; (2) highway transport statistics cover all enterprises and public institutions as well as individuals (including self-employed) registered in Beijing for highway cargo transportation. These data are from Beijing Municipal Commission of Transport.

3. Data on pipeline transport: including the length, capacity and completed traffic of pipelines for transport of crude oil, refined oil, natural gas, and other gases. These data are mainly from Beijing Natural Gas Pipelines Co., Ltd. of Sinopec and CNPC. Statistical data on the pipelines transportation business affiliated to Beijing Yanshan Branch were collected and reviewed by the two corporations mentioned above respectively.

4. Data on civil aviation: excluding non-local and foreign airlines flying and operating in Beijing. Statistics consist of the number, mileage, and traffic volume of regular flight lines for domestic transport, transport from and to Hong Kong, Macao and Taiwan, and international transport. Data for 2009 and earlier are sourced from Air China and Xinhua Airline; from 2010, from corporate entities of civil aviation transport in Beijing area.

5. Data on post and telecommunication: including those on postal and telecom services offered by post and telecom operators, excluding data on services of dedicated networks. Business volume falls into two categories, namely postal service and telecommunication service. Data are mainly sourced from Beijing Post and Telecom Company, Beijing Branch of China Unicom, China Mobile Beijing Company, Beijing Branch of China Tietong, and Beijing Branch of China Telecom.

6. Data on number of civil automobiles: civil automobiles refer to all vehicles registered with traffic administration and granted license plates. In terms of automobile structure, civil automobiles consist of passenger automobiles, cargo automobiles, and so on; in terms of ownership, they include private and company ones. These data are sourced from Beijing Traffic Management Bureau.

13-1 交通运输邮电业基本情况(1978-2013年)
TRANSPORT, POST AND TELECOMMUNICATIONS (1978-2013)

年份 Year	铁路里程(公里) Railway Mileage (km)	公路里程(公里) Highway Mileage (km)	客运量(万人) Passenger Traffic (10000 persons)	铁路 Railway	公路 Highway	民航 Civil Aviation	货运量(万吨) Freight Traffic (10000 tons)	铁路 Railway	公路 Highway	民航 Civil Aviation	管道 Pipeline
1978	699	6562	4431	2264	2120	47	7394	3370	4023	1	
1979	700	7278	4777	2504	2220	53	7764	3485	4277	2	
1980	707	7487	5285	2762	2465	58	7571	3356	4213	2	
1981-1985			**33230**	**17688**	**15058**	**484**	**45456**	**15425**	**29063**	**14**	**954**
1981	858	7566	5877	2982	2824	71	8546	3046	5498	2	
1982	858	7683	6215	3205	2931	79	9097	3065	5812	2	218
1983	860	8058	6662	3546	3038	78	9403	3152	6016	3	232
1984	864	8271	7273	3877	3287	109	9671	3133	6301	3	234
1985	876	8482	7203	4078	2978	147	8739	3029	5436	4	270
1986-1990			**38506**	**21290**	**16160**	**1056**	**121771**	**15518**	**104929**	**41**	**1283**
1986	876	8995	7337	4106	3059	172	22121	3030	18794	6	291
1987	876	9103	7763	4418	3117	228	23068	3125	19734	8	201
1988	876	9124	8491	4782	3460	249	24749	3168	21308	9	264
1989	876	9371	7434	4214	3034	186	25184	3144	21767	8	265
1990	876	9648	7480	3770	3490	220	26648	3051	23326	10	262
1991-1995			**40918**	**20615**	**18010**	**2292**	**147385**	**14923**	**131956**	**79**	**427**
1991	876	10259	7704	4036	3378	289	26804	2983	23739	11	71
1992	875	10827	8158	4196	3593	369	27707	2912	24700	14	80
1993	875	11260	7607	4374	2781	452	29865	3048	26730	17	70
1994	875	11532	8537	3992	4008	537	30825	3006	27700	19	99
1995	875	11811	8913	4017	4250	646	32184	2974	29087	17	106
1996-2000			**62554**	**19683**	**38888**	**3983**	**154376**	**13491**	**140455**	**125**	**304**
1996	922	12084	8801	3650	4395	756	32907	2851	29960	18	78
1997	924	12306	9263	3613	4902	748	32351	2883	29360	20	87
1998	924	12498	11228	3762	6704	762	30127	2563	27490	22	52
1999	997	12825	14866	4201	9878	788	28275	2583	25635	30	27
2000	997	13600	18396	4458	13009	929	30717	2612	28010	35	60
2001-2005			**191964**	**25350**	**157061**	**9553**	**156702**	**11053**	**144049**	**277**	**1323**
2001	987	13891	22469	4750	16630	1090	30607	2505	28007	38	57
2002	987	14359	28384	5032	22103	1249	30961	2348	28375	44	194
2003	964	14453	30520	4352	24940	1228	30925	2265	28361	45	254
2004	964	14630	49750	5437	41463	2850	31700	1959	29256	73	412
2005	966	14696	60841	5779	51925	3137	32509	1976	30050	77	406
2006-2010			**435377**	**37892**	**376377**	**21107**	**121931**	**8820**	**106451**	**508**	**6151**
2006	962	20503	12276	6269	2482	3525	33547	1956	30953	89	549
2007	962	20754	20040	6915	9275	3850	20770	1925	17872	98	875
2008	956	20340	128525	7644	117118	3763	21885	1733	18689	93	1369
2009	956	20755	133872	8161	121373	4339	22017	1635	18753	98	1531
2010	956	21114	140663	8903	126130	5630	23712	1572	20184	130	1827
2011	1067	21347	145773	9755	129918	6100	26849	1380	23276	132	2061
2012	1115	21492	149037	10315	132333	6389	28650	1232	24925	134	2359
2013	1116	21673	71056	11588	52481	6988	28294	1078	24651	136	2429

注：1. 铁路数据为北京市市辖范围，2005年以前取自北京铁路分局，2005年及以后取自北京铁路局。
2. 从2006年开始，公路里程包括村道数据。
3. 2006-2007年公路客运量为持有道路运输经营许可证的客运车辆发生的旅客运输量；从2008年开始，公路客运量根据交通运输部《公路水路运输量专项调查方案》调整旅客运输量统计口径,调整后包括旅游客运、省际客运企业、郊区客运和市郊公交的运输量。2013年公路客运量、公路旅客周转量按照《交通运输部办公厅关于印发公路水路运输量统计试行方案（2014）的通知》，统计范围调整为省际客运、旅游客运和郊区客运，市郊公交不再纳入客运量统计。
4. 从2007年开始,公路货物运输为营业性运量。
5. 民航统计范围为北京地区的民航运输法人单位，不包括在京运输飞行的外省市及外国航空公司。

Note: a) Railway figures are statistics within Beijing's jurisdiction. Figures for years before 2005 were from Beijing Railway Branch, those for 2005 and after were from Beijing Railway Bureau.
b) From 2006, road mileage includes figures of rural roads.
c) In 2006 and 2007, highway passenger traffic refered to numbers of passengers traveled by vehicles with road transportation permit ; From 2008, highway passenger traffic refers to passengers travelled for tourism, cross-provincial, suburban and peri-urban purposes, in line with the adjustments made in Special Survey Program for Highway and Water Way Transportation Volume by the Ministry of Traffic and Transportation. In 2013, according to the Notice by the General Office of the Ministry of Transport on Printing and Issuing Provisional Plan for Counting Highway and Water Way Transportation Volume,the statistical scope of highway passenger traffic and volume of highway transportation was changed to inter-provincial, tourist and suburban transport, and suburban buses are no longer counted.
d) From 2007, highway freight traffic refers to freight for operational purpose.
e) Civil aviation covers legal entities of civil aviation registered in Beijing, excluding airlines of other provinces and other countries with transport and flight in Beijing.

13-1 续表 1 Continued 1

年份 Year	旅客周转量(万人公里) Total Passenger Turnover (10000 passengers-km)	铁路 Railway	公路 Highway	民航 Civil Aviation	货物周转量(万吨公里) Total Freight Turnover (10000 ton-km)	铁路 Railway	公路 Highway	民航 Civil Aviation	管道 Pipeline
1978			59367				92247		
1979			64033				97616		
1980			73692				93899		
1981-1985			**498768**				**540035**		
1981			81879				93254		
1982	755815	641550	90092	24173	3451037	3329450	106767	13530	1290
1983	853655	723200	103742	26713	3794223	3666600	110118	16099	1406
1984	968481	821431	113871	33179	4309798	4171789	115740	20896	1373
1985	1089919	936300	109184	44435	4719663	4576400	114156	27437	1670
1986-1990	**6333894**	**2608550**	**649210**	**3076133**	**13703344**	**11007906**	**2496086**	**191715**	**7637**
1986	1133620	496288	119065	518267	2569579	2133836	405645	28281	1817
1987	1281763	534720	133735	613308	2792589	2282106	471393	37966	1124
1988	1503508	588947	141625	772936	2887270	2344684	498391	42612	1583
1989	1216981	521263	122435	573283	2765660	2179878	546022	38194	1566
1990	1198022	467332	132350	598339	2688246	2067402	574635	44662	1547
1991-1995	**8690001**	**2645880**	**842807**	**5201314**	**15220745**	**11382191**	**3488944**	**346841**	**2769**
1991	1383465	506431	139041	737993	2799731	2153176	591187	54929	439
1992	1666810	531574	161735	973501	2938746	2230406	642200	65614	527
1993	1656130	551392	127461	977277	3143512	2301941	767790	73216	565
1994	1906718	547488	180030	1179200	3107722	2303265	725740	78142	575
1995	2076879	508995	234540	1333344	3231034	2393403	762027	74940	663
1996-2000	**12752549**	**2649587**	**1744526**	**8358436**	**14987253**	**10458031**	**3918017**	**609517**	**1688**
1996	2219196	459514	250488	1509194	3176234	2311011	784888	79983	352
1997	2272177	477538	261204	1533435	3129097	2263274	769190	96202	431
1998	2419787	505554	304592	1609641	2846652	1952602	783237	110470	343
1999	2701471	579759	400597	1721115	2838857	1929269	754264	155171	153
2000	3139918	627222	527645	1985051	2996414	2001875	826438	167691	410
2001-2005	**27318106**	**3454437**	**5282581**	**18581088**	**18786284**	**12470145**	**4130198**	**1121536**	**1064404**
2001	3462571	677146	529776	2255649	3159848	2167201	826437	165832	378
2002	3961623	642676	603510	2715437	3405498	2213728	835873	195792	160105
2003	3933077	619631	693100	2620346	3620777	2409620	789952	208058	213147
2004	7580057	738956	1582441	5258660	4022791	2571459	822992	270182	358158
2005	8380778	776028	1873754	5730996	4577370	3108137	854944	281672	332617
2006-2010	**53738139**	**4632513**	**10259436**	**38846188**	**22812698**	**12714298**	**4414583**	**1906235**	**3777583**
2006	8254536	890691	791947	6571898	4231243	2625719	885991	335693	383840
2007	9603464	908438	1474249	7220776	4490390	2684862	792883	376074	636572
2008	10419977	902281	2409604	7108091	4542168	2535249	840878	356744	809297
2009	11464758	935596	2677144	7852018	4412317	2293902	878887	355257	884271
2010	13995404	995507	2906492	10093405	5136580	2574567	1015944	482467	1063602
2011	15286501	1086609	3036655	11163237	6169272	3113203	1323259	474856	1257955
2012	15957877	1163833	3047757	11746287	6383052	3076143	1397736	489845	1419328
2013	14987719	1179555	1360831	12447333	6809063	3231824	1561929	491861	1523448

13-1 续表 2 Continued 2

年 份 Year	机动车拥有量(万辆) Possession of Motor Vehicles (10000 units)	#民用汽车拥有量 Possession of Civil Motor Vehicles	#私人 Private	邮电业务总量(万元) Business Volume of Post and Telecommunications Service (10000 yuan)	年末固定电话用户数(万户) Number of Fixed Telephone Subscribers (10000 subscribers)	年末移动电话用户数(万户) Number of Mobile Phone Subscribers (10000 subscribers)	固定电话主线普及率(线/百人) Popularization Rate of Landline Telephones (lines/100 persons)	移动电话普及率(户/百人) Popularization Rate of Mobile Phones (subscribers/100 persons)	互联网宽带接入用户数(万户) Subscribers of Broad Band Internet (10000 subscribers)
1978		6.1		24114	7.3		0.8		
1979		7.0		26724	7.8		0.9		
1980		8.1		30047	8.4		0.9		
1981-1985				**204839**					
1981		8.9		31907	9.2		1.0		
1982		9.3		34777	9.8		1.1		
1983		9.8		38525	10.9		1.2		
1984		12.1		45629	12.1		1.3		
1985		16.0		54002	13.6		1.4		
1986-1990				**434582**					
1986		18.6		62079	16.5		1.6		
1987		19.3	0.7	71152	19.5		1.9		
1988		22.2	1.3	84331	23.8		2.2		
1989		24.8	2.4	98124	27.8		2.6		
1990		27.1	2.8	118896	33.3	0.3	3.1	0.03	
1991-1995				**1664508**					
1991		29.7	3.5	157418	39.5	0.7	3.6	0.1	
1992		34.1	4.9	215769	48.0	1.2	4.4	0.1	
1993		41.6	6.7	311251	66.5	3.2	6.0	0.3	
1994		48.1	8.5	418774	100.4	7.7	8.9	0.7	
1995		58.9	12.8	561296	150.5	16.9	12.0	1.4	
1996-2000				**6756754**					
1996		62.2	17.4	729022	195.7	31.0	15.5	2.5	
1997		78.4	29.8	930137	251.2	62.0	20.3	5.0	
1998		89.8	40.7	1290967	313.3	104.2	25.1	8.4	
1999		95.1	44.7	1659133	376.3	186.2	29.9	14.8	
2000	157.8	104.1	49.4	2147496	451.2	347.2	33.1	25.5	
2001-2005				**15331552**					
2001	169.9	114.5	62.4	2182782	525.7	629.4	38.0	45.4	
2002	189.9	133.9	81.1	2540454	585.5	919.5	41.1	64.6	
2003	212.4	163.1	107.1	3040327	682.7	1109.0	46.9	76.1	
2004	229.6	187.1	129.8	3438376	847.4	1340.7	56.8	89.8	
2005	258.3	214.6	154.0	4129614	943.5	1459.8	61.3	94.9	228.9
2006-2010				**40044606**					
2006	287.6	244.1	181.0	5046014	905.2	1571.1	56.5	98.1	281.2
2007	312.8	277.8	212.1	6726273	914.5	1598.3	54.6	95.4	347.2
2008	350.4	318.1	248.3	8008147	884.9	1616.2	50.0	91.3	382.7
2009	401.9	372.1	300.3	9175072	893.1	1825.4	48.0	98.1	451.7
2010	480.9	452.9	374.4	11089100 (4284217)	885.6	2129.8	45.1	108.6	545.6
2011	498.3	473.2	389.7	4878792	883.9	2575.9	43.8	127.6	523.4
2012	520.0	495.7	407.5	5464681	883.1	3168.0	42.7	153.1	572.0
2013	543.7	518.9	426.5	6524689	867.6	3373.8	41.0	159.5	534.7

注：1．邮电业务总量2000年及以前按1990年不变价格计算，2001-2010年按2000年不变价格计算，2011年开始按2010年不变价格计算。表内2010年邮电业务总量是按2000年价格计算,()内数据是按2010年价格计算。

2．2006-2010年主线普及率和移动电话普及率根据第六次人口普查数据进行了调整。

Note: a) Business volume of post and telecommunications before 2000 was calculated at 1990's constant prices; that of 2001-2010 was calculated at 2000's constant prices; and from 2011, the volume was calculated at 2010's constant prices. In this table, the volume of post and telecommunication service in 2010 was calculated at 2000's price, and figures in () were calculated at 2010's price.

b) Data of popularization rate of landline telephones and mobile phones for 2006-2010 were adjusted based on the results from the 6th population census .

13-2 社会客货运总量(换算周转量)
PASSENGER AND FREIGHT TRAFFIC (CONVERTED TURNOVER)

单位：万吨公里 (10000 tons-km)

项目	Item	2013	2012	2013年为2012年% 2013 as % of 2012	构成(%) Composition(%) 2013	2012
运输总量	**Total**	**9281235.4**	**8895413.6**	**104.3**	**100.0**	**100.0**
铁路	Railway	4411379.5	4239975.4	104.0	47.5	47.7
公路	Highway	1698012.1	1702511.3	99.7	18.3	19.1
民航	Civil Aviation	1648395.7	1533598.7	107.5	17.8	17.2
管道	Pipeline	1523448.1	1419328.1	107.3	16.4	16.0

13-3 运输线路
TRANSPORTATION ROUTES

项目	Item	条数(条) Number (line) 2013	2012	长度(公里) Length (km) 2013	2012
铁路	Railway	55	56	1115.5	1115.1
公路	Highway	10289	10145	21673.3	21491.8
民航	Civil Aviation				
#中国国际航空公司	Air China	298	284		
中国新华航空有限责任公司	China Xinhua Airlines	331	327		
管道	Pipeline	16	15	3825.5	3496.9

注：铁路长度为营业里程，管道长度为管输里程。

Note: Railway length refers to operating mileage, and pipeline length refers to transportation mileage.

13-4 铁路、民航主要技术经济指标
MAIN TECHNICAL AND ECONOMIC INDICATORS OF RAILWAY AND CIVIL AVIATION

项目	Item	2013	2012	2013年为2012年% 2013 as % of 2012
铁 路	**Railway**			
内燃机车每万吨公里耗柴油 (千克)	Diesel Consumption of Diesel Locomotives per 10 000 Ton-km (kg)	34.5	34.3	100.6
电力机车每万吨公里耗电 (千瓦小时)	Electricity Consumption of Electric Locomotives per 10000 Ton-km (kwh)	95.4	92.9	102.7
民 航	**Civil Aviation**			
每吨公里耗航空油 (千克)	Aviation-oil Consumption per Ton-km (kg)	0.29	0.24	118.5

13-5 机动车拥有量
NUMBER OF CIVIL MOTOR VEHICLES

单位：万辆 (10000 units)

项目	Item	2013	2012	2013年为2012年% 2013 as % of 2012
机动车	**Motor Vehicles**	**543.7**	**520.0**	**104.6**
#民用汽车	Civil Automobiles	518.9	495.7	104.7
#载货汽车	Trucks	25.7	23.7	108.4
载客汽车	Passanger Cars	486.1	464.9	104.6
#私人汽车	Private Cars	426.5	407.5	104.7
#轿 车	Sedans	311.0	298.2	104.3

资料来源：北京市公安局公安交通管理局。
Source: Beijing Traffic Management Bureau.

13-6 邮电业务主要指标
MAIN INDICATORS OF POST AND TELECOMMUNICATION SERVICE

项　目		Item		2013	2012	2013年为2012年% 2013 as % of 2012
邮电业务量	**(万元)**	**Business Volume of Post and Telecommunications**	**(10000 yuan)**			
(2010年不变价)		**(at 2010's constant prices)**		**6524689**	**5464681**	**119.4**
邮　政		Post		584585	584535	100.0
电　信		Telecommunications		5940104	4880146	121.7
邮电业务总量		**Total Amount of Post and Telecommunication Businesses**				
函　件	(万件)	Letters	(10000 pcs)	71559	67219	106.5
包　件	(万件)	Parcels	(10000 pcs)	582	597	97.5
特快专递	(万件)	EMS	(10000 pcs)	4792	3984	120.3
汇　票	(万件)	Money Orders	(10000 pcs)	620	763	81.2
订销报纸累计	(万份)	Newspapers Subscribed	(10000 copies)	81970	83133	98.6
订销杂志累计	(万份)	Magazines Subscribed	(10000 copies)	4695	6076	77.3
邮政储蓄期末余额	(亿元)	Post Savings Deposit Balance	(100 million yuan)	748.8	713.8	104.9
长途电话通话量(固定)	(亿分钟)	Long-distance Calls (Fixed-line Telephone)	(100 million minutes)	42.2	44.0	95.8
本地电话通话量(固定)	(亿次)	Local Calls (Fixed-line Telephone)	(100 million times)	131.0	142.5	91.9
移动电话通话量	(亿分钟)	Calls of Mobile Phones	(100 million minutes)	1536.0	1478.5	103.9
移动短信业务量	(亿条)	Short Message Services	(100 million messages)	459.0	447.9	102.5
年末移动电话用户	(万户)	Mobile Phone Subscribers	(10000 subscribers)	3373.8	3168.0	106.5
#3G移动电话用户数	(万户)	3G Mobile Phone Subscribers	(10000 subscribers)	1461.0	855.5	170.8
年末固定电话用户	(万户)	Fixed Telephone Subscribers	(10000 subscribers)	867.6	883.1	98.2
#住宅电话用户	(万户)	Household Telephone Subscribers	(10000 subscribers)	525.8	563.8	93.3
长途光缆纤芯长度	(芯公里)	Fiber Core Length of Long-distance Optic Cable	(core-km)	180658.7	172857.0	104.5
长途电话交换机容量	(万路端)	Capacity of Long-distance Telephone Exchanges	(10000 roadheads)	56.6	55.1	102.7
局用交换机容量	(万门)	Capacity of Office Telephone Exchanges	(10000 units)	1678.4	1581.1	106.2
移动电话交换机容量	(万户)	Capacity of Mobile Phone Exchanges	(10000 subscribers)	4820	4734	101.8
固定电话主线普及率	(线/百人)	Popularization Rate of Fixed-line Telephones	(lines/100 persons)	41.0	42.7	
移动电话普及率	(户/百人)	Popularization Rate of Mobile Phones	(subscribers/100 persons)	159.5	153.1	
互联网宽带接入用户数	(万户)	Subscribers of Broad Band Internet	(10000 subscribers)	534.7	572.0	93.5
互联网上网人数	(万人)	Number of Internet Users	(10000 persons)	1556.0	1458.0	106.7

注：1. 固定电话用户包括市内电话用户和农村电话用户。
2. "互联网上网人数"来源于中国互联网络信息中心（CNNIC)发布的《中国互联网络发展状况统计报告》。

Note: a) Data of fixed-line telephone subscribers covered urban and rural areas.
b) "Number of Internet Users" was sourced from the Statistical Report on Internet Development in China issued by CNNIC.

主要统计指标解释

货（客）运量 指在一定时期内，各种运输工具实际运送的货物（旅客）数量。是反映运输业为国民经济和人民生活服务的数量指标，也是制定和检查运输生产计划，研究运输发展规模和速度的重要指标。货运按吨计算，客运按人计算。货物不论运输距离长短，货物类别，均按实际重量统计；旅客不论行程远近或票价多少，均按一人一次作为客运量统计。半价票、小孩票也按一人统计。

货物（旅客）周转量 指在一定时期内，由各种运输工具运送的货物（旅客）数量与其相应运输距离的乘积之总和，是反映运输业生产总成果的重要指标，也是编制和检查运输生产计划、计算运输效率、劳动生产率以及核算运输单位的主要基础资料。计算货物周转量通常按发出站与到达站之间的最短距离，也就是计费距离计算。

邮电业务总量 是以货币形式表示的邮政电信企业为社会提供各类邮政通信服务的总数量。计算公式为：

$$\text{邮电业务总量}=\sum\left(\begin{array}{l}\text{各类邮政通信业务量}\times\text{不变}\\\text{单价}\end{array}\right)$$

$$+\text{出租代维及其他业务收入}$$

函件 是指邮政部门为用户传递以书面信息为主的邮件，包括信件、印刷品和邮送广告。

包件 指符合包裹准寄范围，通过邮政渠道寄递的物品。包括国内普通包裹、国内快递包裹、国际及港澳台包裹。

长途电话交换机容量 是指用于接入长途电话网的电话交换机的设备额定容量。

局用交换机容量 是指安装在本地电信企业内用于接续本地固定电话的电话交换机容量。包括现用和备用的人工或自动交换机（含远端模块）的全部容量，包括接入网设备容量。

移动电话交换机容量 分为 GSM、CDMA 两种。指移动电话交换机根据一定话务模型和交换机处理能力计算出来的最大同时服务用户的数量。

主线普及率 是指报告期行政区域常住人口中，平均每百人拥有的固定电话主线数。计算公式为：

$$\text{主线普及率}=\frac{\text{电话主线数(本地电话用户)}}{\text{行政区域常住人口数}}$$

移动电话普及率 是指报告期行政区域常住人口中，平均每百人拥有的移动电话的用户数。计算公式为：

$$\text{移动电话普及率}=\frac{\text{移动电话用户总数}}{\text{行政区域常住人口数}}$$

联网宽带接入用户数 指报告期末在电信企业登记注册，通过 xDSL、FTTx+LAN 以及其他宽带接入方式和普通专线接入公众互联网的用户。

Explanatory Notes on Main Statistical Indicators

Freight (Passenger) Traffic refers to the volume of freight (passenger) transported with various means during a certain period of time. It is a quantitative measure to show how the transport industry serves the national economy and people's life, and is also an important indicator for preparing and reviewing transport plan and studying the development scale and speed of the transport industry. Freight transport is calculated in tons and passenger traffic is calculated in the number of persons. Regardless of the types or traveling distance of freight, freight transport is calculated in the actual weight of goods: and regardless of the traveling distance or ticket price, passenger traffic is calculated following the principle that one person can be counted only once in one travel. The passenger who travels with a half-price ticket or a child ticket is also calculated as one person.

Freight (Passenger) Turnover refers to the sum of the transported cargo (passengers) multiplyed by the transport distance during a certain period of time. This is an important indicator to show the total results of the transport industry, and also serves as main basic data for preparing and reviewing transport plans and measuring transport efficiency, labor productivity and the unit cost of transport. Freight Turnover is usually calculated by the shortest distance between the departure station and the arrival station, namely the charging distance.

Business Volume of Post and Telecommunications refers to the total amount of post and telecommunication services, expressed in monetary terms, provided by the post and telecommunication sectors for the society. The formula is as follows:

Business Volume of Post and Telecommunications

=∑(Transactions of Post and Telecommunication Service x Constant Price) + Income from Leasing, Maintenance and other Services

Correspondences mean mails mainly in the form of written information delivered by postal authorities, including letters, prints and delivered advertisements.

Parcels means articles permitted for mailing, and mailed through postal channels, including domestic express parcels,

international parcels, and parcels from and to Hong Kong, Macao and Taiwan.

Capacity of Long-distance Phone Exchanges means the rated capacity of phone exchangers used for connecting to the long-distance phone network.

Capacity of Local Exchanges means the capacity of phone exchangers installed in local telecom businesses and used for linking local fixed telephones. It is the sum of all capacity of existing and backup manual or automatic exchangers (with far-end modules), including the capacity of network access equipment.

Capacity of Mobile Phone Exchanges, divided into GSM and CDMA, means the maximum number of users receiving services simultaneously from mobile phone exchangers, calculated from certain traffic model and exchanger processing capacity.

Popularization Rate of Fixed-line Telephones means the average number of main lines of fixed-line telephones owned by one hundred persons of permanent population in administrative areas in the reporting period. It is calculated with the following formula:

Popularization Rate of Landline= Number of Main Lines of Telephone (Local Phone Users) / Number of Permanent Population in Administrative Areas

Popularization Rate of Mobile Phones means the number of mobile phones owned by average 100 persons among permanent population in administrative areas in the reporting period. It is calculated with the following formula:

Popularization Rate of Mobile Phones = Total Number of Mobile Phone Users / Permanent Population in Administrative Areas

Subscribers of Broadband Internet means subscribers registered at telecom companies to connect with public Internet through xDSL, FTTx+LAN as well as other broadband connections and general special lines at the end of reporting period.

北京统计年鉴2014 BEIJING STATISTICAL YEARBOOK

批发和零售业、住宿和餐饮业

WHOLESALE AND RETAIL TRADE, ACCOMMODATION AND RESTAURANTS

简要说明

一、本章资料的主要内容

本章资料反映北京市商品流通市场发展及批发和零售业、住宿和餐饮业经营情况。主要内容有社会消费品零售总额；批发和零售业商品购进、销售、库存总值、商品分类销售情况及主要商品销售情况；住宿业和餐饮业经营情况；机动车销售情况；限额以上批发和零售业、住宿业和餐饮业财务状况；连锁企业基本情况；商品交易市场基本情况、成交额；消费者投诉处理情况。

二、本章的统计范围

社会消费品零售总额指标于1993年、1997年和2003年做了较大调整。1993年起不再包括对农民的农业生产资料；1997年起不再包括居民购买住房；2003年起不再包括由各种经济类型的制造业法人企业、产业活动单位直接售给城乡居民（包括本企业职工）和社会集团的商品以及农民对非农业居民的零售额。

限额以上批发和零售业、住宿业和餐饮业统计限额标准：2008年以前，批发业为年销售额2000万元及以上；零售业为年销售额500万元及以上；住宿业为星级饭店和星级以外年营业收入500万元及以上；餐饮业为年营业额200万元及以上。2008年调整后，批发业为年主营业务收入2000万元及以上；零售业为年主营收入500万元及以上；住宿业为星级饭店和星级以外年主营业务收入200万元及以上；餐饮业为年主营业务收入200万元及以上。

三、本章的资料来源

本章资料中消费者投诉处理情况由北京市消费者协会提供，其它资料由北京市统计局、国家统计局北京调查总队提供。

四、本章的统计调查方法

限额以上批发和零售业、住宿和餐饮业单位采用全面调查的方法；连锁企业、商品交易市场采取全数调查；限额以下批发和零售业、住宿和餐饮业法人单位及个体户采用抽样调查方法。

五、有关统计标准的变化说明

2010年以前企业大中小型划分执行2003年《统计上大中小型企业划分办法（暂行）》标准；自2011年开始，大中微型企业划分标准执行国家统计局《关于统计上大中小微型企业划分办法》（国统字[2011]75号）。

六、本章中关于历史数据调整的问题

按照国家统计局统一要求和统一方法，本章中1978年至2003年的社会消费品零售总额数据，根据2004年第一次经济普查结果，采用“速度推算法”进行了修正。2004年数据为第一次经济普查数据。2005-2007年数据根据2008年第二次经济普查结果，采用“趋势离差法”进行了修正。2008年数据为第二次经济普查数据。

Brief Introduction

I. Main Content

Statistics in this chapter show the development of commodity circulation market and the operations of wholesale and retail trades, accommodation and restaurants. Figures mainly include retail sales of consumer goods, total value of commodity purchase, sales and inventory in wholesale and retail trades, sales of commodities by category, and sales of main commodities; situation of accommodation and restaurants; sales of mobile vehicles; financial status of wholesale, retail, accommodation and restaurants enterprises above designated size; basic situation of chain businesses; basic situation and turnover of commodity transaction markets, and trading volume of main commodities; and settlement of consumer complaints.

II. Scope of Statistics

Major adjustments were made to the indicators of Retail Sales of Consumer Goods for 1993, 1997 and 2003. From 1993, the indicator did not cover agricultural capital goods for farmers any longer; from 1997, it did not cover houses bought by residents any longer; from 2003, it did not cover goods sold by corporate manufacturing enterprises and industrial activity entities of various economic types to urban and rural residents (including enterprises' own employees) and social groups as well as retail sales by farmers to non-agricultural residents any longer.

As for standards for wholesale and retail trades, accommodation and restaurants above designated size, before 2008, for wholesale trades, the standard was annual sales of RMB 20 million or more; for retail trades, annual sales of RMB 5 million or more; for accommodation, star-rated hotels and non-star-rated hotels with annual turnover of RMB 5 million or more; for restaurants, annual turnover of RMB 2 million or more. After adjustments were made in 2008, the designated size is, for whole sale trades, annual sales of RMB 20 million or more; for retail trades, annual sales of RMB 5 million or more; for accommodation, star-rated hotels and non-star-rated hotels with annual main business income of RMB 2 million or more; for restaurants, annual main business income of RMB 2 million or more.

III. Source of Data

Data in settlement of consumer complaints are sourced Beijing Customer Institution. The other Data are sourced from Beijing Municipal Bureau of Statistics and NBS Survey Office in Beijing.

IV. Survey Methodology

The method of comprehensive survey was used for statistics of wholesale and retail trades, accommodation, and restaurants service enterprises above designated size; complete enumeration was used for chain businesses, and commodity trading markets; sample survey was used for wholesale and retail trades, accommodation, and restaurants corporate enterprises below designated size as well as self-employed businesses.

Ⅴ. Changes in Relevant Statistical Standards

Before 2010，the classification of small, medium and large-sized enterprises should comply with the standard of Measures for Statistical Classification of Small, Medium and Large-sized Enterprises (Temporary) 2003. From 2011, the classification of micro, small, medium and large-sized enterprises should comply with the Notification of National Bureau of Statistics on Printing and Issuing the Measures for Statistical Classification of Micro, Small, Medium and Large-sized Enterprises (GTZ[2011]No.75).

Ⅵ. Adjustment to Historical Data

In accordance with the unified requirements and methods put forward by the National Bureau of Statistics, data for 1978-2003 on retail sales of consumer goods were adjusted with the "speed calculation method" according to the first economic census results in 2004. Data for 2004 are gathered from the first economic census. Data for 2005-2007 were revised with the "trend deviation method" in accordance with the second economic census results in 2008. Data for 2008 are gathered from the second economic census.

14-1 历年社会消费品零售总额(1978-2013年)
TOTAL RETAIL SALES OF CONSUMER GOODS (1978-2013)

单位：亿元 (100 million yuan)

年 份 Year	社会消费品零售总额 Retail Sales of Consumer Goods	按商品类别分 By Category of Commodity			
		吃类商品 Food	穿类商品 Clothing	用类商品 Daily Supplies	烧类商品 Fuels
1978	44.2	18.0	8.9	16.0	1.3
1979	53.3	20.8	11.3	19.7	1.5
1980	62.8	24.9	13.4	22.9	1.6
1981-1985	**472.7**	**180.9**	**85.1**	**196.2**	**10.5**
1981	70.7	28.0	14.5	26.5	1.7
1982	75.4	29.7	13.7	30.3	1.7
1983	86.4	34.0	15.7	34.8	1.9
1984	105.8	39.6	18.7	45.2	2.3
1985	134.4	49.6	22.5	59.4	2.9
1986-1990	**1239.8**	**494.9**	**166.7**	**551.8**	**26.4**
1986	155.0	60.7	22.8	68.0	3.5
1987	188.9	77.4	27.4	80.2	3.9
1988	256.0	100.6	36.0	114.9	4.5
1989	294.8	119.4	34.9	134.1	6.4
1990	345.1	136.8	45.6	154.6	8.1
1991-1995	**3239.5**	**1261.4**	**481.3**	**1422.2**	**74.6**
1991	408.3	158.2	53.7	187.6	8.8
1992	503.0	193.6	66.9	230.5	12.0
1993	611.2	220.7	96.5	277.6	16.4
1994	766.6	283.2	125.3	338.6	19.5
1995	950.4	405.7	138.9	387.9	17.9
1996-2000	**6811.7**	**2177.0**	**858.9**	**3576.5**	**199.3**
1996	1061.6	427.5	152.5	461.8	19.8
1997	1208.5	447.9	161.6	565.6	33.4
1998	1373.6	399.8	167.2	764.2	42.4
1999	1509.3	430.4	178.8	852.9	47.2
2000	1658.7	471.4	198.8	932.0	56.5
2001-2005	**11671.8**	**3061.2**	**1218.6**	**6722.7**	**669.3**
2001	1831.4	528.7	221.9	1016.9	63.9
2002	2005.2	540.2	219.9	1167.4	77.7
2003	2296.9	596.4	252.3	1356.4	91.8
2004	2626.6	644.9	242.1	1538.3	201.3
2005	2911.7	751.0	282.4	1643.7	234.6
2006-2010	**23315.2**	**5343.5**	**2107.9**	**14019.4**	**1844.4**
2006	3295.3	818.8	314.7	1852.6	309.2
2007	3835.2	940.4	359.3	2205.2	330.3
2008	4645.5	1073.3	411.7	2799.4	361.1
2009	5309.9	1180.0	473.8	3278.2	377.9
2010	6229.3	1331.0	548.4	3884.0	465.9
2011	6900.3	1561.4	665.2	4080.1	593.6
2012	7702.8	1679.1	718.0	4678.4	627.3
2013	8375.1	1672.6	727.3	5367.8	607.4

注：1978-2003年社会消费品零售额按2004年第一次经济普查数据进行了修订，2004年为第一次经济普查数据，2005-2007年数据按第二次经济普查进行了修订，2008年数据为第二次经济普查数据。

Note: Retail sales of consumer goods for 1978-2003 were revised according to the first economic cencus in 2004.Figures for 2004 were gathered from the first economic census. Figures for 2005-2007 were revised based on the results of the second economic census. Figures for 2008 were gathered from the second economic census.

14-2 社会消费品零售总额(2009-2013年)
TOTAL RETAIL SALES OF CONSUMER GOODS (2009-2013)

单位：亿元 (100 million yuan)

项目	Item	2009	2010	2011	2012	2013	2013年为2012年% 2013 as % of 2012
社会消费品零售总额	**Total Retail Sales of Consumer Goods**	**5309.9**	**6229.3**	**6900.3**	**7702.8**	**8375.1**	**108.7**
按商品类别分	**By Category of Commodity**						
吃类商品	Food	1180.0	1331.0	1561.4	1679.1	1672.6	102.5
穿类商品	Clothing	473.8	548.4	665.2	718.0	727.3	101.0
用类商品	Daily Supplies	3278.3	3884.0	4080.1	4678.4	5367.8	113.5
烧类商品	Fuels	377.9	465.9	593.6	627.3	607.4	97.4
按销售单位所在地分	**By Location of Seller**						
城镇	Urban	5221.7	6128.8	6789.6	7580.4	8231.0	108.6
农村	Rural	88.1	100.5	110.7	122.4	144.1	117.7
按消费品形态分	**By Form of Consumer Goods**						
餐饮收入	Food and Beverage Income	590.3	666.6	765.9	824.4	783.1	95.0
商品零售	Retail Sales of Commodities	4719.6	5562.7	6134.4	6878.4	7592.0	110.4

注：本表中2013年为2012年发展速度指标是按可比口径计算的数据。
Note:Statistis for 2013 are the 2012 olevelopment speed indicator calculated on comparable basis.

14-3 按登记注册类型分限额以上批发和零售企业商品零售额（2013年）
RETAIL SALES OF GOODS IN WHOLESALE AND RETAIL ENTERPRISES ABOVE DESIGNATED SIZE BY REGISTRATION TYPE（2013）

单位：万元 (10000 yuan)

项目	Item	合计 Total Sales	批发业 Wholesale	零售业 Retail Trade
总计	**Total**	**71592656**	**7348633**	**64244023**
内资企业	Domestic Funded Enterprises	56949746	5273574	51676172
#国有	State-owned Enterprises	1374813	93926	1280888
集体	Collectively-owned Enterprises	496593	4965	491628
股份有限公司	Companies Limited by Shares	9861891	1304388	8557503
港澳台商投资企业	Hong Kong, Macao and Taiwan-invested Enterprises	4698838	523607	4175231
外商投资企业	Foreign-invested Enterprises	9944072	1551452	8392620

注：本表统计范围为限额以上批发和零售业法人单位、产业活动单位和个体经营户。
Note: Figures in this table cover corporate entities in wholesale and retail trade above designated size, activity entities and individual entities .

14-4 批发和零售业商品购进、销售、库存情况
TOTAL VALUE OF PURCHASES, SALES AND INVENTORY OF COMMODITIES IN WHOLESALE AND RETAIL TRADE

单位：万元 (10000 yuan)

项目	Item	2013	2012	2013年为2012年% 2013 as % of 2012
商品购进额	**Total Purchases of Commodities**	**561123793**	**501985637**	**111.8**
市内购进	In the City	119523940	102283271	116.9
市外购进	From Outside Beijing	355111921	316570502	112.2
进口	Imported	86487931	83131864	104.0
商品销售额	**Total Sales of Commodities**	**598003037**	**536925945**	**111.4**
批发额	**Wholesale**	**523754692**	**469294051**	**111.6**
市内批发	In the City	120356469	107488128	112.0
市外批发	To Outside Beijing	380000857	342804730	110.9
出口	Exported	23397367	19001193	123.1
零售额	**Retail**	**74248345**	**67631894**	**109.8**
期末商品库存额	**Inventory (Year-end)**	**50333816**	**49904492**	**100.9**

注：本表统计范围为批发和零售业法人单位、产业活动单位和个体经营户。
Note: Figures in this table cover corporate entities in wholesale and retail trade above designated size, activity entities and individual entities .

14-5 限额以上批发和零售业商品购进、销售、库存情况(2013年)
TOTAL VALUE OF PURCHASES, SALES AND INVENTORY IN WHOLESALE AND RETAIL CORPORATE ENTITIES (2013)

单位：万元 (10000 yuan)

项目	Item	合计 Total Sales	批发业 Wholesale	零售业 Retail
商品购进额	**Total Purchases of Commodities**	**546183082**	**475076283**	**71106798**
市内购进	In the City	109660910	75419604	34241305
市外购进	From Outside Beijing	350960283	315739338	35220945
进口	Imported	85561889	83917341	1644548
商品销售额	**Total Sales of Commodities**	**579045127**	**500588780**	**78456347**
批发额	**Wholesale**	**507452471**	**493240147**	**14212324**
市内批发	In the City	108078026	101227197	6850829
市外批发	To Outside Beijing	376546611	369223052	7323559
出口	Exported	22827834	22789898	37936
零售额	**Retail**	**71592656**	**7348633**	**64244023**
期末商品库存额	**Inventory (Year-end)**	**49505831**	**41594243**	**7911588**

注：本表统计范围为限额以上批发和零售业法人单位、产业活动单位和个体经营户。
Note: Figures in this table cover corporate entities in wholesale and retail trade above designated size, activity entities and individual entities .

14-6 限额以上批发和零售业商品销售类值(2013年)
SALES BY CATEGORY FOR CORPORATE WHOLESALE AND RETAIL ENTITIES(2013)

单位：万元 (10000 yuan)

项目	Item	商品销售额 Total Sales	批发额 Wholesale	零售额 Retail
合计	**Total**	**579045127**	**507452471**	**71592656**
粮油、食品、饮料、烟酒类	Cereal, Oil, Food, Beverages, Tobacco and Liquor	31663358	24832262	6831096
粮油、食品类	Cereal, Oil, and Food	19601426	14486518	5114907
#粮油类	Cereal and Oil	8931613	8175946	755667
肉禽蛋类	Meat, Poultry and Eggs	1733304	1021954	711351
饮料类	Beverages	3776778	3206362	570417
烟酒类	Tobacco and Liquor	8285154	7139382	1145772
服装鞋帽、针、纺织品类	Clothing, Shoes, Hats and Textiles	11308753	4464042	6844711
服装类	Clothing	7644907	2398595	5246312
鞋帽类	Shoes and Hats	2292018	1076940	1215078
针、纺织品类	Knitwear and Textiles	1371828	988508	383321
化妆品类	Cosmetics	2619651	967195	1652456
金银珠宝类	Gold, Silver and Jewelry	13706603	9886642	3819961
日用品类	Articles for Daily Use	6272693	3127706	3144987
#洗涤用品类	Cleaning Products	1062477	509864	552613
儿童玩具类	Children's Toys	223712	107189	116522
五金、电料类	Hardware and Electrical Materials	1277828	1131060	146768
体育、娱乐用品类	Sports and Recreation Goods	5487253	4369868	1117385
书报、杂志类	Newspapers and Magazines	1997550	900957	1096593
电子出版物及音像制品类	E-Journals and Video Products	504942	209570	295372
家用电器和音像器材类	Household Appliances and Audiovisual Products	11155645	7873000	3282645
中西药品类	Traditional Chinese and Western Medicines	15051319	7834360	7216959
#西药类	Western Medicines	10214983	5228807	4986176
中草药及中成药类	Chinese Herbal Medicines and Chinese Patent Medicines	2458585	1155284	1303300
文化、办公用品类	Cultural and Office Goods	21057559	16768383	4289176
家具类	Furniture	1100954	143775	957178
通讯器材类	Communication Devices	36555687	31618635	4937052
煤炭及制品类	Coal and Coal Products	32491214	32454390	36824
木材及制品类	Wood and Wooden Products	3940133	3940133	
石油及制品类	Petroleum and Its Products	66740267	61004967	5735299
化工材料及制品类	Raw Chemical Materials	68501803	68501803	
#化肥类	Fertilizer	11607856	11607856	
金属材料类	Metal Materials	115502577	115502577	
建筑及装潢材料类	Building and Decoration Materials	3532723	3286298	246425
机电产品及设备类	Electric-mechanic Products and Equipment	27503521	26957895	545626
#农机类	Agricultural Machinery	332608	332608	
汽车类	Automobiles	79488470	61429252	18059218
种子饲料类	Seed and Feedstuff	1273430	1273430	
棉麻类	Cotton and Hemp	3490309	3489912	397
其他类	Others	16820886	15484359	1336527

注：本表统计范围为限额以上批发和零售业法人单位、产业活动单位和个体经营户。

Note: Figures in this table cover corporate entities in wholesale and retail trade above designated size, activity entities and individual entities .

14-7 限额以上批发和零售业商品销售情况(2013年)
COMMODITY SALES OF WHOLESALE AND RETAIL ENTERPRISES ABOVE DESIGNATED SIZE (2013)

项目		Item		商品销售量 Total Sales	批发量 Wholesale Volume	零售量 Retail Volume
大米(稻米)	(百公斤)	Rice	(100 kg)	23843422	21297604	2545818
白面(小麦面)	(百公斤)	Flour (Wheat Flour)	(100 kg)	3296644	2615815	680829
杂粮	(百公斤)	Coarse Cereals	(100 kg)	25903504	25217559	685945
食用植物油	(百公斤)	Edible Vegetable Oil	(100 kg)	43879605	42892427	987178
猪肉	(百公斤)	Pork	(100 kg)	3508139	2817557	690582
牛肉	(百公斤)	Beef	(100 kg)	649941	503979	145962
羊肉	(百公斤)	Mutton	(100 kg)	171901	64425	107476
禽肉	(百公斤)	Poultry	(100 kg)	1898595	1674293	224303
鲜蛋	(百公斤)	Fresh Eggs	(100 kg)	657402	164675	492727
鲜菜	(百公斤)	Fresh Vegetable	(100 kg)	5301490	2411360	2890130
鲜瓜果	(百公斤)	Fresh Melons and Fruits	(100 kg)	4825510	2789500	2036010
水产品	(百公斤)	Aquatic Products	(100 kg)	3088830	2325750	763080
食糖	(百公斤)	Sugar	(100 kg)	33255930	32828150	427780
卷烟	(万支)	Cigarettes	(10000 units)	9750920	9304102	446818
酒	(百升)	Wine	(100 liter)	31827640	30505592	1322048
#白酒	(百升)	Distillate Spirit	(100 liter)	3220089	2556607	663482
啤酒	(百升)	Beer	(100 liter)	28031733	27607383	424350
茶叶	(百公斤)	Tea	(100 kg)	152260	58060	94200
各种服装	(百件)	Clothing	(100 units)	4616258	2687790	1928468
鞋	(百双)	Shoes	(100 pairs)	1201677	772626	429051
数码照相机	(台)	Digital Cameras	(unit)	11992325	11062879	929446
自行车	(辆)	Bicycles	(unit)	458601	281502	177099
彩色电视机	(台)	Color TV Sets	(unit)	8082028	6274034	1807994
摄像机	(台)	Video Cameras	(unit)	1337485	1233299	104186
家用电风扇	(台)	Household Electrical Fans	(unit)	667618	385602	282016
电冰箱（家用电冰箱）	(台)	Household Refrigerators	(unit)	2162814	1426199	736615
洗衣机（家用洗衣机）	(台)	Household Washing Machines	(unit)	6839079	6131780	707299
家用空调器（房间空调器）	(台)	Household Air Conditioners (Roon	(unit)	5018338	4076196	942142
微波炉	(台)	Microwave Ovens	(unit)	1450448	1057939	392509
热水淋浴器	(台)	Showers	(unit)	1096374	596078	500296
吸尘器	(台)	Vacuum Cleaners	(unit)	1575273	1429490	145783
抽油烟机	(台)	Range Hoods	(unit)	584878	341912	242966
电脑（微型计算机）	(台)	Computers (Micro Computers)	(unit)	18089520	13594422	4495098
移动电话机	(部)	Mobile Phones	(unit)	240277500	219483441	20794059
煤炭	(吨)	Coal	(ton)	588070743	587830063	240680
汽油	(吨)	Gasoline	(ton)	11978312	7658730	4319582
煤油	(吨)	Kerosene	(ton)	17459456	17459406	50
柴油	(吨)	Diesel	(ton)	20834053	19644945	1189108
钢材	(吨)	Steel Products	(ton)	201957906	201941976	15930
水泥	(吨)	Cement	(ton)	37169209	36660849	508360
汽车	(辆)	Motor Vehicles	(unit)	2503222	1736438	766784
#轿车	(辆)	Sedan Cars	(unit)	1435292	808140	627152
化学肥料	(吨)	Chemical Fertilizers	(ton)	62277301	62277301	
化学农药	(吨)	Chemical Pesticides	(ton)	213825	213825	
铜	(吨)	Copper	(ton)	6181038	6181038	
铝	(吨)	Aluminium	(ton)	5243778	5243778	

注：本表统计范围为限额以上批发和零售业法人单位、产业活动单位和个体经营户。
Note: Figures in this table cover corporate entities in wholesale and retail trade above designated size, activity entities and individual entities .

14-8 机动车销售情况(2001-2013年)
SALES OF MOTOR VEHICLES (2001-2013)

单位：万辆 (10000 units)

项　目	Item	2001	2002	2003	2004	2005	2006	2007	2008	2009	2010	2011	2012	2013
机动车销售量	**Sales of Motor Vehicles**	**22.9**	**26.0**	**40.8**	**44.7**	**57.0**	**71.4**	**79.8**	**87.8**	**114.8**	**143.2**	**79.7**	**128.5**	**128.2**
#轿　车	Sedan Cars	11.4	15.1	25.2	27.2	38.0	46.2	52.7	54.5	70.6	92.4	49.0	83.2	80.5
新　车	**New Vehicles**	**16.4**	**17.7**	**29.3**	**30.4**	**37.2**	**39.1**	**44.3**	**49.3**	**70.2**	**91.6**	**40.0**	**58.6**	**58.5**
#轿　车	Sedan Cars	10.0	12.0	19.7	20.6	27.7	30.3	34.8	34.9	50.6	66.6	26.2	39.4	37.9
旧　车	**Second-hand Vehicles**	**6.6**	**8.3**	**11.5**	**14.3**	**19.8**	**32.3**	**35.5**	**38.5**	**44.6**	**51.6**	**39.7**	**69.9**	**69.7**
#轿　车	Sedan Cars	1.4	3.0	5.6	6.6	10.2	15.9	17.9	19.5	19.9	25.8	22.8	43.8	42.6

资料来源：北京市工商行政管理局。
Source: Beijing Administration For Industry & Commerce.

14-9 限额以上住宿和餐饮业经营情况(2013年)
STATISTICS FOR ACCOMODATION AND RESTAURANTS ABOVE DESIGNATED SIZE (2013)

项　目	Item	合计 Total	住宿业 Accomodation Industry	餐饮业 Catering Industry
客房数（间）	**Number of Rooms (room)**	**246067**	**239558**	**6509**
床位数（个）	**Number of Beds (unit)**	**412422**	**400992**	**11430**
餐位数（位）	**Number of Tables (table)**	**1486209**	**357027**	**1129182**
营业额（万元）	**Turnover (10000 yuan)**	**9803747**	**4470319**	**5333428**
客房收入	Income from Rooms	2374612	2333458	41153
餐费收入	Income from Table Money	6409935	1297103	5112831
商品销售额	Sales of Commodities	132686	63258	69429
其他收入	Other Incomes	886515	776500	110015

注：本表统计范围为限额以上住宿和餐饮业法人单位、产业活动单位和个体经营户。
Note:This table covers legal entities in accomodation and Restaurants above designated size, activity entities and individual entities .

14-10 限额以上批发和零售企业财务状况(2013年)

单位：万元

项目	Item	企业单位个数(个) Number of Enterprises (unit)	资产总计 Total Assets	流动资产合计 Total Current Assets
合计	**Total**	**7462**	**320256693**	**235060232**
按隶属关系分	**By Affiliation**			
中央	Central	473	144577147	104362519
地方	Local	6989	175679547	130697714
按企业登记注册类型分	**By Registration Type**			
内资	Domestically-invested Enterprises	6918	263513970	192246951
国有	State-owned Enterprises	284	31411818	22294516
集体	Collectively-owned Enterprises	95	1215737	778803
股份合作	Joint-equity Cooperative Enterprises	86	891985	706789
联营	Associate Enterprises	10	120106	81475
有限责任公司	Limited Liability Companies	2392	164643921	126424542
股份有限公司	Companies Limited by Shares	121	39680818	20151994
私营	Private Enterprises	3930	25549585	21808831
其他	Other			
港澳台商投资	Hong Kong, Macao and Taiwan-invested Enterprises	197	10453251	7877859
外商投资	Foreign-invested Enterprises	347	46289472	34935423
按国民经济行业分	**By Sector**			
批发业	**Wholesale**	**4978**	**281992974**	**205806007**
农、林、牧产品批发	Wholesale of Agricultural or Livestock Products	77	15933788	8079107
食品、饮料及烟草制品批发	Wholesale of Foods, Beverage and Tobaccos	372	17007574	13612751
纺织、服装及家庭日用品批发	Wholesale of Textile, Clothes and Household Commodities	450	12330567	9375328
文化、体育用品及器材批发	Wholesale of Cultural and Sports Goods and Equipment	254	7767137	5154630
医药及医疗器材批发	Wholesale of Medicine and Medical Devices	353	8517543	6529491
矿产品、建材及化工产品批发	Wholesale of Mineral Products, Building Materials, and Chemical Products	1556	124882928	87704848
机械设备、五金交电及电子产品批发	Wholesale of Mechanical Equipment, Hardware and Electronic Products	1775	65807698	50896134
贸易经纪与代理	Trade Broker and Agent	67	22317265	20171025
其他批发	Others	74	7428475	4282693
零售业	**Retail**	**2484**	**38263719**	**29254226**
综合零售	Integrated Retail	219	11504543	7655251
食品、饮料及烟草制品专门零售	Special Retails of Foods, Beverage and Tobacoos	112	709432	523431
纺织、服装及日用品专门零售	Special Retail of Textile, Clothing and Domestic Commodities	219	1596450	1247656
文化、体育用品及器材专门零售	Special Retail of Cultural and Sports Goods and Equipment	191	2422931	2117175
医药及医疗器材专门零售	Special Retail of Medicine and Medical Devices	380	4437257	2954857
汽车、摩托车、燃料及零配件专门零售	Special Retail of Automobiles, Motorcycles, Fuels and Their Accessories	703	8849438	6950512
家用电器及电子产品专门零售	Special Retail of Household Electrical Appliances and Electronic Products	379	5942510	5376940
五金、家具及室内装修材料专门零售	Special Retail of Hardware, Furniture and Indoor Decoration Materials	107	715276	553401
货摊、无店铺及其他零售业	Stand Retail, Retail Without Shops and Other Retail	174	2085882	1875002
按规模划分	**By Size**			
#大中型企业	Medium-and Large-sized Enterprises	3000	272312907	196556976

注：1. 限额以上批发和零售企业是指年主营业务收入2000万元及以上批发业和年主营业务收入500万元及以上的零售业法人企业。
2. 行业划分执行2011年国民经济行业分类标准（GB/T 4754-2011）。
3. 自2011年开始，大中型企业划分标准执行国家统计局《关于统计上大中小微型企业划分办法》(国统字[2011]75号)（下同）。

FINANCIAL STATUS OF WHOLESALE AND RETAIL ENTERPRISES ABOVE DESIGNATED SIZE (2013)

(10000 yuan)

资产负债 Assets and Liabilities							
#应收账款 Accounts Receivable	固定资产合计 Total Fixed Assets	固定资产原价 Total Original Value of Fixed Assets	负债合计 Total Liabilities	#流动负债合计 Total Current Liabilities	#应付账款 Accounts Payable	所有者权益合计 Total Owner's Equity	#实收资本 Paid-up Capital
44344835	**9062955**	**14153343**	**230677698**	**203154395**	**64026200**	**89578996**	**45175269**
22869978	2363576	3561266	107506873	93659119	32390101	37070274	19024372
21474857	6699379	10592077	123170825	109495276	31636098	52508722	26150898
38145673	7551963	11247168	195595959	170045802	52556537	67918011	36275394
2227947	965674	1383462	21783460	18634540	3009338	9628359	4364898
41521	80106	128180	957778	666049	127678	257959	59478
37058	40453	51916	892728	891478	45716	-743	61614
4364	2232	4346	80223	80223	18551	39883	35299
28127525	4492265	6476256	128333748	113369003	40497326	36310173	22770515
2523647	1174021	1888656	23181652	16973523	3522464	16499166	5180128
5183612	797212	1314354	20366371	19430987	5335465	5183214	3803462
1212282	377470	628008	7021213	6118986	2112353	3432038	1740565
4986880	1133521	2278167	28060526	26989607	9357309	18228947	7159310
40757556	**6019845**	**9216232**	**200792411**	**174915488**	**56226380**	**81200563**	**39776818**
524724	288367	374789	10806217	7841867	1161191	5127570	1516189
1788511	455026	700046	10798147	10414262	1335342	6209427	2292228
1468309	290522	439159	7351696	7225627	2022115	4978871	2696800
699290	270873	417766	5633909	4421340	788784	2133228	1306859
2281991	195859	353688	5885170	5479036	2464087	2632373	1245033
15418059	2895319	4032676	91565756	77368690	19838967	33317171	19882038
8830782	1373485	2503767	43472751	39816245	12842409	22334947	8824316
9328224	147724	207705	19189936	18853363	15242842	3127329	1527495
417667	102671	186635	6088829	3495058	530642	1339646	485861
3587279	**3043109**	**4937111**	**29885287**	**28238908**	**7799819**	**8378432**	**5398451**
227264	1279905	2128961	7808136	6942545	2284624	3696408	1651728
48913	139585	213844	350329	340805	116570	359103	139143
173806	139112	218852	1357640	1305370	578682	238810	371334
325386	146632	198563	1944411	1826218	616961	478520	292149
1227422	102369	165123	3492888	3319123	1086834	944369	379313
416214	1001724	1626354	6809162	6545299	482854	2040276	1568777
648740	88000	141711	4815280	4793958	1126048	1127230	546373
88382	86691	137337	562531	478333	134495	152745	158454
431153	59093	106368	2744910	2687257	1372751	-659028	291181
37608213	7049151	11401634	195957190	172993367	54713579	76355716	34660137

Note: a) Wholesale and retail enterprises above designated size refer to wholesale enterprises with an annual main business income of 20 million yuan or above and retail enterprises of 5 million yuan or above.

b) Sectors in this table are classified in accordance with the Standard for Classification of National Economic Sectors 2011 (GB/T 4754-2011).

c) From 2011, the classification of medium and large-sized enterprises should comply with the Notification of National Bureau of Statistics on Printing and Issuing the Measures for Classifcation of Small, Medium, and Large-sized Enterprises. (Guotongzi [2011] No. 75). (the same applies to the table following)

14-10 续表

单位：万元

项目	Item	损益 营业收入 Business Income	#主营业务收入 Main Business Income	营业成本 Business Cost	#主营业务成本 Main Business Cost
合 计	**Total**	**493525095**	**483269929**	**460249475**	**453583046**
按隶属关系分	**By Affiliation**				
中央	Central	206264085	200966866	199314259	194740754
地方	Local	287261009	282303064	260935216	258842292
按企业登记注册类型分	**By Registration Type**				
内 资	Domestically-invested Enterprises	403410880	394712510	383959408	377505092
国 有	State-owned Enterprises	46832039	46652519	44545999	44520106
集 体	Collectively-owned Enterprises	1160540	1134968	1069597	1065789
股份合作	Joint-equity Cooperative Enterprises	934380	931144	898047	897809
联 营	Associate Enterprises	173465	173154	162794	162756
有限责任公司	Limited Liability Companies	273222480	265662661	262089926	255944100
股份有限公司	Companies Limited by Shares	36133807	35679288	33844913	33765820
私 营	Private Enterprises	44954169	44478778	41348132	41148713
其 他	Other				
港澳台商投资	Hong Kong, Macao and Taiwan-invested Enterprises	14470783	14285998	11945032	11897444
外商投资	Foreign-invested Enterprises	75643432	74271422	64345036	64180510
按国民经济行业分	**By Sector**				
批发业	**Wholesale**	**426095506**	**417415117**	**401116668**	**394680367**
农、林、牧产品批发	Wholesale of Agricultural or Livestock Products	8985458	8926121	8618771	8604463
食品、饮料及烟草制品批发	Wholesale of Foods, Beverage and Tobaccos	16223725	16083316	13815129	13789401
纺织、服装及家庭日用品批发	Wholesale of Textile, Clothes and Household Commodities	15941211	15735342	12891541	12831776
文化、体育用品及器材批发	Wholesale of Cultural and Sports Goods and Equipment	12863493	12747557	12106347	12060922
医药及医疗器材批发	Wholesale of Medicine and Medical Devices	11801705	11650399	10227056	10196727
矿产品、建材及化工产品批发	Wholesale of Mineral Products, Building Materials, and Chemical Products	246319788	244338785	241432296	239779237
机械设备、五金交电及电子产品批发	Wholesale of Mechanical Equipment, Hardware and Electronic Products	104383108	98462887	93462706	88877670
贸易经纪与代理	Trade Broker and Agent	5063718	5002087	4471121	4466637
其他批发	Others	4513301	4468623	4091701	4073534
零售业	**Retail**	**67429589**	**65854813**	**59132807**	**58902679**
综合零售	Integrated Retail	15741231	14870228	12704551	12667216
食品、饮料及烟草制品专门零售	Special Retails of Foods, Beverage and Tobacoos	924843	871786	632945	627737
纺织、服装及日用品专门零售	Special Retail of Textile, Clothing and Domestic Commodities	2454411	2382569	1641070	1624524
文化、体育用品及器材专门零售	Special Retail of Cultural and Sports Goods and Equipment	2185575	2102043	1727648	1713847
医药及医疗器材专门零售	Special Retail of Medicine and Medical Devices	4491496	4461762	3902938	3900370
汽车、摩托车、燃料及零配件专门零售	Special Retail of Automobiles, Motorcycles, Fuels and Their Accessories	23488513	23228794	21933355	21859774
家用电器及电子产品专门零售	Special Retail of Household Electrical Appliances and Electronic Products	12249165	12118456	11317192	11292765
五金、家具及室内装修材料专门零售	Special Retail of Hardware, Furniture and Indoor Decoration Materials	704939	687680	461747	459468
货摊、无店铺及其他零售业	Stand Retail, Retail Without Shops and Other Retail	5189414	5131496	4811362	4756979
按规模划分	**By Size**				
#大中型企业	Medium-and Large-sized Enterprises	423382034	413732652	394056291	387759922

注：应交税金合计包括应交增值税、应交所得税、营业税金及附加和管理费用中的税金。

14-10 Continued

(10000 yuan)

Profits and Loss				应交税金合计				
销售费用 Sales Expenses	管理费用 Management Expenses	财务费用 Financial Expenses	利润总额 Total Profits	Total Tax Payable	#营业税金及附加 Business Tax and Surcharges	#主营业务税金及附加 Business Tax and Surtax	#应交增值税 Value Added Tax Payable	#应交所得税 Income Tax Payable
16853251	**8396459**	**1007317**	**10530886**	**7777405**	**923057**	**869238**	**4398954**	**2220088**
2685971	1766871	291603	4031148	1962038	241882	223185	882014	749911
14167280	6629588	715713	6499739	5815367	681175	646053	3516940	1470178
9373042	5127123	1198106	6222441	4540663	631698	582964	2383976	1349000
781550	565273	106552	1099144	574335	147646	143650	169427	230359
42778	35516	13886	31023	16067	2982	2437	10206	1403
16177	17813	20208	-18531	7794	788	756	6224	618
7493	2534	1114	6600	2497	266	261	1853	274
5444535	2713546	682687	3831448	2810815	308471	286040	1520868	869547
1150598	530803	163988	1050217	432829	97901	80398	176177	137076
1929912	1261638	209671	222540	696325	73645	69422	499223	109724
1488904	500726	42858	852581	582865	63762	61393	339085	170375
5991305	2768610	-233648	3455865	2653878	227596	224881	1675893	700714
11883287	**6248369**	**692619**	**9407691**	**6084605**	**660188**	**627417**	**3380945**	**1852820**
135175	183637	170891	743941	56023	9183	8873	9438	32320
1523098	350530	-23428	863157	557083	146216	145488	261984	139640
1927243	701796	-34242	629873	533927	49061	47893	356891	117951
416063	242301	70512	97194	212626	22135	21872	113901	66973
830769	351324	26276	425081	329090	26796	26264	206434	90505
1904084	1374532	600002	1930711	1549266	157420	138994	891031	417253
4855126	2773944	-28336	4055188	2614183	216590	206908	1494283	842600
133575	149855	-122126	506236	166263	24775	24693	22747	113705
158154	120450	33070	156311	66144	8011	6433	24237	31873
4969964	**2148090**	**314698**	**1123195**	**1692800**	**262869**	**241821**	**1018009**	**367268**
1738351	721216	74718	606548	617171	135073	120913	310069	152403
172880	50640	2230	64084	70032	6029	5804	43153	19553
608184	177623	5539	155	138375	19396	17180	101049	15948
254883	142687	14668	49923	62931	10508	10237	32460	17892
262337	171035	68836	145123	153111	14015	13818	106961	29868
753784	462859	144386	224070	318545	34284	32041	205538	70212
573579	218661	890	214475	211285	25828	24966	150368	31169
135945	53623	6185	51484	43107	8007	7437	21638	11910
470021	149746	-2753	-232666	78243	9729	9426	46773	18313
15218895	7281324	905648	9261152	6392190	800889	750717	3539587	1844240

Note: Total tax payable mainly includes VAT payable, income tax payable, business tax and surtax, and tax in management expenses.

14-11 限额以上住宿业企业财务状况(2013年)

单位：万元

项 目	Item	企业单位个数(个) Number of Enterprises (unit)	资产负债 Assets and Liabilities 资产总计 Total Assets	流动资产合计 Total Current Assets	#应收账款 Accounts Receivable	固定资产合计 Total Fixed Assets	固定资产原价 Total Original Value of Fixed Assets	负债合计 Total Liabilities	#流动负债合计 Total Current Liabilities	#应付账款 Accounts Payable
合 计	Total	1110	12284824	4149954	145481	4970281	8122222	9052668	6350120	424513
按隶属关系分	By Affiliation									
中央	Central	197	1976309	564645	23369	985238	1734760	1084475	750308	62968
地方	Local	913	10308515	3585309	122112	3985043	6387462	7968192	5599812	361545
按登记注册类型分	By Registration Type									
内 资	Domestically-invested Enterprises	1042	9064500	3019223	119065	3984309	5699420	7030616	5287832	364070
国 有	State-owned Enterprises	270	2467981	637183	24410	1359559	1877363	1678208	1120320	70253
集 体	Collectively-owned Enterprises	48	326816	94705	1342	189962	293928	234968	126316	7807
股份合作	Joint-equity Cooperative Enterprises	33	97408	40652	2967	37014	65324	72162	54088	5710
联 营	Associate Enterprises	2	4521	3028	-551	826	4606	6873	6473	4883
有限责任公司	Limited Liability Companies	401	5058489	1664432	83276	2133533	3076401	3953994	3164400	204150
股份有限公司	Companies Limited by Shares	8	291623	153031	1522	72619	79675	246178	172556	9189
私 营	Private Enterprises	280	817662	426192	6098	190796	302124	838233	643678	62079
其 他	Others									
港澳台商投资	Hong Kong, Macao and Taiwan-invested Enterprises	40	2132938	621347	19520	611559	1554328	1229148	716855	35817
外商投资	Foreign-invested Enterprises	28	1087386	509384	6897	374414	868475	792904	345433	24626
按国民经济行业分	By Sector									
旅游饭店	Tourism Hotels	660	10481612	3439034	124807	4600757	7557392	7939848	5477807	365616
一般旅馆	Common Inns	429	1688758	680528	20299	323669	520039	994533	782466	55257
其他住宿服务	Other Accomodation Services	21	114454	30393	375	45855	44792	118287	89847	3640

注：1. 限额以上住宿业企业是指年主营业务收入200万元及以上的住宿业法人企业。
2. 应交税金合计包括应交增值税、应交所得税、营业税金及附加和管理费用中的税金。

FINANCIAL STATUS OF ACCOMODATION ENTERPRISES ABOVE DESIGNATED SIZE(2013)

(10000 yuan)

所有者权益合计 Total Owner's Equity	#实收资本 Paid-up Capital	损益 Profits and Loss: 营业收入 Business Income	#主营业务收入 Main Business Income	营业成本 Business Cost	#主营业务成本 Main Business Cost	销售费用 Sales Expenses	管理费用 Manage-ment Expenses	财务费用 Financial Expenses	利润总额 Total Profits	应交税金合计 Total Tax Payable	营业税金及附加 Business Tax and Surcharges	#主营业务税金及附加 Main Business Tax and Surtax	#应交增值税 Value Added Tax Payable	#应交所得税 Income Tax Payable
3232156	**3710317**	**3568211**	**3543805**	**938717**	**934335**	**1082226**	**1274112**	**138923**	**-577**	**320822**	**195249**	**194718**	**3357**	**53756**
891833	778583	705596	700575	213856	212254	205237	248302	3728	2089	62185	38411	38250	716	8976
2340323	2931735	2862615	2843230	724861	722081	876989	1025810	135195	-2666	258637	156838	156468	2641	44779
2033885	2513121	2630109	2607280	707020	702848	866841	970000	101134	-126618	212180	143580	143052	2331	20085
789773	785385	740689	731121	212394	210500	237160	289164	18666	-44057	59144	40526	40230	978	3528
91848	51239	108221	107330	20429	20416	24372	51494	389	6335	10930	5951	5951	107	2071
25246	18527	35397	35326	8491	8338	13923	12271	1148	372	2819	1948	1948	26	513
-2352	3922	5022	5022	1654	1654	1075	2635	23	-656	307	281	281		
1104495	1455765	1329315	1318897	346998	345070	435097	490769	57366	-61576	110917	72139	71926	1066	12945
45445	43431	48984	48773	24470	24468	4649	12564	7167	-704	4282	2621	2619	98	119
-20571	154852	362481	360811	92585	92404	150565	111102	16374	-26333	23781	20115	20097	56	910
903790	877203	619993	619063	179981	179782	139609	188952	20766	82134	68715	33967	33964	869	19918
294482	319993	318109	317461	51716	51705	75776	115160	17023	43907	39927	17702	17702	157	13753
2541764	3102936	2937587	2919144	764045	760800	864416	1082223	124438	-16839	271422	160174	159757	2727	46023
694225	588298	603542	597880	166345	165207	209052	180865	8734	22866	47409	33646	33532	523	7675
-3834	19084	27083	26781	8327	8327	8758	11025	5750	-6604	1991	1430	1430	106	57

Note: a) Accomodation enterprises above designated size refer to corporate enterprises with an annual main business income of 2 million yuan or above.

b) Total tax payable mainly includes VAT payable, income tax payable, business tax and surtax, and tax in management expenses.

14-12 限额以上餐饮业企业财务状况(2013年)

单位：万元

项目	Item	企业单位个数(个) Number of Enterprises (unit)	资产负债 Assets and Liabilities							
			资产总计 Total Assets	流动资产合计 Total Current Assets	#应收账款 Accounts Receivable	固定资产合计 Total Fixed Assets	固定资产原价 Total Original Value of Fixed Assets	负债合计 Total Liabilities	#流动负债合计 Total Current Liabilities	#应付账款 Accounts Payable
合计	**Total**	**1817**	**4167361**	**2289407**	**135978**	**613474**	**1164265**	**3366639**	**2836931**	**493938**
按隶属关系分	**By Affiliation**									
中央	Central	17	85522	65467	3733	7011	22087	62496	61468	21120
地方	Local	1800	4081838	2223940	132244	606463	1142178	3304143	2775463	472819
按登记注册类型分	**By Registration Type**									
内资	Domestically-invested Enterprises	1677	3111500	1811971	116764	424632	813694	2665495	2227050	381499
国有	State-owned Enterprises	31	42405	27182	569	6275	13409	24307	18392	1983
集体	Collectively-owned Enterprises	31	12453	5600	843	4244	7092	11632	11345	1712
股份合作	Joint-equity Cooperative Enterprise	54	27731	17996	981	3183	7179	25182	24067	2299
联营	Associated Enterprises									
有限责任公司	Limited Liability Companies	452	1406216	779793	53293	205839	348519	1272144	1040818	165777
股份有限公司	Companies Limited by Shares	34	555438	303058	6161	61793	112465	287482	163915	13499
私营	Private Enterprises	1075	1067258	678344	54917	143298	325030	1044748	968513	196228
其他	Others									
港澳台商投资	Hong Kong, Macao and Taiwan-invested Enterprises	65	483212	310664	7241	62332	108994	320764	256809	46159
外商投资	Foreign-invested Enterprises	75	572648	166772	11973	126510	241577	380380	353071	66281
按国民经济行业分	**By Sector**									
正餐	Dinner	1629	3148970	1840052	107301	445404	864167	2586574	2242760	385699
快餐	Fast Food	119	603210	246724	11886	139507	247698	376923	356721	74251
饮料及冷饮	Beverage and Cold Drink	23	96851	55291	3438	14383	24863	63262	59925	11884
其他餐饮业	Others	46	318330	147339	13352	14179	27537	339879	177525	22104

注：1. 限额以上餐饮业企业是指年主营业务收入200万元及以上的餐饮业法人企业。
2. 应交税金合计包括应交增值税、应交所得税、营业税金及附加和管理费用中的税金。

FINANCIAL STATUS OF CATERING ENTERPRISES ABOVE DESIGNATED SIZE (2013)

(10000 yuan)

所有者权益合计 Total Owner's Equity	#实收资本 Paid-up Capital	损益 Profits and Loss: 营业收入 Business Income	#主营业务收入 Main Business Income	营业成本 Business Cost	#主营业务成本 Main Business Cost	销售费用 Sales Expenses	管理费用 Management Expenses	财务费用 Financial Expenses	利润总额 Total Profits	应交税金合计 Total Tax Payable	#营业税金及附加 Business Tax and Surtax	#主营业务税金及附加 Main Business Tax and Surcharges	#应交增值税 Value Added Tax Payable	#应交所得税 Income Tax Payable
800722	**845695**	**5263262**	**5206851**	**2235499**	**2227079**	**2085146**	**650772**	**48691**	**-12686**	**351336**	**281538**	**279438**	**7583**	**53914**
23027	10546	127663	123797	50608	49561	26852	36766	-9	7631	9468	6590	6385	65	2317
777695	835149	5135599	5083053	2184891	2177518	2058294	614006	48700	-20317	341868	274948	273053	7518	51597
446005	568596	3315520	3270916	1421505	1417843	1296529	459861	41775	-53921	222413	179712	177651	3169	32671
18098	7181	49079	43864	20502	19427	17923	7315	23	2233	3442	2553	2313	222	554
821	1403	22663	22663	11808	11808	7477	2699	71	-572	1256	1180	1179		63
2549	3385	44891	44890	24297	24297	14411	3553	279	-142	2634	2513	2511	10	89
134072	213949	1331991	1302354	540749	539080	530412	195330	13381	-12899	98351	72354	70766	1157	21600
267956	137510	234468	231913	85043	84981	95448	39663	10092	10357	17494	11948	11933	778	3971
22510	205170	1632428	1625232	739106	738251	630859	211302	17930	-52898	99235	89165	88950	1003	6394
162448	122770	638718	636973	237321	237048	281444	68663	5023	13093	43288	32947	32944	1684	7655
192269	154329	1309024	1298962	576673	572189	507174	122248	1893	28142	85636	68878	68843	2730	13587
562396	663298	3625842	3588396	1529106	1526433	1398517	501512	43343	-18664	250715	198677	197068	2375	42477
226287	127586	1319474	1300944	549724	543987	564760	113132	1321	21788	80583	67957	67466	3229	8535
33589	23367	137605	137593	40373	40373	72121	13570	476	3791	10155	7034	7034	503	2524
-21549	31446	180341	179918	116295	116286	49748	22558	3551	-19600	9883	7870	7870	1477	378

Note: a) Catering enterprises above designated size refer to corporate enterprises with an annual main business income of 2 million yuan or above.
b)Total tax payable mainly includes VAT payable, income tax payable, business tax and surtax, and tax in management expenses.

14-13 连锁企业基本情况(2001-2013年)
STATISTICS FOR CHAIN ENTERPRISES (2001-2013)

年份 Year	连锁总店 (个) Number of General Chain Stores (unit)	门店总数 (个) Number of Chain Stores (unit)	从业人员年末人数 (人) Number of Employed Persons Year-end (person)	营业面积 (平方米) Operational Area (sq.m)	商品销售总额 (营业额) (万元) Total Sales of Commodities (Turnover) (10000 yuan)	#零售额 Retail Sales
2001	129	2123	139470	1605808	4831168	2186540
2002	146	3523	109089	2356266	6621975	6487185
2003	153	4519	132030	3405562	8404232	7601221
2004	196	5432	153942	3783507	8603560	8337829
2005	188	5973	166598	4376383	10612658	9507168
2006	205	6730	170007	5546003	11229026	9514297
2007	210	7645	185114	6677266	13890913	11573838
2008	240	8611	223954	6745802	15720473	12954839
2009	240	8928	218024	6995047	17366414	13816796
2010	234	9299	228292	7268786	21329783	16255496
2011	233	9845	280798	7953891	25742536	19507890
2012	220	10014	287975	8339674	26758403	20140433
2013	241	11111	299445	9026207	27834646	21495798

14-14 连锁企业基本情况(按登记注册类型、经营业态分)(2013年)
STATISTICS FOR CHAIN ENTERPRISES (BY REGISTRATION TYPE OF ENTERPRISES AND OPERATION FORMS) (2013)

项 目	Item	门店总数 (个) Number of Chain Stores (unit)	从业人员年末人数 (人) Year-end Employed Persons (person)	营业面积 (平方米) Operational Area (sq.m)	商品销售额(营业额) (万元) Total sales of Commodities (10000 yuan)	#零售额 Retail Sales
合计	**Total**	**11111**	**299445**	**9026207**	**27834646**	**21495798**
按登记注册类型分	**By Registration Type**					
内资	Domestically-invested Enterprises	7716	179849	6950710	22431064	16359522
国有	State-owned Enterprises	76	1336	18036	44644	38860
集体	Collectively-owned Enterprises	303	1280	83585	84899	82971
股份合作	Joint-equity Cooperative Enterprises	7	179	5410	3697	3697
联营	Associate Enterprises	5	43	928	918	918
有限责任公司	Limited Liability Companies	3350	89929	3260690	9931766	6725765
股份有限公司	Companies Limited by Shares	1596	54416	2777758	11208892	8443508
私营	Private Enterprises	2325	30492	780383	1113533	1021088
其他	Others					
港、澳、台商投资	Hong Kong, Macao and Taiwan-invested Enterprises	1305	28533	440248	1173881	1004134
外商投资	Foreign-invested Enterprises	2090	91063	1635249	4229701	4132141
按经营业态分	**By Operation Form**					
零售业态	**Retail**	**7388**	**158217**	**7150127**	**25157851**	**18930539**
便利店	Convenient Stores	880	4226	92584	217088	209242
折扣店	Discount Stores	47	933	87719	190454	190454
超市	Supermarkets	1521	61170	2249813	5157680	3768954
大型超市	Large Supermarkets	93	19349	860741	1737831	1704296
仓储会员店	Warehouse Club Stores	7	2833	131974	370659	370659
百货店	Department Stores	69	17073	1872320	3487022	3487022
专业店	Specialty Stores	2197	27327	1210177	5218741	4660202
加油站	Gas Stations	692	8345	341965	7767956	3659439
专卖店	Boutiques	1873	15960	234692	784171	654020
家居建材商店	Furniture and Building Material Stores	9	1001	68142	226251	226251
餐饮业态	**Chain Catering Enterprises**	**3596**	**137637**	**1867230**	**2574492**	**2562768**
中式正餐	Chinese Dinner	668	49845	1032925	879164	877327
中式快餐	Chinese Fast Food	1229	19116	266028	497806	490481
外国风味正餐	Exotic Dinner	484	30335	194658	381959	381878
外国风味快餐	Exotic Fast Food	877	34819	316507	686311	683831
茶馆	Teahouses	9	45	910	426	426
咖啡店	Cafés	301	3021	53259	114870	114870
其他	Others	28	456	2943	13957	13957
住宿业态	**Chain Accomodation Enterprises**	**127**	**3591**	**8850**	**102302**	**2490**
旅游饭店	Tourism Hotels	59	1919	3548	51886	946
一般旅馆	Common Inns	68	1672	5302	50416	1544

14-15 商品交易市场基本情况（2013年）
STATISTICS FOR COMMODITY TRANSACTION MARKETS (2013)

项　目	Item	市场数量（个）Number of Markets (unit)	摊位数（个）Number of Booths (unit)	成交额（亿元）Turnover (100 million yuan)
全市合计	**Total**	**821**	**274300**	**3486.0**
按经营方式分	**Grouped by Business Practice**			
批发市场	Wholesale Market	149	105553	2217.0
零售市场	Retail Market	672	168747	1269.0
按经营环境分	**Grouped by Business Environment**			
露天式	Open-air	160	65616	1332.0
封闭式	Closed	600	183536	1768.0
其他	Others	61	25148	386.0
按市场地理环境分	**Grouped by Market Place**			
二环以内	Inside the Second Ring Road	63	12433	54.0
二环至三环以内	Between the Second and Third Ring Road	109	48515	114.0
三环到四环以内	Between the Third and Fourth Ring Road	112	46876	1190.0
四环至五环以内	Between the Fourth and Fifth Ring Road	117	41956	1204.0
五环至六环以内	Between the Fifth and Sixth Ring Road	188	51530	621.0
六环以外	Outside the Sixth Ring Road	232	72990	303.0
按功能区分	**Grouped by Functional Area**			
首都功能核心区	Capital Core Functional Area	104	39770	130.9
城市功能拓展区	Urban Function Extension Area	360	125158	2541.8
城市发展新区	Uban Development New Area	257	79137	714.3
生态涵养发展区	Ecological Conservation Area	100	30235	98.6

14-16 亿元及以上商品交易市场基本情况（2013年）
STATISTICS FOR COMMODITY TRANSACTION MARKETS OVER 100 MILLION YUAN(2013)

项　目	Item	市场数量（个）Number of markets (unit)	总摊位数（个）Number of Booths (unit)	#出租摊位数 Number of Booths on Lease	成交额（亿元）Turnover (100 million yuan)
全市合计	**Total**	**140**	**129132**	**113914**	**3353.0**
按经营方式分	**Grouped by Business Practice**				
批发市场	Wholesale Market	62	83712	71555	2188.6
零售市场	Retail Market	78	45420	42359	1164.1
按经营环境分	**Grouped by Business Environment**				
露天式	Open-air	22	26744	17177	1304.2
封闭式	Closed	108	88456	83668	1675.5
其他	Others	10	13932	13069	373.0
按市场地理环境分	**Grouped by Market Place**				
二环以内	Inside the Second Ring Road	7	4172	3926	44.2
二环至三环以内	Between the Second and Third Ring Road	21	28941	28195	94.1
三环到四环以内	Between the Third and Fourth Ring Road	33	29237	27891	1168.9
四环至五环以内	Between the Fourth and Fifth Ring Road	25	23529	22251	1189.7
五环至六环以内	Between the Fifth and Sixth Ring Road	25	18947	17086	593.5
六环以外	Outside the Sixth Ring Road	29	24306	14565	262.3
按功能区分	**Grouped by Functional Area**				
首都功能核心区	Capital Core Functional Area	19	23756	22967	113.4
城市功能拓展区	Urban Function Extension Area	76	66501	62832	2485.6
城市发展新区	Uban Development New Area	28	28745	20344	674.2
生态涵养发展区	Ecological Conservation Area	17	10130	7771	79.4

14-17 商品交易市场经营情况(2013年)
STATISTICS FOR COMMODITY TRANSACTION MARKETS (2013)

项 目	Item	市场数量（个）Number of Markets (unit)	出租摊位数（个）Number of Booths (unit)	营业面积（万平方米）Operating Area (10,000 sq.m)	成交额（亿元）Turnover (100 million yuan)
合 计	**Total**	**821**	**231645**	**1409.8**	**3486.0**
一、综合市场	**Comprehensive Markets**	**399**	**114064**	**592.0**	**1735.0**
综合贸易市场	**Comprehensive Trade Market**	**399**	**114064**	**592.0**	**1735.0**
生产资料综合市场	Comprehensive Market of Capital Goods	2	457	8.3	0.8
工业消费品综合市场	Comprehensive Market of Industrial Consumer Goods	56	24028	51.4	100.4
农产品综合市场	Comprehensive Market of Agricultural Products	234	57560	365.8	1387.9
其他综合市场	Other Comprehensive Markets	107	32019	167.0	246.0
二、专业市场	**Specialized Markets**	**422**	**117581**	**818.4**	**1751.2**
生产资料市场	**Market of Capital Goods**	**49**	**8959**	**83.2**	**74.2**
农业生产用具市场	Market of Agricultural Production Tools				
农用生产资料市场	Market of Agricultural Production Means				
煤炭市场	Coal Market				
木材市场	Timber Market	2	268	6.0	1.1
建材市场	Building Material Market	42	7732	63.6	47.6
化工材料及制品市场	Chemical Material and Product Market				
金属材料市场	Metal Material Market	3	417	8.2	3.1
机械设备市场	Mechanical Equipment Market	1	262	3.3	13.5
其他生产资料市场	Other Markets of Capital Goods	1	280	2.1	8.9
农产品市场	**Agricultural Product Market**	**71**	**16969**	**111.3**	**454.6**
粮油市场	Foodstuff and Oil Market	5	2315	22.4	172.6
肉禽蛋市场	Meat, Poultry and Egg Market	6	808	5.4	5.7
水产品市场	Aquatic Product Market	3	1545	6.7	105.2
蔬菜市场	Vegetable Market	16	3577	22.1	31.1
干鲜果品市场	Dried and Fresh Fruit Market	3	1279	27.1	18.4
棉麻土畜、烟叶市场	Cotton, Linen, Local and Livestock Product, and Tobacco Leaf Market				
其他农产品市场	Other Agricultural Product Markets	38	7445	27.6	121.6
食品、饮料及烟酒市场	**Food, Beverage, Tobacco and Wine Market**	**19**	**3162**	**13.3**	**5.1**
食品饮料市场	Food and Beverage Market	7	344	1.8	0.4
茶叶市场	Tea Market	6	974	4.0	4.2
烟酒市场	Tobacco and Wine Market				
其他食品饮料及烟酒市场	Other Food, Beverage, Tobacco and Wine Markets	6	1844	7.5	0.5
纺织、服装、鞋帽市场	**Textile, Costume, Shoe and Hat Market**	**78**	**37050**	**222.8**	**56.7**
布料及纺织品市场	Cloth and Textile Market	9	1977	8.0	2.6
服装市场	Clothing Market	57	29098	75.0	47.7
鞋帽市场	Shoe and Hat Market	2	736	2.9	0.5
其他纺织服装鞋帽市场	Other Textile, Costume, Shoe and Cap Markets	10	5239	136.9	5.9
日用品及文化用品市场	**Domestic Commodity and Cultural Article Market**	**17**	**9807**	**22.5**	**50.0**
小商品市场	Small Commodity Market	10	8205	13.4	31.3

14-17 续表 Continued

项目	Item	市场数量（个）Number of Markets (unit)	出租摊位数（个）Number of Booths (unit)	营业面积（万平方米）Operating Area (10,000 sq.m)	成交额（亿元）Turnover (100 million yuan)
箱包市场	Case and Bag Market				
玩具市场	Toy Market				
文具市场	Stationary Market	1	798	5.5	16.0
图书、报刊杂志市场	Book, Newspaper, and Magazine Market	1	196	1.2	1.9
音像制品及电子出版物市场	Audiovisual Product and E-journal Market	1	18	0.8	0.3
体育用品市场	Sports Good Market				
其他日用品及文化用品市场	Other Domestic Commodity and Cultural Article Market	4	590	1.5	0.6
黄金、珠宝、玉器等首饰市场	**Market of Gold, Jewelry, and Jade**	**13**	**2942**	**13.3**	**30.1**
电器、通讯器材、电子设备市场	**Market of Electrical Appliances, Communication Devices, and Electronic Equipment**	**20**	**6170**	**20.4**	**102.3**
家电市场	Household Appliance Market	2	111	0.2	0.2
通讯器材市场	Communication Device Market	5	1167	3.1	2.1
照相、摄像器材市场	Photographic and Camera Shooting Equipment Market	2	364	1.5	4.0
计算机及辅助设备市场	Computer and Supporting Equipment Market	6	3474	13.2	82.9
其他电器、通讯器材、电子设备市场	Other Electrical Appliance, Communication Device and Electronic Equipment Market	5	1054	2.3	13.0
医药、医疗用品及器材市场	**Medicine, Medial Article and Equipment Market**				
中药材市场	Chinese Herb Market				
其他医药、医疗用品及器材市场	Other Medicine, Medial Article and Equipment Market				
家具、五金及装饰材料市场	**Furniture, Hardware, and Decoration Material Market**	**74**	**15088**	**152.7**	**129.1**
家具市场	Furniture Market	32	5434	74.0	58.9
装饰材料市场	Decoration Materials Market	21	5080	35.9	33.1
灯具市场	Lamp and Lantern Market	4	713	10.0	2.7
厨具、盥洗设备市场	Kitchen and Washroom Equipment Market				
五金材料市场	Hardware Market	12	2268	11.1	4.2
其他装修市场	Other Decoration Market	5	1593	21.7	30.2
汽车、摩托车及零配件市场	**Automobile, Autobike, and Part and Fitting Market**	**26**	**6164**	**105.8**	**829.6**
汽车市场	Automobile Market	10	1422	65.4	767.0
摩托车市场	Autobike Market				
机动车零配件市场	Automobile Part and Fitting Market	16	4742	40.4	62.5
花、鸟、鱼、虫市场	**Flower, Bird, Fish and Insect Market**	**17**	**1904**	**5.2**	**3.2**
花卉市场	Flower Market	16	1806	5.0	3.2
鸟市场	Bird Market				
观赏鱼市场	Fish Market				
其他花鸟鱼虫市场	Other Flower, Bird, Fish and Insect Market	1	98	0.2	0.0
旧货市场	**Secondhand Goods Market**	**15**	**6749**	**15.0**	**5.2**
古玩、古董、字画市场	Curio, Antique, Calligraphy and Painting Market	6	1670	7.2	1.3
邮票、硬币市场	Stamp and Coin Market	1	887	0.8	0.8
其他旧货市场	Other Secondhand Goods Market	8	4192	7.0	3.1
其他专业市场	**Other Specialized Market**	**23**	**2617**	**53.1**	**11.1**

14-18 消费者投诉与处理
CONSUMER'S COMPLAINTS AND HANDLING

单位：件 (unit)

项目	Item	2013		2012	
		受理投诉件数 Number of Complaints Accepted	构成(%) Composition (%)	受理投诉件数 Number of Complaints Accepted	构成(%) Composition (%)
合计	**Total**	**18291**	**100.0**	**16892**	**100.0**
按行业分	**Grouped by Sector**				
家用电器类	Household Appliances	2899	15.8	2866	17.0
#电视机	TV Sets	483	2.6	298	1.8
空调类	Air Conditioners	267	1.5	286	1.7
洗衣机类	Washing Machines	105	0.6	80	0.5
电冰箱(柜)	Refrigerators	114	0.6	119	0.7
厨房电器及设备	Kitchen Electrical Appliances and Equipment	207	1.1	178	1.1
通讯类	Communication Equipment	1190	6.5	1313	7.8
计算机类	Computers	279	1.5	410	2.4
家用机械类	Household Machines	450	2.5	562	3.3
#汽车	Automobiles	288	1.6	323	1.9
热水器	Water Heaters	86	0.5	100	0.6
百货类	General Merchandise	4130	22.6	3763	22.3
#家具类	Furniture	543	3.0	492	2.9
服装鞋帽	Clothes, Shoes and Hats	1565	8.6	1238	7.3
日用杂品	Daily Groceries	251	1.4	362	2.1
食品	Foods	918	5.0	975	5.8
房屋及装修建材	Housing and Decoration and Building Materials	776	4.2	525	3.1
#房屋	Housing	179	1.0	141	0.8
装饰材料	Decoration Materials	480	2.6	334	2.0
农用生产资料	Capital Goods for Agricultural Use	6	…	26	0.2
服务类	Service	9712	53.1	8905	52.8
#美容美发	Hairdressing	439	2.4	596	3.5
食宿娱乐庆典	Catering, Accommodation, Entertainment and Celebration	692	3.8	657	3.9
洗衣业	Laundry	379	2.1	416	2.5
装修物业	Decoration and Realty Management	214	1.2	167	1.0
教育或培训	Education or Training	505	2.8	453	2.7
咨询中介	Consultating Agencies	1657	9.1	1675	9.9
其他商品类	Others	318	1.7	245	1.5
按内容分	**Grouped by Content**				
#质量	Quality	9191	50.2	9161	54.2
安全	Safety	90	0.5	59	0.3
价格	Price	281	1.5	306	1.8
计量	Measurement	23	0.1	36	0.2
广告	Advertisements	109	0.6	95	0.6
假冒	Counterfeit Goods	200	1.1	56	0.3
虚假品质表示	Inveracious Quality	157	0.9	82	0.5
营销合同	Marketing and Contracts	6734	36.8	5025	29.7
人格尊严	Personality and Dignity	213	1.2	37	0.2

注：总解决率为98.8%。
资料来源：北京市消费者协会。
Note: Total rate of settlement is 98.8%.
Source: Beijing Customer Institution.

主要统计指标解释

社会消费品零售总额 指企业（单位、个体户）通过交易直接售给个人、社会集团非生产、非经营用的实物商品金额，以及提供餐饮服务所取得的收入金额。个人包括城乡居民和入境人员，社会集团包括机关、社会团体、部队、学校、企事业单位、居委会或村委会等。

批发和零售业单位 指在流通环节从事商品批发活动和零售活动的单位。

商品购进额 指从本企业（单位）以外的单位和个人购进(包括从国外直接进口)作为转卖或加工后转卖的商品金额（含增值税）。本指标反映批发和零售业从国内外市场上购进商品的总量。

商品销售额 指对本企业以外的单位和个人出售的商品金额（包括售给本单位消费用的商品，含增值税）。本指标反映批发和零售业在国内市场上销售商品以及出口商品的总量。

期末商品库存额 对于批发和零售业法人企业和个体经营户，是指取得所有权的全部商品金额（含增值税）；对于批发和零售业产业活动单位，是指期末实际在库且归属法人具有所有权的全部商品金额（含增值税）。这个指标反映批发和零售业的商品库存情况，以及对市场商品供应的保证程度。

连锁总店（总部） 负责连锁企业资源（商号、商誉、经营模式、服务标准、管理模式等）的开发、配置、控制或使用等功能的企业核心管理机构。连锁经营是指经营同类商品或服务，使用统一商号的若干店铺，在同一总店（总部）的管理下，采取统一采购或特许经营等方式,实现规模效益的组织形式，包括直营连锁、特许连锁和自愿连锁三种形式。直营连锁是指连锁店铺由连锁公司全资或控股开设，在总部的直接控制下，开展统一经营的连锁经营形式；特许连锁是指拥有注册商标、企业标志、专利、专有技术等经营资源的企业（特许人），以合同形式将其拥有的经营资源许可其他经营者（被特许人）使用，被特许人按合同约定在统一的经营模式下开展经营，并向特许人支付特许经营费用的连锁经营形式；自愿连锁是指若干个店铺或企业自愿组合起来，在不改变各自资产所有权关系的情况下，以同一个品牌形象面对消费者，以共同进货为纽带开展的连锁经营形式。

连锁门店 在连锁企业经营管理的基础上，按照总店（总部）的指示和服务规范要求，承担日常销售业务的店铺，称连锁门店，包括直营店（控股店）和加盟店。

（1）直营店（控股店） 是指由连锁企业总部投资开设，按连锁经营管理模式，由总部统一管理的店铺。

（2）加盟店 是指在特许连锁中，被特许人获得特许人授权后，使用其商标、商号、经营模式、专利和专有技术等经营资源建立的店铺，也包括自愿连锁的成员店。

门店总数 指该连锁企业所拥有的全部门店（包括直营店和加盟店）数量。其中，总店（如果总公司有门店的话）作为一个直营店处理。此外，有的地区分出控股店，控股店按直营店统计。

餐饮业企业 指在一定场所，专门从事对食物进行现场烹饪、调制，并出售给顾客主要供现场消费服务活动的企业。如各种饭馆、中西餐厅、酒馆、茶馆和火车餐车、车站食堂、飞机场餐厅等。

住宿业企业 指有偿为顾客提供临时住宿服务活动的单位。如旅游饭店、宾馆、酒店和旅馆、旅店等。

商品交易市场 指经有关部门和组织批准设立，有固定场所、设施，有经营管理部门和监管人员，若干市场经营者入内，常年或实际开业三个月以上，集中、公开、独立地进行生活消费品、生产资料等现货商品交易以及提供相关服务的交易场所，包括各类消费品市场，生产资料市场等。

Explanatory Notes on Main Statistical Indicators

Total Retail Sales of Consumer Goods refer to the total prices of physical commodities sold by enterprises (entities or self-employed businesses) through transaction directly to individuals and social groups to be used for non-productive and non-operating purposes, combined with the amount of income from provision of food and beverage services. Individuals include urban and rural residents and persons entering China. Social groups include government agencies, social organizations, armies, schools, enterprises and public institutions, residents' committee or villagers' committee, and so on.

Wholesale and Retail Entities refer to entities engaged in commodity wholesale and retail activities in circulation.

Total Purchases of Commodities refer to the total value (including value added tax) of purchases (including direct imports from foreign countries) of commodities by the enterprises (entities) from other entities or individuals for the purpose of re-selling, either with or without further processing of the commodities purchased. This indicator is used to show the total value of purchases of retail and wholesale commodities from domestic and overseas markets.

Total Sales of Commodities refer to value of commodities sold by the enterprises to other entities and individuals (including the commodities consumed by the enterprises themselves, including value added tax). This indicator is used to show the total value of wholesale and retail commodities sold in domestic markets and exported.

Inventory (year-end) refer to, for wholesale and retail enterprises and self-employed businesses, the value of all commodities with ownership gained (VAT included); for wholesale and retail entities, refer to the value of all commodities with ownership, actually in storage at the end of a period, and owned by the legal person (VAT included). This indicator shows the commodity inventory in wholesale and retail trades, and to what extent the commodities will be supplied to the market.

General Chain Store (Headquarter) means the core management organization in an enterprise, responsible for the development, deployment, control or use of resources (trade name, goodwill, operating model, service standards, and management model, etc.) of the chain enterprise. Chain operation means an organization form in which several stores using unified trade name merchandise the same commodities or provide the same services through uniform purchase or franchise operation under the management of the same general store (headquarters) to achieve benefits of scale. Chain operation falls into direct-sale chain, franchised chain and voluntary chain. Direct-sale chain is a form of chain operation that chain stores are wholly funded or controlled by chain companies, carrying out uniform operation under the direct control of headquarters; franchised chain is a form of chain operation that any enterprise (the franchiser) owning operating resources, such as trademarks, logos, patents and proprietary technologies, authorize such operating resources to any other operator (the franchisee) by contract, and the franchisee operates under uniform operating model as stated in the contract, and pays franchise fees to the franchiser; voluntary chain is a form of chain operation that several stores or enterprises combine together voluntarily to face consumers with the same brand image without changing their own asset ownership relations, and link together through joint purchase.

Chain Stores Based on the operation and management of chain enterprises, stores carrying out daily sales business by following the general store's (headquarters) instruction and required service standards are called chained stores. They include direct-sale stores (controlled stores) and franchise stores.

Direct-sale Stores (Controlled Stores) refer to stores opened with funds from the headquarters of chain enterprises, using the chain operation and management model, and under the uniform management of the headquarters.

Franchised Stores refer to, in franchise chains, stores established after the franchisee is authorized by the franchiser to use its trademark, trade name, operating mode, patent and proprietary technologies and other operating resources. Voluntary chain members are also included.

Total Number of Stores refers to the number of all stores owned by the chain enterprises (including direct-sale stores and franchised stores). The general store (if the parent company has stores) is regarded as a direct-sale store. In addition, controlled stores are considered separately in some areas, which are regarded as direct-sale stores.

Restaurants Enterprises refer to enterprises specialized in cooking and seasoning food which is sold to clients for on-site consumption at a specific site, such as various restaurants, Chinese food and Western food restaurants, pubs, teahouses, dining compartments on trains, canteens at railway stations, and restaurants at airports.

Accommodation Enterprises refer to entities providing clients with temporary accommodation services, such as tourist hotels, guesthouses, rest houses and inns.

Commodity Transaction Markets refer to transaction sites approved by competent authorities and organizations, with fixed places and facilities. There are operation management departments and regulating personnel in the markets, where several operators stay over years or open for over three months, conducting transactions of on-hand commodities such as living consumables and capital goods, and offering relevant services in a concentrated, open and independent manner. Commodity transaction markets include various markets of consumer goods and capital good market.

15

对外经济贸易
FOREIGN ECONOMY AND TRADE

简要说明

一、本章资料的主要内容

本章资料主要反映北京市对外经济贸易的发展状况，包括对外贸易、利用外资、对外经济合作的历年概况，以及对外友好交往情况。

二、本章资料的统计范围和数据来源

1.对外贸易情况

对外贸易统计的范围是凡能引起北京市海关境内物质资源存量增加或减少的进出口货物，除制度另有规定者外，均列入该项统计，调查方法采用全面调查。主要内容包括北京地区进出口总值；主要产品进出口数量等。数据来源于中华人民共和国北京海关。

2.口岸运营情况

口岸运营情况的统计范围是北京首都国际机场空港口岸、北京丰台货运口岸、北京朝阳口岸、北京西站铁路口岸、北京平谷国际陆港、北京天竺综合保税区。主要内容包括旅客吞吐量、货邮吞吐量、监管货物的数量、征收关税等。数据来源于北京市人民政府口岸办公室。

3.利用外资情况

利用外资情况的统计范围是凡经工商行政管理机关核准登记，在中华人民共和国北京地域内所有使用外资（包括港澳台地区投资）的单位和部门，经批准设立的中外合资经营企业、合作经营企业、外资企业、外商投资股份制企业、合作开发项目等具有法人资格的独立核算企业(包括港澳台地区投资企业)，在华从事经营活动的外国及港澳台地区企业及外国公司在中国境内设立的分支机构。主要内容包括实际利用外商直接投资，外商投资企业经营情况，调查方法采用全面调查。数据来源于北京市商务委员会(原北京市商务局)和北京市统计局。

4.对外经济合作

对外经济合作的统计范围是经各级商务部门批准的从事对外承包、劳务合作和设计咨询业务并具有法人资格的对外承包劳务企业；调查方法采用全面调查。主要内容包括对外承包工程、劳务合作和设计咨询。数据来源于北京市商务委员会(原北京市商务局)。

5.友好城市

主要内容包括与北京市建立友好关系的城市名录。数据来源于北京市人民政府外事办公室。

Brief Introduction

I. Main Content

Data in this chapter show the development of foreign economic relations and trade in Beijing, including foreign trade, foreign capital utilization, and foreign economic cooperation in Beijing over the years, as well as friendly exchanges.

II. Scope of Statistical and Source of Data

1. Foreign trade

Foreign trade statistics apply for: any imports and exports that lead to increase or decrease in the stock of physical resources at Beijing customs, except for those otherwise stated in regulations, and were obtained through comprehensive survey. Foreign trade data include: total volume of import and export in Beijing, and quantity of main import and export products, and so on.. Foreign trade data are from Beijing Customs, P.R.C..

2. Statistics for Port Operation

The statistical scope of port operation covers the Port of Beijing Capital International Airport, Beijing Fengtai Cargo Transport Port, Beijing Chaoyang Transport Port, Railway Port at Beijing West Railway Station, Beijing Pinggu International Land Port, and Beijing Tianzhu Comprehensive Bonded Zone. Statistics in this chapter, which is sourced from Port Administration Office of the People's Government of Beijing Municipality, mainly include passenger throughput, cargo throughput, cargos under customs regulation and duties levied.

3. Foreign capital utilization

Scope of statistics: all entities and organizations registered with administration for industry and commerce upon approval, and using foreign capital (including investment from Hong Kong, Macao and Taiwan region) within the jurisdiction of Beijing, P.R.C, enterprises with legal person statues and independent accounting system (including enterprises invested by companies from Hong Kong, Macao and Taiwan region), including joint ventures, cooperative enterprises and foreign-invested enterprises, foreign-invested joint-stock enterprises, and cooperative development projects, and enterprises of foreign countries and Hong Kong, Macao and Taiwan region conducting operations in China as well as branch offices opened by foreign companies in China. Foreign capital utilization data include foreign direct investment, operation of foreign-invested enterprises, and were obtained through comprehensive survey. Data are sourced from Beijing Municipal Commission of Commerce (former Beijing Municipal Bureau of Commerce) and Beijing Municipal Bureau of Statistics.

4. Foreign economic cooperation

Statistics cover foreign labor service enterprises with legal person statues that are engaged in foreign contracting, labor service cooperation and design consulting with approval from departments of commerce at different levels. Comprehensive survey was used. Foreign economic cooperation statistics apply for: foreign contracting projects, labor service cooperation and design consulting. Data are sourced from Beijing Municipal Commission of Commerce (former Beijing Municipal Bureau of Commerce).

5. Sister cities

Data showing the detailed list of sister cities of Beijing are from Foreign Affairs Office of the People's Government of Beijing Municipality.

15-1 北京地区对外经济贸易(1980-2013年)
FOREIGN ECONOMIC RELATIONS AND TRADE (1980-2013)

年份 Year	进出口总值(万美元) Total Value of Imports and Exports (USD 10000)	出口 Exports	#高新技术产品 High-tech Products	#机电产品 Mechanical and Electrical Products	进口 Imports	#高新技术产品 High-tech Products	#机电产品 Mechanical and Electrical Products
1980							
1981-1985							
1981							
1982							
1983	3059926	1468740			1591186		
1984	3559284	1751704			1807580		
1985	3254341	437398			2816943		
1986-1990	**13945243**	**1865234**			**12080009**		
1986	3060236	371282			2688954		
1987	2670466	354374			2316092		
1988	2988576	395887			2592689		
1989	2861489	302343			2559146		
1990	2364476	441348			1923128		
1991-1995	**14305670**	**3547263**			**10758405**		
1991	2424137	457114			1967023		
1992	2498241	561037		157835	1937204	271005	731359
1993	2791700	669930		151133	2121769	302965	885074
1994	2888079	834205		194937	2053873	421071	1121082
1995	3703513	1024977		281810	2678536	407176	1225200
1996-2000	**17397285**	**5011639**		**1609152**	**12385646**	**2242338**	**5049210**
1996	2931833	811975		254450	2119858	240903	733641
1997	3038852	961103		271119	2077749	346166	766288
1998	3050608	1051293		325390	1999315	347556	909222
1999	3435951	990352		320852	2445599	567687	1213857
2000	4940041	1196916	226549	437341	3743125	740026	1426202
2001-2005	**39258570**	**9270820**	**2525916**	**4291246**	**29987748**	**5318558**	**10501427**
2001	5149809	1177236	263382	477568	3972572	992797	1883151
2002	5250529	1261386	314174	570971	3989142	916363	1701504
2003	6850017	1688682	396489	715359	5161335	990357	1949077
2004	9457572	2056926	580929	970117	7400647	1053395	2271805
2005	12550643	3086590	970942	1557231	9464052	1365646	2695890
2006-2010	**113918161**	**24817747**	**8781469**	**14861935**	**89100414**	**11589524**	**25107110**
2006	15803663	3795398	1388925	2170700	12008265	1704997	3786847
2007	19299976	4892639	1797751	2862301	14407337	2360093	4477646
2008	27169290	5749961	1906381	3354179	21419329	2417936	4987666
2009	21479103	4835807	1751571	3080447	16643296	2357239	5194072
2010	30166129	5543942	1936840	3394308	24622187	2749258	6660878
2011	38958314	5899770	1811744	3523452	33058544	3145224	7667795
2012	40810735	5963212	1901750	3737918	34847523	2987939	7217809
2013	42994169	6309757	2035695	3894782	36684413	2923787	7167539

注：进出口总值为海关统计的北京地区进出口数据(包括中央单位)。

资料来源：北京市商务委员会、中华人民共和国北京海关。

Note: Figures of "total value of imports and exports" were imports and exports of Beijing counted by Beijing Customs (including central entities).

Source: Beijing Municipal Commission of Commerce and Beijing Customs of People's Republic of China.

15-1 续表 Continued

Year	外商直接投资项目(合同)个数(个) Number of Direct Projects (Contracts) (unit)	实际利用外商直接投资额(万美元) Actal Vse of Foreign Capital (USD10000)
1980	4	
1981-1985	**124**	
1981	3	
1982	4	
1983	5	
1984	29	
1985	83	
1986-1990	**709**	
1986	63	
1987	72	9534
1988	148	50278
1989	185	31846
1990	241	27696
1991-1995	**10912**	**410896**
1991	724	24482
1992	2208	34984
1993	3753	66693
1994	2675	144460
1995	1552	140277
1996-2000	**4100**	**989794**
1996	868	155290
1997	790	159286
1998	651	206415
1999	644	223004
2000	1147	245799
2001-2005	**7821**	**1231631**
2001	1147	177000
2002	1370	178964
2003	1362	214675
2004	1806	308354
2005	2136	352638
2006-2010	**9232**	**2818387**
2006	2106	455191
2007	2177	506572
2008	1897	608172
2009	1423	612094
2010	1629	636358
2011	1345	705447
2012	1360	804160
2013	1190	852418

15-2 北京地区海关进出口贸易总值(按登记注册类型、贸易方式分)
TOTAL VALUE OF IMPORTS AND EXPORTS AT BEIJING CUSTOMS (BY REGISTRATION TYPE AND COMPOSITION)

项目	Item	金额(万美元) Value (USD 10000)		2013年为2012年% 2013as % of 2012	构成(%) Composition(%)	
		2013	2012		2013	2012
出口	**Local Exports**	**6309757**	**5963212**	**105.8**	**100.00**	**100.00**
按登记注册类型分	**By Registration Type**					
内资企业	Domestically-invested Enterprises	4042999	3828499	105.6	64.08	64.20
国有企业	State-owned Enterprises	3374852	3207836	105.2	53.49	53.79
集体企业	Collectively-owned Enterprises	12156	12306	98.8	0.19	0.21
其他	Others	655990	608357	107.8	10.40	10.20
外商投资企业	Foreign-invested Enterprises	2266758	2134714	106.2	35.92	35.80
中外合资	Joint Ventures	1458547	1294838	112.6	23.12	21.71
中外合作	Cooperatives	4777	8276	57.7	0.08	0.14
外商独资	Solely-funded Enterprises	803434	831600	96.6	12.73	13.95
按贸易方式分	**By Composition**					
#一般贸易	General Trade	2728270	2861663	95.3	43.24	47.99
来料加工装配贸易	Trade of Processing & Assembling Supplied Materials	644232	457138	140.9	10.21	7.67
进料加工贸易	Trade of Processing Imported Materials	1909468	1777013	107.5	30.26	29.80
对外承包工程货物	Contracted Foreign Goods and Projects	654103	503388	129.9	10.37	8.44
出料加工贸易	Trade of Processing Exported Materials	3703	1488	249.0	0.06	0.02
进口	**Imports**	**36684413**	**34847523**	**105.3**	**100.00**	**100.00**
按登记注册类型分	**By Registration Type**					
内资企业	Domestically-invested Enterprises	31472011	29534324	106.6	85.79	84.75
国有企业	State-owned Enterprises	24900054	25392602	98.1	67.88	72.87
集体企业	Collectively-owned Enterprises	108791	148699	73.2	0.30	0.43
其他	Other	6463167	3993022	161.9	17.62	11.46
外商投资企业	Foreign-invested Enterprises	5212401	5313199	98.1	14.21	15.25
中外合资	Joint Ventures	1194042	1045059	114.3	3.25	3.00
中外合作	Cooperatives	5265	4950	106.4	0.01	0.01
外商独资	Solely-funded Enterprises	4013095	4263190	94.1	10.94	12.23
按贸易方式分	**By Composition**					
#一般贸易	General Trade	32705792	31140187	105.0	89.15	89.36
来料加工装配贸易	Trade of Processing and Assembling Supplied Materials	1346798	1009828	133.4	3.67	2.90
进料加工贸易	Trade of Processing Imported Materials	718996	661672	108.7	1.96	1.90
外商投资企业进口设备、物品	Equipment and Goods Imported by Foreign-invested Enterprises	31403	41633	75.4	0.09	0.12
租赁贸易	Leasing Trade	171932	244142	70.4	0.47	0.70

资料来源：中华人民共和国北京海关。
Source: Beijing Customs of People's Republic of China.

15-3 北京地区海关进出口贸易总值(按国别、地区分)

TOTAL VALUE OF IMPORTS AND EXPORTS AT BEIJING CUSTOMS (BY COUNTRY AND REGION)

项目	Item	金额（万美元）Value (USD 10000)		2013年为2012年% 2013as % of 2012	构成（%）Composition(%)	
		2013	2012		2013	2012
出口合计	**Total Exports**	**6309757**	**5963212**	**105.8**	**100.00**	**100.00**
按国别(地区)分	**By Country (Region)**					
#中国香港	Hong Kong, China	607756	478361	127.0	9.63	8.02
中国澳门	Macao, China	34501	34788	99.2	0.55	0.58
中国台湾	Taiwan, China	128041	116659	109.8	2.03	1.96
日本	Japan	482935	473689	102.0	7.65	7.94
新加坡	Singapore	162107	119907	135.2	2.57	2.01
韩国	Korea	226633	200287	113.2	3.59	3.36
越南	Vietnam	202705	182520	111.1	3.21	3.06
伊朗	Iran	110431	113798	97.0	1.75	1.91
印度	India	215731	253408	85.1	3.42	4.25
印度尼西亚	Indonesia	202148	157064	128.7	3.20	2.63
英国	United Kingdom	111990	89216	125.5	1.77	1.50
德国	Germany	125896	153649	81.9	2.00	2.58
法国	France	81682	88877	91.9	1.29	1.49
意大利	Italy	55666	57159	97.4	0.88	0.96
匈牙利	Hungary	95953	64445	148.9	1.52	1.08
俄罗斯联邦	Russian Federation	173167	155925	111.1	2.74	2.61
美国	United States	571241	499105	114.5	9.05	8.37
澳大利亚	Australia	59823	76280	78.4	0.95	1.28
进口合计	**Total Imports**	**36684413**	**34847523**	**105.3**	**100.00**	**100.00**
按国别(地区)分	**By Country (Region)**					
#中国香港	Hong Kong, China	414933	476084	87.2	1.13	1.37
日本	Japan	1210041	1382380	87.5	3.30	3.97
新加坡	Singapore	172814	191048	90.5	0.47	0.55
韩国	Korea	1290432	1436414	89.8	3.52	4.12
沙特阿拉伯	Saudi Arabia	3118808	3085971	101.1	8.50	8.86
英国	United Kingdom	368759	344132	107.2	1.01	0.99
德国	Germany	1818918	2009873	90.5	4.96	5.77
法国	France	326191	285006	114.5	0.89	0.82
意大利	Italy	205565	166330	123.6	0.56	0.48
瑞士	Switzerland	3373473	854275	394.9	9.20	2.45
比利时	Belgium	79254	78587	100.8	0.22	0.23
俄罗斯联邦	Russian Federation	864664	1039310	83.2	2.36	2.98
加拿大	Canada	423888	413133	102.6	1.16	1.19
美国	United States	2970023	2914011	101.9	8.10	8.36
澳大利亚	Australia	1483160	1781719	83.2	4.04	5.11
阿曼	Oman	1648325	1236702	133.3	4.49	3.55
安哥拉	Angola	2658449	2894101	91.9	7.25	8.31

资料来源：中华人民共和国北京海关。
Source: Beijing Customs of People's Republic of China.

15-4 北京地区海关主要商品进口量及金额(2013年)
VOLUME & VALUE OF MAJOR COMMODITIES IMPORTED AT BEIJING CUSTOMS (2013)

项 目		Item		进口数量 Import Volume	进口金额(万美元) Import Value (USD 10000)
粮 食	(万吨)	Grain	(10000 tons)	1119	467778
食用植物油	(万吨)	Edible Vegetabl	(10000 tons)	99	119999
食 糖	(万吨)	Sugar	(10000 tons)	120	59483
酒 类	(万升)	Wine	(10000 liters)	9429	37467
合成橡胶(包括胶乳)	(万吨)	Synthetic Rubbe	(10000 tons)	4	12119
纸 浆	(万吨)	Paper Pulp	(10000 tons)	53	35664
羊 毛	(万吨)	Wool	(10000 tons)	4	26012
棉 花	(万吨)	Cotton	(10000 tons)	82	160088
纺织用合成纤维	(万吨)	Synthetic Fiber	(10000 tons)	5	11966
铁矿砂及其精矿	(万吨)	Iron Sand and Ir	(10000 tons)	8106	1044990
原 油	(万吨)	Crude Oil	(10000 tons)	20454	15895368
成品油	(万吨)	Product Oil	(10000 tons)	932	761397
液化石油气及其他烃类气	(万吨)	LPG and Other	(10000 tons)	739	657494
医药品	(万吨)	Medicines	(10000 tons)	2	310114
肥 料	(万吨)	Fertilizers	(10000 tons)	516	230850
非泡沫塑料的板、片、膜、箔	(万吨)	Non-foam Plasti	(10000 tons)	1	13168
纸及纸板(未切成形的)	(万吨)	Paper and Pressl	(10000 tons)	22	37366
纺织纱线、织物及制品		Textile Yarn, Fabric and Products			161060
服装及衣着附件		Clothes and Clothing Accessories			39352
钢 材	(万吨)	Steel Products	(10000 tons)	73	122831
建筑及采矿用机械及零件		Building and Mining Machinery and Parts			44886
印刷、装订机械及零件		Printing and Binding Machinery and Parts			96498
自动数据处理设备及其部件		Automatic Data Processing Equipment and Their Components			217640
电动机及发电机	(万台)	Electromotors ai	(10000 sets)	961	35781
变压、整流、电感器及零件		Voltage Transformer, Rectifier, Inductor and Parts			97308
电视摄像机、数字照相机及视频摄录一体机	(万台)	Television Cameras, Digital Cameras and Integrated Video Cameras	(10000 sets)	710	163109
印刷电路	(万块)	Printed Circuits	(10000 pieces)	105097	14200
集成电路	(万个)	Integrated Circu	(10000 units)	747386	405666
电线和电缆	(万吨)	Wires and Cable	(10000 tons)	1	21118
汽 车		Automobiles			2276970
汽车零件		Auto Parts			340806
飞 机		Aircrafts			270255
船 舶		Ships and Boats			47474
医疗仪器及器械		Medical Instruments and Devices			197372
计量检测分析自控仪器及器具		Automatically-controlled Measuring, Testing and Analyzing Instruments			475387

15-5 北京地区海关主要商品出口量及金额(2013年)
VOLUME & VALUE OF MAIN COMMODITIES EXPORTED AT BEIJING CUSTOMS (2013)

项目		Item		出口数量 Export Volume	出口金额 Export Value (万美元) (USD 10000)
粮食	(万吨)	Grain	(10000 tons)	46	38154
果蔬汁	(万吨)	Fruit and Veget:	(10000 tons)	11	16745
肥料	(万吨)	Fertilizers	(10000 tons)	429	138029
煤	(万吨)	Coal	(10000 tons)	280	34287
焦炭、半焦炭	(万吨)	Coke and Semi-(	(10000 tons)	151	36071
原油	(万吨)	Crude Oil	(10000 tons)	60	61152
成品油	(万吨)	Product Oil	(10000 tons)	855	794801
医药品	(万吨)	Medicines	(10000 tons)	2	28011
纺织纱线、织物及制品		Textile Yarn, Fabric and Products			69545
铁合金	(万吨)	Ferroalloy	(10000 tons)	1	18913
钢材	(万吨)	Steel Products	(10000 tons)	317	311683
未锻造的铝及铝材	(万吨)	Non-forged Alu	(10000 tons)	2	9133
纺织机械及零件		Textile Machinery and Parts			24335
金属加工机床	(万台)	Metal Processin;	(10000 sets)	1	15719
自动数据处理设备及其部件		Automatic Data Processing Equipment and Their Components			65665
液晶显示板	(万个)	LCD Plates	(10000 units)	2602	59041
电动机及发电机	(万台)	Electromotors a	(10000 sets)	220	8801
变压器	(万个)	Voltage Transfo	(10000 units)	35	18021
蓄电池	(万个)	Storage Cells	(10000 units)	5270	20398
电话机	(万台)	Telephone Sets	(10000 sets)	13770	1109878
二极管及类似半导体器	(万个)	Diode and Simil	(10000 units)	120566	33003
集成电路	(万个)	Integrated Circu	(10000 units)	451444	181775
电线和电缆	(万吨)	Wires and Cable	(10000 tons)	4	40466
汽车(包括整套散件)	(万辆)	Automobiles (In	(10000 sets)	4	101808
汽车零件		Auto Parts			147919
船舶		Boats and Ships			233116
医疗仪器及器械		Medical Instruments and Devices			54477
家具及其零件		Furnitures and Their Parts			19630
服装及衣着附件		Clothes and Clo			187289
鞋类	(万吨)	Footwear	(10000 tons)	1	15019
塑料制品	(万吨)	Plastic Products	(10000 tons)	5	21094

资料来源：中华人民共和国北京海关。
Source: Beijing Customs of People's Republic of China.

15-6 北京口岸运营情况
STATISTICS FOR PORT OPERATION IN BEIJING

项 目		Item		2013	2012	2013年为2012年% 2013 as % of 2012
北京首都国际机场空港口岸		**Port of Beijing Capital International Airport**				
旅客吞吐量	(万人次)	Passenger Throughput	(10000 person-times)	8371.24	8192.93	102.2
进出境人员	(万人次)	Inbound/Outbound Visitors	(10000 person-times)	2102.52	2034.70	103.3
#外籍人员进出境	(万人次)	Inbound/Outbound Foreign Visitors	(10000 person-times)	822.36	892.50	92.1
货邮吞吐量	(万吨)	Cargos Carried	(10000 tons)	184.37	174.50	105.7
飞机起降	(架次)	Takeoff and Landing of Airplanes	(unit)	567759	557168	101.9
#进出境飞机起降	(架次)	Takeoff and Landing of Airplanes Inbound/Outbound	(unit)	123562	121507	101.7
海关监管货物	(万吨)	Cargos under Customs Regulation	(10000 tons)	50.59	51.25	98.7
海关征收关税及代征税	(万元)	Duties Levied and Collected by Custo	(10000 yuan)	3066200	3342931	91.7
北京丰台货运口岸		**Beijing Fengtai Cargo Transport Port**				
海关监管货物	(吨)	Cargos under Customs Regulation	(ton)	17642	9263	190.5
海关征收关税及代征税	(万元)	Duties Levied and Collected by Custo	(10000 yuan)	5033	3756	134.0
北京朝阳口岸		**Beijing Chaoyang Transport Port**				
海关监管货物	(标箱)	Cargos under Customs Regulation	(standard container)	120920	132922	91.0
海关监管货物	(吨)	Cargos under Customs Regulation	(ton)	900766	867860	103.8
海关征收关税及代征税	(万元)	Duties Levied and Collected by Custo	(10000 yuan)	1173486	1418290	82.7
北京西站铁路口岸		**Railway Port at Beijing West Railway Station**				
进出境人员	(人次)	Inbound/Outbound Visitors	(person-times)	98705	116563	84.7
#外籍人员进出境	(人次)	Inbound/Outbound Foreign Visitors	(person-times)	7487	7438	100.7
北京平谷国际陆港		**Beijing Pinggu International Land Port**				
海关监管货物	(标箱)	Cargos under Customs Regulation	(standard container)	27316	21260	128.5
海关监管货物	(吨)	Cargos under Customs Regulation	(ton)	198261	152821	129.7
海关征收关税及代征税	(万元)	Duties Levied and Collected by Custo	(10000 yuan)	202858	170992	118.6
北京天竺综合保税区		**Beijing Tianzhu Comprehensive Bonded Zone**				
实际进出货物	(吨)	Cargos under Customs Regulation	(ton)	40016	31271	128.0
海关征收关税及代征税	(万元)	Duties Levied and Collected by Custo	(10000 yuan)	720113	644270	111.8

注：自2013年起，北京朝阳口岸海关监管货物统计口径调整为按实际报关量统计的监管货物表箱总量，2012年为同口径数据。
资料来源：北京市人民政府口岸办公室。

Note: Since 2013,the statistical scope of cargos under customs regulation of Chaoyang Transport Port has been the actual number of cargoes that went through custom clearance.Data for 2012 covered the same scope.

Source: Port Administration Office of the People's Government of Beijing Municipality.

15-7 外商投资企业实际利用外资情况(2006-2013年) ACTUAL USE OF FOREIGN CAPITAL BY FOREIGN INVESTED ENTERPRISES (2006-2013)

单位：万美元 (USD 10000)

项目	Item	2006	2007	2008	2009	2010	2011	2012	2013
实际利用外商直接投资额	**Actual Use of Foreign Capital**	**455191**	**506572**	**608172**	**612094**	**636358**	**705447**	**804160**	**852418**
按登记注册类型分	**By Registration Type**								
合资经营	Joint Ventures	80570	77887	90916	91049	91335	78983	191944	190667
合作经营	Cooperatives	33039	18037	21372	32249	22890	15068	14184	22887
独资经营	Solely-funded Enterprises	341367	408754	490252	448912	516766	594890	592310	593258
外商投资股份制	Companies Limited by Shares	215	1894	5632	39884	5367	16506	5722	45606
按产业分	**By Industry**								
第一产业	Primary Industry	544	4774	2032	3833	1246	214	733	1717
第二产业	Secondary Industry	109380	93391	162515	88536	71899	80798	112326	149687
第三产业	Tertiary Industry	345267	408407	443625	519725	563213	624435	691101	701014
按行业分	**By Sector**								
农、林、牧、渔业	Agriculture, Forestry, Animal Production and Hunting, Fishing	544	4774	2032	3833	1246	214	733	1717
制造业	Manufacturing	105590	89618	150056	75364	68496	63303	86378	106848
建筑业	Construction	1254	878	1715	2493	411	2343	383	193
信息传输、计算机服务和软件业	Information Transmission, Computer Services and Software	44341	78470	105396	94752	95453	109246	135121	119547
批发与零售业	Wholesale and Retail Trade	24378	33318	34677	55411	66032	115437	74311	92739
住宿和餐饮业	Accommodation and Restaurants	1882	5824	3357	8427	3525	1705	2877	1822
房地产业	Real Estate	72242	119476	78787	79682	141728	112539	87739	148057
租赁和商务服务业	Renting and Leasing Activities, Business Services	174342	92896	132541	225888	175580	190363	161595	171079
其他行业	Other Sectors	30618	81318	99611	66244	83887	110297	255023	210416
按外商国别(地区)分	**By Country (Region) of Foreign Investors**								
#中国香港	Hongkong,China	86600	149291	173292	270295	312863	323041	440357	360481
英属维尔京群岛	Virgin Islands	78445	104154	125045	123201	76255	112981	28882	51111
开曼群岛	Cayman Islands	27596	68646	75463	41389	45209	35982	59320	43982
日本	Japan	67580	30386	47174	23905	40692	77196	59022	44781
韩国	Korea	35357	24420	27841	17601	14725	22372	70959	21029
美国	United States	20043	18280	17888	18628	21370	30221	21097	38882
新加坡	Singapore	17616	15328	10520	12600	24888	12898	31656	19383
巴巴多斯	Barbados	7278	13789	15803	2384	941	821	200	2839
德国	Germany	47797	11476	26654	14308	22344	17939	25763	107467
毛里求斯	Mauritius	10166	8068	7780	5615	7179	1311	1392	3297
百慕大	Bermuda	1658	7540	1699	4441	4860	813	1483	265
萨摩亚	Samoan	1483	6189	2468	1310	1705	893	1163	589
荷兰	Netherlands	4610	4876	28520	4906	10639	3677	8542	14619
法国	France	3578	3824	2583	6349	3700	6642	2286	1409
英国	United Kingdom	2977	3304	4897	4242	1120	6245	3828	2387

资料来源：北京市商务委员会。
Source: Beijing Municipal Commission of Commerce.

15-8 外商投资企业基本情况

项 目	Item	企业单位数（个）Number of Enterprises (unit) 2013	2012
合 计	**Total**	**4360**	**4334**
按登记注册类型分	**By Registration Type**		
港澳台商投资企业	Hong Kong, Macao and Taiwan-invested Enterprises	1615	1567
与港澳台商合资	Joint Ventures	528	527
与港澳台商合作	Cooperatives	128	136
港澳台商独资	Solely-funded Enterprises	926	874
港澳台商投资股份有限公司	Companies Limited by Shares	33	30
其他港澳台投资企业	Others		
外商投资企业	Foreign-invested Enterprises	2745	2767
中外合资	Joint Ventures	808	818
中外合作	Cooperatives	114	118
外商独资	Solely-funded Enterprises	1779	1781
外商投资股份有限公司	Companies Limited by Shares	42	49
其他外商投资企业	Others	2	1
按国民经济行业分	**By Sector**		
农、林、牧、渔业	Agriculture, Forestry, Animal Production and Hunting, Fishing		
制造业	Manufacturing	875	911
建筑业	Construction	89	93
批发与零售业	Wholesale and Retail Trade	544	529
住宿和餐饮业	Accommodation and Restaurants	208	214
信息传输、软件和信息技术服务业	Information Transmission, Software and Information Technology Services	580	598
房地产业	Real Estate	424	428
租赁和商务服务业	Renting and Leasing Activities, Business Services	791	749
其他行业	Other Sectors	849	812
按三次产业分	**By Industry**		
第一产业	Primary Industry		
第二产业	Secondary Industry	970	1011
第三产业	Tertiary Industry	3390	3323

注：1. 本表统计范围为限额以上法人企业。
2. 行业划分执行2011年国民经济行业分类标准(GB/T 4754-2011)。

STATISTICS FOR FOREIGN-INVESTED ENTERPRISES

从业人员平均人数(人) Average Number of Persons Employed (person)		主营业务收入 Operating Income		利润总额 Total Profits		应交税金合计 Total Taxes Paid	
2013	2012	2013	2012	2013	2012	2013	2012
1332263	**1298578**	**242367954**	**215074562**	**29844224**	**25055724**	**9045355**	**7743904**
488513	479876	63622202	56774419	6835132	5239482	2207459	2425660
150675	152096	13918810	11182539	2134209	1059468	777635	520910
22388	23269	2515151	3408334	618611	822650	227366	552196
258055	248026	37553296	32598098	3653282	2625229	1110145	1140283
57395	56485	9634945	9585448	429030	732134	92313	212271
843750	818702	178745753	158300144	23009093	19816242	6837896	5318244
293492	290606	59543126	50233264	6413106	5198304	2873787	2272252
19895	20040	2084745	1493559	367371	200260	140491	90360
493943	476056	115351147	105186514	15899323	14260113	3686866	2852320
31906	27638	1530301	1320074	312251	161724	124161	100786
***	***	***	***	***	***	***	***
392796	387469	70656413	61596575	5270268	4051768	3420155	2685055
11832	17247	1955321	2084522	45936	80590	53752	61073
189701	188558	88557419	83984267	4308445	3790105	2365653	1601477
95975	94453	2872459	2836435	167276	232552	182652	182712
215862	203680	18164534	16636743	9397331	8709491	793776	845363
63192	63785	7917483	6340299	2229144	2057550	966216	1008262
120540	110729	29824725	21473819	2891679	1884459	572394	655025
242365	232657	22419600	20121903	5534145	4249209	690758	704937
408005	407845	74823199	65564311	5755038	4508446	3651295	2794063
924258	890733	167544756	149510251	24089187	20547279	5394060	4949841

Note: a) Statistics in this table cover corporate enterprises above designated size.

b) Sectors in this table are classified in accordance with the Standard for Classification of National Economic Sectors 2011 (GB/T 4754-2011).

15-9 境外投资情况(2003-2012年)
STATISTICS FOR OVERSEAS INVESTMENT (2003-2012)

单位：万美元 (USD 10000)

年 份 Year	中方投资额 Mount of Investment by China Side	截至到各年期末直接投资存量 Diret Investment Stock by the Year End
2003	30054	44844
2004	15739	70086
2005	11306	92940
2006	5612	91873
2007	15295	159195
2008	47299	251019
2009	45185	375865
2010	76614	480882
2011	117503	603380
2012	168900	757800

资料来源：北京市商务委员会。
Source: Beijing Municipal Commission of Commerce.

15-10 对外经济合作(1984-2013年)
STATISTICS FOR FOREIGN ECONOMIC COOPERATION (1984-2013)

年 份 Year	合同数 (份) Number of Contracts (unit)	#对外承包工程 Foreign Contracted Works	合同额 (万美元) Contract Value (USD 10000)	#对外承包工程 Foreign Contracted Works	完成营业额 (万美元) Turnover (USD 10000)	#对外承包工程 Foreign Contracted Works	年末在外人数 (人) Year-end Workers Staying Abroad (person)	对外承包工程 Foreign Contracted Works	对外劳务合作 Foreign Labor Service Cooperation
1984	9	2	2801	2768	502	331	541	163	378
1985	12	2	852	736	2083	355	2401	18	2383
1986	30	7	446	319	1535	90	837	71	766
1987	37	5	547	354	696	186	690	20	670
1988	46	5	885	344	802	281	819	104	715
1989	111	7	1685	235	1018	459	600	83	517
1990	105	16	3756	2253	1056	625	336	25	311
1991	114	9	3202	1671	1897	1469	980	306	674
1992	130	16	8889	7762	3140	2543	952	264	688
1993	143	48	29397	27625	9748	8871	1555	532	1023
1994	114	34	15715	15089	18783	17822	2720	1694	1026
1995	116	35	15613	14014	12789	12156	2604	1297	1307
1996	116	49	67689	62945	43057	38124	2516	1559	957
1997	107	37	35640	23374	29629	17945	3122	1993	1129
1998	180	48	25526	19292	31009	24930	3647	2239	1408
1999	90	28	25232	18715	26167	19690	3476	2199	1277
2000	104	54	16285	9936	19799	13543	3205	1660	1545
2001	105	54	21439	14758	18628	11680	3494	2141	1353
2002	73	42	27949	19376	23160	14453	2134	1112	1022
2003	117	99	48271	30761	34926	17334	2097	1270	827
2004	128	116	81185	51136	59630	29241	2552	1629	923
2005	272	238	93732	56709	71281	35554	4424	2528	1896
2006	232	166	176752	160328	83518	70062	8962	6760	2202
2007	317	143	236881	211560	94077	71727	11299	7060	4239
2008	486	197	558714	520973	168416	131686	11422	6366	5056
2009	190	182	336223	296851	226893	185017	17121	11805	5316
2010	199	170	286179	251114	259794	222514	22499	17145	5354
2011	229	229	264019	262078	252951	249146	17821	12393	5428
2012	340	340	405885	403475	295639	289902	16747	12143	4604
2013	349	349	564383	562440	341046	335854	21036	16549	4487

注：1984-2008年，对外承包工程统计中含对外设计咨询统计数据。
资料来源：北京市商务委员会。
Note: In 1984-2008, statistics for foreign contracted projects included statistics for consultation on foreign design.
Source: Beijing Municipal Commission of Commerce.

15-11 北京市市级友好城市
MUNICIPAL-LEVEL SISTER CITIES OF BEIJING

顺序 No.	城市	City	所在国家	Contury	所属洲	Continent	缔结日期 Date of Conclusion
1	东京都	Tokyo	日本	Japan	亚洲	Asia	1979.03.14
2	纽约市	New York	美国	USA	北美洲	North America	1980.02.25
3	贝尔格莱德市	Belgrade	塞尔维亚	Serbia	欧洲	Europe	1980.10.14
4	利马市	Lima	秘鲁	Peru	南美洲	South America	1983.11.21
5	华盛顿特区	Washington, DC	美国	USA	北美洲	North America	1984.05.15
6	马德里市	Madrid	西班牙	Spain	欧洲	Europe	1985.09.16
7	里约热内卢市	Rio De Janeiro	巴西	Brazil	南美洲	South America	1986.11.24
8	巴黎大区	Greater Parisian Re[illegible]	法国	France	欧洲	Europe	1987.07.02
9	科隆市	Cologne	德国	Germany	欧洲	Europe	1987.09.14
10	安卡拉市	Ankara	土耳其	Turkey	亚洲	Asia	1990.06.20
11	开罗省	Cairo	埃及	Egypt	非洲	Africa	1990.10.28
12	雅加达省	Jakarta	印度尼西亚	Indonesia	亚洲	Asia	1992.08.04
13	伊斯兰堡市	Islamabad	巴基斯坦	Pakistan	亚洲	Asia	1992.10.08
14	曼谷市	Bangkok	泰国	Thailand	亚洲	Asia	1993.05.26
15	布宜诺斯艾利斯市	Buenos Aires	阿根廷	Argentina	南美洲	South America	1993.07.13
16	首尔特别市	Seoul Special City	韩国	South Korea	亚洲	Asia	1993.10.23
17	基辅市	Kiev	乌克兰	Ukraine	欧洲	Europe	1993.12.13
18	柏林市	Berlin	德国	Germany	欧洲	Europe	1994.04.05
19	布鲁塞尔大区	Greater Brussels Re	比利时	Belgium	欧洲	Europe	1994.09.22
20	河内市	Hanoi	越南	Viet Nam	亚洲	Asia	1994.10.06
21	阿姆斯特丹市	Amsterdam	荷兰	Holland	欧洲	Europe	1994.10.29
22	莫斯科市	Moscow	俄罗斯	Russia	欧洲	Europe	1995.05.16
23	巴黎市	Paris	法国	France	欧洲	Europe	1997.10.23
24	罗马市	Rome	意大利	Italy	欧洲	Europe	1998.05.28
25	豪登省	Gauteng	南非	South Africa	非洲	Africa	1998.12.06
26	渥太华市	Ottawa	加拿大	Canada	北美洲	North America	1999.10.18
27	首都地区	The Capital Region	澳大利亚	Australia	大洋洲	Oceania	2000.09.14
28	马德里自治区	Madrid Autonomou	西班牙	Spain	欧洲	Europe	2005.01.17
29	雅典市	Athens	希腊	Greece	欧洲	Europe	2005.05.10
30	布达佩斯市	Budapest	匈牙利	Hungary	欧洲	Europe	2005.06.16
31	布加勒斯特市	Bucharest	罗马尼亚	Rumania	欧洲	Europe	2005.06.21
32	哈瓦那市	Havana	古巴	Cuba	南美洲	South America	2005.09.24
33	马尼拉市	Manila	菲律宾	Philippines	亚洲	Asia	2005.11.14
34	伦敦市	London	英国	UK	欧洲	Europe	2006.04.11
35	亚的斯亚贝巴市	Addis Abeba	埃塞俄比亚	Ethiopia	非洲	Africa	2006.04.17
36	惠灵顿市	Wellington	新西兰	New Zealand	大洋洲	Oceania	2006.05.10
37	赫尔辛基市	Helsinki	芬兰	Finland	欧洲	Europe	2006.07.14
38	阿斯塔纳市	Astana	哈萨克斯坦	Kazakstan	亚洲	Asia	2006.11.16
39	特拉维夫市	Tel Aviv	以色列	Israel	亚洲	Asia	2006.11.21
40	首都大区	The Greater Capital	智利	Chile	南美洲	South America	2007.08.06
41	里斯本市	Lisbon	葡萄牙	Portugal	欧洲	Europe	2007.10.22
42	地拉那市	Tirana	阿尔巴尼亚	Albania	欧洲	Europe	2008.03.21
43	多哈市	Doha	卡塔尔	Qatar	亚洲	Asia	2008.06.23
44	圣何塞市	San Jose	哥斯达黎加	Costarica	北美洲	North America	2009.10.17
45	墨西哥城	Mexican City	墨西哥	Mexico	北美洲	North America	2009.10.19
46	都柏林市	Dublin	爱尔兰	Ireland	欧洲	Europe	2011.06.02
47	哥本哈根市	Copenhagen	丹麦	Denmark	欧洲	Europe	2012.06.28
48	新南威尔士州	New South Wales	澳大利亚	Australia	大洋洲	Oceania	2012.08.03
49	德里邦	Delhi	印度	India	亚洲	Asia	2013.10.23

资料来源：北京市人民政府外事办公室。
Sourse: Foreign Affairs Office of the People's Government of Beijing Municipality.

主要统计指标解释

进出口总值 指实际进、出我国海关并能引起我国境内物质资源增加或减少的进出口货物总金额。包括我国境内法人和其他组织以一般贸易、易货贸易、加工贸易、补偿贸易、寄售代销贸易等方式进出口的货物、租赁期一年及以上的租赁进出口货物、边境小额贸易货物、国际援助物资或捐赠品、保税区和保税仓库进出口货物等的金额合计。进出口总值用以观察一个国家在对外贸易方面的总规模。我国规定出口货物按离岸价格统计，进口货物按到岸价格统计。

一般贸易 指我国境内有进出口经营权的企业单边进口或单边出口的货物。

来料加工装配贸易 指由外商提供全部或部分原材料、辅料、零部件、元器件、配套件和包装物料，必要时提供设备，由我方按对方的要求进行加工装配，成品交对方销售，我方收取工缴费；或对方提供的作价设备价款，我方用工缴费偿还的交易形式。

进料加工贸易 指我方用外汇购买进口的原料、材料、辅料、元器件、零部件、配套件和包装物料，加工成品或半成品后再外销出口的交易形式。

旅客吞吐量 指经乘航班进出北京民用运输机场的中国公民、港澳台同胞、华侨及外国人等旅客数量的总和。

货邮吞吐量 指通过民用运输机场的航班运输的货物、邮寄物品和随身携带的行李物品重量总和。

飞机起降架次 指进出民用运输机场的正常航班架次，不包括包机和其他非正常航班。

海关征收关税 指进出口商品在经过国家关境时，由政府设置的海关向进出口国所征收的税收。

批准外商直接投资企业项目个数 指外商直接投资中批准设立的外商投资企业个数、批准的合作开发项目个数。

实际利用外商直接投资额 指批准的合同外资金额的实际执行数，外国投资者根据批准外商投资企业的合同（章程）的规定实际缴付的出资额和企业投资总额内外国投资者以自己的境外自有资金实际直接向企业提供的贷款。

对外承包工程 指企业按照国际通行做法，在国（境）外承揽和实施各类工程项目的经济活动。企业承揽的我国对外经济援助项目、我国驻外使（领）馆等建设项目视同对外承包工程项目。

对外劳务合作 指企业按照与国（境）外政府有关机构、团体、企业、私人雇主所签合同规定，向国（境）外派遣各类劳务人员的经济活动。企业自带设备以提供技术服务的形式在国（境）外承揽的项目视同对外劳务合作项目。

对外设计咨询 指企业在国（境）外承揽的工程设计、工程监理、技术咨询和人员培训等经济活动。

Explanatory Notes on Main Statistical Indicators

Total Value of Imports and Exports refer to the total value of goods actually imported and exported at China's customs, which lead to increase or decrease in the physical resources in China, including goods imported/exported by China domestic legal persons and other organizations in such manners as general trade, barter trade, processing trade, compensation trade, commission-based sales trade, leasing imports/exports with a lease period of one year and more, small-sum border trade goods, international aid goods and donations, imports/exports in bonded zones and bonded warehouses. The indicator of the Total Value of Imports and Exports can be used to observe the total size of foreign trade in a country. In accordance with the stipulation of the Chinese government, imports are calculated at CIF, while exports are calculated at FOB.

General Trade means goods imported and exported unilaterally by domestic enterprises with import/export rights.

Trade of Processing and Assembling Supplied Materials is a form of transaction in which all or part of raw materials, auxiliary materials, parts and components, elements, fittings, and packaging materials, and equipment if necessary are provided by the foreign party, processed or assemble by Chinese party according to requirements of the foreign party, and the finished products are sold by the foreign party. The Chinese party charges processing fees and pays back the money of priced equipment provided by the foreign party with processing charges.

Trade of Processing Imported Materials is a form of transaction in which the Chinese party purchases raw materials, auxiliary materials, parts and components, elements, fittings, and packaging materials with foreign exchange, processing them into finished or semi-finished products and export them.

Passenger Throughput means the total number of Chinese citizens, compatriots form Hong Kong, Macao and Taiwan, oversea Chinese and foreigners that take off and land at civil airports in Beijing by flights.

Cargos Throughput means the sum of goods, mailed articles and luggage transported by flights taking off from and landing at civil airports in Beijing.

Takeoff and Landing of Airplanes means the number of regular flights taking off from and landing at civil airports in Beijing, excluding chartered flights and other non-regular flights.

Duties Levied and Collected by Customs means the sum of duties actually levied from the imported and exported by customs established by the government when imported and exported goods are going through national borders.

Number of Direct Foreign-invested Enterprises Approved means the number of foreign-invested enterprises and joint development projects approved in foreign direct investment (FDI).

Actual Use of Foreign Capital means the value of approved contractual foreign investment actually used, the amount of actual capital contribution by foreign investors according to the contract (articles of incorporation) of the foreign-invested enterprise approved and, in the total investment of an enterprise, the amount of loans provided directly by foreign investor with its own overseas money.

Foreign Contracted Projects refer to economic activities in which enterprises undertake and implement various projects in foreign (overseas) countries in line with international practices. Foreign economic aid projects and construction projects of Chinese Embassies (Consulates) undertaken by enterprises are deemed as foreign contracted projects.

Foreign Labor Service Cooperation means any economic activity in which enterprises dispatch labors to foreign (overseas) countries as stated in contracts signed with foreign (overseas) government agencies, groups, enterprises, and private employers. Projects undertaken by enterprises in foreign (overseas) countries in a manner of providing technical service with their own equipment are deemed as foreign labor service cooperation projects.

Foreign Design Consulting means any economic activity of project design, project supervision, technical consulting and personnel training undertaken in foreign (overseas) countries by enterprises.

16

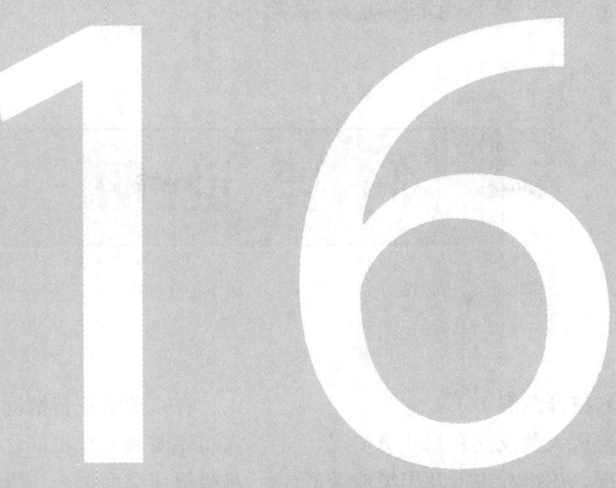

北京统计年鉴2014 BEIJING STATISTICAL YEARBOOK

旅游业
TOURISM

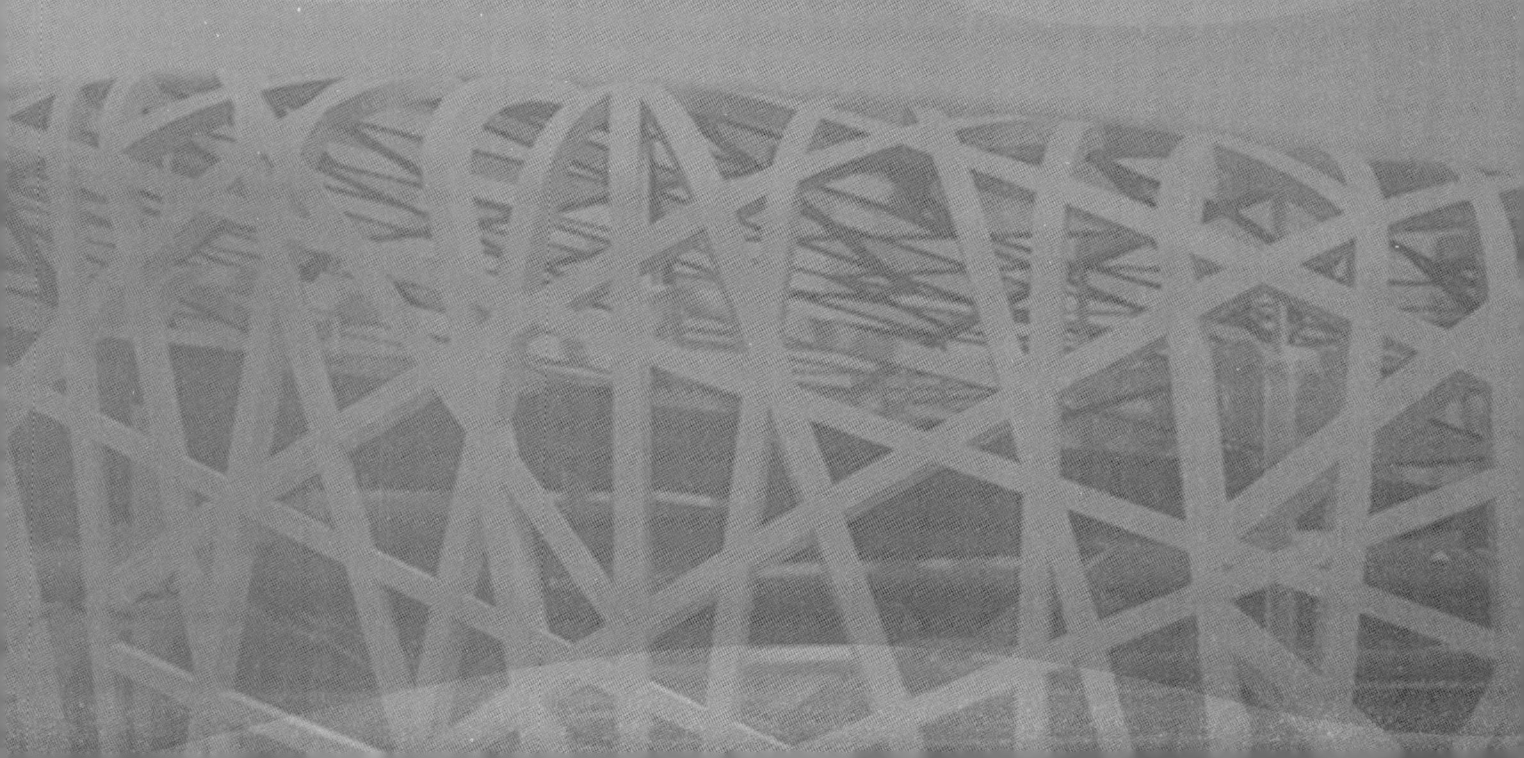

简要说明

一、本章资料的主要内容和统计范围

本章内容主要包括来京旅游者人数及其在京花费情况、星级饭店经营及接待住宿者情况、旅行社接待及出境旅游情况、A级及以上重点旅游景区活动情况等。

统计范围包括国际旅游和国内旅游。

二、本章资料的数据来源

本章中的旅游外汇收入、国内旅游者人数、国内旅游收入、在京旅游花费情况资料来源于北京市旅游发展委员会。入境旅游者人数根据北京市统计局的星级饭店、限额以上非星级饭店全面调查、限额以下饭店抽样调查，以及北京市旅游发展委员会的其他住宿设施抽样调查结果汇总得出。星级饭店、旅行社、A级及以上和重点旅游景区有关数据通过全面调查取得，由北京市统计局、国家统计局北京调查总队提供。

Brief Introduction

I. Main Content and Scope of Statistics

This chapter includes statistics for the number and cost of tourists to Beijing, operation and reception of star-rated hotels, reception and outbound tours made through travel agencies, activities at Level A-or-above key scenic spots, and so on.

Statistics include international and domestic tours.

II. Source of Data

Data of foreign exchange income from tourism, number of domestic tourists, domestic tourism income, and cost of tourists in Beijing are sourced from Beijing Municipal Commission of Tourism Development. The number of inbound tourists is summed from the results of comprehensive survey of star-rated hotels and non-star-rated hotels above designated size, sample survey of hotels below designated size conducted by Beijing Municipal Bureau of Statistics, as well as the results of sample survey of other accommodation facilities conducted by Beijing Municipal Commission of Tourism Development. Data concerning star-rated hotels, travel agencies, Level A-or-above key scenic spots were obtained through comprehensive survey, and provided by Beijing Municipal Bureau of Statistics and NBS Survey Office in Beijing.

16-1 国际、国内旅游情况(1978-2013年)

STATISTICS FOR INTERNATIONAL AND DOMESTIC TOURISM (1978-2013)

年　份 Year	来京旅游者人数（万人次） Number of Tourists to Beijing (10000 person-times)	入境旅游者人数 Inbound Tourists	国内旅游者人数 Domestic Tourists	旅游外汇收入总额（万美元） Foreign Exchange Earnings of Tourism (USD 10000)	国内旅游收入（亿元） Revenue from Domestic Tourism (100 million yuan)
1978		18.7		10000	
1979		25.2		9000	
1980		28.6		12000	
1981-1985		**295.4**		**94000**	
1981		39.4		12000	
1982		45.7		13000	
1983		50.9		14000	
1984		65.7		23000	
1985		93.7		32000	
1986-1990		**492.0**		**280901**	
1986		99.0		46000	
1987		108.1		55000	
1988		120.4		67000	
1989		64.5		47195	
1990		100.0		65706	
1991-1995		**919.6**		**735519**	
1991		132.0		85001	
1992		174.8		107286	
1993		202.8		124128	
1994	6913.0	203.0	6710.0	200904	298.0
1995	6527.0	207.0	6320.0	218200	352.6
1996-2000	**45284.7**	**1203.3**	**44081.4**	**1214800**	**2388.4**
1996	7901.9	218.9	7683.0	225200	359.6
1997	8450.8	229.8	8221.0	224800	391.3
1998	8951.5	220.1	8731.4	238400	424.5
1999	9512.4	252.4	9260.0	249600	530.0
2000	10468.1	282.1	10186.0	276800	683.0
2001-2005	**57116.7**	**1459.7**	**55657.0**	**1475000**	**4968.7**
2001	11292.8	285.8	11007.0	295000	887.7
2002	11810.4	310.4	11500.0	311000	930.0
2003	8885.1	185.1	8700.0	190000	706.0
2004	12265.5	315.5	11950.0	317000	1145.0
2005	12862.9	362.9	12500.0	362000	1300.0
2006-2010	**77925.4**	**2107.4**	**75818.0**	**2247000**	**9712.9**
2006	13590.3	390.3	13200.0	402600	1482.7
2007	14715.5	435.5	14280.0	458000	1753.6
2008	14560.0	379.0	14181.0	446000	1907.0
2009	16669.5	412.5	16257.0	436000	2144.5
2010	18390.1	490.1	17900.0	504400	2425.1
2011	21404.4	520.4	20884.0	541600	2864.3
2012	23134.6	500.9	22633.7	514900	3301.3
2013	25189.0	450.1	24738.8	479468	3666.3

资料来源：旅游外汇收入总额、国内旅游者人数、国内旅游收入来源于北京市旅游发展委员会。

Source: Data of "Foreign Exchange Earnings of Tourism, Number of Domestic Tourists, Revenue from Domestic Tourism" were provided by Beijing Municipal Commission of Tourism Development.

16-2 按客源地分入境旅游者人数(1978-2013年)
NUMBER OF INBOUND TOURISTS BY COUNTRY/REGION(1978-2013)

单位：万人次 (10000 person-times)

年份 Year	入境旅游者人数 Number of Inbound Tourists	港澳台同胞 Hong Kong, Macao and Taiwan Tourists	外国人 Foreigner	#香港 Hong Kong	#日本 Japan	#韩国 Korea	#美国 United States	#英国 United Kingdom	#法国 France	#德国 Germany	#俄罗斯 Russia
1978	18.7	3.3	15.4								
1979	25.2	4.1	21.1								
1980	28.6	5.8	21.7		6.0		3.7	1.3	0.9	0.9	
1981-1985	**295.4**	**47.5**	**233.0**		**68.3**		**47.1**	**10.1**	**9.2**	**10.6**	
1981	39.4	6.8	31.3		5.3		3.8	1.1	1.1	1.0	
1982	45.7	8.2	35.9		8.2		6.6	1.3	1.3	1.4	
1983	50.9	8.9	39.7		10.0		9.4	1.5	1.5	1.7	0.1
1984	65.7	10.0	52.1		17.2		12.5	2.3	2.1	2.5	0.1
1985	93.7	13.6	74.0		27.6		14.8	3.9	3.2	4.0	0.2
1986-1990	**492.0**	**117.7**	**357.0**		**110.0**		**63.8**	**18.1**	**15.7**	**22.4**	**3.8**
1986	99.0	15.8	79.0		25.5		14.7	4.1	3.1	4.6	0.3
1987	108.1	21.8	81.7		26.3		16.5	4.5	4.3	5.1	0.3
1988	120.4	28.8	86.5		27.8		16.7	4.2	4.2	5.4	0.7
1989	64.5	16.6	46.0		12.2		7.3	2.4	2.1	3.3	1.0
1990	100.0	34.7	63.8	11.4	18.2		8.6	2.9	2.0	4.0	1.5
1991-1995	**919.6**	**217.9**	**683.4**	**122.7**	**188.0**	**47.2**	**68.9**	**25.2**	**30.1**	**45.9**	**27.4**
1991	132.0	38.2	91.4	17.6	27.6	4.3	9.5	4.3	3.7	6.0	3.5
1992	174.8	51.2	120.5	24.6	37.6	5.6	12.3	4.4	6.6	9.4	5.1
1993	202.8	52.8	145.0	29.4	39.3	7.3	14.3	5.3	6.9	12.0	7.7
1994	203.0	39.4	160.0	25.7	41.1	12.7	15.4	5.4	6.7	9.7	4.9
1995	207.0	36.3	166.5	25.4	42.4	17.3	17.4	5.8	6.2	8.8	6.2
1996-2000	**1203.3**	**206.2**	**984.3**	**128.3**	**229.4**	**92.6**	**118.6**	**43.8**	**37.5**	**53.0**	**28.1**
1996	218.9	38.6	176.2	25.5	43.0	18.0	18.5	7.5	6.6	10.0	6.9
1997	229.8	40.3	186.9	26.3	43.0	19.4	21.7	9.0	6.5	9.1	6.5
1998	220.1	39.1	178.2	25.0	43.5	8.2	23.2	8.8	6.9	11.3	6.2
1999	252.4	44.1	205.0	26.5	45.6	19.2	24.1	8.8	7.9	10.5	4.6
2000	282.1	44.1	238.0	25.0	54.3	27.8	31.1	9.7	9.6	12.1	3.9
2001-2005	**1459.7**	**220.9**	**1238.8**	**133.2**	**233.7**	**182.9**	**173.8**	**57.8**	**51.7**	**56.9**	**33.2**
2001	285.8	45.9	239.9	26.9	50.7	32.7	33.1	11.1	10.2	12.3	4.9
2002	310.4	43.9	266.5	25.5	56.5	38.0	37.4	12.9	11.3	12.2	5.2
2003	185.1	32.4	152.7	21.7	29.2	24.5	19.4	8.1	5.5	6.3	5.2
2004	315.5	47.4	268.1	27.7	52.3	42.4	37.4	11.8	11.1	11.5	8.2
2005	362.9	51.3	311.6	31.4	45.0	45.3	46.5	13.9	13.6	14.6	9.7
2006-2010	**2107.4**	**286.2**	**1821.1**	**174.4**	**248.2**	**207.9**	**291.8**	**82.4**	**72.3**	**85.7**	**85.2**
2006	390.3	52.0	338.3	30.3	50.6	42.4	49.8	14.8	14.2	15.3	15.0
2007	435.5	52.9	382.6	31.3	58.8	44.4	60.3	17.0	16.4	17.5	18.3
2008	379.0	43.3	335.7	28.1	40.0	35.3	53.8	17.5	14.5	16.0	17.9
2009	412.5	69.6	342.9	44.4	46.2	35.2	57.9	16.3	12.9	16.8	15.0
2010	490.1	68.4	421.6	40.3	52.6	50.6	70.0	16.8	14.3	20.1	19.0
2011	520.4	73.0	447.4	43.4	51.0	53.4	78.9	18.8	15.0	22.2	20.5
2012	500.9	66.5	434.4	37.6	43.7	44.2	75.1	18.5	15.1	24.5	20.0
2013	450.1	62.5	387.6	35.4	24.9	37.7	74.7	17.5	13.4	23.0	16.7

注：1. 1980-1999年的入境旅游者人数由外国游客、港澳台游客、华侨三部分组成。
2. 1990-1999年香港游客人数为香港、澳门合计。

Note: a) "Number of inbound tourists" in 1980-1999 consisted of foreign visitors, visitors from Hong Kong, Macao and Taiwan, and overseas Chinese.
b) Tourists from Hong Kong in 1990-1999 were the total number of tourists from Hong Kong and Macao.

16-3 来京旅游者人数
NUMBER OF TOURISTS TO BEIJING

单位：万人次 (10000 person-times)

项 目	Item	2013	2012	2013年为2012年% 2013 as % of 2012
合 计	**Total**	**25189.0**	**23134.6**	**109.0**
国内旅游人数	**Number of Domestic Tourists**	**24738.8**	**22633.7**	**109.3**
外地来京旅游者人数	Number of Tourists to Beijing from Outside Beijing	14755.5	13620.2	108.3
市民在京游人数	Number of Beijing Citizens Touring in Beijing	9983.3	9013.6	110.8
入境旅游者人数	**Number of Inbound Tourists**	**450.1**	**500.9**	**89.9**
港澳台同胞	Hong Kong, Macao and Taiwan Tourists	62.5	66.5	94.1
中国香港	Hong Kong, China	35.4	37.6	94.2
中国澳门	Macao, China	1.8	1.4	124.9
中国台湾	Taiwan, China	25.3	27.4	92.2
外国人	Foreigners	387.6	434.4	89.2
亚 洲	Asia	139.0	171.4	81.1
#日 本	Japan	24.9	43.7	56.9
韩 国	Korea	37.7	44.2	85.4
菲律宾	Philippines	2.3	2.6	89.0
印度尼西亚	Indonesia	6.2	6.7	92.6
马来西亚	Malaysia	13.4	16.1	83.1
新加坡	Singapore	13.0	15.4	84.1
泰 国	Thailand	5.8	6.4	90.4
印 度	India	7.2	7.1	101.8
蒙 古	Mongolia	6.3	7.3	86.7
美 洲	America	102.0	101.6	100.4
#美 国	United States	74.7	75.1	99.4
加拿大	Canada	15.9	17.2	92.3
欧 洲	Europe	117.9	130.7	90.3
#英 国	United Kingdom	17.5	18.5	94.9
法 国	France	13.4	15.1	89.1
德 国	Germany	23.0	24.5	94.1
意大利	Italy	6.7	8.2	82.4
西班牙	Spain	4.4	5.2	83.7
瑞 典	Sweden	5.0	5.8	85.1
瑞 士	Switzerland	3.4	3.6	95.0
俄罗斯	Russia	16.7	20.0	83.3
大洋洲	Oceania	18.4	19.8	92.9
#澳大利亚	Australia	15.5	16.9	91.9
新西兰	New Zealand	2.2	2.5	90.6
非 洲	Africa	9.4	8.6	109.4
其 他	Others	0.9	2.4	35.9

资料来源：表中“国内旅游人数”的相关资料来自北京市旅游发展委员会。
Source: Data related to "Number of Domestic Tourists" in this table were provided by Beijing Municipal Commission of Tourism Development.

16-4 在京旅游花费构成情况(2005-2013年)
COMPOSITION OF EXPENDITURES FOR TOURISM IN BEIJING (2005-2013)

单位：% (%)

项 目	Item	2005	2006	2007	2008	2009	2010	2011	2012	2013
入境旅游者花费构成	**Compositition of Expenditures for Inbound Tourists**	**100.0**	**100.0**	**100.0**	**100.0**	**100.0**	**100.0**	**100.0**	**100.0**	**100.0**
长途交通费	Long-distance Transportation Expenses	35.3	30.0	29.0	31.1	37.4	28.1	26.4	28.0	26.9
民 航	Air	30.9	29.6	24.4	25.3	27.1	19.8	20.5	22.3	21.2
铁 路	Railway	1.1	0.3	3.0	3.6	5.5	5.3	3.4	3.3	3.7
公 路	Highway	3.3	0.1	1.6	2.2	4.8	3.0	2.5	2.4	2.0
市内交通费	Local Transportation Expenses	1.1	1.7	2.6	2.4	2.7	3.4	3.5	3.5	2.5
住 宿	Accommodation	17.3	32.0	16.9	16.4	14.5	14.4	15.5	16.5	16.9
餐 饮	Foods and Beverage	9.2	11.7	8.7	8.7	7.5	8.7	6.8	7.4	7.3
购 物	Shopping	19.9	15.9	22.5	19.1	20.4	25.1	25.3	23.5	27.6
邮电通讯	Post and Telecommunications	3.4	0.8	2.7	3.8	2.7	3.2	2.0	2.2	1.7
景区游览	Scenic Spot Sightseeing	4.7	2.3	4.2	4.8	3.9	4.7	4.2	5.0	4.2
文化娱乐	Culture and Entertainment	4.6	3.2	5.0	4.5	4.6	5.0	6.0	5.4	3.8
其 他	Others	4.5	2.4	8.4	9.2	6.3	7.4	10.3	8.5	9.1
外地来京游客花费构成	**Compositition of Expenditures for Tourists from Outside Beijing**	**100.0**	**100.0**	**100.0**	**100.0**	**100.0**	**100.0**	**100.0**	**100.0**	**100.0**
长途交通费	Long-distance Transportation Expenses	12.8	15.1	16.3	15.4	12.9	12.8	13.5	15.5	17.0
民 航	Air		8.0	9.2	9.1	6.6	6.0	6.2	7.7	7.5
铁 路	Railway		6.1	6.4	4.5	1.3	5.8	6.9	7.5	9.1
公 路	Highway		1.1	0.7	1.8	5.0	1.0	0.3	0.3	0.4
市内交通费	Local Transportation Expenses	5.7	5.1	5.5	5.6	4.9	5.0	4.5	4.0	3.8
住 宿	Accommodation	17.2	14.9	17.3	15.1	17.7	19.6	20.0	19.8	19.5
餐 饮	Foods and Beverage	19.8	18.7	20.5	23.2	21.8	20.2	20.9	21.4	21.4
购 物	Shopping	24.1	22.2	25.8	32.7	34.5	34.5	34.3	32.1	30.9
邮电通讯	Post and Telecommunications	1.0	1.2	1.8	1.0	0.6	0.5	0.3	0.2	0.2
景区游览	Scenic Spot Sightseeing	9.1	9.5	7.2	4.5	6.1	6.2	5.7	6.1	6.6
文化娱乐	Culture and Entertainment	3.1	2.5	1.9	1.6	1.2	1.0	0.8	0.7	0.5
其 他	Others	7.1	10.8	3.7	0.9	0.3	0.2	0.1	0.1	0.1

资料来源：北京市旅游发展委员会。
Source: Beijing Municipal Commission of Tourism Development.

16-5 旅游服务设施情况(1978-2013年)
TOURISM SERVICE FACILITIES (1978-2013)

年 份 Year	饭店个数(个) Number of Hotels (unit)	五星 5-star	四星 4-star	三星 3-star	二星 2-star	一星 1-star	饭店客房数(万间) Number of Hotel Guest Rooms (10,000 rooms)	旅行社家数(个) Number of Travel Agencies (unit)	#国际社 International Travel Agencies	A级及以上景区个数(个) Number of Scenic Spots at Grade-A and Above (unit)	5A	4A	3A	2A	1A
1978	11						0.39								
1979	13						0.44								
1980	20						0.49								
1981	35						0.69								
1982	39						1.00								
1983	41						1.03								
1984	50						1.30								
1985	63						1.66								
1986	80						2.10								
1987	97						2.40								
1988	96						2.80	30							
1989	101						3.50	77							
1990	122						3.95	77							
1991	213						4.40	69							
1992	226						5.20	69							
1993	226						5.20	55							
1994	175	14	20	32	72	37	5.40	297	113						
1995	197	15	25	43	79	35	5.90	310	125						
1996	204	15	25	46	82	36	6.10	349	128						
1997	248	16	26	60	109	37	6.80	350	130						
1998	258	16	32	65	113	32	7.00	380	135						
1999	268	17	32	71	117	31	7.20	419	144						
2000	409	21	34	132	176	46	8.40	456	150						
2001	506	21	43	154	230	58	9.30	490	160	47		17	4	22	4
2002	572	26	56	175	252	63	10.30	505	161	86		25	9	43	9
2003	614	30	62	195	267	60	10.90	530	165	93		28	9	46	10
2004	613	34	70	207	260	42	9.10	585	170	93		28	9	46	10
2005	652	36	79	224	267	46	10.97	714	196	124		36	26	50	12
2006	700	37	91	228	292	52	11.20	790	212	124		36	26	50	12
2007	806	42	114	257	338	55	13.00	844	239	154	4	41	35	54	20
2008	836	52	127	272	334	51	13.40	860	266	158	4	44	36	54	20
2009	757	54	129	268	269	37	12.95	888	265	179	4	55	53	51	16
2010	729	64	139	262	237	27	13.05	819		201	4	66	72	44	15
2011	598	63	127	207	181	20	11.64	919		211	6	63	80	46	16
2012	612	62	130	207	191	22	11.71	1021		203	8	64	78	40	13
2013	614	62	131	207	193	21	11.64	1147		213	8	67	86	42	10

注：1. 1993年及以前饭店数为涉外饭店口径,1994年以后为星级饭店口径。

2. 1994-1996年国际旅行社为一、二类旅行社合计。从2010年起，旅行社不再按国际旅行社和国内旅行社分组。

资料来源：北京市旅游发展委员会。

Note: a) Number of hotels in 1993 and before was the number of hotels for foreign tourists, and in 1994-2011,the number of star-rated hotels.

b) International travel agencies were the total number of travel agencies of categories I and II after 1994.From 2010, statistics of travel agencies were no more grouped into international and domestic angencies.

Source: Beijing Municipal Commission of Tourism Development.

16-6 星级饭店接待及经营情况(1995-2013年)
RECEPTION AND OPERATION OF STAR-RATED HOTELS (1995-2013)

年份 Year	企业个数 (个) Number of Enterprises (unit)	接待住宿人数 (万人次) Tourists Received (10000 person-time)	接待住宿人天数 (万人天) Persons-Day Received (10000 person-day)	出租率 (%) Renting Rate (%)	平均房价 (元/间天) Average Prices (yuan/room.day)	营业收入 (万元) Business Income (10000 yuan)	利润总额 (万元) Total Profits (10000 yuan)	从业人员平均人数 (人) Average Number of Employed Persons (person)
1995	191	484.6	1843.4	67.0	491	1136136	188095	98535
1996-2000		**3168.1**	**10110.0**			**5388348**	**286868**	
1996	207	485.3	1691.6	63.0	483	1132827	153145	94352
1997	235	541.8	1801.4	59.0	463	1145884	104918	103255
1998	262	605.0	1867.7	55.0	397	1038991	-24239	104391
1999	263	681.5	1918.6	57.0	352	970907	22383	103827
2000	294	854.5	2830.6	61.0	394	1099739	30661	96115
2001-2005		**5931.5**	**14152.9**			**7243160**	**316031**	
2001	363	1038.5	3191.7	62.0	384	1202746	50466	105792
2002	390	1071.2	2437.6	62.0	392	1307094	27212	107091
2003	441	1007.4	2497.2	52.0	389	1227956	-33471	105994
2004	464	1270.8	2798.9	65.0	409	1654198	117541	107386
2005	594	1543.6	3227.5	62.0	425	1851166	154283	126817
2006-2010		**8761.5**	**17721.0**			**11799293**	**650440**	
2006	597	1578.5	3284.5	61.3	460	2055300	194460	126430
2007	638	1664.2	3403.6	60.2	494	2369964	219891	129523
2008	694	1566.1	3206.6	52.0	605	2504849	232746	130609
2009	815	1827.3	3652.8	49.2	430	2261411	-76121	134159
2010	729	2125.4	4173.5	56.4	450	2607769	79464	130050
2011	598	2111.1	4119.6	59.9	482	2853358	162374	128609
2012	612	2101.0	4085.2	60.0	523	3031116	179495	122379
2013	614	1958.8	3769.5	58.4	530	2727974	111669	112512

注：1. 表中企业个数为全市星级宾馆饭店数，其余指标1995-1999年为涉外饭店数据，2000年及以后为星级宾馆饭店数据。
2. 从2011年开始北京市旅游发展委员会每年对全市星级饭店进行重新评定，对未达标饭店取消星级。

Note: a) Number of Enterprises refer to the number of star-rated hotels in Beijing, Other indicators covered hotels for foreign tourists for 1995-1999, and star-rated hotels after 2000.

b) From 2011 Beijing Municipal Tourism Development Commission reevalutaed star-rated hotels across the city , and cancelled the rating of hotels that did not meet the standard.

16-7 星级饭店经营情况
OPERATION OF STAR-RATED HOTELS

项目	Item	企业个数(个) Number of Enterprises (unit)		出租率(%) Renting Rate (%)		平均房价(元/间天) Average Prices (yuan/room.day)	
		2013	2012	2012	2011	2013	2012
合　计	**Total**	**614**	**612**	**58.4**	**60.0**	**530**	**523**
四星、五星合计	**Hotels of 4 and 5 Star Grade**	**193**	**192**	**61.6**	**63.0**	**669**	**670**
五　星	5-Star	62	62	62.2	63.5	858	871
四　星	4-Star	131	130	61.0	62.6	500	500
一星至三星合计	**Hotels of 1 to 3-Star Grade**	**421**	**420**	**54.0**	**56.8**	**335**	**323**
三　星	3-Star	207	207	55.5	57.1	361	362
二　星	2-Star	193	191	51.6	55.6	252	239
一　星	1-Star	21	22	41.3	37.9	217	260

16-7 续表 Continued

项目	Item	营业收入(万元) Business Income (10000 yuan)		利润总额(万元) Total Profits (10000 yuan)		从业人员平均人数(人) Average Number of Employed Persons (person)	
		2013	2012	2013	2012	2013	2012
合　计	**Total**	**2727974**	**3031116**	**111669**	**179495**	**112512**	**122379**
四星、五星合计	**Hotels of 4 and 5 Star Grade**	**2052400**	**2264272**	**123904**	**186966**	**75875**	**79764**
五　星	5-Star	1169186	1316408	93325	133711	35947	39278
四　星	4-Star	883214	947864	30579	53255	39928	40486
一星至三星合计	**Hotels of 1 to 3-Star Grade**	**675574**	**766844**	**-12235**	**-7471**	**36637**	**42615**
三　星	3-Star	548796	618315	-13084	-8730	29381	33871
二　星	2-Star	121045	143089	635	956	6849	8337
一　星	1-Star	5734	5440	214	303	407	407

16-8 星级饭店接待住宿者情况(按住宿者类别分)
TOURSITS RECEIVED BY STAR-RATED HOTELS (BY TYPE OF TOURISTS)

项目	Item	2013 接待量 Tourists Received	2013 构成(%) Composition (%)	2012 接待量 Tourists Received	2012 构成(%) Composition (%)	2013年为2012年% 2013 as % of 2012
接待住宿人数 (万人次)	**Tourists Received (10000 person-times)**	**1958.8**	**100.0**	**2101.0**	**100.00**	**93.2**
国内住宿者	Domestic Tourists	1693.6	86.46	1811.3	86.21	93.5
外国人	Foreigners	233.5	11.92	255.8	12.17	91.3
香港同胞	Compatriots from Hong Kong, China	18.0	0.92	20.7	0.99	86.9
澳门同胞	Compatriots from Macao, China	0.8	0.04	0.7	0.03	114.7
台湾同胞	Compatriots from Taiwan, China	13.0	0.66	12.6	0.60	102.9
接待住宿人天数 (万人天)	**Persons-day Received (10000 persons-day)**	**3769.5**	**100.00**	**4085.2**	**100.00**	**92.3**
国内住宿者	Domestic Tourists	3181.1	84.39	3407.6	83.41	93.4
外国人	Foreigners	518.5	13.76	599.2	14.67	86.5
香港同胞	Compatriots from Hong Kong, China	38.1	1.01	46.7	1.14	81.5
澳门同胞	Compatriots from Macao, China	2.0	0.05	1.7	0.04	119.1
台湾同胞	Compatriots from Taiwan, China	29.8	0.79	30.0	0.74	99.2

16-9 星级饭店接待住宿者情况(按饭店星级分)
TOURSITS RECEIVED BY STAR-RATED HOTELS (BY STAR RATING)

单位：万人次 (10000 person-times)

项目	Item	2013 接待量 Tourists Received	2013 构成(%) Composition (%)	2012 接待量 Tourists Received	2012 构成(%) Composition (%)	2013年为2012年% 2013 as % of 2012
接待住宿人数	**Tourists Received**	**1958.8**	**100.0**	**2101.0**	**100.0**	**93.2**
五星级	5-Star	541.6	27.6	543.5	25.9	99.7
四星级	4-Star	624.8	31.9	633.5	30.2	98.6
三星级	3-Star	563.0	28.7	640.4	30.5	87.9
二星级	2-Star	215.2	11.0	270.1	12.9	79.7
一星级	1-Star	14.1	0.7	13.6	0.6	104.0
接待入境住宿人数	**Inbound Tourists Received**	**265.2**	**100.0**	**289.7**	**100.0**	**91.5**
五星级	5-Star	150.4	56.7	158.8	54.8	94.7
四星级	4-Star	89.8	33.9	98.6	34.0	91.1
三星级	3-Star	18.4	6.9	23.8	8.2	77.1
二星级	2-Star	6.6	2.5	8.5	2.9	77.6
一星级	1-Star	0.1	0.04	0.1	0.04	97.0

16-10 旅行社接待及经营情况(1990-2013年) RECEPTION AND OPERATION OF TRAVEL AGENCIES (1990-2013)

年 份 Year	企业个数(个) Number of Enterprises (unit)	外联(组团)人数(万人次) Number of Inbound Tourists (Organized) (10000 person-times)	接待人数(万人次) Tourists Received (10000 person-times)	国内居民出境人数(万人次) Number of Outbound Chinese Tourists (10000 person-times)	营业收入(万元) Business Income (10000 yuan)	利润总额(万元) Total Profits (10000 yuan)	从业人员平均人数(人) Average Number of Employed Persons (person)
1990		32.5	54.7				
1991-1995		**355.6**	**451.7**				
1991		53.3	69.1				
1992		61.2	100.7				
1993		71.3	103.6				
1994		84.1	91.0	1.0			
1995	100	85.7	87.4	1.2	290987.9	107654.6	
1996-2000		**487.1**	**417.5**	**37.9**	**2187374.9**	**106167.0**	
1996	105	88.0	78.6	2.7	351634.7	13520.8	
1997	110	87.3	76.0	3.8	386254.1	16009.6	
1998	131	85.0	69.0	6.6	387562.7	21319.9	
1999	120	103.1	92.9	11.1	485678.8	26572.0	
2000	127	123.7	101.0	13.7	576244.6	28744.7	6280
2001-2005		**986.2**	**919.6**	**185.4**	**4453919.0**	**51899.5**	
2001	140	143.4	130.1	21.9	700529.0	18682.5	8259
2002	151	179.4	176.3	28.5	823551.0	23362.0	9350
2003	147	80.2	82.4	31.9	553787.0	-11829.0	8382
2004	147	274.8	252.6	51.4	1059989.0	11444.0	7760
2005	147	308.4	278.2	51.7	1316063.0	10240.0	8752
2006-2010		**2036.3**	**1852.4**	**515.9**	**11530195.8**	**82083.6**	
2006	147	343.9	315.7	79.2	1610265.0	7012.0	8659
2007	189	424.1	377.9	100.2	2101874.5	28409.2	11597
2008	245	359.6	310.1	102.0	2166898.1	18121.6	14369
2009	265	370.6	306.6	84.9	2134058.8	5904.6	15262
2010	819	538.1	542.2	149.6	3517099.4	22636.2	21454
2011	919	593.9	552.3	184.3	4436713.3	20879.2	23871
2012	1021	684.5	519.1	272.5	5415692.9	35274.4	28022
2013	1147	661.3	441.6	331.0	6103603.4	64177.5	31694

注：1．本表2009年及以前为国际旅行社口径，从2010年起调整为全部旅行社口径。
2．国内居民出境人数为旅行社组织出境游客的实际人次数，不重复统计。

Note: a) Figures in this table refer to international travel agencies in and before 2009, and all travel agencies after 2010.
b) Number of outbound Chinese visitors is the actual number of tourists going abroad that were organized by travel agencies, which has not been calculated repeatedly.

16-11 旅行社外联(组团)及接待情况
TOURISTS GROUPED (ORGANIZED) AND RECEIVED BY TRAVEL AGENCIES

项目	Item	2013	2012	2013年为2012年% 2013 as % of 2012
外联(组团)人数 (万人次)	**Tourists Grouped (Organized) (10000 person-times)**	**661.3**	**684.5**	**96.6**
国内旅游者	Domestic Tourists	470.8	473.6	99.4
港澳同胞	Compatriots from Hong Kong and Macao, China	4.9	6.5	74.9
台湾同胞	Compatriots from Taiwan, China	4.0	5.1	77.6
外国人	Foreigners	181.7	199.3	91.1
接待人数 (万人次)	**Tourists Received (10000 person-times)**	**441.6**	**519.1**	**85.1**
国内旅游者	Domestic Tourists	319.5	350.7	91.1
港澳同胞	Compatriots from Hong Kong and Macao, China	6.5	7.9	81.9
台湾同胞	Compatriots from Taiwan, China	3.5	3.3	106.6
外国人	Foreigners	112.1	157.2	71.3
外联(组团)人天数 (万人天)	**Persons-day of Tourists Grouped (Organized) (10000 persons-day)**	**2435.1**	**2979.0**	**81.7**
国内旅游者	Domestic Tourists	1781.8	1956.6	91.1
港澳同胞	Compatriots from Hong Kong and Macao, China	18.7	28.3	66.0
台湾同胞	Compatriots from Taiwan, China	19.3	28.2	68.5
外国人	Foreigners	615.3	965.9	63.7
接待人天数 (万人天)	**Persons-day of Tourists Received (10000 persons-day)**	**1701.5**	**1975.8**	**86.1**
国内旅游者	Domestic Tourists	1161.6	1224.7	94.8
港澳同胞	Compatriots from Hong Kong and Macao, China	29.0	33.1	87.7
台湾同胞	Compatriots from Taiwan, China	18.2	17.9	101.5
外国人	Foreigners	492.7	700.1	70.4

16-12 旅行社组织国内居民出境旅游情况
OUTBOUND CHINESE TOURISTS ORGANIZED BY TRAVEL AGENCIES

单位：万人次 (10000 person-times)

项　　目	Item	2013	2012	2013年为2012年% 2013 as % of 2012
旅行社个数(个)	**Number of Travel Agencies (unit)**	**259**	**212**	**122.2**
国内居民出境人数	**Number of Outbound Chinese Tourists**	**331.0**	**272.5**	**121.5**
前往国别及地区	**Countries and Regions of Destination**			
#中国香港	Hong Kong, China	29.6	30.7	96.6
中国澳门	Macao, China	11.3	12.7	89.4
中国台湾	Taiwan, China	18.3	14.6	125.3
泰　国	Thailand	64.8	40.5	159.7
新加坡	Singapore	16.6	23.6	70.1
马来西亚	Malaysia	17.1	17.6	96.7
菲律宾	Philippines	3.7	2.3	162.8
韩　国	Korea	41.1	28.4	144.6
日　本	Japan	18.7	21.4	87.6
澳大利亚	Australia	11.3	9.6	118.0
新西兰	New Zealand	6.3	5.8	108.8

注：1. 本表统计范围为有特许经营出境旅游业务权的旅行社。
2. 国内居民出境人数为旅行社组织出境游客的实际人次数，不重复统计。
3. 前往国别及地区统计中，游客一次出境旅游去往多个国家及地区的，分别计入前往国家及地区。

Note: a) Figures in this table cover the travel agencies that are franchised to operate outbound travelling business.
b) Number of outbound Chinese tourists is the actual number of tourists going abroad who were organized by travel agencies, which has not been calculated repeatedly.
c) In the statistics for "countries and regions of destination", if a tourist went to several countries and regions, he/she would be included in each country and region.

16-13 旅行社经营情况
OPERATION OF TRAVEL SERVICES

单位：万元 (10000 yuan)

项目	Item	2013	2012	2013年为2012年% 2013 as % of 2012
企业个数 （个）	Number of Enterprises (unit)	1147	1021	112.3
营业收入	Business Income	6103603.4	5415692.9	112.7
主营业务成本	Main Business Cost	5684509.5	5064662.7	112.2
营业费用	Business Expenses	193978.6	153000.6	126.8
主营业务税金及附加	Main Business Tax and Surtax	24865.8	21098.7	117.9
主营业务利润	Main Business Profits	389009.4	326800.4	119.0
管理费用	Management Expenses	186359.8	174599.4	106.7
营业利润	Business Profits	57391.3	26962.9	212.9
利润总额	Total Profits	64177.5	35274.4	181.9
从业人员平均人数 （人）	Average Number of Employed Persor (person)	31694	28022	113.1

16-14 A级及以上和重点旅游景区活动情况
STATISTICS FOR KEY SIGHT SPOTS ABOVE GRADE A

项目	Item	2013	2012	2013年为2012年% 2013 as % of 2012
A级及以上和重点旅游景区数 （个）	Number of Key Sight Spots Above Grade A (unit)	215	217	99.1
收入合计 （万元）	Total Income (10000 yuan)	621561	586395	106.0
门票收入	Ticket Income	398495	380993	104.6
商品销售收入	Commodity Sales	13445	15454	87.0
其他收入	Other Income	209621	189948	110.4
接待人数 （万人次）	Tourists Received (10000 person-times)	26726	24276	110.1
#入境旅游者人数	Inbound Tourists	947	1055	89.8

主要统计指标解释

入境旅游者 指来中国（大陆）观光、度假、探亲访友、就医疗养、购物、参加会议或从事经济、文化、体育、宗教活动，且在中国（大陆）的旅游住宿设施内至少停留一夜的外国人、港澳台同胞等游客。入境旅游者不包括以下人员：（1）应邀来华访问的政府部长以上官员及其随行人员；（2）外国驻华使领馆官员、外交人员以及随行的家庭服务人员和受赡养者；（3）常住中国（大陆）一年以上的外国专家、留学生、记者、商务机构人员等；（4）乘坐国际航班过境不需要通过护照检查进入中国（大陆）口岸的中转旅客；（5）边境地区往来的边民；（6）回大陆定居的港澳台同胞；（7）已在中国（大陆）定居的外国人和原已出境又返回在中国（大陆）定居的外国侨民；（8）归国的中国（大陆）出国人员。

国内旅游者 指中国（大陆）居民离开惯常居住地在境内其他地方的旅游住宿设施内至少停留一夜，最长不超过12个月的国内游客。

旅游外汇收入 指入境游客在中国（大陆）境内旅行、游览过程中用于交通、参观游览、住宿、餐饮、购物、娱乐等全部花费。

国内旅游收入 指国内游客在国内旅行、游览过程中用于交通、参观游览、住宿、餐饮、购物、娱乐等全部花费。

外联（组团）入境旅游者人数 指报告期内旅行社自组外联的入境旅游者人数，反映旅行社对外招徕的能力。旅行社按以下要求统计外联人数：入境游客不论其停留时间多少、旅游线路长短，只统计一次；旅行社只统计本社自组外联团的实到人数，不包括非本社外联、仅由本社接受委托办理签证的人数。

接待入境旅游者人数 指报告期内本旅行社派地陪接待的入境人数。

出境旅游总人数 指中国（大陆）公民因公或因私出境前往其他国家、中国香港特别行政区、澳门特别行政区和台湾省观光、度假、探亲访友、就医疗养、购物、参加会议或从事经济、文化、体育、宗教活动的人数。统计时，出境游客按每出境一次统计1人次。

Explanatory Notes on Main Statistical Indicators

Inbound Tourists refer to tourists from foreign countries, Hong Kong, Macao and Taiwan to (mainland of) China for sightseeing, holidays, visiting relatives and friends, medical service and rehabilitation, shopping, conferences, or economic, cultural, sports and religious activities, and staying in a tour accommodation facility in (the mainland of) China for at least one night. They do not include: (1) officials above the rank of governmental ministers, and their accompanying persons who visit China upon invitation; (2) officials in foreign embassies and consulates in Beijing, diplomatic personnel, and their accompanying family service personnel and dependents; (3) foreign experts, students, reporters, and personnel in business institutions who have been in China for more than one year; (4) transit passengers via China by international flights without passport checking; (5) people living on the frontiers who pass through borders; (6) compatriots from Hong Kong, Macao and Taiwan who settle down in the mainland of China; (7) Foreigners that have settled down in China and foreign nationals that have left the country and then come back to settle down in China; (8) Chinese (Mainland) people who have gone abroad and returned to China.

Domestic Tourists refer to domestic visitors as residents in (the mainland of) China who leave their regular dwelling places to stay at least one night and at most 12 months in a travel accommodation facility of other domestic places.

Foreign Exchange Earnings of Tourism means the total spending of international tourists on traffic, tour, accommodation, food and drink, shopping, entertainment and so on during their tour and travel in (the mainland of) China.

Revenue from Domestic Tourism means the total spending of domestic tourists on traffic, tour, accommodation, food and drink, shopping, entertainment and so on during their tour and travel in China.

Number of Inbound Tourists Organized by Travel Agencies means the number of inbound tourists organized by travel agencies in the reporting period. It shows the capacity of travel agencies in attracting inbound tourists; travel agencies shall count the tourists organized as follows: an inbound tourist is regarded as one visit regardless of the duration and distance of the tour; only the actual tourists organized by travel agencies are included. Those organized by other travel agencies or those who have visa submitted by the travel agencies are not included.

Number of Inbound Tourists Received means the number of inbound tourists received by local guides dispatched by travel agencies in the reporting period.

Total Number of Outbound Tourists means the number of citizens from (mainland of) China who visit other countries, Hong Kong Special Administrative Region of PRC, Macao Special Administrative Region of PRC, and Taiwan for sightseeing, holiday, visiting relatives and friends, medical service and rehabilitation, shopping, conferences, or economic, cultural, sport and religious activities for official or private purpose. One visit is calculated as one person-time.

17

北京统计年鉴2014 BEIJING STATISTICAL YEARBOOK

金融和保险
FINANCE AND INSURANCE

简要说明

一、本章资料的主要内容

本章反映北京地区金融业发展情况。主要包括以下四个部分:

1. 金融机构信贷收支情况;
2. 证券市场交易情况;
3. 保险业务情况;
4. 上市公司基本情况。

二、本章资料的数据来源

1. 信贷收支数据来源于中国人民银行营业管理部。
2. 证券市场交易量数据来源于北京市统计局。
3. 银行、保险系统机构及人员数据来源于北京市统计局。
4. 保险业务数据来源于中国保险监督管理委员会北京监管局。
5. 上市公司数据来源于中国证券监督管理委员会北京证监局。

Brief Introduction

I. Main Content

This chapter reflects the development of the financial industry in Beijing, mainly consisting of four parts:

1. Balance of credit for financial institutions;
2. Transactions in securities market;
3. Insurance business;
4. Basic information of listed companies.

II. Source of Data

1. Figures of balance of credit are gathered from the Banking Management Department of the People's Bank of China.
2. Data of transactions in securities market are gathered from Beijing Municipal Bureau of Statistics.
3. Data of banks, insurance institutions and personnel are gathered from Beijing Municipal Bureau of Statistics.
4. Data of insurance business are gathered from Beijing Bureau of China Insurance Regulatory Commission.
5. Data of basic information of listed companies are gathered from Beijing Securities Regulatory Bureau of China Securities Regulatory Commission.

17-1 北京市金融机构(含外资)存贷款余额(1978-2013年)
DEPOSIT AND LOAN BALANCE OF FINANCIAL INSTITUTIONS (INCLUDING FOREIGN BANKS)(1978-2013)

单位：亿元 (100 million yuan)

年份 Year	金融机构本外币存款 Balance of Savings Deposit in Domestic and Foreign Currencies in Financial Institutions	#个人储蓄存款 Individual Saving Deposits	#人民币存款 RMB Deposits	#个人储蓄存款 Individual Saving Deposits	金融机构本外币存款 Deposits in Domestic and Foreign Currencies in Financial Institutions 中资金融机构 Chinese Financial Institutions 存款合计 Total Deposits	人民币存款 RMB Deposits	外汇(亿美元) Foreign Exchange (USD 100 million)	外资银行 Foreign-funded Financial Bank 存款合计 Total Deposits	人民币存款 RMB Deposits	外汇(亿美元) Foreign Exchange (USD 100 million)
1978						114.7				
1979						139.1				
1980						168.0				
1981						220.5				
1982						279.2				
1983						321.3				
1984						375.5				
1985						411.0				
1986						508.8				
1987						610.8				
1988						609.9				
1989						717.6				
1990						893.9				
1991						1244.1				
1992						1528.3				
1993						1873.1				
1994						2677.3				
1995						3527.2				
1996						4378.9				
1997						5228.0				
1998						6666.8				
1999						8267.2				
2000	11526.0					9759.8	205.6			…
2001	14109.2	4599.8			14042.1	12223.4	219.8			7.3
2002	17438.4	5559.5			17369.9	15392.7	238.9			8.3
2003	20476.0	6441.4			20398.2	18321.9	250.9			9.4
2004	23781.3	7154.3	21625.9	6122.3	23679.3	21625.9	248.1			12.3
2005	28969.9	8315.8	26785.9	7477.7	28800.9	26731.3	256.4		54.6	14.2
2006	33793.3	9515.0	31313.8	8705.1	33484.1	31179.2	295.2		134.5	22.4
2007	37700.3	9743.5	35369.7	9155.3	37087.5	35014.1	283.8		355.6	35.2
2008	43980.7	12538.1	42107.6	11955.2	43094.4	41500.0	233.3	886.3	607.5	40.8
2009	56960.1	15329.2	54275.5	14672.1	55804.8	53428.8	348.0	1155.3	846.6	45.2
2010	66584.6	17585.2	64453.9	17003.1	64897.6	63025.2	282.7	1687.0	1428.7	39.0
2011	75001.9	19690.6	72655.4	19126.1	73018.9	70985.1	322.8	1983.1	1670.3	49.6
2012	84837.3	22298.6	81389.6	21644.9	82615.9	79620.6	476.5	2221.4	1769.1	72.0
2013	91660.5	23747.6	87990.6	23086.4	89187.4	85897.2	539.6	2473.1	2093.4	62.3

资料来源：中国人民银行营业管理部。
Source: Banking Management Department of People's Bank of China.

17-1 续表 Continued

单位：亿元 (100 million yuan)

年份 Year	金融机构本外币贷款余额 Balance of Loans in Domestic and Foreign Currencies in Financial Institutions	#人民币贷款 RMB Loans	#中长期贷款 Medium-term &Long-term Loans	金融机构本外币贷款 Loans in Domestic and Foreign Currencies in Financial Institutions					
				中资金融机构 Chinese Financial Institutions			外资银行 Foreign-funded Financial Bank		
				贷款合计 Total Loans	人民币贷款 RMB Loans	外汇（亿美元） Foreign Exchange (USD 100 million)	贷款合计 Total Loans	人民币贷款 RMB Loans	外汇（亿美元） Foreign Exchange (USD 100 million)
1978					53.9				
1979					74.2				
1980					87.3				
1981					91.3				
1982					109.1				
1983					149.5				
1984					174.3				
1985					249.8				
1986					299.2				
1987					346.1				
1988					415.7				
1989					487.1				
1990					573.1				
1991					735.8				
1992					894.7				
1993					1128.1				
1994					1429.0				
1995					1779.1				
1996					2082.8				
1997					2720.7				
1998					3326.6				
1999					4007.8				
2000	6407.9		3106.7	6306.3	6008.2	27.7			9.0
2001	7612.2		3797.3	7514.9	7202.9	37.4			10.8
2002	9704.3		5026.9	9602.6	9230.8	44.9			12.1
2003	12057.7		6352.0	11884.4	11314.7	68.8			20.9
2004	13577.7		7506.4	13312.3	12600.2	86.0			32.0
2005	15335.5		8632.4	14996.6	13792.2	149.2		42.3	36.8
2006	18131.6	15632.7	11142.8	17631.7	15486.9	274.7		145.8	45.4
2007	19861.5	17812.5	12217.6	19053.9	17360.2	231.9	807.5	452.3	48.6
2008	23010.7	19985.0	14688.9	22160.5	19431.1	399.4	850.2	554.0	43.3
2009	31052.9	25421.8	21163.8	30151.6	24805.1	783.0	901.3	616.7	41.7
2010	36479.6	29563.8	26180.2	35352.0	28748.1	997.2	1127.6	815.6	47.1
2011	39660.5	33367.0	24886.3	38410.3	32434.6	948.4	1250.2	932.5	50.4
2012	43189.5	36441.3	26333.5	41839.8	35441.7	1017.9	1349.7	999.6	55.7
2013	47880.9	40506.7	28171.7	46539.5	39557.5	1145.2	1341.4	949.2	64.3

资料来源：中国人民银行营业管理部。
Source: Banking Management Department of People's Bank of China.

17-2 北京市金融机构(含外资)本外币信贷收支表
BALANCE OF CREIT IN DOMESTIC AND FOREIGN CURRENCIES FOR FINANCIAL INSTITUTIONS (INCLUDE FOREIGN BANKS)

单位：万元，汇率：6.0969 (10000 yuan,at an exchange rate of 6.0969)

项 目	Item	余 额 Balance		2013年为2012% 2013 as % of 2012	比年初增减额(+、-) Increase or Decrease than the Beginning of the Year	
		2013	2012		2013	2012
各项存款	**Total Deposits**	**916605365**	**848373099**	**108.0**	**65888214**	**98438114**
#人民币存款	RMB	879905968	813896227	108.1	63869315	87426084
单位存款	Corporate Deposits	576116247	515808083	111.7	59626838	44305791
个人存款	Individual Deposits	255520029	250463256	102.0	4837783	36545139
#储蓄存款	Saving Deposits	237475704	222986186	106.5	15134441	26080411
财政性存款	Fiscal Deposits	14008775	13618685	102.9	390090	2915584
临时性存款	Provisional Deposits	1164507	985822	118.1	166488	-43362
委托存款	Entrusted Deposits	5230118	5287999	98.9	-57881	1875969
其他存款	Other Deposits	64565688	62209254	103.8	924897	12838993
各项贷款	**Total Loans**	**478809245**	**431895276**	**110.9**	**45786988**	**35080493**
#人民币贷款	RMB Loans	405066994	364413476	111.2	39540595	30533282
境内贷款	Domestic Loans	450521555	403437235	111.7	45928488	33765350
短期贷款	Short-term Loans	156937975	128081061	122.5	28085372	16384672
中长期贷款	Medium-term&Long-term Loans	281717190	263335138	107.0	18568762	14087028
融资租赁	Financial Lease	439723	504856	87.1	-65132	36973
票据融资	Bill Financing	11372481	11457861	99.3	-656380	3270973
各项垫款	Advances	54186	58319	92.9	-4133	-14296
境外贷款	Oversea Loans	28287690	28458041	99.4	-141500	1315144

资料来源：中国人民银行营业管理部。
Source: Banking Management Department of People's Bank of China.

17-3 北京市中资金融机构本外币信贷收支表
BALANCE OF CREDIT IN DOMESTIC AND FOREIGN CURRENCIES FOR DOMESTICALLY-FUNDED FINANCIAL INSTITUTIONS

单位：万元，汇率：6.0969 (10000 yuan ,at an exchange rate of 6.0969)

项目	Item	余额 Balance 2013	2012	2013年为2012% 2013 as % of 2012	比年初增减额(+、-) Increase or Decrease than Year-beginning 2013	2012
各项存款	**Total Deposits**	**891873927**	**826158788**	**108.0**	**65397100**	**96054365**
#人民币存款	RMB	858972033	796205663	107.9	62458926	86438776
单位存款	Corporate Deposits	555774582	496710871	111.9	59214062	42275957
个人存款	Individual Deposits	252388346	247361169	102.0	4808788	36142745
#储蓄存款	Saving Deposits	235173334	219884099	107.0	15070962	25678016
财政性存款	Fiscal Deposits	14008775	13618685	102.9	390090	2915584
临时性存款	Provisional Deposits	1151010	985822	116.8	165188	-43362
委托存款	Entrusted Deposits	5230118	5287999	98.9	-57881	1875969
其他存款	Other Deposits	63321096	62194243	101.8	876853	12887472
各项贷款	**Total Loans**	**465395030**	**418398382**	**111.2**	**46001668**	**34085718**
#人民币贷款	RMB Loans	395575414	354417270	111.6	40175609	29861623
境内贷款	Domestic Loans	437801840	390633717	112.1	46173144	40858690
短期贷款	Short-term Loans	150488145	121530811	123.8	28569063	20204292
中长期贷款	Medium-term&Long-term Loans	276796332	258256752	107.2	18503870	21619306
融资租赁	Financial Lease	439723	504856	87.1	-65132	222431
票据融资	Bill Financing	10023454	10282979	97.5	-830524	-1183270
各项垫款	Advances	54186	58319	92.9	-4133	-4068
境外贷款	Oversea Loans	27593189	27764665	99.4	-171476	-8433444

资料来源：中国人民银行营业管理部。
Source: Banking Management Department of People's Bank of China.

17-4 银行、保险系统机构及人员(2013年)
INSTITUTIONS AND PERSONNEL OF BANKING AND INSURANCE SYSTEMS (2013)

项目	Item	银行系统 Banking System 机构(个) Institutions (unit)	人员(人) Personnel (person)	保险系统 Insurance System 机构(个) Institutions (unit)	人员(人) Personnel(person)
全市	**Total**	**3897**	**169305**	**655**	**104606**
首都功能核心区	Capital Core Funtional Area	729	91151	160	38602
城市功能拓展区	Urban Function Extension Area	1935	57487	235	41466
城市发展新区	Urban Development New Area	826	14775	167	15077
生态涵养发展区	Ecological Conservation Area	407	5892	93	9461

注：1. 本表口径为在北京地区经营的银行、保险公司的总行(总公司)、分行(分公司)及所属分支机构。
2. 保险系统人员构成中含营销员。

Note: a) Figures in this table cover the headquarters (head offices), branches banks (branch companies) and subsidiaries of banks and insurance companies operating in Beijing.
b) Personnel of insurance system includes marketing personnel.

17-5 上市公司基本情况(1993-2013年)
LISTED COMPANIES (1993-2013)

年 份 Year	年末 上市公司 (家) Companies Listed by Year-end (unit)	上市公司 总股本 (万股) Total Equity of Listed Companies (10000 Shares)	股票 首发数量 (万股) Initial Public Offering Shares (10000 Shares)	首发 募集资金 (亿元) Funds Raised Through IPO (10000 yuan)	增发 募集资金 (亿元) Funds Raised Through Right Offerings (10000 yuan)	配股 募集资金 (亿元) Funds Raised Through Seasoned Equity Offerings (10000 yuan)
1993	3	24592	3924	58.0		28.8
1994	7	124038	20300	11.7		0.5
1995	7	133309				3.8
1996-2000			**439955**	**304.4**	**33.0**	**85.8**
1996	13	198956	29763	12.8		1.9
1997	26	470026	80200	52.2		7.0
1998	33	723561	52750	32.9		20.2
1999	43	1439894	121242	63.0	10.8	10.7
2000	54	2015049	156000	143.5	22.2	46.0
2001-2005			**764200**	**413.8**	**49.2**	**26.3**
2001	63	9764783	345500	191.6		17.0
2002	68	11929954	23800	16.8	14.9	
2003	74	11493598	373600	188.7	2.8	2.2
2004	83	12553074	21300	16.7	28.4	7.1
2005	83	13159721			3.1	
2006-2010			**11456582**	**6506.1**	**1665.5**	**852.8**
2006	92	58156652	2667911	1073.4	79.4	
2007	104	86151941	2428976	2433.3	304.7	12.1
2008	109	90486962	698853	546.9	502.0	63.8
2009	126	97911881	2179290	1154.2	430.7	
2010	165	137726461	3481552	1298.3	348.7	777.0
2011	194	143088054	420483	462.0	661.7	175.6
2012	217	146788089	211752	191.4	436.2	69.1
2013	219	151694399			183.9	32.5

注：1. 此表数据统计口径由辖区统计转变为注册地统计。

2. 1995年、2005年和2013年没有新股发行。

资料来源：中国证券监督管理委员会北京证监局。

Note: a) Statistics in this table are counted in terms of registered area instead of the formerly used jurisdiction.

b) There were no shares issued in 1995, 2005 and 2013.

Source: Beijing Regulatory Bureau of China Securities Regulatory Commission.

17-6 证券市场交易额情况(1994-2013年)
TRADE VOLUME OF STOCK MARKETS(1994-2013)

单位: 亿元 (100 million yuan)

年 份 Year	证券市场交易额 Trading Volume of Stock Market	#股票交易 Stock Trading	#基金交易 Fund Trading	#债券交易 Bond Trading	年末证券市场累计开户数(万户) Total Investors in Stock Markets (year-end) (10000 investors)
1994	183.26	135.51		47.75	
1995	1619.04	520.48		152.31	
1996	5224.77	2900.63		2324.06	
1997	7934.42	3900.93		3844.82	
1998	10241.50	3426.37	187.02	6435.43	
1999	10694.46	5268.19	341.74	5005.52	88.93
2000	14456.98	9136.52	346.02	4825.91	115.18
2001	12596.50	5339.61	400.61	6729.69	148.95
2002	12565.91	3788.22	485.77	8216.53	154.99
2003	23369.83	5041.40	110.45	18048.37	162.39
2004	18512.92	7247.72	78.94	10928.92	166.21
2005	9322.49	4343.65	91.30	4567.28	169.83
2006	19557.06	14851.55	298.27	2075.20	189.37
2007	97978.66	77487.83	1534.96	2060.09	314.92
2008	62773.56	46231.27	1389.37	4052.52	373.62
2009	92148.02	78339.50	2253.54	1791.32	426.10
2010	87575.38	79843.07	1714.94	3384.28	475.14
2011	79103.13	61743.17	1494.81	15275.31	521.53
2012	85412.95	44993.38	2355.87	37388.61	551.50
2013	145932.74	61596.27	4104.79	69625.37	563.61

17-7 证券市场交易额情况
TRADE VOLUME OF STOCK MARKETS

项目	Item	2013	2012	2013年为2012年% 2013 as % of 2012
成交额合计 （亿元）	**Total Trade Volume (100 million yuan)**	**145932.7**	**85412.9**	**170.9**
股票交易	Stock Trading	61596.3	44993.4	136.9
债券交易	Bond Trading	69625.4	37388.6	186.2
债券现货	Bonds in Stock	1270.7	1073.7	118.3
债券回购	Bond Repurchasing	68354.7	36314.9	188.2
募集资金交易	Trading of Funds Raised	92.9	45.4	204.6
其他交易	Other Tradings	14618.2	2985.5	489.6
年末证券市场累计开户数 （万户）	**Total Investors in Stock Markets (year-end) (10000 investors)**	**563.6**	**551.5**	**102.2**

17-8 保险业务情况(1997-2013年)
INSURANCE BUSINESS (1997-2013)

单位：亿元 (100 million yuan)

年份 Year	原保险保费收入 Premium Income of Original Insurance	人身险 Life Insurance	财产险 Property Insurance	赔付支出 Compensation Expenses	人身险 Life Insurance	财产险 Property Insurance
1997	102.5					
1998	88.6					
1999	91.8			29.9		
2000	93.4			28.4		
2001	141.3			32.0		
2002	234.1			46.9		
2003	282.5			48.0		
2004	279.3			55.3		
2005	498.2			75.4		
2006	411.5	327.2	84.4	84.0	45.1	38.9
2007	498.1	386.3	111.8	135.4	85.7	49.7
2008	585.9	451.8	134.1	188.9	121.0	67.9
2009	697.6	533.2	164.4	196.0	110.6	85.4
2010	966.5	754.2	212.3	199.7	105.9	93.7
2011	820.9	588.4	232.6	232.8	113.8	119.0
2012	923.1	656.1	267.0	286.2	133.9	152.3
2013	994.4	706.4	288.0	318.2	152.9	165.3

资料来源：中国保险监督管理委员会北京监管局。
Source: Beijing Regulatory Bureau of China Insurance Regulatory Commission.

17-9 保险业务情况
STATISTICS FOR INSURANCE BUSINESS

单位：亿元 (100 million yuan)

项　　目	Item	原保险保费收入 Premium Income of Original Insurance		赔付支出 Compensation Expenses	
		2013	2012	2013	2012
合　计	**Total**	**994.4**	**923.1**	**318.2**	**286.2**
人身险业务小计	**Subtotal of Life Insurance**	**706.4**	**656.1**	**152.9**	**133.9**
人寿保险	Life Insurance	570.8	554.3	108.1	100.2
非分红产品	Non-participating Products	53.0	46.6	18.3	24.0
分红产品	Participating Products	513.5	503.6	88.9	75.3
投资连接产品	Investment-linked Products	0.5	0.5	0.1	0.2
万能产品	Universal Products	3.9	3.6	0.9	0.6
意外伤害保险	Accident Insurance	29.9	21.7	6.6	5.0
健康保险	Health Insurance	105.7	80.1	38.2	28.7
财产险业务小计	**Subtotal of Property Insurance**	**288.0**	**267.0**	**165.3**	**152.3**
#企业财产保险	Enterprise Property Insurance	30.6	30.2	15.3	12.3
家庭财产保险	Household Property Insurance	0.7	0.6	0.2	0.3
机动车辆及第三者责任保险	Motor Vehicle and Automobile Liability Insurance	205.3	183.0	131.8	119.6
货物运输保险	Freight Transport Insurance	11.6	12.6	3.8	4.0
责任保险	Liability Insurance	15.0	15.2	5.9	4.4
工程险	Construction Insurance	7.2	5.6	1.9	2.5

资料来源：中国保险监督管理委员会北京监管局。
Source: Beijing Regulatory Bureau of China Insurance Regulatory Commission.

主要统计指标解释

存款 企业、机关、团体或居民根据必须收回的原则，把货币资金存入银行或其他信贷机构保管并取得一定利息的一种信用活动形式。根据存款对象或性质的不同可以划分为单位存款、个人存款、财政性存款、临时性存款、委托存款、其它存款等科目。它是银行信贷资金的主要来源。

贷款 银行或其他信贷机构根据必须归还的原则，按一定利率，为企业、个人等提供资金的一种信用活动形式。我国银行贷款分为短期贷款、中长期贷款、融资租赁、票据融资、各项垫款、境外贷款等。

原保险保费收入 是指保险企业确认的原保险合同保费收入。是投保人根据保险合同的有关规定，为被保险人取得因约定危险事故发生所造成的经济损失补偿（或给付）权利，付给保险人的代价。包括财产险和人身险收入。

保险赔付支出 公司按保险合同约定支付给被保险人（或受益人）的赔款、保险金、给付等。包括赔款支出、死伤医疗给付、满期给付和年金给付。

股票交易额 指投资者在市场买卖各种股票的总金额。包括A股、B股。不含认购新股及认购中签。

基金交易额 指投资者在市场买卖各种基金的总金额。包括封闭式基金、开放式基金等。

债券交易额 指投资者在市场买卖各种债券的总金额。包括债券现货、债券回购。

债券现货交易额 指投资者在市场买卖各种债券现货的总金额。包括国债、金融债、企业债、可转债等。

债券回购额 指投资者在市场债券回购的总金额。包括国债回购、企业债回购等。回购交易只记录单边交易额。

Explanatory Notes on Main Statistical Indicators

Deposit is a form of credit activity, in which enterprises, public institutions, groups or residents save their money, on a reclaimable basis, in banks or other credit institutions and receive certain interest. Based on different depositors, deposit can be divided into enterprise deposit, individual deposit, fiscal deposit,, provisional deposit, entrusted deposit and other deposits based on different depositors. It constitutes a main source of bank funds for extending credit..

Loan is a form of credit activity in which banks or other credit institutions provide funds that must be repaid for enterprises and individuals at a given interest rate. In China, bank loans are classified as short-, medium-, and long-term loans, financial lease, notes financing, advances, oversea loans and so on..

Premium Income of Original Insurance means the income of insurance premium of original insurance contracts confirmed by insurance companies. It is the price paid by policy holders to the insurer for the right to receive compensation (claim settlement) for any economic loss caused by agreed dangerous accidents pursuant to relevant provisions in the insurance contract. There is property insurance income and life insurance income.

Insurance Compensation Expenses refer to indemnity, insurance money, and claim settlement, etc. paid by insurance companies to the insurants (or beneficiaries) as agreed in the insurance contract, including indemnity payment, settlement for medical costs of death and injury, maturity payment and annuity payment.

Stock market Turnover means the total value of shares traded by investors in the market, including: RMB ordinary shares and special Renminbi denominated shares, excluding IPO subscription and IPO lot-winning.

Fund Turnover means the total value of funds traded by investors in the market, including closed-end funds and open-end funds, etc.

Bond Turnover means the total value of bonds traded by investors in market, including cash bonds and bonds repurchased.

Cash Bond Turnover means the total amount of cash bonds traded by investors in market, including treasury bonds, financial bonds, corporate bonds and convertible bonds, etc.

Value of Bond Buyback means the value of bonds repurchased by investors in the market. It includes the repurchase of treasury bonds and corporate bonds. Only unilateral transaction value is recorded in repurchase

18

北京统计年鉴2014 BEIJING STATISTICAL YEARBOOK

教育、文化
EDUCATION AND CULTURE

简要说明

一、教育部分的主要内容和资料来源

教育统计资料包括高等教育（研究生教育、普通本专科教育、成人本专科、其他各类高等学历教育）、中等教育(高中阶段、初中阶段)、小学教育、学前教育、特殊教育(盲聋哑和弱智儿童学校等)、工读学校等资料。主要指标包括学校数、在校学生数、招生数、毕业生数、教职工数、专任教师数等内容。

教育统计资料由北京市教育委员会提供。

二、文化部分的主要内容和资料来源

文化部分主要包括专业艺术剧团、公共图书馆、博物馆、文化馆、档案馆、文化站、广播、电影、电视以及新闻等文化单位的机构、人员和业务活动情况。

文化部分数据中，专业艺术剧团、公共图书馆和群众文化活动的资料主要来自北京市文化局；档案馆资料来自北京市档案局；博物馆资料来自北京市文物局；广播、电影和电视，报纸、期刊、图书出版资料来自北京市新闻出版广电局。

Brief Introduction

I. Main Content and Sources of Data for the Part of Education

Educational statistics include those for higher education (postgraduate education, undergraduate and junior college education, undergraduate and junior college education for adults, and other kinds of higher education for diplomas); secondary education (senior high school, junior high school); primary education; preschool education; special education (schools for the blind, deaf and mute, and mentally handicapped children, etc.); work-study schools for delinquent children. Main indicators include the number of schools, student enrollment, , number of new enrollment, number of teachers and staff, and number of full-time teachers, etc.

Educational data were provided by Beijing Municipal Commission of Education.

II. Main Content and Sources of Data for the Part of Culture

Cultural statistics include the number, personnel and activities of professional art troupes, public libraries, museums, cultural centers, archives, broadcast, films, television and press, and other cultural organizations.

In Cultural data, figures of art, libraries, and mass culture are from Beijing Municipal Bureau of Culture; data of archives are from Beijing Municipal Bureau of Archives; data of museums are from Beijing Municipal Administration of Cultural Heritage; radio, film and television, newspaper, magazine and book publications data are from Beijing Municipal Administration of Press, Publication, Radio, Film and Television.

18-1 教育基本情况(1978-2013年)
BASIC STATISTICS FOR EDUCATION (1978-2013)

年 份 Year	全市各类学校数(个) Total Number of Various Schools (unit)	#普通高等学校 General Institutions of Higher Education	#普通中等学校 General Middle Schools	#高中 Senior Middle Schools	#小学 Primary Schools	全市各类学校在校学生数(人) Enrolled Students in Various Schools (person)	#普通高等学校 General Institutions of Higher Education	#普通中等学校 General Middle Schools	#高中 Senior Middle Schools	#小学 Primary Schools
1978		35			4666		48618		415612	937336
1979		48			4534		55073		299974	968723
1980		50			4485		83032		312188	951763
1981		51			4445		98044		175180	900350
1982		51			4381		93878		92401	854516
1983		54			4269		90894		88657	838078
1984		57			4168		102962		110916	763204
1985		61			4059		122791		119876	733605
1986		66			3995		129647		109862	749101
1987		67			3875		136694		109023	777982
1988		67			3793		145134		108106	850577
1989		67			3703		141625		110745	934696
1990		67			3611		139646		100669	995831
1991	8496	67	1168	282	3482	2142085	136940	565357	93728	1013268
1992	8052	67	1150	279	3306	2194268	139978	617847	82894	1001762
1993	7789	66	1145	280	3190	2266932	158906	679821	78261	1022166
1994	7574	67	1150	280	3035	2348406	175203	758310	86584	1024503
1995	7158	65	1170	286	2867	2380096	182173	834903	102522	1007301
1996	7121	65	1189	296	2780	2388002	189953	881912	118476	999740
1997	6858	65	1181	288	2696	2361438	195842	887644	133461	977323
1998	6456	63	1190	282	2511	2325043	212984	895042	145966	919531
1999	5807	64	1182	275	2352	2297673	234033	931029	161473	836655
2000	5458	59	1159	302	2169	2299433	282585	972930	179002	743109
2001	4873	61	1111	289	1960	2297107	340284	988985	194283	664443
2002	4447	62	998	325	1824	2294947	398573	984117	220667	594241
2003	4158	74	977	329	1652	2299416	458898	968035	250959	546530
2004	3971	77	945	338	1504	2291594	500245	919178	274803	516042
2005	3782	79	917	335	1403	2264004	536724	859132	278358	494482
2006	3751	82	888	335	1310	2910228	554702	799074	259414	473275
2007	3593	83	863	328	1235	3195763	567875	839038	243818	666617
2008	3508	82	838	325	1202	3208704	575639	782866	219163	659500
2009	3425	88	804	305	1160	3214354	577154	740396	203477	647101
2010	3330	89	779	289	1104	3299555	577828	727741	198415	653255
2011	3367	89	769	290	1090	3426025	578633	711130	195072	680457
2012	3314	91	760	289	1081	3568273	581844	732224	193505	718655
2013	3439	89	757	291	1093	3736003	589234	706713	187586	789276

注：1. 从2007年开始，普通中学、小学、工读学校、特殊教育、学前教育在校学生数包括外省市户口借读学生。
2. 1991-2005年，普通中等学校包括普通中专、技工学校、职业中学、普通中学和工读学校。2006年及以后普通中等学校为中等教育口径，包括普通中专、成人中专、技工学校、职业高中和普通中学。

资料来源：北京市教育委员会。

Note: a) From 2007, enrolled students in general high schools, primary schools, work-study schools for delinquent children, special education schools, and pre-school education included those from outside Beijing and studying in Beijing on temporary basis.
b) In 1991-2005, general middle schools included technical secondary schools, technician training schools, vocational schools, general high schools, and work-study schools. In and after 2006, middle schools included technical secondary schools, technical secondary schools for adults, technician training schools, vocational senior high schools and general high schools.

Source: Beijing Municipal Commission of Education.

18-1 续表

年份 Year	全市各类学校招生数(人) New Enrollment in Various Schools (person)	#普通高等学校 General Institutions of Higher Education	#普通中等学校 General Middle Schools	#高中 Senior Middle Schools	#小学 Primary Schools	全市各类学校毕业生数(人) Number of Graduates in Various Schools (person)	#普通高等学校 General Institutions of Higher Education
1978		17445		161288	199076		10881
1979		15848		160340	154809		8585
1980		17972		131961	138751		8233
1981		17921		54296	121744		2289
1982		21936		35212	104357		25753
1983		27988		40282	96028		31009
1984		31805		47068	103482		20110
1985		40670		35265	135048		21442
1986		35390		27863	160513		26953
1987		41163		41186	156954		34894
1988		42187		35429	184516		33066
1989		33557		33254	184609		35863
1990		36275		30596	161742		36171
1991	571685	37700	205107	28589	148300	487740	37702
1992	622142	41517	232765	25790	157145	520787	37075
1993	651729	52205	242274	26275	175853	526982	32888
1994	704933	51884	287642	34704	186315	528199	34855
1995	691972	52868	308786	40803	168903	554690	45094
1996	628772	55269	289612	42603	156898	575969	46471
1997	581091	56884	289719	49566	124231	584120	49973
1998	581786	62264	308157	52956	100415	600662	49322
1999	603332	78354	320731	56998	94358	603027	49936
2000	635328	99397	324862	65890	92002	604900	51556
2001	641432	116344	313257	69195	91230	617889	55831
2002	671956	128320	326835	84679	86406	624329	67621
2003	662877	143483	302071	94894	82631	610826	83816
2004	635842	147298	271396	93519	73577	614137	99637
2005	630515	156124	259133	88605	71020	622974	117367
2006	851808	154969	234524	76375	73138	787596	132488
2007	927144	156222	252709	71590	109203	851126	138834
2008	938891	157238	236714	68397	110440	832585	149459
2009	962648	158992	240937	65983	102414	865025	152336
2010	1002141	155228	238954	65649	113728	834340	150156
2011	1050131	157543	243754	64146	132719	838521	151277
2012	1108574	162042	254790	63381	141738	881804	152980
2013	1182301	163081	239010	59983	165807	923050	148689

18-1 Continued

#普通中等学校 General Middle Schools	#高中 Senior Middle Schools	#小学 Primary Schools	学龄儿童入学率(%) Enrollment Rate of Children at School-age (%)	专任教师数(人) Full-time Teachers (person)	平均每一专任教师负担学生数(人) Average Number of Students Instructed by a Full-time Teacher(person) 高等学校 Institutions of Higher Education	普通中学 General Middle Schools	小学 Primary Schools
	174899	151950	99.00			19.9	20.7
	239813	114047	98.50			16.1	21.3
	145501	144025	98.70			14.8	21.7
	170992	162306	98.90			13.4	19.7
	111153	135562	98.90			12.3	19.5
		95919	99.10			11.5	19.6
	24498	169251	99.30			13.2	18.2
	24720	156035	99.10			13.9	17.4
	36942	138350	99.50			14.1	17.3
	43589	121599	99.50			12.8	16.8
	36127	105948	99.50			11.4	17.6
	29267	97208	99.70			11.0	19.1
	40369	102782	99.50			10.1	18.6
	34428	132544	99.17	168485		10.5	18.0
	32471	156306	99.65	169249		11.3	17.4
	27428	157838	99.88	170361		12.1	17.4
	24112	184566	99.92	175025		13.1	16.9
	23353	183894	99.93	176591		13.6	16.5
	25170	162030	99.93	178006		13.7	16.1
	33010	146023	99.95	179080		13.2	15.7
	39683	156194	99.96	178210		12.8	14.9
	40660	175656	99.95	175496	12.0	13.2	13.7
	47569	185059	99.95	167040	14.0	14.1	12.8
	51263	167076	99.62	168080	17.0	14.3	12.1
	51180	156683	99.63	166490	19.0	14.2	11.2
	56601	123580	99.95	166510	19.0	13.7	11.0
	66556	100139	99.92	172055	17.1	12.9	10.6
	73260	93486	99.90	174589	17.0	11.8	10.3
290047	78037	90799	99.96	191365	17.0	10.8	9.8
272651	78408	112332	100.00	195568	15.4	11.5	13.8
262871	78468	112268	100.00	199114	17.1	10.9	13.5
253067	70132	110730	100.00	203825	16.5	10.0	13.0
233837	62305	102971	99.96	206602	16.6	10.2	13.2
223955	58275	101678	99.99	199789	17.1	9.8	13.4
224938	55657	109492	99.99	204812	17.0	9.7	13.7
240225	58072	111839	99.99	216463		9.5	14.4

18-2 幼儿园基本情况(1978－2013年)
BASIC STATISTICS FOR KINDERGARTENS (1978-2013)

单位：人 (person)

年 份 Year	园数(所) Number of Kindergartens (unit)	班数(个) Number of Classes (unit)	离园人数 Children Leaving	入园人数 Children Entering	在园人数 Children Enrollment	教职工数 Teachers and Staff	#专任教师 Full-time Teachers
1978	5074				235923	39982	8369
1979	4623				237037	40424	8777
1980	3991				219407	38475	7765
1981	3888				233089	38832	8814
1982	3849				254458	42663	9271
1983	1999				306975	48666	8234
1984	3682				295427	47721	9499
1985	2955				316024	47033	10523
1986	3503				342824	52654	12690
1987	3732				364011	54211	14449
1988	3563				354367	52105	14705
1989	3509				344394	50280	17208
1990	3798				372555	49587	17972
1991	3761		133788	172884	402699	49472	18788
1992	3510		158740	181299	404779	48007	18513
1993	3369		165963	170580	372368	44741	18114
1994	3301		113652	167267	352979	42118	17413
1995	3024		103355	148272	315277	38549	16084
1996	3056		135376	112449	271752	33586	14792
1997	2892		110345	95140	253478	32811	14596
1998	2662		99279	93819	245046	30362	13841
1999	2180		91996	89463	237055	29367	13216
2000	2047		85301	91724	229012	27257	12595
2001	1719	8259	85842	87892	217521	26106	12479
2002	1540	8494	79447	91092	213794	25402	12127
2003	1430	7733	76879	86465	199390	26324	13056
2004	1422	8087	71677	86672	205532	28326	14208
2005	1358	8148	71926	83485	202301	28026	14813
2006	1361	8051	70400	68299	197546	28958	15632
2007	1306	8132	70681	83969	214423	30465	17013
2008	1266	8382	72119	85938	226681	32535	18176
2009	1253	9036	65684	89761	247778	34973	17952
2010	1245	9883	68135	105048	276994	37227	21677
2011	1305	11213	76790	115539	311417	44458	24170
2012	1266	11882	79131	115248	331524	48080	26330
2013	1384	12580	88322	128106	348681	53049	28806

资料来源：北京市教育委员会。
Source: Beijing Municipal Commission of Education.

18-3 各类学校基本情况
BASIC STATISTICS FOR VARIOUS SCHOOLS

单位：人 (person)

项目	Item	校数(所) Number of Schools (unit)		教职工数 Teachers and Staff		专任教师 Full-time Teachers	
		2013	2012	2013	2012	2013	2012
合计	**Total**	**3439**	**3314**	**354704**	**346555**	**216463**	**204812**
高等教育	**Higher Education**	**177**	**179**	**146264**	**146801**	**69625**	**64052**
研究生培养机构(不计校数)	Institutions Providing Postgraduate Programs (Number of Schools Not Counted)	(136)	(135)			(47841)	(45052)
高等学校	Institutions of Higer Education	(56)	(56)			(38747)	(36539)
科研机构	Research Institutes	(80)	(79)			(9094)	(8513)
普通高等学校	General Institutions of Higher Education	89	91	137825	137277	66026	60004
成人高等学校	Adult Institutions of Higher Education	19	19	3403	3407	1523	1527
民办的其他高等教育机构	Privately-funded Institutions of Higher Education	69	69	5036	6117	2076	2521
中等教育	**Secondary Education**	**757**	**760**	**96012**	**94433**	**68175**	**66537**
高中阶段教育	Senior Secondary Education	410	419	96012	94433	47704	46569
普通高中	General Middle Schools	291	289	80511	78730	38492	37411
中等职业教育	Secondary Vocational Schools	119	130	15501	15703	9212	9158
普通中专	General Technical Secondary Schools	31	31	3701	3738	1995	1984
成人中专	Technical Secondary Schools for Adults	11	11	572	592	313	342
职业高中	Vocational Senior High Schools	55	54	7653	7834	4872	4928
技工学校	Technician Training Schools	22	34	3575	3539	2032	1904
初中阶段教育	Junior Secondary Education	347	341			20471	19968
小学教育	**Primary Schools**	**1093**	**1081**	**57832**	**55710**	**48726**	**46783**
工读学校	**Work-Study Schools for Delinquent Children**	**6**	**6**	**294**	**300**	**196**	**212**
特殊教育	**Special Education**	**22**	**22**	**1253**	**1231**	**935**	**898**
学前教育	**Pre-school Education**	**1384**	**1266**	**53049**	**48080**	**28806**	**26330**

注：1．普通高中的教职工数中包含普通初中的教职工数。
2．表中带()数据不计入“校数”的合计数据中。
资料来源：北京市教育委员会。
Note: a) Number of "Teachers and Staff" in general senior high schools includes those in general junior high schools.
b) In this table data with () were not be calculated in the total number of schools.
Source: Beijing Municipal Commission of Education.

18-3 续表 Continued

单位：人 (person)

项目	Item	毕业生数 Graduates 2013	毕业生数 Graduates 2012	招生数 New Enrollment 2013	招生数 New Enrollment 2012	在校学生数 Total Enrollment 2013	在校学生数 Total Enrollment 2012
合计	**Total**	**923050**	**881804**	**1182301**	**1108574**	**3736003**	**3568273**
高等教育	**Higher Education**	**480612**	**466202**	**647871**	**595309**	**1882237**	**1777024**
研究生	Postgraduates	73357	70491	91399	87044	265656	252175
高等学校	Institutions of Higher Education	68965	66438	85759	81613	249225	236926
科研机构	Scientific Research Institutions	4392	4053	5640	5431	16431	15249
普通本专科	General Undergraduates and College Students	148689	152980	163081	162042	589234	581844
中央部委属高校	Under Central Ministries and Commissions	71725	71152	79225	77825	304179	299717
市属高校	Under Municipal Government	76964	81828	83856	84217	285055	282127
公办高校	Public Colleges and Universities	58149	59410	63877	63691	217293	214448
民办高校	Privately-funded Colleges and Universities	18815	22418	19979	20526	67762	67679
成人本专科	Adult Undergraduates and College Students	94519	94728	101654	107082	258278	265049
成人高等学校	Adult Institutions of Higher Education	9223	9664	9152	10024	23598	24605
普通高等学校	General Institutions of Higher Education	85296	85064	92502	97058	234680	240444
在职人员攻读硕士学位	Employees Enrolled in Graduate Programes Leading to Master Degrees			22744	19140	80492	70076
网络本专科生	Students Enrolled in Internet-based Courses	164047	148003	268993	220001	688577	607880
中等教育	**Secondary Education**	**240225**	**224938**	**239010**	**254790**	**706713**	**732224**
高中阶段教育	Senior Secondary	147852	129156	132284	146657	396145	426714
普通高中	General Middle Schools	58072	55657	59983	63381	187586	193505
#北京市户籍	Registered Residents of Beijing	53837	52208	51730	55728	166221	174089
中等职业教育	Secondary Vocational Schools	89780	73499	72301	83276	208559	233209
普通中专	General Technical Secondary Schools	17002	16111	14029	14753	56275	59895
成人中专	Technical Secondary Schools for Adults	40786	23523	34392	27398	59871	64858
职业高中	Vocational High Schools	17999	19281	7162	21925	49255	64987
技工学校	Technical Schools	13993	14584	16718	19200	43158	43469
初中阶段教育	Junior Secondary Education	92373	95782	106726	108133	310568	305510
#北京市户籍	Registered Residents of Beijing	71077	79250	65697	71109	207098	212437
小学教育	**Primary Education**	**111839**	**109492**	**165807**	**141738**	**789276**	**718655**
#北京市户籍	Registered Residents of Beijing	65651	71313	90917	74550	419693	394472
工读学校	**Work-study School for Delinquent Children**	**346**	**294**	**351**	**299**	**748**	**728**
特殊教育	**Special Education Schools**	**1706**	**1747**	**1156**	**1190**	**8348**	**8118**
学前教育	**Preschool Education**	**88322**	**79131**	**128106**	**115248**	**348681**	**331524**

18-4 全市高等教育学生情况(2013年)
STATISTICS FOR STUDENTS IN INSTITUTIONS OF HIGHER EDUCATION (2013)

单位：人 (person)

项目	Item	毕(结)业生人数 Number of Graduates	招生数 New Enrollment	在校学生数 Total Enrollment
普通本科、专科生	General Undergraduates and Junior College Students	148689	163081	589234
专科	Enrolled in Specialized Courses Education	36780	37581	107128
本科	Enrolled in Full Undergraduate Courses	111909	125500	482106
成人本科、专科生	Adult Undergraduates and Junior College Students	94519	101654	258278
专科	Enrolled in Specialized Courses Education	42712	44571	104623
本科	Enrolled in Full Undergraduate Courses	51807	57083	153655
网络本科、专科生	Students Enrolled in Internet-based Courses	164047	268993	688577
专科	Enrolled in Specialized Courses	99249	159499	375880
本科	Enrolled in Full Undergraduate Courses	64798	109494	312697
研究生	Postgraduates	73357	91399	265656
硕士	Master Degree	59552	73437	193452
博士	Doctor Degree	13805	17962	72204
在职人员攻读硕士学位	Employees Enrolled in Graduate Programes Leading to Master Degrees		22744	80492
自考助学班	Classes for Self-Learning Programs	1770		2771
普通预科生	College Preparatory Courses			2333
研究生课程进修班	Postgraduate Courses for Advanced Study	12980		14982
进修及培训	In-Service Training Courses	710414		687555
留学生	Overseas Students	26333	29781	43180

资料来源：北京市教育委员会。
Source: Beijing Municipal Commission of Education.

18-5 普通高等学校本专科基本情况(2013年)
BASIC STATISTICS FOR GENERAL INSTITUTIONS OF HIGHER EDUCATION(2013)

单位：人 (person)

项 目	Item	校 数(所) Number of Schools (unit)	毕业生数 Graduates	招生数 New Enrollment	在 校 学生数 Total Enrollment	教职工数 Teachers and Staff	#专任教师 Full-time Teachers
合 计	**Total**	**89**	**148689**	**163081**	**589234**	**137825**	**66026**
#女 性	Females		77053	84316	303788	67089	29686
综合大学	Comprehensive Universities	5	19118	20486	74041	25142	12282
理工院校	Science and Engineering	29	61289	67853	244970	51436	25970
农业院校	Agriculture	3	6411	6316	23386	4890	2471
林业院校	Forestry	1	3195	3441	13282	1781	1180
医药院校	Medicine	4	3021	3697	13244	16538	3069
师范院校	Teacher Training	2	4530	5400	19930	5870	3542
语文院校	Literature	9	11242	11825	42629	7285	4048
财经院校	Finance and Economics	16	22128	23037	83633	11076	6376
政法院校	Politics and Law	8	9118	11462	37513	6526	2943
体育院校	Physical Culture	3	2555	3092	11343	1684	1012
艺术院校	Art	8	3359	3623	13951	3654	2027
民族院校	Minorities Colleges	1	2723	2849	11312	1943	1106

资料来源：北京市教育委员会。
Source: Beijing Municipal Commission of Education.

18-6 全市分学科研究生情况(2013年)
BASIC STATISTICS FOR POSTGRADUATES BY SUBJECT OF STUDY (2013)

单位：人 (person)

项目	Item	毕业生 Graduates			招生数 New Enrollment			在校学生数 Student Enrollment		
		合计 Total	硕士 Master Degree	博士 Doctor Degree	合计 Total	硕士 Master Degree	博士 Doctor Degree	合计 Total	硕士 Master Degree	博士 Doctor Degree
合计	**Total**	**73357**	**59552**	**13805**	**91399**	**73437**	**17962**	**265656**	**193452**	**72204**
#女性	Females	36138	30889	5249	44473	37619	6854	125197	98524	26673
学术型学位	**Academic Degree**	**54375**	**41119**	**13256**	**60596**	**43043**	**17553**	**194360**	**123936**	**70424**
哲学	Philosophy	635	425	210	693	430	263	2300	1356	944
经济学	Economics	3821	3113	708	4025	3055	970	11646	7941	3705
法学	Law	4875	3848	1027	5012	3851	1161	15064	10434	4630
教育学	Education	1729	1479	250	1683	1358	325	5469	4140	1329
文学	Literature	3710	3140	570	3677	3002	675	11505	8658	2847
历史学	History	550	357	193	560	365	195	1847	1133	714
理学	Science	6473	3671	2802	9599	5500	4099	29900	15283	14617
工学	Engineering	20933	16267	4666	23157	16699	6458	78664	50115	28549
农学	Agriculture	1835	1235	600	1979	1292	687	6262	3639	2623
医学	Medicine	3059	2103	956	3546	2446	1100	9863	6494	3369
军事学	Military	25	19	6	26	14	12	120	70	50
管理学	Management	4749	3752	997	5025	3754	1271	16228	10361	5867
艺术学	Art	1981	1710	271	1614	1277	337	5492	4312	1180
专业学位	**Professional Degree**	**18982**	**18433**	**549**	**30803**	**30394**	**409**	**71296**	**69516**	**1780**

资料来源：北京市教育委员会。
Source: Beijing Municipal Commission of Education.

18-7 高等教育外国留学生情况(2013年)

STATISTICS FOR FOREIGN STUDENTS STUDYING IN BEIJING FOR HIGHER EDUCATION (2013)

单位：人 (person)

项 目	Item	毕(结)业生数 Graduates	授予学位人数 Number of Students Conferred with Degree	招生数 New Enrollment	在校学生数 Total Enrollment
合 计	**Total**	**26333**	**4720**	**29781**	**43180**
#女 性	Females	12736	2218	15051	20044
按学历划分	**By Educational Background**				
专 科	Enrolled in Specialized Courses	73		80	120
本 科	Enrolled in Full Undergraduate Courses	3522	3009	4163	15408
硕 士	Master Degree	1521	1443	2273	4932
博 士	Doctor Degree	279	268	761	2359
培 训	Training	20938		22504	20361
按地区划分	**By Region**				
亚 洲	Asia	13849	3467	16075	27851
非 洲	Africa	1096	365	1593	2749
欧 洲	Europe	6394	401	6990	7641
北美洲	North America	3919	310	3737	3382
南美洲	South America	561	118	834	928
大洋洲	Oceania	514	59	552	629
按经费来源	**By Source of Funds**				
国际组织资助	From International Organizations	66	4	97	178
中国政府资助	From Chinese Government	2691	1045	3945	6810
本国政府资助	From the Government of the Students' Home Country	185	72	284	825
学校间交换	Interscholastic Exchange	2718	165	3337	2634
自 费	Self Funding	20673	3434	22118	32733

资料来源：北京市教育委员会。
Source: Beijing Municipal Commission of Education.

18-8 普通中专分科情况(2013年) BASIC STATISTICS FOR SPECIALIZED SECONDARY SCHOOLS BY MAJOR (2013)

单位：人 (person)

项　　目	Item	毕业生数 Graduates	招生数 New Enrollment	在校学生数 Total Enrollment
合　　计	**Total**	**17002**	**14029**	**56275**
#女　生	Females	8352	6171	26421
按类别分	**By Category**			
农林牧渔类	Agriculture, Forestry, Animal Production and Hunting, Fishing	236	201	610
资源环境类	Resources and Environment	89	66	283
能源与新能源类	Energy and New Energy	510	71	856
土木水利类	Construction and Water Conservancy	947	815	3248
加工制造类	Processing and Manufacturing	1914	1438	5693
石油化工类	Petroleum and Chemicals	42		105
轻纺食品类	Light Industry, Textile and Foods	69	111	413
交通运输类	Transportation	2271	2488	9454
信息技术类	IT	1248	999	3866
医药卫生类	Medicine and Health	3625	2623	11654
休闲保健类	Recreation and Healthcare			
财经商贸类	Finance, Business and Trade	2201	1484	5642
旅游服务类	Tourism Services	381	224	842
文化艺术类	Culture and Arts	1704	1801	7995
体育与健身	Sports and Fitness	548	591	1754
教育类	Education	408	359	1363
司法服务类	Judicial Services	253	143	500
公共管理与服务类	Public Management and Services	183	252	769
其　他	Others	373	363	1228

资料来源：北京市教育委员会。
Source: Beijing Municipal Commission of Education.

18-9 职业高中分科情况(2013年)
BASIC STATISTICS FOR VOCATIONAL SCHOOLS BY MAJOR (2013)

单位：人 (person)

项 目	Item	毕业生数 Graduates	招生数 New Enrollment	在校学生数 Total Enrollment
合 计	**Total**	**17999**	**7162**	**49255**
#女 生	Females	8780	3267	24924
按类别分	**By Category**			
农林牧渔类	Agriculture, Forestry, Animal Production and Hunting, Fishing	325	140	694
资源环境类	Resources and Environment			
能源与新能源类	Energy and New Energy			1
土木水利类	Construction and Water Conservancy	153	29	270
加工制造类	Processing and Manufacturing	1457	257	2095
石油化工类	Petroleum and Chemicals			
轻纺食品类	Light Industry, Textile and Foods	151	40	219
交通运输类	Transportation	2147	1117	5136
信息技术类	IT	2776	912	6902
医药卫生类	Medicine and Health	563	154	939
休闲保健类	Recreation and Healthcare	283	102	2081
财经商贸类	Finance, Business and Trade	3036	1021	8464
旅游服务类	Tourism Services	2225	786	6630
文化艺术类	Culture and Arts	2138	1103	7311
体育与健身	Sports and Fitness	281	224	819
教育类	Education	2103	1053	6410
司法服务类	Judicial Services	81	16	304
公共管理与服务类	Public Management and Services	254	138	897
其 他	Others	26	70	83

资料来源：北京市教育委员会。
Source: Beijing Municipal Commission of Education.

18-10 校外教育情况(2013年)
STATISTICS FOR AFTER-SCHOOL EDUCATION (2013)

单位：人 (person)

项 目	Item	单位数(个) Number of Organizations(unit)	活动小组数(个) Activity Groups(unit)	参加小组学生数 Participating Students	教职工人数 Teachers and Staff	#专职辅导员 Full-time Coaches	兼职辅导员 Part-time Coaches
合 计	**Total**	**635**	**9058**	**471201**	**2853**	**1847**	**2068**
少年宫	Children's Palaces	22	6585	246604	1388	832	724
少年科技馆	Children's Scientific Museums	6	675	46799	201	152	149
少年之家	Children's Homes	28	1005	132699	383	235	515
少年活动站	Children's Clubs	579	793	45099	881	628	680

资料来源：北京市教育委员会。
Source: Beijing Municipal Commission of Education.

18-11 幼儿园基本情况(2013年)
STATISTICS FOR KINDERGARTENS (2013)

单位：人 (person)

项 目	Item	总计 Total	#女 Females	城区 In City	镇区 In Counties and Towns	乡村 In Villages
园 数 (所)	Number of Kindergartens (unit)	1384		970	208	206
班 数 (个)	Number of Classes (unit)	12580		10260	1487	833
在园幼儿数	Children Enrollment	348681	165226	287577	40986	20118
教职工数	Teachers and Staff	53049	48803	45642	5328	2079
#园 长	Headmasters	2079	1999	1647	262	170
专任教师	Full-time Teachers	28806	28212	24443	3083	1280
保健医	Health Workers	1958	1928	1725	167	66

注：从2007年开始,基础教育(普通中小学、工读学校、特殊教育、学前教育)的城乡划分按照国家统计局新的标准进行统计。
资料来源：北京市教育委员会。
Note: From 2007, urban and rural division of fundamental education (general primary and middle shcools, work-study schools for delinquent children, special education and pre-school education) are in line with the new standard of National Statistics Bureau.
Source: Beijing Municipal Commission of Education.

18-12 高等教育自学考试情况
STATISTICS FOR HIGHER EDUCATION SELF-STUDY EXAMINATION

项　　目	Item	2013	2012
报考人次 (人次)	Number of Registered Person-times (person-time)	137528	136864
报考科次 (科次)	Number of Registered Subject-times (person-time)	376699	399989
发出专科毕业证书 (个)	Number of Junior College Diplomas Issued (unit)	3803	8866
发出本科毕业证书 (个)	Number of General College Diplomas Issued (unit)	6764	4753
开考专业 (个)	Number of Majors Examined (unit)	106	113

资料来源：北京市教育委员会。
Source: Beijing Municipal Commission of Education.

18-13 特殊教育情况(2013年)
STATISTICS FOR SPECIAL EDUCATION (2013)

单位：人 (person)

项　　目	Item	毕业生 Graduates	招生数 New Enrollment	在校学生数 Total Enrollment
合　计	**Total**	**1706**	**1156**	**8348**
#女　性	Females	575	406	3015
特殊教育学校	Special Education Schools	336	365	2963
小学附设特教班	Special Classes Attached to Primary Schools	29	18	154
小学随班就读	Studying in Primary Schools	645	204	3014
普通(职业)初中随班就读	Studying in General Junior Secondary (Vocational) Classes	696	569	2217

资料来源：北京市教育委员会。
Source: Beijing Municipal Commission of Education.

18-14 职业技术培训机构基本情况(2013年)
BASIC STATISTICS FOR VOCATIONAL AND TECHNICAL TRAINING INSTITUTIONS(2013)

项　目	Item	学校数(所) Schools (unit)	教学班(点、个) Teaching Classes (site,unit)	结业生数(人次) Students Completing Courses (person-time)	
				合　计 Total	#女 性 Females
合　计	**Total**	**3595**	**64954**	**3201775**	**1487870**
#少数民族	National Miniorities			15908	6615
按培训机构分	**By Training Institution**				
职工技术培训学校(机构)	**Technical Training Schools (Institutions) for Employees**	**26**	**490**	**55044**	**23975**
教育部门和集体办	Run by Education Authorities and Collectively-run	3	113	25735	12353
其他部门办	Run by Other Authorities	13	368	28335	11421
民　办	Privately-funded	10	9	974	201
农村成人文化技术培训学校(机构)	**Cultural and Technical Training Schools (Institutions) for Rural Adults**	**2086**	**8782**	**902247**	**520077**
#教育部门和集体办	Run by Education Authorities and Collectively-run	2081	8760	899376	518662
县　办	Run by Counties	13	339	69901	34795
乡　办	Run by Townships	150	4881	444533	252277
村　办	Run by Villages	1918	3540	384942	231590
其他培训机构(含社会培训机构)	**Other Training Institutions (Including Social Training Institutions)**	**1483**	**55682**	**2244484**	**943818**
教育部门和集体办	Run by Education Authorities and Collectively-run	70		80644	41153
其他部门办	Run by Other Authorities	188	232	730489	410938
民　办	Privately-funded	1225	55450	1433351	491727
按培训时间分	**By Training Duration**				
一个月以内	within 1 month			1742557	708626
一个月至三个月以内	1-3 months			442546	251093
三个月至半年以内	3-6 months			601463	306989
半年至一年以内	6 months to 1 year			323578	167743
一年及以上	over 1 year			91631	53419
按培训形式分	**Group by Form of Training**				
#资格证书培训	Qualification Certificate Training			389605	188119
岗位证书培训	Job Post Certificate Training			776486	161935

资料来源：北京市教育委员会。
Source: Beijing Municipal Commission of Education.

18-14 续表 Continued

单位：人 (person)

项 目	Item	注册学生数 Student Enrollment 合 计 Total	#女 性 Females	教职工数 Teachers and Staff 合 计 Total	#专任教师 Full-time Teachers	聘请校外教 师 External Teachers Retained
合 计	**Total**	**2928858**	**1261914**	**56304**	**19032**	**17869**
#少数民族	National Miniorities	16504	7133	92	48	19
按培训机构分	**By Training Institution**					
职工技术培训学校(机构)	**Technical Training Schools (Institutions) for Employees**	**31800**	**14919**	**858**	**505**	**279**
教育部门和集体办	Run by Education Authorities and Collectively-run	6915	4682	514	313	185
其他部门办	Run by Other Authorities	23781	10026	175	89	94
民 办	Privately-funded	1104	211	169	103	
农村成人文化技术培训学校(机构)	**Cultural and Technical Training Schools (Institutions) for Rural Adults**	**453666**	**257603**	**1449**	**807**	**2846**
#教育部门和集体办	Run by Education Authorities and Collectively-run	453666	257603	1449	807	2846
县 办	Run by Counties	66990	33380	99	59	227
乡 办	Run by Townships	199040	116159	655	402	1051
村 办	Run by Villages	187636	108064	695	346	1568
其他培训机构(含社会培训机构)	**Other Training Institutions (Including Social Training Institutions)**	**2443392**	**989392**	**53997**	**17720**	**14744**
教育部门和集体办	Run by Education Authorities and Collectively-run	106913	53728	2558	910	932
其他部门办	Run by Other Authorities	825203	422038	16226	4897	4924
民 办	Privately-funded	1511276	513626	35213	11913	8888
按培训时间分	**By Training Duration**					
一个月以内	within 1 month	1334855	430158			
一个月至三个月以内	1-3 months	413777	220125			
三个月至半年以内	3-6 months	643986	323366			
半年至一年以内	6 months to 1 year	409742	219867			
一年及以上	over 1 year	126498	68398			
按培训形式分	**Group by Form of Training**					
#资格证书培训	Qualification Certificate Training	356165	163172			
岗位证书培训	Job Post Certificate Training	796105	159478			

18-15 民办教育基本情况(2013年)
STATSTICS FOR PRIVATELY-FUNDED EDUCATION (2013)

单位：人 (person)

项目	Item	校数(所) Number of Schools (unit)	毕业生数 Graduates	招生数 New Enrollment	在校学生数 Total Enrollment	教职工数 Teachers and Staff	#专任教师 Full-time Teachers	聘请校外教师数 External Teachers Retained
合计	**Total**	**762**	**71603**	**94255**	**256460**	**46393**	**24509**	**4090**
民办高等教育	**Privately-funded Higher Education**	**84**	**18815**	**19979**	**67762**	**11678**	**5454**	**3681**
普通高校	General Institutions of Higher Education	15	18815	19979	67762	6642	3378	1843
民办高等教育机构	Other Privately-funded Higher Education Institutions	69				5036	2076	1838
民办中等教育	**Privately-funded Secondary Education**	**99**	**14340**	**17203**	**53017**	**9431**	**5801**	**296**
高中阶段教育	Senior High School Education	79	6458	8298	26502	9431	5801	296
民办普通高中	Privately-funded Senior High Schools	56	4631	7323	20743	8246	5188	45
民办中等职业教育	Privately-funded Secondary Vocational Education	23	1827	975	5759	1185	613	251
初中阶段教育	Junior High School Education	20	7882	8905	26515			
民办小学	**Privately-funded Primary Schools**	**61**	**10502**	**14120**	**13994**	**3046**	**2245**	**11**
民办幼儿园	**Privately-funded Kindergartens**	**518**	**27946**	**42953**	**121687**	**22238**	**11009**	**102**

注：普通中学教职工数、专任教师及聘请校外教师数为初中高中合计数。
资料来源：北京市教育委员会。
Note: Number of teachers,staff,full-time teachers,substitutive and part-time teachers in regular secondary schools includes those in junior and senior middle schools.
Source: Beijing Municipal Commission of Education.

18-16 高校办学条件(2013年)
SCHOOL CONDITIONS OF HIGHER EDUCATION INSTITUTIONS (2013)

项目	Item	合计 Total	中央 Central	市属市管 Municipal
普通高校	**General Institutions of Higher Education**			
校舍建筑面积 (平方米)	Building Area (sq.m)	33529230	23443831	10085399
占地面积 (平方米)	Floor Space (sq.m)	41785605	26198857	15586748
图书 (万册)	Books (10000 volumes)	10650	6817	3833
电子图书藏量 (千兆字节)	E-books Collections (Gigabyte)	6177880	6018979	158902
拥有教学用计算机 (台)	Computers for Teaching (unit)	388706	198197	190509
上网课程数 (门)	Number of Online Courses (sort)	52398	31928	20470
成人高校	**Institutions of Higher Education for Adults**			
校舍建筑面积 (平方米)	Building Area (sq.m)	868994	236280	632714
占地面积 (平方米)	Floor Space (sq.m)	1284775	302865	981910
图书 (万册)	Books (10000 volumes)	220	43	177
电子图书藏量 (千兆字节)	E-books Collections (Gigabyte)	35410	27628	7783
拥有教学用计算机 (台)	Computers for Teaching (unit)	10105	1551	8554
上网课程数 (门)	Number of Online Courses (sort)	5523	1354	4169

资料来源：北京市教育委员会。
Source: Beijing Municipal Commission of Education.

18-17 基础教育办学条件(2013年)
SCHOOL CONDITIONS OF BASIC EDUCATION (2013)

单位：平方米 (sq.m)

项　目	Item	普通中学 General Middle Schools	小　学 Primary Schools
学校占地面积	Floor Space	22632980	14179335
校舍建筑面积	Building Area	12141289	6536187
#当年新增	Newly Added in the Year	620807	425780
#危房面积	Area of Dangerous Buildings	1750	569
教学及辅助用房	Teaching and Auxiliary Houses	4368984	3009179
普通教室	Classrooms	2564408	2338580
实验室	Laboratories	757059	220862
图书室	Libraries	326767	150293
微机室	Computer Rooms	197222	137260
语音室	Language Labs	36184	17578
体育馆	Gymnasiums	487344	144606
行政办公用房	Administrative Houses	1364809	790558
生活用房	Houses for Life (Residencial Houses)	3403309	1105083
其他用房	Houses for Other Purposes	3004187	1631367
计算机 (台)	Computers (unit)	242938	203772
图书藏量 (册)	Books Collections (volume)	27321077	26562318
电子图书藏量 (千兆字节)	E-book Collections (Gigabyte)	150265	107038

资料来源：北京市教育委员会。
Source: Beijing Municipal Commission of Education.

18-18 非本市户籍、外国籍学生情况(2013年)
STATISTICS FOR STUDENTS FROM OTHER PROVINCES, MUNICIPALITIES AND AUTONOMOUS REGIONS ALONG WITH OTHER COUNTRIES (2013)

单位：人 (person)

项　目	Item	非本市户籍学生数 Students from Other Provinces, Municipalities and Autonomous Regions	#民办学校 Privately-funded Schools	外国留学生 Overseas Students	#民办学校 Privately-funded Education
合　计	**Total**	**663396**	**142217**	**6589**	**2566**
普通中学	General Middle Schools	124835	21701	2588	623
初　中	Junior Secondary Schools	103470	15036	1038	194
高　中	Senior Secondary Schools	21365	6665	1550	429
中等职业教育	Vocational Secondary Schools	72596	5513	111	
小　学	Primary Schools	369583	67507	2134	671
特殊教育	Special Education Schools	737	35	5	
幼儿园	Kindergartens	95645	47461	1751	1272

资料来源：北京市教育委员会。
Source: Beijing Municipal Commission of Education.

18-19 图书馆、文化馆、档案馆情况(1978-2013年)
LIBRARIES, CULTURAL CENTERS AND ARCHIVES (1978-2013)

年 份 Year	公共图书馆 Public Libraries				群众艺术馆、文化馆 Mass Art Centers, Cultural Centers		档案馆 Archiving Institutions			
	个数 (个) Number (unit)	总藏数 (万册、万件) Total Collections (10000 volumes)	建筑面积 (万平方米) Building Area (10000 sq.m)	书刊文献外借人次 (万人次) Person-times Borrowing Books, Magazines, and Documents (10000 person-times)	个数 (个) Number (unit)	组织文艺活动 (次) Art Activities Organized (times)	个数 (个) Number (unit)	建筑面积 (平方米) Building Area (10000 sq.m)	利用档案资料人次 (万人次) Persons of Using Files (10000 person-times)	案卷 (万卷件) Records (10000 rolls)
1978	18	1423		168.5	19	516				
1979	21	1502		173.7	19	1033				
1980	20	1606	1.8	210.4	19	778				
1981	21	1614	1.9	211.0	19	1131				
1982	21	1676	2.0	228.4	20	1334				
1983	21	1733	1.9	243.0	20	1015				
1984	22	1824	2.3	223.7	22	489				
1985	22	1860	3.0	219.9	23	469				
1986	23	1874	6.0	219.9	23	883				
1987	23	1959	20.6	169.8	23	1067	20	10695	1.30	86.13
1988	23	2050	23.4	300.4	23	647	20	21472	1.46	115.98
1989	23	2128	24.5		23	1411	20	31280	1.48	156.28
1990	23	2205	25.0		23	1429	20	23618	2.51	167.37
1991	23	2281	25.3		23	1128	20	33491	3.24	177.45
1992	23	2397	25.4	147.0	23	978	20	35950	2.64	181.31
1993	23	2461	25.5	212.0	23	764	20	37650	1.73	192.39
1994	23	2548	23.8	383.8	23	1034	20	42641	1.50	192.35
1995	23	2629	24.1	139.3	23	1127	20	65489	1.42	204.06
1996	22	2652	25.3	145.6	23	2277	20	62994	3.03	223.70
1997	23	2789	25.7	188.0	23	1875	20	64147	2.69	227.42
1998	24	2848	25.6	189.0	23	2554	20	67759	2.71	240.78
1999	24	2934	26.4	607.0	23	1490	20	72597	2.52	259.50
2000	26	3020	27.0	283.0	23	1809	20	72596	3.01	278.29
2001	26	3133	31.4	287.7	23	1822	20	72730	4.17	297.02
2002	26	3248	30.7	337.5	20	1817	20	72946	4.53	328.42
2003	26	3355	30.9	334.8	20	2023	20	81519	6.27	358.95
2004	26	3451	30.9	405.0	22	1826	20	83162	7.03	379.13
2005	26	3626	31.7	480.0	22	3697	20	84656	6.97	404.69
2006	25	3776	31.0	515.0	21	2200	20	93773	10.59	436.70
2007	25	3940	31.5	479.0	21	4752	20	93463	9.51	461.67
2008	25	4100	33.4	450.0	20	3007	20	97605	9.00	495.70
2009	25	4368	41.9	471.0	20	3470	20	97605	9.88	523.84
2010	25	4613	42.4	441.0	20	3564	18	97611	13.45	557.99
2011	25	5049	42.1	333.0	20	3401	18	97976	12.30	582.92
2012	25	5556	47.6	317.0	20	3848	18	98879	12.37	602.54
2013	25	5316	48.4	325.0	20	4769	18	101896	23.85	636.10

注：1978-1981年，群众艺术馆、文化馆数据不包括群众艺术馆。

资料来源：北京市文化局、国家图书馆、北京市档案局。

Note: In 1978-1981, the data of mass art centers and cultural centers didn't include those of mass art centers.

Source: Beijing Municipal Bureau of Culture, National Library of China, and Beijing Municipal Bureau of Archives.

18-20 博物馆情况(1982-2013年)
STATISTICS FOR MUSEUMS(1982-2013)

年 份 Year	北京地区博物馆数 (个) Number of Museums in Beijing (unit)	文 物 藏品数 (万件) Cultural Relic Collections (10000 units)	博物馆及其他文物保护机构(文物局系统内) Museums and Other Cultural Relic Protection and Administration Organizations (under the jurisdiction of Beijing Municipal Administration of Cultural Heritage)				
			个数 (个) Number (unit)	#博物馆 Museums	文物藏品数 (万件) Cultural Relic Collections (10000 units)	#一级品 (件) Grade-I Collections (unit)	参观人次 (万人次) Visitors (10000 person-times)
1982			28		8.4	294	9.7
1983			29		4.0		58.0
1984							
1985			32		9.0		20.0
1986			39	7	21.0		905.0
1987							
1988			42	11	21.0		1098.0
1989			46	12	14.0		992.0
1990							
1991			46	12	11.7	2901	6629.1
1992							
1993			50	16	17.4	479	2423.4
1994			51	17	16.7	447	955.0
1995			51	17	16.7	447	2100.3
1996			51	17	18.0	443	2009.3
1997			54	24	18.2	443	935.8
1998			56	26	18.3	387	697.8
1999			54	26	18.5	374	5641.8
2000			53	25	18.2	367	702.7
2001			58	26	17.3	366	99.1
2002			48	27	20.1	716	170.8
2003			55	27	112.4	716	119.2
2004			66	31	370.4	656	599.9
2005			73	34	115.1	620	1370.9
2006			70	33	115.5	643	1416.7
2007			69	34	113.5	439	1493.0
2008	148	331	71	37	116.0	678	1368.4
2009	151	331	76	40	117.0	722	1647.9
2010	156	332	79	41	117.0	725	1712.1
2011	162	430	78	41	117.0	852	1373.4
2012	165	430	78	41	117.0	903	1887.9
2013	167	430	78	41	117.0	903	1760.0

资料来源：北京市文物局。
Source: Beijing Municipal Administration of Cultural Heritage.

18-21 博物馆及其他文物保护管理机构情况(2013年)
STATISTICS FOR MUSEUMS AND OTHER CULTURAL RELIC PROTECTION AND ADMINISTRATION ORGANIZATIONS (2013)

项目		Item		合计 Total	市属 Under the Jurisdiction of the City	区县属 Under the Jurisdiction of a District/County
全市按行业管理登记的博物馆		**Museums Registered by Industry Administration**				
博物馆数	(个)	Museums	(unit)	**167**	**42**	**42**
#免费开放的博物馆数	(个)	Museums Open for Free	(unit)	52	18	20
文物藏品数	(万件)	Cultural Relic Collections	(10000 units)	430		
参观人次	(万人次)	Visitors	(10000 person-times)	3500		
文物古迹个数	(处)	Cultural Relics and Historical Sites	(unit)	3840		
文物拍卖机构数	(个)	Organizations of Cultural Relic Auctions	(unit)	131		
举办文物艺术品拍卖场次	(场)	Cultural Relic Auctions	(time)	260		
文物拍卖标的数	(件、套)	Auction Targets	(unit)	185191		
文物拍卖标的成交金额	(万元)	Turnover of Cultural Relic Auctions	(10000 yuan)	2567794		
文物局系统内博物馆及文物保护管理机构	**(个)**	**Museums and Cultural Relic Protection and Administration Organizations under the Municipal Administration of Cultural Heritage**	**(unit)**	**78**	**31**	**47**
#博物馆	(个)	Museums	(unit)	41	17	24
博物馆按类别分		Grouped by Category				
综合性	(个)	Comprehensive	(unit)	11	2	9
历史性	(个)	Historical	(unit)	17	7	10
艺术性	(个)	Art	(unit)	6	5	1
自然科技类	(个)	Natural Science	(unit)	2	1	1
其他类	(个)	Others	(unit)	5	2	3
从业人员	(人)	Employment	(person)	5264	1848	3416
文物藏品数	(万件)	Cultural Relic Collections	(10000 units)	117	113	4
#一级品	(件)	Grade-I Collections	(unit)	903	609	294
参观人次	(万人次)	Visitors	(10000 person-times)	1760.0	316.4	1443.5
本年收入	(万元)	Revenues in the Year	(10000 yuan)	260288	107259	153029
#财政收入	(万元)	Fiscal Revenue	(10000 yuan)	190113	82845	107268
门票收入	(万元)	Ticket Revenue	(10000 yuan)	43176	1809	41367
本年支出	(万元)	Expenditures in the Year	(10000 yuan)	239758	93285	146473

注：全市博物馆数为北京地区按行业管理登记的博物馆数。
资料来源：北京市文物局。
Note: Number of museums in the city means the number of museums registered by industrial administration in Beijing.
Source: Beijing Municipal Administration of Cultural Heritage.

18-22 公共图书馆(2013年)
PUBLIC LIBRARIES (2013)

项目		Item		合计 Total	中央属 Under Central Jurisdiction	市属 Under the Jurisdiction of the City	区县属 Under the Jurisdiction of a District/ County
个数	(个)	Number	(unit)	25	1	1	23
从业人员	(人)	Employed Persons	(person)	2981	1727	370	884
总藏数	(万册、万件)	Total Collections	(10000 volumes)	5316	3244	688	1384
#图书	(万册、万件)	Books	(10000 volumes)	2954	1112	553	1289
建筑面积	(万平方米)	Building Area	(10000 sq.m)	48.4	24.4	9.4	14.6
阅览座席	(个)	Seating Capacity of Reading Rooms	(unit)	20413	4411	2799	13203
总流通人次	(万人次)	Total Number of Visitors	(10000 person-times)	1452	419	454	579
#书刊文献外借人次	(万人次)	Person-times Borrowing Books, Magazines and Documents	(10000 person-times)	325		67	258
#书刊文献外借册次	(万册次)	Volume-times of Borrowed Books, Magazines and Documents	(10000 volunme-times)	893		273	620

资料来源：北京市文化局、国家图书馆。
Source: Beijing Municipal Bureau of Culture, and National Library of China.

18-23 群众艺术馆、文化馆和文化站情况(2013年)
STATISTICS FOR MASS ART CENTERS, CULTURAL CENTERS AND CULTURAL STATIONS(2013)

项目	Item	合计 Total	群众艺术馆 Mass Art Centers	文化馆 Cultural Centers	文化站 Cultural Stations
个数 （个）	Number (unit)	346	1	19	326
从业人员 （人）	Employed Persons (person)	2549	57	774	1718
举办展览个数 （个）	Exhibitions Held (unit)	2200	12	254	1934
组织文艺活动 （次）	Art Activities Organized (times)	29787	51	4718	25018

资料来源：北京市文化局。
Source: Beijing Municipal Bureau of Culture.

18-24 档案事业基本情况(2013年)
STATISTICS FOR ARCHIVING INSTITUTIONS (2013)

项 目		Item		合 计 Total	市 属 Under the Jurisdiction of the City	区县属 Under the Jurisdiction of a District/County
档案馆个数	**(个)**	**Number of Archives**	**(unit)**	**18**	**2**	**16**
建筑面积	**(平方米)**	**Building Areas**	**(sq.m)**	**101896**	**30962**	**70934**
馆藏档案情况		**Files Collected in Archives**				
全 宗	(个)	Full Archives	(unit)	3184	805	2379
案 卷	(万卷件)	Records	(10000 rolls)	636.10	287.94	348.16
建国前档案	(万卷件)	Files Prior to the Foundation of PRC	(10000 rolls)	100.43	98.84	1.59
建国后档案	(万卷件)	Files After the Foundation of PRC	(10000 rolls)	535.66	189.10	346.56
录音、录像、影片档案	(盘)	Tape, Video, and Film Files	(piece)	42814	34996	7818
照片档案	(张)	Photo Files	(disc)	660236	335524	324712
缩微胶片		Microfiches				
平片、开窗卡	(张)	Flat and Window-open Microfiches	(disc)	289067	289067	
卷 片	(万幅)	Rolled Microfiches	(10000 rolls)	5394	5344	50
档案利用情况		**File Utilization**				
本年利用档案人次	(人次)	Person-times Using Files in the Year	(person-times)	235616	15433	220183
本年利用档案	(万卷件次)	Files Used in the Year	(10000 roll.times)	30.41	7.07	23.34
本年利用资料册次	(册次)	Data Books Used in the Year	(volume-times)	4980	2926	2054
本年利用资料人次	(人次)	Person-times Using Data in the Year	(person-times)	2869	2371	498
本年编研档案、资料	(万字)	Files and Data Edited and Studied in the Year	(10000 Chinese characters)	575.4	265.8	309.6
档案馆网站来访IP次数	**(万次)**	**IPs Visiting Archive Websites**	**(10000 times)**	**81.02**	**50.11**	**30.91**

资料来源：北京市档案局。
Source: Beijing Municipal Bureau of Archives.

18-25 专业艺术剧团、艺术表演场所情况(1978-2013年)
STATISTICS FOR PROFESSIONAL ART TROUPES AND ART PERFORMANCE VENUES (1978-2013)

年份 Year	专业艺术剧团 Professional Art Troupes					艺术表演场所 Art Performance Venues				
	个数(个) Number (unit)	从业人员(人) Employed Perons (person)	演出场次(场次) Perfor-mances (time)	#国内演出场次 Domestic Performances	国内观众人数(万人次) Domestic Audience (10000 person-times)	个数(个) Number (unit)	从业人员(人) Employed Perons (person)	演出场次(场次) Perfor-mances (time)	#艺术演出场次 Art Shows	观众人数(万人次) Audience (10000 person-times)
1978						35	933		3430	
1979						29	792		3354	
1980	42	10035		16544	2092.0	30	850		4106	
1981	42	10150		16298	1860.0	33	887	25963	3234	
1982	43	10674		16656	1721.0	31	833	24367	3641	
1983	41	10424		13997	1596.0	32	849	28603	3680	
1984	41	10645		13470	1443.0	32	898	32460	3407	
1985	42	10390		11380	1105.0	32	892	36021	2883	
1986	42	10871		10907	1086.0	32	1085	33582	3001	2362.8
1987	42	10752		10652	1035.0	26	765	29695	2840	1866.5
1988	41	10228		8194	889.0	25	809	34731	2633	2044.3
1989	43	9865		7544	756.0	25	813	37030	1340	1913.9
1990	43	9847		7527	839.0	25	833	49444	1331	1782.4
1991	44	10116		6623	1612.0	25	849	44846	1147	1463.2
1992	43	9734		6850	682.0	25	810	49259	1195	1070.5
1993	42	9701		6538	529.0	25	831	37406	989	615.9
1994	42	9182		7290	554.0	23	745	30468	895	525.9
1995	43	8925		6728	447.0	23	724	28316	720	429.9
1996	38	7679		7615	638.0	24	761	33356	1411	371.2
1997	38	8090		8426	696.0	22	709	32412	1851	352.3
1998	37	5388		8105	495.0	22	720	32218	1800	270.4
1999	37	6959		8564	1275.0	24	784	32666	2294	264.7
2000	31	5089		7610	926.0	24	739	25922	2088	272.9
2001	37	6786		8466	1668.9	23	709	20373	2302	237.1
2002	36	6911		9528	678.7	24	715	18434	2950	257.8
2003	36	6965		8797	586.1	24	698	13956	2461	216.2
2004	36	6939		8731	846.4	36	1223	24310	7085	538.3
2005	36	6986	11059	8934	758.7	39	1313	26931	7160	542.9
2006	33	7363	10929	9790	866.0	42	1291	31408	8253	504.2
2007	33	7364	11720	10076	720.0	43	1803	34946	9288	553.3
2008	33	7146	11417	10663	877.0	54	2245	45014	11293	750.0
2009	35	7504	10131	9684	863.0	73	1798	59464	14061	791.0
2010	35	7415	10983	10483	1108.0	73	2879	54376	16941	1035.0
2011	35	6713	11757	11069	1173.0	68	2954	54905	16625	931.0
2012	35	7826	12672	11675	1204.0					
2013	35	7835	13016	12084	959.0					

注：1. 专业艺术剧团包括中央、市属及区县属专业院团。
2. 1978年艺术表演场所范围含中央属；1979—2003年包括文化部门主管直属剧场；2004—2011年包括全行业主要剧场。
资料来源：北京市文化局。

Note: a) Professional art troupes include professional troupes at the central, municipal, district and county levels.
b) In 1978, art performance venues included central ones; in 1979-2003 they included theaters directly under the Ministry of Culture; in 2004-2011 they included main theaters across the sector.

Source: Beijing Municipal Bureau of Culture.

18-26 专业艺术剧团(2013年)
STATISTICS FOR PROFESSIONAL ART TROUPES (2013)

项目	Item	个数(个) Number (unit)	从业人员(人) Employed Perons (person)	演出场次(场次) Performances (time)	#国内演出场次 Domestic Performances	#农村演出场次 Performances in Rural Areas	国内观众人数(万人次) Domestic Audience (10000 person-times)	演出收入(万元) Performance Revenues (10000 yuan)
合计	**Total**	**35**	**7835**	**13016**	**12084**	**1294**	**959**	**48814**
按隶属关系分组	**By Affiliation**							
中央属	Central	17	5299	3373	3189	656	539	28287
市属	Municipal	11	2390	8662	8275	624	397	20163
区县属	District and County	7	146	981	620	14	23	364
按剧种分	**By Type of Drama**							
话剧、儿童剧团、滑稽剧团	Stage Play, Children's Drama, and Farce Troupes	4	1133	1970	1937	127	136	8534
歌剧、舞剧、歌舞剧团	Opera, Ballet and Dance Troupes	2	813	341	329	7	85	5054
歌舞团、轻音乐团	Song and Dance Troupes and Light Music Troupes	4	1424	1631	1585	224	181	8009
乐团、合唱团	Philharmonic Troupes and Glee Club	4	782	440	385	7	46	6380
戏曲剧团	Local Opera Troupes	10	1499	2425	2329	377	131	7587
曲、杂、木、皮影剧团	Recitation and Ballad Troupes,Acrobatics and Circus Troupes,Puppet Show Troupes and Shadow Play Troupes	5	624	5293	4627	52	139	6092
综合艺术表演团体	General Art Performance Groups	6	1560	916	892	500	241	7158

资料来源：北京市文化局。
Source: Beijing Municipal Bureau of Culture.

18-27 电影、电视、广播电台情况(1978-2013年)

年份 Year	电影 Films 放映场次 (万场次) Show Times (10000 Times)	电影 Films 观众人次 (万人次) Audience (10000 Person-times)	电影 Films 票房收入 (亿元) Ticket Revenue (100 million yuan)	电视 TVs 电视节目套数 (套) Number of TV Programs (unit)	电视 TVs 平均每日电视节目播出时间 (小时) Daily Show Hours of TV Programs (hour)	电视 TVs 电视综合覆盖率 (%) Comprehensive Coverage Rate of TVs (%)
1978	31.9	29924.1				
1979	35.5	34626.0				
1980	33.1	31189.5		1	4.25	
1981	31.9	30067.0		1	5.46	100.00
1982	32.8	28743.5		1	6.85	91.00
1983	30.1	27345.5		1	7.07	90.00
1984	27.8	23966.7		1	7.15	98.00
1985	23.0	18875.0		1	7.54	98.00
1986	20.6	15904.4		2	19.07	98.00
1987	19.0	13517.7		2	13.64	98.00
1988	19.2	13269.4		2	19.39	98.00
1989	21.5	14492.6		4	25.43	98.00
1990	20.7	12771.2		4	29.43	98.00
1991	21.3	12558.3		4	27.79	98.00
1992	22.1	11587.4		6	45.02	98.00
1993	11.9	5369.8		7	58.18	98.00
1994	10.6	2166.5	0.51	9	77.79	98.30
1995	9.2	1598.6	0.93	12	98.36	98.30
1996	11.5	1644.1	1.07	12	101.01	98.81
1997	12.6	1742.3	1.17	12	111.00	99.12
1998	12.3	1443.5	1.28	12	110.68	99.60
1999	11.7	964.7		12	118.36	99.80
2000	12.2	873.2		12	122.45	99.80
2001	12.6	804.7	0.92	16	200.15	99.91
2002	12.3	827.4	1.09	18	329.40	99.82
2003	11.8	683.0	1.35	19	259.32	99.90
2004	18.1	814.4	1.86	24	244.17	99.50
2005	22.6	873.8	2.29	25	329.81	99.99
2006	28.0	1221.0	3.02	25	294.23	99.99
2007	38.0	1711.0	3.70	25	309.12	99.99
2008	46.8	1767.3	5.37	24	309.06	99.99
2009	62.4	2451.5	8.19	26	319.13	99.99
2010	74.3	2923.3	11.81	26	319.24	99.99
2011	97.4	3235.9	13.52	25	334.22	100.00
2012	120.0	3954.6	16.23	26	343.68	100.00
2013	137.8	4288.5	18.60	26	347.89	100.00

资料来源：北京市新闻出版广电局。

STATISTICS FOR FILMS, TELEVISIONS, AND BROADCASTING STATIONS (1978-2013)

电视 TVs				广播电台 Broadcasting Stations			
农村电视综合覆盖率 (%) Comprehensive Coverage Rate of TVs in Rural Area (%)	无线电视综合覆盖率 (%) Comprehensive Coverage Rate of Wireless TVs (%)	有线电视注册用户数 (万户) Subscnbers of Cable Televisions (10000 households)	有线广播电视入户率 (%) Access Rate of Cable Televisions (%)	广播节目套数 (套) Number of Radio Programs (unit)	平均每日广播节目播出时间 (小时) Daily Show Hours of Radio Programs (hour)	广播综合覆盖率 (%) Comprehensive Coverage Rate of Broadcast (%)	广告收入 (万元) Advertising Income (10000 yuan)
				4	56.08		
				4	57.22	100.00	139
				4	59.37	98.00	166
				5	61.97	98.00	117
				5	73.67	98.00	668
				5	65.87	98.00	645
				5	66.17	98.00	555
				6	68.75	98.00	771
				6	76.33	98.00	964
				7	78.67	98.00	1668
				7	77.87	98.00	2885
				7	77.87	98.00	5115
				10	94.75	98.00	9680
				12	134.75	98.00	15225
		52.71		12	134.85	98.00	26480
		82.21		13	148.25	91.00	45398
		182.97		13	150.25	96.97	93428
		202.75		15	156.05	98.44	100546
		230.97		16	174.67	99.98	106773
		165.78	43.24	16	178.20	99.96	115072
		175.71	45.80	16	188.90	97.7	149661
		205.95	51.76	16	192.43	99.91	136451
		231.24	57.05	16	197.43	99.88	154317
		243.00	58.39	16	197.86	99.91	157210
	97.57	265.50	62.09	16	229.55	100.00	212091
	99.99	282.00	64.12	17	281.88	100.00	236334
99.97	94.90	319.58	70.75	17	282.88	100.00	240146
99.97	93.13	345.06	74.43	17	288.92	99.98	317437
99.97	93.19	383.13	81.00	17	297.40	99.98	385231
99.97	94.38	413.50	85.90	18	316.58	99.99	453932
99.97	98.72	448.12	91.68	18	324.82	99.99	613672
100.00	99.74	475.92	95.90	18	329.56	100.00	796113
100.00	99.75	495.70	99.13	25	471.69	100.00	1081857
100.00	99.75	524.59	103.00	25	473.62	100.00	1689443

Source: Beijing Municipal Bereau Of Press,Publication,Radio,Film and Television.

18-28 电影、电视剧制作情况
STATISTICS FOR PRODUCTION OF FILMS AND TV PLAYS

项目		Item		2013 全国 National Total	2013 北京 Beijing	2013 占全国比重(%) As % of National Total	2012 全国 National Total	2012 北京 Beijing	2012 占全国比重(%) As % of National Total
生产故事片	(部)	Feature Films	(Piece)	638	222	34.8	893	243	27.2
制作电视剧	(部)	TV Plays	(Piece)	441	87	19.7	506	98	19.4
	(集)		(Episode)	15770	2952	18.7	17703	3408	19.3
电视剧出口量部	(部)	TV Plays Exported	(Piece)	243	40	16.5	326	98	30.1
	(集)		(Episode)	11180	1529	13.7	15329	3253	21.2
电视剧出口额	(万元)	Value of TV Plays Exported	(10000 yuan)	9250	2290	24.8	15020	2549	17.0

资料来源：北京市新闻出版广电局。
Source: Beijing Municipal Administration of Press, Publication, Radio, Film and Television.

18-29 电影放映单位情况(2013年)
STATISTICS FOR MOVIE PROJECTION ORGANIZATIONS (2013)

项目	Item	放映单位数(个) Number of Projection Organizations (unit)	总银幕数(块) Total Screens (Piece)	#3D银幕数 3D Screens	#IMAX巨幕数 IMAX Large Screens	放映场次(万场次) Show Times (10000 Times)	观影人次(万人次) Audience (10000 Person-times)	票房收入(亿元) Ticket Revenues (100 million yuan)
合计	**Total**	**150**	**820**	**296**	**5**	**137.82**	**4288.46**	**18.6**
院线影院	Cinema Chains	150	820	296	5	137.69	4250.30	18.5
二级市场	Secondary Market					0.13	38.16	0.1

资料来源：北京市新闻出版广电局。
Source: Beijing Municipal Administration of Press, Publication, Radio, Film and Television.

18-30 电视台情况
STATISTICS FOR TELEVISION STATIONS

项目		Item		2013 中央 Central	2013 地方 Local	2012 中央 Central	2012 地方 Local
基本情况		**Basic Statistics**					
电视台	(座)	Television Stations	(unit)	1	1	1	1
公共节目套数	(套)	Number of Public Programs	(unit)	34	26	32	26
全年公共节目播出时间	(小时)	Annual Broadcast Time of Public Programs	(hour)	270113	126983	268458	125444
播放节目情况		**Shows of TV Programs**					
新闻咨询类节目	(小时)	News and Consulting Programs	(hour)	69008	22538	67995	22112
专题服务类节目	(小时)	Special Service Programs	(hour)	81855	52342	92092	50093
综艺益智类节目	(小时)	Entertainment and Education Programs	(hour)	37647	6876	40538	8893
影视剧类节目	(小时)	Movie and TV Play Programs	(hour)	48976	26055	56371	23314
广告类节目	(小时)	Commercial Programs	(hour)	7490	9945	9301	11767
其他类节目	(小时)	Other Programs	(hour)	25137	9226	2158	9262

注：电视台数不包括区县电视台。
资料来源：北京市新闻出版广电局。
Note: Number of television stations excludes TV stations of districts and counties.
Source: Beijing Municipal Administration of Press, Publication, Radio, Film and Television.

18-31 广播电台情况
STATISTICS FOR BROADCASTING STATIONS

项 目		Item		2013 中 央 Central	2013 地 方 Local	2012 中 央 Central	2012 地 方 Local
基本情况		**Basic Statistics**					
电台数	(座)	Number of Broadcasting Stations	(unit)	2	1	2	1
公共节目套数	(套)	Number of Public Programs	(unit)	34	25	27	25
全年公共节目播出时间	(小时)	Annual Broadcast Time of Public Programs	(hour)	432014	172870	292062	172170
播放节目情况		**Shows of Radio Programs**					
新闻咨询类节目	(小时)	News and Consulting Programs	(hour)	150206	18448	91255	18950
专题服务类节目	(小时)	Special Service Programs	(hour)	163562	35423	111099	39666
综艺类节目	(小时)	Entertainment and Education Programs	(hour)	92581	88267	64294	73536
广播剧类节目	(小时)	Radio Plays	(hour)	4686	10513	2815	8535
广告类节目	(小时)	Commercial Programs	(hour)	16518	12705	14984	14753
其他类节目	(小时)	Other Programs	(hour)	4462	7515	7614	16728

注：1. 广播电台数不包括区县电台。

2. 公共节目套数中含县级广播电视台的广播节目套数。

资料来源：北京市新闻出版广电局。

Note: a) Number of broadcasting stations excluded those of districts and counties.

b) Public programs included broadcast programs of radio stations at county levels.

Source: Beijing Municipal Administration of Press, Publication, Radio, Film and Television.

18-32 广播电视综合覆盖率(2013年)
COMPREHENSIVE COVERAGE RATE OF BROADCASTS AND TELEVISIONS (2013)

项 目		Item		2013
广播综合覆盖率	(%)	Comprehensive Coverage Rate of Broadcasts	(%)	100.0
农村广播综合覆盖率	(%)	Comprehensive Coverage Rate of Broadcasts in Rural Areas	(%)	100.0
无线广播综合覆盖率	(%)	Comprehensive Coverage Rate of Radios	(%)	100.0
电视综合覆盖率	(%)	Comprehensive Coverage Rate of Televisions	(%)	100.0
农村电视综合覆盖率	(%)	Comprehensive Coverage Rate of Televisions in Rural Areas	(%)	100.0
无线电视综合覆盖率	(%)	Comprehensive Coverage Rate of Wireless Televisions	(%)	99.75
有线广播电视入户率	(%)	Access Rate of Wire Broadcasting and Cable TVs	(%)	103.00
有线电视注册用户数	(万户)	Registered Subscribers of Cable TVs	(10000 households)	524.59
#高清交互数字电视用户数	(万户)	Subscribers of High-definition Interactive Digital Televisions	(10000 households)	380.01
付费电视用户数	(万户)	Subscribers of Pay TVs	(10000 households)	11.42
农村有线广播电视用户数	(万户)	Subscribers of Wire Broadcasting and Cable TVs in Rural Areas	(10000 households)	72.11

资料来源：北京市新闻出版广电局。

Source: Beijing Municipal Bereau Of Press,Publication,Radio,Film and Television.

18-33 报纸、期刊、图书出版情况(1978-2013年)
NEWSPAPER, MAGAZINE AND BOOK PUBLICATIONS (1978-2013)

年份 Year	报纸出版 Newspaper Publications				期刊出版 Magazines Publications				图书出版 Books Publications		
	种数(种) Types (kind)	平均期印数(万份) Average Printed Copies Per Issue (10000 copies)	总印数(亿份) Total Printed Copies (100 million copies)	总印张(亿印张) Total Sheets Printed (100 million pieces)	种数(种) Types (kind)	平均期印数(万册) Average Printed Copies Per Issue (10000 copies)	总印数(亿册) Total Printed Copies (100 million copies)	总印张(亿印张) Total Sheets Printed (100 million pieces)	种数(种) Types (kind)	总印数(亿册、亿张) Total Sheets Printed (100 million copies)	总印张(亿印张) Total Sheets Printed (100 million pieces)
1978	11		68.50		468		4.50		5253	5.12	
1979	16		81.60		697		5.92		6723	5.91	
1980	41		84.50		839		5.80		9534	6.28	
1981	55		83.10		886		6.69		11139	7.84	
1982	57		78.30		882		6.67		13862	8.71	
1983	61		79.90		940		6.84		14384	8.49	
1984	73		83.00		987		7.89		15636	8.43	
1985	99		86.00		1098		8.21		17178	9.01	
1986	126		82.00		1206		7.95		19362	5.82	
1987	129		86.00		1409		8.24		21843	6.94	
1988	151		87.00		1514		8.23		23689	7.28	
1989	161		66.00		1580		6.24		25980	6.31	
1990	148		68.00		1415		5.90		27345	6.17	
1991	157		76.70		1499		6.83		29609	7.05	
1992	164	3886	81.38	88.39	1594	6043	7.79	22.30	31320	7.83	58.67
1993	170	3965	81.70	87.71	1597	6037	7.80	22.36	34393	8.60	70.96
1994	233	3759	69.98	92.59	1854	5328	6.29	19.11	38498	8.28	71.71
1995	240	3823	72.92	108.32	1884	5018	6.38	19.62	38819	8.33	70.15
1996	242		70.52		2129		6.13		41572	9.45	
1997	242	3624	71.80	122.17	2162	5396	6.61	22.87	45775	9.93	78.62
1998	247	3561	71.70	130.01	2274	5797	7.28	26.54	50155	10.95	86.05
1999	247	3520	71.65	144.65	2273	6116	8.04	35.18	54783	11.34	93.38
2000	240	3343	68.67	149.58	2352	5909	7.91	32.96	57821	9.63	92.98
2001	243	3339	69.35	153.22	2374	5761	8.09	32.61	63928	10.27	105.06
2002	247	3364	71.02	169.87	2377	5708	8.23	34.34	73836	12.16	127.48
2003	250	3393	72.45	190.35	2382	5702	8.18	34.25	85244	13.82	140.77
2004	253	3405	70.40	206.53	2791	5233	7.97	35.53	98312	15.22	157.17
2005	255	3169	66.16	227.22	2809	4957	7.72	40.80	108152	17.07	180.51
2006	256	3651	74.01	240.39	2809	5077	8.29	47.39	113232	17.19	186.10
2007	256	3454	73.09	218.55	2809	5340	9.17	54.21	125412	18.68	195.30
2008	259	3328	73.21	241.27	2898	5392	9.36	55.39	136284	20.78	220.00
2009	260	3232	71.63	232.50	3030	5373	9.70	59.35	144211	21.04	220.21
2010	262	3406	77.54	275.62	3063	5519	10.03	69.61	155209	21.45	251.18
2011	254	3453	83.07	293.72	3044	5991	10.19	76.74	167942	22.60	243.05
2012	257	3725	89.49	300.17	3064	5940	10.31	76.68	179634	22.54	250.70
2013	254	3737	91.72	298.20	3053	6094	10.36	78.02	192137	24.01	269.54

注：1991年及以前，报纸、期刊、图书为出版数；1992年及以后均为总印数。

资料来源：北京市新闻出版广电局。

Note: Figures on newspaper, magazines and books before 1991 were figures of publications; after 1992, they were total sheet printed.

Source: Beijing Municipal Administration of Press, Publication, Radio, Film and Television.

18-34 报纸出版情况
NEWSPAPER PUBLICATION

项 目	Item	种数(种) Types of Publications (kind)		平均期印数(万份) Average Printed Copies Per Issue (10000 copies)		总印数 (亿份) Total Printed Copies (100 million copies)		总印张 (亿印张) Total Sheets Printed (100 million pieces)	
		2013	2012	2013	2012	2013	2012	2013	2012
合 计	**Total**	**254**	**257**	**3737**	**3725**	**91.7**	**89.5**	**298.2**	**300.2**
综合报	Comprehensive	30	30	1436	1382	47.2	46.0	177.3	178.2
专业报	Professional	224	227	2301	2343	44.5	43.5	120.9	121.9

资料来源：北京市新闻出版广电局。
Source: Beijing Municipal Administration of Press, Publication, Radio, Film and Television.

18-35 期刊出版情况
MAGAZINES PUBLICATION

项 目	Item	种 数 (种) Types of Publications (kind)		平均期印数 (万册) Average Copies Per Issue (10000 copies)		总 印 数 (亿册) Total Printed Copies (100 million copies)		总 印 张 (亿印张) Total Sheets Printed (100 million pieces)	
		2013	2012	2013	2012	2013	2012	2013	2012
合 计	**Total**	**3053**	**3064**	**6094**	**5940**	**10.36**	**10.31**	**78.02**	**76.68**
综 合	Comprehensive	70	70	150	167	0.37	0.40	2.67	3.19
哲学、社会科学	Philosophy and Social Sciences	906	906	3759	3484	6.43	6.20	34.61	32.82
自然科学技术	Natural Sciences and Technology	1568	1580	1280	1335	1.79	1.88	20.40	19.92
文化、教育	Culture and Education	368	369	712	761	1.37	1.46	17.46	18.14
文学、艺术	Literature and Art	141	139	194	193	0.40	0.38	2.87	2.61

资料来源：北京市新闻出版广电局。
Source: Beijing Municipal Administration of Press, Publication, Radio, Film and Television.

18-36 图书出版情况
BOOK PUBLICATION

项 目	Item	出版图书种数合计(种) Types of Publications (kind)		#新书 New Publications		总印数(万册、万张) Total Printed Copies (10000 volumes, 10000 pieces)		总印张(万印张) Total Sheets Printed (10000 print sheets)	
		2013	2012	2013	2012	2013	2012	2013	2012
合 计	**Total**	**192137**	**179634**	**111865**	**107013**	**240142**	**225411**	**2695355**	**2506987**
书籍合计	**Books**	**192047**	**179569**	**111789**	**106971**	**238106**	**223445**	**2683793**	**2490769**
马列主义、毛泽东思想	Maxism, Leninism, Mao Zedong Thought	426	318	297	203	1175	969	23225	18408
哲 学	Philosophy	5183	4993	3599	3561	3172	3388	47664	51042
社会科学总论	General Social Sciences	3287	3140	2019	1974	1845	1923	32873	34300
政治、法律	Politics and Law	13180	12239	10122	9464	13550	11407	182810	155462
军 事	Military Science	986	760	802	603	540	542	7919	7452
经 济	Economics	21520	20775	13488	13635	10875	11360	189657	194531
文化、科学、教育、体育	Culture,Science,Education and Sports	38084	34881	18644	17958	126301	121643	1010837	942051
语言、文字	Languages	12706	11979	5906	5853	21447	12809	322320	222689
文 学	Literature	15512	13938	11761	10559	14450	14615	191311	193013
艺 术	Art	8051	7408	5560	5065	4861	4732	46411	62674
历史、地理	History and Geography	8263	8029	5936	6112	8461	6282	93373	78955
自然科学总论	General Natural Sciences	381	296	257	157	252	202	2849	2589
数学科学、化学	Mathematics and Chemistry	5326	4736	2001	1870	3016	2885	49736	50102
天文学、物理科学	Astronomy and Physics	1608	1434	1129	972	555	598	7253	7375
生物科学	Biology	1629	1516	917	882	871	997	12581	12474
医药、卫生	Medicine and Healthcare	11687	10483	6726	6078	7019	7948	132823	126241
农业科学	Agricultural Sciences	3269	3453	1931	1997	1316	2060	16174	21294
工业技术	Industrial Technologies	34462	33321	16911	16609	14657	15520	261873	261673
交通运输	Transportation	3892	3334	1982	1664	2588	2059	35118	28466
航空、航天	Aeronautics and Aerospace	305	301	236	212	107	113	1545	1565
环境科学	Environmental Sciences	1289	1269	868	883	456	566	6257	7299
综合性图书	General Books	1001	966	697	660	593	827	9181	11116
图片及小件印品合计	**Pictures and Small Printed Publications**	**90**	**65**	**76**	**42**	**2036**	**1966**	**11563**	**16218**

资料来源：北京市新闻出版广电局。
Source: Beijing Municipal Administration of Press, Publication, Radio, Film and Television.

18-37 录音制品出版情况
PUBLICATION OF AUDIO PRODUCTS

项目 Item	录音带 Audio-tapes				激光唱盘 CDs				高密度激光唱盘 DVDs-A			
	种数(种) Types (kind)		数量(万盒) Number (10000 cassettes)		种数(种) Types (kind)		数量(万张) Number (10000 pieces)		种数(种) Types (kind)		数量(万张) Number (10000 pieces)	
	2013	2012	2013	2012	2013	2012	2013	2012	2013	2012	2013	2012
合计 Total	**1310**	**1267**	**15243.3**	**13904.0**	**2128**	**2014**	**2345.1**	**1345.1**	**917**	**965**	**738.7**	**1070.8**
#市属 Municipal	69	17	7.8	4.2	64	56	60.6	59.3	10	44	2.4	12.4

资料来源：北京市新闻出版广电局。
Source: Beijing Municipal Administration of Press, Publication, Radio, Film and Television.

18-38 录像制品出版情况
PUBLICATION OF VIDEO PRODUCTS

项目 Item	录像带 Videotapes				激光视盘 VCDs				高密度激光视盘 DVD-Vs			
	种数(种) Types (kind)		数量(万盒) Number (10000 cassettes)		种数(种) Kind (kind)		数量(万张) Number (10000 pieces)		种数(种) Types (kind)		数量(万张) Number (10000 pieces)	
	2013	2012	2013	2012	2013	2012	2013	2012	2013	2012	2013	2012
合计 Total	**117**	**46**	**49.8**	**20.3**	**1003**	**964**	**2590.7**	**3261.7**	**2703**	**3282**	**3459.7**	**3421.8**
#市属 Municipal	5		38.5		1	4	…	0.5	83	124	201.1	133.4

资料来源：北京市新闻出版广电局。
Source: Beijing Municipal Administration of Press, Publication, Radio, Film and Television.

18-39 电子出版物出版情况(2013年)
PUBLICATION OF E-PUBLICATIONS (2013)

项目	Item	只读光盘CD-ROMs		交互式光盘CD-Is		高密度只读光盘DVD-ROMs	
		种数(种) Types (kind)	数量(万盒) Number (10000 cassettes)	种数(种) Types (kind)	数量(万张) Number (10000 pieces)	种数(种) Types (kind)	数量(万张) Number (10000 pieces)
合计	**Total**	**4455**	**22097.8**	**1071**	**1601.4**	**2603**	**3574.1**
#市属	Municipal	19	14.96	17	0.1	35	23.6

资料来源：北京市新闻出版广电局。
Source: Beijing Municipal Administration of Press, Publication, Radio, Film and Television.

18-40 引进版权量情况
NUMBER OF IMPORTED COPYRIGHTS

项目		Item		2013	2012
引进版权量	**(件)**	**Number of Imported Copyrights**	**(set)**	**9391**	**9587**
软件和电子出版物	(件)	Softwares and E-Publications	(set)	176	233
图书	(件)	Books	(set)	9215	9354

注：2012年引进图书版权量含期刊。
资料来源：北京市新闻出版广电局。
Note: Data on number of imported copyrights in 2012 include magzines.
Source: Beijing Municipal Administration of Press, Publication, Radio, Film and Television.

主要统计指标解释

教　育

研究生培养机构　指经国家批准按国家计划招收和培养硕士、博士和其他研究生的高等学校和科学研究机构。

普通高等学校　指按国家规定的设置标准和审批程序批准举办的，通过国家统一招生考试，招收高中毕业生为主要培养对象，实施高等教育的全日制大学、独立设置的学院和高等专科学校、短期职业大学。

成人高等学校　指按国家规定的设置标准和审批程序批准举办的，通过全国成人高等教育统一招生考试，招收具有高中毕业或同等学历的人员为主要培养对象，利用函授、业余、脱产等多种形式对其实施高等学历教育的学校。包括：职工高等学校、农民高等学校、管理干部学院、教育学院、独立函授学院、广播电视大学和其他机构。

高等教育机构　指经省、自治区、直辖市教育行政部门审批并颁发办学许可证，不具有颁发学历文凭资格的实施高等教育的单位。

民办学校　指经有关主管部门批准，公民个人、社会团体及其他社会组织等利用非国家财政性教育经费，面向社会举办的学校及其他教育机构。

学历文凭考试机构　经教育行政部门专门批准，进行全日制高等教育的民办其他高等教育机构。

专科教育　应当使学生掌握本专业必备的基础理论、专门应用技术知识，具有从事本专业实际工作的基本技能和技术应用能力。全日制专科教育的基本修业年限为二至三年。

本科教育　应当使学生比较系统地掌握本学科、专业必需的基础理论、基本知识，掌握本专业必要的基本技能、方法和相关知识，具有从事本专业实际工作和研究工作的初步能力。全日制本科教育的基本修业年限为四至五年。

硕士研究生教育　应当使学生掌握本学科坚实的基础理论、系统的专业知识，掌握相应的技能、方法和相关知识，具有从事本专业实际工作和科学研究工作的能力。硕士研究生教育的基本修业年限为二至三年。

博士研究生教育　应当使学生掌握本学科坚实宽广的基础理论、系统深入的专业知识、相应的技能和方法，具有独立从事本学科创造性科学研究工作和实际工作的能力。博士研究生教育的基本修业年限为三至四年。

网络学生　指经教育部批准的现代远程教育试点学校设立的网络教育学院，基于互联网上实施高等学历教育所招收的普通和成人本科、专科学生。

在职人员攻读博士、硕士学位学生　指经国务院学位委员会批准的，为提高在职人员业务水平，通过攻读博士、硕士学位入学全国联考所招收的学生。培养的学生只有学位没有学历。

证书教育　指由各类高等教育机构举办的，招收具有高中毕业文化程度，从事专业技术工作或专业性较强的管理工作人员，经过学校学习及考试合格，取得达到岗位要求的专业知识水平证明的非学历教育。证书教育形式包括单科班和专业证书班。

单科班　指学生在学校只学一个科目中的一门或几门课程，考试合格可获得单科结业证书。

专业证书班　学生在学校学习 8 至 10 门课程，考试合格可获得岗位要求的大专层次专业知识水平的证书。

岗位培训　指由各类高等教育机构举办的，以提高本职工作能力为目的的非学历教育和培训活动。接受培训的各类人员按要求经考核合格，颁发岗位合格证书和上岗任职聘任书。岗位培训形式包括资格性培训和适应性培训。

资格性培训　指学生按照岗位规范要求取得上岗(在岗)、转岗、晋升等资格的培训。

适应性培训　指学生根据本岗位工作的发展需要而进行各种适应性的培训。

进修及培训　指对具有大学专科以上学历和中级以上职称的专业人员和管理人员进行扩展知识，提高技能的非学历教育。

外国留学生　指接受来中国学习的外籍学生。

毕业生数　指上学年度内，具有学籍的学生学完教学计划规定的全部课程，考试及格，取得毕业证书，实际毕业的学生数。不包括结业生和肄业生数。

招生数　指新学年开始时，按照国家计划实际招收入学的新生数。不包括留级生和复读学生数。

在校学生数　指学年初开学以后，具有学籍的注册学生数。

结业生数　指具有学籍的学生学习期满，有一门以上主要课程(包括毕业论文或毕业设计)不及格或其他方面不合格，未予毕业而发给结业证书的学生数。不包括短训班和单科结业学生。

教职工数　指在学校(机构)工作并由学校(机构)支付工资的教职工人数。教职工数包括校本部教职工、科研机构人员、校办企业职工、其他附设机构人员。

专任教师　指主要从事教育工作的人员。包括临时（一年以内）调去帮助做其他工作的教学人员。不包括调离教学岗位，担任行政领导工作或其他工作的原教学人员；不包括兼任教师和代课教师。

特殊教育学校 指招收盲聋哑青少年进行初中等教育的学校。

校舍建筑面积 指产权归学校所有，已经使用的各种用房的建筑面积。不包括尚未竣工的在建工程和借用、租用的房舍或临时搭用的棚舍。

危房面积 指年久失修、结构构件受到严重损坏，有倒塌危险，经房管部门鉴定属于危房的面积。

学校占地面积 指学校校园内的土地面积，不包括校园外学校拥有的农场、林场及校办工厂等的土地面积。

文 化

公共图书馆藏书 指各级文化部门举办的面向社会服务的独立的图书馆（不包括文化馆的图书室，也不包括文化系统以外的图书馆）藏书数量。

艺术剧团 指从事戏曲、音乐、舞蹈、杂技等专业艺术表演，有独立账户、实行独立核算的团体。不包括半工半艺和民间职业剧团。

广播电视

广播综合覆盖率 根据国家广电总局制定的《广播电视人口覆盖率统计技术标准和方法》进行统计调查的，在对象区内能接收到广播节目的覆盖人口数占本行政区域内人口总数的比率。

农村广播综合覆盖率 根据国家广电总局制定的《广播电视人口覆盖率统计技术标准和方法》进行统计调查的，在对象区内能接收到广播节目的农村人口数占本行政区域内农村人口总数的比率。农村是指经国家批准设立的乡镇人民政府的乡和农村建制镇所辖区，不包括县政府驻地镇。

无线广播综合覆盖率 根据国家广电总局制定的《广播电视人口覆盖率统计技术标准和方法》进行统计调查的，在对象区内能接收到用中、短波、调频等无线传输技术发射转播的广播节目的人口数占本行政区域内人口总数的比率。包括中央、省、地市、县四级无线广播综合覆盖人口。

电视综合覆盖率 根据国家广电总局制定的《广播电视人口覆盖率统计技术标准和方法》进行统计调查的，在对象区内能接收到电视节目的人口数占本行政区域内人口总数的比率，包括中央、省、地市、县电视节目综合覆盖人口。

农村电视综合覆盖率 根据国家广电总局制定的《广播电视人口覆盖率统计技术标准和方法》进行统计调查的，在对象区内能接收到电视节目的农村人口数占本行政区域内农村人口总数的比率，包括中央、省、地市、县电视节目综合覆盖农村人口。农村是指经国家批准设立的乡镇人民政府的乡和农村建制镇所辖区，不包括县政府驻地镇。

无线电视综合覆盖率 根据国家广电总局制定的《广播电视人口覆盖率统计技术标准和方法》进行统计调查的，在对象区内能接收到用中、短波、调频等无线传输技术发射转播的电视节目的人口数占本行政区域内人口总数的比率。包括中央、省、地市、县四级无线电视综合覆盖人口。

有线电视入户率 指通过广播电视有线传输网收看电视节目的家庭用户数（包括接收模拟信号和接收数字信号的有线电视用户数，不包括宾馆、单位、写字楼等集体用户）与本行政区域内总户数的比率。

数字电视用户数 指通过广播电视有线传输网收看数字信号电视节目的家庭用户数。

付费电视用户数 指通过广播电视有线传输网收看数字信号的电视节目，并交纳收看费的有线电视家庭用户数。

Explanatory Notes on Main Statistical Indicators

Education

Institutions Providing Postgraduate Programs refer to colleges and universities, research institutions recruiting and educating postgraduates of master's degree, doctor's degree and other degree upon approval by the government and under the State Plan.

Regular Institutions of Higher Education refer to educational establishments set up according to the government evaluation and approval procedures, recruiting graduates from senior secondary schools as the main target by National Matriculation Test. They include full-time universities, independent colleges and higher professional schools, short-term vocational colleges.

Adult Institutions of Higher Education refer to educational establishments, set up in line with relevant rules approved by the government, recruiting personnel with senior high school or equivalent educational diploma through national college entrance test for adults, and providing higher education courses in many forms of correspondence, spare-time, or full-time teaching for adults. Institutions of higher learning for adults include schools of higher education for staff and workers, schools of higher education for farmers, colleges for management cadres, pedagogical colleges, independent correspondence colleges, Radio and TV universities and other educational establishments.

Higher Education Institutions refer to institutions offering higher education upon examination and approval by administrative departments in charge of education in provinces, autonomous regions and municipalities, with an education license, which are not eligible for conferring diploma.

Civilian-run Schools refer to schools and other educational institutions run by individuals, social groups and other social organizations upon approval by relevant competent authorities, by using educational funds not from state revenues.

Diploma Test Institutions refer to other civilian-run higher education institutions offering full-time higher education upon special approval by educational administration.

Undergraduate Education shall enable students to understand necessary basic theories and knowledge of a subject or specialty, have necessary basic skills, methodology and relevant knowledge of the specialty, and have preliminary skills for practical work and research of the specialty. Full-time undergraduate education offers a basic study term of 4-5 years.

Secondary Technical Education shall enable students to understand necessary basic theories and special knowledge on applied technologies of a specialty, have basic skills and technical application ability for practice of the specialty. Full-time secondary technically education offers a basic study term of 2-3 years.

Master's-degree Postgraduate Education shall enable students to understand solid basic theories, systematic professional knowledge of a subject, have relevant skills, methodology and relevant knowledge of the specialty, and have preliminary skills for practical work and research of the specialty. Master's-degree postgraduate education offers a basic study term of 2-3 years.

Doctor's-degree Postgraduate Education shall enable students to understand solid and extensive basic theories, systematic and in-depth professional knowledge, relevant skills and methodology of a subject, have relevant skills, methodology and relevant knowledge of the specialty, and have preliminary skills for independent creative research and practical work of the specialty. Doctor's-degree postgraduate education offers a basic study term of 3-4 years.

Online Students refer to students for Internet-based general higher courses, undergraduate courses for adults, and secondary technical courses recruited in online education colleges opened in schools as modern remote education pilots approved by the Ministry of Education.

Employees Enrolled in Graduate Programs refer to students recruited through national joint test for studies of Doctor's and Master's degrees approved by the Academic Degree Commission of the State Council, in order to improve the practical skills of on-the-job personnel. Graduated students will be conferred academic degree only, without academic credentials.

Certificate Education refers education not for academic credentials, run by various higher education institutions that recruit management personnel who are graduated from senior high schools and engaged in professional technical work or strongly professional management work, and receive a certificate for professional knowledge level meeting the requirements of their job position after studying in the school and pass the test. It consists of single-subject program and professional certificate program.

Single-subject Program means that students study only one or more courses of one subject, and will be awarded a certificate of completion of single subject.

Professional Certificate Program means that students study 8-10 courses in the school, and will be awarded a certificate for professional knowledge at junior college level required for their job.

Occupational Training refers to educational and training activities not for academic credentials, aiming to improve the competence, run by various higher education institutions. Various trainees will be awarded Occupational

Incumbency Certification and Engagement Certification. The occupational training is in the form of qualification training and adaptability training.

Qualification Training means any training for students to become qualified for being employed (reemployed) on a job, transfer of job, and promotion as required by job criterion.

Adaptability Training means that students receive training for adaptability in line with needs of their own job.

Advanced Studies and Trainings means education not for academic credentials, offered for professional and managers with educational background of college and above, and technical title above middle rank, to expand their knowledge and improve their skill.

Foreign Students Studying in China refers to foreign students who study in China.

Number of Graduated Students means the number of enrolled students who are actually graduated after passing all exams and receiving a diploma upon completing all courses stated in the teaching plan within the last academic year. This does not include the number of students completing all courses with any one course not passed, and students not completing all courses or discontinuing their schooling.

Number of New Students refers to the number of students actually recruited at the beginning of an academic year in line with State plan, excluding the number of students failing to go up to the next grade and those resuming their interrupted studies.

Number of Enrolled Students means the number of students enrolled at the beginning of a new academic year.

Number of Students Completing Courses means the number of enrolled students completing their schooling with one and more courses not passed (including the graduation paper or graduation design) or other aspects not passed, who are not granted for graduation and awarded a certificate of completion, excluding the number of students completing short-term training courses and single-subject programs.

Faculty Number means the number of faculty working in and paid by schools (institutions). It includes the number of teachers and workers in the principal campus, in research institutions, school-run enterprises and other subsidiaries.

Teachers refer to full-time teaching personnel, including persons temporarily transferred to other jobs, excluding persons transferred from teaching to administrative leadership.

Full-time Teachers refer to personnel mainly engaged in teaching, including persons temporarily (within one year) transferred to other jobs, excluding persons transferred from teaching to administrative leadership or other jobs; excluding part-time teachers and teachers taking over a class for absent teachers.

Schools for Special Education mean schools recruiting blind, deaf and mute teenagers for primary and secondary education.

Floor Space of Schoolhouse refers to the building area of various houses of which the property right is owned by the school and which have been used, excluding houses not completed and under construction, borrowed and rented, or temporarily built sheds and houses.

Area of Dilapidated Houses refers to the area of those houses that have not been repaired for many years, have seriously damaged components, are at the risk of collapse, and are identified by the house administration authority as dilapidated houses.

Area of Land Occupied by School means the area of land within campus, excluding the area of land for farms and forest land outside schools and school-run factories.

Culture

Collection of Books in Public Libraries means the number of books collected in independent libraries open to the public and run by all-level cultural bodies (excluding book rooms in culture centers, and books collected in libraries not included in the cultural system).

Art Troupes refer to groups engaged drama and opera, music, dancing, acrobatics, and other professional art performance, keeping independent accounts. They exclude spare-time and folk vocational art performance troupes.

Radio and Television

Comprehensive Coverage Rate of Broadcast means the share of population who can receive broadcasting programs in the target area, calculated in line with Statistical Standard and Method on Television and Radio Coverage of Population established by the State Administration of Broadcasting, Film and Television, of the total population in the administrative area.

Comprehensive Coverage Rate of Broadcast in Rural Area means the share of rural population who can receive broadcasting programs in the target area, calculated in line with Statistical Standard and Method on Television and Radio Coverage of Population established by the National Administration of Broadcasting, Film and Television, of the total rural population in the administrative area. Rural area means villages of towns with people's governments approved by the State and areas under the jurisdiction of rural towns with organizational system, excluding towns where people's governments of counties are located.

Comprehensive Coverage Rate of Radio means the share of population who can receive broadcasting programs transmitted with short-wave, medium-wave, FM and other radio transmission technologies in the target area, calculated in line with Statistical Standard and Method on Television and Radio Coverage of Population established by the National Administration of Broadcasting, Film and Television, of the total population in the administrative area, including the population covered by broadcasting programs from central, provincial, prefectural cities and county radio stations.

Comprehensive Coverage Rate of TV means the share of population who can receive TV programs in the target area, calculated in line with Statistical Standard and Method on Television and Radio Coverage of Population established by the

National Administration of Broadcasting, Film and Television, of the total population in the administrative area, including the population covered by TV programs from central, provincial, prefectural cities and county TV stations.

Comprehensive Coverage Rate of TV in Rural Area means the share of rural population who can receive TV programs in the target area, calculated in line with Statistical Standard and Method on Television and Radio Coverage of Population established by the National Administration of Broadcasting, Film and Television, of the total rural population in the administrative area, including the population covered by TV programs from central, provincial, prefectural cities and county TV stations. Rural area means villages of towns with people's governments approved by the State and areas under the jurisdiction of rural towns with organizational system, excluding towns where people's governments of counties are located.

Comprehensive Coverage Rate of Wireless TV means the share of population who can receive TV programs transmitted with short-wave, medium-wave, FM and other radio transmission technologies in the target area, calculated in line with Statistical Standard and Method on Television and Radio Coverage of Population established by the National Administration of Broadcasting, Film and Television, of the total population in the administrative area, including the population covered by radio television programs from central, provincial, prefectural cities and county TV stations.

Access Rate of CATV refers to the percentage of households which can watch television programs by cable broadcasting and television transmission network (including cable TV households receiving analog signals and digital signals, excluding collective subscribers such as hotels, companies and entities, office buildings), to the total households in the administrative area).

Number of Digital Broadcast/TV Subscribers means the number of households watching digital-signal TV programs through the TV and radio cable transmission network.

Number of Pay TV Subscribers means the number of cable TV households watching digital-signal TV programs through the TV and radio cable transmission network and paying fees for watching.

19

北京统计年鉴2014　BEIJING STATISTICAL YEARBOOK

科　技
SCIENCE AND TECHNOLOGY

简要说明

一、本章资料的主要内容

本章主要包括：研究与试验发展（R&D）人员情况，研究与试验发展（R&D）经费情况，研究与试验发展（R&D）项目（课题）情况，研究机构情况，规模以上工业企业 R&D 活动基本情况，限额以上信息传输、软件和信息技术服务业企业研究与试验发展(R&D)活动基本情况，规模以上高技术制造业主要科技指标，高等学校科技活动情况、研究与开发机构研发活动、专利申请及授权情况等。

二、本章资料的统计范围

国民经济中研究与试验发展（R&D）活动相对密集行业的法人单位。2013 年主要数据包括：农、林、牧、渔业，采矿业，制造业，电力、热力、燃气及水的生产和供应业，建筑业，交通运输、仓储和邮政业，信息传输、软件和信息技术服务业，金融业，租赁和商务服务业，科学研究和技术服务业，水利、环境和公共设施管理业，教育，卫生和社会工作，文化、体育和娱乐业，公共管理、社会保障和社会组织等。

三、本章资料的数据来源

本章由北京市统计局、北京市科学技术委员会、北京市教育委员会、北京市经济和信息化委员会、北京市人力资源和社会保障局、北京市知识产权局、北京市质量技术监督局、北京市科学技术协会、北京技术市场管理办公室等部门提供。

四、有关统计标准的变化说明

（一）关于行业划分。根据国家统计局规定，自 2012 年开始执行《国民经济行业分类》（GB/T 4754-2011）标准。

（二）关于三次产业划分。根据国家统计局《三次产业划分规定》（国统字[2012]108 号），该规定对三次产业的范围进行了调整。其中第一产业是指农、林、牧、渔业（不含农、林、牧、渔服务业）；第二产业是指采矿业（不含开采辅助活动），制造业（不含金属制品、机械和设备修理业），电力、热力、燃气及水生产和供应业，建筑业；第三产业是指除第一产业、第二产业以外的其他行业。自 2012 年开始执行此规定。

（三）关于高技术制造业。根据国家统计局《关于印发高技术产业（制造业）分类（2013）的通知》（国统字〔2013〕55 号）。本分类在《高技术产业统计分类目录》（国统字〔2002〕33 号）的基础上修订完成，采用了原分类的基本结构框架。自 2013 年开始执行此标准。

Brief Introduction

I. Main Content

Data in this chapter reflect the situation of scientific and technological activities and patents, R&D personnel, R&D funds, R&D projects (tasks), research institutions, basic information on R&D of industrial enterprises above the designated size, basic information on R&D of information transmission, software and information technology service enterprises, scientific and technological activities of colleges and universities, R&D of research institutions and personnel, patent application and licensing, etc.

II. Scope of Statistics

Included in this chapter are the corporate entities in sectors with relatively intensive R&D activities in national economy, such as agriculture, forestry, animal husbandry, fishery, mining, manufacturing, generation and distribution of electricity, heat, gas and water, construction, transport, storage and post, scientific research and development, technology services, information transmission, software and information technology services, finance, renting and leasing activities and business services, management of water conservancy, environment and public facilities, education, healthcare and social works, culture, sports and entertainment, public administration, social security and social organizations, etc.

III. Source of Data

Data in this chapter are from Beijing Municipal Bureau of Statistics, Beijing Municipal Science & Technology Commission, Beijing Municipal Commission of Education, Beijing Municipal Commission of Economy and Information Technology, Beijing Municipal Bureau of Human Resources and Social Security, Beijing Intellectual Property Bureau, Beijing Municipal Bureau of Quality and Technology Supervision, Beijing Municipal Association of Science and Technology, and Beijing Technical Market Management Office, etc.

Ⅳ. Changes in Relevant Statistical Standards

(I) Classification of Sectors. According to relevant provisions of National Bureau of Statistics, the Standard for Classification of National Economic Sectors (GB/T4754-2011) became effective in 2012.

(II) Classification of Primary, Secondary, and Tertiary Industries. According to the provision of National Bureau of Statistics on Classification of Three Industries (GTZ[2012]No.108), the scope of three industries has changed. The primary industry includes agriculture, forestry, animal husbandry and fishery (excluding agricultural, forestry, animal husbandry and fishery services); the secondary industry includes mining (excluding mining support activities), manufacturing (excluding metal products, machinery and equipment repairing), production and distribution of electricity, heat, natural gas and water and construction industry; the tertiary industry means industries other than the primary and secondary industries. The Provisions of the National Bureau of Statistics on Classification of Three Industries (GTZ [2012] No. 108) came into effect in 2012.

(III) High-tech Manufacturing. According to the Circular of National Bureau of Statistics on Printing and Issuing the Classification of High-tech Industry (Manufacturing) 2013 (GTZ [2013], No. 55). This Classification is revised on the basis of Classified Catalog of High-tech Industry Statistics (GTZ [2002], No. 33), following the structure of the original classification. The standard has been put in place since 2013.

19-1 科技活动及专利情况(1985-2013年)
SCIENCE AND TECHNOLOGY ACTIVITIES AND PATENTS (1985-2013)

年 份 Year	科技活动人员 (人) Personnel Engaged in Science and Technology Activities (person)	研究与试验发展(R&D)人员折合全时当量 (人年) Full-time Equivalent of R&D Professionals (person-year)	研究与试验发展(R&D)经费内部支出 (万元) Internal R&D Expenditures (10000 yuan)	研究与试验发展(R&D)经费内部支出相当于地区生产总值比例(%) Internal R&D Expenditures as Percentage of GDP (%)
1985				
1986-1990				
1986				
1987				
1988				
1989				
1990				
1991-1995				
1991	228167			
1992	247525			
1993	252811			
1994	240386			
1995	252232			
1996-2000			**4307457**	
1996	265552	84793	418614	2.34
1997	273161	84913	532257	2.56
1998	237127	86602	861138	3.62
1999	229584	85740	938437	3.50
2000	261113	98723	1557011	4.92
2001-2005			**13434129**	
2001	240609	95255	1711696	4.62
2002	257326	114919	2195402	5.09
2003	270921	110358	2562518	5.12
2004	301202	152132	3169064	5.25
2005	383153	177765	3795450	5.45
2006-2010			**30706037**	
2006	382756	168875	4329878	5.33
2007	450331	204668	5270591	5.35
2008	450147	200080	6200983	5.58
2009	529985	191779	6686351	5.50
2010	529811	193718	8218234	5.82
2011	605980	217255	9366440	5.76
2012	651003	235493	10633640	5.95
2013	681346	242175	11850469	6.08

资料来源：北京市统计局、北京市科学技术委员会、北京市教育委员会、北京市经济和信息化委员会、北京市知识产权局。

Source: Beijing Municipal Bureau of Statistics, Beijing Municipal Science & Technology Commission, Beijing Municipal Commission of Education, Beijing Municipal Commission of Economy and Information Technology, Beijing Intellectual Property Office.

19-1 续表 Continued

年 份 Year	专 利 申请量 (件) Patent Applications (unit)	发 明 Inventions	实用新型 Utility Models	外观设计 Industrial Designs	专 利 授权量 (件) Patents Granted (unit)	发 明 Inventions	实用新型 Utility Models	外观设计 Industrial Designs
1985	1540	754	720	66				
1986-1990	**15087**	**3332**	**11003**	**752**	**6700**	**737**	**5614**	**349**
1986	1692	535	1091	66	491	43	408	40
1987	2425	523	1796	106	776	102	630	44
1988	3342	702	2494	146	1376	169	1147	60
1989	3344	742	2408	194	1789	207	1497	85
1990	4284	830	3214	240	2268	216	1932	120
1991-1995	**31126**	**6604**	**21787**	**2736**	**19379**	**1801**	**15835**	**1743**
1991	4624	1023	3324	277	2369	263	1917	189
1992	6316	1340	4493	483	3265	312	2724	229
1993	6972	1483	4931	558	5806	530	4780	496
1994	6852	1506	4666	680	3914	368	3245	301
1995	6362	1252	4372	738	4025	328	3169	528
1996-2000	**37296**	**10344**	**20395**	**6557**	**22156**	**2483**	**14836**	**4837**
1996	6595	1441	4255	899	3295	246	2563	486
1997	6313	1678	3667	968	3327	281	2340	706
1998	6321	1754	3444	1123	3800	309	2522	969
1999	7723	2062	4045	1616	5829	573	3948	1308
2000	10344	3409	4984	1951	5905	1074	3463	1368
2001-2005	**83993**	**39312**	**30960**	**13721**	**39944**	**10960**	**20019**	**8965**
2001	12174	4984	5114	2076	6246	946	3600	1700
2002	13842	5785	5920	2137	6345	1061	3721	1563
2003	17003	7833	6665	2505	8248	2261	4244	1743
2004	18402	8608	6321	3473	9005	3216	3956	1833
2005	22572	12102	6940	3530	10100	3476	4498	2126
2006-2010	**209275**	**124175**	**62237**	**22863**	**100371**	**35532**	**48350**	**16489**
2006	26555	14226	8200	4129	11238	3864	5490	1884
2007	31680	18763	8819	4098	14954	4824	7364	2766
2008	43508	28394	11157	3957	17747	6478	8776	2493
2009	50236	29326	15424	5486	22921	9157	10141	3623
2010	57296	33466	18637	5193	33511	11209	16579	5723
2011	77955	45057	26615	6283	40888	15880	19628	5380
2012	92305	52720	32609	6976	50511	20140	24672	5699
2013	123336	67554	47586	8196	62671	20695	36301	5675

19-2 研究与试验发展(R&D)活动人员情况

项　目	Item	研究与试验发展(R&D)人员(人) R&D Personnel (person)	
		2013	2012
合　计	**Total**	**334194**	**322417**
按执行部门分	**By Executive Department**		
企　业	Enterprises	142522	138601
工业企业	Industrial Enterprises	79368	75543
非工业企业	Non-industrial Enterprises	63154	63058
科研机构	Scientific Research Institutions	107796	103017
高等学校	Institutions of Higher Education	72905	69615
事业单位	Public Institutions	10971	11184
按隶属关系分	**By Affiliation**		
中　央	Central	200192	193523
地　方	Local	134002	128894
按行业门类分	**By Sector**		
#制造业	Manufacturing	73710	70458
信息传输、软件和信息技术服务业	Information Transmission, Software and Information Technology Services	36242	30944
科学研究和技术服务业	Scientific Research and Development, Technical Services	126994	121502
教　育	Education	72905	69951

注：行业划分执行2011年国民经济行业分类标准(GB/T 4754-2011)。
资料来源：北京市统计局、北京市科学技术委员会、北京市教育委员会、北京市经济和信息化委员会。

RESEARCH AND DEVELOPMENT PERSONNEL

#本科及以上学历 Bachelor Degree or above		研究与试验发展(R&D)人员折合全时当量(人年) Full-time Equivalent of R&D Professionals (person-year)							
				基础研究 Basic Research		应用研究 Applied Research		试验发展 Experimental Development	
2013	2012	2013	2012	2013	2012	2013	2012	2013	2012
217982	**218303**	**242175**	**235493**	**35933**	**34603**	**59253**	**57824**	**146991**	**143066**
52478	60098	107245	105506	487	499	3125	4169	103636	100838
25869	26659	58036	53510	120	163	578	1198	57337	52149
26609	33439	49209	51996	366	336	2547	2971	46299	48689
93649	88739	96249	92577	22432	21309	34834	33325	38983	37943
66780	64161	32307	31239	12212	11878	19076	18276	1020	1085
5075	5305	6373	6171	803	917	2218	2054	3353	3200
159131	153798	150139	146005	31491	30407	49085	47026	69563	68572
58851	64505	92036	89488	4442	4196	10168	10798	77428	74494
25045	25925	54158	49616	118	116	578	528	53462	48972
10652	12173	28324	27032		57	848	881	27476	26094
111032	105082	112978	108027	23053	21883	37235	35285	52690	50859
66780	64493	32307	31438	12212	11941	19076	18340	1020	1157

Note: Sectors in this table are classified in accordance with the Standard for Classification of National Economic Sectors 2011 (GB/T 4754-2011).

Source: Beijing Municipal Bureau of Statistics, Beijing Municipal Science & Technology Commission, Beijing Municipal Commission of Education, Beijing Municipal Commission of Economy and Information Technology.

19-3 研究与试验发展(R&D)经费情况

单位：万元

项目	Item	研究与试验发展(R&D)经费内部支出 Internal R&D Expenditures		按活动类型分 Group by Type of Activity			
				基础研究 Basic Research		应用研究 Applied Research	
		2013	2012	2013	2012	2013	2012
合　计	**Total**	**11850469**	**10633640**	**1372366**	**1258199**	**2580388**	**2418132**
按执行部门分	**By Executive Department**						
企　业	Enterprises	4283298	4213920	28035	20833	182563	208350
工业企业	Industrial Enterprises	2130618	1973442	3086	1883	22176	28952
非工业企业	Non-industrial Enterprises	2152681	2240478	24950	18950	160387	179398
科研机构	Scientific Research Institutions	6023924	4885351	841732	750378	1545116	1404913
高等学校	Institutions of Higher Education	1366460	1369404	481664	467476	805499	767061
事业单位	Public Institutions	176787	164965	20934	19512	47210	37808
按隶属关系分	**By Affiliation**						
中　央	Central	8815089	7592953	1305688	1193367	2351800	2154411
地　方	Local	3035380	3040687	66678	64832	228588	263721
按行业门类分	**By Sector**						
#制造业	Manufacturing	2035064	1880965	2911	1180	22176	20759
信息传输、软件和信息技术服务业	Information Transmission, Software and Information Technology Services	1103590	1117841		1264	43565	57578
科学研究和技术服务业	Scientific Research and Development, Technical Services	6949711	5753870	880682	778661	1683657	1523888
教　育	Education	1366460	1375309	481664	469415	805499	768834

注：行业划分执行2011年国民经济行业分类标准(GB/T 4754-2011)。

资料来源：北京市统计局、北京市科学技术委员会、北京市教育委员会、北京市经济和信息化委员会。

RESEARCH AND EXPERIMENTAL DEVELOPMENT FUNDS

(10000 yuan)

试验发展 Experimental Development		按支出用途分 Group by Purpose of Payment							
		日常性支出 Routine Expenses		#人员劳务费 Labor Cost		资产性支出 Expenditures for Assets		#仪器和设备 Instruments and Equipment	
2013	2012	2013	2012	2013	2012	2013	2012	2013	2012
7897716	**6957309**	**10020407**	**8967244**	**3222578**	**2806947**	**1830062**	**1666396**	**1340780**	**1239551**
4072700	3984737	3907659	3797012	1969387	1705844	375639	416908	348254	383855
2105356	1942607	2032446	1870499	808964	729277	98172	102943	95693	102007
1967344	2042130	1875214	1926513	1160423	976567	277467	313965	252562	281848
3637076	2730060	4775244	3879542	1037646	882732	1248680	1005809	794287	642531
79296	134867	1179844	1150016	156457	170283	186616	219388	180260	189532
108643	107645	157660	140674	59089	48088	19127	24291	17979	23633
5157602	4245175	7218325	6210491	1686837	1492357	1596765	1382462	1115950	960681
2740114	2712134	2802082	2756753	1535741	1314590	233298	283934	224830	278870
2009977	1859026	1942951	1782478	778704	702954	92113	98487	89675	97613
1060025	1058999	999386	972055	780215	587117	104204	145786	102685	145315
4385372	3451321	5552943	4618021	1355924	1167692	1396768	1135849	919061	747487
79296	137060	1179844	1155921	156457	171487	186616	219388	180260	189532

Note: Sectors in this table are classified in accordance with the Standard for Classification of National Economic Sectors 2011 (GB/T 4754-2011).

Source: Beijing Municipal Bureau of Statistics, Beijing Municipal Science & Technology Commission, Beijing Municipal Commission of Education, Beijing Municipal Commission of Economy and Information Technology.

19-3 续表 Continued

单位：万元 (10000 yuan)

项目	Item	按资金来源分 Group by Fund Source							
		政府资金 Governmental Funds		企业资金 Enterprise Funds		国外资金 Foreign Funds		其他资金 Others	
		2013	2012	2013	2012	2013	2012	2013	2012
合计	**Total**	**6795421**	**5659921**	**4011290**	**3686332**	**381571**	**478994**	**662188**	**808393**
按执行部门分	**By Executive Department**								
企业	Enterprises	409748	386104	3446361	3226816	338223	433438	88967	167562
工业企业	Industrial Enterprises	227527	178377	1819635	1736105	16765	8983	66691	49977
非工业企业	Non-industrial Enterprises	182220	207727	1626726	1490711	321458	424455	22277	117585
科研机构	Scientific Research Institutions	5317749	4208980	156745	75393	19098	15298	530332	585680
高等学校	Institutions of Higher Education	925233	929647	397842	378033	22680	29157	20705	32567
事业单位	Public Institutions	142691	135190	10342	6090	1570	1101	22183	22584
按隶属关系分	**By Affiliation**								
中央	Central	6442980	5297809	1705465	1480270	45100	46089	621545	768785
地方	Local	352441	362112	2305825	2206062	336471	432905	40643	39608
按行业门类分	**By Sector**								
#制造业	Manufacturing	220221	169302	1731395	1652919	16757	8767	66691	49977
信息传输、软件和信息技术服务业	Information Transmission, Software and Information Technology Services	25395	38008	808298	758512	256185	307552	13712	13769
科学研究和技术服务业	Scientific Research and Development, Technical Services	5587077	4440143	723820	475917	80124	132190	558690	705620
教育	Education	925233	931744	397842	379175	22680	29157	20705	35233

19-4 单位内部办研发机构情况
STATISTICS FOR IN-HOUSE RESEARCH INSTITUTIONS

项 目	Item	机构数 (个) Number of Institutions (unit)		机构研究与试验发展(R&D)人员 (人) R&D Personnel (Person)		机构研究与试验发展(R&D)经费支出 (万元) R&D Expenditures (10000 yuan)	
		2013	2012	2013	2012	2013	2012
合 计	**Total**	**2362**	**2482**	**175098**	**175322**	**8570151**	**7460008**
按机构所属学科分	**By Subject of Institution**						
自然科学	Natural Science	151	142	28698	27394	1091631	969224
农业科学	Agricultural Science	75	68	5427	5088	205308	194797
医药科学	Medical Science	104	99	9753	8686	263555	234875
工程与技术科学	Engineering and Techical Science	1689	1807	120352	124002	6815392	5885848
人文与社会科学	Humanities and Social Science	343	366	10868	10152	194265	175264
按机构组成类型分	**By Institution Composition**						
政府部门办	Run by Government Agency	531	531	119291	116778	6638914	5485454
与国内高校合办	Jointly Run with Domestic Colleges and Universities	29	38	568	809	35590	30436
与国内独立研究机构合办	Jointly Run with Domestic Independent Research Institutions	13	8	242	112	1361	574
与境外机构合办	Jointly Run with Overseas Institutions	10	7	110	78	3514	801
与境内注册外商独资企业合办	Jointly Run with Solely Foreign-invseted Enterprises Registered in China						
与境内注册其他企业合办	Jointly Run with Other Enterprises Registered in China	62	56	1186	904	31968	35412
单位自办	Self Run	1714	1837	53620	56532	1858526	1907047
其 他	Others	3	5	81	109	279	284

资料来源：北京市统计局、北京市科学技术委员会、北京市教育委员会、北京市经济和信息化委员会。
Source: Beijing Municipal Bureau of Statistics, Beijing Municipal Science & Technology Commission, Beijing Municipal Commission of Education, Beijing Municipal Commission of Economy and Information Technology.

19-5 研究与试验发展(R&D)项目(课题)情况
R&D PROJECTS (TASKS)

项　目	Item	项目(课题)数 (项) Number of Projects (Tasks) (unit)		项目(课题)人员折合全时当量 (人年) Full-time Equivalent of Project (Task) Personnel (person-year)		项目(课题)经费内部支出 (万元) Internal Project (Task) Expenditures (10000 yuan)	
		2013	2012	2013	2012	2013	2012
合　计	**Total**	**118710**	**109514**	**221745**	**217963**	**8976148**	**8427518**
按项目(课题)来源分	**By Source**						
国家科技项目	National Science and Technology Projects	50858	48100	99271	99000	4824349	4553968
地方科技项目	Local Science and Technology Projects	10741	9743	10661	9789	204324	167292
企业委托科技项目	Science and Technology Projects Entrusted by Enterprises	27103	24731	18460	16463	713566	574382
自选科技项目	Self-chosen Science and Technology Projects	24926	21991	72307	71691	2178371	2030674
来自国外的科技项目	Science and Technology Projects from Foreign Countries	1983	2050	9649	9982	486664	585921
其它科技项目	Other Science and Technology Projects	3098	2899	11398	11038	568875	515281
按项目(课题)合作形式分	**By Form of Cooperation**						
与境外机构合作	Cooperating with Overseas Institutions	1693	1618	7142	6961	294901	325760
与国内高校合作	Cooperating with Domestic Colleges and Universities	6517	5843	14378	14702	465650	582329
与国内独立研究机构合作	Cooperating with Domestic Independent Research Institutions	8419	7921	17846	19050	672088	779987
与境内注册外商独资企业合作	Cooperating with solely Foreign-invested Enterprises Registered in China	273	231	544	584	19835	43102
与境内注册其他企业合作	Cooperating with Other Enterprises Registered in China	6036	6124	11125	13413	494328	460438
独立完成	Independent	92661	84992	163614	157504	6727168	6026612
其　他	Others	3110	2785	7098	5749	302179	209290
按项目(课题)活动类型分	**By Type of Project (Task) Activity**						
基础研究	Basic Research	38584	35704	33562	32564	981414	927333
应用研究	Applied Research	57202	52504	55987	54607	1926244	1813321
试验发展	Experimental Development	22924	21306	132196	130792	6068491	5686864
按项目(课题)社会经济目标分	**By Social and Economic Objective**						
#环境保护及污染防治	Environmental Protection and Pollution Prevention and Control	5309	4541	7237	5483	214590	171020
促进能源的生产、分配和合理利用	Promotion of Production, Allocation and Reasonable Utilization of Energy	6990	6195	12026	10848	518601	404666
促进卫生事业的发展	Promotion of Public Health	8074	6893	15742	14884	218153	194113
促进教育事业的发展	Promotion of Education	9832	8916	2878	2714	47538	39841
基础设施以及城市和农村规划	Infrastructure,Urban and Rural Planning	6750	6672	10196	11042	341234	418050

资料来源：北京市统计局、北京市科学技术委员会、北京市教育委员会、北京市经济和信息化委员会。
Source: Beijing Municipal Bureau of Statistics, Beijing Municipal Science & Technology Commission, Beijing Municipal Commission of Education, Beijing Municipal Commission of Economy and Information Technology.

19-5 续表 Continued

项　目	Item	项目(课题)数 (项) Number of Projects (Tasks) (unit)		项目(课题)人员折合全时当量 (人年) Full-time Equivalent of Project (Task) Personnel (person-year)		项目(课题)经费内部支出 (万元) Internal Project (Task) Expenditures (10000 yuan)	
		2013	2012	2013	2012	2013	2012
社会发展和社会服务	Social Development and Social Service	13908	14832	9274	14024	228562	308029
地球和大气层的探索和利用	Exploration and Exploitation of Earth and Aerosphere	3273	2865	5948	5022	173489	157189
民用空间的探测及开发	Exploration and Exploitation of Civil Space	833	930	1158	1747	69894	73494
促进农林牧渔业发展	Promotion of Agriculture, Forestry, Animal Production and Hunting, Fishing	6569	5609	6870	7076	223512	231423
促进工商业发展	Promotion of Industry and Commerce	24312	21662	85126	82659	2958249	2941252
非定向研究	Non-oriented Research	24374	22357	21442	20463	730887	655626
按项目(课题)服务的国民经济行业分	**By Sector of National Economy Served**						
农、林、牧、渔业	Agriculture, Forestry, Animal Production and Hunting, Fishing	5891	4926	5838	6082	189682	194268
采矿业	Mining and Quarrying	2803	2932	6490	6741	262905	240969
制造业	Manufacturing	23094	20395	60229	58466	2183949	2123530
电力、热力、燃气及水生产和供应业	Production and Distribution of Electricity, Heating Power, Gas, Water	1919	1549	2934	2113	83077	64070
建筑业	Construction	2826	2893	6642	6738	182137	161132
批发和零售业	Wholesale and Retail Trade	255	121	167	59	7053	1037
交通运输、仓储和邮政业	Transport, Storage and Post	2664	2968	2452	3206	85699	137945
住宿和餐饮业	Accommodation and Restaurants	173	243	48	109	650	2938
信息传输、软件和信息技术服务业	Information Transmission,Software and Information Technology Services	4196	3591	28150	27281	1029484	1057285
金融业	Finance	1077	981	355	364	6633	6006
房地产业	Real Estate	438	413	116	123	1937	1751
租赁和商务服务业	Renting and Leasing Activities and Business Services	2672	2448	2068	4232	81412	105375
科学研究和技术服务业	Scientific Research and Development, Technical Services	40856	38487	80909	77989	4401848	3946028
水利、环境和公共设施管理业	Management of Water Conservancy, Environment and Public Falicities	3909	3630	4651	3911	155291	121078
居民服务、修理和其他服务业	Resident Services, Repair and Other Services	2217	1694	709	557	11923	10215
教　育	Education	8035	7703	2495	2400	55278	50486
卫生和社会工作	Healthcare and Social Works	6506	4603	11520	10039	144923	119774
文化、体育和娱乐业	Culture, Sports and Entertainment	4875	5737	3883	4611	33616	35154
公共管理、社会保障和社会组织	Public Administration, Social Security and Social Organizations	4198	4062	2056	2904	57395	47872
国际组织	International Organizations	106	138	34	38	1258	605

注：行业划分执行2011年国民经济行业分类标准(GB/T 4754-2011)。

Note: Sectors in this table are classified in accordance with the Standard for Classification of National Economic Sectors 2011 (GB/T 4754-2011).

19-6 规模以上工业企业研究与试验发展(R&D)活动基本情况(2013年)

项目	Item	企业数(个) Number of Enterprises (unit)	#有研究与试验发展(R&D)活动的企业数 Enterprises with R&D Activities	研究与试验发展(R&D)人员(人) R&D Personnel (person)	研究与试验发展(R&D)人员折合全时当量(人年) Full-time Equivalent of R&D Personnel (person-year)	研究与试验发展(R&D)经费内部支出(万元) Internal R&D Expenditures (10000 yuan)
合计	**Total**	**3641**	**1059**	**79368**	**58036**	**2130618**
按企业规模分	**By Size of Enterprise**					
#大中型企业	Medium and Large-sized	775	381	61204	44909	1734465
按隶属关系分	**By Affiliation**					
中央	Central	234	130	16857	12327	593761
地方	Local	3407	929	62511	45709	1536857
按登记注册类型分	**By Registration Type**					
内资企业	Domestically-invested Enterprises	2753	851	61391	45186	1542017
#国有企业	State-owned Enterprises	98	34	4248	3306	103472
港澳台商投资企业	Hong Kong, Macao and Taiwan-invested Enterprises	223	60	4149	3002	158749
外商投资企业	Foreign-invested Enterprises	665	148	13828	9848	429852
按重点产业分	**By Key Sector**					
#高技术制造业	High-tech Manufacturing	782	417	31646	23707	1065430
#现代制造业	Modern Manufacturing	598	299	21360	15613	579629

BASIC INFORMATION ON R&D ACTIVITIES OF INDUSTRIAL ENTERPRISES ABOVE DESIGNATED SIZE (2013)

				专利申请数(件) Patent Applications (unit)		新产品产值(万元) Output Value of New Products (10000 yuan)	新产品销售收入(万元) Sales Income of New Products (10000 yuan)	
政府资金 Governmental Funds	企业资金 Enterprise Funds	国外资金 Foreign Funds	其他资金 Others		#发明专利 Inventions			#出口 Exports
227527	**1819635**	**16765**	**66691**	**19210**	**9240**	**36775653**	**36727656**	**5396851**
188161	1473234	14892	58178	14817	7622	27792818	27728969	5106203
132565	406650	1239	53307	3692	1833	8021703	8123363	67399
94963	1412985	15526	13383	15518	7407	28753950	28604293	5329452
210524	1265624	2468	63401	13260	5998	21208304	20952190	662017
14662	76776		12034	738	362	1128349	1088876	10290
5353	151932	1313	151	2910	2219	6238417	6542946	334517
11650	402079	12984	3139	3040	1023	9328932	9232521	4400317
176270	833376	1824	53961	8308	5358	15668061	15844619	4416106
37590	526666	514	14859	4994	3521	14087665	14256675	3825494

19-7 规模以上工业企业研究与试验发展(R&D)活动基本情况(按行业分)(2013年)

项目	Item	企业数(个) Number of Enterprises (unit)	#有研究与试验发展(R&D)活动的企业数 Enterprises with R&D Activities	研究与试验发展(R&D)人员(人) R&D Personnel (person)
合计	**Total**	**3641**	**1059**	**79368**
采矿业	**Mining and Quarrying**	**22**	**9**	**4456**
煤炭开采和洗选业	Mining and Washing of Coal	4	2	3281
石油和天然气开采业	Extraction of Petroleum and Natural Gas	2	2	170
黑色金属矿采选业	Mining and Processing of Ferrous Metal Ores	7	1	37
有色金属矿采选业	Mining and Processing of Non-Ferrous Metal Ores			
非金属矿采选业	Mining and Processing of Nonmetal Ores	4		
开采辅助活动	Mining Support Service Activities	5	4	968
其他采矿业	Mining of Other Ores			
制造业	**Manufacturing**	**3518**	**1042**	**73710**
农副食品加工业	Processing of Food from Agriculture Products	140	18	765
食品制造业	Manufacture of Foods	121	18	826
酒、饮料和精制茶制造业	Manufacture of Wine, Beverage and Refined Tea	43	5	1085
烟草制品业	Manufacture of Cigarettes and Tobacco	1	***	***
纺织业	Manufacture of Textile	36	9	109
纺织服装、服饰业	Manufacture of Textile Wearing Apparel and Ornament	153	4	326
皮革、毛皮、羽毛及其制品和制鞋业	Manufacture of Leather, Fur, Feather and Its Products, and Footwear	18		
木材加工和木、竹、藤、棕、草制品业	Processing of Timbers, Manufacture of Wood, Bamboo, Rattan, Palm, and Straw Products	20	2	16
家具制造业	Manufacture of Furniture	66	2	262
造纸和纸制品业	Manufacture of Paper and Paper Products	41	1	64
印刷和记录媒介复制业	Printing, Reproduction of Recording Media	119	10	942
文教、工美、体育和娱乐用品制造业	Manufacture of Articles for Culture,Education, Artwork, Sport and Entertainment Activities	33	3	47
石油加工、炼焦和核燃料加工业	Processing of Petroleum, Coking, Processing of Nuclear Fuel	22	2	198
化学原料和化学制品制造业	Manufacture of Raw Chemical Materials and Chemical Products	217	71	2282
医药制造业	Manufacture of Medicines	188	97	6838
化学纤维制造业	Manufacture of Chemical Fibers	3	3	154
橡胶和塑料制品业	Manufacture of Rubber and Plastics Products	119	16	805
非金属矿物制品业	Manufacture of Non-Metallic Mineral Products	252	46	3259
黑色金属冶炼和压延加工业	Smelting and Pressing of Ferrous Metals	32	4	305
有色金属冶炼和压延加工业	Smelting and Pressing of Non-Ferrous Metals	36	14	971
金属制品业	Manufacture of Fabricated Metal Products	226	35	2128
通用设备制造业	Manufacture of General-Purpose Machinery	256	94	6228
专用设备制造业	Manufacture of Special-Purpose Machinery	318	144	8381
汽车制造业	Manufacture of Motor Vehicles	216	40	7564
铁路、船舶、航空航天和其他运输设备制造业	Manufacture of Railway Locomotives, Building of Ships and Boats, Manufacture of Air and Spacecrafts and Other Transportation Equipment	64	37	4043
电气机械和器材制造业	Manufacture of Electrical Machinery and Equipment	260	97	5703
计算机、通信和其他电子设备制造业	Manufacture of Computers, Communication Equipment and Other Electronic Equipment	296	155	14333
仪器仪表制造业	Manufacture of Measuring Instruments and Meters	170	99	4211
其他制造业	Other Manufacturing	29	10	768
废弃资源综合利用业	Recycling and Disposal of Waste	8	1	25
金属制品、机械和设备修理业	Repair of Fabricated Metal Products, Machinery and Equipment	15	4	1047
电力、热力、燃气及水的生产和供应业	**Production and Distribution of Electricity, Heating Power, Gas and Water**	**101**	**8**	**1202**
电力、热力生产和供应业	Production and Distribution of Electricity and Heating Power	59	3	586
燃气生产和供应业	Production and Distribution of Gas	23	2	330
水的生产和供应业	Production and Distribution of Water	19	3	286

注：行业划分执行2011年国民经济行业分类标准(GB/T 4754-2011)。

BASIC INFORMATION ON R&D ACTIVITIES OF INDUSTRIAL ENTERPRISES ABOVE DESIGNATED SIZE (BY SECTOR)(2013)

研究与试验发展(R&D)人员折合全时当量(人年) Full-time Equivalent of R&D Personnel (person-year)	研究与试验发展(R&D)经费内部支出(万元) Internal R&D Expenditures (10000 yuan)	政府资金 Governmenta; Funds	企业资金 Enterprise Funds	国外资金 Foreign Funds	其他资金 Others	专利申请数(件) Applications Patents (unit)	#发明专利 Inventions	新产品产值(万元) Output Value of New Products (10000 yuan)	新产品销售收入(万元) Sales Income of New Products (10000 yuan)	#出口 Exports
58036	**2130618**	**227527**	**1819635**	**16765**	**66691**	**19210**	**9240**	**36775653**	**36727656**	**5396851**
2927	**77466**	**6513**	**70945**	**8**		**359**	**234**	**3705745**	**3705745**	
2130	17135		17135			22	6	3705745	3705745	
113	13291	6007	7276	8		18	10			
10	1128		1128			230	174			
674	45913	506	45407			89	44			
54161	**2035064**	**220221**	**1731395**	**16757**	**66691**	**17710**	**8565**	**33049663**	**33002187**	**5396851**
411	25316	1562	23018	312	424	120	96	290809	286110	3223
627	21955	686	21227		42	63	37	237013	231906	27970
816	17137	129	17008			27	8	249852	296051	3390
***	***		***					***	***	
84	3592	507	2996		89	26	17	98518	126629	3369
128	8051	335	7677		39	31	1	220010	188059	217
3	529		529			11				
92	2234		2234			223	13	48553	50100	15
29	702		702			3	3	33821	35517	14202
518	12261		12261			55	13	153006	146667	2260
37	1664	700	964			29	2	6699	13380	2040
143	2642	9	2634			26	25	239352	435677	
1600	39138	1110	38028			310	240	640423	607397	57060
4930	134259	9298	124115	28	818	465	333	1654021	1690636	10786
75	837	137	700			4	3	5775	4430	
639	12676	103	12422		151	91	27	257416	254152	29015
2048	57965	5088	52850		28	687	250	1458618	1551307	31366
262	4051	479	3573			7	7	164423	162665	4387
854	19223	2377	16752		93	109	92	319628	305249	110250
1771	38493	3146	35179	72	96	349	129	713368	744660	49044
4279	130484	5306	124462	380	337	691	169	1848340	1877901	315024
6131	236967	28881	207613		473	2755	1232	2317728	2212173	194046
5670	215820	5808	204786	5038	189	2676	510	3609597	3209547	1734
3595	225165	82080	93741	337	49007	555	232	1209616	1159437	2870
4498	162213	2549	146988	9132	3545	1398	531	3669761	3653104	175297
10709	531628	51931	473226		6470	6235	4308	12303040	12429525	4319523
3242	94940	14740	76935	1459	1807	649	238	1092080	1113408	37461
458	21790	3242	15464		3085	90	47	164135	173209	2303
25	300	20	280			6	2	7074	6713	
467	11670		11670			19		2945	2537	
951	**18088**	**793**	**17295**			**1141**	**441**	**20244**	**19724**	
491	9791	213	9578			1079	418			
207	5134	294	4840			18	6	10339	10339	
253	3163	287	2877			44	17	9906	9385	

Note: Sectors in this table are classified in accordance with the Standard for Classification of National Economic Sectors 2011 (GB/T 4754-2011).

19-8 规模以上高技术制造业主要科技指标

项目	Item	R&D人员折合全时当量(人年) Full-time Equivalent of R&D Personnel (person-year)	
		2013	2012
高技术制造业	**High-tech Manufacturing**	**23707**	**20409**
医药制造业	Manufacture of Medicines	4930	4027
#化学药品制造	Manufacture of Chemical Medicine	2166	1959
生物药品制造	Manufacture of Biological Medicine and Biochemical Chemical Products	1447	935
航空、航天器及设备制造业	Manufacture of Aircrafts and Spacecrafts	3055	2501
#航空航天器修理	Repair of Air and Spacecrafts	460	87
电子及通信设备制造业	Manufacture of Electronic Equipment and Communication Equipment	9580	8318
#通信设备制造	Manufacture of Communication Equipment	4328	3651
电子器件制造	Manufacture of Electronic Appliances	2379	913
电子元件制造	Manufacture of Electronic Components	893	689
其他电子设备制造	Manufacture of Other Electronic Equipment	1231	951
计算机及办公设备制造业	Manufacture of Computers and Office Equipments	1416	1453
#计算机整机制造	Manufacture of Entired Computer	888	825
医疗仪器设备及仪器仪表制造业	Manufacture of Medical Equipments and Meters	4727	4111
医疗仪器设备及器械制造	Manufacture of Medical Equipment and Appliances	1485	1236
仪器仪表制造	Manufacture of Measuring Instrument and Meter	3242	2876

MAJOR SCIENCE AND TECHNOLOGY INDICATORS OF HIGH-TECH MANUFACTURING ABOVE DESIGNATER SIZE

R&D经费支出 (亿元) R&D Expenditures (100 million yuan)		新产品销售收入 (亿元) Sales Income of New Products (100 million yuan)		专利申请数 (件) Patent Applications (unit)		发明专利 Inventions	
2013	2012	2013	2012	2013	2012	2013	2012
106.5	**92.2**	**1584.5**	**1315.3**	**8308**	**9972**	**5358**	**6314**
13.4	9.9	169.1	127.1	465	367	333	259
6.1	4.9	55.6	37.6	154	129	131	108
4.4	3.0	47.7	38.0	145	139	102	74
20.8	19.0	35.3	24.6	262	250	139	144
1.2	0.2			10	23		1
42.4	36.4	900.6	661.3	3649	5529	2273	3172
15.8	13.7	705.2	480.7	779	792	643	682
15.9	5.4	118.0	25.4	2081	2669	1157	1496
2.5	1.9	24.4	20.0	95	103	40	44
4.6	4.1	24.9	21.8	458	378	322	245
13.0	15.5	349.3	376.9	2687	2439	2103	2124
11.3	13.6	311.1	312.4	2339	2200	1941	1990
16.9	11.4	130.2	125.3	1245	1387	510	615
7.4	4.7	18.9	19.7	596	582	272	239
9.5	6.7	111.2	105.7	649	805	238	376

19-9 限额以上信息传输、软件和信息技术服务业企业研究与试验发展(R&D)活动基本情况(2013年)

项目	Item	企业数(个) Number of Enterprises (unit)	#有研究与试验发展(R&D)活动的企业数 Enterprises with R&D Activities	研究与试验发展(R&D)人员(人) R&D Personnel (person)	研究与试验发展(R&D)人员折合全时当量(人年) Full-time Equivalent of R&D Personnel (person-year)
合计	**Total**	**2746**	**327**	**36242**	**28324**
按隶属关系分	**By Affiliation**				
中央	Central	138	35	3668	2940
地方	Local	2608	292	32574	25385
按登记注册类型分	**By Registration Type**				
内资企业	Domestically-invested Enterprises	2167	274	18958	13398
#国有企业	State-owned Units	30	6	546	321
港澳台商投资企业	Hong Kong, Macao and Taiwan-invested Enterprises	181	17	2265	1892
外商投资企业	Foreign-invested Enterprises	398	36	15019	13035
按行业分	**By Sector**				
电信、广播电视和卫星传输服务	Telecommunications, Broadcasting, Television and Satellite Transmission services	251	30	5813	4617
互联网和相关服务	Internet and Related Services	253	14	5495	4410
软件和信息技术服务业	Software and Information Technology Services	2242	283	24934	19297

注：行业划分执行2011年国民经济行业分类标准(GB/T 4754-2011)。

BASIC INFORMATION ON R&D ACTIVITIES OF INFORMATION TRANSMISSIOM, SOFTWARE AND INFORMATION TECHNICIAL SERVICE ENTERPRISES ABOVE DESIGNATED SIZE (2013)

研究与试验发展(R&D)经费内部支出(万元) Internal R&D Expenditures (10000 yuan)	政府资金 Governmental Funds	企业资金 Enterprise Funds	国外资金 Foreign Funds	其他资金 Others	专利申请数(件) Patent Applications (unit)	#发明专利 Inventions
1103590	**25395**	**808298**	**256185**	**13712**	**9736**	**8382**
101116	10478	83827		6812	2652	2444
1002474	14917	724471	256185	6901	7084	5938
401824	22275	366229		13320	8299	7117
26004	1591	21137		3276	1479	1414
59615	50	59208		357	485	399
642151	3070	382861	256185	35	952	866
273091	3613	162552	104721	2205	1791	1667
189730	312	189410		9	2396	2223
640769	21470	456336	151464	11499	5549	4492

Note: Sectors in this table are classified in accordance with the Standard for Classification of National Economic Sectors 2011 (GB/T 4754-2011).

19-10 研究与开发机构研发活动情况(2007-2013年)

项目		Item		2007
研究与开发机构基本情况		**Basic Information on R&D Institutions**		
机构数	(个)	Number	(unit)	265
中 央	(个)	Central	(unit)	221
地 方	(个)	Local	(unit)	44
研究与试验发展(R&D)投入情况		**R&D Input**		
R&D人员	(万人)	R&D Personnel	(10000 persons)	4.6
按隶属关系分		By Affiliation		
中 央	(万人)	Central	(10000 persons)	4.4
地 方	(万人)	Local	(10000 persons)	0.2
R&D人员折合全时当量	(万人年)	Full-time Equivalent of R&D Personnel	(10000 persons-year)	3.8
基础研究	(万人年)	Basic Research	(10000 persons-year)	1.2
应用研究	(万人年)	Applied Research	(10000 persons-year)	1.6
试验发展	(万人年)	Experimental Development	(10000 persons-year)	1.0
R&D经费内部支出	(亿元)	Internal R&D Expenditures	(100 million yuan)	103.1
按隶属关系分		By Affiliation		
中 央	(亿元)	Central	(100 million yuan)	99.0
地 方	(亿元)	Local	(100 million yuan)	4.1
按活动类型分		By Type of Activity		
基础研究	(亿元)	Basic Research	(100 million yuan)	26.4
应用研究	(亿元)	Applied Research	(100 million yuan)	45.2
试验发展	(亿元)	Experimental Development	(100 million yuan)	31.5
按资金来源分		By Source of Funds		
政府资金	(亿元)	Governmental Funds	(100 million yuan)	88.6
企业资金	(亿元)	Enterprise Funds	(100 million yuan)	3.2
境外资金	(亿元)	Foreign Funds	(100 million yuan)	1.3
其他资金	(亿元)	Others	(100 million yuan)	10.0
研究与试验发展(R&D)项目(课题)情况		**R&D Projects (Tasks)**		
R&D项目(课题)数	(项)	Number of R&D Projects (Tasks)	(unit)	15079
R&D项目(课题)人员折合全时当量	(万人年)	Full-time Equivalent of R&D Personnel	(10000 persons-year)	2.2
R&D项目(课题)经费内部支出	(亿元)	Internal R&D Expenditures	(100 million yuan)	57.1
科技产出及成果情况		**Science & Technology Output and Achievement**		
发表科技论文	(篇)	Published Articles on Science and Technology	(unit)	37232
#国外发表	(篇)	Published Abroad	(unit)	9005
出版科技著作	(种)	Published Writings on Science and Technology	(Sort)	1489
专利申请数	(件)	Number of Patents Applications	(unit)	1993
#发明专利	(件)	Invention Patents	(unit)	1784
专利授权数	(件)	Number of Patents Granted	(unit)	985
#发明专利	(件)	Invention Patents	(unit)	752

注：研究与开发机构范围是北京市政府部门属的科学研究与技术开发机构、科技情报与文献机构。
资料来源：北京市科学技术委员会。

STATISTICS FOR R&D ACTIVITIES IN R&D INSTITUTIONS (2007-2013)

2008	2009	2010	2011	2012	2013
266	275	281	280	288	287
225	228	231	231	238	237
41	47	50	49	50	50
4.8	5.2	5.7	5.9	6.3	6.6
4.5	4.9	5.4	5.6	5.9	6.2
0.3	0.3	0.3	0.3	0.4	0.4
3.9	4.2	4.6	4.7	5.3	5.5
1.3	1.4	1.5	1.6	1.8	1.9
1.6	1.7	2.0	2.1	2.2	2.3
1.0	1.1	1.1	1.0	1.3	1.3
123.8	150.3	187.0	195.1	222.0	246.8
117.4	143.9	178.9	185.1	211.5	236.3
6.4	6.4	8.1	10.0	10.5	10.5
28.3	39.2	49.9	58.5	65.1	73.6
49.0	61.5	78.0	84.0	92.0	102.2
46.5	49.6	59.1	52.6	64.9	71.0
106.6	126.3	164.4	168.0	192.6	220.0
4.0	4.4	3.6	6.6	6.5	8.2
1.8	2.0	1.5	2.5	1.5	1.9
11.4	17.6	17.5	18.0	21.4	16.7
16383	17816	19545	20333	22842	23949
2.3	3.8	4.1	4.3	4.9	5.0
70.9	87.1	107.2	115.0	142.7	156.8
37149	39380	39384	41442	44218	45509
9184	12011	11696	13361	14003	17216
1636	1873	1601	1828	1670	1921
2488	3182	3879	4880	5456	6192
2119	2772	3450	4373	4798	5144
1146	1574	1879	2260	3251	3646
922	1299	1455	1756	2635	2763

Note: R&D institutions cover scientific research and technological development institutions, scientific and technological information institutions subordinate to government authorities of Beijing.

Source: Beijing Municipal Science & Technology Commission.

19-11 高等学校研发活动情况
STATISTICS FOR R&D ACTIVITIES IN COLLEGES & UNIVERSITIES

项目		Item		2013	2012
高等学校基本情况		**Basic Information of Colleges & Universities**			
学校数	(个)	Number of Colleges and Universities	(unit)	95	93
#理工农医	(个)	Colleges & Universities of Science, Engineering, Agriculture, Medical Science	(unit)	65	64
#人文社科	(个)	Colleges & Universities of Arts and Social Sciences	(unit)	65	64
研究与试验发展(R&D)机构数	(个)	Number of R&D Institutions	(unit)	776	767
研究与试验发展(R&D)投入情况		**R&D Input**			
R&D人员	(万人)	R&D Personnel	(10000 person)	7.29	6.96
R&D人员折合全时当量	(万人年)	Full-time Equivalent of R&D Personnel	(10000 persons-year)	3.23	3.12
基础研究	(万人年)	Basic Research	(10000 persons-year)	1.22	1.19
应用研究	(万人年)	Applied Research	(10000 persons-year)	1.91	1.83
试验发展	(万人年)	Experimental Development	(10000 persons-year)	0.10	0.11
R&D经费内部支出	(亿元)	Internal R&D Expenditures	(100 million yuan)	136.65	136.94
按活动类型分		By Type of Activity			
基础研究	(亿元)	Basic Research	(100 million yuan)	48.17	46.75
应用研究	(亿元)	Applied Research	(100 million yuan)	80.55	76.71
试验发展	(亿元)	Experimental Development	(100 million yuan)	7.93	13.49
按资金来源分		By Source of Funds			
#政府资金	(亿元)	Governmental Funds	(100 million yuan)	92.52	92.96
企业资金	(亿元)	Enterprise Funds	(100 million yuan)	39.78	37.80
研究与试验发展(R&D)项目(课题)情况		**R&D Projects (Tasks)**			
R&D项目(课题)数	(项)	Number of R&D Projects (Tasks)	(unit)	76331	69557
R&D项目(课题)人员折合全时当量	(万人年)	Full-time Equivalent of R&D Personnel	(10000 persons-year)	3.22	3.12
R&D项目(课题)经费内部支出	(亿元)	Internal R&D Expenditures	(100 million yuan)	112.93	113.48
科技产出及成果情况		**Science & Technology Output and Achievement**			
发表科技论文	(篇)	Published Articles on Science and Technology	(unit)	113220	112949
#国外发表	(篇)	Published Abroad	(unit)		
出版科技著作	(种)	Published Writings on Science and Technology	(Sort)	5410	5431
专利申请数	(件)	Number of Patent Applications	(unit)	12024	10327
#发明专利	(件)	Invention Patents	(unit)	10291	8755
专利授权数	(件)	Number of Patents Granted	(unit)	7745	7132
#发明专利	(件)	Invention Patents	(unit)	5919	5667

资料来源：北京市教育委员会。
Source: Beijing Municipal Commission of Education.

19-12 科学技术协会及所属学会工作情况(2013年)
STATISTICS FOR SCIENCE AND TECHNOLOGY ASSOCIATION AND SUBORDINATE INSTITUTES (2013)

项目		Item		合计 Total	市科协 Municipal Science and Technology Association	市级学会 Institutes at Municipal Level
基本情况		Basic Information				
机构数	(个)	Number of Institutions	(unit)	160	1	159
机构从业人员	(人)	Number of Employed Persons in the Institutions	(person)	229506	367	229139
学术交流活动		Academic Exchange Activities				
国内学术会议	(次)	Domestic Academic Meetings	(time)	1095	3	1092
参加人数	(人次)	Number of Participants	(person-time)	140693	300	140393
交流论文	(篇)	Number of Papers Exchagned	(unit)	18305	34	18271
境内国际学术会议	(次)	Domestically-held International Academic Meetings	(time)	110		110
参加人数	(人次)	Number of Participants	(person-time)	11631		11631
交流论文	(篇)	Number of Papers Exchagned	(unit)	2716		2716
港澳台地区学术会议	(次)	Academic Meetings Held in Kong Kong, Macao and Taiwan	(time)	17		17
参加人数	(人次)	Number of Participants	(person-time)	2483		2483
交流论文	(篇)	Number of Papers Exchagned	(unit)	467		467
科技期刊		Science and Technology Journals				
主办科技期刊种数	(种)	Types of Science and Technology Journals Sponsored	(sort)	32	3	29
科技期刊总印数	(万册)	Number of Total Printings of Science and Technology Journals	(10000 copies)	402.2	282.5	119.6
科技期刊发表论文数	(篇)	Papers Published on Science and Technology Journals	(unit)	5844	34	5810
科普活动		Activities to Popularize Scientific Knowledge				
举办科普宣讲活动	(次)	Scientific Knowledge Lectures	(time)	3379	1465	1914
播放科技广播、影视节目	(分钟)	Playing Radio, Films and TV Programs on Science and Technology	(minute)	10170	1756	8414
举办实用技术培训	(次)	Holding Practical Technology Trainings	(time)	616	218	398
推广新技术、新品种	(项)	Promoting New Technologies and New Varieties	(unit)	199	54	145
参加活动科技人员总数	(人次)	Participating in Science and Technology Personnel	(person-time)	31296	15527	15769
参加活动的学会、协会、研究会	(个次)	Participating in Socieities, Associations and Research Institutes	(unit-time)	1267	742	525
科技传播		Science and Technology Dissemination				
主办科技报纸种数	(种)	Types of Science and Technology Newspaper Sponsored	(sort)	1	1	
制作科普挂图种数	(种)	Types of Scientific Knowlede Flip Charts Produced	(sort)	141	10	131
制作科技广播、影视节目套数	(套)	Science and Technology Raido, Films and TV Programs Produced	(unit)	41	15	26
制作科技光盘种数	(种)	Types of Science and Technology CDs Produced	(sort)	22	1	21
制作科普动漫作品套数	(套)	Scientific Knowledge Animation Works Produced	(unit)	3005	3000	5
主办科技网站	(个)	Science and Technology Websites Sponsored	(unit)	52	11	41
科技开放与交流		Science and Technology Opening-up and Exchange				
加入国际民间科技组织	(个)	International Cilvilian Science and Technology Organizations Joined	(unit)	1		1
促成科技合作项目	(项)	Scientific and Technological Cooperation Projects Facilitated	(unit)	4		4
参加国外科技活动人数	(人次)	Number of Persons Participating in Foreign Science and Technology Activities	(person-time)	313	40	273
参加港澳台地区科技活动人数	(人次)	Number of Persons Participating in Science and Technology Activities in Hong Kong, Macao and Taiwan	(person-time)	439	56	383
接待国外专家学者	(人次)	Foreign Experts and Scholars Received	(person-time)	605	152	453
接待港澳台地区专家学者	(人次)	Experts and Scholars from Kong Kong, Macao and Taiwan Received	(person-time)	339	115	224
科技服务		Science and Technology Service				
提供决策咨询报告	(篇)	Providing Policy-making Consulting Reports	(unit)	145	26	119
举办决策咨询活动	(次)	Holding Policy-making Consulting Activities	(time)	162	13	149

注：本表统计范围是北京市科学技术协会所属学会、研究会。
资料来源：北京市科学技术协会。
Note: Figures in this table cover societies and research institutes affiliated with Beijing Municipal Science & Technology Association.
Source: Beijing Municipal Science and Technology Association

19-13 公有经济企事业单位专业技术人员(2013年)
NUMBER OF PORFESSIONAL TECHNICAL PERSONNEL IN PUBLIC ENTERPRISES AND INSTITUTIONS (2013)

单位：人 (person)

项　目	Item	合　计 Total	#高　级 Senior	#中　级 Intermediate	#初　级 Junior
合　计	**Total**	**490906**	**62965**	**166808**	**184853**
#工程技术人员	Engineering Technicians	118439	12436	30387	38209
农业技术人员	Agricultural Technicians	4738	510	1406	2285
科学研究人员	Science Research Personnel	6989	1792	2735	1171
卫生技术人员	Medical Technicians	93611	10370	30641	49309
教学人员	Teaching Personnel	163925	30516	75197	53727
经济人员	Economic Personnel	48111	2729	11307	15094
会计人员	Accountants	26712	1451	6333	13210
统计人员	Statisticians	3302	122	705	1388

注：公有经济是指北京市属国有和集体企事业单位,不包含在京中央属企事业单位。

资料来源：北京市人力资源和社会保障局。

Note: Public sector means state-owned and collectively-owned enterprises and institutions in Beijing, excluding central enterprises and institutions located in Beijing.

Source: Beijing Municipal Bureau of Human Resources and Social Security.

19-14 技术合同成交情况(1990-2013年)
STATISTICS FOR CONCLUSION OF TECHNOLOGICAL CONTRACTS (1990-2013)

年 份 Year	合同数(项) Number of Contracts (unit)	技术合同成交总额(亿元) Total Volume of Transaction of Technological Contracts Concluded (100 million yuan)	#技术交易额 Total Volume of Transaction of Technology	#流向外省市技术合同额 Amount of Transaction Flowing to Other Provinces and Municipalities	实现合同总金额(亿元) Total Volume of Transaction Achieved in Contracts (100 million yuan)	#技术交易实现金额 Amount of Technological Transactions Achieved
1990	18588	20.3	10.5		15.4	8.4
1991-1995	**93970**	**167.7**	**120.0**		**115.4**	**83.8**
1991	18547	22.4	13.1		15.3	9.1
1992	23395	31.3	22.2		20.0	14.4
1993	20461	35.6	25.6		24.9	17.6
1994	15220	37.2	26.9		26.9	20.4
1995	16347	41.2	32.2		28.4	22.3
1996-2000	**91421**	**414.2**	**375.9**		**206.7**	**188.1**
1996	14850	45.8	39.2		29.6	25.4
1997	13866	54.3	48.1		31.1	27.8
1998	20724	81.6	73.9		42.1	37.6
1999	20711	92.2	88.5		43.6	41.0
2000	21270	140.3	126.3	65.5	60.3	56.3
2001-2005	**156114**	**1443.8**	**1217.2**	**688.9**	**669.5**	**628.1**
2001	23921	191.0	164.8	85.4	97.6	93.0
2002	27037	221.1	181.0	100.4	101.9	97.2
2003	32173	265.5	226.8	132.4	119.9	113.9
2004	35478	331.8	294.3	165.8	148.7	143.4
2005	37505	434.4	350.4	204.9	201.4	180.6
2006-2010	**256074**	**5422.8**	**3984.7**	**2372.7**	**2226.7**	**2006.7**
2006	51575	697.3	572.6	325.3	349.5	319.7
2007	50972	882.6	660.3	407.4	418.1	353.5
2008	52742	1027.2	778.1	487.0	406.2	375.0
2009	49938	1236.2	906.9	498.2	516.8	452.9
2010	50847	1579.5	1066.7	654.8	536.0	505.6
2011	53552	1890.3	1268.3	635.9	580.4	563.3
2012	59969	2458.5	2048.6	1385.0	739.8	707.0
2013	62743	2851.2	2252.4	1615.9	684.0	659.3

资料来源：北京技术市场管理办公室。
Source: Beijing Technical Market Management Office.

19-15 技术合同成交情况
CONCLUSION OF TECHNICAL CONTRACTS

项目	Item	合同数(项) Number of Contracts (unit)		成交额(万元) Volume of Transaction (10000 yuan)	
		2013	2012	2013	2012
合计	**Total**	**62743**	**59969**	**28511954.3**	**24585033.6**
按合同类别分类	**By Type of Contract**				
技术开发合同	Technological Development	24000	22965	6104492.5	5916931.8
技术转让合同	Technology Transfer	1570	2015	579535.1	1731277.5
技术咨询合同	Technical Consultation	4938	4364	488438.2	385822.3
技术服务合同	Technical Service	32235	30625	21339488.4	16551002.1
按合同卖方类别分类	**By Type of Seller**				
机关法人	Government Organisations	8	17	2545.0	4800.3
事业法人	Public Institutions	10274	10575	1024315.5	989849.9
社团法人	Mass Organisations	23	32	1999.0	879.5
企业法人	Enterprises	52388	49286	27460488.6	23563262.9
自然人	Natural Persons	32	42	9623.7	4037.1
其他组织	Other Organizations	18	17	12982.5	22204.0
按合同买方类别分类	**By Type of Buyer**				
机关法人	Government Organisations	5133	4664	2119154.5	1065051.0
事业法人	Public Institutions	10625	8648	1932410.8	1308925.3
社团法人	Mass Organisations	270	240	48030.3	19143.5
企业法人	Enterprises	45448	45600	21828387.3	20751332.9
自然人	Natural Persons	457	306	18822.6	24745.0
其他组织	Other Organizations	810	511	2565148.7	1415835.8
按服务社会经济目标分类	**By Social and Economic Service Objectives**				
农业、林业和渔业的发展	Development of Agriculture Forestry and Fishing	1828	703	400904.0	79450.2
促进工业的发展	Promoting Industrial Development	1678	6201	305843.5	2119161.2
能源的生产和合理利用	Production and Reasonable Utilization of Energy	5051	4739	2844638.8	5611694.8
基础设施的发展	Development of Infrastructure	5816	6786	9872781.4	6057361.2
环境治理与保护	Environmental Control and Protection	2838	1860	2230069.5	1390700.8
卫生(不包括污染)	Health (Excluding Pollution)	1349	1345	343370.4	248148.4
社会发展和社会服务	Social Development and Service	23403	18906	8043129.7	5776773.1
地球和大气层的探索与利用	Exploration and Utilization of Earth and Aerosphere	144	138	12363.1	30783.4
知识的发展	Development of Knowledge	2048	2449	264688.3	351444.1
民用空间	Civil Space	1021	966	187550.4	170219.4
国防	National Defence	2343	1830	772094.7	340648.1
其他	Others	15224	14046	3234520.2	2408649.1
按技术流向分类	**By Spread Area of Technology**				
流向本市	To Beijing	28059	26264	5817097.7	6556372.1
流向外省市	To Other Provinces and Municipalities	33538	32433	16158755.0	13850055.3
技术出口	Exports	1146	1272	6536101.6	4178606.2

资料来源：北京技术市场管理办公室。
Source: Beijing Technical Market Management Office.

19-16 科技成果及获奖情况(2001-2013年)
STATISTICS FOR SCIENTIFIC AND TECHNOLOGICAL ACHIEVEMENTS AND AWARDS (2001-2013)

单位：项 (unit)

年 份 Year	科技成果登记数 Registered Number of Scientific and Technological Achievements	#国家技术发明奖 National Awards of Technical Invention	#国家科学技术进步奖 National Awards of Scientific and Technological Advancement
2001-2005	**3063**	**25**	**233**
2001	326	1	38
2002	275	5	48
2003	468	5	52
2004	976	6	43
2005	1018	8	52
2006-2010	**5081**	**56**	**257**
2006	1002	12	64
2007	1010	9	44
2008	1016	13	42
2009	1023	11	54
2010	1030	11	53
2011	1035	5	56
2012	1040	22	53
2013	1043	19	38

资料来源：北京市科学技术委员会。
Source: Beijing Municipal Science & Technology Commission.

19-17 专利申请及授权情况
APPLICATIONS AND GRANTING OF PATENTS

单位：件 (unit)

项目	Item	申请量 Patent Applications 2013	申请量 Patent Applications 2012	授权量 Patents Granted 2013	授权量 Patents Granted 2012
合计	**Total**	**123336**	**92305**	**62671**	**50511**
按种类分	**By Type**				
发明	Inventions	67554	52720	20695	20140
实用新型	Utility Models	47586	32609	36301	24672
外观设计	Industrial Designs	8196	6976	5675	5699
按对象分	**By Applicant**				
工矿企业	Industrial and Mining Enterprises	79698	54727	40538	29983
大专院校	Universities & Colleges	13028	11842	6731	6841
科研单位	Scientific Research Institutes	12287	10773	6423	5311
机关团体	Government Organizations	1308	953	658	1098
个人	Individuals	17015	14010	8321	7278

资料来源：北京市知识产权局。
Source: Beijing Intellectual Property Office.

19-18 有效发明专利情况
STATISTICS FOR VALID INVENTION PATENTS

单位：件 (unit)

项目	Item	2013	2012
合计	**Total**	**85434**	**69554**
按对象分	**By Applicant**		
工矿企业	Industrial and Mininig Enterprises	42992	33601
大专院校	Universities & Colleges	19623	16874
科研单位	Scientific Research Institutes	16373	13260
机关团体	Government Organizations	847	571
个人	Individuals	5599	5248

资料来源：北京市知识产权局。
Source: Beijing Intellectual Property Office.

主要统计指标解释

科技活动人员 指报告年度调查单位直接从事科技活动、以及从事科技活动管理和为科技活动提供直接服务的人员。直接从事科技活动人员包括：在单位办的研究室、实验室、技术开发中心及中试车间（基地）等机构中从事科技活动的人员；虽不在上述机构工作，但编入科技活动项目（课题）组的人员等。从事科技活动管理和为科技活动提供直接服务的人员包括：与科技活动相关的行政管理人员，以及直接为科技活动提供资料文献、材料供应、设备维护等服务的人员。

研究与试验发展（R&D） 指在科学技术领域，为增加知识总量、以及运用这些知识去创造新的应用而进行的系统的创造性的活动，包括基础研究、应用研究、试验发展三类活动。

研究与试验发展（R&D）人员 指单位内部从事基础研究、应用研究和试验发展三类活动的人员。包括直接参加上述三类项目活动的人员以及这三类项目的管理人员和直接服务人员。为研发活动提供直接服务的人员包括直接为研发活动提供资料文献、材料供应、设备维护等服务的人员。

研究与试验发展（R&D）人员折合全时当量 是国际上通用的、用于比较科技人力投入的指标。指 R&D 全时人员（全年从事 R&D 活动累积工作时间占全部工作时间的 90% 及以上人员）工作量与非全时人员按实际工作时间折算的工作量之和。

研究与试验发展（R&D）内部支出 指调查单位在报告年度用于内部开展 R&D 活动（基础研究、应用研究和试验发展）的实际支出。包括用于 R&D 项目（课题）活动的直接支出，以及间接用于 R&D 活动的管理费、服务费、与 R&D 有关的基本建设支出以及外协加工费等，不包括生产性活动支出、归还贷款支出以及与外单位合作或委托外单位进行 R&D 活动而转拨给对方的经费支出。

专业技术人员 指从事专业技术工作的人员以及从事专业技术管理工作且已在 1983 年以前评定了专业技术职称或在 1984 年以后聘任了专业技术职务的人员。从事专业技术工作的人员具体指工程技术人员，农业技术人员，科学研究人员（含自然科学研究及实验技术人员），卫生技术人员，教学人员（含高等院校、中等专业学校、技工学校、中学、小学），民用航空飞行技术人员，船舶技术人员，经济专业人员，会计人员，统计人员，翻译人员，图书资料、档案、文博人员，新闻、出版人员，律师、公证人员，广播电视播音人员，工艺美术人员，体育人员，艺术人员及企业政治思想工作人员。从事专业技术管理工作的人员是指企业、事业单位领导；企业、事业单位下设的职能机构、企业的生产车间的辅助车间（或附属辅助生产单位）中从事生产、技术、经济管理和政治工作的人员；按照公务员管理或参照公务员管理的人员不统计为专业技术人员。

专利 是专利权的简称，是对发明人的发明创造经审查合格后，由专利局依据专利法授予发明人和设计人对该项发明创造享有的专有权。包括发明、实用新型和外观设计。

发明专利 指专利法及其实施细则所称的发明，指对产品、方法或者改进所提出的新的技术方案。

实用新型专利 指专利法及其实施细则所称的实用新型，指对产品的形状、构造或者其结合所提出的适于实用的新的技术方案。

外观设计专利 指专利法及其实施细则所称的外观设计，指对产品的形状、图案、色彩或者其结合所做出的富有美感并适于工业上应用的新设计。

Explanatory Notes on Main Statistical Indicators

Personnel Engaged in Science and Technology Activities refer to persons directly engaged in science and technology activities as well as persons engaged in science and technology management and persons offering direct services to science and technology activities in the surveyed entities in the reporting year. Persons directly engaged in science and technology activities include: persons engaged in science and technology activities in such institutions as research labs of entities, laboratories, technical development centers and middle-stage test workshops (bases); persons not working in the above-mentioned institutions but included in the science and technology activity project (task) team, etc. Persons engaged in science and technology management and persons offering direct services for science and technology activities include administrative staff related to science and technology activities, as well as persons directly providing information and literature, supply of materials, equipment maintenance and other services.

R&D refers to systematic and creative activities in the field of science and technology to increase the total knowledge, and apply such knowledge to create new applications, including three kinds of activities, i.e. basic research, applied research, and experimental development.

R&D Personnel refer to persons in the surveyed entities who are engaged in three kinds of activities, i.e. basic research, applied research, and development. They include those who participate in the above-mentioned three kinds of activities directly, research management personnel and persons directly serving these activities. Persons providing direct services include those who provide information and literature, supply of materials, equipment maintenance and other services.

Full-Time Equivalent of R&D Personnel is the sum of the full-time equivalent of personnel participating in R&D projects plus the full time equivalent of management and direct service personnel that should be allocated to R&D projects.

Internal R&D Expenditure means the actual disbursement of investigated entities on internal R&D in the reporting year, including direct spending on R&D project (task) activities, and management expenses and service fees indirectly spent on R&D, R&D related capital construction spending, and external assisting processing charges, etc.

Professional Technical Personnel refer to persons engaged in professional technological work and professional technological management whose professional technological titles were assessed and granted before 1983 or who have been retained at professional technological positions after 1984. Persons engaged in professional technological work refer to engineering technicians, agricultural technicians, research personnel (including natural science research and experiment technicians), medical technicians, teaching staff (including those in colleges and universities, technical secondary schools, vocational schools, high schools, and elementary schools), civil aviation flight technicians, watercraft technicians, economics professionals, accountants, statisticians, translators and interpreters, librarians, archivists, cultural expo personnel, journalists, publishers , lawyers, notaries, TV and radio broadcasters, industrial arts staff, sportspersons, artists, as well as personnel responsible for political ideology work in enterprises.. The professional technological management refer to leaders of enterprises and public institutions; persons engaged in management of production, technology and economy as well as political work in functional organs under enterprises and public institutions, auxiliary workplaces (or affiliated auxiliary production entities) of production workplaces of enterprises; persons managed as civil servants or with reference to civil servants are not counted as professional technicians.

Patent is the abbreviation of patent right, referring to the exclusive right granted by patent authorities upon examination and approval of inventions and creations to the inventors and designers with regard to the invention, including inventions, utility models and industrial designs.

Invention means the invention mentioned in the Patent Law and its detailed rules for implementation, i.e. the new technological solutions presented for the product, methodology, or improvement.

Utility Model means the utility model mentioned in the Patent Law and its detailed rules for implementation, i.e. the new practical technological solutions presented for the product shape, structure, color or combination.

Industrial Design means the industrial design mentioned in the Patent Law and its detailed rules for implementation, i.e. new designs of product shape, pattern, color or combination which are aesthetic and suitable for industrial applications.

卫生、体育
HEALTH AND SPORTS

简要说明

一、本章资料的主要内容

本章主要反映卫生、体育的发展情况。

卫生部分主要内容包括卫生总费用、卫生机构、卫生技术人员、床位数，医院诊疗人次及入院人数，主要疾病死亡原因及构成，全市主要健康指标等情况。体育部分主要包括群众体育活动情况、体育场地情况、运动员获奖情况、体育彩票情况等。

二、本章资料的数据来源

卫生部分的资料由北京市卫生和计划生育委员会提供，体育部分的资料由北京市体育局提供。

Brief Introduction

I. Main Content

This chapter mainly reflects the development of health and sports.

Health statistics include the total health expenditures, the number of health institutions, health technicians, ward beds, patients treated and hospitalized persons, major causes of death and composition, main health indicators of Beijing, and so on. Sports statistics include public sports and sports venues, awards received by athletes, and sports lottery tickets, etc.

II. Source of Data

Health data are from Beijing Municipal Commission of Health and Family Planning. Sports data are from Beijing Municipal Bureau of Sports.

20-1 卫生事业基本情况(1978-2013年)
BASIC STATISTICS ON HEALTH CARE (1978-2013)

年份 Year	卫生机构 (个) Healthcare Institutions (unit)	#医院(卫生院) Hospitals (Health Centers)	#医院 Hospitals	#疾病预防控制中心(防疫站) Centers for Disease Control and Prevention	#妇幼保健院(所、站) Maternity and Child Care Centers(Stations)	#社区卫生服务中心(站) Community Health Services Centers (Stations)
1978	3263	389		22	15	
1979	3614	387		22	17	
1980	3818	393		22	19	
1981	4135	403		22	19	
1982	4389	413		22	18	
1983	4312	412		22	19	
1984	4173	423		22	18	
1985	4248	376		22	18	
1986	4483	371		22	20	
1987	4744	398		22	19	
1988	4342	445		22	17	
1989	4398	470		22	17	
1990	4953	512		22	17	
1991	4970	525	337	22	17	
1992	4868	535	345	22	16	
1993	4962	548	364	32	16	
1994	4958	629	387	33	16	
1995	4955	629	387	33	15	
1996	6470	645	405	33	13	
1997	6577	673	435	33	13	
1998	5723	676	449	32	11	
1999	5990	686	460	32	8	
2000	6176	674	458	30	8	
2001	5969	673	458	30	9	
2002	4998	647	461	24	19	35
2003	5075	646	459	29	19	36
2004	4835	657	503	29	19	43
2005	4818	692	519	28	18	93
2006	4878	705	541	28	18	90
2007	6189	686	535	31	18	1126
2008	6523	660	537	31	19	1282
2009	6603	638	522	31	19	1395
2010	6539		550	31	19	1587
2011	9699		569	32	19	1744
2012	9974		608	32	19	1897
2013	10141		647	32	19	1926

注：1. 2010年及以前，本表中所有数据都不包含村卫生室及驻京部队医院情况。2011年开始，包含村卫生室情况。2012年开始，卫生机构数、卫生技术人员数据中包含驻京部队医院，床位数不包含。2013年开始，本表所有数据均包含驻京部队医院情况。
2. 2010年开始，原卫生院数据并入到社区卫生服务中心(站)等其他卫生机构。

资料来源：北京市卫生和计划生育委员会。

Note: a) Before 2010, figures in this table did not include village health clinics and hospitals of troops stationed in Beijing. From 2011, Figures included village health clinics.From 2012, health institutions and medical technical personnel included hospitals of troops stationed in Beijing,while the number of beds does not include those hospitals. Since 2013, figures included hospitals of troops stationed in Beijing.

b) From 2010, data on health centers were incorporated into other health institutions such as community health service centers (stations).

Source: Beijing Municipal Commission of Health and Family Planning.

20-1 续表 Continued

年 份 Year	卫生机构人员(人) Employed Persons in Healthcare Institutions (person)	#卫生技术人员 Medical Technical Personnel	#执业(助理)医师 Certified (Assistant) Physicians	#注册护士 Registered Nurses	实有床位数(张) Beds (unit)	#医院(卫生院) Hospitals (Health Centers)	#医院 Hospitals	每千户籍人口执业(助理)医师数(人) Certified Physicians Per 1000 Persons(person)	每千户籍人口注册护士数(人) Registered Nurses Per 1000 Persons(person)	每千人口户籍医院床位数(张) Beds Per 1000 Persons (unit)
1978	90174	65943	28435	16085	29767	26432		3.35	1.89	3.11
1979	97942	72131	31842	17398	30231	26808		3.66	1.87	3.08
1980	102601	74753	34365	17492	32453	28495		3.88	1.97	3.22
1981	110774	81183	37886	20025	33666	29783		4.20	2.20	3.30
1982	114420	83843	39385	20389	34574	30940		4.30	2.23	3.40
1983	119222	86593	41216	21181	35987	32242		4.40	2.26	3.50
1984	124664	89362	42112	22286	38580	34602		4.40	2.33	3.70
1985	127771	90831	42216	23782	41603	38180		4.44	2.48	3.99
1986	132865	94433	43403	25383	43956	40903		4.47	3.72	4.21
1987	142556	101829	46007	27786	47538	44407		4.66	2.81	4.49
1988	145362	105237	48216	30250	53078	48711		4.82	3.02	4.87
1989	150062	108108	49361	32056	55623	51877		4.83	3.14	5.08
1990	156304	111614	50934	34565	59036	55474		4.93	3.35	5.37
1991	161103	114342	52309	35714	61744	58744	54888	5.03	3.44	5.65
1992	164213	115825	53254	36768	63230	59833	55858	5.10	3.52	5.73
1993	165170	116173	53906	36687	65621	62340	58605	5.13	3.49	5.93
1994	164867	116818	53865	36608	67112	64416	60661	5.07	3.45	6.07
1995	164436	115967	54114	36719	66925	64211	60337	5.06	3.43	6.00
1996	164981	116849	54091	37712	66760	64902	60997	5.02	3.50	6.02
1997	167090	119256	54909	38630	67946	65826	61865	5.06	3.56	6.06
1998	162609	115976	51902	38883	69095	66954	63144	4.76	3.56	6.13
1999	161823	116597	52646	39625	69465	67684	63660	4.79	3.60	6.15
2000	160258	115510	51570	39900	71245	69183	65138	4.66	3.60	6.25
2001	158185	115935	52100	40537	73053	70837	66537	4.64	3.61	6.31
2002	144021	109564	47236	38879	75188	71967	67750	4.18	3.44	6.46
2003	148406	112212	47887	39912	74298	71173	66990	4.21	3.51	5.89
2004	153154	116610	48988	41547	77359	73811	69850	4.25	3.60	6.54
2005	157133	119874	50617	42897	79067	76031	72329	4.32	3.66	6.65
2006	166278	126904	52795	45647	81440	78588	74762	4.41	3.84	6.77
2007	182475	139275	54989	50890	83736	80158	76915	4.53	4.19	6.34
2008	193799	149916	58773	55349	86196	81937	79089	4.78	4.50	6.43
2009	208156	160435	62348	61604	90100	84896	82471	5.00	4.94	6.62
2010	219762	171093	65954	67308	92871		85935	5.24	5.35	6.83
2011	235708	181938	69749	72812	94735		87596	5.46	5.70	6.85
2012	276654	219714	82192	95202	100167		92610	6.33	7.34	7.14
2013	294012	229720	85819	100652	122754		115278	6.52	7.65	8.76

注：表中每千人口拥有执业(助理)医师数、每千人口拥有注册护士数、每千人口拥有医院床位数按年末户籍人口计算。2013年上述指标按年末常住人口计算分别为4.06人、4.76人和5.45张。

Note:The data of "Certified Physicians per 1000 Persons", "Registered Nurses per 1000 Persons", "Beds per 1000 Persons" were calculated by year-end registered population. These indicators for 2013 calculated by year-end permanent population were 4.06 persons, 4.76 persons and 5.45 units.

20-2 卫生总费用(2000-2012年)
TOTAL HEALTH EXPENDITURES(2000-2012)

年份 Year	卫生总费用(亿元) Total Health Expenditures (100 million yuan)	政府卫生支出 Health Expenditures by Governments		社会卫生支出 Social Health Expenditures		个人现金卫生支出 Health Expenditures in Cash by Individuals		相当于地区生产总值比例(%) Total Health Expenditure as % of GDP Total(%)
		绝对数(亿元) Absolute Number (100 million yuan)	占卫生总费用比重(%) As % of Total(%)	绝对数(亿元) Absolute Number (100 million yuan)	占卫生总费用比重(%) As % of Total(%)	绝对数(亿元) Absolute Number (100 million yuan)	占卫生总费用比重(%) As % of Total(%)	
2000	166.72	34.70	20.81	61.78	37.05	70.25	42.13	5.27
2001	201.12	45.28	22.52	73.18	36.39	82.65	41.10	5.42
2002	262.36	48.51	18.49	99.61	37.97	114.23	43.54	6.08
2003	314.16	65.80	20.94	132.04	42.03	116.33	37.03	6.27
2004	357.19	69.35	19.41	150.72	42.20	137.12	38.39	5.92
2005	432.80	85.73	19.81	187.84	43.40	159.22	36.79	6.21
2006	497.41	115.89	23.30	208.00	41.82	173.52	34.88	6.13
2007	523.20	142.03	27.15	212.00	40.52	169.17	32.33	5.31
2008	668.52	180.01	26.93	271.26	40.58	217.25	32.50	6.01
2009	689.60	201.14	29.17	296.25	42.96	192.21	27.87	5.67
2010	814.74	226.84	27.84	385.10	47.27	202.80	24.89	5.77
2011	977.26	275.48	28.19	453.16	46.37	248.62	25.44	6.01
2012	1190.01	320.40	26.92	600.96	50.50	268.65	22.58	6.66

资料来源：北京市卫生和计划生育委员会。
Source: Beijing Municipal Commission of Health and Family Planning.

20-3 卫生机构基本情况
BASIC STATISTICS FOR HEALTHCARE INSTITUTIONS

项目	Item	2013	2012	构成(%) Composition(%) 2013	构成(%) Composition(%) 2012
卫生机构 (个)	**Health Care Institutions (unit)**	**10141**	**9974**	**100.0**	**100.0**
#医院	Hospitals	647	608	6.4	6.1
社区卫生服务中心(站)	Health Service Centers (Stations) for Community	1926	1897	19.0	19.0
门诊部	Outpatient Departments	946	890	9.3	8.9
妇幼保健院(所、站)	Maternity and Child Care Hospitals	19	19	0.2	0.2
疾病预防控制中心(防疫站)	Disease Prevention and Control Center (Epidemic Prevention Station)	32	32	0.3	0.3
专科疾病防治院(所、站)	Specific Disease Prevention and Cure Centers	28	28	0.3	0.3
诊所、卫生所、医务室、护理站	Clinics, Health Centers, Infirmaries, Nursing Stations	3471	3373	34.2	33.8
床位 (张)	**Beds (unit)**	**122754**	**100167**	**100.0**	**100.0**
#医院	Hospitals	115278	92610	93.9	92.5
社区卫生服务中心(站)	Health Service Centers (Stations) for Community	4548	4745	3.7	4.7
妇幼保健院(所、站)	Maternity and Child Care Hospitals	1912	1770	1.6	1.8
专科疾病防治院(所、站)	Specific Disease Prevention and Cure Centers	539	565	0.4	0.6
卫生技术人员 (人)	**Medical Technical Personnel (person)**	**229720**	**219714**	**100.0**	**100.0**
#医院	Hospitals	170571	162783	74.3	74.1
社区卫生服务中心(站)	Health Service Centers (Stations) for Community	25122	24003	10.9	10.9
妇幼保健院(所、站)	Maternity and Child Care Hospitals	4662	4336	2.0	2.0
专科疾病防治院(所、站)	Specific Disease Prevention and Cure Centers	622	602	0.3	0.3
#执业(助理)医师	Certified Doctors	85819	82192	37.4	37.4
注册护士	Registered Nurses	100652	95202	43.8	43.3

注：本表2012年数据中,床位数不包括驻京部队医院情况,其它都包括。从2013年起本表所有数据均包含驻京部队医院情况。
资料来源：北京市卫生和计划生育委员会。
Note: In this table, apart from number of beds,all the data for 2012 covered hospitals of troops stationed in Beijing.
Since 2013, all the statistics in this table cover the hospitals of troops stationed in Beijing.
Source: Beijing Municipal Commission of Health and Family Planning.

20-4 全市医院基本情况(2013年) BASIC STATISTICS ON HOSPITALS (2013)

项目	Item	医院数 (个) Hospitals (unit)	床位数 (张) Beds (unit)	职工人数 (人) Employed Persons (person)	#卫生技术人员 Medical Technical Personnel	#执业医师 Certified Doctors	#中医 Doctors of Traditional Chinese Medicine
合计	**Total**	**647**	**115278**	**215262**	**170571**	**57658**	**8332**
按隶属关系分	**By Affiliation**						
#市	Municipal	30	20944	42326	34158	11087	760
区县	Districts and Counties	106	29727	51460	41554	14518	2640
按专业分	**By Specialty**						
#综合医院	General Hospitals	336	77312	151651	122246	41437	2267
中医医院	Hospital Specialized in Traditional Chinese Medicine	140	12346	23417	18519	7325	5099
中西医结合医院	Hospitals Combining Western Medicine with Traditional Chinese Medicine	15	4868	4816	3858	1402	519
民族医院	Nationality Hospitals	3	121	435	236	93	41
口腔医院	Stomatology Hospitals	18	355	3813	3058	1134	4
眼科医院	Ophthalmology Hospitals	10	492	733	429	132	5
肿瘤医院	Tumor Hospitals	8	2865	4639	3425	1031	52
心血管病医院	Hospitals for Cardiovascular Diseases	2	1022	2937	2445	644	5
胸科医院	Thorax Hospitals	1	533	795	591	136	1
妇(产)科医院	Hospitals for Gynecology and Obstetrics	9	743	2471	1818	533	23
儿童医院	Children's Hospitals	7	1685	4078	3172	902	53
精神病医院	Psychiatric Hospital	22	7575	5676	4120	846	46
传染病医院	Infectious Disease Hospitals	3	1338	2845	2228	743	37
骨科医院	Hospitals of Orthopedics	9	657	871	592	174	38
整形外科医院	Orthopaedics Hospitals	1	328	701	497	161	
其他专科医院	Other Specialized Hospitals	31	1817	3040	2020	591	83
护理院	Nursing Hospitals	6	70	26	19	6	

注：2013年开始本表数据均包含驻京部队医院情况。
资料来源：北京市卫生和计划生育委员会。
Note: Since 2013, Figures in this fable included hospitals of troops stationed in Beijing.
Source: Beijing Municipal Commission of Health and Family Planning.

20-4 续表 Continued

单位：人 (person)

项 目	Item	#执业助理医师 Certified Assistant Doctors	#中医 Doctors of Traditional Chinese Medicine	#注册护士 Registered Nurses	#药师(士) Pharmacists (Assistant Pharmacists)	#技师(士) Technicians (Assistant Technicians)	#检验师(士) Laboratorians (Assistant Laboratorians)
合 计	**Total**	**1384**	**298**	**83530**	**7951**	**7409**	**4732**
按隶属关系分	**By Affiliation**						
#市	Municipal	61	1	16755	1691	1844	1078
区 县	Districts and Counties	549	83	18752	2484	2013	1430
按专业分	**By Specialty**						
#综合医院	General Hospitals	827	121	61900	4822	5028	3147
中医医院	Hospital Specialized in Traditional Chinese Medicine	270	132	6872	1835	924	626
中西医结合医院	Hospitals Combining Western Medicine with Traditional Chinese Medicine	58	20	1671	226	170	119
民族医院	Nationality Hospitals	10	3	85	15	19	12
口腔医院	Stomatology Hospitals	24		1294	34	71	20
眼科医院	Ophthalmology Hospitals	6	1	201	17	27	21
肿瘤医院	Tumor Hospitals	5	1	1699	141	205	93
心血管病医院	Hospitals for Cardiovascular Diseases	1		1360	60	69	45
胸科医院	Thorax Hospitals			348	30	51	24
妇(产)科医院	Hospitals for Gynecology and Obstetrics	2		948	66	105	82
儿童医院	Children's Hospitals	4		1523	193	221	160
精神病医院	Psychiatric Hospitals	78	3	2353	204	131	98
传染病医院	Infectious Disease Hospitals	2		1149	104	153	128
骨科医院	Hospitals of Orthopedics	13	5	255	33	29	18
整形外科医院	Orthopaedics Hospitals			253	9	14	7
其他专科医院	Other Specialized Hospitals	56	6	989	100	127	84
护理院	Nursing Hospitals			9	2	2	1

注：2013年开始本表数据均包含驻京部队医院情况。
资料来源：北京市卫生和计划生育委员会。
Note: Since 2013, Figures in this fable included hospitals of troops stationed in Beijing.
Source: Beijing Municipal Commission of Health and Family Planning.

20-5 医院工作情况(2013年)
WORKS OF HOSPITALS (2013)

项 目	Item	诊疗人次数(千人次) Patients Treated (1000 person times)	#门诊 Out-patients	健康检查人数(千人次) Health Check (1000 person times)	平均开放病床数(张) Beds in Use (unit)	入院人数(千人次) In-patients (1000 person times)	出院人数(千人次) Discharged Patients (1000 person times)
合 计	**Total**	**147071.1**	**123436.6**	**2988.7**	**92354.2**	**2325.0**	**2785.2**
#综合医院	General Hospitals	100322.2	78688.7	2355.7	56020.9	1618.5	2076.3
中医医院	Hospital Specialized in Traditional Chinese Medicine	28084.5	27077.6	338.0	11883.8	236.2	234.4
中西医结合医院	Hospitals Combining Western Medicine with Traditional Chinese Medicine	3671.8	3408.5	106.7	4663.4	47.8	47.6
民族医院	Nationality Hospitals	118.7	118.7	2.8	116.2	1.0	1.0
口腔医院	Stomatology Hospitals	2236.5	2153.8	23.8	322.5	8.6	8.5
眼科医院	Ophthalmology Hospitals	225.7	224.1	31.0	467.5	10.2	9.9
肿瘤医院	Tumor Hospitals	1205.1	1192.8	87.6	2725.0	97.5	97.5
心血管病医院	Hospitals for Cardiovascular Diseases	602.1	575.8	3.8	1022.4	50.0	49.8
胸科医院	Thorax Hospitals	216.9	211.2		533.0	11.1	11.0
妇(产)科医院	Hospitals for Gynecology and Obstetrics	1455.8	1420.8	8.9	732.3	39.3	39.6
儿童医院	Children's Hospitals	5512.8	5075.8	11.1	1634.3	95.0	93.7
精神病医院	Psychiatric Hospitals	1083.2	1071.2	7.6	7494.4	16.7	17.2
传染病医院	Infectious Disease Hospitals	1012.6	946.1		1338.0	43.6	43.4
骨科医院	Hospitals of Orthopedics	230.1	219.0	0.6	645.8	8.5	8.3
整形外科医院	Orthopaedics Hospitals	110.2	107.8	0.2	328.0	11.4	11.4
其他专科医院	Other Specialized Hospitals	623.9	585.7	9.4	1611.1	24.3	24.4
护理院	Nursing Centers	2.0	2.0		24.9	0.1	0.1

注：2013年开始本表数据均包含驻京部队医院情况。
资料来源：北京市卫生和计划生育委员会。
Note: Since 2013, Figures in this fable included hospitals of troops stationed in Beijing.
Source: Beijing Municipal Commission of Health and Family Planning.

20-5 续表 Continued

项　目	Item	病死率 (%) Case Fatality Rate (%)	病床周转次数 (次) Turnover Beds (time)	病床使用率 (%) Utilization Rate of Beds (%)	出院者平均住院日 (日) Average Hospitalization Period (day)
合　计	**Total**	**1.24**	**25.18**	**82.05**	**11.00**
#综合医院	General Hospitals	1.34	28.86	81.22	10.70
中医医院	Hospital Specialized in Traditional Chinese Medicine	1.48	19.72	75.22	13.39
中西医结合医院	Hospitals Combining Western Medicine with Traditional Chinese Medicine	2.10	10.20	74.65	32.25
民族医院	Nationality Hospitals	1.50	8.63	54.07	21.61
口腔医院	Stomatology Hospitals		26.42	62.57	8.61
眼科医院	Ophthalmology Hospitals	0.01	21.18	57.91	7.09
肿瘤医院	Tumor Hospitals	0.50	35.79	95.99	9.97
心血管病医院	Hospitals for Cardiovascular Diseases	0.24	48.68	106.83	8.01
胸科医院	Thorax Hospitals	1.54	20.70	100.33	17.70
妇(产)科医院	Hospitals for Gynecology and Obstetrics	0.02	54.07	80.77	5.31
儿童医院	Children's Hospitals	0.14	57.31	103.69	6.47
精神病医院	Psychiatric Hospital	1.07	2.29	98.78	144.86
传染病医院	Infectious Disease Hospitals	2.28	32.42	106.84	11.95
骨科医院	Hospitals of Orthopedics	0.34	12.83	53.05	13.69
整形外科医院	Orthopaedics Hospitals	0.01	34.72	76.97	12.46
其他专科医院	Other Specialized Hospitals	2.67	15.16	62.67	12.38
护理院	Nursing Centers	11.11	2.89	85.13	18.76

注：2013年开始本表数据均包含驻京部队医院情况。

Note: Since 2013, Figures in this fable included hospitals of troops stationed in Beijing.

20-6 全市居民前十位死因顺位、死亡率及构成(2013年)
DEATH RATE AND COMPOSITION OF 10 MAJOR DISEASE (2013)

顺 位 No.	死因名称	Cause of Death	死亡率(1/10万) Death Rate (1/100 thousands)	构 成(%) Composition(%)
	全 市	**Total**		
1	恶性肿瘤	Malignant Tumour	165.04	26.92
2	心脏病	Heart Disease	156.60	25.55
3	脑血管病	Cerebrovasular Disease	131.98	21.53
4	呼吸系统疾病	Disease of the Respiratory System	57.92	9.45
5	损伤和中毒	Trauma and Toxicosis	22.39	3.65
6	内分泌、营养、代谢及免疫疾病	Endocrine, Nutrition, Metabolite and Immunity Disease	18.43	3.01
7	消化系统疾病	Disease of the Gigestive System	16.43	2.68
8	神经系统疾病	Neurological Disease	7.61	1.24
9	泌尿生殖系统疾病	Disease of the Genitourinary System	5.04	0.82
10	传染病	Infectious Disease	4.66	0.76
	男 性	**Male**		
1	恶性肿瘤	Malignant Tumour	194.91	28.48
2	心脏病	Heart Disease	166.07	24.27
3	脑血管病	Cerebrovasular Disease	146.62	21.43
4	呼吸系统疾病	Disease of the Respiratory System	65.83	9.62
5	损伤和中毒	Trauma and Toxicosis	27.30	3.99
6	消化系统疾病	Disease of the Gigestive System	18.87	2.76
7	内分泌、营养、代谢及免疫疾病	Endocrine, Nutrition, Metabolite and Immunity Disease	17.96	2.62
8	神经系统疾病	Neurological Disease	8.22	1.20
9	传染病	Infectious Disease	6.36	0.93
10	泌尿生殖系统疾病	Disease of the Genitourinary System	5.17	0.76
	女 性	**Female**		
1	心脏病	Heart Disease	147.05	27.17
2	恶性肿瘤	Malignant Tumour	134.93	24.93
3	脑血管病	Cerebrovasular Disease	117.21	21.66
4	呼吸系统疾病	Disease of the Respiratory System	49.95	9.23
5	内分泌、营养、代谢及免疫疾病	Endocrine, Nutrition, Metabolite and Immunity Disease	18.91	3.50
6	损伤和中毒	Trauma and Toxicosis	17.44	3.22
7	消化系统疾病	Disease of the Gigestive System	13.97	2.58
8	神经系统疾病	Neurological Disease	6.99	1.29
9	泌尿生殖系统疾病	Disease of the Genitourinary System	4.92	0.91
10	传染病	Infection Disease	2.95	0.55

资料来源：北京市卫生和计划生育委员会。
Source: Beijing Municipal Commission of Health and Family Planning.

20-7 全市主要健康指标情况(1978-2013年)
MAJOR HEALTH INDICATIONS OF BEIJING(1978-2013)

年份 Year	婴儿死亡率(‰) Infant Mortality (‰)	城郊 Suburban Districts	远县 Counties	新生儿死亡率(‰) Newborn Baby Mortality (‰)	城郊 Suburban Districts	远县 Counties	孕产妇死亡率(1/10万) Pregnant & Lying-in Women Mortality (1/100000)	城郊 Suburban Districts	远县 Counties	甲乙类传染病发病率(1/10万) Incidence Rate of Catogory A and B Epidemics (1/100000)
1978	17.11	10.34	21.15	12.21	7.35	15.60	31.00	5.00	53.00	
1979	16.97	12.81	19.43	10.08	8.00	12.77	34.70	13.10	41.30	1584.25
1980	14.79	10.40	17.73	10.24	7.12	12.81	26.30	12.50	34.60	2165.23
1981	13.84	9.69	17.26	9.22	6.00	11.85	48.50	18.70	76.10	2225.71
1982	12.97	9.95	15.19	8.02	6.20	9.76	24.50	21.70	32.60	2193.16
1983	13.79	10.54	17.24	8.78	6.22	11.84	28.10	24.30	45.10	1904.55
1984	10.98	10.33	12.49	7.78	6.72	9.20	16.80	11.40	41.50	1666.68
1985	13.94	10.02	18.85	10.41	6.40	15.97	22.90	24.30	35.10	1335.23
1986	16.05	13.42	19.24	12.13	8.97	15.41	30.50	22.90	43.10	1120.19
1987	15.56	12.63	18.23	11.08	8.01	14.02	26.60	14.80	33.30	826.51
1988	14.98	11.71	17.92	10.48	7.96	13.20	24.80	25.40	32.40	640.98
1989	14.96	11.59	18.30	10.53	8.08	13.23	34.50	3.90	55.80	547.61
1990	11.66	10.12	12.55	8.49	7.43	9.38	25.00	13.00	30.50	509.55
1991	12.46	11.94	13.11	8.56	7.83	9.47	24.00	23.80	24.20	448.23
1992	12.12	10.81	14.43	8.93	7.72	11.18	30.10	30.20	29.80	385.98
1993	10.38	10.68	9.93	7.21	7.28	7.10	16.50	21.10	9.60	356.66
1994	10.93	12.09	9.43	7.29	7.57	6.94	18.94	21.02	16.26	374.31
1995	11.45	14.23	8.20	7.52	8.91	5.90	22.27	23.89	20.36	309.99
1996	10.05	11.57	8.13	6.97	7.61	6.17	15.32	11.45	20.19	340.24
1997	9.45	10.49	8.05	6.36	6.75	5.83	23.69	25.25	21.60	294.41
1998	7.58	9.07	5.75	5.53	6.46	4.39	10.46	10.87	9.97	306.37
1999	7.95	7.78	8.38	5.94	5.74	6.45	17.53	15.69	22.06	308.10
2000	5.36	6.29	4.05	3.70	4.26	2.91	9.70	7.10	13.38	301.19
2001	6.01	6.26	5.62	4.05	4.16	3.89	11.71	13.85	8.45	276.85
2002	5.56	5.57	5.54	3.70	3.65	3.77	15.12	16.24	13.29	282.95
2003	5.89	5.91	5.83	3.83	3.56	4.33	15.60	6.92	31.35	228.00
2004	4.61	4.51	4.79	3.49	3.42	3.62	15.19	17.69	10.66	408.03
2005	4.35	4.08	4.84	3.29	3.03	3.79	15.91	7.33	31.95	445.91
2006	4.66	3.96	6.04	3.42	2.99	4.26	7.87	7.12	9.36	448.70
2007	3.89	3.50	4.72	2.65	2.31	3.39	16.74	18.92	12.10	421.02
2008	3.70	3.49	4.21	2.45	2.41	2.52	18.52	15.86	24.76	312.99
2009	3.49	3.28	4.02	2.47	2.37	2.73	14.55	12.56	19.49	339.89
2010	3.29	2.95	4.25	2.06	1.94	2.42	12.14	8.95	21.23	268.99
2011	2.84	2.62	3.43	1.88	1.77	2.17	9.09	9.99	6.67	226.76
2012	2.87	2.48	3.87	1.91	1.65	2.60	6.05	4.20	10.82	174.45
2013	2.33	2.19	2.69	1.52	1.48	1.63	9.45	6.51	17.20	155.87

注：城郊包括东城区、西城区、朝阳区、丰台区、石景山区、海淀区、门头沟区、房山区；远县包括通州区、昌平区、顺义区、大兴区、怀柔区、平谷区、密云县、延庆县。

资料来源：北京市卫生和计划生育委员会。

Note: Suburban districts include Dongcheng, Xicheng, Chaoyang, Fengtai, Shijingshan, Haidian, Mentougou, and Fangshan Districts. Counties include Tongzhou, Changping, Shunyi, and Daxing Districts, Huairou, Pinggu, Miyun and Yanqing Counties.

Source: Beijing Municipal Commission of Health and Family Planning.

20-8 主要年份体育场地情况
SITUATION OF THE GYMNASIUMS AND STADIUMS IN MAIN YEARS

单位：个 (unit)

年份 Year	合计 Total	#体育场 Stadiums	#体育馆 Gymnasiums	#游泳场馆 Natatoriums	#室内 Indoor	#各种训练房 Exercise Rooms
1950	19	1				2
1955	61	1			2	10
1960	124	2		4	3	19
1970	188	2	2	8	3	24
1975	234	3	2	11	4	28
1980	293	3	2	12	4	32
1985	405	4	2	20	8	54
1990	780	12	12	49	26	153
1995	1381	18	18	88	56	291
2000	2815	35	24	214	161	863
2001	3500	42	27	283	216	1101
2002	4176	57	33	334	263	1358
2003	6100	93	36	443	371	1729
2004	6104	93	36	443	371	1729
2005	6112	93	36	446	374	1731
2006	6122	93	36	446	374	1734
2007	6146	94	37	446	374	1736
2008	6149	94	37	446	374	1739
2009	6149	94	37	446	374	1739
2010	6151	94	37	446	374	1741
2011	6151	94	37	446	374	1741
2012	6156	94	37	447	375	1742
2013	6156	94	37	447	375	1742

资料来源：北京市体育局。
Source: Beijing Municipal Bureau of Sports.

20-9 群众体育活动情况
ACTIVITIES OF MASS SPORTS

项目	Item	2013	2012
晨晚练辅导站 (个)	Instruction Stations of Morning and Evening Exercises (unit)	6360	6622
青少年体育俱乐部数 (个)	Number of Teenager Sport Clubs (unit)	203	203
社会体育指导员 (人)	Social Sport Instructors (person)	38915	30814
专项球类场地设施 (个)	Special Ball Game Venues and Facilities (unit)	326	280
社区健身俱乐部 (个)	Community Fitness Clubs (unit)	129	117
体育生活化社区 (个)	Life-oriented Sports Communities (unit)	1453	821

资料来源：北京市体育局。
Source: Beijing Municipal Bureau of Sports.

20-10 运动员、裁判员情况
ATHLETES AND REFEREES

单位：人 (person)

项目	Item	2013	#女性 Females	2012	#女性 Females
分等级运动员发展人数	**Number of Graded Athletes**	**1676**	**612**	**1880**	**744**
国际级运动健将	World-class Athletes	5	2	11	6
国家级运动健将	National Grade Athletes	69	26	106	38
一级	First Grade Athletes	325	129	426	175
二级	Second Grade Athletes	1277	455	1337	525
分等级裁判员发展人数	**Number of Graded Referees**	**1122**	**335**	**1135**	**289**
国家级	National Grade Referees			32	13
一级	First Grade Referees	289	99	152	67
二级	Second Grade Referees	833	236	951	209

资料来源：北京市体育局。
Source: Beijing Municipal Bureau of Sports.

20-11 运动员获奖牌情况(2013年)
STATISTICS FOR MEDALS WON (2013)

单位：块 (piece)

项　目	Item	金 牌 Gold	银 牌 Silver	铜 牌 Copper
合　计	**Total**	**48**	**48**	**48**
国际比赛	International Competitions	8	8	7
国内比赛	Domestic Competitions	40	40	41

资料来源：北京市体育局。
Source: Beijing Municipal Bureau of Sports.

20-12 体育彩票
SPORTS LOTTERY

项　目		Item		2013	2012
电脑体育彩票销售个数	(个)	Number of Computer Sports Lottery Tickets Sold	(unit)	2607	2420
体育彩票发行额	(万元)	Circulation of Sports Lottery	(10000 yuan)	538876	382996
#足　彩	(万元)	Football Lottery	(10000 yuan)	336968	187998
体育彩票公益金提取额	(万元)	Public Welfare Funds Drawn from Sports Lottery	(10000 yuan)	131328	93566
#足　彩	(万元)	Football Lottery	(10000 yuan)	70727	41515

资料来源：北京市体育局。
Source: Beijing Municipal Bureau of Sports.

主要统计指标解释

卫 生

卫生机构 指从卫生行政部门取得《医疗机构执业许可证》，或从民政、工商行政、机构编制管理部门取得法人单位登记证书，为社会提供医疗保健、疾病控制、卫生监督服务或从事医学科研和医学在职培训等工作的单位。

卫生技术人员 指由卫生机构支付工资的全部固定职工和合同制职工中现任职务为卫生技术工作的专业人员，不包括从事管理工作的人员。

执业医师和注册护士 指领取医师执业证书和注册护士证书的人员，不包括从事管理工作的医师和护士。

死亡率（死因死亡率） 是指某种原因（如疾病）所致的死亡人数占户籍人口比重。

婴儿死亡率 指某地区一年内每 1000 名活产婴儿与未满 1 岁的婴儿死亡人数之比。婴儿死亡率可以衡量一个国家或地区经济文化、居民健康状况和卫生保健事业发展情况，同时也是人口平均期望寿命研究的重要内容。

5岁以下儿童死亡率 指某地区一年内每1000名活产婴儿与未满 5 岁儿童死亡人数之比。5 岁以下儿童死亡率是目前国际上公认的反映儿童生存状况的重要指标。

孕产妇死亡率 指某年某地每十万活产中的孕产妇死亡比例。同婴儿死亡率一样，孕产妇死亡率是评价某一地区社会发展状况的重要指标，它的高低与社会经济状况、孕产妇社会环境及卫生保健服务有直接的联系。

体 育

体育场地 指专门用于体育训练、比赛和健身活动的，有一定投资的公益性或经营性体育建筑设施。

晨晚练辅导站 是指本市公民自愿参加，在本市体育场馆、公园、街道、街心花园等公共场所设立的，利用早晚时间，以开展健身活动为目的的群众体育健身场所。

青少年体育俱乐部数 指创建单位利用自己所拥有的体育场馆、人才等资源建立起来的具有社会公益性的新型社会化青少年体育组织。

社会体育指导员 指在竞技体育、学校体育、部队体育以外的群众性体育活动中从事技能传授、锻炼指导和组织管理的工作人员。

专项球类活动场地 为满足不同人群特别是青少年的健身需求，而建设的专项球类活动场地，分篮球广场、笼式多功能球场、乒乓球长廊三种类型。

社区健身俱乐部 指“城市社区居民根据共同的目的和兴趣自愿组成的，以辖区内特定的体育场地设施为依托，经常开展体育活动，且隶属于街道办事处或社区居委会的公益性群众体育组织。”

等级运动员人数 指经考核正式批准授予等级运动员称号的人数。运动员等级分为国际级运动健将、国家级运动健将、一级运动员、二级运动员、三级运动员、少年级运动员。

等级裁判员人数 指经考核正式批准授予等级裁判员称号的人数。裁判员等级分为国际级裁判、国家级裁判、一级裁判、二级裁判、三级裁判。

运动员获奖牌情况 指当年北京市运动员在世界比赛、亚洲比赛、全国比赛中获得金、银、铜牌的数量。

Explanatory Notes on Main Statistical Indicators

Health

Healthcare Institutions refer to institutions granted with License for Medical Institution by the health administration authority, or granted with certificate of corporate unit by the civil affair, administration for industry and commerce, management authority of institutional organization, and providing medical service and healthcare, disease control, health supervision service or carrying out medical research and education, and so on.

Medical Technical Personnel refer to all fixed employees and of contract-based employees, professional personnel in health technology, who receive pays from health institutions, excluding personnel engaged in management.

Certified Doctors and Registered Nurses refer to personnel who have received a physician practicing certificate and certified nurse certificate, excluding physicians and nurses engaged in management. The statistical range is basically the same as that in the yearbook 2002.

Mortality (Cause-specific Death Rate) means the proportion of persons dead due to certain cause (such as disease) in the permanent population.

Infant Mortality means the rate of dead infants under 1 year old to 1000 live infants. Infant death rate measures the development of economy, culture, citizen health and health care in a country or region. It is also an important component of study on average life expectancy of population.

Mortality of Children under 5 means the rate of dead children under 5 years old to 1000 live infants. This is an important indicator now internationally recognized to reflect the survival status of children.

Pregnant and Lying-in Women Mortality refers to the rate of dead pregnant and lying-in women to 100,000 live pregnant and lying-in women in an area in a year. This is an important indicator to evaluate the social development status in an area. The figure of this indicator is directly related to the social and economic status, social environment and health care service for pregnant and lying-in women.

Sports

Sports Venues refer to sports building facilities for public welfare or operating purpose, specially used for sports training, games and fitness activities, and with certain investment.

Instruction Station of Morning and Evening Exercise refer to public sports and fitness sites located in sports gyms and stadiums, parks, streets, street parks and other public sites in a city, where the citizens in the city participate in voluntarily fitness activities in the morning or evening.

Number of Teenager Sports Clubs means the number of new-type social sports organizations for teenagers in the nature of socialistic public welfare, which are established by the builder with its own resources such as sports gyms and stadiums and human resource.

Social Sports Instructors refer to working personnel who carry out skill teaching, exercise instruction, organization and management in mass sports activities other than athletic sports, school sports, and army sports.

Special Ball Game Venue and Facilities are special venues for ball activities built to meet the fitness need of different population, especially teenagers, consisting of three types, i.e. basketball squares, multi-purpose cage-shaped courts, and table tennis corridors.

Community Fitness Clubs refer to "mass sports organizations in the nature of public welfare, which are formed by residents in urban communities voluntarily according to their common purpose and interest, based on specific sports venue facilities in the jurisdiction, for frequent sports activities, and under the jurisdiction of sub-district administrative office or community neighborhood committee."

Number of Graded Athletes means the number of athletes formally granted with the title of graded athlete upon examination. Grades of athletes include international master sportsman, national maser sportsman, grade-I athlete, grade-II athlete, grade-III athlete, and juvenile athlete.

Number of Graded Referees means the number of referees formally granted with the title of graded referees upon examination. Grades of referees include international referee, national referee, grade-I referee, grade-II referee, and grade-III referee.

Medals Won by Athletes mean the number of gold, silver and copper medals won by athletes of Beijing in world games, Asian games and national games.

北京统计年鉴2014　BEIJING STATISTICAL YEARBOOK

社会福利、社区、政法及其他

SOCIAL WELFARE, COMMUNITY, LAW AND OTHERS

简要说明

一、本章资料的主要内容

本章资料主要包括社会活动参与、公检法司、民政事业、劳动保障、残疾人事业、妇女及儿童发展规划监测情况等内容。

二、本章资料的数据来源

1.社会活动参与的内容主要包括历届北京市人大代表和政协委员人数及议案情况、妇联组织和工会组织情况等。资料分别由北京市人民代表大会常务委员会、中国人民政治协商会议北京市委员会、北京市妇女联合会和北京市总工会提供。

2.公检法司的资料主要包括公安机关的刑事案件立案情况和治安案件查处情况，交通、火灾事故情况，检察机关的办案情况，人民法院审理案件和收结案情况，以及司法局提供的律师、公证、调解工作等情况。资料分别由北京市公安局、北京市高级人民法院、北京市人民检察院和北京市司法局提供。

3.民政事业和劳动保障统计资料主要包括社会福利企事业机构、人员、优抚和社会救济情况、婚姻登记情况。资料分别由北京市民政局、北京市人力资源和社会保障局提供。

4.残疾人资料主要包括残疾人康复、教育、就业、扶贫和残联组织建设等情况。资料由北京市残疾人联合会提供。

5.妇女与儿童发展规划监测资料主要包括妇女参与决策和管理、就业、教育、健康、法律保护等情况；儿童的健康、教育、法律保护社会生活环境等情况。资料由北京市统计局依据部门统计报表资料整理提供。

6.安全生产情况由北京市行政工商管理局、北京市食品药品监督管理局、北京市公安交通管理局、北京市安全生产监督管理局提供。

Brief Introduction

I. Main Content

This chapter consists of statistics for social activity participation, public security institutions, procuratorates, courts, judicial authorities, civil affairs, labor security, undertakings for disabled people, women and children development planning and monitoring.

II. Data Sources

1. Statistics for social activity participation consist of the numbers of deputies and proposals at people's congress and political consulting conferences of Beijing in previous years, women's federation and organizations, and trade unions. Data were provided respectively by the Standing Committee of Beijing Municipal People's Congress, Beijing Committee of CPPCC, Beijing Women's Federation, and Beijing Federation of Labor Unions.

2. Statistics for public security institutions, procuratorates, courts, and judicial authorities cover criminal cases put on the record of public security organs as well as public security investigation and punishments, traffic accidents and fires, case settlements in procuratorates, cases accepted and settled by people's courts, information on lawyers, notary, mediation provided by juridical bureaus. Data were provided by Beijing Municipal Bureau of Public Security, People's High Court of Beijing, People's Procuratorate of Beijing, and Beijing Municipal Bureau of Justice.

3. Statistics for civil affairs and labor security mainly consist of social welfare institutions, personnel, social relief, special care, and marriage registration. Data were provided by Beijing Municipal Bureau of Civil Affairs, and Beijing Municipal Bureau of Human Resources and Social Security.

4. Statistics for disabled persons mainly include information on rehabilitation, education, employment and poverty reduction, and building of federations for disabled persons, etc. Data were provided by Beijing Disabled Persons' Federation.

5. Supervision data on women and children development are composed of women's participation in decision making and management, employment, education, health, legal protection, and so on; children's health, education, legal protection, social living environment, etc. Data were provided respectively by Beijing Municipal Bureau of Statistics in accordance with statistic reporting system of different departments.

6. Safe production data were provided by Beijing Administration for Industry and Commerce, Beijing Municipal Food and Drug Administration, Beijing Municipal Bureau of Traffic Management, Beijing Administration of Work Safety.

21-1 北京市历年社会保障相关待遇标准(1994-2013年)
HISTORICAL SOCIAL WELFARE TREATMENT STANDARD IN BEIJING (1994-2013)

单位: 元/月 (yuan/month)

标准 Standard / 年份 Year		职工最低工资 Minimum Wages of Employed Persons	失业保险金最低标准 Minimum Standard of Unemployment Insurance	城市居民最低生活保障标准 Urban Lowest Cost-of-living	企业退休人员基本养老金最低标准 Minimum Standard of Basic Old-age Pensions for Retired Persons	企业退职人员基本养老金最低标准 Minimum Standard of Basic Old-age Pensions for Resigned Persons	企业退养人员基本养老金最低标准 Minimum Standard of Basic Old-age Pensions for Early-retired Persons
1994		210					
1995		240	174				
1996		270	189	170	263	202	170
1997		290	203	190	293	232	200
1998		310	217	200	336	265	233
1999年第一次	First-time in 1999	320	224	210			
1999年第二次	Second-time in 1999	400	291	273	396	335	288
2000		412	300	280	421	360	308
2001		435	305	285	441	380	317
2002		465	326	290	466	405	367
2003		465	326	290	466	405	367
2004年第一次	First-time in 2004	495					
2004年第二次	Second-time in 2004	545	347	290	510	443	402
2005		580	382	300	563	488	443
2006		640	392	310	620	537	487
2007		730	422	330	675	592	527
2008		800	502	390	775	682	607
2009		800	562	410	900	800	700
2010		960	632	430	1000	900	800
2011		1160	782	500	1100	1000	900
2012		1260	842	520	1210	1100	1000
2013		1400	892	580	1330	1210	1100

资料来源：城市居民最低生活保障标准由北京市民政局提供，本表其他资料由北京市人力资源和社会保障局提供。

Source: Data on urban minimum standard of living were provided by Beijing Municipal Bureau of Civil Affairs,others were provided by Beijing Municipal Bureau of Human Resources and Social Security.

21-2 北京市历年参加社会保障情况(1995-2013年)

单位：万人

年 份 Year	参加基本养老保险人数 Employed Persons Participating in Basic Pension Insurance	参加基本医疗保险人数 Staff and Workers Participating in Basic Medical Care Insurance	参加失业保险人数 Employed Persons Participating in Unemployment Insurance	参加工伤保险人数 Employed Persons Participating in Work-related Injury Insurance	参加生育保险人数 Employed Persons Participating in Maternity Insurance
1995	261.1		219.8		
1996	252.0		214.5		
1997	264.3		214.0		
1998	359.2		222.9		
1999	379.0		289.0		
2000	391.6		287.8	212.0	
2001	425.9	210.2	287.2	212.7	
2002	436.2	353.8	299.5	221.0	
2003	448.5	436.1	306.6	242.9	
2004	460.0	484.0	308.0	259.0	
2005	520.0	574.8	394.6	328.9	226.1
2006	604.1	679.5	482.2	465.3	263.3
2007	671.7	783.0	535.3	609.2	290.6
2008	758.1	871.0	614.3	666.5	324.1
2009	827.7	938.4	675.7	747.1	346.8
2010	982.5	1063.7	774.2	823.8	372.2
2011	1091.9	1188.0	881.0	862.4	395.3
2012	1206.4	1279.7	1006.7	897.2	844.7
2013	1311.3	1354.8	1025.1	920.3	883.2

注：1. 2001年开始设置基本医疗保险指标，以前年份称为大病统筹，2000年参加大病统筹人数为232.6万人。
2. 2005年7月1日《北京市企业职工生育保险规定》开始实施。全市农村社会养老保险1992年试点，1996年全市正式实施。
3. 从2006年起，农村最低生活保障人数不含农村五保供养人员。
4. 农村居民参加城乡居民养老保险人数在2007年及以前为参加农村社会养老保险人数口径；2008年为参加新型农村社会养老保险人数；2009年及以后为参加城乡居民养老保险人数中农村参保人数。

资料来源：城乡居民享受最低生活保障人数来源于北京市民政局；参加农村新型医疗人数和参合率来源于北京市卫生和计划生育委员会；其他资料来源于北京市人力资源和社会保障局。

SOCIAL SECURITY PARTICIPATION(1995-2013)

(10000 persons)

参加城乡居民养老保险人数 Residents Participating in Basic Pension Insurance	#农村居民 Rural Residents	参加城镇居民医疗保险人数 Residents Participating in Basic Urban Medical Insurance	参加新型农村合作医疗人数 Residents Participating in New-type Rural Cooperative Medicare	城市居民最低生活保障人数 Persons Receiving Subsistence Allowances in Urban Areas	农村最低生活保障人数 Persons Receiving Subsistence Allowances in Rural Areas	新型农村合作医疗参合率(%) Percentage of Persons Participating in New-type Rural Cooperative Medicare
	29.2			0.9		
	37.4			0.9		
	41.2			2.8		
	34.4			4.3	1.2	
	38.5			6.7	1.6	
	34.7			7.6	1.8	
	32.0			12.0	5.4	
	33.6			16.1	6.7	
	36.8		234.0	16.1	7.5	71.9
	40.6		250.4	15.5	7.8	80.3
	44.8		261.0	15.2	7.6	86.9
	49.1		268.5	14.8	7.8	88.9
	127.5		272.5	14.5	7.9	92.9
	153.9		274.9	14.7	8.0	95.7
168.5	159.3	143.7	278.5	13.7	7.7	96.7
173.4	163.7	159.8	276.8	11.7	7.0	97.7
177.3	167.0	151.9	267.5	11.0	6.3	98.1
180.1	168.7	160.1	254.4	10.4	6.0	98.0

Note: a) The basic medicare indicator was set from 2001. Before that it was called general healthcare program for major diseases which covered 2.326 million people in 2000.

b) Regulations of Beijing on Maternity Insurance for Enterprise Employed Persons became effective from July 1st, 2005. Pilots were made for social pension program in rural area of Beijing in 1992. The program was formally effective in 1996 across the city.

c) Rural persons receiving lowest cost-of-living excluded rural persons enjoying five guarantees from 2006.

d) In and before 2007, the number of rural people participating in urban and rural pension insurance covered the people participating in rural social pension insurance; in 2008, this figure covered the people participating in new-type rural social pension insurance; since 2009, this figure covered the rural people of those participating in the urban and rural pension insurance.

Source: Figures on persons receiving subsistence allowances in urban and rural areas are from Beijing Municipal Bureau of Civil Affairs; Figures on persons participating in new-type rural medicare and percentage of these persons are from Beijing Municipal Commission of Health and Family Planning; other data are from Beijing Municipal Bureau of Human Resources and Social Security.

21-3 城镇职工参加社会保险情况(2013年)
PARTICIPATION OF EMPLOYED PERSONS FOR SOCIAL SECURITY INSURANCE PROGRAMS IN THE URBAN AREA (2013)

项 目	Item	基本养老保险 Basic Pension Insurance		基本医疗保险 Basic Medical Insurance	
		单位个数(个) Number of Entities (unit)	人 数(人) Number of Persons (person)	单位个数(个) Number of Entities (unit)	人 数(人) Number of Persons (person)
合 计	**Total**	**354645**	**13112997**	**351029**	**13547669**
按登记注册类型分	**By Registration Type**				
国 有	State-owned	7497	2037757	6299	1933967
集 体	Collectively-owned	7065	284428	6181	270828
其 他	Others	340083	10790812	338549	11342874
按隶属关系划分	**By Affiliation**				
中央单位	Central	7635	1851378	7079	1768267
地方单位	Local	347010	11261619	343950	11779402

资料来源：北京市人力资源和社会保障局。
Source: Beijing Municipal Bureau of Human Resources and Social Security.

21-3 续表 Continued

项 目	Item	失业保险 Unemployment Insurance		工伤保险 Industrial Injury Insurance		生育保险 Maternity Insurance	
		单位个数(个) Number of Entities (unit)	人 数(人) Number of Persons (person)	单位个数(个) Number of Entities (unit)	人 数(人) Number of Persons (person)	单位个数(个) Number of Entities (unit)	人 数(人) Number of Persons (person)
合 计	**Total**	**355442**	**10250919**	**366749**	**9202740**	**354181**	**8831613**
按登记注册类型分	**By Registration Type**						
国 有	State-owned	7200	1052213	7373	1048759	7256	1017338
集 体	Collectively-owned	6961	146180	7302	149885	7114	136117
其 他	Others	341281	9052526	352074	8004096	339811	7678158
按隶属关系划分	**By Affiliation**						
中央单位	Central	7466	1483200	7794	1387601	7612	1228606
地方单位	Local	347976	8767719	358955	7815139	346569	7603007

资料来源：北京市人力资源和社会保障局。
Source: Beijing Municipal Bureau of Human Resources and Social Security.

21-4 城乡居民参加社会保险情况(2010-2013年) PARTICIPATION OF RURAL AND URBAN RESIDENTS FOR SOCIAL SECURITY INSURANCE PROGRAMS (2010-2013)

单位：万人 (10000 persons)

年 份 Year	城乡居民基本养老保险人数 Basic Pension Insurance		城镇居民医疗保险人数 Basic Medical Care Insurance			
	合计 Total	#农村居民 Rural Residents	合计 Total	学生儿童 Students and Children	无保障老人 Unguaranteed Aged Persons	无业居民 Unemployed Residents
2010	168.5	159.3	143.7	121.3	17.7	4.7
2011	173.4	163.7	159.8	135.5	19.1	5.3
2012	177.3	167.0	151.9	128.6	18.5	4.8
2013	180.1	168.7	160.1	137.5	18.8	3.7

资料来源：北京市人力资源和社会保障局。
Source: Beijing Municipal Bureau of Human Resources and Social Security.

21-5 优抚及主要救助对象情况 STATISTICS FOR PERSONS RECEIVING SPECIAL CARE AND RELIEF

单位：人 (person)

项 目	Item	人数 Number of Persons 2013	2012	2013年为2012年% 2013 as % of 2012
抚恤、补助优抚对象总人数	**Total Number of Persons Receiving Pensions, Subsidies, and Special Care Treatment**	**43427**	**42556**	**102.0**
定期抚恤人数	Number of Persons Receiving Regular Pensions	1775	1829	97.0
定期补助人数	Number of Persons Receiving Regular Subsidies	30477	29816	102.2
伤残人数	Total Number of Disabled Persons	11175	10911	102.4
医疗救助人次数	**Total Number of Persons Receiving Medical Assistance**	**143196**	**112925**	**126.8**
城市医疗救助人次数	Number of Persons Receiving Medical Assistance in the Urban Area	81730	80534	101.5
农村医疗救助人次数	Number of Persons Receiving Medical Assistance in the Rural Area	61466	32391	189.8
社会救助对象总人数	**Total Number of Persons Receiving Social Relief**	**167333**	**176825**	**94.6**
城市居民最低生活保障人数	Number of Persons Receiving Subsistence Allowances in Urban Areas	103682	109743	94.5
农村居民最低生活保障人数	Number of Persons Receiving Subsistence Allowances in Rural Areas	59575	62979	94.6
农村五保供养人数	Rural Residents Enjoying Five Guarantees	4076	4103	99.3
农村集中五保供养人数	Collective Rural Residents Enjoying Five Guarantees	2039	2097	97.2
农村分散五保供养人数	Scattered Rural Residents Enjoying Five Guarantees	2037	2006	101.5

注："农村最低生活保障人数"不含"农村五保供养人数"。
资料来源：北京市民政局。
Note: Number of persons receiving subsistence allowances in rural areas excludes "Rural Residents Enjoying the Five Guarantees".
Source: Beijing Municipal Bureau of Civil Affairs.

21-6 社会福利事业情况
STATISTICS FOR SOCIAL WELFARE

项目		Item		2013	2012	2013年为2012年% 2013 as % of 2012
社区服务机构数	(个)	Number of Service Facilities in Urban Communities	(unit)	6525	6244	104.5
#社区服务中心	(个)	Community Service Centers	(unit)	192	186	103.2
社区服务志愿者组织数	(个)	Number of Community Service Volunteer Organizations	(unit)	11090	9751	113.7
城市便民利民服务网点数	(个)	Number of Urban Convenient Service Outlets	(unit)	11004	11169	98.5
社会福利企业单位数	(个)	Number of Social Welfare Enterprises	(unit)	612	664	92.2
社会福利企业年末职工人数	(人)	Year-end Employed Persons in Social Welfare Enterprises	(person)	28384	31260	90.8
#残疾职工	(人)	Disabled Employed Persons	(person)	11200	12078	92.7

资料来源：北京市民政局。
Source: Beijing Municipal Buresu of Civil Affairs.

21-7 收养性单位情况(2013年)
STATISTICS ON ADOPTING INSTITUTIONS (2013)

项目		Item		合计	#光荣院 Homes for Disabled Veterans	#社会福利院 Social Welfare Institutions	#儿童福利院 Children's Welfare Institutions	#福利类精神病院和医院 Welfare Mental Hospitals and Hospitals	#城市养老服务机构 Urban Elderly Care Agencies	#农村养老服务机构 Rural Elderly Care Agencies
单位数	(个)	Institutions	(unit)	442	10	8	12	2	148	259
职工人数	(人)	Employed Persons	(person)	11486	197	1159	492	361	4344	4770
床位数	(张)	Beds	(unit)	84734	656	3388	1500	557	29491	48259
收养人数	(人)	Persons Received	(person)	33893	161	2733	984	423	13117	16135
#自费	(人)	Self-supported	(person)	29565	19	2168	28	413	12776	13826

资料来源：北京市民政局。
Source: Beijing Municipal Buresu of Civil Affairs.

21-8 离婚、青少年刑事案犯情况
STATISTICS FOR DIVORCE AND JUVENILE CRIMINAL CASES

项目		Item		2013	2012
婚姻家庭纠纷案件数(结案)	(件)	Marriage and Family Disputes (Closed)	(case)	28592	35201
#离婚案件数	(件)	Divorce Cases	(case)	20607	20825
#调离案件数	(件)	Cases of Divorce Reconciled		7099	7531
#判离案件数	(件)	Cases of Divorce Judged	(case)	2977	2801
建立少年法庭个数	(个)	Juvenile Courts Established	(unit)	20	20
青少年罪犯人数	(人)	Teenager Offenders	(person)	9342	8209
#18岁以下青少年罪犯人数	(人)	Teenager Offenders under 18	(person)	1053	1223
青少年刑事案犯占全部刑事案犯的比重	(%)	Teenager Criminal Offenders as % of Total Criminal Offenders	(%)	31.96	34.21
男性	(%)	Male	(%)	88.51	87.62
女性	(%)	Female	(%)	11.49	12.38

资料来源：北京市高级人民法院。
Source: The People's High Court of Beijing.

21-9 婚姻登记(1981-2013年)
BASIC STATISTICS FOR MARRIAGE AND DIVORCE REGISTRATIONS (1981-2013)

年 份 Year	结婚对数(对) Registered Marriages (couple)	#涉外及华侨、港澳台居民登记结婚对数 Registered Marriages Involving Foreigners and Citizens of Hong Kong, Macao and Taiwan	初婚总人数(人) First Marriages (person)	离婚对数(对) Registered Divorces (couple)	#民政部门登记离婚对数 Divorces Registered in the Civil Affair Department (couple)
1981	200352		392855	5170	1780
1982	141253		265834	5359	1581
1983	117976			5322	1465
1984	113362		218009	5654	1387
1985	134462		258256	5874	1746
1986	143105		273634	7541	2474
1987	149952		285803	8916	3218
1988	113333		212070	10664	4198
1989	103829		190978	12515	5174
1990	92988		168304	14748	5791
1991	91979		166579	15287	6483
1992	89095		159588	15567	6477
1993	89938		160127	17829	7589
1994	90379		161972	19928	8327
1995	85511		149878	20160	8096
1996	86803		147855	20716	8225
1997	84208		145099	22257	8628
1998	85534		148026	23708	9381
1999	83312		141740	23922	8502
2000	80212		135620	26616	6384
2001	79385	873	133259	27683	5425
2002	76136	606	126371	27691	5810
2003	93526	761	158729	30637	10142
2004	126436	974	214443	32657	21013
2005	96596	937	158736	34244	23991
2006	171286	1172	294223	35505	24954
2007	117926	991	193387	36622	26432
2008	147516	1165	246309	37619	27277
2009	181771	1176	305803	41299	29998
2010	138104	1085	222269	43970	32595
2011	173238	1260	288406	43521	32999
2012	174114	1242	287436	48575	38243
2013	163676	1070	251636	64610	54536

注：离婚对数包括在民政部门登记的对数和经法院调离和判离的对数。

资料来源：北京市民政局、北京市高级人民法院。

Note: Registered divorces include those registered in the civil affair department and those mediated and judged in courts.

Source: Beijing Municipal Bureau of Civil Affairs, and The People's High Court of Beijing.

21-10 婚姻登记情况
BASIC STATISTICS ON MARRIAGE AND DIVORCE REGISTRATIONS

项　目		Item		2013	2012	2013年为2012年% 2013 as % of 2012
登记结婚对数	**(对)**	**Registered Marriages**	**(couple)**	**163676**	**174114**	**94.0**
按婚前状况分		**By Pre-marriage Status**				
初婚人数	(人)	First Marriages	(person)	251636	287436	87.5
再婚人数	(人)	Remarriages	(person)	75716	60792	124.5
#女　性	(人)	Females	(person)	35954	28368	126.7
按居住地分		**By Place of Residence**				
内地居民登记结婚对数	(对)	Registered Marriages in Mainland	(couple)	162606	172872	94.1
涉外及华侨、港澳台居民登记结婚对数	(对)	Registered Marriages with involving Foreigner and the Citizens of Hong Kong, Macao and Taiwan	(couple)	1070	1242	86.2
内地居民	(人)	Mainland Residents	(person)	1002	1160	86.4
#女　性	(人)	Females	(person)	725	854	84.9
香港居民	(人)	Hong Kong Residents	(person)	59	67	88.1
澳门居民	(人)	Macao Residents	(person)	8	10	80.0
台湾居民	(人)	Taiwan Residents	(person)	129	128	100.8
华　侨	(人)	Overseas Chinese	(person)	28	51	54.9
外国人	(人)	Foreigners	(person)	914	1068	85.6
离婚登记对数	**(对)**	**Registered Divorces**	**(couple)**	**54536**	**38243**	**142.6**
内地居民登记离婚对数	(对)	Mainland Residents	(couple)	54363	38080	142.8
涉外及华侨、港澳台居民登记离婚对数	(对)	Overseas Chinese,Hongkong,Macao, Taiwan Residents	(couple)	173	163	106.1

注：离婚对数不含法院判离数。
资料来源：北京市民政局。
Note: Number of registered divorces excludes the divorces ruled by courts.
Source: Beijing Municipal Bureau of Civil Affairs.

21-11 残疾人事业基本情况
BASIC INFORMATION OF UNDERTAKINGS FOR DISABLED PERSONS

项　目		Item		2013	2012
康　复		**Rehabilitation**			
白内障复明手术	(例)	Sight-Rrestoring Cataract Surgeries	(case)	11124	10356
人工晶体植入率	(%)	Artificial Intra-ocular Lens Implantation Rate	(%)	96	96
低视力配用助视器	(人)	Vision-aids Provided for Individuals with Low-vision	(person)	1514	362
聋儿康复		Rehabilitation of Children with Hearing Disability			
年收训聋儿	(人)	Hearing and Speech Training	(person)	302	332
聋儿入普幼普小率	(%)	Enrollment Rate of Trained Children to Ordinary Kindergartens and Primary Schools	(%)	80	80
培训家长	(人)	Parents Trained	(person)	330	498
精神病防治康复		Prevention and Treatment of Psychiatric Diseases			
开展精神病防治康复工作区县数	(个)	Counties Carried on the Works of Prevention and Treatment of Psychiatric Diseases	(unit)	16	16
综合防治康复精神病人数	(人)	Prevention and Treatment Provided for Patients with Severe Psychiatric Diseases	(person)	24972	29642
监护率	(%)	Guardianship Rate	(%)	86.31	99.79
显好率	(%)	Significant Improvement Rate	(%)	49.97	63.74
社会参与率	(%)	Social Involvement Rate	(%)	36.9	39.47
肇事率	(%)	Violent Events Rate	(%)	0.02	0.03
康复训练与服务		Rehabilitation Training and Service			
肢体残疾康复训练人次	(人次)	Function Training Provided to Persons with Physical Disability	(person-time)	5954	5142
智残儿童康复训练人次	(人次)	Rehabilitation Training Provided to Children with Intellectual Disability	(person-time)	477	361
脑瘫儿童康复训练人次	(人次)	Rehabilitation Training Provided to Children with Cerebral Palsy	(person-time)	267	262
教　育		**Education**			
未入学适龄残疾儿童少年	(人)	School-age Disabled Children Without Schooling	(person)	243	419
职业教育与培训机构数	(个)	Vocational Education and Training Facilities	(unit)	62	45
教育与培训人数	(人次)	Number of Educated and Trained	(person-time)	10471	4111
就　业		**Employment**			
城镇残疾人就业状况		Employment of Urban Disabled Persons			
当年安排就业人数	(人)	Persons Employed by Arrangement in the Year	(person)	3244	2907
#按比例就业人数	(人)	Employed by Quota Scheme	(person)	1221	1181
集中就业人数	(人)	Disalbed Persons Employed in Concentrated Way	(person)	75	285
个体就业人数	(人)	Self-employed	(person)	1233	803
残疾人就业服务机构数	(个)	Employment Placement Service Facilities for Disabled Jobseekers	(unit)	17	17
盲人按摩		Massage by Persons with Visual Disability			
保健按摩机构	(家)	Healthcare Massage Institutions	(unit)	409	498
医疗按摩机构	(家)	Medical Massage Institutions	(unit)	2	2
保健按摩员培训人次	(人次)	Massage Therapists Training	(person-time)	1115	509
医疗按摩员培训人次	(人次)	Keep-fit Massager Training	(person-time)	23	98
扶　贫		**Poverty Alleviation**			
享受城镇廉租住房的残疾人户数	(户)	Number of Households with Disabled Persons Enjoying Low-cost Urban House Leasing	(household)	1185	1540
扶持农村残疾人数	(人)	Number of Disabled Persons Supported in Rural Areas	(person)	9197	5064
社会保障		**Social Securtity**			
城　镇		Urban Areas			
已纳入最低生活保障范围人数	(人)	Covered by the Basic Living System	(person)	19887	47477
集中供养人数	(人)	Covered by Concentrated Supporting	(person)	83	302
享受生活补助的重残人数	(人)	Severely Disabled Persosn Qualified for Living Subsidies	(person)	17813	17236
其他救助救济人数	(人)	With Other Aids	(person)	7333	5036
农　村		Rural Areas			
已纳入最低生活保障范围人数	(人)	Covered by the Basic Living System	(person)	22026	23414
五保供养人数	(人)	Supported by the Five Guarantees	(person)	881	859
享受生活补助的重残人数	(人)	Severely Disabled Persosn Qualified for Living Subsidies	(person)	23809	24447
其他救助救济人数	(人)	With Other Aids	(person)	13943	14022
残联组织建设		**Organization Building of Disabled Persons'Federation**			
残疾人工作者数	(人)	Workers for Disabled Perons	(person)	1202	1432

资料来源：北京市残疾人联合会。
Source: Beijing Disabled Persons Federation.

21-12 残疾人就业、维权援助情况
STATISTICS FOR EMPLOYMENT AND AID FOR RIGHT PROTECTION OF DISABLED PERSONS

项 目		Item		2013	2012
残疾人职业培训人数	(人)	Number of Disabled Persons Trained for Employment	(person)	12989	11763
#女 性	(人)	Females	(person)	5591	6859
新安置残疾人员就业人数	(人)	New Employment of Disabled Persons	(person)	3885	4384
#女 性	(人)	Females	(peoson)	1270	1422
维权信访咨询件数	(件)	Right Protection Letters, Visits and Consulting	(case)	18856	16627
维权法律服务件数	(件)	Right Protection Legal Aid	(case)	4251	4955

资料来源：北京市残疾人联合会。
Source: Beijing Disabled Persons Federation.

21-13 律师工作
STATISTICS FOR LAWYERS

项 目		Item		2013	2012	2013年为2012年% 2013 as % of 2012
律师事务所	(个)	Law Firms	(unit)	1782	1672	106.6
执业律师	(人)	Number of Practicing Lawyers	(person)	23761	22796	104.2
专职律师	(人)	Full-time Lawyers	(person)	22222	21419	103.7
兼职律师	(人)	Part-time Lawyers	(person)	1068	1056	101.1
公司律师	(人)	Company Lawyers	(person)	349	243	143.6
公职律师	(人)	Government Lawyers	(person)	62	17	364.7
法律援助律师	(人)	Legal Aid Lawyers	(person)	60	61	98.4
担任法律顾问	(家)	Legal Counsel	(unit)	21713	21907	99.1
民事诉讼代理	(件)	Civil Case Litigation Agencies	(case)	98630	66341	148.7
行政诉讼代理	(件)	Administrative Case Litigation Agencies	(case)	4815	4031	119.4
刑事诉讼辩护及代理	(件)	Criminal Case Litigation Agencies	(case)	28062	18174	154.4
非诉讼法律事务	(件)	Off-court Cases	(case)	72530	73352	98.9

资料来源：北京市司法局。
Source: Beijing Municipal Bureau of Justice.

21-14 调解工作
MEDIATION

项目		Item		2013	2012	2013年为2012年% 2013 as % of 2012
人民调解委员会个数	(个)	People's Mediation Committees	(unit)	7646	7770	98.4
调解员人数	(万人)	Mediators	(10000 persons)	7.75	7.48	103.7
调解各类纠纷件数	(万件)	Disputes Mediated	(10000 cases)	22.85	23.11	98.9
#调解各类纠纷成功件数	(万件)	Succeed Disputes Mediated	(10000 cases)	21.71	22.26	97.5
防止民间纠纷激化件数	(件)	Civil Disputes Prevented from Intensifica	(case)	1036	1742	59.5
防止民间纠纷激化人数	(人次)	Persons Involved in Civil Disputes Prever	(person)	16071	38420	41.8

资料来源：北京市司法局。
Source: Beijing Municipal Bureau of Justice.

21-15 公证工作
NOTARIZATIONS

项目		Item		2013	2012	2013年为2012年% 2013 as % of 2012
公证处个数	(个)	Notary Offices	(unit)	25	25	100.0
执业公证员人数	(人)	Certified Notaries	(person)	274	275	99.6
总办证数	(件)	Certificates Issued	(case)	814088	633963	128.4

资料来源：北京市司法局。
Source: Beijing Municipal Bureau of Justice.

21-16 法律援助工作情况
STATISTICS FOR LEGAL AID

项　　目		Item		2013	2012	2013年为2012年% 2013 as % of 2012
法律援助机构个数	(个)	Number of Legal Aid Agencies	(unit)	26	26	100
法律援助机构人员数	(人)	Number of Legal Aid Persons	(person)	260	209	124.4
承办民事法律援助案件数	(件)	Civil Cases Aided	(case)	15760	13804	114.2
承办刑事法律援助案件数	(件)	Criminal Cases Aided	(case)	4421	3587	123.3
承办行政法律援助案件数	(件)	Administrative Cases Aided	(case)	24	28	85.7
法律援助机构接待咨询人次	(万人次)	Consultations by Legal Aid Agencies	(10000 person-times)	23.5	26.0	90.5
得到法律援助机构援助的妇女人数	(人次)	Females Receiving Aids from Legal Aid Agencies	(person)	4928	3370	146.2
得到法律援助机构援助的儿童人数	(人次)	Children Receiving Aids from Legal Aid Agencies	(person)	2453	1175	208.8

资料来源：北京市司法局。
Source: Beijing Municiapl Bureau of Justice.

21-17 司法鉴定工作情况
STATISTICS FOR JUDICIAL APPRAISAL

项　　目		Item		2013	2012
司法鉴定机构个数	(个)	Judicial Appraisal Organizations	(unit)	111	109
司法鉴定人员数	(人)	Judicial Appraisal Personnel	(person)	1740	1675
司法鉴定业务量	(件)	Judicial Appraisal Cases Proceeded	(case)	48348	36451

注：本表中司法鉴定机构数为“北京市司法局审核登记的全部司法鉴定机构”个数。
资料来源：北京市司法局。
Note: In the table, the number of judicial appraisal organizations is the number of "all judicial appraisal organizations approved by and registered with Beijing Municipal Bureau of Justice".
Source: Beijing Municipal Bureau of Justice.

21-18 公安、法院、检察院收案、结案情况(2005-2013年)
CASES ACCEPTED AND SETTLED BY PUBLIC SECURITY DEPARTMENTS, COURTS AND PROCURATORATES (2005-2013)

项 目		Item		2005	2006	2007
公安部门侦破刑事案件		**Criminal Cases Detected by Public Security Departments**				
立 案	(起)	Cases Put on File	(case)	107988	120554	127446
破 案	(起)	Cases Settled	(case)	59035	66399	74232
法院刑事案件收、结案情况		**Criminal Cases Accepted and Settled in Courts**				
收 案	(件)	Cases Accepted	(case)	17488	17725	19592
结 案	(件)	Cases Settled	(case)	17624	17701	19536
法院婚姻家庭、继承纠纷案件收、结案情况		**Marriage and Inheritance Dispute Cases Accepted and Settled in Courts**				
收 案	(件)	Cases Accepted	(case)	26739	27860	28089
结 案	(件)	Cases Settled	(case)	27002	27845	27916
法院合同纠纷案件收、结案情况		**Contract Dispute Cases Accepted and Settled in Courts**				
收 案	(件)	Cases Accepted	(case)	133534	141485	135099
结 案	(件)	Cases Settled	(case)	135612	141439	134829
法院权属、侵权纠纷及其他民事案件收、结案情况		**Ownership, Infringement Dispute and Other Civil Cases Accepted and Settled in Courts**				
收 案	(件)	Cases Accepted	(case)	42690	44890	46892
结 案	(件)	Cases Settled	(case)	43166	45005	46372
检察机关办理反贪污贿赂案件		**Anti-Corruption and Bribery Cases Handled by Procuratorates**				
受 案	(件)	Cases Accepted	(case)	1202	1330	1276
立 案		Cases Put on File				
件 数	(件)	Number of Cases	(case)	292	321	322
人 数	(人)	Number of Persons Involved	(person)	356	363	372
挽回经济损失	(万元)	Economic Losses Redeemed	(10000 yuan)	30701	29545	14703
检察机关办理渎职侵权案件		**Misconduct and Infringement Cases Handled by Procuratorates**				
受 案	(件)	Cases Accepted	(case)	218	162	205
立 案		Cases Put on File				
件 数	(件)	Number of Cases	(case)	37	30	34
人 数	(人)	Number of Persons Involved	(person)	38	31	36
挽回经济损失	(万元)	Economic Losses Redeemed	(10000 yuan)	1320	458	71

资料来源：北京市公安局、北京市人民检察院、北京市高级人民法院。
Source: Beijing Municipal Bureau of Public Security, the People's Procuratorate of Beijing, and the People's High Court of Beijing.

21-18 续表 Continued

项 目		Item		2008	2009	2010	2011	2012	2013
公安部门侦破刑事案件		**Criminal Cases Detected by Public Security Departments**							
立 案	(起)	Cases Put on File	(case)	90045	98750	104327	142835	145724	140498
破 案	(起)	Cases Settled	(case)	63294	71950	80401	89156	101776	112594
法院刑事案件收、结案情况		**Criminal Cases Accepted and Settled in Courts**							
收 案	(件)	Cases Accepted	(case)	20024	18819	19824	19574	22168	19109
结 案	(件)	Cases Settled	(case)	20004	18773	19870	19423	22084	19012
法院婚姻家庭、继承纠纷案件收、结案情况		**Marriage and Inheritance Dispute Cases Accepted and Settled in Courts**							
收 案	(件)	Cases Accepted	(case)	30402	33056	36799	35251	35418	37347
结 案	(件)	Cases Settled	(case)	29499	32902	37160	35149	35201	35296
法院合同纠纷案件收、结案情况		**Contract Dispute Cases Accepted and Settled in Courts**							
收 案	(件)	Cases Accepted	(case)	144948	153766	148655	144433	145017	149237
结 案	(件)	Cases Settled	(case)	140512	152128	153130	144766	143153	141642
法院权属、侵权纠纷及其他民事案件收、结案情况		**Ownership, Infringement Dispute and Other Civil Cases Accepted and Settled in Courts**							
收 案	(件)	Cases Accepted	(case)	53864	58057	64379	65972	62736	64747
结 案	(件)	Cases Settled	(case)	51668	57135	65763	66405	62235	61688
检察机关查办贪污贿赂案件		**Anti-Corruption and Bribery Cases Handled by Procuratorates**							
受 案	(件)	Cases Accepted	(case)	1060	1113	1138	988	1070	871
立 案		Cases Put on File							
件 数	(件)	Number of Cases	(case)	282	319	356	343	379	299
人 数	(人)	Number of Persons Involved	(person)	333	369	418	425	459	357
挽回经济损失	(万元)	Economic Losses Redeemed	(10000 yuan)	21148	62542	14634	36469	29955	16171
检察机关办理渎职侵权案件		**Misconduct and Infringement Cases Handled by Procuratorates**							
受 案	(件)	Cases Accepted	(case)	150	206	213	193	351	443
立 案		Cases Put on File							
件 数	(件)	Number of Cases	(case)	29	48	57	55	77	74
人 数	(人)	Number of Persons Involved	(person)	31	53	60	66	94	81
挽回经济损失	(万元)	Economic Losses Redeemed	(10000 yuan)	3019	25	16	58	735	962

21-19 法院行政案件收、结案情况(2013年)
STATISTICS FOR ADMINISTRATIVE CASES ACCEPTED AND SETTLED BY COURT (2013)

单位：件 (case)

项 目	Item	收 案 Cases Accepted	结 案 Cases Settled	#判 决 Judgment	#裁 定 Mediation
合 计	**Total**	**7121**	**6964**	**4310**	**2647**
公 安	Public Security	251	231	120	107
资 源	Resources	70	68	34	34
城 建	City Construction	487	488	167	320
工 商	Industry and Commerce	131	126	55	71
专 利	Patents	652	708	644	64
劳动和社会保障	Labor and Social Security	126	113	60	53
教 育	Education	8	10	1	7
其 他	Others	5396	5220	3229	1991

资料来源：北京市高级人民法院。
Source: The People's High Court of Beijing.

21-20 法院刑事案件收、结案情况(2013年)
STATISTICS FOR CRIMINAL CASES ACCEPTED AND SETTLED BY COURT (2013)

项 目	Item	收 案 (件) Cases Accepted (case)	结 案 (件) Cases Settled (case)	判决发生法律效力 Judgment with Legal Forces	
				件 数(件) Number of Cases (case)	人 数(人) Number of Persons (person)
合 计	**Total**	**19109**	**19012**	**22597**	**29157**
#危害公共安全罪	Offences against Public Security	2160	2152	2432	2550
破坏社会主义市场经济秩序罪	Offences against the Socialist Market Economy Order	2030	2034	2602	3440
侵犯公民人身权利、民主权利罪	Offences against Civil Personal Rights and Democratic Rights	4139	4097	4494	5383
侵犯财产罪	Offences against Property	6478	6468	8051	10504
妨害社会管理秩序罪	Offences against Social Administration	3971	3960	4667	6820
危害国防利益罪	Offences against National Defense Interest	40	40	49	60
贪污贿赂罪	Crimes of Corruption and Bribery	261	241	275	364
渎职罪	Crimes of Misconduct in Office	25	20	27	36

资料来源：北京市高级人民法院。
Source: The People's High Court of Beijing.

21-21 法院婚姻家庭、继承纠纷案件收、结案情况(2013年)
STATISTICS FOR MARRIAGE AND FAMILY AND INHERITANCE DISPUTE CASES ACCEPTED AND SETTLED BY COURT (2013)

单位：件 (case)

项目	Item	收案 Cases Accepted	结案 Cases Settled	#判决 Judgment	#调解 Mediation
合计	**Total**	**37347**	**35296**	**11380**	**14066**
婚姻家庭纠纷	**Marriage and Family Disputes**	**29780**	**28592**	**9407**	**10645**
离婚	Divorces	21298	20621	6827	7606
解除非法同居关系	Relieving the Relation of Illicit Cohabitation	331	313	94	131
抚养、扶养关系纠纷	Child-support Disputes	1015	994	247	521
抚育费纠纷	Child-support Payment Disputes	1170	1158	514	356
赡养纠纷	Support Disputes	1148	1109	496	275
分家析产	Family Property Division	2548	2270	480	1210
其他	Others	2270	2127	749	546
继承纠纷	**Inheritance Disputes**	**7567**	**6704**	**1973**	**3421**
法定继承	Legal Inheritance	4754	4326	931	2477
遗嘱继承	Testamentary Inheritance	873	747	306	284
继承权确认纠纷	Inheritance Right Dispute	1	1		1
其他	Others	1939	1630	736	659

资料来源：北京市高级人民法院。
Source: The People's High Court of Beijing.

21-22 法院合同纠纷案件收、结案情况(2013年)
STATISTICS FOR CONTRACT CASES ACCEPTED AND SETTLED BY COURT (2013)

单位：件 (case)

项目	Item	收案 Cases Accepted	结案 Cases Settled	#判决 Judgment	#调解 Mediation
合计	**Total**	**149237**	**141642**	**50656**	**32131**
#买卖合同纠纷	Trade Contracts	19302	18077	7025	4768
房地产开发经营合同纠纷	Real Estate Development & Operation Contracts	6836	6627	3362	1610
供用电、水、气、热力合同纠纷	Electricity, Water, Gas, Heating Supply contracts	15495	15375	1556	3919
借款合同纠纷	Loan Contracts	15984	15061	6156	3664
租赁合同纠纷	Lease Contracts	10479	9848	4188	1706
建设工程合同纠纷	Construction Contracts	4170	3881	1546	870
承揽合同纠纷	Contracts for Hire of Work	2803	2587	790	753
运输合同纠纷	Transportation Contracts	790	745	327	182
经营合同纠纷	Management Contracts	1198	1061	380	234
农村承包合同纠纷	Rural Contracts	107	104	27	20
劳动争议	Labor Disputes	20287	19312	9916	4508

资料来源：北京市高级人民法院。
Source: The People's High Court of Beijing.

21-23 法院权属、侵权纠纷及其他民事案件收、结案情况(2013年)
STATISTICS FOR OWNERSHIP, TORTIOUS DISPUTES AND OTHER CIVIL CASES ACCEPTED AND SETTLED BY COURT (2013)

单位：件 (case)

项 目	Item	收 案 Cases Accepted	结 案 Cases Settled	#判 决 Judgment	#调 解 Mediation
合 计	**Total**	**64747**	**61688**	**26406**	**12625**
所有权及与所有权相关权利纠纷	Ownership and Related Rights	17891	16797	5918	4321
票据、证券权益纠纷	Bill and Securities Rights	299	300	142	68
股东权纠纷	Shareholder's Rights	1141	1029	463	76
不正当竞争纠纷	Unfair Competition	147	120	65	15
人身权纠纷	Personal Rights	9910	9356	5021	2087
特殊侵权纠纷	Special Infringements	19929	19118	10936	4508
适用特别程序案件	Special-poceeding Cases	5142	5002	1316	
其 他	Others	10288	9966	2545	1550

资料来源：北京市高级人民法院。
Source: The People's High Court of Beijing.

21-24 检察机关办理各类案件情况(2013年)
STATISTICS FOR CASES HANDLED BY PROCURATORIAL ORGANS (2013)

项 目	Item	受案(受理) Cases Accepted		审结案合计 Cases Settled	
		件 Case	人 Person	件 Case	人 Person
审查逮捕	**Arrests to Be Examined and Approved**	**16861**	**21966**	**16860**	**21977**
批准逮捕	Approved			12982	16387
不批准逮捕	Disapproved			3878	5590
审查起诉	**Prosecution to Be Reviewed and Made**	**21798**	**27385**	**20684**	**25904**
起 诉	Prosecuted			18802	23272
不起诉	Non-prosecution			1837	2562
附条件不起诉	Conditional Non-prosecution			45	70
举报案件	**Reported Cases**	**3778**		**3767**	
控告案件	**Complaints**	**1670**		**1652**	
申诉案件	**Appeal Cases**	**3443**		**3434**	
民事、行政案件	**Civil and Administrative Cases**				
民事检察案件	Civil Cases	1176		1556	
行政检察案件	Administrative Cases	123		166	

资料来源：北京市人民检察院。
Source: The People's Procuratorate of Beijing.

21-25 查办贪污贿赂、渎职侵权案件情况(2013年)
STATISTICS FOR CORRUPTION, BRIBERY, MALPRACTICE AND INFRINGEMENT CASES (2013)

项目		Item		查办贪污贿赂案件 Corruption and Bribery Cases	贪污案 Corruption Cases	贿赂案 Bribery Cases	挪用公款案 Misappropriation of Public Funds	其他 Others	渎职侵权案件 Malpractice and Infringement Cases
受案	**(件)**	**Cases Accepted**	**(case)**	**871**	**374**	**434**	**28**	**35**	**443**
立案		**Cases Registered**							
件数	(件)	Number of Cases	(case)	299	103	177	13	6	74
人数	(人)	Persons involved	(person)	357	132	200	13	12	81
大案	**(件)**	**Major Cases**	**(case)**	**246**	**80**	**153**	**13**		**21**
按查办贪污贿赂案件类型分		**By Type of Corruption and Bribery Case**							
5至10万元(不含)	(件)	50000-100000 Yuan	(case)	49	18	31			
10至50万元(不含)	(件)	100000-500000 Yuan	(case)	91	32	54	5		
50至100万元(不含)	(件)	500000-1000000 Yuan	(case)	45	12	32	1		
100至1000万元(不含)	(件)	1000000-10000000 Yuan	(case)	52	17	31	4		
1000万元及以上	(件)	Above 10000000 Yuan	(case)	9	1	5	3		
按查办渎职侵权案件类型分		**By Type of Malpractice and Infringement Case**							
重大	(件)	Serious Cases	(case)						11
特大	(件)	Extraordinary Serious Cases	(case)						10
要案	**(人)**	**Important Cases**	**(person)**	**64**	**17**	**36**	**3**	**8**	**10**
县处级	(人)	County Level	(person)	52	13	30	2	7	7
地厅级	(人)	Departmental Level	(person)	11	4	5	1	1	3
省部级以上	(人)	Above Provincial Level	(person)	1		1			
侦结		**Cases Closed**							
件数	(件)	Number of Cases	(case)	317	95	195	23	4	78
人数	(人)	Number of Persons	(person)	374	123	219	24	8	84
#移送起诉		Handed over to Law Suit							
件数	(件)	Number of Cases	(case)	303	93	185	21	4	75
人数	(人)	Number of Persons	(person)	355	121	204	22	8	81
#移送不起诉		Handed over yet Immunity from Suit							
件数	(件)	Number of Cases	(case)	6		5	1		2
人数	(人)	Number of Persons	(person)	7		6	1		2
挽回经济损失	**(万元)**	**Economic Losses Redeemed**	**(10000 yuan)**	**16171**	**9310**	**5833**	**978**	**50**	**962**

资料来源：北京市人民检察院。
Source: The People's Procuratorate of Beijing.

21-26 刑事案件情况
STATISTICS FOR CRIMINAL CASES

单位：起 (case)

项　　目	Item	2013	2012	2013年为2012年% 2013 as % of 2012
刑事案件	**Criminal Cases**			
立　案	Cases Registered	140498	145724	96.4
破　案	Cases Settled	112594	101776	110.6

资料来源：北京市公安局。
Source: Beijing Municipal Bureau of Public Security.

21-27 消防建设情况(1996-2013年)
STATISTICS FOR FIRECONTROL (1996-2013)

年　份 Year	公安消防队数 (支) Number of Fire Brigades of Public Security (unit)	公安消防车辆 (辆) Number of Fire-fighting Vehicles of Public Security (unit)	企业专职消防队队数 (支) Number of Full-time Fire Brigades in Enterprises (unit)	企业专职消防队人数 (人) Persons of Full-time Fire-fighters in Enterprises (person)
1996	36	180	101	1865
1997	38	190	104	1885
1998	41	210	108	1993
1999	44	236	120	2447
2000	47	259	120	2447
2001	50	266	120	2447
2002	52	296	112	2228
2003	56	303	112	2147
2004	57	381	120	2477
2005	57	342	120	2477
2006	64	357	109	2269
2007	69	401	109	2269
2008	77	558	109	2269
2009	86	572	109	2269
2010	91	664	109	2269
2011	98	604	87	1766
2012	107	670	76	1405
2013	122	735	76	1405

资料来源：北京市公安局消防局。
Source: Fire Department of Beijing Municipal Bureau of Public Security.

21-28 火灾及损失
FIRE ACCIDENTS AND LOSSES

项目	Item	数量 Number 2013	数量 Number 2012	直接经济损失(万元) Direct Pecuniary Losses (10000 yuan) 2013	直接经济损失(万元) Direct Pecuniary Losses (10000 yuan) 2012
火灾起数 (起)	**Fire Accidents (case)**	**4214**	**3409**	**5265.9**	**2967.9**
特别重大火灾	Extraordinarily Serious				
重大火灾	Serious	1		200.0	
较大火灾	Big Fire	3	1	1434.5	47.5
一般火灾	Relatively Big Fire	4210	3408	3631.4	2920.4
起火原因	**Cause of Fire**				
电　气	Electricity and Gas	1348	1235	3110.8	1572.5
生产作业	Violation of Operation	165	112	526.2	113.2
生活用火不慎	Carelessness in Fire Use	634	540	179.9	475.3
吸　烟	Smoking	105	148	74.7	32.7
玩　火	Fire Playing	56	111	40.1	71.6
自　燃	Spontaneous Combustion	111	126	87.1	76.1
雷　击	Thunderstroke	14	2	9.5	0.2
静　电	Static	3	1	3.2	0.2
放　火	Incendiarism	135	71	211.8	52.4
其　他	Others	1643	1062	1022.7	573.8
受伤人数 (人)	**Number of Injur (person)**	**18**	**6**		
死亡人数 (人)	**Number of Deatl (person)**	**53**	**26**		

资料来源：北京市公安局消防局。
Source: Fire Department of Beijing Municipal Bureau of Public Security.

21-29 安全生产情况
STATISTICS FOR SAFE PRODUCTION

项目	Item	2013	2012
亿元地区生产总值生产安全事故死亡率 (人/亿元)	Death Rate of Work Accidents Per 100 million yuan GDP (person/100 million yuan)	0.053	0.060
工矿商贸企业从业人员10万人生产安全事故死亡率 (人/10万人)	Death Rate of Work Accidents in the Mining, Commercial and Trade Industries Per 100,000 Persons (1/100000)	0.94	0.98
煤矿百万吨死亡率 (人/百万吨)	The Death Rate of Coal Mines Per Million Tons (Person/million tons)	0.40	0.41
道路交通万车死亡率 (人/万车)	Road Traffic Death Rate Per 10000 Vehicles (person/10000 vehicles)	1.58	1.77
食品安全监测抽查合格率(含烟酒等) (%)	Up-to-standard Rate of Food Security Monitor Spot Check (tobacco and wine included) (%)	96.94	95.29
#重点食品安全监测抽检合格率 (%)	Up-to-standard Rate of Key Foods Security Monitor Spot Checks (%)	98.35	98.23
药品抽验合格率 (%)	Up-to-standard Rate of Drug Spot Checks (%)	99.88	99.76

数据来源：北京市食品药品监督管理局、北京市公安交通管理局、北京市安全生产监督管理局。
Source: Beijing Municipal Food and Drug Administration, Beijing Municipal Bureau of Traffic Management, Beijing Administration of Work Safety.

21-30 交通事故及损失
STATISTICS FOR TRAFFIC ACCIDENTS AND LOSSES

项　目		Item		2013	2012	2013年为2012年% 2013 as % of 2012
交通事故		**Traffic Accidents**				
交通事故发生数	(起)	Number of Traffic Accidents	(case)	3063	3196	95.8
受伤人数	(人)	Number of Injuries	(person)	3359	3615	92.9
死亡人数	(人)	Number of Deaths	(person)	860	918	93.7
机动车事故		**Motor Vehicle Accidents**				
机动车事故发生数	(起)	Number of Motor Vehicle Accidents	(case)	2466	2556	96.5
受伤人数	(人)	Number of Injuries	(person)	2773	3006	92.2
死亡人数	(人)	Number of Deaths	(person)	737	781	94.4
直接经济损失	**(万元)**	**Direct Economic Losses**	**(10000 yuan)**	**2805.2**	**3017.9**	**93.0**
每万辆机动车死亡人数	**(人)**	**Persons Died Per 10,000 Motor Vehicles**	**(person)**	**1.58**	**1.77**	**89.3**

资料来源：北京市公安局公安交通管理局。
Source: Beijing Municipal Bureau of Traffic Management.

21-31 地震应急避难场所情况
EMERGENT EARTHQUAKE REFUGES

项　目		Item		2013	2012
地震应急避难场所累计个数	(个)	Total Number of Emergent Earthquake Refuges	(unit)	92	81
地震应急避难场所累计面积	(万平方米)	Total Area of Emergent Earthquake Refuges	(10000 sq.m)	1648	1521

资料来源：北京市地震局。
Source: Beijing Municipal Bureau of Earthquake.

21-32 妇联组织状况
STATISTICS FOR WOMEN'S FEDERATIONS AND ORGANIZATIONS

单位：个，人 (unit,person)

项　目	Item	2013	2012	2013年为2012年% 2013 as % of 2012
妇联组织状况	**Status of Women's Federations and Organizations**			
区妇联数	Number of Women's Federations in Districts	14	14	100.0
县妇联数	Number of Women's Federations in Counties	2	2	100.0
乡、镇妇联组织数	Number of Women's Federations in Townships	115	181	63.5
街道妇联组织数	Number of Women's Federations in Subdistricts	214	140	152.9
妇联干部状况	**Status of Cadres in Women's Federation**			
区妇联干部数	Cadres in Women's Federations in Districts	253	253	100.0
县妇联干部数	Cadres in Women's Federations in Counties	35	28	125.0
乡、镇、街道妇联干部数	Cadres in Women's Federations in Townships, Towns and Subdistricts	321	321	100.0
妇联基层妇代会组织个数	**Number of Grass-root Women Congresses of Women's Federations**			
城　市	Urban	2719	2646	102.8
农　村	Rural	3941	3944	99.9
各类妇女联谊组织数	**Women's Sodalities**	**31**	**30**	**103.3**

资料来源：北京市妇女联合会。
Source: Beijing Women's Federation.

21-33 工会组织建设情况(2013年)
STATISTICS FOR LABOR UNIONS (2013)

项 目	Item	基层工会组织 (个) Grassroot Labor Unions (unit)	职工人数 (人) Number of Employed Persons (person)	会员人数 (人) Number of Members (person)
合 计	**Total**	**32064**	**4434073**	**4015696**
按单位类别划分	**By Registration Type**			
国有企业	State-owned Enterprises	1390	560562	539651
集体企业	Collectively-owned Enterprises	1659	156254	134240
股份合作企业	Joint-equity Cooperative Enterprises	661	73532	64287
联营企业	Associated Enterprises	65	4052	3847
国有独资公司	Solely State-owned Enterprises	425	176110	170953
其他有限责任公司	Other Limited-Liability Companies	9308	921764	794295
国有控股公司	State-holding Companies	353	313439	300744
其他股份有限公司	Other Holding Companies	1072	181618	155664
私营企业	Private Enterprises	6275	472056	372443
其他内资企业	Other Domestically-invested Enterprises	89	6051	4805
港澳台商投资企业	Hong Kong, Macao and Taiwan-invested Enterprises	348	88473	81122
外商投资企业	Foreign-invested Enterprises	843	288073	263221
事业单位	Public Institutions	3180	439843	421099
机 关	Governmental Agencies and Organizations	1390	219277	217532
其 他	Others	5006	532969	491793
按系统分	**By System**			
工业国防工会	Labor Unions for Industry and National Defence	693	366972	353946
工 业	Industry	676	355038	342137
国 防	National Defence	17	11934	11809
建筑工会	Construction	1453	609318	462366
本 市	Local	462	195196	188154
市 外	Non-local	991	414122	274212
服务业工会	Services	793	254555	237291
交通运输工会	Transportation	196	285359	281026
机关事业部	Governmental Institutions	200	96626	94499
教育工会	Education	91	146628	137461
金融工会	Finance	65	117123	113230
市直机关工会	Institutions under Direct Municipal Leadership	383	45943	43600
区县工会	Labor Unions in Districts and Counties	28190	2511549	2292277

资料来源：北京市总工会。
Source: Beijing Federation of Labor Unions.

21-34 北京市妇女发展规划监测统计资料
SUPERVISORY STATISTICS ON WOMEN DEVELOPMENT PROGRAMS OF BEIJING

项 目		Item		2013	2012
城镇单位就业人员数	(万人)	Employed Persons in Urban Entites	(10000 persons)	742.3	717.4
#女 性		Females		298.3	287.6
城镇登记失业人员总数	(万人)	Urban Registered Unemployment	(10000 persons)	24.8	27.4
#女 性		Females		9.9	10.6
城镇登记失业人员就业人数	(万人)	Employed Persons from Urban Registered Unemployment	(10000 persons)	16.9	19.0
#女 性		Females		6.8	7.6
女性接受再就业技能培训后就业率	(%)	Employment Rate of Women Receiving Trainings on Re-imployement Skills	(%)	46.5	41.6
参加基本养老保险人数	(万人)	Number of Participants in Basic Pension Insurance	(10000 persons)	1311.3	1206.4
#女 性		Females		595.5	546.9
参加基本医疗保险人数	(万人)	Number of Participants in Basic Medical Insurance	(10000 persons)	1354.8	1279.7
#女 性		Females		624.8	588.0
参加失业保险人数	(万人)	Number of Participants in Unemployment Insurance	(10000 persons)	1025.1	1006.7
#女 性		Females		450.1	442.1
参加工伤保险人数	(万人)	Number of Participants in Work Injury Insurance	(10000 persons)	920.3	897.2
#女 性		Females		388.5	376.5
城乡居民养老保险参保人数	(万人)	Number of Urban and Rural Residents Participating in Basic Pension Insurance for Urban and Rural Residents		180.1	177.3
#女 性		Females		92.8	91.2
城镇居民基本医疗保险参保人数	(万人)	Number of Urban and Rural Residents Participating in Basic Medical Insurance		160.1	151.9
#女 性		Females		84.9	81.0
市人大女代表领衔提出的议案数	(件)	Number of Proposals Put Forward by Women Deputies of Beijing Municipal People's Congress(BMPC)	(case)	8	12
市政协女委员提出的提案数	(件)	Number of Proposals Put Forward by Women Deputies of Beijing Committee of Chinese People's Political Consultative Conference	(case)	585	597
普通高校在校学生人数	(万人)	Enrollment in Institutions of Higher Education	(10000 persons)	58.9	58.2
#女 性		Females		30.4	29.9
在读研究生人数	(万人)	Number of Enrolled Postgraduates	(10000 persons)	26.6	25.2
#女 性		Females		12.5	11.8
成人本专科在校生人数	(万人)	Enrollment of Technical Higher and Secondary Education for Adults	(10000 persons)	25.8	26.5
#女 性		Females		14.5	15.2
妇科病普查率	(%)	Rate of Gynaopathy General Surveys	(%)	15.6	29.4
乳腺癌检出率	(1/10万)	Detection Rate of Breast Cancer	(1/100000)	20.0	20.0
宫颈癌检出率	(1/10万)	Detection Rate of Cervical Cancer	(1/100000)	5.0	4.5
高危孕产妇住院分娩率	(%)	Birth-giving Rate of High-risk Lying-in Women in Hospitals	(%)	100.0	100.0
已婚育龄妇女综合避孕率	(%)	Practising Contraception Rate of Married Women of Child Bearing Age	(%)	77.1	82.7
抓获刑事作案成员中女性比例	(%)	Share of Females in Criminal Suspects Captured	(%)	17.7	18.5
得到法律援助机构援助的妇女人数	(人)	Number of Women Receiving Aids from Law Aid Institutions	(person)	4928	3370

21-35 北京市儿童发展规划监测统计资料
SUPERVISORY STATISTICS FOR CHILDREN DEVELOPMENT IN BEIJING

项目		Item		2013	2012
婚前医学检查率	(%)	Rate of Premarital Medical Checks	(%)	7.2	7.1
新生儿遗传代谢性疾病筛查率	(%)	Screening Rate of Genic Metabolic Diseases for Newborn	(%)	99.8	98.4
出生缺陷监测率	(%)	Monitoring Rate of Birth Deficiencies	(%)	100.0	100.0
新生儿听力筛查率	(%)	Screening Rate of Hearing for Newborns	(%)	96.95	95.06
出生缺陷发生率	(‰)	Rate of Birth Deficiencies	(‰)	14.70	14.83
7岁以下儿童保健管理率	(%)	Rate of Health Management for Children Under 7 Years Old	(%)	98.37	96.56
0-6个月婴儿纯母乳喂养率	(%)	Rate of Exclusive Breast Breeding for Infants of 0-6 Months	(%)	70.01	68.38
婴儿死亡率	(‰)	Mortality Rate of Infants	(‰)	2.33	2.87
5岁以下儿童死亡率	(‰)	Mortality Rate of Children below 5 Years Old	(‰)	2.89	3.29
儿童肥胖率	(%)	Rate of Obesity for Children	(%)	5.06	4.26
儿童龋齿率	(%)	Rate of Decayed Teeth for Children	(%)	36.74	35.36
卡介苗疫苗接种率	(%)	Rate of Inoculation of BCG Vaccines	(%)	99.84	99.90
脊髓灰质炎疫苗接种率	(%)	Rate of Inoculation of Poliomyelities Polio Vaccines	(%)	99.87	99.72
百白破疫苗接种率	(%)	Rate of Inoculation of Pertussis, Diphtheria and Tetanus Vaccines	(%)	99.87	99.74
含麻疹成分疫苗接种率	(%)	Rate of Inoculation of Vaccines with Measle Ingredients	(%)	99.84	99.84
孕产妇系统管理率	(%)	Rate of Systematic Management for Pregnant and Lying-in Women	(%)	97.06	97.74
城市		Urban		96.57	97.45
农村		Rural		98.03	98.30
孕产妇健康教育普及率	(%)	Popularization Rate of Health Education for Pregnant and Lying-in Women	(%)	99.94	99.93
孕产妇住院分娩率	(%)	Birth-giving Rate of Pregnant and Lying-in Women in Hospital	(%)	100.00	100.00
孕产妇死亡率	(1/10万)	Mortality Rate of Pregnant and Lying-in Women	(1/100000)	9.45	6.05

21-36 北京市历届人代会代表人数性别构成及议案、建议数

NUMBER AND SEX COMPOSITION OF DEPUTIES，NUMBERS OF PROPOSALS AND SUGGESTIONS AT PREVIOUS SESSIONS OF PEOPLE'S CONGRESS OF BEIJING

单位：人、%、件 (person,%,case)

项 目 Item	代表人数 Number of Deputies			性别比例 Sex Percentage		议案立案数 Number of Proposals on Record	建议数 Suggestions
	合 计 Total	女 性 Females	男 性 Males	女 性 Females	男 性 Males		
第 一 届 1st	564	106	458	18.8	81.2		
第 二 届 2nd	619	142	477	22.9	77.1		
第 三 届 3rd	618	162	456	26.2	73.8		
第 四 届 4th	745	202	543	27.1	72.9		
第 五 届 5th	751	203	548	27.0	73.0		
第 七 届 7th	1195	325	870	27.1	72.9		
第 八 届 8th	973	252	721	25.9	74.1	55	6644
第 九 届 9th	880	217	663	24.7	75.3	86	7921
第 十 届 10th	885	224	661	25.3	74.7	156	7281
第十一届 11th	763	197	566	25.8	74.2	166	9717
第十二届 12th	762	235	527	30.8	69.2	276	9859
第十三届 13th	779	237	542	30.4	69.6	153	7576
第十四届 14th	771	257	514	33.3	66.7	22	1261

注：1. 北京市人大常委会是经北京市七届三次人民代表大会选举成立的，故一至七届人代会无议案及建议数。
2. 代表人数为届首选举数，议案及建议数均是本届五年会上及平时议案及建议的合计数。
3. 第十四届议案立案及建议数截止到2013年12月底。

资料来源：北京市人民代表大会常务委员会。

Note: a) Standing Committee of Beijing People's Congress was established upon election at the 3rd Session of Beijing 7th People's Congress. As a result, there were no proposals and suggestions at the 1st-7th People's Congresses.

b) Deputies were those first elected for that term. Proposals and suggestions at other terms of Congress included those at the meeting of the term and/or at ordinary times.

c) Data of proposals and suggestions of 14th Congress was counted by the end of december of 2013.

Source: Standing Committee of Beijing Municipal People's Congress (BMPC).

21-37 北京市历届政协会委员人数及提案立案数
NUMBER OF MEMBERS AND PROPOSALS AT HISTORICAL BEIJING CPPCC

单位：人、件 (person,case)

届别 Term	起止年月 Beginning-ending Month	委员人数 Number of Members 合计 Total	女性 Females	男性 Males	提案立案数 Number of Proposals on Record
第一届 1st	1955.04-1959.09	270	40	230	37
第二届 2nd	1959.09-1962.12	463	84	379	13
第三届 3rd	1962.12-1965.09	519	92	427	884
第四届 4th	1965.09-1977.11	529	88	441	23
第五届 5th	1977.11-1983.03	779	161	618	1610
第六届 6th	1983.03-1988.01	766	168	598	3122
第七届 7th	1988.01-1993.01	703	179	524	4276
第八届 8th	1993.01-1998.01	740	185	555	4975
第九届 9th	1998.01-2003.01	782	203	579	6240
第十届 10th	2003.01-2008.01	824	226	598	6871
第十一届 11th	2008.01-2013.01	737	233	504	5354
第十二届 12th	2013.01-2014.01	758	236	522	2274

资料来源：中国人民政治协商会议北京市委员会。
Source: The Chinese People's Political Consultative Conference Beijing Committe.

主要统计指标解释

优抚对象 依照法律和政策的规定，享受国家、社会和群众抚恤优待的人员，包括中国人民解放军（包括中国人民武装警察部队）现役军人、革命伤残人员、复员退伍军人、革命烈士家属、因公牺牲军人家属、病故军人家属、现役军人家属。

社会救助对象总人数 指在报告期末生活在当地规定的最低生活保障线以下的家庭人员及国家规定由民政部门救济的特殊人员和60年代精简退职老职工救济人员等。

城市居民最低生活保障人数 指报告期末家庭平均收入在当地规定的最低生活保障线以下的城镇居民数。包括"三无"对象、失业人员和在职、下岗、退休人员等。

农村居民最低生活保障人数 指报告期末在建立农村最低生活保障制度的地区，得到当地政府或集体给予最低生活保障的农业人口家庭人数。

参加基本养老保险人数 指报告期末按照国家法律、法规和有关政策规定参加基本养老保险并在社保经办机构已建立缴费记录档案的职工人数，包括中断缴费但未终止养老保险关系的职工人数和参加基本养老保险的离休、退休和退职人员的人数。不包括只登记未建立缴费记录档案的人数。

参加基本医疗保险人数 指报告期末按国家有关规定参加基本医疗保险的人数。包括参加保险的职工人数和退休人员数。

参加失业保险人数 指报告期末按照国家法律、法规和有关政策规定参加了失业保险的城镇企业事业单位的职工及地方政府规定参加失业保险的其他人员的人数。参加失业保险人数为参加失业保险的职工人数。

参加工伤保险人数 指报告期末参加工伤保险的职工人数。

参加生育保险人数 指报告期末参加生育保险的职工人数。

农村居民参加城乡居民养老保险人数 指截止报告期末参加城乡居民养老保险的农村居民人数。

参加农村新型合作医疗人数 指截止报告期末乡镇已参加农村新型合作医疗的总人数。农村新型合作医疗制度是由政府组织、引导、支持，农民自愿参加，集体、个人和政府多方筹资，以大病统筹为主的农民医疗互助共济制度。

社区服务机构数 指报告期末社区服务站、社区服务中心、其它社区服务设施的总和。

律师 指受聘参加律师事务所工作，提任法律顾问、刑（民）事代理人、刑事辩护人，办理非诉讼事件、解答法律询问，代写法律事务文书等主要从事律师业务的专职法律工作者和兼职律师。

公证人员 指在国家公证机关依法办理公证事务的司法人员。包括公证员、助理公证员和在公证处工作的其他人员。

办理公证文书 指公证处在一定时期内办结的公证文书件数。公证文书系按司法部规定或批准的格式制作。

调解人员 指人民调解委员会担负调解民间一般民事纠纷和轻微违法行为所引起的纠纷的工作人员。包括调解委员会的委员和调解小组调解员。

调解民间纠纷 指调解委员会依照法律规定，根据自愿原则，用说服教育的方法调解民间发生的有关民事权利和义务的争执，促成当事双方达到协议和谅解，解决纠纷。包括婚姻家庭纠纷，财产权益纠纷等。不包括法院受理调解的民事案件数。

地震应急避难场所 指适用于地震等自然灾害，也适用于其他事件应急状态下，供居民紧急疏散的公园、公共绿地、城市广场、体育场、学校运动场等场地数量。

Explanatory Notes on Main Statistical Indicators

Persons Receiving Special Care refer to persons receiving special treatment from the country, society and the public in accordance with provisions in laws and policies, including active servicemen of PLA (including the People's Armed Policy Army), persons wounded and disabled due to revolution, veterans, military dependents of revolutionary martyrs, military dependents of servicemen who sacrificed on duty, military dependents of servicemen who died of illness, military dependents of active servicemen.

Total Number of Persons Receiving Social Relief refer to the number of family members living under the minimum living standard provided by local governments, special persons receiving relief by civil affair authorities in line with national regulations, as well as employed persons retired because of streamlining in the 1960s, at the end of the reporting period.

Number of Persons Receiving Subsistence Allowances in Urban Areas refers to the number of urban residents whose average family income is below locally provided minimum living standard, including elderly persons, minors, psychotic patients and disables who have no statutory guardian, no fixed pocketbook, no labor ability, unemployed persons, on-the-job persons, laid-off persons, and retired persons, etc.

Number of Persons Receiving Subsistence Allowances in Rural Areas refers to the number of persons in agricultural families covered by subsistence allowances of local government or collective entities in an area where rural minimum living standard guarantee system is established, at the end of reporting period.

Number of People Participating in Basic Pension Insurance refers to the number of employed persons participating in basic pension insurance and keeping insurance premium payment records with social security organizations in accordance with provisions in national laws, rules and relevant policies at the end of reporting period, including the number of employed persons suspending the payment of insurance premium without terminating the pension insurance relation as well as retired employed persons participating in basic endowment insurance, excluding the number of persons only registered but having no insurance premium payment records.

Number of People Participating in Basic Medical Insurance refers to the number of persons participating in medical insurance programs at the end of the reporting period in accordance with relevant national regulations, including the number of employed persons and retired persons participating in the insurance.

Number of People Participating in Unemployment Insurance refers to the number of employed persons in urban enterprises and public institutions participating in unemployment insurance programs at the end of the reporting period in accordance with provisions in national laws, rules and relevant policies, as well as other persons specified by local governments to participate in unemployment insurance. The number of persons participating in unemployment insurance program is the number of persons who participate in unemployment insurance.

Number of People Participating in Work-related Injury Insurance refers to the number of persons participating in work injury insurance programs at the end of the reporting period.

Number of People Participating in Maternity Insurance refers to the number of persons participating in maternity insurance programs at the end of the reporting period.

Number of People Participating in Rural Basic Pension Insurance refers to the number of rural residents who had participated in urban and rural old-age insurance programs by the end of the reporting period.

Number of People Participating in New-type Rural Cooperative Medicare refers to the total number of persons who had participated in the rural new-type cooperative medical service by the end of reporting period. The rural new-type cooperative medical service system is a mutual aid medical system for farmers, focusing on general health care programs for major diseases, organized, guided and supported by government, with farmers' voluntary participation.

Number of Service Facilities in Urban Communities refers to the total number of community service stations, service centers, and other service facilities, by the end of reporting period.

Lawyer refers to a full-time legal worker and part-time lawyer joining a law firm, serving as a legal consultant, criminal (civil) proxy, criminal counsel, handling non-lawsuit events, answering legal questions, writing legal documents for others, and other lawyer business.

Notary refers to any judicial person handling notarization matters in national notarization agencies according to laws, including notaries, assistant notaries, and other personnel working in notarization offices.

Notarization Documents Executed refers to the number of notarization documents executed at notarization offices within a given period of time. Notarization documents are prepared in the format specified or approved by the Ministry of Justice. Notarization includes domestic notarization and foreign notarization. Domestic notarization falls into economic notarization and civil legal relation notarization.

Mediator refer to working personnel responsible for mediating general civil disputes as well as disputes caused by slightly illegal acts in any people's mediation committee, including members of people's mediation committees and mediators of mediation teams.

Mediation of Civil Disputes refers to the mediation of disputes against civil rights and obligations by mediation committees on voluntary basis and in accordance with provisions in laws in order to urge both parties to reach an agreement and understanding to resolve the dispute, including marriage and family disputes, property rights and interest disputes, etc., excluding the number of civil cases accepted by courts.

Emergent Earthquake Refuges refer to the number of parks, public green land, city squares, gyms, school playgrounds for residents' emergent evacuation in the event of natural disasters such as earthquake, and under the condition of other emergent events.

北京统计年鉴2014 BEIJING STATISTICAL YEARBOOK

第三产业
TERTIARY INDUSTRY

简要说明

一、本章资料的主要内容

本章主要内容包括第三产业主要指标、规模以上第三产业主要指标、规模以上第三产业企业财务状况、北京地区服务贸易、文化创意产业、物流业、会展活动和体育及相关产业活动情况等。

二、本章资料的数据来源

本章除北京地区服务贸易情况由北京市商务委员会提供外，其他资料由北京市统计局、国家统计局北京调查总队提供。

三、本章资料的统计范围

本章规模以上第三产业是指除国际组织以外的各行业限额以上的法人单位。2013 年具体为金融业、房地产开发业的全部法人单位；批发业为年主营业务收入 2000 万元及以上的企业；零售业为年主营业务收入 500 万元及以上的企业；住宿业为星级饭店和星级以外年主营业务收入 200 万元及以上企业；餐饮业为年主营业务收入 200 万元及以上的企业；其余行业为年营业收入或收入合计 500 万元及以上的法人单位。

文化创意产业资料根据文化创意产业法人单位的统计年报等有关资料测算取得。

物流业统计范围包括限额（规模）以上铁路运输业、道路运输业、水上运输业、航空运输业、管道运输业、装卸搬运和运输代理业、仓储业、邮政业、包装服务业、批发业、零售业和工业企业。

会展业统计对象涉及会展活动的举办服务单位和接待单位。具体包括星级宾馆饭店及年主营业务收入 200 万元及以上的宾馆饭店、从事各种会展活动的场馆、大型会展活动的主办单位（名单由北京市公安局提供）以及为会展活动提供各类专业服务的单位。2013 年会展业数据由统计年报资料和相关部门资料汇总测算取得，由于每年的统计对象单位范围不完全相同（有新增和消亡单位），为保持数据的可比性，同时列出统计对象本年和上年数据。

体育及相关产业情况根据体育及相关产业单位的统计年报等有关资料汇总计算，执行国家体育总局、国家统计局颁布的《体育及相关产业分类（试行）》标准。

四、有关统计标准的变化说明

（一）关于行业划分。根据国家统计局规定，自 2012 年开始执行《国民经济行业分类》GB/T 4754-2011 标准。

（二）关于三次产业划分。根据国家统计局《三次产业划分规定》（国统字[2012]108 号），该规定对三次产业的范围进行了调整。其中第一产业是指农、林、牧、渔业（不含农、林、牧、渔服务业）；第二产业是指采矿业（不含开采辅助活动），制造业（不含金属制品、机械和设备修理业），电力、热力、燃气及水生产和供应业，建筑业；第三产业是指除第一产业、第二产业以外的其他行业。自 2012 年开始执行此规定。

Brief Introduction

I. Main Content

This chapter includes: main indicators for tertiary industry, main indicators for tertiary industry above designated size, financial status of tertiary industry above designated size, service trade, cultural and creative industry, logistics industry, exhibition activities, sports and activities in related sectors in Beijing.

II. Date Source

Except for the data on service trade in Beijing, which are acquired from Beijing Municipal Commission of Commerce, other data are provided by Beijing Municipal Bureau of Statistics, and NBS Survey Office in Beijing.

III. Scope of Statistics

In this chapter, the tertiary industry above designated size refers to corporate enterprises above designated size other than international organizations, in details including all corporate enterprises in financcial and real estate development sectors, enterprises with annual main business income of RMB 20 million and more in wholesale sector, enterprises with annual main business income of RMB 5 million and more in retail sector star-level and non-star-level enterprises with annual main business income of RMB 2 million and more in accommodation sector, enterprises with annual main business income of RMB 2 million and more in catering sector, and in other sectors, corporate enterprises with annual business income or total income of RMB 5 million and more.

Data on cultural and creative industry were calculated based on survey data of corporate enterprises in cultural and creative sector.

The statistical scope of logistics include enterprises in railway transport, road transport, water transport, air transport, transport via pipelines, loading, unloading, portage, storage, post, packaging services, wholesale trade, retail trade and industrial enterprises above designated size.

Statistical scope of MICE industry covers service companies and reception companies holding the exhibitions, in details, including: star-level hotels and those hotels with annual main business income of RMB 2 million and more; venues for exhibitions; sponsors of large exhibitions (with the list provided by Beijing Municipal Bureau of Public Security) together with organizations providing various professional services to exhibitions. Statistics for MICE in 2013 is calculated after collecting data from annual statistical report and relevant departments. As the scope of companies under survey is not completely the same (there are companies newly added and phasing out), data in both the current year and previous year are collected from the surveyed companies to keep the data comparable.

Data on sports and related industry were calculated according to the data in annual statistical report. As for the scope of statistics, the standards in the Classification of Sports and Related Industry (Temporary) issued by the State Administration for Sports and National Bureau of Statistics were applied.

Ⅳ. Changes in Relevant Statistical Standards

(I) Classification of Sectors. According to relevant provisions of National Bureau of Statistics, the Standard for Classification of National Economic Sectors (GB/T4754-2011) became effective in 2012.

(II) Classification of Three Industries. According to the Provisions of the National Bureau of Statistics on Classification of Three Industries (GTZ [2012] No. 108), the scope of three industries was changed. The primary industry refers to agriculture, forestry, animal production and hunting, fishing (excluding service for agriculture, forestry, animal production and hunting, fishing); the secondary industry refers to mining and quarrying (excluding mining support activities), manufacturing (excluding metal products, machinery and equipment repair), production and distribution of electricity, heating power, gas and water, and construction; the tertiary industry refers to sectors other than the primary and secondary industries. the Provisions of the National Bureau of Statistics on Classification of Three Industries (GTZ [2012] No. 108) came into effect in 2012.

22-1 第三产业主要指标及占全市比重(2000-2013年)

项 目		Item		2000	2001	2002	2003	2004
增加值	(亿元)	Value Added	(100 million yuan)	2049.1	2484.8	2982.6	3435.9	4092.2
占全市比重	(%)	Percentage of the Total	(%)	64.8	67.0	69.1	68.6	67.8
劳动生产率	(元/人)	Overall Labor Productivity	(yuan/person)	61525	73082	83069	86864	83977
相当于全市比例	(%)	Percentage of the Total	(%)	120.4	123.0	125.9	119.9	108.4
从业人员年末人数	(万人)	Year-end Employed Persons	(10000 persons)	338.2	341.8	376.3	414.8	559.8
占全市比重	(%)	Percentage of the Total	(%)	54.6	54.4	55.4	59.0	65.5
固定资产投资	(亿元)	Investment in Fixed Assets	(100 million yuan)	510.3	1367.9	1621.8	1875.4	2112.7
占全市比重	(%)	Percentage of the Total	(%)	39.3	89.3	89.4	86.9	83.6
实际利用外资金额	(亿美元)	Actual Use of Foreign Capital	(USD 100 million)	22.2	12.8	12.5	14.0	19.2
占全市比重	(%)	Percentage of the Total	(%)	90.5	72.4	69.8	65.3	62.4
能源消费总量	(万吨标准煤)	Energy Consumption	(10000 tons of SCE)	1080.9	1196.2	1334.5	1391.0	1638.0
相当于全市比例	(%)	Percentage of the Total	(%)	26.1	28.3	30.1	29.9	31.9

MAIN INDICATORS OF THE TERTIARY INDUSTRY AND THEIR PERCENTAGES OF BEIJING'S TOTAL (2000-2013)

2005	2006	2007	2008	2009	2010	2011	2012	2013
4854.3	5837.6	7236.1	8375.8	9179.2	10600.8	12363.1	13669.9	14986.5
69.6	71.9	73.5	75.4	75.5	75.1	76.1	76.5	76.9
84828	95800	112388	122794	126872	140968	158613	167852	175066
105.4	106.1	106.3	106.3	103.3	101.4	102.5	102.2	100.9
584.7	634.0	653.7	710.5	736.5	767.5	791.4	837.4	874.7
66.6	68.9	69.3	72.4	73.8	74.4	74.0	75.6	76.7
2405.6	2993.8	3465.8	3434.4	4389.5	4922.3	5101.3	5597.5	6101.7
85.1	88.8	87.4	89.2	90.3	89.6	86.3	86.6	86.8
23.0	34.5	40.8	44.4	52.0	56.3	62.4	69.1	70.1
65.2	75.8	80.6	72.9	84.9	88.5	88.5	85.9	82.2
1918.7	2129.3	2389.5	2610.5	2760.3	2897.4	3100.5	3252.1	3423.0
34.7	36.1	38.0	41.3	42.0	41.7	44.3	45.3	46.5

22-2 北京地区服务贸易情况(2003-2012年)
STATISTICS FOR SERVICE TRADE (2003-2012)

单位：亿美元 (USD 100 million)

项　目	Item	2003	2004	2005	2006	2007	2008	2009	2010	2011	2012
服务贸易总额	**Total Volume of Service Trade**	**162.24**	**235.70**	**300.74**	**393.23**	**503.06**	**691.92**	**644.10**	**798.29**	**895.40**	**1000.20**
运　输	Transportation	42.73	66.79	80.06	107.29	110.96	144.38	140.50	177.11	196.30	223.21
旅　游	Tourism	30.87	48.60	54.93	68.22	94.13	88.66	92.90	108.68	136.10	155.48
通讯服务	Communication Services	8.71	7.41	8.55	11.49	18.39	24.28	17.20	17.62	21.50	26.15
建筑服务	Construction Services	10.66	11.90	19.56	23.69	46.28	79.56	74.30	87.16	92.40	85.23
保险服务	Insurance Services	8.91	11.90	14.91	19.85	23.54	72.85	58.60	92.22	133.10	132.14
金融服务	Financial Services	0.53	0.47	0.53	0.53	1.79	1.93	4.70	8.09	11.70	22.16
计算机和信息服务	Computer and Information Services	9.00	9.76	11.60	18.32	24.74	29.25	28.80	39.83	52.00	60.19
专利使用费和特许费	Patent and Royalty Fee	5.27	7.38	9.40	14.39	16.80	20.38	16.40	21.11	22.60	28.40
咨　询	Consultation	12.22	18.94	28.33	43.28	57.91	84.38	81.10	89.47	99.10	116.36
广告、宣传	Advertisements and Publicity	3.19	5.16	6.26	7.40	10.02	12.90	10.80	13.19	17.80	19.61
电影、音像	Movies and Audio-video Products	0.74	1.33	1.95	1.82	3.85	5.51	2.70	3.56	3.40	4.91
其他商业服务	Other Commercial Services	29.41	46.06	64.66	76.95	94.65	127.82	116.00	140.27	109.50	126.36

资料来源：北京市商务委员会。
Source: Beijing Municipal Commission of Commerce .

22-3 北京地区服务贸易情况
STATISTICS FOR SERVICE TRADE

单位：亿美元 (USD 100 million)

项　目	Item	服务贸易总额 Total Turnover of Service Trade		外汇收入 Forex Income		外汇支出 Forex Payment		顺(逆)差 Surplus (Deficit)	
		2012	2011	2012	2011	2012	2011	2012	2011
合　计	**Total**	**1000.20**	**895.40**	**445.11**	**415.00**	**555.09**	**480.40**	**-109.98**	**-65.40**
运　输	Transportation	223.21	196.30	57.22	53.90	165.99	142.50	-108.76	-88.60
旅　游	Tourism	155.48	136.10	51.49	54.20	103.99	81.90	-52.50	-27.70
通讯服务	Communication Services	26.15	21.50	13.56	12.90	12.59	8.70	0.97	4.20
建筑服务	Construction Services	85.23	92.40	64.80	72.40	20.43	20.00	44.36	52.40
保险服务	Insurance Services	132.14	133.10	19.71	16.50	112.43	116.50	-92.72	-100.00
金融服务	Financial Services	22.16	11.70	4.63	7.10	17.53	4.60	-12.90	2.50
计算机和信息服务	Computer and Information Services	60.19	52.00	49.08	41.00	11.11	11.00	37.97	30.00
专利使用费和特许费	Patent or Royalty Fee	28.40	22.60	5.73	2.90	22.66	19.70	-16.93	-16.80
咨　询	Consultation	116.36	99.10	88.71	75.10	27.65	24.00	61.06	51.10
广告、宣传	Advertisements and Publicity	19.61	17.80	12.73	11.60	6.88	6.20	5.86	5.40
电影、音像	Movies and Audio-video Products	4.91	3.40	0.76	0.70	4.15	2.70	-3.38	-2.00
其他商业服务	Other Commercial Services	126.36	109.50	76.68	66.80	49.68	42.60	26.99	24.20

资料来源：北京市商务委员会。
Source: Beijing Municipal Commission of Commerce .

22-4 规模以上第三产业主要指标(2004-2013年)
MAIN INDICATORS FOR TERTIARY INDUSTRY ENTERPRISES ABOVE DESIGNATED SIZE (2004-2013)

项 目	Item	2004	2005	2006	2007	2008
单位数 (个)	Number of Enterprises (unit)	25725	23661	24921	25651	34820
从业人员平均人数 (万人)	Average Number of Employed Persons (10,000 persons)	301.4	323.3	340.4	373.5	443.6
资产总计 (亿元)	Total Assets (100 million yuan)	184985.5	274180.3	336485.9	422458.7	579095.5
收入合计 (亿元)	Income (100 million yuan)	21467.2	24444.6	29468.7	38361.8	47524.3
应交税金合计 (亿元)	Total Tax Payable (100 million yuan)	908.1	1004.0	1376.0	2360.9	1855.2
企业利润总额 (亿元)	Total Profits (100 million yuan)	1544.8	2696.1	2967.2	4511.2	4577.6

注：应交税金合计主要包括应交增值税、应交所得税、营业税金及附加和管理费用中的税金等。

Note: Total tax payable mainly includes VAT payable, income tax payable, business tax and surtax, and tax in management expenses, etc.

22-4 续表 Continued

项 目	Item	2009	2010	2011	2012	2013
单位数 (个)	Number of Enterprises (unit)	36177	36064	36102	36616	36504
从业人员平均人数 (万人)	Average Number of Employed Persons (10,000 persons)	472.1	487.9	509.9	545.0	565.2
资产总计 (亿元)	Total Assets (100 million yuan)	712313.4	798485.4	909953.5	1022849.7	1093973.1
收入合计 (亿元)	Total Income (100 million yuan)	55390.3	69106.8	79246.0	92138.2	103398.8
应交税金合计 (亿元)	Total Tax Payable (100 million yuan)	2560.8	3122.4	4018.9	4652.8	5415.4
企业利润总额 (亿元)	Total Profits (100 million yuan)	10540.8	10236.3	11413.1	14248.4	18410.6

22-5 规模以上第三产业企业财务状况(按登记注册类型分)(2013年)

单位：万元

项目	Item	企业单位个数(个) Number of Enterprises (unit)	资产负债：资产总计 Total Assets	资产负债：流动资产合计 Total Current Assets	资产负债：#应收账款 Accounts Receivable
合计	**Total**	**31396**	**8827247872**	**1042722771**	**97368320**
按隶属关系分	**By Affiliation**				
中央	Central	2731	6717415592	383585616	37762425
地方	Local	28665	2109832280	659137154	59605896
按登记注册类型分	**By Registration Type**				
内资企业	Domestically-invested Enterprises	28020	8388976662	880915288	76426828
国有企业	State-owned Enterprises	1837	812605702	146507076	6930172
集体企业	Collectively-owned Enterprises	492	11793573	7485289	200702
股份合作企业	Joint-equity Cooperative Enterprises	382	5526250	3793312	399996
联营企业	Associated Enterprises	35	447451	208816	9641
有限责任公司	Limited-Liability Companies	11679	1750135153	522676470	48430194
股份有限公司	Companies Limited by Shares	899	5715293695	131569888	9406167
私营企业	Private Enterprises	12643	92290346	68004532	11004289
其他企业	Others	53	884493	669903	45667
港澳台商投资企业	Hong Kong, Macao and Taiwan-invested Enterprises	1344	132809188	67981514	6384343
外商投资企业	Foreign-invested Enterprises	2032	305462022	93825969	14557149

注：1. 行业划分执行2011年国民经济行业分类标准(GB/T 4754-2011)。
2. 应交税金合计主要包括应交增值税、应交所得税、营业税金及附加和管理费用中的税金。
3. 执行《2006年会计准则》的银行、证券、保险业企业，其"主营营业税金及附加"用"营业税金及附加"代替，"营业成本"和"主营业务成本"用"营业支出-营业税金及附加"代替。

FINANCIAL STATUS OF TERTIARY INDUSTRY ENTERPRISES ABOVE DESIGNATED SIZE(BY REGISTRATION TYPE) (2013)

(10000 yuan)

Assets and Liabilites						
固定资产合计 Total Fixed Assets	固定资产原价 Total Original Value of Fixed Assets	负债合计 Total Liabilities	#流动负债合计 Total Current Liabilities	#应付账款 Accounts Payable	所有者权益合计 Total Owner's Equity	#实收资本 Paid-up Capital
160516128	**225152663**	**6745376297**	**824428113**	**129463874**	**2081871575**	**1047090569**
69145599	98803773	5136843833	321356079	55360322	1580571759	797938633
91370530	126348890	1608532464	503072034	74103552	501299815	249151936
129280505	172213664	6492199950	703314198	103560177	1896776712	975943267
26164624	37687394	464227979	105107381	8933691	348377723	176330441
1892876	2499192	8363864	6667218	322463	3429709	697718
675657	915467	3885849	3348456	275502	1640401	505389
66593	115371	214579	207722	33030	232872	253626
55705641	75306628	983301491	413526464	71694203	766833662	486367191
39623929	48044732	4965613832	114173566	11056027	749679863	287191697
4989492	7453508	66080365	59803024	11183459	26209980	24567784
161693	191372	511992	480368	61802	372501	29423
24900222	41636933	83361643	49654593	8771038	49447546	34966426
6335401	11302066	169814705	71459322	17132660	135647317	36180875

Note: 1) Sectors in this table are classified in accordance with the Standard for Classification of National Economic Sectors 2011 (GB/T 4754-2011).
2) Total tax payable mainly includes VAT payable, income tax payable, business tax and surtax, and tax in management expenses, etc.
3) For banks, security and insurance enterprises implementing 2006 Standard of Accounting System, the indicator "Main Business Tax and Surtax" are replaced with "Business Tax and Surtax".

22-5 续表

单位：万元

项　目	Item	损益及分配			
		营业收入 Business Income	#主营业务收入 Main Business Income	营业成本 Business Cost	#主营业务成本 Main Business Cost
合　计	**Total**	**950771930**	**934375452**	**726230797**	**717066331**
按隶属关系分	**By Affiliation**				
中央	Central	428661940	420058985	310962990	305126708
地方	Local	522109990	514316467	415267807	411939624
按登记注册类型分	**By Registration Type**				
内资企业	Domestically-invested Enterprises	772472120	758426148	591982016	583509389
国有企业	State-owned Enterprises	86154581	83874993	77926131	77351575
集体企业	Collectively-owned Enterprises	2273394	2178200	1632343	1604050
股份合作企业	Joint-equity Cooperative Enterprises	1584689	1556743	1204332	1202567
联营企业	Associated Enterprises	266478	263483	207128	206280
有限责任公司	Limited-Liability Companies	463453461	453423296	360614701	353313511
股份有限公司	Companies Limited by Shares	143505078	142691762	89660093	89419036
私营企业	Private Enterprises	74789328	74001491	60504504	60184954
其他企业	Others	445112	436182	232785	227418
港澳台商投资企业	Hong Kong, Macao and Taiwan-invested Enterprises	49102603	48490330	33716619	33272751
外商投资企业	Foreign-invested Enterprises	129197207	127458973	100532161	100284191

22-5 continued

(10000 yuan)

Profits and Losses							
销售费用 Sales Expenses	管理费用 Management Expenses	财务费用 Financial Expenses	利润总额 Total Profits	应交税金合计 Total Tax Payable	#营业税金及附加 Business Tax and Surtax	#主营业务税金及附加 Business Tax and Surtax	#应交所得税 Income Tax Payable
38688405	**44448812**	**10527279**	**184105599**	**53729348**	**12167347**	**11792994**	**33305646**
5875323	11763197	4674633	134637619	28848133	3732803	3509778	23818702
32813082	32685615	5852646	49467981	24881215	8434544	8283216	9486945
22869960	31035833	10072882	160065871	45221320	10116033	9772687	30169608
1646022	5949941	1123612	23656012	4138731	1094167	945877	3482461
150831	353426	2143	168721	106896	44889	42519	31855
129867	219249	330	25458	53053	22125	21303	12213
27330	31014	513	13100	7126	1608	1485	1451
11971950	14701778	5774251	84838821	14657994	4910407	4767539	6452619
2877977	3685465	2618800	49755233	23782502	3272199	3240035	19687444
5989959	5997511	558064	1573049	2456152	757117	740616	498798
76024	97450	-4831	35477	18867	13520	13314	2767
4746005	4486857	423285	6323628	3270394	1028533	1014479	1415051
11072440	8926123	31112	17716101	5237634	1022781	1005828	1720988

22-6 规模以上第三产业企业财务状况(按行业分)(2013年)

单位：万元

项目	Item	企业单位个数(个) Number of Enterprises (unit)	资产负债 资产总计 Total Assets	流动资产合计 Total Current Assets
合 计	**Total**	**31396**	**8827247872**	**1042722771**
批发和零售业	**Wholesale and Retail Trade**	**7462**	**320256693**	**235060232**
批发业	Wholesale	4978	281992974	205806007
零售业	Retail Trade	2484	38263719	29254226
交通运输、仓储和邮政业	**Transport, Storage and Post**	**1089**	**131615982**	**41180740**
铁路运输业	Railway Transport	16	47413659	4834634
道路运输业	Road Transport	543	17141341	5398629
水上运输业	Water Transport	6	63160	21352
航空运输业	Air Transport	17	23513683	3481576
管道运输业	Transport Via Pipelines	2	***	***
装卸搬运和运输代理业	Loading, Unloading, Portage and Other Transport Services	342	6192699	3872602
仓储业	Storage	132	21063299	20178890
邮政业	Post	31	4869473	3081758
住宿和餐饮业	**Accommodation and Restaurants**	**2927**	**16452185**	**6439360**
住宿业	Accommodation	1110	12284824	4149954
餐饮业	Restaurants	1817	4167361	2289407
信息传输、软件和信息技术服务业	**Information Transmission, Software and Information Technology Services**	**2746**	**247070789**	**79518639**
电信、广播电视和卫星传输服务	Telecommunications, Broadcasting, Television and Satellite Transmission Services	252	190840801	38759236
互联网和相关服务	Internet and Related Services	253	9257902	6737951
软件和信息技术服务业	Software and Information Technology Services	2241	46972086	34021451
金融业	**Finance**	**1753**	**6737066292**	**31949095**
货币金融服务	Monetary Financial Services	517	5593159948	6107401
资本市场服务	Capital Market Services	441	337355207	4740873
保险业	Insurance	453	282850611	763998
其他金融业	Other Financial Services	342	523700527	20336824

FINANCIAL STATUS OF TERTIARY INDUSTRY ENTERPRISES ABOVE DESIGNATED SIZE(BY SECTOR) (2013)

(10000 yuan)

Assets and Liabilites							
#应收账款 Accounts Receivable	固定资产合计 Total Fixed Assets	固定资产原价 Total Original Value of Fixed Assets	负债合计 Total Liabilities	#流动负债合计 Total Current Liabilities	#应付账款 Accounts Payable	所有者权益合计 Total Owner's Equity	#实收资本 Paid-up Capital
97368320	**160516128**	**225152663**	**6745376297**	**824428113**	**129463874**	**2081871575**	**1047090569**
44344835	**9062955**	**14153343**	**230677698**	**203154395**	**64026200**	**89578996**	**45175269**
40757556	6019845	9216232	200792411	174915488	56226380	81200563	39776818
3587279	3043109	4937111	29885287	28238908	7799819	8378432	5398451
3884933	**69836687**	**90157548**	**70274047**	**43409591**	**7458888**	**61341935**	**49220199**
844434	35268280	42886849	16702830	6977132	2648766	30710830	32734810
547426	9956769	13541806	10320015	4732337	643624	6821326	5171107
5116	40103	73758	36673	17823	3496	26487	15868
848408	14049697	20601676	15709275	5861052	1742207	7804408	2787664
***	***	***	***	***	***	***	***
951623	515629	803582	3165517	2706612	926021	3027181	1628463
41874	545297	747251	20400015	20011961	648384	663284	430531
525092	458158	881841	2436976	2309927	405107	2432497	1427756
281459	**5583756**	**9286488**	**12419306**	**9187050**	**918452**	**4032878**	**4556013**
145481	4970281	8122222	9052668	6350120	424513	3232156	3710317
135978	613474	1164265	3366639	2836931	493938	800722	845695
13210944	**13381447**	**27795387**	**63851348**	**53867170**	**10716744**	**183219441**	**76423973**
2978564	8931917	19736868	36448925	28633892	4197073	154391876	65223870
745470	1047196	1961470	4654455	4395972	773109	4603448	1373620
9486910	3402334	6097050	22747968	20837307	5746562	24224118	9826483
3563244	**17449593**	**21612579**	**5622954150**	**22761860**	**1246696**	**1114112143**	**564596146**
2004343	12705129	16408657	5094360675	6072742	275980	498799273	192082151
297538	893622	1336174	139265567	2682053	90209	198089640	188869274
61654	2908844	2392973	206924012	234112	58189	75926600	31070654
1199710	941998	1474774	182403897	13772953	822318	341296630	152574068

22-6 续表 1

单位：万元

项 目	Item	损益及分配 营业收入 Business Income	#主营业务收入 Main Business Income
合　计	**Total**	**950771930**	**934375452**
批发和零售业	**Wholesale and Retail Trade**	**493525095**	**483269929**
批发业	Wholesale	426095506	417415117
零售业	Retail Trade	67429589	65854813
交通运输、仓储和邮政业	**Transport, Storage and Post**	**45403351**	**44667339**
铁路运输业	Railway Transport	10791191	10306447
道路运输业	Road Transport	4704216	4609413
水上运输业	Water Transport	37006	37006
航空运输业	Air Transport	10419256	10360940
管道运输业	Transport Via Pipelines	***	***
装卸搬运和运输代理业	Loading, Unloading, Portage and Other Transport Services	7834823	7802578
仓储业	Storage	7274549	7256770
邮政业	Post	2383625	2352667
住宿和餐饮业	**Accommodation and Restaurants**	**8831473**	**8750655**
住宿业	Accommodation	3568211	3543805
餐饮业	Restaurants	5263262	5206851
信息传输、软件和信息技术服务业	**Information Transmission, Software and Information Technology Services**	**49903265**	**49038602**
电信、广播电视和卫星传输服务	Telecommunications, Broadcasting, Television and Satellite Transmission Services	10665669	10255972
互联网和相关服务	Internet and Related Services	6551576	6518917
软件和信息技术服务业	Software and Information Technology Services	32686020	32263713
金融业	**Finance**	**160419949**	**160276428**
货币金融服务	Monetary Financial Services	50001431	49984605
资本市场服务	Capital Market Services	26598621	26590759
保险业	Insurance	36094057	36090049
其他金融业	Other Financial Services	47725840	47611015

22-6 continued 1

(10000 yuan)

Profits and Losses									
营业成本 Business Cost	#主营业务成本 Main Business Cost	销售费用 Sales Expenses	管理费用 Manage-ment Expenses	财务费用 Financial Expenses	利润总额 Total Profits	应交税金合计 Total Tax Payable	#营业税金及附加 Business Tax and Surtax	#主营业务税金及附加 Business Tax and Surtax	#应交所得税 Income Tax Payable
726230797	**717066331**	**38688405**	**44448812**	**10527279**	**184105599**	**53729348**	**12167347**	**11792994**	**33305646**
460249475	**453583046**	**16853251**	**8396459**	**1007317**	**10530886**	**7777405**	**923057**	**869238**	**2220088**
401116668	394680367	11883287	6248369	692619	9407691	6084605	660188	627417	1852820
59132807	58902679	4969964	2148090	314698	1123195	1692800	262869	241821	367268
39095617	**38498285**	**1837303**	**2709521**	**969297**	**2887643**	**688697**	**521422**	**505167**	**865806**
9014230	8553171	13727	898235	425778	272786	624137	323116	313791	286886
5294981	5250260	213005	521799	332666	218092	210653	56088	52843	54309
25198	25198	2713	5630	1394	3552	1066	48	48	601
8746586	8688771	793904	341698	155020	560476	182165	31028	30137	127222
***	***	***	***	***	***	***	***	***	***
6884704	6880071	288375	477337	12017	340637	149938	20926	20353	64329
7012956	7005647	68981	100929	4970	105119	-1047405	6519	6342	6130
1339410	1335363	433171	310953	6732	252664	150887	56879	56442	68887
3174216	**3161414**	**3167372**	**1924884**	**187614**	**-13263**	**672158**	**476787**	**474156**	**107670**
938717	934335	1082226	1274112	138923	-577	320822	195249	194718	53756
2235499	2227079	2085146	650772	48691	-12686	351336	281538	279438	53914
30571471	**29970035**	**6455935**	**8244369**	**-330709**	**18897419**	**4766064**	**648940**	**634959**	**2651050**
6971600	6595302	1692795	1676198	-258495	13750543	2328912	266190	254487	1975534
3225534	3223237	1111636	918223	-86245	1409778	494169	133886	133475	168464
20374337	20151496	3651504	5649948	14031	3737098	1942983	248864	246998	507052
50235495	**50169202**	**317705**	**1106319**	**236331**	**106126319**	**26396216**	**3718580**	**3705103**	**22458549**
21903992	21902204	47034	122927	108500	24844982	21787555	2972901	2972349	18835890
2918106	2917836	24432	215758	59659	23375665	1756307	222759	222691	1503364
22063519	22063118	56660	177275	-2614	13537528	1589499	276438	276338	1277103
3349879	3286044	189579	590360	70787	44368143	1262854	246482	233724	842192

22-6 续表 2

单位：万元

项目	Item	企业单位个数(个) Number of Enterprises (unit)	资产负债 资产总计 Total Assets
房地产业	**Real Estate**	**4601**	**423750808**
租赁和商务服务业	**Renting and Leasing Activities, Business Services**	**5911**	**815695577**
租赁业	Renting and Leasing	135	2505675
商务服务业	Business Services	5776	813189902
科学研究和技术服务业	**Scientific Research and Development, Technical Services**	**2830**	**101224569**
研究和试验发展	Research and Experimental Development	270	18652302
专业技术服务业	Professional Technical Services	1545	59027464
科技推广和应用服务业	Technique Generalization and Application Services	1015	23544803
水利、环境和公共设施管理业	**Management of Water Conservancy, Environment and Public Facilities**	**320**	**13233793**
水利管理业	Management of Water Conservancy	16	784478
生态保护和环境治理业	Ecological Protection and Environmental Control	50	2065525
公共设施管理业	Management of Public Facilities	254	10383791
居民服务、修理和其他服务业	**Resident Services, Repair and Other Services**	**429**	**1439325**
居民服务业	Resident Services	130	559468
机动车、电子产品和日用产品修理业	Repair of Motor Vehicles, Electronics and Household Appliances	139	522242
其他服务业	Other Services	160	357616
教育	**Education**	**193**	**1852717**
卫生和社会工作	**Healthcare and Social Works**	**141**	**956153**
卫生	Healthcare	137	925168
社会工作	Social Works	4	30986
文化、体育和娱乐业	**Culture, Sports and Entertainment**	**994**	**16632989**
新闻和出版业	Journalism and Publishing	471	9238741
广播、电视、电影和影视录音制作业	Radio Broadcasting, Television, Movies, Videos and Sound Recording	192	4890914
文化艺术业	Culture and Arts	101	565153
体育	Sports Activities	133	1434797
娱乐业	Entertainment	97	503384

22-6 continued 2

(10000 yuan)

Assets and Liabilites								
流动资产合计 Total Current Assets	#应收账款 Accounts Receivable	固定资产合计 Total Fixed Assets	固定资产原价 Total Original Value of Fixed Assets	负债合计 Total Liabilities	#流动负债合计 Total Current Liabilities	#应付账款 Accounts Payable	所有者权益合计 Total Owner's Equity	#实收资本 Paid-up Capital
329832583	**6496050**	**17777038**	**22370360**	**326486836**	**238804884**	**15773869**	**97263972**	**60003642**
237717759	**12510769**	**16329055**	**23222101**	**337922732**	**187906207**	**13438015**	**477772844**	**220661257**
781999	158706	938577	1422676	1800255	927269	91653	705420	405571
236935759	12352064	15390477	21799425	336122477	186978938	13346362	477067425	220255685
63289880	**10706378**	**5771805**	**8950552**	**61798808**	**53496130**	**13161412**	**39425761**	**20212972**
13964809	798279	1098414	1739981	13146099	10932786	2616715	5506203	3139584
35649310	6752589	3110967	4915861	35218363	30489179	7212660	23809101	11846026
13675761	3155510	1562424	2294710	13434345	12074166	3332037	10110458	5227362
4466592	**945304**	**2120753**	**2625481**	**9073151**	**3252272**	**841770**	**4160642**	**1400495**
187147	17645	132406	218605	449930	205885	17854	334548	206354
1323379	330625	294545	420224	1368432	1023912	354488	697093	488178
2956066	597034	1693802	1986652	7254790	2022475	469427	3129001	705964
1093780	**168487**	**170751**	**298124**	**1112561**	**1029467**	**153468**	**326764**	**279432**
396620	23304	55908	113415	483013	460447	41914	76455	73660
419411	69905	72292	125598	363977	340991	74469	158264	111788
277749	75279	42550	59111	265571	228029	37085	92045	93984
1291758	**57490**	**309628**	**528978**	**1186414**	**1110765**	**94844**	**666303**	**247608**
531400	**76600**	**327911**	**507120**	**483630**	**447201**	**172787**	**472523**	**257188**
519506	76298	309353	469480	469821	433391	172735	455347	256449
11894	302	18557	37640	13809	13809	52	17176	739
10350953	**1121828**	**2394752**	**3644602**	**7135617**	**6001121**	**1460732**	**9497372**	**4056375**
6139038	511307	1275848	1873618	3150335	2666780	681038	6088405	2084327
2997848	518446	463485	710062	2039005	1817028	627156	2851909	1349541
328152	26429	101834	146878	299665	280350	46449	265489	121335
596351	47319	431730	719064	1366315	1062154	77312	68482	318792
289564	18327	121855	194981	280297	174810	28777	223087	182380

22-6 续表 3

单位：万元

项目	Item	损益及分配 营业收入 Business Income	#主营业务收入 Main Business Income
房地产业	**Real Estate**	**46946875**	**45993484**
租赁和商务服务业	**Renting and Leasing Activities, Business Services**	**84632925**	**82014330**
租赁业	Renting and Leasing	705238	701471
商务服务业	Business Services	83927686	81312859
科学研究和技术服务业	**Scientific Research and Development, Technical Services**	**46850733**	**46492374**
研究和试验发展	Research and Experimental Development	3419589	3322353
专业技术服务业	Professional Technical Services	31542731	31371288
科技推广和应用服务业	Technique Generalization and Application Services	11888413	11798733
水利、环境和公共设施管理业	**Management of Water Conservancy, Environment and Public Facilities**	**3087623**	**3041645**
水利管理业	Management of Water Conservancy	97689	88734
生态保护和环境治理业	Ecological Protection and Environmental Control	895868	892713
公共设施管理业	Management of Public Facilities	2094066	2060198
居民服务、修理和其他服务业	**Resident Services, Repair and Other Services**	**1691250**	**1657453**
居民服务业	Resident Services	389823	382044
机动车、电子产品和日用产品修理业	Repair of Motor Vehicles, Electronics and Household Appliances	826626	805219
其他服务业	Other Services	474802	470191
教育	**Education**	**1354313**	**1339720**
卫生和社会工作	**Healthcare and Social Works**	**1000367**	**996096**
卫生	Healthcare	994091	991013
社会工作	Social Works	6276	5083
文化、体育和娱乐业	**Culture, Sports and Entertainment**	**7124714**	**6837396**
新闻和出版业	Journalism and Publishing	3973174	3733458
广播、电视、电影和影视录音制作业	Radio Broadcasting, Television, Movies, Videos and Sound Recording	2193645	2161722
文化艺术业	Culture and Arts	310222	307913
体育	Sports Activities	430893	421114
娱乐业	Entertainment	216780	213189

22-6 continued 3

(10000 yuan)

Profits and Losses									
营业成本 Business Cost	#主营业务成本 Main Business Cost	销售费用 Sales Expenses	管理费用 Management Expenses	财务费用 Financial Expenses	利润总额 Total Profits	应交税金合计 Total Tax Payable	#营业税金及附加 Business Tax and Surtax	#主营业务税金及附加 Business Tax and Surtax	#应交所得税 Income Tax Payable
28943640	**28497878**	**1885498**	**4301455**	**2340919**	**8193831**	**6698628**	**4372651**	**4294577**	**2001243**
67125633	**66650456**	**5222007**	**10640344**	**5804945**	**30721689**	**3956982**	**872466**	**691093**	**2119374**
464780	463193	68486	81615	47810	47247	30813	13499	13457	16916
66660854	66187263	5153521	10558729	5757135	30674441	3926169	858966	677636	2102458
37628166	**37478584**	**1394413**	**4740741**	**282316**	**5258309**	**1979671**	**377208**	**366270**	**663425**
2421200	2371657	150442	775021	-43832	332033	182590	21915	19101	58267
25625816	25576571	796508	2835763	134874	4018871	1312262	267971	262220	440154
9581150	9530356	447463	1129957	191274	907405	484819	87323	84949	165004
2361003	**2346022**	**87927**	**327466**	**59312**	**216736**	**116806**	**68891**	**67955**	**33520**
56313	56299	479	30076	8843	6248	2388	964	461	1372
671073	670748	29252	74667	27146	95946	28055	10194	10145	11889
1633616	1618974	58196	222723	23323	114542	86363	57733	57350	20259
1061573	**1050533**	**299211**	**241942**	**9049**	**51201**	**100205**	**38832**	**38139**	**19591**
144869	141996	126495	84555	3892	14822	25170	15435	15327	6725
609234	604096	102898	75191	3097	31356	41268	6081	5815	8313
307471	304441	69818	82196	2060	5024	33767	17316	16997	4553
655307	**648697**	**230576**	**298337**	**-10134**	**141607**	**88372**	**41581**	**41402**	**34662**
649196	**647856**	**108734**	**211573**	**2324**	**61225**	**16281**	**853**	**803**	**14145**
645618	644279	108709	204855	2571	62796	15892	797	747	14143
3577	3577	25	6718	-247	-1571	389	56	56	2
4480004	**4364326**	**828473**	**1305402**	**-31301**	**1031999**	**471863**	**106079**	**104133**	**116524**
2342701	2242551	483624	853438	-38512	647296	288948	44027	42840	44372
1613538	1604425	133542	221761	-3993	396716	111153	23526	22927	55272
210072	208001	37247	56815	1400	20639	17660	5073	5029	6368
201560	198832	123523	132817	8068	-42681	33857	20781	20721	5241
112132	110517	50538	40572	1736	10029	20245	12672	12615	5271

22-7 文化创意产业活动单位基本情况
STATISTICS FOR CULTURAL AND CREATIVE INDUSTRY

单位：亿元 (100 million yuan)

项目	Item	资产总计 Total Assets 2013	资产总计 Total Assets 2012	收入合计 Total Income 2013	收入合计 Total Income 2012	从业人员平均人数(万人) Average Number of Employed Persons (10000 persons) 2013	从业人员平均人数(万人) Average Number of Employed Persons (10000 persons) 2012
合　计	**Total**	**18234.2**	**15575.2**	**11657.1**	**10313.6**	**161.7**	**152.9**
文化艺术	Culture and Arts	676.3	551.2	267.6	237.0	7.4	7.2
新闻出版	Journalism and Publications	1714.5	1514.6	954.6	883.0	15.4	15.6
广播、电视、电影	Radios, Televisions amd Movies	2008.6	1570.7	738.8	680.3	6.1	6.0
软件、网络及计算机服务	Software, Network & Computer Services	7659.3	6529.0	4291.7	3888.1	75.7	69.8
广告会展	Advertisements & Exhibitions	1267.9	1050.0	1388.9	1256.8	13.5	12.5
艺术品交易	Transaction of Artworks	910.2	817.5	1098.5	705.6	2.8	2.8
设计服务	Design Services	1436.4	1163.7	491.6	443.0	13.8	11.9
旅游、休闲娱乐	Tourism and Enterainment	1082.7	934.5	964.5	849.0	11.2	11.1
其他辅助服务	Other Auxiliary Services	1478.4	1444.0	1460.8	1370.8	15.7	16.0

22-8 物流业活动情况
STATISTICS FOR LOGISTICS

项　目		Item		2013	2012	2013年为2012年% 2013 as % of 2012
物流业务收入	**(亿元)**	**Business Income of Logistics Sector**	**(100 million yuan)**	**2267.6**	**2104.4**	**107.8**
运输收入		Transportation Income		1618.8	1517.2	106.7
保管收入		Storage Income		596.2	562.4	106.0
一体化物流业务收入		Integrated Logistics Income		52.7	24.8	212.5
限额以上企业物流基础设施情况		**Logistics Infrastructure in Enterprises above the Designated Size**				
自有仓库和货场面积	(万平方米)	Area of Self-owned Warehouses and Good Yards	(10000 sq.m)	3503.4	3208.8	109.2
货运车辆数	(辆)	Number of Transportation Vehicles	(unit)	42638	42907	99.4
普通货车数		Number of Genreal Trucks		31743	32988	96.2
专业货车数		Number of Special Trucks		10895	9919	109.8
装卸设备台数	(台)	Number of Loading and Unloading Equipment	(unit)	27953	39844	70.2
社会物流总额	**(亿元)**	**Total Amount of Social Logistics**	**(100 million yuan)**	**72298.6**	**65851.1**	**109.8**
农产品		Agricultural Products		360.0	337.8	106.6
工业品		Industrial Products		13875.4	13008.6	106.7
进口货物		Imported Goods		22656.4	21984.3	103.1
再生资源		Renewable Resources		129.7	67.0	193.6
外省市流入物品		Goods from Other Provinces and Cities		35230.3	30284.2	116.3
单位与居民物品		Entities and Residents' Goods		46.8	169.2	27.7
物流业从业人员平均人数	**(万人)**	**Employment in Logistics Sector**	**(10000 persons)**	**48.9**	**51.9**	**94.2**
交通运输、邮政、仓储业		Transportation, Post, Storage		32.9	35.0	94.0
采掘业、制造业、批发和零售业		Excavation, Manufacturing, Wholesale, and Retail Trade		16.0	16.8	95.2

22-9 会展业活动情况
STATISTICS FOR MICE INDUSTRY IN BEIJING

项目		Item		2013	2012	2013年为2012年% 2013 as % of 2012
人员情况		**Employed Persons**				
从业人员年末人数	(万人)	Year-end Employed Persons	(10000 person)	21.8	22.5	96.9
设施情况		**Facilities**				
接待场所会议室个数	(个)	Number of Meeting Rooms	(unit)	5604	5580	100.4
#座位数超过500座的会议室	(个)	Number of Meeting Rooms with More Than 500 Seats	(unit)	204	209	97.6
接待场所会议室使用面积	(万平方米)	Usable Area of Meeting Rooms	(10000 sq.m)	81.7	80.7	101.2
接待场所会议室可容纳人数	(万人)	Capacity of Meeting Rooms	(10000 person)	48.2	47.9	100.6
会议情况		**Meetings**				
接待会议个数	(万个)	Number of Meetings Held in Beijing	(10000 unit)	26.9	31.3	85.9
#国际会议	(万个)	International Meetings	(10000 unit)	0.7	0.8	87.5
接待会议人数	(万人次)	Number of Meeting Participants	(10000 person-times)	1714.6	2010.9	85.3
#国际会议	(万人次)	International Meeting Participants	(10000 person-times)	68.3	77.0	88.7
展览情况		**Exhibitions**				
接待展览个数	(个)	Number of Exhibitions Held in Beijing	(unit)	822	956	86.0
#国际展览	(个)	International Exhibitions	(unit)	283	269	105.2
#展览面积1万(不含)平方米以下的展览个数	(个)	Number of Exhibitions with Exhibition Area under 10,000 sq.m (10,000 sq.m excluded)	(unit)	640	752	85.1
展览面积1万平方米及以上的展览个数	(个)	Number of Exhibitions with Exhibition Area of 10,000 sq.m and over	(unit)	182	204	89.2
接待展览累计面积(含室外展览面积)	(万平方米)	Total Exhibition Area (including outdoor exhibition area)	(10000 sq.m)	775.3	740.9	104.6
#国际展览累计面积	(万平方米)	International Exhibition Area	(10000 sq.m)	497.8	377.7	131.8
接待展览观众人数	(万人次)	Number of Exhibition Visitors	(10000 person-times)	556.3	574.7	96.8
#国际展览观众人数	(万人次)	International Exhibition Visitors	(10000 person-times)	268.9	201.8	133.3
奖励旅游情况		**Incentives**				
服务奖励旅游人数	(万人次)	Number of Incentive Tourists	(10000 person-times)	21.3	24.2	88.0
收入情况		**Revenues**				
会展收入	(万元)	Total Revenues from MICE Industry	(10000 yuan)	2259758.8	2472200.0	91.4
会议收入	(万元)	Revenues from Meetings	(10000 yuan)	1192193.2	1349778.5	88.3
#国际会议收入	(万元)	Revenues from International Meetings	(10000 yuan)	108734.4	93540.7	116.2
展览收入	(万元)	Revenues from Exhibitions	(10000 yuan)	970438.9	1027129.4	94.5
#国际展览收入	(万元)	Revenues from International Exhibition	(10000 yuan)	483603.7	468914.7	103.1
奖励旅游收入	(万元)	Revenues from Incentives	(10000 yuan)	97126.7	95719.9	101.5

22-10 体育及相关产业情况
STATISTICS FOR SPORTS INDUSTRY

项 目	Item	收入合计（亿元）Total Income (100 million yuan)		从业人员平均人数（万人）Average Number of Employed Persons (10000 persons)	
		2013	2012	2013	2012
合 计	**Total**	**863.4**	**777.0**	**13.2**	**12.3**
体育组织管理活动	Sports Organization and Management Activities	120.8	108.3	1.6	1.6
体育场馆管理活动	Gym Management Activities	22.0	18.7	0.7	0.7
体育健身休闲活动	Sports, Body Building and Entertainment Activities	39.7	41.2	3.5	3.0
体育中介活动	Sports Agency Activities	24.5	21.8	0.4	0.4
其他体育活动	Other Sports Activities	92.4	77.7	1.2	1.2
体育用品、服装、鞋帽及相关体育产品的制造	Manufacturing of Sports Supplies, Clothes, Shoes and Caps, and Related Sports Products	67.3	61.7	1.0	0.9
体育用品、服装、鞋帽及相关体育产品的销售	Sales of Sports Supplies, Clothes, Shoes and Caps, and Related Sports Products	484.3	436.5	4.7	4.3
体育场馆建筑活动	Gymnasium Building Activities	12.6	11.2	0.1	0.1

主要统计指标解释

物流业务收入 指通过物流业务活动取得的收入。包括企业完成运输、存储、装卸、搬运、包装、流通加工、配送、信息等物流业务取得的收入之和。反映物流相关行业物流活动的总规模。

物流业从业人员 指企业中直接或间接从事物流活动的人数。直接从事物流活动的人员包括在企业中从事运输、配送、装卸搬运、仓储保管等物流活动并取得劳动报酬的从业人员；间接从事物流活动的人员包括在企业中从事物流管理活动并取得劳动报酬的从业人员，包括采购、销售部门的主管人员，但不包括采购、销售部门内部办事人员。

社会物流总额 指第一次进入市内需求领域，产生从供应地向接受地实体流动的物品的价值总额。包括六个方面的内容：进入需求领域的农产品物流总额、工业品物流总额、进口货物物流总额、外省市调入物品物流总额、再生资源物流总额、单位与居民物品物流总额。.

接待会议个数 指报告期内，接待的各种类型会议的个数。包括国际会议和国内会议。

接待国际会议个数 指报告期内，接待的国际会议的个数。国际会议是指在我国境内举办的，与会者来自 3 个或 3 个以上中国大陆以外国家和地区（含港、澳、台地区）的会议、论坛、研讨会、报告会、交流会等。

接待展览个数 指报告期内，接待的各种类型展览的个数。包括国际展览和国内展览。

接待国际展览个数 指报告期内，接待的国际展览的个数。国际展览指中国大陆以外国家和地区（含港、澳、台地区）的参展商参展面积达到该次展出面积 20%以上的展览个数。

服务奖励旅游人数 指报告期内，服务的奖励旅游人数的总和。

服务贸易 服务贸易包括跨境提供、境外消费、商业存在和自然人移动等内容。

跨境提供 是指服务提供者从中国境内向任何其他国家或地区的服务消费者提供服务以及服务提供者从其他国家或地区向中国境内的服务消费者提供服务。

境外消费 是指在中国境内向其他国家或地区的服务消费者提供服务以及在其他国家或地区向中国境内的服务消费者提供服务。

商业存在 是指中国境内的服务提供者通过在任何其他国家或地区设立的企业或分支机构提供服务以及其他国家或地区的服务提供者通过在中国境内设立企业或分支机构提供服务。

自然人移动 是指中国境内的服务提供者通过在其他国家或地区的自然人提供服务以及其他国家或地区的服务提供者通过在中国境内的自然人提供服务。

体育组织管理活动 指专门为社会公众提供比赛、训练、辅导和管理的组织的活动，如群众性体育组织、专项性体育管理组织的活动。

体育场馆管理活动 指为社会公众提供观赏比赛和专业训练的体育场馆管理活动，如综合性体育场馆，训练用场地的管理活动。

体育健身休闲活动 指社会公众提供的可供参与和选择的各种健身休闲活动场所的管理活动。

体育中介活动 指为社会公众提供的体育中介活动，如各种体育商务代理、经纪、咨询活动。

其他体育活动 指为社会公众提供的其他体育服务活动。包括体育培训服务、体育科研服务、体育彩票服务、体育传媒服务、体育展览服务、体育市场管理服务、体育场馆设计服务、体育场所保洁服务和体育文物及文化保护服务。

体育用品、服装、鞋帽及相关体育产品的制造 指提供体育服务所必须的体育用品、服装、鞋帽及相关体育产品的制造活动。

体育用品、服装、鞋帽及相关体育产品的销售 指提供体育服务所必须的体育用品、服装、鞋帽及相关体育产品的销售活动。

体育场馆管理活动 指提供体育服务所必须的体育场馆建筑活动。

Explanatory Notes on Main Statistical Indicators

Business Income of Logistics Sector refers to the income earned from logistics business activities, which is equal to the sum of incomes from such logistics operations completed by enterprises as transportation, storage, loading and unloading, handling, package, circulation and processing, delivery, and information. It reflects the overall scale of logistics activities in logistics related sector.

Employees in Logistics Sector refers to the number of persons directly and indirectly engaged in logistics activities in enterprises. Persons directly engaged in logistics activities are included in employees engaged in logistics activities such as transportation, delivery, loading and unloading, handling, storage and warehouse keeping in enterprises and receiving labor remuneration; persons indirectly engaged in logistics activities are included in employees engaged in management activities in enterprises and receiving labor remuneration, including executives in purchase and sales departments, but excluding clerks in purchase and sales departments.

Total Amount of Social Logistics refers to the total value of goods entering the demand area in the city for the first time and having physical flow from the supply place to the receiving place, consisting of value on six aspects: total logistics amount of agricultural products, total logistics amount of industrial products, total logistics amount of imported goods, total logistics amount of goods transferred from other provinces and cities, total logistics amount of recycled resources, and total logistics amount of corporate and household supplies entering the demand field.

Number of Meeting Held in Beijing refers to the number of various types of conference held in Beijing in the reporting period, including international and domestic conferences.

Number of International Meeting refers to the number of international conferences held in Beijing in the reporting period. International conference means any conference, forum, seminar, report conference, and workshops, etc. held in our country, with participants coming from 3 or more countries and regions (including Hong Kong, Macao and Taiwan) outside Chinese mainland.

Number of Exhibitions Held in Beijing refers to the number of various types of exhibitions held in Beijing in the reporting period, including international and domestic exhibitions.

Number of International Exhibitions Received refers to the number of international exhibitions received in the reporting period. International exhibition means any exhibition with participants from countries and regions (including Hong Kong, Macao and Taiwan) outside Chinese mainland whose exhibition floorage accounts for more than 20% of the exhibition.

Number of Incentive Projects refers to the sum of incentive tour projects served in the reporting period. Incentive tourism means a tour arrangement in any form fully or partially financed by an enterprise as incentive or encouragement to its employee.

Number of Incentive Tourists refers to the sum of persons of incentive tour served in the reporting period.

Service Trade includes overseas provision, overseas consumption, commercial existence, movement of natural persons, and so on.

Overseas Provision refers to any service provider provides service within China for service consumers in any other country or region, and any service provider provides service in any other country or region to service consumers within China.

Overseas Consumption refers to provision of service in China for service consumers in any other country or region, and provision of service in any other country or region for service consumers in China.

Commercial Existence refers to that any service provider in China provides service through its business or branch set up in any other country or region, and any service provider in any other country or region provides service through its business or branch set up in China.

Movement of Natural Persons means that any service provider in China provides service through any natural person in any other country or region, and any service provider in any other country or region provides service through any natural person in China.

Sports Organization and Management Activities mean activities organized specially for providing games, training, coaching and management for the public, such as activities organized for mass sport organizations and special sport management.

Gym Management Activities mean management activities in gym providing games for view and special trainings for the public, such as management activities in comprehensive sports venues and training fields and courts.

Sports, Body Building and Entertainment Activities mean management activities provided for the public at Sports bodybuilding and entertainment sites, which are to be participated in and chosen. Sports Body Building and Entertainment Activities refer to

Sports Agency Activities refer to sport agency activities provided for the public, such as various sports business agency, broker and consulting activities.

Other Sports Activities refer to activities of other sports service provided for the public, including sports training service, sports research service, sports lottery service, sports communication service, sports exhibition service, sports market management service, sports venue design service, sports site cleaning service, sports cultural relics and cultural protection service.

Manufacturing of Sports Supplies, Clothes, Shoes and Caps, and Related Sports Products refers to manufacturing of sports supplies, clothes, shoes and caps, and related sports products necessary for provision of sports service.

Sales of Sports Supplies, Clothes, Shoes and Caps, and Related Sports Products refers to sales of sports supplies, clothes, shoes and caps, and related sports products necessary for provision of sports service.

Gymnasium Building Activities refer to activities of construction of sports venues necessary for provision of sports service.

北京统计年鉴2014　BEIJING STATISTICAL YEARBOOK

企业景气指数、消费者信心指数

ENTERPRISE PROSPERITY INDEX AND CONSUMER CONFIDENCE INDEX

简要说明

一、本章资料的主要内容

本章资料包括企业景气调查和消费者信心指数调查。

二、本章资料的统计范围和调查方法

企业景气调查包括工业，建筑业，批发和零售业，交通运输、仓储和邮政业，住宿和餐饮业，信息传输、软件和信息技术服务业，房地产业，社会服务业等行业的法人单位和产业活动单位及其负责人（如厂长、总经理等）。

消费者信心指数调查采用计算机辅助电话方式调查，调查对象为居住在北京市半年以上 18-65 周岁的城乡居民，调查范围覆盖全市 16 个区县。

三、本章资料的数据来源

本章资料由国家统计局北京调查总队提供。

四、有关统计标准的变化说明

关于行业划分。根据国家统计局规定，自 2012 年开始执行《国民经济行业分类》(GB/T 4754-2011)标准。

Brief Introduction

I. Main Content of Statistics

This chapter consists of survey on enterprise prosperity index and consumer confidence index.

II. Scope of Statistics and Method of Survey

Enterprise prosperity survey covers business entities and industrial activity entities and their persons-in-charge (such as director or general manager) in the following sectors: industry, construction, wholesale and retail trade, transport, storage and post, accommodation and restaurants, information transmission, software and information technology services, real estate and social services.

Statistics on consumer confidence index were obtained through computer-aided phone calls to urban and rural residents at 18-65 who have been living in Beijing for more than half a year. The survey covers 16 districts and counties in the City.

III. Source of Statistics

Statistics in this chapter are from NBS Survey Office in Beijing.

Ⅳ. Changes in Relevant Statistical Standards

Classification of Sectors. According to relevant provisions of National Bureau of Statistics, the Standard for Classification of National Economic Sectors (GB/T4754-2011) became effective in 2012.

23-1 企业景气指数、企业家信心指数(1999-2013年)
ENTERPRISE PROSPERITY INDEX AND ENTERPRENEUR CONFIDENCE INDEX(1999-2013)

年 份 Year	企业景气指数 Enterprise Prosperity Index				企业家信心指数 Enterpreneur Confidence Index			
	一季度 First Quarter	二季度 Second Quarter	三季度 Third Quarter	四季度 Fourth Quarter	一季度 First Quarter	二季度 Second Quarter	三季度 Third Quarter	四季度 Fourth Quarter
1999	111.0	114.7	112.4	121.0	98.0	97.4	102.4	104.4
2000	113.7	130.0	132.9	138.1	107.7	120.6	123.5	118.6
2001	112.6	123.5	117.7	115.8	124.0	116.1	118.7	111.9
2002	117.6	126.9	128.2	131.8	125.4	125.3	124.9	128.8
2003	124.8	100.9	134.5	137.6	132.5	108.0	136.7	136.1
2004	132.7	135.1	134.0	138.0	136.7	127.2	130.0	129.5
2005	129.5	132.9	131.8	127.9	131.4	128.0	126.2	125.1
2006	131.6	138.9	143.4	150.0	136.7	137.5	134.3	140.4
2007	145.8	153.8	158.5	158.7	138.4	142.6	142.3	136.1
2008	152.0	144.7	128.7	108.9	152.9	138.7	117.4	85.5
2009	110.3	115.4	127.9	133.3	91.5	104.0	121.7	126.2
2010	133.2	138.1	141.5	143.8	131.5	130.1	136.7	141.1
2011	131.6	140.0	139.4	138.8	134.4	137.8	132.7	123.0
2012	127.6	127.5	125.9	128.1	124.0	121.5	116.1	122.9
2013	120.8	125.3	126.0	124.1	125.1	123.6	126.9	123.1

23-2 企业景气指数(2013年)

项目	Item	一季度 First Quarter 本期实际 Actual Index in the Period	一季度 First Quarter 比上年同期增减 Year-on-year Increase or Decrease
企业景气指数	**Enterprise Prosperity Index**	**120.8**	**-6.8**
按登记注册类型分	**By Registration Type**		
国有	State-owned Enterprises	123.9	-1.1
集体	Collectively-owned Enterprises	65.2	-13.8
股份合作	Joint-equity Cooperative Enterprises	118.2	1.5
有限责任公司	Limited Liability Companies	120.7	-8
股份有限公司	Companies Limited by Shares	121.9	-10.3
私营	Private Enterprises	103.8	-7.5
港澳台商投资	Hong Kong, Macao and Taiwan-invested Enterprises	130.3	-8.2
外商投资	Foreign-invested Enterprises	127.4	1.5
按行业分	**By Sector**		
工业	Industry	115	1.7
建筑业	Construction	128.8	5.5
批发和零售业	Wholesale and Retail Trade	113.1	-15.9
交通运输、仓储和邮政业	Transport, Storage, Post	124.2	10
住宿和餐饮业	Accommodation and Restaurants	123.9	-26.8
信息传输、软件和信息技术服务业	Information Transmission, Software and Information Technology Services	127	-31.2
房地产业	Real Estate	129.7	14.1
社会服务业	Social Services	124.2	-13.7
按企业规模分	**By Size of Enterprises**		
大型	Large	131.1	-9.5
中型	Medium	121.3	-6.6
小型	Small	115.8	1.4
微型	Mini	92.9	16.2
按单项指标分	**By Individual Indicator**		
生产总量	Gross Production	84.3	-6.6
盈利(亏损)变化	Changes of Profits (Losses)	75.6	-9.3
流动资金	Working Capital	107.5	-1.3
货款拖欠	Loan Delinquency	104.6	-1
劳动力需求	Demand on Labors	104.2	-8.5
固定资产投资	Investment in Fixed Assets	92.7	-2.5
产品订货	Order Products	84.4	-7.3
企业融资	Financing	98	3.2

注：1. 本表中的企业规模划分执行国家统计局《关于统计上大中小微型企业划分办法》〔国统字(2011)75号〕。
2. 行业划分执行2011年国民经济行业分类标准(GB/T 4754-2011)。

ENTERPRISE PROSPERITY INDEX (2013)

二 季 度 Second Quarter		三 季 度 Third Quarter		四 季 度 Fourth Quarter	
本期实际 Actual Index in the Period	比上年同期增减 Year-on-year Increase or Decrease	本期实际 Actual Index in the Period	比上年同期增减 Year-on-year Increase or Decrease	本期实际 Actual Index in the Period	比上年同期增减 Year-on-year Increase or Decrease
125.3	**-2.2**	**126**	**0.1**	**124.1**	**-4**
125.9	-1.7	127.3	4.8	123.1	-9.1
114.1	33.9	111.6	14.7	100.4	-6.4
90.9	-42.4	100	-8.3	120	3.3
128.9	-0.3	130.1	0.8	127.9	-6.8
123.5	-3.6	120.1	-5.8	122.6	5
112.6	-3.3	106	-14.6	110.9	-3.8
112	-10.2	135	12.4	114.8	-18.6
132.1	4.3	129.6	5.4	126.9	10.1
124.9	13.1	121.5	8.2	121	4
135.8	2.5	134.9	4.1	139.5	2.4
112.1	-15	115.3	-7.8	114.6	-10.1
117.5	2.1	139.9	27.6	124.5	-5.3
124.7	-27	115.4	-34.3	108.2	-35.1
135.1	-27.3	137.2	-21.9	134.1	-18.6
125.5	8.7	126.6	14.6	125.8	8.2
134.2	2.3	130.1	-3.1	129.1	-0.6
131	-7.9	136.5	-1.9	125.3	-18.8
128.9	-0.4	130.8	4.4	126.4	1.4
120.8	9.8	116.5	5.1	123.5	14.6
98.6	8.6	97.1	14	95.7	2.5
120.5	-2.9	123.6	6.6	114	-1.9
80.6	-4.8	83.4	-3.3	84.6	-3.8
110.8	2.3	107.9	-1.5	107.2	-1.1
104	2.9	104.8	4.9	106.2	3.4
109.9	0.3	106.4	-3.9	103.6	-2.1
111.4	0.7	108.4	-1	108.3	-3.6
85.9	-26.4	91.1	-17.2	90.7	-20
97.1	-1.1	95.4	-2.7	94.1	-5.5

Note: a) In this table, enterprises are divided by scale in accordance with the provisions concerning the Statistical Division Standards of Mini-, Small, Mediume and Large Enterprises (GTZ (2011) No.75).

b) Sectors in this table are classified in accordance with the Standard for Classification of National Economic Sectors 2011 (GB/T 4754-2011).

23-3 企业家信心指数(2013年)

项 目	Item	一 季 度 First Quarter 本期实际 Actual Index in The Period	一 季 度 First Quarter 比上年同期增减 Year-on-year Increase or Decrease
企业家信心指数	**Entrepreneur Confidence Index**	**125.1**	**1.1**
按登记注册类型分	**By Registration Type**		
国有	State-owned Enterprises	116.2	-10.6
集体	Collectively-owned Enterprises	59.3	-41.9
股份合作	Joint-equity Cooperative Enterprises	118.2	-6.8
有限责任公司	Limited Liability Companies	130.7	8.0
股份有限公司	Companies Limited by Shares	117.6	-3.1
私营	Private Enterprises	113.8	-3.0
港澳台商投资	Hong Kong, Macao and Taiwan-invested Enterprises	123.6	5.7
外商投资	Foreign-invested Enterprises	128.2	0.5
按行业分	**By Sector**		
工 业	Industry	115.0	0.7
建筑业	Construction	134.4	8.8
批发和零售业	Wholesale and Retail Trade	120.7	-5.1
交通运输、仓储和邮政业	Transport, Storage, Post	114.8	-0.4
住宿和餐饮业	Accommodation and Restaurants	128.9	-27.6
信息传输、软件和信息技术服务业	Information Transmission, Software and Information Technology Services	159.0	4.0
房地产业	Real Estate	113.6	32.6
社会服务业	Social Services	127.0	-12.8
按企业规模分	**By Size of Enterprise**		
大 型	Large	139.7	-1.1
中 型	Medium	121.3	1.8
小 型	Small	116.3	5.7
微 型	Mini	91.4	13.1

注：1. 本表中的企业规模划分执行国家统计局《关于统计上大中小微型企业划分办法》〔国统字(2011)75号〕。
2. 行业划分执行2011年国民经济行业分类标准(GB/T 4754-2011)。

ENTERPRENEUR CONFIDENCE INDEX (2013)

二 季 度 Second Quarter		三 季 度 Third Quarter		四 季 度 Fourth Quarter	
本期实际 Actual Index in The Period	比上年同期增减 Year-on-year Increase or Decrease	本期实际 Actual Index in The Period	比上年同期增减 Year-on-year Increase or Decrease	本期实际 Actual Index in The Period	比上年同期增减 Year-on-year Increase or Decrease
123.6	**2.1**	**126.9**	**10.8**	**123.1**	**0.2**
112.3	-5.9	118.1	3.1	112.2	-10.8
89.3	-6.4	89.3	-7.6	89.3	-5.2
118.2	-6.8	63.6	-28.1	80.0	-28.3
127.4	0.7	133.5	11.0	125.5	-1.0
112.5	3.4	113.0	-0.1	129.3	14.9
117.4	2.4	107.7	-0.5	107.1	-15.8
124.7	14.5	138.9	46.5	110.0	-4.0
129.6	6.1	139.1	26.8	134.1	19.2
121.1	11.9	123.6	19.7	121.5	9.7
123.3	-0.5	130.0	10.6	129.0	14.5
104.4	-14.9	111.6	9.3	110.3	-3.9
105.2	-0.3	124.7	23.5	113.0	-10.0
119.2	-42.0	110.7	-43.5	111.0	-43.9
166.4	9.6	156.9	-4.0	153.3	-7.7
113.6	15.8	123.2	23.8	114.3	4.8
131.0		131.8	4.4	125.7	-0.6
136.3	2.7	144.8	23.7	137.9	9.0
120.0	0.8	123.9	5.6	118.8	-4.0
114.4	5.1	115.6	8.8	114.6	3.5
100.0	15.0	104.3	22.9	92.9	-0.3

Note: a) In this table, enterprises are divided by scale in accordance with the provisions concerning the Statistical Division Standards of Mini-, Small, Mediume and Large Enterprises (GTZ (2011) No.75).

b) Sectors in this table are classified in accordance with the Standard for Classification of National Economic Sectors 2011 (GB/T 4754-2011).

23-4 北京消费者信心指数(2013年)
BEIJING CONSUMER CONFIDENCE INDEX(2013)

项　目	Item	一季度 First Quarter	二季度 Second Quarter	三季度 Third Quarter	四季度 Fourth Quarter
消费者信心指数	**Consumer Confidence Index**	**108.9**	**103.4**	**105.5**	**104.6**
消费者满意指数	**Consumer Satisfaction Index**	**105.7**	**102.4**	**104.7**	**102.9**
就业状况满意指数	Index of Satisfaction with Employment Status	120.1	108.9	115.4	115.9
家庭收入状况满意指数	Index of Satisfaction with Household Income Status	97.3	97.7	96.3	93.9
耐用消费品购买时机满意指数	Index of Satisfaction with Durable Consumer Goods	99.7	100.6	102.3	99.0
消费者预期指数	**Consumer Expectation Index**	**111.1**	**104.1**	**106.0**	**105.8**
就业状况预期指数	Index of Expectation for Employment Status	122.5	109.7	113.6	115.2
家庭收入状况预期指数	Index of Expectation for Household Income Status	99.6	98.4	98.3	96.3

主要统计指标解释

企业景气调查 也称为经济周期调查或短期经济观测调查，是以企业家为调查对象，采用问卷方式，定期收集有关宏观经济和企业生产经营景气状况变动判断的一种统计调查。简言之，企业景气调查就是调查企业家对宏观经济态势，对企业生产经营状况所做出的判断和预期。调查采用重点调查和抽样调查相结合的方法，调查范围覆盖国民经济八个主要行业，即：工业，建筑业，批发和零售业，交通运输、仓储和邮政业，住宿和餐饮业，信息传输、软件和信息技术服务业，房地产业，社会服务业。

景气指数 又称景气度，是对企业景气调查中定性经济指标的定量描述，以直观地反映经济所处的状态。指数的数值介于0和200之间，100为临界值。指数大于100时，表明经济状况趋于上升或改善，处于景气状态；指数小于100时，表明经济状况趋于下降或恶化，处于不景气状态。

企业家信心指数 亦称宏观经济景气指数，是根据企业决策者对本行业发展状况的判断及其未来走势的预期（选择“乐观”、“一般”、“不乐观”）而编制的指数，反映企业决策者对国家宏观经济发展的信心和预期，是企业决策者对当前宏观经济状况及未来走势的一种感受、体验和期望。

企业景气指数 亦称企业综合生产经营景气指数，是根据企业决策者对本企业当前生产经营状况的判断及未来企业生产经营状况的预期（选择“良好”、“一般”、“不佳”）而编制的指数，是企业决策者对企业生产经营现状及未来景气动向的一种综合评价和判断。

消费者信心指数 是综合反映并量化消费者对当前经济形势评价和对经济前景、收入水平、收入预期以及消费心理状态的主观感受，是预测经济走势和消费趋向的一个先行指标，是监测经济周期变化不可缺少的依据。消费者信心指数由消费者满意指数和消费者预期指数构成。其中消费者满意指数反映了消费者对当前经济生活的评价；消费者预期指数反映了消费者对未来一段时期经济发展变化的预期。

指数值的含义：指数取值介于0和200之间，100为指数强弱临界点。指数超过100，表明消费者信心处于强信心区，数值由100趋近200，表明消费者信心逐渐增强；反之，指数小于100时，表示消费者信心处于弱信心区，数值由100趋近0，表明消费者信心逐渐减弱。

Explanatory Notes on Main Statistical Indicators

Enterprise Prosperity Survey is also known as economic cycle survey or short-term economic observation survey. Targeting at entrepreneurs, the survey is conducted in a manner of questionnaires. It is a statistical survey to collect information on judgment of macro-economy and changes in business climate of enterprises.. To be brief, enterprise prosperity survey is to investigate entrepreneurs' judgment and expectation on macro-economic dynamics and enterprise production and operation status. The survey covers 8 major national economic sectors, i.e. industry, construction, wholesale and retail trade, transport, storage and post, accommodation and restaurants, information transmission, software and information technology services, real estate, and social services.

Prosperity Index also called prosperity degree, is a quantitative description of qualitative indicators in enterprise prosperity survey, aiming to visualize the status of economy. The value of index ranges from 0 to 200, with 100 as the critical value. When the index is greater than 100, it indicates that the economic status is rising or improving, and in a prosperous state; when the index is 100, it shows the economic status is declining or deteriorating, and in a non-prosperous state.

Entrepreneur Confidence Index also known as Macroeconomic Climate Index, which is indexed according to the enterprise decision-makers' opinions and expectations (with choices of "optimistic", "moderate" and "non-optimistic") on the development status of the sector and its future trend. It reflects the enterprise decision-makers' confidence about and expectation on the national macroeconomic development. It serves as the enterprise decision-makers' feelings, experience and expectations about current macroeconomic status and its trend.

Enterprise Prosperity Index, also known as Comprehensive Business Climate Index, is indexed according to estimations and expectations of enterprise decision-makers' opinions and expectation on the enterprise's current and future production and operation status (choice of "good", "moderate" and "bad"). It represents the enterprise decision-makers' comprehensive evaluation and judgment on the current situation and future trend of the enterprise production and operation.

Consumer Confidence Index is an indicator reflecting and quantifying the consumers' evaluation on current economic situation, and their personal feeling about the economic prospects, income level, income expectation, and psychological state of consumption. It serves as a leading indicator predicting the trend of economy tendency of consumption, and an essential basis for monitoring the changes in economic cycle and other conditions as well as expectation on the economic prospects in the future. Consumer Confidence Index consists of consumer satisfaction index and consumer expectation index, and the latter one reflects consumers' evaluation on current economic life; consumer expectation index reflects consumers' expectation on the development and changes in the economic prospect in the future.

Indexes range from 0 to 200. 100 represents a critical point between strong and weak confidence. An index greater than 100 indicates the consumers' confidence is strong. An index going toward 200 from 100 shows the consumers' confidence is becoming gradually strong; in contrary, an index smaller than 100 means the consumers' confidence is weak. When the indexes go toward 0 from 100, it means the consumers' confidence is weakening gradually.

开发区
DEVELOPMENT ZONES

简 要 说 明

一、本章资料的主要内容

本章资料主要反映北京市开发区的基本情况，招商、入资，企业生产经营、财务、科技活动和人力资源情况，重点介绍了北京经济技术开发区、中关村国家自主创新示范区及北京天竺综合保税区的主要情况。其中，中关村国家自主创新示范区亦庄园在中关村国家自主创新示范区与北京经济技术开发区中为重叠部分。

二、本章资料的数据来源

本章中关村国家自主创新示范区的统计资料由北京市统计局提供；其他各开发区中涉及招商、土地、投资的统计资料由北京市经信委收集提供，财务资料由北京市统计局提供；北京经济技术开发区的统计资料由北京经济技术开发区统计局、调查队提供；北京天竺综合保税区中涉及招商、土地等方面的统计资料由北京天竺综合保税区管委会提供，其它资料由北京市统计局提供。

三、本章的有关变化说明

根据 2012 年《国务院关于同意调整中关村国家自主创新示范区空间规模和布局的批复》，自 2013 年起，中关村国家自主创新示范区的统计范围在原有的海淀园、丰台园、昌平园、电子城科技园、亦庄园、德胜园、雍和园、石景山园、通州园和大兴生物医药产业基地的基础上，增加了平谷园、门头沟园、顺义园、房山园、密云园、怀柔园和延庆园七个园区。同时，“电子城科技园”更名为“朝阳园”；“德胜园”更名为“西城园”；“雍和园”更名为“东城园”。

Brief Introduction

I. Main Content

Data in this chapter mainly shows the basic condition of development zones in Beijing, including business invitation, investment, production and operation of enterprises, financial status, scientific and technological activities, and human resources. This chapter mainly focuses on the situation of Beijing Economic-Technological Development Area, Zhongguancun National Innovation Demonstration Zone and Beijing Tianzhu Bonded Zone. Data of Zhongguancun Yizhuang Park is counted in both Zhongguancun National Innovation Demonstration Zone and Beijing Economic-Technological Development Area.

II. Source of Data

Data of Zhongguancun National Innovation Demonstration Zone in this chapter are sourced from Beijing Municipal Bureau of Statistics; statistics for other development zones in terms of business innovation, land and investment are gathered and provided by Beijing Municipal Commission of Economy and Information Technology; data for Beijing Economic-Technological Development Area are from the Statistics Bureau and Survey Team of Beijing Economic-Technological Development Area; data for business invitation and land in Beijing Tianzhu Bonded Zone are provided by the Administrative Committee of the Bonded Zone, while other data are from Beijing Municipal Bureau of Statistics.

III. Notes on Changes in This Chapter

According to the Official Reply of the State Council on Approving the Spatial Scale and Layout of Zhongguancun National Innovation Demonstration Area, the statistic scope of Zhongguancun Area has been enlarged to include Pinggu Sub-park, Mentougou Sub-park, Shunyi Sub-park, Fangshan Sub-park, Miyun Sub-park, Huairou Sub-park and Yanqing Sub-park to supplement Haidian Sub-park, Fengtai Sub-park, Changping Sub-park, Tongzhou Sub-park, Electronic Park, E-town Sub-park, Deshengyuan Sub-park, Yonghe Sub-park, Shijingshan Sub-park, Tongzhou Sub-park and Daxing Ecological Sub-park Pharmaceutical Base. At the same time, Electronic Park is changed into Chaoyang Sub-park, Deshengyuan Sub-park into Xicheng Sub-park and Yonghe Sub-park into Dongcheng Sub-park.

24-1 开发区基本情况(2013年)
STATISTICS ON DEVELOPMENT ZONES(2013)

项目	Item	国家级 National	市级 Municipal
开发区个数 (个)	Number of Development Zones (unit)	3	16
区规划总面积 (公顷)	Total Planned Area of Development Zones (hectare)	41290.1	9005.5
累计已开发土地面积 (公顷)	Accumulated Area of Land Development (hectare)	25833.2	6515.0
累计已供应土地面积 (公顷)	Accumulated Area of Supplied Land (hectare)	14447.0	4965.2
累计已建成城镇建设用地面积 (公顷)	Accumulated Area of Land for Urban Development (hectare)	20919.0	4638.6
累计招商项目企业个数 (个)	Accumulated Number of Enterprises of Business Inviting Programs (unit)	38695	10994
累计招商项目总投资 (亿元)	Accumulative Total Investment of Business Inviting (100 million yuan)	11664.0	2191.7
累计招商项目注册资本 (亿元)	Accumulative Registered Capital of Business Inviting Programs (100 million yuan)	10078.3	1149.8
#三资企业 (亿元)	Foreign-funded Enterprises (100 million yuan)	1852.2	324.0
累计招商项目合同外资金额 (亿美元)	Accumulative Contracted Foreign Capital of Business Inviting Programs (USD 100 million)	245.0	53.2
累计招商项目外商实际投资 (亿美元)	Accumulated Actual Foreign Investment of Business Inviting Programs (USD 100 million)	168.7	56.9
固定资产投资 (亿元)	Investment in Fixed Assets (100 million yuan)	1181.1	128.4
总收入 (亿元)	Total Revenue (100 million yuan)	31815.0	3306.7
工业总产值(当年价格) (亿元)	Gross Output Value Of Industry (at current prices) (100 million yuan)	8037.6	937.7
工业销售产值(当年价格) (亿元)	Sales Value of Industry (at current prices) (100 million yuan)	7910.1	914.4
利润总额 (亿元)	Total Profits (100 million yuan)	2321.8	321.0
应缴税金 (亿元)	Total Tax Payable (100 million yuan)	1512.3	101.5

注：1. 本表所指开发区包括北京市级及国家级开发区情况。
2. 表内"累计"指自开始至年末的累计数。
3. 本表"总收入"、"工业总产值(当年价格)"、"工业销售产值"(当年价格)、"利润总额"和"应缴税金"数据的统计范围为注册在开发区内的规模(限额)以上法人单位。

Note: a) Development zones in this table include those at Beijing municipal level and national level.
b) Accumulative data in this table refer to the accumulation from the beginning to the end of this year.
c) The statistical scope of total revenue, gross output value of industry, sales value of industry, total profits and total tax payable in this table cover legal entities above designated size that are registered in the development zones.

24-2 开发区土地开发情况(2013年)
LAND EXPLOITATION OF DEVELOPMENT ZONES(2013)

单位：公顷 (hectare)

名称	Item	规划总面积 Total Planned Area	累计已开发土地面积 Accumulated Area of Developed Land	累计已供应土地面积 Accumulated Area of Supplied Land	累计已建成城镇建设用地 Accumulated Area of Land for Urban Development
国家级开发区					
北京经济技术开发区	Beijing Economic-Technological Development Area	4680.00	3700.00	3807.04	3700.00
中关村国家自主创新示范区	Zhongguancun National Independent Innovation Demonstration Zone	38693.69	24461.15	10326.93	19897.01
中关村示范区海淀园	Zhongguancun Haidian Sub-park	13242.17	10683.92	697.76	9986.16
中关村示范区丰台园	Zhongguancun Fengtai Sub-park	1763.00	289.00	176.63	160.70
中关村示范区昌平园	Zhongguancun Changping Sub-park	5140.00	2068.92	1952.92	1719.67
中关村示范区朝阳园	Zhongguancun Chaoyang Sub-park	2610.00	1471.88	1443.06	1211.00
中关村示范区亦庄园	Zhongguancun E-town Sub-park	2678.00	2678.00		2678.00
中关村示范区西城园	Zhongguancun Xicheng Sub-park	1000.00	1000.00	1000.00	
中关村示范区东城园	Zhongguancun Dongcheng Sub-park	603.00	288.78		288.78
中关村示范区石景山园	Zhongguancun Shijingshan Sub-park	1334.00	127.60	40.99	127.60
中关村示范区通州园	Zhongguancun Tongzhou Sub-park	3434.64	1901.58	1851.59	1587.06
中关村示范区大兴生物工程与医药产业基地	Zhongguancun Daxing Ecological Sub-park and Pharmaceutical Base	1207.35	460.40	359.30	501.00
中关村示范区平谷园	Zhongguancun PingGu Sub-park	508.00	343.31	117.35	107.05
中关村示范区门头沟园	Zhongguancun MenTouGou Sub-park	189.00	120.00	120.00	
中关村示范区房山园	Zhongguancun FangShan Sub-park	1573.00	886.93	855.08	505.77
中关村示范区顺义园	Zhongguancun ShunYi Sub-park	1208.49	905.26	699.19	364.67
中关村示范区密云园	Zhongguancun MiYun Sub-park	1000.84	699.27	598.20	450.99
中关村示范区怀柔园	Zhongguancun HuaiRou Sub-park	711.00	266.30	165.30	17.93
中关村示范区延庆园	Zhongguancun YanQing Sub-park	491.20	270.00	249.55	190.63
北京天竺综合保税区	Beijing Tianzhu Bonded Area	594.40	350.00	313.00	
市级开发区					
北京石龙经济开发区	Shilong Economic Development Zone	189.00	120.00	120.00	
北京良乡经济开发区	Liangxiang Economic Development Zone	240.93	109.24	105.82	102.63
北京大兴经济开发区	Daxing Economic Development Zone	746.48	225.26	217.73	190.14
北京通州经济开发区	Tongzhou Economic Development Zone	960.80	515.60	515.60	354.60
北京雁栖经济开发区	Yanqi Economic Development Zone	1096.00	942.40	712.86	659.53
北京兴谷经济开发区	Xinggu Economic Development Zone	978.79	901.25	656.52	643.49
北京密云经济开发区	Miyun Economic Development Zone	1246.41	1246.41	940.01	890.39
北京林河经济开发区	Linhe Economic Development Zone	416.00	385.00	260.00	349.00
北京天竺空港经济开发区	Tianzhu Economic Development Zone	660.00	660.00	444.11	405.35
北京八达岭经济开发区	Badaling Economic Development Zone	480.79	318.59	209.64	299.37
北京永乐经济开发区	Yongle Economic Development Zone	459.81	329.39	162.98	122.91
北京延庆经济开发区	Yanqing Economic Development Zone	354.00	111.96	81.80	159.76
北京昌平小汤山工业园区	Changping Xiaotangshan Industrial Park	257.34	14.32	14.32	45.32
北京采育经济开发区	Caiyu Economic Development Zone	355.01	327.08	215.94	192.35
北京房山工业园区	Fangshan Industrial Park	218.52	159.51	159.51	112.25
北京马坊工业园区	Mafang Bonded Area Industrial Park	345.58	148.95	148.35	111.53

注：1. 本表所指开发区包括北京市级及国家级开发区情况。
2. 中关村国家自主创新示范区亦庄园数据在中关村国家自主创新示范区与北京经济技术开发区中为重叠部分。
3. 自2013年起，平谷园、门头沟园、房山园、顺义园、密云园、怀柔园和延庆园七个园区纳入中关村国家自主创新示范区统计范围，后表同(详见简要说明)。
4. 除中关村国家自主创新示范区海淀园外，中关村国家自主创新示范区各园“规划总面积”指标均填报批复土地面积，范围较2012年有所变化。
5. 表内“累计”指自开始至年末的累计数。

Note: a) Development zones in this table include those at Beijing municipal level and national level.
b) Data on Yizhuang Park of Zhongguancun Demonstration Zone are overlapped in Zhongguancun National Innovation Demonstration Zone and Beijing Economic and Technological Development Area.
c) Since 2013, the Pinggu Sub-park, Mentougou Sub-park, Fangshan Sub-park, Shunyi Sub-park, Huairou Sub-park and Yanqing Sub-park are incorporated into the statistical scope of Zhongguancun National Independent Innovation Demonstration Zone (the same in the following tables). (For details, please refer to the Brief Introduction of this chapter.)
d) Apart from Haidian Sub-park, the total planned area of all sub-parks of Zhongguancun National Independent Innovation Demonstration Zone refers to the approved area of land. The statistical scope is slightly different from that of 2012.
e) "Accumulated" in this table refers to the accumlation from the beginning to the end of the year.

24-3 开发区招商、入资情况(2013年)

名 称	Item	招商项目企业个数(个) Number of Enterprises Involved in Business Inviting Programs (unit)
国家级开发区		
北京经济技术开发区	Beijing Economic-Technological Development Area	6669
中关村国家自主创新示范区	Zhongguancun National Independent Innovation Demonstration Zone	32529
中关村示范区海淀园	Zhongguancun Haidian Sub-park	19737
中关村示范区丰台园	Zhongguancun Fengtai Sub-park	4798
中关村示范区昌平园	Zhongguancun Changping Sub-park	2104
中关村示范区朝阳园	Zhongguancun Chaoyang Sub-park	1374
中关村示范区亦庄园	Zhongguancun E-town Sub-park	665
中关村示范区西城园	Zhongguancun Xicheng Sub-park	546
中关村示范区东城园	Zhongguancun Dongcheng Sub-park	545
中关村示范区石景山园	Zhongguancun Shijingshan Sub-park	2239
中关村示范区通州园	Zhongguancun Tongzhou Sub-park	176
中关村示范区大兴生物工程与医药产业基地	Zhongguancun Daxing Ecological Sub-park and Pharmaceutical Base	65
中关村示范区平谷园	Zhongguancun PingGu Sub-park	
中关村示范区门头沟园	Zhongguancun MenTouGou Sub-park	71
中关村示范区房山园	Zhongguancun FangShan Sub-park	40
中关村示范区顺义园	Zhongguancun ShunYi Sub-park	
中关村示范区密云园	Zhongguancun MiYun Sub-park	66
中关村示范区怀柔园	Zhongguancun HuaiRou Sub-park	76
中关村示范区延庆园	Zhongguancun YanQing Sub-park	27
北京天竺综合保税区	Beijing Tianzhu Bonded Area	162
市级开发区		
北京石龙经济开发区	Shilong Economic Development Zone	5605
北京良乡经济开发区	Liangxiang Economic Development Zone	82
北京大兴经济开发区	Daxing Economic Development Zone	321
北京通州经济开发区	Tongzhou Economic Development Zone	305
北京雁栖经济开发区	Yanqi Economic Development Zone	1286
北京兴谷经济开发区	Xinggu Economic Development Zone	195
北京密云经济开发区	Miyun Economic Development Zone	230
北京林河经济开发区	Linhe Economic Development Zone	177
北京天竺空港经济开发区	Tianzhu Economic Development Zone	527
北京八达岭经济开发区	Badaling Economic Development Zone	1191
北京永乐经济开发区	Yongle Economic Development Zone	25
北京延庆经济开发区	Yanqing Economic Development Zone	833
北京昌平小汤山工业园区	Changping Xiaotangshan Industrial Park	78
大兴采育经济开发区	Caiyu Economic Development Zone	57
北京房山工业园区	Fangshan Industrial Park	25
北京马坊工业园区	Mafang Industrial Park	57

注：1.中关村国家自主创新示范区亦庄园数据在中关村国家自主创新示范区与北京经济技术开发区中为重叠部分。
2.本表中关村国家自主创新示范区统计口径为注册在园区内的法人单位，其他开发区统计口径为经营在开发区内的法人单位，部分开发区范围较2012年有所变化。

STATISTICS FOR BUSINESS INVITATION AND INVESTMENT IN DEVELOPMENT ZONES (2013)

自开始至报告期累计 Accumulative Number from Beginning				
项目总投资(万元) Total Investment (10000 yuan)	注册资本(万元) Registered Capital (10000 yuan)	#三资企业 Foreign-funded Enterprises	合同外资金额(万美元) Contracted Foreign Capital (USD 10000)	外商实际投资(万美元) Actual Foreign Investment (USD 10000)
29855173	20731984	6718144	948438	611181
100804243	87451806	15655102	1785380	1404055
41585339	36576639	8164934	1141502	747353
11591742	11591742	227253	26905	33239
13383559	13181112	619996	57084	57084
8843383	8843383	1205527	101053	101053
15280431	7996762	4169956	328978	332443
5111775	5111775	460394	75723	75723
748592	748592	92745	1678	1796
1672536	1752034	203504	31308	34210
1205084	459640	172406	16222	16222
393669	249730	23200	4750	4750
27313	27313			
20685	459878	204804	75	75
517900	305407	23192		
392865	123240	86740		
29370	24559	450	102	107
1261162	596243	318822	44796	4533
1933437	1933437	41265	7997	6423
336327	109545	12057	1532	1532
	272524	14256		
2841426	675512	213306	44370	44120
2970448	914645	460489	240471	252780
784886	309676	228143	49545	45491
2325071	489601	125010	23807	43275
835156	518899	113882	13382	8312
5438959	3700953	1950891	142035	157920
716221	520538	27217	75	75
216934	47139			1487
1867915	1622724		5857	6494
52800	34731	6242	989	655
713971	124347	6981	1735	780
236258	115429			
646772	108396	40135		

Note: a) Data on Yizhuang Park of Zhongguancun Demonstration Zone are overlapped in Zhongguancun National Innovation Demonstration Zone and Beijing Economic and Technological Development Area.

b) The statistical scope of Zhongguancun Demonstration Zone covers all legal entities registered in the zone, while the scope for other development zones covers all legal entities operating in them. The scope for some development zones is modified from that of 2012.

24-4 开发区投资、生产情况(2013年)
INVESTMENT AND PRODUCTION OF DEVELOPMENT ZONES (2013)

名称	Item	自年初累计 Accumulative Number from Year-beginning		
		固定资产投资(万元) Investment in Fixed Assets (10000 yuan)	总收入(万元) Total Revenues (10000 yuan)	利润总额(万元) Total Profits (10000 yuan)
国家级开发区				
北京经济技术开发区	Beijing Economic-Technological Development Area	3751544	47861613	2765610
中关村国家自主创新示范区	Zhongguancun National Independent Innovation Demonstration Zone	9098175	304974327	22647561
中关村示范区海淀园	Zhongguancun Haidian Sub-park	3132492	125335753	9384202
中关村示范区丰台园	Zhongguancun Fengtai Sub-park	922336	32955947	1773379
中关村示范区昌平园	Zhongguancun Changping Sub-park	1209279	29434078	2088271
中关村示范区朝阳园	Zhongguancun Chaoyang Sub-park	794573	35511248	3429624
中关村示范区亦庄园	Zhongguancun E-town Sub-park	1482039	35878281	2343902
中关村示范区西城园	Zhongguancun Xicheng Sub-park	764824	10606371	1471834
中关村示范区东城园	Zhongguancun Dongcheng Sub-park	40031	7646107	482180
中关村示范区石景山园	Zhongguancun Shijingshan Sub-park	232637	11836061	651667
中关村示范区通州园	Zhongguancun Tongzhou Sub-park	96758	3461837	114043
中关村示范区大兴生物工程与医药产业基地	Zhongguancun Daxing Ecological Sub-park and Pharmaceutical Base	107504	2341734	240651
中关村示范区平谷园	Zhongguancun PingGu Sub-park	21179	667659	35558
中关村示范区门头沟园	Zhongguancun MenTouGou Sub-park	29976	498710	26738
中关村示范区房山园	Zhongguancun FangShan Sub-park	20685	1703568	6332
中关村示范区顺义园	Zhongguancun ShunYi Sub-park	131594	3968182	290782
中关村示范区密云园	Zhongguancun MiYun Sub-park	67009	1120487	88654
中关村示范区怀柔园	Zhongguancun HuaiRou Sub-park	32368	1494039	183908
中关村示范区延庆园	Zhongguancun YanQing Sub-park	12892	514268	35839
北京天竺综合保税区	Beijing Tianzhu Bonded Area	443013	1192434	149069
市级开发区				
北京石龙经济开发区	Shilong Economic Development Zone	35308	423530	59406
北京良乡经济开发区	Liangxiang Economic Development Zone	31295	1686355	12076
北京大兴经济开发区	Daxing Economic Development Zone	112014	1899844	81572
北京通州经济开发区	Tongzhou Economic Development Zone	141463	421454	17596
北京雁栖经济开发区	Yanqi Economic Development Zone	192203	2987593	302246
北京兴谷经济开发区	Xinggu Economic Development Zone	95209	182910	-21006
北京密云经济开发区	Miyun Economic Development Zone	190270	1078521	67366
北京林河经济开发区	Linhe Economic Development Zone	3220	1265997	58755
北京天竺空港经济开发区	Tianzhu Economic Development Zone	201237	14985858	853862
北京八达岭经济开发区	Badaling Economic Development Zone	73496	1148551	76247
北京永乐经济开发区	Yongle Economic Development Zone	28041	179850	2534
北京延庆经济开发区	Yanqing Economic Development Zone	71741	3373354	1796919
北京昌平小汤山工业园区	Changping Xiaotangshan Industrial Park		384632	27253
大兴采育经济开发区	Caiyu Economic Development Zone	58184	1160250	-163029
北京房山工业园区	Fangshan ındustrial Park	15389	70401	302
北京马坊工业园区	Mafang Industrial Park	34993	1818155	38397

注：1.中关村国家自主创新示范区亦庄园数据在中关村国家自主创新示范区与北京经济技术开发区中为重叠部分。
2.北京经济技术开发区、市级各开发区"总收入"、"利润总额"指标的统计范围为规模(限额)以上法人单位。

Note: a) Data on Yizhuang Park of Zhongguancun Demonstration Zone are overlapped in Zhongguancun National Innovation Demonstration Zone and Beijing Economic and Technological Development Area.

b) The statistical scope of total revenues and total profits for Beijing Economic-Technological Development Area and other municipal-level development zones covers legal entities above designated size.

24-5 北京经济技术开发区主要经济指标
MAIN ECONOMIC INDICATORS FOR BEIJING ECONOMIC-TECHNOLOGICAL DEVELOPMENT AREA

项目		Item		2013	2012	2013年为2012年% 2013 as % of 2012
规划面积	(公顷)	Area Planned	(hectare)	4680.0	4650.0	100.6
开发区生产总值	(亿元)	Gross Output Value	(100 million yuan)	913.5	827.7	110.4
工业总产值 (当年价格)	(亿元)	Gross Output Value of Industry (at current prices)	(100 million yuan)	2292.9	2187.9	104.8
#高新技术企业	(亿元)	High and New Technology Enterprises	(100 million yuan)	2129.0	1993.7	106.8
销售(营业)收入	(亿元)	Sales(Business)Revenue	(100 million yuan)	4786.2	4328.5	110.6
利润总额	(亿元)	Total Profits	(100 million yuan)	276.6	212.1	130.4
进出口总值	(亿美元)	Total Value of Imports and Exports	(USD 100 million)	211.8	219.2	96.6
出口	(亿美元)	Exports	(USD 100 million)	110.3	107.5	102.6
进口	(亿美元)	Imports	(USD 100 million)	101.5	111.7	90.8
公共财政预算收入	(亿元)	Local Public Finance Budget Revenue	(100 million yuan)	100.3	80.5	124.6
公共财政预算支出	(亿元)	Local Public Finance Budget Expenditure	(100 million yuan)	102.0	84.0	121.4
批准企业个数	(个)	Number of Enterprises Ratified	(unit)	1414	1210	116.9
入区企业投资额	(亿美元)	Investment of Enterprises Entering the Area	(USD 100 million)	93.8	60.1	156.0
注册资本	(亿美元)	Registered Capital	(USD 100 million)	56.0	43.3	129.4
合同外资金额	(亿美元)	Contracted Foreign Capital	(USD 100 million)	8.0	7.3	109.9
实际利用外资	(亿美元)	Actual Use of Foreign Capital	(USD 100 million)	6.3	6.7	93.7
固定资产投资	(亿元)	Investment in Fixed Assets	(100 million yuan)	375.2	339.9	110.4
从业人员期末人数	(人)	Number of Employed Persons	(person)	279462	275219	101.5
从业人员工资总额	(万元)	Total Wages of Employed Persons	(10000 yuan)	2597521	2297846	113.0

注：工业总产值(当年价格)、销售(营业)收入和利润总额指标的统计范围是规模(限额)以上法人单位。

资料来源：北京经济技术开发区统计局、调查队。

Note: The statistical scope of gross output value of industry (at current prices), sales (business) revenue and total profits covers legal entities above designated size.

Source: Statistics Bureau and Survey Team of Beijing Economic-Technological Development Area.

24-6 中关村国家自主创新示范区企业经营及科技活动情况(2008-2013年) OPERATING ACTIVITIES AND SCIENCE ACTIVITIES OF ENTERPRISES IN ZHONGGUANCUN NATIONAL INNOVATION DEMONSTRATION ZONE (2008-2013)

项目		Item		2008	2009	2010	2011	2012	2013
总收入	**(亿元)**	**Total Revenue**	**(100 million yuan)**	**10222.4**	**13004.6**	**15940.2**	**19646.0**	**25025.0**	**30497.4**
技术收入	(亿元)	Technological Revenue	(100 million yuan)	1693.4	2093.6	2478.3	2845.9	3403.1	4032.4
产品销售收入	(亿元)	Products Sales Revenue	(100 million yuan)	5229.2	5923.6	6889.6	7809.4	8741.2	10788.4
#新产品销售收入	(亿元)	Sales Revenue of New Products	(100 million yuan)	3327.0	3203.7	3949.2	3405.1	3352.1	4070.4
商品销售收入	(亿元)	Commodity Sales Revenue	(100 million yuan)	2398.9	3689.4	5032.2	7161.9	10077.4	11339.6
其他收入	(亿元)	Other Revenues	(100 million yuan)	900.9	1298.0	1540.1	1828.9	2803.4	4337.0
出口总额	(亿美元)	Total Exports	(USD 100 million)	207.4	208.2	227.4	237.3	261.7	336.2
实缴税费总额	(亿元)	Total Tax Paid	(100 million yuan)	504.0	658.7	767.2	925.8	1445.8	1506.6
利润总额	(亿元)	Total Profits	(100 million yuan)	726.3	1122.4	1298.9	1533.9	1788.6	2264.8
研究与试验发展人员	(人)	R&D Personnel	(person)	174797	152168	96699	111685	125429	152772
研究与试验发展经费内部支出	(亿元)	Internal R&D Expenditures	(100 million yuan)	324.5	235.4	260.4	313.5	381.3	456.3
获奖成果情况		**Statistics on Prize-winning Achievements**							
获奖成果个数	(个)	Number of Prize-winning Achievements	(unit)	1448	1909	1811	2329	2509	2852
#国家级	(个)	National	(unit)	282	276	256	323	377	450
省部级	(个)	Provincial	(unit)	641	1044	1015	1351	1318	1652
专利情况		**Statistics on Patents**							
专利申请数	(件)	Number of Patents Applied	(unit)	17219	17226	18515	24894	34192	44275
拥有有效发明专利数	(件)	Number of Patents in Force	(unit)	9836	11611	13988	15232	23198	35000
专利授权数	(件)	Number of Patents Licensed	(unit)	9050	10512	13151	12951	17969	22308

24-7 中关村国家自主创新示范区企业经营活动情况
OPERATING ACTIVITIES OF ENTERPRISES IN ZHONGGUANCUN NATIONAL INNOVATION DEMONSTRATION ZONE

单位：亿元 (100 million yuan)

项　　目	Item	2013	2012
工业总产值(当年价格)	Gross Output Value of Industry (at current prices)	7890.3	6494.7
工业销售产值(当年价格)	Sales Value of Industry (at current prices)	7769.2	6420.5
#出口交货值	Delivery Value of Exports	929.9	910.0
总收入	Total Revenue	30497.4	25025.0
技术收入	Technological Revenue	4032.4	3403.1
产品销售收入	Products Sales Revenue	10788.4	8741.2
#新产品销售收入	Sales Revenue of New Products	4070.4	3352.1
#出口收入	Export Revenue	1067.7	1021.1
商品销售收入	Commodity Sales Revenue	11339.6	10077.4
其他收入	Other Revenues	4337.0	2803.4
利润总额	Total Profits	2264.8	1788.6
实缴税费总额	Total Tax Paid	1506.6	1445.8
#增值税	Value Added Tax	584.7	443.4
营业税	Business Tax	116.5	148.2
所得税	Corporate Income Tax	403.5	340.2
本年实缴关税	Duties Paid in the Year	143.2	290.5
减免税总额	Reduced and Exempted Tax	224.3	169.1
#增值税	Value Added Tax	90.8	49.3
营业税	Business Tax	4.3	15.5
所得税	Corporate Income Tax	121.7	97.7
应交增值税	Value Added Tax Payable	410.1	444.3
出口总额 (亿美元)	Foreign Exchange Created by Export (USD100 million)	336.2	261.7

24-8 中关村国家自主创新示范区企业科技活动情况
SCIENTIFIC ACTIVITIES OF ENTERPRISES IN ZHONGGUANCUN NATIONAL INNOVATION DEMONSTRATION ZONE

项目		Item		2013	2012
科技活动情况		**Statistics on Scientific and Technological Activities**			
科技活动人员合计	(人)	Total Number of Personnel Engaged in Scientific and Technological Activities	(person)	499870	402330
#全时人员		Full-time Personnel		445849	357559
#研究与试验发展(R&D)人员		R&D Personnel		152772	125429
企业内部用于科技活动的经费支出	(亿元)	Total Expenditures on Research Activities Inside Enterprises	(100 million yuan)	1032.6	811.9
#人员人工费(包括各种补贴)		Labor Cost (Including Various Subsidies)		560.5	431.4
原材料费		Cost of Raw Materials		185.8	129.6
#研究与试验发展(R&D)经费内部支出		R&D Expenditures		456.3	381.3
委托外单位开展科技活动经费支出	(亿元)	Expenditures on Scientific and Technological Activities Institutions Conducted by External Institutes Entrusted	(100 million yuan)	132.5	106.3
#对境内研究机构及高等学校的支出		Spending on Domestic Research Institutes and of Higher Education		85.5	68.3
对境外支出		Overseas Spending		4.2	3.0
本年度R&D项目情况		**R&D Projects in the Year**			
R&D项目数	(项)	Number of R&D Projects	(unit)		12124
项目人员折合全时当量	(人年)	Total Number of Personnel in R&D Projects	(person-year)		77153
研究与试验发展(R&D)项目经费支出	(亿元)	Expenditures on R&D Programs	(100 million yuan)		296.9
企业科技活动产出情况		**Scientific and Technological Output**			
获奖成果情况		**Statistics on Prize-winning Achievements**			
获奖成果个数	(个)	Number of Prize-winning Achievements	(unit)	2852	2509
#国家级	(个)	National	(unit)	450	377
省部级	(个)	Provincial	(unit)	1652	1318
地市级	(个)	Prefecture and City-level	(unit)	747	785
专利情况		**Statistics on Patents**			
专利申请数	(件)	Number of Patents Applied	(case)	44275	34192
#发明专利	(件)	Invention Patents	(case)	26737	20914
拥有有效发明专利数	(件)	Number of Patents in Force	(case)	35000	23198
专利授权数	(件)	Number of Patent Licensed	(case)	22308	17969
论文、著作情况		**Statistics on Papers and Writings**			
发表科技论文篇数	(篇)	Number of Published Scientific Papers	(unit)	13227	10197
技术改造和技术获取情况		**Technical Rennovation and Acquisition**			
技术改造经费支出	(亿元)	Expenditures on Technical Rennovation	(100 million yuan)	13.4	17.7
引进国外技术经费支出	(亿元)	Expenditures on Introduction of Foreign Technologies	(100 million yuan)	16.1	12.8
引进技术的消化吸收经费支出	(亿元)	Expenditures on Absorption of Imported Technologies	(100 million yuan)	5.7	4.3
购买国内技术经费支出	(亿元)	Expenditures on Purchasing Domestic Technologies	(100 million yuan)	14.7	9.9

24-9 中关村国家自主创新示范区企业人力资源情况
HUMAN RESOURCES OF ENTERPRISES IN ZHONGGUANCUN NATIONAL INNOVATION DEMONSTRATION ZONE

单位：人 (person)

项 目	Item	2013	2012
企业人力资源情况	**Statistics on Human Resource**		
从业人员年末人数	**Number of Employeed Persons at the Year End**	**1898756**	**1585950**
#工程技术人员	Engineering Technician	578860	472496
#留学归国人员	Returned Students Studying Abroad	19763	16102
#在岗长期职工	On-the-post Long-term Employed Persons	1723520	1427907
按文化程度分	**By Educational Background**		
博士及以上	Doctor Degree and Above	18426	15193
#留学归国人员	Returned Students Studying Abroad	2185	1890
硕 士	Masters	183350	156736
#留学归国人员	Returned Students Studying Abroad	12613	10529
大 本	Undergraduates	747026	614973
大 专	Junior College	412466	321269
按技术职称分	**By Technical Post**		
高 级	Senior	108358	83488
中 级	Middle	196578	154997
初 级	Junior	219991	173594
按年龄分	**By Age**		
#29岁及以下	Age 29 and Below	881781	762377
30-39岁	30-39	632065	507631
40-49岁	40-49	258292	215710
从业人员平均人数	**Average Number of Empolyed Persons**	**1844792**	**1562830**
在岗职工参加社会保险人数	**Number of Employees Covered by the Social Insurance**	**1638578**	**1311960**

24-10 中关村国家自主创新示范区企业财务状况
FINANCIAL STATUS OF ENTERPRISES IN ZHONGGUANCUN NATIONAL INNOVATION DEMONSTRATION ZONE

单位：亿元 (100 million yuan)

项目	Item	2013	2012
资产总计	Total Assets	50814.4	40386.9
流动资产合计	Total Current Assets	29545.1	22958.8
固定资产合计	Total Fixed Assets	6580.7	4980.9
固定资产原价	Original Value of Fixed Assets	9106.2	7164.2
累计折旧	Accumulative Depreciation	2595.7	2026.6
负债合计	Total Liabilities	28472.4	22393.1
所有者权益合计	Total Owner's Equity	22342.0	17982.2
实收资本	Paid-up Capital	11464.4	9340.1
主营业务收入	Operating Income	29877.8	24588.2
主营业务成本	Operating Cost	24513.1	20228.4
主营业务税金及附加	Business Tax and Surtax	245.2	239.5
利润总额	Total Profits	2264.8	1788.6

主要统计指标解释

已开发土地面积 指在规划范围内达到“七通一平”标准的，具备进行房屋建筑物施工或出让条件的土地面积。

已供应土地面积 指开发区内通过各种方式获得土地使用权的土地面积，包括出让、划拨、租赁等。

已建成城镇建设用地面积 截至报告期，已经建设并通过竣工验收的国有建设用地。包括已建成的住宅用地、工矿仓储用地、多功能用地、交通运输用地、商服用地、公共管理与公共服务用地，以及其他城镇建设用地等。海关特殊监管区域的已建成城镇建设用地包括现状围网范围内已建成的城镇建设用地，及开发区四至范围与围网范围间的海关专属办公用地。

累计招商项目企业个数 指自开始至报告期末累计招商入区，并经工商管理机关注册取得法人营业执照的企业个数。

累计招商项目总投资 指自开始至报告期末累计批准的合同（章程）规定的投资总额。

累计招商项目注册资本 指自开始至报告期末累计为设立经营企业在工商行政管理机关注册的资本总额。

累计招商项目合同外资金额 指自开始至报告期末累计批准的合同（章程）中，外商和港、澳、台商的出资额。

累计招商项目外商实际投资 指自开始至报告期末累计按合同规定的外方和港、澳、台方以现金、实物、工业产权及专有技术的计价实缴资本投资额。

总收入 指企业全年的生产产品销售收入、技术性收入和与本企业产品相关的商品的销售收入、其它收入等各种收入的总和，总收入等于主营业务收入加上其他业务收入。总收入应按不含增值税的价格计算，不包括补贴收入、营业外收入、投资收益。

出口总额 指出售给外贸部门或直接出售给外商的产品或商品的总金额。包括来料加工装配出口，境外技术合同实现金额及在国内以外汇计价的商品出售和技术服务的总额等。

留学归国人员 指出国学习，取得学位的归国人员。

Explanatory Notes on Main Statistical Indicators

Area of Developed Land refers to the area of land that meets the standard of "seven connections and one leveling" and is qualified for construction or sale.

Area of Supplied Land refers to the area of land whose right of use is acquired in the development zones by various means including sale, transfer, and lease.

Area of Land for Urban Development refers to state-owned construction land that has already gone through construction and acceptance check by the end of the reporting period. It includes land for complete residential buildings, land for industrial, mining and storage use, multi-functional land, land for transportation, land for commercial services, land for public administration and services and other lands for urban development. Land for urban development under special administration of customs includes urban development land completed inside the current seine and land for office buildings of customs inside the development zones and between the seines.

Accumulated Number of Enterprises Involved in Business Inviting Programs refers to the total number of enterprises invited to development zones and awarded with business licenses for legal persons from the administration for industry and commerce from the beginning to the end of the reporting period.

Accumulative Investment of Business Inviting Programs refers to the total investment of contracts (articles of incorporation) approved from the beginning to the end of the reporting period.

Accumulative Registered Capital of Business Inviting Programs refers to the total capital registered with the administration for industry and commerce for the purpose of establishment of operating enterprises from the beginning to the end of the reporting period.

Accumulative Contracted Foreign Capital of Business Inviting Programs refers to the cumulative capital contribution of investors from foreign countries, Hong Kong, Macao and Taiwan as approved in contracts (articles of incorporation) from the beginning to the end of the reporting period.

Accumulated Actual Foreign Investment of Business Inviting Programs refers to the cumulative amount of paid-up capital contribution investors from foreign countries, Hong Kong, Macao and Taiwan made in cash, in physical material, industrial property right and proprietary technology, as stated in contracts, from the beginning to the end of the reporting period.

Total Revenue refers to the sum of income earned by enterprises from sales of their own products, technological income, and income from selling commodities related to their own products, and other income. Total income is the sum of main business income and other business income. Total income shall be calculated at VAT-excluded prices, and exclude subsidies, non-operating income and return on investment across the year.

Total Exports refers to the total amount of products or commodities sold to foreign trade organizations or directly sold to foreign traders. It includes the value of export of investor's raw materials processed, the value of technical contracts completed at home and abroad, and the total value of domestic commodity sales and technical services measured in foreign currency.

Returned Students Studying Abroad refer to persons who have come home after studying abroad and been conferred with academic degrees.